ROAD ATLAS
BRITAIN

Free AA Street by Street Z-Map

AA Street by Street Z-Maps are a new series of credit-card size street maps of major towns and cities that combine a clever Z-fold pattern with Britain's clearest street mapping.

- Large-scale street maps
- Easy-to-read road names
- Car parks & one-way streets
- Helpful index
- Ideal size for wallet or purse

Choose from one of these 10 popular titles

Birmingham   Liverpool
Bristol   London The City
Cardiff   London West End
Edinburgh   Manchester
Glasgow   Newcastle upon Tyne

Here's how to get your free AA Street by Street Z-Map:
Simply clip the coupon on the corner of this page and seal it in an envelope (maximum size 114 x 162mm or 4½" x 6⅜"). On the back of this envelope, write your own name and postal address and in the bottom right hand corner, the name of your chosen Z-Map title (all in capitals please). Send to:
Atlas Z-Map Offer, Swift FM, Swift Park, Old Leicester Road, Rugby, Warwicks CV21 1DZ.

Please send me my
Free
Street by Street Z-Map
REF RAB

TERMS AND CONDITIONS
1. Offer open to residents of the UK and Republic of Ireland only. 2. Only the original coupons printed in participating AA atlases are valid. Photocopies are not permitted. 3. No cash alternative is available.
4. Applications must be received by 12 July 2002. Please allow up to 28 days for delivery of your free Z-Map. 5. No liability will be accepted for applications lost, damaged or delayed in the post.
Proof of posting will not be accepted as proof of receipt. 6. Application instructions above form part of the Terms and Conditions.
Promoter: Automobile Association Developments Limited, Norfolk House, Priestley Road, Basingstoke, Hampshire RG24 9NY.

contents

Scale 1:200,000 or 3.15 miles to 1 inch

16th edition July 2001

© Automobile Association Developments Limited 2001

Original edition printed 1986.

Ordnance Survey This product includes mapping data licensed from Ordnance Survey® with the permission of the Controller of Her Majesty's Stationery Office. © Crown copyright 2001. All rights reserved. Licence number 399221.

Northern Ireland mapping reproduced by permission of the Director and Chief Executive, Ordnance Survey of Northern Ireland, acting on behalf of the controller of Her Majesty's Stationery Office © Crown copyright 2001. Permit No. 1674.

Republic of Ireland mapping based on Ordnance Survey Ireland by permission of the Government. Permit No. MP004201 © Government of Ireland.

All rights reserved. No part of this publication may be reproduced, stored in a retrieval system, or transmitted in any form or by any means – electronic, mechanical, photocopying, recording or otherwise – unless the permission of the publisher has been given beforehand.

Published by AA Publishing (a trading name of Automobile Association Developments Limited, whose registered office is Norfolk House, Priestley Road, Basingstoke, Hampshire RG24 9NY. Registered number 1878835).

Mapping produced by the Cartographic Department of The Automobile Association. This atlas has been compiled and produced from the Automaps database utilising electronic and computer technology.

ISBN 0 7495 2973 3

A CIP catalogue record for this book is available from The British Library.

Printed in Italy by Pizzi, Milan.

The contents of this atlas are believed to be correct at the time of the latest revision. However, the publishers cannot be held responsible for loss occasioned to any person acting or refraining from action as a result of any material in this atlas, nor for any errors, omissions or changes in such material. The publishers would welcome information to correct any errors or omissions and to keep this atlas up to date. Please write to the Cartographic Editor, Publishing Division, The Automobile Association, Fanum House, Basing View, Basingstoke, Hampshire RG21 4EA.

Information on National Parks provided by the Countryside Agency for England and the Countryside Council for Wales.

Information on National Scenic Areas in Scotland provided by Scottish Natural Heritage.

Information on Forest Parks provided by the Forestry Commission.

The RSPB sites shown are a selection chosen by the Royal Society for the Protection of Birds.

National Trust properties shown are a selection of those open to the public as indicated in the handbooks of the National Trust and the National Trust for Scotland.

Map pages	inside front cover
Traffic and travel information	IV–V
Route planner	VI–XI
Motorways	**XII–XV**
Restricted junctions	XII–XIII
M25 London orbital motorway	XIV
M60 Manchester orbital motorway	XV
Map symbols	XVI–1
Road maps	**2–174**
Scottish islands	168–169
Ireland	170–173
The Channel Islands & The Isle of Man	174
Town plans	**175–234**
Key to town plans	175
Central London	240–250
Central London street index	251–257
Ports and airports	**235–239**
Major ports	235
Major airports	236–238
Channel Tunnel	239
District maps	**258–269**
London district	258–261
Birmingham district	262–263
Glasgow district	264–265
Manchester district	266–267
Tyne & Wear district	268–269
Index to place names	**270–320**
County map (index opener)	270
Distances and journey times	inside back cover

traffic and travel information

The Automobile Association is Britain's largest motoring organisation, providing accurate and up-to-date information for all motorists. Our information detailing traffic congestion, road conditions and public transport news is collected from more than 8,000 sources, including, among others, local authorities, roadside cameras and our own registered mobile phone service 'Jambusters'. AA Roadwatch operates 24 hours a day, giving traffic information on all UK motorways, major trunk roads and local roads. The result is one of the most comprehensive and up-to-the-minute traffic report services available.

Instant traffic reports
09003 401 100/401 100 mobile
www.theAA.com

These numbers give you direct access to a range of traffic and travel information services, including: the latest traffic reports for your local area, or for any region of the UK; a traffic report on any motorway or A-road of your choice; and local and national five-day weather forecasts.

UK and european routes
0870 5500 600
www.theAA.com

AA routes are available for the UK, Ireland and continental Europe, to help you map out a detailed plan of the best way to get to your destination. Route planning is also available online and, if you tell us your usual routes, we can send you e-mail alerts at times pre-determined by you to let you know what traffic incidents and delays are occurring.

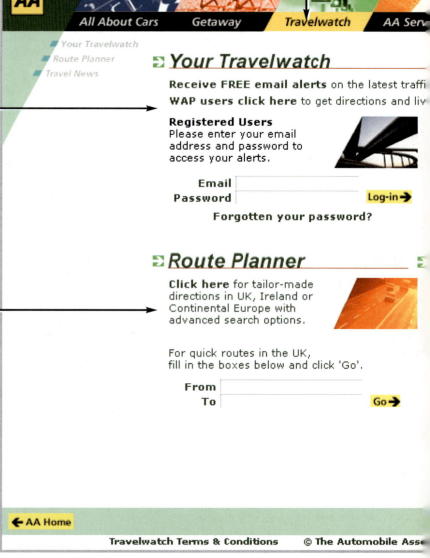

In-car information systems and radio

AA traffic and travel information can also be received by intelligent in-car navigation systems that warn of delays, provide detailed routes and even recommend a suitable hotel for a stopover. Alternatively, use your WAP-enabled mobile device to access this information on the AA's website. AA Roadwatch reports are also available over many local radio stations.

Air ambulance
0800 3899 899

For information about the work of the National Association of Air Ambulance Services, or to make a donation to NAAAS by debit or credit card, call the number above.

Air ambulances are a vital part of emergency services, providing a rapid response and transfer from incident to hospital.

AA The Driving School
0800 60 70 80
www.theAA.com

The AA's Driving School is the only national driving school to use fully qualified instructors exclusively. Attractive packages are available to people pre-paying for 12 hours' tuition.

Petrolbusters
www.theAA.com

Click on the Petrolbusters symbol to locate the cheapest petrol in your area.

Call tariffs
0800 – free to caller, 0845 – charged at BT local rate, 0870 – charged at BT national rate, 09003 – 60p per minute at all times. Availability and prices for mobile calls can vary – contact your service provider for details.

Information correct at time of going to press.

Road user information line (Highways Agency)
0845 750 040 30

For information on motorways and trunk roads, to make a complaint or comment on road conditions or roadworks, for MoT and vehicle licence enquiries.

motorways – restricted junctions

Motorway junctions which have access and exit restrictions,
as shown by [3] on atlas pages
(Motorways and Service Areas booklet also available tel: **0870 5500 600**)

M1 LONDON–LEEDS

Junction		
2 (pg 28)	**Northbound**	No exit. Access only from A1 *(northbound)*
	Southbound	No access. Exit only to A1 *(southbound)*
4 (pg 28)	**Northbound**	No exit. Access only from A41 *(northbound)*
	Southbound	No access. Exit only to A41 *(southbound)*
6A (pg 50)	**Northbound**	No exit. Access only from M25
	Southbound	No access. Exit only to M25
7 (pg 50)	**Northbound**	No exit. Access only from M10
	Southbound	No access. Exit only to M10
17 (pg 60)	**Northbound**	No access. Exit only to M45
	Southbound	No exit. Access only from M45
19 (pg 60)	**Northbound**	Exit only to northbound M6
	Southbound	No access from A14. Access only from M6
21A (pg 60)	**Northbound**	No access. Exit only to A46
	Southbound	No exit. Access only from A46
23A (pg 72)	**Northbound**	No exit. Access only from A42
	Southbound	No access. Exit only to A42
24A (pg 72)	**Northbound**	No exit. Access only from A50
	Southbound	No access. Exit only to A50
34 (pg 84)	Staggered junction; follow signs	
	Northbound	No restriction
	Southbound	No restriction
35A (pg 84)	**Northbound**	No access. Exit only to A616
	Southbound	No exit. Access only from A616
43 (pg 90)	**Northbound**	No access. Exit only to M621
	Southbound	No exit. Access only from M621
48 (pg 90)	**Northbound**	No exit. Access only from A1(M)
	Southbound	No access. Exit only to A1(M)

M2 ROCHESTER–FAVERSHAM

Junction		
1 (pg 29)	**Westbound**	Exit only to A289 *(eastbound)*
	Eastbound	Access only from A289 *(westbound)*

M3 SUNBURY–SOUTHAMPTON

Junction		
8 (pg 26)	**Southwestbound**	No access. Exit only to A303
	Northeastbound	No exit. Access only from A303
10 (pg 26)	**Southwestbound**	No exit. Access only from Winchester & A31
	Northeastbound	No access. Exit only to Winchester & A31
11 (pg 26)	Staggered junction; follow signs	
	Southwestbound	No restriction
	Northeastbound	No restriction
13 (pg 14)	**Southwestbound**	Access only to M27 *(westbound)* & A33
	Northeastbound	No restriction
14 (pg 14)	**Southwestbound**	No access. Exit only to M27 *(eastbound)* & A33
	Northeastbound	No exit. Access only

M4 LONDON–SOUTH WALES

Junction		
1 (pg 28)	**Westbound**	Access only from A4 *(westbound)*
	Eastbound	Exit only to A4 *(eastbound)*
2 (pg 28)	Staggered junction; follow signs	
	Westbound	No restriction
	Eastbound	No restriction
4A (pg 28)	**Southbound**	No exit to A4 *(westbound)*
	Northbound	No restriction
21 (pg 37)	**Westbound**	No access. Exit only to M48
	Eastbound	No exit. Access only from M48
23 (pg 37)	**Westbound**	No exit. Access only from M48
	Eastbound	No access. Exit only to M48
25 (pg 36)	**Westbound**	No access. Exit only to B4596
	Eastbound	No exit. Access only from B4596
25A (pg 36)	**Westbound**	No access. Exit only to A4042
	Eastbound	No exit. Access only from A4042
29 (pg 36)	**Westbound**	No access. Exit only to A48(M)
	Eastbound	No exit. Access only from A48(M)
38 (pg 35)	**Westbound**	No access. Exit only to A48
	Eastbound	No restriction
39 (pg 35)	**Westbound**	No exit. Access only from A48
	Eastbound	No access or exit
41 (pg 35)	Staggered junction; follow signs	
	Westbound	No restriction
	Eastbound	No restriction
42 (pg 35)	Staggered junction; follow signs	
	Westbound	Exit only to A483
	Eastbound	Access only from A483

M5 BIRMINGHAM–EXETER

Junction		
10 (pg 47)	**Southwestbound**	No access. Exit only to A4019
	Northeastbound	No exit. Access only from A4019
11A (pg 38)	**Southwestbound**	Exit only to A417 *(eastbound)*
	Northeastbound	Access only from A417 *(westbound)*
12 (pg 38)	**Southwestbound**	No exit. Access only from A38
	Northeastbound	No access. Exit only
18A (pg 37)	**Southwestbound**	No exit. Access only from M49
	Northeastbound	Exit only to M49

M6 RUGBY–CARLISLE

Junction		
4 (pg 59)	**Northwestbound**	No access from M42 *(southbound)*. No exit to M42 *(northbound)*
	Southeastbound	No access from M42 *(southbound)*. No exit to M42
4A (pg 59)	**Northwestbound**	No exit. Access only from M42 *(southbound)*
	Southeastbound	No access. Exit only to M42
5 (pg 58)	**Northwestbound**	No access. Exit only to A452
	Southeastbound	No exit. Access only from A452
10A (pg 58)	**Northbound**	No access. Exit only to M54
	Southbound	No exit. Access only from M54
20 (with M56) (pg 82)	Staggered junction; follow signs	
	Northbound	No restriction
	Southbound	No restriction
24 (pg 81)	**Northbound**	No exit. Access only from A58
	Southbound	No access. Exit only to A58
25 (pg 81)	**Northbound**	No access. Exit only
	Southbound	No exit. Access only
29 (pg 88)	**Northbound**	No direct access, use adjacent slip road to junction 29A
	Southbound	No direct exit, use adjacent slip road from junction 29A
29A (pg 88)	**Northbound**	No direct exit, use adjacent slip road from junction 29
	Southbound	No direct access, use adjacent slip road to junction 29
30 (pg 88)	**Northbound**	No exit. Access only from M61
	Southbound	No access. Exit only to M61
31A (pg 88)	**Northbound**	No access. Exit only
	Southbound	No exit. Access only

M8 EDINBURGH–GLASGOW–BISHOPTON

Junction		
3A (pg 131)	Staggered junction; follow signs	
	Westbound	No restriction
	Eastbound	No restriction
8 (pg 130)	**Westbound**	No access from M73 *(southbound)* or from A8 *(eastbound)* & A89
	Eastbound	No exit to M73 *(northbound)* or to A8 *(westbound)* & A89
9 (pg 130)	**Westbound**	No exit. Access only
	Eastbound	No access. Exit only
13 (pg 130)	**Westbound**	Access only from M80 *(southbound)*
	Eastbound	Exit only to M80 *(northbound)*
14 (pg 130)	**Westbound**	No exit. Access only
	Eastbound	No access. Exit only
16 (pg 129)	**Westbound**	No access. Exit only to A804
	Eastbound	No exit. Access only from A879
17 (pg 129)	**Westbound**	Exit only to A82
	Eastbound	No restriction
18 (pg 129)	**Westbound**	Access only from A82 *(eastbound)*
	Eastbound	No access. Exit only to A814
19 (pg 129)	**Westbound**	No access from A814 *(westbound)*
	Eastbound	No access. Exit only to A814 *(westbound)*
20 (pg 129)	**Westbound**	No access. Exit only
	Eastbound	No exit. Access only
21 (pg 129)	**Westbound**	No exit. Access only
	Eastbound	No access. Exit only to A8
22 (pg 129)	**Westbound**	No access. Exit only to M77 *(southbound)*
	Eastbound	No exit. Access only from M77 *(northbound)*
23 (pg 129)	**Westbound**	No access. Exit only to B768
	Eastbound	No exit. Access only from B768
25 (pg 129)	**Westbound**	No access/exit from/to A8
	Eastbound	No access/exit from/to A8
25A (pg 129)	**Westbound**	No access. Exit only
	Eastbound	No exit. Access only
28 (pg 129)	**Westbound**	No access. Exit only
	Eastbound	No exit. Access only

M9 EDINBURGH–DUNBLANE

Junction		
1A (pg 131)	**Northwestbound**	No access. Exit only to A8000
	Southeastbound	No exit. Access only from A8000
2 (pg 131)	**Northwestbound**	No exit. Access only
	Southeastbound	No access. Exit only
3 (pg 131)	**Northwestbound**	No access. Exit only
	Southeastbound	No exit. Access only
6 (pg 131)	**Northwestbound**	No exit. Access only from A904
	Southeastbound	No access. Exit only to A905
8 (pg 131)	**Northwestbound**	No access. Exit only to M876 *(southwestbound)*
	Southeastbound	No exit. Access only from M876 *(northeastbound)*

M10 ST ALBANS–M1

Junction		
with M1 (jct 7) (pg 50)	**Northwestbound**	Exit only to M1 *(northbound)*
	Southeastbound	Access only from M1 *(southbound)*

M11 LONDON–CAMBRIDGE

Junction		
4 (pg 29)	**Northbound**	Access only from A406
	Southbound	Exit only to A406
5 (pg 29)	**Northbound**	No access. Exit only to A1168
	Southbound	No exit. Access only from A1168
9 (pg 50)	**Northbound**	No access. Exit only to A11
	Southbound	No exit. Access only from A11
13 (pg 62)	**Northbound**	No access Exit only to A1303
	Southbound	No exit. Access only from A1303
14 (pg 62)	**Northbound**	Exit only to A14 *(eastbound)*
	Southbound	Access only from A14

M20 SWANLEY–FOLKESTONE

Junction		
2 (pg 29)	Staggered junction; follow signs	
	Southeastbound	No access. Exit only to A227
	Northwestbound	No exit. Access only from A227
3 (pg 29)	**Southeastbound**	No exit. Access only from M26 *(eastbound)*
	Northwestbound	No access. Exit only to M26 *(westbound)*
5 (pg 30)	**Southeastbound**	For access follow signs. Exit only to A20
	Northwestbound	No exit. Access only from A20
6 (pg 30)	**Southeastbound**	For exit follow signs
	Northwestbound	No restriction
11A (pg 19)	**Southeastbound**	No access. Exit only
	Northwestbound	No exit. Access only

M23 HOOLEY–CRAWLEY

Junction		
7 (pg 28)	**Southbound**	Access only from A23 *(southbound)*
	Northbound	Exit only to A23 *(northbound)*
10A (pg 16)	**Southbound**	No access. Exit only to B2036
	Northbound	No exit. Access only from B2036

M25 LONDON ORBITAL MOTORWAY

(refer also to atlas pg xiv)

Junction		
1B (pg 29)	**Clockwise**	No access (use slip road via jct 2).Exit only to A225 & A296
	Anticlockwise	No exit (use slip road via jct 2). Access only from A225 & A296
5 (pg 29)	**Clockwise**	No exit to M26
	Anticlockwise	No access from M26
9 (pg 28)	Staggered junction; follow signs	
	Clockwise	No restriction
	Anticlockwise	No restriction
19 (pg 28)	**Clockwise**	No access. Exit only to A41
	Anticlockwise	No exit. Access only from A41
21 (pg 50)	**Clockwise**	Access only from M1 *(southbound)*. Exit only to M1 *(northbound)*
	Anticlockwise	Access only from M1 *(southbound)*. Exit only to M1 *(northbound)*
21A (pg 50)	**Clockwise**	No link from M1 to A405
	Anticlockwise	No link from M1 to A405
31 (pg 29)	**Clockwise**	No exit (use slip road via jct 30)
	Anticlockwise	For access follow signs

M26 SEVENOAKS–WROTHAM

Junction		
with M25 (jct 5) (pg 29)	**Eastbound**	Access only from anticlockwise M25 *(eastbound)*
	Westbound	Exit only to clockwise M25 *(westbound)*
with M20 (jct 3) (pg 29)	**Eastbound**	Exit only to M20 *(southeastbound)*
	Westbound	Access only from M20 *(northwestbound)*

M27 CADNAM–PORTSMOUTH

Junction		
4 (pg 14)	Staggered junction; follow signs	
	Eastbound	Access only from M3 *(southbound)*. Exit only to M3 *(northbound)*
	Westbound	Access only from M3 *(southbound)*. Exit only to M3 *(northbound)*
10 (pg 14)	**Eastbound**	No exit. Access only from A32
	Westbound	No access. Exit only to A32
12 (pg 15)	Staggered junction; follow signs	
	Eastbound	Access only from M275 *(northbound)*
	Westbound	Exit only to M275 *(southbound)*

M40 LONDON–BIRMINGHAM

Junction		
3 (pg 41)	**Northwestbound**	No access. Exit only to A40
	Southeastbound	No exit. Access only from A40
7 (pg 41)	**Northwestbound**	No access. Exit only to A329
	Southeastbound	No exit. Access only from A329

8 (pg 40)	Northwestbound Southeastbound	No access. Exit only to A40 No exit. Access only from A40
13 (pg 48)	Northwestbound Southeastbound	No access. Exit only to A452 No exit. Access only from A452
14 (pg 48)	Northwestbound Southeastbound	No exit. Access only from A452 No access. Exit only to A452
16 (pg 58)	Northwestbound Southeastbound	No exit. Access only from A3400 No access. Exit only to A3400

M42 BROMSGROVE–MEASHAM

Junction		
1 (pg 58)	Northeastbound Southwestbound	No exit. Access only from A38 No access. Exit only to A38
7 (pg 59)	Northeastbound	No access. Exit only to M6 *(northwestbound)*
	Southwestbound	No exit. Access only from M6 *(northwestbound)*
7A (pg 59)	Northeastbound	No access. Exit only to M6 *(southeastbound)*
	Southwestbound	No access or exit
8 (pg 59)	Northeastbound	No exit. Access only from M6 *(southeastbound)*
	Southwestbound	No access. Exit only to M6 *(northwestbound)*

M45 COVENTRY–M1

Junction		
unnumbered (Dunchurch) (pg 60)	Eastbound Westbound	No access. Exit only to A45 & B4429 No exit. Access only from A45 & B4429
with M1 (jct 17) (pg 60)	Eastbound Westbound	Exit only to M1 *(southbound)* Access only from M1 *(northbound)*

M53 MERSEY TUNNEL–CHESTER

Junction		
1 (pg 81)	Southwestbound	No exit. Access only from A554 & A5139
	Northeastbound	No access. Exit only to A554 & A5139
11 (pg 81)	Southeastbound	Access only from M56 *(westbound)*. Exit only to M56 *(eastbound)*
	Northwestbound	Access only from M56 *(westbound)*. Exit only to M56 *(eastbound)*

M54 TELFORD

Junction		
with M6 (jct 10A) (pg 58)	Westbound	No exit. Access only from M6 *(northbound)*
	Eastbound	No access. Exit only to M6 *(southbound)*

M56 NORTH CHESHIRE

Junction		
1 (pg 82)	Westbound	No exit. Access only from M60 *(westbound)*
	Eastbound	No access. Exit only to M60 *(eastbound)* & A34 *(northbound)*
2 (pg 82)	Westbound Eastbound	No access. Exit only to A560 No exit. Access only from A560
3 (pg 82)	Westbound Eastbound	No exit. Access only from A5103 No access. Exit only to A5103 & A560
4 (pg 82)	Westbound Eastbound	No access. Exit only No exit. Access only
7 (pg 82)		Staggered junction; follow signs
	Westbound Eastbound	No restriction No restriction
9 (pg 82)	Westbound	Exit to M6 *(southbound)* via A50 interchange
	Eastbound	Access from M6 *(northbound)* via A50 interchange
15 (pg 81)	Westbound Eastbound	No access. Exit only to M53 No exit. Access only from M53

M57 LIVERPOOL OUTER RING ROAD

Junction		
3 (pg 81)	Northwestbound Southeastbound	No exit. Access only from A526 No access. Exit only to A526
5 (pg 81)	Northwestbound	No exit. Access only from A580 *(westbound)*
	Southeastbound	No access. Exit only to A580

M58 LIVERPOOL–WIGAN

Junction		
1 (pg 81)	Eastbound Westbound	No exit. Access only No access. Exit only

M60 MANCHESTER ORBITAL

(refer also to atlas pg xv)

Junction		
2 (pg 82)	Clockwise Anticlockwise	No exit. Access only from A560 No access. Exit only to A560
3 (pg 82)	Clockwise Anticlockwise	No access from M56 No exit. Access only from A34 *(northbound)*
4 (pg 82)	Clockwise	Access only from A34 *(northbound)*. Exit only to M56
	Anticlockwise	Access only from M56 *(eastbound)*. Exit only to A34 *(southbound)*
5 (pg 82)	Clockwise	Access/exit only from/to A5103 *(northbound)*
	Anticlockwise	Access/exit only from/to A5103 *(southbound)*
7 (pg 82)	Clockwise	No access (use adjacent slip road to junction 8). Exit only to A56
	Anticlockwise	No exit (use adjacent slip road from junction 8). Access only from A56
14 (pg 82)	Clockwise	No exit. Access to M60 from A580 *(eastbound)*. Access to M61 *(westbound)* from A580 *(westbound)*
	Anticlockwise	No access. Exit from M61 *(eastbound)* to A580 *(eastbound)*. No exit from M60
15 (pg 82)	Clockwise	Access only from M61 *(eastbound)*. Exit to M61 *(westbound)*
	Anticlockwise	No access. Exit to M61 *(westbound)* & A580 *(westbound)*
16 (pg 82)	Clockwise Anticlockwise	No exit. Access only from A666 No access. Exit only to A666
20 (pg 82)	Clockwise Anticlockwise	No access. Exit only to A664 No exit. Access only from A664
22 (pg 82)	Clockwise Anticlockwise	No restriction No access. Exit only to A62
25 (pg 82)	Clockwise Anticlockwise	No access. Exit only to A6017 No restriction
26 (pg 82)	Clockwise Anticlockwise	No restriction No access or exit
27 (pg 82)	Clockwise Anticlockwise	No exit. Access only from A626 No access. Exit only to A626

M61 GREATER MANCHESTER–PRESTON

Junction		
1 (pg 82)		No restriction; follow signs
2 (pg 82)		No restriction; follow signs
3 (pg 82)	Northwestbound Southeastbound	No access or exit No access. Exit only to A660
with M6 (jct 30) (pg 82)	Northwestbound Southeastbound	Exit only to M6 *(northbound)* Access only from M6 *(southbound)*

M62 LIVERPOOL–HUMBERSIDE

Junction		
23 (pg 90)	Eastbound Westbound	No access. Exit only to A640 No exit. Access only from A640

M65 PRESTON–COLNE

Junction		
1 (pg 88)	Northeastbound Southwestbound	Access and exit to M6 only Access and exit to M6 only
9 (pg 89)	Northeastbound Southwestbound	No access. Exit only to A679 No exit. Access only from A679
11 (pg 89)	Northeastbound Southwestbound	No exit. Access only No access. Exit only

M66 GREATER MANCHESTER

Junction		
with A56 (pg 89)	Southbound Northbound	Access only from A56 *(southbound)* Exit only to A56 *(northbound)*
1 (pg 89)	Southbound Northbound	No exit. Access only from A56 No access. Exit only to A56

M67 HYDE BYPASS

Junction		
1 (pg 82)	Eastbound Westbound	No access. Exit only to A6017 No exit. Access only from A6017
2 (pg 82)	Eastbound Westbound	No exit. Access only No access. Exit only to A57
3 (pg 82)	Eastbound Westbound	No restriction No access. Exit only to A627

M69 COVENTRY–LEICESTER

Junction		
2 (pg 59)	Northbound Southbound	No exit. Access only from B4669 No access. Exit only to B4669

M73 EAST OF GLASGOW

Junction		
2 (pg 130)	Northbound	No access from or to A89. No access from M8 *(eastbound)*
	Southbound	No access from or to A89. No exit to M8 *(westbound)*
3 (pg 130)	Northbound Southbound	Exit only to A80 *(northeastbound)* Access only from A80 *(southwestbound)*

M74 GLASGOW–ABINGTON

Junction		
2 (pg 120)	Southbound Northbound	No exit. Access only from A763 No access. Exit only to A763
3 (pg 120)	Southbound Northbound	No access. Exit only Exit via junction 4. Access only
7 (pg 120)	Southbound Northbound	No access. Exit only to A72 No exit. Access only from A72
9 (pg 120)	Southbound Northbound	No access. Exit only to B7078 No access or exit
10 (pg 120)	Southbound Northbound	No exit. Access only from B7078 No restrictions
11 (pg 120)	Southbound Northbound	No access. Exit only to B7078 No exit. Access only from B7078
12 (pg 120)	Southbound Northbound	No exit. Access only from A70 No access. Exit only to A70

A74(M) ABINGTON–GRETNA

Junction		
14 (pg 120)		Staggered junction; follow signs
	Southbound Northbound	No restriction No restriction
18 (pg 111)	Southbound Northbound	No exit. Access only from B723 No access. Exit only to B723
21 (pg 111)	Southbound Northbound	No access. Exit only to B6357 No exit. Access only from B6357
with B7076 (pg 111)	Southbound Northbound	No exit. Access only No access. Exit only
Gretna Green (pg 111)	Southbound	No access. Exit only (use B7076 through Gretna to access A75)
	Northbound	No exit. Access only
with A75 (pg 111)	Southbound Northbound	No exit. Access only from A75 No access. Exit only to A75
with A6071 (pg 111)	Southbound Northbound	Exit only to A74 *(southbound)* Access only from A74 *(northbound)*

M77 WEST OF GLASGOW

Junction		
with M8 (pg 119)	Southbound Northbound	No access from M8 *(eastbound)* No exit to M8 *(westbound)*
4 (pg 119)	Southbound Northbound	No access. Exit only No exit. Access only
with A77 (pg 119)	Southbound Northbound	Exit only to A77 *(southbound)* Access only from A77 *(northbound)*

M80 STEPPS BYPASS

Junction		
3 (pg 130)	Northeastbound Southwestbound	No access. Exit only No exit. Access only

M80 BONNYBRIDGE–STIRLING

Junction		
5 (pg 130)	Northbound	No access. Exit only to M876 *(northeastbound)*
	Southbound	No exit. Access only from M876 *(southwestbound)*

M90 FORTH ROAD BRIDGE–PERTH

Junction		
2A (pg 131)	Northbound	No access. Exit only to A92 *(eastbound)*
	Southbound	No exit. Access only from A92 *(westbound)*
7 (pg 131)	Northbound Southbound	No exit. Access only from A91 No access. Exit only to A911
8 (pg 131)	Northbound Southbound	No access. Exit only to A91 No exit. Access only from A91
10 (pg 140)	Northbound	No access from A912. No exit to A912 *(southbound)*
	Southbound	No access from A912 *(northbound)*. No exit to A912

M180 SOUTH HUMBERSIDE

Junction		
1 (pg 84)	Eastbound Westbound	No access. Exit only to A18 No exit. Access only from A18

M606 BRADFORD SPUR

Junction		
2 (pg 90)	Northbound Southbound	No access. Exit only No restriction

M621 LEEDS–M1

Junction		
2A (pg 90)	Eastbound Westbound	No exit. Access only No access. Exit only
4 (pg 90)	Southeastbound Northwestbound	No access. Exit only No restriction
5 (pg 90)	Southeastbound Northwestbound	No exit. Access only No access. Exit only
6 (pg 90)	Southeastbound Northwestbound	No access. Exit only No exit. Access only
with M1 (jct 43) (pg 90)	Southbound Northbound	Exit only to M1 *(southbound)* Access only from M1 *(northbound)*

M876 BONNYBRIDGE–KINCARDINE BRIDGE

Junction		
with M80 (jct 5) (pg 130)	Northeastbound Southwestbound	Access only from M80 *(northbound)* Exit only to M80 *(southbound)*
2 (pg 131)	Northeastbound Southwestbound	No access. Exit only to A9 No exit. Access only from A9
with M9 (jct 8) (pg 131)	Northeastbound Southwestbound	Exit only to M9 *(eastbound)* Access only from M9 (westbound)

A1(M) SOUTH MIMMS–BALDOCK

Junction		
2 (pg 50)	Northbound Southbound	No access. Exit only to A1001 No exit. Access only from A1001
3 (pg 50)	Northbound Southbound	No restriction No access. Exit only to A414
5 (pg 50)	Northbound Southbound	No exit. Access only No access or exit

A1(M) ALCONBURY–PETERBOROUGH

Junction		
14 (pg 61)		Staggered junction; follow signs
	Northbound Southbound	No restriction No restriction
15 (pg 61)		Staggered junction; follow signs
	Northbound Southbound	No restriction No restriction

A1(M) EAST OF LEEDS

Junction		
44 (pg 90)	Northbound Southbound	Access only from M1 *(northbound)* Exit only to M1 *(southbound)*

A1(M) SCOTCH CORNER–TYNESIDE

Junction		
57 (with A66(M)) (pg 106)	Northbound	No access. Exit only to A66(M) *(eastbound)*
	Southbound	No exit. Access only from A66(M) *(westbound)*
65 (with A194(M)) (pg 114)	Northbound	No access. Exit only to A194(M) & A1 *(northbound)*
	Southbound	No exit. Access only from Access only from A194(M) *(southbound)*

A3(M) HORNDEAN–HAVANT

Junction		
1 (pg 15)	Southbound Northbound	No access. Exit only to A3 No exit. Access only from A3
4 (pg 15)	Southbound Northbound	No exit. Access only No access. Exit only

A48(M) CARDIFF SPUR

Junction		
29 (with M4) (pg 37)	Westbound Eastbound	Access only from M4 *(westbound)* Exit only to M4 *(eastbound)*
29A (pg 37)	Westbound Eastbound	Exit only to A48 *(westbound)* Access only from A48 *(eastbound)*

A66(M) DARLINGTON SPUR

Junction		
with A1(M) (jct 57) (pg 106)	Eastbound Westbound	Access only from A1(M) *(northbound)* Exit only to A1(M) *(southbound)*

A194(M) TYNESIDE

Junction		
with A1(M) (jct 65) (pg 114)	Northbound Southbound	Access only from A1(M) *(northbound)* Exit only to A1(M) *(southbound)*

M25 London orbital motorway

Refer also to atlas pages 28–29

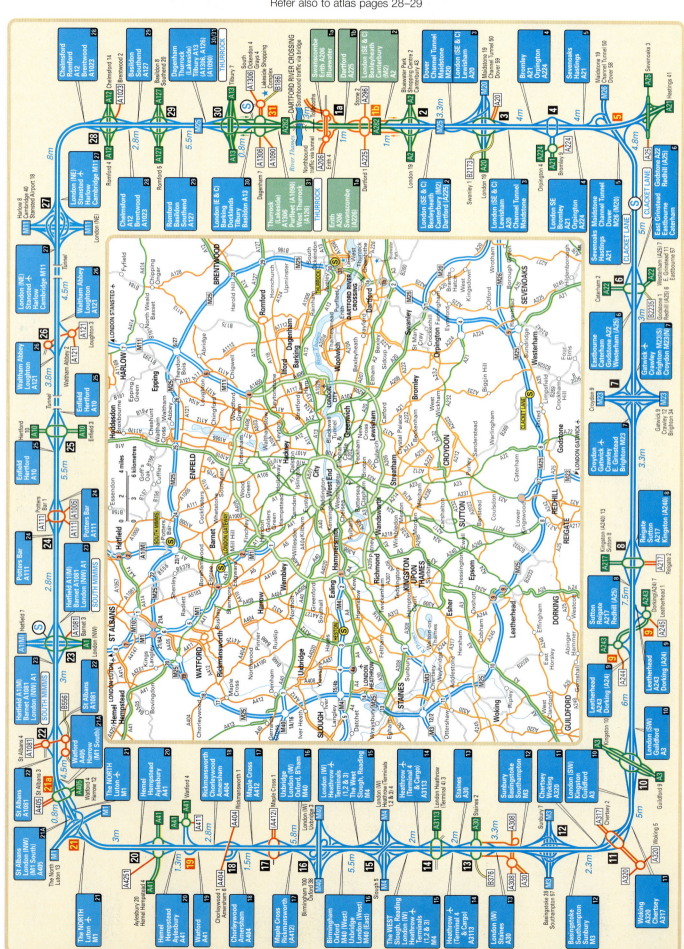

M60 Manchester orbital motorway

Refer also to atlas page 82

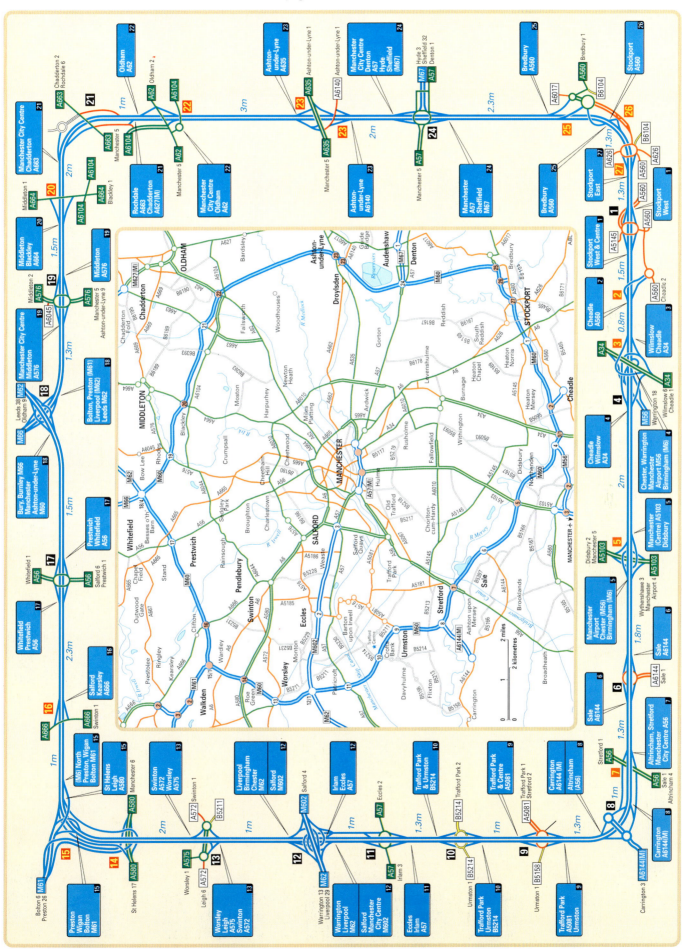

map symbols

Motoring information

Symbol	Description	Symbol	Description	Symbol	Description	Symbol	Description
M4	Motorway with number		Unclassified road single/dual carriageway	St Malo V	Vehicle ferry		AA telephone
11	Motorway junction with and without number		Roundabout		Railway line/in tunnel		Urban area and village
3	Restricted motorway junctions		Interchange/junction		Railway station and level crossing	628	Spot height in metres
S Fleet	Motorway service area		Narrow primary/other A/B road with passing places (Scotland)		Tourist railway	348 Rannoch Moor	Pass
	Motorway and junction under construction		Road under construction		Airport		River, canal, lake
A3	Primary route single/dual carriageway		Road tunnel	H	Heliport		Sandy beach
S Grantham North	Primary route service area		Steep gradient (arrows point downhill)	F	International freight terminal		County/County Borough/Council Area boundary
BATH	Primary route destination	Toll	Road toll	★	Major shopping centre		National boundary
A1123	Other A road single/dual carriageway	5	Distance in miles between symbols	P+R	Park and Ride location (at least 6 days)	23	Page overlap and number
B2070	B road single/dual carriageway						

Tourist information

Places of interest are also shown on town plans. See pages 175–234

Ireland (see pages 170–173) For tourist information see opposite page

Central London (see pages 240–250)

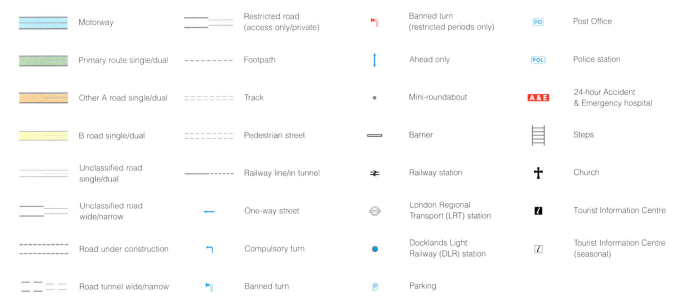

Royal Parks (opening and closing times for traffic)
Green Park   Constitution Hill: closed Sundays, 08.00–dusk
Hyde Park   Open 05.00–midnight
Regent's Park   Open 05.00–midnight
St James's Park   The Mall: closed Sundays, 08.00–dusk

Traffic regulations in the City of London include security checkpoints and restrict the number of entry and exit points.

Note: Oxford Street is closed to through-traffic (except buses & taxis) 07.00–19.00, Monday–Saturday. Restricted parts of Frith Street/Old Compton Street are closed to vehicles 12.00–01.00 daily.

District maps (see pages 258–269) For tourist information see opposite page

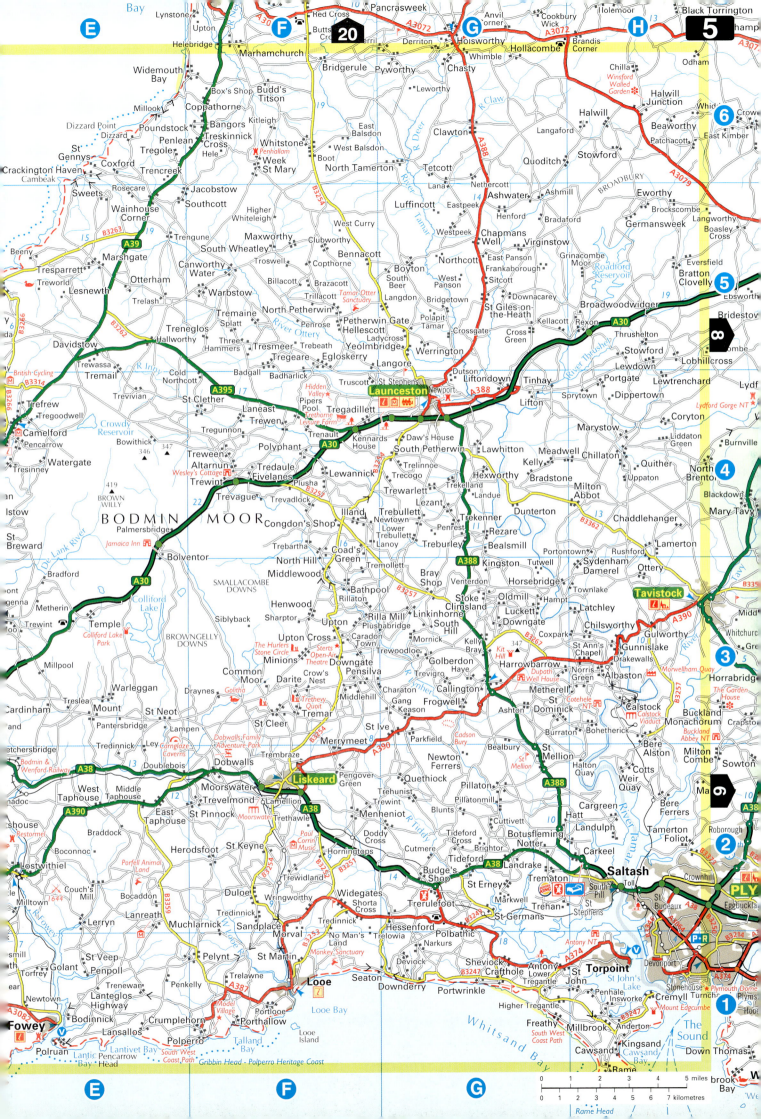

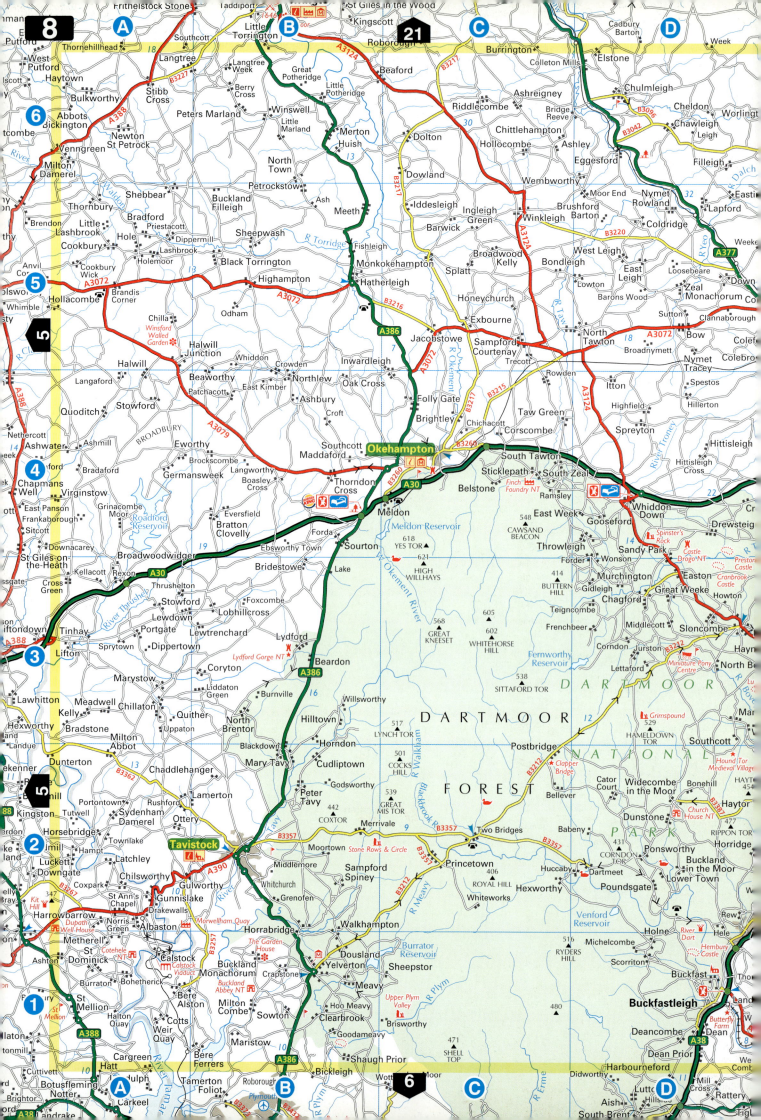

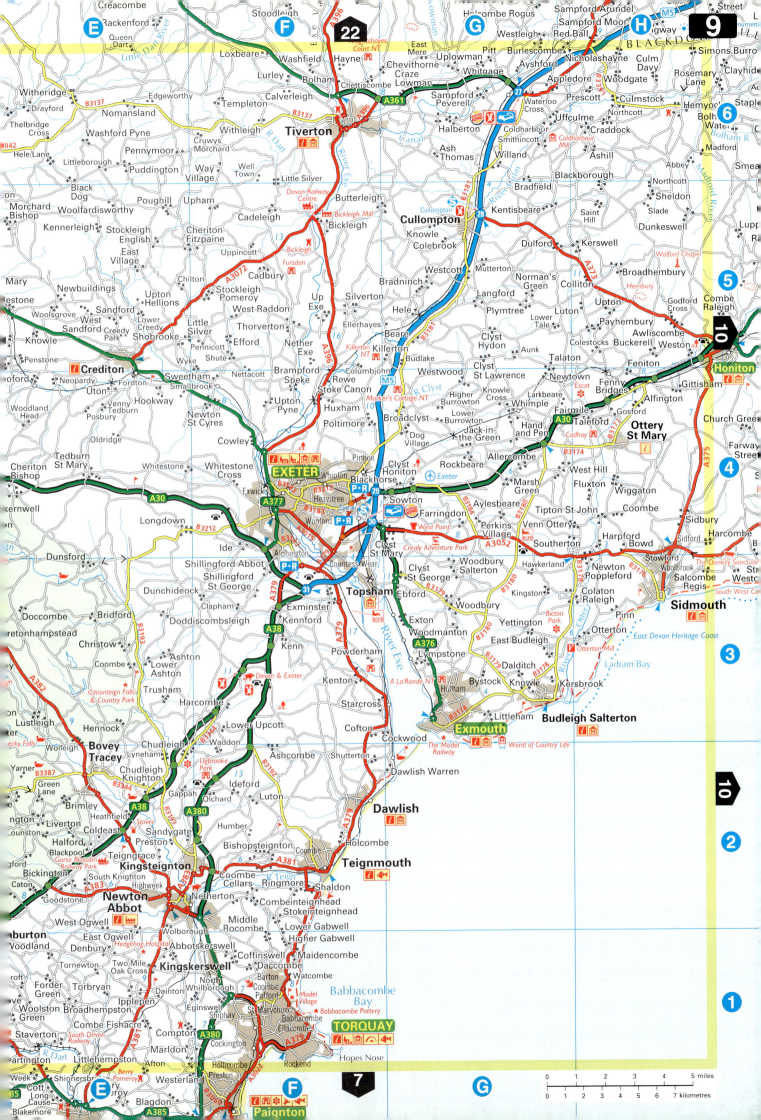

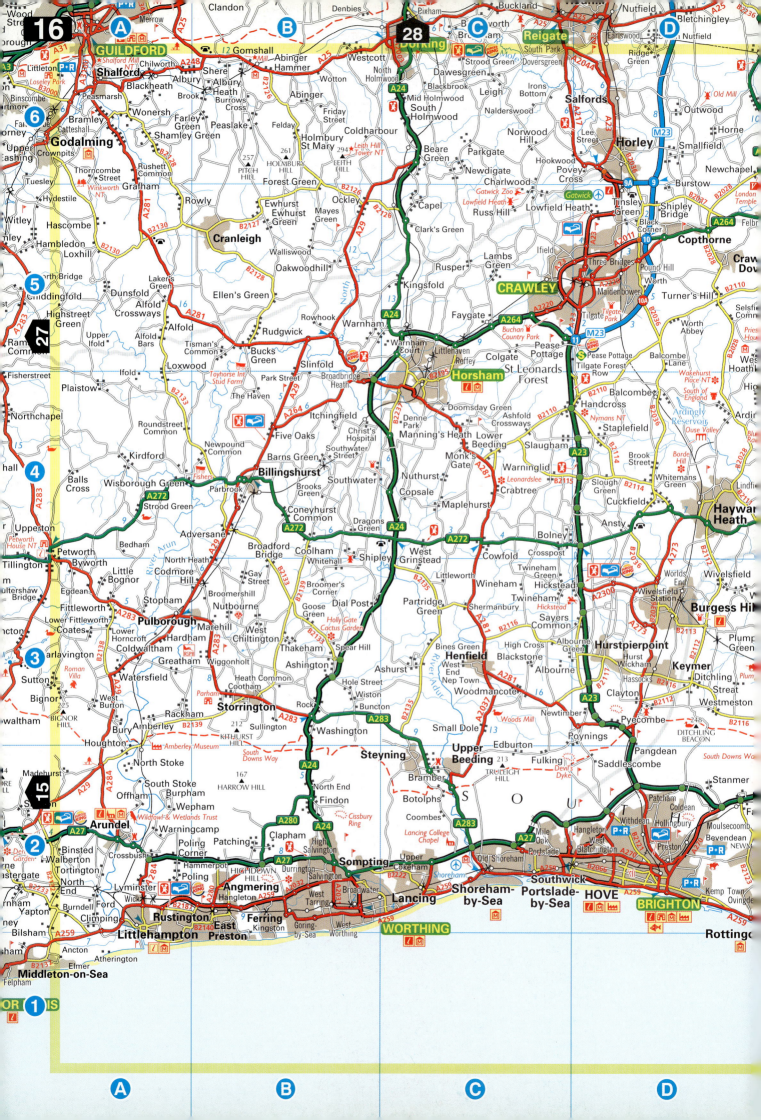

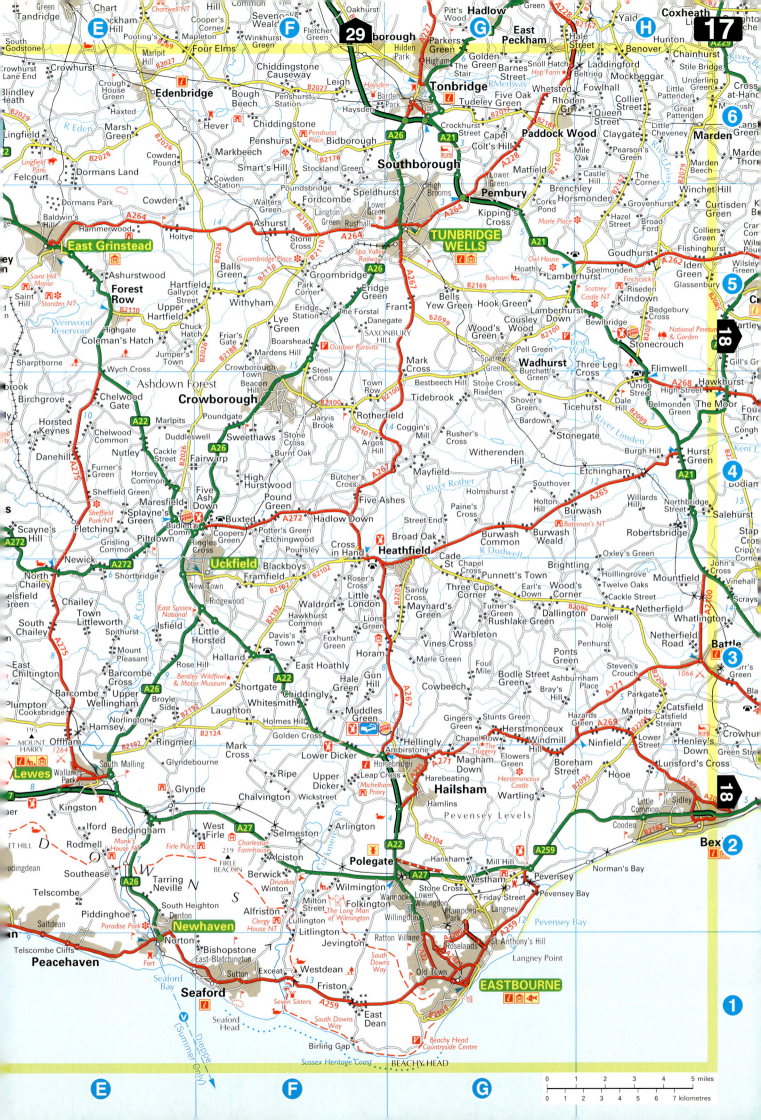

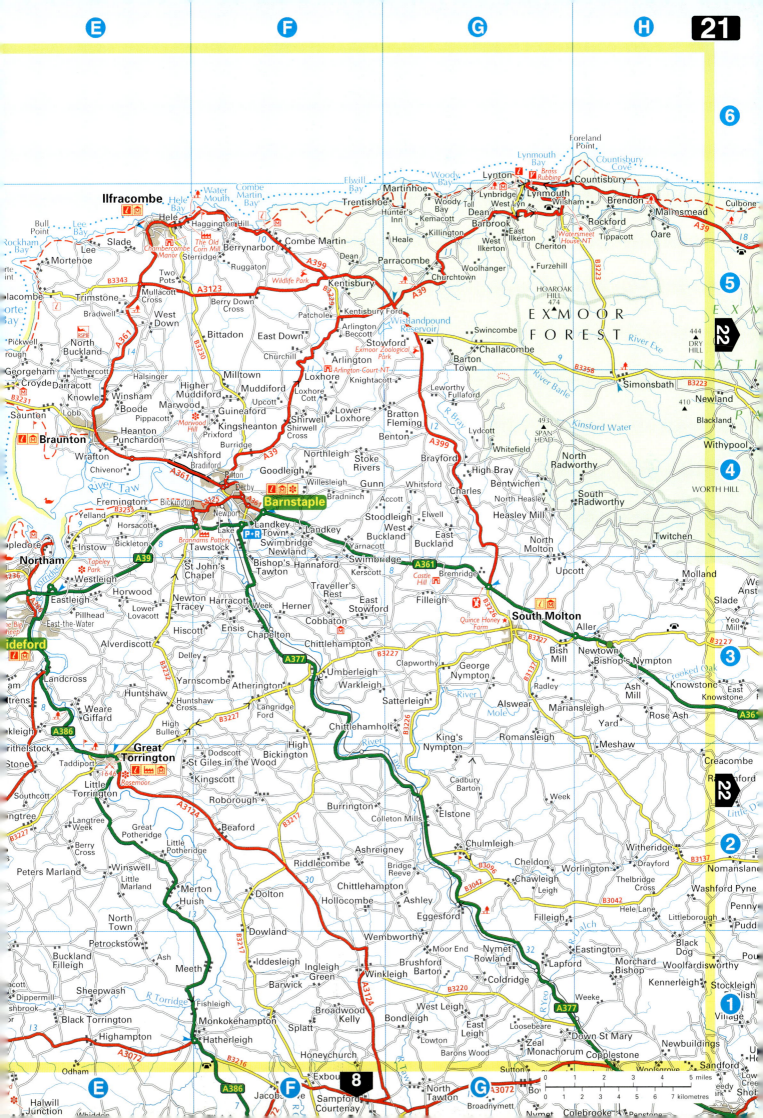

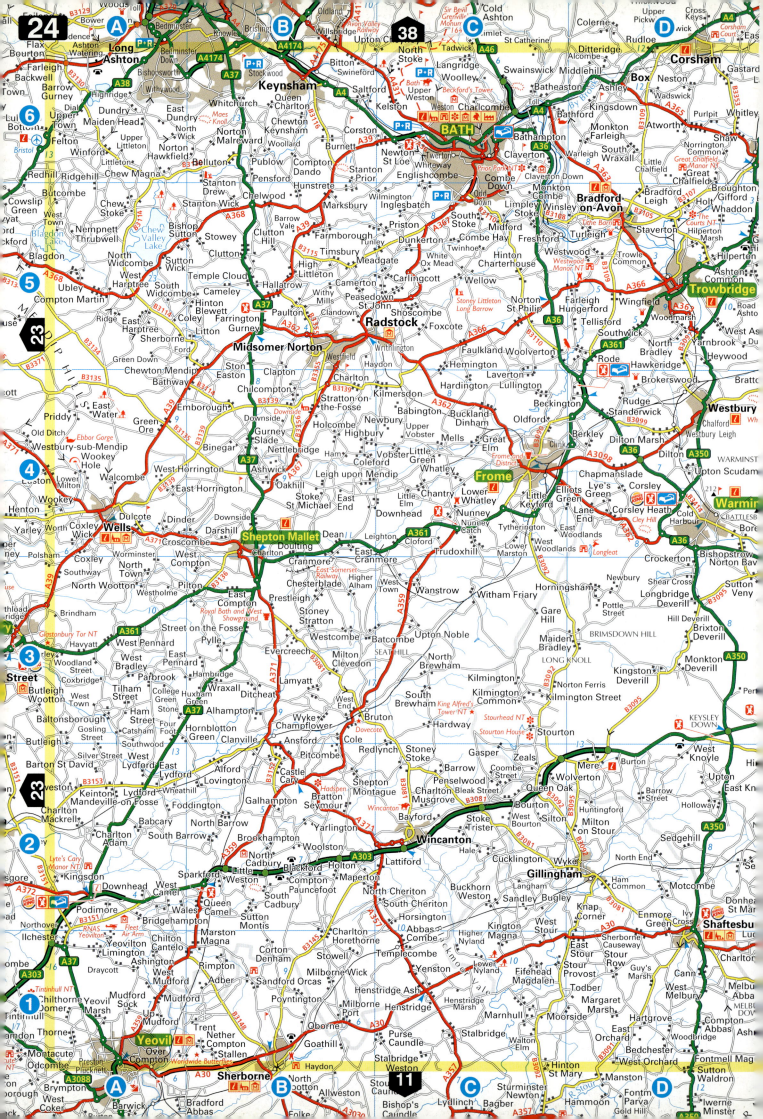

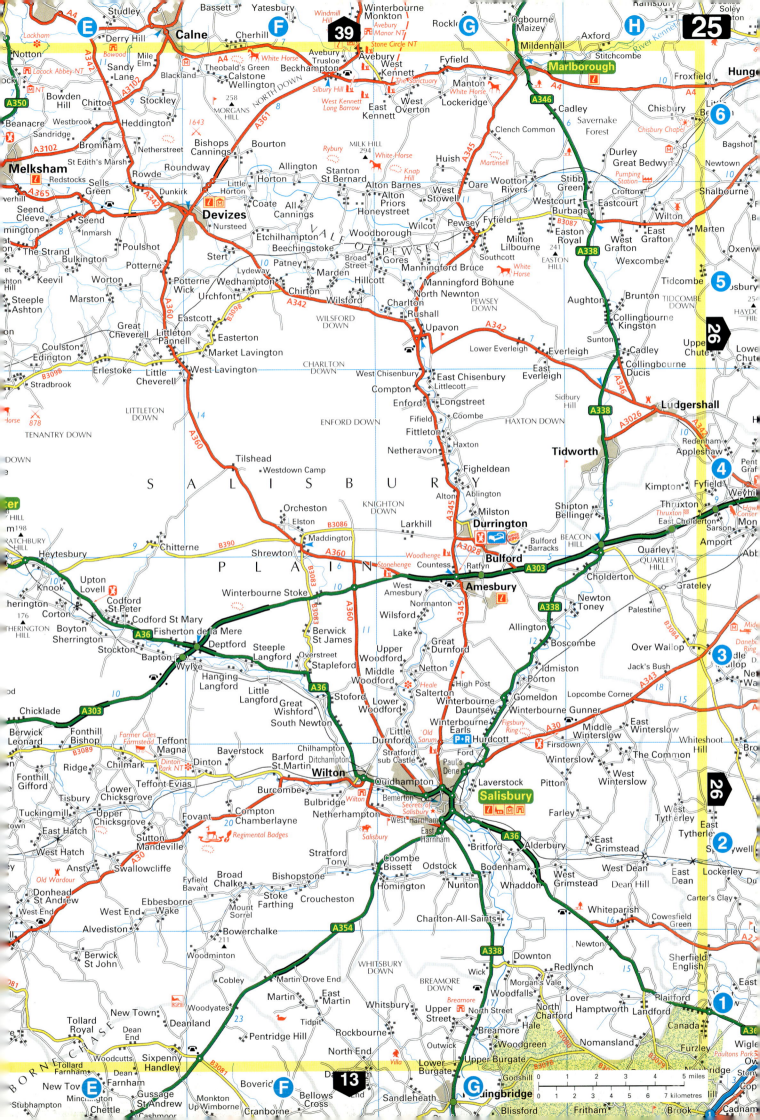

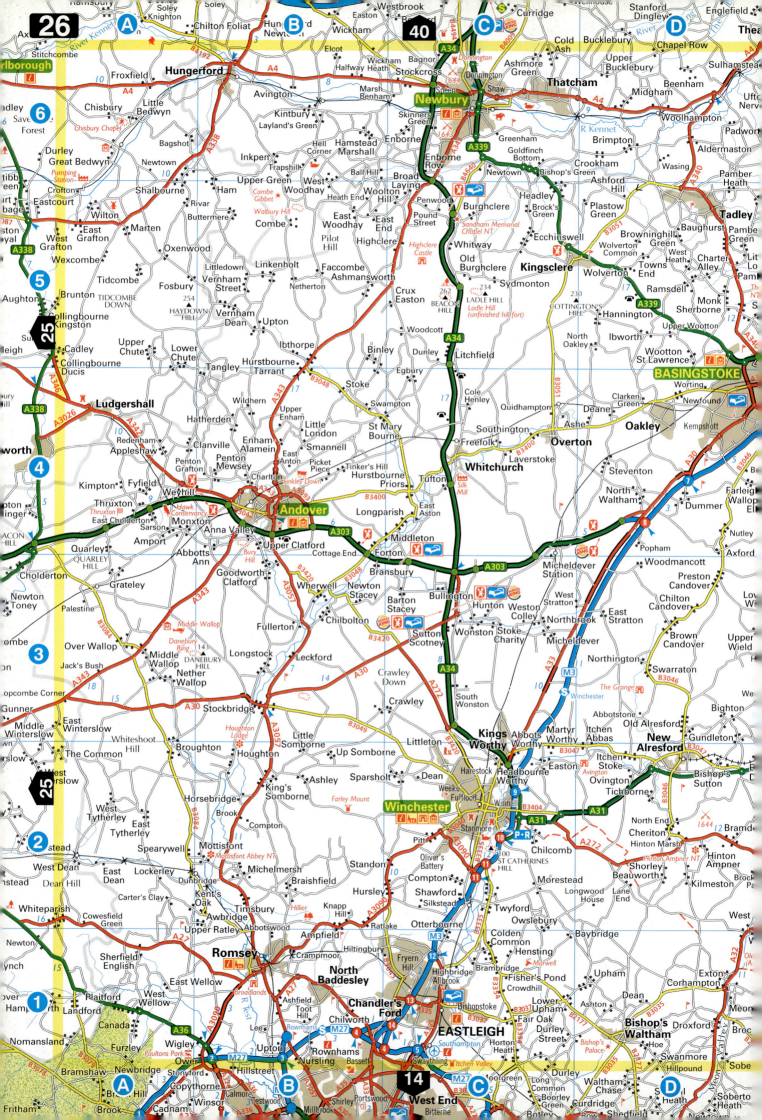

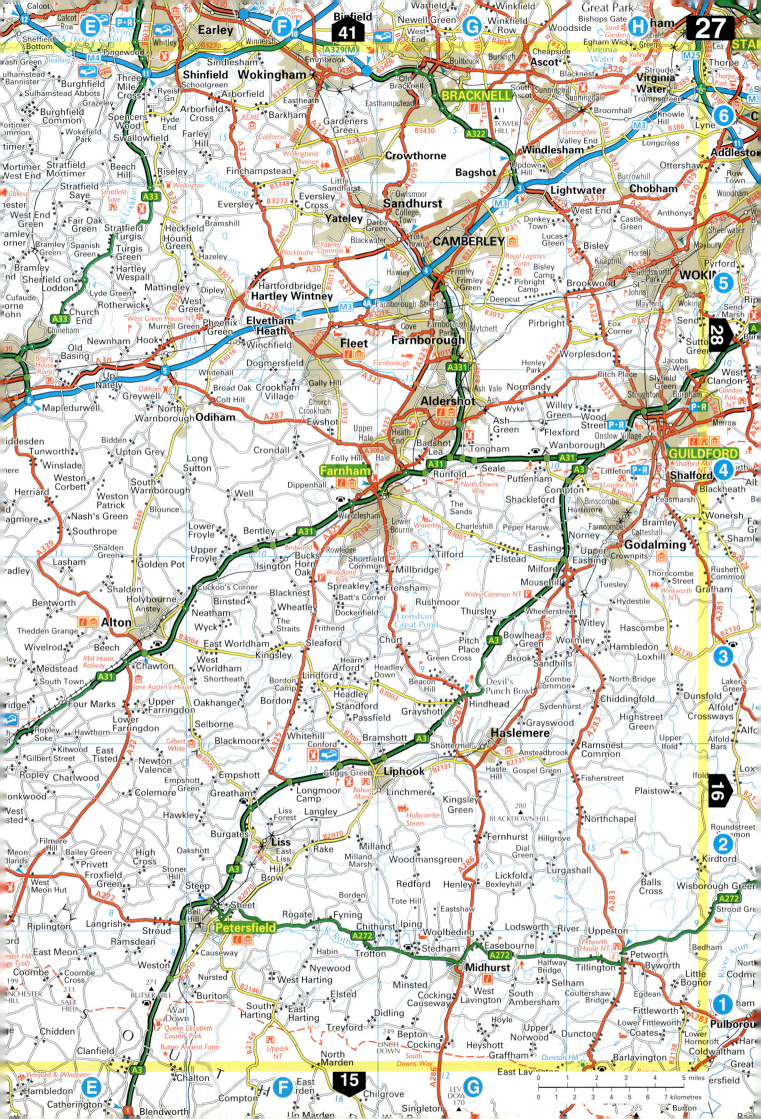

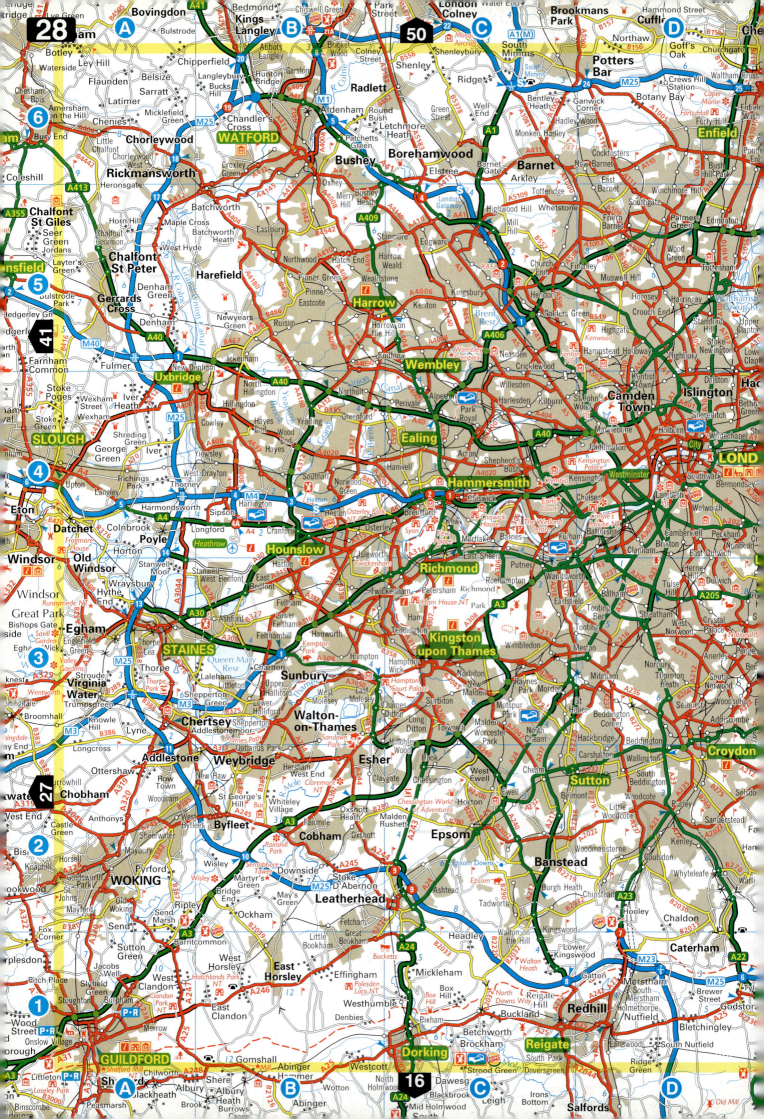

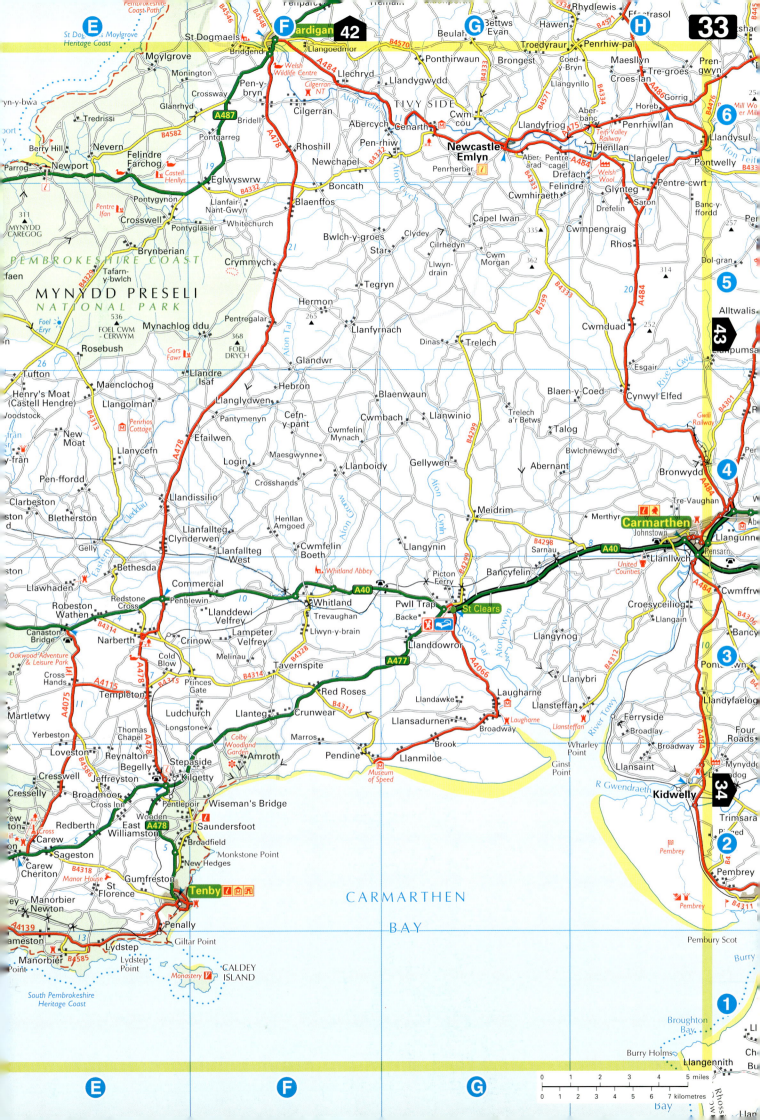

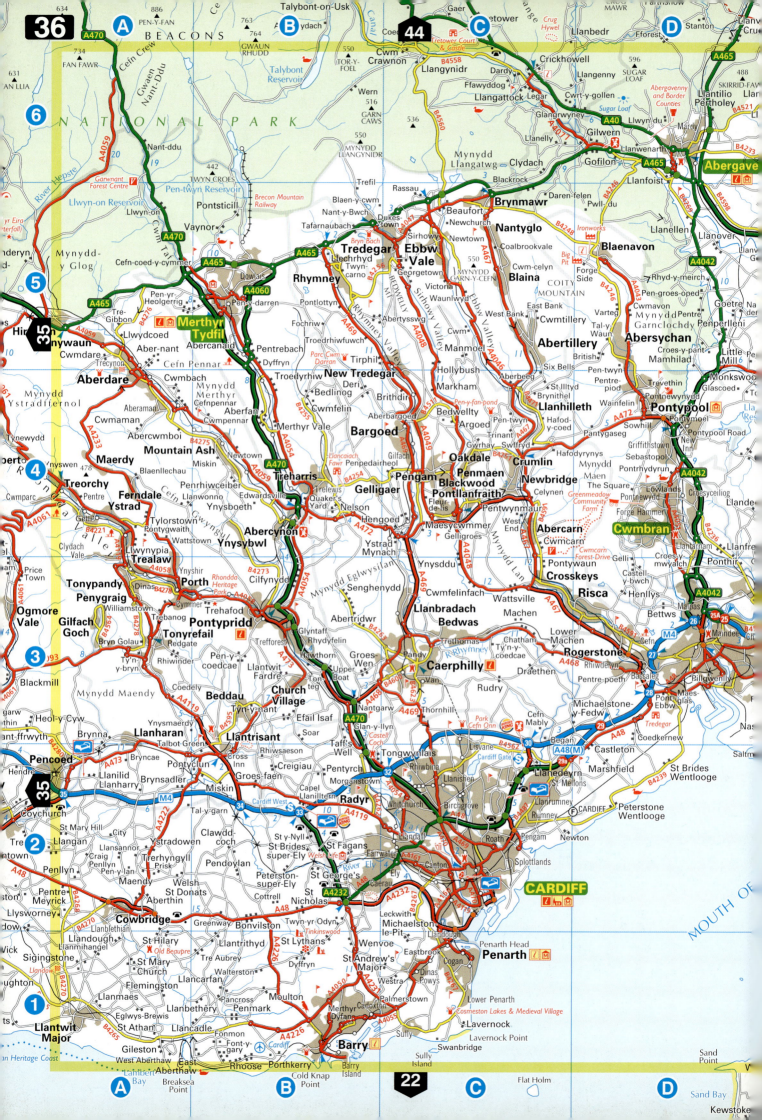

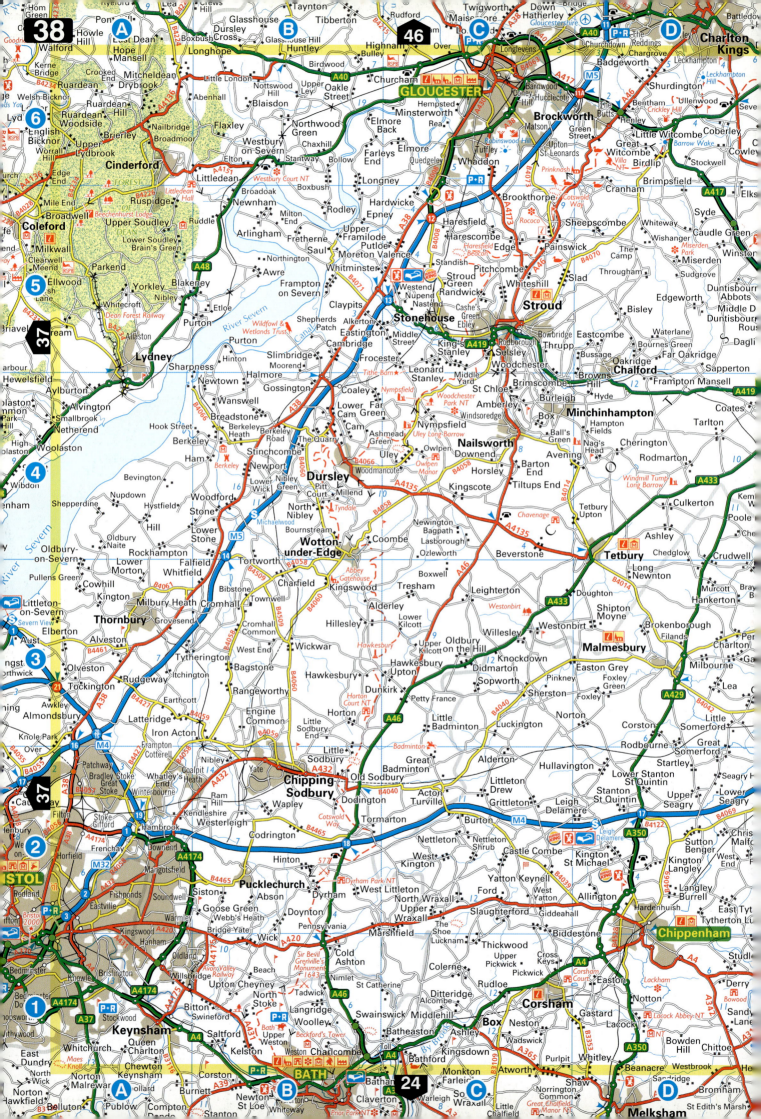

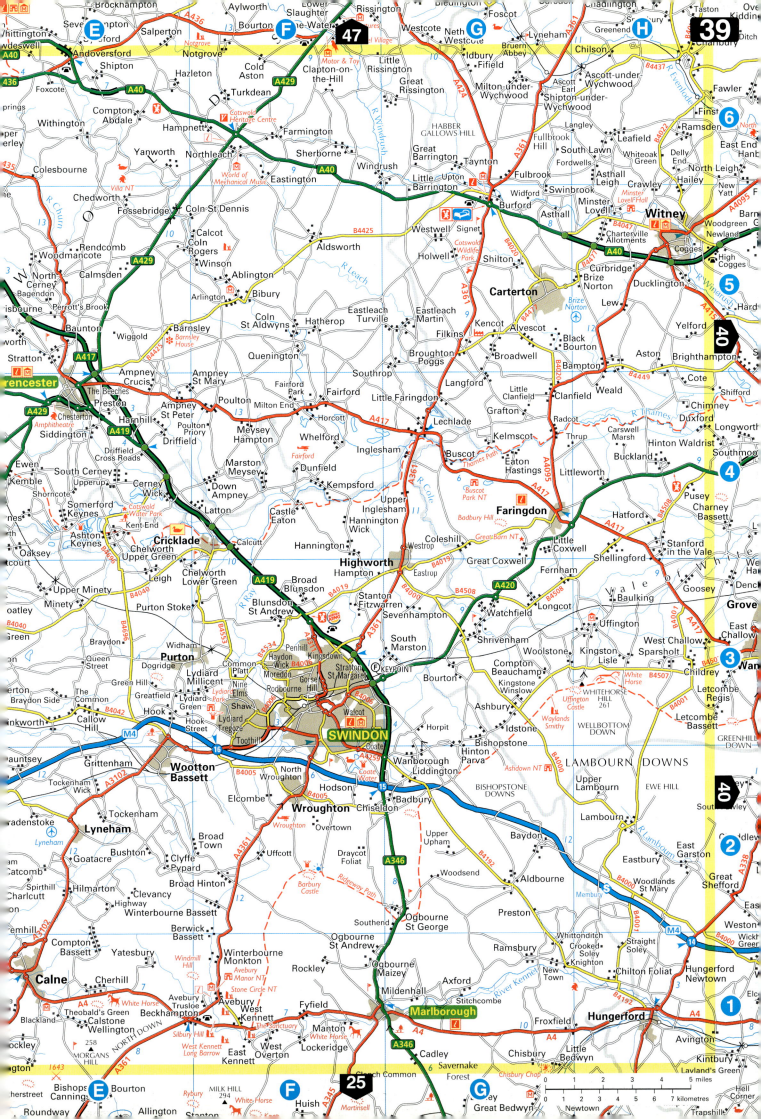

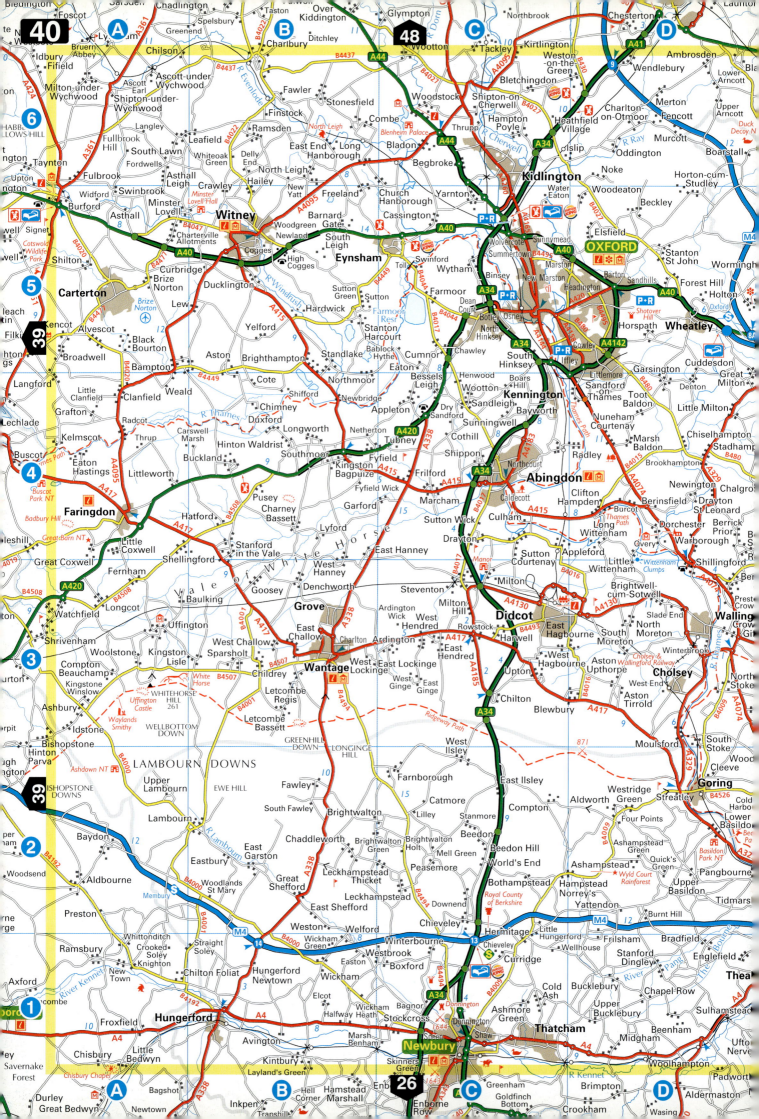

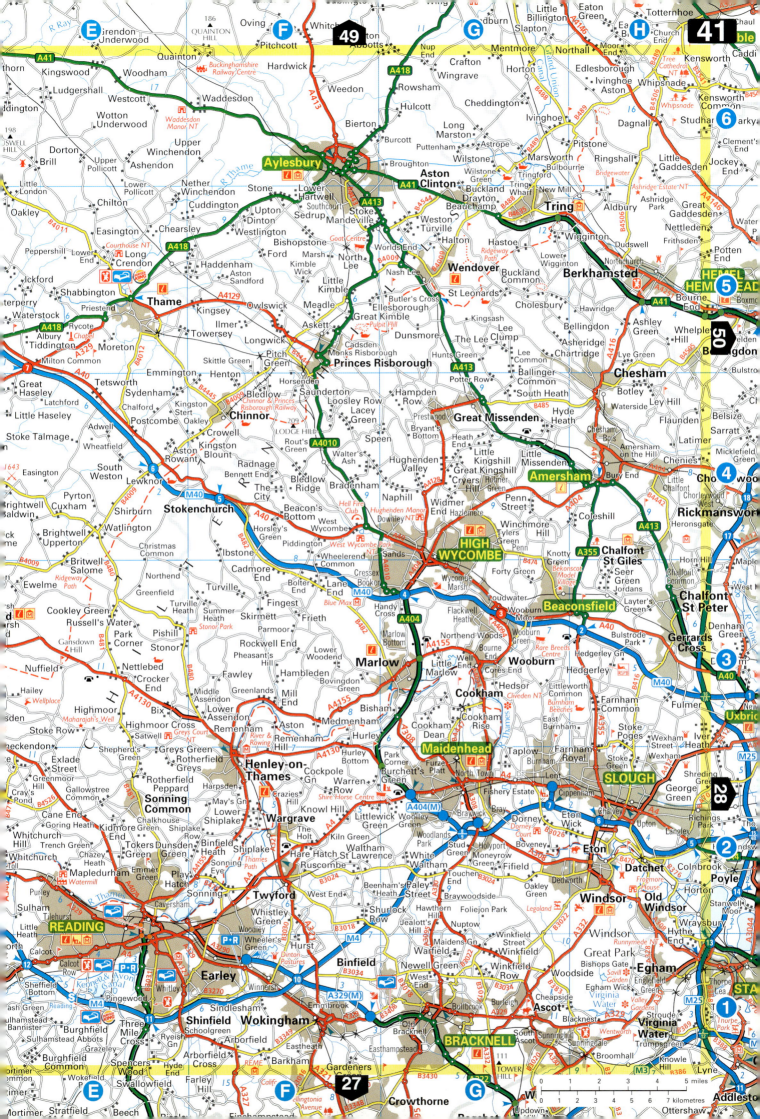

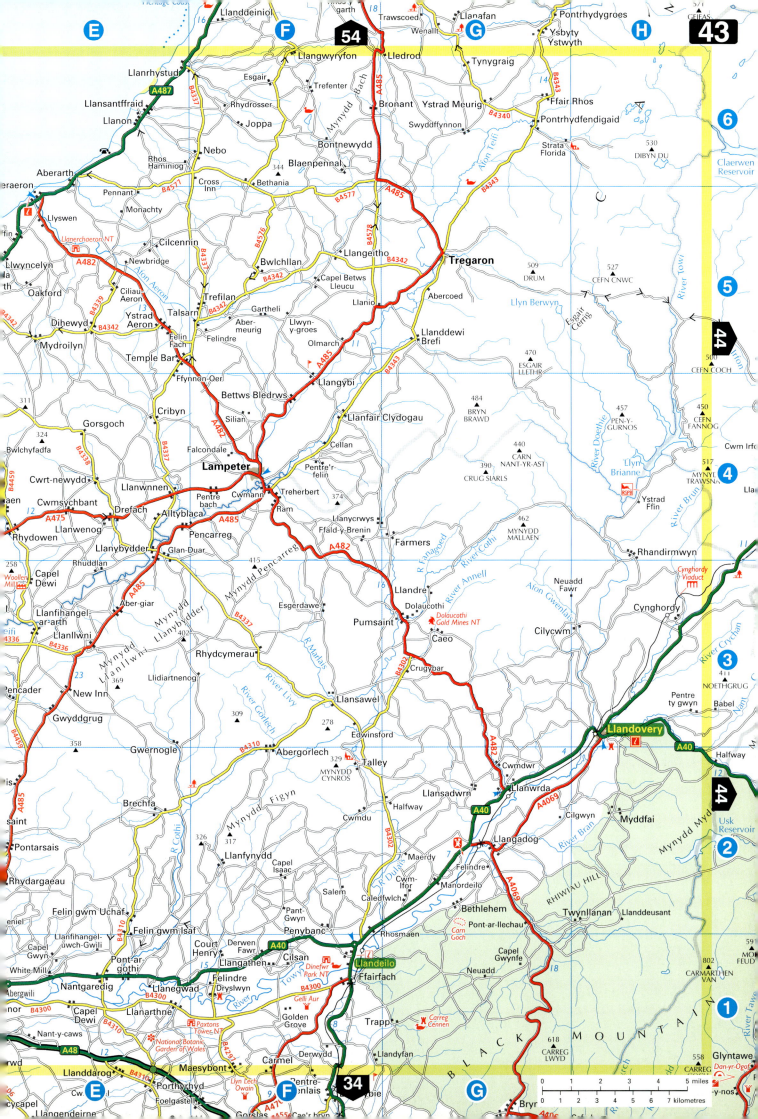

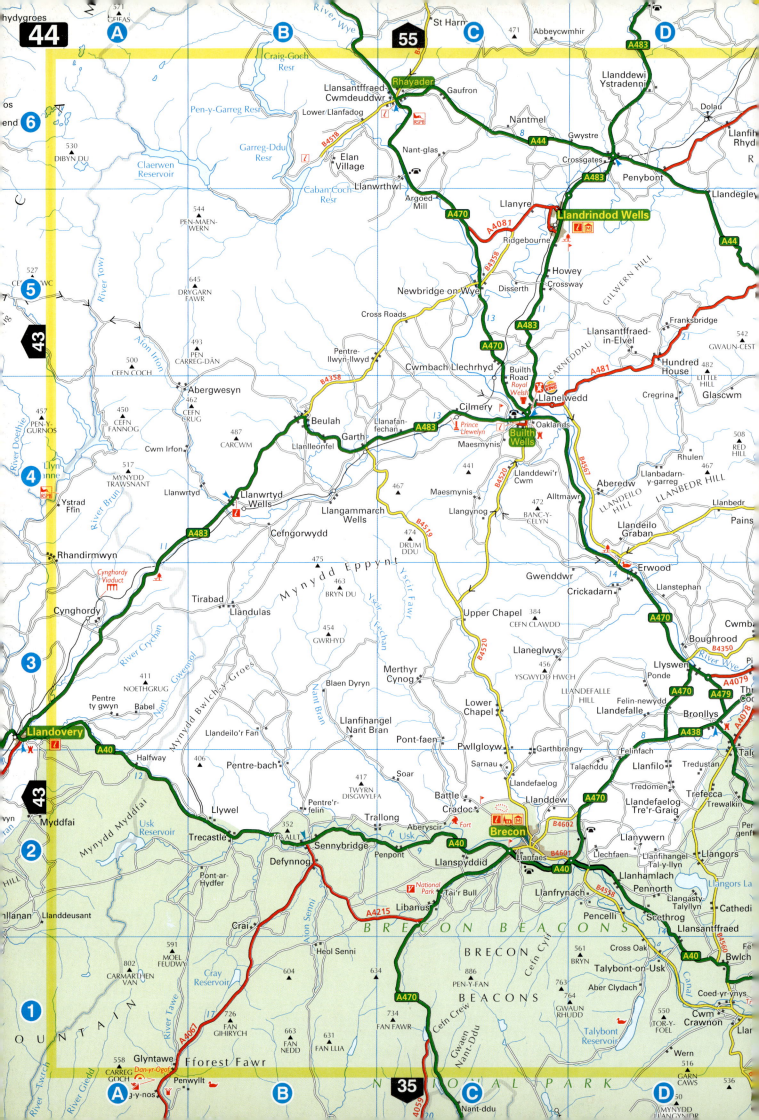

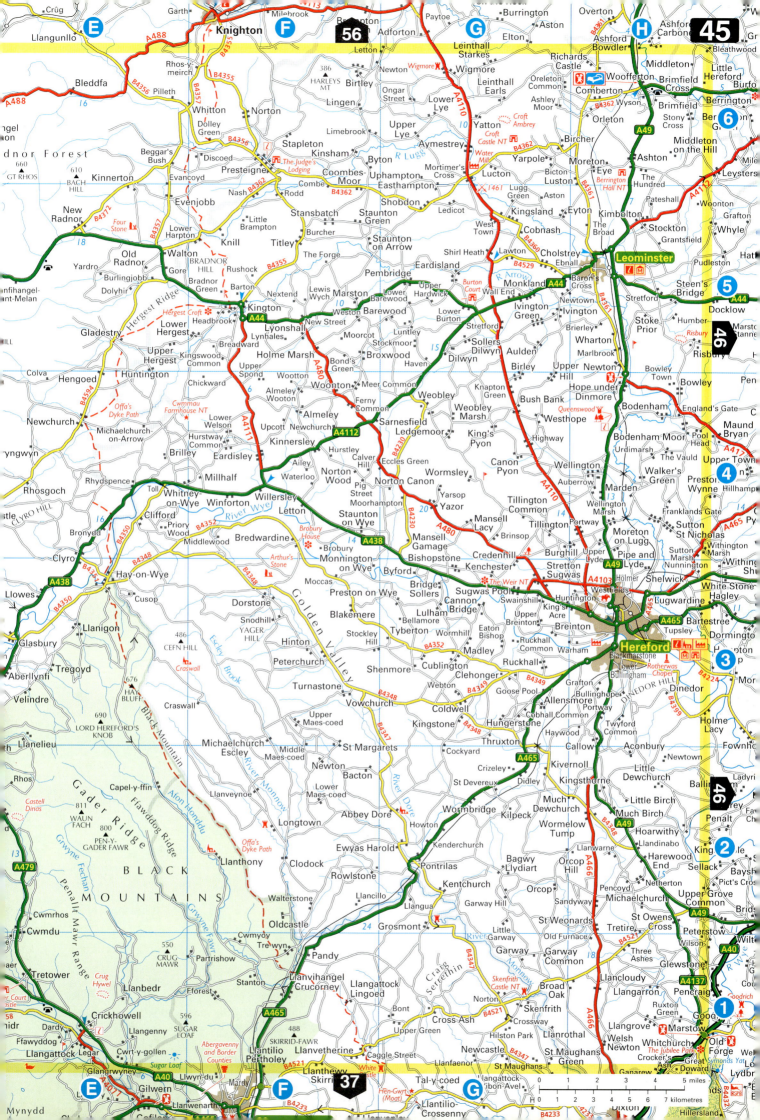

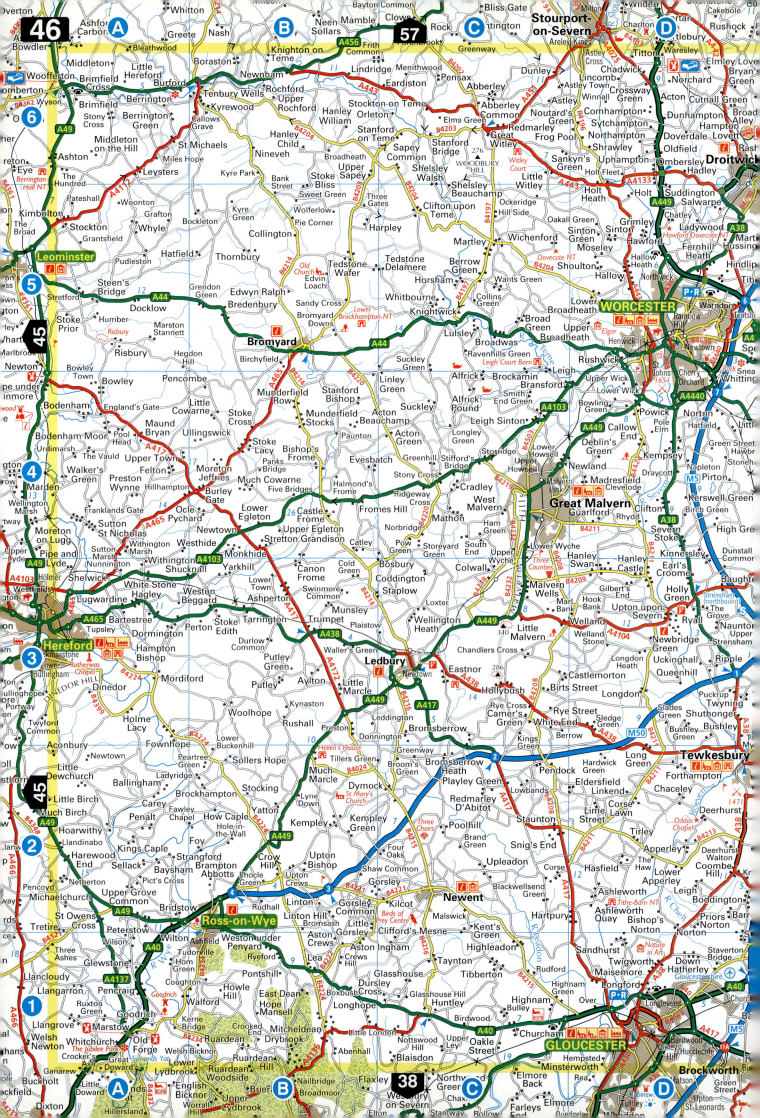

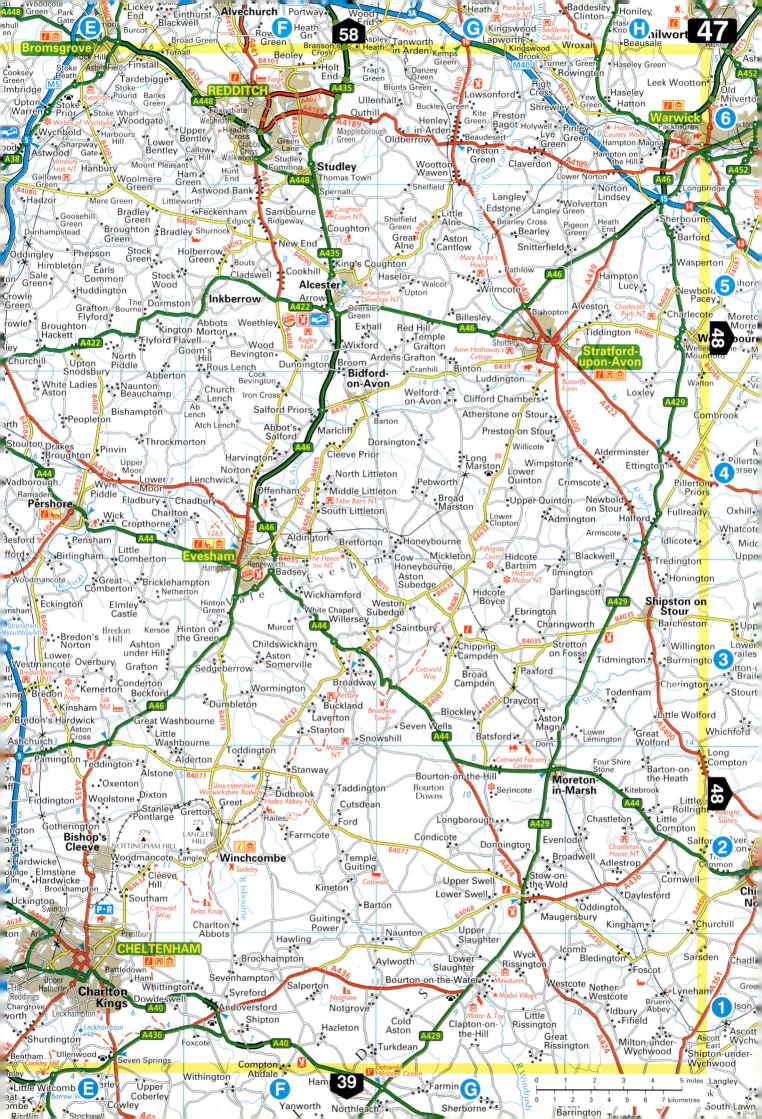

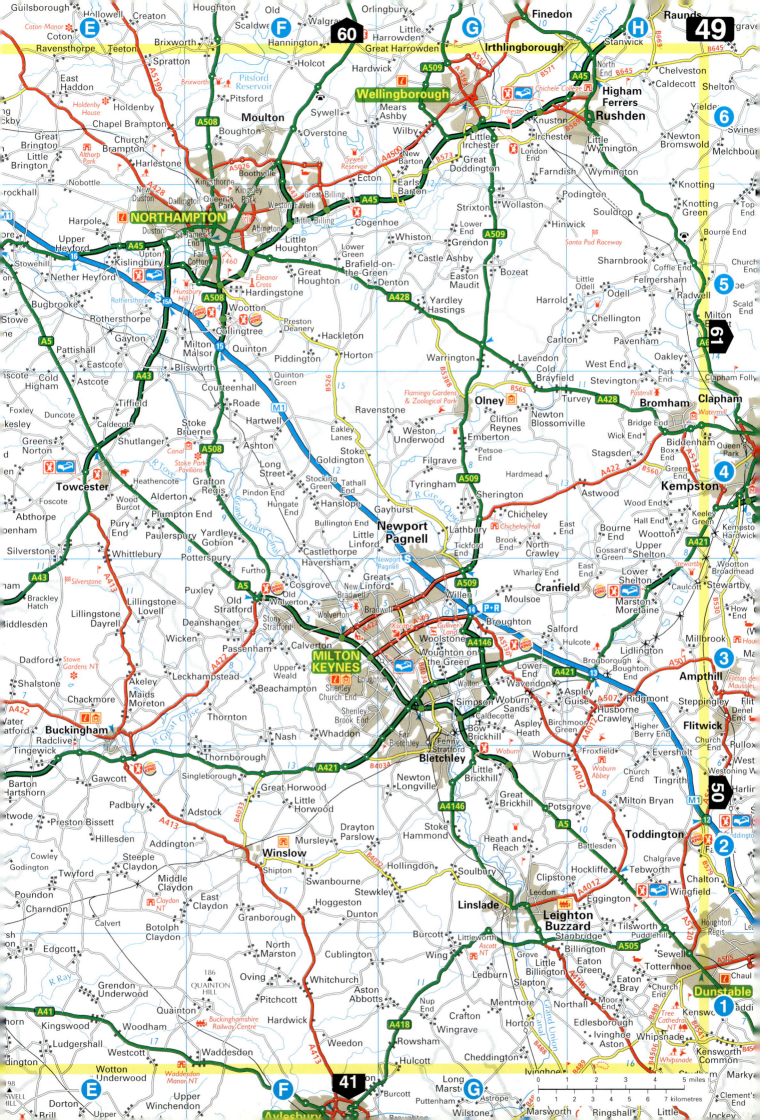

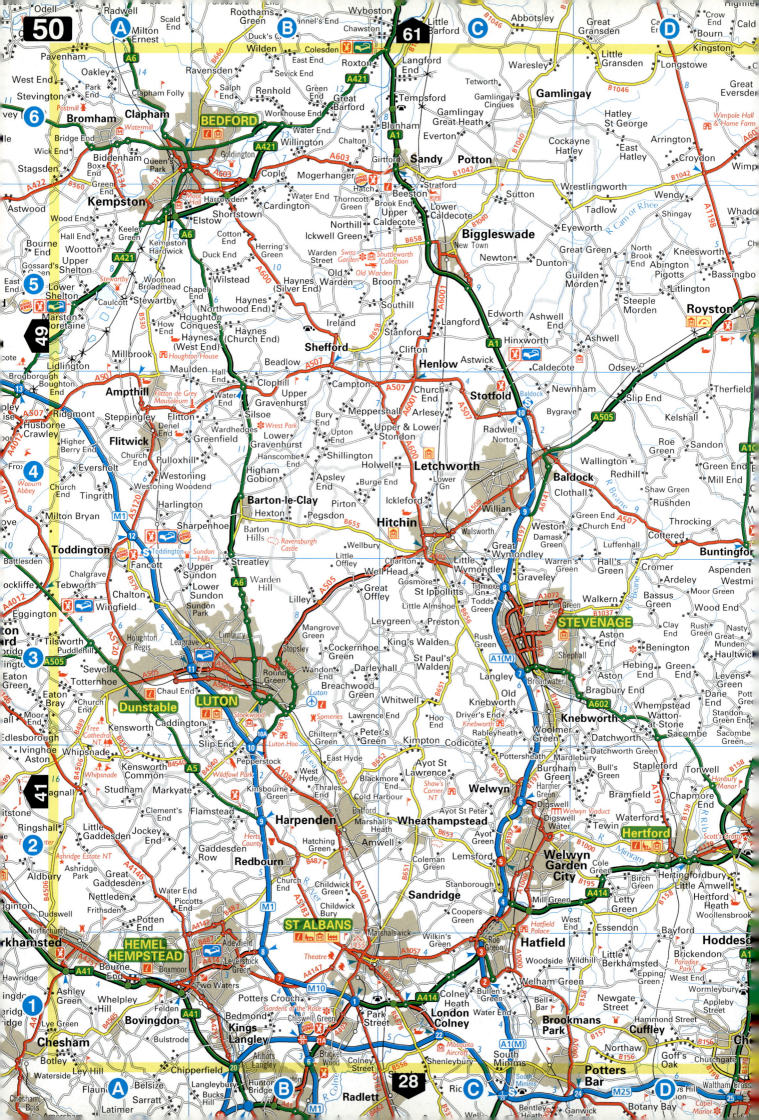

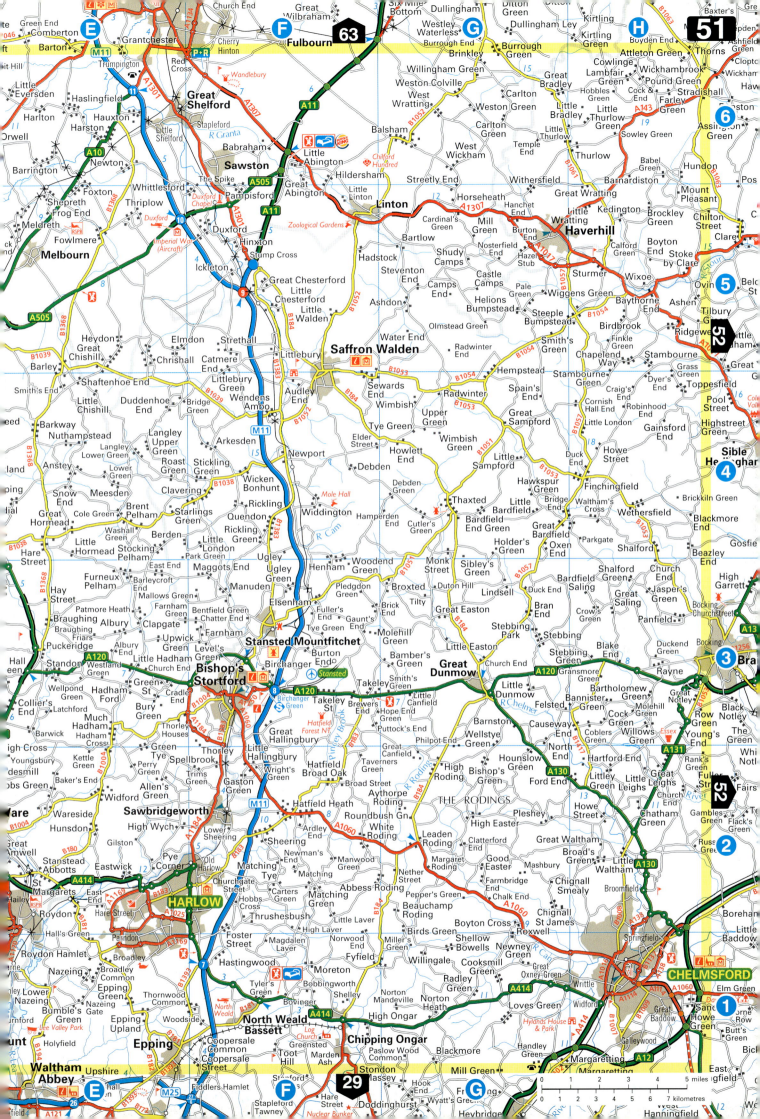

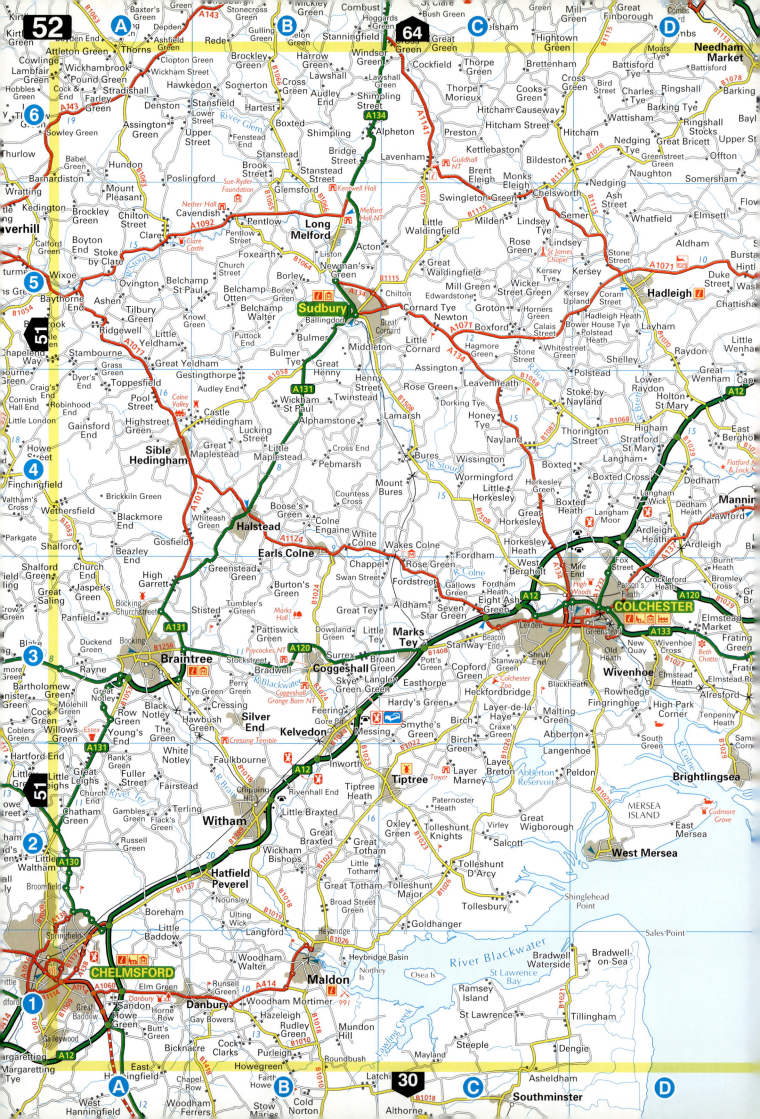

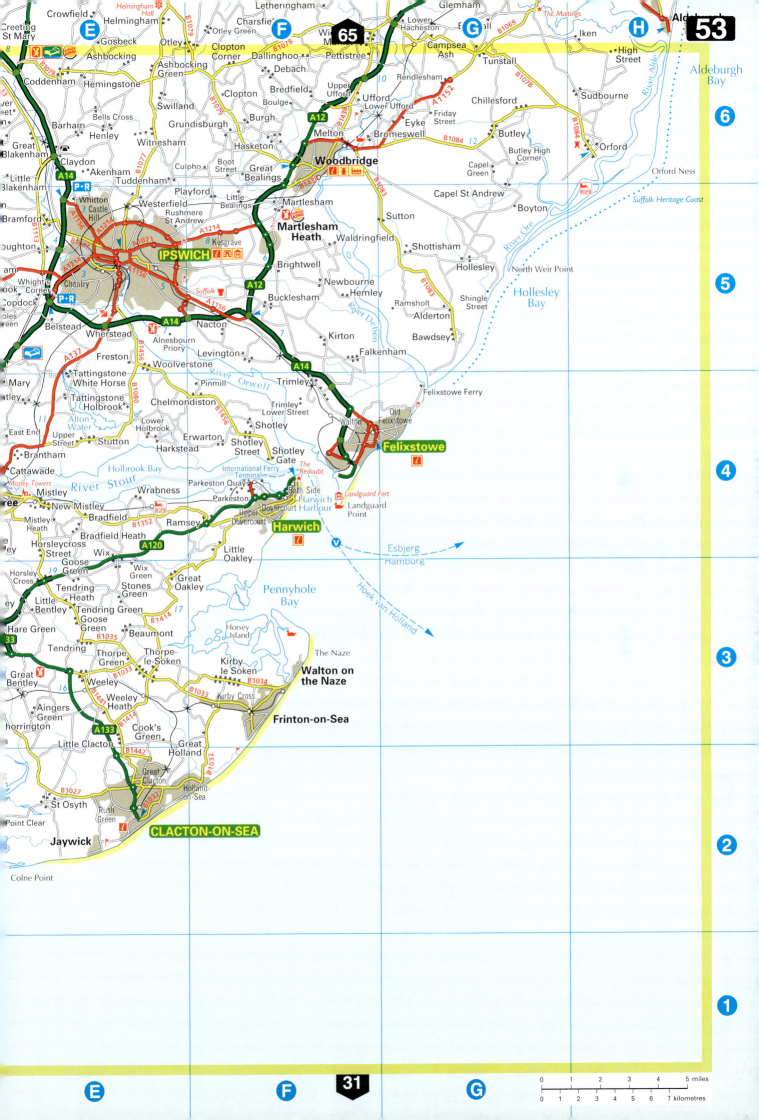

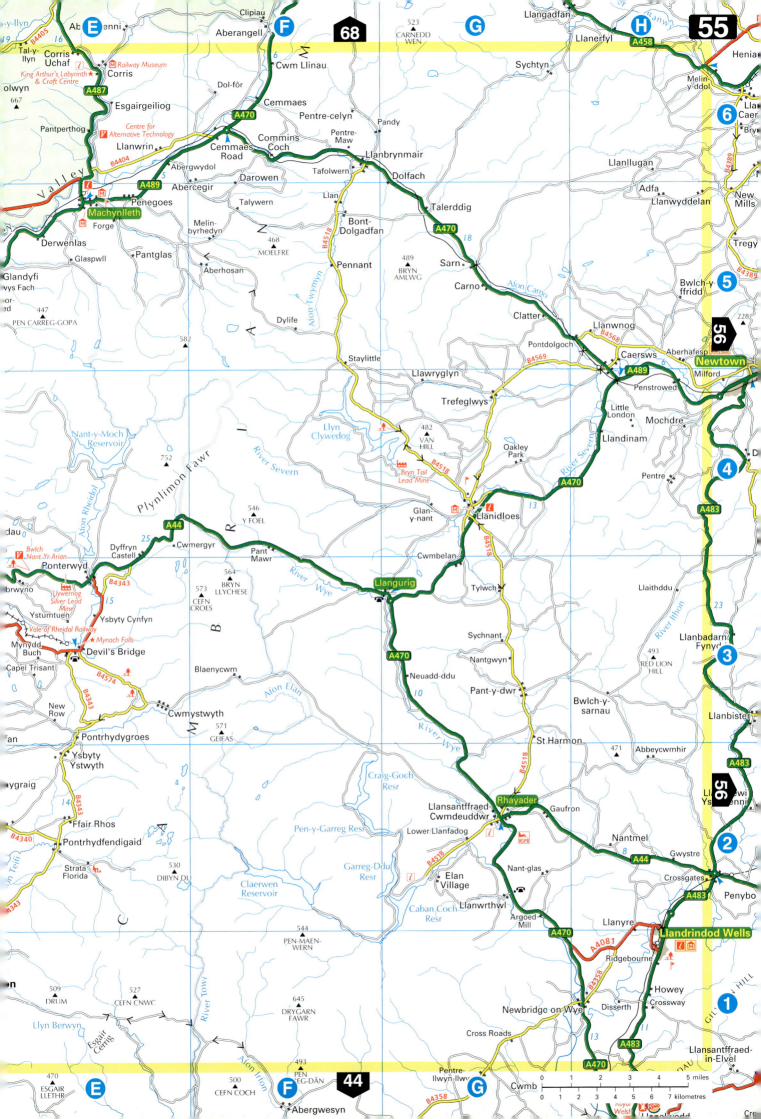

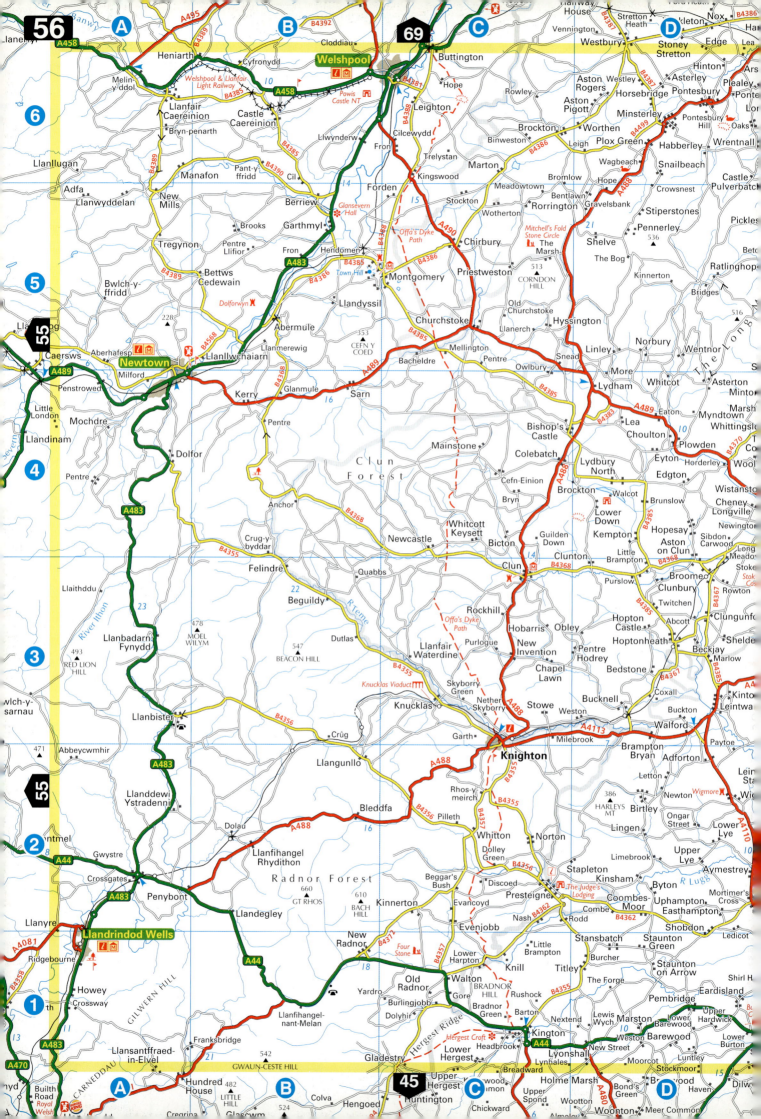

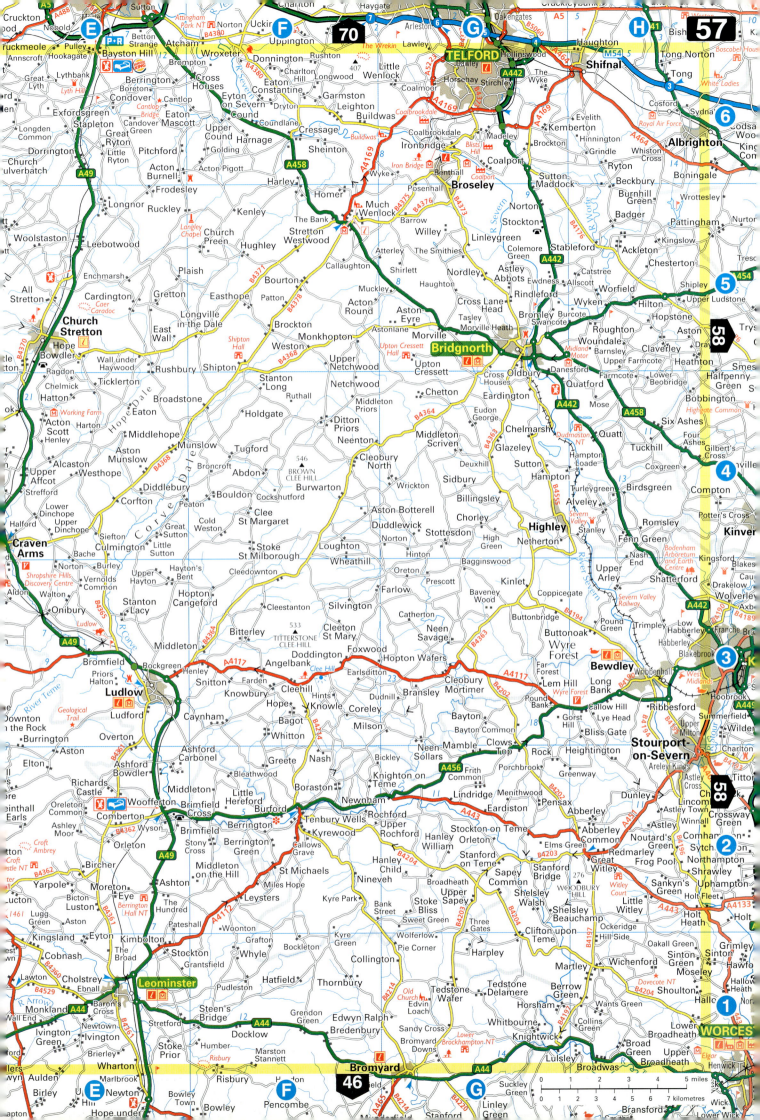

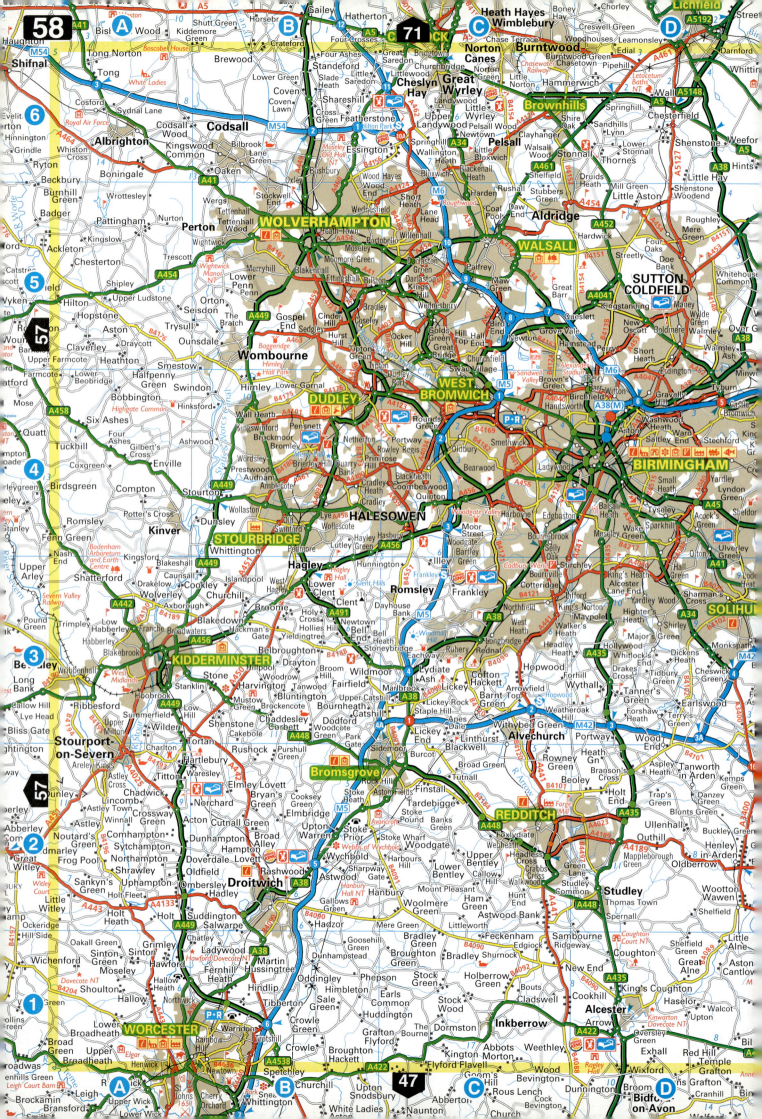

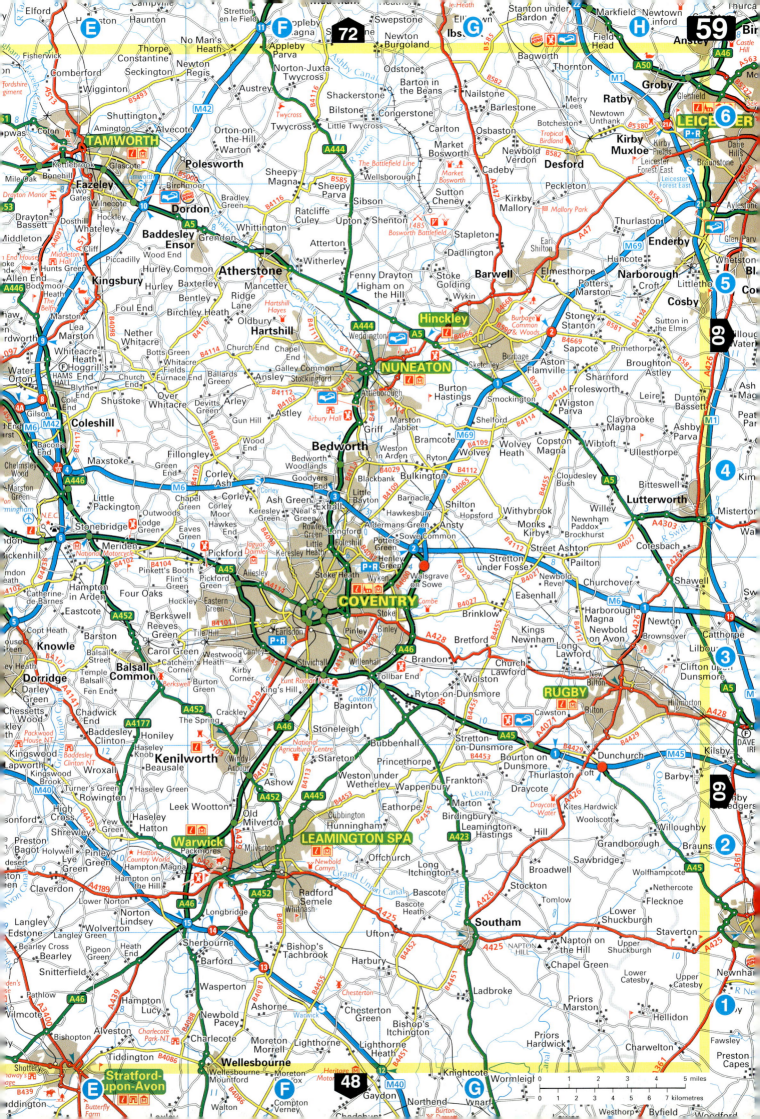

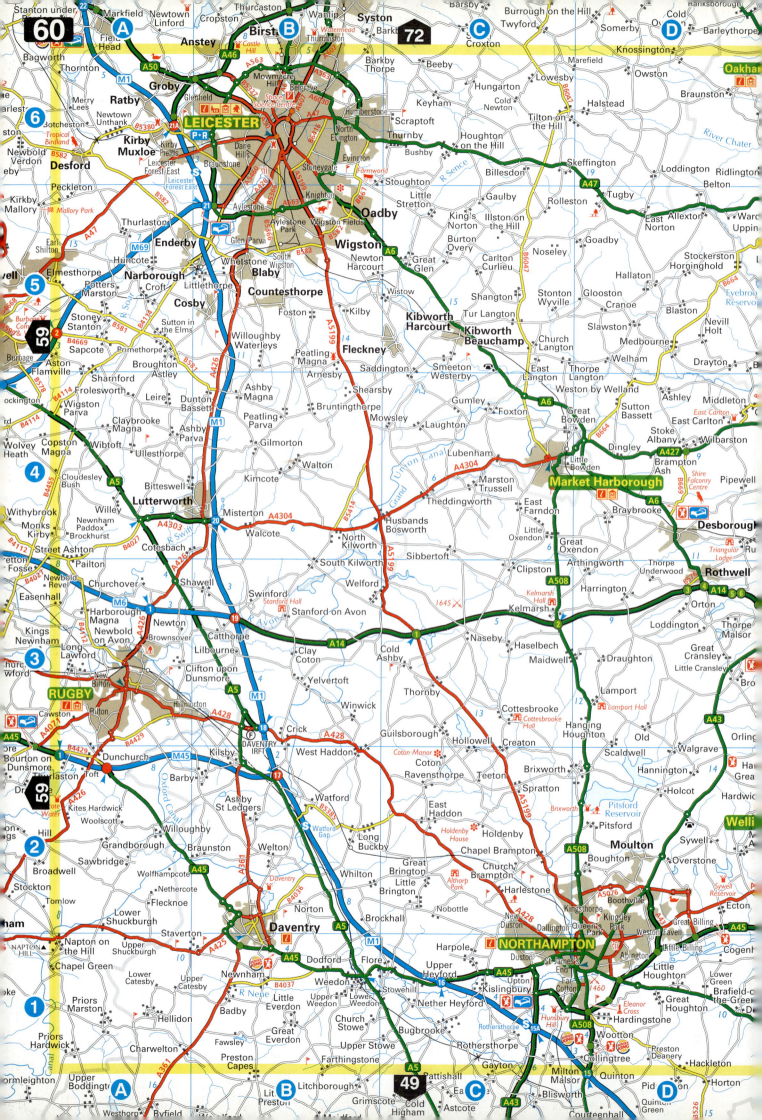

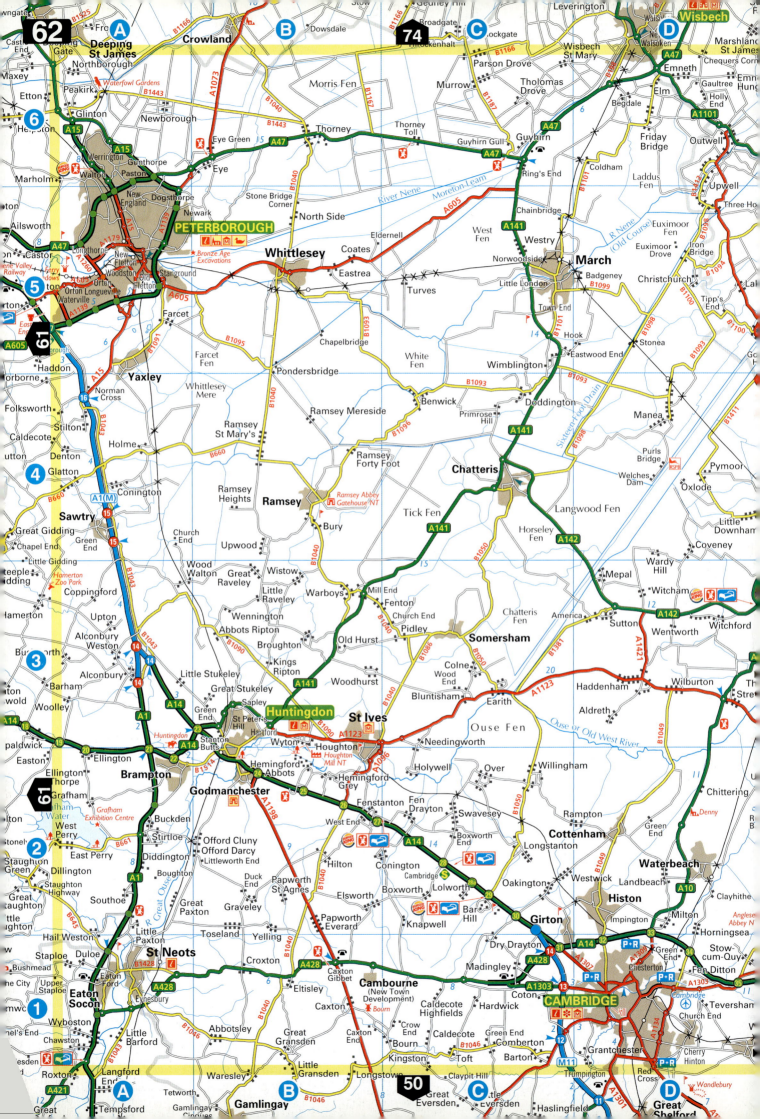

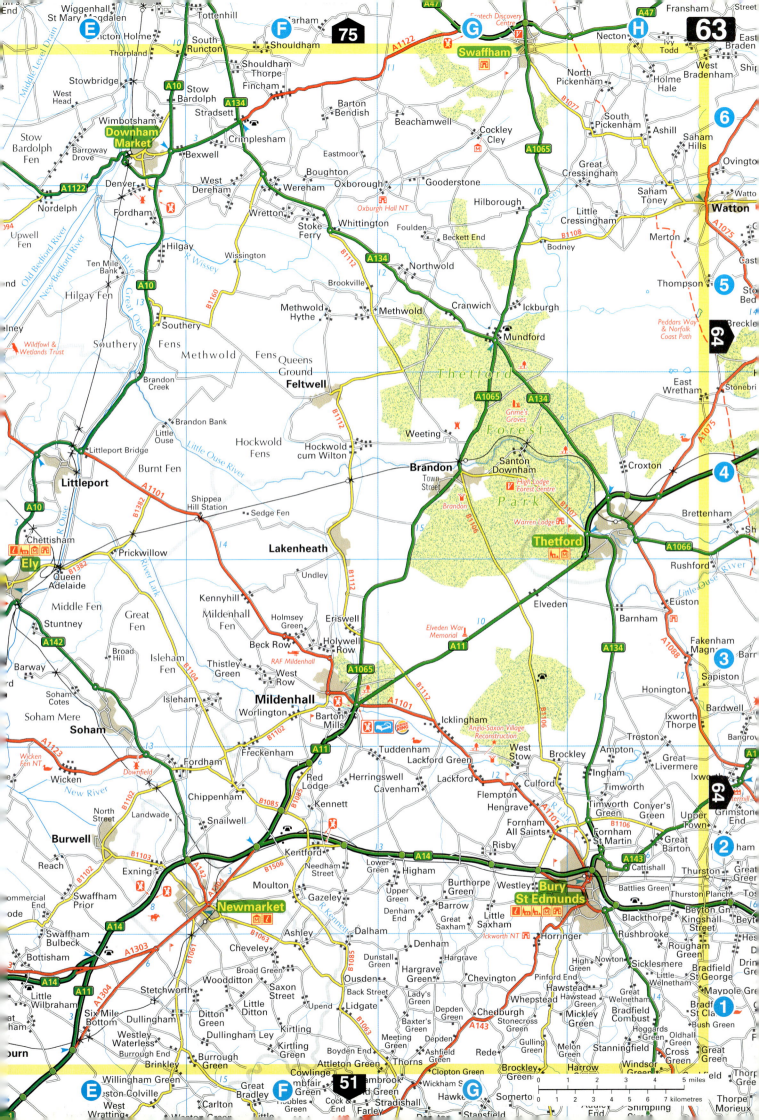

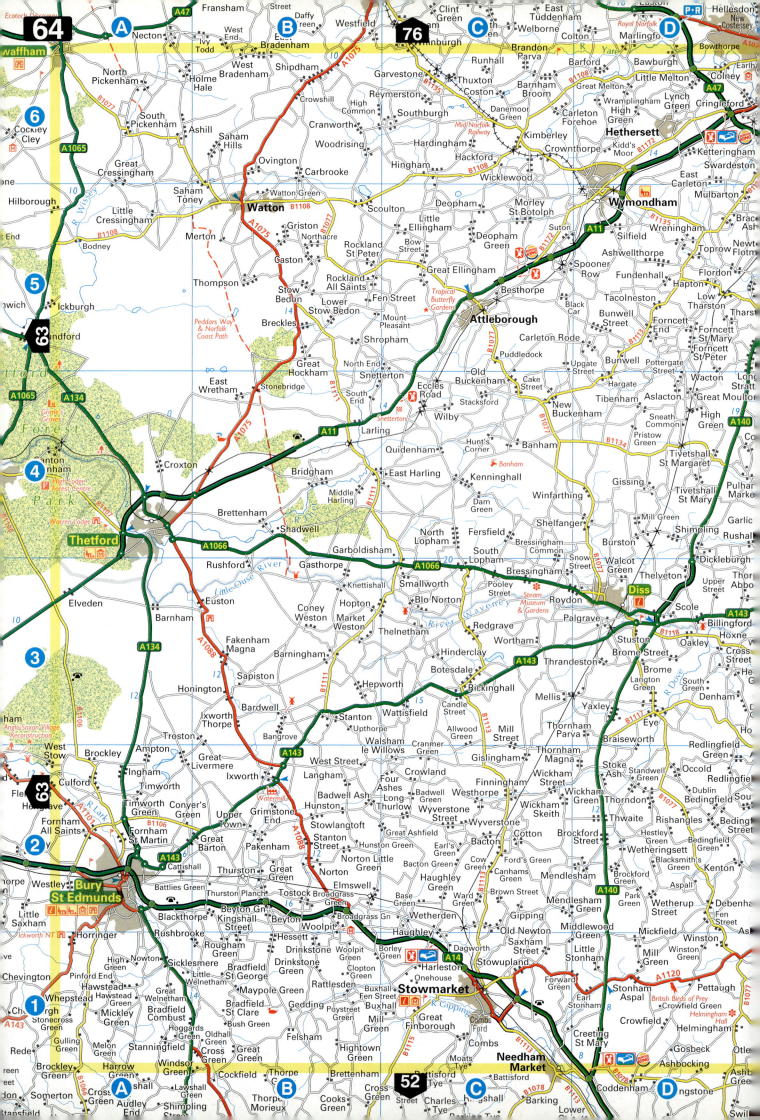

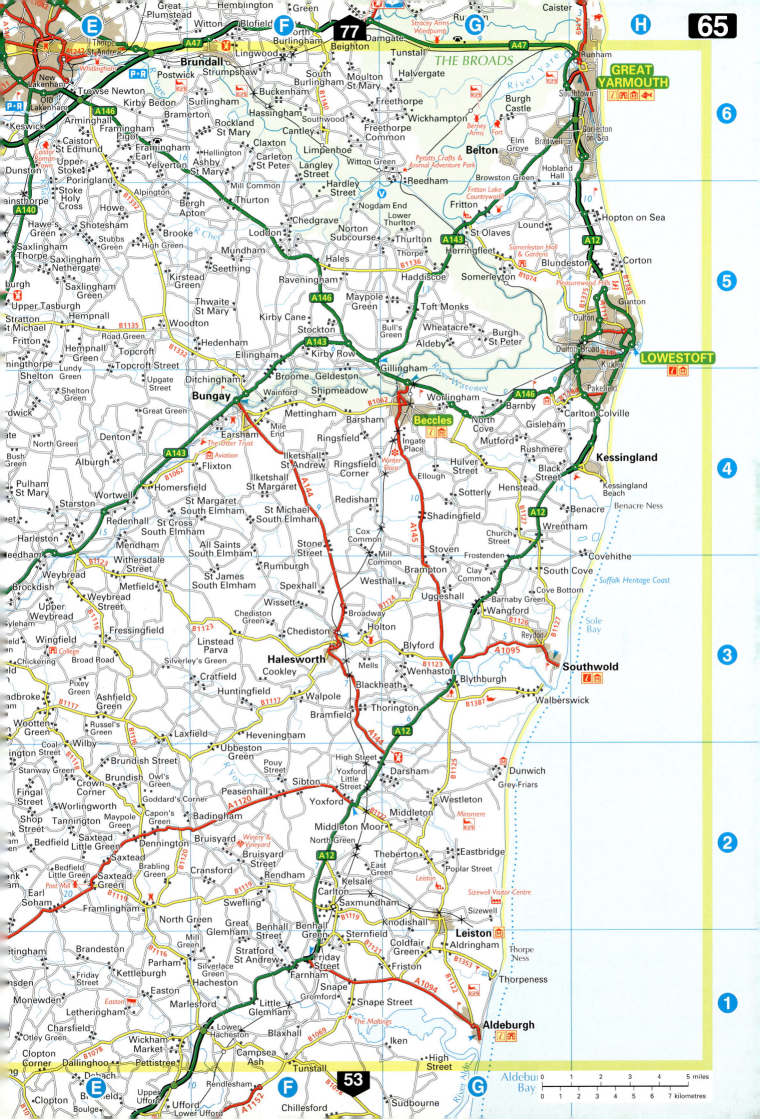

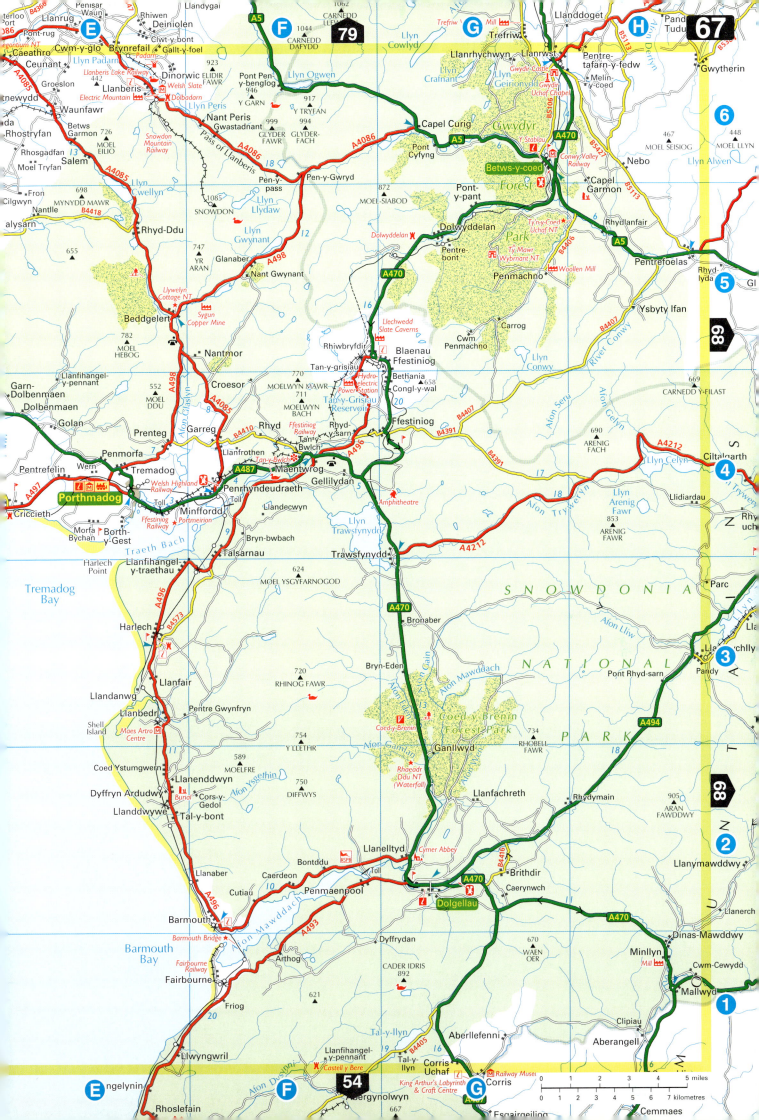

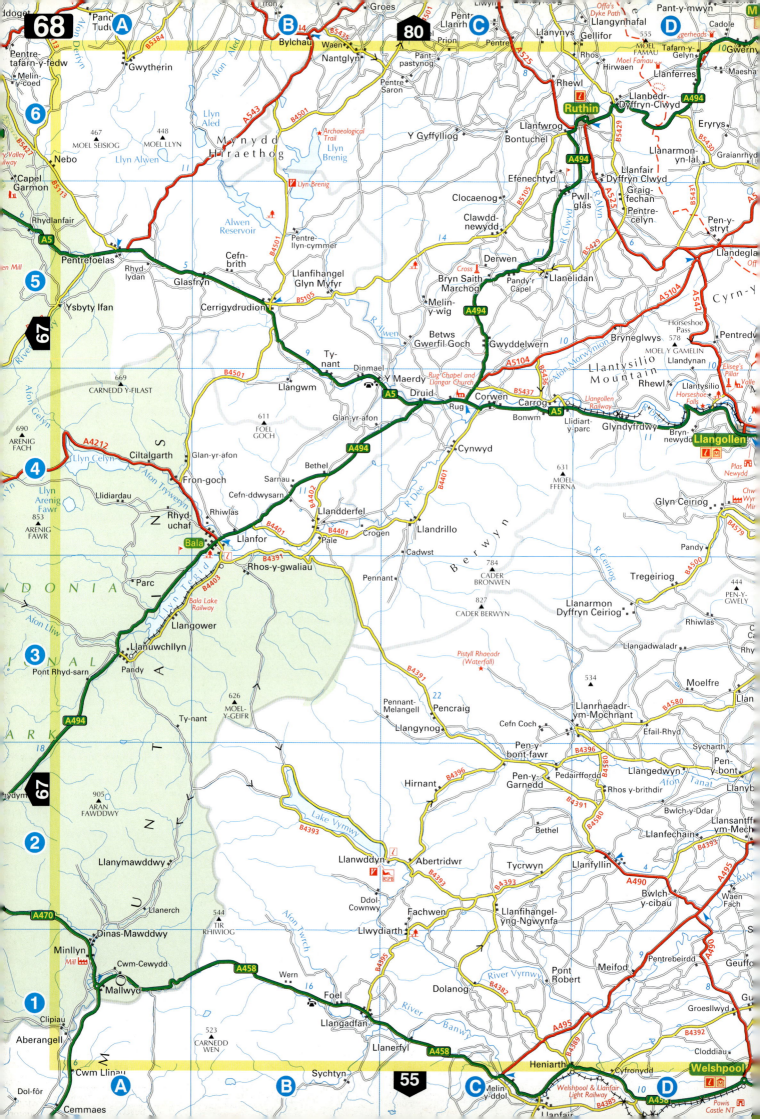

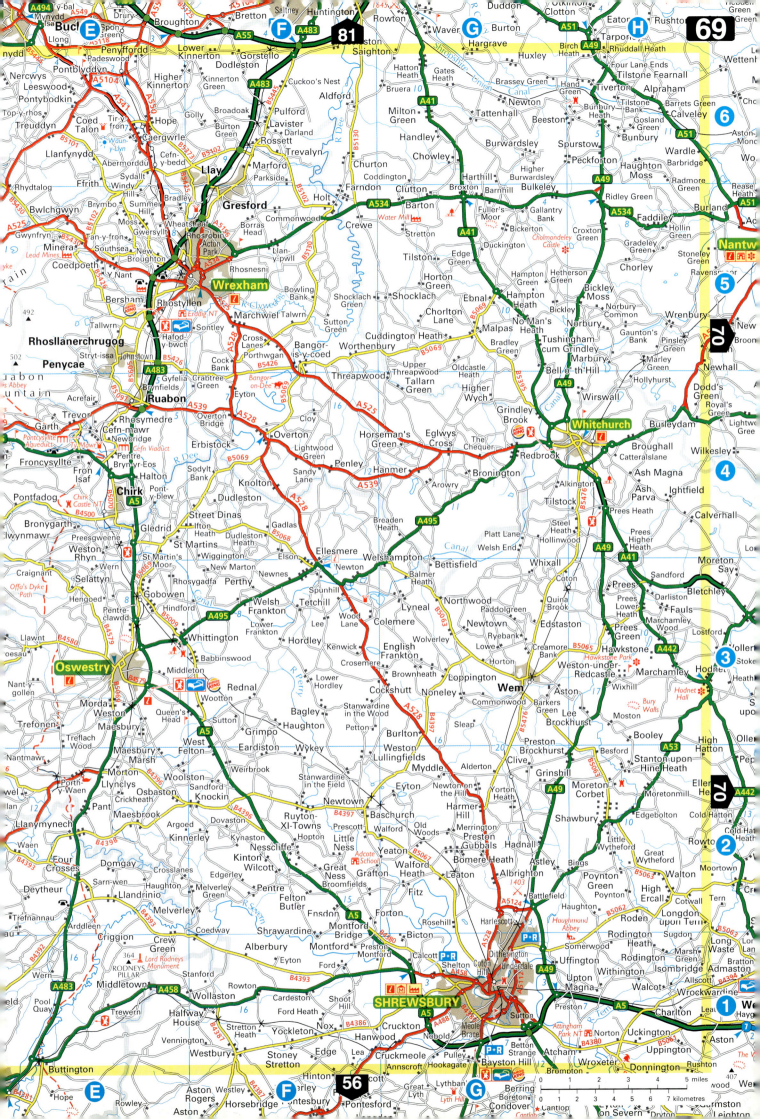

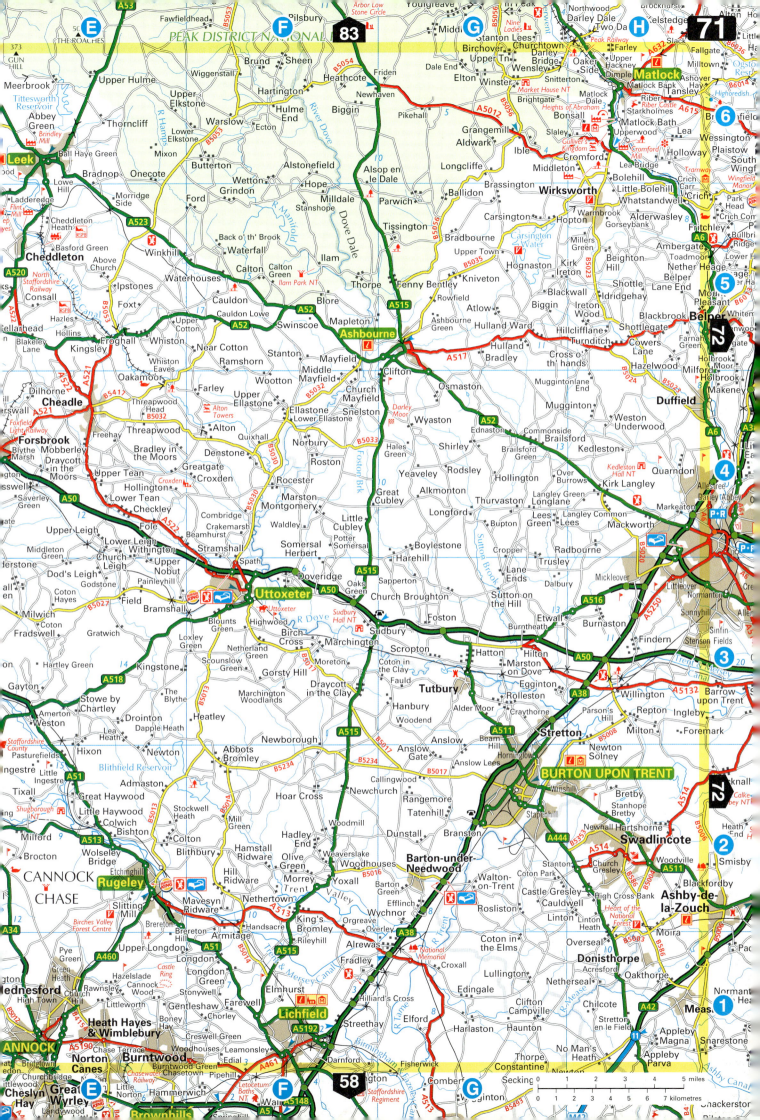

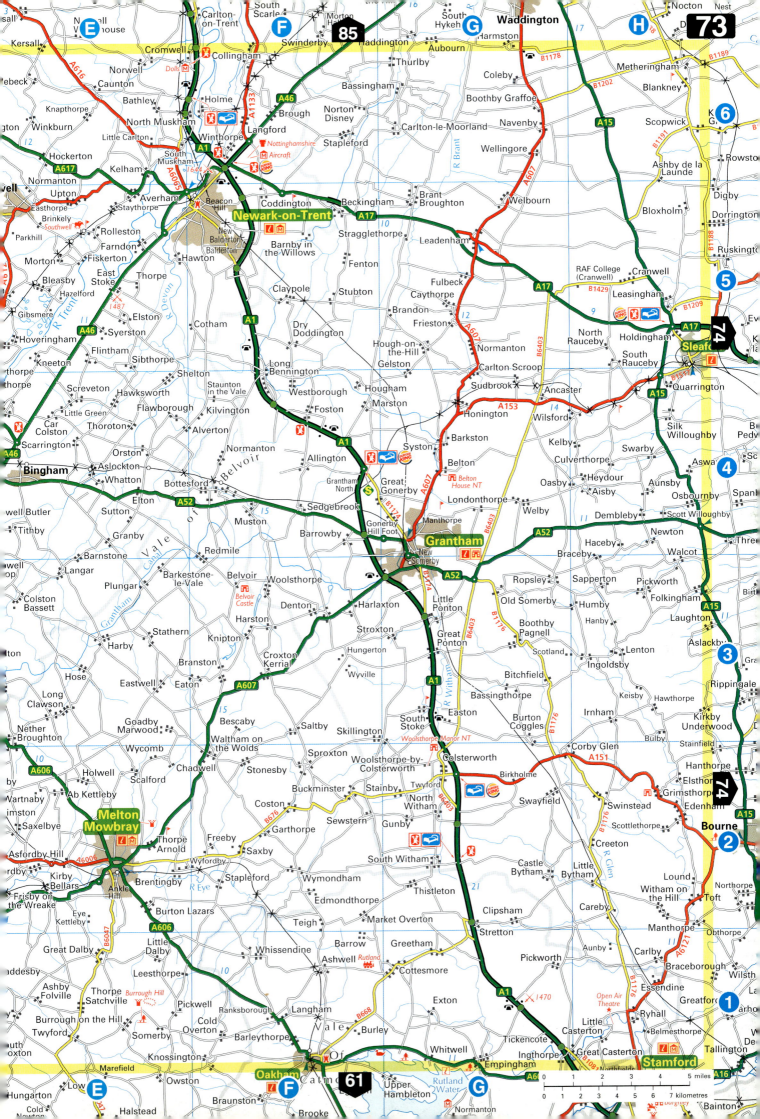

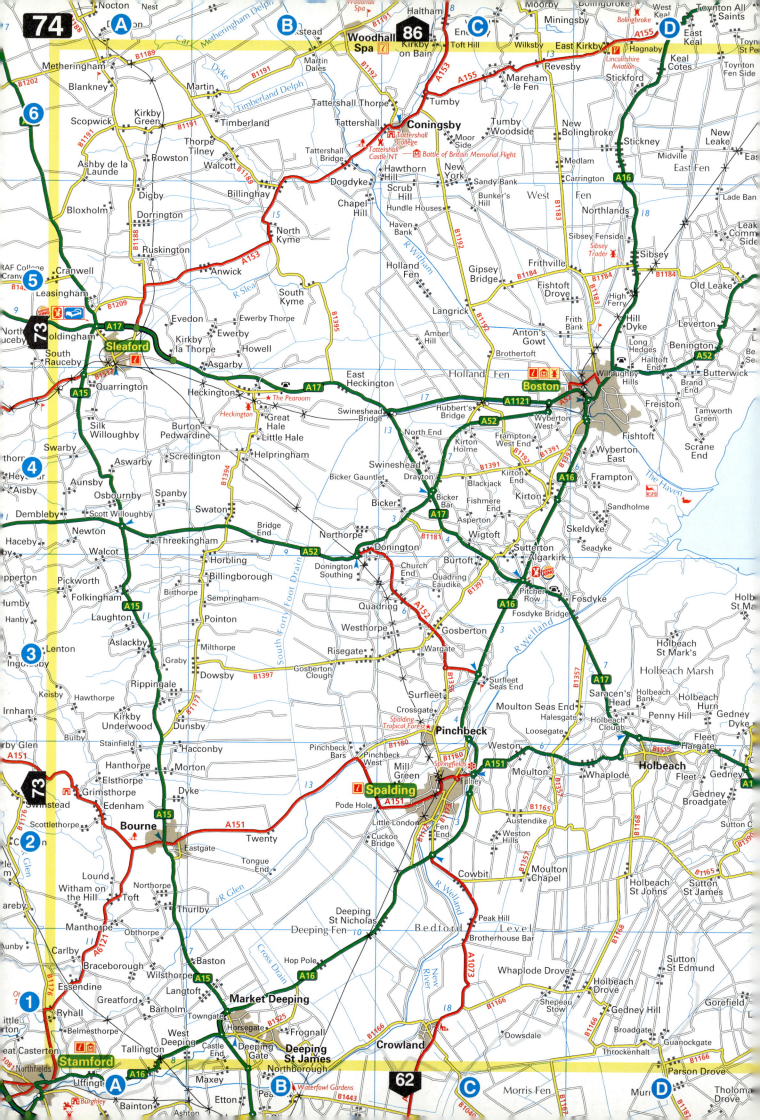

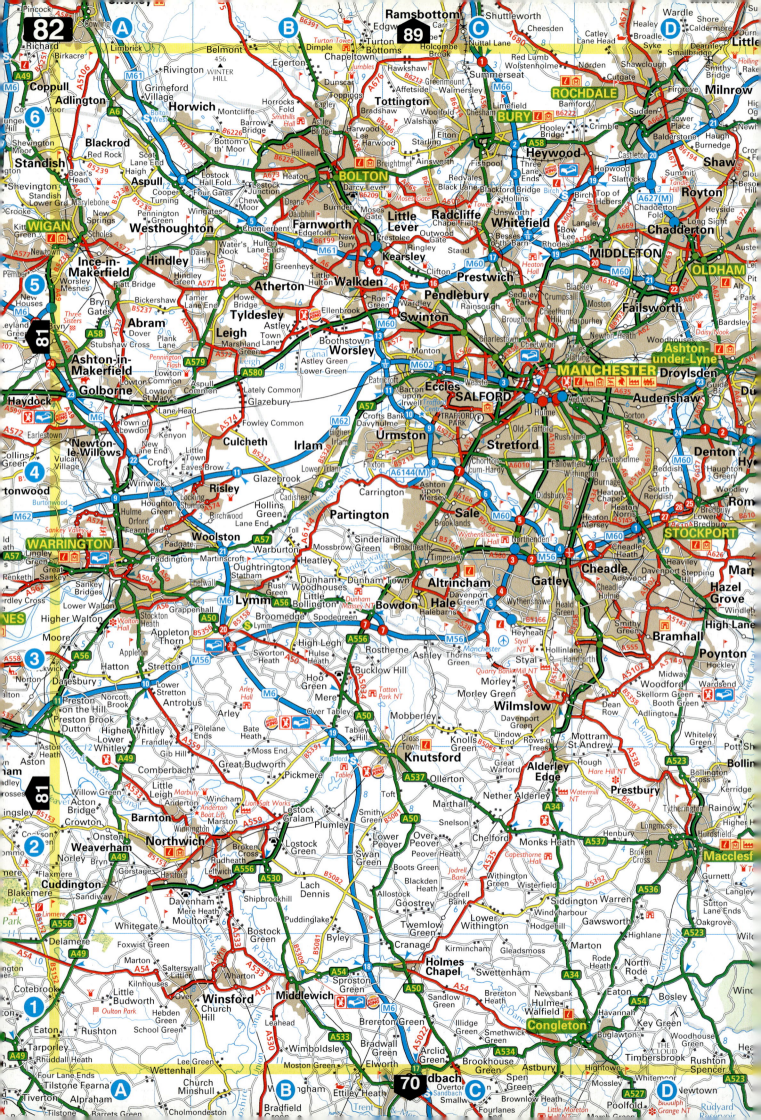

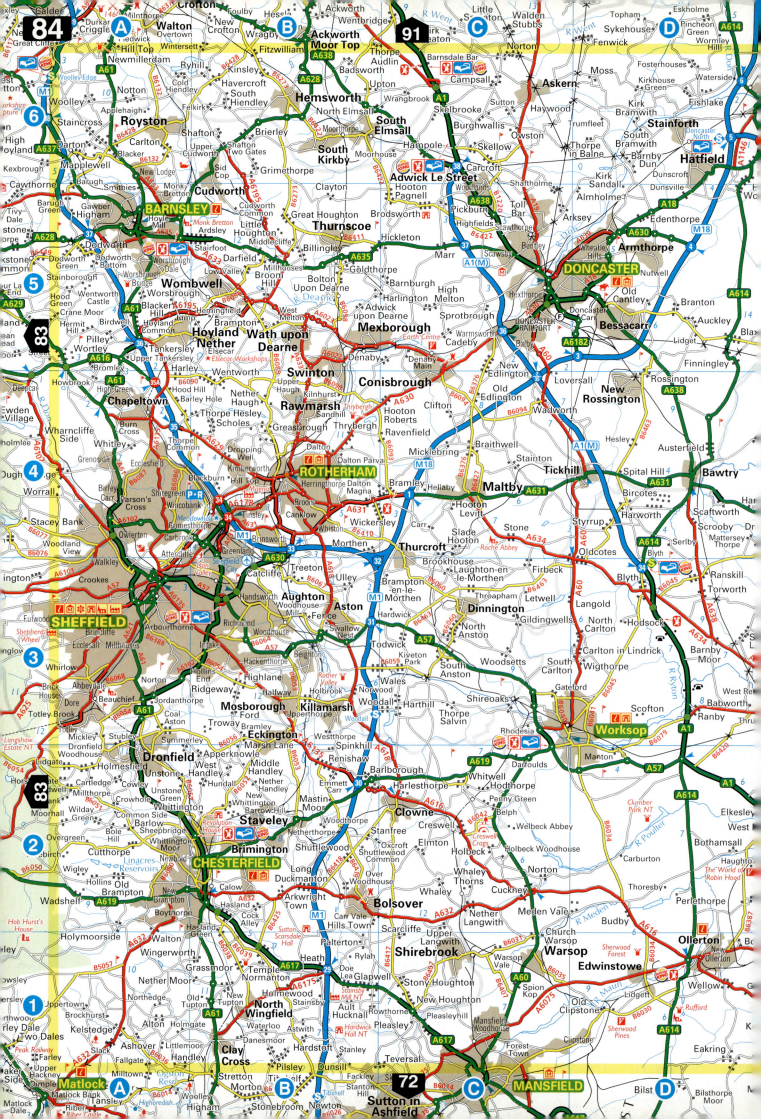

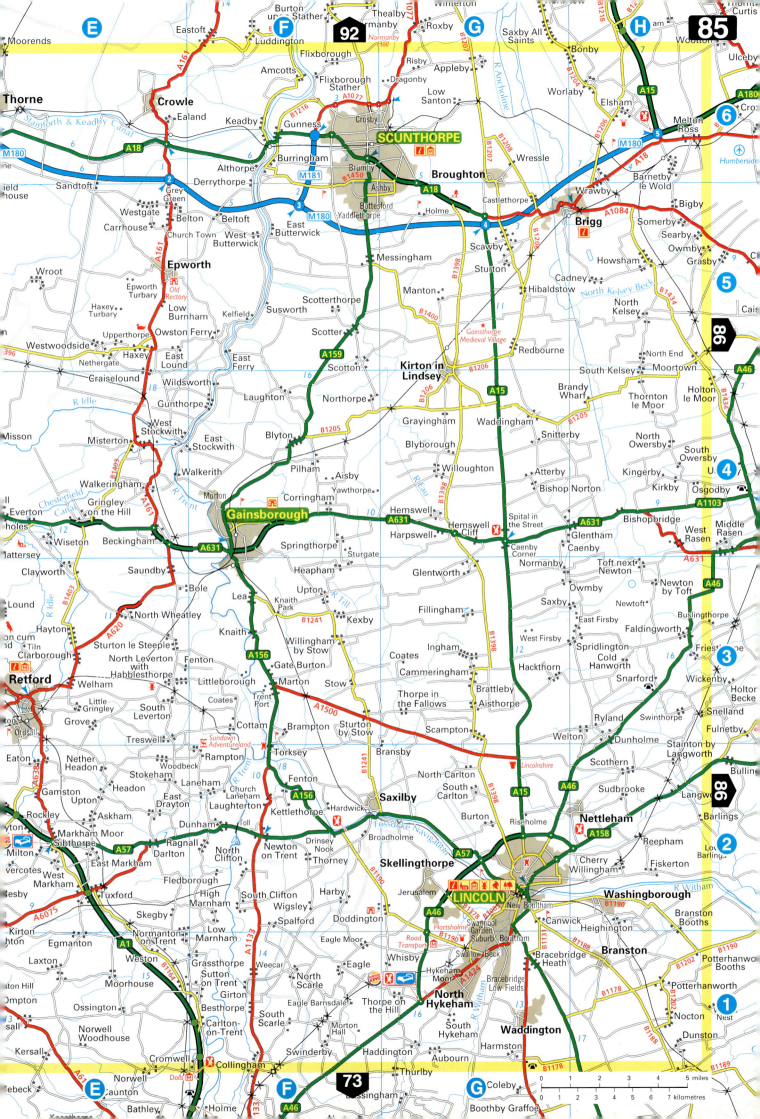

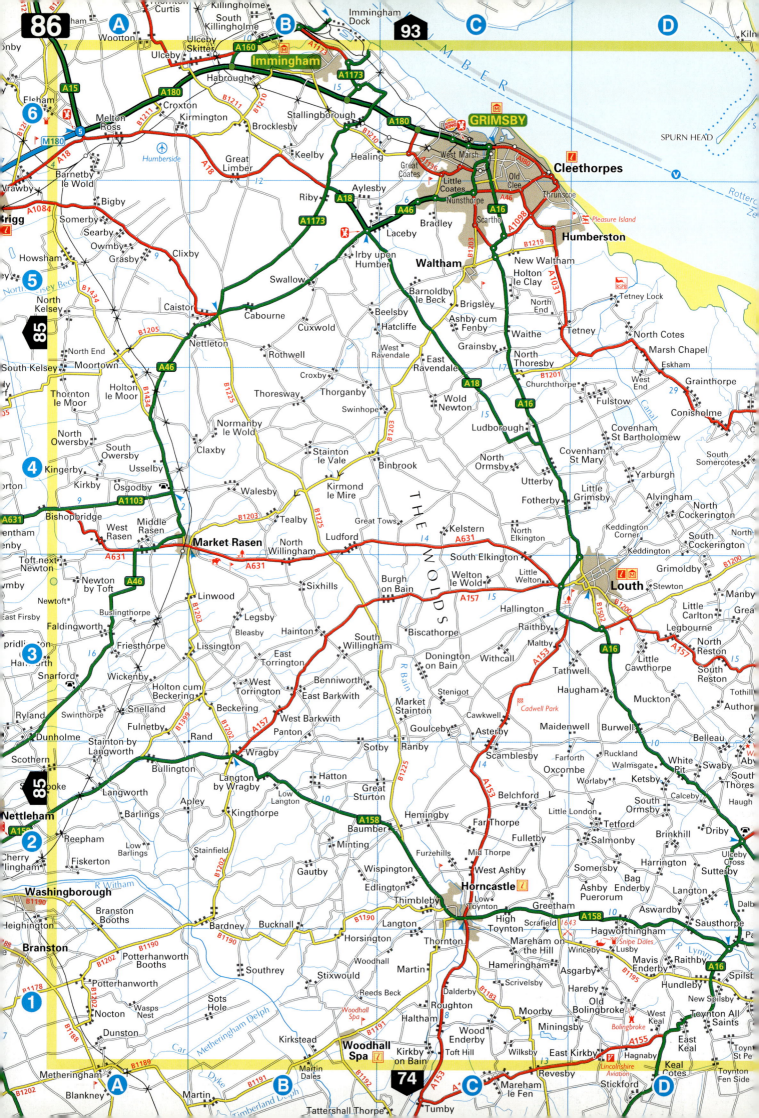

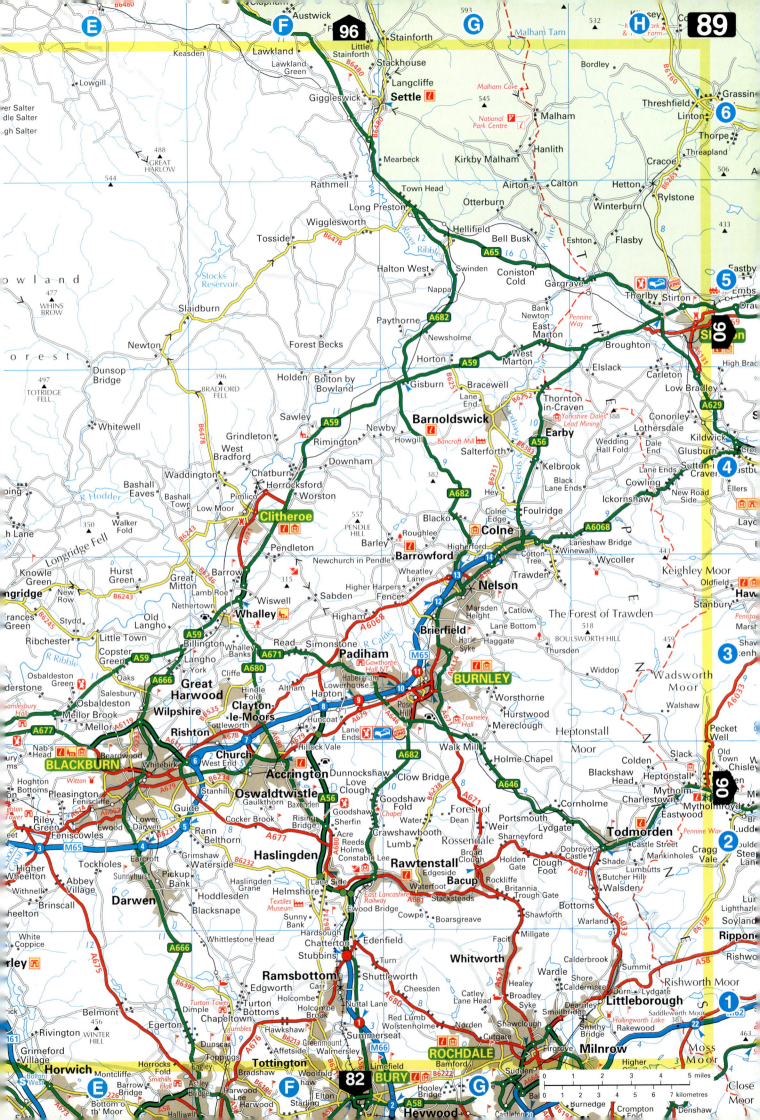

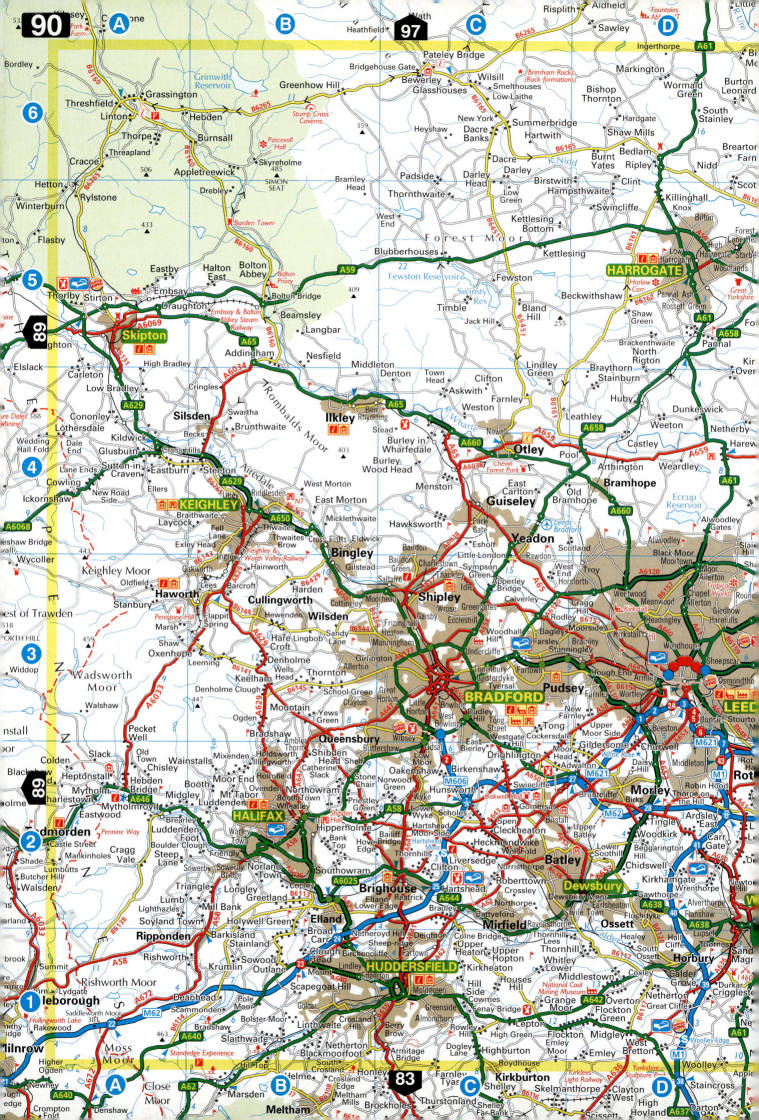

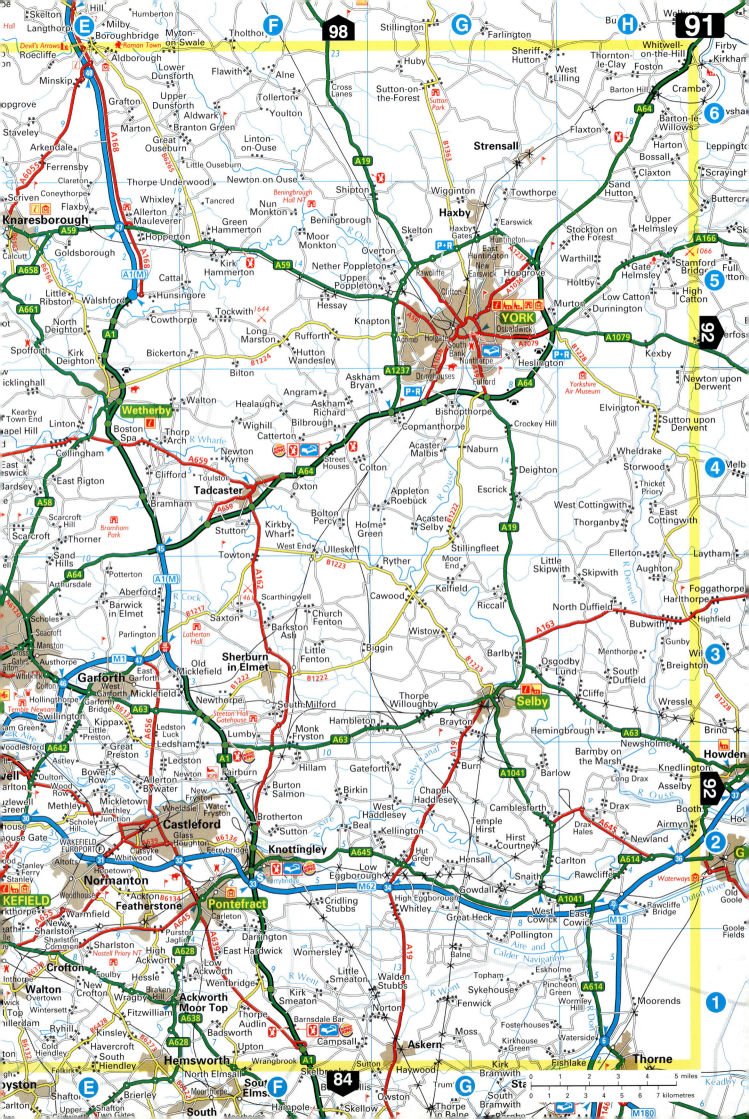

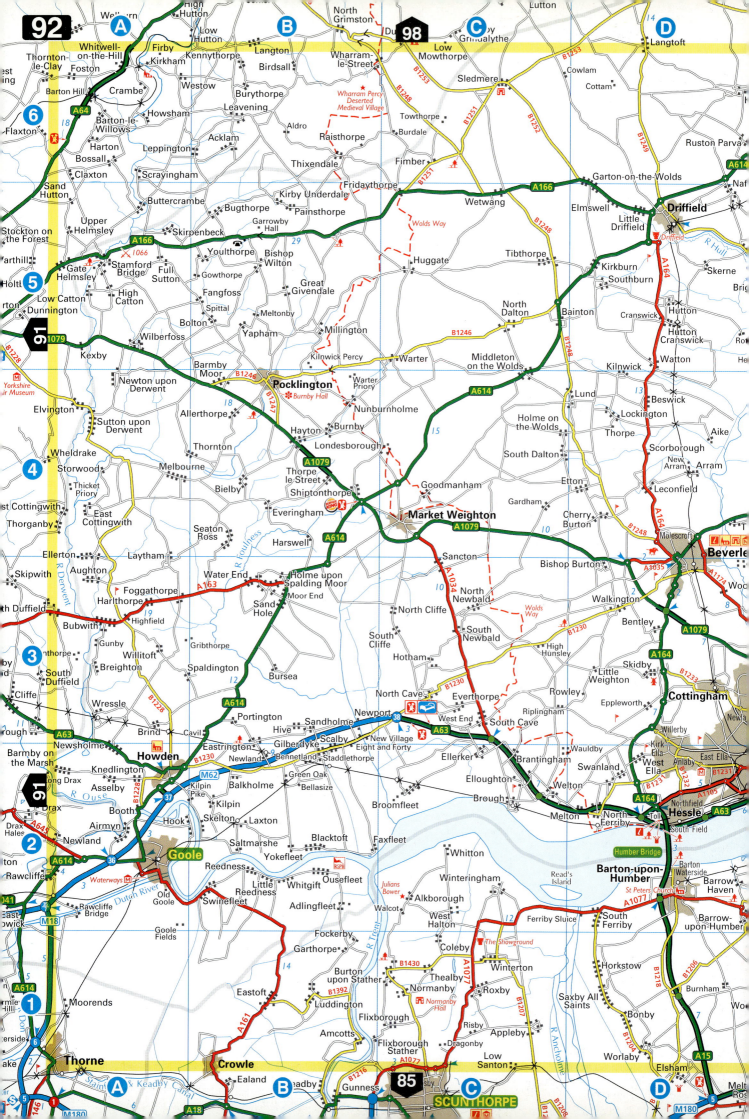

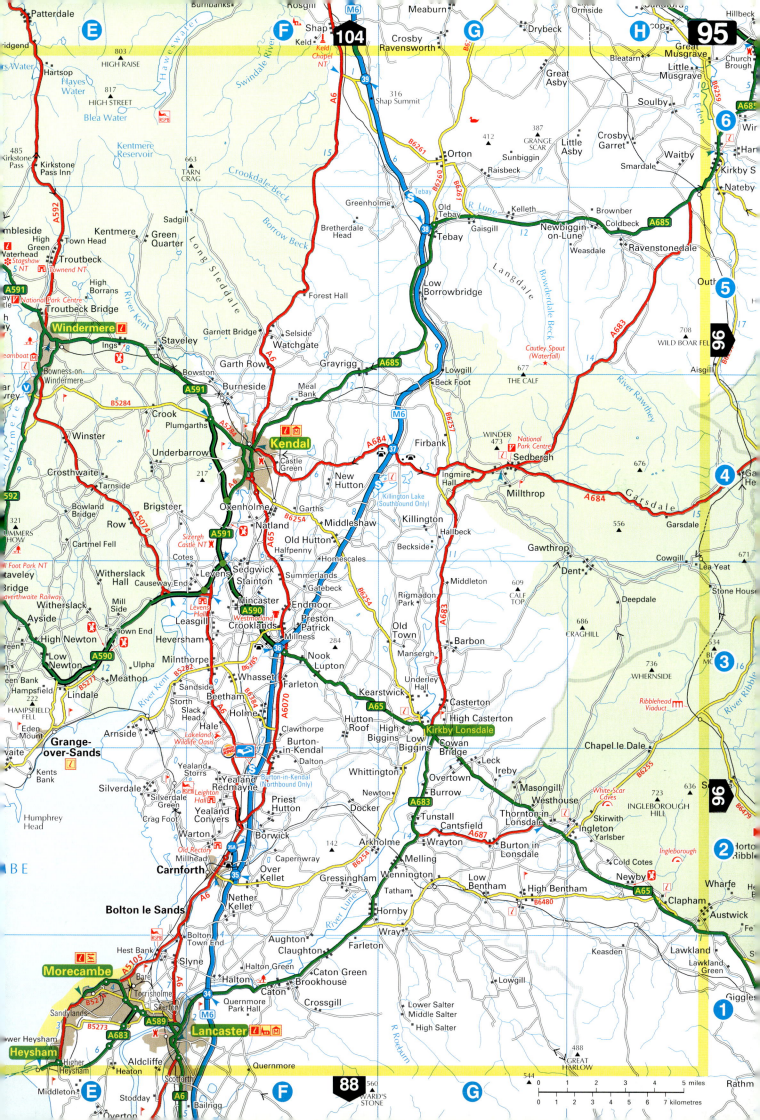

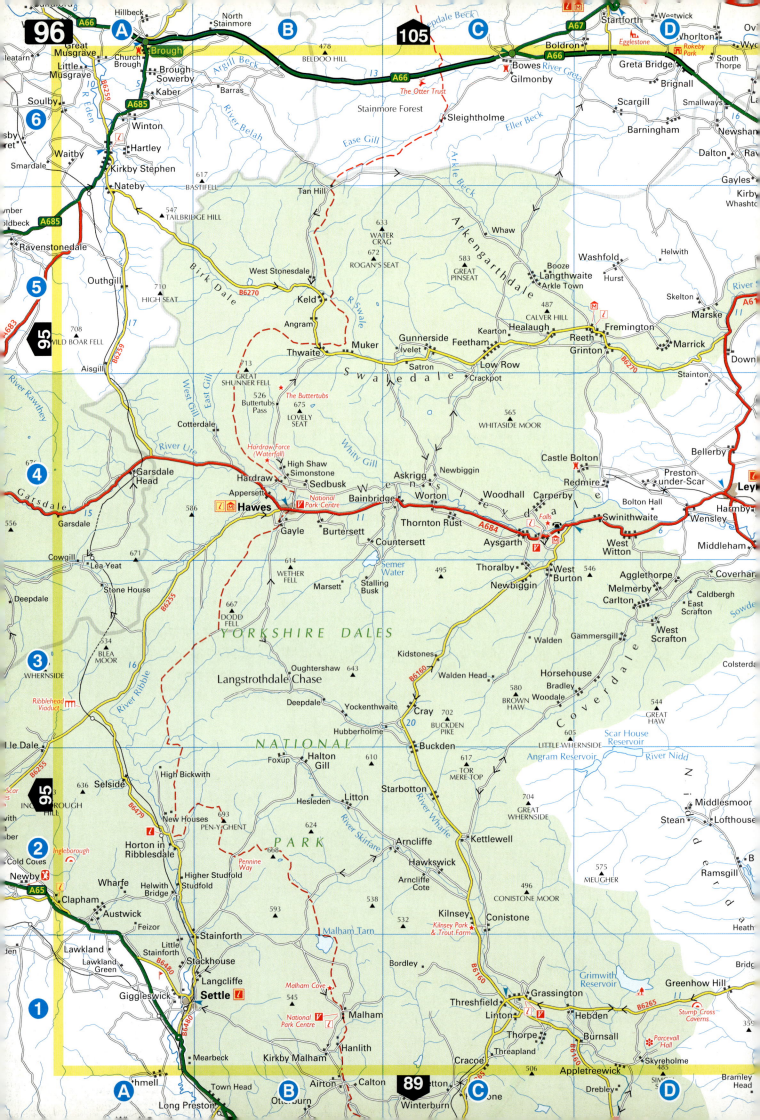

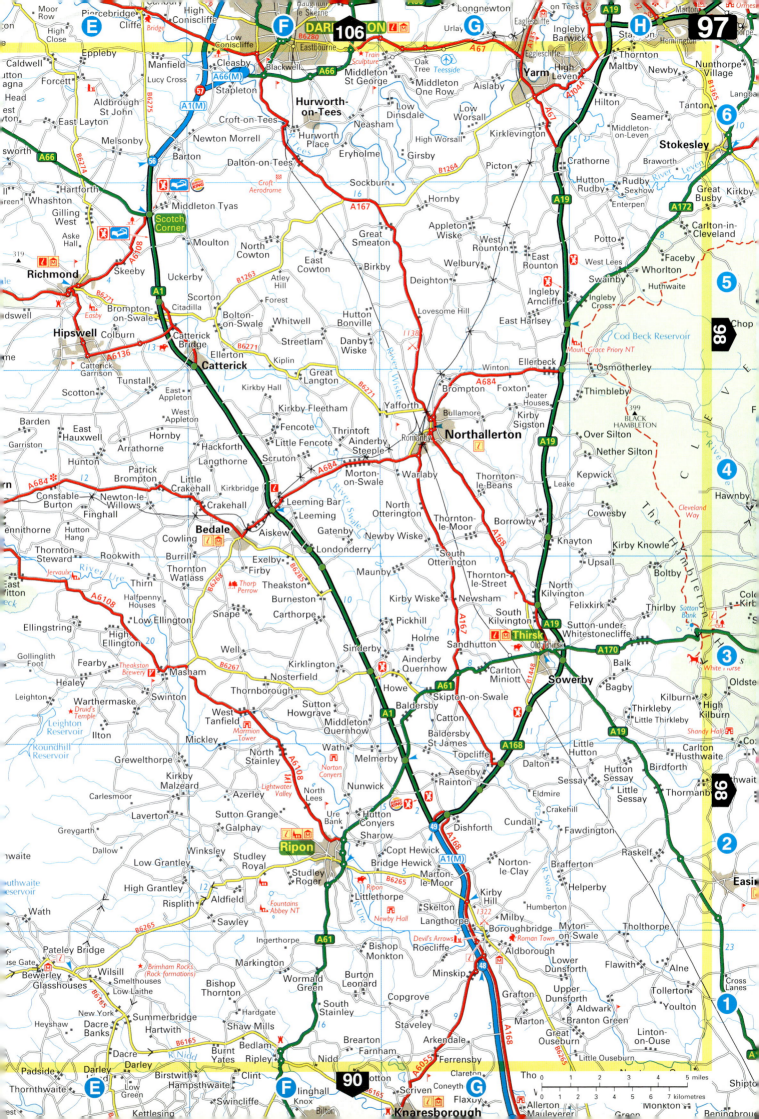

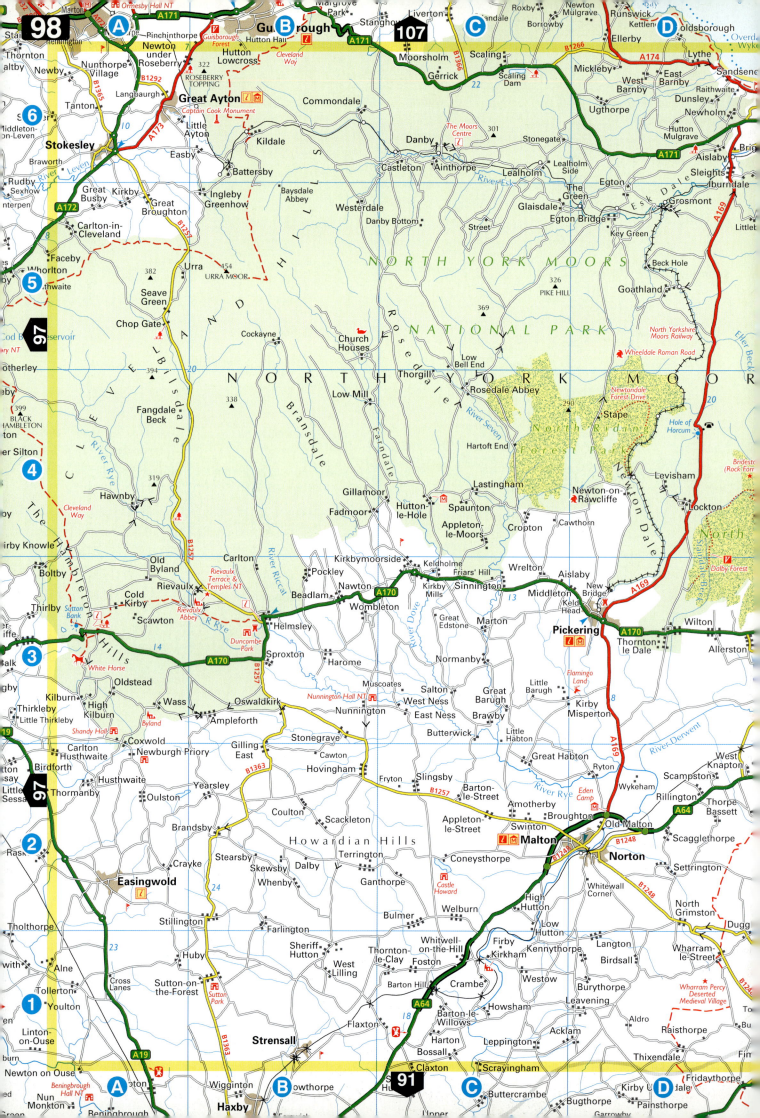

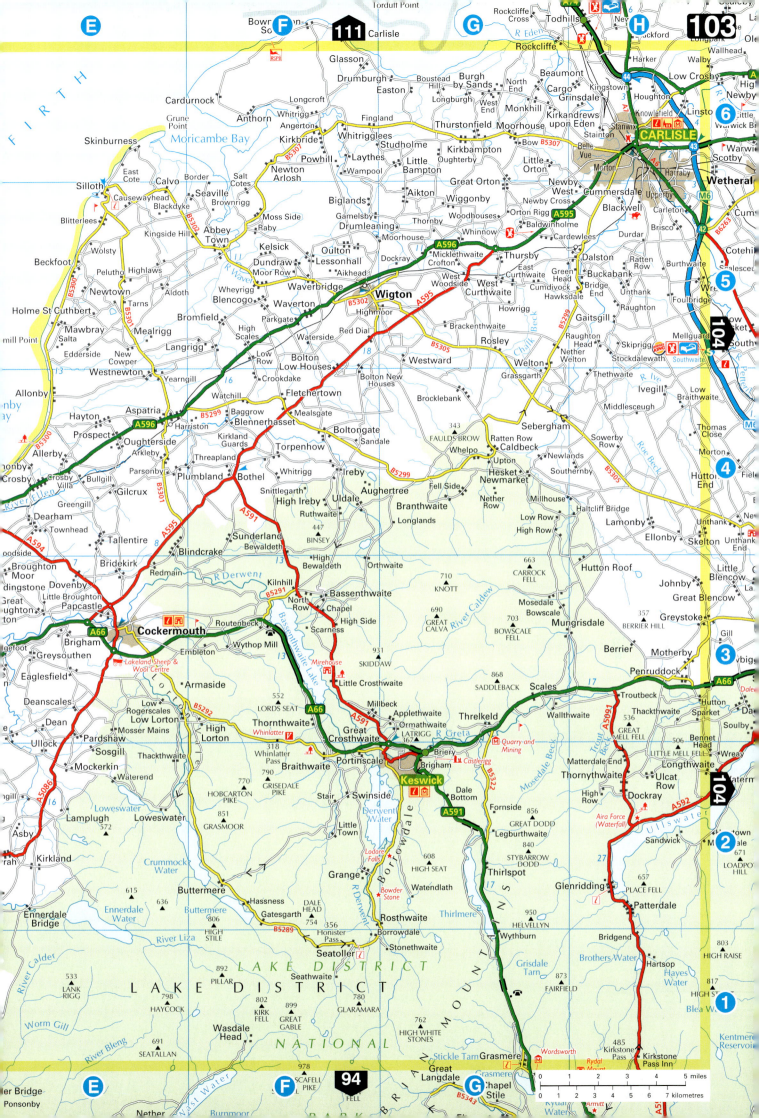

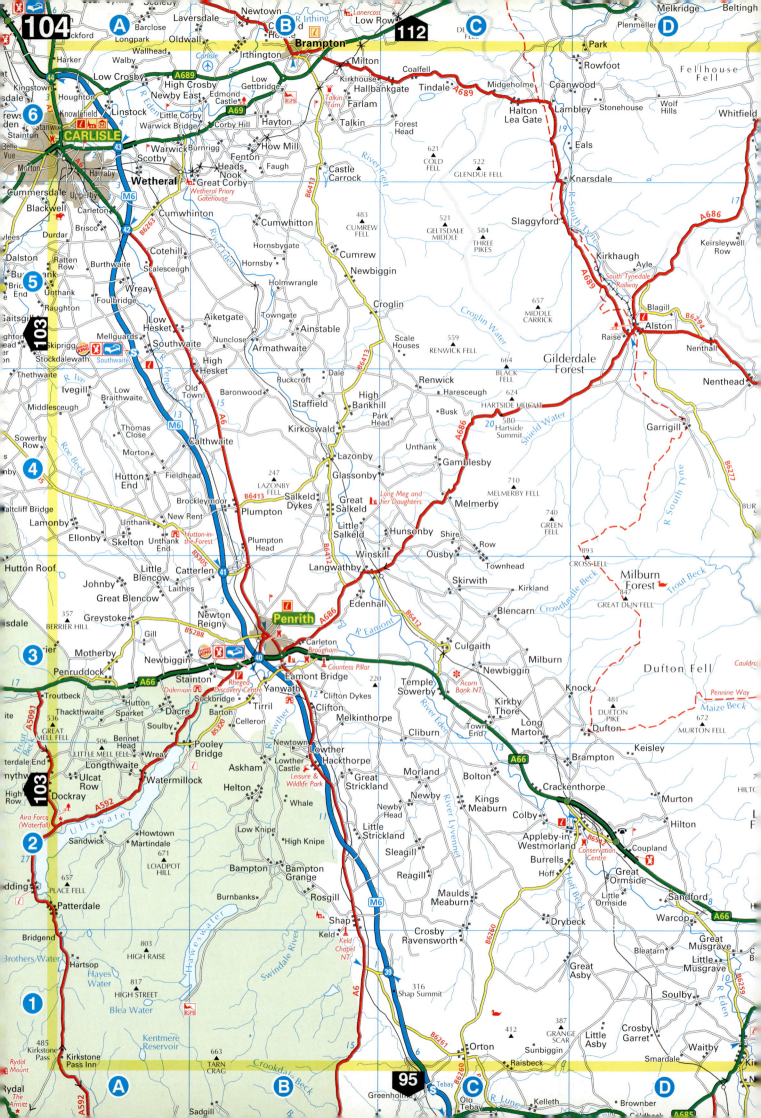

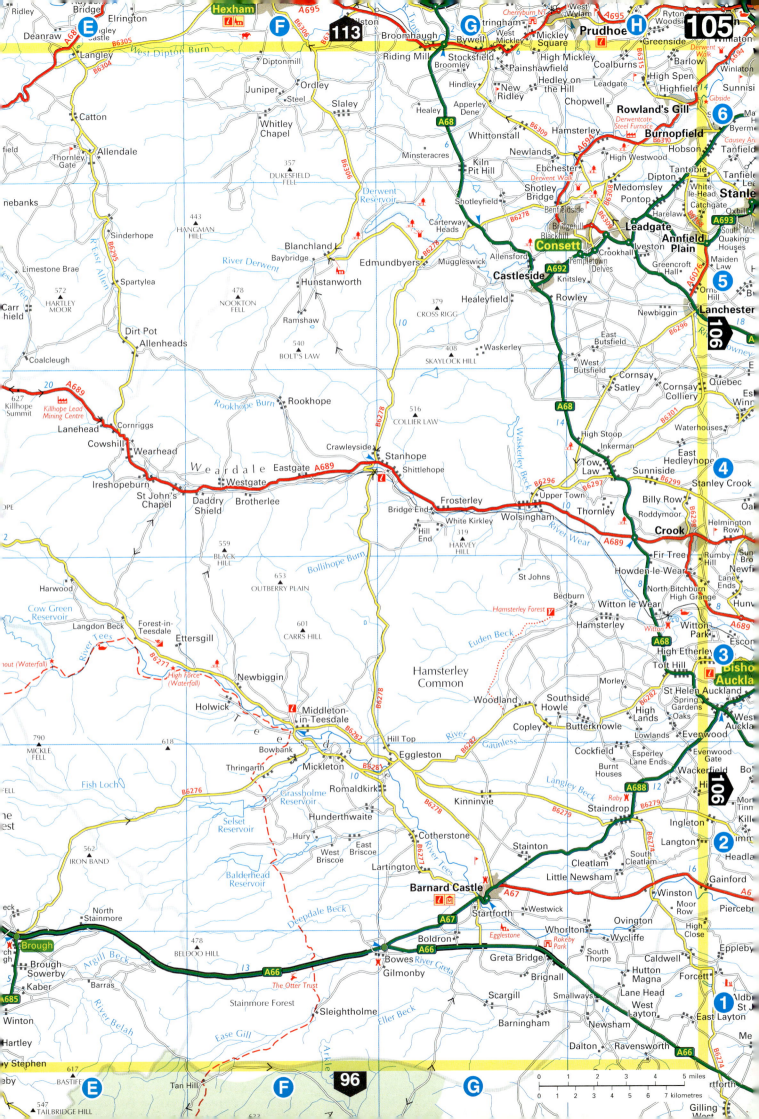

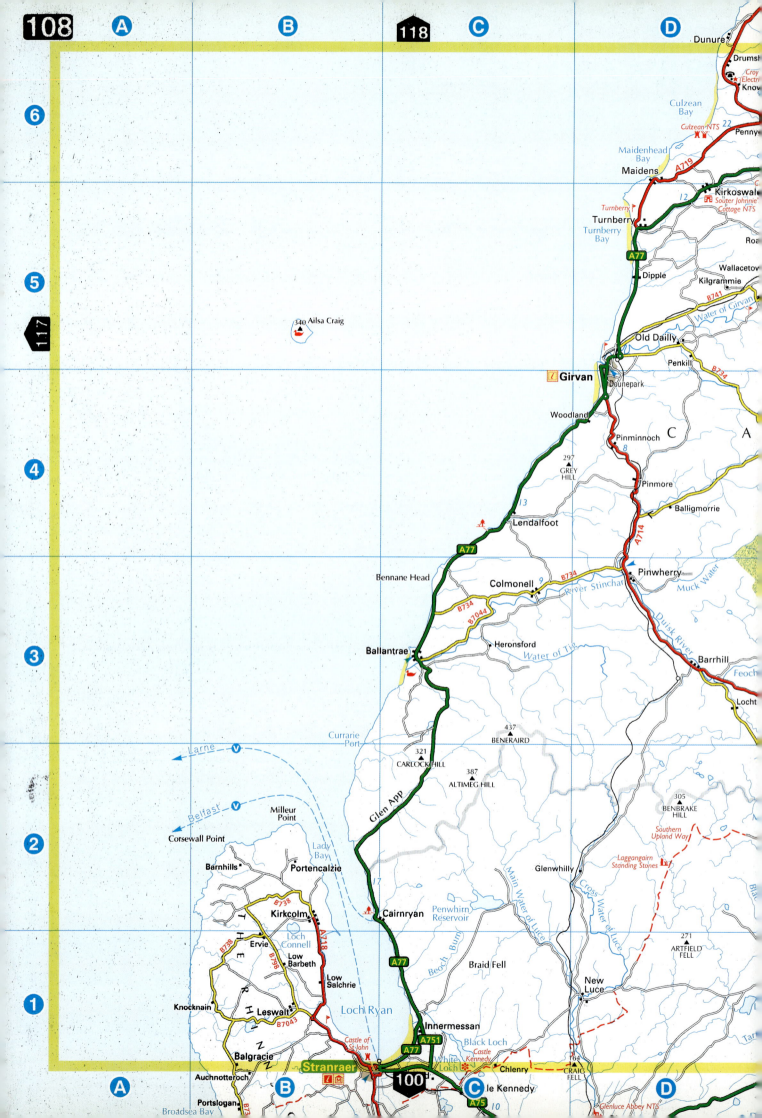

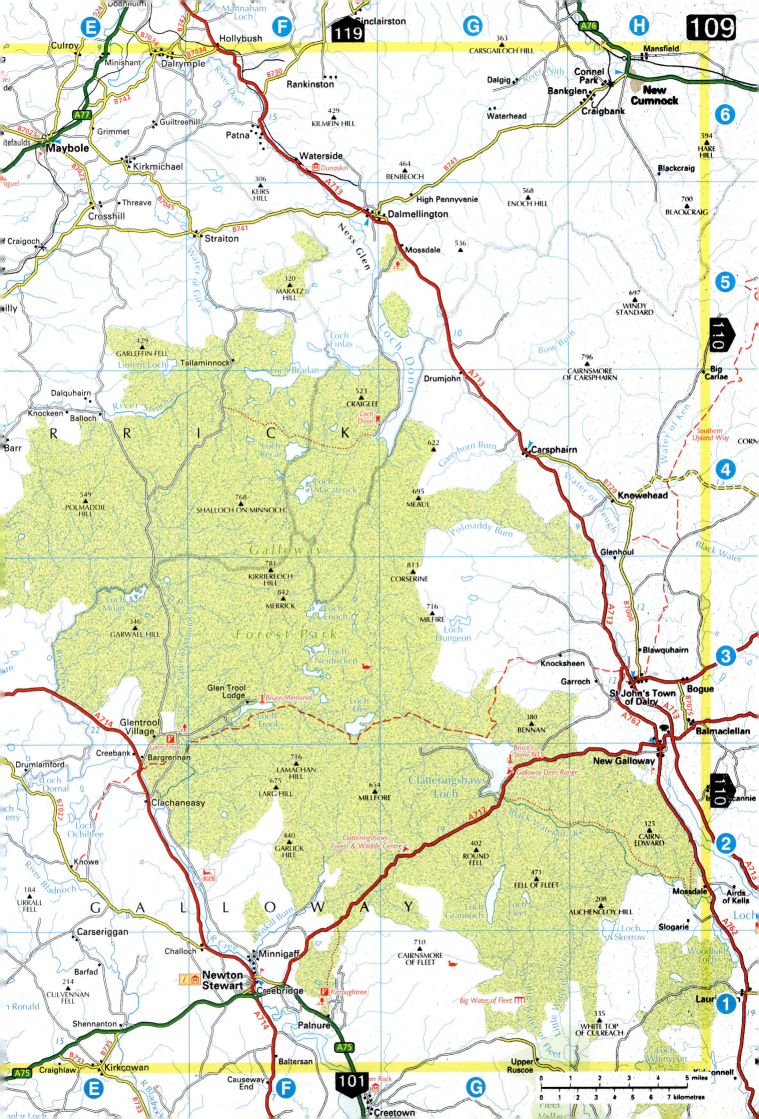

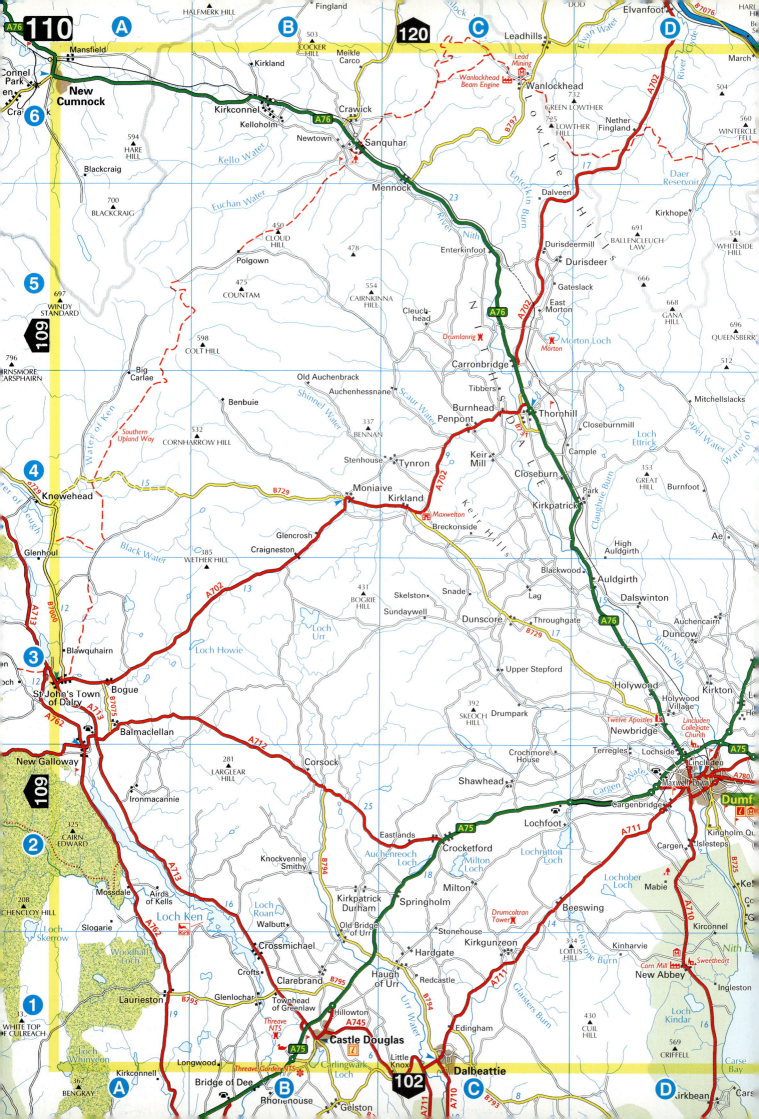

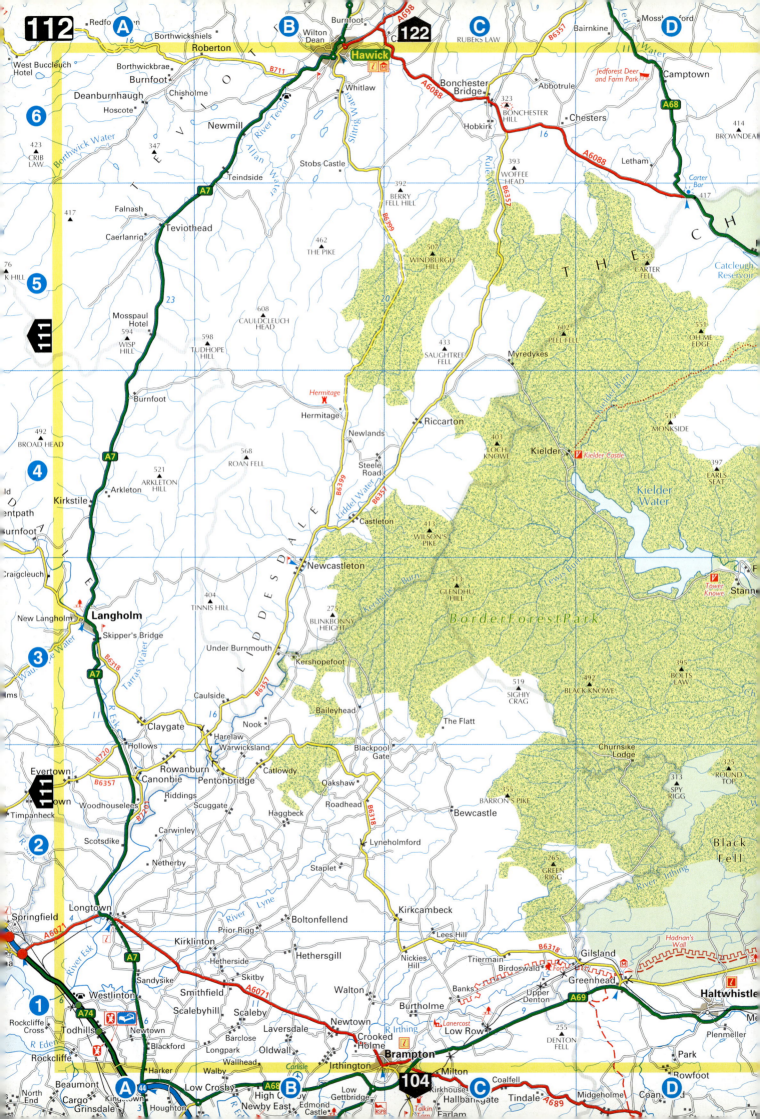

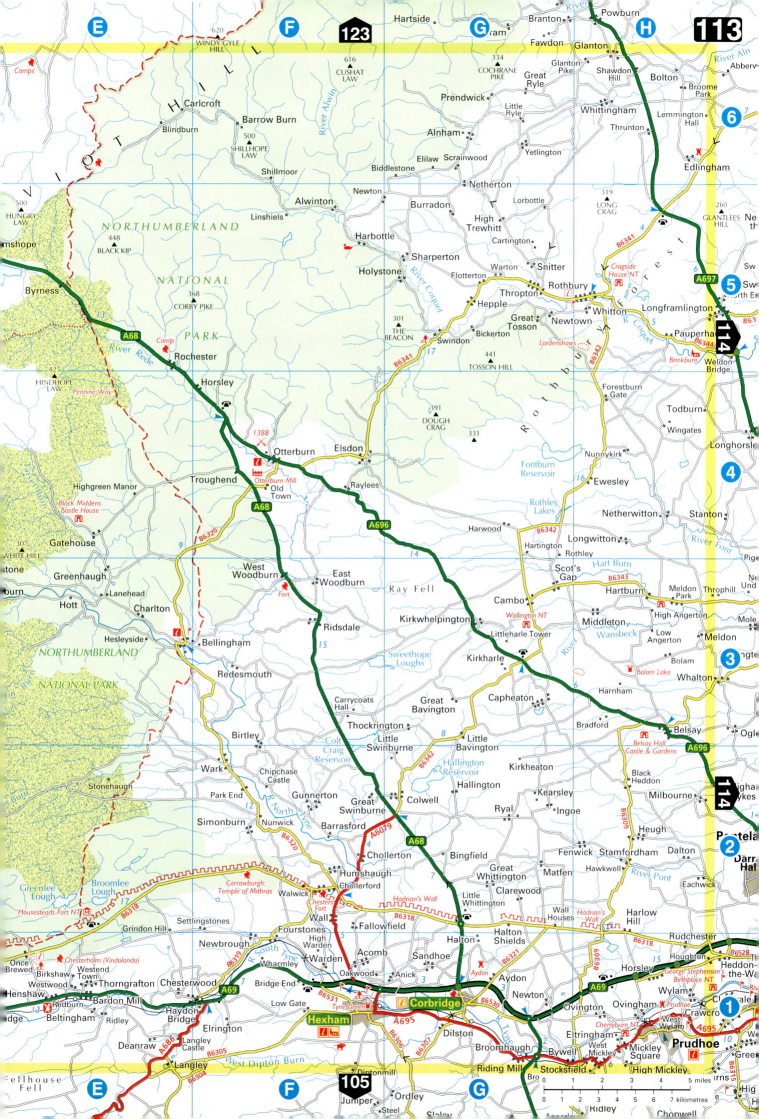

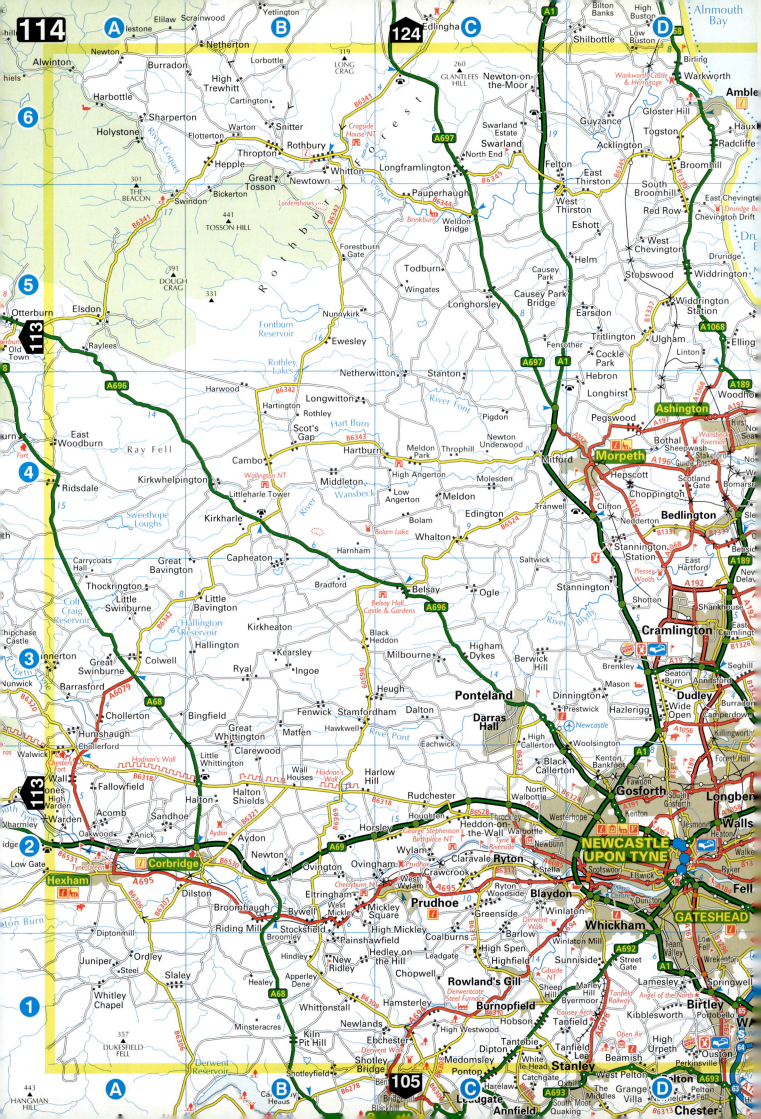

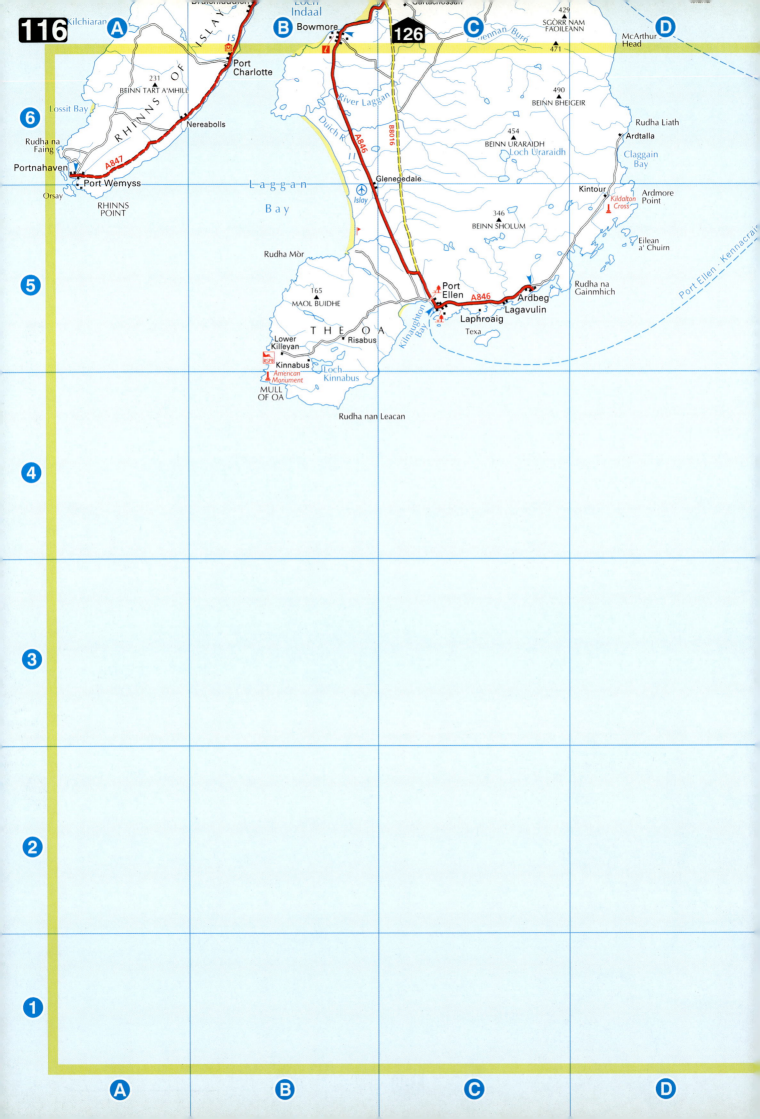

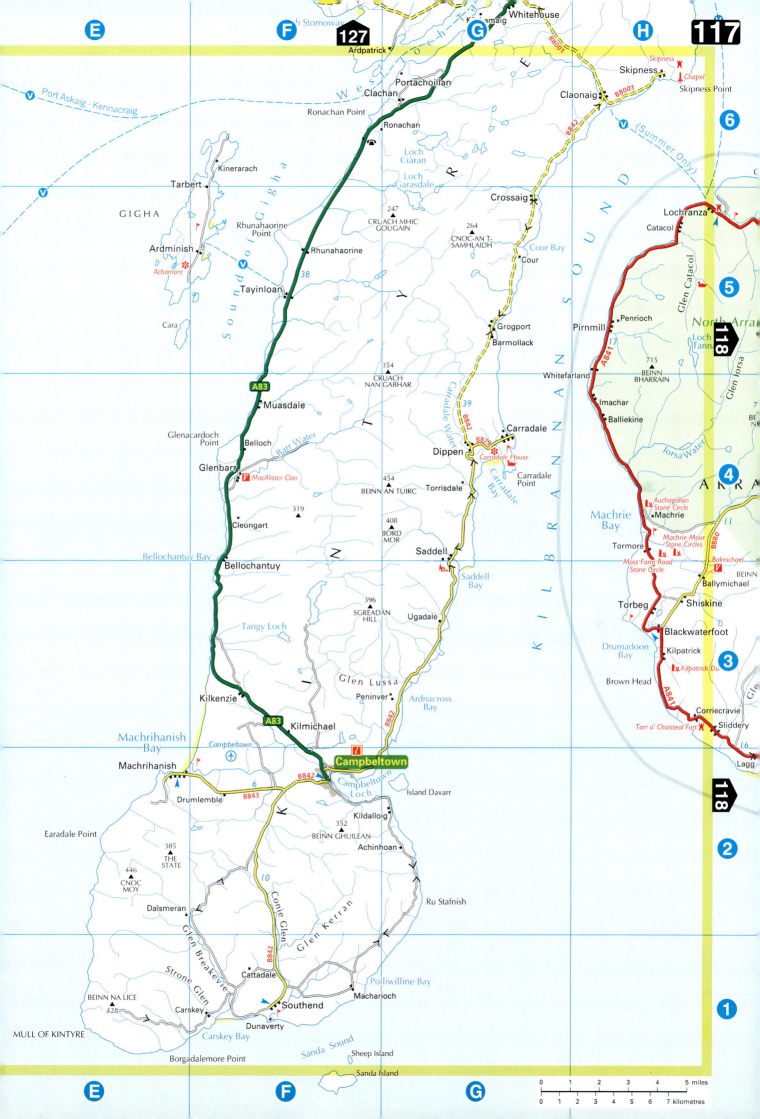

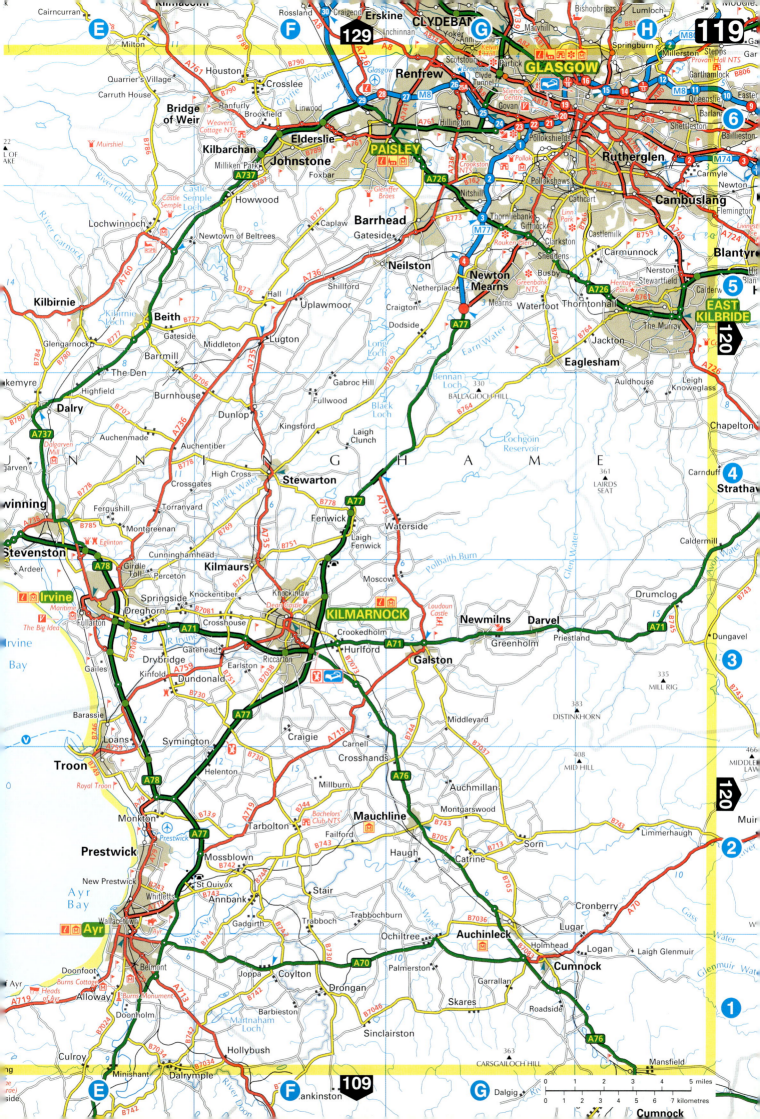

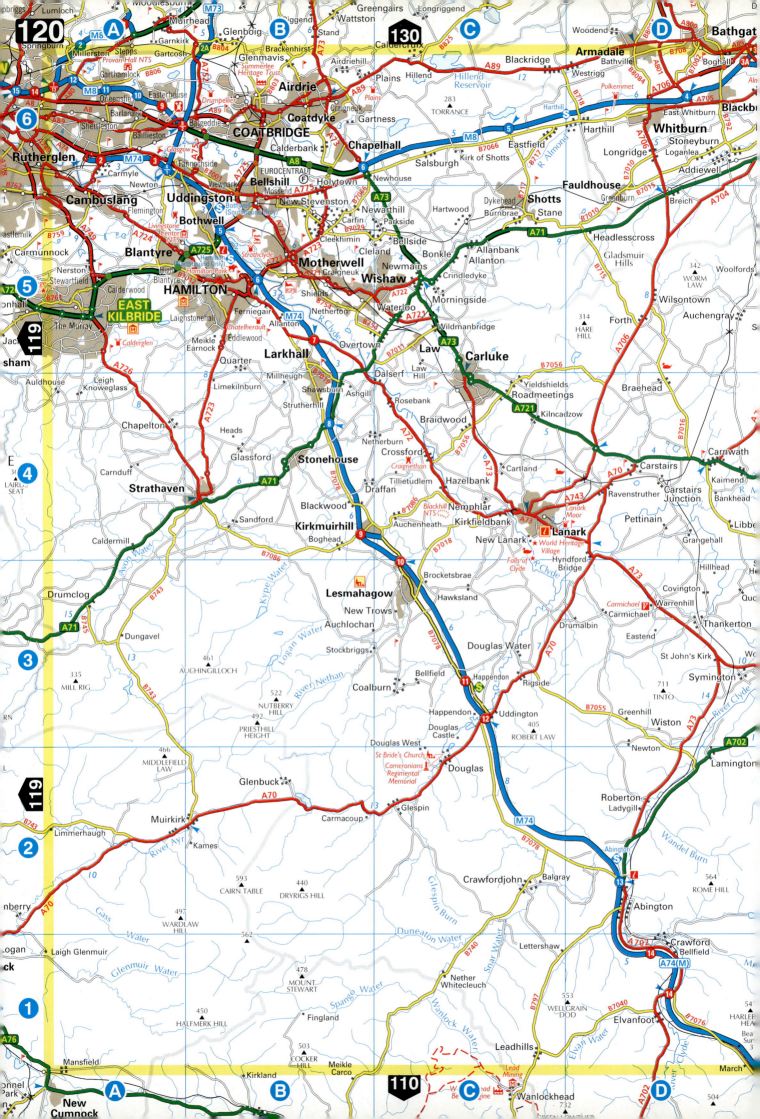

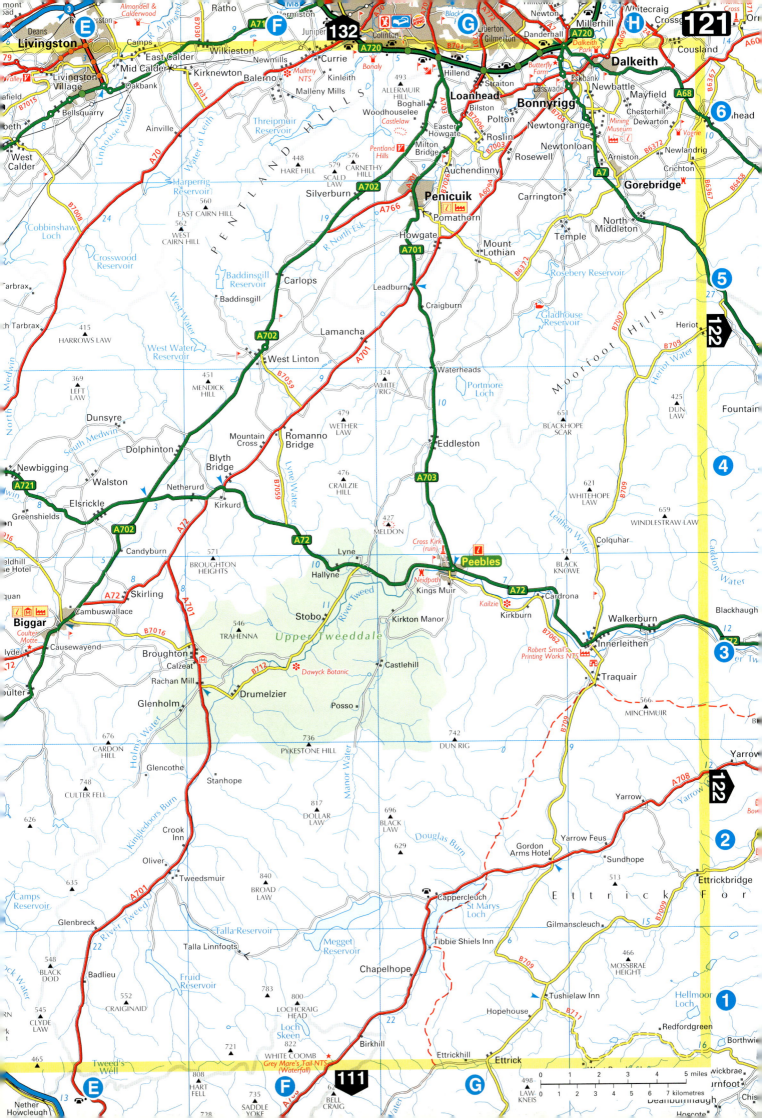

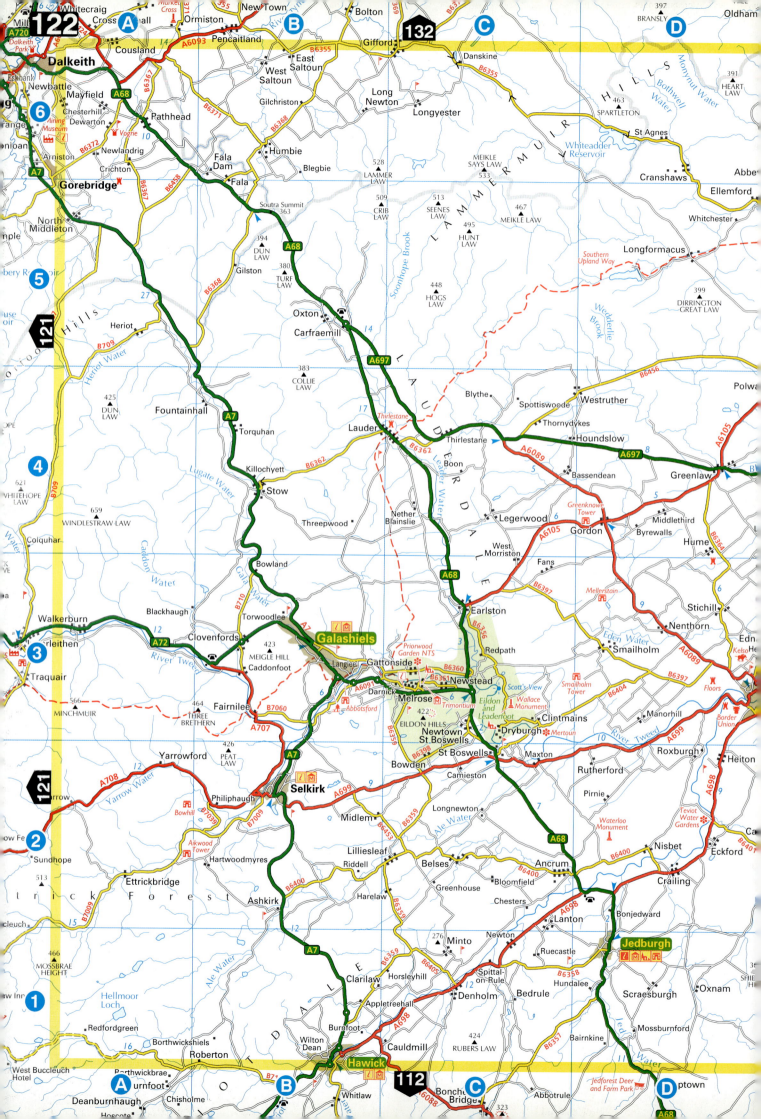

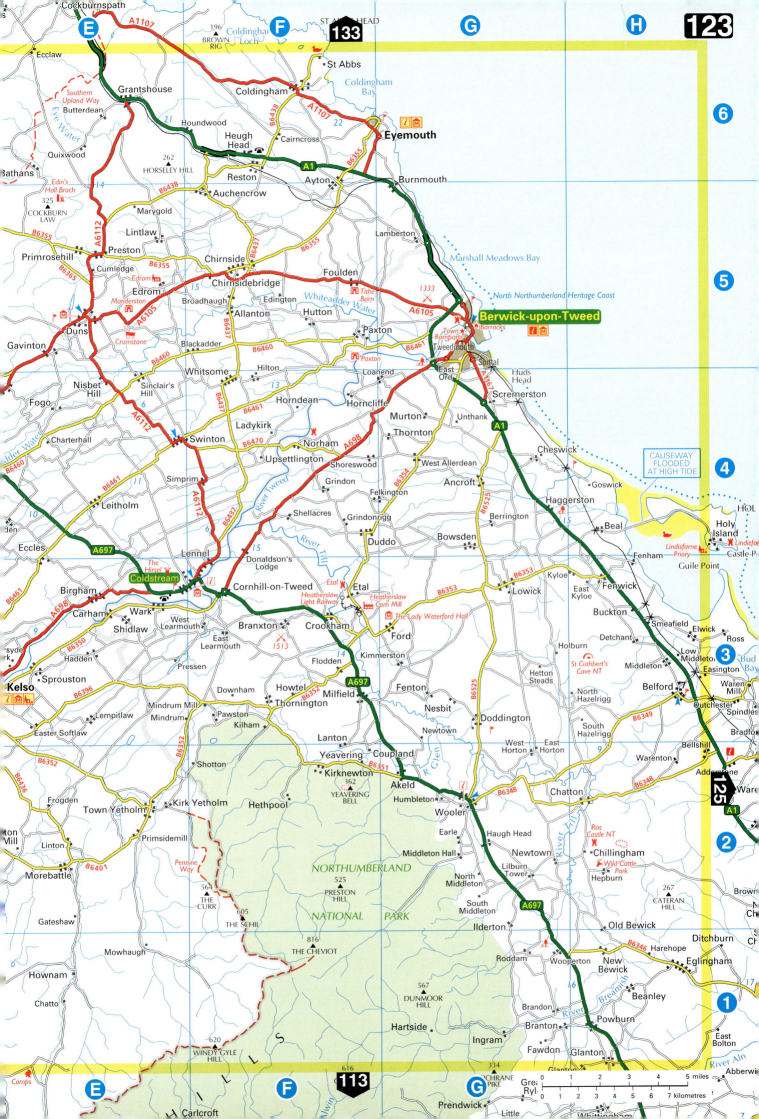

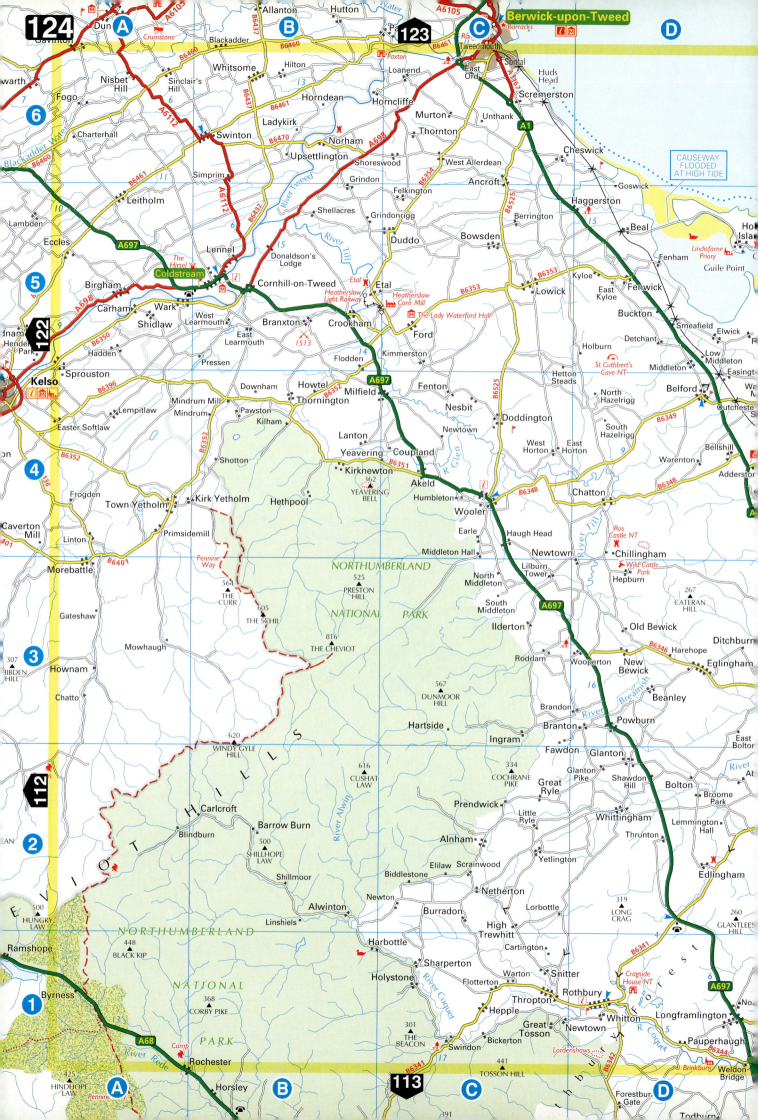

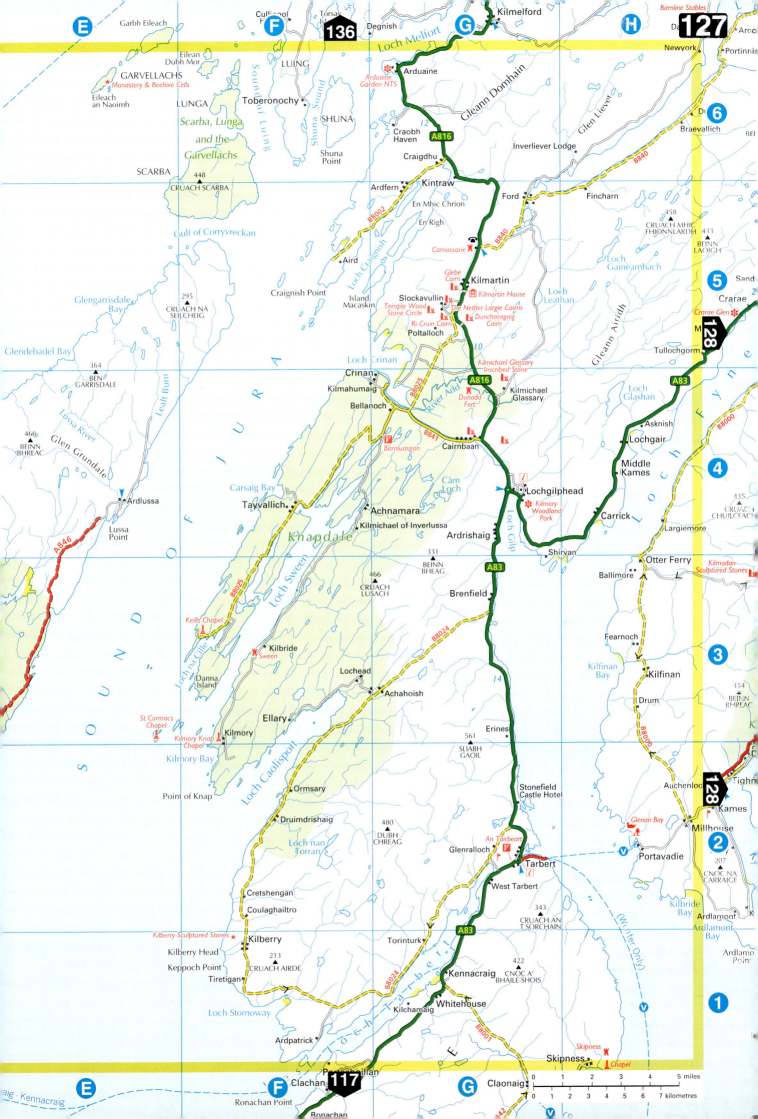

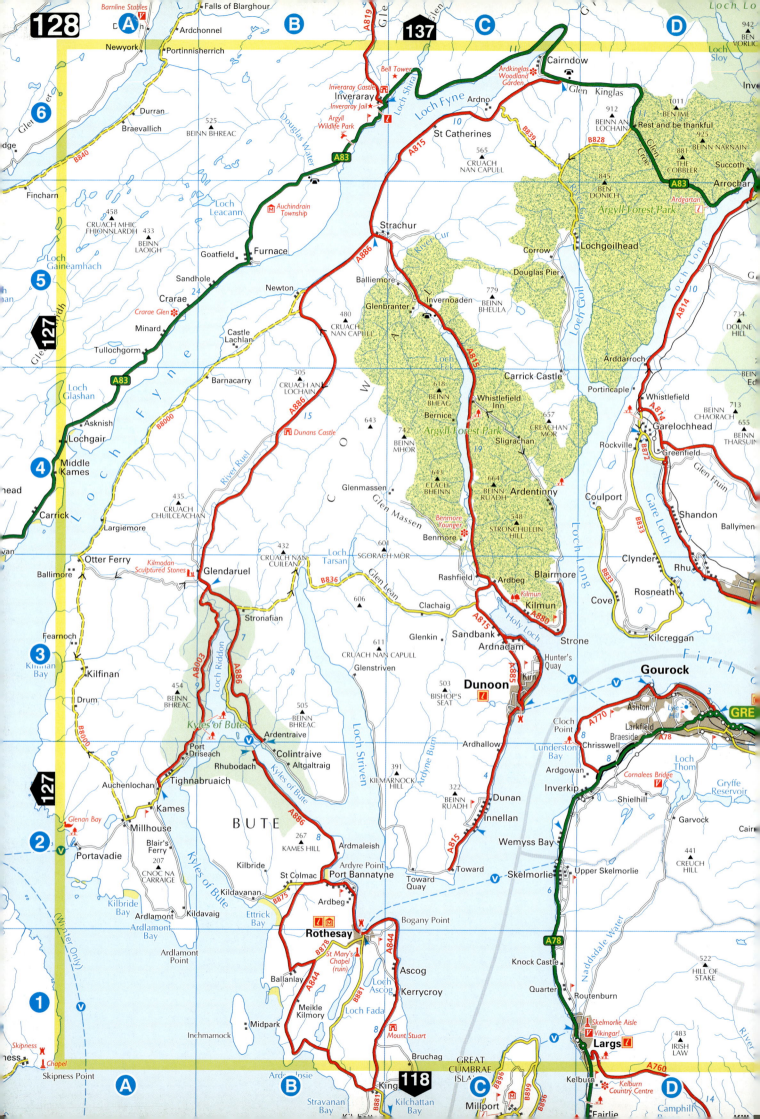

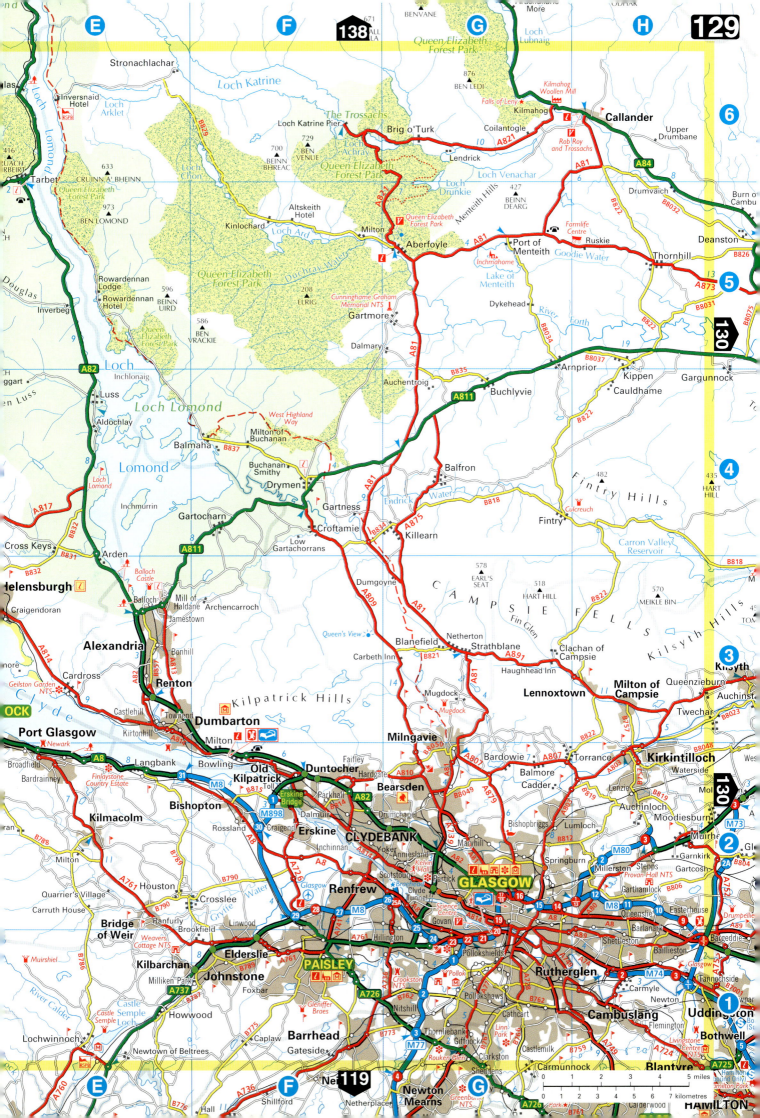

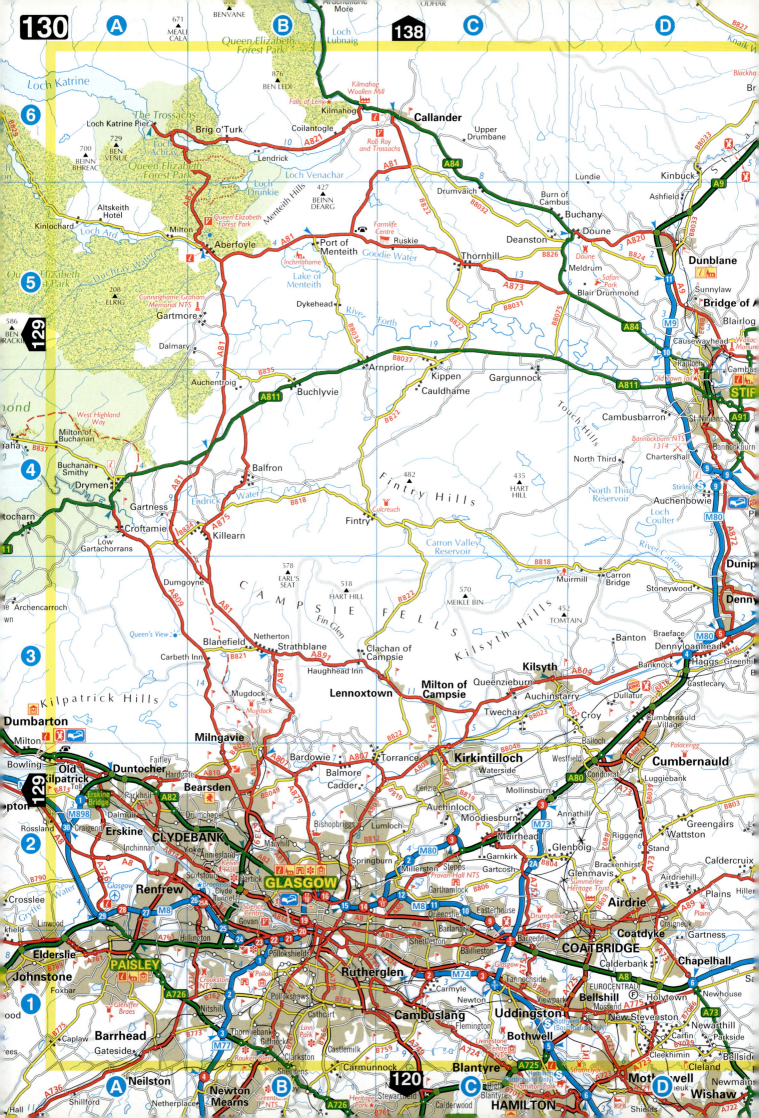

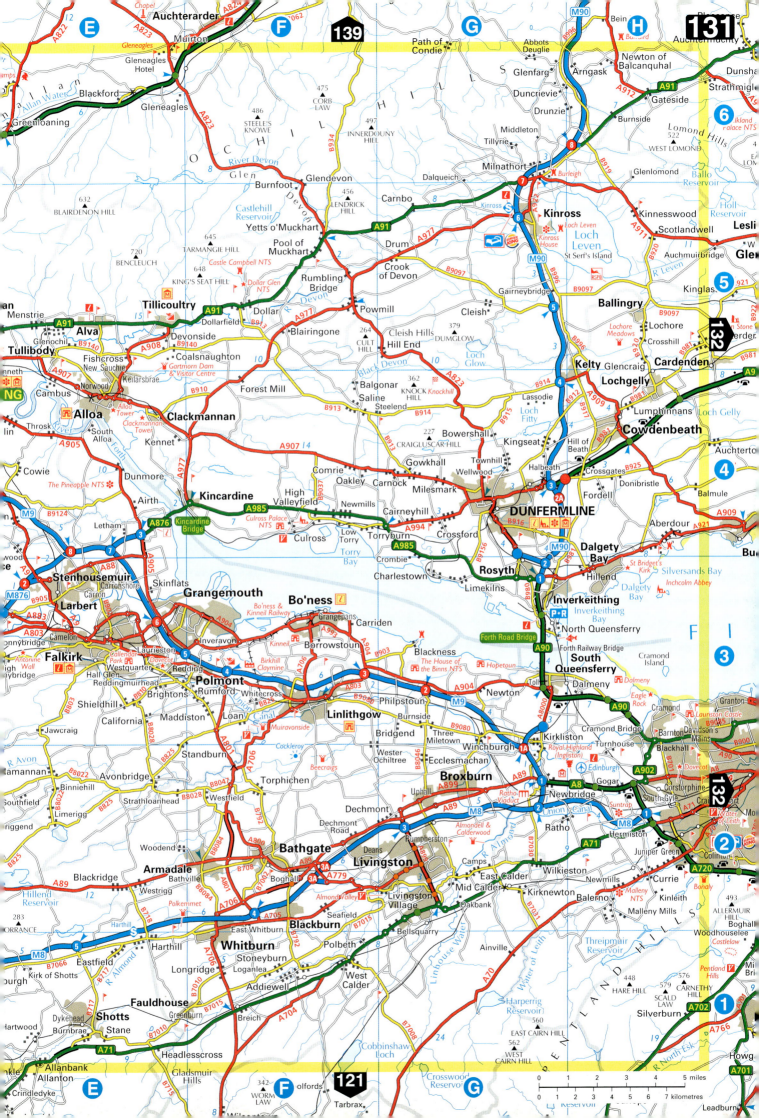

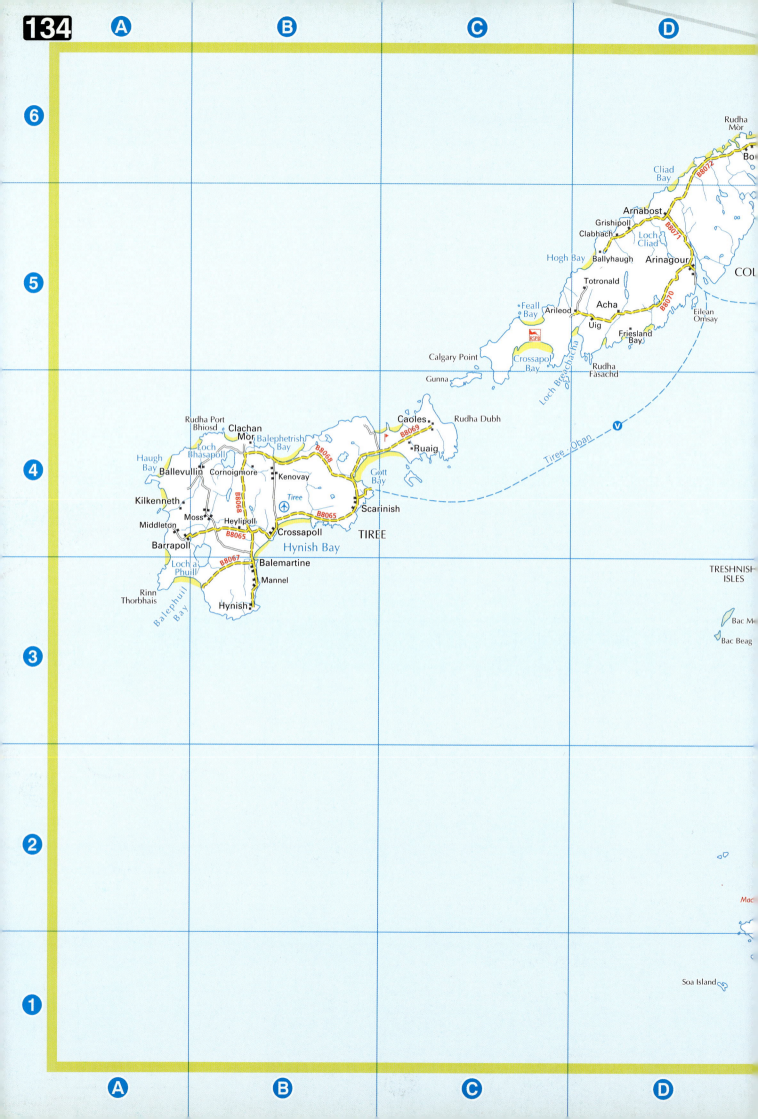

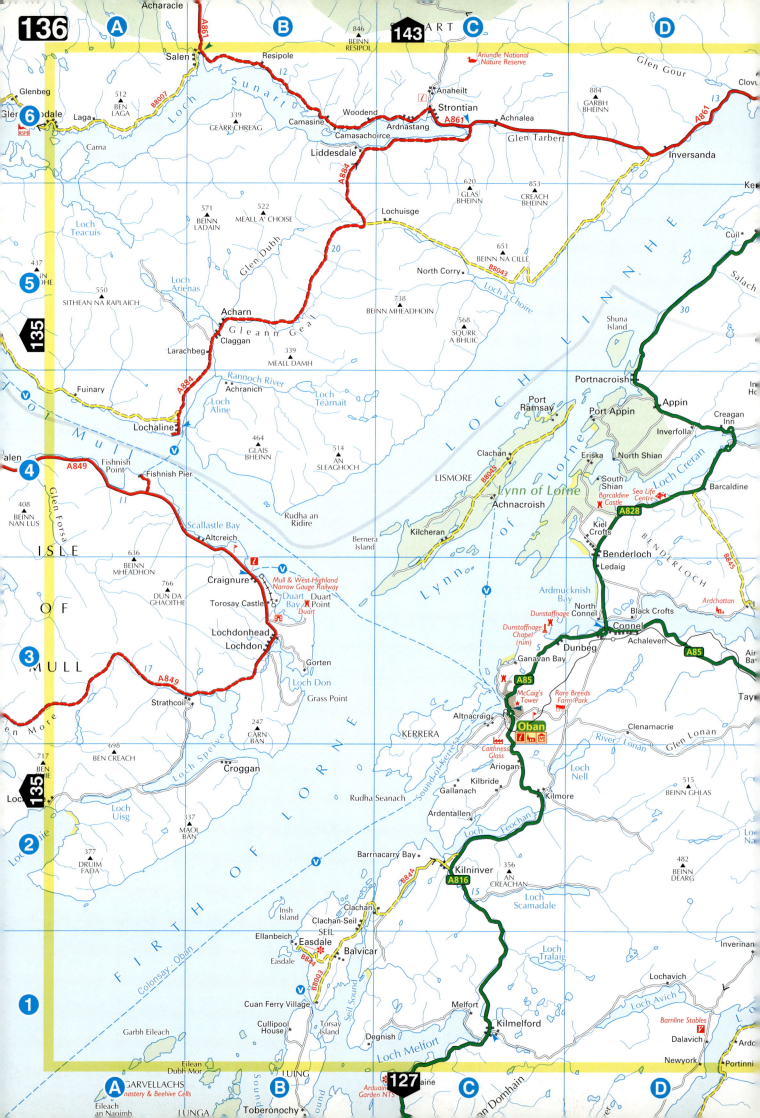

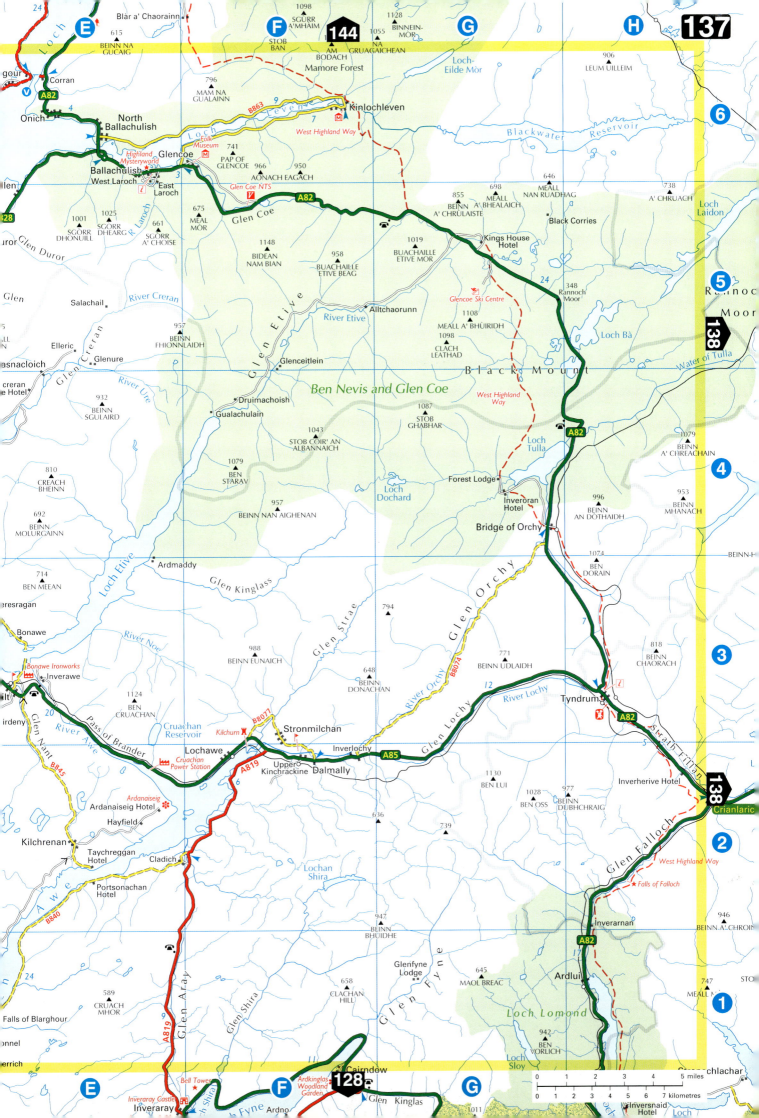

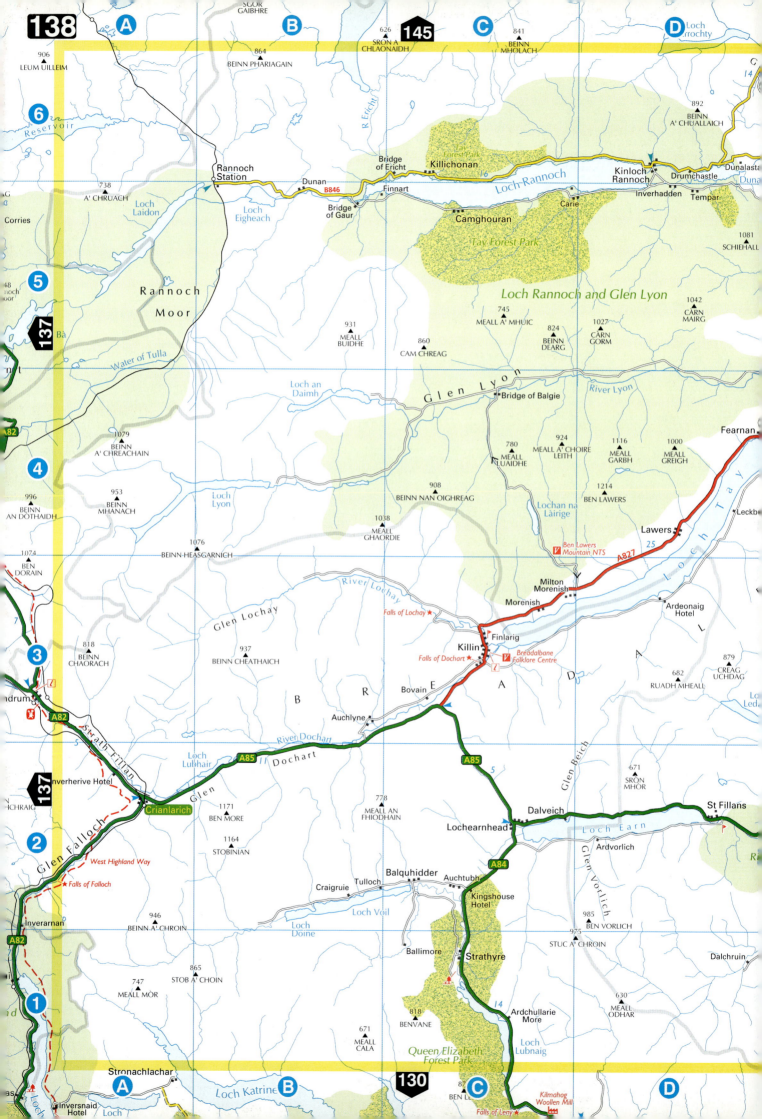

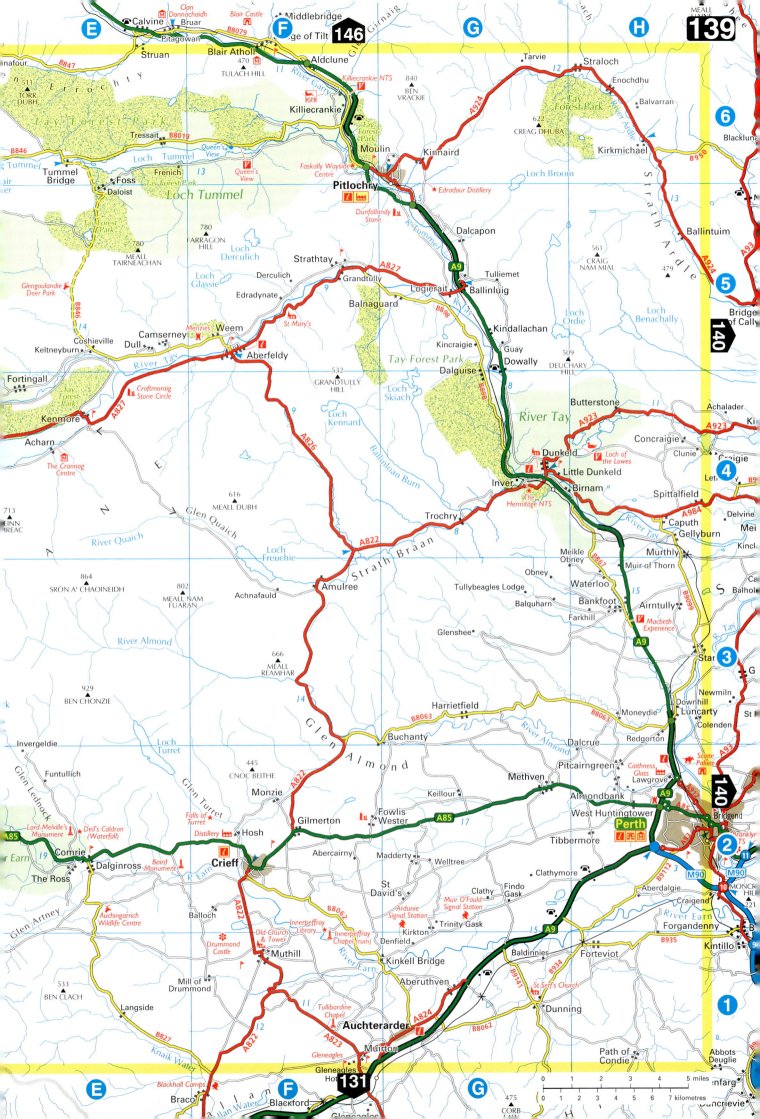

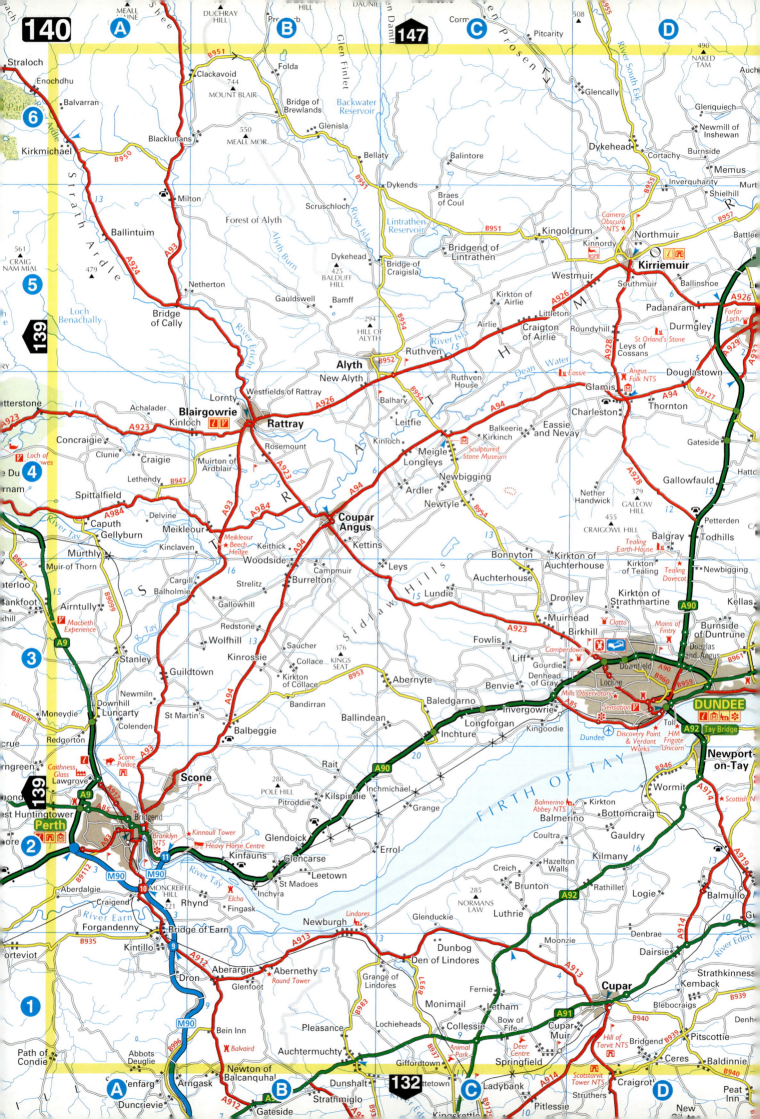

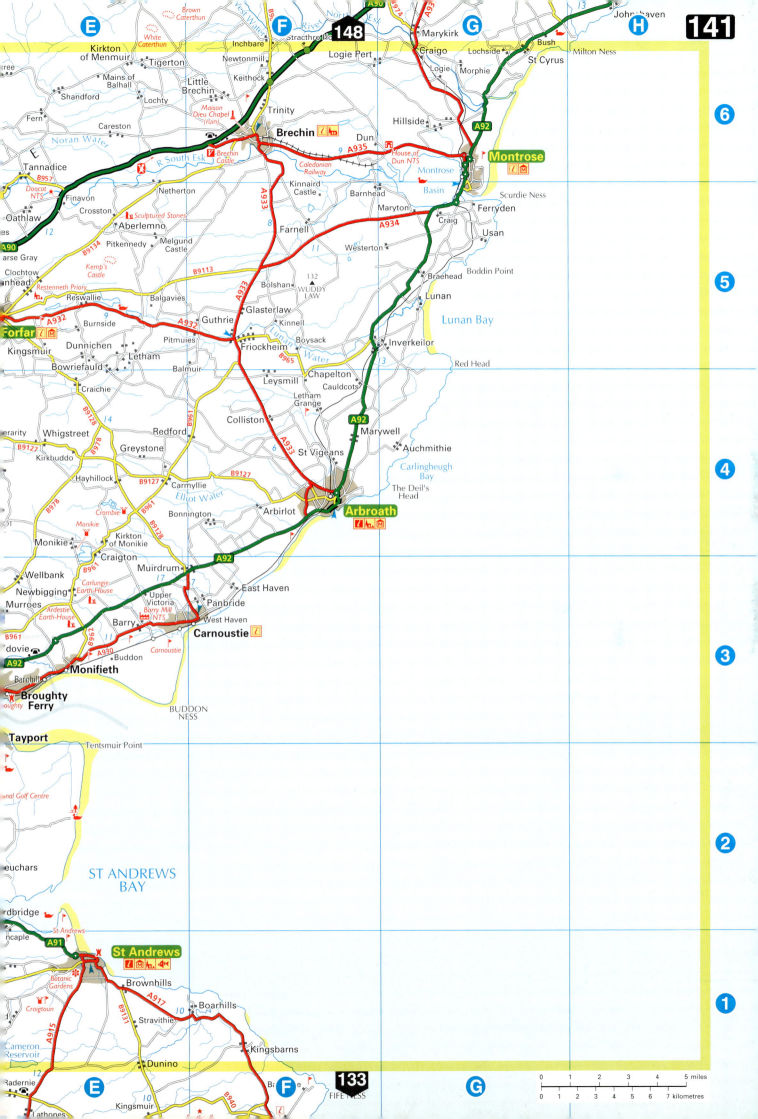

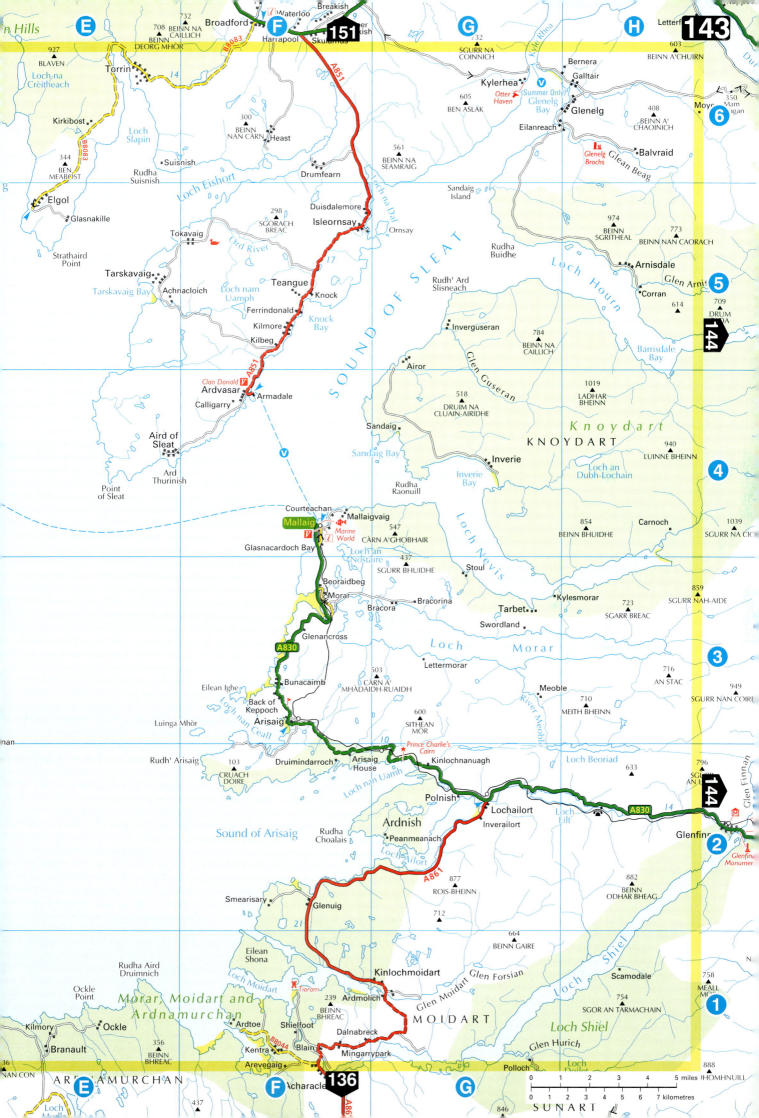

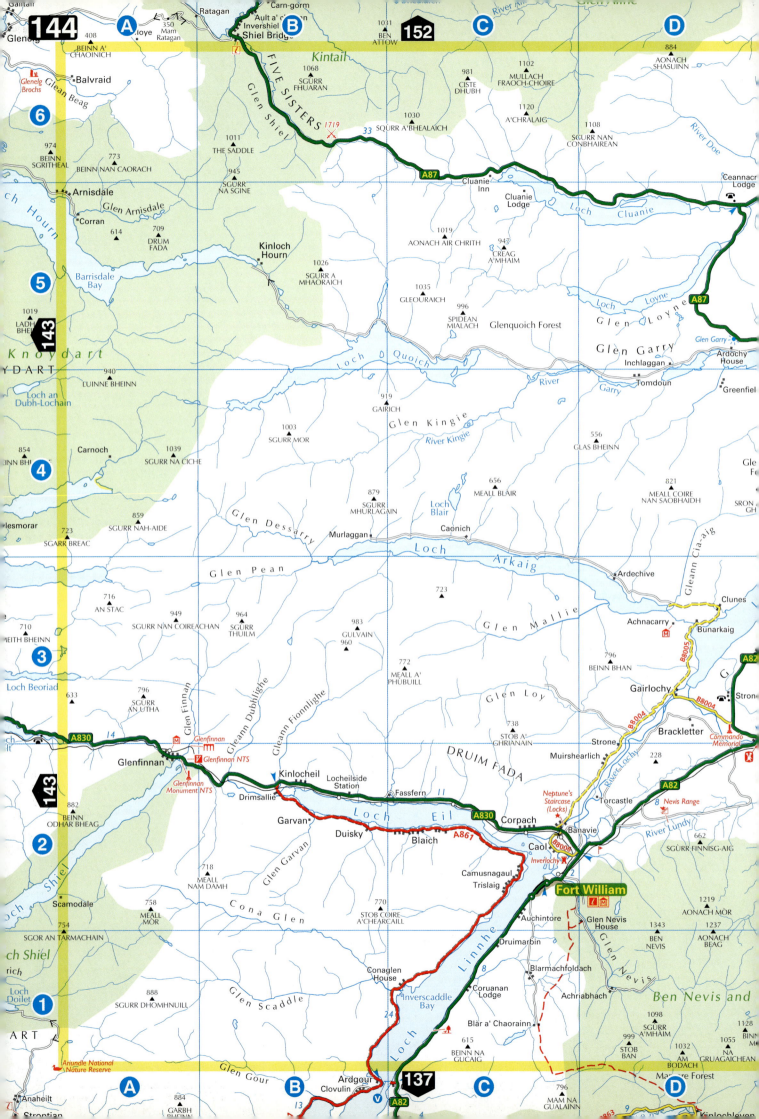

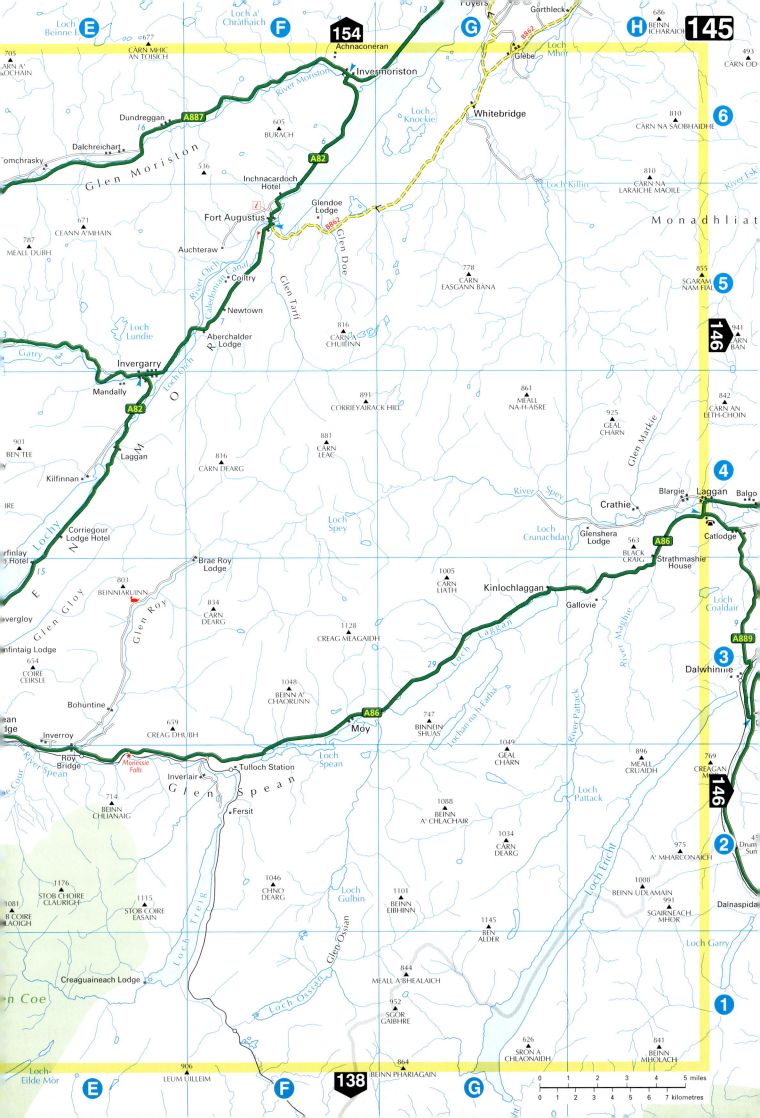

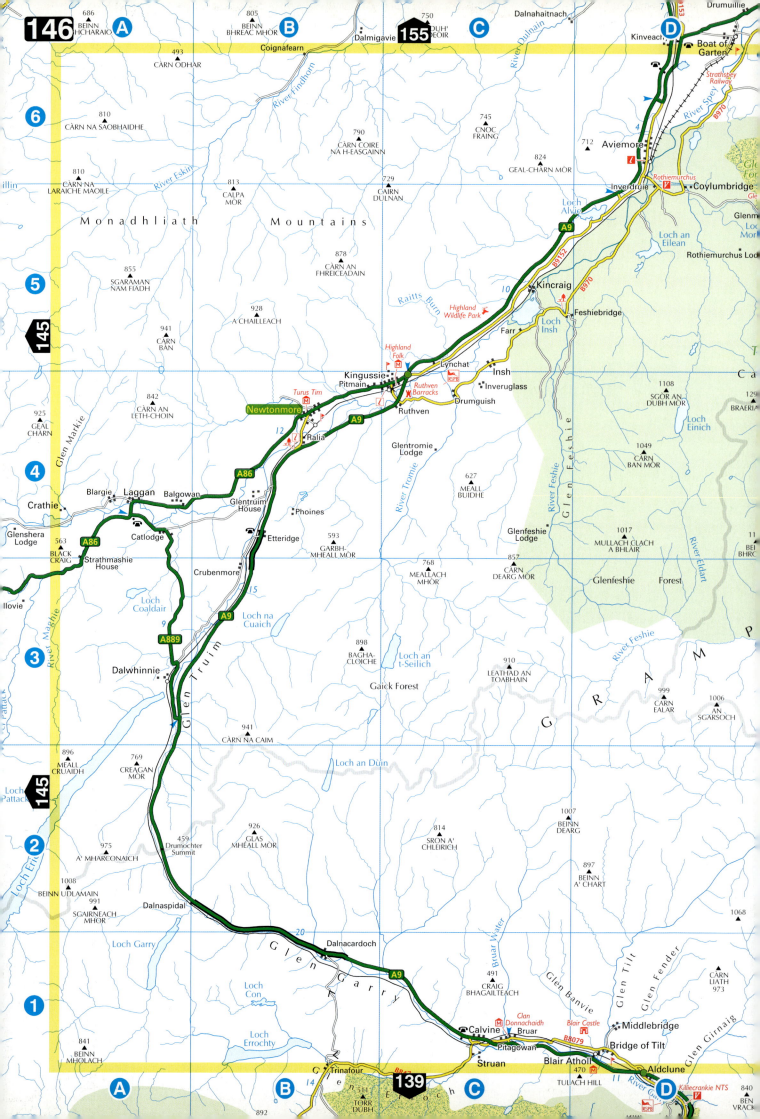

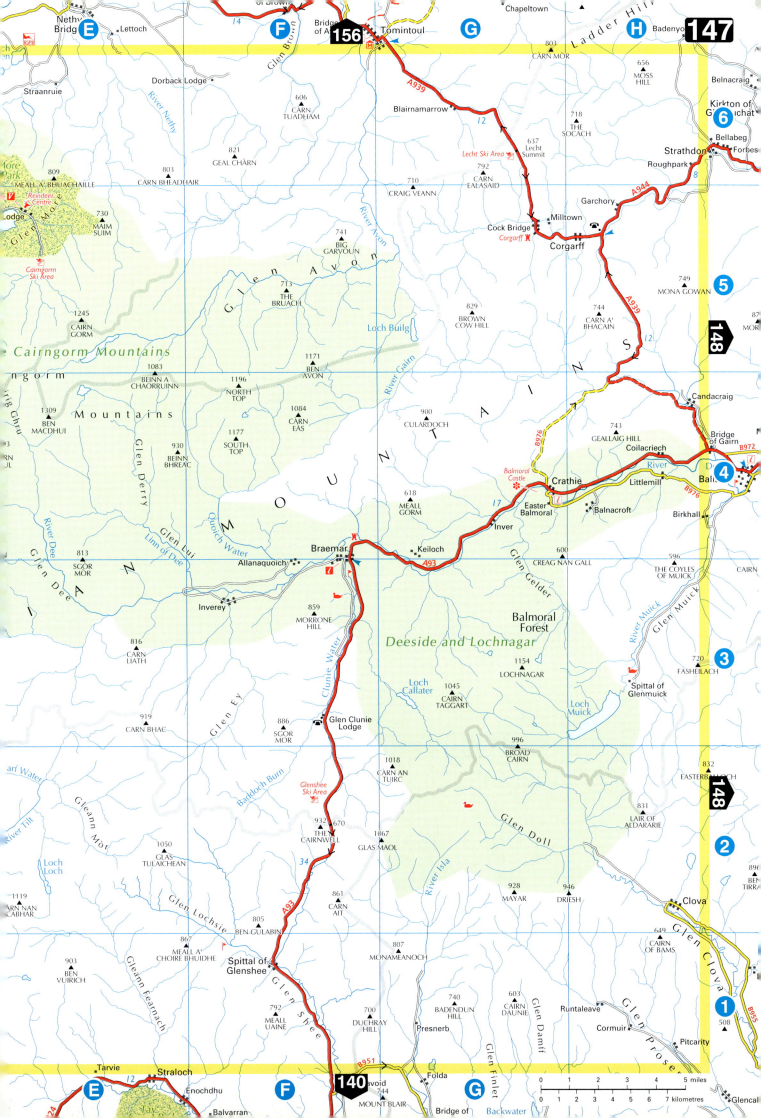

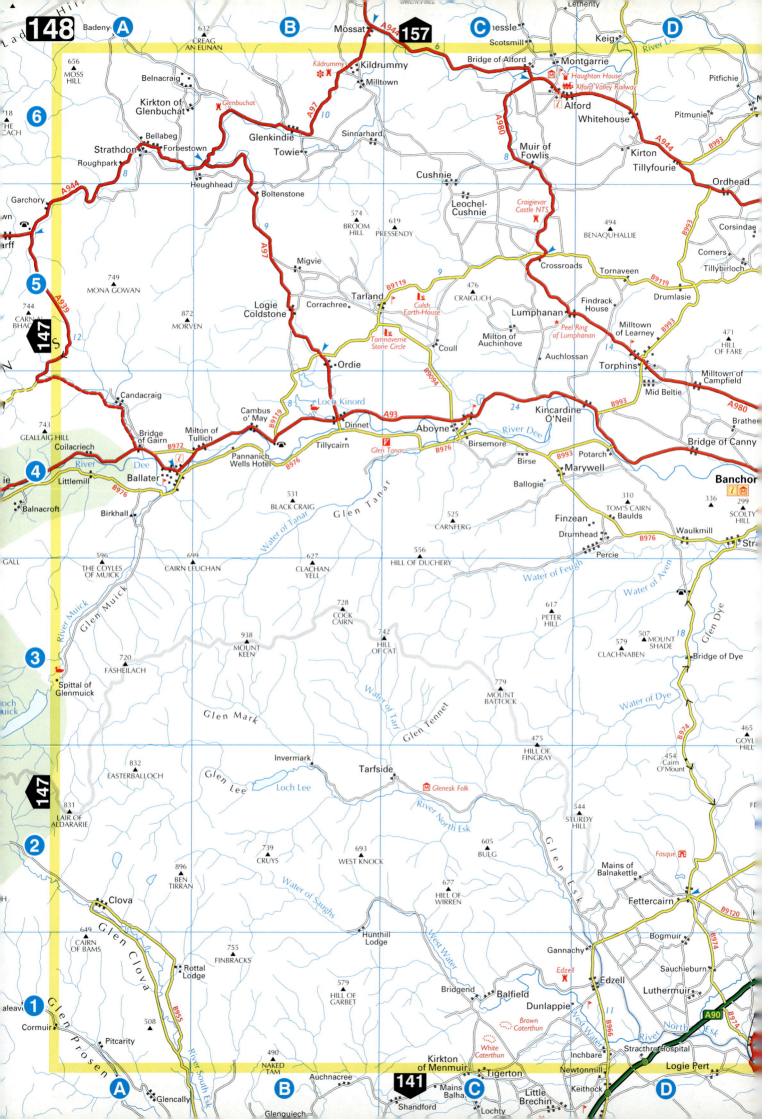

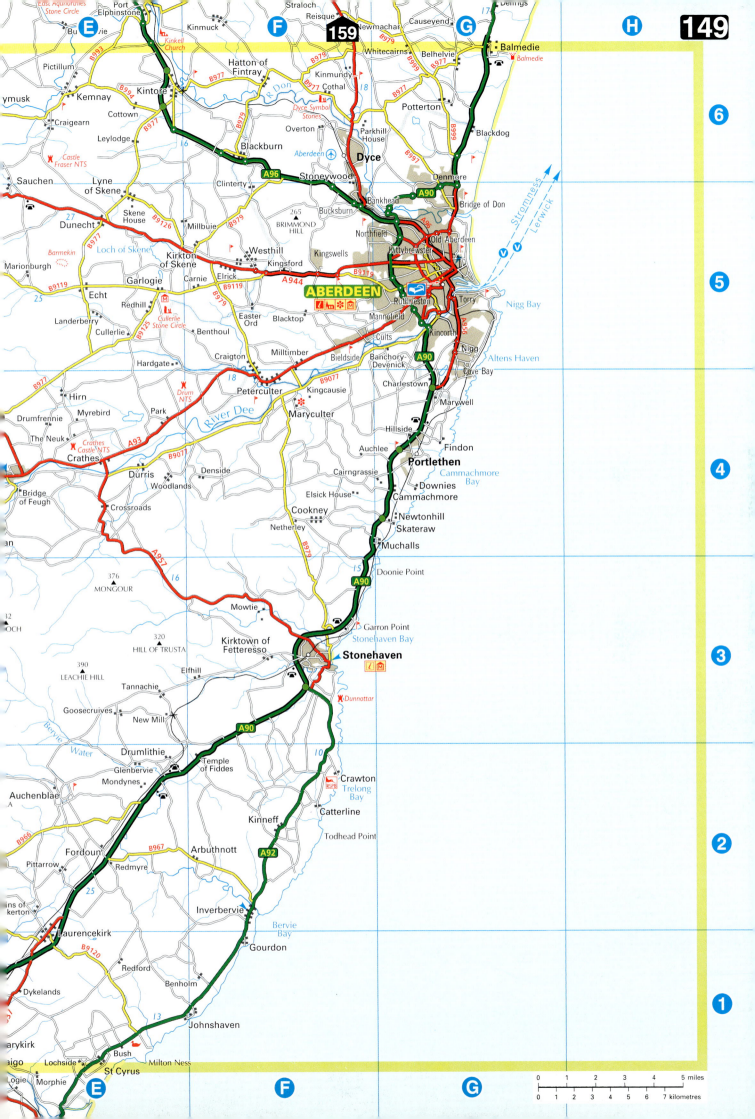

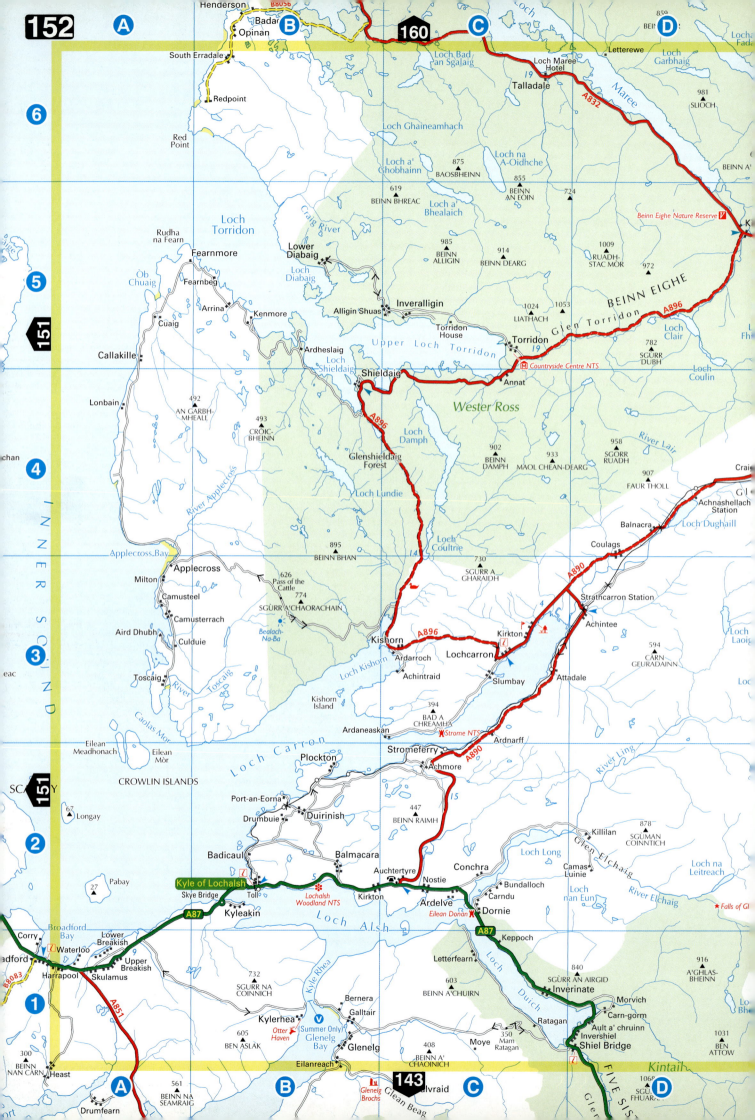

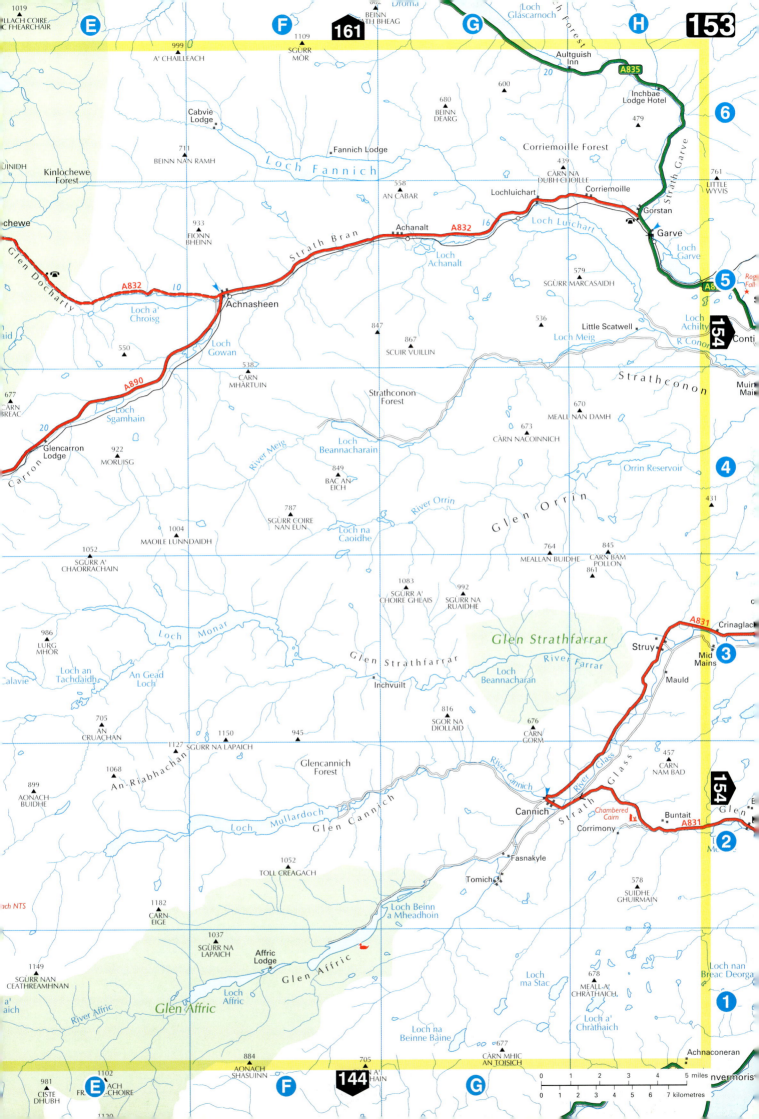

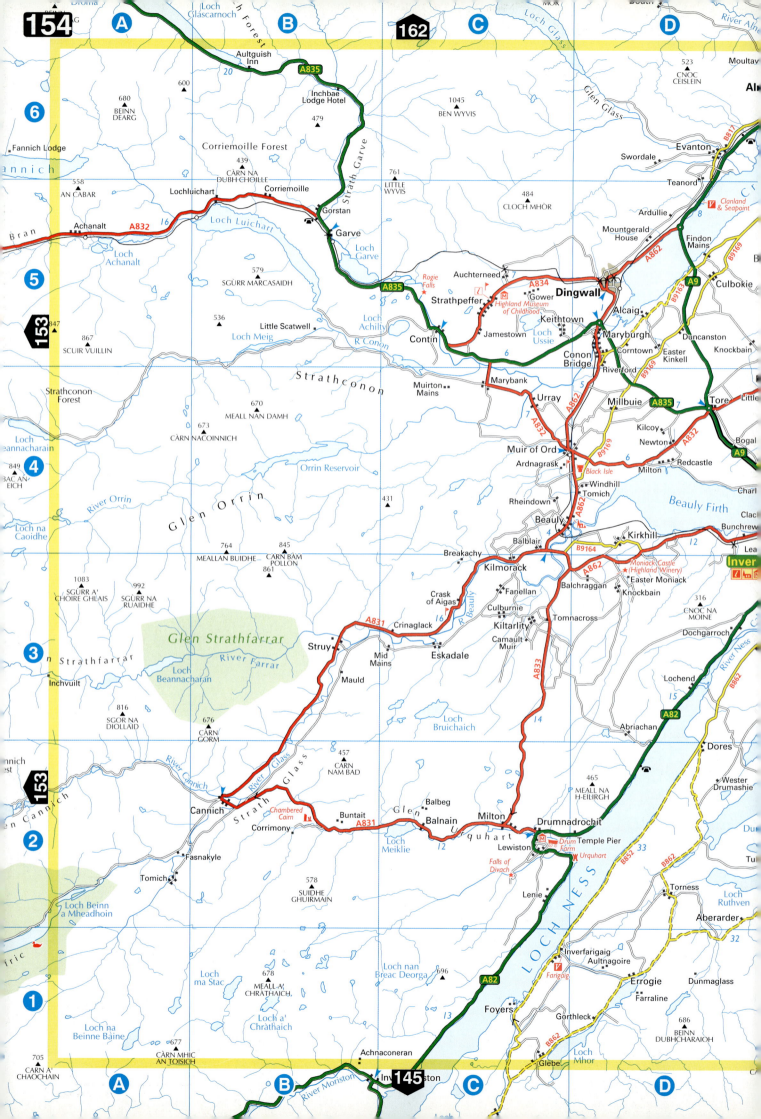

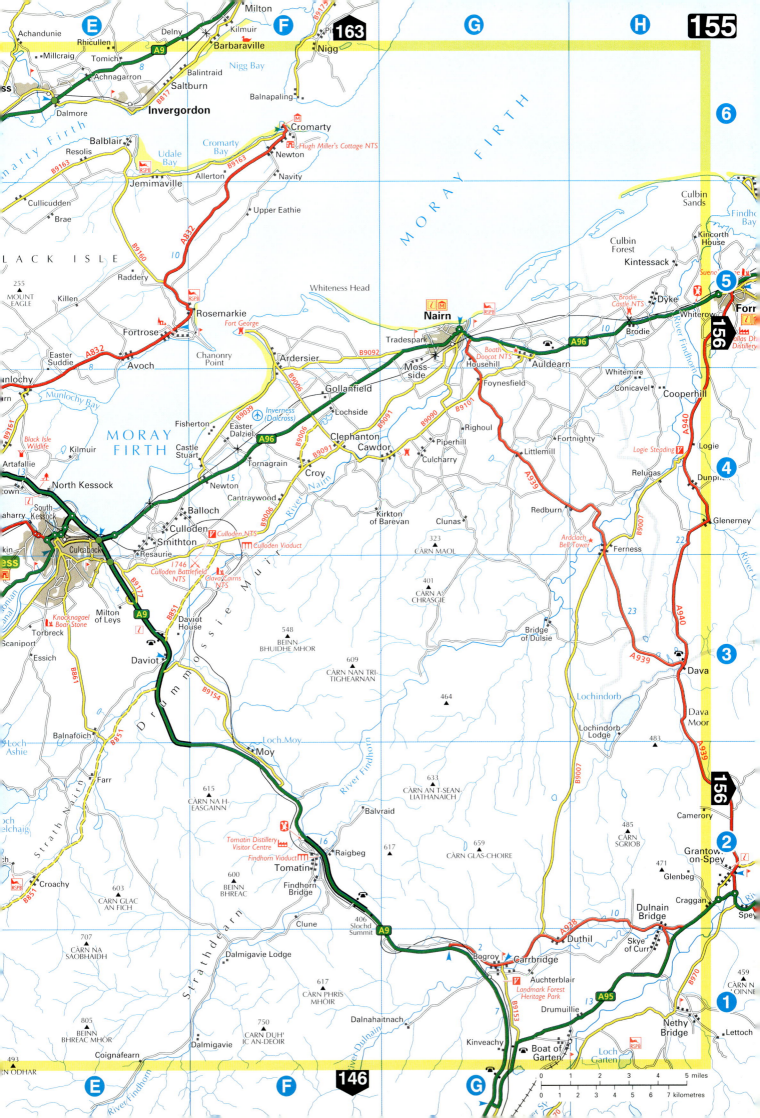

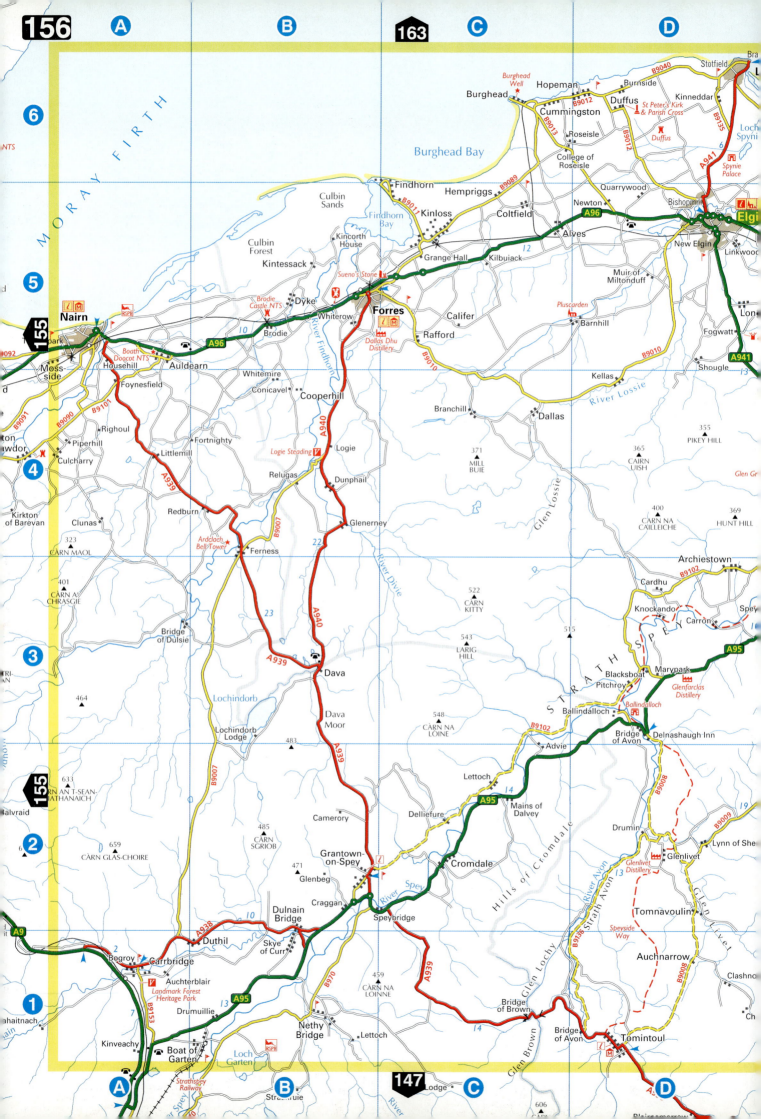

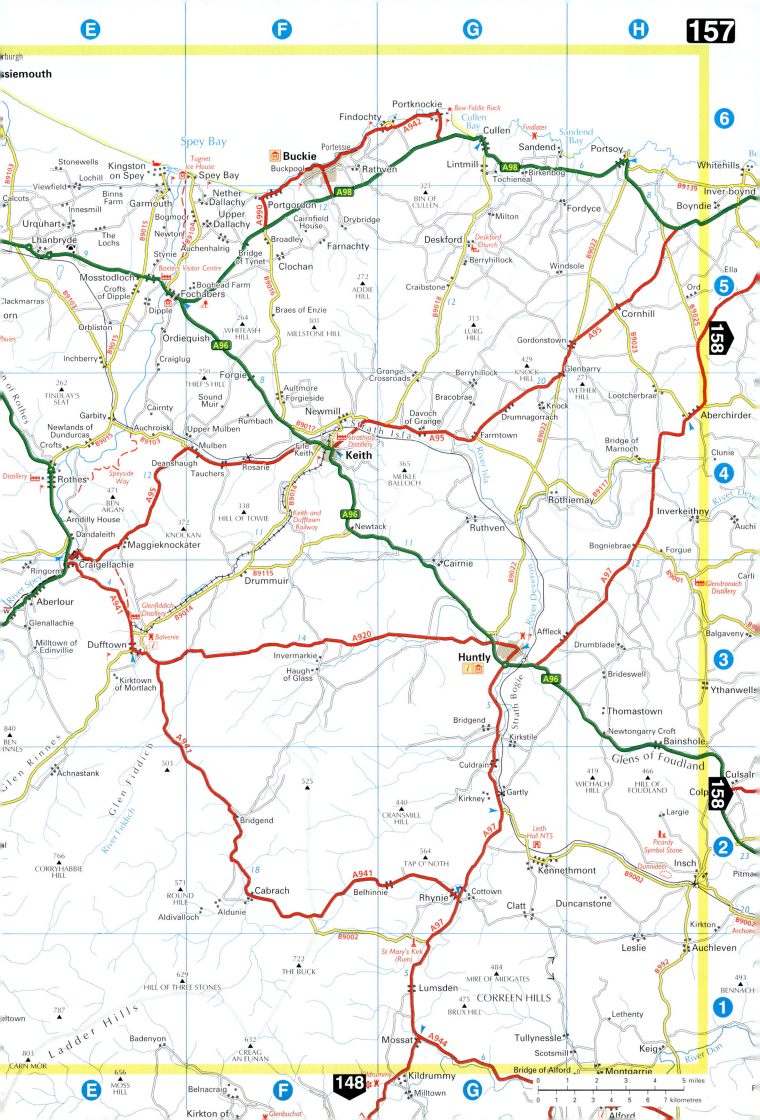

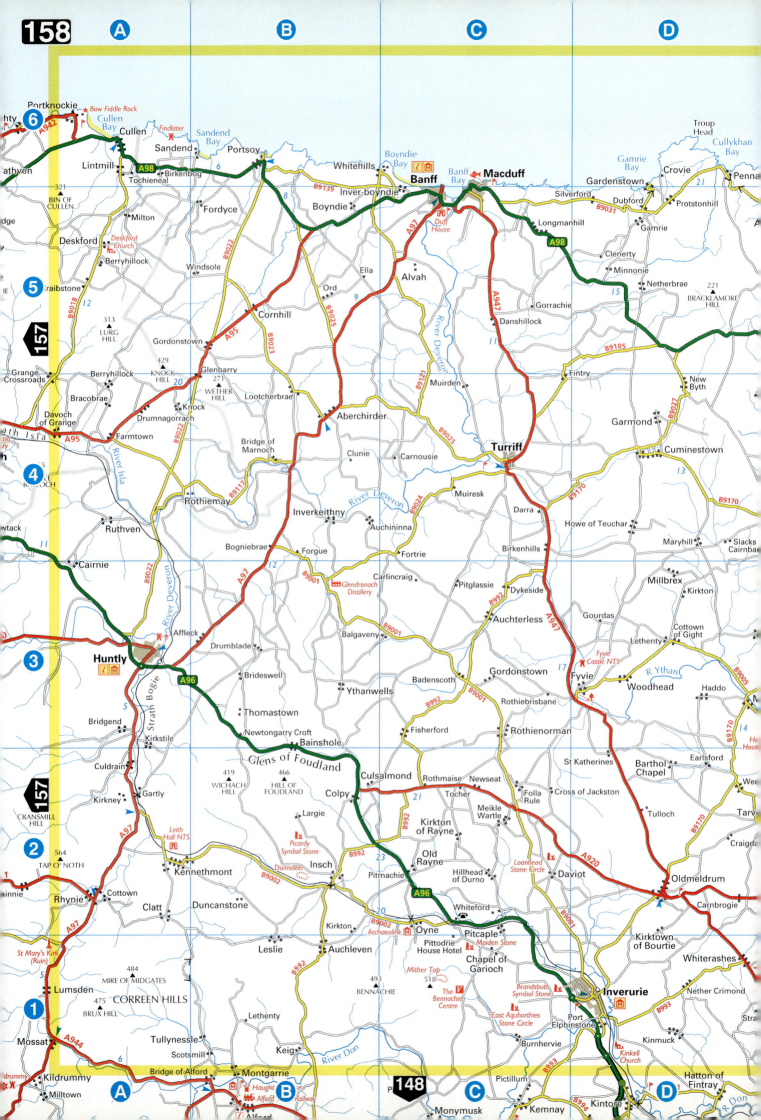

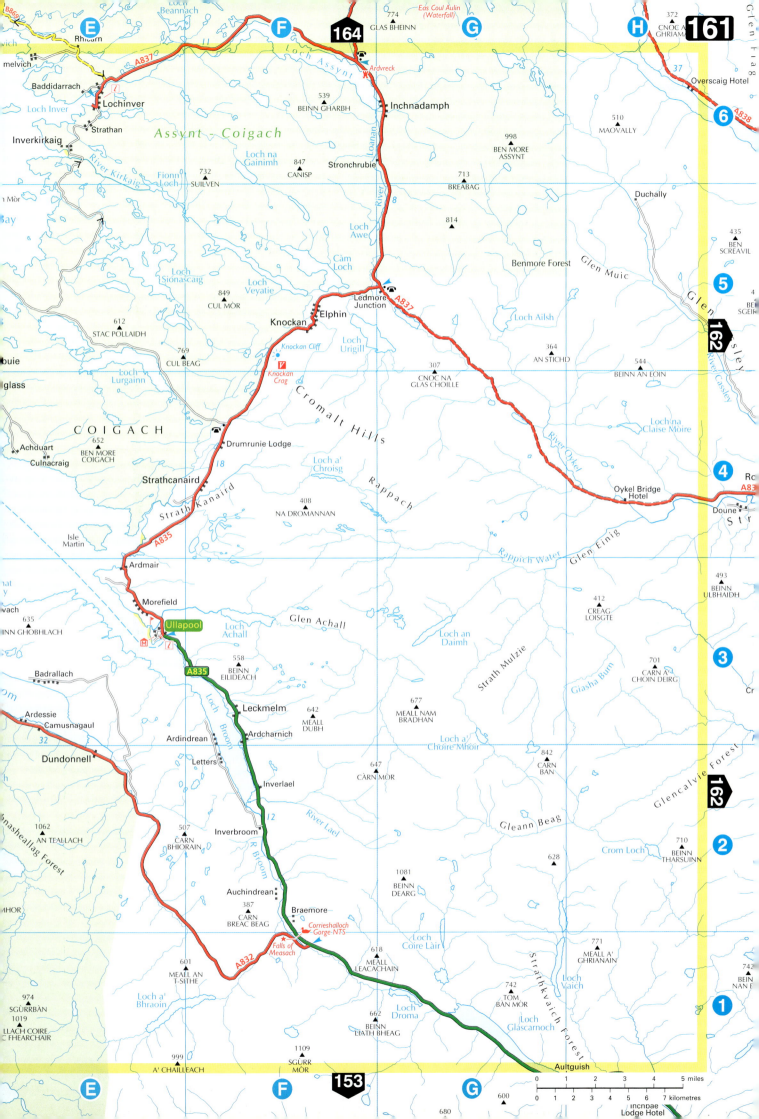

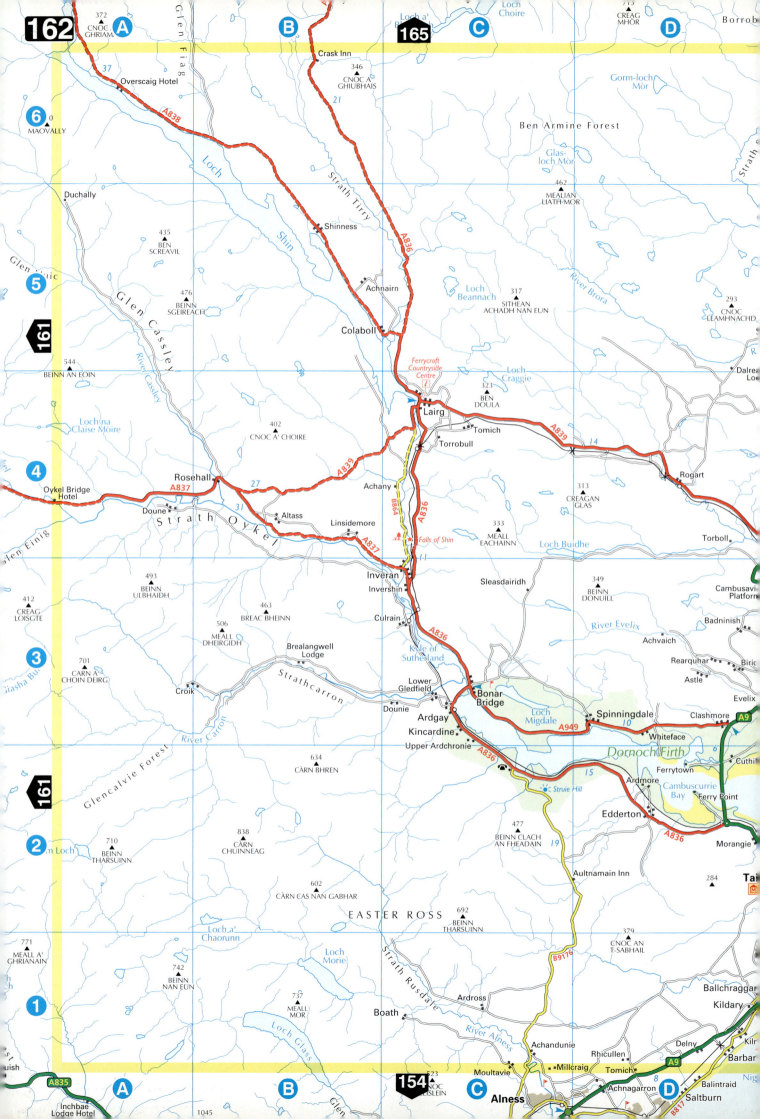

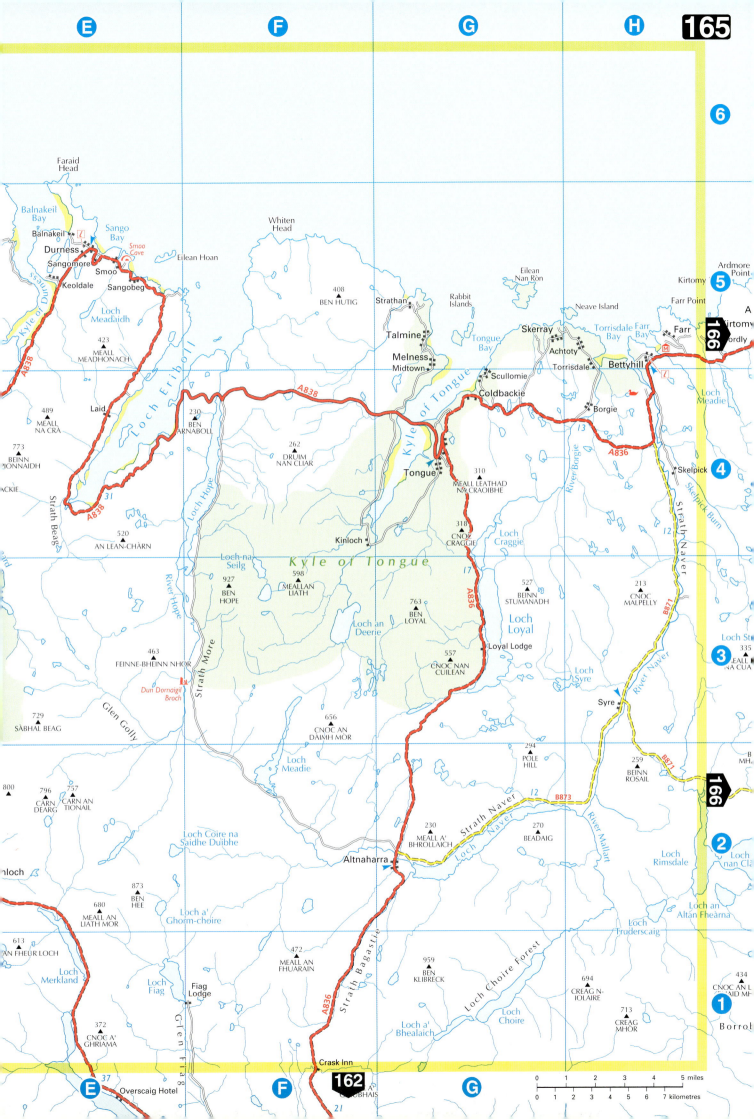

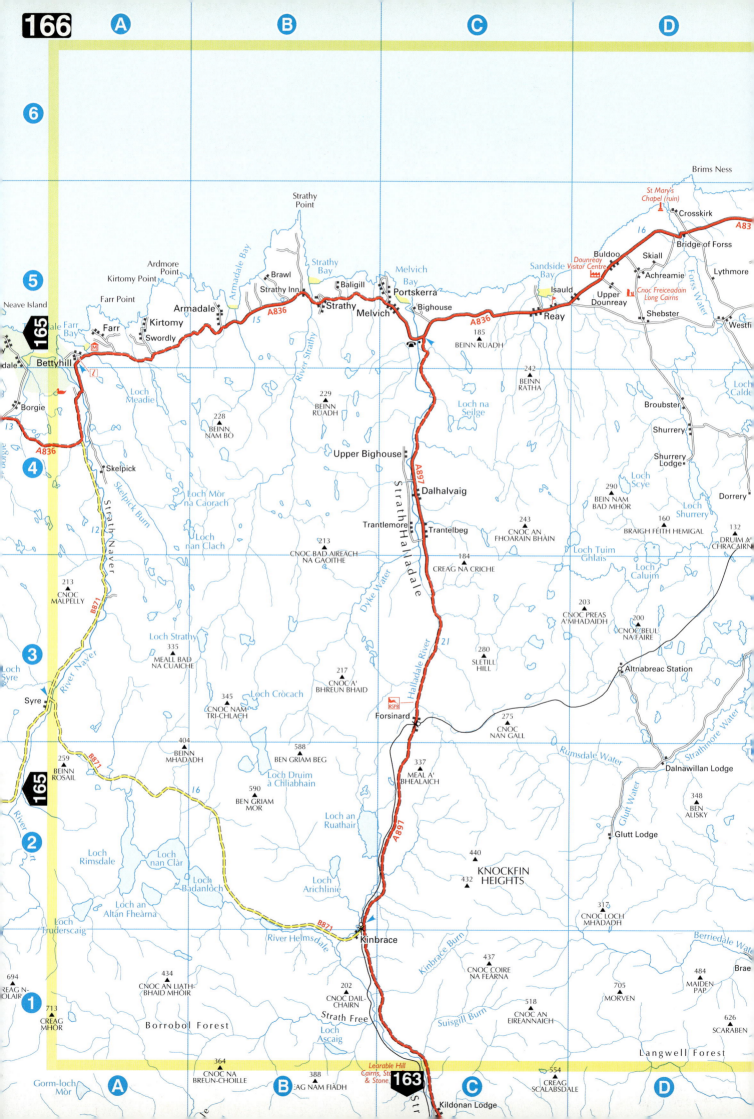

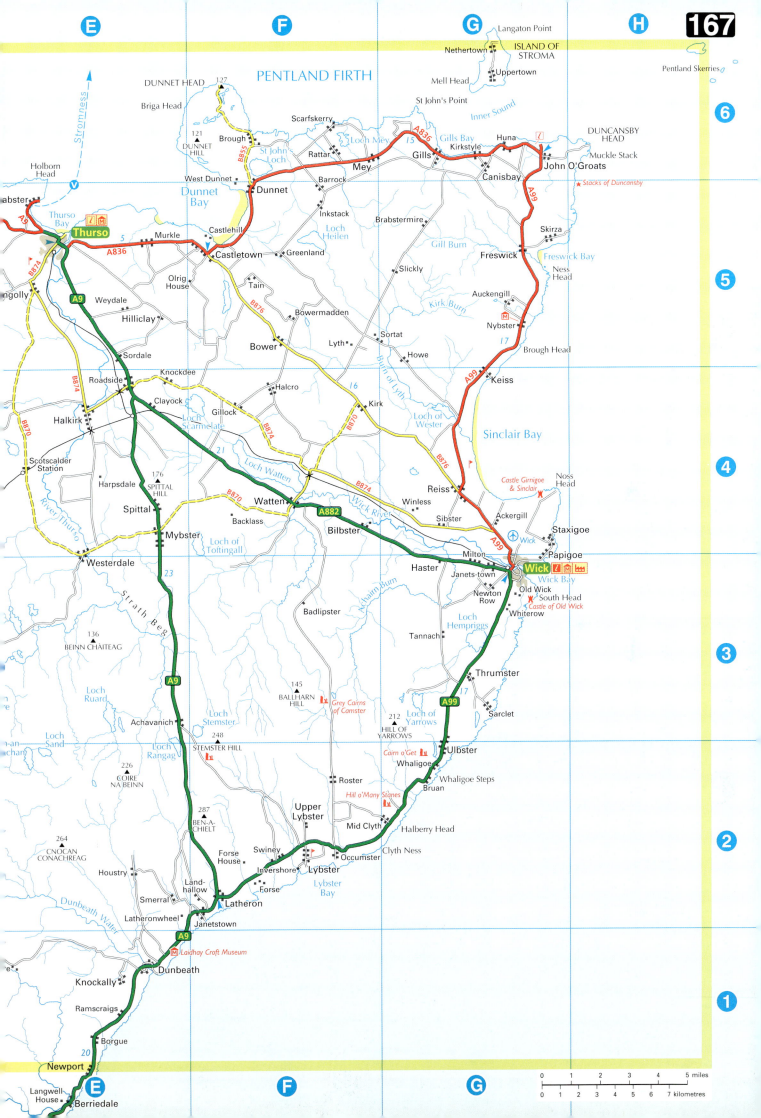

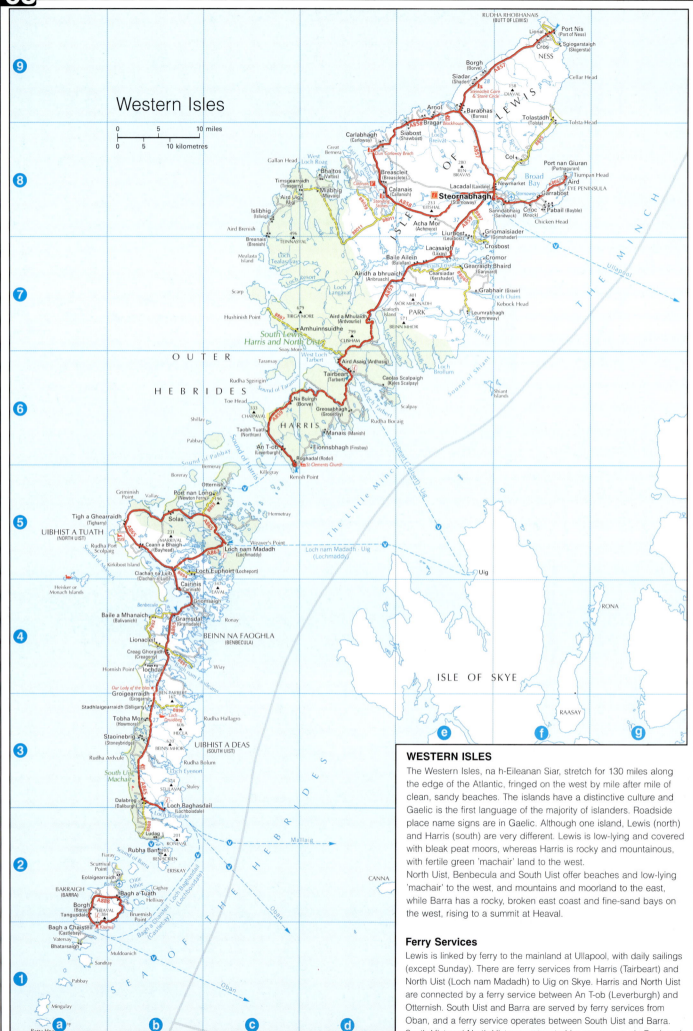

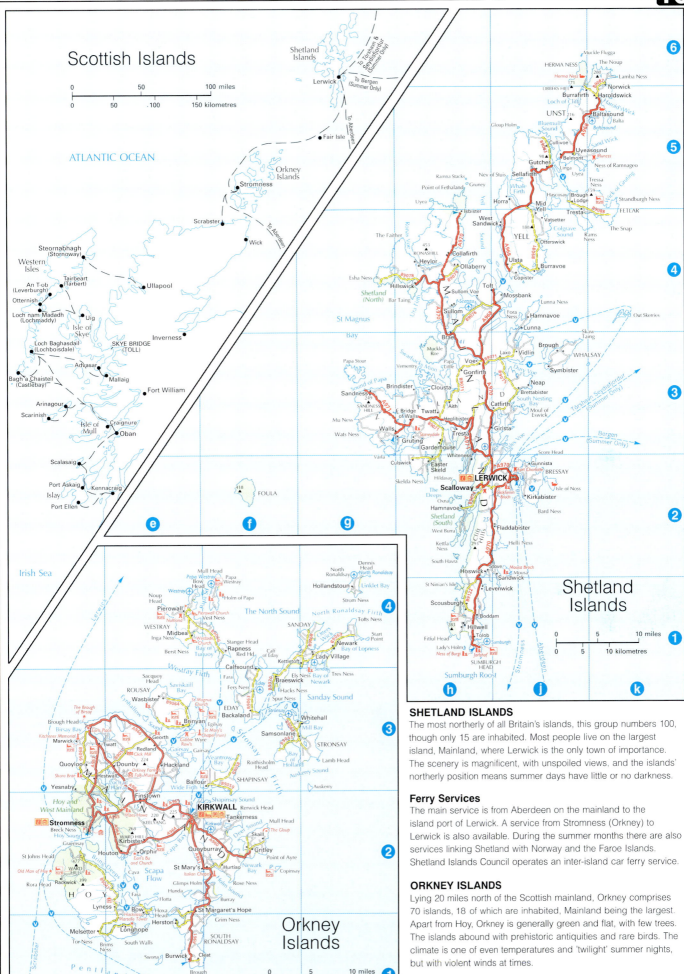

SHETLAND ISLANDS

The most northerly of all Britain's islands, this group numbers 100, though only 15 are inhabited. Most people live on the largest island, Mainland, where Lerwick is the only town of importance. The scenery is magnificent, with unspoiled views, and the islands' northerly position means summer days have little or no darkness.

Ferry Services

The main service is from Aberdeen on the mainland to the island port of Lerwick. A service from Stromness (Orkney) to Lerwick is also available. During the summer months there are also services linking Shetland with Norway and the Faroe Islands. Shetland Islands Council operates an inter-island car ferry service.

ORKNEY ISLANDS

Lying 20 miles north of the Scottish mainland, Orkney comprises 70 islands, 18 of which are inhabited, Mainland being the largest. Apart from Hoy, Orkney is generally green and flat, with few trees. The islands abound with prehistoric antiquities and rare birds. The climate is one of even temperatures and 'twilight' summer nights, but with violent winds at times.

Ferry Services

The main service is from Scrabster on the Caithness coast to the island port of Stromness. A service from Aberdeen to Stromness provides a link to Shetland at Lerwick. Inter-island car ferry services are also operated (advance reservations recommended).

Ireland

Abbeydorney B3	Banteer B2	Clones D5
Abbeyfeale B3	Bantry B2	Clonmany B7
Abbeyleix D3	Beaufort B2	Clonmel C3
Adamstown D3	Belcoo C6	Clonmellon D5
Adare B3	Belfast E6	Clonmore C4
Adrigole B2	Belgooly C2	Clonony C3
Ahascragh C4	Bellaghy D6	Clonoulty C3
Ahoghill E6	Belleek C6	Clonroche D3
Allihies A2	Belmullet B6	Clontibret D5
Anascaul A2	(Béal an Mhuirhead)	Cloondara C5
Annalong E6	Belturbet D5	Cloonlara C5
Annestown D2	Benburb D6	Clough E6
Antrim E6	Bennett's Bridge D3	Cloughjordan C4
Ardagh B3	Beragh D6	Cloyne C2
Ardara C6	Birr C4	Coagh D6
Ardcath E4	Blacklion C6	Coalisland D6
Ardee D5	Blackwater E3	Cobh C2
Ardfert B3	Blarney C2	Coleraine D7
Ardfinnan C3	Blessington D4	Collinstown D5
Ardglass E5	Boherbue B2	Collon D5
Ardgroom A2	Borris D3	Collooney C5
Arklow E3	Borris-in-Ossory C4	Comber E6
Arless D3	Borrisokane C4	Cong B5
Armagh D6	Borrisoleigh C3	Conna C2
Armoy E7	Boyle C5	Cookstown D6
Arthurstown D2	Bracknagh D4	Coole D5
Arvagh D5	Bray E4	Cooraclare B3
Ashbourne E4	Bridgetown D2	Cootehill D5
Ashford E4	Brittas D4	Cork C2
Askeaton B3	Broadford C3	Cornamona B4
Athboy D5	Broadford B3	Corofin B4
Athea B3	Broughshane E6	Courtmacsherry B2
Athenry C4	Bruff C3	Courtown Harbour E3
Athleague C4	Bruree C3	Craigavon E6
Athlone C4	Bunclody D3	Craughwell C4
Athy D4	Buncrana D7	Creeslough C7
Augher D6	Bundoran C6	Creggs C5
Aughnacloy D6	Bunmahon D2	Croagh B3
Aughrim E3	Bunnahowen B6	Crolly (Croithli) C7
Avoca E3	Bunnyconnellan B5	Crookedwood D4
	Burnfort C2	Crookhaven B1
Bagenalstown D3	Bushmills D7	Crookstown B2
(Muine Bheag)	Butler's Bridge D5	Croom B3
Bailieborough D5	Buttevant B3	Crossakeel D5
Balbriggan E4		Cross Barry B2
Balla B5	Cadamstown C4	Crosshaven C2
Ballacolla D3	Caherconlish C3	Crossmaglen D5
Ballaghaderreen C5	Caherdaniel A2	Crossmolina B5
Ballina B3	Cahersiveen A2	Crumlin E6
Ballina B5	Cahir C3	Crusheen B4
Ballinadrid C5	Caledon D6	Culdaff D7
Ballinagh D5	Callan D3	Cullybackey E6
Ballinakill D3	Caltra C4	Curracloe E3
Ballinalee C5	Camp A3	Curraghboy C4
Ballinamallard C5	Cappagh White C3	Curry C5
Ballinascarty B2	Cappamore C3	Cushendall E7
Ballinasloe C4	Cappoquin C2	
Ballindine B5	Carlanstown D5	Daingean D4
Ballineen B2	Calingford E5	Delvin D5
Ballingarry C3	Carndonagh D7	Derrygonnelly C6
Ballingarry B3	Carnew D3	Derrylin D5
Ballingeary B2	Carnlough E7	Dervock E7
(Béal Átha an	Carracastle C5	Dingle A2
Ghaorfthaidh)	Carrick C6	(An Daingean)
Ballinhassig C2	(An Charraig)	Doagh E6
Ballinlough C5	Carrickfergus E6	Donaghadee E6
Ballinrobe B5	Carrickmacross D5	Donaghmore C3
Ballinspittle C2	Carrickmore D6	Donegal C6
Ballintober C5	Carrick-on-Shannon	Doneraile C3
Ballintra C6	C5	Doon C4
Ballivor D4	Carrick-on-Suir D3	Doonbeg B3
Ballon D3	Carrigahorig C4	Douglas C2
Ballybaun C4	Carrigaline C2	Downpatrick E6
Ballybay D5	Carrigallen D5	Downs C5
Ballybofey C6	Carriganimmy B2	Draperstown D6
Ballybunion B3	Carrigans D7	Drimoleague B2
Ballycanew E3	Carrigart C7	Dripsey B2
Ballycarry E6	(Carraig Airt)	Drogheda E5
Ballycastle B6	Carrigtohill C2	Dromahair C6
Ballycastle E7	Carrowkeel D7	Dromcolliher B3
Ballyclare E6	Carryduff E6	Dromod C5
Ballyconneely A4	Cashel C3	Dromore E6
Ballycotton C2	Castlebar B5	Dromore D6
Ballycumber C4	Castlebellingham E5	Dromore West C6
Ballydehob B1	Castleblayney D5	Drum D5
Ballydesmond B2	Castlebridge D3	Drumcliff C6
Ballyduff C2	Castlecomer D3	Drumconrath D5
Ballyduff B3	Castlederg D6	Drumkeeran D5
Ballyfarnan C5	Castledermot D3	Drumlish C5
Ballygalley E6	Castleisland B3	
Ballygar C4	Castlemaine B2	
Ballygawley D6	Castlemartyr C2	
Ballygowan E6	Castleplunket C5	
Ballyhaise D5	Castlepollard D5	
Ballyhale D3	Castlerea C5	
Ballyhaunis C5	Castlerock D7	
Ballyhean B5	Castleshane D5	
Ballyheige B3	Castletown D4	
Ballyjamesduff D5	Castletown	
Ballykeeran C4	Bearhaven A2	
Ballylanders C3	Castletownroche C2	
Ballylongford B3	Castletownshend B1	
Ballylooby C3	Castlewellan E5	
Ballylynan D3	Causeway B3	
Ballymahon C4	Cavan D5	
Ballymakeery B2	Celbridge D4	
Ballymena E6	Charlestown C5	
Ballymoe C5	Charleville B3	
Ballymoney D7	(Rath Luirc)	
Ballymore C4	Clady D6	
Ballymore Eustace D4	Clane D4	
Ballymote C5	Clara C4	
Ballynahinch E6	Clarecastle B3	
Ballynure E6	Claremorris B5	
Ballyporeen C3	Clarinbridge B4	
Ballyragget D3	Clashmore C2	
Ballyroan D4	Claudy D7	
Ballyronan D6	Clifden A4	
Ballysadare C5	Cliffoney C6	
Ballyshannon C6	Clogh D3	
Ballyvaughan B4	Cloghan C4	
Ballywalter E6	Clogheen C3	
Balrothery E4	Clogher D6	
Baltimore B1	Clohamon D3	
Baltinglass D3	Clonakilty B2	
Banagher C4	Clonard D4	
Banbridge E6	Clonaslee D4	
Bandon B2	Clonbulloge D4	
Bangor E6	Clonbur B5	
Bangor Erris B5	(An Fhairche)	
Bansha C3	Clondalkin E4	

Drumquin D6	Glenmore D3	Kilmaganny D3
Drumshanbo C5	Glenties C6	Kilmaine B5
Drumsna C5	Glin B3	Kilmallock C3
Duagh B3	Glinsk B4	Kilmanagh D3
Dublin E4	(Glinsce)	Kilmeadan D2
Duleek E5	Golden C3	Kilmeage B4
Dunboyne D4	Goleen B1	Kilmeedy B3
Duncormick D2	Gorey E3	Kilmichael B2
Dundalk E5	Goresbridge D3	Kilmore Quay D2
Dunderrow C2	Gort B4	Kilnaleck D5
Dundrum E5	Gortin D6	Kilrea D7
Dunfanaghy C7	Gowran D3	Kilrush B3
Dungannon D6	Graiguenamanagh D3	Kilsheelan C3
Dungarvan C2	Granard E5	Kiltealy D3
Dungarvan B3	Grange C6	Kiltegan D3
Dungiven D7	Greyabbey E6	Kiltimagh B5
Dungloe C7	Greystones E4	Kiltoom C4
(An Clochan Liath)	Gulladuff D6	Kingscourt D5
Dungourney C2		Kinlough C6
Dunkineely C6	Hacketstown D3	Kinnegad D4
Dun Laoghaire E4	Headford B4	Kinnitty C4
Dunlavin D3	Herbertstown C3	Kinsale C2
Dunleer E5	Hillsborough E6	Kinvarra B4
Dunloy E7	Hilltown E5	Kircubbin E6
Dunmanway B2	Holycross C3	Kildorrery C2
Dunmore C5	Holywood E6	Knock B5
Dunmore East D2	Howth E4	Knockcroghery C4
Dunmurry E6		Knocklofty C3
Dunshauglin D4	Inch A2	Knocktopher D3
Durrow D3	Inchigeelagh B2	
Durrus B2	Inishannon B2	Lahinch B4
Dysart C4	Irvinestown D6	Laragh E4
		Larne E6
Easky B6	Johnstown C3	Lauragh A2
Edenderry D4		Laurencetown C4
Edgeworthstown D5	Kanturk B2	Leap B2
Eglinton D7	Keadue C5	Leenane B5
Elphin C5	Keady D5	Leighlinbridge D3
Emyvale D6	Keel A5	Leitrim C5
Enfield D4	Keenagh C5	Leixlip D4
Ennis B3	Kells D5	Lemybrien C2
Enniscorthy D3	Kells D5	Letterfrack B5
Enniscrone B6	Kenmare B2	Letterkenny D7
Enniskean B2	Kesh C6	Lifford D6
Enniskillen D6	Kilbeggan D4	Limavady D7
Ennistymon B4	Kilberry D5	Limerick C3
Eyrecourt C4	Kilbrittain B2	Lisbellaw D6
	Kilcar C6	Lisburn E6
Farnaght C5	(Cill Charthaigh)	Liscannor B4
Farnaght C5	Kilcock B4	Liscarroll B3
Feakle C4	Kilcolgan B4	Lisdoonvarna B4
Fenagh C5	Kilconnell C4	Lismore C2
Ferbane C4	Kilcoole E4	Lisnaskea D6
Fermoy C2	Kilcormac C4	Lisryan D5
Ferns D3	Kilcullen D4	Listowel B3
Fethard D2	Kilcurry E5	Loghill B3
Fethard C3	Kildare D4	Londonderry D7
Finnea D5	Kildavin D3	Longford C5
Fintona D6	Kildorrery C2	Loughbrickland E6
Fivemiletown D6	Kilfenora B4	Loughall D6
Fontstown D4	Kilgarvan B2	Loughglinn C5
Foxford B5	Kilkee B3	Loughrea C4
Foynes B3	Kilkeel E5	Louisburgh B5
Freemount B3	Kilkelly C5	Lucan D4
Frenchpark C5	Kilkenny D3	Lurgan E6
Freshford D3	Kilkieran B3	Lusk E4
Fuerty C5	Kilkinlea B3	
	Kill D2	Macroom B2
Galbally C3	Killadysert B3	Maghera E5
Galway B4	Killala B6	Maghera D6
Garrison C6	Killaloe C3	Magherafelt D6
Garristown E4	Killarney B2	Maguiresbridge D6
Garvagh D7	Killashee C5	Malahide E4
Geashill D4	Killeigh D4	Malin D7
Gilford E6	Killenaule C3	Malin More C6
Glandore B1	Killashandra D5	Mallow C2
Glanworth C2	Killimer B3	Manorhamilton C6
Glaslough D6	Killimor C4	Markethill D6
Glassan C4	Killiney E4	Maynooth D4
Glenamaddy C5	Killinick D2	Mazetown E6
Glenarm E7	Killorglin B2	Middletown D6
Glenavy E6	Killough E5	Midleton C2
Glenbeigh A2	Killucan D4	Milford D7
Glencolumbkille C6	Killyleagh E6	Millstreet B2
(Gleann Cholm	Killybegs C6	Milltown B2
Cille)	Kilmacanoge E4	Milltown Malbay B3
Glendalough E4	Kilmacrenan C7	Mitchelstown C3
Glenealy E3	Kilmacthomas D2	Moate C4
Glengarriff B2	Monaghan D5	Mohill C5

Monasterevin D4	Portrane E4	Strandhill C6
Moneygall C3	Portroe C3	Strangford E6
Moneymore D6	Portrush D7	Stranorlar C6
Monivea C4	Portstewart D7	Strokestown C5
Mooncoin D2	Portumna C4	Summerhill D4
Moorfields E6	Poulgorm Bridge B2	Swanlinbar C5
Mount Bellew C4	Poyntzpass E6	Swatragh D6
Mount Charles C6		Swinford B5
Mountmellick D4	Raharney D4	Swords E4
Mountrath D4	Randalstown E6	
Mountshannon C4	Rasharkin E7	Taghmon D3
Moville D7	Rathangan D4	Tagoat D2
Moy D6	Rathcoole E4	Tahilla A2
Moynalty D5	Rathcormack C2	Tallaght E4
Moyvore C4	Rathdowney C3	Tallow C2
Muckross B2	Rathdrum E3	Tallowbridge C2
Muff D7	Rathfriland E5	Tandragee E6
Mullinavat D3	Rathkeale B3	Tang C4
Mullingar D4	Rathmelton D7	Tarbert B3
Mulrany B5	Rathmolyon D4	Templemore C3
Myshall D3	Rathmore B2	Templetouhy C3
	Rathmullan D7	Termonfeckin E5
Naas D4	Rathnew E3	Thomastown D3
Naul E4	Rathowen D5	Thurles C3
Navan D4	Rathvilly D3	Timahoe D4
Neale B5	Ratoath D4	Timoleague B2
Nenagh C3	Ray D7	Tinahely D3
Newbliss D5	Ring (An Rinn) C2	Tipperary C3
Newbridge D4	Ringaskiddy C2	Tobercurry C5
(Droichead Nua)	Rockcorry D5	Tobermore D6
Newcastle E5	Roosky C5	Toomyvara C3
Newcastle West B3	Rosapenna C7	Toormore B1
Newinn C3	Rosbercon D3	Tralee B3
Newmarket B2	Roscommon C5	Tramore B3
Newmarket-on	Roscrea C4	Trim B4
Fergus B3	Ross Carbery B1	Tuam B4
Newport B3	Rosscor C6	Tuamgraney C3
Newport B5	Rosses Point C6	Tulla B3
New Ross D3	Rosslare Harbour D2	Tullamore D4
Newry E5	Rosslea D5	Tullow D3
Newtown D3	Rostrevor E5	Tulsk C5
Newtownabbey E6	Roundstone B4	Turlough B5
Newtownards E6	Roundwood E4	Tyrrellspass D4
Newtownbutler D5	Rush E4	
Newtownhamilton D5		Urlingford C3
Newtown-	St Johnstown D7	
mountkennedy E4	Saintfield E6	Virginia D5
Newtownstewart D6	Sallins D4	
Newtown Forbes C5	Scarriff C4	Warrenpoint E5
Nobber D5	Scartaglen B2	Waterford D2
	Scarva E6	Watergrasshill C2
Oilgate D3	Schull B1	Waterville A2
Oldcastle D5	Scramoge C5	Westport B5
Omagh D6	Seskinore D6	Wexford D3
Omeath E5	Shanagarry C2	Whitegate C2
Oola C3	Shanagolden B3	Whitehead E6
Oranmore B4	Shannonbridge C4	Wicklow E4
Oughterard B4	Shercock D5	Woodenbridge E3
Ovens B2	Shillelagh D3	Woodford C4
	Shinrone C4	
Pallas Grean C3	Shrule B4	Youghal C2
Parknasilla B2	Silvermines C3	
Partry B5	Sion Mills D6	
Passage East D2	Sixmilebridge B3	
Passage West C2	Skerries E4	
Patrickswell C3	Skibbereen B1	
Paulstown D3	Slane D5	
Pettigo C6	Sligo C6	
Plumbridge D6	Smithborough D5	
Pomeroy D6	Sneem A2	
Portadown E6	Spiddal B4	
Portaferry E6	(An Spideal)	
Portarlington D4	Stewartstown D6	
Portavogie E6	Stonyford D3	
Portglenone E6	Strabane D6	
Portlaoise D3	Stradbally D4	
Portmarnock E4	Stradone D5	

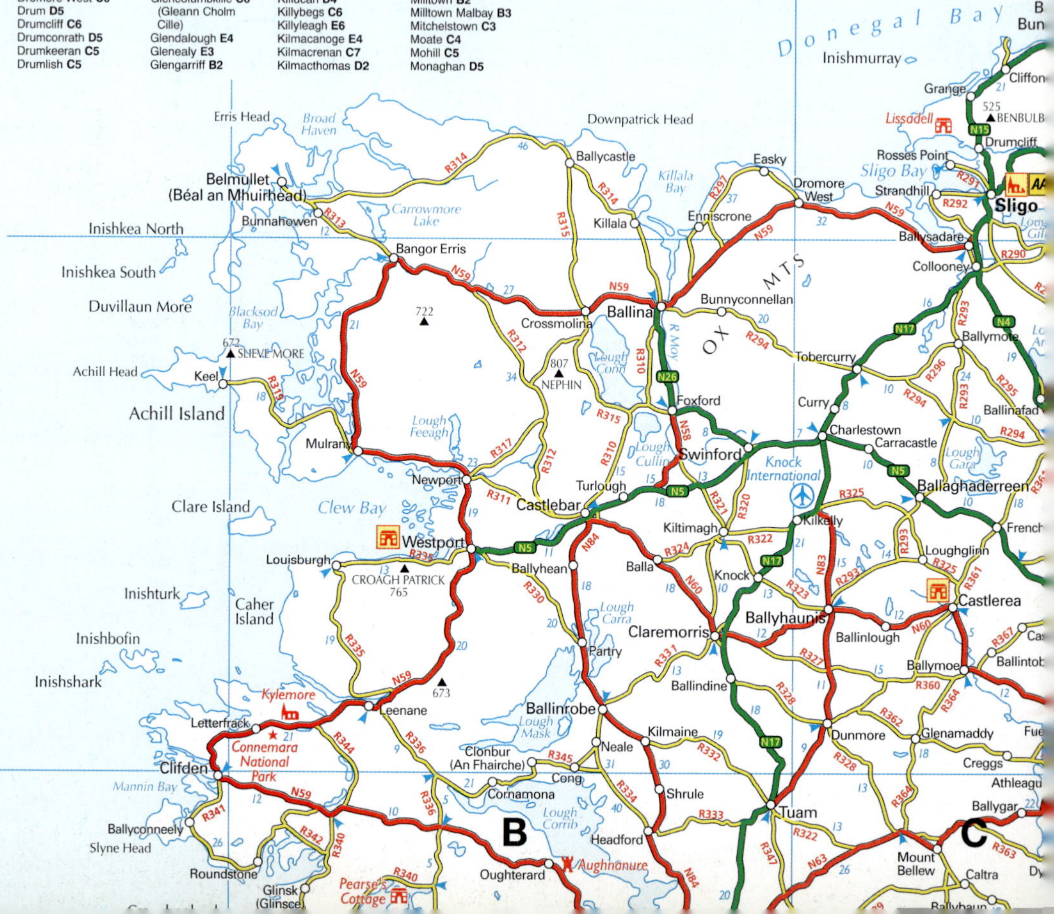

The Isle of Man

The Channel Islands

Guernsey

Jersey

key to town plans

Aberdeen	Page 176	Manchester	Page 205
Aberystwyth	177	Margate	206
Basingstoke	177	Middlesbrough	206
Bath	178	Milton Keynes	207
Birmingham	179	Newcastle-under-Lyme	208
Blackpool	180	Newcastle upon Tyne	209
Bournemouth	178	Newport	208
Bradford	181	Newquay	210
Brighton	181	Northampton	210
Bristol	182	Norwich	211
Brixham	183	Nottingham	212
Cambridge	184	Oldham	213
Canterbury	183	Oxford	214
Cardiff	185	Paignton	213
Carlisle	186	Perth	215
Chatham	186	Peterborough	215
Cheltenham	187	Plymouth	216
Chester	187	Poole	218
Colchester	188	Portsmouth	217
Coventry	188	Preston	218
Darlington	189	Ramsgate	219
Derby	190	Reading	219
Doncaster	189	St Andrews	220
Dover	191	Salisbury	221
Dundee	191	Scarborough	220
Durham	192	Sheffield	222
Eastbourne	192	Shrewsbury	223
Edinburgh	193	Southampton	224
Exeter	194	Southend-on-Sea	223
Glasgow	195	Stirling	225
Gloucester	194	Stockton-on-Tees	225
Great Yarmouth	196	Stoke-on-Trent (Hanley)	226
Guildford	196	Stratford-upon-Avon	226
Harrogate	197	Sunderland	227
Huddersfield	197	Swansea	228
Hull	198	Swindon	228
Inverness	198	Taunton	229
Ipswich	199	Torquay	229
Lancaster	199	Tunbridge Wells	230
Leeds	200	Warwick	230
Leicester	201	Watford	231
Lincoln	202	Weston-Super-Mare	231
Liverpool	203	Winchester	232
Llandudno	202	Windsor	232
LONDON	240–250	Wolverhampton	233
Luton	204	Worcester	233
Maidstone	204	York	234

Aberdeen

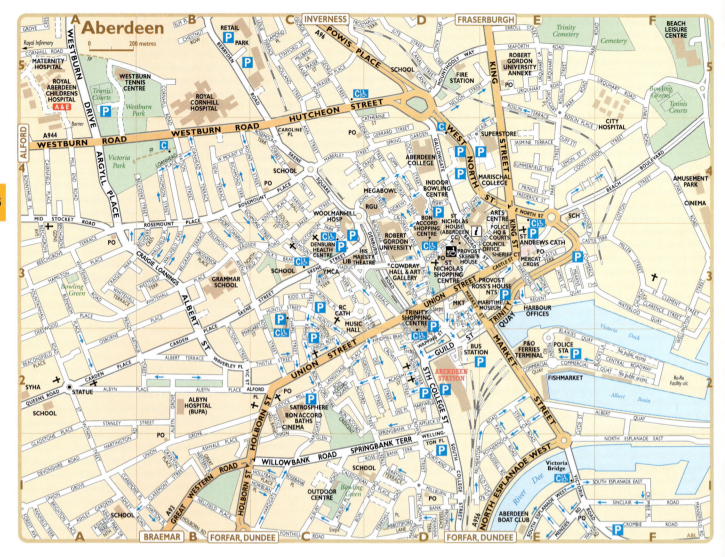

Aberdeen

Aberdeen is found on atlas page **149 G5**

Academy Street	D2
Affleck Street	D2
Albert Quay	E2-F2
Albert Street	B2-B3
Albert Terrace	B2
Albury Place	C1
Albury Road	C1
Albyn Grove	B1-B2
Albyn Place	A2-B2
Alford Place	B2-C2
Ann Street	C4
Annfield Terrace	A1
Argyll Place	A4
Ashley Gardens	A1
Ashley Road	A1-B1
Ashvale Place	B1-B2
Back Wynd	D3
Baker Street	C3-C4
Bank Street	D1
Beach Boulevard	E4-F4
Beechgrove Avenue	A3-A4
Beechgrove Gardens	A3-A4
Beechgrove Terrace	A3
Belgrave Terrace	B3
Belmont Street	D3
Belvidere Street	A4-B4
Berry Street	D4
Berryden Road	B5-C5
Blackfriar Street	D3-D4
Blaikies Quay	E3-E2-F2
Blenheim Place	A2-A3
Bon Accord Crescent	C2
Bon Accord Square	C2
Bon Accord Street	C1-D1-D2-C2
Bon Accord Terrace	C2
Bridge Street	D2-D3
Brighton Place	A1
Broad Street	D3-E3
Cairnfield Place	A4
Caledonian Place	C1-D1
Canal Street	D5
Carden Place	A2-B2-B3
Caroline Place	C4
Castle Street	E3
Castle Terrace	E3-F3
Catherine Street	C5-D5
Central Roadway	F2
Chapel Street	C2-C3
Charlotte Street	C4-D4
Chestnut Row	B5
Church Street	F3
Claremont Place	A1-B1
Claremont Street	B1
Clarence Street	F3
Clyde Street	E2
Commerce Street	E3
Commercial Quay	E2-F2
Constitution Street	E4-F4
Cornhill Road	A5
Cornhill Road	B4-B5
Cotton Street	F3-F4
Craigie Loanings	B3
Craigie Park	A3
Craigie Street	C4-D4
Crimon Place	C3
Crombie Place	F1
Crombie Road	F1
Crooked Lane	D3-D4
Crown Street	D1-D2
Crown Terrace	D2
Dee Place	D2
Dee Street	D2
Deeswood Place	A2-A3
Denburn Road	D3-D4
Devonshire Road	A1
East North Street	E4
Erroll Street	E5
Esslemont Avenue	B4-B3-C3
Exchange Street	D3
Farmers Hall	C4
Ferryhill Road	D1
Ferryhill Terrace	D1
Forbes Street	C4
Fountainhall Road	A2-A3
Fraser Place	C5
Fraser Road	C5
Frederick Street	E4
Gallowgate	D4
George Street	C5-C4-D4
Gerrard Street	D4
Gilcomston Park	C3
Gladstone Place	A1-A2
Gordon Street	C2-C3
Granton Place	B1
Great Western Place	B1
Great Western Road	B1
Grosvenor Place	B3
Guild Street	D2-E3
Hamilton Place	A3
Hanover Street	E3-E4
Hardgate	C1-C2
Hartington Road	A1-A2
Hill Street	C4
Holburn Street	B1-C1-C2
Holland Street	C4
Hollybank Place	C1
Howburn Place	C1
Huntly Street	C2-C3
Hutcheon Street	C4-C5-D5
Jack's Brae	C3
James Street	E3
Jasmine Terrace	E4
John Street	C4-D4
Jopps Lane	D4
Justice Mill Lane	C2
Justice Mill Bank	C2
Jute Street	D5
Kidd Street	C3
King Street	E3-E4-E5
Kintore Place	C4
Lamond Place	C5
Langstane Place	C2-D2
Leadside Road	B3-C3
Lemon Street	E4
Leslie Terrace	C5
Links Road	F3-F4-F5
Littlejohn Street	D4
Loanhead Terrace	B4
Loch Street	D4
Maberley Street	C4-D4
Margaret Street	B2-C3
Marischal Street	E3
Market Street	D3-E3-E2
Marywell Street	D2
Mearns Street	E3
Menzies Road	E1
Mid Stocket Road	A3-A4
Mile End Road	A4
Miller Street	F3
Mount Street	B4-C4
Mounthooly Way	D5-E5
Nellfield Place	B1
Nelson Street	D5-E5
North Esplanade East	E1-F1
North Esplanade West	D1-E1
Northfield Place	B3-C3
Old Ford Road	E1
Osborne Place	A2-A3-B3
Palmerston Road	D1-E1-E2
Park Road	E5-F5
Park Street	E4
Portland Street	D1
Powis Place	C5-D5
Poynernook Road	E1-E2
Prince Arthur Street	A3-A2-B2
Princes Street	E4
Queen Street	D3-E3-E4
Queens Road	A2
Raik Road	E1-E2
Regent Quay	E3
Regent Road	E2
Richmond Street	B4-C4-C3
Richmond Terrace	B4
Rose Street	C2-C3
Rosebank Place	C1
Rosebank Terrace	C1-D1
Rosemount Place	A4-B4-C4
Rosemount Terrace	C4
Rosemount Viaduct	C3
Roslin Place	E4-E5
Roslin Street	E5
Roslin Terrace	E5
Russell Road	E1
St Andrews Street	D4
St Clair Street	D4-E4-E5
St Clement Street	F3
St Swithin Street	A1-A2
School Hill	D3
Seaforth Road	E5
Short Loanings	B3-B4
Silver Street North	C3
Sinclair Road	E1-F1
Skene Square	C4
Skene Street	B3-C3
Skene Terrace	C3
South College Street	D1-D2
South Crown Street	D1
South Esplanade East	E1-F1
South Esplanade West	E1
South Mount Street	C3-C4
Spa Street	C3-C4
Spital Kings Crescent	D5
Spring Garden	D4
Springbank Street	D2
Springbank Terrace	C1-D1
Stafford Street	C5
Stanley Street	A2-B2
Stell Road	E1-E2
Stirling Street	D2-D3
Summer Street	C2-C3
Summerfield Terrace	E4
Thistle Street	C2
Thomson Street	B4
Trinity Quay	E3
Union Glen	C1-C2
Union Grove	A1-B1-B2-C2
Union Row	C2
Union Street	C2-D2-D3
Union Terrace	C3-D3
Union Wynd	C2-C3
Urquhart Lane	E5
Urquhart Place	E5
Urquhart Road	E5-F5
Urquhart Street	E5
Victoria Road	E1-F1
Victoria Street	B2-B3
View Terrace	B4
Wallfield Crescent	B3
Wallfield Place	B3
Wapping Street	D2-D3
Waterloo Quay	F2-F3
Watson Street	B4
Waverley Place	B2
Wellington Place	D1-D2
Wellington Street	F2-F3
West Mount Street	B3
West North Street	D5-D4-E4
Westburn Drive	A4-A5
Westburn Road	A4-B4-C4
Westfield Terrace	B3
Whitehall Place	A3-B3
Whitehall Road	A3
Whitehall Terrace	A3-B3
Willowbank Road	C1
Windmill Brae	D2

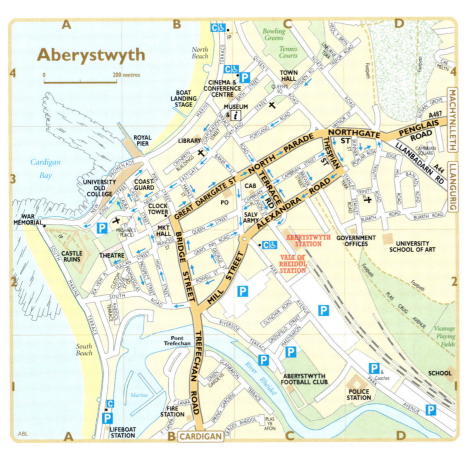

Aberystwyth

Aberystwyth is found on atlas page **54 C3**

Alexandra Road	C2-C3	Poplar Row	D3
Baker Street	B3-C3	Portland Road	C3-C4
Banadl Road	D3	Portland Street	B3-C3-C4
Bath Street	B4-C4	Powell Street	B2
Brewer Street	C3	Princess Street	B2
Bridge Street	B2-B3	Prospect Street	B2
Buarth Road	D3	Queen Street	B2-B3-C3
Cae Melyn	D4	Queen's Road	C3-C4
Cambrian Place	C3	Queen's Square	C4
Cambrian Square	D3	Rheidol Terrace	A2
Cambrian Street	C3	Riverside Terrace	B2-C2-C1
Castle Street	B3	St Michael's Place	B2-B3
Corporation Street	B3-B4	Sea View Place	A2
Crynfryn Buildings	B3	Skinner Street	D3
Custom House Street	A2-B2	South Marine Terrace	A1-A2-A3
Eastgate	B3	South Road	A2-B2
Edge Hill Road	D3	Spring Gardens	B1-C1
Elysian Grove	D4	Stanley Road	D3
George Street	B2	Stanley Terrace	C3-D3
Gerddi Rheidol	B1-C1	Terrace Road	B4-B3-C3
Glanrafon Terrace	B1-C1	Thespian Street	C3
Glyndwr Road	C2	Trefechan Road	B1-B2
Grays Inn Road	B2-C2	Trefor Road	C4-D4
Great Darkgate Street	B3-C3	Trinity Place	D3
Green Gardens	B1	Trinity Road	D3
Greenfield Street	C1-C2	Union Street	C3
Heoly Bryn	C4-D4	Vaynor Street	C3-C4-D4
High Street	B2	Vulcan Street	A2-B2
King Street	A3-B3	Y Lanfa	B1
Laura Place	A3-B3		
Lisburne Terrace	C4		
Llanbadarn Road	D3		
Loveden Road	C4		
Maesyrafon	C1-C2		
Marine Terrace	B3-B4		
Market Street	B3		
Mill Street	B2-C2		
New Promenade	A3-B3		
New Street	B3		
North Parade	C3		
North Road	C4-D4-D3		
Northgate Street	C3-D3		
Park Avenue	C2-C1-D1		
Penglais Road	D3-D4		
Penmaesglas	B2		
Pier Street	B3		
Plas Crug Avenue	D1-D2		
Plas Yr Afon	C1		

Basingstoke

Basingstoke is found on atlas page **27 E4**

Alencon Link	A4-B4-C4	Rayleigh Road	A2-A3
Allnutt Avenue	D3	Red Lion Lane	C2
Basing View	C4-D4	Rochford Road	A3
Beaconsfield Road	B1-C1	St Mary's Court	C3-D3
Bounty Rise	A1	Sarum Hill	A2-B2
Bounty Road	A1-B1	Southend Road	A3
Bramblys Close	A2	Southern Road	B1-C1
Bramblys Drive	A2	Timberlake Road	A3-B3-B2, C3
Budds Close	A2	Victoria Street	B1-B2
Bunnian Place	C4	Vyne Road	B4
Castle Road	C1	White Hart Lane	D2
Chapel Hill	A4-B4	Winchester Road	A1-A2-B2
Chequers Road	C3-D3	Winchester Street	B2
Chester Place	A1	Winterthur Way	A4-B4
Church Hill	B4	Worting Road	A2
Church Square	B3	Wote Street	B2-C2
Church Street	B2-B3		
Churchill Way	A3-B3-B4-C4		
Churchill Way East	C4-D4		
Churchill Way West	A3		
Cliddesden Road	C1		
Clifton Terrace	B4-C4		
Council Road	B1		
Cross Street	B2		
Crossborough Gardens	D1-D2		
Crossborough Hill	D1-D2		
Eastfield Avenue	D2-D3		
Eastrop Lane	D2-D3		
Eastrop Way	D3		
Essex Road	A2-A3		
Fairfields Road	B1-C1		
Flaxfield Court	A2-A3		
Flaxfield Road	A2-B2		
Frances Road	A1		
Frescade Crescent	A1		
Goat Lane	C3-D3		
Hackwood Road	C1-C2		
Hardy Lane	A1		
Jubilee Road	B1		
London Road	C2-D2		
London Street	C2		
Lytton Road	D2		
Mortimer Lane	A3		
New Road	B2-C2-C3		
New Street	B2		
Old Market Square	B2		
Old Reading Road	C4		
Penrith Road	A1-A2		

177

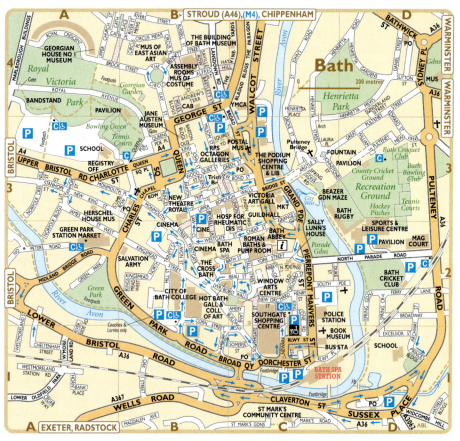

Bath

Bath is found on atlas page **24 C6**

Abbey Square	C2	Lower Oldfield Park	A1
Alfred Street	B4	Manvers Street	C1-C2
Ambury	B1	Midland Bridge Road	A2
Argyle Street	C3	Mill Street	B2
Avon Street	B2	Milsom Street	B3-B4
Barton Street	B3	Monmouth Place	A3-B3
Beau Street	B2-C2	Monmouth Street	B2-B3
Bennett Street	B4	New Bond Street	B3-C3
Bladud Buildings	B4-C4	New King Street	A3-B3
Bridewell Lane	B2-B3	New Orchard Street	C2
Bridge Street	C3	North Parade Road	C2-D2
Bristol Road	A2-A1-B1	Oak Street	B1
Broad Quay	B1-C1	Old Orchard Street	C2
Broad Street	B4-C3	Pierrepont Street	C2
Broadway	D2	Princes Street	B3
Brock Street	A4-B4	Pulteney Road	D1-D2-D3
Chapel Row	B3	Queen Square	B3
Charles Street	A2-B2-B3	Queen Square Place	B3
Charlotte Street	A3-B3	Queen Street	B3
Cheap Street	C2-C3	Quiet Street	B3
Circus Mews	B4	Railway Street	C1
Claverton Street	C1	Royal Avenue	A4-B4-B3
Corn Street	B2	Royal Crescent	A4
Dorchester Street	C1	Russell Street	B4
Edward Street	D3-D4	St John's Road	C4
Ferry Lane	D2	Saw Close	B2-B3
Gay Street	B4	South Parade	C2-D2
George Street	B3-B4	Southgate Street	C1-C2
Grand Parade	C3	Stall Street	C2
Grange Grove	C3	Sussex Place	D1
Great Pulteney Street	C3-D3-D4	Sydney Place	D4
Great Stanhope Street	A3	The Circus	B4
Green Park	A2	The Paragon	C4
Green Park Road	A2-B2-B1	The Vineyards	B4-C4
Green Street	B3-C3	Trim Street	B3
Grove Street	C3-C4	Union Passage	C2-C3
Henrietta Gardens	D4	Union Street	C2-C3
Henrietta Mews	C4-D4	Upper Borough Walls	B3-C3
Henrietta Road	C4-D4	Upper Bristol Road	A3
Henrietta Street	C3-C4	Upper Church Street	A4
Henry Street	C2	Walcot Street	C4
James Street West	A2-A3	Wells Road	A1-B1
John Street	B3	Westgate	B2
Kingsmead North	B2	Westgate Street	B2-C2
Kingsmead Street	B2	Westmoreland Road	A1
Lansdown Road	B4	William Street	D3
Little Stanhope Street	A3	Wood Street	B3
Lower Borough Walls	B2-C2	York Street	C2

Bournemouth

Bournemouth is found on atlas page **13 E4**

Albert Road	B2-B3	Park Road	D4
Avenue Lane	A2	Parsonage Road	C2
Avenue Road	A2-A3-B2	Poole Hill	A2
Bath Road	C2-D2-D3	Post Office Road	B2
Beacon Road	B1	Priory Road	A1-B1-B2
Bodorgan Road	B3-B4	Purbeck Road	A2
Bourne Avenue	A3-B3-B2	Richmond Gardens	B3
Bradburne Road	A3	Richmond Hill	B3
Braidley Road	B3-B4	Richmond Hill Drive	B3
Branksome Wood Road	A3-A4	Russell Cotes Road	C2
Cavendish Road	C4	St Michael's Road	A1-A2
Central Drive	A3-A4	St Paul's Lane	D4
Christchurch Road	D3	St Paul's Place	D3
Coach House Place	D4	St Paul's Road	D4
Commercial Road	A2-B2	St Peter's Road	B2-B3-C3-C2
Cumnor Road	C3	St Stephens Road	A3-B3
Cotlands Road	D3	St Stephens Way	B3
Cranborne Road	A2-B2	St Valerie Road	B4
Crescent Road	A3	South Cliff Road	B1
Dean Park Crescent	B3-C3	South View Place	A2
Dean Park Road	B3-B4-C4-C3	Stafford Road	C3-D3
Durley Road	A2	Suffolk Road	A3
Durrant Road	A3	Terrace Road	A2-B2
East Overcliff Drive	C2-D2	The Square	B2
Exeter Crescent	B2	The Triangle	A2
Exeter Park Road	B2	Tregonwell Road	A1-A2
Exeter Road	B1-B2	Trinity Road	C3
Fir Vale Road	C3	Upper Hinton Road	B2-C2
Gervis Place	B2	Upper Norwich Road	A2
Gervis Road	C2-D2	Upper Terrace Road	A2-B2
Glen Fern Road	C3	Wessex Way	A3-B3-C3-D3
Grove Road	C2-D2	West Cliff Gardens	A1
Hahnemann Road	A2	West Cliff Road	A1
Hinton Road	B2-C2	West Hill Road	A1-A2
Holdenhurst Road	D3-D4	Westover Road	B2-C2
Kerley Road	A1-B1	Wimborne Road	B3-B4
Landsowne Gardens	C4-D4	Wootton Mount	C3-D3
Lansdowne Road	C4-D4-D3	Wychwood Close	B4
Lorne Park Road	C3	Wychwood Drive	B4
Madeira Road	C3	Yelverton Road	B3
Merlewood Close	B4	York Road	D3
Meyrick Road	D2-D3		
Norwich Avenue	A2-A3		
Norwich Road	A2		
Old Christchurch Road	B2-B3-C3-D3		
Orchard Street	A2-B2		
Oxford Road	D3-D4		

178

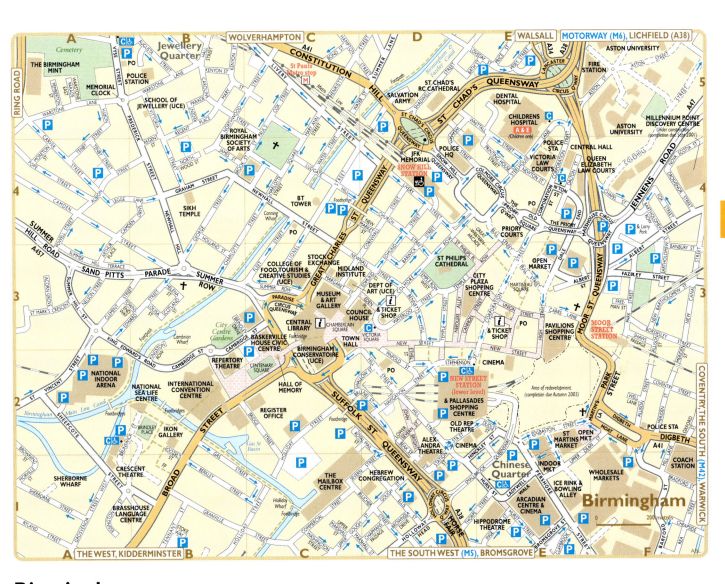

Birmingham

Birmingham is found on atlas page **58 D4**

Acorn Grove	A3	Carrs Lane	E3	Freeman Street	F3	Loveday Street	D5-E5	Pinfold Street	D2	Summer Lane	D5
Albert Street	E3-F3-F4	Carver Street	A4-A5	Gas Street	B2-B1-C1	Lower Severn Street	D2	Pope Street	A4	Summer Row	B3-C3
Albion Street	A4-B4	Centenary Square	C2	George Street	B3-B4	Ludgate Hill	C4	Powell Street	A3-A4	Swallow Street	C2-D2
Allison Street	F2-F3	Chamberlain Square	C3	Gough Street	D1	Margaret Street	C3	Price Street	E5	Temple Row	D3-E3
Arthur Place	A3-A4	Chapel Street	F4	Graham Street	B4	Marshall Street	C1-D1	Printing House Street	E4	Temple Row West	D3
Aston Street	E5-F5	Chapmans Passage	D1	Granville Street	B1-C1	Martin's Lane	E2-F2	Rea Street	F1	Temple Street	D3
Augusta Street	B5	Charlotte Street	B3-B4-C4	Great Charles Street		Mary Ann Street	C5	Regent Parade	B5	Tenby Street	A4
Banbury Street	F3	Cheapside	F1	Queensway	C3-C4-D4	Mary Street	B5-C5	Regent Place	B5	Tenby Street North	A4-A5
Barford Street	F1	Church Street	D3-D4	Grosvenor Street	F4	Masshouse Circus		Regent Street	B4-B5	Tennant Street	B1
Bartholomew Row	F4	Claybrook Street	E1	Grosvenor Street West	A1	Queensway	E3-E4-F4-F3	Royal Mail Street	C2-D2	The Priory Queensway	E4
Bartholomew Street	F3-F4	Clement Street	A3-B3	Hall Street	B5	Meriden Street	F2	Ryland Street	A1	Thorpe Street	D1-E1
Barwick Street	D3-D4	Coleshill Street	F4-F5	Hampton Street	C5-D5	Mill Lane	F1-F2	St Chad's Circus		Townsend Way	A3-B3
Bath Street	D5-E5	Colmore Circus		Helena Street	B3	Moat Lane	F2	Queensway	D4-D5	Union Street	E3
Beak Street	D1-D2	Queensway	D4-E4	Henrietta Street	C5-D5	Moor Street Queensway	E3-F3	St Chad's Queensway	D5-E5	Upper Dean Street	E1-F2
Bennetts Hill	D3	Colmore Row	D3-D4	High Street	E2-E3	Moreton Street	A4	St Mark's Crescent	A3	Upper Gough Street	C1-D1
Berkley Street	B1-C1	Commercial Street	C1	Hill Street	C2-D2	Morville Street	A1	St Paul's Square	C4-C5	Upper Marshall Street	C1
Blucher Street	C1-D1	Constitution Hill	C5-D5	Hinckley Street	D1-E2	Navigation Street	D2	St Philips Place	D4-D3-E3	Vesey Street	E5
Bond Street	C5	Cornwall Street	C3-D3-D4	Holland Street	B3-B4	Needless Alley	D3	St Vincent Street	A2-A3	Victoria Square	D3
Bordesley Street	F2-F3	Corporation Street	E3-E4-E5	Holliday Street	B1-C1-C2	Nelson Street	A3	Sand Pitts	A3	Vittoria Street	B4-B5
Bradford Street	F1	Coventry Street	F2	Holloway Circus Queensway	D1	New Bartholomew Street	F3-F4	Scotland Street	B3	Vyse Street	A5
Bridge Street	B2-C2-C1	Cox Street	C5	Holloway Head	D1	New Canal Street	F3-F4	Severn Street	C1-D1	Warstone Lane	A5-B5
Brindley Drive	B3	Dale End	E3-E4	Horse Fair	D1	New Market Street	C4-D4	Shadwell Street	D5	Warstone Parade East	A5
Brindley Place	B2	Dalton Street	E4	Hurst Street	E1	New Street	D3-E3-E2	Shaws Passage	F2-F3	Washington Street	C1
Broad Street	A1-B1-B2-C2	Digbeth	F2	Inge Street	E1	Newhall Hill	B3-B4	Sheepcote Street	A1-A2	Water Street	C4-C5-D5
Bromsgrove Street	E1	Dudley Street	E2	James Street	B4	Newhall Street	B4-C4-C3-D3	Sherborne Street	A1	Waterloo Street	D3
Brook Street	B4-C4	Eden Place	C3-D3	Jennens Road	F4-F5	Newton Street	E4	Smallbrook Queensway	D1-E1-E2	Weaman Street	D4-D5
Browning Street	A1-A2	Edgbaston Street	E2	John Bright Street	D1-D2	Northwood Street	B4-B5-C5	Snow Hill Queensway	D4	Well Lane	F2
Brownsea Drive	D1	Edmund Street	C3-D3-D4	Kenyon Street	B5	Nova Scotia Street	F4	Station Street	D1-D2	Whittall Street	D5-E5-E4
Brunel Street	C2-D2	Edward Street	A3-B3	King Edward's Road	A3-A2-B2	Old Square	E4	Steelhouse Lane	E4-E5		
Brunswick Street	A1-A2-B2	Ellis Street	D1	Kingston Row	B2-B3	Oozel's Street	B1-B2	Stephenson Street	D2-E2		
Bull Street	E3-E4	Essington Street	A1	Ladywell Walk	E1	Oxford Street	F2	Stoke Way	B1		
Cambridge Street	B2-B3-C3	Ethel Street	D2	Lancaster Circus Queensway	E5	Parade	B3	Suffolk Street			
Camden Drive	A4-B4	Fazeley Street	F3	Legge Lane	A4-B4	Paradise Circus Queensway	C3	Queensway	C2-D2-D1		
Camden Street	A4-B3	Fleet Street	C3-C4	Lionel Street	C3-C4	Park Street	F2-F3	Summer Hill Road	A3-A4		
Cannon Street	D3-E3	Fox Street	F4	Livery Street	C5-C4-D4	Pemberton Street	A5	Summer Hill Street	A3		
Caroline Street	B5-C5	Frederick Street	A5-B5-B4	Louisa Street	B3	Pershore Street	E1-E2	Summer Hill Terrace	A3-B3		

Blackpool

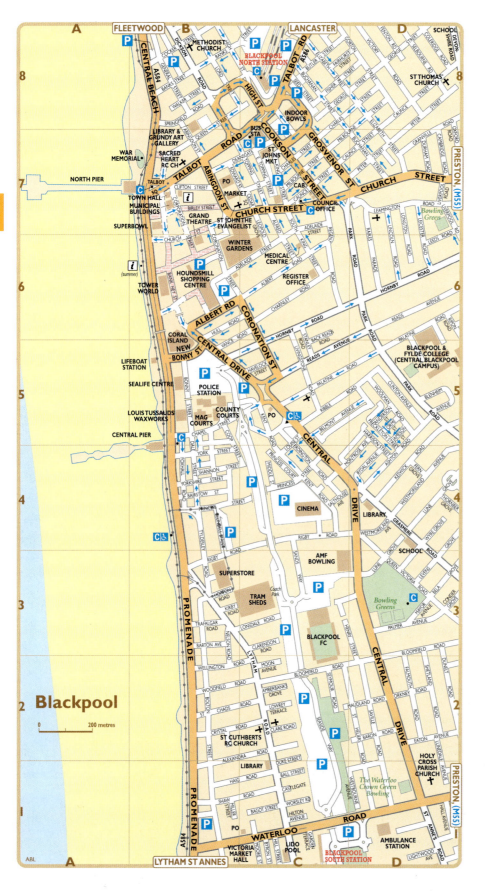

Blackpool is found on atlas page **88 B3**

Abingdon Street	B7-B8
Adelaide Street	B6-C6-C7
Albert Road	B6-C6
Alexandra Road	B1-B2-C2
Alfred Street	C6-C7
Amberbanks Grove	C2
Anderson Street	D5
Ashton Road	D4-D5
Back Reads Road	C5-C6
Bagot Street	C1
Bairstow Street	B4
Ball Street	C1
Bank Hey Street	B6
Banks Street	B8-C8
Baron Road	D2
Barton Avenue	B3
Bela Grove	D3
Belmont Avenue	C5-D5
Birley Street	B7
Blenheim Avenue	D5
Bloomfield Road	C2-D2-D3
Blundell Street	B3-B4
Bolton Street	B2
Bonny Street	B5
Buchanan Street	C8-C7-D7
Butler Street	C8
Byron Street	C1
Cambridge Road	D7
Castlegate	C1
Caunce Street	C7-D7-D8
Cedar Square	C7
Central Beach	B8
Central Drive	B6-C5-D3-D1
Chapel Street	B5
Charles Street	C7-C8-D8
Charnley Road	C6
Church Street	B6-B7-C7-D7
Clare Road	C2
Clarendon Road	C3
Clifton Street	B7
Clinton Avenue	D5
Cocker Street	B8
Coleridge Road	D8
Conder Grove	D3
Cookson Street	C7-C8
Coop Street	B4-B5
Coronation Street	B7-B6-C6-C5
Corporation Street	B6-B7
Crystal Road	B2-C2
Dale Street	B4-B5
Deansgate	B7-C7
Devonshire Road	D8
Dickson Road	B8
Duke Street	C1-C2
Dunelt Road	D2-D3
Durham Road	D7
East Topping Street	C7
Eaton Avenue	D2
Edward Street	B7
Elizabeth Street	C8-D8-D7
Erdington Road	C4-C5
Fairhurst Street	C8
Falmouth Road	D2
Fenton Road	D8
Fern Grove	D4
Fisher Street	C8-D8
Foxhall Road	B4
Freckleton Street	D5
Garden Terrace	C1
General Street	B8
George Street	C8-D8
Gorton Street	C8-D8
Granville Road	D7-D8
Grasmere Road	D3-D4
Grosvenor Street	C7
Haig Road	B1-C1
Hall Avenue	D1
Harrison Street	D4-D5
Havelock Street	C5
Henry Street	C3-D3
High Street	B8-C8
Hill Street	C1
Hilton Avenue	C1
Hopton Road	B3
Hornby Road	C5-C6-D6
Hull Road	B6
Jameson Street	D5
Kent Road	C4-C5
Keswick Road	D4-D5
King Street	C7
Kirby Road	B3
Leamington Road	D7
Leeds Road	D6-D7
Leicester Road	D6-D7
Leopold Grove	C6-C7
Levens Grove	D3-D4
Lightwood Avenue	D1
Lincoln Road	D6-D7
Liverpool Road	D6-D7
Livingstone Road	C5-C6
Longton Road	D6-D7
Lonsdale Road	B3-C3
Lord Street	B8
Louise Street	C4-C5
Lowrey Terrace	C2
Lune Grove	D3-D4
Lunedale Avenue	D1-D2
Lytham Road	B3-C3-C2-C1
Maudland Road	C2-D2
Mayor Avenue	D3
Middle Street	C4
Milbourne Street	C7-D8
Miller Street	B1
Montrose Avenue	C4-D4-D5
Moon Avenue	C2
Moore Street	C1
Nelson Road	B2-B3
New Bonny Street	B5
Orkney Road	D2
Orme Street	D5
Oxford Road	D7-D8
Palatine Road	C5-D5-D6
Palmer Avenue	D3
Park Road	C7-D6-D5
Peter Street	C7-D7-D8
Princess Court	C4
Princess Street	B4-C4
Promenade	B1-B2-B3
Queen Street	B7-B8
Queen Victoria Road	D3
Raikes Parade	D6-D7
Reads Avenue	C5-C6-D6
Regent Road	C6-C7
Ribble Road	C5-D5
Rigby Street	B3-C4
Ripon Road	D6
Rydal Avenue	D4
St Anne's Road	D1
St Chads Road	B2-C2
St Heliers Road	C2-D2-D1
Salthouse Avenue	C4
Sands Way	C3-C4
Saville Road	D1-D2
Seaside Way	C1-C2
Seed Street	C8
Selbourne Road	D7
Seymour Road	C2
Shannon Street	B4
Shaw Road	B1-C1
Shetland Road	D2-D3
South King Street	C6-C7
Springfield Road	B8
Stanley Road	C5-C6
Talbot Road	B7-C8
Talbot Square	B7
Thornber Grove	D4
Topping Street	C7
Trafalgar Road	B3
Tyldesley Road	B3-B4
Vance Road	B5-B6-C6
Victory Road	D8
Walker Street	B8
Waterloo Road	B1-C1-D1
Wellington Road	B2-C2
Westbourne Avenue	C1-D1
Westmoreland Avenue	D4
Woodfield Road	B2-C2
Woolman Road	D5
Worsley Road	C1
Wyre Grove	D4
York Street	B4
Yorkshire Street	B4

180

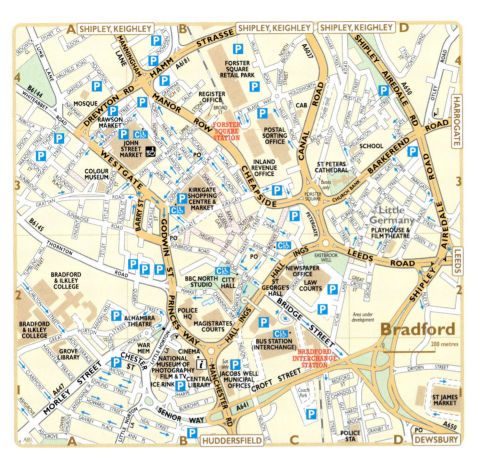

Bradford

Bradford is found on atlas page **90 C3**

Bank Street	B3-C3-C2	Manchester Road	B1
Barkerend Road	D3-D4	Manningham Lane	A4-B4
Barry Street	B3	Mannville Terrace	A1
Bolton Road	C3-C4	Manor Row	B3-B4
Bridge Street	B2-C2-C1	Market Street	B2-C2-C3
Broadway	C2-C3	Melbourne Place	A1
Burnett Street	D3	Morley Street	A1-B1-B2
Canal Road	C3-C4	Neal Street	B1
Captain Street	C3-C4-D4	Nelson Street	C1-C2
Carlton Street	A2	Norfolk Gardens	B2-C2
Channing Way	B2	North Brook Street	C4
Chapel Street	D2-D3	North Parade	B3-B4
Charles Street	C2-C3	North Street	D4
Cheapside	B3-C3	Northgate	B3-B4
Chester Street	A2-A1-B1	Otley Road	D4
Church Bank	C3-D3	Peckover Street	D3
Claremont	A1	Petergate	C3
Croft Street	C1	Piccadilly	B3
Currer Street	C3-D3	Princes Way	B1-B2
Dale Street	B3-C3	Quebec Street	B2
Darfield Street	A4	Rawson Place	B3
Darley Street	B3	Rawson Road	A3-A4-B4
Drake Street	C2	Rawson Square	B3
Drewton Road	A4-B4	St Blaise Way	B3-C3
Dryden Street	D1	St Thomas Road	A3-A4
Duke Street	B3	Salem Street	B4
East Parade	D2-D3	Sawrey Place	A1
Edmund Street	A1-B1	Sedgwick Close	A4
Edward Street	C1	Senior Way	B1
Forester Square	C3	Sharpe Street	B1
Godwin Street	B2-B3	Shipley Airedale Road	D1-D3-D4
Grammar School Street	B4	Simes Street	A3-A4-B4
Grattan Road	A3-B3	Stott Hill	C4-C3-D3
Great Horton Street	A1-A2-B2	Sunbridge Road	A3-B3-B2
Guy Street	C1	Sylhet Close	A4
Hall Ings	B1-B2-C2	Tetley Street	A2-A3
Halfield Road	A4	Thornton Road	A3-A2-B2
Hamm Strasse	B4-C4	Tumbling Hill Street	A2
Holdsworth Street	C4	Tyrrel Street	B2-B3
Houghton Place	A4	Upper Parkgate	D3
Howard Street	A1	Upper Piccadilly	B3-B4
Ivegate	B2-B3	Valley Road	C3-C4
James Street	B3	Well Street	C2-C3
John Street	B3	Wellington Street	D3-D4
Kirkgate	B2-B3-C3	Westgate	A3-B3
Leeds Road	C2-D2	Wharf Street	C4
Little Horton Lane	A1-B1-B2	Whiteabbey Road	A4
Lumb Lane	A4	Wigan Street	A3

Brighton

Brighton is found on atlas page **16 D2**

Ashton Rise	D4	Marlborough Place	C3
Bartholomews	B2-C2	Meeting House Lane	B2
Black Lion Street	B1-B2	Middle Street	B2
Blenheim Place	C4	Morley Street	D4
Bond Street	B3	New Dorset Street	B4
Brighton Square	B2	New Road	C2-C3
Broad Street	D1-D2	Nile Street	B2
Buckingham Road	A4	North Gardens	B4
Camelford Street	D1-D2	North Road	B4-C4
Cannon Place	A2-A3	North Street	B3-B2-C2
Carlton Hill	D3	Old Steine	C1-C2
Castle Square	C2	Palace Place	C2
Centurion Road	A4-B4	Pavilion Buildings	C2
Charles Street	D1-D2	Pavilion Parade	C2-C3
Cheltenham Place	C4	Pool Valley	C1
Church Street	A4-B3-C3	Portland Street	B3
Circus Street	D3-D4	Powis Grove	A4
Clifton Terrace	A4	Prince Albert Street	B2
Dorset Gardens	D2	Prince's Place	C2
Duke Street	B2	Princes Street	C2-D2
Duke's Lane	B2	Queen Square	A3-B3
Dyke Road	A3-A4	Queens Gardens	B4-C4
East Street	C1-C2	Queens Road	B3-B4
Edward Street	D2	Regency Road	A2-A3
Foundry Street	B4	Regent Arcade	B2-C2
Frederick Street	B4	Regent Hill	A3
Gardner Street	C3-C4	Regent Street	C3-C4
George Street	D2	Robert Street	C4
Gloucester Place	C4-D4	Russell Road	A2
Gloucester Road	B4-C4	St James's Street	C2-D2
Gloucester Street	C4-D4	St Nicholas Road	A4-B4
Grand Junction Road	B1-C1	Ship Street	B1-B2-B3
Grand Parade	C3-D3-D4	Ship Street Gardens	B2
High Street	D2	Spring Gardens	B3-B4
Ivory Place	D4	Steine Lane	C2
John Street	D2-D3-D4	Steine Street	C1-C2
Kensington Gardens	C4	Tichborne Street	B3-B4-C4
Kensington Street	C4	Union Street	B2
Kew Street	B4	Upper Gardner Street	C4
King's Road	A2-B1-C1	Upper Gloucester Road	A4-B4
Leopold Road	A4	Upper North Street	A3
Little East Street	C1	Vine Street	C4
Madeira Drive	C1-D1	Wentworth Street	D1-D2
Madeira Place	D1-D2	West Street	A2-B2-B3
Manchester Street	D1-D2	Western Road	A3
Margaret Street	D1-D2	White Street	D2-D3
Marine Parade	C1-D1	William Street	D3
Market Street	B2-C2	Windsor Street	B3

Bristol

Bristol
Bristol is found on atlas page 37 G1

Acraman's Road	B1-C1
Albert Road	F1-F2
Alfred Hill	C5
Allington Road	B1
Alpha Road	C1
Anchor Road	A3-B3-C3
Avon Street	E3-F3-F2
Baldwin Street	C3-D3
Barton Manor	F4
Barton Road	F3
Beauley Road	A1-B1
Bell Lane	C4
Bellevue Crescent	A3
Bellevue Road	E1-F1
Berkeley Place	A4
Berkeley Square	A4-B4
Birkin Street	F3
Bond Street	D5-E5-E4
Braggs Lane	E4-F4-F5
Brandon Hill Lane	A4
Brandon Steep	B3
Bridewell Street	C4
Broad Mead	D4-D5
Broad Plain	E4
Broad Quay	C3-C4
Broad Street	C4
Broad Weir	D4-E4
Bruton Place	A4
Caledonian Road	A2-B2
Cambridge Street	E1-F1
Canons Road	C3
Canons Way	B2
Canynge Street	D2
Castle Street	D4-E4
Cattle Market Road	E2-F2
Chapel Street	F2
Charles Street	C5-D5
Charlotte Street	B4
Charlotte Street South	B3-B4
Christmas Steps	C4
Church Street	E3
Clare Street	C3-C4
Clarence Road	D1-E1-E2
Clarence Road	F5
College Green	B3-C3
Colston Avenue	C4
Colston Street	C4
Commercial Road	C1-D1
Constitution Hill	A3
Corn Street	C4
Coronation Road	A1-B1-C1-D1
Cottage Place	C5
Countesslip	D3
Cumberland Road	A1-B2-B1-C1
Dale Street	E5
Dean Lane	B1
Deanery Road	B3
Denmark Street	B3-C3
Dighton Street	C5
Earl Street	C5
East Street	C1-D1
Edgeware Road	B1
Elmdale Road	A4-A5
Elton Road	A5-B5
Eugene Street	C5
Eugene Street	F5
Fairfax Street	D4
Feeder Road	F2
Ferry Street	D3
Frederick Place	A4
Frog Lane	B3
Frogmore Street	B3-B4-C4
Gas Ferry Road	A2
Gas Lane	F3
Great George Street	A3-B3-B4
Great George Street	E5
Guinea Street	C2-D2
Harbour Way	B2
Haymarket	D5
High Street	D4
Hill Street	E1
Horfield Road	C5
Horton Street	F4
Hotwell Road	A2-A3
Houlton Street	E5
Howard Road	A1-B1
Islington Road	A1-B1
Jacob Street	E4
Jacob's Well Road	A3
John Street	C4
King Street	C3
Kingsland Road	F3
Kingston Road	B1
Lamb Street	E4-E5-F5
Lawfords Gate	F5
Leighton Road	A1
Lewins Mead	C4-C5
Little Ann Street	F5
Little George Street	E5-F5
Little King Street	C3
Lodge Street	B4-C4
Lower Castle Street	E4
Lower Clifton Hill	A4
Lower Guinea Street	C1-C2
Lower Maudlin Street	C5
Lower Park Row	C4
Marlborough Hill	C5
Marlborough Street	C5-D5
Marsh Street	C3
Mead Street	E1
Merchant Street	D4-D5
Meridian Place	A4
Middle Avenue	C3
Midland Road	F4
Mitchell Lane	D3
Montague Street	C5
Myrtle Road	B5
Narrow Plain	E4
Nelson Street	C4-D4
New Charlotte Street	C1
New Kingsley Road	E3-F3-F4
Newfoundland Street	E5
Newgate	D4
Newton Street	F5
Oakfield Place	A5
Old Bread Street	E3
Old Market Street	E4
Osborne Road	B1
Oxford Street	F3
Park Place	A4
Park Road	A1
Park Row	B4
Park Street	B3-B4
Park Street Avenue	B4
Pembroke Road	B1
Pembroke Street	D5-E5
Penn Street	D5-E5-E4
Pennywell Road	F5
Perry Road	C4
Pipe Lane	C4
Prewett Street	D2
Prince Street	C2-C3
Princess Street	D1
Priory Road	A5-B5
Pritchard Street	E5
Pump Lane	D2
Quakers Friars	D4-D5
Quay Street	C4
Queen Charlotte Street	C3
Queen Square	C2-C3
Queen Street	D4-E4
Queen's Avenue	A5
Queen's Road	A4-A5
Queens Parade	A3-B3
Raleigh Road	A1
Redcliff Mead Lane	D2-E2
Redclife Parade East	D2
Redcliff Street	D2-D3
Redcliffe Backs	D2
Redcliffe Hill	D1-D2
Redcliffe Parade West	C2-D2
Redcliffe Way	D2
Redcross Street	E4
Richmond Hill	A4-A5
River Street	E5
Royal Fort Road	B5
Rupert Street	C4-D5
Russ Street	E3-E4
St Augustine's Parade	C3-C4
Saint George's Road	A3-B3
St John's Road	C1
St Luke's Road	E1
St Mathias Park	E4-E5
St Michael's Hill	B5-C5-C4
St Michael's Park	B5
St Nicholas Street	C4-C3-D4
St Paul's Street	E5
St Pauls Road	A5
St Phillips Road	F4
St Stephen's Street	C3-C4
St Thomas Street	D2-D3
Ship Lane	D1-D2
Silver Street	D4-D5
Silverthorne Lane	F2
Small Street	C4
Somerset Street	D2-E2-E1
Southville Road	B1-C1
Spring Street	D1-E1
Stackpool Road	B1
Stapleton Road	F5
Stoke's Croft	D5
Stratton Street	E5
Surrey Street	D5-E5
Sydney Row	A2
Telephone Avenue	C3
Temple Back	D3-E3
Temple Street	D3
Temple Way	E2-E3-E4
Terrell Street	C5
The Grove	C2
The Horsefair	D5
Three Queens Lane	D3
Thrissell Street	F5
Tower Hill	E4
Tower Lane	C4-D4
Trenchard Street	C4
Triangle South	A4
Triangle West	A4
Trinity Road	F5
Trinity Street	F4-F5
Tyndall Avenue	B5
Tyndall's Park Road	A5
Union Road	F3
Union Street	D4-D5
Unity Street	B3
University Road	A4-B4-B5
Upper Byron Place	A4
Upper Maudlin Street	C4-C5
Upper Perry Hill	B1
Victoria Grove	D1
Victoria Road	F2
Victoria Road	D3-E3-E2
Wade Street	E5-F5
Wapping Road	C1-C2
Waterloo Road	F4
Waterloo Street	F4
Wellington Road	F5
Welsh Back	D2-D3
West Street	F4-F5
Whitehouse Street	D1
Whiteladies Road	A5
Wilson Street	E5
Wine Street	D4
Woodland Road	B4-B5
York Road	D1-E1
York Street	D5

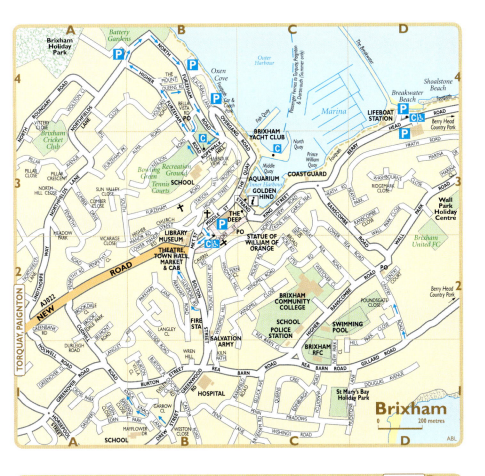

Brixham

Brixham is found on atlas page **7 G3**

Alma Road	A3-B3-B4	Lindthorpe Way	A2
Barnfield Road	B1-C1	Lower Manor Road	B2-B3
Bella Vista Road	B4	Lower Rea Road	C3-C2-D2
Berry Head Road	C3-D3-D4	Lytes Road	C2
Blackball Lane	B4	Marina Drive	D3
Bolton Street	B1-B2	Market Street	B2-B3
Briseham Road	C1	Middle Street	B3
Broadacre Road	C2	Mount Pleasant Road	B2
Burton Street	B1	Mount Road	C2
Castor Road	B1	Mudstone Lane	D1
Cavern Road	B2	Nelson Road	B3
Centry Court	D2	New Park Close	C1
Centry Road	D1-D2	New Road	A2-B2
Church Street	B3	North Boundary Road	A3-A4
Cross Park	A1	North Furzeham Road	B3-B4
Cudhill Road	A1-A2	North View Road	C3
Cumber Drive	A2-A3	Northfields Lane	A2,A3-A4
Dashpers	A1	Overgang Road	B4-C3
Doctors Road	B1	Parkham Lane	B2
Douglas Avenue	D1	Parkham Road	B2
Drew Street	B1	Peasditch	C1
Eden Park	A1-B1	Penn Lane	B1-C1
Edinburgh Road	C1	Penn Meadows	B1-C1
Elkins Hill	C3	Penpethy Road	A2-A3
Fore Street	B2-B3-C3	Pillar Avenue	A3
Furzeham Park	A3	Prospect Road	B3-C3
Garlic Rea	C3	Queens Crescent	C1
Gillard Road	D1	Queens Road	B4
Glenmore Road	B2	Ranscombe Road	C3-D3-D2
Great Rea Road	C3-C2-D2	Rea Barn Close	C1-C2
Greenbank Road	A2	Rea Barn Road	B1-C1-D1
Greenover Road	A1	Ropewalk Hill	B3
Greenwood Road	B1	Sellick Avenue	C1
Harbour View Close	B3	South Furzeham Road	A3-B3
Heath Park	D3	Station Hill	B3
Heath Road	C2	Strand	B3-C3
Higher Furzeham Road	B3-B4	The Close	A3-A4
Higher Manor Road	B2-B3	The Mount	B4
Higher Ranscombe Road	C1-D2	The Quay	B3-C3
Higher Street	B3	Wall Park Close	D2-D3
Hill Park Close	D1-D2	Wall Park Road	D2-D3
Hillside Road	B1-B2	Washbourne Close	D3
Holborn Road	B4	Westover Close	C2
Holwell Road	A1-A2	Windmill Close	B2-C2
Horsepool Street	A1	Windmill Hill	B1-B2
King Street	C3	Windmill Road	C2
Knick Knack Lane	A1-B1	Wishings Road	C1
Langley Avenue	A1-A2-B2	Wolston Close	A4

Canterbury

Canterbury is found on atlas page **31 E2**

Albion Place	C3-D3	Oaten Hill	C1-D1
Artillery Street	C4-D4-D3	Old Dover Road	C1-D1
Beer Cart Lane	B2	Orange Street	B3-C3
Best Lane	B3	Orchard Street	A3-A4
Black Griffin Way	A2-B2-B3	Palace Street	C3
Blackfriars Street	B3	Parade	C2
Broad Street	C3-D3-D2	Pound Lane	B3-B4
Burgate	C2	Rheims Way	A1-A2-A3
Butchery Lane	C2	Rhodaus Town	B1-C1
Canterbury Lane	C2	Roper Road	A4-B4
Castle Row	B1	Rose Lane	B2-C2
Castle Street	B1-B2	Roseacre Close	A4
Church Street	D2	Rosemary Lane	B1-B2
Cross Street	A3-A4	St Alphege Street	C3
Dover Street	C2-C1-D1	St Dunstan's Street	A4-A3-B3
Duck Lane	C4	St George's Street	C2
Edward Road	D1-D2	St John's Lane	B1-B2
Forty Acres Road	A4	St John's Place	C4
George's Lane	C1-C2	St Margaret's Street	B2-C2
Gordon Road	A1-B1	St Mary's Street	B1-B2
Gravel Walk	C2	St Peter's Grove	B2-B3
Guildhall Street	B2-B3-C3	St Peter's Lane	B3-B4
Havelock Street	D3	St Peter's Place	A2-A3-B3
Hawks Lane	B2	St Peter's Street	B3
High Street	B3-B2-C2	St Radigund's Street	C3-C4
Hospital Lane	B2	St Stephen's Road	B4
Iron Bar Lane	C2	Simmonds Road	A1
Ivy Lane	C2-D2	Station Road East	B1
Jewry Lane	B2	Stour Street	B2-B3
King Street	B3-C3	Sun Street	C3
Kingsmead Road	C4-D4	The Causeway	B4
Kirby's Lane	A3-B3-B4	The Borough	C3
Lansdown Road	C1	The Friars	B3
Linden Grove	A3	Tourtel Road	D4
Longport	D2	Tower Way	B3
Lower Bridge Street	C2	Union Street	D3-D4
Lower Chantry Lane	D1-D2	Upper Bridge Street	C1-C2
Marlowe Avenue	B1-B2	Upper Chantry Lane	D1
Mercery Lane	C2	Vernon Place	C1
Mill Lane	B3-C3-C4	Victoria Row	C4-D4
Monastery Street	D2-D3	Watling Street	B2-C1
New Dover Road	C2-D2-D1	Westgate Grove	A3-B3
New Ruttington Lane	D4	White Horse Lane	B2
New Street	A3-A4	Whitehall Bridge Road	A3
North Holmes Road	D3	Whitehall Close	A2-A3
North Lane	B3-B4	Whitehall Gardens	A3
Northgate	C4-D4	Whitehall Road	A3
Notley Street	D4	Worthgate Place	B1

Cambridge

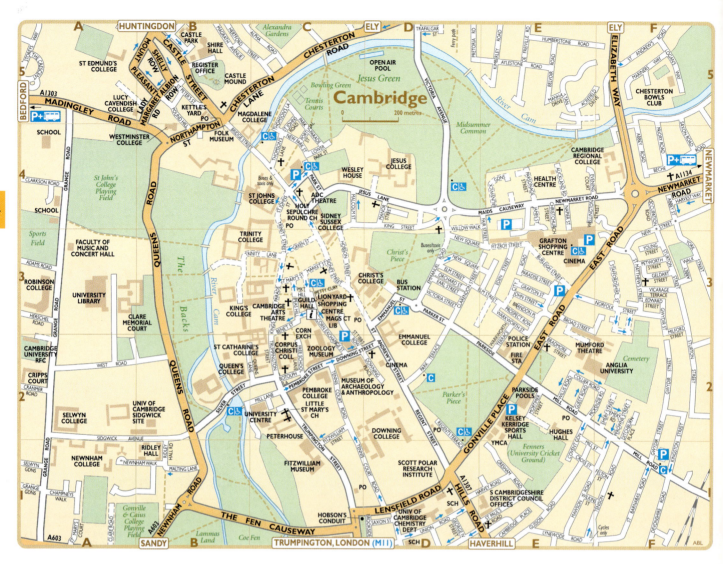

Cambridge
Cambridge is found on atlas page **62 D1**

Abbey Road	F4-F5
Abbey Street	F4
Abbey Walk	F3
Acrefield Drive	E5
Adams Road	A3
Albion Row	B5
Alpha Road	B5-C5
Auckland Road	E4
Aylestone Road	E5
Beche Road	F4
Belvoir Road	E5
Bene't Street	C3
Botolph Lane	C2
Bradmore Street	E2
Brandon Place	E3
Bridge Street	B5-B4-C4
Broad Street	E3
Brookside	D1
Brunswick Gardens	E4
Burleigh Street	E3
Cambridge Place	E1
Castle Street	B5
Champneys Walk	A1
Chesterton Lane	B5-C5
Chesterton Road	C5-D5
Christchurch Street	E4
City Road	E3
Clare Road	A1
Clarendon Street	D3-E3
Clarkson Road	A4
Collier Road	E2-F2
Corn Exchange Street	C2-C3
Covent Garden	E1-E2
Cranmer Road	A2
Cross Street	E1
De Freville Road	E5
Devonshire Road	F1
Ditchburn Place	F2
Downing Place	C2-D2
Downing Street	C2-D2
Earl Street	D3
East Road	E2-E3-F3-F4
Eden Street	E3
Edward Street	F3
Elizabeth Way	F5
Elm Street	D3-E3
Emery Road	F2
Emery Street	F2
Emmanuel Road	D3-D4
Emmanuel Street	D3
Evening Court	E4
Fair Street	D4-E3
Felton Street	F1
Fitzroy Street	E3
Fitzwilliam Street	C2
Free School Lane	C2
Geldart Street	F3
George IV Street	D1
Glisson Road	E1
Gonville Place	D1-D2-E2
Grafton Street	E3
Grange Gardens	A1
Grange Road	A1-A3-A5
Green Street	C3
Gresham Road	E1
Guest Road	E2
Gwydir Street	F1-F2-F3
Harvest Way	F4
Harvey Road	D1-E1
Herschel Road	A3
Hertford Street	B5-C5
Hills Road	D1-E1
Hobson Street	C3
Humberstone Road	E5-F5
James Street	E4
Jesus Lane	C4-D4
John Street	E3
Kimberley Road	E5
King Street	C4-D4
Kings Parade	C3
Kingston Street	F1-F2
Lady Margaret Road	B5
Lensfield Road	C1-D1
Logan's Way	F5
Lower Park Street	C4
Lynewode Road	E1
Madingley Road	A5-B5-B4
Magrath Avenue	B5
Maids Causeway	D4-E4
Malcolm Street	C4
Malting Lane	B1
Manhattan Drive	E5
Manor Street	D4
Mariners Way	F5
Market Hill	C3
Market Street	C3
Mawson Road	E1
McKenzie Road	E2-F2
Milford Street	F3
Mill Lane	B2-C2
Mill Road	E2-F2-F1
Mill Street	E2-E1-F1
Mortimer Street	E2
Mount Pleasant	A5-B5
Napier Street	E4
New Park Street	C4
New Square	D3
New Street	F3-F4
Newmarket Road	E4-F4
Newnham Road	B1
Newnham Walk	A1-B1
Norfolk Street	E3-F3
Northampton Street	B4-B5
Occupation Road	F4
Orchard Street	D3
Paradise Street	E3
Park Parade	C4-C5
Park Street	C4
Park Terrace	D2-D3
Parker Street	D3
Parkside	D3-D2-E2
Parsonage Street	E4
Peas Hill	C3
Pembroke Street	C2
Perowne Street	F2
Petty Cury	C3
Petworth Street	F3
Portugal Street	C4
Pound Hill	B5
Pretoria Road	D5
Priory Road	F4-F5
Prospect Row	E3
Queens Lane	B2
Queens Road	B1-B2-B3-B4
Regent Street	D1-D2
Regents Terrace	D1-D2
Ridley Hall Road	B1
St Andrew's Street	D2-D3
St Andrew's Road	F5
St Barnabas Road	F1
St Johns Road	C4-C5
St Johns Street	C4
St Mary's Court	A1
St Mary's Street	C3
St Matthew's Street	F3
St Paul's Road	E1
St Peter's Street	B5
St Tibbs Row	C2-C3
Saxon Road	F4-F5
Saxon Street	D1
Selwyn Gardens	A1
Shelly Row	B5
Sidgwick Avenue	A2-B2
Sidney Street	C3
Silver Street	B2-C2
Staffordshire Street	F3
Storeys Way	A5
Sturton Street	F2-F3
Tenison Road	E1-F1
Tennis Court Road	C2-C1-D1
The Crescent	A5
The Fen Causeway	B1-C1
Thomson's Lane	C4-C5
Trafalgar Street	D5
Trinity Lane	B3-C3
Trinity Street	C3-C4
Trumpington Street	C1-C2
Union Road	D1
Vicarage Terrace	F3
Victoria Avenue	D4-D5
Victoria Road	D3
Warkworth Street	E3
Warkworth Terrace	E2-E3
Wellington Street	E4
West Road	A2-B2
Wilkins Street	E1
Willis Road	E2
Willow Walk	D4
York Street	F3-F4
Young Street	F3

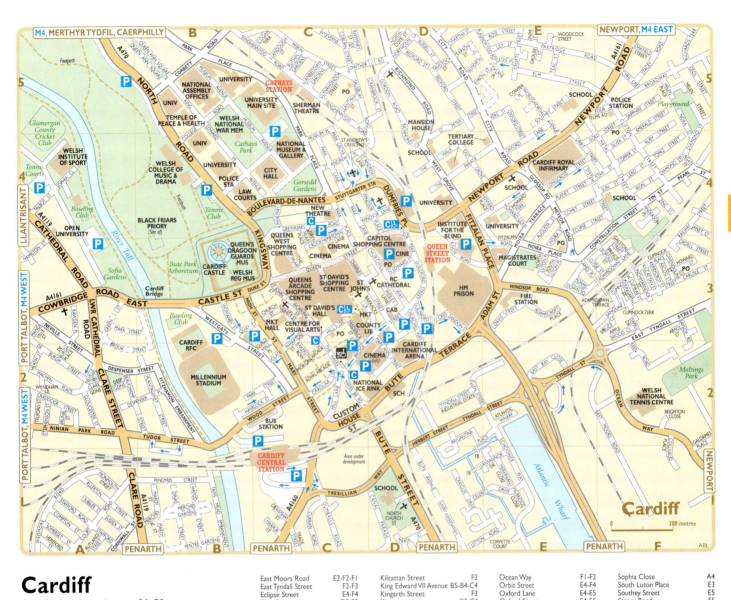

Cardiff

Cardiff is found on atlas page **36 C2**

Adam Street	D3-E3
Adamscroft Place	E3
Adamsdown Lane	F3
Adamsdown Square	E3
Adamsdown Terrace	F3
Allerton Street	A1
Ascog Street	F3
Atlantic Wharf	E2
Augusta Street	E3-E4
Bakers Row	C2
Barracks Lane	C3-D3
Bayside Road	F2-F3
Beauchamp Street	A2-B2
Bedford Street	D5
Boulevard de Nantes	B4-C4
Bridge Street	C2-D3
Brigantine Place	D2-E2
Broadway	F5
Brook Street	A3-A2-B2
Bute Avenue	D1
Bute Street	D1-D2
Bute Terrace	D2-D3
Byron Street	D5-E5
Canal Parade	D1
Carlisle Street	F3
Caroline Street	C2
Castle Street	B3
Cathedral Road	A3-A4
Celerity Drive	D1-E1
Charles Street	C3-D3
Church Street	C3
Churchill Way	D2-D3
City Road	D5-E5-E4
Clare Road	A2-A1-B1
Clare Street	A2
Clifton Street	F4-F5
Clive Place	E5
Clyde Street	E3-F3
Coburn Street	C5
College Road	B4-B5
Comet Street	E4-F4
Compton Street	A1
Constellation Street	E3-F3-F4
Copper Street	F4
Corbett Road	B5
Cornwall Street	A1
Court Road	A1
Cowbridge Road East	A3-B3
Cowper Place	E5
Craddock Street	A2
Cranbrook Street	D5
Craiglee Drive	D1
Crockherbtown Lane	C3-C4
Crofts Street	E5
Cumnock Place	F3
Cumnock Terrace	F3
Cumrae Street	F3
Curran Road	C1
Custom House Street	C2
Cyril Crescent	F5
Davis Street	E3
De Burgh Street	A2-A3
Despenser Gardens	A2
Despenser Place	A2-B2
Despenser Street	A2-B2
Diamond Street	F4
Dinas Street	B1
Duke Street	B3-C3
Dumballs Road	C1
Dumfries Place	D4
East Bay Close	E2
East Grove	D4-E4
East Moors Road	E2-F2-F1
East Tyndall Street	F2-F3
Eclipse Street	E4-F4
Ellen Street	D2-E2
Elm Street	E5-F5
Emerald Street	F4-F5
Fitzalan Place	D4-D3-E3
Fitzalan Road	E3
Fitzhamon Embankment	B2
Four Elms Road	E5-F5
Frederick Street	C2-C3
Galston Street	F3
Glossop Road	E4
Gloucester Street	A2
Glynrhondda Street	C5
Golate	C3
Gold Street	E4-F4-F5
Gordon Road	D5
Green Street	A3
Greyfriars Place	C3-C4
Greyfriars Road	C3-C4
Guildford Crescent	D3
Guildford Street	D3
Guildhall Place	C2
Gwendoline Street	F3
Hafod Street	B1
Havelock Street	B2-C2
Hayes Bridge Road	C2
Heath Street	A2
Helen Street	F5
Herbert Street	D1-D2
High Street	B3-C3
Hill's Street	C3
Howard Gardens	E4
Howard Place	E4
Howard Terrace	E4
Inchmarnock Street	F3
Iron Street	F4
Kames Place	E3
Keen Road	F2
Kerrycroy Street	F3
Kilcattan Street	F3
King Edward VII Avenue	B5-B4-C4
Kingarth Street	F3
Kingsway	C3-C4
Knox Road	D3
Lead Street	F4
Letton Road	D1-E1
Lily Street	E5
Llanbeddian Gardens	C5
Llandough Street	C5
Llansannor Drive	D1-E1
Llantwit Street	C5
Longcross Street	E4
Lower Cathedral Road	A2-A3
Lowther Road	C5-D5
Machen Place	A2
Mardy Street	B1
Mark Street	A3-B3
Mary Ann Street	D2
Merches Gardens	B1
Mervinian Close	E1
Metal Street	F4
Meteor Road	E3-E4
Mill Lane	C3
Miskin Street	C5
Moira Place	E3
Moira Street	E3-E4
Moira Terrace	E3-E4
Monmouth Street	A1
Morgan Arcade	C3
Museum Avenue	B5-C4
Museum Place	C4
Neville Place	A2
Neville Street	A2-A3
Newport Road	D4-E4-E5-F5
Ninian Park Road	A2
Nora Street	F4-F5
North Edward Street	D3
North Luton Place	E3
North Road	A5-B5-B4
Northcote Lane	D5
Ocean Way	F1-F2
Orbit Street	E4-F4
Oxford Lane	E4-E5
Oxford Street	E4-E5
Park Grove	C4
Park Lane	C4-D3
Park Place	B5-C5-C4-C3
Park Street	B2-C2
Partridge Road	E5-F5
Pearl Street	F4
Pearson Street	D5
Pendyris Street	B1
Planet Street	E4
Plantaganet Street	B2
Plasnewydd Road	D5-E5
Prince Leopold Street	F3
Quay Street	B3-C3
Queen Ann Square	A5-B5
Queen Street	C3
Rawden Place	A3
Richmond Crescent	D4-D5
Richmond Road	D4-D5
Royal Arcade	C2
Ruby Street	F4-F5
Russell Street	D5
Ruthin Gardens	C5
St Andrews Crescent	C4
St Andrews Lane	C4-D4
St Andrews Place	C4
St John Street	C3
St Mary Street	C2-C3
St Peter's Street	D5
Salisbury Road	C5-D5-D4
Sandon Street	D3
Sanquar Street	E3-F3
Sapele Drive	F3
Sapphire Street	F5
Schooner Way	E1-E2
Senghennydd Road	B5-C5-D4
Silver Street	F4
Somerset Street	A1
Sophia Close	A4
South Luton Place	E3
Southey Street	E5
Stacey Road	F5
Stafford Road	A1
Star Street	F4
Station Terrace	D3-D4
Stuttgarter Strasse	C4-D4
Sun Street	F4
System Street	E4-F4
Taffs Mead Embankment	B1
Talbot Street	A4
Talworth Street	D5
Teal Street	E5
The Friary	C3
The Hayes	C2
The Parade	D4-E4
The Walk	D4
Tin Street	F4
Topaz Street	F4
Tresillian Way	C1-D1
Trinity Street	C3
Tudor Street	A2-B2-B1
Tyndall Street	D2-E2
Tyndall Street Industrial Estate	D2
Vere Street	E5
Wedmore Road	A1
Wesley Lane	D3
West Canal Wharf	C1
West Grove	D4
Westgate Street	B3-B2-C2
Wharton Street	C2-C3
Windsor Lane	C4-D4
Windsor Place	C4-D4
Windsor Road	E3
Womanby Street	B3
Wood Street	B2-C2
Wordsworth Avenue	E4-E5
Working Street	C3
Wyndham Street	A2
Zinc Street	F4

Carlisle

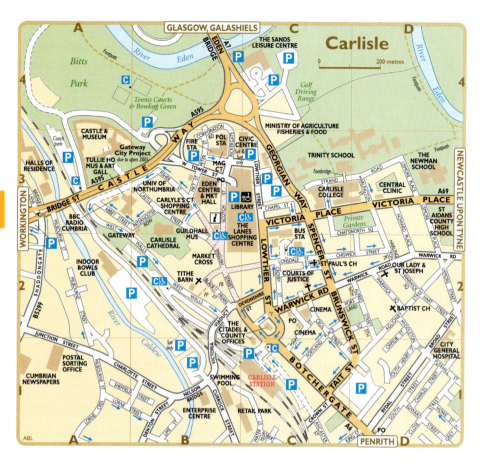

Carlisle is found on atlas page **103 H6**

Abbey Street	A3
Aglionby Street	D1-D2
Alfred Street North	D2
Alfred Street South	D2
Blackfriars Street	B2
Botchergate	C1-D1
Bridge Lane	A3
Bridge Street	A3
Broad Street	D1-D2
Brunswick Street	C2-D1
Castle Street	B2-B3
Castle Way	A3-B3-B4
Cecil Street	C1-C2
Chapel Street	C3
Charles Street	D1
Charlotte Street	A1-B1
Chatsworth Square	C3-D3
Chiswick Street	C2-D2
Close Street	D1
Corporation Road	B3-B4
Crosby Street	C2
Crown Street	C1
Currock Street	B1
Denton Street	B1
Devonshire Street	B2-C2
Eden Bridge	B4
Edward Street	D1
English Street	B2
Fisher Street	B3
Fusehill Street	D1
Georgian Way	C3-C4
Grey Street	D1
Harlington Place	D2
Harlington Street	D3
Hart Street	D2
Howard Place	D2-D3
Howe Street	D1
Junction Street	A1-A2
King Street	C1-D1
Lancaster Street	C1
Lime Street	B1
Lismore Place	D2-D3
Lismore Street	D2
Lonsdale Street	C2
Lorne Crescent	A1
Lorne Street	A1-B1
Lowther Street	C2-C3
Market Street	B3
Mary Street	C1-C2
Milbourne Street	A1-A2-A3
Myddleton Street	D1-D2
Nelson Bridge	B1
Orfeur Street	D1-D2
Paternoster Row	B3
Peter Street	B3
Portland Place	C1-C2
Portland Square	C2-D2
Rickergate	B3
Robert Street	C1
Rydal Street	D1
Scotch Street	B2-B3
Shaddongate	A2
Sheffield Street	A1-B1
South Henry Street	D1
South Street	D1
Spencer Street	C2-C3
Strand Road	C3-D3
Tait Street	C1-D1
Victoria Place	C3-D3
Victoria Viaduct	B1-B2
Warwick Road	C2-D2
Warwick Square	D2
Water Street	B1-C1
West Tower Street	B3
West Walls	A3-A2-B2

Chatham

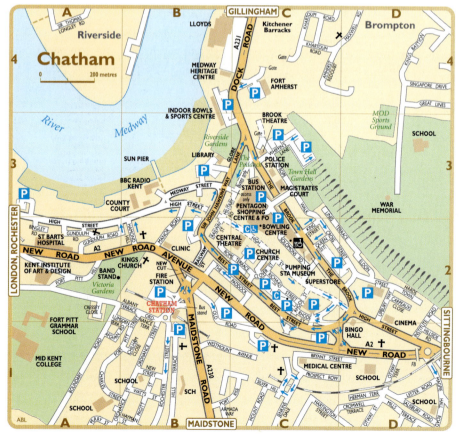

Chatham is found on atlas page **30 A3**

Afghan Road	A1-B1
Albany Terrace	B2
Amherst Redoubt	C4
Armada Way	B1
Best Street	B2-C2-C1
Bingley Road	A2
Boundary Road	A1-A2
Bryant Street	C1-D1
Carpeaux Close	D2
Charles Street	A1
Chilham Close	B1
Clover Street	C2
Cressey Close	A2
Cromwell Terrace	C1-D1
Cross Street	C2-D2
Dock Road	B4-C4
Eldon Street	D2
Fort Pitt Hill	A2
Fort Pitt Street	A1-B1-B2
Globe Lane	C3
Great Lines	D4
Gundulph Road	A2-B2
Hamond Hill	B2
Hards Town	D2
Hartington Street	C1-D1
Hayman Street	B1
Herman Terrace	D1
High Street	A2-B3-C2-D1
Hills Terrace	B1
Hillside Road	D1
Institute Road	D1-D2
Jenkins Dale	C1
Khartoum Road	C4
King Street	C2
Kings Bastion	D4
Lester Road	D1
Lines Terrace	C3-C2-D2
Lumsden Terrace	A2-B1
Magpie Hall Road	D1
Maidstone Road	B1-B2
Manor Road	B2-B3
Maxwell Road	D4
Medway Street	B3
Military Road	B3-C3
Mills Terrace	D1
Mount Road	C1
New Road	A2, B2-C1-D1
New Road Avenue	A2-B2
New Street	B1
Old Road	B2-B1-C1
Ordnance Street	A1-B1
Ordnance Terrace	B2
Otway Street	D1
Otway Terrace	D1
Pagitt Street	B1
Perry Street	A1
Port Rise	B1-C1
Prospect Row	C1-D1
Queen Street	C2
Railway Street	B2
Rhode Street	C2
Richard Street	C2
Rochester Street	B1
Rome Terrace	B2-C2
Rope Way	C3
Salisbury Road	D1
Silver Hill	C1
Singapore Drive	D4
Sir John Hawkins Way	B2-B3
Sir Thomas Longley Road	A4
Solomons Road	C2
The Brook	C3-C2-D2
The Paddock	B2-C2
Upbury Way	C2
Watts Street	B1
Westmount Avenue	B1-C1
Whiffin's Lane	C3

Cheltenham

Cheltenham is found on atlas page **47 E1**

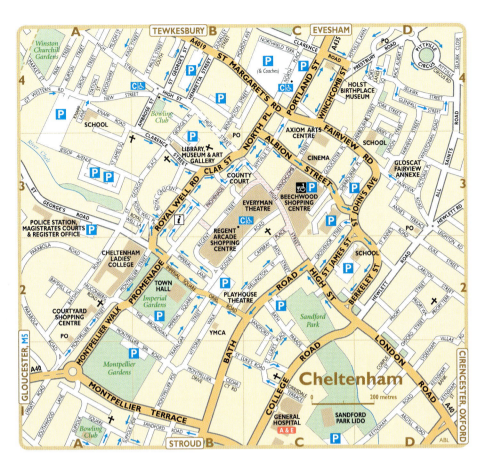

Albion Street	C3	Oxford Street	D1-D2
All Saints Road	D3-D4	Parabola Road	A1-A2
Ambrose Street	B4	Park Street	A4
Argyll Road	D1	Pittville Circus	D4
Back Albert Place	D4	Pittville Circus Road	D4
Bath Parade	C1-C2	Pittville Lawn	C4-D4
Bath Road	B1-B2-C2	Pittville Street	C3
Bath Street	C2	Portland Square	D4
Bayshill Road	A2-A3	Portland Street	C4
Bennington Street	B3-B4-C4	Prestbury Road	C4-D4
Berkeley Street	C2-D2	Priory Street	D2
Burton Street	A4	Priory Terrace	D2
Cambray Place	C2-C3	Priory Walk	D2
Carlton Street	D2	Promenade	A2-B2-B3
Clarence Road	C4	Regent Street	B2-B3
Clarence Street	B3-B4	Rodney Road	B2-C2-C3
College Road	C1-C2	Royal Crescent	B3
Devonshire Street	A4	Royal Well Place	B3
Duke Street	D2	Royal Well Road	B3
Fairview Road	C4-C3-D3	St Anne's Road	D2-D3
Fairview Street	D3-D4	St Anne's Terrace	D3
Fauconberg Road	A2	St George's Place	A3-B3-B4
Glenfall Street	D4	St George's Road	A3
Gloucester Place	C3	St George's Street	B4
Great Western Road	A4	St James Square	A3
Grosvenor Street	C2-C3	St James Street	C2
Grove Street	A4	St John's Avenue	C3-D3
Henrietta Street	B4	St Luke's Place	C1-C2
Hewlett Road	D2-D3	St Luke's Road	B1-C1
High Street	A4-B4-C3-C2	St Margaret's Road	B4-C4
Imperial Lane		St Paul's Street South	B4
Imperial Square	B2	Sandford Road	B1
Jessop Avenue	A3	Sandford Street	C2
Keynsham Road	D1	Selkirk Street	D4
King Street	A4-B4	Sherbourne Place	C3-D3
Knapp Road	A4	Sherbourne Street	D3-D4
London Road	D1-D2	Southwood Lane	A1
Monson Avenue	B4-C4	Suffolk Square	A1
Montpellier Drive	B1	Sydenham Villas Road	D1-D2
Montpellier Parade	B1	The Broadwalk	A2-B2-B1
Montpellier Spa Road	A2-B2-B1	Trafalgar Street	B1-B2
Montpellier Street	A1-A2-B2	Union Street	D3-D4
Montpellier Walk	A1-A2	Victoria Place	D3
Montpellier Terrace	A1-B1	Vittoria Walk	B1-B2
New Street	A4-B4	Wellington Street	B2-C2
North Place	C3-C4	Winchcomb Street	C3-C4
Northfield Terrace	C4	Winstonian Road	D3-D4
Oriel Road	B2	York Street	D4

Chester

Chester is found on atlas page **81 F1**

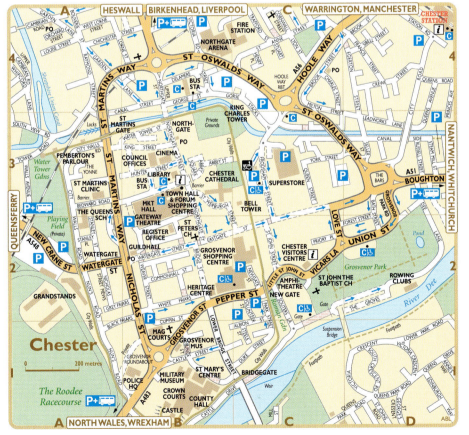

Abbey Square	B3	New Crane Street	A2
Abbey Street	B3	Newgate Street	C2
Albion Street	B1-C1-C2	Nicholas Street	B1-B2
Bath Street	D2-D3	Nicholas Street Mews	A2
Bedward Road	A3	Northgate Street	B2-B3-B4
Black Friars	A1-B2	Nun's Road	A2-A1-B1
Bridge Street	B2	Park Street	C1-C2
Bunce Street	B1	Pepper Street	B2-C2
Canal Side	D3	Queen Street	C3
Canal Street	A3-B4	Queens Avenue	D3-D4
Castle Drive	B1-C1	Queens Drive	D1
Castle Street	B1	Queens Park Road	C1-D1
Charles Street	C4	Queens Road	D4
Chichester Street	A4-B4	Raymond Street	A4
City Road	D3-D4	Russell Street	D3
City Walls Road	A2-A3	St Anne Street	C4
Commonhall Street	B2	St John Street	C2
Crewe Street	D4	St Johns Road	D1
Cuppin Street	B1-B2	St Martins Way	B2-A3-A4-B4
Dee Lane	D2-D3	St Oswalds Way	B4-C4-C3-D3
Delamere Street	B4	St Werburgh Street	B3-C2
Duke Street	C1	Seller Street	D3
Eastgate Street	B2-C2	Sibell Street	D4
Edinburgh Way	D1	Souters Lane	C1-C2
Egerton Street	D3-D4	South Crescent Road	D1
Forest Street	C2-D2-D3	South View Road	A3
Francis Street	C4	Stanley Street	A2
Frodsham Street	C3	Station Road	D4
Garden Lane	A4-B4	Steam Mill Street	D3
George Street	B4	Steele Street	C1
Gorse Stacks	B4-C4-C3	Stuart Place	C4
Granville Street	A4	The Bars	D3
Grey Friars	A2-B2	The Groves	C2-D2
Grosvenor Park Road	D3	Tower Road	A3
Grosvenor Street	B1-B2	Trafford Street	C4
Hoole Way	C4-D4	Union Street	D2
Hunter Street	A3-B3	Upper Northgate Street	B4
King Street	A3-B3	Vicars Lane	C2
Leadworks Lane	D3	Victoria Crescent	D1
Little St John Street	C2	Victoria Road	B4
Lorne Street	A4-B4	Volunteer Street	C4
Louise Street	A4	Walls Avenue	A2-A3
Love Street	C2-C3	Water Tower Street	A3-B3
Lower Bridge Street	B2-B1-C1	Watergate Street	A2-B2
Lower Park Road	D1-D2	Weaver Street	B2
Lyon Street	C4	West Lorne Street	A4
Mason Street	B4	Whipcord Lane	A3-A4
Milton Street	C4-C3-D3	York Street	C3-D3

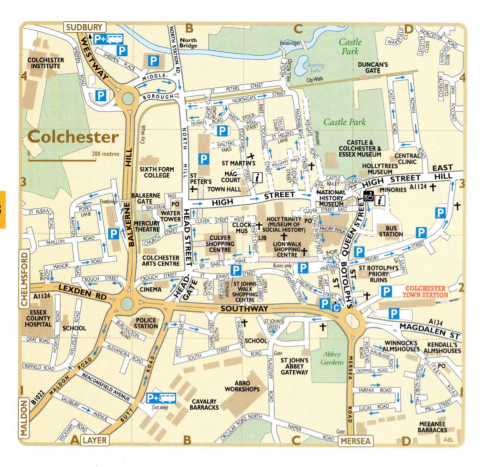

Colchester

Colchester is found on atlas page **52 D3**

Abbey Gate Street	C2	Museum Street	C3
Alexandra Road	A1-B1	Napier Road	C1
Art Street	C2	North Hill	B3-B4
Balkerne Hill	A2-A3-A4	North Station Road	B4
Balkerne Passage	B3	Northgate Street	B4-C4
Beaconsfield Avenue	A1	Nunn's Road	B4
Burlington Road	A2-B2-B1	Osborne Street	C2
Butt Road	A1-B1-B2	Papillon Road	A2
Castle Bailey	C3	Pope's Lane	A3
Castle Road	D3-D4	Portland Road	D1-D2
Chapel Street North	B2	Priory Street	C2-D2-D3
Chapel Street South	B1-B2	Priory Walk	C3
Church Street	B2-B3	Queen Street	C2-C3
Circular Road North	B1-C1	Rawston Road	A2-A3
Coventry Close	D4	Roman Road	D3-D4
Cowdray Crescent	C3-D3	Ryegate Road	C3-C4
Creffield Road	A1	St Alban's Road	A2-A3
Cromwell Road	D1	St Botolph's Street	C2
Crouch Street	A2-B2	St Helen's Lane	C3-C4
Culver Street East	C3-D3	St John's Avenue	B2
Culver Street West	B3-C3	St John's Green	C2
East Hill	D3	St John's Street	B2-C2
East Stockwell Street	C3-C4	St Julian Grove	D2
Fairfax Road	D1	St Peters Street	B4-C4
Flagstaff Road	C1	Salisbury Avenue	A1
George Street	C3	Sheepen Place	A4-B4
Golden Noble Hill	D1	Sheepen Road	A4
Gray Road	A1	Short Cut Road	B4
Head Street	B2-B3	Short Wyre Street	C2
Headgate	B2	Shrubland Road	D1
High Street	B3-C3, D3	Sir Isaac's Walk	B2-C2
Hospital Lane	A2	South Street	B1
Hospital Road	A1-A2	Southway	B2-C2
Inverness Close	D4	Stanwell Street	C2
Leicester Close	D4	Stockwell Street	B4-C4
Lexden Road	A2	Taylor Court	C3-C4
Lincoln Way	D4	Trinity Street	C2-C3
Long Wyre Street	C2-C3	Vineyard Street	C2
Lucas Road	D1	Wakefield Close	D4
Magdalen Street	D2	Walsingham Road	B2-B1-C1
Maidenburgh Street	C3-C4	Walters Yard	B3
Maldon Road	A1-A2	Wellesley Road	A1-A2
Manor Road	A2	West Stockwell Street	B4-B3-C3
Mersea Road	C1-D1	West Street	B1-B2
Middle Mill Road	C4	Westway	A4
Middleborough	A4-B4	Wickham Road	A1
Military Road	D1-D2	William's Walk	C3
Mill Street	D1	Worcester Road	D4

Coventry

Coventry is found on atlas page **59 F3**

Abbotts Lane	A4	Meriden Street	A3-A4
Acacia Avenue	D1	Middleborough Road	A4-B4
Alma Street	D3	Mile Lane	C1
Barras Lane	A3	Much Park Street	C2
Bayley Lane	C2-C3	New Buildings	C3
Bird Street	C4	New Union Street	B2-C2
Bishop Street	B3-B4	Norfolk Street	A3
Bond Street	B3	Park Road	B1-C1
Broadgate	B3-C3	Parkside	C1-D1
Burges	B3	Primrose Hill Street	C4-D4
Butts Road	A2	Priory Row	C3
Canterbury Street	D3-D4	Priory Street	C3
Chantry Place	C3-C4	Puma Way	C1-D1
Charles Street	D4	Quarryfield Lane	D1
Colchester Street	D4	Queen Victoria Road	B2-B3
Cook Street	C4	Queens Road	A2
Corporation Street	B3	Quinton Road	C1
Coundon Road	A4	Radford Road	B4
Cox Street	C4-D3-C3-C2	Raglan Street	D3
Croft Road	A2-B2	Regent Street	A1-A2
Cross Cheaping	B3-C3	Ringway Hill Cross	A3-B3-B4
Drapers Fields	B4	Ringway Queens	A2-B1
Earl Street	C2	Ringway Rudge	A2-A3
Eaton Road	B1	Ringway St Johns	C1-C2
Fairfax Street	C3	Ringway St Nicholas	B4
Ford Street	C3-D3	Ringway St Patrick	B1-C1
Friars Road	B1-B2-C2	Ringway Swanswell	C4-C3-D3
Gosford Street	C2-D2	Ringway Whitefriars	D2-D3
Greyfriars Lane	B2	St John's Street	C2
Greyfriars Road	B2	St Nicholas Street	B4
Grosvenor Road	A1	St Patrick's Road	B1-C1-C2
Gulson Road	D2	Salt Lane	B2-C2
Hales Street	B3-C3	Silver Street	B3-B4-C4
Hay Lane	C2-C3	Spon Street	A3-B3
Hertford Street	B2	Stoney Road	B1-C1
High Street	B3-C2	Stoney Stanton Road	C4
Hill Street	A3-B3	Strathmore Avenue	D1-D2
Holyhead Road	A3	Swanswell Gate	C3
Hood Street	D3	Tower Street	B4
Jordan Well	C2	Trinity Street	C3
King William Street	D4	Upper Well Street	B3
Lamb Street	B3-B4	Victoria Road	D4
Little Park Street	C2	Vine Street	D3-D4
London Road	D1	Warwick Road	B1-B2
Lower Ford Street	D3	Westminster Road	A1
Manor House Drive	B1-B2	White Street	C4
Manor Road	B1	Whitefriars Street	C2-D2
Meadow Street	A2-A3	Yardley Street	D4

Darlington

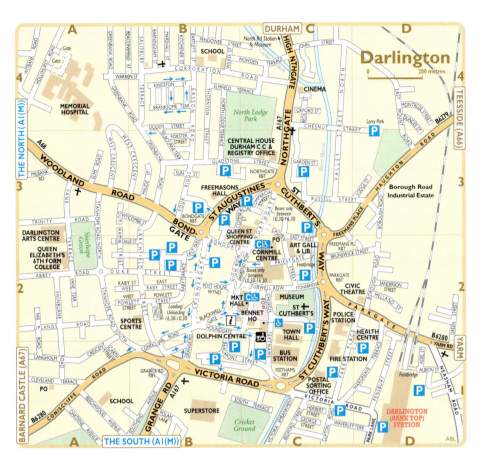

Darlington is found on atlas page **106 B2**

Abbey Road	A2	Larchfield Street	B2-B3
Albion Street	D1	Marshall Street	B4
Barningham Street	B4	Maude Street	B3
Bartlett Street	B4	Melland Street	D2
Beaconsfield Street	A4	Mowden Terrace	B4-C4
Beaumont Street	B2-B1-C1	Neasham Road	D1
Beck Street	C4	North Lodge Terrace	B3-B4
Bedford Street	C1	Northgate	C2-C3-C4
Beechwood Avenue	A1	Oakdene Avenue	A1
Blackwell Gate	B2	Outram Street	A2-A3
Bondgate	B2-B3	Oxford Street	C4
Borough Road	D2-D3	Park Lane	D1
Branksome Terrace	B4	Park Place	C1-D2
Brunswick Street	C2-D2	Parkgate	C2-D2
Chesnut Street	C4-D4-D3	Pendower Street	B4-C4
Church Row	C2	Pensbury Street	D1
Cleveland Terrace	A1	Post House Wynd	B2
Clifton Road	C1	Powlett Street	B2
Commercial Street	B3-C3	Prebend Row	B2-C2
Coniscliffe Road	A1-B1-B2	Priestgate	C2
Corporation Road	B4-C4	Raby Terrace	B2
Crown Street	C2-C3	Russell Street	C3-D3
Dodd's Street	B4	St Augustines Way	B3-C3
Duke Street	A2-B2	St Cuthbert's Way	C1-C2-C3
Easson Road	B3-B4	Salisbury Terrace	B4
East Mount Road	D3-D4	Salt Yard	B2
East Raby Street	B2	Selbourne Terrace	B3
East Street	C2	Skinnergate	B2
Elmfield Terrace	B4-C4	South Terrace	B1-C1
Eskale Street	A2-B2	Southend Avenue	A1-B1
Feethams	C1-C2	Stanhope Road North	A2-A3
Forster Street	B3	Stanhope Road South	A2-A1-B1
Four Riggs	B3	Stonebridge	C2
Freemans Place	C2-C3-D3	Swinburne Road	A1-A2
Garden Street	C3	Thornton Street	B3-B4
Gladstone Street	B3-C3	Trinity Road	A3
Grange Road	B1	Tubwell Row	C2
Greenbank Road	A4-B4-B3	Uplands Road	A2
Hargreave Terrace	C1-D1-D2	Valley Street North	C3-C4
Haughton Road	D3-D4	Vane Terrace	A2-A3
High Northgate	C4	Victoria Embankment	C1
High Row	B2	Victoria Road	B1-C1-D1
Hollyhurst Road	A4	Waverley Terrace	C1-D1
Houndgate	B2-C2	West Crescent	A4-A3-B3
John Street	C4	Wilkes Street	B4
Kingston Street	B4	Woodland Road	A3-B3
Kitchener Street	B4	Wycombe Street	A3-B3
Langholm Crescent	A1-A2	Yarm Road	D1

Doncaster

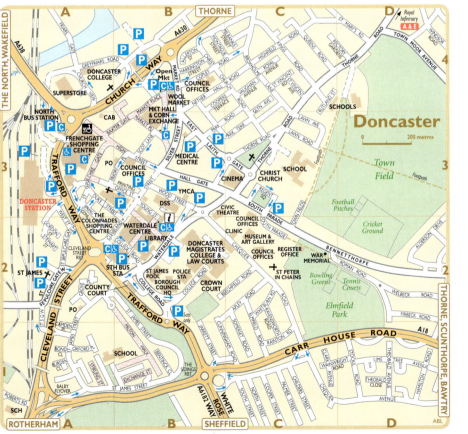

Doncaster is found on atlas page **84 C5**

Alderson Drive	D2	Montague Street	B4-C4
Allerton Street	B4	Nether Hall Road	B4-C4
Apley Road	C2	North Street	C1
Baxter Gate	A3-B3	Oxford Place	A1
Beechfield Road	B2-C2	Palmer Street	C1
Bennetthorpe	C2-D2	Park Road	B3-C3-C4
Bentinck Close	B1	Park Terrace	B3-C3
Bond Close	A1	Printing Office Street	B3
Broxholme Lane	C4	Priory Place	B3
Camden Place	A1	Queens Road	C4
Carr House Road	B1-C1-D1	Rainton Road	C1
Chequer Avenue	C1-D1	Ravensworth Road	C1-C2
Chequer Road	B2-C2-C1	Rectory Gardens	C4-D4
Childers Street	C1	Regent Square	C3
Christ Church Road	B4-C4-C3	Roberts Road	A1
Church View	A4	Roman Road	D2
Church Way	A4-B4	Royal Avenue	C4
Clark Avenue	C1	Rutland Street	C4
Cleveland Street	A1-A2-B2-B3	St James Street	A1-A2-B2-B1
College Road	B2	St Mary's Road	D4
Cooper Street	C1	St Sepulchre Gate	A3
Coopers Terrace	B4-C4	St Sepulchre Gate West	A1-A2
Copley Road	B4-C4	St Vincent Avenue	C4
Cunningham Road	B2-B1-C1	St Vincent Road	C4
Duke Street	A3-B3	Scot Lane	B3
East Laith Gate	B3-C3	Silver Street	B3
Elmfield Road	C1-C2	Somerset Road	C1-C2
Exchange Street	B1	South Parade	C2-C3
Firbeck Road	D2	South Street	C1
Friars Gate	A4	Spring Gardens	A3
Glyn Avenue	C4	Sterling Street	A1
Gordon Street	A2	Stewart Street	A2
Greyfriars Road	A4-B4	Stockil Road	D1
Grove Place	A2	Theobald Avenue	D1
Hall Gate	B3	Thorne Road	C3-C4-D4
Hamilton Road	D1	Town Fields	C2-C3
Harrington Street	B4	Town Moor Avenue	D4
High Street	B3	Trafford Way	A3-A2-B2-B1
Highfield Road	C4	Vaughan Avenue	C4
Jarrett Street	B1	Wainwright Road	C1-D1
Kings Road	C4	Waterdale	B2-B3
Lawn Avenue	C3	Welbeck Road	D2
Lawn Road	C3	West Street	A2-A3
Lime Tree Avenue	D1	Whitburn Road	C2
Market Place	B3-B4	White Rose Way	B1-C1
Market Road	B4	Windsor Road	D4
Milbanke Street	C4	Wood Street	B3
Milton Walk	B1-B2	Young Street	B2-B3

Derby

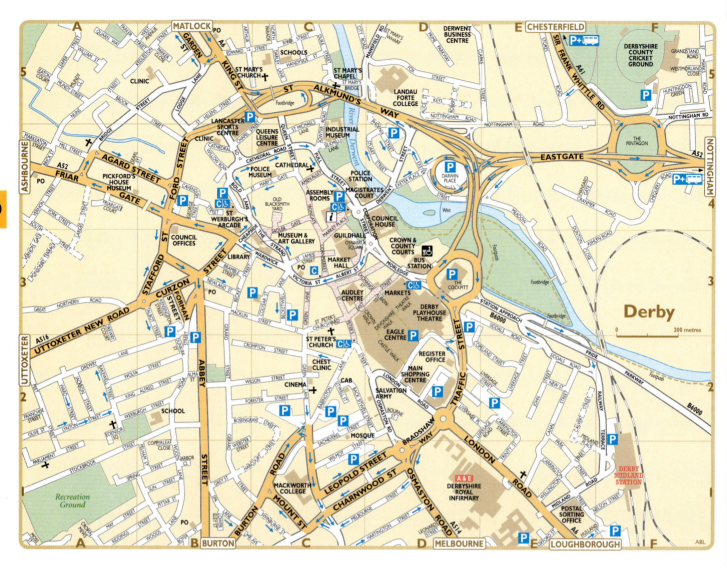

Derby
Derby is found on atlas page **72 A4**

Abbey Street	B1-B2-B3	Colyear Street	C3	Gerard Street	B3-B2-B1-C1	Meadow Road	E3-E4	River Street	C5	Uttoxeter New Road	A2-A3
Agard Street	A4-B4	Copeland Street	D3-D2-E2	Grandstand Road	F5	Melbourne Street	C1-D1	Robert Street	D5	Vernon Gate	A3
Albert Street	C3	Copperleaf Close	B1	Great Northern Road	A3	Midland Place	E1-E2	Rosengrave Street	B2-C2	Vernon Street	A4
Albion Street	D3	Cornmarket	C3	Green Lane	C2-C3	Midland Road	E1	Sacheverel Street	C1-C2	Victoria Street	C3
Alice Street	D5	Corporation Street	C4-D3	Grey Street	B1	Mill Street	A4	Sadler Gate	C3-C4	Ward Street	A2
Alma Street	B2	Cranmer Road	E4-F4	Handyside Street	C5	Monk Street	B2-B3	St Alkmund's Way	C5-D5	Wardwick	B3-C3
Amen Alley	C4	Crompton Street	B2-C2	Hansard Gate	E4	Morledge	D3	St Helens Street	B5	Webster Street	B1-B2
Arbor Close	B1	Crown Mews	A1	Harcourt Street	B1-C1	Moss Street	A1	St James Street	C3	Wellington Street	E1
Arthur Street	B5-C5	Crown Walk	C3-D3	Hartington Street	C1-D1	Mount Street	C1	St Marks Road	F5	Werburgh Street	A2-B2
Ashlyn Road	E3-F3-F4	Curzon Street	B3	Hulland Street	E1-F1	Mundy Close	A5	St Mary's Bridge	C5	West Avenue	B5
Babington Lane	C2	Darley Lane	C5	Huntingdon Green	F5	Mundy Street	A5	St Mary's Wharf	D5	Westmorland Close	F5
Back Sitwell Street	C2-D2	Derwent Street	D4	Irongate	C4	Nelson Street	E1-F1	St Marys Gate	B4-C4	William Street	A5
Bakewell Street	A2	Devonshire Walk	D3	Jackson Street	A2	New Street	E2	St Michael's Lane	C4-C5	Willow Row	B4
Becket Street	B3-C3	Drewry Court	A2-A3	John Street	E2	Newland Street	B3	St Peter's Churchyard	C3	Wilmot Street	C1-D2
Becketwell Lane	C3	Drewry Lane	A2-B2-B3	Kedleston Street	A5-B5	North Parade	C5	St Peter's Street	C3-C2-D2	Wilson Street	B2-C2
Bold Lane	B4	Duke Street	C5	Kensington Street	B3	Nottingham Road	D5-E5, F5	Searl Street	A4-B4	Wolfa Street	A2-B2
Bourne Street	D2	Dunkirk Street	B2	Keys Street	D5	Nuns Street	A4-A5	Siddals Road	D3-E3-E2	Woods Lane	B1-B2
Boyer Street	B1	Dunton Close	E3-E4	King Alfred Street	A2-B2	Olive Street	A2	Silkmill Lane	C4	York Street	A4
Bradshaw Way	D1-D2	East Street	C3-D3	King Street	B5	Osmaston Road	D1-D2	Sir Frank Whittle Road	E5-F5		
Bramble Street	B3	Eastgate	E4	Larges Street	A3-A4	Osnabrük Square	C3	Sitwell Street	C2		
Brick Street	A4	Eaton Court	A5	Leaper Street	A5	Oxford Street	E1	South Street	A3-A4		
Bridge Street	A4-A5-B5	Edensor Square	A1-A2	Leonard Street	D1	Park Street	E1-E2	Sowter Road	C4-C5		
Brook Street	A5-B5-B4	Edward Street	B5-C5	Leopold Street	C1-D1	Parker Close	B5	Spa Lane	B1		
Burton Road	B1-C1-C2	Exchange Street	C3-D3	Lime Avenue	B1-C1	Parker Street	A5-B5	Spring Street	A1-B1		
Calvert Street	E2	Exeter Place	D4	Liversage Place	D2-E2	Parliament Street	A1	Stafford Street	B3-B4		
Canal Street	E2	Exeter Street	D4	Liversage Road	D2-E2	Peet Street	A1-A2	Station Approach	D3-E3		
Carrington Street	E1, E2	Ford Street	B4	Liversage Street	D2-E2	Pelham Street	B1	Stockbrook Street	A1-B1-B2		
Castle Walk	D2	Forester Street	B2-C2	Lodge Lane	B4-B5	Phoenix Street	D4-D5	Stores Road	E5		
Cathedral Road	B4-C4	Forman Street	B3	London Road	D2-D1-E1	Pittar Street	B1	Stuart Street	D4		
Cavendish Street	B4	Fox Street	D5	Lower Eley Street	A3	Ponsonby Terrace	B1	Sun Street	B1		
Chapel Street	B4-C5	Franchise Street	A2	Lynton Street	A2	Pride Parkway	E3-E2-F2	Swinburne Street	C1		
Charnwood Street	C1-D1	Friar Gate	A4-B4	Macklin Street	B3-C3	Prime Parkway	B2-B3	Talbot Street	B2-B3		
Cheapside	B3-C4	Friargate Court	B4	Mansfield Road	D5	Quarn Way	A5	The Strand	C3-C4		
Chequers Road	F4	Full Street	C4	Markeaton Street	A4	Queen Street	C4-C5	Theatre Walk	D3		
City Road	C5	Garden Street	B5	Market Place	C3-C4	Railway Terrace	E2-F2-F1	Traffic Street	D2-D3		
Clarke Street	D5-E5	George Street	B4	May Street	A1-B1	Riddings Street	A1-B1	Trinity Street	E1		

Dover

Dover is found on atlas page **19 G6**

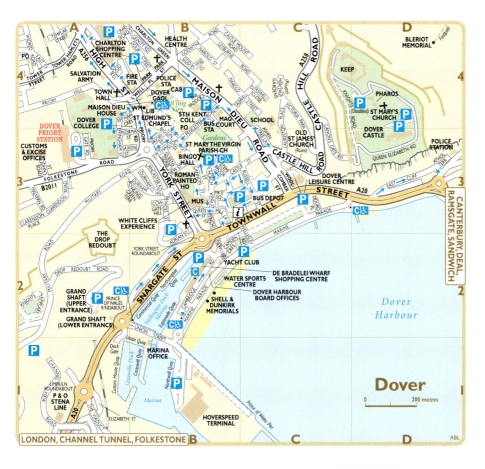

Adrian Street	B2-B3	Mill Lane	B3
Ashen Tree Lane	C3-C4	New Bridge	B2
Athol Terrace	D3	New Street	B3
Bench Street	B3	Norman Street	A3-B3
Biggin Street	B3-B4	Park Place	B4
Bowling Green Terrace	B3	Park Street	B4
Cambridge Road	B2	Pencester Road	B3-B4
Camden Crescent	B2-C2	Princes Street	B3
Cannon Street	B3	Priory Gate Road	A3
Canon's Gate Road	C3-C4	Priory Hill	A4
Castle Hill Road	C3-C4	Priory Road	B3-B4
Castle Mount Road	B4-C4	Priory Street	B3
Castle Street	B3-C3	Queen Elizabeth Road	D3
Channel View Road	A1	Queen Street	B3
Charlton Green	B4	Queens Gardens	B3
Church Street	B3	Russell Street	C3
Clarendon Road	A3	St John's Road	A3
Cowgate Hill	B3	Saxon Street	A3-B3
Crafford Street	A4-B4	Snargate Street	B2
Dour Street	A4-B4	Stem Brook	B3
Douro Place	C3	Taswell Close	C4
Drop Redoubt Road	A2	Taswell Street	B4-C4
Durham Close	B3	Templar Street	A4
Durham Hill	B3	The Paddock	B4
East Cliff	D3	The Viaduct	A1
East Street	A4	Tower Hamlets Road	A4
Effingham Crescent	A4-B4	Tower Street	A4
Effingham Street	A3-A4	Townwall Street	B3-C3
Elizabeth Street	A1	Union Street	B1-B2
Folkestone Road	A3-B3	Victoria Park	C3-C4
Godwyne Close	B4	Wellesley Road	C2-C3
Godwyne Road	B4	Widred Road	A4
Harold Street	B4-C4	Wood Street	A4
Heritage Gardens	C4	Woolcomber Street	C3
Hewitt Road	B4	Worthington Street	B3
High Street	A4-B4	York Street	B3
King Street	B3		
Knights Road	C4-D3		
Knights Templars	A2		
Ladywell	B4		
Lancaster Road	B3		
Laureston Place	C3-C4		
Leyburne Road	B4-C4		
Maison Dieu Road	B4-C4-C3		
Malvern Road	A3		
Marine Parade	B2-C2-C3		
Market Square	B3		
Military Road	A2-A3-B3		

Dundee

Dundee is found on atlas page **140 D3**

Airlie Place	A1	Nicoll Street	B3
Balfour Street	A2	North Lindsay Street	B2-B3
Bank Street	B3	North Marketgait	A4-B4-C4
Barrack Road	A4	Panmure Street	B3-C3-C4
Barrack Street	B3	Park Place	A2-A1-B1
Bell Street	B3-B4-C4	Park Wynd	A2
Blackscroft	D4	Perth Road	A1
Blinshall Street	A2-A3	Prospect Place	A4-B4
Brown Street	A2-A3	Queen Street	C4-D4
Candle Lane	C3-D3	Rattray Street	B3
Castle Street	C2-C3	Reform Street	B3-C3
Commercial Street	C3	Riverside Drive	B1-C1-C2
Constable Street	D4	Roseangle	A1
Constitution Road	A4-B4-B3	St Andrews Street	C4
Cowgate	C4	St Roques Lane	D4
Crichton Street	C2	Seabraes Court	A1
Cross Lane	A2-B2	Seagate	C3-C4-D4
Dens Street	D4	Session Street	A2-A3
Dock Street	C2-C3	Small's Lane	A2
Douglas Street	A3	Small's Wynd	A1-A2
Dudhope Street	B4	South Marketgait	B2-C2-D3
Dudhope Terrace	A4	South Tay Street	A2-B2
East Dock Street	D3-D4	South Victoria Dock Road	D3
East Marketgait	C4-D4-D3	South Ward Road	B2-B3
Euclid Crescent	B3	Trades Lane	C3-D3
Euclid Street	B3	Union Street	B2-C2
Exchange Street	C2-C3	Union Terrace	A4
Foundry Lane	D4	Victoria Road	B4-C4
Gellatly Street	C3-D3	Ward Road	A3-B3
Greenmarket	B1-B2	West Bell Street	A3-B3
Guthrie Street	A3	West Marketgait	A3-A2-B2
Hawkhill	A2	West Port	A2
High Street	C2-C3	Whitehall Crescent	C2
Hilltown	B4-C4	Whitehall Street	C2
Hilltown Terrace	B4	Willison Street	B2-B3
Horsewater Wynd	A2		
Irvine's Square	B4		
Johnston Street	A3-B3		
King Street	C4-D4		
Ladywell Avenue	C4-D4		
Laurel Bank	B4		
Lochee Road	A4		
Mary Anne Lane	D3-D4		
McDonald Street			
Meadowside	B3-C3-C4-B4		
Middle Street	D4		
Miln Street	A3		
Nethergate	A1-B1-B2		

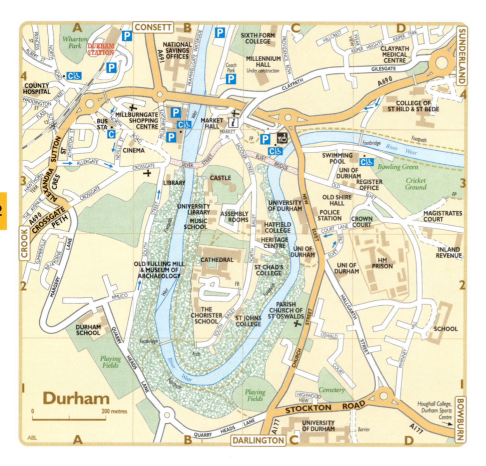

Durham

Durham is found on atlas page **106 B5**

Albert Street	A4
Alexandra Crescent	A3
Allergate	A3
Atherton Street	A3-A4
Briardene	A2
Church Street	C1-C2
Claypath	C4
Court Lane	C3-D3
Crossgate	A3-B3
Crossgate Peth	A2-A3
Elvet Bridge	C3
Elvet Crescent	C2-C3
Flass Street	A3-A4
Framwellgate	B4
Gilesgate	D4
Hallgarth Street	C2-D2-D1
Hawthorn Terrace	A3
Highwood View	C1
Hillcrest	C4
Keiper Heights	C4-D4
Keiper Terrace	D4
Margery Lane	A2-A3
Market Place	B3-B4
Millburngate	B3-B4
Neville Street	A3
New Elvet	C2-C3
North Bailey	C2-C3
North Road	A4-A3-B3
Old Elvet	C3-D3
Oswald Court	C2-C1-D1
Pimlico	A2
Princess Street	A4
Providence Row	C4
Quarry Heads Lane	A2-A1-B1-C1
Saddler Street	B3-C3
Silver Street	B3
South Bailey	B1-B2
South Street	B2-B3
Stockton Road	C1-D1
Summerville	A2-A3
Sutton Street	A3-A4
The Avenue	A3
Waddington Street	A4
Wear View	D4
Whinney Hill	D1-D2

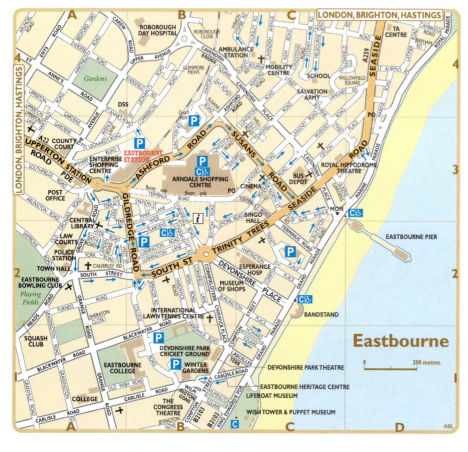

Eastbourne

Eastbourne is found on atlas page **17 G1**

Arlington Road	A2-A3	Lascelles Terrace	B1-C1
Ashford Road	B3-B4-C4	Latimer Road	D4
Ashford Square	B4	Leaf Road	B4
Bedford Grove	A4	Lismore Road	B2-B3-C3
Belmore Road	C4-D4	Longstone Road	B3-C3-C4
Blackwater Road	A1-B1-B2	Lushington Lane	B2
Bolton Road	B2-B3	Lushington Road	B2
Bourne Street	C4-C3-D3	Marine Parade	D3
Burlington Place	B2-C2-C1	Marine Road	D3-D4
Burlington Road	C2-C3	Mark Lane	B2-B3
Camden Road	A2	Meads Road	A1-A2
Carew Road	A4-B4	Melbourne Road	C4
Carlisle Road	A1-B1-C1	New Road	C4
Cavendish Avenue	C4	North Street	C3
Cavendish Bridge	B4	Old Orchard Road	A2-A3
Cavendish Place	C3-C4	Old Wish Road	A1-B1
Ceylon Place	C3-D3-D4	Pevensey Road	C3-C4-D3
Chiswick Place	B1-B2	Queens Gardens	C3-D3
College Road	B1-B2	Royal Parade	D4
Commercial Road	B3-B4	St Anne's Road	A4-A3-B3
Compton Street	B1-C1-C2	St Aubyn's Road	D4
Connaught Road	B2	St Leonard's Road	A3-B3-B4
Cornfield Lane	B2	Saffrons Road	A3
Cornfield Road	B2-B3	Seaside	D4
Cornfield Terrace	B2	Seaside Road	C3-D3
Devonshire Place	B2-C2	South Street	A2-B2
Dursley Road	C4	Southfields Road	A3
Elms Avenue	C2-C3	Spencer Road	B2
Elms Road	C2-C3	Station Parade	A3
Enys Road	A4	Station Street	B3
Eversfield Road	A4-B4	Susans Road	B4-B3-C3
Furness Road	A2-B2	Sydney Road	A3
Gildredge Road	A3-B2	Terminus Road	B3-C3-C2
Grand Parade	C1-C2	The Avenue	A3-A4
Grange Road	A1-A2	Tideswell Road	B3-C3-C2
Granville Road	A1	Trinity Place	C2
Grassington Road	A1-A2	Trinity Trees	B2-C2
Grove Road	A2-A3	Upper Avenue	A4-B4
Hardwick Road	B1-B2	Upperton Gardens	A3-A4
Hartfield Road	A3-A4	Upperton Road	A3
Hartington Place	C2	West Street	A2-B2
Howard Square	C1	West Terrace	A2-A3
Hyde Gardens	B2-B3	Wharf Road	A3
Hyde Road	A2	Willowfield Road	C4-D4
Ivy Terrace	A3	Wilmington Gardens	B1
Junction Road	B3	Wilmington Square	B1
King Edward's Parade	B1-C1	Wish Road	B2
Langney Road	C3-C4-D4	York Road	A2

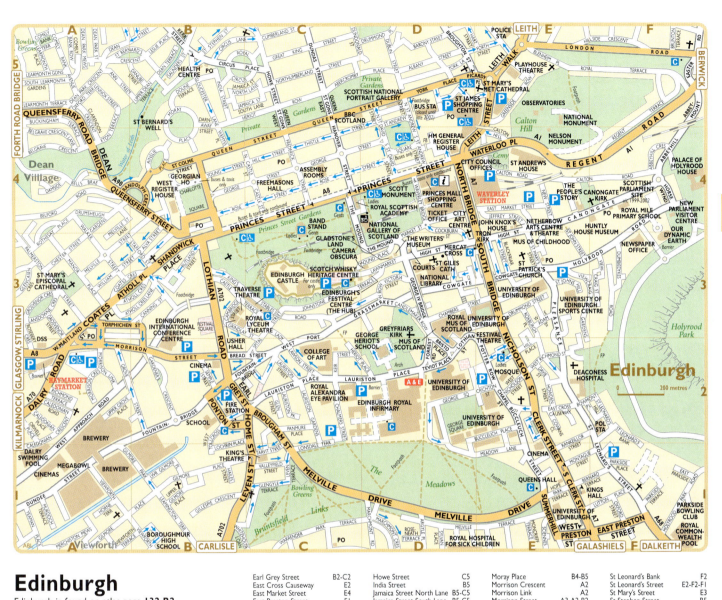

Edinburgh

Edinburgh is found on atlas page 132 B2

Abbeyhill	F4	Castle Terrace	B3-C3	Earl Grey Street	B2-C2	Howe Street	C5	Moray Place	B4-B5	St Leonard's Bank	F2
Abbeyhill Crescent	F4	Chalmers Street	C2	East Cross Causeway	E2	India Street	B5	Morrison Crescent	A2	St Leonard's Street	E2-F2-F1
Abbeymount	F5	Chambers Street	D3-E3	East Market Street	E4	Jamaica Street North Lane	B5-C5	Morrison Link	A2	St Mary's Street	E3
Abercromby Place	C5-D5	Chapel Street	E2	East Preston Street	F1	Jamaica Street South Lane	B5-C5	Morrison Street	A3-A2-B2	St Stephen Street	B5
Ainslie Place	B4	Charlotte Square	B4	Eton Terrace	A4-A5	Jeffrey Street	E4	Mound Place	C3-D3	Semple Street	B2
Albany Street	D5	Chester Street Gardens	A3-A4	Festival Square	B3	Johnstone Terrace	C3-D3	Murdoch Terrace	A1	Shandwick Place	B3
Alva Street	B3-B4	Circus Lane	B5-C5	Forrest Road	D2-D3	Keir Street	C2	New Street	E4	South Bridge	E3
Ann Street	A5-B5	Circus Place	B5-C5	Forth Street	D5-E5	Kerr Street	B5	Nicholson Street	E2-E3	South Clerk Street	E1-F1
Argyle Place	D1	Clarendon Crescent	A4-A5	Fountainbridge	A2-B2-C2	King's Stables Road	B3-C3	North Bridge	D4-E4	South Learmonth Gardens	A5
Atholl Crescent	A3-B3	Clerk Street	E1-E2	Frederick Street	C4	Lady Lawson Street	C2-C3	North Castle Street	B4-C4	South St Andrew Street	D4
Atholl Crescent Lane	A3-B3	Coates Crescent	A3-B3	Gardener's Crescent	B2	Lansdowne Crescent	A3	North St Andrew Street	D5	South St David Street	D4
Atholl Place	A3-B3	Coates Place	A3	George IV Bridge	D3	Lauriston Gardens	C2	North St David Street	D4-D5	Spital Street	C2-C3
Barony Street	D5	Cockburn Street	D3-D4	George Square	D2	Lauriston Park	C2	Northumberland Street	C5	Stafford Street	B3
Belford Road	A4	Comely Bank Avenue	A5	George Street	B4-C4-D4	Lauriston Place	C2-D2	Oxford Street	F1	Summerhill	E1
Belgrave Crescent	A4	Cowgate	D3-E3	Gillespie Crescent	B1	Lauriston Street	C2	Palmerston Street	A3-A4	Tarvit Street	C1-C2
Belgrave Crescent Lane	A4-A5	Crichton Street	E2	Gilmore Park	A2-A1-B1	Lawnmarket	D3	Panmure Place	C2	Teviot Place	D2
Bells Brae	A4	Dalkeith Road	F1	Gilmore Place	A1-B1-C1	Leamington Terrace	B1	Parkside Terrace	F1	The Mound	C4-D3
Bernard Terrace	E1-F1	Dalry Road	A2	Gladstone Terrace	C2	Learmonth Terrace	A5	Picardy Place	D5-E5	Thistle Street	C4-C5-D5
Blackfriar Street	E3	Damside	A4	Glen Street	C2	Leith Street	D4-E5	Pleasance	E2-E3	Torphichen Street	A3-B3
Bowmont Place	E2-F2	Danube Street	A5-B5	Glengyle Terrace	C1	Leith Walk	E5	Ponton Street	B2	Upper Dean Terrace	B5
Bread Street	B2-C2	Darnaway Street	B5	Gloucester Lane	B4-B5	Lennox Street	A5	Potter Row	E2-E3	Upper Gilmore Place	B1
Bristo Place	D2-D3	Davie Street	E2	Grassmarket	C3-D3	Leslie Place	B5	Princes Street	B4-C4-D4	Upper Grove Place	A2
Brougham Street	C2	Dean Bridge	A4	Great King Street	C5	Leven Street	B1-C1	Queen Street	B4-C4-C5-D5	Valleyfield Street	C1
Broughton Street	D5	Dean Park Crescent	A5	Greenside Row	E5	Leven Terrace	C1	Queen Street Gardens East	C5	Victoria Street	D3
Buccleuch Place	D2-E2	Dean Park Mews	A5	Grindlay Street	B3-C3	Livingstone Place	E1	Queen Street Gardens West	C5	Viewcraig Gardens	F3
Buccleuch Street	E1-E2	Dean Park Street	A5	Grosvenor Crescent	A3	Lochrin Place	B2	Queensferry Road	A4-A5	Viewcraig Street	F3
Buckingham Terrace	A4-A5	Dean Street	A5-B5	Grosvenor Street	A3	London Road	E5-F5	Queensferry Street	A4-B4	Viewforth	A1-B1
Caledonian Crescent	A2	Dean Terrace	B5	Grove Street	A2-B2	Lonsdale Terrace	C1-C2	Randolph Crescent	A4-B4	Walker Street	A3-A4
Caledonian Place	A2	Doune Terrace	B5	Hanover Street	C4-C5	Lothian Road	B2-B3	Rankeillor Street	E2	Warrender Park Terrace	C1-D1
Caledonian Road	A2	Drummond Place	D5	Heriot Place	C2-D2	Lothian Street	D2-D3	Regent Road	E4-F4-F5	Waterloo Place	D4-E4
Calton Hill	E4-E5	Drummond Street	E3	Heriot Row	B5-C5	Lutton Place	E1-F1	Regent Terrace	F4-F5	Waverley Bridge	D4
Calton Road	E4-F4	Drumsheugh	A4	High Street	D3-E3-E4	Manor Place	A3-A4	Rose Street	B4-C4-D4	West Approach Road	A1-A2-B2
Cambridge Street	B3	Dublin Street	D5	Hill Place	E2-E3	Marchmont Crescent	D1	Rothesay Place	A3-A4	West Bow	D3
Candlemaker Row	D3	Dumbiedykes Road	F3	Hill Street	C4	Marchmont Road	D1	Royal Circus	B5-C5	West Maitland Street	A2-A3
Canongate	E4-F4	Dundas Street	C5	Hillside Crescent	E5-F5	Market Street	D3-D4	Royal Terrace	F4-F5	West Nicholson Street	E2
Castle Street	C4	Dundee Street	A1	Holyrood Park Road	F1	Meadow Lane	E1-E2	Rutland Street	B3	West Port	C2-C3
				Holyrood Road	E3-F3-F4	Melville Drive	C1-D1-E1	St Andrew Square	D4-D5	West Preston Street	E1
				Home Street	C1-C2	Melville Street	A3-B4	St Bernard's Crescent	A5-B5	West Richmond Street	E2
				Hope Park Terrace	E1	Melville Street Lane	A4	St Colme Street	B4	William Street	A3-B3
				Horse Wynd	F4	Melville Terrace	D1-E1	St John Street	E3-E4	York Place	D5
				Howden Street	E2	Montague Street	E1-F1	St Johns Hill	E3	Young Street	B4

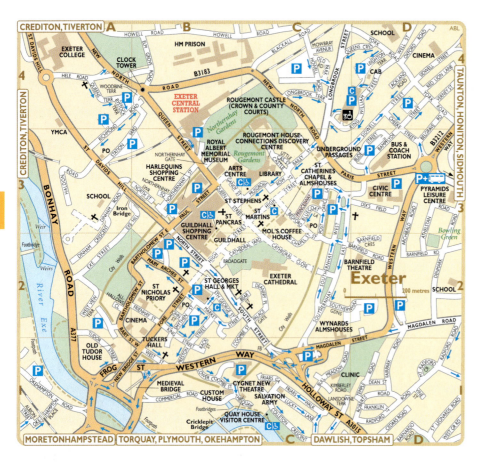

Exeter

Exeter is found on atlas page **9 F4**

Archibald Road	D2-D3	Leighton Terrace	D4
Athelstan Road	D2-D3	Little Castle Street	C3
Bailey Street	C3	Longbrook Street	C3-C4
Bampfylde Street	D3-D4	Longbrook Terrace	C4
Barnfield Road	C2-D2	Lower Coombe Street	B1
Bartholomew Street	A2-B2	Lower North Street	B3
Bartholomew Street East	B2-B3	Lucky Lane	C1
Bartholomew Street West	A2-A1-B1	Magdalen Road	D2
Bedford Street	C2-C3	Magdalen Street	C1-D1-D2
Belgrave Road	D3-D4	Market Street	B2
Blackall Road	C4	Mary Arches Street	A1-B1
Bluecoat Lane	C3	Musgrove Row	B3-C3
Bonhay Road	A1-A2-A3	New Bridge Street	A1-B1
Broadgate	B2	New North Road	A4-B4-C4-C3
Bude Street	D3	North Street	B2-B3
Bull Meadow Road	C1	Northernhay Street	B3
Castle Street	C3	Okehampton Road	A1
Cathedral Close	C2-C3	Oxford Road	D4
Cathedral Yard	B2-C2	Palace Gate	C2
Chapel Street	C2-C3	Paris Street	C3-D3
Cheeke Street	D3-D4	Paul Street	B3
Colleton Crescent	C1	Post Office Lane	C2-C3
Commercial Road	B1	Preston Street	B1-B2
Coombe Street	B1-B2-C2	Princesway	C3
Dean Street	D1	Queen Street	B4-B3-C3
Deanery Place	C2	Queens Terrace	A4
Denmark Road	D2-D3	Radford Road	D1-D2
Dinham Crescent	A2-A3	Red Lion Lane	D4
Dinham Road	A3	Richmond Road	A3-A4-B4
Dix's Field	D3	Roberts Road	C1
Elm Grove Road	B4	St Davids Hill	A4-A3-B3
Exe Hill	A3-B3	St Leonards Road	D1
Exe Street	A2	Sidwell Street	C3-D3-D4
Fairpark Road	D1-D2	Smythen Street	B2
Fore Street	B1-B2	South George Street	B2
Friars Walk	C1	South Street	B2-C1
Frienhay Street	B2	Southernhay East	C1-C2-C3
Frog Street	A1-B1	Southernhay Gardens	C2-D2
Gandy Street	B3-C3	Southernhay West	C2-C3
Haldon Road	A3	Station Yard	A3-B3-B4
Hele Road	A4	Temple Road	D1
High Street	B2-B3-C3	The Quay	B1-C1
Holloway Street	C1-D1	Tudor Street	A1-A2
Howell Road	A4-B4-C4	West Street	B1
John Street	B2	West View Terrace	A2
King Street	B1-B2	Western Way	B1-C1
King William Street	C4-D4	Western Way	D2-D3-D4
		York Road	C4-D4

Gloucester

Gloucester is found on atlas page **46 D1**

Albion Street	B1	Market Parade	C2-C3
All Saints Road	D1	Merchants Road	A1-B1
Alvin Street	C3-D3	Mercia Road	B4
Archdeacon Street	B3	Metz Way	D2
Arthur Street	C1-D1	Montpelier	C1
Barbican Road	B2	Mount Street	B3
Barbican Way	B2	Napier Street	D1
Barton Street	D1	North Street	B1
Belgrave Road	C1	Northgate Street	C2-C3
Berkeley Street	B2-B3	Old Tram Road	B1
Blackdog Way	C3	Oxford Road	D3-D4
Blackfriars	B2	Oxford Street	D3
Blenheim Road	D1	Park Road	C1
Brunswick Road	B1-C1-C2	Park Street	C3
Brunswick Square	B1-C1	Parliament Street	B2-B1-C1
Bruton Way	C3-D2-D1	Pembroke Street	D1
Bull Lane	B2	Pitt Street	B3-C3
Clare Street	B3	Priory Road	B4
Claremont Road	D3	Quay Street	A3-B3
Clarence Row	C3	Royal Oak Road	A3
Clarence Street	C2	Russell Street	C2-D2
College Court	B3	St Aldate Street	C2-C3
College Street	B3	St Catherine Street	C4
Commercial Road	B2	St John's Lane	B2-C2-C3
Cromwell Street	C1	St Mark Street	C4
Dean's Walk	C4	St Mary's Square	B3
Dean's Way	D4	St Mary's Street	B3
Denmark Road	D4	St Michael's Square	C1
Eastgate Street	C2-D1	St Oswald's Road	B3-B4
Gouda Way	B3-B4-C3	Sebert Street	C4-D4
Great Western Road	D2-D3	Serlo Road	B4
Greyfriars	B2-C2	Severn Road	A1-A2
Guinea Street	C4-D4	Sherbourne Street	D3-D4
Hampden Way	C1-C2	Sinope Street	D1
Hare Lane	C2	Southgate Street	B1-B2-C2
Heathville Road	D3-D4	Spa Road	B1-C1
Hempsted Lane	A1	Station Road	D2
Henry Road	D3-D4	Swan Road	C4
High Orchard Street	A1-B1	Sweetbriar Street	C4-D4
Honyatt Road	D4	The Oxbode	C2
Kimbrose Way	B2	The Quay	A2-A3
Kings Barton Street	C1-D1	Union Street	C4-D4
Kings Square	C2	Upper Quay Street	B2-B3
Kingsholme Road	C3-C4	Victoria Street	D1
Ladybellgate Street	B2	Wellington Street	C1-C2
Llanthony Road	A1-B1	Westgate Street	A3-B3-B2
London Road	D3	Widden Street	D1
Longsmith Street	B2	Worcester Street	C3,C4

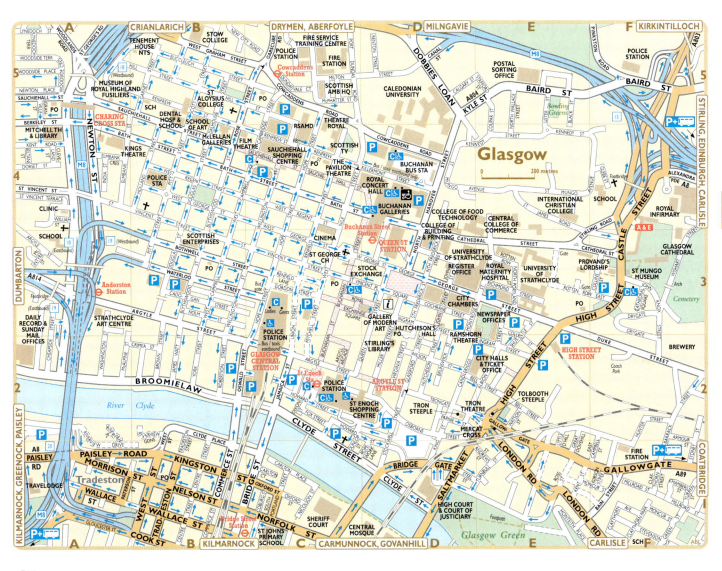

Glasgow

Glasgow is found on atlas page **130 B2**

Albion Street	D2-E2-E3
Alexandra Parade	F4
Argyll Arcade	C2
Argyle Street	A3-B3-C2-D2
Armour Street	F1-F2
Bain Street	E1-F1
Baird Street	E5-F5
Barrack Street	F1-F2
Bath Street	A4-B4-C4-D4
Bell Street	D2-E2
Beltane Street	A4
Berkeley Street	A4-A5
Black Street	E4-E5
Blythswood Street	B3-B4
Bothwell Street	B3-C3
Bridge Gate	D1
Bridge Street	B1-C1
Broomielaw	A2-B2
Brown Street	B2-B3
Brunswick Street	D2
Buccleuch Street	B5-C5
Buchanan Street	C2-C3
Cadogan Street	B3-C3
Calgary Street	D5
Cambridge Street	C4-C5
Canal Street	D5
Candleriggs	D2-E2
Carlton Court	C1
Carlton Place	C1
Castle Street	F3-F4
Cathedral Square	F3
Cathedral Street	D3-E3-F3
Centre Street	B1
Chambers Street	F1
Cheapside Street	A2-A3
Claythorn Avenue	F1
Claythorn Park	F1
Claythorn Street	F1
Cleveland Street	A4
Clyde Place	B1-B2
Clyde Street	C2-C1-D1
Coburg Street	C1
Cochrane Street	D3
College Street	E2-E3
Collins Street	F3
Commerce Street	B1
Coupar Street	E4-E5
Cowcaddens Road	C5-C4-D4
Crimea Street	A2-B2
Dalhousie Street	B4-B5
Dixon Street	C2
Dobbies Loan	D4-D5
Dorset Street	A4
Douglas Street	B3-B4
Drygate	F2-F3
Duke Street	E3-E2-F2
Dundasvale Court	C5
Dunlop Street	C1
East Campbell Street	F1
Elmbank Crescent	A4
Elmbank Street	A4-A5
Fox Street	C2
Gallowgate	E2-E1-F1
Garnet Street	B5
Garscube Road	C5
George Square	D3
George Street	D3-E3
Gibson Street	F1
Glassford Street	D2-D3
Glebe Street	F4
Gloucester Street	A1
Gordon Street	C3
Granville Street	A5
Great Dovehill	E1-E2
Green Street	F1
High Street	E2-E3-F3
Hill Street	A5-B5-C5
Holland Street	B4
Holm Street	B3
Hope Street	C2-C3-C4-C5
Howard Street	C2-D1
Hunter Street	F1-F2
Hutcheson Street	D2
India Street	A4
Ingram Street	D3-D2-E2
Jamaica Street	C2
James Watt Street	B2-B3
John Knox Street	F2-F3
John Street	D3
Kennedy Street	D4-E4
Kent Road	A4
Kent Street	E1
Killermont Street	C4-D4
King Street	D1-D2
Kingston Street	B1
Kyle Street	D5-E5
Lister Street	E4-E5
Little Dovehill	E1-E2
London Road	E1-F1
Lynedoch Street	A5
Lynedoch Terrace	A5
McAlpine Street	A2-A3
McIntyre Street	A3
McPhatter Street	C5
Miller Street	D2-D3
Millroad Street	F1
Milton Street	C5-D5
Mitchell Street	C2-C3
Moncur Street	E1-F1
Monteith Place	E1
Montrose Street	D3-E3
Morrison Street	A1-B1
Nelson Street	B1
New City Road	B5-C5
Newton Place	A5
Nicholson Street	C1
Nile Street	C3-C4
Norfolk Street	B1-C1
North Frederick Street	D3
North Hanover Street	D3-D4-D5
North Portland Street	E3
North Wallace Street	E4-E5
Osborne Street	D1-D2
Oswald Street	B2
Oxford Street	C1
Paisley Road	A1-B1
Parnie Street	D2
Paterson Street	A1
Pinkston Road	F5
Pitt Street	B3-B4
Port Dundas Road	C5
Queen Street	C2-D2-D3
Renfield Street	C3-C4
Renfrew Street	A5-B5-B4-C4
Renton Street	D5
Richmond Street	E3
Riverview Drive	A2-A1-B1
Riverview Gardens	B2
Riverview Place	A2-A1
Robertson Street	B2
Ropework Lane	C1-D1
Rose Street	B4-B5-C5
Ross Street	E1
Rotten Row	E3
Rotten Row East	E3-F3
Royal Exchange Square	C3-D3
St Andrews Street	D1-E1
St Georges Road	A5
St James Road	E3-E4
St Mungo Avenue	D4-E4-F4
St Vincent Place	C3-D3
St Vincent Street	A4-B4-B3-C3
St Vincent Terrace	A4
Saltmarket	D1
Sauchiehall Street	A5-B5-B4-C4-D4
Scott Street	B4-B5
Shuttle Street	E2-E3
South Frederick Street	D3
South Portland Street	C1
Stafford Street	E5
Steel Street	D1
Stevenson Street	F1
Stirling Road	E3-F4
Stockwell Street	D1-D2
Sydney Street	F1-F2
Tradeston Street	B1-B2
Trongate	D2
Turnbull Street	D1-E1
Union Street	C2-C3
Virginia Street	D2
Wallace Street	A1-B1
Washington Street	A2-A3
Waterloo Street	B3-C3
Watson Street	E2
Wellington Street	B3-C3-C4
West Campbell Street	B3-B4-C4
West George Street	B4-C4-D3
West Graham Street	B5-C5
West Nile Street	C3-C4-D4
West Regent Street	B4-C4
West Street	B1-B2
William Street	A4
Wilson Street	D2
Wishart Street	F3
Woodlands Road	A5
Woodside Crescent	A5
Woodside Place	A5
Woodside Terrace	A5
York Street	B2-B3

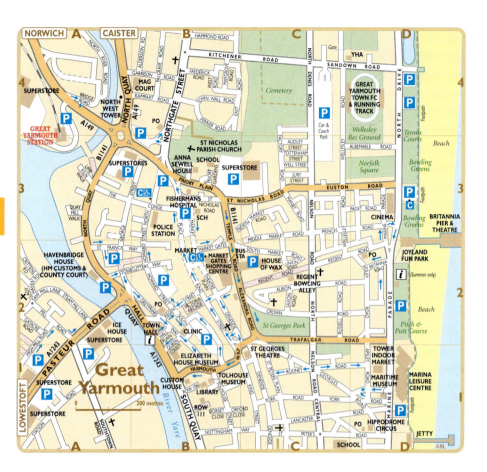

Great Yarmouth

Great Yarmouth is found on atlas page **65 H6**

Albemarle Road	C3-D3	Nottingham Way	B1-C1
Albion Road	C2-D2	Orford Close	B1-C1
Alderson Road	B4	Paget Road	C3-D3
Alexandra Road	C2	Palgrave Road	B4
Apsley Road	D1-D2	Pasteur Road	A1-A2
Audley Street	C3	Princes Road	C3-D3
Bridge Road	A4	Priory Gardens	B3
Britannia Road	D2	Priory Plain	B3
Crittens Road	A2	Quay Mill Walk	A3
Crown Road	C2-D2	Queen Street	B1-B2
Deneside	B2-C1	Rampart Road	B4
Dorset Close	B1	Regent Road	C2-D2
East Road	B4	Regent Street	B2
Euston Road	C3-D3	Rodney Road	C1-D1
Factory Road	C3-C4	Row 106	B1
Ferrier Road	B4	Russell Road	C2
Frederick Road	B4	St Francis Way	A2-B2
Garrison Road	A4-B4	St Georges Road	C1-D1
Gatacre Road	A2	St Nicholas Road	B3-C3
George Street	A2-A3-B3	St Peter's Road	C1-D1
Greyfriars Way	A2-B2-B1	St Peters Plain	C1
Hall Plain	B2	Sandown Road	C4-D4
Hall Quay	B2	Saw Mill Lane	A2
Hammond Road	B4	Saxon Road	C2
High Mill Road	A1-A2	South Market Road	B2-C2
Howard Street North	B2-B3	South Quay	B1
Howard Street South	B2	Southtown Road	A1
Jury Street	C3	Station Road	A1
King Street	B2-C1	Steam Mill Lane	A2
Kitchener Road	B4-C4	Stonecutters Way	A2-B2
Lady Haven Road	A2	Temple Road	B3-B2
Lancaster Road	C1-D1	The Conge	A3-B3
Lime Kiln Walk	A3	Theatre Plain	B2
Manby Road	C3	Tolhouse Street	B1
Marine Parade	D1-D2-D3	Tottenham Street	C3
Market Gates	B2	Town Wall Road	B4
Market Place	B2-B3	Trafalgar Road	C2-D2
Maygrove Road	B4	Union Road	C2
Middle Market Road	C2-C3	Victoria Arcade	B2
Mill Road	A2	Well Street	C3
Nelson Road Central	C1	Wellesley Road	C2-C3-C4
Nelson Road North	C2-C3	West Road	B4
North Denes Road	C4	Yarmouth Way	B1-C1-C2
North Drive	D3-D4	York Road	C1-D1
North Market Road	B3-C3		
North Quay	A2-A3-A4		
North River Road	A4		
Northgate Street	B3-B4		

Guildford

Guildford is found on atlas page **27 H4**

Abbot Road	C1	Millmead Terrace	A1-B1
Angel Gate	B2	Mount Pleasant	A1-A2
Artillery Road	B4	Nightingale Road	D4
Artillery Terrace	B4-C4	North Street	B2-B3-C3
Bedford Road	A3	Onslow Street	B3
Bridge Street	A2-A3-B3	Oxford Road	C2
Bright Hill	C2-D2	Oxford Terrace	C2
Brodie Road	D2-D3	Park Street	A2-B2
Bury Fields	B1	Pewley Bank	D2
Bury Street	A1-B1-B2	Pewley Hill	C2-D2-D1
Castle Hill	C1-C2	Pewley Way	D2
Castle Street	B2-C2	Portsmouth Road	A1-A2-B2
Chapel Street	B2-C2	Poyle Road	D1-D2
Chelsdon Road	D2-D3	Quarry Street	B2-B1-C1
Chertsey Street	C3	Sandfield Terrace	C3-C4
Church Road	B4	Semaphore Road	D1-D2
College Road	B3-B4	South Hill	C1-C2
Commercial Road	B2-B3	Springfield Road	C4-D4
Dene Road	D3-D4	Station View	A3
Eagle Road	C4	Stoke Fields	C4
Eastgate Gardens	D3	Stoke Road	C3-C4
Epsom Road	D3	Swan Lane	B2
Falcon Road	C4	Sydenham Road	C2-D2-D3
Finch Road	C4	Testard Road	A2
Flower Walk	B1	The Bars	C2
Fort Road	C1-D1	The Mount	A1-A2
Foxenden Road	D4	Tuns Gate	C2
Friary Street	B2	Victoria Road	D4
George Road	B4	Walnut Tree Close	A3-A4
Great Quarry	C1	Ward Street	C3
Guildford Park Road	A2-A3	Warwicks Bench	C1
Harvey Road	C2-D2-D3	White Lion Walk	B2
Haydon Place	C3-B3-B4-C4	William Road	A4
High Pewley	D1	Woodbridge Road	B3-B4
High Street	C3-D3	York Road	B4-C4-D4
Jenner Road	D2-D3		
Lawn Road	A1-B1		
Leapale Lane	B3-C3		
Leapale Road	B3		
Leas Road	B4		
London Road	D3-D4		
Mareschal Road	A1-A2		
Margaret Road	B4		
Market Street	C2-C3		
Martyr Road	C3		
Mary Road	A4		
Millbrook	B2-B1-C1		
Millmead	B1-B2		

Harrogate

Harrogate is found on atlas page **90 D5**

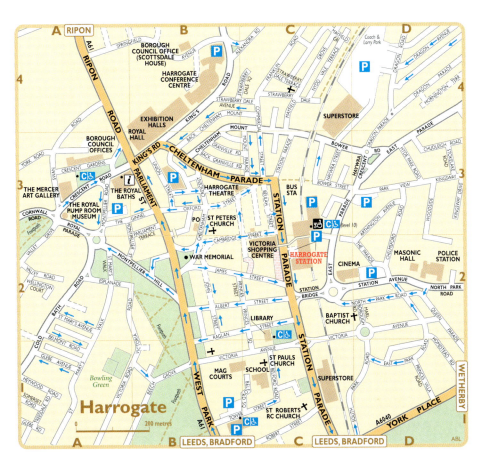

Albert Street	B2-C2	Mornington Terrace	D4
Alexandra Road	B4-C4	Mount Parade	C3
Arthington Avenue	D2-D3	North Park Road	C2-D2
Back Cheltenham Mount	B3-B4-C4	Nydd Vale Terrace	C4
Back Granville Road	B3	Oxford Street	B3-C3
Beech Grove	A1-B1	Park View	D3
Belford Road	C1	Parliament Street	B3
Belford Square	C1	Parliament Terrace	B3
Belmont Road	A1-A2	Princes Square	B2-C2
Beulah Street	C3	Princes Street	B2-C2
Bower Road	C3-D3	Princes Villa Road	D1
Bower Street	C3	Queen Parade	D1-D2
Cambridge Street	B2-C2	Raglan Street	B1-B2-C2
Chelmsford Road	D2-D3	Ripon Road	A3-A4
Cheltenham Crescent	B2-B3	Robert Street	C1
Cheltenham Mount	B3-B4-C4	Royal Parade	A3
Cheltenham Parade	B3-C3	St Mary's Avenue	A2
Chudleigh Road	D3	St Mary's Walk	A1-A2
Cold Bath Road	A1-A2	Somerset Road	A1
Commercial Street	C3-C4	South Park Road	C1-D1
Cornwall Road	A3	Springfield Avenue	A4-B4
Crescent Gardens	A3	Station Avenue	C2-D2
Crescent Road	A3	Station Bridge	C2
Dragon Avenue	D4	Station Parade	C1-C2-C3
Dragon Parade	D3-D4	Stonelake Road	D3
Dragon Road	D4	Strawberry Dale	C4
East Parade	C2-C3-D3-D4	Strawberry Dale Avenue	B4-C4
East Park Road	D1-D2	Strawberry Dale Square	B4-C4
Esplanade	A2	Strawberry Dale Terrace	C4
Franklin Road	C4	Swan Road	A3-A4
Glebe Avenue	A1	The Ginnel	A3-B3
Glebe Road	A1	The Parade	D2
Granville Road	B3	Tower Street	B1-C1
Haywra Crescent	D3	Treesdale Road	A1
Haywra Street	C3	Union Street	B3
Heywood Road	A1	Valley Drive	A2-A3
Homestead Road	D1-D2	Valley Road	A2
Hyde Park Road	D3	Victoria Avenue	B1-C1-C2-D2
James Street	B2-C2	Victoria Road	A1-B1-B2-A2
John Street	B2	Wellington Court	A2
King's Road	B3-B4	West Park	B1
Kingsway	D3	Woodside	D2-D3
Kingsway Drive	D3	York Place	D1
Marlborough Road	D2	York Road	A3
Mayfield Grove	C4		
Montpellier Hill	A2-B2		
Montpellier Road	A3		
Montpellier Street	A2-A3		

Huddersfield

Huddersfield is found on atlas page **90 C1**

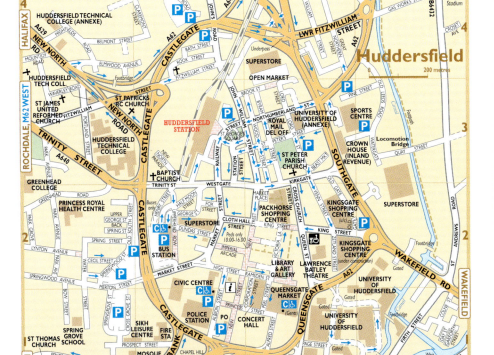

Albion Street	B1-B2	New North Road	A4-A3-B3
Alfred Street	C1	New Street	B1-B2-C2
Back Spring Street	A2	Northumberland Street	C3
Bath Street	B4	Old Leeds Road	D3-D4
Beast Market	C3	Old Gate	C2-C3
Belmont Street	A4-B4	Old South Street	A2
Bow Street	A1-A2	Outcote Bank	A1-B1
Brook Street	B3-C3	Page Street	C1
Byram Street	C3	Park Avenue	A2-A3
Cambridge Road	B4	Peel Street	C1-C2
Castlegate	B1-B2-B3-B4	Pine Street	C3-D3
Cecil Street	A2	Portland Street	A3
Chapel Street	B1-C1	Princess Street	B1-C1
Claremont Street	B4	Prospect Street	A1-B1
Cloth Hall Street	B2-C2	Quay Street	D3
Colne Street	D1	Queen Street	C2
Corporation Street	B1-C1-C2	Queensgate	C1-C2-D2
Cross Church Street	C2	Railway Street	B3
Crossgrove Street	A1	Ramsden Street	C2
Day Street	D1	Rook Street	B4
Dundas Street	B2	St Andrews Road	D2-D3-D4
Elmwood Avenue	A4-B4	St John's Road	B4
Fenton Square	A1	St Peter's Street	C3
Firth Street	D1	Southgate	C3-C2-D2
Fitzwilliam Street	A3-B3-B4	Springrove Street	A1
Fox Street	B2	Spring Street	A2
Garforth Street	D1	Springwood Avenue	A2
Gasworks Street	D4	Springwood Street	A2
George Street	B2	Station Street	B3
Great Northern Street	C4	Trinity Street	A3-A2-B2
Greenhead Road	A2	Westgate	B2-C2
Half Moon Street	B2	Upper George Street	A2
Henry Street	B2	Upperhead Row	B2
High Street	B2	Venn Street	C2-C3
Highfields Road	A4	Victoria Lane	C2
Imperial Arcade	B2	Wakefield Road	D1-D2
John William Street	B3-C3	Water Street	A1-A2
King Street	C2	Watergate	D3
Kings Mill Lane	D1	Waverley Road	A3
Kirkgate	C2-C3	William Street	C4
Lord Street	C3	Wood Street	C3
Lower Fitzwilliam Street	C4-D4	Zetland Street	C2
Lynton Avenue	A2		
Manchester Road	A1-B1		
Market Place	C2		
Market Street	B2		
Merton Street	A1-A2-B2		
New North Parade	B3		

197

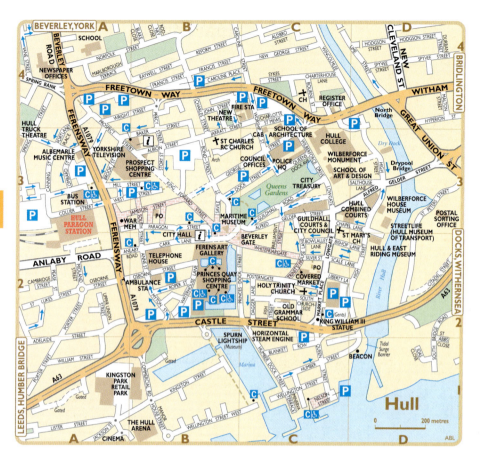

Hull

Hull is found on atlas page **93 E2**

Adelaide Street	A1-A2	Market Place	C2
Albion Street	B3	Marlborough Terrace	A4
Alfred Gelder Street	C3-D3	Midland Street	A2
Anlaby Road	A2-B2	Mill Street	A3-B3
Anne Street	B2	Myton Street	B2
Baker Street	A3-B3-B4	New Cleveland Street	D4
Beverley Road	A4	New George Street	C4
Bishop Lane	C2-D2	Norfolk Street	A4-B4
Blanket Row	C1	Osborne Street	A2-B2
Bond Street	B3	Paragon Street	B3
Bourne Street	C4	Parliament Street	C2-C3
Bowlalley Lane	C2	Pease Street	A2
Brook Street	A3	Percy Street	B3-B4
Canning Street	A3	Porter Street	A1-A2
Caroline Place	B4	Postergate	C2
Caroline Street	B4-C4	Princes Dock Street	B2-C2
Carr Lane	B2	Prospect Street	A4-A3-B3
Castle Street	B2-C2	Queen Street	C1
Chapel Lane	C3-D3	Queens Dock Avenue	C3
Charles Street	B3-B4	Raywell Street	B4
Charlotte Street Mews	C4	Reform Street	B4
Charterhouse Lane	C4	Roper Street	B2
Collier Street	A3	St Lukes Street	A2
Commercial Road	B1	St Peters Street	D3
Dagger Lane	C2	Savile Street	B3
Dock Street	B3-C3	Scale Lane	C2-D2
Ferensway	A2-A3-A4	Silver Street	C2
Fish Street	C2	South Bridge Road	D1-D2
Freetown Way	A4-B4-C4	South Churchside	C2
George Street	B3-C3	South Street	B2-B3
Great Union Street	D3-D4	Spring Bank	A4
Guildhall Road	C3	Spring Street	A3-A4
High Street	D3	Spyvee Street	D4
Hodgson Street	D4	Story Street	B3
Humber Dock Street	C1-C2	Sykes Street	C4
Humber Street	C1-D1	Trinity House Lane	C2-C3
Hyperion Street	D4	Upper Union Street	A2
Jameson Street	A3-B3	Waterhouse Lane	B2
Jarratt Street	B3-C4	Wellington Street	C1
John Street	B4	Wellington Street West	B1-C1
King Edward Street	B3	West Street	A3-B3
Kingston Street	B1	Whitefriargate	C2
Liberty Lane	C2	Wilberforce Drive	C3
Lime Street	C4-D4	William Street	A1
Lister Street	A1	Wincolmlee	C4-D4
Lombard Street	A3	Witham	D4
Lowgate	C2-C3	Worship Street	C3-C4
Manor House Street	B1	Wright Street	A4-B4

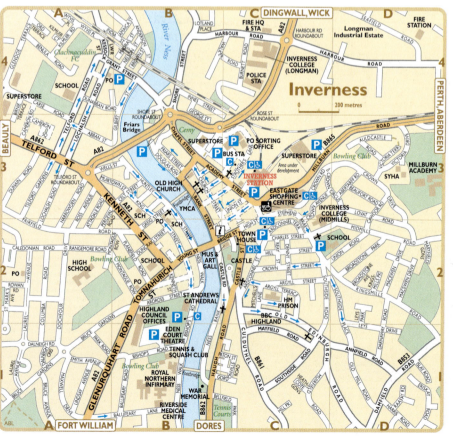

Inverness

Inverness is found on atlas page **155 E4**

Abertarff Road	D3	Glendoe Terrace	A4
Academy Street	B3-C3	Glenurquhart Road	A1-B1-B2
Anderson Street	B4	Grant Street	A4-B4
Annfield Road	D1	Greig Street	B2-B3
Ardconnel Street	C2	Harbour Road	B4-C4-D4
Ardconnel Terrace	C2	Harrowden Road	A2-A3
Ardross Street	B2	Haugh Road	B1-C1-C2
Argyll Street	C2	High Street	C2-C3
Argyll Terrace	C2	Hill Street	C2
Attadale Road	A2-A3	Huntley Street	B2-B3
Auldcastle Road	D3	India Street	A4-B4
Ballifeary Lane	A1-B1	Kenneth Street	A3-B3-B2
Ballifeary Road	B1	King Street	B2-B3
Bank Street	B2-B3	Kingsmills Road	C2-D2-D1
Beaufort Road	D3	Laurel Avenue	A1-A2
Benula Road	A4	Leys Drive	D1-D2
Bishop's Road	B1-B2	Lochalsh Road	A2-A3-A3
Bridge Street	B2-C2	Lovat Road	D2-D3
Broadstone Park	D2	Lower Kessock Street	A4
Bruce Avenue	A1	Macewen Drive	D2
Bruce Gardens	A1-A2-B2	Maxwell Drive	A1
Burnett Road	C4	Mayfield Road	C1
Caledonian Road	A2	Midmills Road	C2-D2
Cameron Road	A3-A4	Millburn Road	C3-D3
Carse Road	A3-A4	Muirfield Road	C1-D1
Castle Road	B2-C2	Muirtown Street	A3-B3
Castle Street	C2	Ness Bank	B1-B2-C2
Cawdor Road	D2-D3	Ness Walk	B1,B2
Celt Street	B3	Old Edinburgh Road	C2-C1-D1
Chapel Street	B3	Old Mill Road	D1
Charles Street	C2	Planefield Road	B2
Church Street	B3	Rangemore Road	A2
Columba Road	A1-A2	Seafield Road	D4
Crown Avenue	C3	Shore Street	B4
Crown Circus	C3-D3	Southside Place	C2-D2-D1
Crown Drive	D2-D3	Southside Road	C1-C2
Crown Road	C3	Stephens Brae	C2-C3
Crown Street	C2	Strother's Lane	C3
Culduthel Road	C1-C2	Telford Gardens	A3
Dalneigh Road	A1	Telford Road	A3-A4
Damfield Road	D1	Telford Street	A3
Darnaway Road	D1-D2	Tomnahurich Street	B2
Dochfour Drive	A1-A2	Union Road	C2-D2
Douglas Row	B3	Union Street	C3
Dunain Road	A3	Victoria Drive	D3
Fairfield Road	A3-A2-B2	Walker Road	B4-C4
Friars Street	B3	Wells Street	A3-B3
Gilbert Street	B3-B4	Young Street	B2

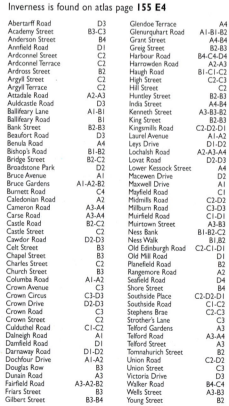

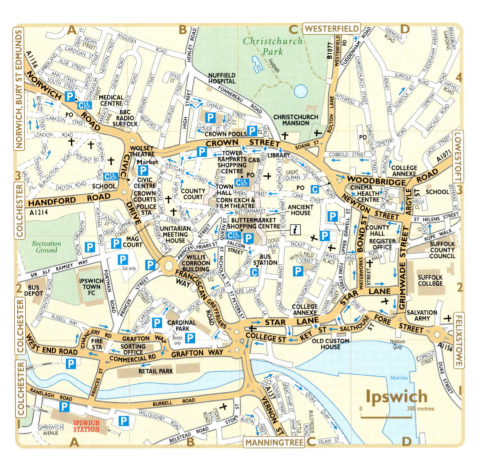

Ipswich

Ipswich is found on atlas page **53 E5**

Alderman Road	A2-A3	High Street	B3-B4
Anglesea Road	A4-B4	Key Street	C1-C2
Ann Street	A4	London Road	A3
Argyle Street	D3	Lower Brook Street	C2
Belstead Road	B1	Museum Street	B3
Berners Street	B4	New Cardinal Street	B2
Black Horse Lane	B3	Newton Street	C3-D3
Bolton Lane	C3-C4	Northgate Street	C3
Bond Street	D2-D3	Norwich Road	A3-A4
Burlington Road	A3	Old Foundary Road	C3
Burrell Road	B1	Orford Street	A4
Buttermarket	B3-C3	Orwell Place	C2
Cardigan Street	A4	Portman Road	A2-A3
Carr Street	C3	Princes Street	A1-A2-B2-B3
Cecil Road	A4-B4	Queen Street	B2-B3
Cecilia Street	B2	Ranelagh Road	A1
Cemetery Road	D3-D4	Rope Walk	D2-D3
Chancery Road	A1-A2	Rose Lane	B2-C2
Charles Street	B4-C4	Russell Way	A2
Christchurch Street	D3-D4	St Georges Street	B3-B4
Civic Drive	A3-B3-B2	St Helens Street	D3
Clarkson Street	A4	St Nicholas Street	B2
Claude Street	B2	St Peters Street	B2-C2
Cobbold Street	C3-D3	Salthouse Street	C2-D2
College Street	C1-C2	Silent Street	B2-C2
Commercial Road	A1-B1	Sir Alf Ramsey Way	A2
Constantine Road	A2	Soane Street	C3
Crown Street	B3-C3	Star Lane	C2-D2
Cumberland Street	A4	Stevenson Road	A3
Cutler Street	B2	Stoke Quay	C1
Dalton Road	A3	Stoke Street	B1
Dock Street	C1	Suffolk Road	D4
Dogs Head Street	C2	Tacket Street	C2
Duke Street	D1	Tavern Street	B3-C3
Elm Street	B3	Tower Street	C3
Falcon Street	B2-C2	Tuddenham Avenue	D4
Fonnereau Road	B4-C4-C3	Tuddenham Road	C4-D4
Fore Street	C2-D2	Turret Lane	C2
Foundation Street	C2	Upper Brook Street	C2-C3
Franciscan Way	B2	Upper Orwell Street	C2-C3
Friars Street	B2	Vernon Street	C1
Geneva Road	A4-B4	Waterworks Street	D2
Grafton Way	A2-B2-B1	West End Road	A1-A2
Greyfriars Road	B2	Westerfield Road	C4
Grimwade Street	D2-D3	Westgate Street	B3
Handford Road	A3	Willoughby Road	B1
Henley Road	B4	Wolsey Street	B2
Hervey Street	D3-D4	Woodbridge Road	C3-D3

Lancaster

Lancaster is found on atlas page **88 C6**

Aberdeen Road	D1	Long Marsh Lane	A2-A3
Albert Road	B4-C4	Lord Street	B3-B4
Aldcliffe Road	B1	Lune Street	B4-C4
Ambleside Road	D4	Market Street	B2
Balmoral Road	D1	Marton Street	B1-C1
Bath Street	D2	Mary Street	C2
Blades Street	A1-A2	Meeting House Lane	A2-B2
Borrowdale Road	D3	Melrose Street	D1
Brewery Lane	C2	Middle Street	B2
Brock Street	C2	Moor Lane	C2
Bulk Street	C2	Moorgate	D1-D2
Cable Street	B3	Nelson Street	C2
Captain's Row	C4	New Road	B2-B3
Castle Hill	B2	North Road	C3
Castle Park	A2-B2	Park Square	D2
Chapel Street	C3	Parliament Street	C3-C4
Cheapside	B2-C2	Patterdale Road	D3-D4
China Street	B2-B3	Penny Street	B1-B2
Church Street	B3-B2-C2	Perth Street	D1
Common Garden Street	B2	Phoenix Street	C3
Dale Street	C1-D1	Portland Street	B1
Dallas Road	B1-B2	Quarry Road	C1-D1
Dalton Square	C2	Queen Street	B1
Damside Street	B3-B2-C2	Regent Street	B1
De Vitre Street	C3-D3	Ridge Lane	D3-D4
Derby Road	C4	Rydal Road	D2
Dumbarton Road	D1	St George's Quay	B3-B4
Dunkeld Street	D1	St Leonard's Gate	C2-C3
Earl Street	C4	St Peter's Road	C1-C2-D2
East Road	D1-D2	Sibsey Street	A1-A2
Edward Street	C2	Spring Garden Street	B1
Elgin Street	D1	Station Road	A2
Fairfield Road	A2	Stirling Road	D1
Friar Street	C2	Sulyard Street	C2
Gage Street	C2	Sun Street	B2
George Street	C1	Sunnyside Lane	A1-A2
Gladstone Terrace	D3	Thurnham Street	C1-C2
Grasmere Road	D2-D3	Troutbeck Road	D3
Great John Street	C2	Ullswater Road	D2-D3
Gregson Road	D1	Water Street	B3
High Street	B1-B2	West Road	A2-A3
Kentmere Road	D3	Westbourne Place	A2
King Street	B2	Westbourne Road	A2
Kingsway	C4-D4	Wheatfield Street	A2-B2
Kirkes Road	D1	Williamson Road	D2
Langdale Road	D4	Wingate Saul Road	A1-A2
Lincoln Road	A1-A2	Wolseley Street	D3
Lodge Street	C2	Wyresdale Road	D1

Leeds

Leeds

Leeds is found on atlas page **90 D3**

Aire Street	C2	Cookridge Street	D4	Kendal Lane	B4	Oatland Court	E5	Templar Street	E3-E4
Albion Place	D3	County Arcade	D3-E3	Kendal Road	B5-C5	Oxford Place	C3-C4	The Close	F2
Albion Street	D2-D3	Cromer Terrace	B5	King Street	C3	Oxford Row	C3-C4	The Drive	F2
Argyle Street	F4	Cromwell Street	F4	Kirkgate	D3-E3-E2	Park Cross Street	C3	The Garth	F2
Armley Road	A2	Cross Kelso Road	B5	Kirkstall Road	A3-A4	Park Lane	A4-B4-B3	The Headrow	C3-D3-E3
Bath Road	C1	Crown Point Road	E1-E2	Lady Lane	E3	Park Place	C3	The Lane	F2
Bedford Street	C3-D3	Cudbear Street	E1	Lands Lane	D3	Park Row	D2-D3-D4	Trafalgar Street	E4
Belle Vue Road	A5	David Street	C1	Leylands Road	E4-F4	Park Square East	C3	Union Street	E3
Benson Road	E5-F5	Dock Street	D2-E2	Lincoln Road	F5	Park Square North	C3	Upper Basinghall Street	D3
Black Bull Street	E1	Dolly Lane	F5	Lisbon Street	B3	Park Square West	C3	Vicar Lane	E3
Boar Lane	D2	Duncan Street	D2-E2	Little Queen Street	C3	Park Street	C3-C4	Victoria Quarter	D3-E3
Braithwaite Street	B1	Duncombe Street	B3	Lovell Park Hill	E5	Portland Crescent	C4-D4	Victoria Street	B4
Bridge End	D2	East Parade	C3	Lower Basinghall Street	D2-D3	Portland Way	C4-D4	Victoria Terrace	A4-B4
Bridge Street	E3-E4	Eastgate	E3-F3	Ludgate Hill	E3	Quebec Street	C3-D2	Wade Lane	D4-E4
Briggate	D2-D3	Ellerby Road	F2	Lyddon Terrace	B5	Queen Street	C3	Water Lane	B1-C1-D1
Bristol Street	F5	Elmwood Road	D4-E4	Mabgate	F4	Regent Street	F4-F5	Waterloo Street	E2
Burley Road	A4-A5	Flax Place	F2	Macauley Street	F4	Rider Street	F3	Well Close Rise	D5
Burley Street	A4-B4-B3	Globe Road	B2-B1-C1	Manor Road	C1-D1	Rillbank Lane	A5	Wellington Street	B3-C3-C2
Butterley Street	E1	Gotts Road	A2-B2	Marlborough Street	B3	Rosebank Road	A5	West Street	B3
Byron Street	E4-F4	Gower Street	E4-F4	Marshall Street	C1	Roseville Road	F5	Westfield Road	A4-A5
Calls	D2-E2	Grafton Street	E4	Meadow Lane	D1-D2	Roseville Way	F5	Westgate	C3
Calverley Street	C4	Great George Street	C4-D4	Melbourne Street	E4	St John's Road	A5-A4-B4	Wharf Street	E2
Carlton Carr	D5-E5	Great Wilson Street	D1-E1	Merrion Street	D4-E4	St Pauls Street	C3	Whitehall Road	A1-B1-B2-C2
Carlton Gate	D5	Greek Street	C3-D3	Merrion Way	D4	St Peter's Street	E3	Whitelock Street	E5-F5
Carlton Hill	D5	Hanover Avenue	B4	Mill Hill	D2	Sayner Road	F1	Woodhouse Lane	C5-D5-D4
Carlton Rise	D5	Hanover Square	B4	Mill Street	F2	Sheaf Street	E1	Woodsley Road	A5-B5
Central Road	D2-E2-E3	Hanover Way	B3-B4	Millwright Street	F4	Sheepscar Grove	E5	Woodsley Terrace	B5
Chadwick Street	E1-F1	Holbeck Lane	A1-B1	Mount Preston Street	B4-B5	Sheepscar Street South	E5-F5	York Place	C3
Chadwick Street South	F1	Hunslet Road	E1	Neville Street	D1-D2	Skinner Lane	E5-F4		
Cherry Row	F4-F5	Hyde Terrace	B4-B5	New Briggate	D3-E3-E4	Skinner Street	B3		
Clarence Street	F1	Infirmary Street	C3-D3	New Lane	D1	South Parade	C3-D3		
Commercial Street	D3	Ingram Row	C1	New Station Street	D2	Sovereign Street	D2		
Concord Street	E4	Kelso Gardens	A5-B5	New York Road	E4	Spence Lane	A1		
Consort Street	A4-B4	Kelso Place	A5	New York Street	E3	Springwell Road	B1		
Consort Terrace	A4	Kelso Road	A5-B5	North Street	E4-E5	Springwell Street	A1-B1		
Consort Walk	A4	Kelso Street	A5-B5	Northern Street	C2-C3	Templar Place	E3		

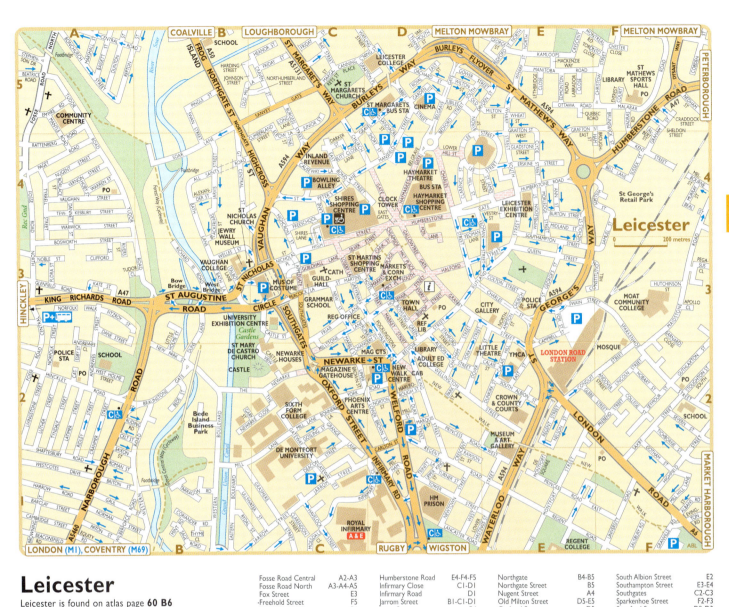

Leicester

Leicester is found on atlas page **60 B6**

Abbey Street	D5	Castle View	C2	Fosse Road Central	A2-A3	Humberstone Road	E4-F4-F5	Northgate	B4-B5	South Albion Street	E2
Albion Street	D2-D3	Causeway Lane	C4	Fosse Road North	A3-A4-A5	Infirmary Close	C1-D1	Northgate Street	B5	Southampton Street	E3-E4
All Saints Road	B4	Chancery Street	C2-D3	Fox Street	E3	Infirmary Road	D1	Nugent Street	A4	Southgates	C2-C3
Andrewes Street	A2-A3	Charles Street	D4-D3-E3	Freehold Street	F5	Jarrom Street	B1-C1-D1	Old Milton Street	D5-E5	Sparkenhoe Street	F2-F3
Applegate	C3	Chatham Street	D2-D3	Freeschool Lane	C4	Jarvis Street	B4	Orchard Street	D5	Stamford Street	D2-D3
Barclay Street	A1	Cheapside	D3-D4	Friar Lane	C3-D3	Kamloops Crescent	E5	Ottawa Road	E5	Sussex Street	F4
Bath Lane	B3-B4	Christow Street	F5	Friday Street	C5	Kent Street	F4	Oxford Street	C2	Swain Street	E3-F3
Battenberg Road	A4-A5	Church Gate	C5-C4-D4	Frog Island	B5	King Richards Road	A3-B3	Paget Road	A4	Swan Street	B4-B5
Bay Street	C5	Clarence Street	D4	Gallowtree Gate	D3-D4	King Street	D1-D2	Peacock Lane	C3	Tarragon Road	B1
Bedford Street North	E5	Clyde Street	E4	Garden Street	D5	Lancaster Road	D1-E1	Pelham Street	D1	Tewkesbury Street	A4
Bedford Street South	D4-D5	College Street	F2	Gateway Street	C1	Latimer Street	A1-A2	Pingle Street	B5	The Gateway	C1-C2
Belgrave Gate	D4-D5	Colton Street	E3	Gaul Street	A1-B1	Lee Street	D4-E4	Pocklingtons Walk	D2-D3	The Newarke	B2-C2
Bell Lane	F4	Conduit Street	E2-F2	Gladstone Street	E4	Lincoln Street	F2	Prebend Street	F2	Tichborne Street	F1-F2
Belvoir Street	D2-D3	Coriander Road	B1	Glebe Street	E2-F2	Livingstone Street	A2	Princess Road East	E1-F1	Tower Street	D1-E1
Bishop Street	D3	Cranmer Street	A1-A2	Glenfield Road	A3	London Road	E2-F2-F1	Princess Road West	D2-E1	Tudor Road	A5-A4-B3
Blackfriars Street	B4	Craven Street	C5	Gotham Street	F1-F2	Loseby Lane	D2	Queen Street	E3	Turner Street	D1
Bonchurch Street	A5	Cumberland Street	C4-C5	Grafton Place	C5-D5	Lower Brown Street	C3	Regent Road	D2-D1-E1-F1	Tyndale Street	A2
Bosworth Street	A3-A4	Dane Street	A3	Grafton Street East	E4-E5-F4	Lower Hill Street	D4	Regent Street	E2	Tyrrell Street	A4
Bowling Green Street	D3	De Montfort Street	E1-E2	Grafton Street West	E4-E5	Luther Street	A2	Repton Street	A5-B5	Ullswater Street	B1-C1
Braunstone Gate	A2-B2	Deacon Street	C1-C2	Graham Street	F4-F5	Maidstone Road	F2-F3-F4	Richard III Road	B3	University Road	F1
Briton Street	A1	Dover Street	D2-E2-E3	Granby Street	D3-E3-E2	Malabar Road	F5	Ridley Street	A1-A2	Upper Brown Street	C2
Brunswick Street	F4-F5	Dryden Street	D5-E5	Grange Lane	C1-C2	Manitoba Road	E5-F5	Rutland Street	D3-E3-E4	Vaughan Street	A4
Burgess Street	C4-C5	Duke Street	D2	Grasmere Street	B1-C1	Mansfield Street	D4-D5	St Augustine Road	B3	Vaughan Way	C3-C4-C5
Burleys Flyover	D5-E5	Dunkirk Street	E2	Gravel Street	C4-C5-D5	Marble Street	C2-C3	St Georges Street	E3	Vernon Street	A4
Burleys Way	C5-D5	Duns Lane	B2-B3	Great Central Street	B4-C4	Market Place	D3	St George's Way	E2-E3-E4	Warwick Street	A4
Burton Street	E4	Dunton Street	A5	Greyfriars	C3	Market Place South	D3	St Margaret's Way	C5	Waterloo Way	E1-E2
Butt Close Lane	C4	Dysart Way	F5	Guildhall Lane	C3	Market Street	D2-D3	St Margarets Street	C5	Welford Road	D1-D2
Byron Street	D4-D5	East Bond Street	C4-D4	Guthlaxton Street	F2	Marlborough Street	D2	St Martins	C3	Welles Street	B3-C3
Calais Hill	E2	East Gates	D4	Halford Street	D3-E3	Melbourne Street	F4	St Mathew's Way	E4-E5	Wellington Street	D2-E2
Cambridge Street	A1	East Street	E2	Harrow Road	A1	Mill Lane	B1-C1-C2	St Nicholas Circle	B3-C3	West Street	D1-E1
Campbell Street	E2-E3	Eastern Boulevard	B1	Havelock Street	C1	Millstone Lane	C2-C3	St Nicholas Place	C3	Westcotes Drive	A1
Cank Street	D3	Edmonton Road	E5	Haymarket		Morledge Street	E4	St Peter's Lane	C4-D4	Western Boulevard	B1-B2
Canning Place	C5	Empire Road	A5	High Street	C3-C4-D4	Narborough Road	A1-A2-B2-B3	Samuel Street	F3-F4	Western Road	B1-A1-B2
Canning Street	C5-D5	Erskine Street	E4	Highcross Street	C3-C4	Nelson Street	E1-E2	Sanvey Gate	B5-C5	Wharf Street North	E5
Carlton Street	D1-D2	Every Street	D3	Highfield Street	F1-F2	New Park Street	B2-B3	Saxby Street	F1-F2	Wharf Street South	E4-E5
Castle Street	C3	Fitzroy Street	A3	Hill Street	D4	New Street	C3	Severn Street	F2	Wilberforce Road	A1
				Hinckley Road	A2	Newarke Close	B2-C2	Seymour Street	F2	William Street	F4
				Hobart Street	F2	Newarke Street	C2-D2	Shaftesbury Road	A1-A2	Wimbledon Street	E4
				Horsefair Street	D3	Newtown Street	D1	Short Street	D1	Yeoman Street	D4-E4-E3
				Hotel Street	C3-D3	Norfolk Street	A2-A3	Silver Street	C3-D3-D4	York Road	C2-D2
				Humberstone Gate	D4-E4	Norman Street	A1-B1	Soar Lane	B4-B5	York Street	D2-D3

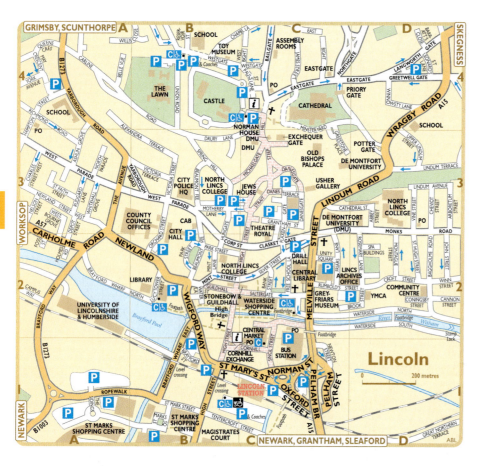

Lincoln

Lincoln is found on atlas page **85 G2**

Abbey Street	D3	Monks Road	D3
Alexandra Terrace	A4-A3-B3	Montague Street	D2
Arboretum Street	D3	Motherby Lane	B3
Ashlin Grove	A3-A4	Newland	A2-B2
Bagholme Road	D2	Newland Street West	A3
Bailgate	C4	Newton Street	C1
Bank Street	C2	Norman Street	C1
Beaumont Fee	B2-B3	North Parade	A3
Brayford Way	A1-A2	Northgate	C4-D4
Brayford Wharf East	B1-B2	Orchard Street	B2-B3
Brayford Wharf North	A2-B2	Oxford Street	C1
Brook Street	C2-D2	Park Street	B2
Carholme Road	A2-A3	Pelham Bridge	C1
Carline Road	A4-B4-B3	Pelham Street	C1
Cathedral Street	C3-D3	Queens Crescent	A4
Charles Street West	A3	Reservoir Street	B4
Cheviot Street	D3	Richmond Road	A3-A4
Clasket Gate	C2	Ropewalk	A1-B1
Coningsby Street	D2	Rosemary Lane	D2
Cornhill	C1	Rudgard Lane	A3
Corporation Street	B2-C2	Rumbold's Street	C2-D2
Croft Street	D2	St Hugh Street	D2
Danesgate	C3	St Mark Street	B1
Depot Street	A2-A3	St Mary's Street	B1-C1
Drury Lane	B3-C3	St Paul's Lane	C4
East Bight	C4	Saltergate	B2-C2
Eastgate	C4-D4	Silver Street	C2
Flaxengate	C2-C3	Sincil Street	C1-C2
Free School Lane	C2	Spring Hill	B3
Friars Lane	C2	Steep Hill	C3-C4
Grantham Street	C3	Strait	C3
Greetwell Gate	D4	Tentercroft Street	B1-C1
Guildhall Street	B2	The Avenue	A3
Hampton Street	A3-A4	Union Road	B4
High Street	B1-B2-C2-C3	Upper Lindum Street	D3
Hungate	B2-B3	Victoria Street	B3
James Street	C4	Victoria Terrace	B3
John Street	D2	Vine Street	D3
Langworth Gate	D4	Waterside North	C2-D2
Lindum Avenue	D3	Waterside South	C2-D2
Lindum Road	C3-D3	West Parade	A3-B3
Lindum Terrace	D3	Westgate	B4-C4
May Crescent	A4	Whitehall Grove	A3
Melville Street	C2-C3	Wigford Way	B1-B2
Michaelgate	B3-C3	Winn Street	D2
Minster Yard	C3-C4	Winnowsty Lane	D4
Mint Lane	B2	Wragby Road	D3-D4
Mint Street	B2	Yarborough Road	A4-A3-B3

Llandudno

Llandudno is found on atlas page **79 G3**

Abbey Road	A3-A4	Jacksons Court	C1
Adelphi Street	C2-C3	James Street	A3
Albert Street	B2	Jubilee Street	B2
Argyll Road	B2-C2	King's Avenue	A1
Arvon Avenue	A3-A4	King's Place	A1
Augusta Street	B2	King's Road	A1
Back Madoc Street	B3	Llewelyn Avenue	A4
Bodafon Street	B3-C3	Lloyd Street	A2-A3-B3
Bodhyfryd Road	A4	Llwynon Gardens	A4
Brookes Street	A3-B3-B2	Madoc Street	A3-B3
Builder Street	B1-B2	Maelgwyn Road	A3
Builder Street West	A1-B1	Maesdu Road	C1
Cae Bach	B1	Market Street	A3
Cae Clyd	D1	Masonic Street	A4
Cae Mawr	A1	Mostyn Broadway	C2-D2
Caroline Road	A3-B3-B2	Mostyn Crescent	C3
Chapel Street	A3	Mostyn Street	A4-B3-C3
Charlotte Road	C1-C2-D2	Nevill Crescent	C3
Charlton Street	B2	New Street	A3
Church Walks	A4-B4	Norman Road	B1-B2
Claremont Road	A2	North Parade	B4
Clarence Crescent	D1-D2	Old Road	A4
Clarence Drive	D1	Oxford Road	B2-C2
Clement Avenue	A3-A4	Penrhyn Crescent	D2-D3
Clifton Road	A3	Plas Road	A4
Clonmell Street	B3	St Andrews Avenue	A1-A2
Conway Road	C2-C1-D1	St David's Place	A2
Council Street West	B1	St David's Road	A2
Court Street	A4	St George's Crescent	B3
Cwm Road	B1-B2	St George's Place	B3
Deganwy Avenue	A3	St Mary's Road	A3-A2-B2
Dyffryn Road	A1	St Seiriol's Road	A2
Ffordd Dewi	C1	Somerset Street	B3
Ffordd Gwynedd	B1	South Parade	A4-B4
Ffordd Las	C1	Taliesin Street	A3
Ffordd Morfa	C1	Thorpe Street	B2
Ffordd Penrhyn	B1-C1	Trinity Avenue	A1-A2-B2
Ffordd Tudno	C1	Trinity Square	B2-B3
Garage Street	B2-C2	Tudno Street	A4
Garden Street	A3	Tudor Crescent	C2
George Street	A4-A3-B3	Tudor Road	C2-D2
Glan Y Mor Parade	B3-B4	Ty Gwyn Road	A4
Gloddaeth Crescent	B3-C3	Ty Isa Road	B3-B4
Gloddaeth Street	A3-A4	Ty'n Y Ffrith Road	D2
Hill Terrace	A4-B4	Vardre Lane	A4
Howard Place	B1	Vaughan Street	B2-C2-C3
Howard Road	B1-B2	Wern Y W Ylan	B1
Hywel Place	B1	York Road	A3

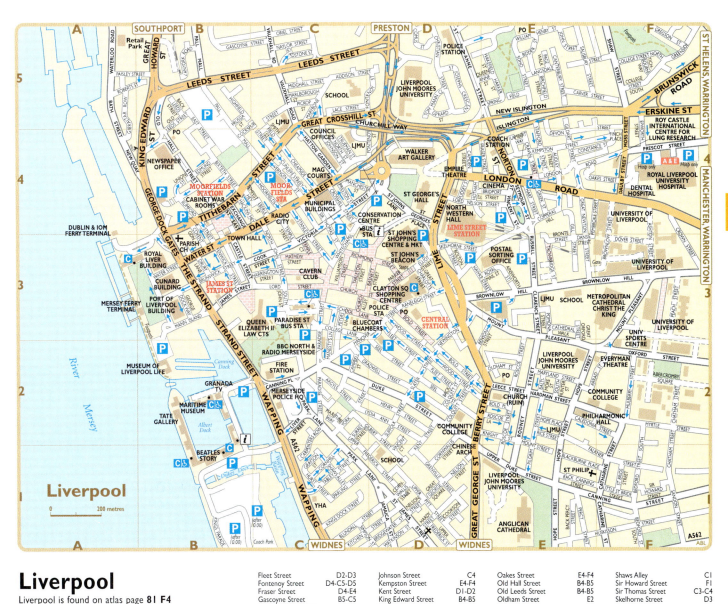

Liverpool

Liverpool is found on atlas page **81 F4**

Abercromby Square	F2
Addison Street	C5-D5
Ainsworth Street	E3
Argyle Street	C2
Arrad Street	E2-F2
Ashton Street	F3-F4
Audley Street	E4
Basnett Street	C3-D3
Bath Street	A4-A5
Bedford Street South	F1-F2
Benson Street	D2-E3
Berry Street	D2-E2
Bixteth Street	B4
Blackburne Place	E1-F1
Blundall Street	C1-D1
Bold Street	D2-D3
Bolton Street	D3
Bridport Street	D4-E4
Bronte Street	E3
Brownlow Hill	D3-E3-F3
Brownlow Street	F3-F4
Brunswick Road	F5
Brunswick Street	B3
Caledonia Street	E2-F2
Camden Street	D4
Campbell Street	C2
Canning Place	C2
Canning Street	E1-F1
Canterbury Street	E5
Carpenters Row	C1-C2
Carver Street	E5-F5
Castle Street	B3-C3
Catharine Street	F1-F2
Chatham Street	F1-F2
Cheapside	C4
Christian Street	D5
Church Alley	C3
Church Street	C3-D3
Churchill Way	C5-C4-D4
Clarence Street	E3
Cockspur Street	B4-C5
College Lane	C3
College Street North	F5
College Street South	F5
Colquitt Street	D2
Constance Street	E4-F4
Cook Street	B3-C3
Cookson Street	D1
Copperas Hill	E4
Cornhill	C1
Cornwallis Street	D1-D2
Covent Garden	B3-B4
Craven Street	E4
Crosshill Street	C5-D5
Crown Street	F3-F4
Cunliffe Street	C4
Dale Street	B3-B4-C4
Dansie Street	E3
Daulby Street	F4
Devon Street	E5-E4-F4
Dover Street	F3
Drury Lane	B3
Duke Street	C2-D2
East Street	B4-B5
Eberle Street	C4
Edmund Street	B4
Elliot Street	D3
Epworth Street	F4-F5
Erskine Street	F5
Exchange Street East	B4
Falkner Street	E2-E1-F1
Fenwick Street	B3
Fleet Street	D2-D3
Fontenoy Street	D4-C5-D5
Fraser Street	D4-E4
Gascoyne Street	B5-C5
George Dock Gates	B3-B4
George Dock Way	B3
Gerard Street	D5
Gibraltar Row	A4-A5
Gilbert Street	C2-D2-D1
Gildart Street	E4-E5
Gill Street	E3-E4
Gladstone Street	C5
Gradwell Street	C2-D2
Great Charlotte Street	D3
Great Crosshill Street	C5-D5
Great George Street	D1
Great Howard Street	B5
Great Newton Street	E3-E4
Greek Street	E4
Greenside	F5
Gregson Street	F5
Grenville Street	D1
Hackins Hey	B4-C4
Hanover Street	C2-D3
Hardman Street	E2
Harker Street	E5
Harrington Street	C3
Hart Street	E4
Hatton Garden	C4
Hawke Street	D3-E3
Henry Street	C2-D2
Highfield Street	B5-C4
Hope Place	E2
Hope Street	E1-E2
Hotham Street	D4
Hurst Street	C1
Huskisson Street	E1-F1
Islington	E4-E5
Jamaica Street	D1
James Street	B3
John Street	E5
Johnson Street	C4
Kempston Street	E4-F4
Kent Street	D1-D2
King Edward Street	B4-B5
Kings Dock Street	C1
Kings Parade	B1
Kitchen Street	C1-D1
Knight Street	E2
Lace Street	C5
Langsdale Street	E5-F5
Leece Street	E2
Leeds Street	B5-C5-D5
Lime Street	D3-D4
Little St Bride Street	F1
Liver Street	C2
London Road	D4-E4-F4
Lord Nelson Street	D4-E4
Lord Street	C3
Lydia Ann Street	C2-D2
Manchester Street	C4-D4
Manesty's Lane	C2-C3
Mann Island	B3
Marlborough Street	C5
Marybone	C5
Maryland Street	E2
Mathew Street	C3
Midghall Street	C5
Moorfields	C4
Moss Street	F4-F5
Mount Pleasant	D3-E3-F2-F3
Mount Street	E1
Mulberry Street	F2
Myrtle Street	F2
Naylor Street	C5
Nelson Street	D1
New Islington	E5
New Quay	A4-B4
Newington	D2-D3
North John Street	C3-C4
North Street	C4
Norton Street	E4
Oakes Street	E4-F4
Old Hall Street	B4-B5
Old Leeds Street	B4-B5
Oldham Street	E2
Oxford Street	F2
Paisley Street	A5-B5
Pall Mall	B5-B4-C4
Paradise Street	C2-C3
Park Lane	C2-C1-D1
Parker Street	D3
Peach Street	F3
Pembroke Street	E3-E4-F4
Peters Lane	C3
Pilgrim Street	E1-E2
Pomona Street	E3
Prescot Street	F4
Preston Street	C4
Prussia Street	B5
Pudsey Street	D4
Ranelegh Street	D3
Rice Street	E2
Richmond Street	C3-D3
Roberts Street	A5-B5
Rodney Street	E1-E2
Roscoe Street	E1-E2
Royal Mail Street	E3
Rumford Street	B3-B4
Russell Street	E4
St Anne Street	D5-E5
St Bride Street	F1
St Georges Place	D4
St James Street	D1
St Johns Lane	D4
St Josephs Crescent	D5
St Vincent Street	E4
Salisbury Street	E5
Sandon Street	F1
School Lane	C3-D3
Seel Street	D2
Seymour Street	E4
Shaw Street	F5
Shaws Alley	C1
Sir Howard Street	F1
Sir Thomas Street	C3-C4
Skelhorne Street	D3
Slater Street	D2
Smithfield Street	C4-C5
Soho Street	E5
South John Street	C3
Sparling Street	C1
Springfield	E5
Stafford Street	E4-E5
Stanley Street	C3-C4
Strand Street	B3-B2-C2
Suffolk Street	D2
Surrey Street	C2
Tabley Street	C1
Tarleton Street	C3
Tempest Hey	B4-C4
Temple Court	C3
Temple Street	C3-C4
The Strand	B3
Tichbourne Way	F5
Tithebarn Street	B4-C4
Tom Mann Close	D5
Trowbridge Street	E3
Trueman Street	C4
Upper Duke Street	D1-E1
Upper Frederick Street	C2-C1-D1
Upper Pitt Street	D1
Vauxhall Road	C5
Vernon Street	C4
Victoria Street	C3-C4-D4
Vincent Court	D1-D2
Wakefield Street	E5
Wapping	C1-C2
Water Street	B3
Waterloo Road	A5
Whitechapel	C3-C4
Williamson Street	C3
Wood Street	D2-D3
York Street	C2

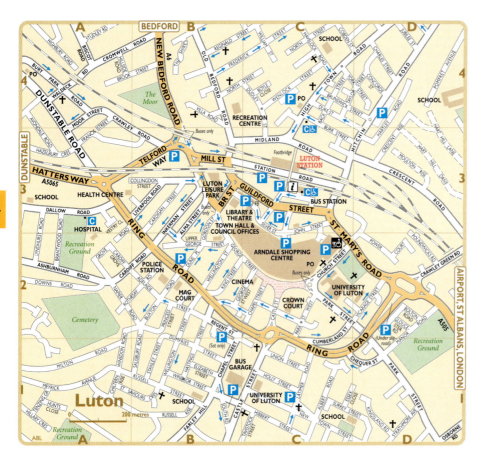

Luton
Luton is found on atlas page **50 B3**

Adelaide Street	B2	Hazelbury Crescent	A3
Albert Road	C1	Hibbert Street	C1
Alma Street	B2-B3	High Town Road	C3-C4-D4
Ashburnham Road	A2	Hitchin Road	C3-D3-D4
Avondale Road	A3-A4	Holly Street	C1
Back Street	C4	Inkerman Street	B2-B3
Biscot Road	A4	John Street	C3
Brantwood Road	A2-A3	Jubilee Street	D4
Bridge Street	B3	King Street	B2
Brook Street	A4-B4	Latimer Road	C1
Brunswick Street	C4-D4	Liverpool Road	B3
Burr Street	C3-C4	Manor Road	D1-D2
Bury Park Road	A4	Meyrick Avenue	A1
Buxton Road	B2	Midland Road	B3-C3
Cardiff Grove	A2	Mill Street	B3
Cardigan Street	B3	Milton Road	A1
Castle Street	B1-C1-C2	Moor Street	A4
Chapel Street	B1-B2-C2	Napier Road	A2-B2
Charles Street	D4	New Bedford Road	B4
Chequer Street	C1-D1	New Town Street	C1-D1
Church Street	C2	Old Bedford Road	B3-B4
Cobden Street	C4	Park Street	C2-D2-D1
Concorde Street	D4	Park Street West	C2
Crawley Green Road	D2	Power Court	D2
Crawley Road	A4-B3	Regent Street	B2
Crescent Rise	D3-D4	Reginald Street	B4-C4
Crescent Road	D2-D3	Ring Road	A3-B2-C1-D2
Cromwell Road	A4-B4	Rothesay Road	A2-B2
Cumberland Street	C1-C2	Russell Rise	B1
Dallow Road	A3	Russell Street	A1-B1
Downs Road	A2	St Mary's Road	C3-C2-D2
Dudley Street	C3-C4	Salisbury Road	B1-B2
Duke Street	C4	Silver Street	C2-C3
Dumfries Street	B1-B2	Stanley Street	B1-B2
Duns Place	B2	Station Road	B3-C3
Dunstable Road	A3-A4	Surrey Street	C1-D1
Farley Hill	B1	Telford Way	A3-B3
Frederick Street	B4-C4	Tenzing Grove	A1
George Street	B2-C2	Union Street	C1
George Street West	B2-C2	Upper George Street	B2
Gordon Street	B2-B3	Vicarage Street	D2
Grove Road	A2-A3	Waldeck Road	A4
Guildford Street	B3-C3	Wellington Street	B1-B2
Hart Hill Drive	D3	Wenlock Street	C4
Hartley Road	D3-D4	William Street	C4
Hastings Street	B1-B2	Windsor Street	B1
Hatters Way	A3	Winsdon Road	A1-A2
Havelock Road	C4	York Street	C4-D4

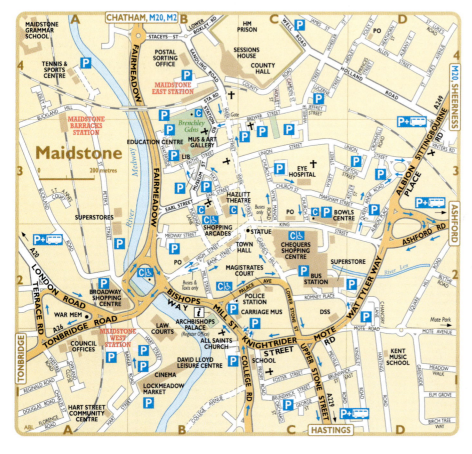

Maidstone
Maidstone is found on atlas page **30 A2**

Albion Place	D2-D3	Market Street	B3
Allen Street	D4	Marsham Street	C3-D3
Ashford Road	D2-D3	Meadow Walk	D1
Astley Street	C3-D3	Medway Street	B2
Bank Street	B2-C2	Melville Road	C1-D1
Barker Road	A1-B1	Mill Street	B2-C1
Birch Tree Way	D1	Mote Avenue	D1
Bishops Way	B2	Mote Road	C1-C2-D2-D1
Blythe Road	D2	Museum Street	B3
Brewer Street	B3-C3-C4	Orchard Street	C1
Brunswick Street	C1	Palace Avenue	B2-C2
Brunswick Street East	C1-D1	Princes Street	D4
Buckland Hill	A3-A4	Priory Road	C1
Buckland Road	A2-A3	Pudding Lane	B2-B3
Camden Street	C4	Queen Anne Road	D2-D3
Chancery Lane	D2	Reginald Road	A1
Charles Street	A1	Romney Place	C2
Church Street	C3	Rowland Close	A1
College Avenue	B1-C1	St Annes Court	A3
College Road	C1	St Faiths Street	B3
County Road	B4-C4	St Luke's Avenue	D4
Cromwell Road	D3	St Luke's Road	D4
Douglas Road	A1	St Peter's Street	A2-A3
Earl Street	B3	Sandling Road	B4
Elm Grove	D1	Sittingbourne Road	D3-D4
Fairmeadow	B2-B3-B4	Square Hill Road	D2
Florence Road	A1	Staceys Street	B4
Foley Street	D4	Station Road	B3-B4
Foster Street	C1	Terrace Road	A1-A2
Gabriel's Hill	C2	Tonbridge Road	A1-A2-B2
George Street	C1	Tufton Street	C3-D3
Greenside	D1	Union Street	C3-D3
Hart Street	A1-B1-B2	Upper Stone Street	C1
Hastings Road	D1	Vinters Road	D3
Heathorn Street	C1	Wat Tyler Way	D2
Hedley Street	C4-D4	Waterside	B3
High Street	B2-C2-C3	Week Street	B4-B3-C3
Holland Road	C4-D4	Well Road	C4
James Street	C4	Westree Road	A1
Jeffrey Street	C3	Wheeler Street	C3-C4-D4
King Street	C3-C2-D2	Wollett Street	C4-D4
Kingsley Road	D1	Wyatt Street	C3
Knightrider Street	C1	Wyke Manor Road	C3
Lesley Place	A4		
London Road	A2		
Lower Boxley Road	B4		
Lower Stone Street	C1-C2		
Lucerne Street	C4		

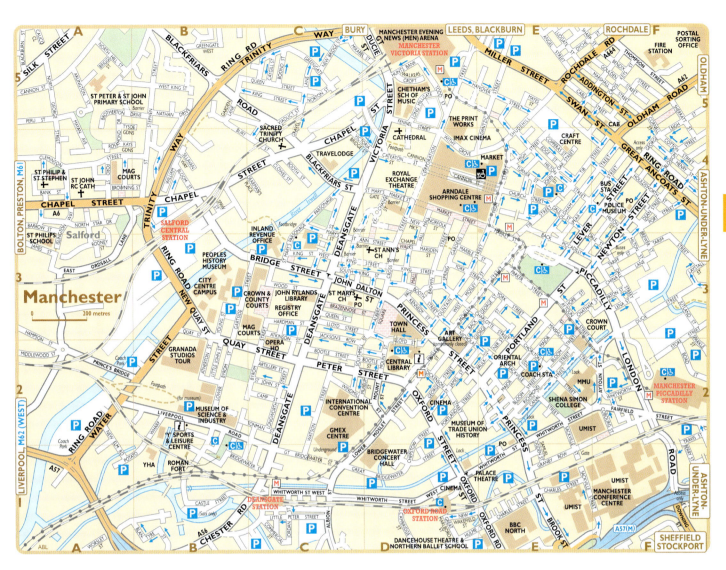

Manchester

Manchester is found on atlas page **82 C4**

Addington Street	E5-F5
Albert Square	D3
Albion Street	C1
Angel Street	E5
Arlington Street	A5
Artillery Street	C2
Atherton Street	B2
Atkinson Street	C2-C3
Aytoun Street	E3-E2-F2
Back George Street	D3-E3
Back Piccadilly	E4-E3-F3
Bank Street	A4
Barrow Street	A4
Bendix Street	F5
Berry Street	F1
Blackburn Street	A5
Blackfriars Road	B5-C5
Blackfriars Street	C4
Blantyre Street	A1-B1
Bloom Street	B4
Bloom Street	E2-E3
Blossom Street	F4
Boad Street	F2
Boond Street	C5
Booth Street	C4
Booth Street	D3
Bootle Street	C2-D2
Brazennose Street	C3-D3
Brewer Street	F3-F4
Bridge Street	B3-C3
Bridgewater Street	B1-C1
Briggs Street	A5
Brook Street	E1
Brotherton Drive	A5-B5
Brown Street	D3-D4
Browning Street	A4-B4
Bury Street	B5-B4-C4
Byrom Street	B2-C2-C3
Cable Street	E5-F5
Calico Close	A5
Cambridge Street	D1
Camp Street	C2
Canal Street	E2
Cannon Street	A5
Cannon Street	D4-E4
Castle Street	B1
Cateaton Street	D4
Caygill Street	C5
Chapel Street	A4-B4-C4-D5
Chapel Walks	D3
Charles Street	E1
Charlotte Street	D3-E3-E2
Chatham Street	E3-F3
Chepstow Street	D1-D2
Chester Road	B1-C1
China Lane	F3
Chorlton Street	E2
Church Street	E4
Cleminson Street	A4-B4
Clowes Street	C4
Cobourg Street	F2
Commercial Street	C1
Copperas Street	E4
Cornell Street	F4-F5
Corporation Street	D4-D5-E5
Cotton Street	F4
Cross Keys Street	F5
Cross Street	D3-D4
Dale Street	E4-F3
Dantzic Street	D4-E4-E5
Dean Street	F4
Deansgate	C2-C3-C4
Dearman's Place	C4
Dickenson Street	D2
Downing Street	F1
Ducie Street	F3
Dyche Street	E5-F5
East Ordsall Lane	A3-A4
Edge Street	E4
Exchange Street	D4
Fairfield Street	F2
Faulkner Street	D2-E2-E3
Fennel Street	D4-D5
Ford Street	A4
Fountain Street	D3-E3-E4
Garden Lane	B5
Gartside Street	B3-C3
George Leigh Street	F4-F5
George Street	D2-D3-E3
Goulden Street	F5
Granby Row	E1
Gravel Lane	C4-C5
Great Ancoats Street	F4
Great Bridgewater Street	C1-D1
Great Ducie Street	D5
Great Marlborough Street	D1
Greengate	C5
Greengate West	B5
Hampson Street	A2-A3
Hanover Street	D5-E5
Hardman Street	C3
Henry Street	F4
High Street	E4
Hilton Street	E4-F4-F3
Hope Street	E3
Houldsworth Street	F4
Hulme Street	D1-E1
Hunts Bank	D5
Islington Way	A3-A4
Jackson's Row	C2-C3
James Street	A3
John Dalton Street	C3-D3
John Street	E4
Jordan Street	C1
Jutland Street	F3
Kays Gardens	A4-B4
Kennedy Street	D3
King Street	B5-C5
King Street	C3-D3
King Street West	C3
Laystall Street	F3
Lena Street	F3
Lever Street	E3-E4-F4
Little John Street	B2
Little Peter Street	C1
Liverpool Road	A2-B2-C1
Lloyd Street	C3-D3-D2
London Road	F1-F2
Long Millgate	D5
Longworth Street	C2
Lower Byrom Street	B2
Lower Mosley Street	C1-D2
Ludgate Street	E5
Major Street	E2-E3
Marble Street	D3-E3
Market Street	D4-E4-E3
Marsden Street	D3
Marshall Street	E5-F5
Mayan Avenue	A4-A5
Mayes Street	E5
Middlewood Street	A2
Miller Street	E5
Minshull Street	E3-E2-F2
Mirabel Street	C5-D5
Mosley Street	D2-D3-E3
Mount Street	D2
Museum Street	C2-D2
Nathan Drive	B5
New Bridge Street	C5
New Elm Road	A1-A2
New Market	D4
New Quay Street	B3
New Wakefield Street	D1
Newton Street	E3-F3-F4
Nicholas Street	D3-D2-E2
Norfolk Street	D4
North George Street	A4-A5
North Hill Street	A5
North Star Drive	A4
Norton Street	C5
Oak Street	E4
Oldham Road	F4-F5
Oldham Street	E4-F4
Oxford Road	E1
Oxford Street	D1-D2
Pall Mall	D3-D4
Parker Street	E3
Parsonage	C4
Paton Street	F3
Peru Street	A5
Peter Street	C2-D2
Piccadilly	E3-F3
Port Street	F4
Portland Street	D2-E2-E3
Potato Wharf	A1-B1-B2
Prince's Bridge	A2-B2
Princess Street	D3-D2-E2-E1
Quay Street	B3-B2-C2
Queen Street	B5-C5
Queen Street	C3
Richmond Street	E2
Rochdale Road	E5-F5
Rodney Street	A3
Rosamond Drive	A4-A5
Sackville Street	E2-E1-F1
St Ann Street	C3-D3
St James Street	D2
St John Street	C2
St Mary's Gate	D4
St Mary's Parsonage	C3-C4
St Mary's Street	C3-C4
St Stephen Street	B4-B5
Samuel Ogden Street	E1-E2
Sharp Street	E5-F5
Sherratt Street	F4-F5
Shudehill	E4-E5
Silk Street	A5
Sillavan Way	B4
South King Street	C3-D3
Southmill Street	C2-D3
Sparkle Street	F2-F3
Spaw Street	B4
Spear Street	E3-E4-F4
Spring Gardens	D3-D4
Store Street	F2-F3
Swan Street	E5-F5-F4
Tariff Street	F3
Thompson Street	F5
Tib Street	E4-F4
Todd Street	D5
Tonman Street	B2-C2
Travis Street	F2
Trinity Way	B3-B4-B5-C5
Turner Street	E4
Tysoe Gardens	A5-B5
Viaduct Street	C5
Victoria Bridge Street	C4-D4
Victoria Street	C4-D4-D5
Walkers Croft	D5
Water Street	A1-A2-B2-B3
Watson Street	C1-C2
West King Street	B5
West Mosley Street	D3-E3
Whitworth Street	D1-E1-E2-F2
Whitworth Street West	C1-D1
William Street	B4
Windmill Street	C2-D2
Withy Grove	D4
Wood Street	C3
York Street	D3-E3
Young Street	B3

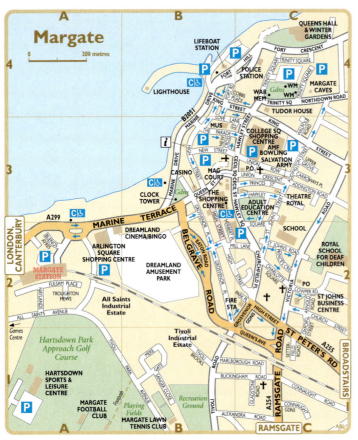

Margate

Margate is found on atlas page **31 G3**

Addington Road	C3	St John's Road	C2
Addington Street	C3	St John's Street	C2-C3
Alexandra Road	B1-C1	St Peter's Road	C1
All Saints Avenue	A2	Sanger Close	B1
Arnold Road	C2	Setterfield Road	C1
Belgrave Road	B2-B3	The Parade	B3
Buckingham Road	B1-C1	Tivoli Brooks	B1
Buenos Ayres	A2	Tivoli Park Avenue	A2-A1-B1
Carroways Place	C3	Tivoli Road	B1
Cecil Square	B3-C3	Trinity Square	C4
Cecil Street	B3-C3	Troughton Mews	A2
Charlotte Square	C2	Union Crescent	C3
Church Street	C1-C2	Union Row	C3
Churchfield Place	C2	Upper Grove	C3
Cobbs Place	B4-C4	Victoria Road	C2-C3
Connaught Gardens	C1	Walpole Road	C3
Connaught Road	C1		
Cowper Road	C2		
Eaton Road	B2		
Fort Crescent	C4		
Fort Hill	B4-C4		
Fort Road	B4		
Fulsam Place	A2		
Gladstone Road	C1		
Grosvenor Gardens	C2		
Grosvenor Place	B2-B3		
Hawley Square	C2-C3		
Hawley Street	C3		
Herbert Place	B2		
High Street	B3-B2-C2		
King Street	B4-C4-C3		
Love Lane	B3-C3		
Marine Drive	B3-B4		
Marine Terrace	A2-B3		
Marlborough Road	B1-C1		
Mere Gate	B1		
Mill Lane	B2-C2		
Naylands	A2		
New Cross Street	B3		
New Street	B3		
Northdown Road	C4		
Oxford Street	C1-C2		
Park Place	C2		
Prince's Crescent	C2		
Princes Street	C3		
Queen Street	B3		
Queens Avenue	C1		
Ramsgate Road	C1		

Middlesbrough

Middlesbrough is found on atlas page **106 D3**

Abingdon Road	C1-C2-C3	Emily Street	C3	Outram Street	A2
Acton Street	C1-C2	Enfield Street	A2	Oxford Street	A1
Aire Street	A1-A2	Errol Street	C1-C2	Palm Street	C2
Albert Mews	C4	Esher Street	C2	Park Lane	B1-C1
Albert Road	B3-B4-C4	Eshwood Square	A3-B3	Park Road North	B1
Albert Street	B4-C4	Essex Street	A1-A2	Park Road South	A1-B1
Albert Terrace	B1	Exchange Square	C4	Park Vale Road	C1-C2
Alwent Road	A3-B3	Fairbridge Street	B3	Parliament Road	A2-A1-B1
Amber Street	B3	Falkland Street	A2	Pelham Street	B2
Ammerston Road	A3	Falmouth Street	C1-C2	Percy Street	B2-B3
Angle Street	C1-C2	Fife Street	C3	Portman Street	B2
Aske Road	A2	Finsbury Street	A2	Princes Road	A2-B2
Athol Street	A2	Fleetham Street	A2-A3	Queens Square	C4
Aubrey Street	C1-C2	Fry Street	C3	Romney Street	A2
Ayresome Park Road	A1	Garnet Street	B2-B3	Roscoe Street	C2
Ayresome Street	A1	Glebe Road	A2	Ruby Street	B3
Baker Street	B3	Grange Road	B3-C3	Russell Street	C3
Bedford Street	B3	Granville Road	B1-B2	St Aidens Drive	B3
Borough Road	B3-C3-C2	Gresham Road	A2-B2	St Pauls Road	A2-A3
Bow Street	A2	Gurney Street	C3-C4	Somerset Street	C2-C3
Brentnall Street	B3	Haddon Street	C1-C2	Southfield Road	B2-C2
Bridge Street	C4	Harford Street	A1-A2	Southfold Lane	B2
Bright Street	C3	Hartington Road	A3-B3	Stamford Street	C2
Brompton Street	A1	Howe Street	A2	Station Street	B4
Byelands Street	C1	Jedburgh Street	C3	Stephenson Street	B2-B3
Cadogan Street	A2	Kensington Road	A1	Stowe Street	A2-B2
Camden Street	C2-C3	Kingston Street	A3-B2	Talbot Street	C2
Cannon Park Road	A3	Laura Street	B1-B2	Tennyson Street	B1-B2
Cannon Park Way	A3-A4	Laurel Street	C2	The Boulevard	C3
Carey Close	A3	Lees Road	A3	The Midfield	A1
Caxton Street	A1	Linthorpe Road	A1-B1-B2-B3	The Turnstile	A1
Chester Street	A1	Lonsdale Street	A2	Union Street	A2-A3-B3
Clairville Road	C1	Lothian Road	C1	Victoria Road	B2-C2
Clarendon Road	B2-C2	Lower Feversham Street	C4	Walpole Street	A2-A3
Clifton Street	A2-B2	Lower Gosford Street	C4	Warren Street	A2-A3
Clive Road	A1	Manor Street	A2	Warwick Street	A1-A2
Colville Street	A2	Maple Street	C2	Waterloo Road	B2-C2-C1
Corporation Road	B4-B3-C3	Marsh Road	A4, A4-B4	Waverley Street	A2
Costa Street	A1-A2	Marsh Street	A3	Wentworth Street	A2
Craven Street	A2	Marton Road	C2-C3	Wilson Street	B4
Crescent Road	A1-A2	Melrose Street	C3	Wilton Street	B2
Croydon Street	C1-C2	Metz Bridge Road	A4	Windsor Street	B3
Derwent Street	A2-A3	Myrtle Street	C2	Windward Way	C4
Diamond Road	B2-B3	Napier Street	A1	Wood Street	C4
Earl Street	B3	Newlands Road	C2	Woodlands Road	B1-B2-C2-C1
Egerton Street	C1-C2	Newport Road	A3-B4	Worcester Street	A1-A2
Egmont Road	C1	Newstead Road	C1	Wylam Street	A2
Emerald Street	B3	North Road	A4-B4	Zetland Road	B4-C4

206

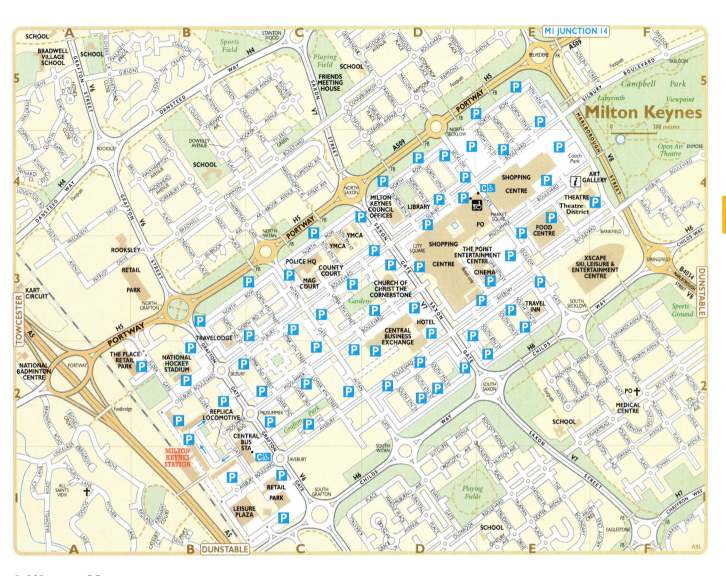

Milton Keynes

Milton Keynes is found on atlas page **49 G3**

Adelphi Street	E5-F5	Downley Avenue	B4	Maynard Close	A4	Ramsons Place	D5
Albion Place	F4	Ebbsgrove	A1-A2	Maypitch Place	B4	Redland Drive	B1
All Saints View	A1	Eelbrook Avenue	B3-B4	Midsummer		Saxon Gate	D4-D3-D2-E2
Arbrook Avenue	C4	Elder Gate	B2-B1-C1	Boulevard	B2-C2-D3-E4	Saxon Street	C5-C4, E2-E1-F1
Arlott Crescent	E1-F1	Evans Gate	D1	Milburn Avenue	D1	School Lane	A1
Athins Close	A4	Fishermead Boulevard	E2-F2	Mullion Place	F1-F2	Secklow Gate	D4-E4-E3
Avebury Boulevard	B1-C2-E3-F4	Forrabury Avenue	B4	North 2nd Street	B2-B3	Shackleton Place	D2-E1
Bignell Croft	A2	Germander Place	C5-D5	North 3rd Street	B3-C3	Silbury Boulevard	B2-C3-D4-F5
Booker Avenue	B4-C4-C5	Gibsons Green	A5-B5	North 4th Street	C3	Skeldon Gate	F5
Bossiney Place	E2-F2	Glovers Lane	A5	North 6th Street	C3	South 5th Street	D2
Boycott Avenue	D1-E1-E2	Grace Avenue	D1	North 7th Street	C3-C4	South 6th Street	D2
Bradwell Common		Grafton Gate	B3-B2-C2-C1	North 8th Street	D4	South 7th Street	D2
Boulevard	B3-B4-C4-C5	Grafton Street	A5-A4-B4-B3	North 9th Street	D4	South 8th Street	E2-E3
Bradwell Road	A1, A2	Gurnards Avenue	F3	North 10th Street	D4	South 9th Street	E3
Brill Place	A4-B4	Hadley Place	B3-B4	North 11th Street	E4	South 10th Street	E3
Burnham Drive	B5-B4-C4	Hampstead Gate	B4-C4-C3	North 12th Street	E4-E5	Speedwell Place	D5
Caruna Place	D5	Harrier Drive	F1	North 13th Street	E4-E5	Stainton Drive	B5
Catesby Court	B1	Helford Place	F2	North 14th Street	E5	Statham Place	E1
Century Avenue	E1	Helston Place	F1-F2	North Row	B3-C3-D4-E5	Stokenchurch Place	B5-C5-C4
Chaffron Way	F1	Honey Pot Close	A5	Oldbrook Boulevard	D1-E1	Stonecrop Place	D5
Chesham Avenue	B5	Hutton Avenue	E1-E2	Padstow Avenue	E2	Streatham Place	B3
Childs Way	C1-D2-E3-F5	Ibstone Avenue	B5-C5	Patriot Drive	A3-B3	Strudwick Drive	E1
Church Lane	A1	Kernow Crescent	F2	Pencarrow Place	F2	Sutcliffe Avenue	D1-D2-E2
Cleavers Avenue	D4-D5	Kirkham Court	B1	Penryn Avenue	F2	Talland Avenue	E2-F2
Coleshill Place	B4-B5	Kirkstall Place	C1-D1	Pentewan Gate	F2	The Boundary	E1
Coltsfoot Place	C5-D4	Lincelade Grove	A2-A1-B1	Perran Avenue	F1-F2	The Craven	B5
Columbia Place	F4	Loughton Road	A4	Pinks Court	B1	Tolcarne Avenue	F2
Conniburrow Boulevard	C5-D5	Lower 2nd Street	C2	Pitcher Lane	A1-B1	Towan Avenue	F1-F2
Coppin Lane	A4	Lower 3rd Street	C2	Plumstead Avenue	C4	Tranlands Brigg	A5
Craddocks Close	A4-A5	Lower 4th Street	C2	Polruan Place	F1-F2	Trueman Place	E1
Cranesbill Place	D5	Lower 10th Street	E3	Porthleven Place	F2-F3	Tylers Green	C4-C5
Dalgin Place	F4	Lucy Lane	A1	Portway	A2-B3-C4-E5	Upper 2nd Street	C2
Dansteed Way	A3-A4-B5-C5	Maidenhead Avenue	B4	Precedent Drive	A3-A4	Upper 4th Street	C2-C3
Deltic Avenue	A3-A4	Mallow Gate	D5	Quintin Drive	A4-A5	Upper 5th Street	C3
Dexter Avenue	E1	Marigold Place	D5	Ramsay Close	A4	Vellan Avenue	F2
Douglas Place	D1	Marlborough Street	E5-F4-F3	Ramsons Avenue	D5-E5	Walgrave Drive	A5
						Walkhampton Avenue	B4
						Wandsworth Place	C4
						Wardle Place	D1
						Whetstone Close	A5
						Wisley Avenue	C4
						Witan Gate	C3-C2-D2
						Woodruff Avenue	D5

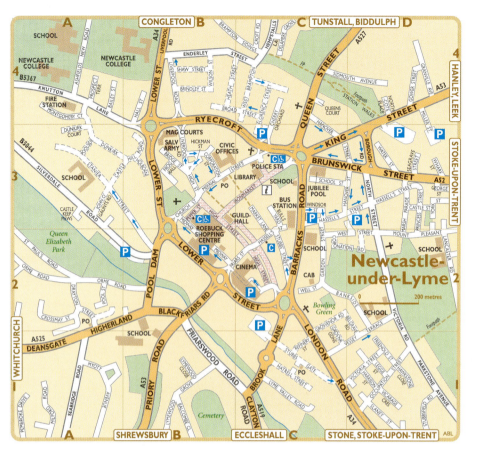

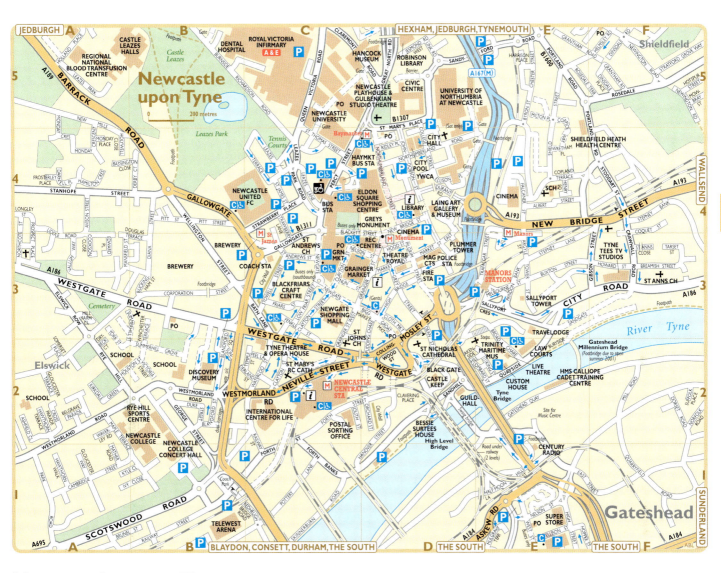

Newcastle upon Tyne

Newcastle upon Tyne is found on atlas page 114 D2

Akenside Hill	D2-E2
Albert Street	E4
Argyle Street	E3
Ashfield Close	A2
Askew Road	D1-E1
Avison Street	A4
Barrack Road	A5-B4
Bassington Close	A4-B4
Bath Lane	C3
Belgrave Parade	A2
Bigg Market	C3-D3
Blackett Street	C4-D4
Blandford Square	B2-B3
Blandford Street	B2
Breamish Street	F3
Broad Chare	E2-E3
Brunel Street	A1-B1
Buckingham Street	B3
Burnside	B5
Buryside	E2
Buxton Street	E3
Byron Street	E5
Cambridge Street	A1
Chester Street	E5
City Road	E3-F3
Claremont Road	C5-D5
Clavering Place	D2
Clayton Street	C2-C3
Cloth Market	D3
College Street	D4-D5
Collingwood Street	D2
Cookson Close	A3
Copland Terrace	E4
Coppice Way	E4-E5
Coquet Street	F4
Corporation Street	B3
Crawhall Road	F3-F4
Cross Parade	A2
Darnell Place	A4
Dean Street	D2-D3
Derby Court	B4
Diana Street	B3-B4
Dinsdale Place	F5
Dinsdale Road	F5
Dorset Road	F2
Douglas Terrace	A4-B3
Drybeck Court	A2-A3
Duke Street	B2
Durant Road	D4
East Street	E1-F1
Edward Place	A3
Ellison Place	D4
Ellison Street	E1
Elswick Row	A3
Falconer Street	E4
Fenckle Street	C3
Forth Banks	C1-C2
Forth Street	C1-C2-D2
Friars Street	C3
Frosterley Place	A4
Gallowgate	B4-C3-C4
Gateshead Quay	E2
George Street	B1-B2
Gibson Street	F3-F4
Gloucester Terrace	A2
Gloucester Way	A1
Grainger Street	C3-D3
Grainger Street West	C2-C3
Grantham Road	E5-F5
Great North Road	D5
Grey Street	D3
Groat Market	D3
Half Moon Lane	E1
Hamilton Crescent	A4
Hanover Street	C1-D1-D2
Harrison Place	E5
Hawthorn Terrace	A2
Hawthorn Walk	A1
Helmsley Road	E5-F5
Henry Square	E4
High Bridge	D3
High Street	E1
Holland Place	A5
Hills Street	E1
Holywell Close	A4
Hood Street	D3
Hopper Street	E1
Hotspur Street	F3
Houston Street	A2-B2
Howard Street	F3
Ivy Close	A1-B1
Jesmond Road West	D5
John Dobson Street	D4
King Street	E2
Kirkdale Green	A2
Kyle Close	A1-B1
Leazes Lane	C4
Leazes Park	A5
Leazes Park Road	C4
Leazes Terrace	C4
Liddle Road	A3-A4
Link Road	D5
Lombard Street	D2-E2
Longley Street	A4
Low Friar Street	C3
Melbourne Street	E3
Mansfield Street	A3
Maple Terrace	A2-B1
Market Street	D3
Market Street East	D3-D4
Mather Road	A1-A2
Mill Farm Close	A3
Mill Road	F2
Milton Place	E5
Monday Crescent	A4-A5
Monday Place	A4
Mosley Street	D3
Mowbray Street	F5
Mulgrave Terrace	E1
Nelson Street	C3-D3
Nelson Street (Gateshead)	E1
New Bridge Street	D4
New Bridge Street	E4-F4
New Mills	A5-A4
Newgate	C3
Newington Road	F5
Norfolk Road	F2
Northcote Street	A3-A4
Northumberland Road	D4-E4
Northumberland Street	D4
Nun Street	C3
Orchard Street	D2
Pandon Bank	E3
Park Road	A1
Peel Lane	C2
Percy Street	C4
Pilgrim Street	D3
Pitt Street	B4
Portland Road	E5-F5-F4
Pottery Lane	C1
Prospect Place	A3-A4
Pudding Chare	D2-D3
Quarryfield Road	F1-F2
Quayside	E2
Queen Victoria Road	C4-C5
Railway Street	A1-B1-C1-C2
Redheugh Bridge Road	B1-C1
Richardson Road	B5-C5-C4
Ridley Place	D4
Rosedale	F5
Rosedale Terrace	E5-F5
Rye Hill	A2-B2
St Andrews Street	C3
St Anns Close	F3
St James Street	C4
St Mary's Place	D5
St Thomas Street	C4-C5
Sallyport Crescent	E3
Sandgate	E3
Sandhill	D2
Sandyford Road	D5-E5
Scotswood Road	A1-B1
Shield Street	E4-E5
Skinnerburn Road	C1
Somerset Place	A2
South Street	C2-D2
Stanhope Street	A4-B4
Stepney Bank	F3-F4
Stepney Lane	E3-E4
Stoddart Street	F4
Stowell Street	C3
Stratford Grove West	F5
Strawberry Lane	C3-C4
Strawberry Place	C4
Suffolk Place	F2
Summerhill Grove	B2
Summerhill Place	A3-B3
Sunderland Street	B2-C2
Tarset Street	F3
Temple Street	B2-C2
Tower Street	E3
Trafalgar Street	E3-E4
Vallum Way	A3
Victoria Street	B2
Waterloo Street	C2
Waverley Road	A2
Wellington Street	B3-B4
West Street	E1
Westgate Road	A3-B3-C3-D2
Westmorland Road	A1-A2-B2-C2
Winchester Terrace	B2-B3
Wretham Place	E4
York Street	A2-A3

Newquay
Northampton

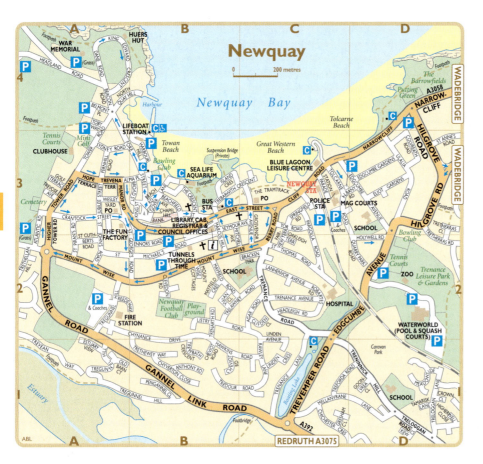

Newquay
Newquay is found on atlas page **4 B2**

Agar Road	C2	Marcus Hill	B2-B3
Albany Road	C3-D3	Mayfield Road	B2
Alma Place	A3-B3	Meadowside	D1
Anthony Road	B1	Mellanvrane Lane	C1-D1
Atlantic Road	A2-A3	Mitchell Avenue	B3-B2-C2
Bank Street	B3	Mount Wise	A2-B2-C2
Beach Road	B3	Narrowcliff	D3-D4
Beachfield Avenue	B3	North Quay Hill	A4-B4
Beacon Road	A4	Pargolla Road	C2-C3
Berry Road	C2-C3	Penganell Close	B1
Bracken Terrace	C2	Quarry Park Road	D2
Broad Street	B3	Rawley Lane	C1
Chapel Hill	B3	Robartes Road	C2
Chichester Crescent	C1-D1	St Cuthberts Road	A2
Chynance Drive	A2-B2-B1	St George's Road	A3-B3-B2
Chyverton Close	D3	St John's Road	A2-A3
Cliff Road	C3	St Michael's Road	A2-B2-B3
Colvreath Road	D3	St Piran's Road	A2-A3
Crantock Street	A3	St Thomas Road	C2
Dane Road	A4	Seymour Avenue	B3-C3
East Street	B3-C3	Springfield Road	C3
Edgcumbe Avenue	C2-D2-D3	Station Parade	C3
Edgcumbe Gardens	D3	Sydney Road	A3
Eliot Gardens	D3	The Crescent	B3
Ennors Road	B2	Tolcarne Road	C3-D3
Fernhill Road	A3	Tor Road	C3
Fore Street	A4-A3-B3	Tower Road	A3-A4
Gannel Link Road	A1-B1-C1	Trebarwith Crescent	B3-C3
Gannel Road	A2	Tredour Road	B1-C1
Gover Lane	B3	Treforda Road	C1-D1
Grosvenor Avenue	C2-C3	Tregunnel Hill	A2-A1-B1
Harbour Hill	B3	Trelawney Road	B2-C2
Hawkins Road	B1-C1	Treloggan Lane	D1
Headland Road	A4	Treloggan Road	D1
Headleigh Road	C2	Trembath Crescent	B1
Higher Tower Road	A2-A3	Trenance Avenue	C2
Hilgrove Road	D3-D4	Trenance Lane	C1-C2
Holywell Road	D2	Trenance Road	C2
Hope Terrace	A3	Trenarth Road	B2
Island Crescent	B3	Treninnick Hill	C1-D1
Jubilee Street	A3	Tretherras Road	D2-D3
King Edward Crescent	A4	Trethewey Way	B1-B2
King Street	B3	Trevean Way	A1-A2
Lanhenvor Avenue	C2	Trevemper Road	C1
Linden Avenue	C1-C2	Trevena Terrace	A3
Linden Crescent	C1	Ulalia Road	D3
Listry Road	B2-C2	Vivian Close	B1
Manor Road	A3	Wesley Yard	A3

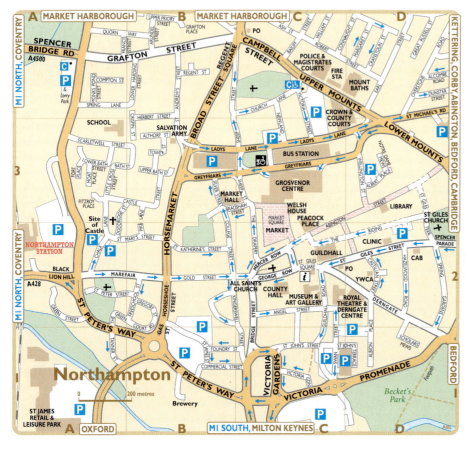

Northampton
Northampton is found on atlas page **49 F5**

Abington Street	C2-C3-D3	Lower Bath Street	A3
Albert Place	D3	Lower Harding Street	B4
Albion Place	D1-D2	Lower Mounts	D3
Alcombe Road	D4	Marefair	A2-B2
Althorp Street	B3	Margaret Street	D4
Angel Street	C2	Mercer Row	C2
Arundel Street	B4	Moat Place	A3
Ash Street	C4	Monks Pond Street	A4
Bailiff Street	C4	Newland	C3-C4
Bath Street	A3-B3	Overstone Road	D4
Black Lion Hill	A2	Pike Lane	B2-B3
Bradshaw Street	B3-C3	Quorn Way	A4-B4
Bridge Street	C1-C2	Regent Square	B4
Broad Street	B3-B4	Regent Street	B4
Campbell Street	C4	Robert Street	C4-D4
Castilian Street	D2	St Andrews Street	B3-B4
Castle Street	A3-B3	St Giles Square	C2
Chalk Lane	A2-A3	St Giles Street	C2-D2
Church Lane	C4	St Giles Terrace	D2-D3
College Street	B2-B3	St James Street	B1
Commercial Street	B1-C1	St John's Street	C1
Compton Street	A4	St John's Terrace	C1-D1
Connaught Street	C4-D4	St Katherine's Street	B2
Court Road	B1-B2	St Mary's Street	A2-B2
Cranstoun Street	D4	St Michael's Road	D3-D4
Crispin Street	B3-B4	St Peter Street	A2-B2
Derngate	C2-D2-D1	St Peter's Way	A2-A1-B1-C1
Doddridge Street	A2-A3-B3	Scarletwell Street	A3-B3
Dunster Street	D4	Sheep Street	B4-B3-C3
Earl Street	D4	Silver Street	B3
Foundry Street	B1-C1	Spencer Bridge Road	A4
Francis Street	A4	Spencer Parade	D2
Freeschool Street	B2	Spring Gardens	D2
Gas Street	B1-B2	Spring Lane	A4
George Row	C2	Swan Street	C1-C2
Gold Street	B2	Tanner Street	A1
Grafton Street	A4-B4	The Drapery	C2-C3
Green Street	A2	The Green	A2
Gregory Street	B2	The Riding	C2-D2-D3
Greyfriars	B3-C3	Tower Street	B3
Guildhall Road	C1-C2	Upper Bath Street	B3
Hazelwood Road	D2	Upper Mounts	C4-D4
Herbert Street	B3-B4	Upper Priory Street	B4
Horsemarket	B2-B3	Victoria Gardens	C1
Horseshoe Street	B2	Victoria Promenade	C1-D1
Kingerswell Street	B2-C1	Victoria Street	C3-C4
Lady's Lane	B3-C3-D3	Wellington Street	D3
Little Cross Street	A3	William Street	C4

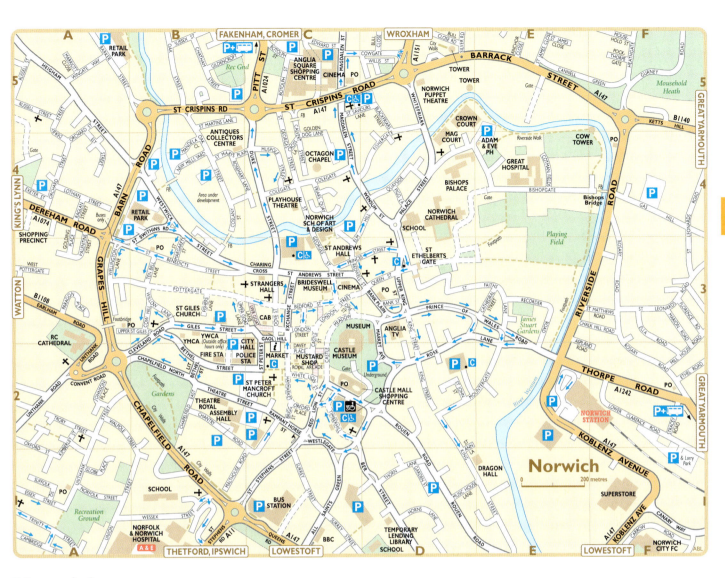

Norwich

Norwich is found on atlas page **77 E1**

All Saints Green	C1	Cow Hill	B3	Johnson Place	A2	Raglan Street	A4	Thorpe Road	E2-F2
Anchor Close	E5	Cowgate	C5-D5	Ketts Hill	F5	Rampant Horse Street	C2	Timberhill	C2
Aspland Road	E3-F2	Cross Lane	C4	Kimberley Street	A1-A2	Recorder Road	E3	Trinity Street	A1
Bank Plain	D3	Davey Place	C2	King Street	D3-D2-D1-E1	Red Lion Street	C2	Trory Street	A2
Bank Street	D3	Derby Street	A4-A5	Koblenz Avenue	E2-F2-F1	Redwell Street	C3-D3	Union Street	A1-B1
Barker Street	A5-B5	Dereham Road	A4	Little Bethel Street	B2	Riverside	E1-E2	Unthank Road	A2-A3
Barn Road	A4-B4-B5	Dove Street	C3	London Street	C3-D3	Riverside Road	E3-F3-F4-F5	Unthank Street	A1-A2
Barrack Street	D5-E5-F5	Duke Street	C3-C4-C5	Lothian Street	A4	Rosary Road	F2-F3-F4	Upper Goat Lane	B3-C3
Bedford Street	C3	Earlham Road	A3	Lower Clarence Road	F1-F2	Rose Lane	D2-D3-E3	Upper King Street	D3
Ber Street	D2-D1	Edward Street	C5	Lower Goat Lane	C3	Rosemark Lane	B4-C4	Upper St Giles Street	A3-B3
Bethel Street	B3-B2-C2	Ella Road	F2-F3	Magdalen Street	C4-C5	Rouen Road	D2-D1-E1	Valentine Street	A3-A4
Bishopgate	E4-F4	Elm Hill	C3-D4	Malthouse Road	B1-C1	Royal Arcade	C2	Walpole Street	A2-B2
Blackfriars Street	D5	Ely Street	A4-A5	Mandela Close	B4	Russell Street	A5	Wellington Lane	A3
Botolph Street	C5	Essex Street	A1	Marion Road	F3	St Andrews Street	C3	Wensum Street	C4-D4
Brigg Street	C2	Ethel Road	F2	Market Avenue	D2-D3	St Ann Lane	D1-D2	Wessex Street	A1-B1
Bull Close	D5	Exchange Street	C3	Marriott Close	A5	St Benedicts Street	B3	West Pottergate	A3
Calvert Street	C4-C5	Exeter Street	A4	Mountergate	D2-E2	St Crispins Road	B5-C5-D5	Westlegate	C1-C2
Canary Way	F1	Fishergate	D4-D5	Music House Lane	D1-E1	St Faiths Lane	D3-E3	Westwick Street	B3-B4
Cambridge Street	A1	Fishers Lane	B3	Muspole Street	C4	St Georges Street	C3-C4-C5	White Lion Street	C2
Cannell Green	E5-F5	Florence Road	F3	New Mills Yard	B4	St James Close	E5	Whitefriars	D4-D5
Carrow Road	F1	Friars Quay	C4	Norfolk Street	A1	St John Street	D2	Willis Street	D5
Castle Meadow	C2-C3-D3	Gaol Hill	C3	Oak Street	B4-B5	St Leonards Road	F3-F4	Willow Lane	B3
Castle Street	C2-C3	Garden Street	D1	Opie Street	C3	St Margarets Street	B3-B4	Wingate Way	A5
Cathedral Street	E3	Gas Hill	F4	Orchard Street	A4-A5	St Martins Lane	B5		
Chalk Hill Road	E3-F3	Gildencroft	B5	Orford Place	C2	St Marys Plain	B4-C4		
Chantry Road	B2-C2-C1	Giles Street	B3-C3	Oxford Street	A1-A2	St Matthews Road	E3-F3		
Chapelfield East	B2	Globe Place	A1	Palace Street	D4	St Peter Street	C2-C3		
Chapelfield North	B2	Golden Dog Lane	C4-C5	Paragon Place	A3	St Saviours Lane	C5-D5		
Chapelfield Road	A2-B2-B1	Golding Place	A3-A4	Pigg Lane	D4	St Stephens Street	B1-C1-C2		
Charing Cross	C3	Grapes Hill	A3	Pitt Street	C5	St Swithins Road	B3-B4		
Chatham Street	B5	Gurney Road	F5	Pockthorpe Gate	F5	Stracey Road	F2		
Cleveland Road	A2-B2-B3	Haymarket	C2	Pottergate	A3-B3-C3	Suffolk Square	A1		
Colegate	C4	Heathgate	F5	Prince of Wales Road	D3-E3	Surrey Street	C1-D1		
Convent Road	A2	Heigham Street	A5-A4-B4	Princes Street	C3-D3	Ten Bell Lane	B3		
Coslany Street	B4	Hill House Road	F2-F3	Quayside	D4	Theatre Street	B2-C2		
Cotman Fields	E4	Horns Lane	D1	Queen Street	D3	Thorn Lane	D1		

Nottingham

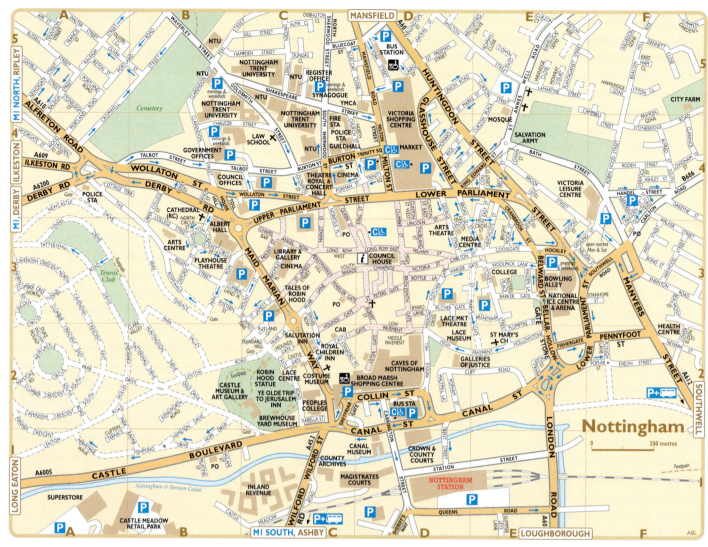

Nottingham

Nottingham is found on atlas page 72 C4

Aberdeen Street	F3-F4	Castle Road	C2	Fiennes Crescent	A1-A2	Lamartine Street	E5-F5	Oliver Street	A5-B5	South Sherwood Street	C4-C5
Albert Street	D3	Cavendish Crescent East	A2-A3	Fishergate	E2	Lennox Street	E3-E4	Oxford Street	B3	Southwell Road	F3
Alfred Street South	F4	Cavendish Crescent North	A3	Fishpond Drive	A1-B1	Lenton Road	A1-A2-B2-C2	Palatine Street	B1	Spaniel Row	C2-C3
Alfreton Road	A4-A5	Cavendish Crescent South	A2	Fletcher Gate	D3	Lincoln Circus	A3	Park Drive	A2-B2	Standard Hill	C2
Alma Close	C5	Chapel Bar	C3	Forman Street	C4-D4	Lincoln Street	D3-D4	Park Ravine	A2-B1	Stanford Street	C2-D2
Angel Row	C3	Chaucer Street	B4-C4	Friar Lane	C2-C3	Lister Gate	D2	Park Row	B3-C3	Station Street	D1-E1
Barker Gate	E3	Cheapside	D3	Gamble Street	A5	Liverpool Street	F4	Park Terrace	B3	Stonebridge Road	F4-F5
Bath Street	E4-F4	Clare Valley	B2-B3	Gedling Street	E3-F3	London Road	E1-E2	Park Valley	B2-B3	Stoneleigh Street	A5
Beacon Hill Rise	F5	Clarence Street	F4	George Street	D3-D4	Long Row East	D3	Peel Street	B5-C5	Stoney Street	E2-E3
Beastmarket Hill	C3	Clarendon Street	B4-B5	Gill Street	B5-C5	Long Row West	C3	Pelham Street	D3	Talbot Street	A4-B4-C4
Beaumont Street	F3	Cliff Road	D2-E2	Glasshouse Street	D4-D5	Longden Street	F3-F4	Pemberton Street	E2	Tattershall Drive	A3-A2-B2
Beck Street	E4	Clifton Terrace	A1	Goldsmith Street	B5-C5-C4	Low Pavement	D2	Pennyfoot Street	F2	Tennis Drive	A3
Bellargate	E2-E3	Clinton Street East	D4	Goosegate	E3	Lowdham Street	F4	Pilcher Gate	D3	Tennyson Street	A5
Belward Street	E3	Clinton Street West	D4	Great Freeman Street	D5	Lower Parliament		Plantaganet Street	E5	The Ropewalk	A4-B4-B3
Bluecoat Close	C5-D5	Clumber Crescent East	A2-A3	Greyfriar Gate	C2	Street	D4-E4-E3-E2	Plough Lane	F2	Thurland Street	D3
Bluecoat Street	C5	Clumber Crescent North	A3	Hamilton Drive	B1-B2	Lytton Close	F5	Plumptre Street	E2-E3	Toll House Hill	B4
Bond Street	F3	Clumber Crescent South	A2	Hampden Street	B5-C5	Maid Marian Way	B3-C3-C2	Popham Street	D2	Trent Street	D1-D2
Boston Street	E3	Clumber Street	D3-D4	Handel Street	F4	Maiden Lane	E3	Poplar Street	F2	Trinity Square	D4
Bottle Lane	D3	College Street	B3-B4	Haslam Street	B1	Mansfield Road	C5-D5	Portland Road	A4-A5-B5	Troman Close	E5
Bridlesmith Gate	D3	Collin Street	D2	Haywood Street	F3	Manvers Street	F2-F3	Postern Street	B3	Tunnel Road	A3
Brightmoor Street	E3-E4	Comyn Gardens	E5	Heathcote Street	E3-E4	Market Street	C3-C4	Queen Street	C4-C3-D3	Union Road	D5
Broad Street	D4-D3-E3	Conuent Street	E4	Hermitage Walk	A1	Middle Hill	D2	Queens Road	D1-E1	Upper College Street	B3-B4
Broadway	E3	Cowan Street	E4	High Cross Street	E3-E4	Middle Pavement	D2	Raleigh Street	A5	Upper Parliament	
Bromley Place	C3	Cranbrook Street	E3-E4	High Pavement	D2-E2	Milton Street	D4	Regent Street	B3	Street	C3-C4-D3
Brook Street	E4-E3-F3	Cromwell Street	A4-A5-B5	High Street	D3	Moorgate Street	A4	Rick Street	D4	Victoria Street	D3
Burton Street	C4	Cumberland Place	B3-C3	Hockley	E3	Mount Street	C3	Risters Place	E3	Walker Street	F3-F4
Byard Lane	D3	Curzon Place	D4-E4-E5	Holles Crescent	A2-B2	Mowray Court	E5	Robin Hood Street	F4	Walter Street	A5
Cairns Street	D5	Curzon Street	E5	Hollowstone	E2	Nelson Street	E3-E4	Roden Street	F4	Warser Gate	D3-E3
Campbell Street	E5-F5-F4	Dakeyne Street	F4	Hope Drive	B1-B2	Newark Street	F2	Russell Street	A5	Wasnidge Close	E5
Canal Street	C2-D2-E2	Dennett Close	F5	Hounds Gate	C2-C3	Newcastle Circus	A2	Rutland Street	C3	Watkin Street	D5
Carlton Road	F3-F4	Derby Road	A4-B4	Howard Street	D4	Newcastle Drive	A3-A4-B3	St Annes Well Road	E4-E5	Waverley Street	B5
Carlton Street	D3-E3	Dryden Street	C5	Huntingdon Drive	B2-B3	Newdigate Street	A5	St James's Street	C3	Weekday Cross	D3
Carrington Street	D1-D2	Duke William Mount	A2	Huntingdon Street	D5-D4-E4	Nile Street	E4	St James's Terrace	B3-C3-C2	Wellington Circus	B3
Castle Boulevard	A1-B1-C1-C2	East Circus Street	B3	Ilkeston Road	A4	Norfolk Place	C3-C4	St Lukes Street	F4	West Street	F3
Castle Gate	C2-D2	East Street	E4	Instow Rise	E5	North Church Street	C4-D4	St Marks Street	D5-E5	Wheeler Gate	C3
Castle Meadow Road	B1-C1	Evelyn Street	F2	Ireton Street	A5	North Circus Street	B3-C3	St Mary's Gate	D3-E3-E2	Wilford Road	C1
				Isabella Street	C2	North Road	A3	St Peters Gate	D3	Wilford Street	C1
				Kenilworth Road	B2	North Sherwood Street	C5	Shakespeare Street	B5-C5-D4	Wollaton Street	A4-B4-C4
				Kent Street	D4-E4	Ogle Drive	B2	Shelton Street	D5-E5	Wood Street	A4
				King Edward Street	D4-E4	Old Lenton Street	D3	Sneinton Road	F3	Woolpack Lane	E3
				King Street	D3-D4	Oliver Close	A5	South Parade	C3-D3	York Street	D5

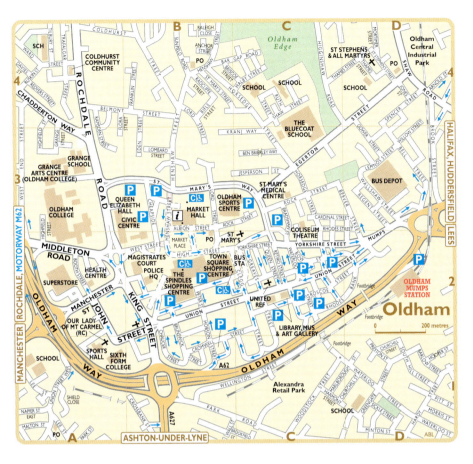

Oldham

Oldham is found on atlas page **82 D5**

Albion Street	B3	Market Place	B2
Bar Gap Road	B4-C4	Marlborough Street	C1-D1
Barlow Street	D1	Middleton Road	A2
Beever Street	C3-D3-D2	Morris Street	D1
Bell Street	D3	Mortimer Street	D4
Belmont Street	A4-B4	Mumps	D2-D3
Ben Brierley Way	C3	Oldham Way	B1-C1-C2-D2
Booth Street	A2	Park Road	B1-C1
Bow Street	C2-D2	Peter Street	B2
Bradshaw Street	C2-C3	Preston Street	D1
Brook Street	D3-D4	Queen Street	C2
Brunswick Street	B1-B2	Radcliffe Street	B4
Cardinal Street	C3-D3	Ramsden Street	A3-A4
Chadderton Way	A3-A4	Redvers Street	A4
Chaucer Street	B1-B2	Regent Street	D3
Cheapside	B2-B3	Retiro Street	C2
Churchill Street	C1-D1, D1	Rhodes Bank	C2-D2
Clegg Street	B2-C2-C1	Rhodes Street	C3-D3
Coldhurst Street	A4-B4	Rifle Street	B1
Cromwell Street	B1-C2	Rochdale Road	A2-A3-A4
Crossbank Street	B1	Rock Street	B3-C3
Eden Street	B3-B4	Roscoe Street	C2-D2
Egerton Street	C3-D4	Ruskin Street	A4
Franklin Street	B4	Ruth Street	C4
Gower Street	D3-D4	Shaw Road	D4
Grange Street	A3	St Mary's Street	B4
Greaves Street	C1-C2	St Mary's Way	A3-B3-C3-C2
Greengate Street	D1	St Stephen's Street	D4
Hardy Street	D1	Shaw Street	C4
Harmony Street	C1-D1	Sickle Street	D1
Henshaw Street	B2-B3-B4	South Hill Street	D1
Higginshaw Road	C4	Spencer Street	D4
High Street	B2	Sunfield Road	B4
Highfield Street	A2-A3, A3-A4	Thames Street	C4-D4
Hobson Street	B1-B2	Tilbury Street	A4
Hooper Street	D1	Trafalgar Street	A4
Horsedge Street	B4-C4-C3	Union Street	B2-C2-D2
Jesperson Street	B3-C3	Union Street West	A1
John Street	A2-A1-B1-B2	Wall Street	B1
Jones Street	D4	Wallshaw Street	D3
King Street	B1-B2	Ward Street	A4
Kranj Way	B3-C3	Waterloo Street	C2-C1-D1
Lee Street	A1	Wellington Street	B1-C1
Lemnos Street	D3	West End Street	A2-A3-A4
Lombard Street	B3	West Street	A2-B2
Lord Street	B2-B3, B3-B4	Willow Street	D3-D4
Malby Street	C4	Woodstock Street	C1
Manchester Street	A1-A2	Yorkshire Street	C2-D2

Paignton

Paignton is found on atlas page **7 F4**

Adelphi Lane	C2	Leighton Road	C3-C4
Adelphi Road	C2	Littlegate Road	A4-B4
Barum Close	B4	Logan Road	B4
Batson Gardens	A1	Lower Polsham Road	B4-C4
Baymount Road	A4	Mabel Place	A2
Beach Road	C3	Marine Drive	C4
Bell Vue Road	C1	Marine Park	C4
Bishops Place	A3-B3	Mead Lane	B4-C4
Brent Street	A3-A4	Midvale Road	A2
Cadwell Road	B4	Mill Lane	A3-A4
Cecil Mews	B4	New Street	A2
Cecil Road	A4-B4	Norman Road	C4
Central Avenue	A4	Oldenburg Park	C4
Church Street	A3-B3	Osney Avenue	A1
Churchward Road	A4	Osney Crescent	A1
Cleveland Road	C1	Palace Avenue	A3
Cliffe Road	C1-D1	Palace Place	A3
Clifton Road	A2-A3	Polsham Park	B4
Climsland Road	A1-A2	Princes Street	A3
Colley End Road	A4	Queens Park Road	B2
Commercial Road	B3	Queens Road	B2-C2
Conway Crescent	A2	Redburn Road	A4
Conway Road	A1-A2	Roundham Road	B1-C1-C2
Courtland Road	B4	St Andrews Road	B1-B2
Coverdale Road	A3	St Michaels Road	A1
Curledge Street	A2-B2	Sands Road	B2-C2
Dartmouth Road	B1-B2	Southfield Road	A4
Dendy Road	B3	Stafford End	B2
Elm Bank Gardens	A2	Station Lane	B2
Elmsleigh Park	A1-B1	Steartfield Road	C3-C4
Elmsleigh Road	A1-B1-B2	Sunbury Road	A1
Esplanade	C2-C3-C4	The Riviera	B1
Esplanade Road	C2-C3-C4	Torbay Road	B3-B2-C2
Fisher Street	A2-A1-B1	Torquay Road	B3-B4
Garfield Road	C3	Totnes Road	A2-A3
Gerston Place	A3-B3	Tower Road	A3
Gerston Road	B2-B3	Victoria Street	B3
Glen Road	B4	Warefield Road	C4
Great Western Road	B2-B3	Well Street	A3-A4
Grosvenor Road	A2-B2	Whitestone Road	B1
Higher Polsham Road	A4-B4	Wilbarn Road	C4
Hill Park Terrace	B1-B2	Winner Hill Road	A3
Hyde Road	B3	Winner Street	A2-A3-A4
Kernou Road	C3	Woodland Park	A4
Keysfield Road	C1	York Road	A1
Killerton Close	A4		
Kings Avenue	C4		
Kirkham Street	A4		

Oxford

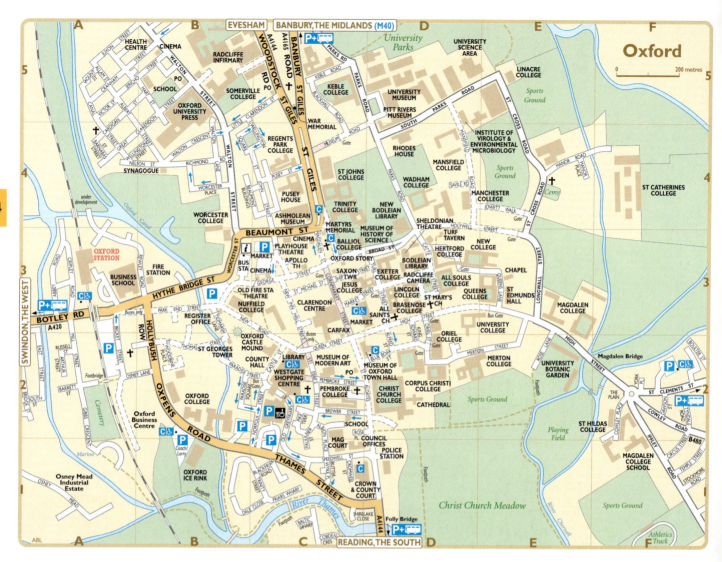

Oxford
Oxford is found on atlas page **40 C5**

Abbey Road	A3	Faulkner Street	C1-C2	Paradise Square	B2	Tyndale Road	F2
Albert Street	A5-B4	Friars Wharf	C1	Paradise Street	B2-C2	Victor Street	A5
Albion Place	C1-C2	George Street	B3-C3	Park End Street	A3-B3	Walton Crescent	B4
Alfred Street	D2-D3	Gibbs Crescent	A1-A2	Parks Road	C5-D5-D4	Walton Lane	B4-B5
Allam Street	A5	Great Clarendon Street	A4-B4-B5	Pembroke Street	C2	Walton Street	B4-B5
Arthur Street	A2	Hart Street	B5	Pike Terrace	C2	Wellington Square	B4-C4
Baltic Wharf	C1	High Street	C2-D3-E2-F2	Pusey Street	C4	Wellington Street	A4-B4
Banbury Road	C5	Hollybush Row	B2-B3	Queen Street	C2	Woodbine Place	B2
Barrett Street	A2	Holywell Street	D4-E4-E3	Queens Lane	E3	Woodstock Road	C5
Beaumont Buildings	B4-C4	Hythe Bridge Street	B3	Rewley Road	A3-B3	Worcester Place	B4
Beaumont Street	B3-C3-C4	Iffley Road	F1-F2	Richmond Road	B4	Worcester Street	B3
Becket Street	A2-A3	Jericho Street	A5-B5	Rose Lane	E2-E3	York Place	F2
Blackfriars Road	C1	Jowett Walk	D4-E4	Rose Place	C2		
Blackhall Road	C4-C5	Juxon Street	A5	Russell Street	A2		
Blue Boar Street	D2	Keble Road	C5	St Aldates	C2-D2-D1		
Botley Road	A3	King Edward Street	D2-D3	St Barnabas Street	A4		
Boulter Street	F2	Little Clarendon Street	B4-B5-C5	St Clements Street	F2		
Brewer Street	C2	Longwall Street	E3	St Cross Road	E3-E4-E5		
Bridge Street	A2	Magdalen Street	C3	St Ebbe's Street	C2		
Broad Street	C3-D3	Manor Place	E4	St Giles	C4-C5		
Butterwyke Place	C1	Manor Road	E4-F4	St John Street	C3-C4		
Canal Street	A4-A5	Mansfield Road	D4-D5	St Michael Street	C3		
Cardigan Street	A4-A5-B5	Market Street	C3-D3	St Thomas Street	B2		
Castle Street	C2	Merton Street	D2-E2-E3	Savile Road	D4		
Cattle Street	D3	Mill Street	A2-A3	Ship Street	C3-D3		
Circus Street	F1-F2	Mount Street	A5	Shirelake Close	C1		
Cobden Crescent	C1	Museum Road	C4	South Parks Road	D4-D5-E5		
Cornmarket Street	C3	Nelson Street	A4-B4	South Street	A2		
Cowley Place	F2	New Inn Hall Street	C2-C3	Speedwell Street	C1-D1		
Cowley Road	F2	New Road	B3-C3-C2	Stockmore Road	F1		
Cranham Street	A5-B5	Norfolk Street	C1-C2	Temple Street	F1-F2		
Cripley Road	A3	Old Greyfriars Street	C1-C2	Thames Street	B1-C1-D1		
Cromwell Street	C1	Oriel Street	D2-D3	The Plain	F2		
Dale Close	B1-C1	Osney Lane	A2-B2	Tidmarsh Lane	B2-B3		
Dawson Street	F2	Osney Mead	A1	Trinity Street	C1		
East Street	A2-A3	Oxpens Road	B1-B2	Turl Street	D3		

Perth

Perth is found on atlas page **140 A2**

Alexandra Road	B2	Rose Terrace	C4
Ardchoillie Gardens	D4	St Andrew Street	B2
Atholl Street	B3-C3	St Catherines Road	A4-A3-B3
Balhousie Street	B4	St John Street	C2-D3
Barossa Place	C4	St Johns Place	C2
Barossa Street	B4-C4	St Leonards Bank	C1
Barrack Street	B4	Scott Street	C1-C2-C3
Caledonian Road	B2-B3	South Methuen Street	B2-B3
Canal Street	B2-C2	South Street	B2-C2-D2
Carpentor Street	C3	South William Street	C1
Cavendish Avenue	A1	Stormont Street	B3-B4
Charlotte Street	C3	Tay Street	D1-D2-D3
Commercial Street	D3	Victoria Street	B2-C2
County Place	B2	Watergate	D2-D3
Cross Street	B1-B2	Whitefriars Crescent	A2-A3
Dunkeld Road	A4-B4	Wilson Street	A1
East Bridge Street	D3	York Place	A2-B2
Edinburgh Road	C1		
Feus Road	A3-A4		
George Street	C3-D3		
Glasgow Road	A2		
Glover Street	A1-A2		
Gowrie Street	D2-D3		
Grey Street	A1-A2		
Hay Street	B4		
High Street	B3-C3-D3		
Isla Road	D4		
James Street	C1-C2		
King Edward Street	C2		
King Street	B1-B2		
Kings Place	B1		
Kinnoull Causeway	A2-B2		
Kinnoull Street	C3		
Longcauseway	A3-B3		
Low Street	B4		
Marshall Place	C1-D1		
Melville Street	B3-B4		
Mill Street	C3		
Milne Street	B2-B3		
Murray Street	B3-C3		
Needless Road	A1		
New Row	B2-B3		
North Methuen Street	B3		
Perth Bridge	D3		
Pickletullum Road	A1		
Princes Street	C1-C2		
Queens Bridge	D2		
Raeburn Park	A1		

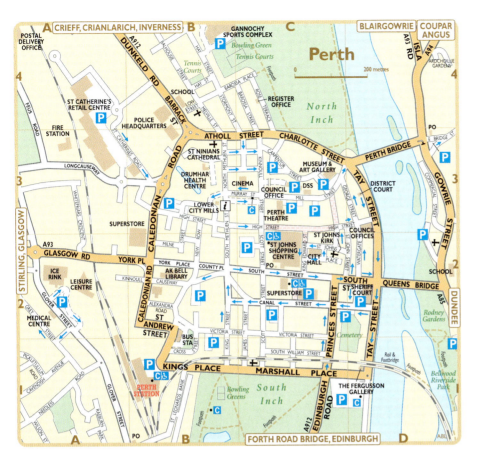

Peterborough

Peterborough is found on atlas page **62 A5**

Bishops Road	C2-C3-D3	South Street	D3
Boongate	D4	Star Road	D3
Bourges Boulevard	A4-A2-B2	Station Road	A3-A4
Bridge Street	B2-B3	Trinity Street	B2-B3
Bright Street	A4-B4	Versen Platz	B1-B2
Broadway	B3-B4	Vineyard Road	C2-C3
Cathedral Square	B3	Wake Road	D3
Church Street	B3	Wellington Street	C4-D4
City Road	C3-C4	Wentworth Street	B2
Cowgate	A3-B3	Westgate	A4-B4-B3
Cromwell Road	A4	Wheel Yard	B3
Cross Street	B3		
Deacon Street	A4		
Dickens Street	D4		
East Station Road	B1-C1		
Eastgate	D3		
Exchange Street	B3		
Fengate Close	D3		
Fitzwilliam Street	B4		
Frank Perkins Parkway	D1-D2		
Geneva Street	B4		
George Street	A1		
Gladstone Street	A4		
Granby Street	C3-D3		
Gravel Walk	C2		
Hereward Street	D3		
Jubilee Street	A1		
Lea Gardens	A2		
Lincoln Road	B4		
Long Causeway	B3		
Manor House Street	B4		
Mayors Walk	A4		
Midgate	B3-C3		
Morris Street	B4		
Nene Street	D3		
New Road	C4		
North Street	B4		
Northminster Road	B4-C4-C3		
Oundle Road	A1-B1		
Park Road	B3-B4		
Potters Way	D1-D2		
Priestgate	A3-B3-B2		
Queen Street	B3		
River Lane	A2-A3		
Rivergate	B1-B2-C2		
Russell Street	A4-B4		
St Johns Street	C3-C4		
St Peters Road	B2		

215

Plymouth

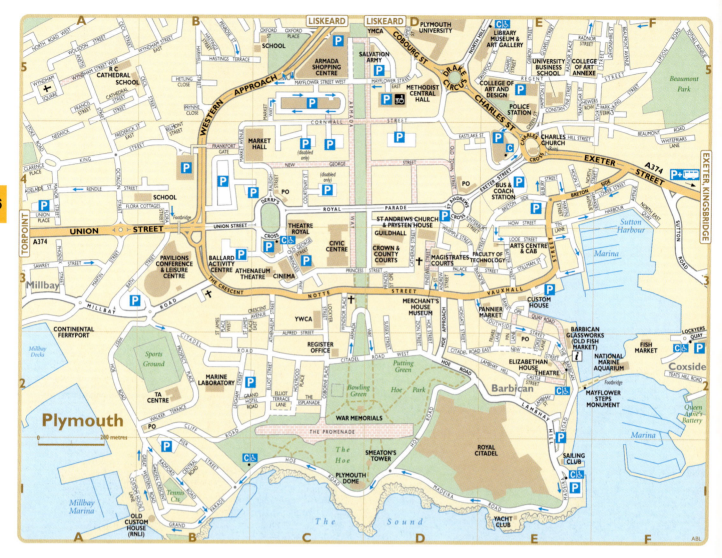

Plymouth
Plymouth is found on atlas page **6 B3**

Adelaide Street	A4	Eastlake Street	D4-E4	Kinterbury Street	D4-D3-E3	Phoenix Street	A3	Union Place	A4
Alfred Street	C2	Elliot Street	C2	Lambhay Hill	D2-E2-E1	Pier Street	B1-B2	Union Street	A3-C3
Anstis Street	A4-A5	Elliot Terrace Lane	C2	Lambhay Street	E2	Pin Lane	E2	Vauxhall Street	E3
Armada Way	C2-C3-D3-D2	Exeter Street	D4-E4-F4	Leigham Street	B2	Princess Street	C3-D3	Walker Terrace	B3
Armada Way	C3-C4-C5	Fineswell Street	D3	Lipson Road	F5	Princess Street Ope	D3	West Hoe Road	A2-A3-B3
Athenaeum Street	C2-C3	Flora Cottages	A4-B4	Lockyer Street	C3	Princess Way	C3	Western Approach	B4-B5-C5
Basket Ope	E3	Flora Street	B4	Lockyers Quay	F2	Prospect Place	B2	Whimple Street	D3
Bath Street	A3-B3	Francis Street	A5	Looe Street	E3	Prynne Close	B5	Whitefriars Lane	F4
Batter Street	E3	Frankfort Gate	B4	Lower Street	F4	Quay Road	E3	Windsor Place	C3
Beaumont Avenue	F5	Frederick Street East	A4-B4	Madeira Road	D1-E1-E2	Radford Road	B1	Wolsdon Street	A5
Beaumont Road	F4-F5	Friars Lane	E2-E3	Manor Street	A3-A4	Radnor Place	E5	Wyndham Square	A5
Belmont Street	B4	Garden Crescent	B1	Market Avenue	B4	Radnor Street	E5-F5	Wyndham Street East	A5-B5
Bilbury Street	E4	Gasking Street	F5	Market Way	C4-C5	Raleigh Street	C4	Wyndham Street West	A5
Breton Side	E4-F4	Gibbon Street	E5	Martin Street	A3	Regent Street	E5-F5	Zion Street	D2-D3
Buckwell Street	D3-E3	Gilwell Street	E4	Martin Street	E4	Rendle Street	A4-B4		
Castle Street	E2	Grand Hotel Road	B2-C2	Mayflower Street East	D5	Royal Parade	C4-D4		
Cathedral Street	A5	Grand Parade	B1	Mayflower Street West	C5	St Andrew Street	D3		
Catherine Street	D3	Great Western Road	B1	Millbay Road	A3-B3	St Andrews Cross	D4		
Cecil Street	A5-B5-B4	Green Street	E4-E5	Moon Street	E4	St James Place East	B2-B3		
Central Road	B1	Hampton Street	E5	Neswick Street	A4-A5-B5	St James Place West	B2-B3		
Chapel Street	E5	Harbour Avenue	F4	New George Street	C4-D4	Sawrey Street	A3		
Charles Cross	E4	Harwell Street	B5	New Street	E2	Southside Street	D3-E3-E2		
Charles Street	D5-E5-E4	Hastings Street	B5	North East Quay	F3-F4	Stillman Street	E3		
Citadel Road	B3-B2-C2-D2	Hastings Terrace	B5-C5	North Hill	D5-E5	Stoke Road	A4-A5		
Citadel Road East	D2-E2	Hawkers Avenue	E4-F4	North Road West	A5	Stokes Lane	E2		
Clarence Place	A4	Hetling Close	B5	North Street	E4-F4-F5	Sussex Street	D2-D3		
Cliff Road	B1-B2-C2	Hewers Row	E5	Notte Street	C3-D3	Sutton Road	F3-F4		
Cobourg Street	D5	Hill Street	E4	Octagon Street	A4	Tavistock Place	D5-E5		
Constantine Street	E5	Hoe Approach	D2-D3	Old George Street	C3	Teats Hill Road	F2		
Cornwall Street	B4-C4-D4-D5	Hoe Road	B1-C1-D1-D2	Old Town Street	D4	The Barbican	E2		
Courtenay Street	C4	Hoe Street	D2-D3	Osborne Place	C2	The Crescent	B3-C3		
Crescent Avenue	B3-C3	Hoegate Street	D2-D3	Oxford Place	C2	The Esplanade	C2		
Custom House Lane	A1-B1	Holyrood Place	C2	Oxford Street	B5-C5	The Promenade	C2-D2		
Derry's Cross	C3-C4	How Street	E3-E4	Palace Street	D3-E3	Tin Lane	E3-E4		
Devonshire Street	F5	James Street	D5	Park Terrace	F5	Tothill Avenue	F5		
Drake Circus	D5	King Street	A4-B4	Penrose Street	B5	Trafalgar Street	E5		

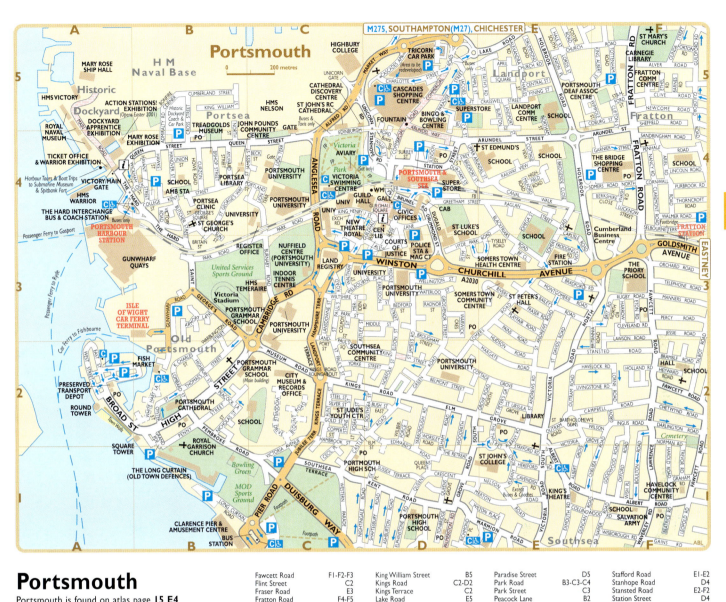

Portsmouth

Portsmouth is found on atlas page 15 E4

Admiralty Road	B4-B5	Canal Walk	E4	Fawcett Road	F1-F2-F3	King William Street	B5	Paradise Street	D5	Stafford Road	E1-E2
Albany Road	E1-E2	Carlisle Road	E3-E4	Flint Street	C2	Kings Road	C2-D2	Park Road	B3-C3-C4	Stanhope Road	D4
Albert Grove	E1-E2	Cascades Approach	D5	Fraser Road	E3	Kings Terrace	C2	Park Street	C3	Stansted Road	E2-F2
Albert Road	E2-E1-F1	Castle Road	C1-C2-D2	Fratton Road	F4-F5	Lake Road	E5	Peacock Lane	B2	Station Street	D4
Alec Rose Lane	D3-D4	Cavendish Road	E1	Garnier Street	F4	Landport Street	C3	Pelham Road	D1-D2	Stone Street	C2
Alexandra Road	E5	Charles Street	E5	Gold Street	C2	Landport Terrace	C2	Pembroke Road	B2-B1-C1	Surrey Street	D4
Alfred Road	C5	Charlotte Street	D5	Goldsmith Avenue	F3	Lansdowne Street	C2	Penhale Road	F4	Sussex Terrace	D1
Alver Road	F5	Chelsea Road	E1-F1-F2	Goodwood Road	F1-F2	Lawrence Road	F1-F2	Penny Street	B2	Telephone Road	F3
Angelsea Close	C4	Chetwynd Road	F2	Great Southsea Street	C2-D2	Lawson Road	F2-F3	Percy Road	F3	Temple Street	D5
April Square	E5	Church Road	E5-F5	Green Road	D2	Lincoln Road	F4	Pier Road	C1	The Hard	A4-B4-B3
Ariel Road	F4	Claremont Road	F4	Greetham Street	D4-E4	Little Southsea Street	C2	Playfair Road	E3	The Retreat	E5
Armory Lane	B3	Cleveland Road	F3	Grosvenor Street	D3	Livingstone Road	E2-F2	Purbrook Road	F4	The Thicket	E2
Arundel Street	D4-E4-F4	Clifton Street	F5	Grove Road North	E2	Lombard Street	B2	Queen Street	A4-B4-C4	Unicorn Road	C5-D5
Arundel Way	D4-D5	Clive Road	F5	Grove Road South	D1-D2	Long Curtain Road	B1	Queens Crescent	D1	Union Place	E5
Ashburton Road	D1	Coburg Street	E5-F5	Guildhall Square	D4	Lords Street	E5	Queens Grove	D1	Upper Arundel Street	D4-E4
Astley Street	C3	Collingwood Road	E1-F1	Guildhall Walk	C3-D4	Lorne Road	F2	Queens Place	D1	Victoria Avenue	C1-C2
Aylward Street	B4	Commercial Road	D4-D5	Gunwharf Road	B3	Lucknow Street	F4	Raglan Street	E4	Victoria Grove	E2-F2
Baileys Road	E3	Cornwall Road	F4	Hambrook Street	C2	Main Road	A4-A5	Railway View	E4	Victoria Road North	E2-E3-F3
Belmont Street	D2	Cottage Grove	D2-E2	Hampshire Terrace	C3	Manners Road	F3	Rugby Road	F3	Victoria Road South	E1-E2
Bishop Street	B4	Cottage View	E4	Hanover Street	B4	Margate Road	D2-E2	St Andrews Road	E2-E3	Victory Road	B4
Blackfriars Road	E3-E4	Crasswell Street	E5	Harold Road	F1	Market Way	C5-D5	St Davids Road	E2-E3	Vivash Road	F4
Bonfire Corner	B5	Cross Street	B4-B5	Havant Street	B4	Marmion Road	D1-E1	St Edward's Road	D1-D2	Walmer Road	F4
Boulton Road	F1-F2	Cumberland Street	B5	Havelock Road	E2-F2	Melbourne Place	C3-D3	St Faith's Road	E5	Waltham Street	C3
Bramble Road	F2	Curzon Howe Road	B4	Hawke Street	B4	Merton Road	D1-E1	Saint George's Road	B3	Warblington Street	B2-B3
Bridgeside Close	F2	Darlington Road	F2	Hereford Road	E1	Middle Street	D3	St George's Way	C4	Warwick Crescent	D3
Bridport Street	D4-E4	Dugald Drummond Street	D3-D4	High Street	B2	Milford Road	E4	St James's Road	D2-D3	Waterloo Street	D3
Britannia Road	F2-F3	Duisburg Way	C1	Highbury Street	B2	Montgomerie Road	E3	St James's Street	B4-C4	Waverley Road	F1
Britannia Road North	F3	Duncan Road	E1-F1	Holbrook Road	E5-E4-F3	Museum Road	C2	St Nicholas Street	B2	Wellington Street	D3
Broad Street	A2-B2	Durham Street	D4	Hudson Road	E2-E3	Nancy Road	F4	St Paul's Road	C3	West Street	A2
Brougham Street	D2-D3	Earlsdon Street	D3	Hyde Park Road	D3-E3-E4	Napier Road	F1	St Paul's Street	C2	Western Parade	C1
Buck Street	D4-D5	East Street	A2	Inglis Road	F2	Nelson Road	D1-E1	St Peter's Grove	E2	White Hart Lane	B2
Buriton Street	E5	Edinburgh Road	C4-D4	Isambard Brunel Road	D4	Newcome Road	F5	St Thomas's Street	B2-B3	Wickham Street	A4-B4
Burnaby Road	C3	Eldon Street	D2-D3	Jacobs Street	D5	Nightingale Road	C1	Sandringham Road	F4	Willis Street	D4
Butcher Street	B3-B4	Elm Grove	D2-E2	Jessie Road	F3	Norfolk Street	D2	Selbourne Terrace	F4	Wilson Grove	E2-F2
Cambridge Road	C3	Elphinstone Road	D1	Jubilee Terrace	C1-C2	Norman Road	F2	Shaftesbury Road	D1	Wiltshire Street	F1
Campbell Road	E2-F2	Exmouth Road	E1	Kent Road	C1-D1	North Street	B4-B5	Sheffield Road	F5	Winston Churchill Avenue	C3-E3
				Kent Street	B4	Orchard Road	F3	Silver Street	C2	Wisborough Road	F1
				King Albert Street	F5	Oxford Road	F1-F2	Slindon Street	D4	Woodpath	D1-D2
				King Charles Street	B2	Oyster Street	B2	Somers Road	D2-D3-E3-E4	Woodville Drive	C2
				King Henry I Street	C4-D4	Pains Road	E2-E3	Somers Road North	E4-E4	Yarborough Road	D2
				King Street	D2	Palmerston Road	D1	Southsea Terrace	C1	Yorke Street	C2-D2

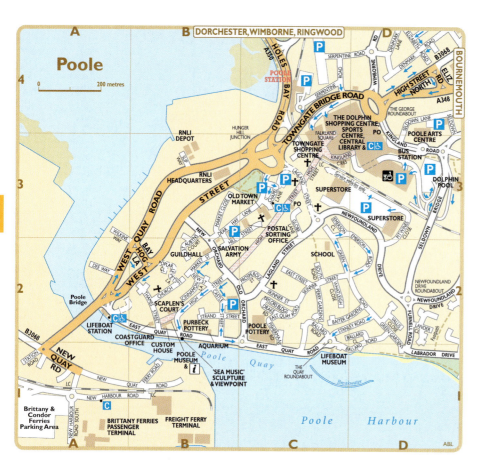

Poole

Poole is found on atlas page 12 D4

Baiter Gardens	C2-D2	Prosperous Street	C2
Ballard Close	C2-D2	St Aubyns Court	B2-B3
Ballard Road	C2-C1-D1-D2	Seldown	D4
Bay Hog Lane	B2	Seldown Bridge	D2-D3
Blandford Road	A1-A2	Seldown Lane	D3-D4
Castle Street	B2	Serpentine Road	C4-D4
Chapel Lane	C3	Skinner Street	C2
Church Street	B2	Slip Way	B3
Cinnamon Lane	B2	South Road	C2
Dear Hay Lane	B3-C3	Stanley Road	C2-D2
Dee Way	A2	Station Road	A1
Denmark Lane	D4	Sterte Road	C4
Denmark Road	D4	Strand Street	B2
Drake Road	C2	Taylors Buildings	C2
East Quay Road	A2-B2-C1-C2	Thames Street	B2
East Street	C2	Towngate Bridge Road	C3-C4-D4
Elizabeth Road	D4	Vallis Close	D2
Emerson Close	C3	West Street	A2-B2-B3-C3
Emerson Road	C3-D3-D2	West Quay Road	A2-B3
Falkland Square	C3-C4	Whatleigh Close	C2
Ferry Road	B1	Wilkins Way	A2-A3
Fishermans Road	C2	Wimborne Road	D4
Furnell Road	D2		
Globe Lane	C3		
Green Gardens	D1-D2		
Green Road	C3-C2-D2		
High Street	B2-C2-D2		
High Street North	D4		
Hill Street	B2-B3-C3		
Holes Bay Road	C4		
Kingland Crescent	C3-D3		
Kingland Road	D3-D4		
Labrador Drive	D1		
Lagland Street	C2-C3		
Lander Close	D2		
Levet's Lane	B2		
Market Close	B3		
Market Street	B2		
New Harbour Road	A1-B1		
New Harbour Road South	A1		
New Orchard	B2-B3		
New Quay Road	A1-B1		
New Street	B2		
Newfoundland Drive	C3-D3-D2		
Old Orchard	B2-C2		
Perry Gardens	C2		
Pitwines Close	D2-D3		
Poplar Close	B2		

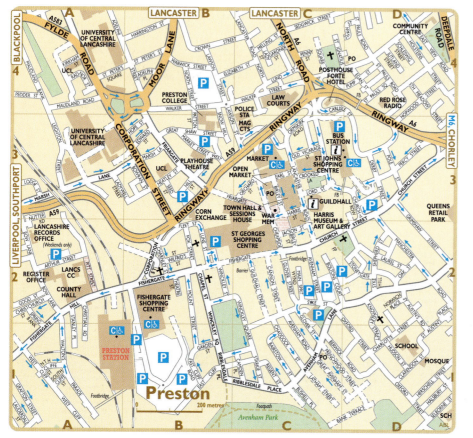

Preston

Preston is found on atlas page 88 D3

Adelphi Street	A4-B4	Jutland Street	D4
Arthur Street	A2	Knowsley Street	D1-D2
Avenham Lane	C1-C2	Ladywell Street	A3-B3
Avenham Road	C1-C2	Lancaster Road	C2-C3
Avenham Street	C2	Lancaster Road North	B4-C4
Bairstow Street	C1	Laurel Street	D2
Berwick Road	C1-D1	Lawson Street	B4-B3-C3
Bow Lane	A2	Leighton Street	A3-A4
Bowran Street	B3	Lord Street	C3
Cannon Street	C2	Lund Street	C4
Carlisle Street	C4-D4-D3	Lune Street	B3
Chaddock Street	C1-C2	Manchester Road	D2-D3
Chapel Street	B2	Market Street West	B3
Charlotte Street	D1-D2	Maudland Bank	A4
Cheapside	C2	Melling Street	C4
Christchurch Street	A2	Moor Lane	B4
Church Row	D3	Mount Street	B1-B2
Church Street	C2-D2-D3	North Road	C4
Clarendon Street	D1	North Street	B4
Corporation Street	A3-B3-B2	Oak Street	D2
Crooked Lane	C3	Old Vicarage Street	C3
Crown Street	B4-C4	Orchard Street	C3
Derby Street	D3	Ormskirk Road	C3
Earl Street	C3	Oxford Street	C2-D2-D1
East Cliff	B1	Percy Street	D3
East Cliff Road	B1	Pitt Street	A2-A3
East View Road	D4	Pole Street	D3
Egan Street	D4	Pump Street	C4-D4
Elizabeth Street	B4-C4	Ribblesdale Place	B1-C1
Fishergate	B2-C2	Ringway	B3-C4-D4-D3
Fishergate Hill	A1-A2	St Austin's Place	D1-D2
Fleet Street	B2	St Austin's Road	D1-D2
Fox Street	B2	St Ignatius Square	C4
Frenchwood Street	C1-D1	St Pauls Road	D4
Friargate	B3-C3	St Pauls Square	D4
Fylde Road	A4	St Peter's Square	A4-B4
Great Avenham Street	C1-D1	St Peter's Street	B4
Great Shaw Street	B3	Seed Street	B3
Grimshaw Street	D2-D3	Shepherd Street	D2
Guildhall Street	C2	South Meadow Street	D3-D4
Harrington Street	A4-B4	Starkie Street	C1
Harris Street	C3	Syke Street	C2
Heatley Street	B3	Walker Street	B4-C4
Herschell Street	D1	Walton's Parade	A1-A2
Hill Street	B3	Warwick Street	B4
Holsteins Street	D4	West Cliff	A1
Hopwood Street	D3-D4	Winckley Square	B1-B2-C2-C1
Jacson Street	C2	Winckley Street	B2

Ramsgate

Ramsgate is found on atlas page 31 **G2**

Abbots Hill	B3	Hardres Road	B4
Addington Street	B2	Hardres Street	B3-B4
Albert Road	C4	Hereson Road	B4
Albert Street	B2	Hibernia Street	B3-C3
Albion Place	B3-C3	High Street	A3-B3
Albion Road	C4	Hollicondane Road	A4
Alma Road	A4	King Street	B3-B4
Anns Road	A4-B4	Lawn Villas	B3
Arklow Square	B4	Leopold Street	B2-B3
Artillery Road	B4-C4	Liverpool Lawn	B2
Augusta Road	C4	London Road	A1
Avenue Road	B4	Madeira Walk	C3
Belgrave Close	A3	Margate Road	A4
Bellevue Avenue	B4	Marlborough Road	A2-B2
Bellevue Road	C4	Meeting Street	B3
Belmont Road	A3	Monkton	A3
Belmont Street	B4	Nelson Crescent	B2
Beresford Road	B2	North Avenue	A2
Boundary Road	A4-B4	Paragon Street	B1-B2
Brights Place	B4	Percy Road	A4
Broad Street	B3	Plains of Waterloo	B3-C3
Brunswick Street	B3	Priory Road	B1
Camden Road	B3	Queen Street	B2
Cannon Road	A3	Richmond Road	A2
Cannonbury Road	A1	Rose Hill	B2
Carlton Avenue	A2	Royal Crescent	B1-B2
Cavendish Street	B3	Royal Esplanade	A1-B1
Chapel Place	A3	Royal Road	B1-B2
Chatham Place	A3-A4	Ryton Road	A2
Chatham Street	A3-B3	St Augustine's Road	B1
Church Road	B3-B4	St Benedict's Lawn	B1
Codrington Road	A2	St Luke's Avenue	A4-B4
Coronation Road	A2	School Lane	B3-B4
Cottage Road	B3-C3	Spencer Square	B1-B2
Crescent Road	A2	Station Approach Road	A4
Denmark Road	B4	Sussex Street	B4
Duncan Road	A2	Townley Street	B2
Eagle Hill	A3	Truro Road	C4
Effingham Street	B3	Turner Street	B3
Elizabeth Road	C3	Upper Dumpton Park Road	A4
Ellington Road	A3	Vale Road	A2
Elms Road	B2	Vale Square	A2-B2
Finsbury Road	A4	Victoria Parade	C4
George Street	B3	Victoria Road	B4-C4
Grange Road	A1	Wellington Crescent	C3-C4
Grove Road	A2-A3	West Cliff Road	A1-A2
Harbour Parade	C3	Willsons Road	A1-A2
Harbour Street	B3-C3	York Street	B3

Reading

Reading is found on atlas page 41 **E2**

Abattoirs Road	A4	Katesgrove Lane	B1
Abbey Square	C2-C3	Kenavon Drive	D3
Abbey Street	C2-C3	Kendrick Road	C1
Abbots Walk	C3	Kennet Side	C2-D2
Addison Road	A4	Kennet Street	D2
Anstey Road	A2	Kings Meadow Road	C4
Barry Place	A4	Kings Road	C2-D2
Betam Road	D2	London Road	C1-D1-D2
Blagrave Street	B3	London Street	C1-C2
Bridge Street	B2	Meadow Road	A4
Broad Street	B2-B3	Minster Street	B2
Brook Street West	A1-B1	Mount Pleasant	C1
Cardiff Road	A4	Napier Road	C4-D4
Carey Street	A1-A2	Northfield Road	A4
Castle Street	A2-B2	Orts Road	D2
Castle Hill	A1	Oxford Road	A2
Chain Street	B2	Pell Street	B1
Chatham Street	A3	Queen Victoria Street	B3
Cheapside	A2-A3	Queens Road	C2-D2
Coley Hill	A1	Redlands Road	D1
Coley Park Road	A1	Rose Walk	B2
Coley Place	A1	Ross Road	A4
Craven Road	D1	St Giles Close	B1-C1
Cross Street	B3	St Johns Road	D2
Crossland Road	B1-C2	St Mary's Butts	B2
Crown Street	C1	Sherman Road	B1
Deansgate Road	B1	Sidmouth Street	C2-C1
Duke Street	C2	Silver Street	C1
East Street	C1-C2	Simmonds Street	B2
Eaton Place	A2-A3	South Street	C2-D2
Eldon Road	D2	Southampton Street	B1-C1
Eldon Terrace	D2	Stanshawe Road	A3
Field Road	A1	Station Road	B3
Fobney Street	B1-B2	Swan Place	B1-B2
Forbury Road	B3-C3	Swansea Road	A4
Friar Street	A3-B3	The Grove	D2
Garnet Hill	A1	Tudor Road	A3-B3
Garnet Street	A1	Union Street	B3
Garrard Street	B3	Upper Brook Street	B1
Gas Works Road	D2-D3	Valpy Street	B3-C3
George Street	C4	Vastern Road	B4
Great Knollys Street	A3	Watlington Street	D1-D2
Greyfriars Road	A3	Waylen Street	A2
Gun Street	B2	Weldale Street	A3
Henry Street	B1	West Street	A3-B2
Hill Street	B1	Wolseley Street	A1
Howard Street	A2	York Road	A4
Jesse Terrace	A1-A2	Zinzan Street	A2

219

St Andrews
Scarborough

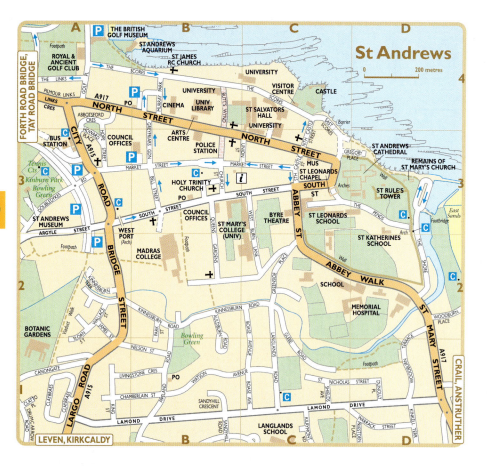

St Andrews
St Andrews is found on atlas page **141 E1**

Abbey Street	C2-C3	St Nicholas Street	C1-D1
Abbey Walk	C2-D2	Sandyhill Crescent	B1
Abbotsford Crescent	A4	Sandyhill Road	B1
Argyle Street	A2-A3	Shields Avenue	C1
Auldburn Road	B1-B2	Sloan Street	A1-A2
Bell Street	B3	South Castle Street	C3
Boase Avenue	C1-C2	South Street	A3-B3-C3
Bridge Street	A1-A2-A3	The Links	A4
Butts Wynd	B4	The Pends	C3-D3
Canongate	A1	The Scores	A4-B4-C4
Chamberlain Street	A1-B1	The Shore	D2-D3
Church Street	B3	Union Street	B3-C3
City Road	A3-A4	Wallace Street	A2
Clatto Place	A1	Warrack Street	C1-D1
Claybraes	A1	Watson Avenue	B1-C1
Doubledykes Road	A3	West Burn Lane	C2-C3
Drumcarrow Road	A1	Woodburn Place	D2
Dunolly Place	D1	Woodburn Terrace	D1-D2
East Scores	C3-C4		
Glebe Road	C1-C2		
Golf Place	A4		
Greenside Place	C2		
Gregory Place	C3-D3		
Greyfriars Garden	B3-B4		
Hope Street	A3-A4		
Howard Place	A3-A4		
James Street	A1-A2		
Kilrymont Road	C1		
King Street	A1		
Kinkell Terrace	D1		
Kinnessburn Road	A2-B2-C2		
Kinnessburn Terrace	A2		
Lamond Drive	A1-B1-C1-D1		
Langlands Road	C1-C2		
Largo Road	A1		
Links Crescent	A4		
Livingstone Crescent	A1-B1		
Market Street	A3-B3-C3		
Murray Park	B4		
Nelson Street	A1-B1		
North Castle Street	C3-C4		
North Street	A4-B4-B3-C3		
Park Street	B1-B2		
Pilmour Links	A4		
Pipeland Road	B1-B2		
Priestden Road	D1		
Queens Gardens	B2-B3		
St Mary Street	D1-D2		

Scarborough
Scarborough is found on atlas page **99 F4**

Aberdeen Walk	A2-B2	Peasholm Crescent	A3-A4
Albemarle Crescent	A1-A2	Peasholm Drive	A4
Albert Road	B3-B4	Princess Street	C3
Alma Square	A1-A2	Prospect Road	A2
Auborough Street	B3	Quay Street	D2
Bar Street	B2	Queen Street	B2-B3
Barwick Street	A1-A2	Queens Parade	A4-B4-B3
Bedford Street	B2	Queens Terrace	B3
Bellevue Parade	A1	Ramshill Road	B1
Bellevue Street	A1	Rutland Terrace	B3-C3
Brook Street	A2	St Mary's Street	C3
Cambridge Street	A2	St Marys Walk	C3
Castle Road	A2-B2-B3-C3	St Nicholas Street	B1-B2
Castlegate	C3-D3	St Sepulchre Street	C2-C3
Church Lane	C3	St Thomas Street	B2-B3
Clark Street	B3	Sandringham Street	A3-B3
Cliff Bridge Terrace	B1	Sandside	C2-D2
Columbus Ravine	A3-A4	Sherwood Street	A1
Cooks Row	C3	Somerset Terrace	A1-B1
Cross Street	B3-B2-C2	Springfield	C2-C3
Dean Road	A2-A3	Sussex Street	B2
Durham Street	A3-B3	Tennyson Avenue	A3-A4
Eastborough	C2	The Crescent	B1
Elders Street	B2	Tindall Street	A1
Falconer's Road	B1	Tollergate	B3-C3
Falsgrave Road	A1	Trafalgar Road	A3-A4
Foreshore Road	B1-C1-C2	Trafalgar Square	A3-B3
Friargate	C2-C3	Trafalgar Street West	A2-A3
Friars Way	B3	Union Street	A2-B2
Graham Close	C3	Valley Bridge Road	A1-B1
Hanover Road	A1	Valley Road	B1
Hope Street	B3	Vernon Road	B1-B2
Hoxton Road	A2	Victoria Park	A4
James Street	A3-B3	Victoria Park Avenue	A4
King Street	B2	Victoria Road	A1-A2
Langdale Road	A3	Victoria Street	A2
Longwestgate	B3-C3	Vine Street	B2
Marlborough Street	B3	Westborough	B1-B2
Melrose Street	A2	Woodall Avenue	A4
Moorland Road	A3-A4	Wrea Lane	A3
Nelson Street	A2	York Place	B1
New Queen Street	B3		
Newborough	B2-C2		
North Marine Road	A4-B4-B3		
North Street	B2-B3		
North Way	A2		
Oxford Street	A3-B2		
Paradise	C3		

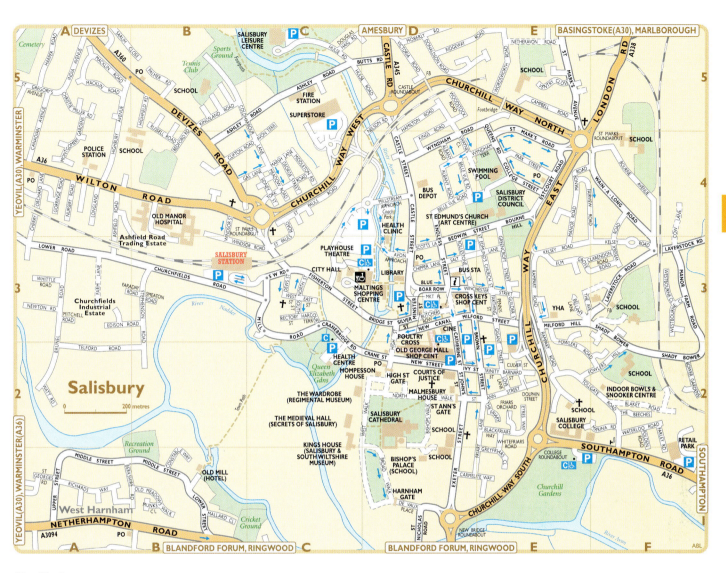

Salisbury

Salisbury is found on atlas page **25 G2**

Albany Road	D4	Churchill Way South	D1-E1	Gorringe Road	A4	Mitchell Road	A3	Shady Bower	F2-F3
Ashfield Road	A3-A4	Churchill Way West	C4-C5-D5	Greencroft Street	E3-E4	Moberly Road	D5	Sidney Street	C4
Ashley Road	B4-B5-C5	Clarendon Road	E3-F3	Greyfriars Close	E1	Montgomery Gardens	A4-A5	Silver Street	D3
Avon Approach	D3	Clifton Road	B4-C4	Guilder Street	E3	Munks Close	B1	Smeaton Road	B3
Avon Terrace	C4-C5	Coldharbour Lane	B5-C4	Hamilton Road	D4-D5	Nelson Road	D4-D5	South Street	C3
Barnard Street	E2	College Street	E4	Harcourt Terrace	C3	Netheravon Road	E5	South West Road	C3
Bedford Road	B4	Constable Way	B1	Harper Road	A5	Netherhampton Road	A1-B1	Southampton Road	E2-E1-F1
Bedwin Street	D3-D4-E4	Cow Lane	F3-F4	High Street	D2-D3	New Canal	D3	Stephenson Road	B2-B3
Bellamy Lane	E3	Crane Street	D2	Highbury Avenue	A4-A5	New Street	D2	Swaynes Close	D4
Belle Vue Road	D4	Cranebridge Road	C2-C3	Highfield Road	B5	Newton Road	A3	Telford Road	A2-B2
Berkshire Road	A1-B1	Culver Street	E2	Hulse Road	C5-D5	North Street	C3	The Avenue	E3
Bishops Walk	D1-D2	De Vaux Place	D1	India Avenue	A5	North Walk	D2	The Beeches	F2
Blackfriars Way	E2	Devizes Road	A5-B5-B4-C4	Ivy Street	D2	Nursery Road	A4	The Friary	E2
Blakey Road	F2	Dews Street	C3	Kelsey Road	E3-F3	Old Meadows Walk	B1	Tollgate Road	E2-F2-F1
Blue Boar Row	D3	Dolphin Street	E2	Kings Road	D4-D5	Palmer Road	B5	Trinity Street	E2
Bourne Avenue	F4	Donaldson Road	D5-E5	Kingsland Road	B5	Park Street	E4	Upper Street	A1
Bourne Hill	E4	Douglas Haig Road	C5-D5	Laverstock Road	F3	Pennyfarthing Street	E3	Ventry Close	E5
Bower Gardens	F2	East Street	C3	London Road	E4-F5	Polden Road	F1-F2	Victoria Road	D5
Bridge Street	D3	Edison Road	A3-B3	Longland	A4	Queens Road	E4	Wain a Long Road	F3-F4
Broad Walk	D1	Elm Grove Road	E3-F3	Love Lane	E2	Rampart Road	E2-E3	Waterloo Road	F2
Brown Street	D3-E2	Endless Street	D3-D4	Lower Road	A3	Rectory Street	C3	Watt Road	A2
Brunel Road	A2-A3	Estcourt Road	E4	Lower Street	B1	Richards Way	A1	Wessex Road	F3-F4
Butchers Row	D3	Exeter Street	D1-D2	Macklin Road	A5	Ridgeway Road	D5-E5	West Street	C3
Butts Road	C5-D5	Eyres Way	E2	Mallard Close	B1	Rollerstone Street	D3	West Walk	D1-D2
Campbell Road	E5	Fairview Road	E4-E3-F3	Manor Farm Road	F3	Russell Road	B4-B5	Westbourne Close	F3
Canadian Avenue	A4-A5	Faraday Road	A3-B3	Manor Road	E3-E4	St Ann Street	D2-E2	Whitefriars Road	E1-E2
Carmelite Way	D1-E1	Farley Road	F1-F2	Marina Road	F2	St Edmund's Church Street	E3	Whittle Road	A3
Castle Road	D5	Farm Lane	A3	Marsh Lane	C4	St Georges Road	A1	Wilton Road	A4-B4-C4
Castle Street	D3-D4-D5	Fisherton Street	C3	Meadow Road	C4	St Gregory's Avenue	A5	Winchester Street	D3-E3
Catherine Street	D2-D3	Fowlers Hill	E2-F2	Middle Street	A1-B1	St John's Street	D2	Windsor Road	B3-C3
Cherry Orchard Lane	A3-A4	Fowlers Road	E3-E2-F2	Middleton Road	C4	St Mark's Avenue	E5	Windsor Street	B3-B4
Chipper Lane	D3	Friars Orchard	E2	Milford Lane	E3	St Mary's Road	E4	Woodstock Road	D5
Christie Miller Road	A5	Friary Lane	D1-E1-E2	Milford Street	D3-E3	St Nicholas Road	D1	Wordsworth Road	E5
Churchfields Road	B3-C3	Gas Lane	B4-C4	Mill Road	C3	St Pauls Road	C3-C4	Wyndham Road	D4-E5
Churchill Way East	E2-E3-E4	George Street	C4	Millstream Approach	D4	Salt Lane	D3-E3	Wyndham Terrace	D4-E4
Churchill Way North	D5-E5-E4	Gigant Street	E2-E3	Minster Street	D3	Scotts Lane	D3	York Road	C4

Sheffield

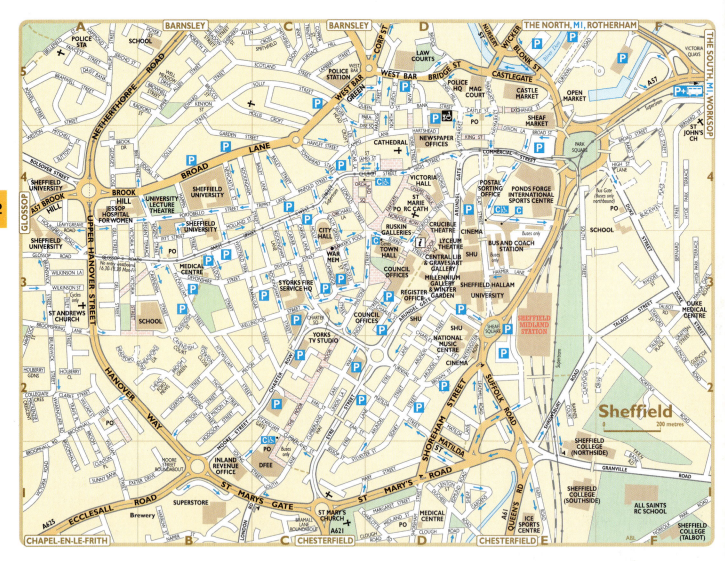

Sheffield

Sheffield is found on atlas page **84 A3**

Allen Street	B5-C5		Carver Lane	C3-C4		Egerton Street	B2		Holberry Close	A2		Nursery Street	D5-E5		Suffolk Road	E2
Arundel Gate	D2-D3-D4		Carver Street	C3-C4		Eldon Street	B3		Holberry Gardens	A2		Old Street	F4		Sunny Bank	A1
Arundel Lane	D2		Castle Street	D5-E5		Ellis Street	B5		Holland Street	B4		Orchard Lane	C4		Surrey Street	D3
Arundel Street	C1-D1-D2-D3		Castlegate	E5		Exchange Street	E5		Hollis Croft	B5-C5		Orchard Square	C4-D4		Sutton Street	A4
Bailey Lane	C4		Cavendish Court	B2		Exeter Drive	A1-B1		Holly Street	C3-C4		Paradise Square	C5-D5		Sylvester Street	C1-D1
Bailey Street	C4		Cavendish Street	B3		Eyre Lane	C1-C2-D2-D3		Hounsfield Road	A3-A4		Paradise Street	D4-D5		Talbot Place	F2-F3
Balm Green	C3-C4		Chapel Walk	D4		Eyre Street	C1-C2-D2		Hyde Park Terrace	F3, F3-F4		Park Square	E4-F4		Talbot Road	F3
Bank Street	D5		Charles Street	D2-D3		Fargate	D4		Jericho Street	A5-B5		Paternoster Row	D2		Talbot Street	F3
Bard Street	F4		Charlotte Road	C1-D1		Farm Bank Road	F1		Jessop Street	C1		Pinfold Street	C4		The Moor	C2
Barker's Pool	C3		Charter Row	C2-C3		Farm Road	E1		Kenyon Street	B5		Pinstone Street	C3-D3		Thomas Street	B2
Barnes Court	E2		Charter Square	C3		Fawcett Street	A5		King Street	D4-E4		Pitt Street	B3		Townhead Street	C4
Beet Street	A4-B4		Church Street	C4-D4		Fitzwilliam Gate	C2		Lambert Street	C5		Portobello Street	A4-B4		Trafalgar Street	B3-C3-C2
Bellefield Street	A5		Clarke Street	A2		Fitzwilliam Street	B3-B2-C2		Leadmill Road	D2-E2		Powell Street	A5		Travis Place	A2
Bernard Street	F3-F4-F5		Claywood Drive	E2-F2		Flat Street	D4-E3		Leavygreave Road	A4		Queen Street	C5-D5		Trinity Street	C5
Blackwell Place	F4		Clinton Place	A1		Furnace Hill	C5		Lee Croft	C4		Queen's Road	E1		Trippet Lane	C4
Blonk Street	E5		Clough Road	C1-D1		Furnival Road	E5-F5		Lenton Street	D1		Radford Street	A5-B5		Tudor Square	D3-D4
Bolsover Street	A4		Collegiate Crescent	A2		Furnival Street	D2		Leopold Street	C4		Regent Street	B3-B4		Union Lane	C2
Bramwell Street	A5		Commercial Street	E4		Garden Street	B5-B4-C4		London Road	B1-C1		Regent Terrace	B3-B4		Union Street	C3-D3
Bridge Street	D5		Copper Street	C5		Gell Street	A3-A4		Mackenzie Crescent	A2		Rhodes Street	F3		Upper Allen Street	B4-B5
Broad Lane	B4-C4		Corporation Street	D5		George Street	D4		Manor Oaks Road	F3		Rockingham Lane	C3-C4		Upper Hanover Street	A3-A4
Broad Street	E4, F4-F5		Cross Smithfield	B5-C5		Glencoe Drive	F2		Mappin Street	B3-B4		Rockingham Street	B4-C4-C3-C2		Vicar Lane	C4
Brocco Street	B5		Cumberland Street	C1-C2		Glencoe Road	F2		Margaret Street	D1		St George's Close	A4		Victoria Road	A1
Brook Drive	A4		Cumberland Way	C1-C2		Glossop Road	A3-B3		Mary Street	C1-D1		St James Street	C4-D4		Victoria Street	A3-A4
Brook Hill	A4		Daisy Bank	A5		Grafton Street	F2-F3		Matilda Lane	D2		St Mary's Gate	B1-C1		Waingate	E5
Broom Green	B2		Devonshire Street	B3		Granville Road	E1-F1		Matilda Street	C2-D2-D1		St Mary's Road	C1-D1		Well Meadow Drive	B5
Broom Street	A1-A2		Division Street	C3		Hammond Street	A5		Meadow Street	B5		St Philip's Street	A5		Wellington Street	B3-C3
Broomhall Place	A1		Dixon Lane	E4		Hanover Way	A2-B2-B1		Midland Street	D1		Scotland Street	B5-C5		West Bar	D5
Broomhall Road	A1-A2		Dover Street	A5-B5		Harmer Lane	E3		Milton Lane	B2		Sheaf Gardens	D1-E1		West Bar Green	C5
Broomhall Street	A2		Duchess Road	D1-E1		Harrow Street	B1		Milton Street	B2-C2		Shepherd Street	B5		West Street	B3-C4
Broomspring Lane	A3		Duke Street	F2-F3-F4		Hartshead	D4		Mitchell Street	A4		Shoreham Street	D1-D2		Westfield Terrace	B3
Brown Street	D2		Earl Street	C2-D2		Havelock Street	A2-A3		Moore Street	B1-B2-C2		Shrewsbury Road	E2		Weston Street	A4-A5
Brownell Street	B5		Earl Way	C2		Hawley Street	C4		Morpeth Street	B5		Siddall Street	B4		Wharncliffe Road	A2
Brunswick Street	A2-A3		Ecclesall Road	A1-B1		Haymarket	D4-D5, E4-E5		Napier Street	B1		Sidney Street	D2		Wilkinson Lane	A3
Burgess Street	C3		Edmund Road	D1		Headford Gardens	A2-B2		Netherthorpe Road	A4-A5-B5		Silver Street Head	C5		Wilkinson Street	A3
Cambridge Street	C3		Edward Street	B5		Headford Grove	B2		New Street	D5		Smithfield	C5		William Street	A1-A2
Campo Lane	C4-D4		Egerton Close	B2		Headford Mews	B2		Newcastle Street	B4		Snig Hill	D5		York Street	D4
						Headford Street	B2		Norfolk Park Road	F1		Snow Lane	C5		Young Street	B1-C1
						High Street	D4		Norfolk Road	F2		Solly Street	B4-B5-C5			
						High Street Lane	F4		Norfolk Row	D4		South Lane	C1			
						Hodgson Street	B1-B2		Norfolk Street	D3-D4		South Street	E3-E4			
									North Church Street	D4-D5		Stafford Street	F3			

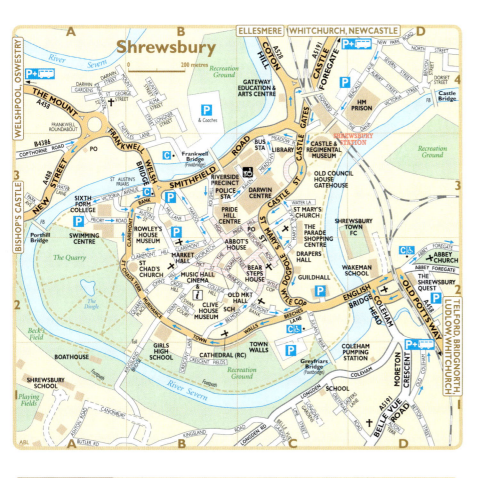

Shrewsbury

Shrewsbury is found on atlas page **69 G1**

Abbey Foregate	D2	Mardol	B3
Albert Street	D4	Market Street	B2
Alma Street	B4	Meadow Place	C3
Alton Terrace	D1	Moreton Crescent	D1
Ashton Road	A1	Mount Street	A4-B4
Beacalls Lane	C4-D4	Murivance	B2
Beeches Lane	C2	Nettles Lane	A4-B3-B4
Belle Vue Gardens	C1	New Park Road	D4
Belle Vue Road	D1	New Street	A3
Belmont	B2-C2	North Street	D4
Belmont Bank	C2	Old Coleham	D1
Benyon Street	D4	Old Potts Way	D1-D2
Betton Street	D1	Park Avenue	A3
Butchers Row	C2-C3	Pride Hill	B3-C3
Butler Road	A1	Princess Street	B2-C2
Canonbury	A1-B1	Priory Road	A3-B3
Castle Foregate	C4	Quarry Place	B2
Castle Gates	C3-C4	Raven Meadows	B3-C3
Castle Street	C3	Roushill	B3
Claremont Bank	B2-B3	St Austin's Friars	A3
Claremont Hill	B2	St Austin's Street	B3
Claremont Street	B2	St Chads Terrace	B2
Coleham Head	D2	St George Street	A4-B4
College Hill	B2	St John's Hill	B2
Copthorne Road	A3	St Julian's Friar	C1-C2
Coton Hill	C4	St Mary's Place	C2-C3
Crescent Fields	B1	St Mary's Street	C2-C3
Crescent Lane	B1-B2	Salters Lane	C1-D1
Cross Hill	B2	Severn Street	D4
Darwin Gardens	A4	Shoplatch	B2
Darwin Street	A4	Smithfield Road	B3-C3-C4
Dogpole	C2	Swan Hill	B2
Dorset Street	D4	Swan Hill Court	B2
Drinkwater Street	A4	The Dana	C4-D4
English Bridge	C2-D2	The Mount	A4
Frankwell	A4-A3-B3	The Square	B2
Greyfriars Road	C1-D1	Town Walls	B2-B1-C2
High Street	B3-B2-C2	Victoria Avenue	A3-B3
Hill Lane	B3	Victoria Street	D4
Howard Street	C4	Water Lane	A3
Hunter Street	B4	Water Lane	C3
Kingsland Bridge	A1-B1-B2	Welsh Bridge	B3
Kingsland Road	B1-C1	Wyle Cop	C2
Lime Street	C1		
Longden Coleham	C1-D1		
Longden Gardens	C1		
Longden Road	B1-C1		
Longner Street	B4		

Southend-on-Sea

Southend-on-Sea is found on atlas page **30 B5**

Albert Road	C2	London Road	A3
Alexandra Road	A2	Lucy Road	C1
Alexandra Street	A2-B2	Luker Road	A3
Ambleside Drive	D3	Marine Parade	C1-D1
Ash Walk	C2	Marks Court	D1
Ashburnham Road	A2-A3	Milton Street	B4
Baltic Avenue	B2	Napier Avenue	A3
Baxter Avenue	A4	Nelson Mews	A2
Beresford Road	D1	Nelson Street	A2
Boscombe Road	C4-D4	Oban Road	D4
Bournemouth Park Road	C4-D4	Old Southend Road	D2
Cambridge Road	A2	Outing Close	D2
Capel Terrace	A2	Pier Hill	B1-C1
Chancellor Road	B2-C2	Pleasant Road	C2-C1-D1
Cheltenham Road	D2-D3	Portland Avenue	B2-C2
Chichester Road	B2-B3-B4	Prittlewell Square	A1-A2
Christchurch Road	D4	Quebec Avenue	B3-C3
Church Road	B1-B2	Queen's Road	A3
Clarence Road	A2	Queensway	A4-B4-C2-D2
Clarence Street	A2-B2	Royal Mews	B1
Clifftown Parade	A1	St Ann's Road	B4
Clifftown Road	A2-B2	St Leonards Road	C2
Coleman Street	B4-C4	Scratton Road	A2
College Way	A3	Short Street	A4-B4
Cromer Road	C2-C3	Southchurch Avenue	D1-D2-D3
Devereux Road	A1-A2	Southchurch Road	B3-C3-C4-D2
Elmer Avenue	A3	Stanley Road	C2-D2
Eastern Esplanade	D1	Sutton Road	C4
Essex Street	B4	Toledo Road	C2-C3
Ferndown Close	D4	Tylers Avenue	B2
Fowler Close	D3	Tyrrel Drive	C3
Gordon Place	A2-A3	Victoria Avenue	A4
Gordon Road	A3	Warrior Square East	B3
Great Eastern Avenue	A4	Warrior Square	B3
Guildford Road	B4	Wesley Road	B3
Hamlet Road	A2	Western Esplanade	A1-B1
Hartington Place	C1	Weston Road	A2-B2
Hartington Road	C1-C2	Whitegate Road	B3
Hastings Road	C2-C3	Wimborne Road	C4-D4
Herbert Grove	C1-C2	Windermere Road	D3
Heygate Avenue	B2-C2	Woodgrange Drive	D2
High Street	A3-B3-B2-B1	York Road	B2-C2-D2
Hillcrest Road	C3		
Honiton Road	D2-D3		
Kilworth Avenue	C3-D3		
Kursaal Way	D1-D2		
Lancaster Gardens	C3		
Leamington Road	D2-D3		

223

Southampton

Southampton

Southampton is found on atlas page 14 B5

Above Bar Street	C3-C4-C5	Coleman Street	D3-E3	John Street	D1-D2	Platform Road	C1-D1	West Park Road	B4-B5
Albert Road North	E2	College Street	D2	Kent Street	F5	Porters Lane	C1	West Quay Road	A4-A3-B3-B2
Albert Road South	E1-E2	Commercial Road	A5-B5-C5	King Street	D2	Portland Street	C3	West Street	C2
Alexandra Road	A5	Cook Street	D3	Kings Park Road	C5	Portland Terrace	B3-B4	Western Esplanade	A4-B4, B2-B3
Andersons Road	E2	Cossack Green	C4-D4	Kingsway	D3-D4	Pound Tree Road	C3	William Street	F5
Anglesea Terrace	E2	Crosshouse Road	E2-F2	Latimer Street	D1-D2	Queens Terrace	D1	Wilson Street	E4-E5
Argyle Road	D5-E5	Cumberland Place	B5-C5	Lime Street	D2	Queensway	C1-C2	Winkle Street	C1
Ascupart Street	D4	Derby Road	E4-E5	London Road	C5	Radcliffe Road	E5	Winton Street	C4-D4
Augustine Road	E5	Devonshire Road	B5	Lower Canal Walk	C1	Richmond Street	D2	Wyndham Place	A4-A5
Back of the Walls	C1-C2	Duke Street	D2	Mandela Way	A5	Roberts Road	A5	York Close	F5
Bargate Street	C3	Durnford Road	E5	Marine Parade	E3	Rochester Street	E4-F4		
Bedford Place	C5	East Park Terrace	C4-C5	Market Place	C2	Royal Crescent Road	E1-E2		
Belvidere Road	E3-E4-F4-F5	East Street	C2-D2-D3	Marsh Lane	D2	St Albans Road	E5		
Belvidere Terrace	F5	Eastgate Street	C2	Maryfield	D2	St Andrews Road	C5-D5-D4		
Bernard Street	C2-D2	Elm Terrace	E2	Melbourne Street	E3	St Marks Road	D5		
Blechynden Terrace	A4-B4	Endle Street	E2	Millbank Street	F5	St Mary Street	D3-D4		
Bond Street	F5	Exmoor Road	D5	Morris Road	A5-B5	St Marys Road	D5		
Brintons Road	D4-D5	Fitzhugh Street	B4	Mountbatten Way	A4	St Michaels Street	C2		
Britannia Road	E4-E5	Floating Bridge Road	E1-F1	Neptune Way	D1	Saltmarsh Road	E1-E2		
Briton Street	C1	French Street	C1	New Road	C4-D4	Shirley Road	A4-A5		
Broad Green	D4	Golden Grove	D4-E4-E3	Newcombe Road	B5	South Front	C3-D3-D4		
Brunswick Place	C5	Granville Street	E3	Nichols Road	D5	Southbrook Road	A4		
Brunswick Square	C1-C2	Grosvenor Square	B5	North Front	C4-D4	Southern Road	A4		
Bugle Street	B1-C2	Hamtun Street	C2	Northam Road	D4-E4-E5-F5	Standford Street	E3		
Canal Walk	C2	Handel Road	B5	Northbrook Road	D5	Sussex Road	C4		
Canute Road	D1-E1	Handel Terrace	A5-B5	Northumberland Road	E4-E5	Terminus Terrace	D1-D2		
Captains Place	D2	Hanover Buildings	C3	Ocean Way	D1-E1	The Polygon	B5		
Castle Way	B3-C3-C2-C1	Harbour Parade	A4-B4-B3-B2	Ogle Road	B3-C4	The Square	C4		
Central Bridge	D2-E2	Hartington Road	E5	Orchard Lane	C2-D2	Threefield Lane	D2		
Central Station Bridge	A4	Havelock Road	B4-B5	Orchard Place	C1-D1-D2	Town Quay	B1-C1		
Channel Way	E1	Herbert Walker Avenue	B2	Oxford Avenue	D5-E5	Trinity Road	D5		
Chapel Road	D3-E3	High Street	C1-C2-C3	Oxford Street	D1-D2	Upper Bugle Street	C2		
Charlotte Place	C5	Hill Lane	A5	Paget Street	E2-E3	Victoria Street	E4		
Civic Centre Road	B4-C4	Houndwell Place	C3-D3	Palmerston Road	C3-C4	Vincents Walk	C3		
Clifford Street	D4	Itchen Bridge	E2-F2	Park Walk	C4-C5	Waterloo Terrace	C5		
Clovelly Road	D5-E5	James Street	D3-E3	Peel Street	E4-F5	West Marlands Road	C4-C5		

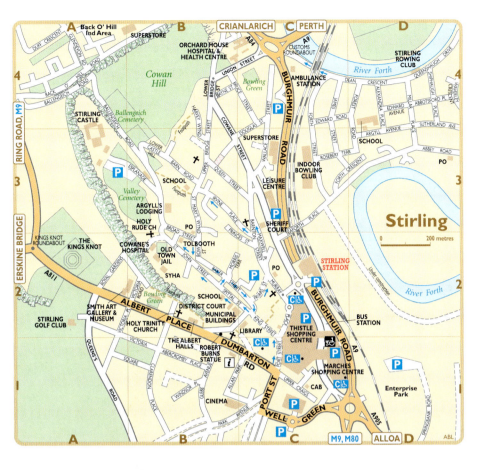

Stirling

Stirling is found on atlas page **130 D4**

Abbey Road	D3	Roseberry Terrace	C3-D3
Abbotsford Place	D4	Royal Gardens	A2
Abercromby Place	B1	St John Street	B2
Albert Place	A2-B2	St Mary's Wynd	B2-B3
Alexandra Place	D4	Seaforth Place	C2-C3
Allan Park	B1-C1	Shiphaugh Place	D4
Argyll Avenue	D3-D4	Spittal Street	B2-C2
Back O' Hill Road	A4-B4	Springbank Road	D1
Baker Street	B2-C2	Sutherland Avenue	D4
Ballengeich Road	A4-A3-B3	Union Street	B4-C4
Barn Road	B3	Upper Bridge Street	B3-B4
Barnton Street	C2-C3	Upper Craigs	C1
Bayne Street	B4	Victoria Place	A2-B2
Bow Street	B2	Victoria Road	B2
Broad Street	B2-B3	Victoria Square	A1-B1
Bruce Street	B4-C4	Wallace Street	C3-C4
Burghmuir Road	C4-C2-D1	Waverley Crescent	D4
Clarendon Place	B1-B2	Well Green	C1
Cowane Street	B4-B3-C3	Windsor Place	B1
Dean Crescent	C4-D4		
Douglas Street	B3-C4		
Duff Crescent	A4		
Dumbarton Road	B1-C1		
Edward Avenue	D4		
Edward Road	C4		
Esplanade	A3-B3		
Forest Road	D3-D4		
Forth Crescent	C3-D3		
Forth Street	C3-C4		
Friars Street	C2		
Glebe Avenue	B1		
Glendevon Road	A4		
Harvey Wynd	B3-B4		
Irvine Place	B3-C2		
James Street	C3-C4		
King Street	C2		
Lower Bridge Street	B4		
Lower Castle Hill	B3		
Maxwell Place	C2-C3		
Millar Place	D3-D4		
Morris Terrace	B2		
Murray Place	C2		
Park Avenue	B1-C1		
Port Street	C1		
Princes Street	B3-B2-C2		
Queen Street	B3-C3		
Queenshaugh Drive	D4		
Queen's Road	A1-A2		

Stockton-on-Tees

Stockton-on-Tees is found on atlas page **106 D3**

Allison Street	B4	Outram Street	A1
Alma Street	B4	Oxbridge Lane	A1
Bath Lane	B4-C4	Palmerston Street	A3
Bedford Street	A4	Park Road	A1
Bishop Street	B3-C3	Parkfield Road	B1
Bishopton Lane	A4-B4	Parkfield Way	B1
Bishopton Road	A4	Parliament Street	A1-B1
Boathouse Lane	C1	Petch Street	A3
Bowesfield Lane	A1-B1	Phoenix Sidings	A4
Bridge Road	B1-B2	Portrack Lane	C4-D4
Bright Street	B3	Prince Regent Street	B2-B3
Brunswick Street	B2	Princess Avenue	B4-C4
Buchanan Street	A1-A2	Princeton Drive	D1
Chalk Close	B1	Radcliffe Crescent	D1-D2
Chapel Street	D1	Riverside	B1-C1-C2-C3
Church Road	B3-C3-C4-D4	Russell Street	B3
Claremont Court	D1	Ryan Avenue	C4
Clarence Row	C4	St Bernard Road	A2
Columbia Drive	C2-C3	St Johns Close	A4-B4
Commercial Street	C3	Shaftesbury Street	A1
Corporation Street	A3-A4	Silver Street	B3
Council of Europe Boulevard	C2-C3	Skinner Street	B2
Cromwell Avenue	B4-C4	Smith Street	B3-B4
Derby Street	A3	Stamp Street	A3-A4
Dixon Street	A3	Stanford Close	D1
Dovecot Street	A2-B2-B3	Station Street	D1
Durham Road	A4	Sydney Street	A3-B3
Durham Street	A4	Tarring Street	A2-A3
Edward Street	A1	The Square	B3-C3
Egglestone Terrace	A2	Thistle Green	B3-C3
Ewbank Drive	A2	Tower Street	B2-C2
Finkle Street	B2	Union Street East	C4
Frederick Street	B4	University Boulevard	C2-D2
Fudan Way	D2	Vasser Way	C2
Garbutt Street	B4-C4	Vicarage Avenue	A4
Hartington Road	A2-B2	Vicarage Street	A4
Harvard Avenue	D1-D2	Wade Avenue	C4
High Street	B2-B3-B4	Webster Close	A2
Hume Street	B3	Wellington Street	A3-B3
Hutchison Street	A3	West Row	B2-B3
Lawrence Street	A1	Westbourne Street	A1
Limeoak Way	D4	Westpoint Road	C2-D2
Mandale Road	D1	William Street	B2
Maritime Road	C4	Woodland Street	A1
Massey Road	D2-D3	Worthing Street	A2
Melbourne Street	A3	Yale Crescent	C1-D1-D2
Mill Street West	A3-B3	Yarm Lane	A1-B2
Norton Road	B4	Yarm Road	A1

Stoke-on-Trent (Hanley)
Stratford-upon-Avon

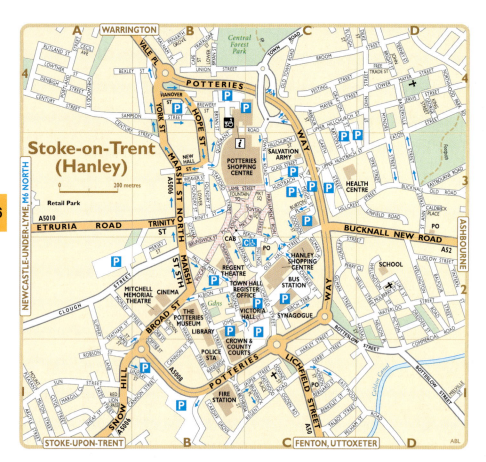

Stoke-on-Trent (Hanley)

Stoke-on-Trent (Hanley) is found on atlas page **70 D5**

Albion Street	B2	Lower Bethesda Street	B1-C1
Bagnall Street	B2	Lower Foundry Street	B3
Balfour Street	D2	Lower Mayer Street	D4
Baskerville Street	D3-D4	Lowther Street	A4
Berkeley Street	C1	Margill Close	A1
Bethesda Street	B1-B2	Market Lane	B3-C3
Birch Terrace	C2	Market Square	C3
Botteslow Street	C2-D1	Marsh Street North	B2-B3
Brewery Street	B4	Marsh Street South	B2
Broad Street	B2	Mayer Street	C4-D4
Broom Street	C4-D4	Meigh Street	C3
Brunswick Street	B2-B3	Morley Street	A2-B2
Bryan Street	B3-B4	Mynors Street	D3-D4
Bucknall New Road	C3-D3-D2	New Hall Street	B3
Bucknall Old Road	D3	Old Hall Street	C2-C3
Cannon Street	A1-B1	Old Town Road	C4
Century Street	A4-B3	Pall Mall	B2
Charles Street	C2	Parliament Row	C3
Cheapside	B2	Percy Street	B3-C3-C2
Clough Street	A2-B2	Piccadilly	B2-B3
Clyde Street	A1	Picton Street	D1-D2
Commercial Road	D1-D2	Portland Street	A4
Denbigh Street	A4	Potteries Way	B1-C2-C4-B4
Derby Street	C1-C2	Quadrant Road	B3-B4-C4
Dresden Street	D2	Regent Road	B1-C1
Eastwood Road	C1-D1	Robson Street	A1
Eaton Street	D3-D4	St Ann Street	D3
Etruria Road	A3	St John Street	D3-D4
Festing Street	C4-D4	Sampson Street	A4-B4
Foundry Street	B3	Slippery Lane	A1-A2
Fountain Square	B3-B2	Snow Hill	A1
Garth Street	C3	Stafford Street	B3-B2-C2
Gilman Street	C2-D2	Statham Street	A1-A2
Gitana Street	B2-B3	Sun Street	A1
Glass Street	C3	Talbot Street	C1
Goodson Street	C3	Tontine Street	C2-C3
Grafton Street	C3-C4	Town Road	C3-C4
Hanover Street	B4	Trinity Street	B3
Hillchurch Street	C3	Union Street	B4-C4
Hillcrest Street	C3-D3	Upper Hillchurch Street	C3-C4-D4
Hope Street	B3-B4	Upper Huntbach Street	C3-D3
Hordley Street	C2-D2	Vale Place	B4
Huntbach Street	C3	Warner Street	B1-B2
Jervis Street	D4	Waterloo Street	D2
John Bright Street	D4	Wellington Road	D2
John Street	B2-C2	Wells Street	C2-D2
Lamb Street	B3-C3	Yates Street	A1
Lichfield Street	C1-C2	York Street	B3-B4

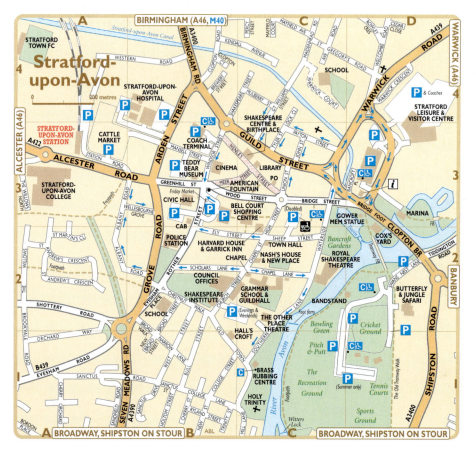

Stratford-upon-Avon

Stratford-upon-Avon is found on atlas page **47 G5**

Albany Road	A3-A2-B2	New Street	B1
Alcester Road	A3-B3	Old Town	B2-B1-C1
Arden Street	B3-B4	Orchard Way	A1-A2
Avenue Road	C4	Payton Street	C3
Bancroft Place	D3	Percy Street	C4
Birmingham Road	B4	Rother Street	B2-B3
Bordon Place	A1	Rowley Crescent	D4
Brewery Street	B4	Ryland Street	B1
Bridge Foot	D3	St Andrew's Crescent	A2
Bridge Street	C3-D3	St Gregory's Road	C4-D4
Broad Street	B2	St Martin's Close	A2
Broad Walk	B1-B2	Sanctus Drive	B1
Brookvale Road	A1-A2	Sanctus Road	A1-B1
Bull Street	B1-B2	Sanctus Street	B1
Cedar Close	D4	Sandfield Road	A1
Chapel Lane	C2	Scholars Lane	B2-C2
Chapel Street	C2	Seven Meadows Road	A1-B1
Cherry Orchard	A1	Shakespeare Street	B4-C4
Cherry Street	B1	Sheep Street	C2
Chestnut Walk	B2	Shipston Road	D1-D2
Church Street	B2-C2	Shottery Road	A2
Clopton Bridge	D2-D3	Southern Lane	C1-C2
Clopton Court	B4	Station Road	A3
Clopton Road	B4	Swans Nest Lane	D2
College Lane	B1	The Willows	A2-A3
College Street	B1	The Willows North	A3
Ely Street	B2-C2	Tiddington Road	D2
Evesham Place	B2	Trinity Street	B1
Evesham Road	A1	Tyler Street	C3
Great Williams Street	C3-C4	Union Street	C3
Greenhill Street	B3	Warwick Court	C4
Grove Road	B2-B3	Warwick Crescent	D4
Guild Street	B3-C3	Warwick Road	D4
Henley Street	B3-C3	Waterside	C2-C3
High Street	C2-C3	Welcombe Road	C4-D4
Holtom Street	B1	Wellesbourne Grove	A3-B3
John Street	C3	West Street	B1-B2
Kendall Avenue	B4-C4	Western Road	A4-B4
Lock Close	C3-C4	Windsor Street	B3
Maidenhead Road	C4	Wood Street	B3-C3
Mansell Street	B4		
Mayfield Avenue	C4		
Mayfield Court	C4		
Meer Street	B3-C3		
Mill Lane	C1		
Mulberry Street	C4		
Narrow Lane	B1		
New Broad Street	B1		

Sunderland

Sunderland is found on atlas page 115 F1

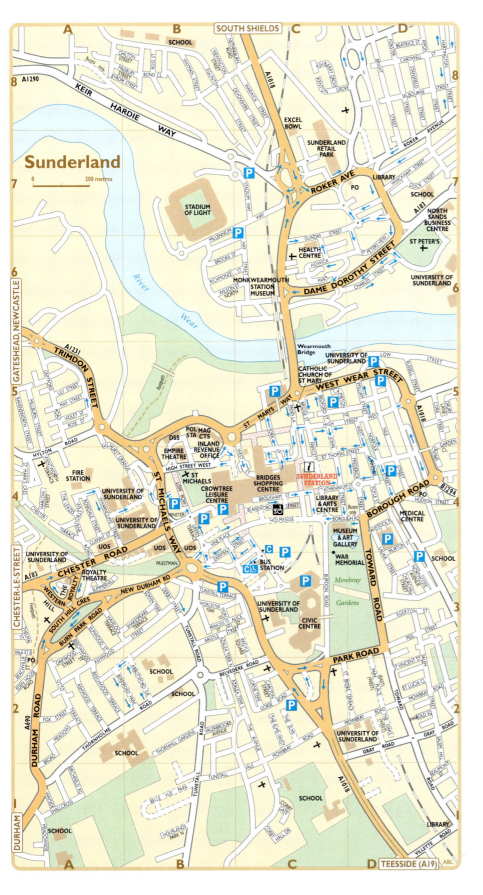

Abbotsford Grove	B2
Alice Street	B3-C3
Argyle Square	C3
Ashberry Grove	C8
Ashwood Street	A2-A3-B3
Ashwood Terrace	A2
Athenaeum Street	C4-D4
Azalea Terrace North	B2-B3
Azalea Terrace South	B2-C2
Beachville Street	A2
Beatrice Street	D8
Beaumont Street	D1-D2
Bedford Street	C5
Beechwood Street	A2-A3
Beechwood Terrace	A2
Belle Vue Park	B1
Belvedere Road	B2-C2-C3
Beresford Park	A2-B2
Birchfield Road	A1
Blandford Street	C4
Bond Close	B8
Borough Road	C4-D4
Bridge Street	C5
Bright Street	D7-D8
Broad Meadows	A1-A2
Brooke Street	B6-C6
Brougham Street	C4
Burdon Road	C3-C4
Burn Park Road	A3
Byrom Street	A8-B8
Cardwell Street	D8
Carlton Street	C2
Charles Street	C6-D6
Chester Road	A3-B4
Chester Terrace	A4
Chilton Street	A8-B8
Churchill Street	D3
Clanny Street	A4
Corby Gate	C1
Corby Hall Drive	C1
Cork Street	D5
Dame Dorothy Street	C6-D6
Deptford Road	A5
Derby Street	B3
Derwent Street	B3-B4-C4
Devonshire Street	B8-C8-C7
Dock Street	D7
Drury Lane	D5
Dundas Street	C6-C7-D7
Durham Road	A1-A2-A3
Eden House Road	A2
Edwin Terrace	B3
Egerton Street	D3
Eglinton Street	B8-C8-C7
Elmwood Street	A3
Fawcett Street	C4-C5
Finsbury Street	A8-B8
Forster Street	D7-D8
Fox Street	A2
Foyle Street	D4
Frederick Street	D4
Gilhurst Grange	A5-A4-B4
Gorse Road	C2
Gray Road	D2
Green Terrace	B4
Harlow Street	A4
Harold Square	D2
Hartington Street	D8
Havelock Terrace	A3
Hay Street	C6-C7
High Street West	B4, C5-D5
Holmlands Park North	B1
Holmside	C4
Howick Park	C6
Hudson Street	D4
Hylton Road	A4-A5
John Street	C4-C5
Keir Hardie Way	A8-B8-B7
Kenton Grove	C8
Lambton Street	C5
Laura Street	D3-D4
Lily Street	A5
Lorne Terrace	C2
Low Row	B4
Low Street	C5-D5
May Street	A5
Meadowside	A1
Millburn Street	A5
Millennium Way	B6-B7-C7
Mowbray Road	C2-D2
Murton Street	D3-D4
Netherburn Road	B8-C8
New Durham Road	A3-B3
Newington Street	B8
Nile Street	D4-D5
Norfolk Street	D4-D5
Northcote Avenue	D3
Oakwood Street	A2-A3
Otto Terrace	A2
Pann Lane	C4-C5
Park Place East	D2
Park Place West	D2
Park Road	C2-C3-D3
Peel Street	D3
Princess Street	B3
Ravensworth Street	A5
Richmond Street	B6-C6
Ripon Street	D8
Roker Avenue	C7-D7-D8
Rose Street	A5
Rosedale Street	A4
Ross Street	B8
Russell Street	D5
St Bedes Terrace	C2-D2
St Lucia Close	D2
St Mark's Crescent	A4
St Marys Way	C5
St Michaels Way	B3-B4
St Peters View	D6-D7
St Thomas Street	C4-C5
St Vincent Street	D2-D3
Salem Hill	D1-D2
Salem Street	D2-D3
Selbourne Street	D8
Shakespeare Terrace	A3-B3
Shallcross	A1
South Hill Crescent	A3
Spring Garden Close	D4-D5
Stadium Way	C7
Stansfield Street	D8
Summerhill	A3
Tavistock Place	D4
The Avenue	C2
The Elms	C2
The Elms West	C2
The Leazes	A4
The Oaks West	D2
The Royalty	A3
Thelma Street	A3
Thornhill Gardens	B2
Thornholme Road	A1-A2-B2
Toward Road	D1-D2-D3-D4
Trimdon Street	A5-A6
Tunstall Road	B1-B2-B3
Tunstall Terrace	B3-C3
Tunstall Vale	B1-C1-C2
Valerbrooke Road	B2
Villette Road	D1
Vine Place	B3-B4-C4
Violet Street	A5
Warwick Street	C8
Wayman Street	B8
Wayside	A1
Wentworth Terrace	A4
West Street	C4-C5
West Sunniside	D4-D5
West Wear Street	C5-D5
Westbourne Road	A3-A4
Western Hill	A3
Wharncliffe Street	A4
Whickham Street	D7
William Street	D5
Wilson Street North	B6-C6
Worcester Street	B3
Worcester Terrace	B3
Yale Street	A3
York Street	C4-C5

227

Swansea
Swansea is found on atlas page **34 D3**

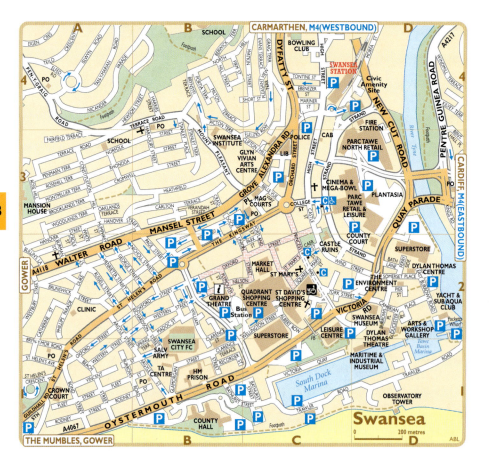

Albert Row	C2	Nicander Parade	A4-B4
Alexandra Road	C3	Nicholl Street	A2-B2
Argyle Street	A2-A1-B1	Norfolk Place	A3-B3
Bath Lane	D2	North Hill	B4-C4
Bathurst Street	B1-C1	Orchard Street	C3
Beach Street	A1	Oxford Street	A1-B2-C2-C3
Belle Vue Way	C3	Oystermouth Road	A1-B1-C1
Bond Street	A1	Page Street	B2
Brooklands Terrace	A3	Pen y Graig Road	A3-A4
Brunswick Street	A2	Penmaen Terrace	A3
Bryn-y-Mor Road	A1	Pentre Guinea Road	D3-D4
Brynsyfi Terrace	B4	Phillips Parade	A1-A2
Burrows Road	A1-B1	Picton Terrace	B3-B4
Cambrian Place	D2	Pier Street	D2
Carlton Terrace	B3	Plymouth Street	B2
Castle Street	C3	Portland Street	C2-C3
Catherine Street	A1-A2	Portia Terrace	B4
Clifton Hill	B4	Princess Way	C2-C3
College Street	C3	Quay Parade	D3
Constitution Hill	A3	Rhondda Street	A3-B3
Cromwell Street	A3-B3	Richardson Street	A2-B2-B1
Duke Street	A2	Rodney Street	A1-B1
Dyfatty Street	C4	Rosehill Terrace	A3
East Burrows Road	D2	Russell Street	A2
Evans Terrace	C4	St Helen's Avenue	A1
Fairfield Terrace	A3	St Helen's Road	A1-A2-B2
Firm Street	B4	St Mary's Square	C2
Fleet Street	A1-B1	Somerset Place	D2
Fullers Row	B3-C3-C4	Stanley Place	B2
George Street	A2-B2	Strand	D4-C3-C2-D2
Glamorgan Street	B1	Tan y Marian Road	A4
Graig Terrace	C4	Teilo Crescent	A4
Grove Place	C3	Terrace Road	A3-B4
Hanover Street	A2-A3-B3	The Kingsway	B2-C3
Harcourt Street	B3-B4	Tontine Street	C4
Heathfield	B3	Trawler Road	C1-D1
Henrietta Street	A2-B2	Union Street	B2-C2
Hewson Street	A4-B4	Victoria Quay	C1
High Street	C3-C4	Victoria Road	C2-D2
Hill Street	B4	Vincent Street	A1-B1
Islwyn Road	A4	Walter Road	A2-B2
Madoc Street	B2	Watkin Street	C4
Mansel Street	B2-B3	Wellington Street	B2-C2
Milton Terrace	B4	Western Street	A1-A2-B2
Montpellier Terrace	A3	William Street	B1-B2
Mount Pleasant	B4-B3	Wind Street	C2-D2
Nelson Street	B2-C2	Woodlands Terrace	A3
New Cut Road	D3-D4	York Street	C2-D2

Swindon
Swindon is found on atlas page **39 F3**

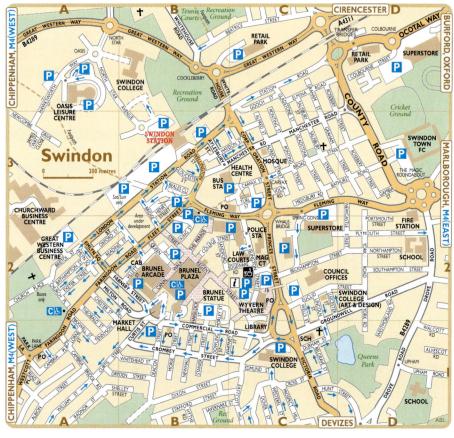

Albion Street	A1	Groundwell Road	C1-C2-D2
Alfred Street	C3	Havelock Street	B1-B2
Aylesbury Street	B3	Hawksworth Way	A3-A4
Bathampton Street	A2	Haydon Street	B3-C3
Bathurst Road	C3-D3	Henry Street	B2-B3
Beales Close	B3	Hunt Street	C1-D1
Beatrice Street	B4-C4	Islington Street	C3
Beckhampton Street	C2-D2	James Watt Close	A3
Belgrave Street	C1	King Street	B2
Bridge Street	B2-B3	Leicester Street	C2
Bristol Street	A2	Lincoln Street	C2
Broad Street	C3-D3	London Street	A2
Cambria Bridge Road	A1	Manchester Road	B3-C3-D4
Cambria Place	A1	Maxwell Street	A1-A2
Canal Walk	B2	Milton Road	A2-B2
Carfax Street	C3	Morley Street	B1-B2
Chester Street	A2	Morse Street	B1
Church Place	A2	Newcastle Street	D2-D3
Colbourne Street	D4	Newcombe Drive	A3
College Street	B2-C2	Newhall Street	C3
Commercial Road	B1-C1	North Star Avenue	A4-B4-B3
Corporation Street	C3	Ocotal Way	D4
County Road	C4-D4-D3	Oxford Street	A2
Crombey Street	B1-C1	Plymouth Street	C2-D2
Cross Street	C1	Ponting Street	C3-C4
Curtis Street	A1-B1	Princes Street	C2
Deacon Street	B1-B2	Queen Street	B2
Dixon Street	B1-C1	Reading Street	A2-B2
Dowling Street	B1	Regent Street	B2-C2
Drove Road	D1-D2-D3	Rosebery Street	C4-C3-D3
Dryden Street	A1-B1	Salisbury Street	C4-C3-D3
Durham Street	C1	Shrivenham Road	D3
Eastcott Hill	C1	Southampton Street	D2
Edgeware Road	B2-C2	Stafford Street	B1-C1
Edmund Street	C1	Stanier Street	B2
Elmina Road	C4	Station Road	B3-C4
Emlyn Square	A2	Tennyson Street	A1-B2
Euclid Street	C2-D2	The Parade	B2
Exeter Street	A1	Theobald Street	A1-A2
Faringdon Road	A1-A2-B2	Upham Road	D1
Farnsby Street	A2-B2	Victoria Road	C1
Fleet Street	B2-B3	Villett Street	B2
Fleming Way	B3-C3-D3	Wellington Street	B3
Gladstone Street	C3-C4	Whitehead Street	A1-B1
Gloucester Street	B3	Whitehouse Road	B4
Gooch Street	C3-C4	Whitney Street	B1-C1
Graham Street	C4-C3-D3	William Street	A1
Great Western Way	A4-B4-C4	York Road	D1-D2-D3

Taunton

Taunton is found on atlas page **23 E2**

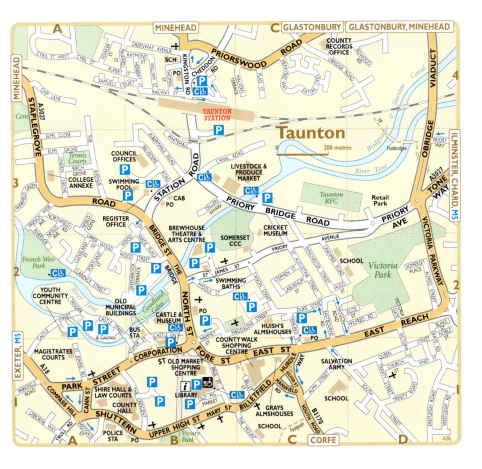

Albermarle Road	B3-B4	Middle Street	B2-C2
Alfred Street	D2	North Street	B2
Alma Street	C1	Northfield Road	A3
Belvedere Road	B3	Obridge Road	C4-D4
Billetfield	C1	Obridge Viaduct	D3-D4
Birch Grove	A3	Old Pig Market	B1
Bridge Street	B2-B3	Park Street	A1
Canal Road	B3-C3	Paul Street	B1
Cann Street	A1	Plais Street	C4
Canon Street	C2	Portland Street	A2
Castle Green	B2	Priorswood Road	B4-C4
Castle Street	A1-A2-B-B1	Priory Avenue	C2-D2-D3
Cheddon Road	B4	Priory Bridge Road	B3-C3-D3
Church Street	D1	Queen Street	D1-D2
Clarence Street	A2	Railway Street	B4
Cleveland Street	A2-A3	Raymond Street	B4
Compass Hill	A1	Rupert Street	A4-B4
Corporation Street	B1	St Augustine Street	C2
Cranmer Road	C2	St James Street	B2-C2
Cyril Street	A4	St Johns Road	A1
Cyril Street West	A4	Shuttern	A1-B1
Dellers Wharf	B3	Silver Street	C1
Duke Street	C2	South Road	C1
East Reach	C1-D1-D2	South Street	C1-D1
East Street	C1	Staplegrove Road	A4-A3-B3
Eastbourne Road	C1-C2	Station Road	B3
Eastleigh Road	D1	Stephen Street	C2
Eaton Crescent	C4	Tancred Street	C1-C2
Elms Grove	A3	Tangier	A2
Fore Street	B1	The Avenue	A3-A4
Fowler Street	A4	The Bridge	B2
French Weir Avenue	A3	The Crescent	A1-B1
Grays Road	D1-D2	Thomas Street	B4
Greenbrook Terrace	B2	Tone Way	D3
Greenway Avenue	B4	Tower Street	B1-B2
Hammet Street	B1-B2	Trinity Road	D1
Haydon Road	C2	Trinity Street	D1
Heavitree Way	C4	Trull Road	A1
Herbert Street	B4	Upper High Street	B1
Hurdle Way	C1	Upper Wood Street	A2-A3
Kingston Road	B4	Victoria Gate	D2
Laburnum Street	C2	Victoria Parkway	D2-D3
Linden Grove	A3	Victoria Street	D1-D2
Magdalene Street	B2-C2	Viney Street	D1
Malvern Terrace	C4	William Street	B4
Mansfield Road	C1	Winchester Street	C2
Mary Street	B1	Wood Street	B3-B2-A2
Maxwell Street	A4-B4	Yarde Place	B2-B3

Torquay

Torquay is found on atlas page **7 F4**

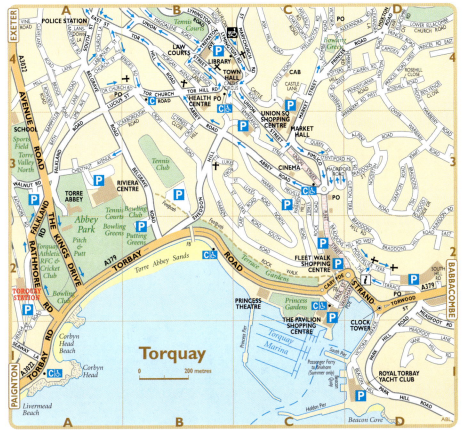

Abbey Road	B4-B3-C3	Melville Street	C2-C3
Alexandra Road	C4-D4	Middle Warberry Road	D3-D4
Alpine Road	C3-D3	Mill Lane	A4
Ash Hill Road	C4	Montpelier Terrace	D2
Avenue Road	A3-A4	Morgan Avenue	B4
Bampfylde Road	A3-A4	Palk Street	C2-D2
Bath Lane	A3-A4	Park Hill Road	D1-D2
Beacon Hill	D1	Pennsylvania Road	D4
Belgrave Road	A4-A3-B3-B2	Pimlico	C3
Braddons Hill Road	D2	Potters Hill	C4-D4
Braddons Hill Road East	D2	Princes Road	C4-D4
Braddons Hill Road West	C2-D2	Princes Road West	D4
Braddons Street	D3	Queen Street	C3
Bridge Road	A3-A4	Rathmore Road	A2-A3
Camden Road	D4	Rock Road	C2-C3
Cary Parade	C2	Rosehill Road	D4
Cary Road	C2-C3	St Efride's Road	A4-B4
Castle Circus	B4-C4	St Lukes Road	B3-C3
Castle Lane	C4	St Lukes Road North	B3-C3-C2
Castle Road	C4	St Lukes Road South	B3-C3-C2
Cavern Road	D4	St Marychurch Road	C4
Chatsworth Road	C4	Scarborough Road	A3-B3
Chestnut Avenue	A3	Seaway Lane	A1
Church Lane	A4	Sheddon Hill	B2-B3
Church Street	A4	South Hill Road	D2
Cleveland Road	A4	South Street	A4
Clifton Terrace	D3	Stentiford Hill Road	C3-D3
Croft Hill	B3	Strand	D2
Croft Road	B3-B4	Temperance Street	C3-C4
East Street	A4	The Kings Drive	A2-A3
Ellacombe Road	C4	The Terrace	D2
Falkland Road	A2-A3-A4	Thurlow Road	B4
Fleet Street	C3-C2-D2	Tor Church Road	A4-B4
Grafton Road	D3	Tor Hill Road	B4
Hennapyn Road	A1-A2	Torbay Road	A1-A2-B2-C2
Higher Union Lane	B4	Torwood Street	D2
Hillesdon Road	D3	Trematon Avenue	B4
Hoxton Road	D4	Union Street	B4-C4-C3
Laburnum Street	A4	Upper Braddons Hill Road	D2-D3
Lower Ellacombe Church Road	D4	Vansittart Road	A4
Lower Warberry Road	D3-D4	Vaughan Parade	C2-D2
Lucius Street	A4-B4	Victoria Parade	D1-D2
Lymington Road	B4-C4	Victoria Road	C4-D4
Madrepore Road	C3-D3	Walnut Road	A3
Magdalene Road	B4	Warberry Road West	C4-C3-D4
Market Street	C3-C4	Warren Hill	C3
Meadfoot Lane	D1	Warren Road	B3-B2-C2-C3
Meadfoot Road	D1-D2	Wellington Road	C4

Tunbridge Wells
Warwick

Tunbridge Wells
Tunbridge Wells is found on atlas page **17 G5**

Arundel Road	C1	Mount Ephraim	A3-A4-B4
Belgrave Road	B4-C4	Mount Ephraim Road	B4
Berkeley Road	B1	Mount Pleasant Road	B2-B3
Boyne Park	A4	Mount Sion	B1
Buckingham Road	C1-C2	Mountfield Gardens	C2
Calverley Road	B4-C4-C3	Mountfield Road	C2
Calverley Street	C4	Nevill Street	A1
Camden Road	C4	Newton Road	B4-C4
Castle Street	B1-B2	Norfolk Road	C1-C2
Chapel Place	A1-B1	Poona Road	C1-C2
Church Road	A3-B3	Rock Villa Road	B4
Clanricarde Gardens	B3	Rodmell Road	B1
Clanricarde Road	B3	Rosehill Walk	B3
Claremont Road	B1-C1-C2	Royal Chase	A4
Clarence Road	A2-B2-B3, B3	Somerville Gardens	A4
Crescent Road	B3-C3	South Grove	B1-B2
Culverden Street	B4	Spencer Mews	B1
Cumberland Gardens	B1	Station Approach	B2
Cumberland Yard	B1	Sutherland Road	B2-C2
Dale Street	C4	The Pantiles	A1
Dudley Road	A4-B4	The Pantiles Lower Walk	A1
Farmcombe Road	C1	Vale Avenue	B2
Frog Lane	B1	Vale Road	B2
Garden Road	C4	Victoria Road	C4
Garden Street	C3-C4	Warwick Road	B1
Goods Station Road	B4-C4	York Road	A3-B3
Grecian Road	C1		
Grosvenor Road	B4		
Grove Avenue	B2		
Grove Hill Gardens	C2		
Grove Hill Road	B2-C2		
Grover Street	C4		
Guildford Road	C2		
Hanover Road	B4		
High Street	B1-B2		
Lansdowne Road	C3-C4		
Lansdowne Square	C3-C4		
Lime Hill Road	B4		
Little Mount Sion	B1		
London Road	A1-B2-A3-B4		
Lonsdale Gardens	B3		
Madeira Park	B1-C1		
Major York's Road	A1		
Meadow Hill Road	C2		
Meadow Road	B4		
Molyneux Park Road	A3-A4		
Monson Road	B3-C3		
Mount Edgcumbe Road	A2		

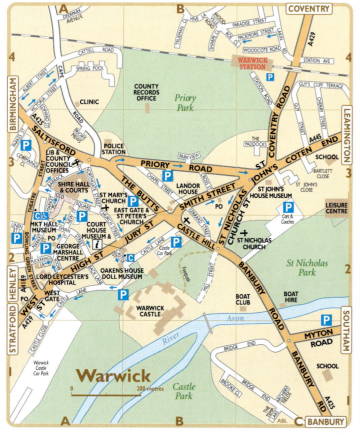

Warwick
Warwick is found on atlas page **59 F2**

Albert Street	A4	St Nicholas Church Street	B2-C3
Archery Fields	C1	Saltisford	A3
Back Lane	A2	Sharpe Close	B4
Banbury Road	B2-C2-C1	Smith Street	B3-C3
Barrack Street	A3	Spring Pool	A4
Bartlett Close	C3	Station Avenue	C4
Bowling Green Street	A2	Station Road	C4
Bridge End	B1-C1	Swan Street	A2
Brook Street	A2	The Butts	A3-B3
Brooke Close	B1-C1	The Paddocks	C3
Cape Road	A3-A4	The Templars	C1
Castle Close	A1-A2	Theatre Street	A2-A3
Castle Hill	B2	Trueman Close	B4
Castle Lane	A2-B2	Victoria Street	A4
Castle Street	A2-B2	Vine Lane	B4
Cattell Road	A4	West Street	A1-A2
Chapel Street	B3	Woodcote Road	C4
Cherry Street	C3-C4	Woodville Road	B4
Church Street	A2-A3		
Commainge Close	A3		
Coten End	C3		
Coventry Road	C3-C4		
Cross Street	B3		
Deerpark Avenue	A4		
Edward Street	A3-A4		
Gerrard Street	B2-B3		
Guy Street	C3-C4		
Guy's Cliff Terrace	C4		
High Street	A2		
Jury Street	B2-B3		
Lakin Road	C4		
Linen Street	A2		
Market Place	A3		
Market Street	A2		
Myton Road	C1		
New Street	A2-A3		
Northgate Street	A3		
Old Square	A3		
Packmore Street	B4-C4		
Paradise Street	B4-C4		
Parkes Street	A3		
Parkview	B3		
Priory Mews	A3		
Priory Road	A3-B3-C3		
Puckerings Lane	A2		
Roe Close	B4-C4		
St John's	C3		
St John's Close	C3		

Watford
Weston-Super-Mare

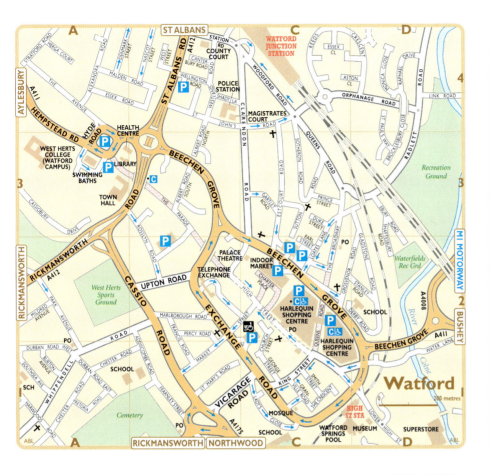

Watford

Watford is found on atlas page **28 B6**

Addiscombe Road	B1-B2	Nascot Street	B4
Albert Road North	B3-B4	Orphanage Road	C4-D4
Albert Road South	B3	Park Avenue	A1-A2
Alexandra Road	A4	Percy Road	B2
Aston Close	C4-D4	Pretoria Road	A1
Beechen Grove	B3-C2-D2-D1	Prince Street	C3
Brocklesbury Close	D3-D4	Queens Road	C1-C2, C3-C4
Burton Avenue	A1	Radlett Road	D3-D4
Canterbury Road	B4	Raphael Drive	D4
Cassio Road	A2-B2-B1	Reeds Crescent	C4-D4
Cassiobury Drive	A3	Rickmansworth Road	A2-A3-B3
Charter Place	C2	Rosslyn Road	B2-B3
Chester Road	A1-B1	St Albans Road	B4
Church Street	C1-C2	St John's Road	B4-C4
Clarendon Road	C3-C4	St Mary's Road	B1
Denmark Street	A4-B4	St Paul's Way	D3-D4
Derby Road	C2-D2	Shady Lane	B4
Duke Street	C3	Shaftesbury Road	D2-D3
Durban Road East	A1	Smith Street	C1
Durban Road West	A1	Sotheron Road	C3-C4
Earl Street	C2	Southsea Avenue	A1
Ebury Road	D2-D3	Stanley Road	C2-D2
Essex Close	C4	Station Road	B4
Essex Road	A4-B4	Stratford Road	A4
Estcourt Road	C2-C3-C4	Sutton Road	C3
Exchange Road	B2-B1-C1	The Avenue	A4
Fearnley Street	B1	The Broadway	C2-C3
Francis Road	B1-B2	The Crescent	C1
Gartlet Road	C3	The Parade	B3
George Street	C1	Upton Road	B2
Gladstone Road	D2-D3	Vicarage Road	B1-C1
Granville Road	C1	Water Lane	D1-D2
Grosvenor Road	C2-D2	Wellington Road	B4
Harwoods Road	A1	West Street	B4
Hempstead Road	A3-A4	Westland Road	B4
Herga Court	A4	Whippendell Road	A1-A2-B2
High Street	B2-C2-C1	Woodford Road	C4
Hyde Road	A3-A4		
King Street	C1		
Lady's Close	C1		
Link Road	D4		
Loates Lane	C2-C3		
Lower High Street	D1		
Malden Road	A4-B4		
Market Street	B1-B2-C2		
Marlborough Road	B2		
Mildred Avenue	A2		
Monica Close	D4		

231

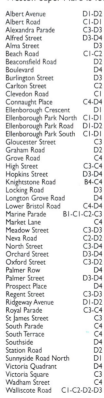

Weston-Super-Mare

Weston-Super-Mare is found on atlas page **23 F5**

Albert Avenue	D1-D2	Waterloo Street	C4-D4
Albert Road	C1-D1	West Street	C4
Alexandra Parade	C3-D3	Whitecross Road	D1
Alfred Street	D3-D4	Wilton Gardens	C2
Alma Street	D3	Worthy Lane	D4
Beach Road	C1-C2	Worthy Place	C4-D4
Beaconsfield Road	D2	York Street	C3
Boulevard	D4		
Burlington Street	D3		
Carlton Street	C2		
Clevedon Road	C1		
Connaught Place	C4-D4		
Ellenborough Crescent	D1		
Ellenborough Park North	C1-D1		
Ellenborough Park Road	D1-D2		
Ellenborough Park South	C1-D1		
Gloucester Street	C3		
Graham Road	D2		
Grove Road	C4		
High Street	C3-C4		
Hopkins Street	D3-D4		
Knightstone Road	B4-C4		
Locking Road	D3		
Longton Grove Road	D4		
Lower Bristol Road	C4-D4		
Marine Parade	B1-C1-C2-C3		
Market Lane	C4		
Meadow Street	C3-D3		
Neva Road	C2-D2		
North Street	C3-D4		
Orchard Street	D3-D4		
Oxford Street	C3-D2		
Palmer Row	D4		
Palmer Street	D3-D4		
Prospect Place	D4		
Regent Street	C3-D3		
Ridgeway Avenue	D1-D2		
Royal Parade	C3-C4		
St James Street	C3		
South Parade	C4		
South Terrace	C4		
Southside	D4		
Station Road	D2		
Sunnyside Road North	D1		
Victoria Quadrant	D4		
Victoria Square	C3		
Wadham Street	C4		
Walliscote Road	C1-C2-D2-D3		

Winchester
Windsor

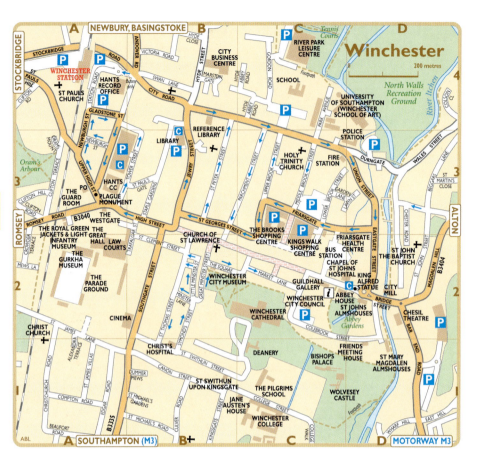

Winchester
Winchester is found on atlas page **26 C2**

Alexandra Terrace	A1-A2	Park Avenue	C3-C4
Andover Road	B4	Romsey Road	A3
Bar End Road	D1-D2	St Clement Street	B2
Beaufort Road	A1	St Georges Street	B3-C2
Beggars Lane	D3	St James Lane	A1-A2
Bridge Street	D2	St James Villas	A1
Canon Street	B1	St John Street	D2-D3
Chester Road	D2-D3	St Martin's Close	D3
Christchurch Road	A1-A2	St Michael's Gardens	B1
City Road	B4	St Michael's Road	A1-B1
Clifton Hill	A3	St Paul's Gate	B3
Clifton Road	A3-A4	St Pauls Hill	A4
Clifton Terrace	A3	St Peter Street	B3-B4
Colebrook Street	C2-D2-D1	St Swithun Street	B1
College Street	C1	St Thomas Street	B1-B2
College Walk	C1	Southgate Street	B1-B2-B3
Colson Close	D4	Staple Gardens	B3
Compton Road	A1	Station Road	A4
Crowder Terrace	A2-A3	Stockbridge Road	A4-B4
Culver Road	B1	Swan Lane	B4
Dummer Mews	A2	Symond's Street	B1-B2
Durngate	D3	The Square	B2-C2
East Hill	D1	Tower Street	A4-B4-B3-A3
Eastgate Street	D2-D3	Trafalgar Street	B2-B3
Edgar Road	A1	Union Street	D3
Friarsgate	C3	Upper Brook Street	C3
Garden Lane	C3	Upper High Street	A3
Gladstone Street	A4	Victoria Road	B4
Gordon Road	C4	Wales Street	D3-D4
Great Minster Street	B2	Wharf Hill	D1
High Street	A3-B3		
Hyde Abbey Road	B4-C4		
Hyde Close	B4		
Hyde Street	B4		
Jewry Street	B3-B4		
Kingsgate Street	B1		
Lawn Street	C3-D3		
Little Minster Street	B2		
Lower Brook Street	C3		
Magdalen Hill	D2-D3		
Market Lane	C2		
Marston Gate	B4		
Mews Lane	A2		
Middle Brook Street	C3		
Minster Lane	B2		
Newburgh Street	A3-A4		
Orams Mount	A3		
Parchment Street	B3-C3-C4		

Windsor
Windsor is found on atlas page **41 H2**

Adelaide Square	C2-D2	High Street, Eton	C4
Albany Road	C3	High Street, Windsor	C3-D3
Albert Street	A3-B3	Imperial Road	A1-A2-A3
Alexandra Road	C2-C3	Kings Road	C1-D1-D2
Alma Road	B2-B3-B4	Lammas Court	C2
Arthur Road	B3-B4	Madeira Walk	C3-D3
Bachelors Acre	C3	Maidenhead Road	A4-B4
Bailey Close	A2	Meadow Lane	C4
Balmoral Gardens	C1	Mill Lane	A4
Barry Avenue	B4-C4	Nightingale Walk	C1
Beaumont Road	C2	Orchard Avenue	A3
Bexley Street	B3	Osborne Road	B2-C2-C1
Bolton Avenue	C1-C2	Oxford Road	B3
Bolton Crescent	C1	Park Street	D3
Bolton Road	B1-C1	Parsonage Lane	A3-A4
Bridgeman Drive	A2	Peascod Street	C3
Brook Street	D2	Peel Close	B1
Bulkeley Avenue	B1-B2	Princes Avenue	A1-B1
Carey Close	B1	Queens Road	B2-C2
Castle Hill	C3-D3	River Street	C4
Cavalry Crescent	B1	Riverside Walk	D4
Charles Street	C3-C4	Russell Street	C3
Claremont Road	B3-C3	St Leonards Avenue	C2
Clarence Crescent	B3-C3	St Leonards Road	B1-C2-C3
Clarence Road	A3-B3-C3	St Marks Place	B2-C2
Clewer Avenue	A2	St Marks Road	B2-C2
Clewer Court Road	A4	Sheet Street	D2-D3
Clewer New Town	A2-A3	Springfield Road	A2-B2
Clewer Park	A4	Stowell Road	B4
College Crescent	B2	Temple Road	C2
Dagmar Road	C2	Thames Street	C3-C4
Datchet Road	C4-D4	The Arches	C4
Devereux Road	C2	Trinity Road	C3
Dorset Road	B3	Upcroft	A1-B1
Duke Street	B4	Vantissart Road	B3
Dyson Close	B1	Victor Road	B1-C1
Elm Road	B2	Victoria Street	C3-D3
Farm Yard	C4-D4	Ward Royal	B3-C3
Fountain Gardens	C1	Westmead	A1-A2
Frances Road	C1-C2-D2	William Street	C3
Gloucester Place	C2-D2	Wood Close	C1
Goslar Way	A3-B3-B2	York Avenue	B2
Goswell Road	C4	York Road	A2-B2
Green Lane	A3-A2-B2		
Grove Road	C2-D2		
Helena Road	C2		
Helston Lane	A3		
Hermitage Lane	A1		

Wolverhampton
Worcester

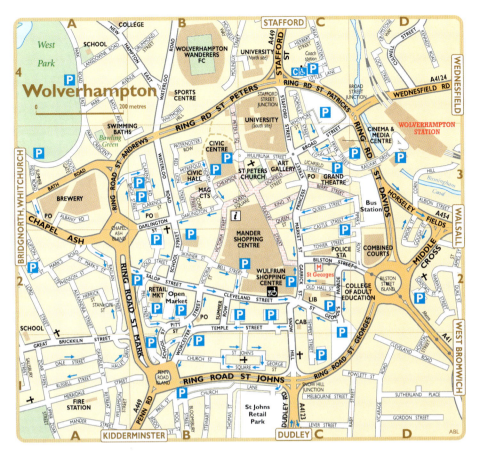

Wolverhampton

Wolverhampton is found on atlas page **58 B5**

Alexandra Street	A1-A2	Penn Road	B1
Bath Avenue	A4-A3-B3	Piper's Row	D2-D3
Bath Road	A3	Pitt Street	B2
Bell Street	B2-C2	Princess Street	C3
Berry Street	C3-D3	Queen Square	B3-C3
Bilston Street	C2-D2	Queen Street	C3-D3
Birch Street	B3	Raby Street	C1-D1
Broad Street	C3-D4	Raglan Street	A2
Castle Street	C2-C3-D3	Railway Drive	D3
Chapel Ash	A2-A3	Red Lion Street	B3
Cheapside	B3-C3	Retreat Street	A1
Church Lane	B1-C1	Ring Road St Andrews	A3-B3
Church Street	B1	Ring Road St Davids	D2-D3
Clarence Road	B3	Ring Road St Georges	C1-D1-D2
Clarence Street	B3	Ring Road St Johns	B1-C1
Cleveland Road	D1	Ring Road St Mark	A2-B2-B1
Cleveland Street	B2-C2	Ring Road St Patricks	C4-D4
Corn Hill	D3	Ring Road St Peters	B3-B4-C4
Corporation Street	B3	Russell Street	A1
Culwell Street	D4	St George's Parade	C2
Dale Street	A1	St John's Square	B1-C1
Darlington Street	B3	St Mark's Road	A2
Dudley Road	C1	St Mark's Street	A2
Dudley Street	C2-C3	St Peter's Square	B4-B3-C3
Fold Street	B2	Salop Street	B2
Fryer Street	C3-D3	School Street	B1-B2, B2-B3
Garrick Street	C2	Skinner Street	B2
Graiseley Street	A1	Snow Hill	C1-C2
Great Brickkiln Street	A1	Stafford Street	C3-C4
Great Western Street	C4	Stephenson Street	A2
Hallet Drive	A1	Stewart Street	B1
Horseley Fields	D3	Summer Row	B2
King Street	C3	Sutherland Place	D1
Lichfield Street	C3-D3	Tempest Street	C1-C2
Littles Lane	C4	Temple Street	B2-C2
Long Street	C3	Thomas Street	B1
Lord Street	A1-A2	Thornley Street	C3-C4
Market Street	C2-C3	Tower Street	C2-D2
Merridale Street	A1-B1	Vicarage Road	D1
Middle Cross	D2	Victoria Street	B2-B3
Mitrefold	B3	Warwick Street	D2
Molineux Street	B4-C4	Waterloo Road	B3-B4
New Hampton East	A4-B4	Wednesfield Road	D4
North Street	B3	Whitmore Hill	B4
Old Hall Street	C2	Whitmore Street	C3-C4
Park Avenue	A4-B4	Worcester Street	B1-B2
Park Road East	A4	Wulfruna Street	C3
Peel Street	B2	Zoar Street	A1

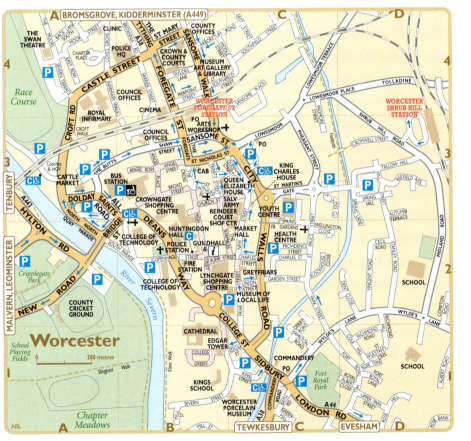

Worcester

Worcester is found on atlas page **46 D5**

All Saints Road	A3	New Road	A2
Angel Place	B3	New Street	C2-C3
Angel Row	B3	North Parade	A2
Angel Street	B3	North Quay	A2-A3
Arboretum Road	B4-C4	Park Street	C1-C2
Bath Road	C1	Pheasant Street	C3
Bridge Street	A2	Pierpoint Street	B4
Britannia Road	B4	Providence Street	C2
Broad Street	B3	Pump Street	B2-C2
Byefield Rise	D3	Queen Street	B3-C3
Castle Street	A4-B4	Richmond Hill	D1-D2
Cecil Road	D2	Richmond Road	D1
Charles Street	C2	Rose Terrace	D1
Charter Place	A4	St James Close	C3
Church Street	B3	St Martin's Gate	C3
City Walls Road	C1-C2-C3	St Mary Street	B4
Cole Hill	D1	St Nicholas Street	B3-C3
College Green	B1	St Paul's Street	C2-C3
College Street	B2-C2-C1	St Swithuns Street	B3
Commandery Road	C1	St Wulstan's Crescent	D1
Copenhagen Street	B2	Sansome Place	C4
Croft Road	A3-A4	Sansome Street	B3-C3
Cromwell Street	D3	Sansome Walk	B3-B4
Deans Way	B2-B3	Severn Street	B1-C1
Dent Close	D2	Severn Terrace	A4
Dolday	A3	Shaw Street	B3
Easy Row	A4	Shrub Hill Road	C4-D4-D3
Farrier Street	B4	Sidbury	C1
Foregate Street	B3-B4	South Parade	A2-B2
Fort Royal Hill	C1-D1	Southfield Street	C4
Friar Street	C1-C2	Spring Gardens	C2-C3
Garden Street	C2	Spring Hill	D3
Green Hill	C1	Spring Lane	D2-D3
Hamilton Road	C1	Stanley Road	D2
High Street	B2-B3	Tallow Hill	D3
Hill Street	D3	Taylors Lane	B4
Hylton Road	A2-A3	The Butts	A3-B3
Infirmary Walk	A4-B4	The Cross	B3
King Street	C1	The Foregate	B3
Little Southfield Street	B4-C4	The Shambles	B3-C3
London Road	C1-D1	The Tything	B4
Love's Grove	A4	Tolladine	D4
Lowesmoor	C3	Trinity Street	B3
Lowesmoor Place	C4-D4	Union Street	C2
Lowesmoor Terrace	C4-D4	Upper Park Street	D1
Middle Street	B4-C4	Vincent Road	D2
Midland Road	D2-D3	Wellington Close	C2
Moor Street	A4	Wylde's Lane	C1-D2

233

York

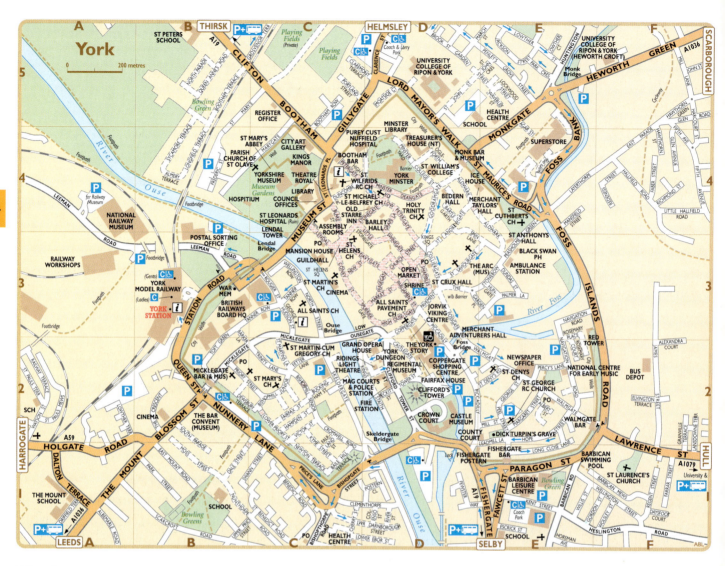

York

York is found on atlas page **91 G5**

Agar Street	E4-E5	Cromwell Road	C1-C2	Goodramgate	D3-D4	Long Close Lane	E1-E2	Park Street	B1	St Saviourgate	D3-E3
Albemarle Road	A1	Dale Street	B1	Gordon Street	E1-F1	Longfield Terrace	B4	Parliament Street	D3	Scarcroft Road	A1-B1
Albert Street	E2	Dalton Terrace	A1	Granville Terrace	F1-F2	Lord Mayor's Walk	D4-D5	Pavement	D3	Shambles	D3
Aldwark	D4-E4-E3	Davygate	C3-D3	Grape Lane	D4	Low Ousegate	C2-D3	Peasholme Green	E3-E4	Skeldergate	C2
Alexandra Court	F2	Daysfoot Court	F1	Grosvenor Terrace	B5-C5	Low Petergate	D3-D4	Peckitt Street	D2	South Parade	B1-B2
Almery Terrace	B4	Deangate	D4	Hallfield Road	F4	Lower Darnborough Street	C1-D1	Peel Street	E2	Spen Lane	D3
Baile Hill Terrace	C1	Dewsbury Terrace	B2-C2	Hampden Street	C2	Lower Ebor Street	C1-D1	Penley's Grove Street	D5-E5	Spurrier Gate	C3-D3
Barbican Mews	F1	Driffield Terrace	A1	Harcourt Street	F4-F5	Lower Priory Street	C2	Percy's Lane	E2	Station Road	B2-B3
Barbican Road	E1	Duncombe Place	C4	Hawthorn Green	F5	Lowther Court	E5	Piccadilly	D1-D2-D3	Stonegate	C3-C4-D4
Barker Lane	B2-B3	Dundas Street	E3	Hawthorn Street	F4	Lowther Street	E5	Portland Street	C5	Swann Street	B1-C1
Bartle Garth	D4	East Mount Road	B1	Heslington Road	E1-F1	Lowther Terrace	A2	Postern Close	D1	Swinegate	D3
Bishopgate Street	C1-D1	East Parade	F4	Heworth Green	E5-F5	Mansfield Street	E4	Price's Lane	C1	Sycamore Terrace	B4-B5
Bishopmill Junior	C2	Elvington Terrace	F2	High Ousegate	D3	March Street	D5-E5	Priory Street	B2-C2	Tanner Row	B3-C3
Bishopmill Senior	C2	Escrick Street	E1	High Petergate	C4	Margaret Street	E2	Queen Anne's Road	B5	The Crescent	B2
Bishopthorpe Road	C1	Faber Street	F4	Holgate Road	A1-B2	Market Street	D3	Queen Street	B2	The Mount	A1-B1
Blake Street	C3-C4	Fairfax Street	C2	Hope Street	E2	Marygate	B4-C4-C5	Railway Terrace	A2	The Stonebow	D3-E3
Blossom Street	B1-B2	Falkland Street	C1-C2	Horsman Avenue	E1	Micklegate	B2-C2	Redeness Street	F4	Toft Green	B2
Bootham	C4-C5	Farrar Street	F1	Hungate	E3	Mill Lane	F5	Regent Street	F1	Tower Street	D2
Bootham Row	C4-C5	Fawcett Street	E1	Huntington Road	E5	Mill Street	F2	Richmond Street	F4	Trinity Lane	C2
Bootham Terrace	B5	Feasegate	D3	Jackson Street	E5	Minster Yard	D4	River Street	D1	Upper Price Street	B1
Brook Street	D5	Fetter Lane	C2	James Street	F1-F2-F3	Moatside Court	D5	Rosemary Court	E2	Victor Street	C1
Buckingham Street	C2	Fewster Way	D1-E1	John Street	F5	Monkgate	D4-E4-E5	Rosemary Place	E2-E3	Walmgate	D2-E2-E2
Castlegate	D2	Fifth Avenue	F4	Kent Street	E1	Moss Street	B1	Rougier Street	C3	Watson Street	E5
Cherry Street	C1	Fishergate	D1-E1	Kings Square	D3	Museum Street	C3-C4	St Andrewgate	D3-D4	Waverley Street	E5
Church Street	D3	Foss Bank	E4-E5	Kings Staith	C2-D2	Navigation Road	E2-E3	St Benedict Road	C1	Wellington Row	C3
Claremont Terrace	C5-D5	Foss Islands Road	E4-E3-F3-F2	Kyme Street	C1-C2	New Street	C3	St Denys Road	E2	Wellington Street	E1-F1
Clarence Street	D5	Fossgate	D3	Lansdowne Terrace	F1-F2	Newton Terrace	C1	St Helen's Square	C3	Willis Street	E1
Clementhorpe	C1-D1	Frederic Street	B4	Lawrence Street	F1-F2	North Parade	B5	St John Crescent	E5	Wolsley Street	F1
Clifford Street	D2	Garden Place	D3-E3	Layerthorpe	E4-F4	North Street	C2-C3	St John Street	D5		
Clifton	B5-C5	Garden Street	D5-E5	Leadmill Lane	E1-E2	Nunnery Lane	B2-C2-C1	St Leonards Place	C4		
Colenso Street	D1	George Hudson Street	C2-C3	Leeman Road	A4-A3-B3	Nunthorpe Road	B1-C1	St Martins Lane	C2		
College Street	D4	George Street	E2	Lendal	C3-C4	Ogle Forth	D4	St Mary's	B4-B5-C5		
Colliergate	D3	Gillygate	C4-C5-D5	Little Hallfield Road	F4	Palmer Lane	E3	St Maurice's Road	D5-E5		
Coney Street	C3-D3	Glen Avenue	F4	Little Stonegate	C4-D3	Paragon Street	E1	St Pauls Mews	A2		
Coppergate	D2-D3	Glen Road	F5	Lockwood Street	E5	Park Crescent	E5	St Pauls Terrace	A2		

ports and airports

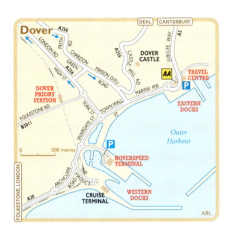

Pay-on-return parking is available at the Dover Eastern Docks and pay-and-display at the Hoverspeed Terminal.
For further information tel: 01304 241427
A long-stay parking facility with a collection and delivery service is also available.
For details tel: 01304 201227

Open-air parking is available at the terminal.
For charge details tel: 01255 242000
Further parking is available 5 miles from Harwich International Port with a collection and delivery service.
For charge details tel: 01255 870217

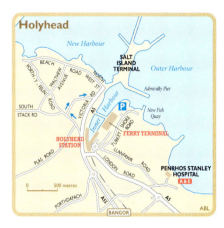

Open-air 'park and ride' car park is available close to the Ferry Terminal.
For charge details tel: 01407 762304 or 606732

Free open-air parking is available at King George Dock (left at owners' risk).
Tel: 01482 795141
Undercover parking is also available.
For charge details tel: 01482 781021

Open-air secure parking is available at the DFDS International Ferry Terminal, Royal Quays.
For charge details tel: 0191 296 0202

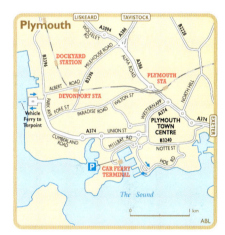

Free open-air parking is available outside the terminal building.
Tel: 0990 360360

Open-air parking for 600 vehicles is available adjacent to the Ferry Terminal.
For charge details tel: 01202 440220

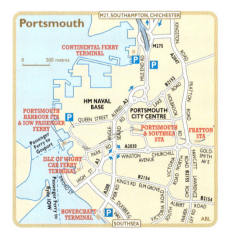

Secure parking facilities are available at the Continental Ferry Terminal and long-stay parking off Mile End Rd.
For charge details tel: 023 9275 1261
Pay-and-display parking is available opposite the Hovercraft Terminal.
Multi-storey parking is available close to the Isle of Wight Passenger Ferry Terminal.
For charge details tel: 023 9282 3153

Covered or fenced compound parking for 2,000 vehicles is available within the Western Docks with a collection and delivery service.
For charge details tel: 023 8022 8001
Fax: 023 8063 5699

major airports

London Heathrow Airport – 16 miles west of London

Telephone: 0870 0000 123 or visit www.baa.co.uk
Parking: short-stay, long-stay and business parking is available.
For charge details tel: 0800 844844
Public Transport: coach, bus, rail and London Underground.
There are several 4-star and 3-star hotels within easy reach of the airport.
Car hire facilities are available.

London Gatwick Airport – 35 miles south of London

Telephone: 01293 535353 or visit www.baa.co.uk
Parking: short and long-stay parking is available at both the North and South terminals.
For charge details tel: 0800 844844
Public Transport: coach, bus and rail.
There are several 4-star and 3-star hotels within easy reach of the airport.
Car hire facilities are available.

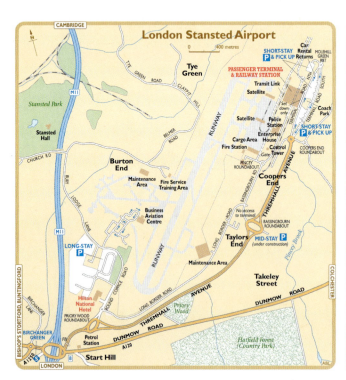

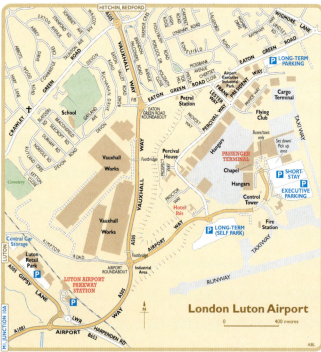

London Stansted Airport – 36 miles north east of London

Telephone: 0870 000 0303 or visit www.baa.co.uk
Parking: short and long-stay open-air parking is available.
For charge details tel: 01279 681192
Public Transport: coach, bus and direct rail link to London on the Stansted Express.
There is one 3-star hotel within easy reach of the airport.
Car hire facilities are available.

London Luton Airport – 33 miles north of London

Telephone: 01582 405100 or visit www.london-luton.com
Parking: short and long-stay open-air parking is available.
For charge details tel: 01582 395249
Public Transport: coach, bus and rail.
There are several 3-star hotels within easy reach of the airport.
Car hire facilities are available.

major airports

London City Airport – 7 miles east of London

Telephone: 020 7646 0088 or visit www.londoncityairport.com
Parking: open-air parking is available.
For charge details tel: 020 7646 0088
Public Transport: shuttle-bus service into London (Liverpool Street). Easy access to the rail network, Docklands Light Railway and the London Underground.
There are 5-star, 4-star and 3-star hotels within easy reach of the airport.
Car hire facilities are available.

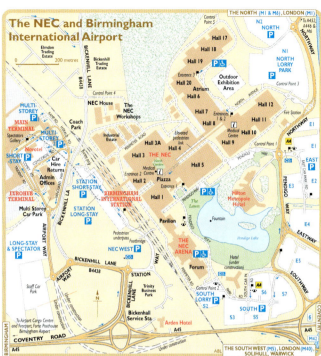

Birmingham International Airport – 8 miles east of Birmingham

Telephone: 0121 767 5511 (Main Terminal), 0121 767 7502 (Eurohub Terminal) or visit www.bhx.co.uk
Parking: short and long-stay parking is available. For charge details tel: 0121 767 7861
Public Transport: shuttle-bus service to Birmingham International railway station and the NEC.
There is one 3-star hotel adjacent to the airport and several 4 and 3-star hotels within easy reach of the airport. Car hire facilities are available.

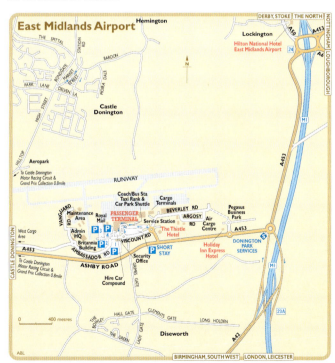

East Midlands Airport – 15 miles south west of Nottingham, next to the M1 at junctions 23A and 24

Telephone: 01332 852852 or visit www.eastmidlandsairport.com
Parking: short and long-stay parking is available.
For charge details tel: 01332 852852 ext 3263
Public Transport: bus and coach services to major towns and cities in the East Midlands.
There are several 3-star hotels within easy reach of the airport.
Car hire facilities are available.

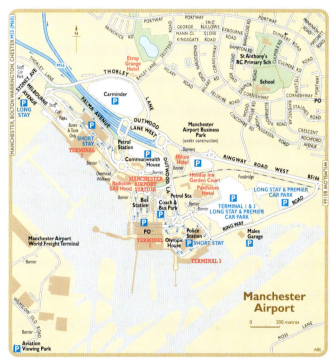

Manchester Airport – 10 miles south of Manchester

Telephone: 0161 489 3000 or visit www.manchesterairport.co.uk
Parking: short and long-stay parking is available. For charge details tel: 0161 489 3723
Public Transport: bus, coach and rail. Manchester airport railway station connects with the rail network.
There are several 4-star and 3-star hotels within easy reach of the airport.
Car hire facilities are available.

major airports

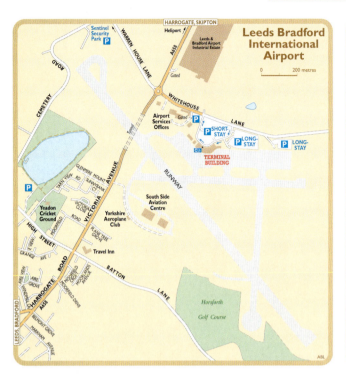

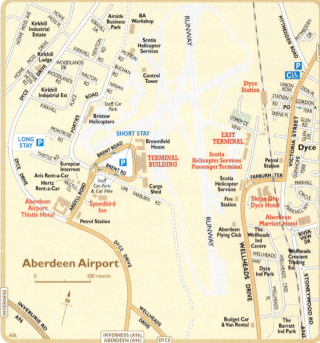

Leeds Bradford International Airport – 7 miles north east of Bradford and 9 miles north west of Leeds

Telephone: 0113 250 9696 or visit www.lbia.co.uk
Parking: short and long-stay parking is available.
For charge details tel: 0113 250 9696 ext 2214
Public Transport: regular bus and coach services operate from Bradford and Leeds.
There is one 4-star and several 3-star hotels within easy reach of the airport.
Car hire facilities are available.

Aberdeen Airport – 7 miles north west of Aberdeen

Telephone: 01224 722331 or visit www.baa.co.uk
Parking: open-air parking is available.
For charge details tel: 01224 722331 ext 5142
Public Transport: regular bus service to central Aberdeen.
There are several 4-star and 3-star hotels within easy reach of the airport.
Car hire facilities are available.

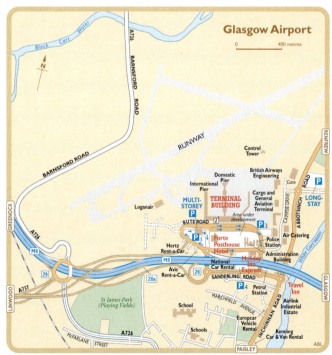

Edinburgh Airport – 7 miles west of Edinburgh

Telephone: 0131 333 1000 or visit www.baa.co.uk
Parking: open-air parking is available.
For charge details tel: 0131 344 3197
Public Transport: regular bus services to central Edinburgh.
There are two 4-star hotels and several 3-star hotels within easy reach of the airport.
Car hire facilities are available.

Glasgow Airport – 8 miles west of Glasgow

Telephone: 0141 887 1111 or visit www.baa.co.uk
Parking: short and long-stay parking is available, mostly open-air.
For charge details tel: 0141 889 2751
Public Transport: regular coach services operate direct to central Glasgow and Edinburgh.
There are several 3-star hotels within easy reach of the airport.
Car hire facilities are available.

the Channel Tunnel

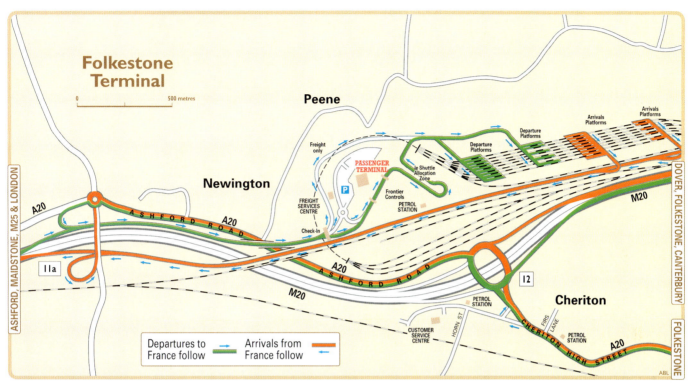

Services to Europe

The Eurotunnel shuttle service for cars, cars towing caravans and trailers, motorcycles, coaches and HGV vehicles runs between terminals at Folkestone and Calais/Coquelles.
It takes just over one hour to travel from the M20 motorway in Kent, via the Channel Tunnel, to the A16 autoroute in France. The service runs 24 hours a day, every day of the year. Call the Eurotunnel Call Centre (tel: 08705 353535) or visit www.eurotunnel.com for the latest ticket and travel information.

There are up to four departures per hour at peak times, with the journey in the tunnel from platform to platform taking just 35 minutes (45 minutes at night). Travellers pass through British and French frontier controls on departure, saving time on the other side of the Channel. Each terminal has bureaux de change, restaurants and a variety of shops. In Calais/Coquelles, the Cité de l'Europe contains numerous shops, restaurants and a hypermarket.

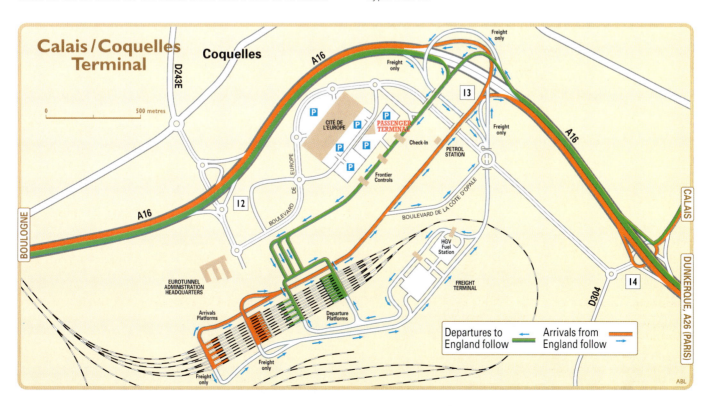

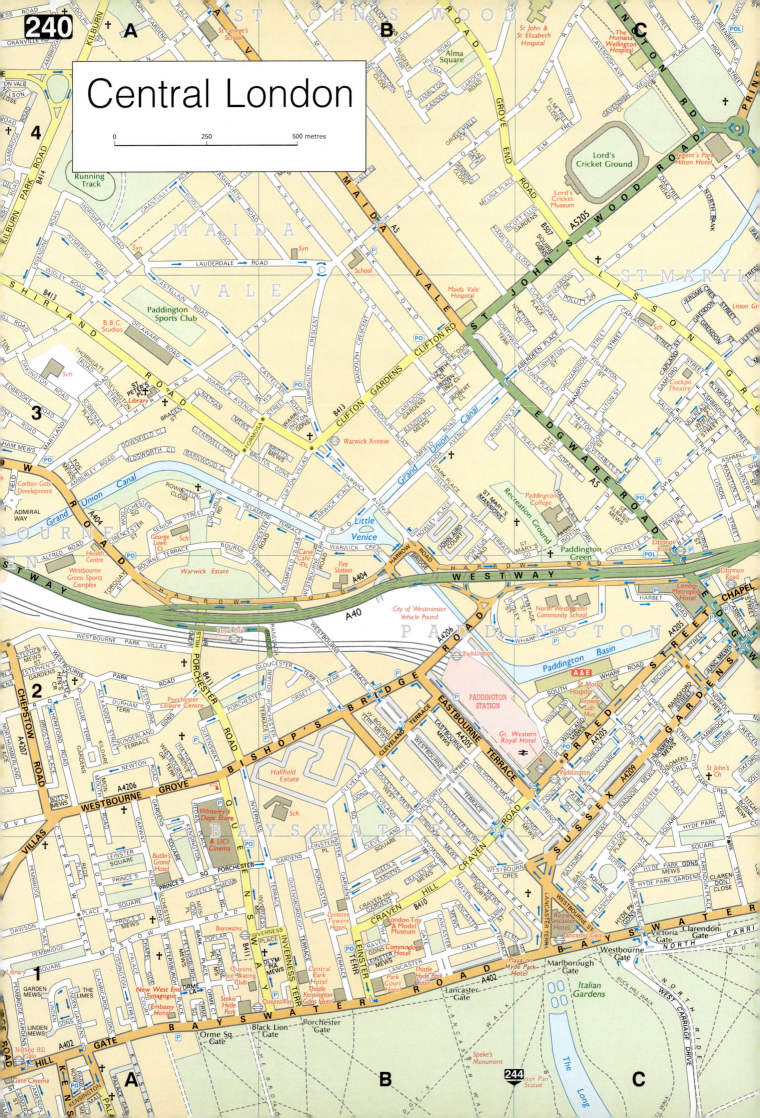

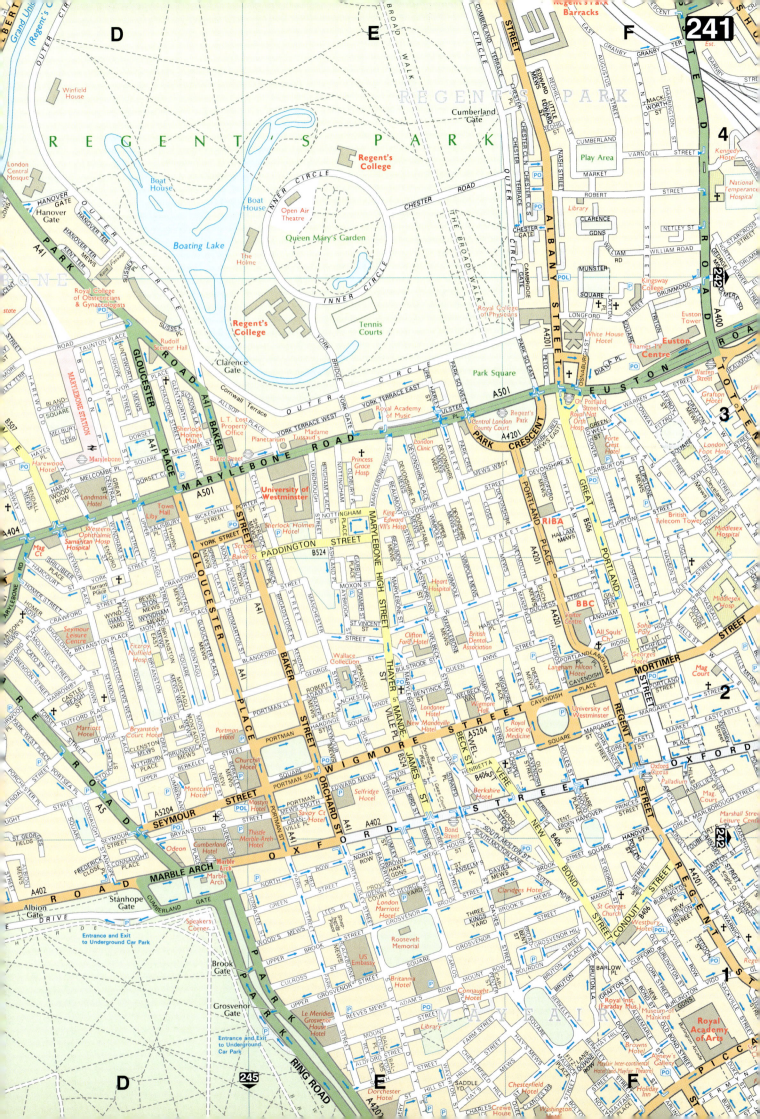

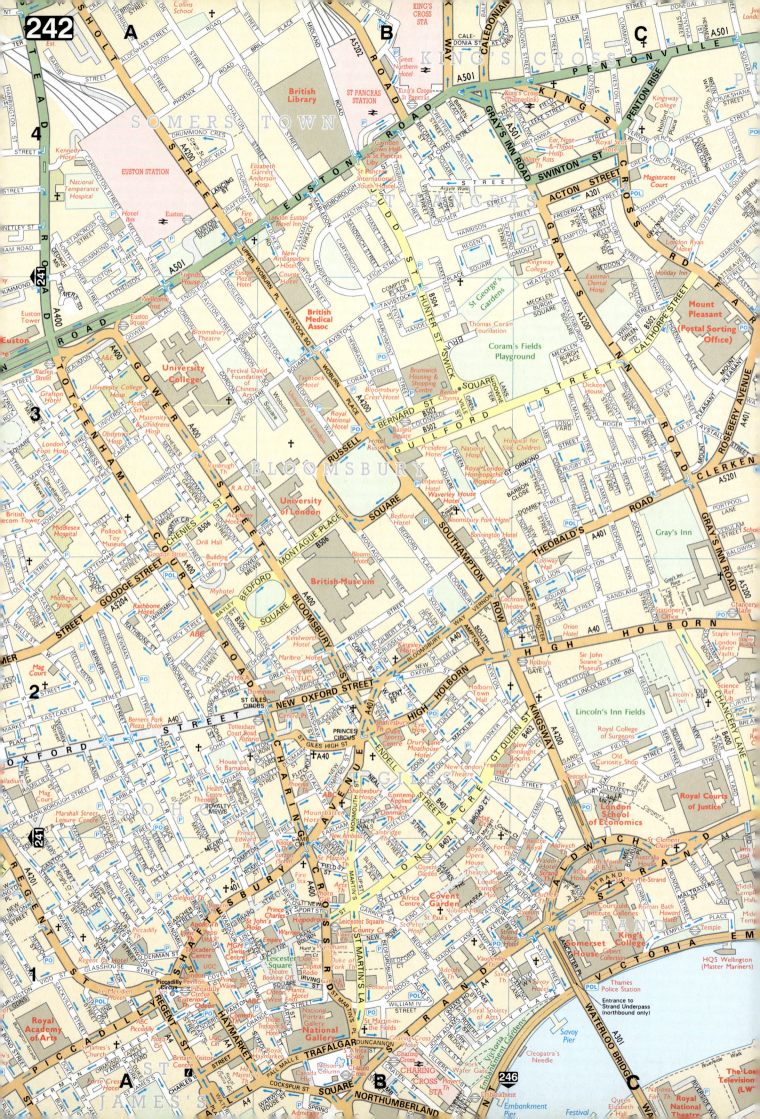

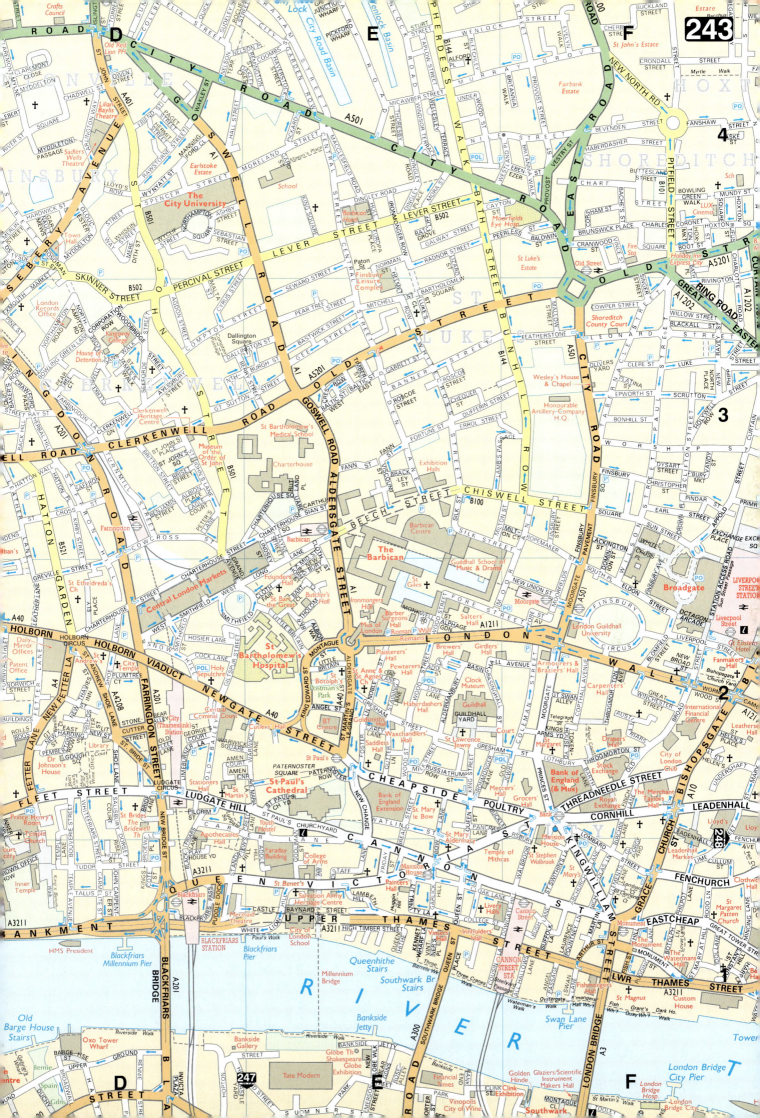

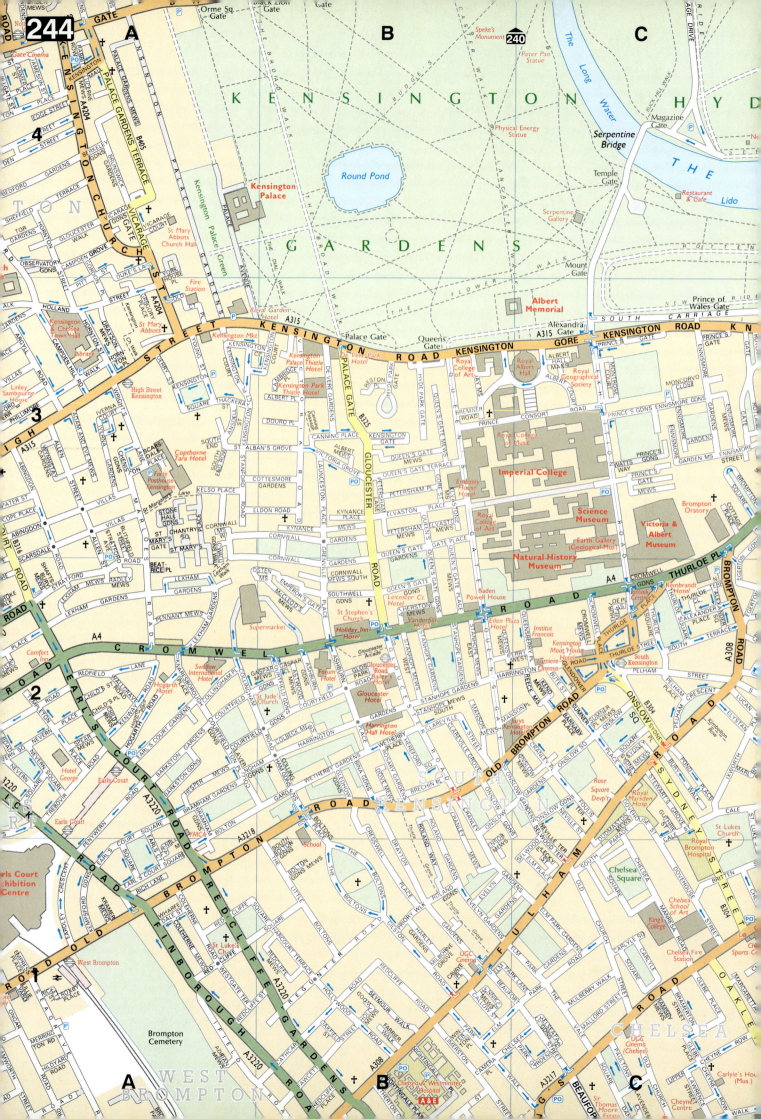

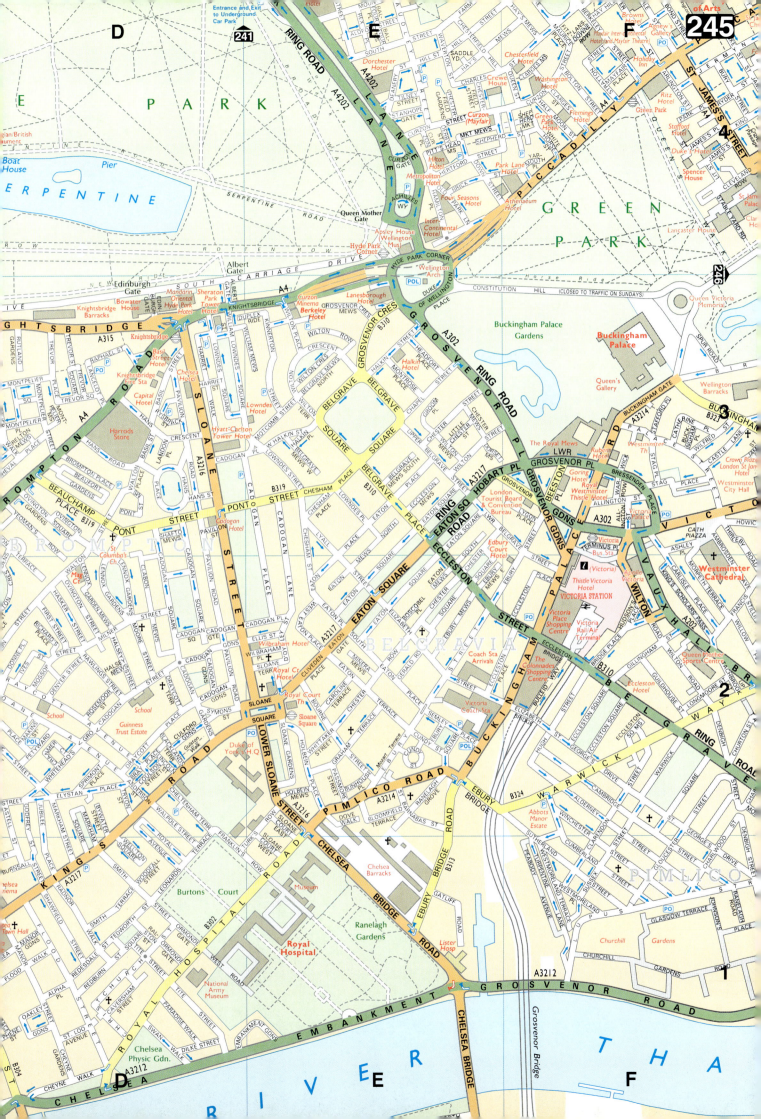

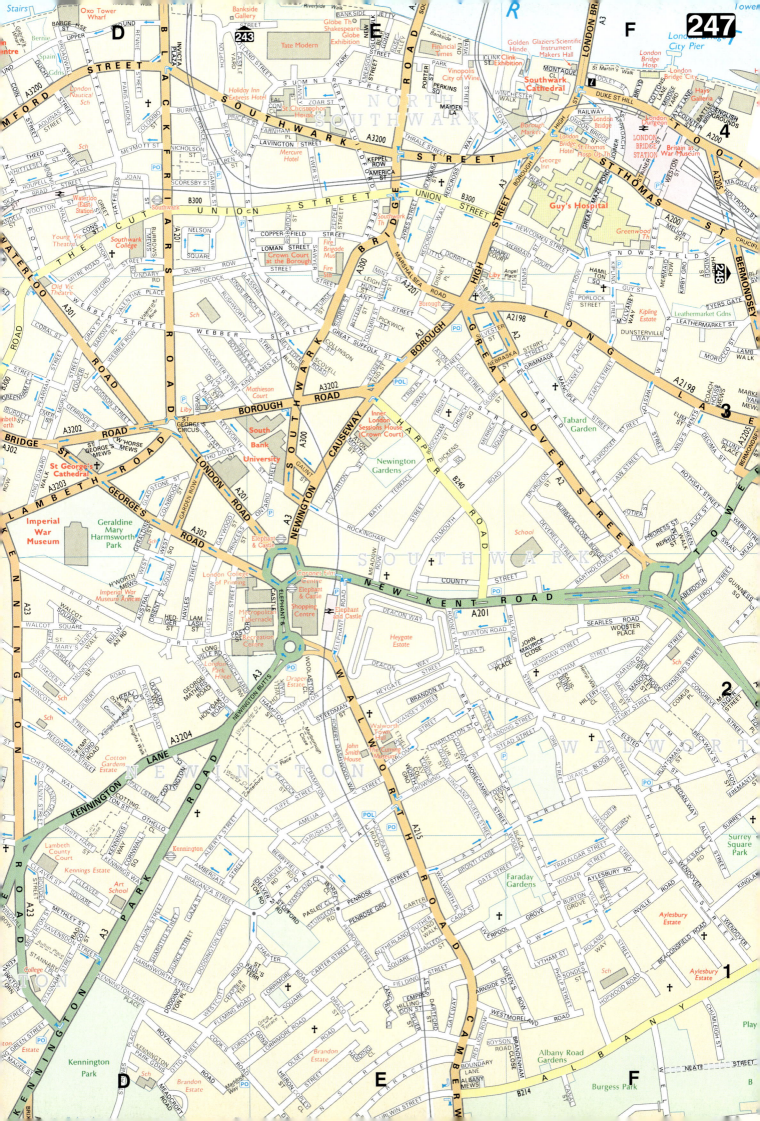

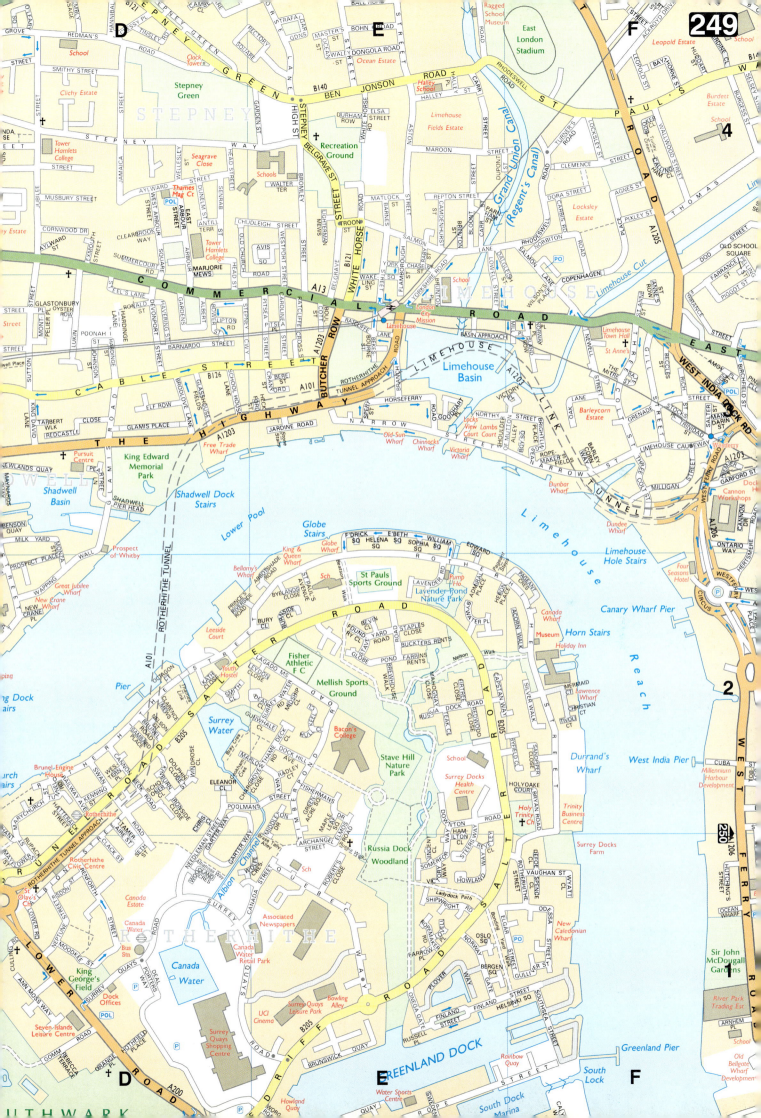

Central London street index

In the index the street names are listed in alphabetical order and written in full, but may be abbreviated on the map. Postal codes are listed where information is available. Each entry is followed by its map page number in bold type, and an arbitrary letter and grid reference number. For example, for Exhibition Road SW7 **244** C3, turn to page 244. The letter 'C' refers to the grid square located at the bottom of the page; the figure '3' refers to the grid square located at the left-hand side of the page. Exhibition Road is found within the intersecting square. SW7 is the postcode. A proportion of street names and their references are also followed by the name of another street in italics. These entries do not appear on the map due to insufficient space but can be located adjacent to the name of the road in italics.

A

Abbey Orchard Street *SW1* **246** B3
Abbey Street *SE1* **248** A1
Abbots Gardens *W8* **244** A3
St Mary's Place
Abbots Lane *SE1* **248** A2
Abbots Walk *W8* **244** A3
St Mary's Place
Abbotshade Road *SE16* **249** E2
Abchurch Lane *EC4* **243** F1
Abercorn Close *NW8* **240** B4
Abercorn Place *NW8* **240** B4
Aberdeen Place *NW8* **240** C3
Aberdour Street *SE1* **247** F2
Abingdon Road *W8* **244** A3
Abingdon Street *SW1* **246** B3
Abingdon Villas *W8* **244** A3
Achilles Way *W1* **245** E4
Ackroyd Drive *E3* **249** F4
Acorn Walk *SE16* **249** F2
Acton Street *WC1* **242** C4
Adam And Eve Mews *W8* **244** A3
Adam and Eve Court *W1* **241** E1
Oxford Street
Adam Street *WC2* **242** B1
Adam's Row *W1* **241** E1
Adams Place *E14* **250** A4
Addington Street *SE1* **246** C3
Addle Hill *EC4* **243** E1
Addle Street *EC2* **243** E2
Adelaide Street *WC2* **242** B1
William IV Street
Adelina Grove *E1* **248** D4
Adeline Place *WC1* **242** B2
Adelphi Terrace *WC2* **242** B1
Adams Street
Adler Street *E1* **248** B4
Admiral Place *SE16* **249** E2
Admiral Way *W9* **240** A3
Admirals Way *E14* **250** A3
Adpar Street *W2* **240** C3
Adrian Mews *SW10* **244** A1
Agar Street *WC2* **242** B1
Agatha Close *E1* **248** C2
Agdon Street *EC1* **243** D3
Agnes Street *E14* **249** F4
Ainstey Street *SE16* **249** D1
Brunel Road
Air Street *W1* **242** A1
Alaska Street *SE1* **246** C4
Albany Mews *SE5* **247** E1
Albany Road *SE5* **247** E1
Albany Street *NW1* **241** F4
Albatross Way *SE16* **249** D1
Albemarle Street *W1* **241** F1
Albemarle Way *EC1* **242** C3
Clerkenwell Road
Albert Court *SW7* **244** C3
Albert Embankment *SE1* **246** B1
Albert Gardens *E1* **249** D3
Albert Hall Mansions *SW7* **244** C3
Albert Mews *W8* **244** B3
Albert Place *W8* **244** B3
Alberta Street *SE17* **247** D1
Albion Close *W2* **241** D1
Albion Mews *W2* **241** D1
Albion Place *EC1* **243** D3
Albion Street *SE16* **249** D1
Albion Street *W2* **241** D1
Albion Way *EC1* **243** E2
Albion Yard *E1* **248** C4
Aldburgh Mews *W1* **241** E2
Marylebone Lane
Aldenham Street *NW1* **242** A4
Aldermanbury *EC2* **243** E2
Aldermanbury Square *EC2* **243** E2
Aldermanbury
Alderney Street *SW1* **245** F2
Aldersgate Street *EC1* **243** E3
Aldford Street *W1* **241** E1
Aldgate *EC3* **248** A3
Aldgate High Street *EC3* **248** A3
Aldsworth Close *W9* **240** A3
Aldwych *WC2* **242** C1
Alexander Place *SW7* **244** C2
Alexander Square *SW3* **244** C2
Alexander Street *W2* **240** A2
Alford Place *N1* **243** E4
Alfred Mews *W1* **242** A3
Alfred Place *WC1* **242** A3
Alfred Road *W2* **240** A2
Alice Street *SE1* **247** F3
Alie Street *E1* **248** B3
All Hallows Lane *EC4* **243** F1
All Soul's Place *W1* **241** F2
Langham Street
Allen Street *W8* **244** A3
Allington Street *SW1* **245** F3
Allsop Place *NW1* **241** D3
Alma Square *NW8* **240** B4
Alpha Grove *E14* **250** A3
Alpha Place *SW3* **245** D1
Alsace Road *SE17* **247** F1
Alscot Road *SE1* **248** B1
Alvey Street *SE17* **247** F2
Ambassador Square *E14* **250** B2
Ambergate Street *SE17* **247** D1
Amberley Road *W9* **240** A3
Ambrosden Avenue *SW1* **246** A3
Amelia Street *SE17* **247** E2
Amen Corner *EC4* **243** D2
Amen Court *EC4* **243** D2
America Square *EC3* **248** A3
America Street *SE1* **247** E4
Amoy Place *E14* **249** F3
Ampton Place *WC1* **242** C4
Ampton Street *WC1* **242** C4
Amsterdam Road *E14* **250** C2
Amwell Street *EC1* **242** C4
Anderson Street *SW3* **245** D2
Andrew Borde Street *WC2* **242** B2
Charing Cross Road
Angel Court *EC2* **243** F2
Angel Court *SW1* **246** A4
King Street
Angel Mews *E1* **248** C3
Angel Passage *EC4* **243** F1
Angel Place *SE1* **247** E4
Angel Street *EC1* **243** E2
Ann Moss Way *SE16* **249** D1
Ansdell Street *W8* **244** A3
Antill Terrace *E1* **249** D4
Apothecary Street *EC4* **243** D2
New Bridge Street
Apple Tree Yard *SW1* **242** A1
Appold Street *EC2* **243** F3
Aquinas Street *SE1* **247** D4
Arbour Square *E1* **249** D4
Archangel Street *SE16* **249** E1
Archer Street *W1* **242** A1
Arden Crescent *E14* **250** A2
Argent Street *SE1* **247** E4
Loman Street
Argyle Square *WC1* **242** B4
Argyle Street *WC1* **242** B4
Argyle Walk *WC1* **242** B4
Argyll Road *W8* **244** A3
Argyll Street *W1* **241** F2
Arlington Street *SW1* **245** F4
Arlington Way *EC1* **243** D4
Arne Street *WC2* **242** B2
Arneway Street *SW1* **246** A2
Arnhem Place *E14* **250** A2
Arnside Street *SE17* **247** E1
Arthur Street *EC4* **243** F1
Artichoke Hill *E1* **248** C3
Artillery Lane *E1* **248** A4
Artillery Passage *E1* **248** A4
Artillery Lane
Artillery Row *SW1* **246** A3
Artizan Street *E1* **248** A4
Harrow Place
Arundel Street *WC2* **242** C1
Ashbridge Street *NW8* **240** C3
Ashburn Gardens *SW7* **244** B2
Ashburn Mews *SW7* **244** B2
Ashburn Place *SW7* **244** B2
Ashby Street *EC1* **243** D4
Ashdown Walk *E14* **250** A2
Asher Drive *E1* **248** B3
Ashfield Street *E1* **248** C4
Ashfield Yard *E1* **249** D4
Ashfield Street
Ashland Place *W1* **240** E3
Ashley Place *SW1* **245** F3
Ashmill Street *NW1* **240** C3
Ashworth Road *W9* **240** A4
Aske Street *N1* **243** F4
Asolando Drive *SE17* **247** E2
King & Queen Street
Aspen Way *E14* **250** B4
Assam Street *E1* **248** B4
Assembly Passage *E1* **249** D4
Aste Street *E14* **250** B3
Astell Street *SW3* **245** D2
Aston Street *E14* **249** E4
Astwood Mews *SW7* **244** B2
Atherstone Mews *SW7* **244** B2
Atterbury Street *SW1* **246** B2
Attneave Street *WC1* **242** C4
Aubrey Place *NW8* **240** B4
Auckland Street *SE11* **246** C1
Augustus Street *NW1* **241** F4
Aulton Place *SE11* **247** D1
Austin Friars *EC2* **243** F2
Austin Friars Square *EC2* **243** F2
Austin Friars
Austral Street *SE11* **247** D2
Ave Maria Lane *EC4* **243** E2
Aveline Street *SE11* **246** C1
Avery Row *W1* **241** F1
Avis Square *E1* **249** E4
Avon Place *SE1* **247** E3
Avonmouth Street *SE1* **247** E3
Aybrook Street *W1* **241** E2
Aylesbury Road *SE17* **247** F1
Aylesbury Street *EC1* **243** D3
Aylesford Street *SW1* **246** A1
Aylward Street *E1* **249** D4
Ayres Street *SE1* **247** E4

B

Babmaes Street *SW1* **246** A4
Jermyn Street
Bacchus Walk *N1* **243** F4
Bache's Street *N1* **243** F4
Back Church Lane *E1* **248** B4
Back Hill *EC1* **243** D3
Bacon Grove *SE1* **248** A1
Baffin Way *E14* **250** C4
Bainbridge Street *WC1* **242** B2
Baker Street *W1 & NW1* **241** D3
Baker's Mews *W1* **241** E2
Baker's Row *EC1* **243** F3
Baker's Yard *EC1* **243** D3
Baker's Row
Bakers Hall Court *EC3* **248** A3
Harp Lane
Balcombe Street *NW1* **241** D3
Balderton Street *W1* **241** E1
Baldwin Street *EC1* **243** F4
Baldwin's Gardens *EC1* **242** C3
Bale Road *E1* **249** F4
Balfe Street *N1* **242** B4
Balfour Mews *W1* **241** E1
Balfour Place *W1* **241** E1
Balfour Street *SE17* **247** F2
Ballast Quay *SE10* **250** C1
Balneil Gate *SW1* **246** A1
Baltic Street East *EC1* **243** E3
Baltic Street West *EC1* **243** E3
Balvaird Place *SW1* **246** B2
Bancroft Road *E1* **246** C1
Bank End *SE1* **247** E4
Bankside *SE1* **247** E4
Bankside Jetty *SE1* **243** E1
Banner Street *EC1* **243** E3
Banyard Road *SE16* **248** C1
Barbon Close *WC1* **242** C3
Barge House Street *SE1* **243** D1
Bark Place *W2* **240** A1
Barkston Gardens *SW5* **244** A2
Barleycorn Way *E14* **249** F3
Barlow Place *W1* **241** F1
Barlow Street *SE17* **247** F2
Barnaby Place *SW7* **244** C2
Barnardo Street *E1* **249** D3
Barnby Street *NW1* **242** A4
Barnes Street *E14* **249** E4
Barnfield Place *E14* **250** A2
Barnham Street *SE1* **248** A2
Barnsdale Avenue *E14* **250** A2
Barnwood Close *W9* **240** A3
Baron's Place *SE1* **247** D3
Barque Mews *SE8* **250** A1
Barrett Street *W1* **241** E2
Barrie Street *W2* **240** B1
Barrow Hill Road *NW8* **240** C4
St Johns Wood High Street
Barter Street *WC1* **242** B2
Barth Lane *EC2* **243** F2
Bartholomew Close *EC1* **243** E2
Bartholomew Square *EC1* **243** E3
Bartholomew Street *SE1* **247** F2
Barton Street *SW1* **246** B3
Basevi Way *SE8* **250** A1
Basil Street *SW3* **245** D3
Basin Approach *E14* **249** E3
Basinghall Avenue *EC2* **243** E2
Basinghall Street *EC2* **243** E2
Bastwick Street *EC1* **243** E3
Bate Street *E14* **249** F3
Bateman Street *W1* **242** A2
Bateman's Buildings *W1* **242** A2
Bath Court *EC1* **242** C3
Warner Street
Bath Place *N1* **243** F4
Bath Street *EC1* **243** E4
Bath Terrace *SE1* **247** E3
Bathurst Mews *W2* **240** C1
Bathurst Street *W2* **240** C1
Battle Bridge Lane *SE1* **247** F4
Batty Street *E1* **248** B4
Bayley Street *WC1* **242** A2
Baylis Road *SE1* **246** C3
Bayswater Road *W2* **240** A1
Baythorne Street *E3* **249** F4
Beaconsfield Road *SE17* **247** F1
Beak Street *W1* **242** A1
Bear Alley *EC4* **243** D2
Farringdon Street
Bear Gardens *SE1* **243** E1
Bear Lane *SE1* **247** D4
Bear Street *WC2* **242** B1
Cranbourn Street
Beatrice Place *W8* **244** A2
Beauchamp Place *SW3* **245** D3
Beauchamp Street *EC1* **243** D3
Brooke Street
Beaufort Gardens *SW3* **245** D3
Beaufort Street *SW3* **244** B1
Beaumont Mews *W1* **241** E2
Beaumont Place *W1* **242** A3
Beaumont Street *W1* **241** E3
Beccles Street *E14* **249** F3
Beckway Street *SE17* **247** F2
Bedale Street *SE1* **247** E3
Borough High Street
Bedford Avenue *WC1* **242** B2
Bedford Court *WC2* **242** B1
Bedford Gardens *W8* **244** A4
Bedford Place *WC1* **242** B3
Bedford Row *WC1* **242** C3
Bedford Square *WC1* **242** B2
Bedford Street *WC2* **242** B1
Bedford Way *WC1* **242** B3
Bedfordbury *WC2* **242** B1
Bedser Close *SE11* **246** C1
Beech Street *EC2* **243** E3
Beeston Place *SW1* **245** F3
Bekesbourne Street *E14* **249** E3
Belgrave Mews North *SW1* **245** E3
Belgrave Mews South *SW1* **245** E3
Belgrave Mews West *SW1* **245** E3
Belgrave Place *SW1* **245** E3
Belgrave Road *SW1* **245** F2
Belgrave Square *SW1* **245** E3
Belgrave Street *E1* **249** E3
Belgrove Street *WC1* **242** B4
Bell Lane *E1* **248** A4
Bell Street *NW1* **240** C3
Bell Yard *WC2* **242** C2
Bellamy Close *E14* **250** A3
Manilla Street
Belvedere Buildings *SE1* **247** E3
Belvedere Road *SE1* **246** C4
Ben Jonson Road *E1* **249** E4
Ben Smith Way *SE16* **248** C1
Benbow Street *SE8* **250** A1
Bendall Mews *W1* **241** D3
Bennet's Hill *EC4* **243** E1
Castle Baynard Street
Benson Quay *E1* **249** D3
Bentinck Mews *W1* **241** E2
Marylebone Lane
Bentinck Street *W1* **241** E2
Bere Street *E1* **249** E3
Bergen Square *SE16* **249** E1
Bering Square *E14* **250** A1
Maritime Quay
Berkeley Gardens *W8* **244** A4
Berkeley Mews *W1* **241** D2
Berkeley Square *W1* **241** F1
Berkeley Street *W1* **241** F1
Bermondsey Square *SE1* **243** E2
Long Lane
Bermondsey Street *SE1* **248** A2
Bermondsey Wall East *SE16* **248** B1
Bermondsey Wall West *SE16* **248** B2
Bernard Street *WC1* **242** B3
Berners Mews *W1* **242** A2
Berners Street *W1* **242** A2
Berry Street *EC1* **243** E3
Berryfield Road *SE17* **247** E1
Berwick Street *W1* **242** A2
Bessborough Gardens *SW1* **246** B2
Bessborough Place *SW1* **246** A1
Bessborough Street *SW1* **246** A1
Betterton Street *WC2* **242** B2
Betts Street *E1* **248** C3
Bevenden Street *N1* **243** F4
Beverston Mews *W1* **241** D2
Bevin Close *SE16* **249** E2
Bevin Way *WC1* **242** C4
Bevington Street *SE16* **248** B1
Bevis Marks *EC3* **248** A4
Bewley Street *E1* **248** C3
Bickenhall Street *W1* **241** D3
Bidborough Street *WC1* **242** B4
Biddulph Road *W9* **240** A4
Bigland Street *E1* **248** C3
Billiter Square *EC3* **248** A3
Fenchurch Avenue
Billiter Street *EC3* **248** A3
Billson Street *E14* **250** C2
Bina Gardens *SW5* **244** B2
Bingham Place *W1* **241** E3
Binney Street *W1* **241** E1
Birchfield Street *E14* **249** E3
Birchin Lane *EC3* **243** F1
Bird Street *W1* **241** E2
Birdcage Walk *SW1* **246** A3
Birkenhead Street *WC1* **242** B4
Bishop's Court *EC4* **243** D2
Old Bailey
Bishop's Court *WC2* **242** C2
Chancery Lane
Bishop's Terrace *SE11* **247** D2
Bishops Bridge Road *W2* **240** B2
Bishopsgate *EC2* **243** F2
Bishopsgate Arcade *EC2* **248** A4
Bishopsgate Churchyard *EC2* **243** F2
Bittern Street *SE1* **247** E3
Black Prince Road *SE1 & SE11* **246** C2
Black Swan Yard *SE1* **248** A2
Blackall Street *EC2* **243** F3
Blackburne's Mews *W1* **241** E1
Blackfriars Bridge *EC4 & SE1* **243** D1
Blackfriars Lane *EC4* **243** D1
Blackfriars Passage *EC4* **243** D1
Blackfriars Road *SE1* **247** D4
Blacklands Terrace *SW3* **245** D2
Blackwall Tunnel *E14 & SE10* **250** C4
Blackwood Street *SE17* **247** F1
Blandford Square *NW1* **241** D3
Blandford Street *W1* **241** F2
Blasker Walk *E14* **250** A1
Bleeding Heart Yard *EC1* **243** D2
Greville Street
Blenheim Street *W1* **241** F1
New Bond Street
Bletchley Street *N1* **243** E4
Blithfield Street *W8* **244** A3
Blomfield Road *W9* **240** A3
Blomfield Street *EC2* **243** F2
Blomfield Villas *W2* **240** B2
Bloomburg Street *SW1* **245** F2
Vauxhall Bridge Road
Bloomfield Place *W1* **241** F1
Bourdon Street
Bloomfield Terrace *SW1* **245** E2
Bloomsbury Court *WC1* **242** B2
High Holborn
Bloomsbury Place *WC1* **242** B3
Southampton Row
Bloomsbury Square *WC1* **242** B2
Bloomsbury Street *WC1* **242** B2
Bloomsbury Way *WC1* **242** B2
Blount Street *E14* **249** E4
Blue Anchor Yard *E1* **248** B3
Blue Ball Yard *SW1* **246** A4
St James's Street
Blyth Close *E14* **250** C2
Boardwalk Place *E14* **250** B4
Bohn Road *E1* **249** F4
Bolsover Street *W1* **241** F3
Bolt Court *EC4* **243** D2
Bolton Gardens *SW5* **244** A2
Bolton Gardens Mews *SW10* **244** B1
Bolton Street *W1* **245** F4
Boltons Place *SW10* **244** B2
Bond Way *SW8* **246** B1
Bonding Yard Walk *SE16* **249** E1
Bonhill Street *EC2* **243** F3
Bonnington Square *SW8* **246** C1
Booker Close *E14* **249** F4
Boot Street *N1* **243** F4
Booth's Place *W1* **241** F2
Wells Street
Boreas Walk *N1* **243** E4
Nelson Place
Borough High Street *SE1* **247** E3
Borough Road *SE1* **247** E3
Borrett Close *SE17* **247** E1
Borthwick Street *SE8* **250** A1
Boscobel Place *SW1* **245** E2
Boscobel Street *NW8* **240** C3
Boss Street *SE1* **248** A2
Boston Place *NW1* **240** D3
Bosun Close *E14* **250** A3
Boswell Court *WC1* **242** B3
Boswell Street
Boswell Street *WC1* **242** B3
Botolph Lane *EC3* **243** F1
Bott's Mews *W2* **240** A2
Boulcott Street *E1* **249** E3
Boundary Lane *SE17* **247** E1
Boundary Road *SE1* **247** D4
Bourdon Street *W1* **241** F1
Bourlet Close *W1* **241** F2
Bourne Street *SW1* **245** E2
Bourne Terrace *W2* **240** A2
Bouverie Street *EC4* **243** D1
Bow Lane *EC4* **243** E1
Bow Street *WC2* **242** B2
Bowden Street *SE11* **247** D1
Bower Street *E1* **249** D3
Bowling Green Lane *EC1* **243** D3
Bowling Green Place *SE1* **247** F4
Newcomen Street
Bowling Green Street *SE11* **246** C1
Bowling Green Walk *N1* **243** F4
Boyd Street *E1* **248** B3
Boyfield Street *SE1* **247** D3
Boyle Street *W1* **241** F1
Savile Row
Boyson Road *SE17* **247** E1
Brackley Street *EC1* **243** E3
Brad Street *SE1* **247** D4
Braden Street *W9* **240** A3
Bradenham Close *SE17* **247** F1
Braganza Street *SE17* **247** D1
Braham Street *E1* **248** B3
Bramerton Street *SW3* **244** C1
Bramham Gardens *SW5* **244** A2
Branch Road *E14* **249** E3
Brandon Street *SE17* **247** E2
Brangton Road *SE11* **246** C1
Brass Tally Alley *SE16* **249** E1
Bray Crescent *SE16* **249** D2
Bray Place *SW3* **245** D2
Bread Street *EC4* **243** E1
Bream's Buildings *EC4* **242** C2
Brechin Place *SW7* **244** B2
Breezer's Hill *E1* **248** C3
Bremner Road *SW7* **244** B3
Brendon Street *W1* **241** D2
Brenton Street *E14* **249** E4
Bressenden Place *SW1* **245** F3
Brettell Street *SE17* **247** F1
Brewer Street *W1* **242** A1
Brewers' Green *SW1* **246** A3
Caxton Street
Brewhouse Lane *E1* **248** C2
Brewhouse Walk *SE16* **249** E2
Brick Court *EC4* **242** C2
Middle Temple Lane
Brick Street *W1* **245** E4
Bride Lane *EC4* **243** D2
Bridewain Street *SE1* **248** B1
Bridewell Place *EC4* **243** D1
Bridford Mews *W1* **241** F3
Bridge House Quay *E14* **250** C4
Bridge Place *SW1* **245** F2
Bridge Street *SW1* **246** B3
Bridge Yard *SE1* **247** F4
Bridgeport Place *E1* **248** B2
Kennet Street
Bridgewater Square *EC2* **243** E3
Beech Street
Bridgewater Street *EC2* **243** E3
Beech Street
Bridgeway Street *NW1* **242** A2
Bridle Lane *W1* **242** A1
Bridstow Place *W2* **240** A2
Brightlingsea Place *E14* **249** F3
Brill Place *NW1* **242** A4
Briset Street *EC1* **243** D3
Bristol Gardens *W9* **240** A3
Bristol Mews *W9* **240** B3
Britannia Road *E14* **250** A2
Britannia Street *WC1* **242** C4
Britannia Walk *N1* **243** F4
Britten Street *SW3* **244** C1
Britton Street *EC1* **243** D3
Broad Court *WC2* **242** B2
Broad Sanctuary *SW1* **246** B3
Broad Walk *W2* **245** E4
Broadbent Street *W1* **241** F1
Broadley Street *NW8* **240** C4
Broadley Terrace *NW1* **241** D3
Broadstone Place *W1* **241** E2
Broadwall *SE1* **247** D4
Broadway *SW1* **246** A3
Broadwick Street *W1* **242** A1
Brockham Street *SE1* **247** E3
Brodlove Lane *E1* **249** D3
Bromley Street *E1* **249** E4
Brompton Place *SW3* **245** D3
Brompton Road *SW3* **245** D3
Brompton Square *SW3* **244** C3
Bronti Close *SE17* **247** E1
Brook Drive *SE11* **247** D2

Brook Gate
Disney Place
252

Brook Gate W1 241 E1
Brook Mews North W2 240 B1
Brook Street W1 241 E1
Brook Street W2 240 C1
Brook's Mews W1 241 F1
Brooke Street EC1 243 D2
Brooke's Court EC1 242 C2
Brooke's Market EC1 243 D2
Brooke Street
Brown Hart Gardens W1 241 E1
Brown Street W1 241 D2
Browning Close W9 240 B3
Browning Street SE17 247 E2
Brownlow Mews WC1 242 C3
Brownlow Street WC1 242 C2
Brune Street E1 248 A4
Brunel Road SE16 249 D1
Brunswick Gardens W8 244 A4
Brunswick Mews W1 241 D2
Brunswick Place N1 243 F4
Brunswick Quay SE16 249 E1
Brunswick Square WC1 242 B3
Brunton Place E14 249 E3
Brushfield Street E1 248 A4
Bruton Lane W1 241 F1
Bruton Place W1 241 F1
Bruton Street W1 241 F1
Bryan Road SE16 249 F2
Bryanston Mews East W1 241 D2
Bryanston Mews West W1 241 D2
Bryanston Place W1 241 D2
Bryanston Square W1 241 D2
Bryanston Street W1 241 D2
Buck Hill Walk W2 240 C1
Buck Street WC2 242 B1
Buckingham Gate SW1 245 F3
Buckingham Palace Road SW1 245 F2
Buckingham Place SW1 245 F3
Buckland Street N1 243 F4
Buckle Street E1 248 B4
Bucklersbury EC4 243 E2
Bucknall Street WC2 242 B2
Buckters Rents SE16 249 E2
Budge's Walk W2 240 B4
Bulleid Way SW1 245 F2
Bulstrode Place W1 241 E2
Marylebone Lane
Bulstrode Street W1 241 E2
Bunhill Row EC1 243 F3
Bunhouse Place SW1 245 E2
Burbage Close SE1 247 F3
Burdett Street SE1 247 D3
Burge Street SE1 247 F3
Burgess Street E14 249 F4
Burgon Street EC4 243 E2
Carter Lane
Burleigh Street WC2 242 B1
Burlington Arcade W1 241 F1
Burlington Gardens W1 241 F1
Burne Street NW1 240 C3
Burnsall Street SW3 245 D1
Burnside Close SE16 249 E2
Burr Cose E1 248 B2
Burrell Street SE1 247 D4
Burrells Wharf Square E14 250 A1
Burrows Mews SE1 247 D4
Bursar Street SE1 248 A2
Tooley Street
Burslem Street E1 248 C3
Burton Grove SE17 247 F1
Burton Street WC1 242 B4
Burwell Close E1 248 C3
Burwood Place W2 241 D2
Bury Close SE16 249 E2
Bury Court EC3 248 A4
Bury Place WC1 242 B2
Bury Street EC3 248 A3
Bury Street SW1 246 A4
Bury Walk SW3 244 C2
Bush Lane EC4 243 E1
Bushell Street E1 248 B2
Wapping High Street
Butcher Row E1 249 E3
Bute Street SW7 244 C1
Butler Place SW1 245 F3
Buckingham Gate
Butterfield Close SE16 248 C1
Buttesland Street N1 243 F4
Byelands Close SE16 249 E2
Byfield Close SE16 249 F2
Byng Place WC1 242 A3
Byng Street E14 250 A3
Byward Street EC3 248 A3
Bywater Place SE16 249 E2
Bywater Street SW3 245 D2

C

Cabbell Street NW1 240 C2
Cable Street E1 248 B3
Cabot Square E14 250 A4
Cadiz Street SE17 247 E1
Cadogan Gardens SW3 245 D2
Cadogan Gate SW1 245 D2
Cadogan Lane SW1 245 E3
Cadogan Place SW1 245 E2
Cadogan Square SW1 245 D2
Cadogan Street SW3 245 D2
Cahill Street EC1 243 E3
Dufferin Street
Cahir Street E14 250 A2
Cale Street SW3 244 C2
Caleb Street SE1 247 E4
Marshalsea Road
Caledonia Street N1 242 B4
Caledonian Road N1 & N7 242 B4
Caledonian Wharf E14 250 C2
Callingham Close E14 249 F4
Callow Street SW3 244 B1
Calthorpe Street WC1 242 C3
Camberwell Road SE5 247 E1
Cambridge Circus WC2 242 B1
Cambridge Gate NW1 241 F3
Cambridge Gate Mews NW1 241 F4
Albany Street
Cambridge Place W8 244 B3
Cambridge Road NW6 240 A4
Cambridge Square W2 240 C2
Cambridge Street SW1 245 F2
Cambridge Terrace Mews NW1 241 F4
Chester Gate
Camdenhurst Street E14 249 E4
Camera Place SW10 244 B1
Cameron Place E1 248 C4
Camomile Street EC3 248 A4
Campden Grove W8 244 A4
Campden Hill Road W8 244 A3
Camperdown Street E1 248 B3
Canada Square E14 250 B4
Canada Street SE16 249 E1
Canal Street SE5 247 F1
Candover Street W1 241 F2
Foley Street
Canning Passage W8 244 B3
Canning Place W8 244 B3
Cannon Beck Road SE16 249 D2
Cannon Drive E14 249 F3
Cannon Row SW1 246 B3
Cannon Street EC4 243 E2
Cannon Street Road E1 248 C3
Canterbury Place SE17 247 E2
Canvey Street SE1 247 E4
Cape Yard E1 248 B3
Capland Street NW8 240 C3
Capper Street WC1 242 A3
Capstan Square E14 250 C3
Capstan Way SE16 249 E2
Caravel Close E14 250 A3
Carbis Road E14 249 F4
Carburton Street W1 241 F3
Cardale Street E14 250 B3
Plevina Street
Cardigan Street SE11 246 C1
Cardington Street NW1 242 A4
Carey Lane EC2 243 E2
Carey Street WC2 242 C2
Carlisle Avenue EC3 248 A3
Carlisle Lane SE1 246 C3
Carlisle Place SW1 245 F2
Carlisle Street W1 242 A2
Carlos Place W1 241 E1
Carlton Gardens SW1 246 A4
Carlton House Terrace SW1 246 A4
Carlton Vale NW6 240 A4
Carlyle Square SW3 244 C1
Carmelite Street EC4 243 D1
Carnaby Street W1 242 A1
Caroline Place Mews W2 240 A1
Caroline Street E1 249 E3
Caroline Terrace SW1 245 E2
Carpenter Street W1 241 E1
Carr Street E14 249 E4
Carrick Mews SE8 250 A1
Carrington Street W1 245 E4
Shepherd Street
Carter Lane EC4 243 E2
Carter Place SE17 247 E1
Carter Street SE17 247 E1
Carteret Street SW1 246 A3
Carthusian Street EC1 243 E3
Cartier Circle E14 250 B4
Carting Lane WC2 242 C1
Cartwright Gardens WC1 242 B4
Cartwright Street E1 248 B3
Casson Street E1 248 B4
Castalia Square E14 250 B3
Castellain Road W9 240 A3
Castle Baynard Street EC4 243 E1
Castle Lane SW1 246 A3
Castle Yard SE1 247 D4
Castlebrook Close SE11 247 D2
Brook Drive
Castlereagh Street W1 241 D2
Castor Lane E14 250 A4
Catesby Street SE17 247 F2
Cathay Street SE16 248 C1
Cathcart Road SW10 244 B1
Cathedral Piazza SW1 245 F3
Cathedral Street SE1 247 F4
Winchester Walk
Catherine Place SW1 245 F3
Catherine Street WC2 242 C1
Catherine Wheel Alley E1 248 A4
Catherine Wheel Yard SW1 246 A4
Little St James's Street
Cato Street W1 241 D2
Catton Street WC1 242 C2
Causton Street SW1 246 B2
Cavaye Place SW10 244 B1
Cavell Street E1 248 C4
Cavendish Avenue NW8 240 C4
Cavendish Close NW8 240 C4
Cavendish Mews North W1 241 F3
Hallam Street
Cavendish Mews South W1 241 F2
Hallam Street
Cavendish Place W1 241 F2
Cavendish Square W1 241 F2
Caversham Street SW3 245 D1
Caxton Street SW1 246 A3
Cayton Place EC1 243 E4
Cayton Street
Cayton Street EC1 243 E4
Cecil Court WC2 242 B1
St Martin's Lane
Centaur Street SE1 246 C3
Central Street EC1 243 E4
Chadwell Street EC1 243 D4
Chadwick Street SW1 246 A3
Chagford Street NW1 241 D3
Chalton Street NW1 242 A4
Chamber Street E1 248 B3
Chambers Street SE16 248 B1
Chancel Street SE1 247 D4
Chancellor Passage E14 250 A4
South Colonnade
Chancellor Passage E14 250 A4
Chancery Lane WC2 242 C2
Chandler Street E1 248 C2
Chandos Place WC2 242 B1
Chandos Street W1 241 F2
Chantry Square W8 244 A3
Chapel Court SE1 247 E4
Chapel House Street E14 250 B1
Chapel Place W1 241 F2
Chapel Side W2 240 A1
Chapel Street NW1 240 C2
Chapel Street SW1 245 E3
Chapman Street E1 248 C3
Chapter Road SE17 247 E1
Chapter Street SW1 246 A2
Chapter Terrace SE17 247 D1
Chargrove Close SE16 249 D2
Charing Cross Road WC2 242 B2
Charles II Street SW1 242 A1
Charles Square N1 243 F4
Charles Street W1 245 F4
Charleston Street SE17 247 E2
Charlie Chaplin Walk SE1 246 C4
Waterloo Road
Charlotte Place W1 242 A2
Goodge Street
Charlotte Place SW1 245 F2
Wilton Road
Charlotte Road EC2 243 F4
Charlotte Street W1 242 A3
Charlwood Street SW1 246 A1
Charnwood Gardens E14 250 A2
Chart Street N1 243 F4
Charterhouse Square EC1 243 E2
Charterhouse Street EC1 243 D2
Chaseley Street E14 249 E4
Chatham Street SE17 247 F2
Cheapside EC4 243 E2
Chelsea Bridge SW1 & SW8 245 E1
Chelsea Bridge Road SW1 245 E1
Chelsea Embankment SW3 245 D1
Chelsea Manor Gardens SW3 245 D1
Chelsea Manor Street SW3 245 D1
Chelsea Park Gardens SW3 244 C1
Chelsea Square SW3 244 C1
Cheltenham Terrace SW3 245 D2
Chenies Mews WC1 242 A3
Chenies Street WC1 242 E3
Cheniston Gardens W8 244 A3
Chepstow Place W2 240 A1
Chepstow Road W2 240 A2
Chequer Street EC1 243 E3
Cherbury Street N1 243 F4
Cherry Garden Street SE16 248 C1
Cherry Tree Terrace SE1 248 A2
Chesham Place SW1 245 E3
Chesham Street SW1 245 E3
Chester Close North NW1 241 F4
Chester Close South NW1 241 F4
Chester Court NW1 241 F4
Albany Street
Chester Gate NW1 241 F4
Chester Mews SW1 245 E3
Chester Place NW1 241 F4
Chester Row SW1 245 E2
Chester Square SW1 245 E2
Chester Street SW1 245 E3
Chester Terrace NW1 241 F4
Chester Way SE11 247 D2
Chesterfield Gardens W1 245 E4
Chesterfield Hill W1 241 E1
Chesterfield Street W1 245 E4
Cheval Place SW7 245 D3
Cheval Street E14 250 A3
Cheyne Gardens SW3 244 D1
Cheyne Walk SW3 & SW10 244 C1
Chicheley Street SE1 246 C4
Chichester Parade E14 250 C2
Chichester Rents WC2 242 C2
Chancery Lane
Chichester Road W2 240 A3
Chichester Street SW1 246 A1
Chicksand Street E1 248 B4
Chigwell Hill E1 248 C3
The Highway
Child's Place SW5 244 A2
Child's Street SW5 244 A2
Childs Mews SW5 244 A2
Chiltern Street W1 241 E3
Chilworth Mews W2 240 B2
Chilworth Street W2 240 B2
Chipka Street E14 250 B3
Chiswell Street EC1 243 E3
Chitty Street W1 242 A3
Christchurch Street SW3 245 D1
Christian Court SE16 249 F2
Christian Street E1 248 C3
Christopher Close SE16 248 D1
Christopher Street EC2 243 F3
Chudleigh Street E1 249 E4
Chumleigh Street SE5 247 F1
Church Place SW1 245 F4
Piccadilly
Church Street NW8 240 C3
Church Yard Row SE11 247 D2
Churchill Gardens Road SW1 245 F1
Churchill Place E14 250 B4
Churchway NW1 242 A4
Churton Street SW1 246 A2
Cinnamon Street E1 248 C2
Circus Mews W1 241 D3
Enford Street
Circus Place EC2 243 F2
Finsbury Circus
Circus Road NW8 240 C4
Cirencester Street W2 240 A3
Citadel Place SE11 246 C2
City Garden Row N1 243 E4
City Road EC1 243 E3
Clabon Mews SW1 245 D2
Clack Street SE16 249 D1
Claire Place E14 250 A3
Clanricarde Gardens W2 240 A1
Clare Market WC2 242 C2
Claremont Close N1 243 D4
Claremont Square N1 243 D4
Clarence Gardens NW1 241 F4
Clarence Mews SE16 249 D2
Clarendon Close W2 240 C1
Clarendon Gardens W9 240 B3
Clarendon Place W2 240 C1
Clarendon Road W11 245 F1
Clarendon Street SW1 245 F1
Clarendon Terrace W9 240 B3
Clareville Grove SW7 244 B2
Clareville Street SW7 244 B2
Clarges Mews W1 245 F4
Clarges Street W1 245 F4
Clark Street E1 248 C4
Clark's Orchard SE16 248 C1
Claude Street E14 250 A2
Clave Street E1 248 C2
Claverton Street SW1 246 A1
Clay Street W1 241 D2
Clayton Street SE11 246 C1
Clearbrook Way E1 249 D4
Clearwell Drive W9 240 A3
Cleaver Square SE11 247 D1
Cleaver Street SE11 247 D1
Clegg Street E1 248 C2
Clemence Street E14 249 F4
Clement's Inn WC2 242 C2
Clement's Road SE16 248 C1
Clements Lane EC4 243 F1
Clenston Mews W1 241 D2
Clere Street EC2 243 F3
Clerkenwell Close EC1 243 D3
Clerkenwell Green EC1 243 D3
Clerkenwell Road EC1 242 C3
Cleveland Gardens W2 240 B2
Cleveland Mews W1 241 F3
Cleveland Place SW1 246 A4
King Street
Cleveland Row SW1 246 A4
Cleveland Square W2 240 B2
Cleveland Street W1 241 F3
Cleveland Terrace W2 240 B2
Clifford Street W1 241 F1
Clifton Gardens W9 240 B3
Clifton Place W2 240 C1
Clifton Road W9 240 B3
Clifton Street EC2 243 F3
Clifton Villas W9 240 B3
Clink Street SE1 247 E4
Clipper Close SE16 249 D2
Kinburn Street
Clipstone Mews W1 241 F3
Clipstone Street W1 241 F3
Cliveden Place SW1 245 E2
Cloak Lane EC4 243 E1
Cloth Fair EC1 243 E2
Cloth Street EC1 243 E3
Clunbury Street N1 243 F4
Cherbury Street
Cluny Place SE1 247 F3
Coach & Horses Yard W1 241 F1
Old Burlington Street
Coach House Mews SE1 247 F3
Cobb Street E1 248 A4
Cobourg Street NW1 242 A4
Cock Lane EC1 243 D2
Cockpit Yard WC1 242 C3
Cockspur Street SW1 246 B4
Codling Close E1 248 C1
Coin Street SE1 247 D4
Coke Street E1 248 B4
Colbeck Mews SW7 244 B2
Colchester Street E1 248 B4
Drum Street
Coldbath Square EC1 242 C3
Coldharbour E14 250 C4
Cole Street SE1 247 E3
Colebrooke Row N1 243 D1
Coleherne Mews SW10 246 A1
Coleherne Road SW10 244 A1
Coleman Street EC2 243 E2
Coley Street WC1 242 C3
College Hill EC4 243 E1
College Street
College Street EC4 243 E1
Collett Road SE16 248 C1
Collier Street N1 242 C4
Collingham Gardens SW5 244 A2
Collingham Place SW4 244 A2
Collingham Road SW5 244 A2
Collinson Street SE1 247 E3
Colnbrook Street SE1 247 D3
Colombo Street SE1 247 D4
Colonnade WC1 242 B3
Colworth Grove SE17 247 E2
Commercial Road E1 & E14 248 B4
Commercial Street E1 248 A4
Compton Passage EC1 243 D3
Compton Place WC1 242 B3
Compton Street EC1 243 D3
Comus Place SE17 247 F2
Concert Hall Approach SE1 246 C4
Conder Street E14 249 E4
Salmon Lane
Conduit Mews W2 240 C4
Conduit Place W2 240 C2
Conduit Street W1 241 F1
Congreve Street SE17 247 F2
Connaught Place W2 241 D1
Connaught Square W2 241 D2
Connaught Street W2 240 C2
Cons Street SE1 247 D4
Constitution Hill SW1 245 E3
Content Street SE17 247 E2
Conway Street W1 241 F3
Cook's Road E15 247 D1
Cookham Crescent SE16 249 D2
Coombs Street N1 243 E4
Cooper Close SE1 247 D3
Cooper's Row EC3 248 A3
Cope Place W8 244 A3
Copeland Drive E14 250 A2
Copenhagen Place E14 249 F3
Copley Close SE17 247 E1
Copperfield Street SE1 247 E4
Copthall Avenue EC2 243 F2
Coptic Street WC1 242 B2
Coral Street SE1 247 D3
Coram Street WC1 242 B3
Cord Way E14 250 A3
Cork Square E1 248 C2
Cork Street W1 241 F1
Corlett Street NW1 240 C3
Bell Street
Corner House Street WC2 246 B4
Northumberland Street
Cornhill EC3 243 F2
Cornwall Gardens SW7 244 B3
Cornwall Gardens Walk SW7 244 A2
Cornwall Mews South SW7 244 B2
Cornwall Mews West SW7 244 A3
Cornwall Road SE1 246 C4
Cornwall Square SE11 247 D1
Cornwall Street E1 248 C3
Cornwall Terrace NW1 241 D3
Cornwood Drive E1 249 D4
Coronet Street N1 243 F4
Corporation Row EC1 243 D3
Corsham Street N1 243 F4
Cosmo Place WC1 242 B3
Cosser Street SE1 246 C3
Cosway Street NW1 241 D3
Cotham Street SE17 247 E2
Cottage Place SW3 244 C3
Cottesloe Mews SE1 247 D3
Cottesmore Gardens W8 244 B3
Cottingham Close SE11 247 D2
Cottington Street SE11 247 D2
Cottons Lane SE1 247 F4
Counter Street SE1 247 F4
County Street SE1 247 E2
Court Street E1 248 C4
Courtenay Square SE11 246 C1
Courtenay Street SE11 246 C1
Courtfield Gardens SW5 244 A2
Courtfield Road SW7 244 B2
Cousin Lane EC4 243 F1
Coventry Street W1 242 A1
Coverley Close E1 248 B4
Cowcross Street EC1 243 D3
Cowley Street SW1 246 B3
Cowper Street EC2 243 F3
Coxon Place SE1 248 A1
Crace Street NW1 242 A4
Crail Row SE17 247 F2
Cramer Street W1 241 E2
Crampton Street SE17 247 C2
Cranbourn Street WC2 242 B1
Crane Street SE10 250 C1
Cranford Street E1 249 E3
Cranley Gardens SW7 244 B2
Cranley Mews SW7 244 B2
Cranley Place SW7 244 C2
Cranmer Court SW3 245 D2
Cranwood Street EC1 243 F4
Craven Hill W2 240 B1
Craven Hill Gardens W2 240 B1
Craven Hill Mews W2 240 B1
Craven Road W2 240 B1
Craven Street WC2 242 B1
Craven Terrace W2 240 B1
Crawford Passage EC1 243 D3
Crawford Place W1 241 D2
Crawford Street W1 241 D2
Creasy Street SE1 247 F3
Swan Mead
Creechurch Lane EC3 248 A3
Creechurch Place EC3 248 A3
Creed Lane EC4 243 E2
Crescent EC3 248 A3
America Square
Crescent Place SW3 245 D2
Crescent Row EC1 243 E3
Cresswell Place SW10 244 B1
Cressy Place E1 249 D4
Crestfield Street WC1 242 B4
Cricketers' Court SE11 247 D1
Kennington Park Road
Crimscott Street SE1 248 A1
Cripplegate Street EC1 241 E3
Viscount Street
Crispin Street E1 248 A4
Crofts Street E1 248 B3
Cromer Street WC1 242 B3
Crompton Street W2 240 B3
Cromwell Mews SW7 244 C2
Cromwell Place SW7 244 C2
Cromwell Road SW7 & SW5 244 A1
Crondall Street N1 243 F4
Crosby Row SE1 247 F3
Crosby Square EC3 243 F2
Great St Helen's
Cross Keys Close W1 241 E2
Marylebone Lane
Cross Lane EC3 248 A3
St Dunstan's Hill
Crosslet Street SE17 247 F2
Crosswall EC3 248 A3
Crowder Street E1 248 C3
Crown Court WC2 242 B2
Crown Office Row EC4 243 D1
Crown Passage SW1 246 A4
Crown Place EC2 243 F3
Crucifix Lane SE1 248 A2
Cruikshank Street WC1 242 C4
Crutched Friars EC3 248 A3
Cuba Street E14 250 A2
Cubitt Steps E14 250 A4
Cubitt Street WC1 242 C4
Cubitts Yard WC2 242 B1
James Street
Culford Gardens SW3 245 D2
Culling Road SE16 249 D1
Cullum Street EC3 248 A3
Culross Street W1 241 E1
Culworth Street NW8 240 C4
Cumberland Gardens WC1 242 C4
Great Percy Street
Cumberland Gate W1 & W2 241 D1
Cumberland Market NW1 241 F4
Cumberland Street SW1 245 F1
Cumberland Terrace NW1 241 E4
Cumberland Terrace Mews NW1 241 F4
Albany Street
Cumming Street N1 242 C4
Cundy Street SW1 245 E2
Cunningham Place NW8 240 C3
Cureton Street SW1 246 B2
Curlew Street SE1 248 B2
Cursitor Street EC4 242 C2
Curzon Gate W1 245 E4
Curzon Place W1 245 E4
Curzon Street W1 245 E4
Cuthbert Street W2 240 C3
Cutler Street E1 248 A4
Cutlers Square E14 250 A2
Cyclops Mews E14 250 A2
Cynthia Street N1 242 C4
Cypress Place W1 242 A3
Cyrus Street EC1 243 D3
Czar Street SE8 250 A1

D

D'Arblay Street W1 242 A2
D'Oyley Street SW1 245 E2
Da Gama Place E14 250 A1
Maritime Quay
Dacre Street SW1 246 A3
Dalgleish Street E14 249 E4
Dallington Square EC1 243 E3
Dallington Street EC1 243 D3
Damien Street E1 248 C4
Dane Street WC1 242 C2
Dante Road SE11 247 D2
Daplyn Street E1 248 B4
Dark House Walk EC3 243 F1
Dartford Street SE17 247 E1
Dartmouth Street SW1 246 A3
Darwin Street SE17 247 F2
Date Street SE17 247 E1
Davenant Street E1 248 B4
Daventry Street NW1 240 C3
Davidge Street SE1 247 D3
Davies Mews W1 241 E1
Davies Street W1 241 E1
Dawes Street SE17 247 F2
Dawson Place W2 240 A1
De Laune Street SE17 247 D1
De Vere Gardens W8 244 B3
De Walden Street W1 241 E2
Westmorland Street
Deacon Way SE17 247 E2
Deal Porters Way SE16 249 D1
Deal Street E1 248 B4
Dean Bradley Street SW1 246 B2
Dean Close SE16 249 E2
Dean Farrar Street SW1 246 A3
Dean Ryle Street SW1 246 B2
Dean Stanley Street SW1 246 B2
Millbank
Dean Street W1 242 A2
Dean Trench Street SW1 246 B3
Dean's Buildings SE17 247 F2
Dean's Court EC4 243 E2
Carter Lane
Dean's Mews W1 241 F2
Deancross Street E1 248 C3
Deanery Street W1 245 E4
Decima Street SE1 247 F3
Deck Close SE16 249 E2
Defoe Close SE16 249 F1
Delamere Terrace W2 240 A3
Delaware Road W9 240 A3
Dellow Street E1 248 C3
Delverton Road SE17 247 E1
Denbigh Street SW1 246 A2
Denman Street W1 242 A1
Denmark Place WC2 242 B2
Charing Cross Road
Denmark Street WC2 242 B2
Denning Close NW8 240 B4
Denny Crescent SE11 247 D2
Denny Street SE11 247 D2
Denyer Street SW3 245 D2
Deptford Green SE8 250 A1
Derby Gate SW1 246 B3
Derby Street W1 245 E4
Dering Street W1 241 F2
Deverell Street SE1 247 F3
Devereux Court WC2 242 B1
Strand
Devonport Street E1 249 D3
Devonshire Close W1 241 F3
Devonshire Mews South W1 241 E3
Devonshire Mews West W1 241 E3
Devonshire Place W1 241 E3
Devonshire Place W8 244 A3
St Mary's Place
Devonshire Place Mews W1 241 E3
Devonshire Row EC2 248 A4
Devonshire Square EC2 248 A4
Devonshire Street W1 241 E3
Devonshire Terrace W2 240 B1
Diadem Court W1 242 A2
Dean Street
Dickens Square SE1 247 E3
Dilke Street SW3 245 D1
Dingle Gardens E14 250 A4
Dingley Place EC1 243 E4
Dingley Road EC1 243 E4
Disney Place SE1 247 E3

Disney Street
Hanover Terrace Mews
253

Disney Street SE1 247 E4
Redcross Way
Distaff Lane EC4 243 E1
Distin Street SE11 246 C2
Dixon's Alley SE16 248 C1
West Lane
Dock Hill Avenue SE16 249 E2
Dock Street E1 248 B3
Dockers Tanner Road E14 250 A2
Dockhead SE1 248 B1
Dockley Road SE16 248 B1
Dod Street E14 249 F4
Doddington Grove SE17 247 D1
Doddington Place SE17 247 D1
Dodson Street SE1 247 D3
Dolben Street SE1 247 D4
Dolland Street SE11 246 C1
Dolphin Close SE16 249 D2
Dombey Street WC1 242 C3
Domingo Street EC1 243 E3
Old Street
Dominion Street EC2 243 F2
Donegal Street N1 242 C4
Dongola Road E1 249 F4
Donne Place SW3 245 D2
Doon Street SE1 246 C4
Dora Street E14 249 F4
Doric Way NW1 242 A4
Dorrington Street EC1 243 D3
Brooke Street
Dorset Close NW1 241 D3
Dorset Mews SW1 245 E3
Dorset Rise EC4 243 D1
Dorset Square NW1 241 D3
Dorset Street W1 241 D2
Doughty Mews WC1 242 C3
Doughty Street WC1 242 C3
Douglas Place SW1 246 A2
Douglas Street
Douglas Street SW1 246 A2
Douro Place W8 244 B3
Dove Mews SW5 244 B2
Dove Walk SW1 245 E2
Dovehouse Street SW3 244 C1
Dover Street W1 241 F1
Dowgate Hill EC4 243 F1
Down Street W1 245 E4
Downfield Close W9 240 A3
Downing Street SW1 246 B4
Downton Road SE16 249 E2
Doyce Street SE1 247 E4
Draco Street SE17 247 E1
Drake Street WC1 242 C2
Drawdock Road SE10 250 C4
Draycott Avenue SW3 245 D2
Draycott Place SW3 245 D2
Draycott Terrace SW3 245 D2
Drayson Mews W8 244 A3
Drayton Gardens SW10 244 B1
Druid Street SE1 248 A2
Drum Street E1 248 B4
Drummond Crescent NW1 242 A4
Drummond Gate SW1 246 A1
Drummond Road SE16 248 C1
Drummond Street NW1 241 F3
Drury Lane WC2 242 B2
Dryden Court SE11 247 D2
Duchess Mews W1 241 F2
Duchess Street W1 241 F2
Duchy Street SE1 247 D4
Duck Lane W1 242 A2
Dudley Street W2 240 B2
Dudmaston Mews SW3 244 C2
Dufferin Street EC1 243 E3
Dufour's Place W1 242 A4
Dugard Way SE11 247 D2
Renfrew Road
Duke of Wellington Place SW1 245 E3
Duke of York Street SW1 242 A1
Duke Street W1 241 E2
Duke Street Hill SE1 247 F4
Duke's Lane W8 244 A4
Duke's Place EC3 248 A4
Duke's Road WC1 242 B4
Duke's Yard W1 241 E2
Duke Street
Duncannon Street WC2 242 B1
Dundee Street E1 248 C2
Dundee Wharf E14 249 F3
Dunelm Street E1 249 D4
Dunlop Place SE16 248 B1
Dunraven Street W1 241 E1
Dunstable Mews W1 241 E3
Dunster Court EC3 248 A3
Dunsterville Way SE1 247 F3
Duplex Ride SW1 245 E3
Dupont Street E14 249 E4
Durham House Street WC2 242 B1
Durham Row E1 249 E4
Durham Street SE11 246 C1
Durham Terrace W2 240 A2
Durward Street E1 248 C4
Durweston Street W1 241 D2
Crawford Street
Duthie Street E14 250 C4
Dyott Street WC1 242 B2
Dysart Street EC2 243 F3

E

Eagle Court EC1 243 D3
Eagle Place SW1 246 A4
Piccadilly
Eagle Street WC2 242 C2
Eardley Crescent SW5 244 A1
Earl Street EC2 243 F3
Earl's Court Gardens SW5 244 A2
Earl's Court Square SW5 244 A1
Earlham Street WC2 242 B2
Earls Court Road W8 244 A2
Earlstoke Street EC1 243 D4
Spencer Street
Earnshaw Street WC2 242 B2
Easley's Mews W1 241 E2
Wigmore Street
East Arbour Street E1 249 D4
East Ferry Road E14 250 B2
East Harding Street EC4 243 D2
East India Dock Wall Road E14 243 D2
East Lane SE16 248 B1
East Mount Street E1 248 C4
East Road N1 243 F4
East Smithfield E1 248 B3
East Street SE17 247 E1
East Tenter Street E1 248 B3
Eastbourne Mews W2 240 B2
Eastbourne Terrace W2 240 B2
Eastcastle Street W1 242 A2
Eastcheap EC3 243 F1
Eastney Street SE10 250 C1
Easton Street WC1 242 C3
Eaton Gate SW1 245 E2
Eaton Mews North SW1 245 E2
Eaton Mews South SW1 245 E2
Eaton Place SW1 245 E2
Eaton Square SW1 245 E2
Eaton Terrace SW1 245 E2
Ebbisham Drive SW8 246 C1
Ebenezer Street N1 243 F4
Ebury Bridge SW1 245 E2
Ebury Bridge Road SW1 245 E1
Ebury Mews SW1 245 E2
Ebury Mews East SW1 245 E2
Ebury Square SW1 245 E2
Ebury Street SW1 245 E2
Eccleston Bridge SW1 245 F2
Eccleston Mews SW1 245 E3
Eccleston Place SW1 245 E2
Eccleston Square SW1 245 F2
Eccleston Square Mews SW1 245 F2
Eccleston Street SW1 245 E2
Edbrooke Road W9 240 A3
Edge Street W8 244 A4
Edgware Road W2 240 C3
Edward Mews NW1 241 F4
Edward Mews W1 241 E2
Edward Square SE16 249 F3
Egerton Crescent SW3 245 D2
Egerton Gardens SW3 244 C2
Egerton Terrace SW3 245 D3
Elba Place SE17 247 E2
Eldon Road W8 244 B3
Eldon Street EC2 243 F2
Eleanor Close SE16 249 D2
Elephant and Castle SE1 247 E2
Elephant Lane SE16 248 C2
Elephant Road SE17 247 E2
Elf Row E1 249 D3
Elgar Street SE16 249 F1
Elgin Avenue W9 240 A3
Elgin Mews North W9 240 A4
Elgin Mews South W9 240 B4
Elia Street N1 243 D4
Elim Street SE1 247 F3
Eliot Mews NW8 240 B4
Elizabeth Bridge SW1 245 F2
Elizabeth Close W9 240 B3
Elizabeth Square SE16 249 E3
Elizabeth Street SW1 245 E2
Ellen Street E1 248 B3
Elliott Road SE9 247 D2
Ellis Street SW1 245 E2
Elm Park Gardens SW10 244 C1
Elm Park Lane SW3 244 B1
Elm Park Road SW3 244 B1
Elm Place SW7 244 C1
Elm Street WC1 242 C3
Elm Tree Close NW8 240 C4
Elm Tree Road NW8 240 C4
Elmfield Way W9 240 A3
Elmos Road SE16 249 E1
Elms Mews W2 240 C1
Elnathan Mews W9 240 A3
Elsa Street E1 249 E4
Elsted Street SE17 247 F2
Elvaston Mews SW7 244 B3
Elvaston Place SW7 244 B3
Elverton Street SW1 246 A2
Ely Place EC1 243 D2
Elystan Place SW3 245 D2
Elystan Street SW3 244 C2
Emba Street SE16 248 C1
Embankment Gardens SW3 245 D1
Embankment Place WC2 246 B4
Emerald Street WC1 242 C3
Emerson Street SE1 247 E4
Emery Hill Street SW1 246 A2
Emery Street SE1 247 D3
Emmett Street E14 249 F3
Emperor's Gate SW7 244 B2
Empire Wharf Road E14 250 C2
Empress Place SW6 244 A1
Empress Street SE17 247 E1
Endell Street WC2 242 B2
Endsleigh Gardens WC1 242 A3
Endsleigh Place WC1 242 A3
Endsleigh Street WC1 242 A3
Enford Street W1 241 D3
English Grounds SE1 248 A2
Enid Street SE16 248 B1
Ennismore Garden Mews SW7 244 C3
Ennismore Gardens SW7 244 C3
Ennismore Mews SW7 244 C3
Ennismore Street SW7 244 C3
Ensign Street E1 248 B3
Ensor Mews SW7 244 B1
Epping Close E14 250 A2
Epworth Street EC2 243 F3
Erasmus Street SW1 246 B2
Errol Street EC1 243 E3
Essendine Road W9 240 A4
Essex Street WC2 242 C1
Esterbrooke Street SW1 246 A2
Ethel Street SE17 247 E2
Europa Place EC1 243 E4
Euston Road NW1 241 F3
Euston Square NW1 242 A4
Euston Street NW1 242 A4
Evelyn Gardens SW7 246 B1
Evelyn Walk N1 243 F4
Evelyn Yard W1 242 A2
Gresse Street
Eversholt Street NW1 242 A4
Ewer Street SE1 247 E4
Exchange Place EC2 248 A4
Exchange Square EC2 248 A4
Exeter Street WC2 242 B1
Exhibition Road SW7 244 C3
Exmouth Market EC1 243 D3
Exmouth Street E1 249 D4
Exon Street SE17 247 F2
Exton Street SE1 246 C4
Eyre Street Hill EC1 243 D3

F

Factory Place E14 250 B1
Ferry Street
Fair Street SE1 248 A2
Fairclough Street E1 248 B3
Falcon Close SE1 247 E4
Falcon Way E14 250 B2
Falconberg Mews W1 242 A2
Sutton Row
Falmouth Road SE1 247 E3
Fann Street EC1 243 E3
Fanshaw Street N1 243 F4
Fareham Street W1 242 B1
Dean Street
Farm Street W1 241 E1
Farmer Street W8 244 A4
Farncombe Street SE16 248 C1
Farnell Mews SW5 244 A1
Farnham Place SE1 247 E4
Farnham Royal SE11 246 C1
Farrance Street E14 249 F3
Farrier Walk SW10 244 B1
Farringdon Lane EC1 243 D3
Farringdon Road EC1 242 C3
Farringdon Street EC4 243 D2
Farrins Rents SE16 249 E2
Farrow Place SE16 249 E1
Farthing Alley SE1 248 B1
Wolseley Street
Farthing Fields E1 248 C2
Raine Street
Fashion Street E1 248 B4
Faunce Street SE17 247 D1
Fawcett Street SW10 244 B1
Feather's Place SE10 250 C1
Featherstone Street EC1 243 F3
Felstead Gardens E14 250 B1
Fen Court EC3 248 A3
Fenchurch Avenue EC3 248 A3
Fenchurch Buildings EC3 243 F1
Fenchurch Street
Fenchurch Place EC3 243 F1
Fenchurch Street
Fenchurch Street EC3 243 F1
Fendall Street SE1 248 A1
Fenning Street SE1 247 F4
St Thomas Street
Fennings Circus W1 242 A2
Ferguson Close E14 250 A2
Fernsbury Street WC1 242 C4
Ferry Street E14 250 B1
Fetter Lane EC4 243 D2
Field Street WC1 242 C4
Fieldgate Street E1 248 B4
Fielding Street SE17 247 E1
Finborough Road SW10 244 A1
Finch Lane EC3 243 F2
Finland Street SE16 249 E1
Finsbury Avenue EC2 243 F2
Finsbury Circus EC2 243 F2
Finsbury Market EC2 243 F3
Finsbury Pavement EC2 243 F3
Finsbury Square EC2 243 F3
Finsbury Street EC2 243 F3
First Street SW3 245 D2
Firtree Close SE16 249 E2
Fish Street Hill EC3 243 F1
Fish Wharf EC3 243 F1
Fisher Street WC1 242 C2
Fisherman's Walk E14 250 A4
Fishermans Drive SE16 249 E2
Fisherton Street NW8 240 C3
Fishmongers' Hall Wharf EC4 243 F1
Fitzalan Street SE11 246 C2
Fitzhardinge Street W1 241 E2
Fitzmaurice Place W1 241 F1
Fitzroy Square W1 241 F3
Fitzroy Street WC1 241 F3
Flamborough Street E14 249 E3
Flank Street E1 248 B3
Flaxman Terrace WC1 242 B4
Fleet Square WC1 242 C4
Fleet Street EC4 243 D2
Fleming Road SE17 247 D1
Fletcher Street E1 248 B3
Flint Street SE17 247 F2
Flitcroft Street WC2 242 B2
Flood Street SW3 245 D1
Flood Walk SW3 245 D1
Floral Street WC2 242 B1
Flower and Dean Walk E1 248 B4
Thrawl Street
Foley Street W1 241 F2
Folly Wall E14 250 C3
Forbes Street E1 248 B3
Ford Square E1 248 C4
Fordham Street E1 248 C4
Fore Street EC2 243 E2
Fore Street Avenue EC2 243 E2
Formosa Street W9 240 A3
Forset Street W1 241 D2
Forsyth Gardens SE17 247 D1
Fort Street E1 248 A4
Artillery Lane
Fortune Street EC1 243 E3
Foscote Mews W9 240 A3
Foster Lane EC2 243 E2
Foubert's Place W1 241 F1
Foulis Terrace SW7 244 C2
Foundry Close SE16 249 E2
Fountain Green Square SE16 248 C1
Fournier Street E1 248 B4
Fowey Close E1 248 C2
Fox and Knot Street EC1 243 E2
Charterhouse Square
Frampton Street NW8 240 C3
Francis Close E14 250 C2
Francis Street SW1 246 A2
Franklin's Row SW3 245 D1
Frazier Street SE1 246 C3
Frean Street SE16 248 B1
Frederick Close W2 241 D1
Frederick Road SE17 247 E1
Frederick Square SE16 249 E3
Frederick Street WC1 242 C4
Fredericks Row EC1 243 D4
Goswell Road
Fremantle Street SE17 247 F2
French Ordinary Court EC3 248 A3
Hart Street
Friar Street EC4 243 E2
Carter Lane
Friars Mead E14 250 B2
Friday Street EC4 243 E1
Friend Street EC1 243 D4
Frigate Mews SE8 250 A1
Frith Street W1 242 A2
Frobisher Passage E14 250 A4
North Collonade
Frobisher Passage E14 250 A4
Frostic Walk E1 248 B4
Frying Pan Alley E1 248 A4
Fulbourne Street E1 248 C4
Fulford Street SE16 248 C1
Fulham Road SW3, SW6 & SW10 244 C1
Fulwood Place WC1 242 C2
Furnival Street EC4 243 D2
Fynes Street SW1 246 A2

G

Gabriels Wharf SE1 247 D4
Gainsford Street SE1 248 A2
Galbraith Street E14 250 B3
Galen Place WC1 242 B2
Galleon Close SE16 249 D2
Kinburn Street
Galleons View E14 250 C3
Galway Street EC1 243 E4
Gambia Street SE1 247 D4
Ganton Street W1 242 A1
Garbutt Place W1 241 E2
Gard Street EC1 243 E4
Garden Mews W2 240 A1
Garden Road NW8 240 B4
Garden Row SE1 247 D3
Garden Street E1 249 E4
Gardeners Lane EC4 243 E1
High Timber Street
Garford Street E14 249 F3
Garlick Hill EC4 243 F1
Garnault Mews EC1 243 D4
Garnet Street E1 248 C3
Garrett Street EC1 243 E3
Garrick Street WC2 242 B1
Garter Way SE16 249 D1
Garway Road W2 240 A2
Gaselee Street E14 250 C4
Gasholder Place SE11 246 C1
Gaspar Close SW5 244 B2
Gaspar Mews SW5 244 B2
Gate Street WC2 242 C2
Gateway SE17 247 E1
Gatliff Road SW1 245 E1
Gaunt Street SE1 247 E3
Gavel Street SE17 247 F2
Gayfere Street SW1 246 B3
Gaywood Street SE1 247 D3
Gaza Street SE17 247 D1
Gedling Place SE1 248 B1
Gee Street EC1 243 E3
Gees Court W1 241 E2
George Mathers Road SE11 247 D2
George Mews NW1 242 A4
George Row SE16 248 B1
George Street W1 241 D2
George Yard EC3 243 F1
George Yard W1 241 E1
Gerald Road SW1 245 E2
Geraldine Street SE11 247 D3
Gerrard Place W1 242 B1
Gerrard Street
Gerrard Street W1 242 A1
Gerridge Street SE1 247 D3
Gibson Road SE11 247 D3
Gilbert Place WC1 242 B2
Gilbert Road SE11 247 D2
Gilbert Street W1 241 E1
Gildea Street W1 241 F2
Gill Street E14 249 F3
Gillingham Street SW1 245 F2
Gillison Walk SE16 248 C1
Gilpin Close W2 240 B2
Porteus Road
Gilston Road SW10 244 B1
Giltspur Street EC1 243 D2
Gladstone Street SE1 247 D3
Glamis Place E1 249 D3
Glamis Road E1 249 D3
Glangarnock Avenue E14 250 C2
Glasgow Terrace SW1 245 F1
Glasshill Street SE1 247 E3
Glasshouse Fields E1 249 D3
Glasshouse Street W1 242 A1
Glasshouse Walk SE11 246 B1
Glastonbury Place E1 249 D3
Glebe Place SW3 244 C1
Gledhow Gardens SW5 244 B2
Glenaffric Avenue E14 250 C2
Glendower Place SW7 244 C2
Glengall Grove E14 250 B3
Glentworth Street NW1 241 D3
Glenworth Avenue E14 250 C2
Globe Pond Road SE16 249 E2
Globe Street SE1 247 E3
Gloucester Arcade SW7 244 B2
Gloucester Court EC3 248 A3
Gloucester Gate Mews NW1 242 F4
Albany Street
Gloucester Mews W2 240 B2
Gloucester Mews West W2 240 B2
Gloucester Park SW7 244 B2
Gloucester Place NW1 & W1 241 D3
Gloucester Place Mews W1 241 D2
Gloucester Road SW7 244 B3
Gloucester Square W2 240 C2
Gloucester Street SW1 245 F1
Gloucester Terrace W2 240 B2
Gloucester Walk W8 244 A4
Gloucester Way EC1 243 D4
Glyn Street SE11 246 C1
Goat Street SE1 248 A2
Lafone Street
Godfrey Street SW3 245 D2
Goding Street SE11 246 B1
Godliman Street EC4 243 E1
Golden Lane EC1 243 E3
Golden Square W1 242 A1
Golding Street E1 248 C3
Gomm Road SE16 249 D1
Goodge Place W1 242 A2
Goodge Street W1 242 A2
Goodhart Place E14 249 E3
Goodman's Stile E1 248 B4
Goodman's Yard E1 248 B3
Goodwin Close SE16 248 B1
Gophir Lane EC4 243 F1
Bush Lane
Gordon Place W8 244 A4
Gordon Square WC1 242 A3
Gordon Street WC1 242 A3
Gore Street SW7 244 B3
Goring Street E1 248 A4
Bevis Marks
Gosfield Street W1 241 F2
Goslett Yard WC2 242 B2
Goswell Road EC1 243 D4
Gough Square EC4 243 D2
Gough Street WC1 242 C3
Goulston Street E1 248 B4
Gower Mews WC1 242 A2
Gower Place WC1 242 A3
Gower Street WC1 242 A3
Gowers Walk E1 248 B3
Grace's Alley E1 248 B3
Gracechurch Street EC3 243 F1
Graces Mews NW8 240 B4
Grafton Mews W1 241 F3
Grafton Place NW1 242 A4
Grafton Street W1 241 F1
Grafton Way W1 241 A3
Graham Street N1 243 E4
Graham Terrace SW1 245 E2
Granby Terrace NW1 241 F4
Grand Avenue EC1 243 D2
Grand Junction Wharf N1 243 E4
Grange Court WC2 242 C2
Grange Road SE1 248 A1
Grange Walk SE1 248 A1
Grange Yard SE1 248 A1
Grant's Quay Wharf EC3 243 F1
Grantully Road W9 240 A4
Granville Place W1 241 E2
Granville Road NW6 240 A4
Granville Square WC1 242 C4
Granville Street WC1 242 C4
Granville Square
Grape Street WC2 242 B2
Gravel Lane E1 248 A4
Gray Street SE1 247 D3
Gray's Inn Place WC1 242 C2
Gray's Inn Road WC1 242 B4
Great Castle Street W1 241 F2
Great Central Street NW1 241 D3
Great Chapel Street W1 242 A2
Great College Street SW1 241 D1
Seymour Street
Great Cumberland Place W1 241 D2
Great Dover Street SE1 247 F3
Great Eastern Street EC2 243 F3
Great George Street SW1 246 B3
Great Guildford Street SE1 247 E4
Great James Street WC1 242 C3
Great Marlborough Street W1 241 F2
Great Maze Pond SE1 247 F4
Great New Street EC4 243 D2
Great Newport Street WC2 242 B1
Charing Cross Road
Great Ormond Street WC1 242 C3
Great Percy Street WC1 242 C4
Great Peter Street SW1 246 A3
Great Portland Street W1 241 F3
Great Pulteney Street W1 242 A1
Great Queen Street WC2 242 B2
Great Russell Street WC1 242 B2
Great Scotland Yard SW1 246 B4
Great Smith Street SW1 246 B3
Great St Helen's EC3 243 F2
Great St Thomas Apostle EC4 243 E1
Queen Street
Great Suffolk Street SE1 247 E3
Great Sutton Street EC1 243 D3
Great Swan Alley EC2 243 F2
Great Tower Street EC3 248 A3
Great Trinity Lane EC4 243 E1
Garlick Hill
Great Turnstile WC1 242 B2
High Holborn
Great Winchester Street EC2 243 F2
Great Windmill Street W1 242 A1
Greatorex Street E1 248 B4
Greek Street W1 242 B2
Green Bank E1 248 C2
Green Dragon Court SE1 247 F4
Green Dragon Yard E1 248 B4
Green Street W1 241 E1
Green Walk SE1 247 F3
Green Yard WC1 242 C3
Greenacre Square SE16 249 E2
Greenberry Street NW8 240 C4
Greencoat Place SW1 246 A2
Greencoat Row SW1 246 A2
Greenfield Road E1 248 B4
Greenham Close SE1 247 D3
Greenwell Street W1 241 F3
Greenwich Park Street SE10 250 C1
Greenwich View Place E14 250 C3
Greet Street SE1 247 D4
Gregory Place W8 244 A3
Greig Terrace SE17 247 E1
Grenade Street E14 249 F3
Grendon Street NW8 240 C3
Grenville Place SW7 244 B2
Grenville Street WC1 242 B3
Gresham Street EC2 243 E2
Gresse Street W1 242 A2
Greville Street EC1 243 D2
Greycoat Place SW1 246 A3
Greycoat Street SW1 246 A2
Greystoke Place EC4 243 D2
Fetter Lane
Grigg's Place SE1 248 A1
Groom Place SW1 245 E3
Grosvenor Crescent SW1 245 E3
Grosvenor Crescent Mews SW1 245 E3
Grosvenor Gardens SW1 245 F3
Grosvenor Gate W1 241 E1
Park Lane
Grosvenor Hill W1 241 F1
Grosvenor Place SW1 245 E3
Grosvenor Road SW1 245 F1
Grosvenor Square W1 241 E1
Grosvenor Street W1 241 E1
Grosvenor Wharf Road E14 250 C2
Grove End Road NW8 240 B4
Grove Gardens NW8 241 D4
Grove Hall Court NW8 240 B4
Guildhall Buildings EC2 243 E2
Basinghall Street
Guildhall Yard EC2 243 E2
Guildhouse Street SW1 245 F2
Guilford Place WC1 242 B3
Guilford Street
Guilford Street WC1 242 B3
Guinness Square SE1 247 F2
Gulliver Street SE16 249 F1
Gulston Walk SW3 245 D2
Gun Street E1 248 A4
Gunthorpe Street E1 248 B4
Gunwhale Close SE16 249 E2
Guthrie Street SW3 244 C2
Gutter Lane EC2 243 E2
Guy Street SE1 247 F3
Gwynne Place WC1 242 C4

H

Haberdasher Street N1 243 F4
Hainton Close E1 248 C3
Halcrow Street E1 248 C4
Half Moon Court EC1 243 E2
Bartholomew Close
Half Moon Street W1 245 F4
Halkin Place SW1 245 E3
Halkin Street SW1 245 E3
Hall Gate NW8 240 B4
Hall Place W2 240 C3
Hall Road NW8 240 B4
Hall Street EC1 243 D4
Hallam Mews W1 241 F3
Hallam Street W1 241 F3
Halley Place E14 249 E4
Halley Street E14 249 E4
Halsey Mews SW3 245 D2
Halsey Street SW3 245 D2
Hamilton Close NW8 240 B4
Hamilton Close SE16 249 E1
Hamilton Gardens NW8 240 B4
Hamilton Place W1 245 E4
Hamilton Square SE1 247 F3
Hamilton Terrace NW8 240 B4
Hammett Street EC3 248 A3
America Square
Hampstead Road NW1 241 F4
Hampton Street SE1 & SE17 247 E2
Hanbury Street E1 248 B4
Handel Street WC1 242 B3
Hankey Place SE1 247 F3
Hannibal Road E1 249 D4
Hanover Place WC2 242 B1
Long Acre
Hanover Square W1 241 F2
Hanover Street W1 241 F2
Hanover Terrace NW1 241 D4
Hanover Terrace Mews NW1 241 D4

Hans Crescent Margaret Street
254

Hans Crescent SW1 245 D3
Hans Place SW1 245 D3
Hans Road SW3 245 D3
Hans Street SW1 245 D3
Hanson Street W1 241 F2
Hanway Place W1 242 A2
Hanway Street W1 242 A2
Harbert Road W2 240 C2
Harbinger Road E14 250 A2
Harbour Exchange Square E14 250 B3
Harcourt Street W1 241 D2
Harcourt Terrace SW10 244 B1
Harding Close SE17 247 E1
Hardinge Lane E1 249 D3
Hardinge Street
Hardinge Street E1 249 D3
Hardwick Street EC1 243 D4
Hardwicke Mews WC1 242 C4
Lloyd Baker Street
Hardwidge Street SE1 247 F4
Harewood Avenue NW1 241 D3
Harewood Place W1 241 F2
Harley Gardens SW10 244 B1
Harley Place W1 241 E2
Harley Street W1 241 E3
Harleyford Road SE11 246 C1
Harmsworth Mews SE11 247 D2
West Square
Harmsworth Street SE17 247 D1
Harp Alley EC4 243 D2
Farringdon Street
Harp Lane EC3 248 A3
Harper Road SE1 247 E3
Harpur Street WC1 242 C3
Harriet Street SW1 245 D3
Harriet Walk SW1 245 D3
Harrington Gardens SW7 244 B2
Harrington Road SW7 244 C2
Harrington Street NW1 241 F4
Harrison Street WC1 242 B4
Harrow Place E1 248 A4
Harrow Road W2,W9,W10 & NW10 240 B2
Harrow Road Bridge W2 240 B2
Harrowby Street W1 241 D2
Hart Street EC3 248 A3
Harwich Lane EC2 248 A4
Harwood Row NW1 241 D3
Hasker Street SW3 245 D2
Hastings Street WC1 242 B4
Hatfields SE1 247 D4
Hatherley Grove W2 240 A2
Hatherley Street SW1 246 A2
Hatteraick Street SE16 249 D2
Hatton Garden EC1 243 D3
Hatton Place EC1 243 D3
Hatton Place EC1 243 D3
Hatton Street NW8 240 C3
Hatton Wall EC1 243 D3
Haunch of Venison Yard W1 240 C1
Brook Street
Havannah Street E14 250 A3
Havering Street E1 249 D3
Haverstock Street N1 243 E4
Hawkesmoor Mews E1 248 C3
Hay Hill W1 241 F1
Hay's Lane SE1 247 F4
Hay's Mews W1 241 F1
Hayes Place NW1 241 D3
Hayles Street SE11 247 D2
Haymarket SW1 242 A1
Hayne Street EC1 243 E3
Hayward's Place EC1 243 D3
Headfort Place SW1 245 E3
Heathcote Street WC1 242 C3
Heckford Street E1 249 E3
Heddon Street W1 241 F1
Hedger Street SE11 247 D2
Heiron Street SE17 247 E1
Helena Square SE16 249 E3
Hellings Street E1 248 B2
Helmet Row EC1 243 E3
Helsinki Square SE16 249 E3
Hemp Walk SE17 247 F2
Henderson Drive NW8 240 C3
Heneage Lane EC3 248 A4
Heneage Place EC3 248 A4
Heneage Street E1 248 B4
Henniker Mews SW3 244 B1
Henrietta Close SE8 250 A1
Henrietta Place W1 241 E2
Henrietta Street WC2 242 B1
Henriques Street E1 248 B4
Henshaw Street SE17 247 F2
Herald's Place SE11 247 D2
Herbal Hill EC1 243 D3
Herbrand Street WC1 242 B3
Hercules Road SE1 246 C3
Hereford Road W2 240 A2
Hereford Square SW7 244 B2
Hermes Street N1 242 C4
Hermit Street EC1 243 D4
Hermitage Street W2 240 C2
Hermitage Wall E1 248 B2
Heron Place SE16 249 E2
Heron Quays E14 250 A4
Herrick Street SW1 246 B2
Hertford Street W1 245 E4
Hertsmere Road E14 250 A4
Hesper Mews SW5 244 A2
Hesperus Crescent E14 250 B2
Hessel Street E1 248 C3
Heygate Street SE17 247 E2
Hickin Street E14 250 B3
Hide Place SW1 246 A2
High Holborn WC1 242 B2
High Timber Street EC4 243 E1
Highbridge SE10 250 C1
Hildyard Road SW6 244 A1
Hill Road W9 240 B4
Hill Street W1 241 F2
Hillery Close SE17 247 F2
Hilliard's Court E1 248 C2
Hillingdon Street SE5 & SE17 247 E1
Pelier Street
Hind Court EC4 243 D2
Hinde Street W1 241 E2
Hindmarsh Close E1 248 B3
Hobart Place SW1 245 F3
Hogarth Court EC3 243 F1
Fenchurch Street
Hogarth Place SW5 244 A2
Hogarth Road SW5 244 A2
Holbein Mews SW1 245 E2
Holbein Place SW1 245 E2
Holborn EC1 243 D2
Holborn Circus EC1 243 D2
Holborn Viaduct EC1 243 D2
Holford Place WC1 242 C4
Holford Street WC1 242 C4
Holland Street SE1 247 D4
Holland Street W8 244 A3
Hollen Street W1 242 A2
Wardour Street
Holles Street W1 241 F2
Holley Mews SW10 244 B1
Drayton Gardens
Hollywood Mews SW10 244 B1
Hollywood Road SW10 244 B1
Holyoak Road SE11 247 D2
Holyoake Court SE16 249 F2
Holyrood Street SE1 247 F4
Holywell Row EC2 243 F3
Homer Drive E14 250 A2
Homer Row W1 241 D2
Homer Street W1 241 D2
Honduras Street EC1 243 E3
Old Street
Hooper Street E1 248 B3
Hop Gardens WC2 242 B1
St Martin's Lane
Hope Wharf SE16 249 D2
Hopetown Street E1 248 B4
Hopkins Street W1 242 A1
Hopton Street SE1 247 D4
Hopwood Road SE17 247 F1
Horatio Place E14 250 C4
Horley Crescent SE16 249 D2
Marlow Way
Hornton Place W8 244 A3
Hornton Street W8 244 A3
Horse Guards Avenue SW1 246 B4
Horse Guards Road SW1 246 B4
Horse Ride SW1 245 F3
Horseferry Road E14 249 E3
Horseferry Road SW1 246 A3
Horselydown Lane SE1 248 A2
Horseshoe Close E14 250 B2
Hosier Lane EC1 243 D2
Hoskins Street SE10 250 C1
Hothfield Place SE16 249 D1
Hotspur Street SE11 246 C2
Houghton Street WC2 242 C1
Aldwych
Houndsditch EC3 248 A4
Howard Place SW1 242 A2
Carlisle Street
Howell Walk SE1 247 E2
Howick Place SW1 246 A3
Howland Street W1 242 A3
Howland Way SE16 249 E1
Howley Place W2 240 B3
Hoxton Market N1 243 F4
Hoxton Square N1 243 F4
Huddart Street E3 249 F4
Hudson's Place SW1 245 F2
Huggin Hill EC4 243 E1
Hugh Street SW1 245 F2
Hull Close SE16 249 E2
Hull Street EC1 243 E4
Hunt's Court WC2 242 B1
Hunter Close SE1 247 F3
Prioress Street
Hunter Street WC1 242 B3
Huntley Street WC1 242 A3
Huntsman Street SE17 247 F2
Huntsworth Mews NW1 241 D3
Hutching's Street E14 250 A3
Hutton Street EC4 243 D1
Hyde Park Corner W1 245 E4
Hyde Park Crescent W2 240 C2
Hyde Park Gardens W2 240 C1
Hyde Park Gardens Mews W2 240 C1
Hyde Park Gate SW7 244 B3
Hyde Park Square W2 240 C2
Hyde Park Street W2 240 C2

I

Idol Lane EC3 248 A3
Ifield Road SW10 244 A1
Ilchester Gardens W2 240 A1
Iliffe Street SE17 247 E2
Indescon Court E14 250 A3
India Place WC2 242 C1
Montreal Place
India Street EC3 248 A3
Ingestre Place W1 242 A1
Inglebert Street EC1 243 D4
Inglewood Close E14 250 A2
Ingram Close SE11 246 C2
Inigo Place WC2 242 B1
Bedford Street
Inner Temple Lane EC4 243 D2
Inverness Gardens W8 244 A4
Palace Garden Terrace
Inverness Mews W2 240 B1
Inverness Place W2 240 B1
Inverness Terrace W2 240 B1
Invicta Plaza SE1 247 D4
Inville Road SE17 247 F1
Ireland Yard EC4 243 D1
St Andrew's Hill
Ironmonger Lane EC2 243 E2
Ironmonger Place E14 250 A2
Ironmonger Row EC1 243 E4
Ironside Close SE16 249 D2
Irving Street WC2 242 B1
Isambard Place SE16 249 D2
Island Row E14 249 F3
Iverna Court W8 244 A3
Iverna Gardens W8 244 A3
Ives Street SW3 245 D2
Ivor Place NW1 241 D3
Ixworth Place SW3 244 C2

J

Jacob Street SE1 248 B2
Jamaica Road SE1 & SE16 248 B1
Jamaica Street E1 249 D4
James Street W1 241 E2
James Street WC2 242 B1
Long Acre
Jameson Street W8 244 A4
Janet Street E14 250 A3
Janeway Place SE16 248 C1
Janeway Street SE16 248 C1
Jardine Road E1 249 E3
Jay Mews SW7 244 B3
Jermyn Street SW1 242 A1
Jerome Crescent NW8 240 C3
Jewry Street EC3 248 A3
Joan Street SE1 247 D4
Jockey's Fields WC1 242 C3
John Adams Street WC2 242 B1
John Aird Court W2 240 B3
John Carpenter Street EC4 243 D1
John Felton Road SE16 248 B1
John Fisher Street E1 248 B3
John Islip Street 246 B2
John Maurice Close SE17 247 F2
John Princes Street W1 241 F2
John Roll Way SE16 248 C1
John Street WC1 242 C3
John's Mews WC1 242 C3
Johnson Street E1 249 D3
Johnson's Place SW1 246 A1
Joiner Street SE1 247 F4
Jonathan Street SE11 246 C2
Jones Street W1 241 A3
Bourdon Street
Jubilee Crescent E14 250 C2
Jubilee Place SW3 245 D2
Jubilee Street E1 249 D4
Judd Street WC1 242 B4
Julian Place E14 250 B1
Junction Mews W2 240 C2
Juxon Street SE11 246 C2

K

Katherine Close SE16 249 D2
Kean Street WC2 242 C2
Keel Close SE16 249 E2
Keeley Street WC2 242 C2
Keeton's Road SE16 248 C1
Kelso Place W8 244 A3
Kemble Street WC2 242 C2
Kempsford Gardens SW5 244 A1
Kempsford Road SE11 247 D2
Kempton Court E1 248 C4
Durward Street
Kendal Street W2 241 C2
Kendall Place W1 241 D2
Kendrick Mews SW7 244 C2
Kendrick Place SW7 244 C2
Reece Mews
Kennet Street E1 248 B2
Kennet Wharf Lane EC4 243 E1
Kenning Street SE16 249 D2
Kennings Way SE11 247 D1
Kennington Green SE11 247 D1
Kennington Grove SE11 246 C1
Kennington Lane SE11 246 C1
Kennington Oval SE11 246 C1
Kennington Park Gardens SE11 247 D1
Kennington Park Place SE11 247 D1
Kennington Park Road SE11 247 D1
Kennington Road SE1 & SE11 246 C3
Kenrick Place W1 241 E2
Kensington Church Street W8 244 A4
Kensington Church Walk W8 244 A3
Kensington Court W8 244 A3
Kensington Court Place W8 244 A3
Kensington Gardens Square W2 240 A2
Kensington Gate W8 244 B3
Kensington Gore SW7 244 B3
Kensington High Street W8 & W14 244 A3
Kensington Mall W8 244 A4
Kensington Palace Gardens W8 244 A4
Kensington Road W8 & SW7 244 B3
Kensington Square W8 244 A3
Kent Passage NW1 241 D4
Kent Terrace NW1 241 D4
Kenton Street WC1 241 B3
Kenway Road SW5 243 A2
Keppel Row SE1 247 E4
Keppel Street WC1 242 B3
Keyse Road SE1 248 B1
Keystone Crescent N1 242 B4
Keyworth Street SE1 247 D3
Kilburn Park Road NW6 240 A4
Kildare Gardens W2 240 A2
Kildare Terrace W2 240 A2
Kimbolton Row SW3 244 C2
Fulham Road
Kinburn Street SE16 249 D2
Kinder Street E1 248 C3
King and Queen Street SE17 247 E2
King Charles Street SW1 246 B3
King David Lane E1 249 D3
King Edward III Mews SE16 248 C1
Paradise Street
King Edward Street EC1 243 E2
King Edward Walk SE1 247 D3
King James Street SE1 247 E3
King Square EC1 243 E4
King Street EC2 243 E2
King Street SW1 246 A4
King Street WC2 242 B1
King William Street EC4 243 F1
King's Bench Walk EC4 243 D1
King's Cross Road WC1 242 C4
King's Mews WC1 242 C3
King's Road SW3, SW6 & SW10 245 D1
King's Scholars' Passage SW1 245 F2
King's Stairs Close SE16 248 C2
Kingfield Street E14 250 C2
Kinghorn Street EC1 243 E3
Kinglake Street SE17 247 F2
Kingly Court W1 242 A1
Kingly Street W1 241 F1
Kings Arms Yard EC2 243 F2
Kings Bench Street SE1 247 D3
Kingscote Street EC4 243 D1
Kingsway WC2 242 C2
Kinnerton Street SW1 245 E3
Kipling Street SE1 247 F4
Kirby Grove SE1 247 F3
Kirby Street EC1 243 D3
Knaresborough Place SW5 244 A2
Knight's Walk SE11 247 D2
Knighten Street E1 248 C2
Knightrider Street EC4 243 E1
Godliman Street
Knightsbridge SW1 & SW7 245 D3
Knightsbridge Green SW1 245 D3
Brompton Road
Knox Street W1 241 D3
Kramer Mews SW5 244 A1
Kynance Mews SW7 244 B3

L

Lackington Street EC2 243 F3
Lafone Street SE1 248 A2
Lagado Mews SE16 249 E2
Lamb Street E1 248 A4
Lamb Walk SE1 247 F3
Lamb's Conduit Street WC1 242 C3
Lamb's Passage EC1 243 F3
Lambeth Bridge SW1 & SE11 246 B2
Lambeth High Street SE1 246 C2
Lambeth Hill EC4 243 E1
Lambeth Palace Road SE1 246 C2
Lambeth Road SE1 246 C2
Lambeth Walk SE11 246 C2
Lamlash Street SE11 247 D2
Lanark Place W9 240 B3
Lanark Road W9 240 A4
Lanark Square E14 250 B3
Lancaster Drive E14 250 B4
Lancaster Gate W2 240 B1
Lancaster Mews W2 240 B1
Lancaster Place WC2 245 D3
Lancaster Street SE1 247 D3
Lancaster Terrace W2 240 C1
Lancaster Walk W2 240 B1
Lancelot Place SW7 245 D3
Lancing Street NW1 242 A4
Landon Place SW1 245 D3
Landon's Close E14 250 B4
Langbourne Place E14 250 B1
Langdale Close SE17 247 E1
Langham Place W1 241 F2
Langham Street W1 241 F2
Langley Lane SW8 246 B1
Langley Street WC2 242 B1
Langton Close WC1 242 C3
Lansdowne Row W1 241 F1
Lansdowne Terrace WC1 242 B3
Lant Street SE1 247 E3
Lanterns Court E14 250 A3
Larcom Street SE17 247 E2
Lassell Street SE10 250 C1
Lauderdale Road W9 240 A4
Launcelot Street SE1 246 C3
Lower Marsh
Launceston Place W8 244 B3
Launch Street E14 250 B3
Laurence Pountney Lane EC4 243 F1
Lavender Close SW3 244 C1
Lavender Road SE16 249 E2
Laverton Place SW5 244 A2
Lavington Street SE1 247 E4
Law Street SE1 247 F3
Lawn House Close E14 250 B3
Lawn Lane SW8 246 B1
Lawrence Lane EC2 243 E2
Trump Street
Lawrence Street SW3 244 C1
Laxton Place NW1 241 F3
Laystall Street EC1 242 C3
Layton's Buildings SE1 247 E4
Borough High Street
Leadenhall Place EC3 243 F1
Leadenhall Street EC3 243 F2
Leake Street SE1 246 C3
Leather Lane EC1 243 D3
Leathermarket Court SE1 247 F3
Leathermarket Street
Leathermarket Street SE1 247 F3
Lecky Street SW7 244 C1
Leerdam Drive E14 250 C2
Lees Place W1 241 E1
Leicester Court WC2 242 B1
Cranbourn Street
Leicester Place WC2 242 A1
Lisle Street
Leicester Square WC2 242 B1
Leicester Street WC2 242 B1
Leigh Hunt Street SE1 247 E3
Leigh Street WC1 242 B4
Leinster Gardens W2 240 B1
Leinster Mews W2 240 B1
Leinster Place W2 240 B1
Leinster Square W2 240 A1
Leinster Terrace W2 240 B1
Leman Street E1 248 B3
Lennox Gardens SW1 245 D2
Lennox Gardens Mews SW1 245 D2
Leonard Street EC2 243 F3
Leopold Street E3 249 F4
Leroy Street SE1 247 F2
Lever Street EC1 243 E4
Leverett Street SW3 245 D2
Mossop Street
Lewisham Street SW1 246 B3
Lexham Gardens W8 244 A2
Lexham Mews W8 244 A2
Lexham Walk W8 244 A2
Lexington Street W1 242 A1
Leyden Street E1 248 A4
Leydon Close SE16 249 E2
Library Place E1 248 C3
Library Street SE1 247 D3
Lighterman Mews E1 249 E4
Lightermans Road E14 250 A3
Lilestone Street NW8 240 C3
Lilley Close E1 248 B2
Lillie Yard SW6 244 A1
Lime Close E1 248 B2
Lime Street EC3 243 F1
Lime Street Passage EC3 243 F1
Lime Street
Limeburner Lane EC4 243 D2
Limeharbour E14 250 B3
Limehouse Causeway E14 249 F3
Limehouse Link Tunnel E14 249 E3
Limerston Street SW10 244 B1
Lincoln Street SW3 245 D2
Lincoln's Inn Fields WC2 242 C2
Linden Gardens W2 240 A1
Linden Mews W2 240 A1
Lindley Street E1 248 C4
Lindsay Square SW1 246 B2
Lindsey Street EC1 243 E3
Linhope Street NW1 240 D3
Links Yard E1 248 B4
Linsey Street SE16 248 B1
Lipton Road E1 249 D3
Lisle Street W1 242 A1
Lisson Grove NW1 & NW8 240 C3
Lisson Street NW1 240 C3
Litchfield Street WC2 242 B1
Little Argyll Street W1 246 A2
Regent Street
Little Britain EC1 243 E2
Little Chester Street SW1 245 E3
Little College Street SW1 246 B3
Little Dorrit Close SE1 247 E4
Little Edward Street NW1 241 F4
Little George Street SW1 246 B3
Great George Street
Little London Court SE1 248 B1
Mill Street
Little Marlborough Street W1 241 F1
Kingly Street
Little New Street EC4 243 D2
New Street Square
Little Newport Street WC2 242 B1
Little Portland Street W1 241 F2
Little Russell Street WC1 242 B2
Little Sanctuary SW1 246 B3
Broad Sanctuary
Little Smith Street SW1 246 B3
Little Somerset Street E1 248 A3
Little St James's Street SW1 246 A4
Little Titchfield Street W1 241 F2
Little Trinity Lane EC4 243 E1
Liverpool Grove SE17 247 E1
Liverpool Street EC2 243 F2
Livingstone Place E14 250 B1
Livonia Street W1 242 A2
Lizard Street EC1 243 E4
Llewellyn Street SE16 248 B1
Lloyd Baker Street WC1 242 C4
Lloyd Square WC1 242 C4
Lloyd Street WC1 242 C4
Lloyd's Avenue EC3 248 A3
Lloyd's Row EC1 243 D4
Lockesfield Place E14 250 B1
Locksley Street E14 249 F4
Lockwood Square SE16 248 C1
Lodge Road NW8 240 C4
Loftie Street SE16 248 B1
Lolesworth Close E1 248 B4
Lollard Street SE11 246 C2
Loman Street SE1 247 E4
Lomas Street E1 248 C4
Lombard Court EC4 243 F1
Lombard Lane EC4 243 A2
Temple Lane
London Bridge EC4 & SE1 243 F1
London Bridge Street SE1 247 F4
London Road SE1 247 D3
London Street EC3 248 A3
London Street W2 240 C2
London Wall EC2 243 E2
Long Acre WC2 242 B1
Long Lane EC1 243 E2
Long Lane SE1 247 F3
Long Walk SE1 248 A1
Long Yard WC1 242 C3
Longford Street NW1 241 F3
Longmoore Street SW1 245 F2
Longville Road SE11 247 D2
Lord Hill's Bridge W2 240 A2
Lord Hill's Road W2 240 A3
Lord North Street SW1 246 B3
Lordship Place SW3 244 C1
Lawrence Street
Lorenzo Street WC1 242 C4
Lorrimore Road SE17 247 E1
Lorrimore Square SE17 247 E1
Lothbury EC2 243 F2
Loughborough Street SE11 246 C1
Lovat Lane EC3 243 F1
Love Lane EC2 243 E2
Lovegrove Walk E14 250 B4
Lovell Place SE16 249 E1
Lovers' Walk W1 245 E4
Lowell Street E14 249 E4
Lower Belgrave Street SW1 245 E3
Lower Grosvenor Place SW1 245 F3
Lower James Street W1 242 A1
Lower John Street W1 242 A1
Lower Marsh SE1 246 C3
Lower Road SE8 & SE16 249 D1
Lower Robert Street WC2 242 B1
Savoy Place
Lower Sloane Street SW1 245 E1
Lower Thames Street EC3 243 F1
Lowndes Place SW1 245 E3
Lowndes Square SW1 245 D3
Lowndes Street SW1 245 E3
Lowood Street E1 248 C3
Bewley Street
Loxham Street WC1 242 B3
Cromer Street
Lucan Place SW3 244 C2
Lucerne Mews W8 244 A4
Lucey Road SE16 248 B1
Ludgate Broadway EC4 243 D2
Pilgrim Street
Ludgate Circus EC4 243 D2
Ludgate Square EC4 243 D2
Luke Street EC2 243 F3
Lukin Street E1 249 D3
Lumley Street W1 241 E1
Brown Hart Garden
Lupus Street SW1 245 F1
Luralda Gardens E14 250 C1
Luton Street NW8 240 C3
Luxborough Street W1 241 E3
Lyall Street SW1 245 E3
Lygon Place SW1 245 F3
Lynch Walk SE8 250 A1
Lyons Place NW8 240 C3
Lytham Street SE17 247 F1

M

Mabledon Place WC1 242 B4
Macclesfield Road EC1 243 E4
Mackenzie Walk E14 250 A4
Macklin Street WC2 242 B2
Mackworth Street NW1 241 F4
Macleod Street SE17 247 E1
Maconochies Road E14 250 B1
Macquarie Way E14 250 B2
Maddock Way SE17 247 D1
Maddox Street W1 241 F1
Magdalen Street SE1 248 A2
Magee Street SE11 247 D1
Magellan Place E14 250 A1
Maritime Quay
Maguire Street SE1 248 B2
Mahognay Close SE16 249 E2
Maida Avenue W2 240 B3
Maida Vale W9 240 B4
Maiden Lane WC2 242 B1
Maiden Lane SE1 247 E4
Makins Street SW3 248 D2
Malabar Street E14 250 A3
Malet Street WC1 242 A3
Mallord Street SW3 244 C1
Mallory Street NW8 240 C3
Mallow Street EC1 243 F3
Malta Street EC1 243 D3
Maltby Street SE1 248 A1
Maltravers Street WC2 242 C1
Managers Street E14 250 C4
Manchester Grove E14 250 B2
Manchester Road E14 250 B3
Manchester Square W1 241 E2
Manchester Street W1 241 E2
Manciple Street SE1 247 F3
Mandarin Street E14 249 F3
Mandeville Place W1 241 E2
Manette Street W1 242 B2
Manilla Street E14 250 A3
Manningford Close EC1 243 D4
Manningtree Street E1 248 B4
Commercial Road
Manor Place SE17 247 E1
Manresa Road SW3 244 C1
Mansell Street E1 248 B3
Mansfield Mews W1 241 F2
Mansfield Street
Mansfield Street W1 241 F2
Mansion House Place EC4 243 A1
St Swithun's Lane
Manson Mews SW7 244 B2
Manson Place SW7 244 C2
Maple Leaf Square SE16 249 E2
Maple Street W1 241 F3
Maples Place E1 248 C4
Marble Arch W1 241 D1
Marchmont Street WC1 242 B3
Margaret Court W1 241 F2
Margaret Street
Margaret Street W1 241 F2

Margaretta Terrace
Prince's Gardens
255

Margaretta Terrace *SW3* 244 C1
Margery Street *WC1* 242 C4
Marigold Street *SE16* 248 C1
Mariners Mews *E14* 250 C2
Maritime Quay *E14* 250 A1
Marjorie Mews *E1* 249 D4
Mark Lane *EC3* 248 A3
Market Court *W1* 241 E1
Oxford Street
Market Mews *W1* 245 E4
Market Place *W1* 241 F2
Market Yard Mews *SE1* 248 A1
Markham Place *SW3* 245 D2
Elystan Place
Markham Square *SW3* 245 D2
Markham Street *SW3* 245 D2
Marlborough Close *SE17* 247 E2
Marlborough Road *SW1* 246 A4
Marlborough Street *SW3* 244 C2
Marloes Road *W8* 244 A3
Marlow Way *SE16* 249 D2
Marne Street *W10* 248 B1
Maroon Street *E14* 249 E4
Marsh Street *E14* 250 A2
Marsh Wall *E14* 250 A3
Marshall Street *W1* 242 A1
Marshall's Place *SE16* 248 B1
Marshalsea Road *SE1* 247 E4
Marsham Street *SW1* 246 B3
Marshfield Street *E14* 250 B3
Marsland Close *SE17* 247 E1
Martha Street *E1* 248 C3
Martin Lane *EC4* 243 F1
Martin's Street *WC2* 242 B1
Martlett Court *WC2* 242 B2
Marylands Road *W9* 240 A3
Marylebone High Street *W1* 241 E3
Marylebone Lane *W1* 241 E2
Marylebone Mews *W1* 241 E2
Marylebone Road *NW1* 241 D3
Marylebone Street *W1* 241 E2
Marylee Way *SE11* 246 C2
Mason Street *SE17* 247 F2
Mason's Arms Mews *W1* 241 F1
Maddox Street
Mason's Place *EC1* 243 E4
Mason's Yard *SW1* 241 E2
Duke Street
Massinger Street *SE17* 247 F2
Mast House Terrace *E14* 250 A2
Master's Street *E1* 249 E4
Mastmaker Road *E14* 250 A2
Matlock Street *E14* 249 E4
Matthew Parker Street *SW1* 246 B3
Maunsel Street *SW1* 246 A2
May's Court *WC2* 242 B1
St Martin's Lane
Mayfair Place *W1* 245 F4
Mayflower Street *SE16* 249 D1
Maynards Quay *E1* 248 C3
McAuley Close *SE1* 246 C3
McCleod's Mews *SW7* 244 B2
Mead Row *SE1* 247 D3
Meadcroft Road *SE11* 247 D1
Meadow Row *SE1* 247 E2
Meard Street *W1* 242 A2
Mecklenburgh Place *WC1* 242 C3
Mecklenburgh Square *WC1* 242 C3
Mecklenburgh Street *WC1* 242 C3
Mecklenburgh Square
Medway Street *SW1* 246 A2
Melbury Terrace *NW1* 241 D3
Melcombe Place *NW1* 241 D3
Melcombe Street *NW1* 241 D3
Melina Place *NW8* 240 B4
Melior Place *SE1* 247 F4
Snowsfields
Mellish Street *E14* 250 A3
Melon Place *W8* 244 A4
Kensington Church Street
Melton Street *NW1* 242 A4
Memel Court *EC1* 243 E3
Baltic Street
Mepham Street *SE1* 246 C4
Mercator Place *E14* 250 A1
Napier Avenue
Mercer Street *WC2* 242 B1
Meredith Street *EC1* 243 D4
Meridian Place *E14* 250 B3
Merlin Street *WC1* 243 D4
Mermaid Court *SE1* 247 F4
Mermaid Court *SE16* 249 F2
Mermaid Row *SE1* 247 F3
Merrick Square *SE1* 247 E3
Merrington Road *SW6* 244 A1
Merrow Street *SE17* 247 E1
Methley Street *SE11* 247 D1
Mews Street *E1* 248 B2
Meymott Street *SE1* 247 D4
Micawber Street *N1* 243 E4
Middle Street *EC1* 243 E2
Middle Temple Lane *EC4* 242 C2
Middle Yard *SE1* 247 F4
Middlesex Street *E1* 248 A4
Middleton Drive *SE16* 249 E2
Midford Place *W1* 242 A3
Tottenham Court Road
Midhope Street *WC1* 242 B4
Midland Place *E14* 250 B1
Midland Road *NW1* 242 B4
Midship Close *SE16* 249 E2
Milborne Grove *SW10* 244 B1
Milcote Street *SE1* 247 D3
Mile End Road *E1* 248 C4
Miles Street *SW8* 246 B1
Milford Lane *WC2* 242 C1
Milk Street *EC2* 243 E2
Milk Yard *E1* 249 D3
Mill Place *E14* 249 F3
Mill Street *SE1* 248 B1
Mill Street *W1* 241 F1
Millbank *SW1* 246 B2
Millennium Drive *E14* 250 C2
Millennium Square *SE1* 248 B2
Millharbour *E14* 250 A3
Milligan Street *E14* 249 F3
Millman Street *WC1* 242 C3
Millstream Road *SE1* 248 A1
Millwall Dock Road *E14* 250 A3
Milner Street *SW3* 245 D2
Milton Court *EC2* 243 F3
Milton Street *EC2* 243 F3
Milverton Street *SE11* 247 D1
Milward Street *E1* 248 C4
Mincing Lane *EC3* 248 A3
Minera Mews *SW1* 245 E2
Minories *EC3* 248 A3
Mint Street *SE1* 247 E4
Miranda Close *E1* 248 C4
Mitali Passage *E1* 248 B4
Mitchell Street *EC1* 243 E3
Mitre Road *SE1* 247 D3
Mitre Square *EC3* 248 A3
Mitre Street
Mitre Street *EC3* 248 A3
Molyneux Street *W1* 241 D2
Monck Street *SW1* 246 B3
Moncorvo Close *SW7* 244 C3
Monkton Street *SE11* 247 D2
Monkwell Square *EC2* 243 E2
Monmouth Road *W2* 240 A2
Monmouth Street *WC2* 242 B1
Montagu Mansions *W1* 241 D3
Montagu Mews North *W1* 241 D2
Montagu Mews South *W1* 241 D2
Montagu Mews West *W1* 241 D2
Montagu Place *W1* 241 D2
Montagu Row *W1* 241 D2
Montagu Square *W1* 241 D2
Montagu Street *W1* 241 D2
Montague Close *SE1* 247 F4
Montague Place *WC1* 242 D3
Montague Street *EC1* 243 E2
Montague Street *WC1* 242 B3
Montford Place *SE11* 246 C1
Montpelier Mews *SW7* 245 D3
Montpelier Place *SW7* 245 D3
Montpelier Place *E1* 249 D3
Montpelier Square *SW7* 245 D3
Montpelier Street *SW7* 245 D3
Montpelier Walk *SW7* 245 D3
Montreal Place *WC2* 242 C1
Montrose Court *SW7* 244 C3
Montrose Place *SW1* 245 E3
Monument Street *EC3* 243 F1
Monza Street *E1* 249 D3
Moodkee Street *SE16* 249 D1
Moor Lane *EC2* 243 F2
Moor Place *EC2* 243 F2
Moorfields
Moore Street *SW3* 242 A1
Old Compton Street
Moorfields *EC2* 243 F2
Moorgate *EC2* 243 F2
Mora Street *EC1* 243 E4
Morecambe Close *E1* 249 D4
Morecambe Street *SE17* 247 E2
Moreland Street *EC1* 243 E4
Moreton Place *SW1* 246 A2
Moreton Street *SW1* 246 A2
Moreton Terrace *SW1* 246 A1
Morley Street *SE1* 247 D3
Morocco Street *SE1* 247 F3
Morpeth Terrace *SW1* 245 F2
Morris Street *E1* 248 C3
Morshead Road *W9* 240 A4
Mortimer Market *WC1* 242 A3
Capper Street
Mortimer Street *W1* 241 F2
Morton Mews *SW5* 244 A2
Earl's Court Gardens
Morwell Street *WC1* 242 A2
Moscow Place *W2* 240 A1
Moscow Road *W2* 240 A1
Moss Close *E1* 248 B4
Mossop Street *SW3* 245 D2
Motcomb Street *SW1* 245 E3
Mount Pleasant *WC1* 242 C3
Mount Row *W1* 241 E1
Mount Street *W1* 241 E1
Mount Terrace *E1* 248 C4
Moxon Street *W1* 241 E2
Mozart Terrace *SW1* 245 E2
Muirfield Crescent *E14* 250 B3
Mulberry Street *E1* 248 B4
Mulberry Walk *SW3* 244 C1
Mulready Street *NW8* 240 C3
Mulvaney Way *SE1* 247 F3
Mumford Court *EC2* 243 E2
Milk Street
Mundy Street *N1* 243 F4
Munster Square *NW1* 241 F4
Munton Road *SE17* 247 E2
Murphy Street *SE1* 246 C3
Murray Grove *N1* 243 E4
Musbury Street *E1* 249 D4
Muscovy Street *EC3* 248 A3
Museum Street *WC1* 242 B2
Myddelton Passage *EC1* 243 D4
Myddelton Square *EC1* 243 D4
Myddelton Street *EC1* 243 D4
Mylne Street *EC1* 243 D4
Myrdle Street *E1* 248 C4
Myrtle Walk *N1* 243 F4

N

Naoroji Street *WC1* 242 C4
Napier Avenue *E14* 250 A1
Narrow Street *E14* 249 E3
Nash Place *E14* 250 A4
Nash Street *NW1* 241 F4
Nassau Street *W1* 241 F2
Nathaniel Close *E1* 248 B4
Thrawl Street
National Terrace *SE16* 248 C1
Bermondsey Wall East
Neal Street *WC2* 242 B2
Neathouse Place *SW1* 245 F2
Wilton Road
Nebraska Street *SE1* 247 E3
Neckinger *SE1* 248 B1
Neckinger Street *SE1* 248 B1
Nelson Court *SE16* 249 D2
Nelson Passage *EC1* 243 E4
Mora Street
Nelson Place *N1* 243 E4
Nelson Square *SE1* 247 D4
Nelson Street *E1* 248 C4
Nelson Terrace *N1* 243 D4
Nelson Walk *SE16* 249 E2
Neptune Street *SE16* 249 D1
Nesham Street *E1* 248 B3
Netherton Grove *SW10* 244 B1
Netley Street *NW1* 241 F4
Nevern Place *SW5* 244 A2
Nevern Square *SW5* 244 A2
Neville Court *EC4* 243 D2
Neville Street *SW7* 244 C2
Neville Terrace *SW7* 244 C1
New Bond Street *W1* 241 F1
New Bridge Street *EC4* 243 D2
New Broad Street *EC2* 243 F2
New Burlington Mews *W1* 248 A3
Hart Street
New Burlington Place *W1* 241 F1
New Burlington Street *W1* 241 F1
New Cavendish Street *W1* 241 E2
New Change *EC4* 243 E2
New Compton Street *WC2* 242 B2
New Crane Place *E1* 249 D2
New Fetter Lane *EC4* 243 D2
New Globe Walk *SE1* 247 E4
New Goulston Street *E1* 248 A4
New Kent Road *SE1* 247 E2
New King Street *SE8* 250 A1
New North Place *EC2* 243 F3
New North Road *N1* 243 F4
New North Street *WC1* 242 C3
New Oxford Street *WC1* 242 B2
New Quebec Street *W1* 241 D2
New Ride *SW7* 244 C3
New Road *E1* 248 C4
New Row *WC2* 242 B1
New Spring Gardens Walk *SE11* 246 B1
Goding Street
New Square *WC2* 242 C2
New Street *EC2* 248 A4
New Street Square *EC4* 243 D2
New Turnstile *WC1* 242 B2
High Holborn
New Union Close *E14* 250 C3
New Union Street *EC2* 243 F2
Newark Street *E1* 248 C4
Newburgh Street *W1* 242 F1
Foubert's Place
Newburn Street *SE11* 246 C1
Newbury Street *EC1* 243 E2
Newcastle Place *W2* 240 C3
Newcomen Street *SE1* 247 F4
Newell Street *E14* 249 F3
Newgate Street *EC1* 243 D2
Newington Butts *SE1 & SE11* 247 D2
Newington Causeway *SE1* 247 E3
Newlands Quay *E1* 249 D3
Newman Street *W1* 242 A2
Newman's Row *WC2* 242 C2
Lincoln's Inn Fields
Newnham Terrace *SE1* 246 C3
Newnhams Row *SE1* 248 A1
Newport Place *WC2* 242 B1
Newport Street *SE11* 246 C2
Newton Road *W2* 240 A2
Newton Street *WC2* 242 B2
Nicholas Lane *EC4* 243 F1
Nicholson Street *SE1* 247 D4
Nightingale Place *SW10* 244 B1
Nile Street *N1* 243 E4
Nine Elms Lane *SW8* 246 A1
Noble Street *EC2* 243 E2
Noel Street *W1* 242 A2
Norbiton Road *E14* 249 F4
Norfolk Crescent *W2* 240 C2
Norfolk Place *W2* 240 C2
Norfolk Square *W2* 240 C2
Norman Street *EC1* 243 E4
Norris Street *SW1* 242 A1
North Audley Street *W1* 241 E1
North Bank *NW8* 240 C4
North Colonnade *E14* 250 A4
North Crescent *WC1* 242 A3
North Flockton Street *SE16* 248 B1
Chambers Street
North Gower Street *NW1* 242 A4
North Mews *WC1* 242 C3
North Ride *W2* 240 C1
North Row *W1* 241 E1
North Tenter Street *E1* 248 B3
North Terrace *SW3* 244 C2
North Wharf Road *W2* 240 B2
Northampton Road *EC1* 243 D3
Northampton Row *EC1* 243 D3
Exmouth Market
Northampton Square *EC1* 243 D4
Northburgh Street *EC1* 243 D3
Northchurch *SE17* 247 F2
Northdown Street *N1* 242 C4
Northington Street *WC1* 242 C3
Northumberland Alley *EC3* 248 A3
Northumberland Avenue *WC2* 246 B4
Northumberland Street *WC2* 246 B4
Northwick Close *NW8* 240 C3
Northwick Terrace *NW8* 240 B3
Northy Street *E14* 249 E3
Norton Folgate *E1* 248 A4
Norway Gate *SE16* 249 E1
Norway Place *E14* 249 F3
Norwich Street *EC4* 243 D2
Notting Hill Gate *W11* 240 A1
Nottingham Place *W1* 241 E3
Nottingham Street *W1* 241 E3
Nugent Terrace *NW8* 240 B4

O

O'Leary Square *E1* 249 D4
O'Meara Street *SE1* 247 E4
Oak Lane *E14* 249 F3
Oak Tree Road *NW8* 240 C4
Oakden Street *SE11* 247 D2
Oakfield Street *SW10* 244 B1
Oakington Road *W9* 240 A3
Oakley Crescent *EC1* 243 E4
Oakley Gardens *SW3* 245 D1
Oakley Street *SW3* 244 C1
Oat Lane *EC2* 243 E2
Observatory Gardens *W8* 244 A4
Observatory Mews *E14* 250 C2
Storers Quay
Occupation Road *SE17* 247 E1
Ocean Street *E1* 249 E4
Ocean Wharf *E14* 250 A3
Octagon Arcade *EC2* 243 F2
Octagon Court *SE16* 249 D2
Odessa Street *SE16* 249 F1
Ogle Street *W1* 241 F2
Old Bailey *EC4* 243 D2
Old Bond Street *W1* 241 F1
Old Broad Street *EC2* 243 F2
Old Brompton Road *SW5 & SW7* 244 A1
Old Burlington Street *W1* 241 F1
Old Castle Street *E1* 248 B4
Old Cavendish Street *W1* 241 F2
Old Church Road *E1* 249 D4
Old Church Street *SW3* 244 C1
Old Compton Street *W1* 242 A1
Old Court Place *W8* 244 A3
Old Fleet Lane *EC4* 243 D2
Old Gloucester Street *WC1* 242 B3
Old Jamaica Road *SE16* 248 B1
Old Jewry *EC2* 243 F2
Old Marylebone Road *NW1* 241 D2
Old Mitre Court *EC4* 243 D2
Fleet Street
Old Montagu Street *E1* 248 B4
Old North Street *WC1* 242 C3
Theobalds Road
Old Palace Yard *SW1* 246 B3
Old Paradise Street *SE11* 246 C2
Old Park Lane *W1* 245 E4
Old Pye Street *SW1* 246 A3
Old Quebec Street *W1* 241 D2
Old Queen Street *SW1* 246 A3
Old School Square *E14* 249 F4
Old Square *WC2* 242 C2
Old Street *EC1* 243 E3
Old Theatre Court *SE1* 246 E4
Park Street
Old Woolwich Road *SE10* 250 C1
Oldbury Place *W1* 241 E3
Olivers Yard *EC1* 243 F3
Olliffe Street *E14* 250 C2
Olney Road *SE7* 247 E1
Olympia Mews *W2* 240 B1
Omega Close *E14* 250 A3
Onega Gate *SE16* 249 E1
Ongar Road *SW6* 244 A1
Onslow Gardens *SW7* 244 B2
Onslow Mews *SW7* 244 C2
Onslow Square *SW7* 244 C2
Onslow Street *EC1* 243 D3
Saffron Street
Ontario Street *SE1* 247 E3
Ontario Way *E14* 250 A4
Opal Street *SE11* 247 D2
Orange Place *SE16* 249 D1
Orange Street *WC2* 242 B1
Orb Street *SE17* 247 F2
Orchard Street *W1* 241 E2
Orchardson Street *NW8* 240 C3
Orde Hall Street *WC1* 242 C3
Orient Street *SE11* 247 D2
Orme Court *W2* 240 A1
Orme Lane *W2* 240 A1
Orme Square *W2* 240 A1
Ormond Yard *SW1* 242 A1
Ormonde Gate *SW3* 245 D1
Orsett Street *SE11* 246 C2
Orsett Terrace *W2* 240 B2
Orton Street *E1* 248 B2
Wapping High Street
Osbert Street *SW1* 246 A2
Osborne Street *E1* 248 B4
Oslo Square *SE16* 249 E1
Osnaburgh Street *NW1* 241 F3
Osnaburgh Terrace *NW1* 241 F4
Albany Street
Ossington Buildings *W1* 241 E2
Moxon Street
Ossington Street *W2* 240 A1
Ossulston Street *NW1* 242 A4
Osten Mews *SW7* 244 B2
Oswin Street *SE11* 247 D2
Othello Close *SE1* 247 D2
Otto Street *SE17* 247 D1
Oval Way *SE11* 246 C1
Ovex Close *E14* 250 C3
Ovington Gardens *SW3* 245 D3
Ovington Square *SW3* 245 D3
Ovington Street *SW3* 245 D2
Owen Street *EC1* 243 D4
Oxendon Street *SW1* 242 A1
Coventry Street
Oxford Circus *W1* 241 F2
Regent Street
Oxford Square *W2* 240 C2
Oxford Street *W1* 241 E1
Oyster Row *E1* 249 D3
Oystergate Walk *EC4* 243 F1

P

Paddington Green *W2* 240 C3
Paddington Street *W1* 241 E3
Page Street *SW1* 246 B2
Pageant Crescent *SE16* 249 F2
Pageant Steps *SE16* 249 E2
Pageantmaster Court *EC4* 243 D2
Ludgate Hill
Paget Street *EC1* 243 D4
Pakenham Street *WC1* 242 C3
Palace Avenue *W8* 244 A4
Palace Court *W2* 240 A1
Palace Gardens Mews *W8* 244 A4
Palace Gardens Terrace *W8* 244 A4
Palace Gate *W8* 244 B3
Palace Street *SW1* 245 F3
Pall Mall *SW1* 246 A4
Pall Mall East *SW1* 242 B1
Pall Mall Place *SW1* 246 A4
Palmer Street *SW1* 246 A3
Pancras Lane *EC4* 243 E2
Panton Street *SW1* 242 A1
Paradise Street *SE16* 248 C1
Paradise Walk *SW3* 245 D1
Paragon Mews *SE1* 247 F2
Searles Road
Pardoner Street *SE1* 247 F3
Parfetts Street *E1* 248 C4
Paris Garden *SE1* 247 D4
Park Approach *SE16* 248 C1
Park Crescent *W1* 241 E3
Park Crescent Mews East *W1* 241 F3
Park Crescent Mews West *W1* 241 E3
Park Lane *W1* 241 E1
Park Place *SW1* 245 F4
Park Place *E14* 250 A4
Park Place Villas *W2* 240 B3
Park Road *NW1 & NW8* 241 D4
Park Row *SE10* 250 C1
Park Square East *NW1* 241 F3
Park Square Mews *W1* 241 E3
Harley Street
Park Square West *NW1* 241 E3
Park Street *SE1* 247 E4
Park Street *W1* 241 E1
Park Walk *SW10* 244 B1
Park West Place *W2* 241 D2
Parker Street *WC2* 242 B2
Parkers Row *SE1* 248 B1
Parliament Square *SW1* 246 B3
Parliament Street *SW1* 246 B4
Parnham Street *E14* 249 E4
Parry Street *SW8* 246 B1
Parsonage Street *E14* 250 C2
Pasley Close *SE17* 247 E1
Passmore Street *SW1* 245 E2
Pastor Street *SE11* 247 D2
Pater Street *W8* 244 A3
Paternoster Row *EC4* 243 E2
Paternoster Square *EC4* 243 E2
Paton Street *EC1* 243 E3
Paul Julius Close *E14* 250 C4
Paul Street *EC2* 243 F3
Paul's Walk *EC4* 243 E1
Paultons Square *SW3* 244 C1
Paveley Street *NW8* 240 C4
Pavilion Road *SW1* 245 D2
Pavilion Street *SW1* 245 D3
Peabody Avenue *SW1* 245 F1
Peacock Street *SE17* 247 E2
Pear Tree Court *EC1* 243 D3
Pear Tree Street *EC1* 243 E3
Pearl Street *E1* 248 C2
Pearman Street *SE1* 247 D3
Peartree Lane *E1* 249 D3
Peerless Street *EC1* 243 E4
Pelham Crescent *SW7* 244 C2
Pelham Place *SW7* 244 C2
Pelham Street *SW7* 244 C2
Pelier Street *SE17* 247 E1
Pelling Street *E14* 249 F4
Pemberton Row *EC4* 243 D2
Pembridge Gardens *W2* 240 A1
Pembridge Place *W2* 240 A1
Pembridge Road *W11* 240 A1
Pembridge Square *W2* 240 A1
Pembroke Mews *W8* 244 A2
Earls Court Road
Penang Street *E1* 248 C2
Penfold Place *NW1* 240 C3
Penfold Street *NW1 & NW8* 240 C3
Pennant Mews *W8* 244 A2
Pennington Street *E1* 248 C3
Penrose Grove *SE17* 247 E1
Penrose Street *SE17* 247 E1
Penryn Street *NW1* 244 A2
Penton Place *SE17* 247 D2
Penton Rise *WC1* 242 C4
Pentonville Road *N1* 242 C4
Pepper Street *SE1* 247 E4
Pepper Street *E14* 250 B3
Pepys Street *EC3* 248 A3
Percival Street *EC1* 243 D3
Percy Circus *WC1* 242 C4
Percy Street *W1* 242 A2
Perkin's Rents *SW1* 246 A3
Perkins Square *SE1* 247 E4
Perry's Place *W1* 242 A2
Perryn Road *SE16* 248 C1
Peter Street *W1* 242 A1
Peter's Hill *EC4* 243 E2
Peter's Lane *EC1* 243 D3
Petersham Lane *SW7* 244 B3
Petersham Mews *SW7* 244 B3
Petersham Place *SW7* 244 B3
Peto Place *NW1* 241 F3
Petticoat Lane *E1* 248 B4
Petticoat Square *E1* 248 A4
Petty France *SW1* 246 A3
Petyward *SW3* 245 D2
Phelp Street *SE17* 247 F1
Phene Street *SW3* 245 D1
Philchurch Place *E1* 248 B3
Phillimore Walk *W8* 244 A3
Philpot Lane *EC3* 243 F1
Philpot Street *E1* 248 C4
Phipp Street *EC2* 243 F3
Phoenix Place *WC1* 242 C3
Phoenix Road *NW1* 242 A4
Phoenix Street *WC2* 242 B2
Charing Cross Road
Piccadilly *W1* 245 F4
Piccadilly Arcade *SW1* 246 A4
Piccadilly
Piccadilly Circus *W1* 242 A1
Piccadilly Place *W1* 242 A1
Vine Street
Pickard Street *EC1* 243 E4
Pickford Wharf *N1* 243 E4
Pickwick Street *SE1* 247 E3
Picton Place *W1* 241 E2
Pier Street *E14* 250 C2
Piggot Street *E14* 249 F3
Pilgrim Street *EC4* 243 D2
Pilgrimage Street *SE1* 247 F3
Pimlico Road *SW1* 245 E2
Pinchin Street *E1* 248 B3
Pindar Street *EC2* 243 F3
Pindock Mews *W9* 240 A3
Pine Street *EC1* 243 D3
Pitfield Street *N1* 243 F4
Pitsea Place *E1* 249 E3
Pitsea Street *E1* 249 E3
Pitt Street *W8* 244 A3
Pitt's Head Mews *W1* 245 E4
Pixley Street *E14* 249 F4
Platina Street *EC2* 243 F3
Playhouse Yard *EC4* 243 D1
Plevina Street *E14* 250 B3
Pleydell Street *EC4* 243 D1
Bouverie Street
Plough Place *EC4* 243 D2
Fetter Lane
Plover Way *SE16* 249 E1
Plumber's Row *E1* 249 B4
Plumtree Court *EC4* 243 D2
Plymouth Wharf *E14* 250 C2
Plympton Street *NW8* 240 C3
Pocock Street *SE1* 247 D3
Pointers Close *E14* 250 B1
Poland Street *W1* 242 A2
Pollen Street *W1* 241 F1
Pollitt Drive *NW8* 240 C3
Polygon Road *NW1* 242 A4
Pomwell Way *E1* 248 B4
Pond Place *SW3* 244 C2
Ponler Street *E1* 248 C3
Ponsonby Place *SW1* 246 B2
Ponsonby Terrace *SW1* 246 B2
Pont Street *SW1* 245 D3
Pont Street Mews *SW1* 245 D3
Poolmans Street *SE16* 249 D2
Poonah Street *E1* 249 D3
Pope Street *SE1* 248 A1
Poplar Place *W2* 240 A1
Poppins Court *EC4* 243 D2
Fleet Street
Porchester Gardens *W2* 240 A1
Porchester Place *W2* 241 D2
Porchester Road *W2* 240 A2
Porchester Square *W2* 240 A2
Porchester Terrace *W2* 240 B1
Porlock Street *SE1* 247 F3
Porter Street *W1* 241 E3
Porter Street *SE1* 247 E4
Porteus Road *W2* 240 B2
Portland Mews *W1* 242 A2
D'Arblay Street
Portland Place *W1* 241 F2
Portland Square *E1* 248 C2
Portland Street *SE17* 247 F1
Portman Close *W1* 241 E2
Portman Mews South *W1* 241 E2
Portman Square *W1* 241 E2
Portman Street *W1* 241 E2
Portpool Lane *EC1* 242 C3
Portsea Place *W2* 241 D2
Portsmouth Street *WC2* 242 C2
Portugal Street
Portsoken Street *EC3* 248 B3
Portugal Street *WC2* 242 C2
Potier Street *SE1* 247 F3
Pottery Street *SE16* 248 C1
Poultry *EC2* 243 E2
Praed Street *W2* 240 C2
Pratt Walk *SE11* 246 C2
Premier Place *E14* 250 A4
Prescot Street *E1* 248 B3
President Street *EC1* 243 E4
Central Street
Presidents Drive *E1* 248 C2
Prestage Way *E14* 250 C4
Prestons Road *E14* 250 C4
Prestwood Street *N1* 243 E4
Wenlock Road
Price's Street *SE1* 247 D4
Prideaux Place *WC1* 242 C4
Primrose Hill *EC4* 243 D1
Hutton Street
Primrose Street *EC2* 248 A4
Prince Albert Road *NW1 & NW8* 240 C4
Prince Consort Road *SW7* 244 C3
Prince of Wales Terrace *W8* 244 B1
Kensington Road
Prince's Gardens *SW7* 244 C3

Prince's Gate
Strathmore Gardens
256

Prince's Gate SW7 244 C3
Prince's Gate Mews SW7 244 C3
Prince's Mews W2 240 A1
Prince's Square W2 240 A1
Princelet Street E1 248 B4
Princes Arcade SW1 246 A4
Piccadilly
Princes Circus WC2 242 B2
Princes Court E1 248 C3
Princes Riverside Road SE16 249 D2
Princes Street EC2 243 F2
Princes Street W1 241 F2
Princess Street SE1 247 D3
Princeton Street WC1 242 C2
Printer Street EC4 243 D2
Prioress Street SE1 247 F3
Priory Walk SW10 244 B1
Procter Street WC1 242 C2
Prospect Place E1 249 D2
Prospect Street SE16 248 C1
Providence Court W1 241 E1
Providence Square SE1 248 B2
Provost Street N1 243 F4
Prusom Street E1 248 C2
Pudding Lane EC3 243 F1
Puddle Dock EC4 242 D1
Puma Court E1 248 B4
Purbrook Street SE1 248 A1

Q

Quarley Way SE15 241 D2
New Quebec Street
Quebec Way SE16 249 E1
Queen Anne Mews W1 241 F2
Chandos Street
Queen Anne Street W1 241 E2
Queen Anne's Gate SW1 246 A3
Queen Elizabeth Street SE1 248 A2
Queen Square WC1 242 B3
Queen Street EC4 243 E1
Queen Street W1 243 F4
Queen Street Place EC4 243 E1
Queen Victoria Street EC4 243 D1
Queen's Gardens SW1 245 F3
Queen's Gardens W2 240 B1
Queen's Gate SW7 244 B3
Queen's Gate Gardens SW7 244 B2
Queen's Gate Mews SW7 244 B3
Queen's Gate Place SW7 244 B3
Queen's Gate Place Mews SW7 244 B2
Queen's Gate Terrace SW7 244 B3
Queen's Mews W2 240 A1
Queen's Row SE17 247 E1
Queen's Walk SW1 245 F4
Queenhithe EC4 243 E1
Queensberry Mews West SW7 244 B2
Queensberry Place SW7 241 F4
Harrington Street
Queensborough Terrace W2 240 B1
Queensway W2 240 A2
Quick Street N1 243 D4

R

Rabbit Row W8 244 A4
Raby Street E14 249 E4
Radcliffe Road SE1 248 A1
Radcot Street SE11 247 D1
Radley Court SE16 249 E2
Radley Mews W8 244 A2
Radnor Mews W2 240 C2
Radnor Place W2 240 C2
Radnor Street EC1 243 D3
Radnor Walk SW3 245 D1
Railway Approach SE1 247 F4
Railway Avenue SE16 249 D2
Rainbow Avenue E14 250 B1
Raine Street E1 248 C2
Rainsford Street W2 240 C2
Raleana Road E14 250 C4
Ralston Street SW3 245 D1
Ramillies Place W1 241 F2
Ramillies Street W1 242 A2
Rampart Street E1 248 C4
Rampayne Street SW1 246 A2
Ramsey Mews SW3 244 C1
Randall Road SE11 246 C2
Randall Row SE11 246 C2
Randolph Avenue W9 240 A4
Randolph Crescent W9 240 B3
Randolph Mews W9 240 B3
Randolph Road W9 240 B3
Ranelagh Bridge W2 240 B2
Ranelagh Grove SW1 245 E2
Ranelagh Road SW1 246 A1
Ranston Street NW1 240 C3
Raphael Street SW7 245 D3
Ratcliff Grove EC1 243 E4
Ratcliffe Cross Street E1 249 E3
Ratcliffe Lane E14 249 E3
Rathbone Place W1 242 A2
Raven Row E1 248 C4
Ravensdon Street SE11 247 D1
Ravent Road SE11 246 C2
Ravey Street EC2 243 F3
Rawlings Street SW3 245 D2
Rawstorne Place EC1 243 D4
Rawstorne Street
Rawstorne Street EC1 243 D4
Ray Street EC1 243 D3
Reardon Path E1 248 C2
Reardon Street E1 248 C2
Rebecca Terrace SE16 249 D1
Rectory Square E1 249 E4
Red Lion Row SE17 247 E1
Red Lion Square WC1 242 C2
Red Lion Street WC1 242 C2
Redan Place W2 240 A2
Redburn Street SW3 245 D1
Redcastle Close E1 249 D3
Redcliffe Gardens SW10 & SW5 244 A1
Redcliffe Mews SW10 244 B1
Redcliffe Place SW10 244 B1
Redcliffe Road SW10 244 B1
Redcliffe Square SW10 244 A1
Redcliffe Street SW10 244 A1
Redcross Way SE1 247 E4
Rede Place W2 240 A1
Redesdale Street SW3 245 D1
Redfield Lane SW5 244 A2
Redhill Street NW1 241 F4
Redman's Road E1 249 D4
Redmead Lane E1 248 B2
Wapping High Street
Redriff Road SE16 249 E1
Redwood Close SE16 249 E2
Reece Mews SW7 244 C1
Reedworth Street SE11 247 D2
Reeves Mews W1 241 E1
Regal Close E1 248 C4
Regan Way N1 243 F4
Regency Street SW1 246 A2
Regent Square WC1 242 B4
Regent Street W1 & SW1 241 F2
Regnart Buildings NW1 242 A4
Euston Street
Relton Mews SW7 245 D3
Remington Street N1 243 E4
Remnant Street WC2 242 C2
Kingsway
Renforth Street SE16 249 D1
Renfrew Road SE11 247 D2
Rennie Street SE1 243 E1
Rephidim Street SE1 247 F3
Repton Street E14 249 E4
Reston Place SW7 244 B3
Reveley Close SE16 249 E1
Rex Place W1 241 E1
Rhodeswell Road E14 249 F4
Rich Lane SW5 244 A1
Rich Street E14 249 F3
Richard's Place SW3 245 D2
Richbell Place WC1 242 C3
Emerald Street
Richmond Buildings W1 242 A2
Dean Street
Richmond Mews W1 242 A2
Richmond Terrace SW1 246 B4
Rickett Street SW6 244 A1
Ridgmount Gardens WC1 242 A3
Ridgmount Street WC1 242 A3
Riding House Street W1 241 F2
Riley Road SE1 248 A1
Ringwood Gardens E14 250 A2
Risborough Street SE1 247 E4
Risdon Street SE16 249 D1
River Barge Close E14 250 C3
River Street EC1 243 D4
Riverside Walk SE1 246 C4
Rivington Street EC2 243 F3
Robert Adam Street W1 241 E2
Robert Close W9 240 B3
Robert Dashwood Way SE17 247 E2
Robert Street NW1 241 F4
Robert Street WC2 242 B1
Roberts Close SE16 249 E1
Roberts Place EC1 243 D3
Bowling Green Lane
Robinson Street SW3 245 D1
Flood Street
Rochester Row SW1 246 A2
Rochester Street SW1 246 A2
Rockingham Street SE1 247 E3
Rocliffe Street N1 243 E4
Roding Mews E1 248 B2
Rodmarton Street W1 241 D2
Rodney Place SE17 247 E2
Rodney Road SE17 247 E2
Roffey Street E14 250 B3
Roger Street WC1 242 C3
Roland Gardens SW7 244 B1
Roland Way SE17 247 F1
Roland Way SW7 244 B1
Rolls Buildings EC4 243 D2
Rolls Passage EC4 242 C2
Romford Street E1 248 C4
Romilly Street W1 242 A1
Romney Mews W1 241 E3
Chiltern Street
Romney Street SW1 246 B2
Ronald Street E1 249 D3
Rood Lane EC3 243 F1
Rope Street SE16 249 E1
Ropemaker Road SE16 249 E1
Ropemaker Street EC2 243 F3
Ropemaker's Fields E14 249 F3
Roper Lane SE1 248 A1
Rosary Gardens SW7 244 B2
Roscoe Street EC1 243 E3
Rose & Crown Yard SW1 246 A4
King Street
Rose Alley SE1 247 E4
Rose Street WC2 242 B1
Rosebery Avenue EC1 245 D3
Rosemoor Street SW3 245 D2
Roserton Street E14 250 B3
Rosoman Place EC1 243 D4
Rosoman Street
Rosoman Street EC1 243 D4
Rossmore Road NW1 241 D3
Rotary Street SE1 247 D3
Rotherhithe Street SE16 249 D2
Rotherhithe Tunnel Approach E14 249 E3
Rotherhithe Tunnel Approach SE16 249 F1
Rothsay Street SE1 247 F3
Rotten Row SW7 & SW1 244 C4
Rotterdam Drive E14 250 C2
Rouel Road SE16 248 B1
Roupell Street SE1 247 D4
Rowington Close W2 240 A3
Roxby Place SW6 244 A1
Roy Square E14 249 F3
Royal Avenue SW3 245 D1
Royal Exchange Buildings EC3 243 F2
Cornhill
Royal Hospital Road SW3 245 D1
Royal Mint Place E1 248 B3
Royal Mint Street E1 248 B3
Royal Opera Arcade SW1 246 A4
Royal Road SE17 247 D1
Royal Street SE1 246 C3
Royalty Mews W1 242 A2
Royalty Mews W1 242 A2
Rudolf Place SW8 246 B1
Rudolph Road NW6 240 A4
Rufus Street N1 243 F4
Rugby Street WC1 242 C3
Rugg Street E14 249 F3
Rum Close E1 248 C3
Rupack Street SE16 249 D1
Rupert Street W1 242 A1
Rushworth Street SE1 247 D3
Russell Court SW1 246 A4
Cleveland Row
Russell Place SE16 249 E1
Russell Square WC1 242 B3
Russell Street WC2 242 C1
Russia Dock Road SE16 249 E2
Russia Row EC2 243 E2
Russia Walk SE16 249 E1
Rutherford Street SW1 246 A2
Rutland Gardens SW7 245 D3
Rutland Gate SW7 244 C3
Rutland Gate Mews SW7 244 C3
Rutland Gate
Rutland Mews East SW7 244 C3
Ennismore Street
Rutland Mews South SW7 244 C3
Ennismore Street
Rutland Place EC1 243 E3
Rutland Street SW7 244 C3
Rysbrack Street SW3 245 D3

S

Sackville Street W1 242 A1
Saddle Yard W1 245 E4
Saffron Hill EC1 243 D3
Saffron Street EC1 243 D3
Sage Street E1 248 C3
Sage Way WC1 242 C4
Sail Street SE11 246 C2
St Agnes Place SE11 247 D1
St Alban's Grove W8 244 A3
St Alban's Street SW1 242 A1
St Albans Mews W2 240 C3
St Alphage Garden EC2 243 E2
St Andrew Street EC4 243 D2
St Andrew's Hill EC4 243 D1
St Ann's Lane SW1 246 A3
St Ann's Row E14 249 F3
St Ann's Street SW1 246 B3
St Anne Street E14 249 F3
St Anne's Court W1 242 A2
St Anselm's Place W1 241 E1
St Anthony's Close E1 248 B2
St Barnabas Street SW1 245 E2
St Botolph Street EC3 248 A4
St Bride Street EC4 243 D2
St Catherines Mews SW3 245 D2
Milner Street
St Chad's Place WC1 242 B4
St Chad's Street WC1 242 B4
St Christoper's Place W1 241 E2
St Clare Street EC3 248 A3
St Clement's Lane WC2 242 C2
St Clements Court EC4 243 F1
St Cross Street EC1 243 D3
St David's Square E14 250 B1
St Dunstan's Court EC4 243 D2
Fleet Street
St Dunstan's Lane EC3 243 F1
St Mary at Hill
St Dunstans Alley EC3 248 A3
St Dunstans Hill
St Dunstans Hill EC3 248 A3
St Ermins Hill SW1 246 A3
St George Street W1 241 F1
St George's Circus SE1 247 D3
St George's Court EC4 243 D2
St George's Drive SW1 245 F2
St George's Mews SE1 247 D3
St George's Road SE1 247 D3
St George's Square SW1 246 A1
St George's Square E14 249 E3
St George's Square Mews SW1 246 A1
St Georges Fields W2 241 D1
St Giles High Street WC2 242 B2
St Helen's Place EC3 243 F2
St Helena Street WC1 242 C4
St James's Court SW1 246 A3
St James's Market SW1 242 A1
Haymarket
St James's Place SW1 245 F4
St James's Road SE1 & SE16 248 B1
St James's Row EC1 243 D3
St James's Walk
St James's Square SW1 246 A4
St James's Street SW1 246 A4
St James's Walk EC1 243 D3
St John Street EC1 243 D4
St John's Lane EC1 243 D3
St John's Place EC1 243 D3
St John's Square EC1 243 D3
St John's Villas W8 244 A3
St Mary's Place
St John's Wood High Street NW8 240 C4
St John's Wood Road NW8 240 C4
St Katherine's Row EC3 243 F1
Fenchurch Street
St Katherine's Way E1 248 B1
St Lawrence Street E14 250 C4
St Leonard's Terrace SW3 245 D1
St Loo Avenue SW3 245 D1
St Luke's Close EC1 243 E3
St Luke's Street SW3 244 C1
St Margaret's Lane W8 244 A3
St Margaret's Street SW1 246 B3
St Mark Street E1 248 B3
St Martin's Court WC2 242 B1
St Martin's Lane
St Martin's Lane WC2 242 B1
St Martin's Place WC2 242 B1
St Martin's Street WC2 242 B1
St Martin's-le-Grand EC1 243 E2
St Mary Axe EC3 248 A3
St Mary at Hill EC3 243 F1
St Mary's Gardens SE11 247 D2
St Mary's Gate W8 244 A3
St Mary's Mansions W2 240 B3
St Mary's Place W8 244 A3
St Mary's Square W2 240 C3
St Mary's Terrace W2 240 B3
St Mary's Walk SE11 247 D2
St Marychurch Street SE16 249 D1
St Matthew Street SW1 246 A3
St Michael's Street W2 240 C2
St Olav's Square SE16 249 D1
Lower Road
St Oswald's Place SE11 246 C1
St Paul's Avenue SE16 249 E2
St Paul's Churchyard EC4 243 E2
St Paul's Terrace SE17 247 E1
St Paul's Way E3 249 F4
St Peter's Place W9 240 A3
St Petersburgh Mews W2 240 A1
St Petersburgh Place W2 240 A1
St Stephen's Crescent W2 240 A2
St Stephen's Gardens W2 240 A2
St Stephen's Mews W2 240 A2
St Swithin's Lane EC4 243 F1
St Thomas Street SE1 247 F4
St Vincent Street W1 241 E2
Salamanca Place SE1 246 C2
Salamanca Street SE1 & SE11 246 C2
Salem Road W2 240 A1
Salisbury Close SE17 247 F2
Salisbury Court EC4 243 D2
Salisbury Place W1 241 D3
Salisbury Square EC4 243 D2
Salisbury Court
Salisbury Street NW8 240 C3
Salmon Lane E14 249 E4
Salter Road SE16 249 E1
Salter Street E14 249 F3
Samford Street NW8 240 C3
Sampson Street E1 248 C2
Sancroft Street SE11 246 C2
Sanctuary Street SE1 247 E4
Marshalsea Road
Sandell Street SE1 247 D4
Sandland Street WC1 242 C2
Sandpiper Close SE16 249 F2
Sandwich Street WC1 242 B4
Sandys Row E1 248 A4
Sans Walk EC1 243 D3
Saracens Head Yard EC3 248 A3
Sardinia Street WC2 242 C2
Saunders Court E14 249 F3
Limehouse Causeway
Saunders Ness Road E14 250 C2
Savage Gardens EC3 248 A3
Pepys Street
Savernake Close E14 250 A2
Savile Row W1 241 F1
Savoy Buildings WC2 242 C1
Savoy Hill WC2 242 C1
Savoy Way
Savoy Place WC2 242 B1
Savoy Row WC2 242 C1
Savoy Street
Savoy Steps WC2 242 C1
Savoy Way
Savoy Street WC2 242 C1
Savoy Way WC2 242 C1
Sawyer Street SE1 247 E4
Scala Street W1 242 A2
Scandrett Street E1 248 C2
Scarborough Street E1 248 B3
Scarsdale Place W8 244 A3
Scarsdale Villas W8 244 A3
School House Lane E1 249 D3
Schooner Close SE16 249 D2
Schooner Close E14 250 C2
Scoresby Street SE1 247 D4
Scotswood Street EC1 245 D3
Sans Walk
Scott Ellis Gardens NW8 240 B4
Scott Lidgett Crescent SE16 248 B1
Scott Russell Place E14 250 B1
Scovell Road SE1 247 E3
Scrutton Street EC2 243 F3
Seagrave Road SW6 244 A1
Searles Road SE1 247 F2
Sebastian Street EC1 243 D4
Secker Street SE1 246 C4
Sedan Way SE17 247 F2
Sedding Street SW1 245 E2
Sloane Square
Seddon Street WC1 242 C4
Sedley Place W1 241 F2
Woodstock Street
Seething Lane EC3 248 A3
Sekforde Street EC1 243 D3
Sellon Mews SE11 246 C2
Selsdon Way E14 250 B2
Selsey Street E14 249 F4
Selwood Place SW7 244 C1
Selwood Terrace SW7 244 C2
Semley Place SW1 245 E2
Senior Street W2 240 A3
Senrab Street E1 249 D4
Serle Street WC2 242 C2
Serpentine Road W2 244 C1
Seth Street SE16 249 D1
Settles Street E1 248 C4
Seven Dials WC2 242 B2
Seville Street SW1 245 D3
Knightsbridge
Sevington Street W9 240 A3
Seward Street EC1 243 E3
Sextant Avenue E14 250 C2
Seymour Mews W1 241 E2
Seymour Place W1 241 D2
Seymour Street W2 241 D1
Seymour Walk SW10 244 B1
Seyssel Street E14 250 C2
Shad Thames SE1 248 A2
Shadwell Pier Head E1 249 D3
Shadwell Place E1 248 C3
Shaftesbury Avenue W1 & WC2 242 A1
Shaftesbury Mews W8 244 A2
Shafto Mews SW1 245 D3
Shand Street SE1 248 A2
Sharsted Street SE17 247 D1
Shawfield Street SW3 245 D1
Sheffield Street WC2 242 C2
Portugal Street
Sheffield Terrace W8 244 A4
Shelmerdine Close E3 249 F4
Shelton Street WC2 242 B2
Shepherd Market W1 245 F4
Shepherd Street W1 245 E4
Shepherd's Place W1 241 E1
Shepherdess Place N1 243 E4
Shepherdess Walk
Shepherdess Walk N1 243 E4
Sheraton Street W1 242 A2
Wardour Street
Sherlock Mews W1 241 E3
Sherwood Gardens E14 250 A2
Sherwood Street W1 242 A1
Shillibeer Place W1 241 D2
Ship Yard E14 250 A1
Shipwright Road SE16 249 E1
Shirland Road W9 240 A3
Shoe Lane EC4 243 D2
Short Street SE1 247 D4
Short's Gardens WC2 242 B2
Shorter Street E1 248 B3
Shoulder of Mutton Alley E14 249 F2
Shouldham Street W1 241 D2
Shroton Street NW1 240 C3
Sicilian Avenue WC1 242 B2
Vernon Place
Siddons Lane NW1 241 D3
Sidford Place SE1 246 C2
Sidmouth Street WC1 242 C4
Sidney Square E1 249 D4
Sidney Street E1 248 C4
Silex Street SE1 247 D3
Silk Street EC2 243 E3
Silver Walk SE16 249 F2
Silvester Street SE1 247 E3
Simpson's Road E14 250 B4
Singer Street EC2 243 F3
Sise Lane EC4 243 E2
Pancras Lane
Skinner Street EC1 243 D3
Skinners Lane EC4 243 F4
Queen Street
Sleaford Street SW8 242 B4
Slingsby Place WC2 242 B1
Slippers Place SE16 248 C1
Sloane Avenue SW3 245 D2
Sloane Court East SW3 245 E2
Sloane Court West SW3 245 E1
Sloane Gardens SW1 245 E2
Sloane Square SW1 245 E2
Sloane Street SW1 245 D3
Sloane Terrace SW1 245 E2
Sly Street E1 248 C3
Cannon Street Road
Smart's Place WC2 242 B2
Smeaton Street E1 248 C2
Smith Close SE16 249 D2
Smith Square SW1 246 B3
Smith Street SW3 245 D1
Smith Terrace SW3 245 D1
Smithfield Street EC1 243 D2
Smithy Street E1 249 D4
Snow Hill EC1 243 D2
Snowsfields SE1 247 F4
Soho Square W1 242 A2
Soho Street W1 242 A2
Somerford Way SE16 249 E1
Somers Crescent W2 240 C2
Somers Mews W2 240 C2
Sondes Street SE17 247 F1
Sophia Square SE16 249 E3
South Audley Street W1 241 E1
South Bolton Gardens SW5 244 B1
South Carriage Drive SW1 & SW7 244 C3
South Collonnade E14 250 A4
South Crescent WC1 242 A2
Store Street
South Eaton Place SW1 245 E2
South End W8 244 A3
South End Row W8 244 A3
South Lambeth Place SW8 246 B1
South Molton Lane W1 241 E1
South Molton Street W1 241 E2
South Parade SW3 244 C1
South Place EC2 243 F2
South Street W1 245 E4
South Tenter Street E1 248 B3
South Terrace SW7 244 C2
South Wharf Road W2 240 C2
Southall Place SE1 247 F3
Long Lane
Southampton Buildings WC2 242 C2
Southampton Place WC1 242 B2
Southampton Row WC1 242 B3
Southampton Street WC2 242 B1
Southsea Street SE16 249 F1
Southwark Bridge EC4 & SE1 243 E1
Southwark Bridge Road SE1 247 E3
Southwark Park Road SE16 248 C1
Southwark Street SE1 247 D4
Southwell Gardens SW7 244 B2
Southwick Street W2 240 C2
Hyde Park Crescent
Sovereign Close E1 248 C3
Spa Road SE16 248 B1
Spanish Place W1 241 E2
Spear Mews SW5 244 A2
Spelman Street E1 248 B4
Spence Close SE16 249 F1
Spencer Street EC1 243 D4
Spenser Street SW1 246 A3
Spert Street E14 249 E3
Spindrift Avenue E14 250 A2
Spital Square E1 248 A4
Spital Street E1 248 B4
Sprimont Place SW3 245 D2
Spring Gardens SW1 246 B4
Spring Mews W1 241 D3
Spring Street W2 240 C2
Spur Road SW1 245 F3
Spur Road SE1 246 C3
Lower Marsh
Spurgeon Street SE1 247 F3
Squire Gardens NW8 240 C4
Stable Yard Road SW1 246 A4
Stables Way SE11 246 C1
Stacey Street WC2 242 B2
Staff Street EC1 243 F4
Vince Street
Stafford Place SW1 245 F3
Stag Place SW1 245 F3
Stainer Street SE1 247 F4
Staining Lane EC2 243 E2
Stalbridge Street NW1 240 C3
Stalham Street SE16 248 C1
Stamford Street SE1 246 C4
Stanford Road W8 244 A3
Stanford Street SW1 246 A2
Stanhope Gardens SW7 244 B2
Stanhope Gate W1 245 E4
Hertford Street
Stanhope Mews East SW7 244 B2
Stanhope Mews South SW7 244 B2
Stanhope Mews West SW7 244 B2
Stanhope Place W2 244 B2
Stanhope Street NW1 241 F4
Stanhope Terrace W2 240 C1
Stannary Place SE11 247 D1
Stannary Street SE11 247 D1
Stanworth Street SE1 248 B1
Staple Inn Buildings WC1 242 C2
Staple Street SE1 247 F3
Staples Close SE16 249 E2
Star Place E1 248 B3
Star Street W2 240 C2
Star Yard WC2 242 C2
Starboard Way E14 250 A3
Starcross Street NW1 242 A3
Station Acces Road EC2 243 F2
Stave Yard Road SE16 249 E2
Stead Street SE17 247 E2
Stebondale Street E14 250 C2
Stedham Place WC1 242 B2
New Oxford Street
Steedman Street SE17 247 E2
Steel's Lane E1 249 D3
Steelyard Passage EC4 243 E1
Steers Way SE16 249 E1
Stephen Mews W1 242 A2
Gresse Street
Stephen Street W1 242 A2
Stephen's Row EC4 243 F1
Walbrook
Stephenson Way NW1 242 A3
Stepney Causeway E1 249 D3
Stepney Green E1 249 D4
Stepney High Street E1 249 E4
Stepney Way E1 248 C4
Sterling Street SW7 245 D3
Montpelier Place
Sterry Street SE1 247 F3
Stevedore Street E1 248 C2
Stevens Street SE1 248 A1
Steward Street E1 248 A4
Stewart Street E14 250 C3
Stewart's Grove SW3 244 C2
Stillington Street SW1 246 A2
Stockholm Way E1 248 B2
Vaughan Way
Stocks Place E14 249 F3
Stone Buildings WC2 242 C2
Chancery Lane
Stone Hall Gardens W8 244 A3
Stone Hall Place W8 244 A3
Stone Hall Gardens
Stone Stairs E1 249 E3
Stonecutter Street EC4 243 D2
Stones End Street SE1 247 E3
Stoney Lane E1 248 A4
Stoney Street SE1 247 F4
Stopford Road SE17 247 E1
Store Street WC1 242 A2
Storers Quay E14 250 C2
Storey's Gate SW1 246 B3
Stork's Road SE16 248 C1
Stoughton Close SE11 246 C2
Stourcliffe Street W1 241 D2
Strafford Street E14 250 A3
Strand WC2 242 B1
Stratford Avenue W8 244 A3
Stratford Place W1 241 E2
Stratford Road W8 244 A2
Strathearn Place W2 240 C2
Hyde Park Square
Strathmore Gardens W8 244 A4
Palace Gardens Terrace

Stratton Street Zoar Street

Stratton Street W1 245 F4
Strattondale Street E14 250 B3
Streatham Street WC1 242 B2
Dyott Street
Strutton Ground SW1 246 A3
Strype Street E1 248 A4
Stukeley Street WC2 242 B2
Sturge Street SE1 247 E3
Sturgeon Road SE17 247 E1
Sturt Street N1 243 E4
Stutfield Street E1 248 B3
Sudeley Street N1 243 D4
Sudrey Street SE1 247 E3
Suffolk Lane EC4 243 F1
Suffolk Place SW1 242 B1
Suffolk Street
Suffolk Street SW1 242 B1
Sugar Quay Walk EC3 248 A3
Sullivan Road SE1 247 D2
Summercourt Road E1 249 D4
Summers Street EC1 243 D3
Back Hill
Sumner Place SW7 244 C2
Sumner Place Mews SW7 244 C2
Sumner Street SE1 247 E4
Sun Street EC2 243 F3
Sun Street Passage EC2 243 F2
Sun Walk E1 248 B3
Sunderland Terrace W2 240 A2
Sunningdale Gardens W8 244 A2
Stratford Road
Surrenale Place W9 240 A3
Surrey Quays Road SE16 249 D1
Surrey Row SE1 247 D4
Surrey Square SE17 247 F2
Surrey Street WC2 242 C1
Surrey Water Road SE16 249 E2
Sussex Gardens W2 240 C1
Sussex Place NW1 241 D4
Sussex Place W2 240 C2
Sussex Square W2 240 C1
Sussex Street SW1 245 F1
Sutherland Avenue W9 240 A3
Sutherland Row SW1 245 F1
Sutherland Street
Sutherland Square SE17 247 E1
Sutherland Street SW1 245 F1
Sutherland Walk SE17 247 E1
Sutton Row W1 242 B2
Swallow Street W1 242 A1
Swan Lane EC4 243 F1
Swan Mead SE1 247 F3
Swan Road SE16 249 D2
Swan Street SE1 247 E3
Swan Walk SW3 245 D1
Sweden Gate SE16 249 E1
Swedenborg Gardens E1 248 C3
Sweeney Crescent SE1 248 B1
Swinton Street WC1 242 C4
Swiss Court WC2 242 B1
Leicester Square
Sycamore Street EC1 243 E3
Old Street
Sydney Close SW3 244 C2
Sydney Mews SW3 244 C2
Sydney Street SW3 244 C2
Symons Street SW3 245 D2

T

Tabard Street SE1 247 F3
Tabernacle Street EC2 243 F3
Tachbrook Street SW1 246 A2
Taeping Street E14 250 B2
Tailworth Street E1 248 B4
Chicksand Street
Talbot Square W2 240 C2
Talbot Yard SE1 247 F4
Tallis Street EC4 243 D1
Tameraire Street SE16 249 D2
Tamworth Street SW6 243 A1
Tankerton Street WC1 242 B4
Cromer Street
Tanner Street SE1 248 A1
Taplow Street N1 243 E4
Tarbert Walk E1 249 D3
Tarling Street E1 248 C3
Tarver Road SE17 247 E1
Tatum Street SE17 247 F2
Taunton Mews NW1 241 D3
Balcombe Street
Taunton Place NW1 241 D3
Tavistock Place WC1 242 B3
Tavistock Square WC1 242 B3
Tavistock Street WC2 242 B1
Taviton Street WC1 242 A3
Tavy Close SE11 247 D2
Teak Close SE16 249 E2
Tedworth Square SW3 245 D1
Telegraph Place E14 250 A2
Telegraph Street EC2 243 F2
Temple Avenue EC4 243 D1
Temple Lane EC4 243 A2
Temple Place WC2 242 C1
Templeton Place SW5 243 D1
Tench Street E1 248 C2
Tenison Court W1 241 F2
Regent Street
Tenison Way SE1 246 C4
Tennis Street SE1 247 F3
Tenter Ground E1 248 A4
White's Row
Tenterden Street W1 241 F2
Terminus Place SW1 245 F3
Thackeray Street W8 244 A3
Thalia Close SE10 250 C1
Thame Road SE16 249 E2
Thames Circle E14 250 A2
Thames Link SE16 249 D2
Thames Street SE10 250 B1
Thanet Street WC1 242 B4
Thavies Inn EC4 243 D2
Thayer Street W1 241 E2
The Boltons SW10 244 B1
The Broad Walk NW1 241 E4
The Broad Walk W8 244 B4
The Cut SE1 247 D4
The Dial Walk W8 244 B4
The Economist Plaza SW1 246 A4
Bury Street
The Flower Walk SW7 244 B3
The Grange SE1 248 A1
The Highway E1 & E14 248 C3
The Limes W2 240 A1
The Little Boltons SW10 & SW5 243 B1
The Mall SW1 246 A4
The Mitre E14 249 F3
The Piazza WC2 242 B1
The Quarterdeck E14 250 A3
The Vale SW3 244 C1
Theed Street SE1 247 D4
Theobald Street SE1 247 F2
New Kent Road
Theobald's Road WC1 242 C3
Thermopylae Gate E14 250 B2
Theseus Walk N1 243 E4
Rocliffe Street
Thirleby Road SE1 246 A3
Thistle Grove SW10 244 B1
Thomas Doyle Street SE1 247 D3
Thomas More Street E1 248 B2
Thomas Place W8 244 A3
St Mary's Place
Thomas Road E14 249 F4
Thoresby Street N1 243 E4
Thorney Street SW1 246 B2
Thorngate Road W9 240 A3
Thornton Place W1 241 D3
Thrale Street SE1 247 E4
Thrawl Street E1 248 B4
Threadneedle Street EC2 243 F2
Three Colt Street E14 249 F3
Three Cranes Walk EC4 243 E1
Three Kings Yard W1 241 E1
Three Oak Lane SE1 248 A2
Throgmorton Avenue EC2 243 F2
Throgmorton Street EC2 243 F2
Thrush Street SE17 247 E1
Thurland Road SE16 248 B1
Thurloe Close SW7 244 C2
Thurloe Place SW7 244 C2
Thurloe Place Mews SW7 244 C2
Thurloe Square SW7 244 C2
Thurloe Street SW7 244 C2
Thurlow Street SE17 247 F2
Tiller Road E14 250 A3
Tillman Street E1 248 C3
Tilney Street W1 245 E3
Timber Street EC1 243 E3
Timberland Road E1 248 C3
Timberpond Road SE16 249 E2
Tinsley Road E1 249 D4
Tinworth Street SE11 246 B2
Titchborne Row W2 240 C2
Tite Street SW3 245 D1
Tiverton Street SE1 247 E3
Tivoli Court SE16 249 F2
Tobago Street E14 250 A3
Tokenhouse Yard EC2 243 F2
Tolmers Square NW1 242 A3
Tonbridge Street WC1 242 B4
Took's Court EC4 242 C2
Tooley Street SE1 248 A2
Topham Street EC1 243 D3
Tor Gardens W8 244 A4
Torquay Street W2 240 A2
Torrens Street EC1 243 D4
Torres Square E14 250 A1
Maritime Quay
Torrington Place E1 248 C1
Torrington Place WC1 242 A3
Tothill Street SW1 246 A3
Tottenham Court Road W1 242 A3
Tottenham Street W1 242 A3
Toulmin Street SE1 247 E3
Toussaint Walk SE16 248 B1
Tower Bridge E1 & SE1 248 A2
Tower Bridge Approach E1 248 B2
Tower Bridge Road SE1 248 A1
Tower Court WC2 242 B1
Monmouth Street
Tower Hill EC3 248 A3
Tower Hill Terrace EC3 248 A3
Gloucester Close
Tower Street WC2 242 B1
Townley Street SE17 247 E2
Townsend Street SE17 247 F2
Toynbee Street E1 248 B4
Tracey Street SE11 246 C2
Trafalgar Gardens E1 249 E4
Trafalgar Gardens W8 244 A3
South End Row
Trafalgar Grove SE10 250 C1
Trafalgar Road SE10 250 C1
Trafalgar Square WC2 242 B1
Trafalgar Street SE17 247 F1
Trafalgar Way E14 250 B4
Transom Square E14 250 B1
Tranton Road SE16 248 C1
Trebeck Street W1 245 E4
Curzon Street
Trebovir Road SW5 244 A2
Tregunter Road SW10 244 B1
Trenchard Street SE10 250 C1
Tresham Crescent NW8 240 C4
Treveris Street SE1 247 D4
Bear Lane
Trevithick Street SE8 250 A1
Trevor Place SW7 245 D3
Trevor Square SW7 245 D3
Trevor Street SW7 245 D3
Trinidad Street E14 249 F3
Trinity Church Square SE1 247 E3
Trinity Place EC3 248 A3
Trinity Square
Trinity Square EC3 248 A3
Trinity Street SE1 247 E3
Trio Place SE1 247 E3
Triton Square NW1 241 F3
Troon Street E1 249 E4
Trumans Street SE16 248 C1
Trump Street EC2 243 E2
Tryon Street SW3 245 D2
Tudor Street EC4 243 D1
Tufton Street SW1 246 B3
Tunley Green E14 249 F4
Tunnel Avenue SE10 250 C3
Tunnel Road SE16 249 D2
Turk's Row SW3 245 D2
Turner Street E1 248 C4
Turnmill Street EC1 243 D3
Turpentine Lane SW1 245 F1
Turquand Street SE17 247 E2
Twine Court E1 248 C3
Twyford Place WC2 242 C2
Kingsway
Tyers Gate SE1 247 F3
Tyers Street SE11 246 C1
Tyers Terrace SE11 246 C1
Tyne Street E1 248 B4
Tysoe Street EC1 243 D4

U

Udall Street SW1 246 A2
Ufford Street SE1 247 D3
Ulster Place NW1 241 E3
Umberston Street E1 248 C4
Undershaft EC3 243 F2
Underwood Row N1 243 E4
Shepherdess Walk
Underwood Street N1 243 E4
Undine Road E14 250 B2
Union Street SE1 247 D4
University Street WC1 242 A3
Upbrook Mews W2 240 B2
Upper Belgrave Street SW1 245 E3
Upper Berkeley Street W1 241 D2
Upper Brook Street W1 241 E1
Upper Cheyne Row SW3 244 C1
Upper Grosvenor Street W1 241 E1
Upper Ground SE1 243 D1
Upper Harley Street NW1 241 E3
Upper James Street W1 242 A1
Upper John Street W1 242 A1
Upper Marsh SE1 246 C3
Upper Montagu Street W1 241 D3
Upper St Martin's Lane WC2 242 B1
Upper Tachbrook Street SW1 246 A2
Upper Thames Street EC4 243 E1
Upper Wimpole Street W1 241 E3
Upper Woburn Place WC1 242 B3

V

Valcan Square E14 250 A2
Vale Close W9 240 B4
Valentine Place SE1 247 D3
Valentine Row SE1 247 D3
Vandon Passage SW1 246 A3
Vandon Street SW1 246 A3
Vandy Street EC2 243 F3
Vane Street SW1 246 A2
Vantage Mews E14 250 C4
Managers Street
Varden Street E1 248 C4
Varndell Street NW1 241 F4
Vauban Street SE16 248 B1
Vaughan Street SE16 249 F1
Vaughan Way E1 248 B2
Vauxhall Bridge SW1 & SE1 246 B2
Vauxhall Bridge Road SW1 245 F2
Vauxhall Grove SW8 246 B1
Vauxhall Street SE11 246 C1
Vauxhall Walk SE11 246 C2
Venables Street NW8 240 C3
Vere Street W1 241 E2
Vernon Place WC1 242 B2
Vernon Rise WC1 242 C4
Vernon Square WC1 242 C4
Penton Rise
Vernon Street W14 242 C4
Verulam Street WC1 242 C3
Vestry Street N1 243 F4
Vicarage Court W8 244 A4
Vicarage Gardens W8 244 A4
Vicarage Gate W8 244 A4
Victoria Avenue EC2 248 A4
Victoria Embankment SW1, WC2 & EC4 242 C1
Victoria Grove W8 244 B3
Victoria Road W8 244 B3
Victoria Street SW1 245 F3
Victory Place SE17 247 F2
Victory Place E14 249 E3
Victory Way SE16 249 E1
Vigo Street W1 242 A1
Villa Street SE17 247 F1
Villiers Street WC2 242 B1
Vince Street EC1 243 F4
Vincent Close SE16 249 E1
Vincent Square SW1 246 A2
Vincent Street SW1 246 A2
Vine Court E1 248 C4
Vine Lane SE1 248 A2
Vine Street EC3 248 A3
Vine Street W1 242 A1
Vine Street Bridge EC1 243 D3
Farringdon Lane
Vinegar Street E1 248 C2
Vinegar Yard SE1 247 F4
St Thomas Street
Vineyard Walk EC1 243 D3
Pine Street
Vintner's Place EC4 243 E1
Violet Hill NW8 240 B4
Virgil Place W1 241 D2
Seymour Place
Virgil Street SE1 246 C3
Virginia Street E1 248 B3
Viscount Street EC1 243 E3

W

Wadding Street SE17 247 E2
Waithman Street EC4 243 D2
Pilgrim Street
Wakefield Mews WC1 242 B4
Wakefield Street
Wakefield Street WC1 242 B4
Wakeling Street E14 249 E3
Wakley Street EC1 243 D4
Walbrook EC4 243 F1
Walburgh Street E1 248 C3
Walcorde Avenue SE17 247 E2
Walcot Square SE11 247 D2
Walden Street E1 248 C4
Waley Street E1 249 E4
Wallgrave Road SW5 244 A2
Wallwood Street E14 249 F4
Walmer Street W1 241 D3
Seymour Place
Walnut Tree Walk SE11 246 C2
Walpole Street SW3 245 D2
Walter Terrace E1 249 E4
Walton Place SW3 245 D3
Walton Street SW3 245 D2
Walton's Mews W1 241 D2
Walworth Place SE17 247 E1
Walworth Road SE1 & SE17 247 E2
Wansey Street SE17 247 E2
Wapping Dock Street E1 248 C2
Wapping High Street E1 248 B2
Wapping Lane E1 248 C3
Wapping Walk E1 248 C3
Wapping Wall E1 249 D2
Wardour Street W1 242 A2
Warner Street EC1 242 C3
Warren Street W1 241 F3
Warrington Crescent W9 240 B3
Warrington Gardens W9 240 B3
Warwick Avenue W9 240 A3
Warwick Court WC1 242 C2
Warwick Crescent W2 240 B3
Warwick House Street SW1 246 B4
Warwick Lane EC4 243 E2
Warwick Passage EC4 243 D2
Warwick Square
Warwick Place W9 240 B3
Warwick Row SW1 245 F3
Warwick Square SW1 245 F2
Warwick Square EC4 243 D2
Warwick Street W1 242 A1
Warwick Way SW1 245 F2
Water Lane EC3 248 A3
Watergate EC4 243 D2
New Bridge Street
Watergate Street SE8 250 A1
Watergate Walk WC2 242 B1
Villiers Street
Wateridge Close E14 250 A2
West Ferry Road
Waterloo Bridge WC2 & SE1 242 C1
Waterloo Place SW1 246 A4
Waterloo Road SE1 246 C4
Waterman Way E1 248 C2
Waterman's Walk EC4 243 F1
Waterside Close SE16 248 B1
Watling Street EC4 243 E2
Watney Market E1 248 C4
Watney Street E1 248 C3
Watson's Street SE8 248 C2
Watts Way SW7 244 C3
Waveney Close E1 248 B2
Waverton Street W1 245 E4
Weavers Lane SE1 248 A2
Webb Street SE1 247 F3
Webber Row SE1 247 D3
Webber Street SE1 247 D3
Webster Road SE16 248 C1
Weighouse Street W1 241 E1
Welbeck Street W1 241 E2
Welbeck Way W1 241 E2
Well Court EC4 243 E1
Queen Street
Welland Mews E1 248 C1
Wellclose Square E1 248 B3
Wellclose Street E1 248 C3
The Highway
Weller Street SE1 247 E3
Wellesley Street E1 249 D4
Wellesley Terrace N1 243 E4
Wellington Place NW8 240 C4
Wellington Road NW8 240 C4
Wellington Square SW3 245 D1
Wellington Street WC2 242 C1
Wells Mews W1 242 A2
Wells Square WC1 242 C4
Wells Street W1 241 F2
Wendover SE17 247 F1
Wenlock Road N1 243 E4
Wenlock Street N1 243 E4
Wentworth Market E1 248 B4
Wentworth Street
Wentworth Street E1 248 B4
Werrington Street NW1 242 A4
Wesley Close SE17 247 D2
Wesley Street W1 241 E2
Weymouth Street
West Arbour Street E1 249 D4
West Central Street WC1 242 B2
West Eaton Place SW1 245 E2
West Ferry Road E14 250 A3
West Gardens E1 248 C3
West Halkin Street SW1 245 E3
West India Avenue E14 250 A4
West India Dock Road E14 249 F3
West Lane SE16 248 C1
West Mews SW1 245 F2
Warwick Way
West Poultry Avenue EC1 243 D2
West Smithfield
West Road SW4 245 D1
West Smithfield EC1 243 D2
West Square SE11 247 D2
West Street WC2 242 B1
West Tenter Street E1 248 B3
Westbourne Crescent W2 240 B1
Westbourne Gardens W2 240 A2
Westbourne Grove W2 & W11 240 A2
Westbourne Grove Terrace W2 240 A2
Westbourne Park Road W2 & W11 240 A1
Westbourne Park Villas W2 240 A1
Westbourne Street W2 240 C1
Westbourne Terrace W2 240 B2
Westbourne Terrace Mews W2 240 B2
Westbourne Terrace Road W2 240 B2
Westcott Road SE17 247 D1
Western Place SE16 249 D2
Westferry Circus E14 250 A4
Westgate Terrace SW10 244 A1
Westland Place N1 243 F4
Westminster Bridge SW1 & SE1 246 B3
Westminster Bridge Road SE1 246 C3
Westmoreland Place SW1 245 F1
Westmoreland Road SE17 247 E1
Westmoreland Street W1 241 E2
Westmoreland Terrace SW1 245 F1
Weston Rise WC1 242 C4
Weston Street SE1 247 F3
Westport Street E1 249 E4
Westway W12 240 B2
Wetherby Gardens SW5 244 B2
Wetherby Mews SW5 244 A2
Earls Court Road
Wetherby Place SW7 244 B2
Weymouth Mews W1 241 F2
Weymouth Street W1 241 E2
Wharf Road N1 243 E4
Wharfedale Street SW10 244 A1
Wharton Street WC1 242 C4
Wheat Sheaf Close E14 250 A2
Wheatley Street W1 241 E2
Marylebone Street
Whetstone Park WC2 242 C2
Whidborne Street WC1 242 B4
Whiskin Street EC1 243 D4
Whitcomb Street WC2 242 A1
White Church Lane E1 248 B4
White Hart Street SE11 247 D2
White Horse Lane E1 249 E4
White Horse Mews SE1 247 D3
White Horse Road E1 249 E3
White Horse Street W1 245 F4
White Kennet Street E1 248 A4
White Lion Hill EC4 243 E1
White's Grounds SE1 248 A1
White's Row E1 248 A4
Whiteadder Way E14 250 B2
Whitechapel High Street E1 248 B4
Whitechapel Road E1 248 B4
Whitecross Place EC2 243 F3
Whitecross Street EC1 243 E3
Whitefriars Street EC4 243 D2
Whitehall SW1 246 B4
Whitehall Court SW1 246 B4
Whitehall Place SW1 246 B4
Whitehaven Street NW8 240 C3
Whitehead's Grove SW3 245 D2
Whitfield Place W1 242 A3
Whitfield Street
Whitfield Street W1 242 A3
Whitgift Street SE11 246 C2
Whittaker Street SW1 245 E2
Whittington Avenue EC3 243 F2
Leadenhall Street
Whittlesey Street SE1 247 D4
Wickham Street SE11 246 C1
Wicklow Street WC1 242 C4
Widegate Street E1 248 A4
Middlesex Street
Widley Road W9 240 A4
Wigmore Place W1 241 E2
Wigmore Street W1 241 E2
Wilbraham Place SW1 245 E2
Wilcox Place SW1 246 A3
Wild Court WC2 242 C2
Wild Street WC2 242 B2
Wild's Rents SE1 247 F3
Wilfred Street SW1 245 F3
Wilkes Street E1 248 B4
William IV Street WC2 242 B1
William Mews SW1 245 E3
William Road NW1 241 F4
William Square SE16 249 E3
William Street SW1 245 D3
Willoughby Passage E14 250 A4
Willoughby Street WC1 242 B2
Streatham Street
Willow Place SW1 246 A2
Willow Street EC2 243 F3
Wilmington Square WC1 243 D4
Wilmington Street WC1 243 D4
Wilson Grove SE16 248 C1
Wilson Street EC2 243 F2
Wilson's Place E14 249 F3
Wilton Crescent SW1 245 E3
Wilton Mews SW1 245 E3
Wilton Place SW1 245 E3
Wilton Road SW1 245 F2
Wilton Row SW1 245 E3
Wilton Street SW1 245 E3
Wilton Terrace SW1 245 E3
Wimpole Mews W1 241 E2
Wimpole Street W1 241 E2
Winchester Close SE17 247 D2
Winchester Square SE1 247 F4
Winchester Walk
Winchester Street SW1 245 F2
Winchester Walk SE1 247 F4
Wincott Street SE11 247 D2
Windmill Row SE11 247 D1
Windmill Street W1 242 A2
Windmill Walk SE1 247 D4
Windrose Close SE16 249 D2
Windsor Terrace N1 243 E4
Wine Close E1 248 C2
Wine Office Court EC4 243 D2
Winnett Street W1 242 A1
Rupert Street
Winsland Mews W2 240 C2
Winsland Street W2 240 C2
Winsley Street W1 242 A2
Winterton Place SW10 244 B1
Woburn Place WC1 242 B3
Woburn Square WC1 242 B3
Woburn Walk WC1 242 B3
Upper Woburn Place
Wolfe Crescent SE16 249 D1
Wolseley Street SE1 248 B1
Wood Street EC2 243 E2
Wood's Mews W1 241 E1
Wood's Place SE1 248 A1
Woodbridge Street EC1 243 D3
Woodchester Square W2 240 A3
Woodfall Street SW3 245 D1
Woodland Crescent SE16 249 D1
Woodstock Mews W1 241 E2
Westmoreland Street
Woodstock Street W1 241 F2
Woolaston Close SE1 247 E2
Wooler Street SE17 247 F1
Wooster Place SE1 247 F2
Wootton Street SE1 247 D4
Worgan Street SE11 246 C2
Wormwood Street EC2 243 F2
Worship Street EC2 243 F3
Wren Landing E14 250 A4
Wren Street WC1 242 C3
Wright's Lane W8 244 A3
Wyatt Close SE16 249 F1
Wybert Street NW1 241 F3
Laxton Place
Wyclif Street EC1 243 D4
Wymering Road W9 240 A4
Wynan Road E14 250 B1
Wyndham Mews W1 241 D2
Wyndham Place W1 241 D2
Wyndham Street W1 241 D2
Wyndham Yard W1 241 D2
Wynnstay Gardens W8 244 A3
Wynyard Terrace SE11 246 C1
Wynyatt Street EC1 243 D4
Wythburn Place W1 241 D2

Y

Yabsley Street E14 250 C4
Yardley Street WC1 242 C4
Yarmouth Place W1 245 E4
Yeoman's Row SW3 245 D3
York Buildings WC2 242 B1
York Gate NW1 241 E3
York House Place W8 244 A4
York Road SE1 246 C3
York Square E14 249 E4
York Street W1 241 D3
York Terrace East NW1 241 E3
York Terrace West NW1 241 E3
Yorkshire Road E14 249 E3
Young Street W8 244 A3

Z

Zoar Street SE1 247 E4

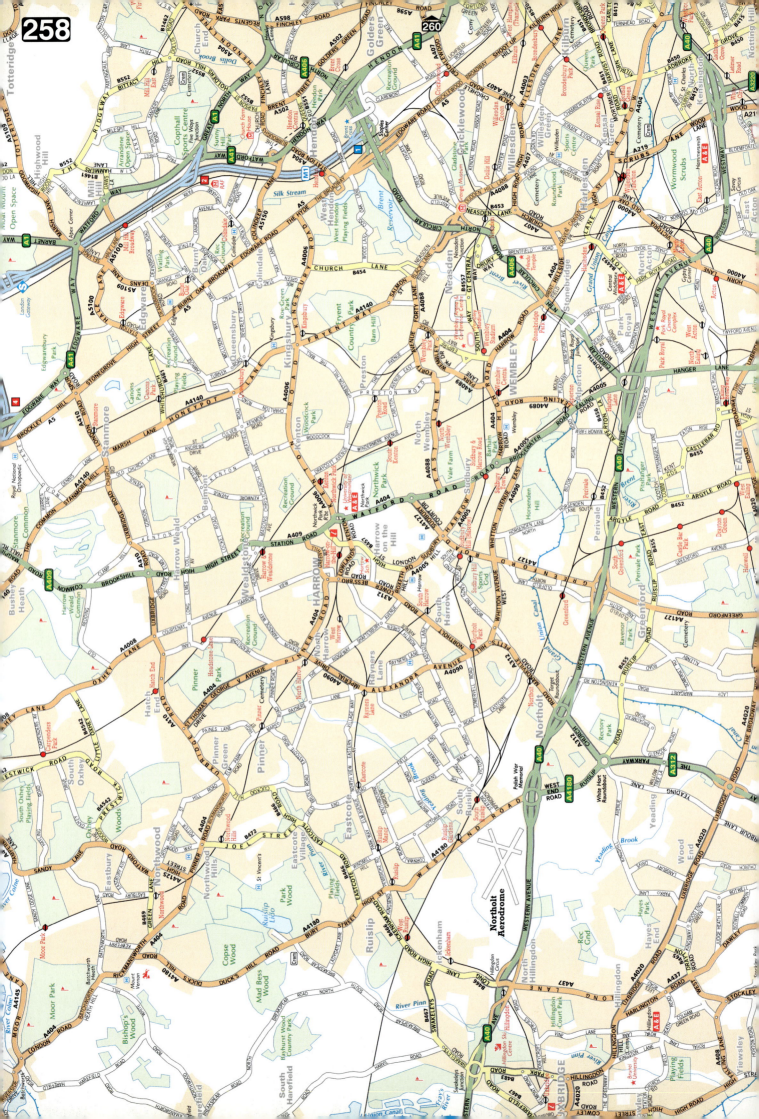

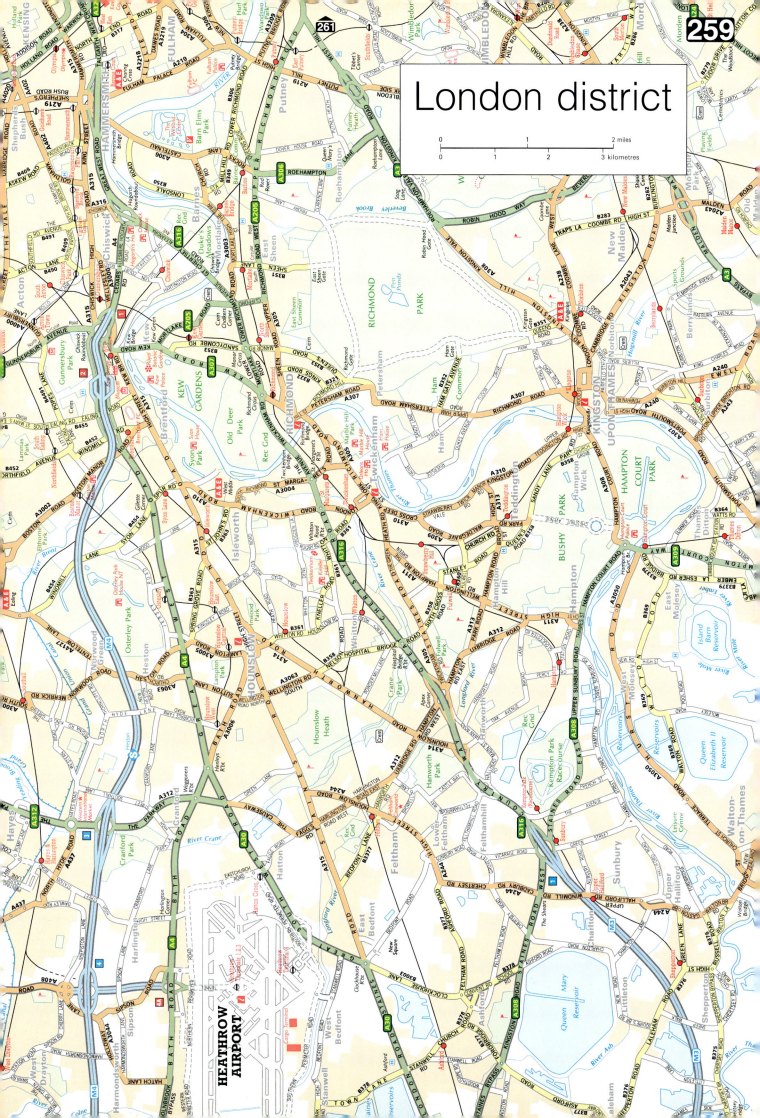

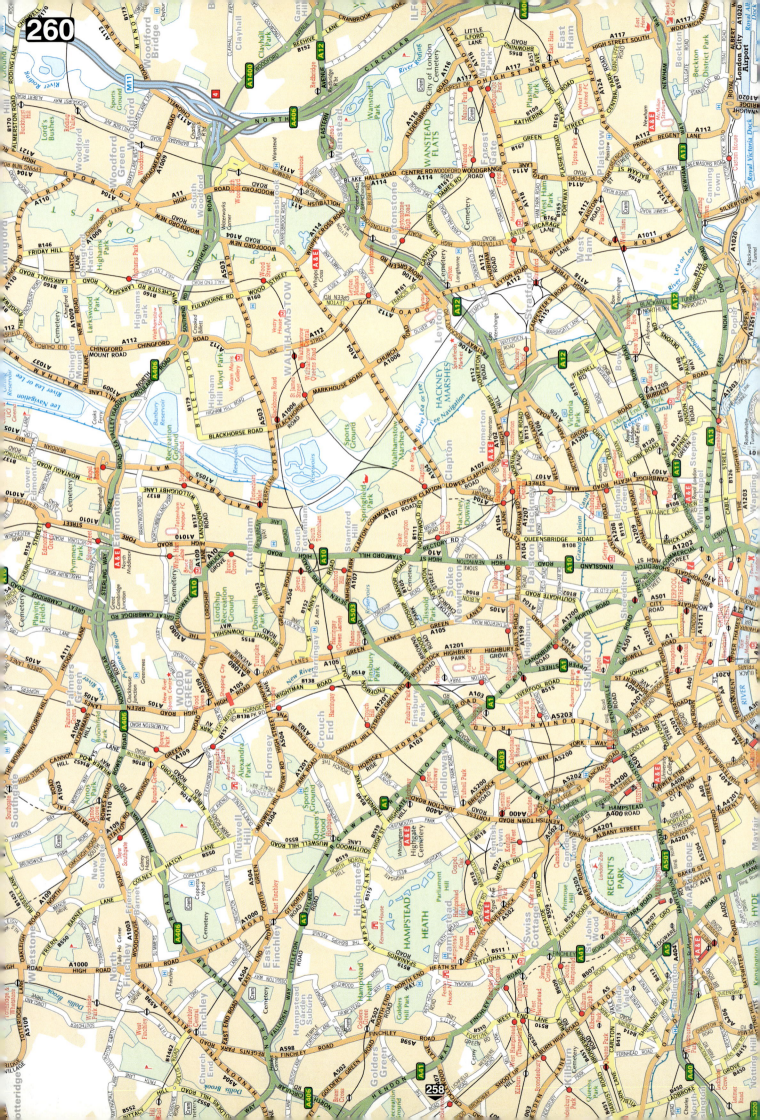

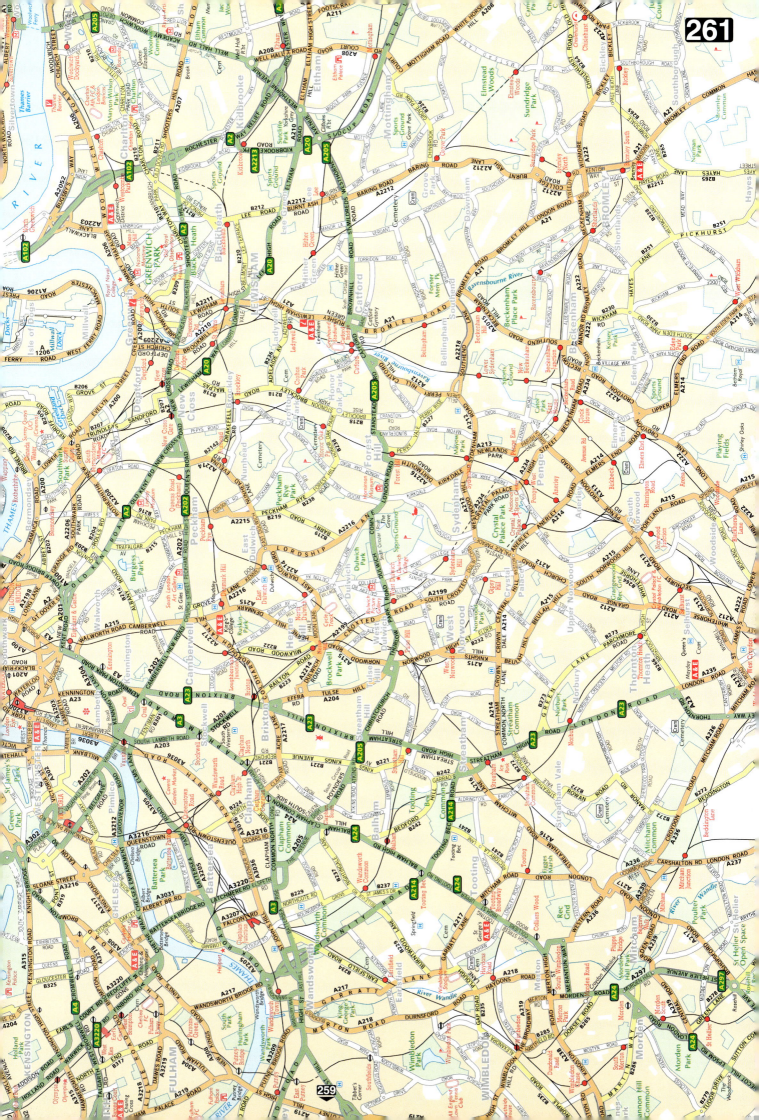

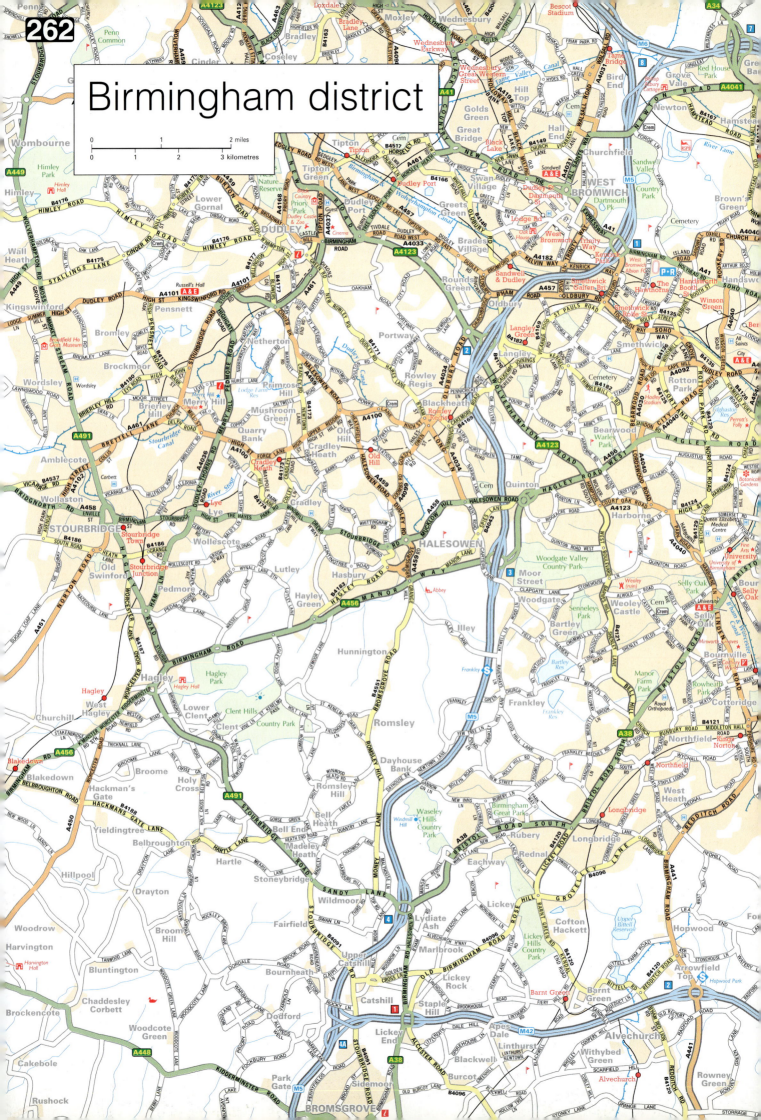

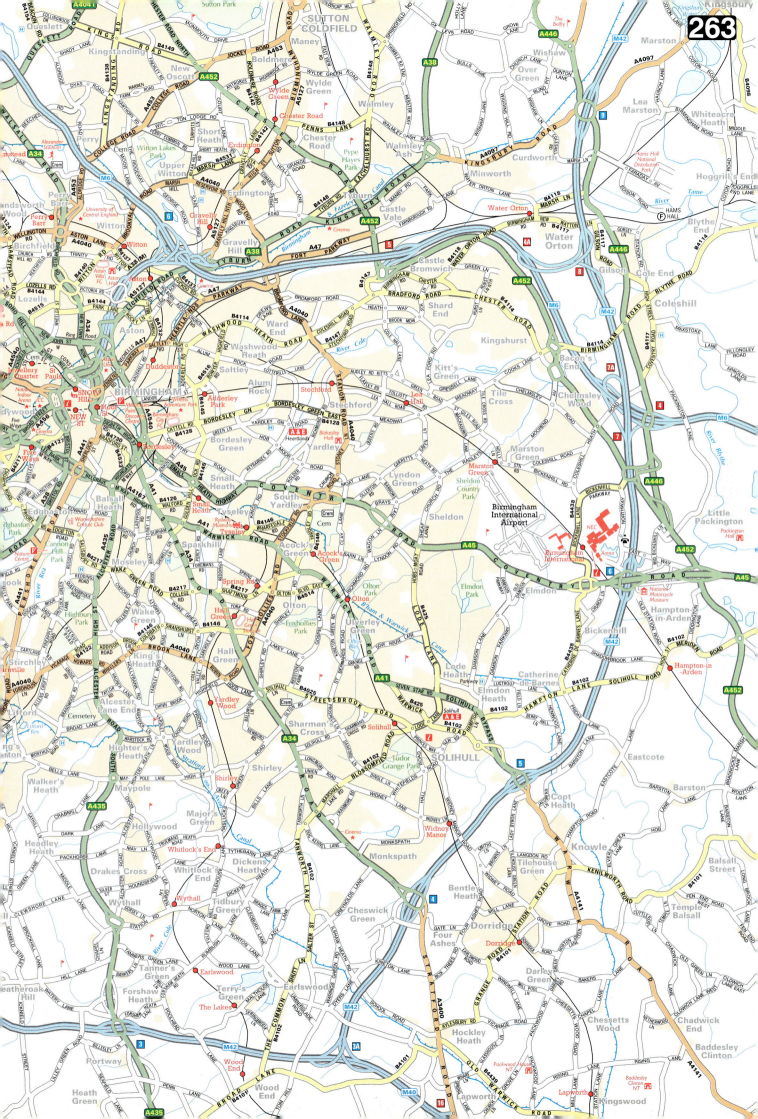

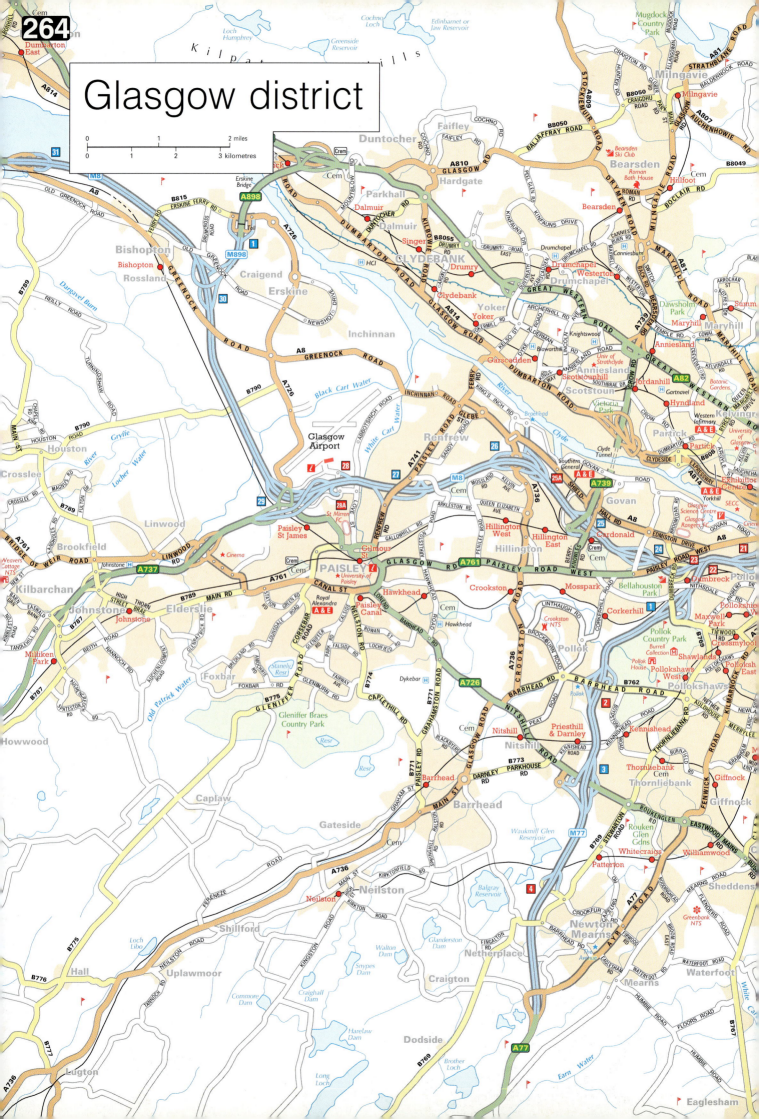

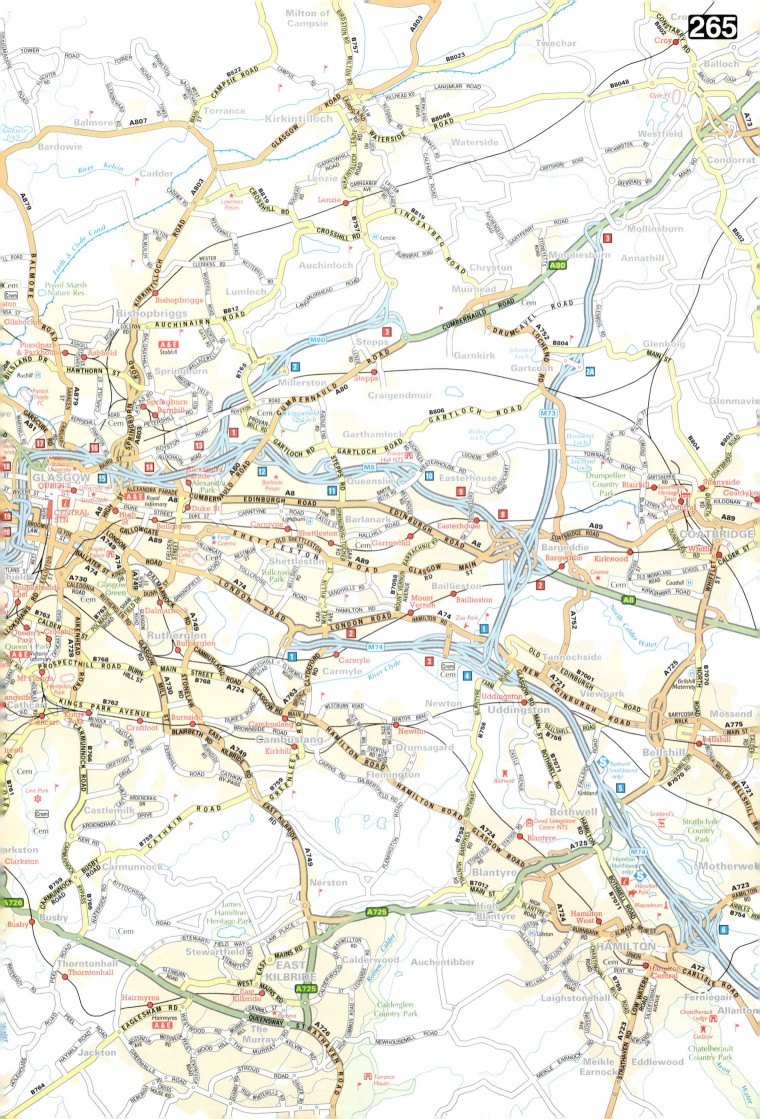

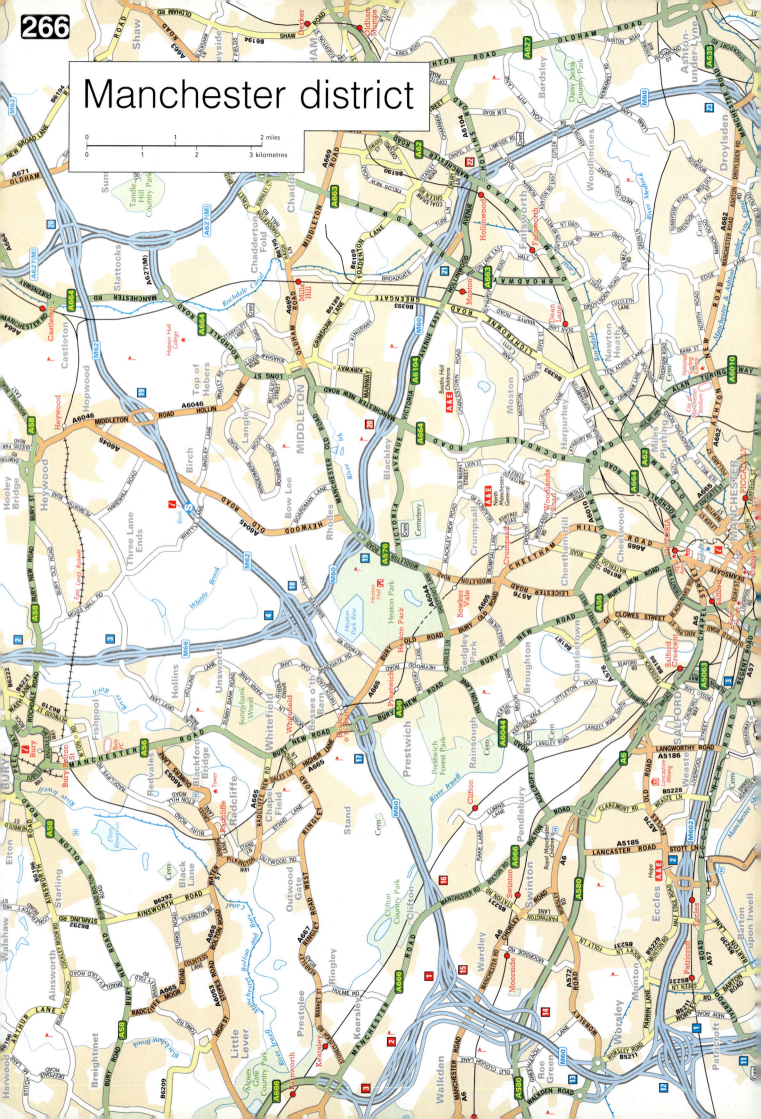

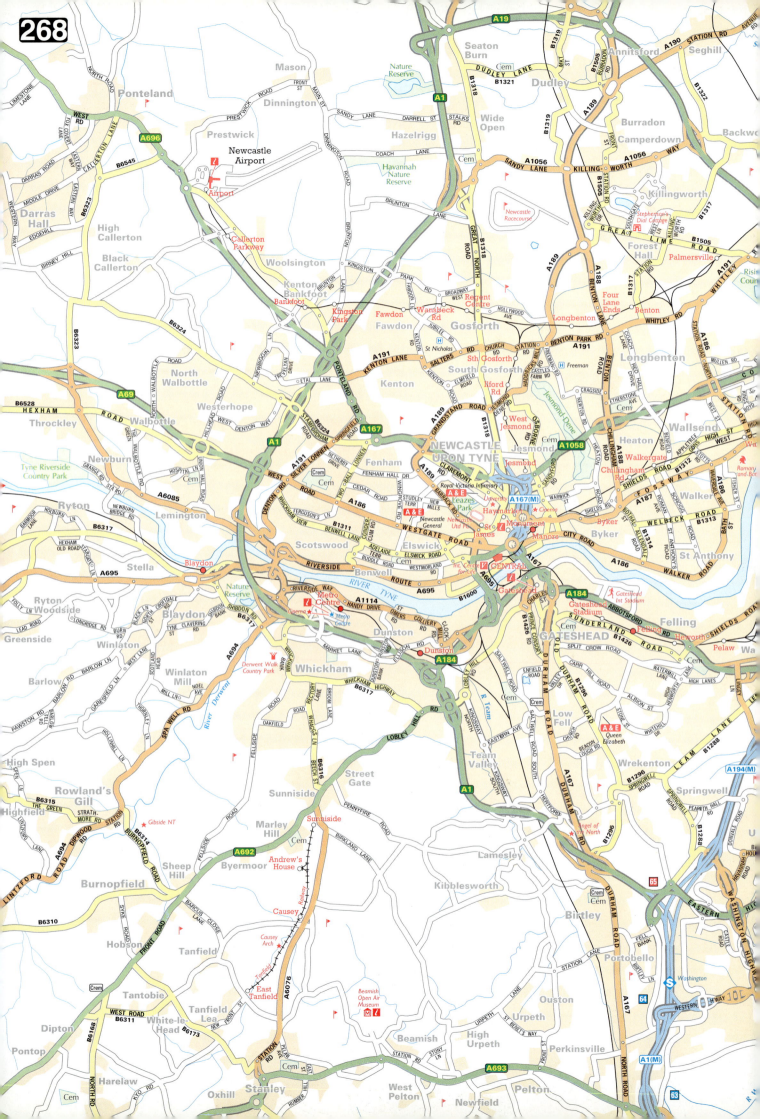

index to place names

Place names are listed alphabetically. Each place name is followed by its County, County Borough or Council Area name, the page number and the reference to the square in which the name is found.

100 places of interest are indexed in red.

Airports are indexed in blue.

Scotland

Aber C	Aberdeen City
Abers	Aberdeenshire
Angus	Angus
Ag & B	Argyll & Bute
Border	Borders (Scottish)
C Edin	City of Edinburgh
C Glas	City of Glasgow
Clacks	Clackmannanshire
D & G	Dumfries & Galloway
Dund C	Dundee City
E Ayrs	East Ayrshire
E Duns	East Dunbartonshire
E Loth	East Lothian
E Rens	East Renfrewshire
Falk	Falkirk
Fife	Fife
Highld	Highland
Inver	Inverclyde
Mdloth	Midlothian
Moray	Moray
N Ayrs	North Ayrshire
N Lans	North Lanarkshire
Ork	Orkney Islands
P & K	Perth & Kinross
Rens	Renfrewshire
Shet	Shetland Islands
S Ayrs	South Ayrshire
S Lans	South Lanarkshire
Stirlg	Stirling
W Isls	Western Isles
W Duns	West Dunbartonshire
W Loth	West Lothian

Wales

Blae G	Blaenau Gwent
Brdgnd	Bridgend
Caerph	Caerphilly
Cardif	Cardiff
Carmth	Carmarthenshire
Cerdgn	Ceredigion
Conwy	Conwy
Denbgs	Denbighshire
Flints	Flintshire
Gwynd	Gwynedd
IOA	Isle of Anglesey
Myr Td	Merthyr Tydfil
Mons	Monmouthshire
Neath	Neath Port Talbot
Newpt	Newport
Pembks	Pembrokeshire
Powys	Powys
Rhondd	Rhondda Cynon Taff
Swans	Swansea
Torfn	Torfaen
V Glam	Vale of Glamorgan
Wrexhm	Wrexham

The Channel Islands & Isle of Man

Guern	Guernsey
Jersey	Jersey
IOM	Isle of Man

England

Beds	Bedfordshire
Berks	Berkshire
Bristl	Bristol
Bucks	Buckinghamshire
Cambs	Cambridgeshire
Ches	Cheshire
Cnwll	Cornwall
Cumb	Cumbria
Derbys	Derbyshire
Devon	Devon
Dorset	Dorset
Dur	Durham
E R Yk	East Riding of Yorkshire
E Susx	East Sussex
Essex	Essex
Gloucs	Gloucestershire
Gt Lon	Greater London
Gt Man	Greater Manchester
Hants	Hampshire
Herefs	Herefordshire
Herts	Hertfordshire
IOW	Isle of Wight
IOS	Isles of Scilly
Kent	Kent
Lancs	Lancashire
Leics	Leicestershire
Lincs	Lincolnshire
Mersyd	Merseyside
Norfk	Norfolk
N York	North Yorkshire
Nhants	Northamptonshire
Nthumb	Northumberland
Notts	Nottinghamshire
Oxon	Oxfordshire
Rutlnd	Rutland
Shrops	Shropshire
Somset	Somerset
S York	South Yorkshire
Staffs	Staffordshire
Suffk	Suffolk
Surrey	Surrey
T & W	Tyne & Wear
Warwks	Warwickshire
W Mids	West Midlands
W Susx	West Sussex
W York	West Yorkshire
Wilts	Wiltshire
Worcs	Worcestershire

A'Chill
Anlaby
271

A

A'Chill Highld 142 B5
Ab Kettleby Leics 73 E2
Ab Lench Worcs 47 F4
Abbas Combe Somset 24 C1
Abberley Worcs 57 H2
Abberley Common Worcs 57 H2
Abberton Essex 52 D3
Abberton Worcs 47 E5
Abberwick Nthumb 124 D2
Abbess Roding Essex 51 F2
Abbey Devon 10 B6
Abbey Dore Herefs 45 G2
Abbey Green Staffs 71 E6
Abbey Hill Somset 23 F1
Abbey St Bathans Border 123 E6
Abbey Town Cumb 103 F5
Abbey Village Lancs 89 E2
Abbey Wood Gt Lon 29 F4
Abbeycwmhir Powys 55 H2
Abbeydale S York 83 H3
Abbeystead Lancs 88 D5
Abbot's Chair Derbys 83 E4
Abbot's Salford Warwks 47 F4
Abbotrule Border 112 C6
Abbots Bickington Devon 20 D2
Abbots Bromley Staffs 71 F2
Abbots Deuglie P & K 131 G6
Abbots Langley Herts 50 B1
Abbots Leigh Somset 37 F2
Abbots Morton Worcs 47 F5
Abbots Ripton Cambs 62 B3
Abbots Worthy Hants 26 C2
Abbotsbury Dorset 11 F3
Abbotsham Devon 20 D3
Abbotskerswell Devon 7 F4
Abbotsleigh Devon 7 E2
Abbotsley Cambs 62 B1
Abbotstone Hants 26 D3
Abbotswood Hants 26 B1
Abbott Street Dorset 12 D5
Abbotts Ann Hants 26 B4
Abcott Shrops 56 D3
Abdon Shrops 57 F4
Abenhall Gloucs 38 A6
Aber Clydach Powys 44 D1
Aber-arad Carmth 42 C3
Aber-banc Cerdgn 42 D3
Aber-giar Carmth 43 E3
Aber-Magwr Cerdgn 54 D3
Aber-meurig Cerdgn 43 F5
Aber-nant Rhondd 35 G5
Aberaeron Cerdgn 43 E5
Aberaman Rhondd 35 G4
Aberangell Gwynd 67 H1
Aberarder Highld 154 D2
Aberargie P & K 140 B1
Aberarth Cerdgn 54 B2
Aberavon Neath 35 E3
Aberbargoed Caerph 36 C4
Aberbeeg Blae G 36 C4
Abercairny P & K 139 F2
Abercanaid Myr Td 36 B5
Abercarn Caerph 36 C4
Abercastle Pembks 32 C5
Abercegir Powys 55 F6
Aberchalder Lodge Highld 145 F5
Aberchirder Abers 158 B4
Abercoed Cerdgn 46 B5
Abercraf Powys 35 F6
Abercregan Neath 35 F4
Abercwmboi Rhondd 36 A4
Abercych Pembks 42 C3
Abercynon Rhondd 36 B4
Aberdalgie P & K 139 H2
Aberdare Rhondd 35 G4
Aberdaron Gwynd 66 A3
Aberdeen Aber C 149 G5
Aberdeen Airport Aber C 149 F6
Aberdesach Gwynd 66 D5
Aberdour Fife 131 H4
Aberdulais Neath 35 E4
Aberdyfi Gwynd 54 D5
Aberedw Powys 44 D4
Abereiddy Pembks 32 B5
Abererch Gwynd 66 D4
Aberfan Myr Td 36 B4
Aberfeldy P & K 139 F5
Aberffraw IOA 78 C2
Aberffrwd Cerdgn 54 D3
Aberford W York 91 E3
Aberfoyle Stirlg 129 G5
Abergarw Brdgnd 35 G3
Abergarwed Neath 35 F4
Abergavenny Mons 36 D6
Abergele Conwy 80 B2
Abergorlech Carmth 43 F2
Abergwesyn Powys 44 A4
Abergwili Carmth 43 E1
Abergwydol Powys 55 E6
Abergwynfi Neath 35 F4
Abergwyngregyn Gwynd 79 F2
Abergynolwyn Gwynd 54 D6
Aberhafesp Powys 56 A5
Aberhosan Powys 55 F5
Aberkenfig Brdgnd 35 F3
Aberlady E Loth 132 D3
Aberlemno Angus 141 E5
Aberllefenni Powys 67 G1
Aberllynfi Powys 45 E3
Aberlour Moray 157 E3
Abermorddu Flints 69 E6
Abermule Powys 56 B5
Abernant Carmth 33 G4
Abernethy P & K 140 B1
Abernyte P & K 140 C3
Aberporth Cerdgn 42 C4
Abersoch Gwynd 66 C3
Abersychan Torfn 36 D5
Aberthin V Glam 35 G2
Abertillery Blae G 36 C5
Abertridwr Caerph 36 B3
Abertridwr Powys 68 C2
Abertysswg Caerph 36 B5
Aberuthven P & K 139 G1
Aberyscir Powys 44 C2
Aberystwyth Cerdgn 54 C3
Abingdon Oxon 40 C4
Abinger Surrey 16 B6
Abinger Hammer Surrey 16 B6
Abington Nhants 49 F5
Abington S Lans 120 D2
Abington Pigotts Cambs 50 D5
Ablington Gloucs 39 F5
Ablington Wilts 25 G4
Abney Derbys 83 G3
Above Church Staffs 71 E5
Aboyne Abers 148 C4
Abram Gt Man 82 A5
Abriachan Highld 154 D3
Abridge Essex 29 E6
Abson Gloucs 38 B2
Abthorpe Nhants 49 E4
Aby Lincs 86 D2
Acaster Malbis N York 91 G4
Acaster Selby N York 91 G4
Accott Devon 21 F4
Accrington Lancs 89 F2
Acha Ag & B 134 D5
Acha Mor W Isls 168 e8
Achahoish Ag & B 127 F3
Achalader P & K 140 A4
Achaleven Ag & B 136 D3
Achanalt Highld 153 G5
Achandunie Highld 162 C1
Achany Highld 162 C4
Acharacle Highld 143 F1
Acharn Highld 136 B5
Acharn P & K 139 E4
Achavanich Highld 167 E3
Achduart Highld 161 E4
Achfary Highld 164 D2
Achiltibuie Highld 160 D5
Achinhoan Ag & B 117 G2
Achintee Highld 152 D3
Achintraid Highld 152 C3
Achmelvich Highld 161 E6
Achmore Highld 152 C2
Achmore W Isls 168 e8
Achnacarnin Highld 164 B2
Achnacarry Highld 144 C2
Achnacloich Highld 143 E5
Achnaconeran Highld 154 B1
Achnacroish Ag & B 136 C4
Achnadrish Lodge Ag & B 135 F5
Achnafauld P & K 139 F3
Achnagarron Highld 155 E6
Achnaha Highld 135 F6
Achnahaird Highld 160 D5
Achnairn Highld 162 B5
Achnalea Highld 136 C6
Achnamara Ag & B 127 F4
Achnasheen Highld 153 F5
Achnashellach Station Highld 152 D4
Achnastank Moray 157 E2
Achosnich Highld 135 F6
Achranich Highld 136 B4
Achreamie Highld 166 D5
Achriabhach Highld 144 D1
Achriesgill Highld 164 D4
Achtoty Highld 165 H5
Achurch Nhants 61 F4
Achvaich Highld 162 D3
Ackergill Highld 167 G4
Acklam N York 106 D3
Acklam N York 92 B6
Ackleton Shrops 57 H5
Acklington Nthumb 114 D6
Ackton W York 91 E2
Ackworth Moor Top W York 91 E1
Acle Norfk 77 G1
Acock's Green W Mids 58 D4
Acol Kent 31 G3
Acomb N York 91 G5
Acomb Nthumb 113 F1
Acombe Somset 10 B6
Aconbury Herefs 45 H2
Acre Lancs 89 F2
Acrefair Wrexhm 69 E4
Acresford Derbys 71 H1
Acton Ches 70 A5
Acton Dorset 12 D2
Acton Gt Lon 28 C4
Acton Staffs 70 C4
Acton Suffk 52 C5
Acton Worcs 58 A2
Acton Beauchamp Herefs 46 B4
Acton Bridge Ches 82 A2
Acton Burnell Shrops 57 E6
Acton Green Herefs 46 C4
Acton Park Wrexhm 69 F5
Acton Pigott Shrops 57 F6
Acton Round Shrops 57 F5
Acton Scott Shrops 57 E4
Acton Trussell Staffs 70 D2
Acton Turville Gloucs 38 C2
Adbaston Staffs 70 C3
Adber Dorset 24 B1
Adbolton Notts 72 D4
Adderbury Oxon 48 C3
Adderley Shrops 70 B4
Adderstone Nthumb 124 D4
Addiewell W Loth 120 D6
Addingham W York 90 B5
Addington Bucks 49 F2
Addington Gt Lon 29 E2
Addington Kent 29 G2
Addiscombe Gt Lon 28 D3
Addlestone Surrey 28 A2
Addlestonemoor Surrey 28 A3
Addlethorpe Lincs 87 F2
Adeney Shrops 70 B2
Adeyfield Herts 50 B1
Adfa Powys 55 H5
Adforton Herefs 56 D2
Adisham Kent 31 F1
Adlestrop Gloucs 47 H2
Adlingfleet E R Yk 92 B2
Adlington Ches 82 D3
Adlington Lancs 82 A6
Admaston Shrops 70 A1
Admaston Staffs 71 E2
Admington Warwks 47 G4
Adsborough Somset 23 F2
Adscombe Somset 23 E3
Adstock Bucks 49 E2
Adstone Nhants 48 D4
Adswood Gt Man 82 D3
Adversane W Susx 16 B4
Advie Highld 156 C2
Adwalton W York 90 C2
Adwell Oxon 41 E4
Adwick Le Street S York 84 C6
Adwick upon Dearne S York 84 B5
Ae D & G 110 D4
Ae Bridgend D & G 111 E3
Affetside Gt Man 82 C6
Affleck Abers 158 B3
Affpuddle Dorset 12 B4
Affric Lodge Highld 153 F1
Afon-wen Flints 80 D2
Afton Devon 7 F4
Agglethorpe N York 96 D3
Aigburth Mersyd 81 F3
Aike E R Yk 92 D4
Aiketgate Cumb 104 B5
Aikhead Cumb 103 F5
Aikton Cumb 103 G5
Ailby Lincs 87 E2
Ailey Herefs 45 F4
Ailsworth Cambs 61 G5
Ainderby Quernhow N York 97 G3
Ainderby Steeple N York 97 F4
Aingers Green Essex 53 E3
Ainsdale Mersyd 81 E6
Ainsdale-on-Sea Mersyd 81 E6
Ainstable Cumb 104 B5
Ainsworth Gt Man 82 C6
Ainthorpe N York 107 F2
Aintree Mersyd 81 F4
Ainville W Loth 131 G1
Aird Ag & B 127 F5
Aird D & G 100 B6
Aird W Isls 168 f8
Aird a Mhulaidh W Isls 168 d7
Aird Asaig W Isls 168 d6
Aird Dhubh Highld 151 G3
Aird of Kinloch Ag & B 135 G2
Aird of Sleat Highld 143 E4
Aird Uig W Isls 168 d8
Airdeny Ag & B 137 E3
Airdrie N Lans 130 D2
Airdriehill N Lans 130 D2
Airds Bay Ag & B 137 E3
Airds of Kells D & G 110 A2
Airidh a bhruaich W Isls 168 e7
Airieland D & G 102 B6
Airlie Angus 140 C5
Airmyn E R Yk 92 A2
Airntully P & K 140 A3
Airor Highld 143 G5
Airth Falk 131 E4
Airton N York 89 G5
Aisby Lincs 85 F4
Aisby Lincs 73 H4
Aisgill Cumb 96 A5
Aish Devon 6 D4
Aish Devon 7 F3
Aisholt Somset 23 E3
Aiskew N York 97 F4
Aislaby Dur 106 C2
Aislaby N York 107 H2
Aislaby N York 98 C3
Aisthorpe Lincs 85 G3
Aith Shet 169 h3
Akeld Nthumb 123 G2
Akeley Bucks 49 E3
Akenham Suffk 53 E6
Albaston Devon 5 H3
Alberbury Shrops 69 F1
Albourne W Susx 16 C3
Albourne Green W Susx 16 D3
Albrighton Shrops 69 G2
Albrighton Shrops 58 A6
Alburgh Norfk 65 E4
Albury Herts 51 E3
Albury Oxon 41 E5
Albury Surrey 16 A6
Albury End Herts 51 E3
Albury Heath Surrey 16 B6
Alby Hill Norfk 77 E3
Alcaig Highld 154 D5
Alcaston Shrops 57 E4
Alcester Warwks 47 F5
Alcester Lane End W Mids 58 D3
Alciston E Susx 17 F2
Alcombe Wilts 38 C1
Alconbury Cambs 61 H3
Alconbury Weston Cambs 61 H3
Aldborough N York 97 G1
Aldborough Norfk 77 E3
Aldbourne Wilts 39 G2
Aldbrough E R Yk 93 F3
Aldbrough St John N York 106 A2
Aldbury Herts 41 H5
Aldcliffe Lancs 88 C6
Aldclune P & K 139 F6
Aldeburgh Suffk 65 G1
Aldeby Norfk 65 G5
Aldenham Herts 28 B6
Alder Moor Staffs 71 G3
Alderbury Wilts 25 G2
Aldercar Derbys 72 B5
Alderford Norfk 76 D2
Alderholt Dorset 13 E6
Alderley Gloucs 38 B3
Alderley Edge Ches 82 C2
Aldermans Green W Mids 59 F4
Aldermaston Berks 26 D6
Alderminster Warwks 47 H4
Aldershot Hants 27 G4
Alderton Gloucs 47 E2
Alderton Nhants 49 F4
Alderton Shrops 69 G2
Alderton Suffk 53 G5
Alderton Wilts 38 C2
Alderwasley Derbys 71 H5
Aldfield N York 97 F2
Aldford Ches 69 F6
Aldgate Rutlnd 61 F6
Aldham Essex 52 C3
Aldham Suffk 52 D5
Aldingbourne W Susx 15 G4
Aldingham Cumb 94 D2
Aldington Kent 18 D5
Aldington Worcs 47 F4
Aldington Corner Kent 18 D5
Aldivalloch Moray 157 F2
Aldochlay Ag & B 129 E4
Aldon Shrops 57 E3
Aldoth Cumb 103 E5
Aldreth Cambs 62 D3
Aldridge W Mids 58 C5
Aldringham Suffk 65 G1
Aldro N York 92 B6
Aldsworth Gloucs 39 F5
Aldsworth W Susx 15 F4
Aldunie Moray 157 F2
Aldwark Derbys 71 G6
Aldwark N York 97 H1
Aldwick W Susx 15 G3
Aldwincle Nhants 61 F3
Aldworth Berks 40 D2
Alexandria W Duns 129 E3
Aley Somset 23 E3
Alfardisworthy Devon 20 C2
Alfington Devon 10 B4
Alfold Surrey 16 A5
Alfold Bars W Susx 16 A5
Alfold Crossways Surrey 16 A5
Alford Abers 148 C6
Alford Lincs 87 E2
Alford Somset 24 B2
Alfreton Derbys 72 B6
Alfrick Worcs 46 C4
Alfrick Pound Worcs 46 C4
Alfriston E Susx 17 F2
Algarkirk Lincs 74 C3
Alhampton Somset 24 B3
Alkborough Lincs 92 C2
Alkerton Gloucs 38 B5
Alkerton Oxon 48 B3
Alkham Kent 19 F6
Alkington Shrops 69 G4
Alkmonton Derbys 71 G4
All Cannings Wilts 25 F5
All Saints South Elmham Suffk 65 F4
All Stretton Shrops 57 E5
Allaleigh Devon 7 E3
Allanaquoich Abers 147 F3
Allanbank N Lans 120 C5
Allanton Border 123 F5
Allanton N Lans 120 C5
Allanton S Lans 120 B5
Allaston Gloucs 37 G5
Allbrook Hants 14 C6
Allen End Warwks 59 E5
Allen's Green Herts 51 E2
Allendale Nthumb 105 E6
Allenheads Nthumb 105 E5
Allensford Dur 105 G5
Allensmore Herefs 45 G3
Allenton Derbys 72 A3
Aller Devon 21 H3
Aller Somset 23 G2
Allerby Cumb 103 E4
Allercombe Devon 9 G4
Allerford Somset 22 B4
Allerston N York 98 D3
Allerthorpe E R Yk 92 B4
Allerton Highld 155 F6
Allerton Mersyd 81 F3
Allerton W York 90 B3
Allerton Bywater W York 91 E2
Allerton Mauleverer N York 91 E5
Allesley W Mids 59 F3
Allestree Derbys 72 A4
Allet Common Cnwll 3 E5
Allexton Leics 60 D5
Allgreave Ches 83 E1
Allhallows Kent 30 B4
Allhallows-on-Sea Kent 30 B4
Alligin Shuas Highld 152 C5
Allimore Green Staffs 70 C2
Allington Dorset 11 E4
Allington Kent 30 A2
Allington Lincs 73 F4
Allington Wilts 38 D2
Allington Wilts 25 F6
Allington Wilts 25 G3
Allithwaite Cumb 95 E2
Alloa Clacks 131 E4
Allonby Cumb 103 E4
Allostock Ches 82 B2
Alloway S Ayrs 119 E1
Allowenshay Somset 10 D6
Allscott Shrops 70 A1
Allscott Shrops 57 G5
Alltami Flints 81 E1
Alltchaorunn Highld 137 F5
Alltmawr Powys 44 D4
Alltwalis Carmth 43 E2
Alltwen Neath 35 E5
Alltyblaca Cerdgn 43 E4
Allweston Dorset 11 G6
Allwood Green Suffk 64 C3
Almeley Herefs 45 F4
Almeley Wooton Herefs 45 F4
Almer Dorset 12 C4
Almholme S York 84 D5
Almington Staffs 70 B3
Almodington W Susx 15 F3
Almondbank P & K 139 H2
Almondbury W York 90 C1
Almondsbury Gloucs 37 G3
Alne N York 97 H1
Alnesbourn Priory Suffk 53 E5
Alness Highld 155 E6
Alnham Nthumb 124 C2
Alnmouth Nthumb 125 E2
Alnwick Nthumb 125 E2
Alperton Gt Lon 28 C4
Alphamstone Essex 52 B4
Alpheton Suffk 52 B6
Alphington Devon 9 F4
Alpington Norfk 65 E5
Alport Derbys 83 G1
Alpraham Ches 69 H6
Alresford Essex 52 D3
Alrewas Staffs 71 G1
Alsager Ches 70 C6
Alsagers Bank Staffs 70 C5
Alsop en le Dale Derbys 71 F5
Alston Cumb 104 D5
Alston Devon 10 C5
Alston Sutton Somset 23 G4
Alstone Gloucs 47 E2
Alstone Somset 23 F4
Alstone Green Staffs 70 D2
Alstonefield Staffs 71 F6
Alswear Devon 21 G3
Alt Gt Man 82 D5
Altandhu Highld 160 D5
Altarnun Cnwll 5 F4
Altass Highld 162 B4
Altcreich Ag & B 136 B4
Altgaltraig Ag & B 128 B2
Altham Lancs 89 F3
Althorne Essex 30 C6
Althorpe Lincs 85 F6
Altnabreac Station Highld 166 D3
Altnacraig Ag & B 136 C3
Altnaharra Highld 165 G2
Altofts W York 91 E2
Alton Derbys 84 A1
Alton Hants 27 E3
Alton Staffs 71 F4
Alton Wilts 25 G4
Alton Barnes Wilts 25 F5
Alton Pancras Dorset 11 G5
Alton Priors Wilts 25 G5
Alton Towers Staffs 71 F4
Altrincham Gt Man 82 C3
Altskeith Hotel Stirlg 129 F5
Alva Clacks 131 E5
Alvah Abers 158 C5
Alvanley Ches 81 G2
Alvaston Derbys 72 B3
Alvechurch Worcs 58 C3
Alvecote Warwks 59 E6
Alvediston Wilts 25 E2
Alveley Shrops 57 H4
Alverdiscott Devon 21 E3
Alverstoke Hants 14 D3
Alverstone IOW 14 D2
Alverthorpe W York 90 D2
Alverton Notts 73 E4
Alves Moray 156 C5
Alvescot Oxon 39 G5
Alveston Gloucs 37 G3
Alveston Warwks 47 H5
Alvingham Lincs 86 D4
Alvington Gloucs 37 G4
Alwalton Cambs 61 G5
Alwinton Nthumb 113 F5
Alwoodley W York 90 D4
Alwoodley Gates W York 90 D4
Alyth P & K 140 B5
Amber Hill Lincs 74 C5
Amber Row Derbys 72 B6
Ambergate Derbys 72 A5
Amberley Gloucs 38 C4
Amberley W Susx 16 A3
Amberstone E Susx 17 G2
Amble Nthumb 125 F1
Amblecote W Mids 58 B4
Ambler Thorn W York 90 B2
Ambleside Cumb 94 D5
Ambleston Pembks 32 D4
Ambrosden Oxon 48 D1
Amcotts Lincs 85 F6
America Cambs 62 D3
Amersham Bucks 41 H4
Amersham on the Hill Bucks 41 H4
Amerton Staffs 71 E3
Amesbury Wilts 25 G3
Amhuinnsuidhe W Isls 168 c7
Amington Staffs 59 E6
Amisfield Town D & G 110 D3
Amlwch IOA 78 D4
Ammanford Carmth 34 D5
Amotherby N York 98 C2
Ampfield Hants 26 B2
Ampleforth N York 98 B3
Ampney Crucis Gloucs 39 E4
Ampney St Mary Gloucs 39 F4
Ampney St Peter Gloucs 39 E4
Amport Hants 26 A4
Ampthill Beds 50 A4
Ampton Suffk 63 H2
Amroth Pembks 33 F2
Amulree P & K 139 F3
Amwell Herts 50 C2
An T-ob W Isls 168 c6
Anaheilt Highld 136 C6
Ancaster Lincs 73 G4
Anchor Shrops 56 B4
Ancroft Nthumb 123 G4
Ancrum Border 122 C2
Ancton W Susx 15 H4
Anderby Lincs 87 F2
Andersea Somset 23 F3
Andersfield Somset 23 E3
Anderson Dorset 12 C4
Anderton Ches 82 B2
Anderton Cnwll 6 B3
Andover Hants 26 B4
Andoversford Gloucs 47 F1
Andreas IOM 174 m5
Anelog Gwynd 66 A3
Anerley Gt Lon 28 D3
Anfield Mersyd 81 F4
Angarrack Cnwll 2 C4
Angarrick Cnwll 3 E3
Angelbank Shrops 57 F3
Angersleigh Somset 23 E1
Angerton Cumb 103 F6
Angle Pembks 32 C2
Angmering W Susx 16 B2
Angram N York 96 B5
Angram N York 91 F4
Angrouse Cnwll 2 D2
Anick Nthumb 113 G1
Ankerville Highld 163 E1
Ankle Hill Leics 73 E2
Anlaby E R Yk 92 D2

Anmer Avoch

Anmer Norfk 75 H3
Anmore Hants 15 E5
Anna Valley Hants 26 B4
Annan D & G 111 F1
Annaside Cumb 94 B3
Annat Highld 152 C4
Annathill N Lans 130 D2
Annbank S Ayrs 119 F2
Anne Hathaway's Cottage Warwks 47 G5
Annesley Notts 72 C5
Annesley Woodhouse Notts 72 C5
Annfield Plain Dur 106 A6
Anniesland C Glas 129 G2
Annitsford T & W 114 D3
Annscroft Shrops 57 E6
Ansdell Lancs 88 B2
Ansford Somset 24 B2
Ansley Warwks 59 F4
Anslow Staffs 71 G2
Anslow Gate Staffs 71 G2
Anslow Lees Staffs 71 G2
Ansteadbrook Surrey 27 G2
Anstey Hants 27 E3
Anstey Herts 51 E4
Anstey Leics 60 B6
Anstruther Fife 133 E5
Ansty W Susx 16 D4
Ansty Warwks 59 G4
Ansty Wilts 25 E2
Ansty Cross Dorset 12 B5
Anthill Common Hants 15 E5
Anthonys Surrey 28 A2
Anthorn Cumb 103 F6
Antingham Norfk 77 E3
Anton's Gowt Lincs 74 C5
Antony Cnwll 5 G1
Antrobus Ches 82 A3
Antron Cnwll 2 D2
Anvil Corner Devon 20 D1
Anvil Green Kent 31 E1
Anwick Lincs 74 B5
Anwoth D & G 101 G6
Aperfield Gt Lon 29 E2
Apes Dale Worcs 58 C3
Apethorpe Nhants 61 F5
Apeton Staffs 70 C2
Apley Lincs 86 A2
Apperknowle Derbys 84 B2
Apperley Gloucs 46 D2
Apperley Bridge W York 90 C3
Apperley Dene Nthumb 114 B1
Appersett N York 96 B4
Appin Ag & B 136 D4
Appleby Lincs 92 C1
Appleby Magna Leics 71 H1
Appleby Parva Leics 71 H1
Appleby Street Herts 50 D1
Appleby-in-Westmorland Cumb 104 D2
Applecross Highld 151 G3
Appledore Devon 21 E4
Appledore Devon 10 A6
Appledore Kent 18 C4
Appledore Heath Kent 18 C4
Appleford Oxon 40 C4
Applegarth Town D & G 111 E3
Applehaigh S York 84 A6
Appleshaw Hants 26 A4
Applethwaite Cumb 103 G3
Appleton Ches 81 G3
Appleton Ches 82 A3
Appleton Oxon 40 C4
Appleton Roebuck N York 91 G4
Appleton Thorn Ches 82 A3
Appleton Wiske N York 97 G5
Appleton-le-Moors N York 98 C4
Appleton-le-Street N York 98 C2
Appletreehall Border 122 B1
Appletreewick N York 90 B6
Appley Somset 22 D1
Appley Bridge Lancs 81 G6
Apse Heath IOW 14 D2
Apsley End Beds 50 B4
Apuldram W Susx 15 G4
Arabella Highld 163 E1
Arbirlot Angus 141 F4
Arboll Highld 163 F2
Arborfield Berks 27 F6
Arborfield Cross Berks 27 F6
Arbourthorne S York 84 A3
Arbroath Angus 141 F4
Arbuthnott Abers 149 F2
Arcadia Kent 18 B5
Archddu Carmth 34 B4
Archdeacon Newton Dur 106 B2
Archencarroch W Duns 129 F3
Archiestown Moray 156 D3
Archirondel Jersey 174 d2
Arclid Green Ches 70 C6
Ardanaiseig Hotel Ag & B 137 E2
Ardaneaskan Highld 152 C3
Ardarroch Highld 152 C3
Ardbeg Ag & B 116 C5
Ardbeg Ag & B 128 B2
Ardbeg Ag & B 128 C3
Ardcharnich Highld 161 F3
Ardchiavaig Ag & B 135 F1
Ardchonnel Ag & B 136 D1
Ardchullarie More Stirlg 138 C1
Arddarroch Ag & B 128 D5
Arddleen Powys 69 E2
Ardechive Highld 144 D3
Ardeer N Ayrs 119 E3
Ardeley Herts 50 D3
Ardelve Highld 152 C2
Arden Ag & B 129 E3
Ardens Grafton Warwks 47 G5
Ardentallen Ag & B 136 C2
Ardentinny Ag & B 128 C4
Ardentraive Ag & B 128 B2
Ardeonaig Hotel Stirlg 138 D3
Ardersier Highld 155 F5
Ardessie Highld 161 E3
Ardfern Ag & B 127 G5
Ardgay Highld 162 C3
Ardgour Highld 137 E6
Ardgowan Inver 128 D2
Ardhallow Ag & B 128 C2
Ardhasig W Isls 168 d6
Ardheslaig Highld 152 B5
Ardindrean Highld 161 F3
Ardingly W Susx 16 D4
Ardington Oxon 40 C3
Ardington Wick Oxon 40 C3
Ardlamont Ag & B 128 A2
Ardleigh Essex 52 D4
Ardleigh Heath Essex 52 D4
Ardler P & K 140 C4
Ardley Oxon 48 D2
Ardley End Essex 51 F2
Ardlui Ag & B 137 H1
Ardlussa Ag & B 127 E4
Ardmaddy Ag & B 137 E3
Ardmair Highld 161 E3
Ardmaleish Ag & B 128 B2
Ardminish Ag & B 117 F5
Ardmolich Highld 143 G1
Ardmore Ag & B 129 E3
Ardmore Highld 162 D2
Ardnadam Ag & B 128 C3
Ardnagrask Highld 154 C4
Ardnarff Highld 152 C3
Ardnastang Highld 136 C6
Ardno Ag & B 128 C6
Ardochy Lodge Hotel Highld 144 D5
Ardpatrick Ag & B 127 F1
Ardrishaig Ag & B 127 G4
Ardross Highld 162 C1
Ardrossan N Ayrs 118 D4
Ardsley S York 84 B5
Ardsley East W York 90 D2
Ardslignish Highld 135 G5
Ardtalla Ag & B 116 D6
Ardtoe Highld 143 F1
Arduaine Ag & B 127 G6
Ardullie Highld 154 D5
Ardvasar Highld 143 F4
Ardvorlich P & K 138 D2
Ardvourlie W Isls 168 d7
Ardwell D & G 100 B5
Ardwick Gt Man 82 D4
Areley Kings Worcs 58 A2
Arevegaig Highld 143 F1
Arford Hants 27 F3
Argoed Caerph 36 C4
Argoed Shrops 69 E2
Argoed Mill Powys 55 G2
Argos Hill E Susx 17 F4
Aribruach W Isls 168 e7
Aridhglas Ag & B 135 E2
Arileod Ag & B 134 D5
Arinagour Ag & B 134 D5
Ariogan Ag & B 136 C2
Arisaig Highld 143 F3
Arisaig House Highld 143 F2
Arkendale N York 91 E6
Arkesden Essex 51 F4
Arkholme Lancs 95 F2
Arkle Town N York 96 C5
Arkleby Cumb 103 E4
Arkleton D & G 112 A4
Arkley Gt Lon 28 C6
Arksey S York 84 C5
Arkwright Town Derbys 84 B2
Arle Gloucs 47 E2
Arlecdon Cumb 102 D2
Arlescote Warwks 48 B4
Arlesey Beds 50 C4
Arleston Shrops 70 B1
Arley Ches 82 B3
Arley Warwks 59 F4
Arlingham Gloucs 38 B5
Arlington Devon 21 F5
Arlington E Susx 17 F2
Arlington Gloucs 39 F5
Arlington Beccott Devon 21 F5
Armadale Highld 166 B5
Armadale Highld 143 F4
Armadale W Loth 131 F2
Armaside Cumb 103 E3
Armathwaite Cumb 104 B5
Arminghall Norfk 65 E6
Armitage Staffs 71 F2
Armitage Bridge W York 83 F6
Armley W York 90 D3
Armscote Warwks 47 H4
Armshead Staffs 70 D5
Armston Nhants 61 G4
Armthorpe S York 84 D5
Arnabost Ag & B 134 D5
Arnaby Cumb 94 C3
Arncliffe N York 96 C2
Arncliffe Cote N York 96 C2
Arncroach Fife 132 D6
Arndilly House Moray 157 E4
Arne Dorset 12 D3
Arnesby Leics 60 B5
Arnfield Derbys 83 E4
Arngask P & K 131 H6
Arnisdale Highld 143 H5
Arnish Highld 151 F3
Arniston Mdloth 121 H6
Arnol W Isls 168 e9
Arnold E R Yk 93 E4
Arnold Notts 72 D5
Arnprior Stirlg 130 B5
Arnside Cumb 95 E3
Aros Ag & B 135 G4
Arowry Wrexhm 69 G4
Arrad Foot Cumb 94 D3
Arram E R Yk 92 D4
Arrathorne N York 97 E4
Arreton IOW 14 D2
Arrina Highld 152 B5
Arrington Cambs 50 D6
Arrochar Ag & B 128 D5
Arrow Warwks 47 F5
Arrowfield Top Worcs 58 C3
Arscott Shrops 57 E6
Artafallie Highld 154 D4
Arthington W York 90 D4
Arthingworth Nhants 60 D3
Arthog Gwynd 67 F1
Arthrath Abers 159 F3
Arthursdale W York 91 E3
Artrochie Abers 159 F2
Arundel W Susx 16 A2
Asby Cumb 103 E2
Ascog Ag & B 118 C6
Ascot Berks 41 G1
Ascott Warwks 48 B3
Ascott Earl Oxon 48 A1
Ascott-under-Wychwood Oxon 48 A1
Asenby N York 97 G2
Asfordby Leics 73 E2
Asfordby Hill Leics 73 E2
Asgarby Lincs 74 B5
Asgarby Lincs 86 D1
Ash Devon 8 B5
Ash Devon 7 F3
Ash Dorset 12 C6
Ash Kent 29 G2
Ash Kent 31 F2
Ash Somset 23 F1
Ash Somset 23 G1
Ash Surrey 27 G4
Ash Green Surrey 27 G4
Ash Green Warwks 59 F4
Ash Magna Shrops 69 H4
Ash Mill Devon 21 H3
Ash Parva Shrops 69 H4
Ash Priors Somset 22 D2
Ash Street Suffk 52 D5
Ash Thomas Devon 9 G6
Ash Vale Surrey 27 G4
Ashampstead Berks 40 D2
Ashampstead Green Berks 40 D2
Ashbocking Suffk 53 E6
Ashbocking Green Suffk 53 E6
Ashbourne Derbys 71 G5
Ashbourne Green Derbys 71 G5
Ashbrittle Somset 22 C1
Ashburnham Place E Susx 17 H3
Ashburton Devon 7 E5
Ashbury Devon 8 B4
Ashbury Oxon 39 G3
Ashby Lincs 85 G6
Ashby by Partney Lincs 87 E1
Ashby cum Fenby Lincs 86 C5
Ashby de la Launde Lincs 73 H6
Ashby Folville Leics 73 E1
Ashby Magna Leics 60 B4
Ashby Parva Leics 60 A4
Ashby Puerorum Lincs 86 D2
Ashby St Ledgers Nhants 60 B2
Ashby St Mary Norfk 65 F6
Ashby-de-la-Zouch Leics 72 A2
Ashchurch Gloucs 47 E2
Ashcombe Devon 9 F2
Ashcombe Somset 23 F5
Ashcott Somset 23 G3
Ashdon Essex 51 G5
Ashe Hants 26 D4
Asheldham Essex 30 C6
Ashen Essex 52 A5
Ashendon Bucks 41 E6
Asheridge Bucks 41 G5
Ashfield Hants 14 B5
Ashfield Herefs 46 B1
Ashfield Stirlg 130 D5
Ashfield Suffk 65 E2
Ashfield Green Suffk 63 G1
Ashfield Green Suffk 65 E3
Ashfields Shrops 70 B3
Ashfold Crossways W Susx 16 C4
Ashford Devon 21 E4
Ashford Devon 6 D2
Ashford Kent 18 D6
Ashford Surrey 28 B3
Ashford Bowdler Shrops 57 E2
Ashford Carbonel Shrops 57 E2
Ashford Hill Hants 26 D5
Ashford in the Water Derbys 83 G2
Ashgill S Lans 120 B4
Ashill Devon 10 A6
Ashill Norfk 64 A6
Ashill Somset 23 F1
Ashingdon Essex 30 B5
Ashington Dorset 12 D4
Ashington Nthumb 114 D4
Ashington Somset 24 A1
Ashington W Susx 16 B3
Ashkirk Border 122 B2
Ashlett Hants 14 C4
Ashleworth Gloucs 46 D2
Ashleworth Quay Gloucs 46 D2
Ashley Cambs 63 F1
Ashley Ches 82 C3
Ashley Devon 21 G2
Ashley Dorset 13 E5
Ashley Gloucs 38 D4
Ashley Hants 26 B2
Ashley Hants 13 F4
Ashley Kent 31 G1
Ashley Nhants 60 D4
Ashley Staffs 70 C4
Ashley Wilts 38 C1
Ashley Green Bucks 41 H5
Ashley Heath Dorset 13 E5
Ashley Moor Herefs 57 E2
Ashmansworth Hants 26 B5
Ashmansworthy Devon 20 D2
Ashmead Green Gloucs 38 B4
Ashmill Devon 5 G5
Ashmore Dorset 25 E1
Ashmore Green Berks 40 C1
Ashorne Warwks 48 A5
Ashover Derbys 84 A1
Ashover Hay Derbys 72 A6
Ashow Warwks 59 F2
Ashperton Herefs 46 B3
Ashprington Devon 7 E3
Ashreigney Devon 21 F2
Ashridge Park Herts 41 H5
Ashtead Surrey 28 C2
Ashton Cambs 61 G6
Ashton Ches 81 G2
Ashton Cnwll 2 D3
Ashton Cnwll 5 G3
Ashton Devon 9 E3
Ashton Hants 14 D5
Ashton Herefs 57 E2
Ashton Inver 128 D3
Ashton Nhants 49 F4
Ashton Nhants 61 F4
Ashton Somset 23 G4
Ashton Common Wilts 24 D5
Ashton Hill Wilts 24 D5
Ashton Keynes Wilts 39 E4
Ashton under Hill Worcs 47 E3
Ashton upon Mersey Gt Man 82 C4
Ashton Watering Somset 37 F1
Ashton-in-Makerfield Gt Man 81 H5
Ashton-under-Lyne Gt Man 82 D5
Ashurst Hants 13 G6
Ashurst Kent 17 F5
Ashurst W Susx 16 C3
Ashurstwood W Susx 17 E5
Ashwater Devon 5 G5
Ashwell Herts 50 D5
Ashwell Rutlnd 73 F1
Ashwell Somset 10 D6
Ashwell End Herts 50 C5
Ashwellthorpe Norfk 64 D5
Ashwick Somset 24 B4
Ashwicken Norfk 75 G2
Ashwood Staffs 58 B4
Askam in Furness Cumb 94 C3
Aske Hall N York 97 E5
Askern S York 84 C6
Askerswell Dorset 11 F4
Askett Bucks 41 F5
Askham Cumb 104 B2
Askham Notts 85 E2
Askham Bryan N York 91 G4
Askham Richard N York 91 F4
Asknish Ag & B 127 H4
Askrigg N York 96 C4
Askwith N York 90 C4
Aslackby Lincs 74 A3
Aslacton Norfk 64 D4
Aslockton Notts 73 E4
Asney Somset 23 G3
Aspall Suffk 64 D2
Aspatria Cumb 103 E4
Aspenden Herts 50 D3
Aspenshaw Derbys 83 E3
Asperton Lincs 74 C4
Aspley Staffs 70 C3
Aspley Guise Beds 49 G3
Aspley Heath Beds 49 G3
Aspley Heath Warwks 58 D2
Aspull Gt Man 82 A5
Aspull Common Gt Man 82 A4
Asselby E R Yk 92 A2
Asserby Lincs 87 E2
Asserby Turn Lincs 87 E2
Assington Suffk 52 C4
Assington Green Suffk 52 A6
Astbury Ches 70 C6
Astcote Nhants 49 E4
Asterby Lincs 86 C3
Asterley Shrops 56 D6
Asterton Shrops 56 D4
Asthall Oxon 39 G5
Asthall Leigh Oxon 39 H6
Astle Highld 162 D3
Astley Gt Man 82 B5
Astley Shrops 69 G2
Astley W York 91 E2
Astley Warwks 59 F4
Astley Worcs 57 H2
Astley Abbots Shrops 57 G5
Astley Bridge Gt Man 82 B6
Astley Cross Worcs 58 A2
Astley Green Gt Man 82 B5
Astley Town Worcs 57 H2
Aston Berks 41 F3
Aston Ches 81 H2
Aston Ches 70 A5
Aston Derbys 83 G3
Aston Flints 81 E1
Aston Herefs 57 E2
Aston Herefs 57 E2
Aston Herts 50 D3
Aston Oxon 40 B5
Aston S York 84 B3
Aston Shrops 69 G3
Aston Shrops 70 A1
Aston Shrops 58 A5
Aston Staffs 70 C4
Aston Staffs 70 D2
Aston Staffs 70 D3
Aston W Mids 58 D4
Aston Abbotts Bucks 49 G1
Aston Botterell Shrops 57 F4
Aston Cantlow Warwks 47 G5
Aston Clinton Bucks 41 G5
Aston Crews Herefs 46 B1
Aston Cross Gloucs 47 E3
Aston End Herts 50 D3
Aston Fields Worcs 58 C2
Aston Flamville Leics 59 G5
Aston Heath Ches 81 H3
Aston Ingham Herefs 46 B1
Aston juxta Mondrum Ches 70 B6
Aston le Walls Nhants 48 C4
Aston Magna Gloucs 47 G3
Aston Munslow Shrops 57 E4
Aston on Clun Shrops 56 D3
Aston Pigott Shrops 56 D6
Aston Rogers Shrops 56 D6
Aston Rowant Oxon 41 E4
Aston Sandford Bucks 41 F5
Aston Somerville Worcs 47 F3
Aston Subedge Gloucs 47 G3
Aston Tirrold Oxon 40 D3
Aston Upthorpe Oxon 40 D3
Aston-Eyre Shrops 57 G5
Aston-upon-Trent Derbys 72 B3
Astonlane Shrops 57 G5
Astrop Nhants 48 C3
Astrope Herts 41 G6
Astwick Beds 50 C5
Astwith Derbys 84 B1
Astwood Bucks 49 H4
Astwood Worcs 58 B2
Astwood Bank Worcs 47 F5
Aswarby Lincs 74 A4
Aswardby Lincs 86 D2
Atch Lench Worcs 47 F4
Atcham Shrops 69 H1
Athelhampton Dorset 12 B4
Athelington Suffk 65 E2
Athelney Somset 23 F2
Athelstaneford E Loth 132 D3
Atherfield Green IOW 14 C1
Atherington Devon 21 F3
Atherington W Susx 16 A1
Atherstone Somset 23 G1
Atherstone Warwks 59 F5
Atherstone on Stour Warwks 47 G4
Atherton Gt Man 82 B5
Atley Hill N York 97 F5
Atlow Derbys 71 G5
Attadale Highld 152 C3
Attenborough Notts 72 C3
Atterby Lincs 85 G4
Attercliffe S York 84 B3
Atterley Shrops 57 F5
Atterton Leics 59 F5
Attleborough Norfk 64 C5
Attleborough Warwks 59 G4
Attlebridge Norfk 76 D2
Attleton Green Suffk 52 A6
Atwick E R Yk 93 F5
Atworth Wilts 24 D6
Auberrow Herefs 45 H4
Aubourn Lincs 85 G1
Auchedly Abers 159 E2
Auchenblae Abers 149 E2
Auchenbowie Stirlg 130 D4
Auchencairn D & G 102 B5
Auchencairn D & G 110 D3
Auchencairn N Ayrs 118 B2
Auchencrow Border 123 F5
Auchendinny Mdloth 121 G6
Auchengray S Lans 120 D5
Auchenhalrig Moray 157 F5
Auchenheath S Lans 120 C4
Auchenhessnane D & G 110 C4
Auchenlochan Ag & B 128 A2
Auchenmade N Ayrs 119 E4
Auchenmalg D & G 100 D5
Auchentiber N Ayrs 119 E4
Auchentroig Stirlg 129 G4
Auchindrean Highld 161 F2
Auchininna Abers 158 B4
Auchinleck E Ayrs 119 G2
Auchinloch N Lans 130 C2
Auchinstarry N Lans 130 C3
Auchintore Highld 144 C2
Auchiries Abers 159 G3
Auchlee Abers 149 F4
Auchleven Abers 158 B1
Auchlochan S Lans 120 C3
Auchlossan Abers 148 C5
Auchlyne Stirlg 138 B3
Auchmillan E Ayrs 119 G2
Auchmithie Angus 141 G4
Auchmuirbridge Fife 132 A5
Auchnacree Angus 141 E6
Auchnagatt Abers 159 E3
Auchnarrow Moray 156 D1
Auchnotteroch D & G 100 A6
Auchroisk Moray 157 E4
Auchterarder P & K 139 G1
Auchteraw Highld 145 F5
Auchterblair Highld 155 G1
Auchtercairn Highld 160 B1
Auchterderran Fife 132 A5
Auchterhouse Angus 140 C3
Auchterless Abers 158 C3
Auchtermuchty Fife 140 B1
Auchterneed Highld 154 C5
Auchtertool Fife 132 A4
Auchtertyre Highld 152 C2
Auchtubh Stirlg 138 C2
Auckengill Highld 167 G5
Auckley S York 84 D5
Audenshaw Gt Man 82 D4
Audlem Ches 70 B4
Audley Staffs 70 C5
Audley End Essex 51 F4
Audley End Essex 51 F4
Audley End Essex 52 B4
Audley End Suffk 52 B6
Audmore Staffs 70 C2
Audnam W Mids 58 B4
Aughertree Cumb 103 F4
Aughton E R Yk 91 H3
Aughton Lancs 81 F5
Aughton Lancs 95 F2
Aughton S York 84 B3
Aughton Wilts 25 H5
Aughton Park Lancs 81 F5
Auldearn Highld 155 G5
Aulden Herefs 45 G5
Auldgirth D & G 110 D3
Auldhouse S Lans 119 H4
Ault a' chruinn Highld 152 D1
Ault Hucknall Derbys 84 B1
Aultbea Highld 160 C3
Aultgrishin Highld 160 B2
Aultguish Inn Highld 154 B6
Aultmore Moray 157 F4
Aultnagoire Highld 154 D1
Aultnamain Inn Highld 162 D2
Aunby Lincs 73 H1
Aunk Devon 9 G5
Aunsby Lincs 73 H4
Aust Gloucs 37 G3
Austendike Lincs 74 C2
Austerfield S York 84 D4
Austerlands Gt Man 83 E5
Austhorpe W York 91 E3
Austonley W York 83 F5
Austrey Warwks 59 F6
Austwick N York 96 A2
Authorpe Lincs 86 D3
Authorpe Row Lincs 87 F2
Avebury Wilts 39 F1
Avebury Trusloe Wilts 39 F1
Aveley Essex 29 F4
Avening Gloucs 38 D4
Averham Notts 73 E5
Aveton Gifford Devon 6 D2
Aviemore Highld 146 D6
Avington Berks 26 B6
Avoch Highld 155 E5

Avon
Bath
273

Avon Dorset 13 E4
Avon Dassett Warwks 48 B4
Avonbridge Falk 131 E2
Avonmouth Bristl 37 F2
Avonwick Devon 6 D3
Awbridge Hants 26 B2
Awkley Gloucs 37 G3
Awliscombe Devon 10 B5
Awre Gloucs 38 B5
Awsworth Notts 72 C4
Axborough Worcs 58 B3
Axbridge Somset 23 G5
Axford Hants 26 D4
Axford Wilts 39 G1
Axminster Devon 10 C4
Axmouth Devon 10 C4
Axton Flints 80 C3
Aycliffe Dur 106 B3
Aydon Nthumb 113 G1
Aylburton Gloucs 37 G4
Ayle Cumb 104 D5
Aylesbeare Devon 9 G4
Aylesbury Bucks 41 F6
Aylesby Lincs 86 B5
Aylesford Kent 29 H2
Aylesham Kent 31 F1
Aylestone Leics 60 B5
Aylestone Park Leics 60 B5
Aylmerton Norfk 77 E4
Aylsham Norfk 77 E3
Aylton Gloucs 46 B3
Aylworth Gloucs 47 F1
Aymestrey Herefs 56 D2
Aynho Nhants 48 C2
Ayot Green Herts 50 C2
Ayot St Lawrence Herts 50 C2
Ayot St Peter Herts 50 C2
Ayr S Ayrs 119 E2
Aysgarth N York 96 C4
Ayshford Devon 9 G6
Ayside Cumb 95 E3
Ayston Rutlnd 61 E5
Aythorpe Roding Essex 51 G2
Ayton Border 123 F5
Azerley N York 97 F2

B

Babbacombe Devon 7 G4
Babbington Notts 72 C4
Babbinswood Shrops 69 F3
Babbs Green Herts 51 E2
Babcary Somset 24 A2
Babel Carmth 44 A3
Babel Green Suffk 51 H6
Babell Flints 80 D2
Babeny Devon 8 D2
Babington Somset 24 C4
Bablock Hythe Oxon 40 C5
Babraham Cambs 51 F6
Babworth Notts 84 D3
Bachau IOA 78 D3
Bache Shrops 57 E4
Bacheldre Powys 56 C5
Bachelor's Bump E Susx 18 B3
Back o' th' Brook Staffs 71 F5
Back of Keppoch Highld 143 F3
Back Street Suffk 63 G1
Backaland Ork 169 c3
Backbarrow Cumb 94 D3
Backe Carmth 33 G3
Backfolds Abers 159 F4
Backford Ches 81 F2
Backford Cross Ches 81 F2
Backies Highld 163 E4
Backlass Highld 167 F4
Backwell Somset 37 F1
Backworth T & W 115 E3
Bacon's End W Mids 59 E4
Baconsthorpe Norfk 76 D4
Bacton Herefs 45 F2
Bacton Norfk 77 F3
Bacton Suffk 64 C2
Bacton Green Suffk 64 C2
Bacup Lancs 89 G2
Badachro Highld 160 B1
Badbury Wilts 39 G2
Badby Nhants 48 D5
Badcall Highld 164 C3
Badcall Highld 164 C4
Badcaul Highld 160 D3
Baddeley Edge Staffs 70 D5
Baddeley Green Staffs 70 D5
Baddesley Clinton Warwks 59 E3
Baddesley Ensor Warwks 59 F5
Baddidarrach Highld 161 E6
Baddinsgill Border 121 F5
Badenscoth Abers 158 C3
Badenyon Abers 157 E1
Badgall Cnwll 5 F5
Badgeney Cambs 62 D5
Badger Shrops 57 H5
Badger's Cross Cnwll 2 B3
Badgers Mount Kent 29 F2
Badgeworth Gloucs 47 E1
Badgworth Somset 23 G4
Badharlick Cnwll 5 F5
Badicaul Highld 152 B2
Badingham Suffk 65 E2
Badlesmere Kent 30 D1
Badlieu Border 121 E1
Badlipster Highld 167 F3
Badluachrach Highld 160 D3
Badninish Highld 162 D3
Badrallach Highld 161 E3
Badsey Worcs 47 F3
Badshot Lea Surrey 27 G4
Badsworth W York 91 F1
Badwell Ash Suffk 64 B2
Badwell Green Suffk 64 C2
Bag Enderby Lincs 86 D2
Bagber Dorset 12 A6
Bagby N York 97 H3
Bagendon Gloucs 39 E5
Bagginswood Shrops 57 G3
Baggrow Cumb 103 F4
Bagh a Chaisteil W Isls 168 a1
Bagh a Tuath W Isls 168 b2
Bagham Kent 30 D1
Bagillt Flints 80 D2
Baginton Warwks 59 F3
Baglan Neath 35 E3
Bagley Shrops 69 F3
Bagley Somset 23 G4
Bagley W York 90 C3
Bagmore Hants 27 E4
Bagnall Staffs 70 D5
Bagnor Berks 40 C1
Bagot Shrops 57 F3
Bagshot Surrey 27 G6
Bagshot Wilts 26 A6
Bagstone Gloucs 38 B3
Bagthorpe Notts 72 B5
Bagworth Leics 59 G6
Bagwy Llydiart Herefs 45 G2
Baildon W York 90 C4
Baildon Green W York 90 C3
Baile a Mhanaich W Isls 168 b4
Baile Ailein W Isls 168 e7
Baile Mor Ag & B 135 E2
Bailey Green Hants 27 E2
Baileyhead Cumb 112 B3
Bailiff Bridge W York 90 C2
Baillieston C Glas 130 C1
Bailrigg Lancs 88 C5
Bainbridge N York 96 C4
Bainshole Abers 158 B3
Bainton Cambs 61 G6
Bainton E R Yk 92 C5
Bainton Oxon 48 D2
Baintown Fife 132 C5
Bairnkine Border 122 D1
Baker Street Essex 29 G4
Baker's End Herts 51 E2
Bakewell Derbys 83 G1
Bala Gwynd 68 B4
Balallan W Isls 168 e7
Balbeg Highld 154 C2
Balbeggie P & K 140 B3
Balblair Highld 154 C4
Balblair Highld 155 E6
Balby S York 84 C5
Balcary D & G 102 B5
Balchraggan Highld 154 D3
Balchreick Highld 164 C4
Balcombe W Susx 16 D4
Balcombe Lane W Susx 16 D5
Balcomie Links Fife 133 E6
Baldersby N York 97 G3
Baldersby St James N York 97 G2
Balderstone Gt Man 82 D6
Balderstone Lancs 89 E3
Balderton Notts 73 F5
Baldhu Cnwll 3 E4
Baldinnie Fife 132 C6
Baldinnies P & K 139 G1
Baldock Herts 50 C4
Baldovie Dund C 140 D3
Baldrine IOM 174 m3
Baldslow E Susx 18 B3
Baldwin IOM 174 l3
Baldwin's Gate Staffs 70 C4
Baldwin's Hill Surrey 17 E5
Baldwinholme Cumb 103 G5
Bale Norfk 76 C4
Baledgarno P & K 140 C3
Balemartine Ag & B 134 B3
Balerno C Edin 131 H2
Balfarg Fife 132 B5
Balfield Angus 148 C1
Balfour Ork 169 c3
Balfron Stirlg 129 G4
Balgaveny Abers 158 C3
Balgavies Angus 141 E5
Balgonar Fife 131 F4
Balgowan D & G 100 C4
Balgowan Highld 146 A4
Balgown Highld 150 D6
Balgracie D & G 100 A6
Balgray Angus 140 D4
Balgray S Lans 120 C2
Balham Gt Lon 28 D3
Balhary P & K 140 C4
Balholmie P & K 140 B3
Baligill Highld 166 B5
Balintore Angus 140 C6
Balintore Highld 163 E1
Balintraid Highld 155 E6
Balivanich W Isls 168 b4
Balk N York 97 H3
Balkeerie Angus 140 C4
Balkholme E R Yk 92 B2
Ball Green Staffs 70 D5
Ball Haye Green Staffs 71 E6
Ball Hill Hants 26 B6
Ball's Green Gloucs 38 C4
Ballabeg IOM 174 k2
Ballachulish Highld 137 E6
Ballafesson IOM 174 k2
Ballakilpheric IOM 174 k2
Ballamodha IOM 174 k2
Ballanlay Ag & B 118 B6
Ballantrae S Ayrs 108 C3
Ballards Gore Essex 30 C5
Ballards Green Warwks 59 F4
Ballasalla IOM 174 l2
Ballater Abers 148 A4
Ballaugh IOM 174 l4
Ballchraggan Highld 162 D1
Ballencrieff E Loth 132 D3
Ballevullin Ag & B 134 B4
Ballidon Derbys 71 G5
Balliekine N Ayrs 117 H4
Balliemore Ag & B 128 C5
Balligmorrie S Ayrs 108 D4
Ballimore Ag & B 127 H3
Ballimore Stirlg 138 C1
Ballindalloch Moray 156 D3
Ballindean P & K 140 C3
Ballingdon Essex 52 B5
Ballinger Common Bucks 41 G5
Ballingham Herefs 46 A2
Ballingry Fife 131 H5
Ballinluig P & K 139 G5
Ballinshoe Angus 140 D5
Ballintuim P & K 140 A5
Balloch Highld 155 E4
Balloch N Lans 130 D2
Balloch P & K 139 F2
Balloch S Ayrs 109 E4
Balloch W Duns 129 E3
Ballogie Abers 148 C4
Balls Cross W Susx 27 H2
Balls Green E Susx 17 F5
Ballygown Ag & B 135 F4
Ballygrant Ag & B 126 C2
Ballyhaugh Ag & B 134 D5
Ballymenoch Ag & B 128 D4
Ballymichael N Ayrs 118 A2
Balmacara Highld 152 B2
Balmaclellan D & G 110 A3
Balmae D & G 102 A5
Balmaha Stirlg 129 F4
Balmalcolm Fife 132 B6
Balmangan D & G 101 H5
Balmedie Abers 159 E1
Balmer Heath Shrops 69 G3
Balmerino Fife 140 D2
Balmerlawn Hants 13 G5
Balmoral Castle Grounds Abers 147 G4
Balmore E Duns 130 B2
Balmuchy Highld 163 F1
Balmuir Angus 141 F5
Balmule Fife 132 A4
Balmullo Fife 140 D2
Balnacoil Lodge Highld 163 E5
Balnacra Highld 152 D4
Balnacroft Abers 147 H4
Balnafoich Highld 155 E3
Balnaguard P & K 139 G5
Balnahard Ag & B 135 F3
Balnahard Ag & B 126 C5
Balnain Highld 154 C2
Balnakeil Highld 165 E5
Balnapaling Highld 155 F6
Balne N York 91 G1
Balquharn P & K 139 G3
Balquhidder Stirlg 138 C2
Balsall Common W Mids 59 E3
Balsall Heath W Mids 58 D4
Balsall Street W Mids 59 E3
Balscote Oxon 48 B3
Balsham Cambs 51 G6
Baltasound Shet 169 k5
Baltasound Airport Shet 169 k5
Balterley Staffs 70 C5
Balterley Green Staffs 70 C5
Balterley Heath Staffs 70 B5
Baltersan D & G 109 F1
Baltonsborough Somset 24 A3
Balvarran P & K 139 H6
Balvicar Ag & B 136 B1
Balvraid Highld 143 H6
Balvraid Highld 155 F2
Balwest Cnwll 2 C3
Bamber Bridge Lancs 88 D2
Bamber's Green Essex 51 G3
Bamburgh Nthumb 125 E4
Bamburgh Castle Nthumb 125 E5
Bamff P & K 140 B5
Bamford Derbys 83 G3
Bamford Gt Man 82 D6
Bampton Cumb 104 B2
Bampton Devon 22 B1
Bampton Oxon 40 A5
Bampton Grange Cumb 104 B2
Banavie Highld 144 C2
Banbury Oxon 48 C3
Banc-y-ffordd Carmth 42 D3
Bancffosfelen Carmth 34 B5
Banchory Abers 149 E4
Banchory-Devenick Abers 149 G5
Bancycapel Carmth 34 B6
Bancyfelin Carmth 33 G3
Bandirran P & K 140 B3
Bandrake Head Cumb 94 D4
Banff Abers 158 C5
Bangor Gwynd 79 E2
Bangor's Green Lancs 81 F6
Bangor-is-y-coed Wrexhm 69 F5
Bangors Cnwll 5 F6
Bangrove Suffk 64 B3
Banham Norfk 64 C4
Bank Hants 13 G5
Bank Ground Cumb 94 D5
Bank Newton N York 89 G5
Bank Street Worcs 57 F2
Bank Top Lancs 81 G5
Bank Top W York 90 B2
Bankend D & G 111 E2
Bankfoot P & K 139 H3
Bankglen E Ayrs 109 H6
Bankhead Aber C 149 G5
Bankhead S Lans 120 D4
Banknock Falk 130 D3
Banks Cumb 112 C1
Banks Lancs 88 B2
Banks Green Worcs 58 C2
Bankshill D & G 111 F3
Banningham Norfk 77 E3
Bannister Green Essex 51 H3
Bannockburn Stirlg 130 D4
Banstead Surrey 28 C2
Bantham Devon 6 D2
Banton N Lans 130 D3
Banwell Somset 23 G5
Bapchild Kent 30 C2
Bapton Wilts 25 E3
Bar Hill Cambs 62 C2
Barabhas W Isls 168 e9
Barassie S Ayrs 119 E3
Barbaraville Highld 162 D1
Barber Booth Derbys 83 F3
Barber Green Cumb 95 E3
Barbieston S Ayrs 119 F1
Barbon Cumb 95 G3
Barbridge Ches 70 A6
Barbrook Devon 21 G5
Barby Nhants 60 B2
Barcaldine Ag & B 136 D4
Barcheston Warwks 47 H3
Barclose Cumb 112 B1
Barcombe E Susx 17 E3
Barcombe Cross E Susx 17 E3
Barcroft W York 90 B3
Barden N York 97 E4
Barden Park Kent 17 G6
Bardfield End Green Essex 51 G4
Bardfield Saling Essex 51 H3
Bardney Lincs 86 B2
Bardon Leics 72 B1
Bardon Mill Nthumb 113 E1
Bardowie E Duns 130 B2
Bardown E Susx 17 G4
Bardrainney Inver 129 E2
Bardsea Cumb 94 D2
Bardsey W York 91 E4
Bardsley Gt Man 82 D5
Bardwell Suffk 64 B3
Bare Lancs 95 E1
Bareppa Cnwll 3 E3
Barewood Herefs 45 G5
Barfad D & G 109 E1
Barford Norfk 64 D6
Barford Warwks 48 A5
Barford St John Oxon 48 C2
Barford St Martin Wilts 25 F2
Barford St Michael Oxon 48 C2
Barfrestone Kent 31 F1
Bargate Derbys 72 A5
Bargeddie N Lans 130 C1
Bargoed Caerph 36 C4
Bargrennan D & G 109 E2
Barham Cambs 61 G3
Barham Kent 31 F1
Barham Suffk 53 E6
Barholm Lincs 74 A1
Barkby Leics 72 D1
Barkby Thorpe Leics 72 D1
Barkers Green Shrops 69 G3
Barkestone-le-Vale Leics 73 E3
Barkham Berks 27 F6
Barking Gt Lon 29 E4
Barking Suffk 52 D6
Barking Tye Suffk 52 D6
Barkingside Gt Lon 29 E5
Barkisland W York 90 B1
Barkla Shop Cnwll 3 E5
Barkston Lincs 73 G4
Barkston Ash N York 91 F3
Barkway Herts 51 E4
Barlanark C Glas 130 C1
Barlaston Staffs 70 D4
Barlavington W Susx 15 H5
Barlborough Derbys 84 B2
Barlby N York 91 G3
Barlestone Leics 59 G6
Barley Herts 51 E5
Barley Lancs 89 G4
Barley Hole S York 84 A4
Barleycroft End Herts 51 E3
Barleythorpe Rutlnd 73 F1
Barling Essex 30 C5
Barlings Lincs 86 A2
Barlochan D & G 102 B6
Barlow Derbys 84 A2
Barlow N York 91 G2
Barlow T & W 114 C2
Barmby Moor E R Yk 92 B4
Barmby on the Marsh E R Yk 91 H2
Barmer Norfk 76 A3
Barming Heath Kent 29 H1
Barmollack Ag & B 117 G5
Barmouth Gwynd 67 F2
Barmpton Dur 106 C3
Barmston E R Yk 93 E5
Barnaby Green Suffk 65 G3
Barnacarry Ag & B 128 B4
Barnack Cambs 61 G6
Barnacle Warwks 59 G4
Barnard Castle Dur 105 G2
Barnard Gate Oxon 40 B5
Barnardiston Suffk 51 H6
Barnbarroch D & G 102 B6
Barnburgh S York 84 C5
Barnby Suffk 65 G4
Barnby Dun S York 84 D6
Barnby in the Willows Notts 73 F5
Barnby Moor Notts 84 D3
Barncorkrie D & G 100 B4
Barnehurst Gt Lon 29 F4
Barnes Gt Lon 28 C4
Barnes Street Kent 17 G6
Barnet Gt Lon 28 C6
Barnet Gate Gt Lon 28 C6
Barnetby le Wold Lincs 86 A6
Barney Norfk 76 C3
Barnham Suffk 64 A3
Barnham W Susx 15 H4
Barnham Broom Norfk 64 C6
Barnhead Angus 141 G5
Barnhill Ches 69 G5
Barnhill Dund C 141 E3
Barnhill Moray 156 D5
Barnhills D & G 108 B2
Barningham Dur 96 D6
Barningham Suffk 64 B3
Barnoldby le Beck Lincs 86 C5
Barnoldswick Lancs 89 G4
Barns Green W Susx 16 B4
Barnsdale Bar N York 91 F1
Barnsley Gloucs 39 E5
Barnsley S York 84 A5
Barnsley Shrops 57 H5
Barnsole Kent 31 F2
Barnstaple Devon 21 F4
Barnston Essex 51 G3
Barnston Mersyd 81 E3
Barnstone Notts 73 E4
Barnt Green Worcs 58 C3
Barnton C Edin 131 H3
Barnton Ches 82 A2
Barnwell All Saints Nhants 61 F4
Barnwell St Andrew Nhants 61 F4
Barnwood Gloucs 46 D1
Baron's Cross Herefs 45 G5
Barons Wood Devon 8 D5
Baronwood Cumb 104 B4
Barr S Ayrs 109 E4
Barrachan D & G 101 E5
Barrapoll Ag & B 134 A4
Barra Airport W Isls 168 b2
Barras Cumb 105 E1
Barrasford Nthumb 113 F2
Barrets Green Ches 69 H6
Barrhead E Rens 119 G5
Barrhill S Ayrs 108 D3
Barrington Cambs 51 E6
Barrington Somset 23 G1
Barripper Cnwll 2 D4
Barrmill N Ayrs 119 E5
Barrnacarry Bay Ag & B 136 C2
Barrock Highld 167 F5
Barrow Gloucs 46 D2
Barrow Lancs 89 F3
Barrow Rutlnd 73 F1
Barrow Shrops 57 G5
Barrow Somset 24 C2
Barrow Suffk 63 G2
Barrow Bridge Gt Man 82 B6
Barrow Burn Nthumb 113 F6
Barrow Gurney Somset 37 F1
Barrow Haven Lincs 92 D2
Barrow Hill Derbys 84 B2
Barrow Island Cumb 94 C2
Barrow Nook Lancs 81 G5
Barrow Street Wilts 24 D2
Barrow upon Soar Leics 72 C2
Barrow upon Trent Derbys 72 A3
Barrow Vale Somset 24 B5
Barrow's Green Ches 81 G3
Barrow's Green Ches 70 B6
Barrow-in-Furness Cumb 94 C2
Barrow-upon-Humber Lincs 92 D2
Barroway Drove Norfk 63 E6
Barrowby Lincs 73 F4
Barrowden Rutlnd 61 E5
Barrowford Lancs 89 G3
Barry Angus 141 E3
Barry V Glam 36 B1
Barry Island V Glam 22 D6
Barsby Leics 73 E1
Barsham Suffk 65 F4
Barston W Mids 59 E3
Bartestree Herefs 46 A3
Barthol Chapel Abers 158 D2
Bartholomew Green Essex 51 H3
Barthomley Ches 70 C5
Bartley Hants 13 G6
Bartley Green W Mids 58 C4
Bartlow Cambs 51 G5
Barton Cambs 62 C1
Barton Ches 69 G5
Barton Cumb 104 B3
Barton Devon 7 F4
Barton Gloucs 47 F2
Barton Herefs 45 F5
Barton Lancs 81 F6
Barton Lancs 88 D3
Barton N York 106 B2
Barton Oxon 40 D5
Barton Warwks 47 F4
Barton Bendish Norfk 63 F6
Barton End Gloucs 38 C4
Barton Green Staffs 71 G2
Barton Hartshorn Bucks 49 E2
Barton Hill N York 98 C1
Barton in Fabis Notts 72 C3
Barton in the Beans Leics 59 G6
Barton Mills Suffk 63 F3
Barton Seagrave Nhants 61 E3
Barton St David Somset 24 A2
Barton Stacey Hants 26 C3
Barton Town Devon 21 G5
Barton Turf Norfk 77 F2
Barton upon Irwell Gt Man 82 C4
Barton Waterside Lincs 92 D2
Barton-le-Clay Beds 50 B4
Barton-le-Street N York 98 C2
Barton-le-Willows N York 92 A6
Barton-on-Sea Hants 13 F4
Barton-on-the-Heath Warwks 47 H2
Barton-under-Needwood Staffs 71 G2
Barton-upon-Humber Lincs 92 D2
Barugh S York 83 H5
Barugh Green S York 83 H5
Barvas W Isls 168 e9
Barway Cambs 63 E3
Barwell Leics 59 G5
Barwick Devon 8 C5
Barwick Herts 51 E3
Barwick Somset 11 F6
Barwick in Elmet W York 91 E3
Baschurch Shrops 69 F2
Bascote Warwks 59 G2
Bascote Heath Warwks 59 G2
Base Green Suffk 64 C2
Basford Green Staffs 71 E5
Bashall Eaves Lancs 89 E4
Bashall Town Lancs 89 E4
Bashley Hants 13 F4
Basildon Essex 29 H5
Basingstoke Hants 27 E4
Baslow Derbys 83 G2
Bason Bridge Somset 23 F4
Bassaleg Newpt 36 D3
Bassendean Border 122 C4
Bassenthwaite Cumb 103 F3
Bassett Hants 14 B5
Bassingbourn Cambs 50 D5
Bassingfield Notts 72 D4
Bassingham Lincs 73 G6
Bassingthorpe Lincs 73 G3
Bassus Green Herts 50 D3
Basted Kent 29 G2
Baston Lincs 74 B1
Bastwick Norfk 77 G2
Batch Somset 23 F5
Batchworth Herts 28 B5
Batchworth Heath Herts 28 B5
Batcombe Dorset 11 F5
Batcombe Somset 24 B3
Bate Heath Ches 82 B3
Batford Herts 50 B2
Bath Somset 24 C6

Bath Side
Birchgrove
274

Bath Side Essex 53 F4
Bathampton Somset 24 C6
Bathealton Somset 22 D2
Batheaston Somset 24 C6
Bathford Somset 24 C6
Bathgate W Loth 131 F2
Bathley Notts 73 E6
Bathpool Cnwll 5 F3
Bathpool Somset 23 E2
Bathville W Loth 131 F2
Bathway Somset 24 B4
Batley W York 90 C2
Batsford Gloucs 47 G3
Batson Devon 7 E1
Batt's Corner Surrey 27 F3
Battersby N York 107 E2
Battersea Gt Lon 28 D4
Battisborough Cross Devon 6 C2
Battisford Suffk 52 D6
Battisford Tye Suffk 52 D6
Battle E Susx 18 A3
Battle Powys 44 C2
Battle of Britain Memorial Flight Lincs 74 C6
Battleborough Somset 23 F4
Battledown Gloucs 47 E1
Battledykes Angus 140 D5
Battlefield Shrops 69 G2
Battlesbridge Essex 30 A5
Battlesden Beds 49 H2
Battleton Somset 22 B2
Battlies Green Suffk 64 B2
Battramsley Cross Hants 13 G4
Battyeford W York 90 C2
Baughton Worcs 46 D3
Baughurst Hants 26 D5
Baulds Abers 148 D4
Baulking Oxon 40 A3
Baumber Lincs 86 C2
Baunton Gloucs 39 E5
Baveney Wood Shrops 57 G3
Baverstock Wilts 25 F2
Bawburgh Norfk 64 D6
Bawdeswell Norfk 76 C2
Bawdrip Somset 23 F3
Bawdsey Suffk 53 G5
Bawsey Norfk 75 G2
Bawtry S York 84 D4
Baxenden Lancs 89 F2
Baxter's Green Suffk 63 G1
Baxterley Warwks 59 F5
Bay Highld 150 C4
Bay Horse Lancs 88 C5
Bayble W Isls 168 f8
Baybridge Hants 26 C1
Baybridge Nthumb 105 F5
Baycliff Cumb 94 D2
Baydon Wilts 39 G2
Bayford Herts 50 D1
Bayford Somset 24 C2
Bayhead W Isls 168 b5
Bayley's Hill Kent 29 F1
Baylham Suffk 53 E6
Baynard's Green Oxon 48 D2
Baysdale Abbey N York 98 B5
Baysham Herefs 46 A2
Bayston Hill Shrops 69 G1
Baythorne End Essex 51 H5
Bayton Worcs 57 G3
Bayton Common Worcs 57 G3
Bayworth Oxon 40 C4
Beach Gloucs 38 B1
Beachampton Bucks 49 F3
Beachamwell Norfk 63 G6
Beachborough Kent 19 E5
Beachley Gloucs 37 F3
Beacon Devon 10 B5
Beacon End Essex 52 C3
Beacon Hill E Susx 17 F4
Beacon Hill Kent 18 B5
Beacon Hill Notts 73 F5
Beacon Hill Surrey 27 G3
Beacon's Bottom Bucks 41 F4
Beaconsfield Bucks 41 H3
Beadlam N York 98 B3
Beadlow Beds 50 B5
Beadnell Nthumb 125 E4
Beaford Devon 21 F2
Beal N York 91 F2
Beal Nthumb 123 H4
Bealbury Cnwll 5 G3
Bealsmill Cnwll 5 G4
Beam Hill Staffs 71 G3
Beamhurst Staffs 71 E4
Beaminster Dorset 11 E5
Beamish Dur 106 B6
Beamsley N York 90 B5
Bean Kent 29 G3
Beanacre Wilts 25 E6
Beanley Nthumb 124 D3
Beardon Devon 8 B3
Beardwood Lancs 89 E2
Beare Devon 9 G5
Beare Green Surrey 16 C6
Bearley Warwks 47 G5
Bearley Cross Warwks 47 G5
Bearpark Dur 106 B5
Bearsden W Duns 129 G2
Bearsted Kent 30 B2
Bearstone Shrops 70 B4
Bearwood Dorset 12 D4
Bearwood W Mids 58 C4
Beattock D & G 111 E5
Beauchamp Roding Essex 51 G2
Beauchief S York 84 A3
Beaudesert Warwks 58 D2
Beaufort Blae G 36 C5
Beaulieu Hants 14 B4
Beaulieu House Hants 14 B4
Beaulieu Road Station Hants 13 G5
Beauly Highld 154 C4
Beaumaris IOA 79 F2
Beaumont Cumb 103 G6
Beaumont Essex 53 E3
Beaumont Jersey 174 b2
Beaumont Hill Dur 106 B3
Beausale Warwks 59 E2
Beauworth Hants 26 D2
Beaver Kent 18 D5
Beaver Green Kent 18 D6
Beaworthy Devon 8 B4
Beazley End Essex 52 A4
Bebington Mersyd 81 F3
Bebside Nthumb 114 D4
Beccles Suffk 65 G4
Becconsall Lancs 88 C2
Beck Foot Cumb 95 G4
Beck Hole N York 98 D5
Beck Row Suffk 63 F3
Beck Side Cumb 94 C3
Beck Side Cumb 94 D3
Beckbury Shrops 57 H5
Beckenham Gt Lon 29 E3
Beckering Lincs 86 B3
Beckermet Cumb 94 A5
Beckett End Norfk 63 G5
Beckfoot Cumb 103 E5
Beckfoot Cumb 94 B5
Beckfoot Cumb 94 C4
Beckford Worcs 47 E3
Beckhampton Wilts 39 F1
Beckingham Lincs 73 F5
Beckingham Notts 85 E4
Beckington Somset 24 D4
Beckjay Shrops 56 D3
Beckley E Susx 18 B4
Beckley Hants 13 F4
Beckley Oxon 40 D5
Becks W York 90 B4
Beckside Cumb 95 G4
Beckton Gt Lon 29 E4
Beckwithshaw N York 90 D5
Becontree Gt Lon 29 F5
Becquet Vincent Jersey 174 c2
Bedale N York 97 F4
Bedburn Dur 105 H3
Bedchester Dorset 24 D1
Beddau Rhondd 36 B3
Beddgelert Gwynd 67 E5
Beddingham E Susx 17 E2
Beddington Gt Lon 28 D3
Beddington Corner Gt Lon 28 D3
Bedfield Suffk 65 E2
Bedfield Little Green Suffk 65 E2
Bedford Beds 50 A6
Bedgebury Cross Kent 17 H5
Bedham W Susx 16 A4
Bedhampton Hants 15 E4
Bedingfield Suffk 64 D2
Bedingfield Green Suffk 64 D2
Bedingfield Street Suffk 64 D2
Bedlam N York 90 D6
Bedlam Lane Kent 18 B6
Bedlington Nthumb 114 D4
Bedlinog Myr Td 36 B4
Bedminster Bristl 37 G1
Bedminster Down Bristl 37 G1
Bedmond Herts 50 B1
Bednall Staffs 70 D2
Bedrule Border 122 C1
Bedstone Shrops 56 D3
Bedwas Caerph 36 C3
Bedwellty Caerph 36 C4
Bedworth Warwks 59 F4
Bedworth Woodlands Warwks 59 F4
Beeby Leics 60 C6
Beech Hants 27 E3
Beech Staffs 70 C4
Beech Hill Berks 27 E6
Beechingstoke Wilts 25 F5
Beedon Berks 40 C2
Beedon Hill Berks 40 C2
Beeford E R Yk 93 E5
Beeley Derbys 83 G1
Beelsby Lincs 86 B5
Beenham Berks 40 D1
Beenham's Heath Berks 41 F2
Beeny Cnwll 5 E5
Beer Devon 10 C3
Beer Somset 23 G2
Beer Hackett Dorset 11 F6
Beercrocombe Somset 23 F1
Beesands Devon 7 E2
Beesby Lincs 87 E3
Beeson Devon 7 E2
Beeston Beds 50 C6
Beeston Ches 69 H6
Beeston Norfk 76 B2
Beeston Notts 72 C4
Beeston W York 90 D3
Beeston Regis Norfk 77 E4
Beeswing D & G 110 C2
Beetham Cumb 95 F3
Beetham Somset 10 C6
Beetley Norfk 76 C2
Began Cardif 36 C3
Begbroke Oxon 40 C6
Begdale Cambs 62 D6
Begelly Pembks 33 E2
Beggar's Bush Powys 56 C2
Beggarington Hill W York 90 D2
Beguildy Powys 56 B3
Beighton Norfk 65 F6
Beighton S York 84 B3
Beighton Hill Derbys 71 H5
Bein Inn P & K 140 B1
Beith N Ayrs 119 E5
Bekesbourne Kent 31 E2
Bekesbourne Hill Kent 31 E2
Belaugh Norfk 77 F2
Belbroughton Worcs 58 B3
Belchalwell Dorset 12 B6
Belchalwell Street Dorset 12 B5
Belchamp Otten Essex 52 B5
Belchamp St Paul Essex 52 B5
Belchamp Walter Essex 52 B5
Belchford Lincs 86 C2
Belford Nthumb 124 D4
Belgrave Leics 60 B6
Belhaven E Loth 133 F3
Belhelvie Abers 149 G6
Belhinnie Abers 157 G2
Bell Bar Herts 50 C1
Bell Busk N York 89 G5
Bell End Worcs 58 B3
Bell Heath Worcs 58 B3
Bell Hill Hants 27 F2
Bell o' th' Hill Ches 69 G5
Bellabeg Abers 148 A6
Bellamore Herefs 45 G3
Bellanoch Ag & B 127 G4
Bellasize E R Yk 92 B2
Bellaty Angus 140 B6
Belle Vue Cumb 103 H6
Belle Vue W York 91 E1
Belleau Lincs 86 D2
Bellerby N York 96 D4
Bellever Devon 8 C2
Bellfield S Lans 120 C3
Bellfield S Lans 120 D1
Bellingdon Bucks 41 H5
Bellingham Nthumb 113 E3
Belloch Ag & B 117 F4
Bellochantuy Ag & B 117 F4
Bellows Cross Dorset 13 E6
Bells Cross Suffk 53 E6
Bells Yew Green E Susx 17 G5
Bellshill N Lans 120 B5
Bellshill Nthumb 124 D4
Bellside N Lans 120 C5
Bellsquarry W Loth 131 G2
Belluton Somset 24 B6
Belmesthorpe Rutlnd 73 H1
Belmont Gt Lon 28 C2
Belmont Lancs 89 E1
Belmont S Ayrs 119 E1
Belmont Shet 169 j5
Belnacraig Abers 148 A6
Belowda Cnwll 4 C2
Belper Derbys 72 A5
Belper Lane End Derbys 72 A5
Belph Derbys 84 C2
Belsay Nthumb 114 C3
Belses Border 122 C2
Belsford Devon 7 E3
Belsize Herts 28 A6
Belstead Suffk 53 E5
Belstone Devon 8 C4
Belthorn Lancs 89 F2
Beltinge Kent 31 E3
Beltingham Nthumb 113 E1
Beltoft Lincs 85 F5
Belton Leics 72 B2
Belton Lincs 85 E5
Belton Lincs 73 G4
Belton Norfk 65 G6
Belton Rutlnd 60 D5
Beltring Kent 17 G6
Belvedere Gt Lon 29 F4
Belvoir Leics 73 F3
Belvoir Castle Leics 73 F3
Bembridge IOW 15 E2
Bemersley Green Staffs 70 D5
Bemerton Wilts 25 G2
Bempton E R Yk 99 G2
Ben Rhydding W York 90 C4
Benacre Suffk 65 G4
Benbecula Airport W Isls 168 b4
Benbuie D & G 110 B4
Benderloch Ag & B 136 D4
Benenden Kent 18 B5
Benfieldside Dur 105 G5
Bengates Norfk 77 F3
Bengeworth Worcs 47 F3
Benhall Green Suffk 65 F1
Benhall Street Suffk 65 F1
Benholm Abers 149 F1
Beningbrough N York 91 F5
Benington Herts 50 D3
Benington Lincs 74 D5
Benington Sea End Lincs 74 D5
Benllech IOA 79 E3
Benmore Ag & B 128 C4
Bennacott Cnwll 5 F5
Bennan N Ayrs 118 B1
Bennet Head Cumb 104 A2
Bennetland E R Yk 92 B2
Bennett End Bucks 41 F4
Benniworth Lincs 86 B3
Benover Kent 29 H1
Benson Oxon 40 D3
Bentfield Green Essex 51 F3
Benthall Shrops 57 G6
Bentham Gloucs 38 D6
Benthoul Aber C 149 F5
Bentlawn Shrops 56 D5
Bentley E R Yk 92 D3
Bentley Hants 27 F4
Bentley S York 84 C5
Bentley Suffk 53 E4
Bentley Warwks 59 F5
Bentley Heath Herts 28 C6
Bentley Heath W Mids 59 E3
Benton Devon 21 G4
Bentpath D & G 111 G4
Bentwichen Devon 21 G4
Bentworth Hants 27 E3
Benvie Angus 140 C3
Benville Dorset 11 F5
Benwick Cambs 62 C4
Beoley Worcs 58 D2
Beoraidbeg Highld 143 F3
Bepton W Susx 15 G5
Berden Essex 51 E4
Bere Alston Devon 6 B4
Bere Ferrers Devon 6 B4
Bere Regis Dorset 12 B4
Berea Pembks 32 B5
Berepper Cnwll 2 D2
Bergh Apton Norfk 65 E5
Berhill Somset 23 G3
Berinsfield Oxon 40 D4
Berkeley Gloucs 38 B4
Berkeley Heath Gloucs 38 B4
Berkeley Road Gloucs 38 B4
Berkhamsted Herts 41 H5
Berkley Somset 24 D4
Berkswell W Mids 59 E3
Bermondsey Gt Lon 28 D4
Bernera Highld 143 G6
Bernice Ag & B 128 C4
Bernisdale Highld 150 D4
Berrick Prior Oxon 40 D4
Berrick Salome Oxon 40 D4
Berriedale Highld 163 H6
Berrier Cumb 103 H3
Berriew Powys 56 B5
Berrington Nthumb 123 G4
Berrington Shrops 57 E6
Berrington Worcs 57 F2
Berrington Green Worcs 57 F2
Berrow Somset 23 F4
Berrow Worcs 46 C3
Berrow Green Worcs 46 C5
Berry Brow W York 83 F6
Berry Cross Devon 21 E2
Berry Down Cross Devon 21 F5
Berry Hill Gloucs 37 G5
Berry Hill Pembks 33 E6
Berry Pomeroy Devon 7 F4
Berry's Green Gt Lon 29 E2
Berryhillock Moray 157 G4
Berryhillock Moray 157 G5
Berrynarbor Devon 21 F5
Bersham Wrexhm 69 E5
Berthengam Flints 80 C3
Berwick E Susx 17 F2
Berwick Bassett Wilts 39 F2
Berwick Hill Nthumb 114 C3
Berwick St James Wilts 25 F3
Berwick St John Wilts 25 E1
Berwick St Leonard Wilts 25 E2
Berwick-upon-Tweed Nthumb 123 G5
Bescaby Leics 73 F3
Bescar Lancs 81 F6
Besford Shrops 69 H2
Besford Worcs 47 E4
Besom Hill Gt Man 83 E5
Bessacarr S York 84 D5
Bessels Leigh Oxon 40 C4
Besses o' th' Barn Gt Man 82 C5
Bessingby E R Yk 99 G1
Bessingham Norfk 77 E4
Bestbeech Hill E Susx 17 G4
Besthorpe Norfk 64 C5
Besthorpe Notts 85 F1
Beswick E R Yk 92 D4
Betchcott Shrops 57 E5
Betchworth Surrey 28 C1
Beth Chatto Garden Essex 52 D3
Bethania Cerdgn 54 C2
Bethania Gwynd 67 G4
Bethel Gwynd 79 E1
Bethel Gwynd 68 B4
Bethel IOA 78 D2
Bethel Powys 68 C2
Bethersden Kent 18 C5
Bethesda Gwynd 79 F1
Bethesda Pembks 33 E3
Bethlehem Carmth 43 G2
Bethnal Green Gt Lon 28 D4
Betley Staffs 70 C5
Betsham Kent 29 G3
Betteshanger Kent 31 G1
Bettiscombe Dorset 10 D5
Bettisfield Wrexhm 69 G3
Betton Shrops 70 B4
Betton Strange Shrops 69 G1
Bettws Newpt 36 D3
Bettws Bledrws Cerdgn 43 F4
Bettws Cedewain Powys 56 B5
Bettws Evan Cerdgn 42 C4
Bettws-Newydd Mons 37 E5
Bettyhill Highld 165 H5
Betws Brdgnd 35 F3
Betws Carmth 34 D5
Betws Garmon Gwynd 67 E6
Betws Gwerfil Goch Denbgs 68 C5
Betws-y-coed Conwy 67 G6
Betws-yn-Rhos Conwy 80 A2
Beulah Cerdgn 42 C4
Beulah Powys 44 B4
Bevendean E Susx 16 D2
Bevercotes Notts 85 E2
Beverley E R Yk 92 D3
Beverstone Gloucs 38 C4
Bevington Gloucs 37 H4
Bewaldeth Cumb 103 F4
Bewcastle Cumb 112 C2
Bewdley Worcs 57 H3
Bewerley N York 97 E1
Bewholme E R Yk 93 E5
Bewlbridge Kent 17 H5
Bexhill E Susx 18 A2
Bexley Gt Lon 29 F3
Bexleyheath Gt Lon 29 F4
Bexleyhill W Susx 27 G2
Bexon Kent 30 C2
Bexwell Norfk 63 E6
Beyton Suffk 64 B2
Beyton Green Suffk 64 B2
Bhaltos W Isls 168 d8
Bhatarsaigh W Isls 168 a1
Bibstone Gloucs 38 B3
Bibury Gloucs 39 F5
Bicester Oxon 48 D1
Bickenhill W Mids 59 E4
Bicker Lincs 74 C4
Bicker Bar Lincs 74 C4
Bicker Gauntlet Lincs 74 C4
Bickershaw Gt Man 82 A5
Bickerstaffe Lancs 81 G5
Bickerton Ches 69 G5
Bickerton Devon 7 E1
Bickerton N York 91 F5
Bickerton Nthumb 113 G5
Bickford Staffs 70 D1
Bickington Devon 21 E4
Bickington Devon 7 E5
Bickleigh Devon 9 F5
Bickleigh Devon 6 C4
Bickleton Devon 21 E4
Bickley Ches 69 G5
Bickley Gt Lon 29 E3
Bickley N York 99 E4
Bickley Worcs 57 F2
Bickley Moss Ches 69 H5
Bicknacre Essex 52 B1
Bicknoller Somset 22 D3
Bicknor Kent 30 B2
Bickton Hants 13 E6
Bicton Herefs 57 E2
Bicton Shrops 69 G1
Bicton Shrops 56 C4
Bidborough Kent 17 F6
Bidden Hants 27 E4
Biddenden Kent 18 B5
Biddenden Green Kent 18 C6
Biddenham Beds 50 A6
Biddestone Wilts 38 C2
Biddisham Somset 23 G5
Biddlesden Bucks 49 E3
Biddlestone Nthumb 124 C2
Biddulph Staffs 70 D6
Biddulph Moor Staffs 70 D6
Bideford Devon 21 E3
Bidford-on-Avon Warwks 47 F4
Bidston Mersyd 81 E4
Bielby E R Yk 92 B4
Bieldside Aber C 149 F5
Bierley IOW 14 C1
Bierton Bucks 41 F6
Big Balcraig D & G 101 E4
Big Carlae D & G 110 A4
Big Pit Blaenavon Torfn 36 D5
Big Sand Highld 160 B2
Bigbury Devon 6 D2
Bigbury-on-Sea Devon 6 D2
Bigby Lincs 86 A5
Biggar Cumb 94 C1
Biggar S Lans 121 E3
Biggin Derbys 71 G5
Biggin Derbys 71 F6
Biggin N York 91 F3
Biggin Hill Gt Lon 29 E2
Biggin Hill Airport Gt Lon 29 E2
Biggleswade Beds 50 C5
Bigholms D & G 111 G3
Bighouse Highld 166 C5
Bighton Hants 26 D3
Bigland Hall Cumb 94 D3
Biglands Cumb 103 F5
Bignor W Susx 15 H5
Bigrigg Cumb 102 D1
Bilborough Notts 72 C4
Bilbrook Somset 22 C3
Bilbrook Staffs 58 B6
Bilbrough N York 91 F4
Bilbster Highld 167 F4
Bildershaw Dur 106 A3
Bildeston Suffk 52 D6
Billacott Cnwll 5 F5
Billericay Essex 29 G5
Billesdon Leics 60 C6
Billesley Warwks 47 G5
Billingborough Lincs 74 B3
Billinge Mersyd 81 G5
Billingford Norfk 76 C2
Billingford Norfk 64 D3
Billingham Dur 106 D3
Billinghay Lincs 74 B5
Billingley S York 84 B5
Billingshurst W Susx 16 B4
Billingsley Shrops 57 G4
Billington Beds 49 G1
Billington Lancs 89 F3
Billington Staffs 70 D2
Billockby Norfk 77 G1
Billy Row Dur 106 A5
Bilsborrow Lancs 88 D4
Bilsby Lincs 87 E2
Bilsham W Susx 15 H4
Bilsington Kent 18 D5
Bilsthorpe Notts 72 D6
Bilsthorpe Moor Notts 72 D6
Bilston Mdloth 132 B1
Bilston W Mids 58 B5
Bilstone Leics 59 F6
Bilting Kent 30 D1
Bilton E R Yk 93 E3
Bilton N York 91 F5
Bilton N York 90 D5
Bilton Nthumb 125 E2
Bilton Warwks 59 H3
Bilton Banks Nthumb 125 E2
Binbrook Lincs 86 B4
Binchester Blocks Dur 106 B4
Bincombe Dorset 11 G3
Binegar Somset 24 B4
Bines Green W Susx 16 C3
Binfield Berks 41 G1
Binfield Heath Oxon 41 F2
Bingfield Nthumb 113 G2
Bingham Notts 73 E4
Bingham's Melcombe Dorset 12 B5
Bingley W York 90 B3
Bings Shrops 69 H2
Binham Norfk 76 C4
Binley Hants 26 B5
Binley W Mids 59 G3
Binnegar Dorset 12 C3
Binniehill Falk 131 E2
Binns Farm Moray 157 E5
Binscombe Surrey 27 H4
Binsey Oxon 40 C5
Binstead IOW 14 D3
Binsted Hants 27 F3
Binsted W Susx 15 H4
Binton Warwks 47 G5
Bintree Norfk 76 C2
Binweston Shrops 56 C6
Birch Essex 52 C3
Birch Gt Man 82 C5
Birch Close Dorset 12 C5
Birch Cross Staffs 71 F3
Birch Green Essex 52 C3
Birch Green Herts 50 D2
Birch Green Worcs 46 D4
Birch Heath Ches 69 H6
Birch Hill Ches 81 G2
Birch Vale Derbys 83 E3
Birch Wood Somset 10 C6
Bircham Newton Norfk 75 H3
Bircham Tofts Norfk 75 H3
Birchanger Essex 51 F3
Birchencliffe W York 90 B1
Bircher Herefs 57 E2
Birchfield W Mids 58 D4
Birchgrove Cardif 36 C2
Birchgrove E Susx 17 E4

Birchgrove

Bosley

275

Birchgrove Swans 35 E4
Birchington Kent 31 F3
Birchley Heath Warwks 59 F5
Birchmoor Warwks 59 E5
Birchmoor Green Beds 49 H3
Birchover Derbys 83 G1
Birchwood Ches 82 B4
Birchyfield Herefs 46 B5
Bircotes Notts 84 D4
Bird End W Mids 58 C5
Bird Street Suffk 52 D6
Birdbrook Essex 51 H5
Birdforth N York 97 H2
Birdham W Susx 15 F4
Birdingbury Warwks 59 G2
Birdlip Gloucs 38 D6
Birdoswald Cumb 112 C1
Birds Edge W York 83 G5
Birds Green Essex 51 G2
Birdsall N York 98 D1
Birdsgreen Shrops 57 H4
Birdsmoorgate Dorset 10 D5
Birdwell S York 84 A5
Birdwood Gloucs 46 C1
Birgham Border 123 E3
Birichin Highld 162 D3
Birkacre Lancs 88 D1
Birkby N York 97 F5
Birkdale Mersyd 88 B1
Birkenbog Abers 157 G6
Birkenhead Mersyd 81 E3
Birkenhills Abers 158 C4
Birkenshaw W York 90 C2
Birkhall Abers 148 A4
Birkhill Angus 140 C3
Birkhill D & G 121 F1
Birkholme Lincs 73 G2
Birkin N York 91 F2
Birks W York 90 D2
Birkshaw Nthumb 113 E1
Birley Herefs 45 G4
Birley Carr S York 84 A4
Birling Kent 29 H2
Birling Nthumb 125 F2
Birling Gap E Susx 17 F1
Birlingham Worcs 47 E3
Birmingham W Mids 58 D4
Birmingham Airport W Mids 59 E4
Birnam P & K 139 G4
Birness Abers 159 F2
Birse Abers 148 C4
Birsemore Abers 148 C4
Birstall Leics 72 D1
Birstall W York 90 C2
Birstwith N York 90 D6
Birthorpe Lincs 74 A3
Birtley Herefs 56 D2
Birtley Nthumb 113 F3
Birtley T & W 114 D1
Birts Street Worcs 46 C3
Bisbrooke Rutlnd 61 E5
Biscathorpe Lincs 86 C3
Biscovey Cnwll 3 H5
Bish Mill Devon 21 G3
Bisham Berks 41 G3
Bishampton Worcs 47 E4
Bishop Auckland Dur 106 B4
Bishop Burton E R Yk 92 D3
Bishop Middleham Dur 106 C4
Bishop Monkton N York 97 F1
Bishop Norton Lincs 85 G4
Bishop Sutton Somset 24 A5
Bishop Thornton N York 97 F1
Bishop Wilton E R Yk 92 B5
Bishop's Castle Shrops 56 C4
Bishop's Caundle Dorset 11 G6
Bishop's Cleeve Gloucs 47 E2
Bishop's Frome Herefs 46 B4
Bishop's Green Essex 51 G2
Bishop's Green Hants 26 C6
Bishop's Itchington Warwks 48 B5
Bishop's Norton Gloucs 46 D2
Bishop's Nympton Devon 21 H3
Bishop's Offley Staffs 70 C3
Bishop's Stortford Herts 51 F3
Bishop's Sutton Hants 26 D2
Bishop's Tachbrook Warwks 48 A5
Bishop's Tawton Devon 21 F4
Bishop's Waltham Hants 14 D5
Bishop's Wood Staffs 70 C1
Bishopbridge Lincs 85 H4
Bishopbriggs E Duns 130 B2
Bishopmill Moray 156 D5
Bishops Cannings Wilts 25 F6
Bishops Gate Surrey 41 H1
Bishops Hull Somset 23 E2
Bishops Lydeard Somset 23 E2
Bishopsbourne Kent 31 E1
Bishopsteignton Devon 7 F5
Bishopstoke Hants 14 C6
Bishopston Swans 34 C3
Bishopstone Bucks 41 F5
Bishopstone E Susx 17 F1
Bishopstone Herefs 45 G3
Bishopstone Kent 31 F3
Bishopstone Wilts 25 F2
Bishopstone Wilts 39 G3
Bishopstrow Wilts 24 D4
Bishopswood Somset 10 C6
Bishopsworth Bristl 37 G1
Bishopthorpe N York 91 G4
Bishopton Dur 106 C3
Bishopton Rens 129 F2
Bishopton Warwks 47 G5
Bishton Newpt 37 E3
Bishton Staffs 71 E2
Bisley Gloucs 38 D5
Bisley Surrey 27 H5
Bisley Camp Surrey 27 G5
Bispham Lancs 88 B4
Bispham Green Lancs 81 G6
Bissoe Cnwll 3 E4
Bisterne Hants 13 E5
Bitchet Green Kent 29 F1
Bitchfield Lincs 73 G3
Bittadon Devon 21 F5
Bittaford Devon 6 D3
Bittering Norfk 76 B2
Bitterley Shrops 57 F3
Bitterne Hants 14 C5
Bitteswell Leics 60 A4
Bitton Gloucs 38 B1
Bix Oxon 41 E3
Blaby Leics 60 B5
Black Bourton Oxon 39 G5
Black Callerton T & W 114 C2
Black Car Norfk 64 C5
Black Corner W Susx 16 D5
Black Corries Highld 137 G5
Black Crofts Ag & B 136 D3
Black Cross Cnwll 4 C2
Black Dog Devon 9 E6
Black Heddon Nthumb 114 B3
Black Lane Gt Man 82 C5
Black Lane Ends Lancs 89 H4
Black Moor W York 90 D4
Black Notley Essex 52 A3
Black Pill Swans 34 D3
Black Street Suffk 65 G4
Black Tar Pembks 32 D3
Black Torrington Devon 8 B5
Blackadder Border 123 F5
Blackawton Devon 7 E3
Blackbank Warwks 59 F4
Blackbeck Cumb 94 A6
Blackborough Devon 10 A5
Blackborough End Norfk 75 G1
Blackboys E Susx 17 F3
Blackbrook Derbys 72 A5
Blackbrook Staffs 70 C4
Blackbrook Surrey 16 C6
Blackburn Abers 149 F6
Blackburn Lancs 89 E2
Blackburn S York 84 B4
Blackburn W Loth 131 F2
Blackcraig E Ayrs 109 H6
Blackden Heath Ches 82 C2
Blackdog Abers 149 G6
Blackdown Devon 8 B2
Blackdown Dorset 10 D5
Blackdyke Cumb 103 E5
Blackenall Heath W Mids 58 C6
Blacker S York 84 A6
Blacker Hill S York 84 A5
Blackfen Gt Lon 29 E3
Blackfield Hants 14 C4
Blackford Cumb 112 A1
Blackford P & K 131 E6
Blackford Somset 23 G4
Blackford Somset 24 B2
Blackford Bridge Gt Man 82 C5
Blackfordby Leics 72 A2
Blackgang IOW 14 C1
Blackhall C Edin 131 H3
Blackhall Dur 106 D5
Blackhall Colliery Dur 106 D5
Blackhaugh Border 122 A3
Blackheath Essex 52 D3
Blackheath Gt Lon 29 E4
Blackheath Suffk 65 G3
Blackheath Surrey 16 A6
Blackheath W Mids 58 C4
Blackhill Abers 159 F3
Blackhill Abers 159 G5
Blackhill Abers 159 G3
Blackhill Dur 105 G5
Blackhill of Clackriach Abers 159 E4
Blackhorse Devon 9 G4
Blackhorse Hill E Susx 18 A3
Blackjack Lincs 74 C4
Blackland Somset 22 A3
Blackland Wilts 39 E1
Blacklaw D & G 111 E6
Blackley Gt Man 82 D5
Blacklunans P & K 140 B6
Blackmarstone Herefs 45 H3
Blackmill Brdgnd 35 G3
Blackmoor Hants 27 F3
Blackmoor Somset 23 G5
Blackmoorfoot W York 83 F6
Blackmore Essex 51 G1
Blackmore End Essex 52 A4
Blackmore End Herts 50 C2
Blackness Falk 131 G3
Blacknest Berks 41 H1
Blacknest Hants 27 F3
Blacko Lancs 89 G4
Blackpool Devon 7 F2
Blackpool Devon 7 E5
Blackpool Lancs 88 B3
Blackpool Airport Lancs 88 B3
Blackpool Gate Cumb 112 C2
Blackridge W Loth 131 E2
Blackrock Cnwll 2 D3
Blackrock Mons 36 C5
Blackrock Mons 37 F3
Blackrod Gt Man 82 A6
Blacksboat Moray 156 D3
Blackshaw D & G 111 E1
Blackshaw Head W York 89 H2
Blacksmith's Green Suffk 64 D2
Blacksnape Lancs 89 E2
Blackstone W Susx 16 C3
Blackthorn Oxon 48 D1
Blackthorpe Suffk 64 B2
Blacktoft E R Yk 92 B2
Blacktop Aber C 149 F5
Blackwall Derbys 71 G5
Blackwater Cnwll 3 E4
Blackwater Hants 27 G5
Blackwater IOW 14 C2
Blackwater Somset 10 C6
Blackwaterfoot N Ayrs 117 H3
Blackwell Cumb 103 H5
Blackwell Derbys 83 F2
Blackwell Derbys 72 B6
Blackwell Dur 106 B2
Blackwell Warwks 47 H3
Blackwell Worcs 58 C3
Blackwellsend Green Gloucs 46 C2
Blackwood Caerph 36 C4
Blackwood D & G 110 D3
Blackwood S Lans 120 B4
Blackwood Hill Staffs 70 D6
Blacon Ches 81 F1
Bladbean Kent 19 E6
Bladnoch D & G 101 E6
Bladon Oxon 40 C6
Bladon Somset 23 G1
Blaen Dyryn Powys 44 B3
Blaen-y-Coed Carmth 33 H4
Blaen-y-cwm Blae G 36 B5
Blaen-y-cwm Rhondd 35 G4
Blaenannerch Cerdgn 42 C4
Blaenau Ffestiniog Gwynd 67 G5
Blaenavon Torfn 36 D5
Blaenffos Pembks 42 B3
Blaengarw Brdgnd 35 F3
Blaengeuffordd Cerdgn 54 D3
Blaengwrach Neath 35 F5
Blaengwynfi Neath 35 F4
Blaenllechau Rhondd 35 G4
Blaenpennal Cerdgn 54 D2
Blaenplwyf Cerdgn 54 C3
Blaenporth Cerdgn 42 C4
Blaenrhondda Rhondd 35 G4
Blaenwaun Carmth 33 F4
Blaenycwm Cerdgn 55 F3
Blagdon Devon 7 F4
Blagdon Somset 23 E1
Blagdon Somset 23 H5
Blagdon Hill Somset 23 E1
Blagill Cumb 104 D5
Blaguegate Lancs 81 G5
Blaich Highld 144 C2
Blain Highld 143 F1
Blaina Blae G 36 C5
Blair Atholl P & K 146 D1
Blair Drummond Stirlg 130 D5
Blair's Ferry Ag & B 128 A2
Blairgowrie P & K 140 B4
Blairingone P & K 131 F5
Blairlogie Stirlg 131 E5
Blairmore Ag & B 128 C3
Blairmore Highld 164 C4
Blairnamarrow Moray 147 G6
Blaisdon Gloucs 38 B6
Blake End Essex 51 H3
Blakebrook Worcs 58 A3
Blakedown Worcs 58 B3
Blakeley Lane Staffs 71 E5
Blakemere Ches 81 H2
Blakemere Herefs 45 F3
Blakemore Devon 7 E4
Blakeney Gloucs 38 B5
Blakeney Norfk 76 C4
Blakenhall Ches 70 B5
Blakenhall W Mids 58 B5
Blakeshall Worcs 58 A3
Blakesley Nhants 48 D4
Blanchland Nthumb 105 F5
Bland Hill N York 90 C5
Blandford Camp Dorset 12 C5
Blandford Forum Dorset 12 C5
Blandford St Mary Dorset 12 C5
Blanefield Stirlg 129 G3
Blankney Lincs 74 A6
Blantyre S Lans 120 A5
Blar a' Chaorainn Highld 144 C1
Blargie Highld 146 A4
Blarmachfoldach Highld 144 C1
Blashford Hants 13 E5
Blaston Leics 60 D5
Blatherwycke Nhants 61 F5
Blawith Cumb 94 D4
Blawquhairn D & G 109 H3
Blaxhall Suffk 65 F1
Blaxton S York 84 D5
Blaydon T & W 114 C2
Bleadney Somset 23 H4
Bleadon Somset 23 F5
Bleak Street Somset 24 C2
Blean Kent 31 E2
Bleasby Lincs 86 B3
Bleasby Notts 73 E5
Bleasdale Lancs 88 D4
Bleatarn Cumb 104 D1
Bleathwood Herefs 57 F2
Blebocraigs Fife 140 D1
Bleddfa Powys 56 B2
Bledington Gloucs 47 H1
Bledlow Bucks 41 F4
Bledlow Ridge Bucks 41 F4
Bleet Wilts 24 D5
Blegbie E Loth 122 B6
Blencarn Cumb 104 C3
Blencogo Cumb 103 F5
Blendworth Hants 15 E5
Blennerhasset Cumb 103 F4
Bletchingdon Oxon 40 C6
Bletchingley Surrey 28 D1
Bletchley Bucks 49 G2
Bletchley Shrops 70 A3
Bletherston Pembks 33 E4
Bletsoe Beds 61 F1
Blewbury Oxon 40 D3
Blickling Norfk 77 E3
Blidworth Notts 72 D6
Blidworth Bottoms Notts 72 D5
Blindburn Nthumb 113 E6
Blindcrake Cumb 103 E4
Blindley Heath Surrey 16 D6
Blisland Cnwll 5 E3
Bliss Gate Worcs 57 H3
Blissford Hants 13 F6
Blisworth Nhants 49 E4
Blithbury Staffs 71 F2
Blitterlees Cumb 103 E5
Blo Norton Norfk 64 C3
Blockley Gloucs 47 G3
Blofield Norfk 77 F1
Bloomfield Border 122 C2
Blore Staffs 70 B3
Blore Staffs 71 F5
Blounce Hants 27 E4
Blounts Green Staffs 71 F3
Blowick Mersyd 88 B1
Bloxham Oxon 48 C3
Bloxholm Lincs 74 A5
Bloxwich W Mids 58 C6
Bloxworth Dorset 12 C4
Blubberhouses N York 90 C5
Blue Anchor Cnwll 4 C2
Blue Anchor Somset 22 C4
Blue Bell Hill Kent 30 A2
Blue John Cavern Derbys 83 F3
Blundellsands Mersyd 81 E5
Blundeston Suffk 65 H5
Blunham Beds 50 B6
Blunsdon St Andrew Wilts 39 F3
Bluntington Worcs 58 B3
Bluntisham Cambs 62 C3
Blunts Cnwll 5 G2
Blunts Green Warwks 58 D2
Blurton Staffs 70 D4
Blyborough Lincs 85 G4
Blyford Suffk 65 G3
Blymhill Staffs 70 C1
Blymhill Lawn Staffs 70 C1
Blyth Notts 84 D3
Blyth Nthumb 115 E4
Blyth Bridge Border 121 F4
Blythburgh Suffk 65 G3
Blythe Border 122 C4
Blythe Bridge Staffs 70 D4
Blythe End Warwks 59 E4
Blythe Marsh Staffs 71 E4
Blyton Lincs 85 F4
Bo'ness Falk 131 F3
Boar's Head Gt Man 81 H6
Boarhills Fife 141 F1
Boarhunt Hants 14 D4
Boarley Kent 30 A2
Boars Hill Oxon 40 C4
Boarsgreave Lancs 89 G2
Boarshead E Susx 17 F5
Boarstall Bucks 40 D6
Boasley Cross Devon 8 B4
Boat of Garten Highld 156 B1
Boath Highld 162 C1
Bobbing Kent 30 B2
Bobbington Staffs 58 A4
Bobbingworth Essex 51 F1
Bocaddon Cnwll 5 E2
Bochym Cnwll 2 D2
Bocking Essex 52 A3
Bocking Churchstreet Essex 52 A3
Bockleton Worcs 46 B5
Boconnoc Cnwll 5 E2
Boddam Abers 159 G3
Boddam Shet 169 h1
Boddington Gloucs 46 D2
Bodedern IOA 78 C3
Bodelwyddan Denbgs 80 B2
Bodenham Herefs 45 H4
Bodenham Wilts 25 G2
Bodenham Moor Herefs 46 A4
Bodewryd IOA 78 D4
Bodfari Denbgs 80 C2
Bodffordd IOA 78 D2
Bodfuan Gwynd 66 C4
Bodham Norfk 76 D4
Bodiam E Susx 18 A4
Bodiam Castle E Susx 18 B4
Bodicote Oxon 48 C3
Bodieve Cnwll 4 D3
Bodinnick Cnwll 5 E1
Bodle Street Green E Susx 17 G3
Bodmin Cnwll 4 D3
Bodnant Garden Conwy 79 G2
Bodney Norfk 63 G5
Bodorgan IOA 78 C1
Bodrean Cnwll 3 F5
Bodsham Green Kent 19 E6
Bodwen Cnwll 4 D2
Bodymoor Heath Warwks 59 E5
Bogallan Highld 155 E4
Bogbrae Abers 159 F3
Boghall Mdloth 132 A2
Boghall W Loth 131 F2
Boghead S Lans 120 B4
Boghead Farm Moray 157 F5
Bogmoor Moray 157 F5
Bogmuir Abers 148 D1
Bogniebrae Abers 158 B4
Bognor Regis W Susx 15 G3
Bogroy Highld 155 G1
Bogue D & G 110 A3
Bohetherick Devon 5 H3
Bohortha Cnwll 3 F3
Bohuntine Highld 145 E3
Bojewyan Cnwll 2 B3
Bokiddick Cnwll 4 D2
Bolam Dur 106 A3
Bolam Nthumb 114 C4
Bolberry Devon 6 D1
Bold Heath Mersyd 81 G4
Boldmere W Mids 58 D5
Boldon Colliery T & W 115 E2
Boldre Hants 13 G4
Boldron Dur 105 G1
Bole Notts 85 E3
Bole Hill Derbys 84 A2
Bolehill Derbys 71 H6
Bolenowe Cnwll 2 D4
Bolham Devon 9 F6
Bolham Water Devon 10 B6
Bolingey Cnwll 3 E5
Bollington Ches 82 D2
Bollington Cross Ches 82 D2
Bollow Gloucs 38 B6
Bolney W Susx 16 C4
Bolnhurst Beds 61 G1
Bolshan Angus 141 F5
Bolsover Derbys 84 B2
Bolster Moor W York 90 B1
Bolsterstone S York 83 H4
Boltby N York 97 H3
Boltenstone Abers 148 B5
Bolter End Bucks 41 F3
Bolton Cumb 104 C2
Bolton E Loth 132 D2
Bolton E R Yk 92 B5
Bolton Gt Man 82 B6
Bolton Nthumb 124 D2
Bolton Abbey N York 90 B5
Bolton Bridge N York 90 B5
Bolton by Bowland Lancs 89 F4
Bolton Hall N York 96 D4
Bolton le Sands Lancs 95 E2
Bolton Low Houses Cumb 103 F4
Bolton New Houses Cumb 103 F4
Bolton Percy N York 91 F4
Bolton Town End Lancs 95 E1
Bolton Upon Dearne S York 84 B5
Bolton-on-Swale N York 97 F5
Boltonfellend Cumb 112 B2
Boltongate Cumb 103 F4
Bolventor Cnwll 5 E4
Bomarsund Nthumb 114 D4
Bomere Heath Shrops 69 G2
Bonar Bridge Highld 162 C3
Bonawe Ag & B 137 E3
Bonby Lincs 92 D1
Boncath Pembks 42 B3
Bonchester Bridge Border 112 C6
Bonchurch IOW 14 D1
Bond's Green Herefs 45 F5
Bondleigh Devon 8 C5
Bonds Lancs 88 C4
Bone Cnwll 2 B3
Bonehill Devon 8 D2
Bonehill Staffs 59 E6
Boney Hay Staffs 71 E1
Bonhill W Duns 129 E3
Boningale Shrops 58 A6
Bonjedward Border 122 D2
Bonkle N Lans 120 C5
Bonnington Angus 141 F4
Bonnington Kent 18 D5
Bonnybank Fife 132 C5
Bonnybridge Falk 130 D3
Bonnykelly Abers 158 D4
Bonnyrigg Mdloth 132 B2
Bonnyton Angus 140 C4
Bonsall Derbys 71 H6
Bonshaw Tower D & G 111 G2
Bont Mons 45 G1
Bont-Dolgadfan Powys 55 F5
Bontddu Gwynd 67 F2
Bonthorpe Lincs 87 E2
Bontnewydd Cerdgn 54 D2
Bontnewydd Gwynd 66 D6
Bontuchel Denbgs 68 C6
Bonvilston V Glam 36 B2
Bonwm Denbgs 68 C4
Bonymaen Swans 34 D4
Boode Devon 21 E4
Boohay Devon 7 F3
Booker Bucks 41 F3
Booley Shrops 69 H3
Boon Border 122 C4
Boon Hill Staffs 70 C5
Boorley Green Hants 14 C5
Boosbeck N York 107 F2
Boose's Green Essex 52 B4
Boot Cnwll 5 F6
Boot Cumb 94 C5
Boot Street Suffk 53 F6
Booth E R Yk 92 A2
Booth W York 90 B2
Booth Green Ches 82 D3
Booth Town W York 90 B2
Boothby Graffoe Lincs 73 G6
Boothby Pagnell Lincs 73 G3
Boothstown Gt Man 82 B5
Boothville Nhants 60 D2
Bootle Cumb 94 B4
Bootle Mersyd 81 F4
Boots Green Ches 82 C2
Booze N York 96 C5
Boraston Shrops 57 F2
Bordeaux Guern 174 h3
Borden Kent 30 B2
Borden W Susx 27 F2
Border Cumb 103 F5
Bordley N York 96 C1
Bordon Hants 27 F3
Bordon Camp Hants 27 F3
Boreham Essex 52 A2
Boreham Wilts 24 D4
Boreham Street E Susx 17 G2
Borehamwood Herts 28 C6
Boreland D & G 111 F4
Boreraig Highld 150 B4
Boreston Devon 7 E3
Boreton Ches 57 E6
Borgh W Isls 168 e9
Borgh W Isls 168 a2
Borgie Highld 165 H4
Borgue D & G 101 G5
Borgue Highld 167 E1
Borley Essex 52 B5
Borley Green Essex 52 B5
Borley Green Suffk 64 B1
Borneskitaig Highld 150 D6
Borness D & G 101 G5
Borough Green Kent 29 G2
Boroughbridge N York 97 G1
Borras Head Wrexhm 69 F5
Borrowash Derbys 72 B3
Borrowby N York 107 G2
Borrowby N York 97 G4
Borrowdale Cumb 103 F1
Borrowstoun Falk 131 F3
Borstal Kent 29 H3
Borth Cerdgn 54 D4
Borth-y-Gest Gwynd 67 E4
Borthwickbrae Border 112 A6
Borthwickshiels Border 122 B1
Borve Highld 151 E3
Borve W Isls 168 e9
Borve W Isls 168 a2
Borve W Isls 168 c6
Borwick Lancs 95 F2
Borwick Lodge Cumb 94 D5
Borwick Rails Cumb 94 C3
Bosavern Cnwll 2 A3
Bosbury Herefs 46 C4
Boscarne Cnwll 4 D3
Boscastle Cnwll 5 E5
Boscombe Dorset 13 E4
Boscombe Wilts 25 G3
Boscoppa Cnwll 3 H5
Bosham W Susx 15 F4
Bosham Hoe W Susx 15 F4
Bosherston Pembks 32 D1
Boskednan Cnwll 2 B3
Boskenna Cnwll 2 B2
Bosley Ches 82 D1

Bosoughan Brimscombe

276

Bosoughan Cnwll 4 B2
Bossall N York 92 A6
Bossiney Cnwll 4 D5
Bossingham Kent 31 E1
Bossington Somset 22 B4
Bostock Green Ches 82 B2
Boston Lincs 74 D4
Boston Spa W York 91 E4
Boswarthan Cnwll 2 B3
Boswinger Cnwll 3 G4
Botallack Cnwll 2 A3
Botanic Gardens C Glas 141 E1
Botany Bay Gt Lon 28 D6
Botcheston Leics 59 H6
Botesdale Suffk 64 C3
Bothal Nthumb 114 D4
Bothampstead Berks 40 C2
Bothamsall Notts 84 D2
Bothel Cumb 103 F4
Bothenhampton Dorset 11 E4
Bothwell S Lans 120 B5
Botley Bucks 41 H4
Botley Hants 14 C5
Botley Oxon 40 C5
Botolph Claydon Bucks 49 E2
Botolph's Bridge Kent 19 E5
Botolphs W Susx 16 C2
Bottesford Leics 73 F4
Bottesford Lincs 85 F5
Bottisham Cambs 63 E1
Bottom o' th' Moor Gt Man 82 B6
Bottom of Hutton Lancs 88 C2
Bottomcraig Fife 140 D2
Bottoms Cnwll 2 A2
Bottoms W York 89 H2
Botts Green Warwks 59 E5
Botusfleming Cnwll 5 H2
Botwnnog Gwynd 66 B3
Bough Beech Kent 17 F6
Boughrood Powys 44 D3
Boughspring Gloucs 37 G4
Boughton Cambs 62 A2
Boughton Nhants 60 D2
Boughton Norfk 63 F6
Boughton Notts 84 D1
Boughton Aluph Kent 18 D6
Boughton End Beds 49 H3
Boughton Green Kent 30 A1
Boughton Malherbe Kent 30 B1
Boughton Monchelsea Kent 30 A1
Boughton Street Kent 30 D2
Boulby N York 107 G3
Boulder Clough W York 90 B2
Bouldnor IOW 14 B2
Bouldon Shrops 57 F4
Boulge Suffk 53 F6
Boulmer Nthumb 125 F2
Boulston Pembks 32 D3
Boultham Lincs 85 G2
Bourn Cambs 62 C1
Bourne Lincs 74 A2
Bourne End Beds 49 H4
Bourne End Beds 61 F1
Bourne End Bucks 41 G3
Bourne End Herts 50 A1
Bournebridge Essex 29 F5
Bournebrook W Mids 58 C4
Bournemouth Dorset 13 E4
Bournemouth Airport Dorset 13 E4
Bournes Green Essex 30 C5
Bournes Green Gloucs 38 D5
Bournheath Worcs 58 B3
Bournstream Gloucs 38 B4
Bournville W Mids 58 C3
Bourton Dorset 24 C2
Bourton Oxon 39 G3
Bourton Shrops 57 F5
Bourton Somset 23 G6
Bourton Wilts 25 F6
Bourton on Dunsmore Warwks 59 G2
Bourton-on-the-Hill Gloucs 47 G2
Bourton-on-the-Water Gloucs 47 G1
Bousd Ag & B 134 D6
Boustead Hill Cumb 103 G6
Bouth Cumb 94 D3
Bouthwaite N York 96 D2
Bouts Worcs 47 F5
Bovain Stirlg 138 C3
Boveney Berks 41 G2
Boveridge Dorset 12 D6
Bovey Tracey Devon 9 E2
Bovingdon Herts 50 A1
Bovingdon Green Bucks 41 F3
Bovinger Essex 51 F1
Bovington Dorset 12 B3
Bovington Camp Dorset 12 B3
Bovington Tank Museum Dorset 12 B3
Bow Cumb 103 G6
Bow Devon 8 D5
Bow Devon 7 E3
Bow Gt Lon 29 E4
Bow Ork 169 b2
Bow Brickhill Bucks 49 G3
Bow Lee Gt Man 82 C5
Bow of Fife Fife 140 C1
Bow Street Cerdgn 54 D4
Bow Street Norfk 64 C5
Bowbank Dur 105 F2
Bowbridge Gloucs 38 C5
Bowburn Dur 106 B5
Bowcombe IOW 14 C2
Bowd Devon 10 B3
Bowden Border 122 C2
Bowden Devon 7 F2
Bowden Hill Wilts 25 E6
Bowdon Gt Man 82 C3
Bower Highld 167 F5
Bower Ashton Bristl 37 G1
Bower Hinton Somset 23 G1
Bower House Tye Suffk 52 C5
Bower's Row W York 91 E2
Bowerchalke Wilts 25 F1
Bowerhill Wilts 25 E5
Bowermadden Highld 167 F5
Bowers Staffs 70 C4
Bowers Gifford Essex 30 A5
Bowershall Fife 131 G4
Bowes Dur 105 G1
Bowgreave Lancs 88 C4
Bowhouse D & G 111 E1
Bowithick Cnwll 5 E4
Bowker's Green Lancs 81 F5
Bowland Border 122 B3
Bowland Bridge Cumb 95 E4
Bowley Herefs 46 A4
Bowley Town Herefs 46 A4
Bowlhead Green Surrey 27 G3
Bowling W Duns 129 F2
Bowling W York 90 C3
Bowling Bank Wrexhm 69 F5
Bowling Green Worcs 46 D4
Bowmanstead Cumb 94 D4
Bowmore Ag & B 126 B1
Bowness-on-Solway Cumb 111 G1
Bowness-on-Windermere Cumb 95 E5
Bowriefauld Angus 141 E5
Bowscale Cumb 103 G3
Bowsden Nthumb 123 G4
Bowston Cumb 95 F4
Bowthorpe Norfk 77 E1
Box Gloucs 38 C4
Box Wilts 38 C1
Box End Beds 50 A6
Box Hill Surrey 28 C1
Box's Shop Cnwll 5 F6
Boxbush Gloucs 46 B1
Boxbush Gloucs 38 B6
Boxford Berks 40 C1
Boxford Suffk 52 C5
Boxgrove W Susx 15 G4
Boxley Kent 30 A2
Boxmoor Herts 50 A1
Boxted Essex 52 D4
Boxted Suffk 52 B6
Boxted Cross Essex 52 D4
Boxted Heath Essex 52 D4
Boxwell Gloucs 38 C3
Boxworth Cambs 62 C2
Boxworth End Cambs 62 C2
Boyden End Suffk 63 F1
Boyden Gate Kent 31 F3
Boylestone Derbys 71 G4
Boyndie Abers 158 B5
Boyndlie Abers 159 E5
Boynton E R Yk 99 G2
Boys Hill Dorset 11 G6
Boysack Angus 141 F5
Boythorpe Derbys 84 B2
Boyton Cnwll 5 G5
Boyton Suffk 53 G5
Boyton Wilts 25 E3
Boyton Cross Essex 51 G2
Boyton End Suffk 51 H5
Bozeat Nhants 49 G5
Braaid IOM 174 l3
Brabling Green Suffk 65 E2
Brabourne Kent 19 E6
Brabourne Lees Kent 18 D5
Brabstermire Highld 167 G5
Bracadale Highld 150 D2
Braceborough Lincs 74 A1
Bracebridge Heath Lincs 85 G1
Bracebridge Low Fields Lincs 85 G1
Braceby Lincs 73 H3
Bracewell Lancs 89 G4
Brackenfield Derbys 72 A6
Brackenhirst N Lans 130 D2
Brackenthwaite Cumb 103 G5
Brackenthwaite N York 90 D5
Bracklesham W Susx 15 F3
Brackletter Highld 144 D3
Brackley Nhants 48 D3
Brackley Hatch Nhants 49 E3
Bracknell Berks 41 G1
Braco P & K 131 E6
Bracobrae Moray 157 G4
Bracon Ash Norfk 64 D5
Bracora Highld 143 G3
Bracorina Highld 143 G3
Bradaford Devon 5 G5
Bradbourne Derbys 71 G5
Bradbury Dur 106 C4
Bradden Nhants 49 E4
Braddock Cnwll 5 E2
Bradeley Staffs 70 D5
Bradenham Bucks 41 F4
Bradenstoke Wilts 39 E2
Bradfield Berks 40 D1
Bradfield Devon 9 G6
Bradfield Essex 53 E4
Bradfield Norfk 77 F3
Bradfield S York 83 G4
Bradfield Combust Suffk 64 A1
Bradfield Green Ches 70 B6
Bradfield Heath Essex 53 E4
Bradfield St Clare Suffk 64 B1
Bradfield St George Suffk 64 B1
Bradford Cnwll 5 E3
Bradford Devon 20 D1
Bradford Nthumb 125 E4
Bradford Nthumb 114 B3
Bradford W York 90 C3
Bradford Abbas Dorset 11 F6
Bradford Leigh Wilts 24 D5
Bradford Peverell Dorset 11 G4
Bradford-on-Avon Wilts 24 D5
Bradford-on-Tone Somset 23 E1
Bradiford Devon 21 F4
Brading IOW 14 D2
Bradley Ches 81 G2
Bradley Derbys 71 G5
Bradley Hants 27 E3
Bradley Lincs 86 C5
Bradley N York 96 D3
Bradley Staffs 70 D2
Bradley W Mids 58 B5
Bradley W York 90 C2
Bradley Worcs 47 E5
Bradley Wrexhm 69 E5
Bradley Green Ches 69 G5
Bradley Green Somset 23 E3
Bradley Green Warwks 59 F5
Bradley Green Worcs 47 E5
Bradley in the Moors Staffs 71 E4
Bradley Stoke Gloucs 37 G2
Bradmore Notts 72 C3
Bradney Somset 23 F3
Bradninch Devon 21 F4
Bradninch Devon 9 G5
Bradnop Staffs 71 E6
Bradnor Green Herefs 45 F5
Bradpole Dorset 11 E4
Bradshaw Gt Man 82 B6
Bradshaw W York 90 B1
Bradshaw W York 90 B3
Bradstone Devon 5 G4
Bradwall Green Ches 82 C1
Bradwell Bucks 49 F3
Bradwell Derbys 83 G3
Bradwell Devon 21 E5
Bradwell Essex 52 B3
Bradwell Norfk 65 G6
Bradwell Waterside Essex 52 D1
Bradwell-on-Sea Essex 52 D1
Bradworthy Devon 20 C2
Brae Highld 155 E5
Brae Shet 169 h3
Brae Roy Lodge Highld 145 F4
Braeface Falk 130 D3
Braehead Angus 141 G5
Braehead D & G 101 E5
Braehead S Lans 120 D4
Braemar Abers 147 F4
Braemore Highld 167 E1
Braemore Highld 161 F2
Braes of Coul Angus 140 C5
Braes of Enzie Moray 157 F5
Braeside Inver 128 D3
Braeswick Ork 169 c3
Braevallich Ag & B 128 A6
Brafferton Dur 106 B3
Brafferton N York 97 G2
Brafield-on-the-Green Nhants 49 F5
Bragar W Isls 168 e9
Bragbury End Herts 50 D3
Braidwood S Lans 120 C4
Brailsford Derbys 71 G4
Brailsford Green Derbys 71 G4
Brain's Green Gloucs 38 A5
Braintree Essex 52 A3
Braiseworth Suffk 64 D2
Braishfield Hants 26 B2
Braithwaite Cumb 103 F2
Braithwaite W York 90 B4
Braithwell S York 84 C4
Braken Hill W York 91 E1
Bramber W Susx 16 C2
Brambridge Hants 26 C1
Bramcote Notts 72 C4
Bramcote Warwks 59 G4
Bramdean Hants 26 D2
Bramerton Norfk 65 E6
Bramfield Herts 50 D2
Bramfield Suffk 65 F3
Bramford Suffk 53 E5
Bramhall Gt Man 82 D3
Bramham W York 91 E4
Bramhope W York 90 D4
Bramley Derbys 84 B3
Bramley Hants 27 E5
Bramley S York 84 C4
Bramley Surrey 16 A6
Bramley W York 90 D3
Bramley Corner Hants 27 E5
Bramley Green Hants 27 E5
Bramley Head N York 90 B5
Bramling Kent 31 F2
Brampford Speke Devon 9 F4
Brampton Cambs 62 A2
Brampton Cumb 104 B6
Brampton Cumb 104 C2
Brampton Lincs 85 F3
Brampton Norfk 77 E2
Brampton S York 84 B5
Brampton Suffk 65 G3
Brampton Abbotts Herefs 46 B2
Brampton Ash Nhants 60 D4
Brampton Bryan Herefs 56 D3
Brampton-en-le-Morthen S York 84 C3
Bramshall Staffs 71 E3
Bramshaw Hants 13 F6
Bramshill Hants 27 F5
Bramshott Hants 27 G2
Bramwell Somset 23 G2
Bran End Essex 51 G3
Branault Highld 143 E1
Brancaster Norfk 75 H4
Brancaster Staithe Norfk 76 A4
Brancepeth Dur 106 B5
Branchill Moray 156 C4
Brand End Lincs 74 D4
Brand Green Gloucs 46 C2
Branderburgh Moray 156 D6
Brandesburton E R Yk 93 E4
Brandeston Suffk 65 E1
Brandis Corner Devon 20 D1
Brandiston Norfk 76 D2
Brandon Dur 106 B5
Brandon Lincs 73 G5
Brandon Nthumb 124 D3
Brandon Suffk 63 G4
Brandon Warwks 59 G3
Brandon Bank Norfk 63 E4
Brandon Creek Norfk 63 E5
Brandon Parva Norfk 64 C6
Brandsby N York 98 B2
Brandy Wharf Lincs 85 H4
Brane Cnwll 2 B3
Branksome Dorset 12 D4
Branksome Park Dorset 12 D4
Bransbury Hants 26 B3
Bransby Lincs 85 F3
Branscombe Devon 10 B3
Bransford Worcs 46 D4
Bransgore Hants 13 F4
Bransholme E R Yk 93 E3
Bransley Shrops 57 G3
Branson's Cross Worcs 58 D2
Branston Leics 73 F3
Branston Lincs 85 H1
Branston Staffs 71 G2
Branston Booths Lincs 86 A2
Branstone IOW 14 D2
Brant Broughton Lincs 73 G5
Brantham Suffk 53 E4
Branthwaite Cumb 103 E3
Branthwaite Cumb 103 G4
Brantingham E R Yk 92 C2
Branton Nthumb 124 D3
Branton S York 84 D5
Branton Green N York 91 E6
Branxton Nthumb 123 F3
Brassey Green Ches 69 G6
Brassington Derbys 71 G5
Brasted Kent 29 F1
Brasted Chart Kent 29 E1
Brathens Abers 148 D4
Bratoft Lincs 87 E1
Brattleby Lincs 85 G3
Bratton Shrops 70 A1
Bratton Somset 22 B4
Bratton Wilts 25 E4
Bratton Clovelly Devon 8 B4
Bratton Fleming Devon 21 G4
Bratton Seymour Somset 24 B2
Braughing Herts 51 E3
Braughing Friars Herts 51 E3
Braunston Nhants 60 B2
Braunston Rutlnd 60 D6
Braunstone Leics 60 B6
Braunton Devon 21 E4
Brawby N York 98 C3
Brawdy Pembks 32 C4
Brawl Highld 166 B5
Braworth N York 106 D2
Bray Berks 41 G2
Bray Shop Cnwll 5 G3
Bray's Hill E Susx 17 G3
Braybrooke Nhants 60 D4
Braydon Wilts 39 E3
Braydon Brook Wilts 39 E3
Braydon Side Wilts 39 E3
Brayford Devon 21 G4
Braystones Cumb 94 A5
Braythorn N York 90 D4
Brayton N York 91 G3
Braywick Berks 41 G2
Braywoodside Berks 41 G2
Brazacott Cnwll 5 F5
Breach Kent 30 B3
Breach Kent 19 E6
Breachwood Green Herts 50 B3
Breaden Heath Shrops 69 G4
Breadsall Derbys 72 A4
Breadstone Gloucs 38 B4
Breadward Herefs 45 F5
Breage Cnwll 2 D3
Breakachy Highld 154 C3
Brealangwell Lodge Highld 162 B3
Bream Gloucs 37 G5
Breamore Hants 25 G1
Brean Somset 23 F5
Breanais W Isls 168 c8
Brearley W York 90 A2
Brearton N York 90 D6
Breascleit W Isls 168 d8
Breasclete W Isls 168 d8
Breaston Derbys 72 B3
Brechfa Carmth 43 E2
Brechin Angus 141 F6
Breckles Norfk 64 B5
Breckonside D & G 110 C4
Brecon Powys 44 C2
Bredbury Gt Man 82 D4
Brede E Susx 18 B3
Bredenbury Herefs 46 B5
Bredfield Suffk 53 F6
Bredgar Kent 30 B2
Bredhurst Kent 30 B2
Bredon Worcs 47 E3
Bredon's Hardwick Worcs 47 E3
Bredon's Norton Worcs 47 E3
Bredwardine Herefs 45 F4
Breedon on the Hill Leics 72 B2
Breich W Loth 120 D5
Breightmet Gt Man 82 B6
Breighton E R Yk 92 A3
Breinton Herefs 45 G3
Bremhill Wilts 38 D1
Bremridge Devon 21 G3
Brenchley Kent 17 H6
Brendon Devon 20 D1
Brendon Devon 21 H5
Brendon Hill Somset 22 C3
Brenfield Ag & B 127 G3
Brenish W Isls 168 c8
Brenkley T & W 114 D3
Brent Eleigh Suffk 52 C5
Brent Knoll Somset 23 F4
Brent Mill Devon 6 D3
Brent Pelham Herts 51 E4
Brentford Gt Lon 28 C4
Brentingby Leics 73 E2
Brentwood Essex 29 G5
Brenzett Kent 18 D4
Brenzett Green Kent 18 D4
Brereton Staffs 71 E2
Brereton Green Ches 82 C1
Brereton Heath Ches 82 C1
Brereton Hill Staffs 71 E1
Bressingham Norfk 64 C3
Bressingham Common Norfk 64 C4
Bretby Derbys 71 H2
Bretford Warwks 59 G3
Bretforton Worcs 47 F4
Bretherdale Head Cumb 95 F5
Bretherton Lancs 88 C2
Brettabister Shet 169 j3
Brettenham Norfk 64 B4
Brettenham Suffk 52 C6
Bretton Derbys 83 G2
Bretton Flints 81 F1
Brewer Street Surrey 28 D1
Brewers End Essex 51 F3
Brewood Staffs 70 D1
Briantspuddle Dorset 12 B4
Brick End Essex 51 F3
Brick Houses S York 83 H3
Brickendon Herts 50 D1
Bricket Wood Herts 50 B1
Brickkiln Green Essex 52 A4
Bricklehampton Worcs 47 E3
Bride IOM 174 m5
Bridekirk Cumb 103 E3
Bridell Pembks 42 B3
Bridestowe Devon 8 B3
Brideswell Abers 158 B3
Bridford Devon 9 E3
Bridge Cnwll 2 D4
Bridge Kent 31 E1
Bridge End Beds 50 A6
Bridge End Cumb 103 H5
Bridge End Cumb 94 C3
Bridge End Devon 6 D2
Bridge End Dur 105 G4
Bridge End Essex 51 G4
Bridge End Lincs 74 B4
Bridge End Nthumb 113 F1
Bridge End Surrey 28 B2
Bridge Green Essex 51 E4
Bridge Hewick N York 97 F2
Bridge of Alford Abers 148 C6
Bridge of Allan Stirlg 130 D5
Bridge of Avon Moray 156 D3
Bridge of Avon Moray 156 D1
Bridge of Balgie P & K 138 C4
Bridge of Brewlands Angus 140 B6
Bridge of Brown Highld 156 C1
Bridge of Cally P & K 140 A5
Bridge of Canny Abers 148 D4
Bridge of Craigisla Angus 140 C5
Bridge of Dee D & G 102 A6
Bridge of Don Aber C 149 G5
Bridge of Dulsie Highld 155 G3
Bridge of Dye Abers 148 D3
Bridge of Earn P & K 140 A2
Bridge of Ericht P & K 138 C6
Bridge of Feugh Abers 149 E4
Bridge of Forss Highld 166 D5
Bridge of Gairn Abers 148 A4
Bridge of Gaur P & K 138 B5
Bridge of Marnoch Abers 158 B4
Bridge of Orchy Ag & B 137 G4
Bridge of Tilt P & K 146 D1
Bridge of Tynet Moray 157 F5
Bridge of Walls Shet 169 h3
Bridge of Weir Rens 129 E2
Bridge Reeve Devon 21 G2
Bridge Sollers Herefs 45 G3
Bridge Street Suffk 52 B6
Bridge Trafford Ches 81 G2
Bridge Yate Gloucs 38 B1
Bridgefoot Cumb 103 E3
Bridgehampton Somset 24 A2
Bridgehill Dur 105 H5
Bridgehouse Gate N York 97 E1
Bridgemary Hants 14 D4
Bridgemere Ches 70 B5
Bridgend Abers 157 G3
Bridgend Ag & B 126 B1
Bridgend Angus 148 C1
Bridgend Brdgnd 35 F2
Bridgend Cerdgn 42 B4
Bridgend Cumb 103 H1
Bridgend D & G 111 E6
Bridgend Devon 6 C2
Bridgend Fife 140 D1
Bridgend Moray 157 F2
Bridgend P & K 140 A2
Bridgend W Loth 131 G3
Bridgend of Lintrathen Angus 140 C5
Bridgerule Devon 5 F6
Bridges Shrops 56 D5
Bridgetown Devon 5 G5
Bridgetown Somset 22 B3
Bridgham Norfk 64 B4
Bridgnorth Shrops 57 G5
Bridgtown Staffs 58 C6
Bridgwater Somset 23 F3
Bridlington E R Yk 99 G1
Bridport Dorset 11 E4
Bridstow Herefs 46 A2
Brierfield Lancs 89 G3
Brierley Gloucs 37 G6
Brierley Herefs 45 H5
Brierley W York 84 B6
Brierley Hill W Mids 58 B4
Brierton Dur 106 D4
Briery Cumb 103 G2
Brig o'Turk Stirlg 129 G6
Brigg Lincs 85 G5
Briggate Norfk 77 F3
Briggswath N York 107 H2
Brigham Cumb 103 E3
Brigham Cumb 103 G2
Brigham E R Yk 93 E5
Brighouse W York 90 C2
Brighstone IOW 14 C2
Brightgate Derbys 71 G6
Brighthampton Oxon 40 B5
Brightholmlee Derbys 83 H4
Brightley Devon 8 C4
Brightling E Susx 17 H3
Brightlingsea Essex 52 D2
Brighton Cnwll 3 F5
Brighton E Susx 16 D2
Brighton le Sands Mersyd 81 E5
Brightons Falk 131 E3
Brightor Cnwll 5 G2
Brightwalton Berks 40 C2
Brightwalton Green Berks 40 B2
Brightwalton Holt Berks 40 C2
Brightwell Suffk 53 F5
Brightwell Baldwin Oxon 41 E4
Brightwell Upperton Oxon 41 E4
Brightwell-cum-Sotwell Oxon 40 D3
Brignall Dur 105 G1
Brigsley Lincs 86 C5
Brigsteer Cumb 95 E4
Brigstock Nhants 61 E4
Brill Bucks 41 E6
Brill Cnwll 3 E3
Brilley Herefs 45 E4
Brimfield Herefs 57 E2
Brimfield Cross Herefs 57 F2
Brimington Derbys 84 B2
Brimley Devon 9 E2
Brimpsfield Gloucs 38 D5
Brimpton Berks 26 D6
Brimscombe Gloucs 38 C4

Brimstage Burn of Cambus
277

Brimstage Mersyd 81 E3
Brincliffe S York 84 A3
Brind E R Yk 92 A3
Brindham Somset 23 H3
Brindister Shet 169 h3
Brindle Lancs 88 D2
Brineton Staffs 70 C1
Bringhurst Leics 60 D5
Brington Cambs 61 G3
Brininghham Norfk 76 C3
Brinkely Notts 73 E5
Brinkhill Lincs 86 D2
Brinkley Cambs 51 G6
Brinklow Warwks 59 G3
Brinkworth Wilts 39 E3
Brinscall Lancs 89 E2
Brinscombe Somset 23 G4
Brinsea Somset 23 G5
Brinsley Notts 72 B5
Brinsop Herefs 45 G4
Brinsworth S York 84 B4
Brinton Norfk 76 C4
Brinyan Ork 169 b3
Brisco Cumb 104 A5
Brisley Norfk 76 C2
Brislington Bristl 37 G1
Brissenden Green Kent 18 C5
Bristol Bristl 37 G1
Bristol Airport Somset 23 H6
Bristol Zoo Bristl 37 G2
Briston Norfk 76 D3
Brisworthy Devon 6 C4
Britannia Lancs 89 G2
Britford Wilts 25 G2
Brithdir Caerph 36 C4
Brithdir Gwynd 67 G2
British Torfn 36 D5
British Legion Village Kent 29 H2
Briton Ferry Neath 35 E4
Britwell Salome Oxon 41 E3
Brixham Devon 7 G3
Brixton Devon 6 C3
Brixton Gt Lon 28 D4
Brixton Deverill Wilts 24 D3
Brixworth Nhants 60 D2
Brize Norton Oxon 39 H5
Brize Norton Airport Oxon 39 H5
Broad Alley Worcs 58 B2
Broad Blunsdon Wilts 39 F3
Broad Campden Gloucs 47 G3
Broad Carr W York 90 B1
Broad Chalke Wilts 25 F2
Broad Clough Lancs 89 G2
Broad Ford Kent 17 H5
Broad Green Essex 52 B3
Broad Green Worcs 46 C5
Broad Green Worcs 58 C2
Broad Haven Pembks 32 C3
Broad Hill Cambs 63 E3
Broad Hinton Wilts 39 F2
Broad Laying Hants 26 C5
Broad Marston Worcs 47 G4
Broad Meadow Staffs 70 C5
Broad Oak Cumb 94 B4
Broad Oak E Susx 18 B3
Broad Oak E Susx 17 G4
Broad Oak Hants 27 F4
Broad Oak Herefs 45 H1
Broad Oak Kent 31 E2
Broad Oak Mersyd 81 G4
Broad Road Suffk 65 E3
Broad Street E Susx 18 B3
Broad Street Essex 51 F2
Broad Street Kent 30 A3
Broad Street Kent 30 B2
Broad Street Wilts 25 F5
Broad Street Green Essex 52 B2
Broad Town Wilts 39 F2
Broad's Green Essex 51 H2
Broadbottom Gt Man 83 E4
Broadbridge W Susx 15 F4
Broadbridge Heath W Susx 16 B4
Broadclyst Devon 9 G4
Broadfield Inver 129 E2
Broadfield Pembks 33 E2
Broadford Highld 151 F1
Broadford Bridge W Susx 16 B3
Broadgairhill Border 111 F6
Broadgate Lincs 74 D1
Broadgrass Green Suffk 64 B2
Broadhaugh Border 123 F5
Broadheath Gt Man 82 C4
Broadheath Worcs 57 G2
Broadhembury Devon 10 A5
Broadhempston Devon 7 E4
Broadholme Notts 85 F2
Broadland Row E Susx 18 B3
Broadlay Carmth 34 A5
Broadley Essex 51 E1
Broadley Gt Man 89 G1
Broadley Moray 157 F5
Broadley Common Essex 51 E1
Broadmayne Dorset 11 G3
Broadmere Hants 26 D4
Broadmoor Gloucs 37 G6
Broadmoor Pembks 33 E2
Broadnymett Devon 8 D5
Broadoak Dorset 11 E4
Broadoak Gloucs 38 B5
Broadoak Wrexhm 69 F6
Broadstairs Kent 31 G3
Broadstone Dorset 12 D4
Broadstone Mons 37 F5
Broadstone Shrops 57 F4
Broadwas Worcs 46 C5
Broadwater Herts 50 C3
Broadwater W Susx 16 B2
Broadwaters Worcs 58 A3
Broadway Carmth 33 G3
Broadway Carmth 34 A5
Broadway Pembks 32 C3
Broadway Somset 10 D6
Broadway Suffk 65 F3
Broadway Worcs 47 F3
Broadwell Gloucs 37 G5
Broadwell Gloucs 47 G2
Broadwell Oxon 39 G5
Broadwell Warwks 59 G2
Broadwey Dorset 11 G3
Broadwindsor Dorset 11 E5
Broadwood Kelly Devon 8 C5
Broadwoodwidger Devon 5 H5
Brobury Herefs 45 F4
Brochel Highld 151 F3
Brock Lancs 88 D4
Brock's Green Hants 26 C5
Brockamin Worcs 46 C5
Brockbridge Hants 14 D5
Brockdish Norfk 65 E3
Brockencote Worcs 58 B3
Brockenhurst Hants 13 G5
Brocketsbrae S Lans 120 C3
Brockford Green Suffk 64 D2
Brockford Street Suffk 64 D2
Brockhall Nhants 60 B2
Brockham Surrey 28 C1
Brockhampton Gloucs 47 E2
Brockhampton Gloucs 47 F1
Brockhampton Hants 15 E4
Brockhampton Herefs 46 B2
Brockhampton Green Dorset 11 G5
Brockholes W York 83 F6
Brockhurst Derbys 84 A1
Brockhurst Warwks 59 G4
Brocklebank Cumb 103 G4
Brocklesby Lincs 86 B6
Brockley Somset 23 G6
Brockley Suffk 63 G2
Brockley Green Suffk 51 H5
Brockley Green Suffk 52 B6
Brockleymoor Cumb 104 B4
Brockmoor W Mids 58 B4
Brockscombe Devon 8 B4
Brockton Shrops 56 C6
Brockton Shrops 57 G6
Brockton Shrops 56 D4
Brockton Shrops 57 E5
Brockton Staffs 70 C3
Brockweir Gloucs 37 F4
Brockwood Park Hants 26 D2
Brockworth Gloucs 38 D6
Brocton Cnwll 4 D3
Brocton Staffs 71 E2
Brodick N Ayrs 118 B3
Brodie Moray 156 B5
Brodsworth S York 84 C5
Brogaig Highld 151 E5
Brogborough Beds 49 H3
Broken Cross Ches 82 B2
Broken Cross Ches 82 D2
Brokenborough Wilts 38 D3
Brokerswood Wilts 24 D4
Bromborough Mersyd 81 F3
Brome Suffk 64 D3
Brome Street Suffk 64 D3
Bromeswell Suffk 53 F6
Bromfield Cumb 103 F5
Bromfield Shrops 57 E3
Bromham Beds 50 A6
Bromham Wilts 25 E6
Bromley Gt Lon 29 E3
Bromley S York 83 H5
Bromley Shrops 57 G5
Bromley W Mids 58 B4
Bromley Common Gt Lon 29 E3
Bromley Cross Essex 52 D3
Bromlow Shrops 56 C6
Brompton Kent 30 A3
Brompton N York 97 G4
Brompton N York 99 E3
Brompton Shrops 57 F6
Brompton Ralph Somset 22 D2
Brompton Regis Somset 22 B2
Brompton-on-Swale N York 97 E5
Bromsash Herefs 46 B2
Bromsberrow Gloucs 46 C3
Bromsberrow Heath Gloucs 46 C2
Bromsgrove Worcs 58 C2
Bromstead Heath Staffs 70 C2
Bromyard Herefs 46 B5
Bromyard Downs Herefs 46 B5
Bronaber Gwynd 67 G3
Bronant Cerdgn 54 D2
Broncroft Shrops 57 F4
Brongest Cerdgn 42 C4
Bronington Wrexhm 69 G4
Bronllys Powys 44 D3
Bronwydd Carmth 42 D1
Bronydd Powys 45 E4
Bronygarth Shrops 69 E4
Brook Carmth 33 G3
Brook Hants 13 F6
Brook Hants 26 B2
Brook IOW 14 B2
Brook Kent 18 D6
Brook Surrey 27 G3
Brook Surrey 16 B6
Brook End Beds 61 G2
Brook End Beds 50 C5
Brook End Bucks 49 G4
Brook End Cambs 61 G3
Brook Hill Hants 13 F6
Brook House Denbgs 80 C1
Brook Street Essex 29 G5
Brook Street Kent 18 C5
Brook Street Suffk 52 B6
Brook Street W Susx 16 D4
Brooke Norfk 65 E5
Brooke Rutlnd 60 D6
Brookfield Rens 129 F1
Brookhampton Oxon 40 D4
Brookhampton Somset 24 B2
Brookhouse Lancs 95 F1
Brookhouse S York 84 C4
Brookhouse Green Ches 70 C6
Brookhouses Derbys 83 E4
Brookland Kent 18 C4
Brooklands Gt Man 82 C4
Brookmans Park Herts 50 C1
Brooks Powys 56 B5
Brooks End Kent 31 F3
Brooks Green W Susx 16 B4
Brooksby Leics 72 D2
Brookthorpe Gloucs 38 C5
Brookville Norfk 63 F5
Brookwood Surrey 27 H5
Broom Beds 50 C5
Broom Dur 106 B5
Broom S York 84 B4
Broom Warwks 47 F5
Broom Green Norfk 76 C2
Broom Hill Dorset 12 D5
Broom Hill Notts 72 C5
Broom Hill S York 84 B5
Broom Hill Worcs 58 B3
Broom Street Kent 30 D2
Broom's Green Gloucs 46 C2
Broome Norfk 65 F4
Broome Shrops 56 D3
Broome Worcs 58 B3
Broome Park Nthumb 124 D2
Broomedge Ches 82 B3
Broomer's Corner W Susx 16 B3
Broomershill W Susx 16 B3
Broomfield Essex 51 H2
Broomfield Kent 30 B1
Broomfield Kent 31 E3
Broomfield Somset 23 E2
Broomfields Shrops 69 F2
Broomfleet E R Yk 92 C2
Broomhall Surrey 27 H6
Broomhaugh Nthumb 114 B2
Broomhill Nthumb 114 D6
Broomhill Green Ches 70 A5
Broomley Nthumb 114 B1
Broomsthorpe Norfk 76 B3
Brora Highld 163 F4
Broseley Shrops 57 G6
Brotherhouse Bar Lincs 74 C1
Brotherlee Dur 105 F4
Brothertoft Lincs 74 C5
Brotherton N York 91 F2
Brotton N York 107 F3
Broubster Highld 166 D4
Brough Cumb 105 E1
Brough Derbys 83 G3
Brough E R Yk 92 C2
Brough Highld 167 F6
Brough Notts 73 F6
Brough Shet 169 j3
Brough Lodge Shet 169 j5
Brough Sowerby Cumb 105 E1
Broughall Shrops 69 H4
Broughton Border 121 F3
Broughton Bucks 41 G6
Broughton Bucks 49 G3
Broughton Cambs 62 B3
Broughton Flints 81 F1
Broughton Gt Man 82 C5
Broughton Hants 26 A2
Broughton Lancs 88 D3
Broughton Lincs 85 G6
Broughton N York 89 H5
Broughton N York 98 C2
Broughton Nhants 60 D3
Broughton Oxon 48 B3
Broughton Staffs 70 C3
Broughton V Glam 35 G1
Broughton Astley Leics 60 A5
Broughton Beck Cumb 94 D3
Broughton Gifford Wilts 24 D6
Broughton Green Worcs 47 E5
Broughton Hackett Worcs 47 E5
Broughton Mains D & G 101 F5
Broughton Mills Cumb 94 C4
Broughton Moor Cumb 103 E3
Broughton Poggs Oxon 39 G5
Broughton Tower Cumb 94 C4
Broughton-in-Furness Cumb 94 C4
Broughty Ferry Dund C 141 E3
Brow End Cumb 94 C2
Brow-of-the-Hill Norfk 75 G2
Brown Candover Hants 26 D3
Brown Edge Lancs 88 B1
Brown Edge Staffs 70 D5
Brown Heath Ches 81 G1
Brown Lees Staffs 70 D6
Brown Street Suffk 64 C2
Brown's Green W Mids 58 C4
Brownber Cumb 95 H5
Brownheath Shrops 69 G3
Brownhill Abers 158 D3
Brownhills Fife 141 E1
Brownhills W Mids 58 C6
Brownieside Nthumb 125 E3
Browninghill Green Hants 26 D5
Brownlow Heath Ches 70 C6
Brownrigg Cumb 102 D2
Brownrigg Cumb 103 F5
Browns Hill Gloucs 38 D4
Brownsham Devon 20 C3
Brownsover Warwks 60 A3
Brownston Devon 6 D3
Brownston Green Norfk 65 G5
Broxa N York 99 E4
Broxbourne Herts 51 E1
Broxburn E Loth 133 F3
Broxburn W Loth 131 G2
Broxfield Nthumb 125 E3
Broxted Essex 51 G3
Broxton Ches 69 G5
Broxwood Herefs 45 F5
Broyle Side E Susx 17 E3
Bruan Highld 167 G2
Bruar P & K 146 C1
Brucefield Highld 163 F2
Bruchag Ag & B 118 C5
Bruera Ches 69 G6
Bruern Abbey Oxon 47 H1
Bruichladdich Ag & B 126 B1
Bruisyard Suffk 65 F2
Bruisyard Street Suffk 65 F2
Brumby Lincs 85 F6
Brund Staffs 71 F6
Brundall Norfk 65 F6
Brundish Suffk 65 E2
Brundish Street Suffk 65 E2
Brunnion Cnwll 2 C3
Brunslow Shrops 56 D4
Bruntcliffe W York 90 D2
Brunthwaite W York 90 B4
Bruntingthorpe Leics 60 B4
Brunton Fife 140 C2
Brunton Nthumb 125 E3
Brunton Wilts 25 H5
Brushford Somset 22 B2
Brushford Barton Devon 8 D5
Bruton Somset 24 B3
Bryan's Green Worcs 58 B2
Bryanston Dorset 12 C5
Bryant's Bottom Bucks 41 G4
Brydekirk D & G 111 F2
Brymbo Wrexhm 69 E5
Brympton Somset 11 E6
Bryn Ches 82 A2
Bryn Gt Man 81 H5
Bryn Neath 35 F3
Bryn Shrops 56 C4
Bryn Du IOA 78 C2
Bryn Gates Lancs 82 A5
Bryn Golau Rhondd 35 G3
Bryn Saith Marchog Denbgs 68 C5
Bryn-bwbach Gwynd 67 F4
Bryn-coch Neath 35 E4
Bryn-Eden Gwynd 67 G3
Bryn-Henllan Pembks 32 D6
Bryn-mawr Gwynd 66 B3
Bryn-newydd Denbgs 68 D4
Bryn-penarth Powys 56 A6
Bryn-y-bal Flints 81 E1
Bryn-y-Maen Conwy 79 H2
Bryn-yr-Eos Wrexhm 69 E4
Brynaman Carmth 35 E6
Brynberian Pembks 42 A3
Brynbryddan Neath 35 E3
Bryncae Rhondd 35 G2
Bryncethin Brdgnd 35 G3
Bryncir Gwynd 66 D4
Bryncroes Gwynd 66 B3
Bryncrug Gwynd 54 D6
Bryneglwys Denbgs 68 D5
Brynfields Wrexhm 69 E4
Brynford Flints 80 D2
Bryngwran IOA 78 C2
Bryngwyn Mons 37 E5
Bryngwyn Powys 45 E4
Brynhoffnant Cerdgn 42 C4
Bryning Lancs 88 C3
Brynithel Blae G 36 C4
Brynmawr Blae G 36 C5
Brynmenyn Brdgnd 35 F3
Brynmill Swans 34 D3
Brynna Rhondd 35 G2
Brynrefail Gwynd 79 E1
Brynrefail IOA 78 D3
Brynsadler Rhondd 36 A2
Brynsiencyn IOA 78 D1
Brynteg IOA 78 D3
Bualintur Highld 142 D6
Buarth-draw Flints 80 D3
Bubbenhall Warwks 59 F3
Bubwith E R Yk 92 A3
Buchanan Smithy Stirlg 129 F4
Buchanhaven Abers 159 G4
Buchanty P & K 139 G3
Buchany Stirlg 130 C5
Buchlyvie Stirlg 130 B4
Buck's Cross Devon 20 D3
Buck's Mills Devon 20 D3
Buckabank Cumb 103 H5
Buckden Cambs 62 A2
Buckden N York 96 C3
Buckenham Norfk 65 F6
Buckerell Devon 10 B5
Buckfast Devon 7 E4
Buckfastleigh Devon 7 E4
Buckhaven Fife 132 C5
Buckholt Mons 37 F6
Buckhorn Weston Dorset 24 C2
Buckhurst Hill Essex 29 E5
Buckie Moray 157 F6
Buckingham Bucks 49 E3
Buckland Bucks 41 G5
Buckland Devon 6 D2
Buckland Gloucs 47 F3
Buckland Hants 13 G4
Buckland Herefs 46 A5
Buckland Kent 19 F6
Buckland Oxon 40 B4
Buckland Surrey 28 C1
Buckland Brewer Devon 20 D3
Buckland Common Bucks 41 G5
Buckland Dinham Somset 24 C4
Buckland Filleigh Devon 8 B5
Buckland in the Moor Devon 7 E5
Buckland Monachorum Devon 6 B4
Buckland Newton Dorset 11 G5
Buckland Ripers Dorset 11 G3
Buckland St Mary Somset 10 C6
Buckland-Tout-Saints Devon 7 E2
Bucklebury Berks 40 D1
Bucklers Hard Hants 14 B4
Bucklesham Suffk 53 F5
Buckley Flints 81 E1
Buckley Green Warwks 58 D2
Buckley Mountain Flints 81 E1
Bucklow Hill Ches 82 B3
Buckminster Leics 73 F2
Bucknall Lincs 86 B2
Bucknall Staffs 70 D5
Bucknell Oxon 48 D2
Bucknell Shrops 56 D3
Buckpool Moray 157 F6
Bucks Green W Susx 16 B5
Bucks Hill Herts 28 B6
Bucks Horn Oak Hants 27 F3
Bucksburn Aber C 149 F5
Buckshead Cnwll 3 F4
Buckton E R Yk 99 G2
Buckton Herefs 56 D3
Buckton Nthumb 123 H3
Buckworth Cambs 61 G3
Budby Notts 84 D2
Budd's Titson Cnwll 5 F6
Buddileigh Staffs 70 C5
Buddon Angus 141 E3
Bude Cnwll 20 B1
Budge's Shop Cnwll 5 G2
Budlake Devon 9 G5
Budle Nthumb 125 E4
Budleigh Salterton Devon 9 G3
Budlett's Common E Susx 17 F4
Budock Water Cnwll 3 E3
Buerton Ches 70 B4
Bugbrooke Nhants 49 E5
Bugford Devon 7 F3
Buglawton Ches 82 D1
Bugle Cnwll 4 D2
Bugley Dorset 24 C2
Bugthorpe E R Yk 92 B5
Buildwas Shrops 57 F6
Builth Road Powys 44 C4
Builth Wells Powys 44 C4
Bulbourne Herts 41 G6
Bulbridge Wilts 25 F2
Bulby Lincs 73 H3
Buldoo Highld 166 D5
Bulford Wilts 25 G4
Bulford Barracks Wilts 25 G4
Bulkeley Ches 69 G5
Bulkington Warwks 59 G4
Bulkington Wilts 25 E5
Bulkworthy Devon 20 D2
Bull Bay IOA 78 D4
Bull's Green Herts 50 D2
Bull's Green Norfk 65 G5
Bullamore N York 97 G4
Bullbridge Derbys 72 A5
Bullbrook Berks 41 G1
Bullen's Green Herts 50 C1
Bulley Gloucs 46 C1
Bullgill Cumb 103 E4
Bullinghope Herefs 45 H3
Bullington Hants 26 C3
Bullington Lincs 86 A2
Bullington End Bucks 49 F4
Bullockstone Kent 31 E3
Bulmer Essex 52 B5
Bulmer N York 98 C2
Bulmer Tye Essex 52 B5
Bulphan Essex 29 G5
Bulstone Devon 10 B4
Bulstrode Herts 50 A1
Bulstrode Park Bucks 41 H3
Bulverhythe E Susx 18 A2
Bulwark Abers 159 E4
Bulwell Notts 72 C4
Bulwick Nhants 61 F5
Bumble's Green Essex 51 E1
Bunacaimb Highld 143 F3
Bunarkaig Highld 144 D3
Bunbury Ches 69 H6
Bunbury Heath Ches 69 H6
Bunchrew Highld 154 D4
Buncton W Susx 16 B3
Bundalloch Highld 152 C2
Bunessan Ag & B 135 F1
Bungay Suffk 65 F4
Bunker's Hill Lincs 74 C5
Bunnahabhain Ag & B 126 C2
Bunny Notts 72 C3
Buntait Highld 154 B2
Buntingford Herts 50 D4
Bunwell Norfk 64 D5
Bunwell Street Norfk 64 D5
Bupton Derbys 71 G4
Burbage Derbys 83 E2
Burbage Leics 59 G5
Burbage Wilts 25 H5
Burcher Herefs 45 F5
Burchett's Green Berks 41 F2
Burchett's Green E Susx 17 G4
Burcombe Wilts 25 F2
Burcot Oxon 40 D4
Burcot Worcs 58 C2
Burcote Shrops 57 H5
Burcott Bucks 41 G6
Burcott Bucks 49 G1
Burdale N York 92 C6
Bures Essex 52 C4
Burford Oxon 39 G5
Burford Shrops 57 F2
Burg Ag & B 135 F4
Burgates Hants 27 F2
Burge End Herts 50 B4
Burgess Hill W Susx 16 D3
Burgh Suffk 53 F6
Burgh by Sands Cumb 103 G6
Burgh Castle Norfk 65 G6
Burgh Heath Surrey 28 C2
Burgh Hill E Susx 17 H4
Burgh le Marsh Lincs 87 E1
Burgh next Aylsham Norfk 77 E2
Burgh on Bain Lincs 86 C3
Burgh St Margaret Norfk 77 G1
Burgh St Peter Norfk 65 G5
Burghclere Hants 26 C5
Burghead Moray 156 C6
Burghfield Berks 41 E1
Burghfield Common Berks 27 E6
Burghill Herefs 45 H4
Burghwallis S York 84 C6
Burham Kent 29 H2
Buriton Hants 15 F6
Burland Ches 70 A5
Burlawn Cnwll 4 D3
Burleigh Berks 41 G1
Burleigh Gloucs 38 C4
Burlescombe Devon 22 D1
Burleston Dorset 12 B4
Burlestone Devon 7 F2
Burley Hants 13 F5
Burley Rutlnd 73 F1
Burley Shrops 57 E3
Burley Gate Herefs 46 B4
Burley in Wharfedale W York 90 C4
Burley Lawn Hants 13 F5
Burley Street Hants 13 F5
Burley Wood Head W York 90 C4
Burleydam Ches 70 A4
Burlingham Green Norfk 77 G1
Burlingjobb Powys 45 E5
Burlington Shrops 70 C1
Burlton Shrops 69 G3
Burmarsh Kent 19 E5
Burmington Warwks 47 H3
Burn N York 91 G2
Burn Cross S York 84 A4
Burn Naze Lancs 88 B4
Burn of Cambus Stirlg 130 C5

Burnage Carlingcott

278

Burnage Gt Man 82 D4
Burnaston Derbys 71 H3
Burnbanks Cumb 104 B2
Burnbrae N Lans 120 C5
Burnby E R Yk 92 B4
Burndell W Susx 15 H4
Burnden Gt Man 82 B5
Burnedge Gt Man 82 D6
Burneside Cumb 95 F4
Burneston N York 97 F3
Burnett Somset 24 B6
Burnfoot Border 112 A6
Burnfoot Border 122 B1
Burnfoot D & G 110 D4
Burnfoot D & G 111 H4
Burnfoot D & G 112 A4
Burnfoot P & K 131 F5
Burnham Bucks 41 G2
Burnham Lincs 92 D1
Burnham Deepdale Norfk 76 A4
Burnham Green Herts 50 D2
Burnham Market Norfk 76 A4
Burnham Norton Norfk 76 A4
Burnham Overy Norfk 76 B4
Burnham Overy Staithe Norfk 76 B4
Burnham Thorpe Norfk 76 B4
Burnham-on-Crouch Essex 30 C6
Burnham-on-Sea Somset 23 F4
Burnhaven Abers 159 G3
Burnhead D & G 110 C4
Burnhervie Abers 158 C1
Burnhill Green Staffs 57 H5
Burnhope Dur 106 A6
Burnhouse N Ayrs 119 F4
Burniston N York 99 F4
Burnley Lancs 89 G3
Burnmoor Dur 106 B6
Burnmouth Border 123 G5
Burnopfield Dur 114 C1
Burnrigg Cumb 104 B6
Burnsall N York 90 B6
Burnside Angus 141 E5
Burnside Angus 140 D6
Burnside Fife 131 H6
Burnside Moray 156 D6
Burnside W Loth 131 G3
Burnside of Duntrune Angus 140 D3
Burnt Heath Essex 52 D3
Burnt Hill Berks 40 D2
Burnt Houses Dur 105 H2
Burnt Oak E Susx 17 F4
Burnt Yates N York 90 D6
Burntcommon Surrey 28 A1
Burntheath Derbys 71 G3
Burnthouse Cnwll 3 E3
Burntisland Fife 132 A4
Burntwood Staffs 71 E1
Burntwood Green Staffs 71 F1
Burnville Devon 8 B3
Burnworthy Somset 10 B6
Burpham Surrey 28 A1
Burpham W Susx 16 A2
Burradon Nthumb 113 G5
Burradon T & W 114 D3
Burrafirth Shet 169 j5
Burras Cnwll 2 D3
Burraton Cnwll 5 H3
Burraton Devon 6 D3
Burravoe Shet 169 j4
Burrells Cumb 104 C2
Burrelton P & K 140 B3
Burridge Devon 21 F4
Burridge Devon 10 D5
Burridge Hants 14 C5
Burrill N York 97 F4
Burringham Lincs 85 F6
Burrington Devon 21 F2
Burrington Herefs 57 E3
Burrington Somset 23 G5
Burrough End Cambs 63 E1
Burrough Green Cambs 63 F1
Burrough on the Hill Leics 73 E1
Burrow Lancs 95 G2
Burrow Somset 22 B3
Burrow Bridge Somset 23 F2
Burrowhill Surrey 27 H6
Burrows Cross Surrey 16 B6
Burry Swans 34 B3
Burry Port Carmth 34 B4
Burrygreen Swans 34 B3
Burscough Lancs 81 G6
Burscough Bridge Lancs 81 G6
Bursea E R Yk 92 B3
Burshill E R Yk 93 E4
Bursledon Hants 14 C4
Burslem Staffs 70 D5
Burstall Suffk 53 E5
Burstock Dorset 11 E5
Burston Norfk 64 D4
Burston Staffs 70 D3
Burstow Surrey 16 D5
Burstwick E R Yk 93 F2
Burtersett N York 96 B4
Burtholme Cumb 112 C1
Burthorpe Green Suffk 63 G2
Burthwaite Cumb 103 H5
Burthy Cnwll 3 G5
Burtle Hill Somset 23 G4
Burtoft Lincs 74 C3
Burton Ches 81 E2
Burton Ches 81 G1
Burton Dorset 11 G4
Burton Dorset 13 E4
Burton Lincs 85 G2
Burton Nthumb 125 E4
Burton Pembks 32 D2
Burton Somset 23 E4
Burton Somset 11 F6
Burton Wilts 38 C2
Burton Wilts 24 D2
Burton Agnes E R Yk 93 E6
Burton Bradstock Dorset 11 E3
Burton Coggles Lincs 73 G3
Burton Constable Hall E R Yk 93 F3
Burton Dassett Warwks 48 B4
Burton End Essex 51 F3
Burton End Suffk 51 G5
Burton Fleming E R Yk 99 F2
Burton Green Warwks 59 F3
Burton Green Wrexhm 69 F6
Burton Hastings Warwks 59 G4
Burton in Lonsdale N York 95 G2
Burton Joyce Notts 72 D4
Burton Latimer Nhants 61 E3
Burton Lazars Leics 73 E2
Burton Leonard N York 97 F1
Burton on the Wolds Leics 72 D2
Burton Overy Leics 60 C5
Burton Pedwardine Lincs 74 B4
Burton Pidsea E R Yk 93 F3
Burton Salmon N York 91 F2
Burton upon Stather Lincs 92 C1
Burton upon Trent Staffs 71 G2
Burton's Green Essex 52 B3
Burton-in-Kendal Cumb 95 F2
Burtonwood Ches 81 H4
Burwardsley Ches 69 G6
Burwarton Shrops 57 F4
Burwash E Susx 17 G4
Burwash Common E Susx 17 G4
Burwash Weald E Susx 17 G4
Burwell Cambs 63 E2
Burwell Lincs 86 D3
Burwen IOA 78 D4
Burwick Ork 169 b1
Bury Cambs 62 B4
Bury Gt Man 82 C6
Bury Somset 22 B2
Bury W Susx 16 A3
Bury End Beds 50 B4
Bury End Bucks 41 H4
Bury Green Herts 51 E3
Bury St Edmunds Suffk 63 H2
Burythorpe N York 98 D1
Busby E Rens 119 G5
Buscot Wilts 39 G4
Bush Abers 149 E1
Bush Cnwll 20 C1
Bush Bank Herefs 45 G4
Bush Green Norfk 65 E4
Bush Green Suffk 64 B1
Bush Hill Park Gt Lon 28 D6
Bushbury W Mids 58 B6
Bushby Leics 60 C6
Bushey Herts 28 B6
Bushey Heath Herts 28 B5
Bushley Worcs 46 D3
Bushley Green Worcs 46 D3
Bushmead Beds 61 G1
Bushton Wilts 39 E2
Busk Cumb 104 C4
Buslingthorpe Lincs 86 A3
Bussage Gloucs 38 D5
Bussex Somset 23 F3
Butcher Hill W York 89 H2
Butcher's Cross E Susx 17 F4
Butcombe Somset 23 H5
Butleigh Somset 23 H3
Butleigh Wootton Somset 23 H3
Butler's Cross Bucks 41 G5
Butler's Hill Notts 72 C5
Butlers Marston Warwks 48 A4
Butley Suffk 53 G6
Butley High Corner Suffk 53 G6
Butt Green Ches 70 B5
Butt Lane Staffs 70 C5
Butt's Green Essex 52 A1
Buttercrambe N York 92 A5
Butterdean Border 133 G1
Butterknowle Dur 105 H3
Butterleigh Devon 9 G5
Butterley Derbys 72 B5
Buttermere Cumb 103 F2
Buttermere Wilts 26 B5
Butters Green Staffs 70 C5
Buttershaw W York 90 C2
Butterstone P & K 139 H4
Butterton Staffs 70 C4
Butterton Staffs 71 F6
Butterwick Dur 106 C4
Butterwick Lincs 74 D4
Butterwick N York 98 C3
Butterwick N York 99 F2
Buttington Powys 69 E1
Buttonbridge Shrops 57 G3
Buttonoak Shrops 57 H3
Butts Ash Hants 14 B4
Buttsbear Cross Cnwll 20 C1
Buxhall Suffk 64 C1
Buxhall Fen Street Suffk 64 C1
Buxted E Susx 17 F4
Buxton Derbys 83 E2
Buxton Norfk 77 E2
Buxton Heath Norfk 77 E2
Bwlch Powys 44 D1
Bwlch-y-cibau Powys 68 D2
Bwlch-y-Ddar Powys 68 D2
Bwlch-y-ffridd Powys 56 A5
Bwlch-y-groes Pembks 42 C3
Bwlch-y-sarnau Powys 55 H3
Bwlchgwyn Wrexhm 69 E5
Bwlchllan Cerdgn 43 F5
Bwlchnewydd Carmth 33 H4
Bwlchtocyn Gwynd 66 C3
Bwlchyfadfa Cerdgn 43 E4
Bwlchymyrdd Swans 34 C4
Byermoor T & W 114 C1
Byers Garth Dur 106 C5
Byers Green Dur 106 B4
Byfield Nhants 48 C4
Byfleet Surrey 28 B2
Byford Herefs 45 G3
Bygrave Herts 50 D4
Byker T & W 114 D2
Bylchau Conwy 80 B1
Byley Ches 82 B2
Bynea Carmth 34 C4
Byrewalls Border 122 D4
Byrness Nthumb 113 E5
Bystock Devon 9 G3
Bythorn Cambs 61 F3
Byton Herefs 56 D2
Bywell Nthumb 114 B2
Byworth W Susx 15 H6

C

Cabbacott Devon 20 D3
Cabourne Lincs 86 B5
Cabrach Ag & B 126 D1
Cabrach Moray 157 F2
Cabus Lancs 88 C4
Cabvie Lodge Highld 153 F6
Cackle Street E Susx 17 E4
Cackle Street E Susx 17 H3
Cackle Street E Susx 18 B3
Cadbury Devon 9 F5
Cadbury Barton Devon 21 G2
Cadder E Duns 130 B2
Caddington Beds 50 B3
Caddonfoot Border 122 B3
Cade Street E Susx 17 G3
Cadeby Leics 59 G6
Cadeby S York 84 C5
Cadeleigh Devon 9 F5
Cadgwith Cnwll 3 E1
Cadham Fife 132 B5
Cadishead Gt Man 82 B4
Cadle Swans 34 D4
Cadley Lancs 88 D3
Cadley Wilts 25 G6
Cadley Wilts 25 H5
Cadmore End Bucks 41 F3
Cadnam Hants 13 G6
Cadney Lincs 85 H5
Cadole Flints 80 D1
Cadoxton V Glam 36 B1
Cadoxton Juxta-Neath Neath 35 E4
Cadsden Bucks 41 F5
Cadwst Denbgs 68 C4
Cae'r bryn Carmth 34 C6
Cae'r-bont Powys 35 E5
Caeathro Gwynd 67 E6
Caehopkin Powys 35 F5
Caenby Lincs 85 G4
Caenby Corner Lincs 85 G4
Caeo Carmth 43 G3
Caer Farchell Pembks 32 B4
Caerau Brdgnd 35 F4
Caerau Cardif 36 B2
Caerdeon Gwynd 67 F2
Caergeiliog IOA 78 C2
Caergwrle Flints 69 E6
Caerhun Conwy 79 G2
Caerlanrig Border 112 A5
Caerleon Newpt 36 D3
Caernarfon Gwynd 78 D1
Caernarfon Airport Gwynd 66 D6
Caernarfon Castle Gwynd 78 D1
Caerphilly Caerph 36 C3
Caersws Powys 55 H5
Caerwedros Cerdgn 42 D5
Caerwent Mons 37 F3
Caerwys Flints 80 D2
Caerynwch Gwynd 67 G2
Caggle Street Mons 37 E6
Caim IOA 79 F3
Cairinis W Isls 168 b4
Cairnbaan Ag & B 127 G4
Cairnbulg Abers 159 F6
Cairncross Border 133 H1
Cairncurran Inver 129 E2
Cairndow Ag & B 128 C6
Cairneyhill Fife 131 G4
Cairnfield House Moray 157 F5
Cairngarroch D & G 100 B5
Cairngrassie Abers 149 G4
Cairnie Abers 157 G3
Cairnorrie Abers 159 E3
Cairnryan D & G 108 B2
Cairnty Moray 157 E4
Caister-on-Sea Norfk 77 H1
Caistor Lincs 86 B5
Caistor St Edmund Norfk 65 E6
Cake Street Norfk 64 C4
Cakebole Worcs 58 B3
Calais Street Suffk 52 C5
Calanais W Isls 168 d8
Calbourne IOW 14 B2
Calceby Lincs 86 D2
Calcot Berks 41 E1
Calcot Flints 80 D2
Calcot Gloucs 39 F5
Calcot Row Berks 41 E1
Calcots Moray 157 E5
Calcott Kent 31 E2
Calcott Shrops 69 G1
Calcutt N York 91 E5
Calcutt Wilts 39 F4
Caldbeck Cumb 103 G4
Caldbergh N York 96 D3
Caldecote Cambs 61 G4
Caldecote Cambs 62 C1
Caldecote Herts 50 C5
Caldecote Nhants 49 E4
Caldecote Highfields Cambs 62 C1
Caldecott Nhants 61 F2
Caldecott Oxon 40 C4
Caldecott Rutlnd 61 E5
Caldecotte Bucks 49 G3
Calder Bridge Cumb 94 A5
Calder Grove W York 90 D1
Calder Vale Lancs 88 D4
Calderbank N Lans 130 D1
Calderbrook Gt Man 89 H1
Caldercruix N Lans 130 D2
Caldermill S Lans 120 A4
Caldermore Gt Man 89 H1
Calderwood S Lans 120 A5
Caldicot Mons 37 F3
Caldwell N York 106 A2
Caldy Mersyd 81 E3
Caledfwlch Carmth 43 G2
Calendra Cnwll 3 G4
Calenick Cnwll 3 F4
Calford Green Suffk 51 H5
Calfsound Ork 169 c3
Calgary Ag & B 135 F4
Califer Moray 156 C5
California Falk 131 E3
California Norfk 77 H1
California Cross Devon 6 D3
Calke Derbys 72 A2
Callakille Highld 151 G4
Callander Stirlg 130 C6
Callanish W Isls 168 d8
Callaughton Shrops 57 F5
Callestick Cnwll 3 E5
Calligarry Highld 143 F4
Callington Cnwll 5 G3
Callingwood Staffs 71 G2
Callow Herefs 45 H3
Callow End Worcs 46 D4
Callow Hill Wilts 39 E3
Callow Hill Worcs 57 H3
Callow Hill Worcs 58 C2
Callows Grave Worcs 57 F2
Calmore Hants 13 G6
Calmsden Gloucs 39 E5
Calne Wilts 39 E1
Calow Derbys 84 B2
Calshot Hants 14 C4
Calstock Cnwll 6 B4
Calstone Wellington Wilts 39 E1
Calthorpe Norfk 77 E3
Calthorpe Street Norfk 77 G2
Calthwaite Cumb 104 A4
Calton N York 89 G5
Calton Staffs 71 F5
Calton Green Staffs 71 F5
Calveley Ches 70 A6
Calver Derbys 83 G2
Calver Hill Herefs 45 F4
Calver Sough Derbys 83 G2
Calverhall Shrops 70 A4
Calverleigh Devon 9 F6
Calverley W York 90 C3
Calvert Bucks 49 E2
Calverton Bucks 49 F3
Calverton Notts 72 D5
Calvine P & K 146 C1
Calvo Cumb 103 E5
Calzeat Border 121 F3
Cam Gloucs 38 B4
Camas Luinie Highld 152 D2
Camasachoirce Highld 136 B6
Camasine Highld 136 B6
Camastianavaig Highld 151 E3
Camault Muir Highld 154 C3
Camber E Susx 18 C3
Camberley Surrey 27 G5
Camberwell Gt Lon 28 D4
Camblesforth N York 91 G2
Cambo Nthumb 114 B4
Cambois Nthumb 115 E4
Camborne Cnwll 2 D4
Camborne Cmbs 62 B1
Cambridge Cambs 62 D1
Cambridge Gloucs 38 B5
Cambridge Airport Cambs 62 D1
Cambrose Cnwll 2 D4
Cambus Clacks 131 E4
Cambus o' May Abers 148 B4
Cambusavie Platform Highld 162 D3
Cambusbarron Stirlg 130 D4
Cambuskenneth Stirlg 130 D4
Cambuslang S Lans 120 A5
Cambuswallace S Lans 121 E3
Camden Town Gt Lon 28 D4
Cameley Somset 24 B5
Camelford Cnwll 5 E4
Camelon Falk 131 E3
Camer's Green Worcs 46 C3
Camerory Highld 156 B2
Camerton Cumb 102 D3
Camerton Somset 24 B5
Camghouran P & K 138 C5
Camieston Border 122 C2
Cammachmore Abers 149 G4
Cammeringham Lincs 85 G3
Camore Highld 163 E3
Campbeltown Ag & B 117 F2
Campbeltown Airport Ag & B 117 F2
Camperdown T & W 114 D3
Cample D & G 110 C4
Campmuir Angus 140 B3
Camps W Loth 131 G2
Camps End Cambs 51 G5
Campsall S York 84 C6
Campsea Ash Suffk 65 F1
Campton Beds 50 B4
Camptown Border 112 D6
Camrose Pembks 32 D4
Camserney P & K 139 E5
Camusnagaul Highld 161 E3
Camusnagaul Highld 144 C2
Camusteel Highld 151 G3
Camusterrach Highld 151 G3
Canada Hants 26 A1
Canal Foot Cumb 94 D3
Canaston Bridge Pembks 33 E3
Candacraig Abers 148 A4
Candle Street Suffk 64 C3
Candlesby Lincs 87 E1
Candover Green Shrops 57 E6
Candyburn Border 121 E4
Cane End Oxon 41 E2
Canewdon Essex 30 C5
Canford Bottom Dorset 12 D5
Canford Cliffs Dorset 12 D3
Canford Heath Dorset 12 D4
Canford Magna Dorset 12 D4
Canhams Green Suffk 64 C2
Canisbay Highld 167 G6
Canklow S York 84 B4
Canley W Mids 59 F3
Cann Dorset 24 D1
Cannich Highld 154 B2
Canning Town Gt Lon 29 E4
Cannington Somset 23 E3
Cannock Staffs 71 E1
Cannock Wood Staffs 71 E1
Cannon Bridge Herefs 45 G3
Canon Frome Herefs 46 B3
Canon Pyon Herefs 45 G4
Canonbie D & G 112 A2
Canons Ashby Nhants 48 D4
Canonstown Cnwll 2 C3
Canterbury Kent 31 E2
Canterbury Cathedral Kent 31 E2
Cantley Norfk 65 F6
Cantlop Shrops 57 E6
Canton Cardif 36 C2
Cantraywood Highld 155 F4
Cantsfield Lancs 95 G2
Canvey Island Essex 30 B4
Canwick Lincs 85 G2
Canworthy Water Cnwll 5 F5
Caol Highld 144 C2
Caolas Scalpaigh W Isls 168 d6
Caoles Ag & B 134 C4
Caonich Highld 144 C4
Capel Kent 17 G6
Capel Surrey 16 C5
Capel Bangor Cerdgn 54 D3
Capel Betws Lleucu Cerdgn 43 F5
Capel Coch IOA 78 D3
Capel Curig Conwy 67 G6
Capel Cynon Cerdgn 42 D4
Capel Dewi Carmth 43 E1
Capel Dewi Cerdgn 43 E3
Capel Garmon Conwy 67 H6
Capel Green Suffk 53 G6
Capel Gwyn Carmth 43 E1
Capel Gwyn IOA 78 C2
Capel Gwynfe Carmth 43 G1
Capel Hendre Carmth 34 C5
Capel Isaac Carmth 43 F2
Capel Iwan Carmth 42 C3
Capel le Ferne Kent 19 F5
Capel Llanilltern Cardif 36 B2
Capel Mawr IOA 78 D2
Capel Seion Cerdgn 54 D3
Capel St Andrew Suffk 53 G5
Capel St Mary Suffk 52 D4
Capel Trisant Cerdgn 55 E3
Capel-Dewi Cerdgn 54 D4
Capel-y-ffin Powys 45 E2
Capel-y-graig Gwynd 79 E2
Capelles Guern 174 g2
Capeluchaf Gwynd 66 D5
Capelulo Conwy 79 G2
Capenhurst Ches 81 F2
Capernwray Lancs 95 F2
Capheaton Nthumb 114 B3
Caplaw E Rens 119 F5
Capon's Green Suffk 65 E2
Cappercleuch Border 121 G2
Capstone Kent 30 A2
Capton Devon 7 F3
Capton Somset 22 D3
Caputh P & K 139 H4
Car Colston Notts 73 E4
Caradon Town Cnwll 5 F3
Carbeth Inn Stirlg 129 G3
Carbis Cnwll 4 D2
Carbis Bay Cnwll 2 C4
Carbost Highld 150 D2
Carbost Highld 150 D3
Carbrook S York 84 B4
Carbrooke Norfk 64 B6
Carburton Notts 84 D2
Carclaze Cnwll 3 H5
Carclew Cnwll 3 E4
Carcroft S York 84 C6
Cardenden Fife 132 A5
Cardeston Shrops 69 F1
Cardewlees Cumb 103 G5
Cardhu Moray 156 D3
Cardiff Cardif 36 C2
Cardiff Airport V Glam 22 D6
Cardigan Cerdgn 42 B4
Cardinal's Green Cambs 51 G5
Cardington Beds 50 B5
Cardington Shrops 57 E5
Cardinham Cnwll 5 E3
Cardrain D & G 100 C3
Cardrona Border 121 G3
Cardross Ag & B 129 E3
Cardryne D & G 100 C3
Cardurnock Cumb 103 F6
Careby Lincs 73 H2
Careston Angus 141 E6
Carew Pembks 33 E2
Carew Cheriton Pembks 33 E2
Carew Newton Pembks 33 E2
Carey Herefs 46 A2
Carfin N Lans 120 B5
Carfraemill Border 122 B5
Cargate Green Norfk 77 G1
Cargen D & G 110 D2
Cargenbridge D & G 110 D2
Cargill P & K 140 B3
Cargo Cumb 103 H6
Cargreen Cnwll 6 B4
Cargurrel Cnwll 3 F3
Carham Nthumb 123 E3
Carhampton Somset 22 C3
Carharrack Cnwll 3 E4
Carie P & K 138 C5
Carinish W Isls 168 b4
Carisbrooke IOW 14 C2
Cark Cumb 94 D2
Carkeel Cnwll 5 H2
Carlabhagh W Isls 168 d8
Carland Cross Cnwll 3 F5
Carlbury Dur 106 B2
Carlby Lincs 73 H1
Carlcroft Nthumb 113 E6
Carlecotes S York 83 G5
Carleen Cnwll 2 D3
Carlesmoor N York 97 E2
Carleton Cumb 104 A5
Carleton Cumb 104 B3
Carleton Cumb 94 A6
Carleton Lancs 88 B3
Carleton N York 89 H4
Carleton W York 91 F2
Carleton Forehoe Norfk 64 C6
Carleton Rode Norfk 64 D5
Carleton St Peter Norfk 65 F6
Carlidnack Cnwll 3 E3
Carlin How N York 107 F3
Carlincraig Abers 158 C3
Carlingcott Somset 24 C5

Carlisle
Cheselbourne
279

Carlisle *Cumb* 103 H6
Carlisle Airport *Cumb* 104 B6
Carloggas *Cnwll* 4 B2
Carlops *Border* 121 F5
Carloway *W Isls* 168 d8
Carlton *Beds* 49 H5
Carlton *Cambs* 51 G6
Carlton *Dur* 106 C3
Carlton *Leics* 59 G6
Carlton *N York* 96 D3
Carlton *N York* 98 B3
Carlton *N York* 91 G2
Carlton *Notts* 72 D4
Carlton *S York* 84 A6
Carlton *Suffk* 65 F2
Carlton *W York* 90 D2
Carlton Colville *Suffk* 65 G4
Carlton Curlieu *Leics* 60 C5
Carlton Green *Cambs* 51 G6
Carlton Husthwaite *N York* 97 H2
Carlton in Lindrick *Notts* 84 D3
Carlton Miniott *N York* 97 G3
Carlton Scroop *Lincs* 73 G4
Carlton-in-Cleveland *N York* 97 H5
Carlton-le-Moorland *Lincs* 73 G6
Carlton-on-Trent *Notts* 85 F1
Carluddon *Cnwll* 3 H5
Carluke *S Lans* 120 C4
Carlyon Bay *Cnwll* 3 H5
Carmacoup *S Lans* 120 B2
Carmarthen *Carmth* 42 D1
Carmel *Carmth* 34 C6
Carmel *Flints* 80 D2
Carmel *Gwynd* 67 E5
Carmichael *S Lans* 120 D3
Carminowe *Cnwll* 2 D2
Carmunnock *C Glas* 119 H5
Carmyle *C Glas* 120 A6
Carmyllie *Angus* 141 E4
Carn Brea *Cnwll* 2 D4
Carn-gorm *Highld* 152 D1
Carnaby *E R Yk* 99 G1
Carnbee *Fife* 132 D6
Carnbo *P & K* 131 G5
Carnbrogie *Abers* 158 D2
Carndu *Highld* 152 C2
Carnduff *S Lans* 120 A4
Carne *Cnwll* 3 E2
Carne *Cnwll* 3 G4
Carne *Cnwll* 4 C2
Carnell *E Ayrs* 119 F3
Carnewas *Cnwll* 4 B3
Carnforth *Lancs* 95 F2
Carnhedryn *Pembks* 32 B4
Carnhell Green *Cnwll* 2 D3
Carnie *Abers* 149 F5
Carnkie *Cnwll* 3 E3
Carnkiet *Cnwll* 3 E5
Carno *Powys* 55 G5
Carnoch *Highld* 144 A4
Carnock *Fife* 131 G4
Carnon Downs *Cnwll* 3 E4
Carnousie *Abers* 158 C4
Carnoustie *Angus* 141 E3
Carnwath *S Lans* 120 D4
Carnyorth *Cnwll* 2 A3
Carol Green *W Mids* 59 E3
Carpalla *Cnwll* 3 G5
Carperby *N York* 96 C4
Carr *Gt Man* 89 F1
Carr *S York* 84 C4
Carr Gate *W York* 90 D2
Carr Shield *Nthumb* 105 E5
Carr Vale *Derbys* 84 B2
Carradale *Ag & B* 117 G4
Carrbridge *Highld* 155 G1
Carrbrook *Gt Man* 83 E5
Carrefour *Jersey* 174 b3
Carreglefn *IOA* 78 C4
Carrhouse *Lincs* 85 E5
Carrick *Ag & B* 127 H4
Carrick Castle *Ag & B* 128 C4
Carriden *Falk* 131 F3
Carrington *Gt Man* 82 B4
Carrington *Lincs* 74 C6
Carrington *Mdloth* 121 H5
Carrismerry *Cnwll* 4 D2
Carrog *Conwy* 67 G5
Carrog *Denbgs* 68 C4
Carron *Falk* 131 E3
Carron *Moray* 156 D3
Carron Bridge *Stirlg* 130 D3
Carronbridge *D & G* 110 C5
Carronshore *Falk* 131 E3
Carrow Hill *Mons* 37 E3
Carruth House *Inver* 129 E2
Carrutherstown *D & G* 111 E2
Carrville *Dur* 106 B5
Carrycoats Hall *Nthumb* 113 F3
Carsaig *Ag & B* 135 G1
Carse Gray *Angus* 140 D5
Carseriggan *D & G* 109 E1
Carsethorn *D & G* 102 D6
Carshalton *Gt Lon* 28 D2
Carsington *Derbys* 71 G5
Carskey *Ag & B* 117 F1
Carsluith *D & G* 101 F6
Carsphairn *D & G* 109 G4
Carstairs *S Lans* 120 D4
Carstairs Junction *S Lans* 120 D4
Carswell Marsh *Oxon* 40 B4
Carter's Clay *Hants* 26 A2
Carters Green *Essex* 51 F2
Carterton *Oxon* 39 G5
Carterway Heads *Dur* 105 G5
Carthew *Cnwll* 3 G5
Carthorpe *N York* 97 F3
Cartington *Nthumb* 124 C1
Cartland *S Lans* 120 C4
Cartledge *Derbys* 83 H2
Cartmel *Cumb* 95 E3
Cartmel Fell *Cumb* 95 E4
Carway *Carmth* 34 B5
Carwinley *Cumb* 112 A2
Cashe's Green *Gloucs* 38 C5
Cashmoor *Dorset* 12 D6
Cassington *Oxon* 40 C5
Cassop Colliery *Dur* 106 C5
Castallack *Cnwll* 2 B2
Castell *Conwy* 79 G2
Castell-y-bwch *Torfn* 36 D3
Casterton *Lancs* 95 G3
Castle *Cnwll* 5 E2
Castle Acre *Norfk* 76 A1
Castle Ashby *Nhants* 49 G5
Castle Bolton *N York* 96 D4
Castle Bromwich *W Mids* 58 D4
Castle Bytham *Lincs* 73 G2
Castle Caereinion *Powys* 56 B6
Castle Camps *Cambs* 51 G5
Castle Carrock *Cumb* 104 B6
Castle Cary *Somset* 24 B2
Castle Combe *Wilts* 38 C2
Castle Donington *Leics* 72 B3
Castle Douglas *D & G* 110 B1
Castle Eaton *Wilts* 39 F4
Castle Eden *Dur* 106 D5
Castle End *Cambs* 61 G6
Castle Frome *Herefs* 46 B4
Castle Gate *Cnwll* 2 B3
Castle Green *Cumb* 95 F4
Castle Green *Surrey* 27 H5
Castle Gresley *Derbys* 71 H2
Castle Hedingham *Essex* 52 B4
Castle Hill *Kent* 17 H6
Castle Hill *Suffk* 53 E5
Castle Kennedy *D & G* 100 B6
Castle Lachlan *Ag & B* 128 B5
Castle Morris *Pembks* 32 C5
Castle O'er *D & G* 111 G4
Castle Pulverbatch *Shrops* 56 D6
Castle Rising *Norfk* 75 G2
Castle Street *W York* 89 H2
Castle Stuart *Highld* 155 F4
Castlebay *W Isls* 168 a1
Castlebythe *Pembks* 32 D5
Castlecary *Falk* 130 D3
Castleford *W York* 91 E2
Castlehill *Border* 121 G3
Castlehill *Highld* 167 F5
Castlehill *W Duns* 129 E3
Castlemartin *Pembks* 32 C1
Castlemilk *C Glas* 119 H5
Castlemorton *Worcs* 46 C3
Castlerigg *Cumb* 103 G2
Castleside *Dur* 105 G5
Castlethorpe *Bucks* 49 F4
Castlethorpe *Lincs* 85 G5
Castleton *Border* 112 B4
Castleton *Derbys* 83 F3
Castleton *Gt Man* 82 D6
Castleton *N York* 107 F2
Castleton *Newpt* 36 D3
Castletown *Dorset* 11 G2
Castletown *Highld* 167 F5
Castletown *IOM* 174 k2
Castletown *T & W* 115 E1
Castley *N York* 90 D4
Caston *Norfk* 64 B5
Castor *Cambs* 61 G5
Caswell Bay *Swans* 34 C3
Cat and Fiddle *Ches* 83 E2
Cat's Ash *Newpt* 37 E3
Catacol *N Ayrs* 118 A4
Catbrook *Mons* 37 F4
Catch *Flints* 80 D2
Catchall *Cnwll* 2 B3
Catchem's Corner *W Mids* 59 E3
Catchgate *Dur* 106 A6
Catcliffe *S York* 84 B3
Catcomb *Wilts* 39 E2
Catcott *Somset* 23 G3
Catcott Burtle *Somset* 23 G3
Catel *Guern* 174 g2
Caterham *Surrey* 28 D1
Catfield *Norfk* 77 G2
Catfield Common *Norfk* 77 G2
Catfirth *Shet* 169 j3
Catford *Gt Lon* 29 E3
Catforth *Lancs* 88 C3
Cathcart *C Glas* 119 H5
Cathedine *Powys* 44 D2
Catherine Slack *W York* 90 B2
Catherine-de-Barnes *W Mids* 59 E3
Catherington *Hants* 15 E5
Catherston Leweston *Dorset* 10 D4
Catherton *Shrops* 57 G3
Catisfield *Hants* 14 D4
Catley *Herefs* 46 B4
Catley Lane Head *Gt Man* 89 G1
Catlodge *Highld* 146 A4
Catlow *Lancs* 89 G3
Catlowdy *Cumb* 112 B2
Catmere End *Essex* 51 F5
Catmore *Berks* 40 C2
Caton *Devon* 7 E5
Caton *Lancs* 95 F1
Caton Green *Lancs* 95 F1
Cator Court *Devon* 8 D2
Catrine *E Ayrs* 119 G2
Catsfield *E Susx* 17 H3
Catsfield Stream *E Susx* 17 H3
Catsgore *Somset* 23 H2
Catsham *Somset* 24 A3
Catshill *Worcs* 58 C3
Catstree *Shrops* 57 H5
Cattadale *Ag & B* 117 F1
Cattal *N York* 91 F5
Cattawade *Suffk* 53 E4
Catterall *Lancs* 88 C4
Catteralslane *Shrops* 69 H4
Catterick *N York* 97 F5
Catterick Bridge *N York* 97 E5
Catterick Garrison *N York* 97 E5
Catterlen *Cumb* 104 B3
Catterline *Abers* 149 F2
Catterton *N York* 91 F4
Catteshall *Surrey* 27 H4
Catthorpe *Leics* 60 B3
Cattishall *Suffk* 64 A2
Cattistock *Dorset* 11 F4
Catton *Cumb* 105 E6
Catton *N York* 97 G3
Catton *Norfk* 77 E1
Catwick *E R Yk* 93 E4
Catworth *Cambs* 61 G3
Caudle Green *Gloucs* 38 D5
Caulcott *Beds* 50 A5
Caulcott *Oxon* 48 C2
Cauldcots *Angus* 141 F4
Cauldhame *Stirlg* 130 C4
Cauldmill *Border* 122 C1
Cauldon *Staffs* 71 F5
Cauldon Lowe *Staffs* 71 F5
Cauldwell *Derbys* 71 G2
Caulkerbush *D & G* 102 C6
Caulside *D & G* 112 B3
Caundle Marsh *Dorset* 11 G6
Caunsall *Worcs* 58 B3
Caunton *Notts* 73 E6
Causeway *Hants* 27 F1
Causeway End *Cumb* 95 F3
Causeway End *D & G* 101 E6
Causeway End *Essex* 51 H3
Causewayend *S Lans* 121 E3
Causewayhead *Cumb* 103 E5
Causewayhead *Stirlg* 130 D5
Causey Park *Nthumb* 114 C5
Causey Park Bridge *Nthumb* 114 D5
Causeyend *Abers* 159 E1
Cavendish *Suffk* 52 B5
Cavenham *Suffk* 63 G2
Caversfield *Oxon* 48 D2
Caversham *Berks* 41 E2
Caverswall *Staffs* 70 D4
Caverton Mill *Border* 123 E2
Cavil *E R Yk* 92 B3
Cawdor *Highld* 155 G4
Cawkwell *Lincs* 86 C3
Cawood *N York* 91 G3
Cawsand *Cnwll* 6 B3
Cawston *Norfk* 76 D2
Cawston *Warwks* 59 H3
Cawthorn *N York* 98 C4
Cawthorne *S York* 83 H5
Cawton *N York* 98 B2
Caxton *Cambs* 62 B1
Caxton End *Cambs* 62 B1
Caxton Gibbet *Cambs* 62 B1
Caynham *Shrops* 57 F3
Caythorpe *Lincs* 73 G5
Caythorpe *Notts* 72 D5
Cayton *N York* 99 F3
Ceann a Bhaigh *W Isls* 168 b5
Ceannacroc Lodge *Highld* 144 D6
Cearsiadar *W Isls* 168 e7
Ceciliford *Mons* 37 F5
Cefn *Newpt* 36 D3
Cefn Berain *Conwy* 80 B2
Cefn Byrle *Powys* 35 F5
Cefn Canel *Powys* 69 E3
Cefn Coch *Powys* 68 C3
Cefn Cribwr *Brdgnd* 35 F2
Cefn Cross *Brdgnd* 35 F2
Cefn Mably *Caerph* 36 C3
Cefn-brith *Conwy* 68 B5
Cefn-bryn-brain *Carmth* 35 E6
Cefn-coed-y-cymmer *Myr Td* 36 A5
Cefn-ddwysarn *Gwynd* 68 B4
Cefn-Einion *Shrops* 56 C4
Cefn-mawr *Wrexhm* 69 E4
Cefn-y-bedd *Wrexhm* 69 E6
Cefn-y-pant *Carmth* 33 F4
Cefneithin *Carmth* 34 C6
Cefngorwydd *Powys* 44 B4
Cefnpennar *Rhondd* 36 B4
Ceint *IOA* 78 D2
Cellan *Cerdgn* 43 F4
Cellardyke *Fife* 133 E5
Cellarhead *Staffs* 70 D5
Celleron *Cumb* 104 B3
Celynen *Caerph* 36 C4
Cemaes *IOA* 78 C4
Cemmaes *Powys* 55 F6
Cemmaes Road *Powys* 55 F6
Cenarth *Cerdgn* 42 C3
Cerbyd *Pembks* 32 B4
Ceres *Fife* 140 D1
Cerne Abbas *Dorset* 11 G5
Cerney Wick *Gloucs* 39 E4
Cerrigceinwen *IOA* 78 D2
Cerrigydrudion *Conwy* 68 B5
Cess *Norfk* 77 G2
Ceunant *Gwynd* 67 E6
Chaceley *Gloucs* 46 D2
Chacewater *Cnwll* 3 E4
Chackmore *Bucks* 49 E3
Chacombe *Nhants* 48 C4
Chadbury *Worcs* 47 F4
Chadderton *Gt Man* 82 D5
Chadderton Fold *Gt Man* 82 D5
Chaddesden *Derbys* 72 B4
Chaddesley Corbett *Worcs* 58 B3
Chaddlehanger *Devon* 8 B2
Chaddleworth *Berks* 40 B2
Chadlington *Oxon* 48 B1
Chadshunt *Warwks* 48 B4
Chadwell *Leics* 73 E2
Chadwell *Shrops* 70 C1
Chadwell End *Beds* 61 G2
Chadwell Heath *Gt Lon* 29 F5
Chadwell St Mary *Essex* 29 G4
Chadwick *Worcs* 58 A2
Chadwick End *W Mids* 59 E3
Chadwick Green *Mersyd* 81 G5
Chaffcombe *Somset* 10 D6
Chafford Hundred *Essex* 29 G4
Chagford *Devon* 8 D3
Chailey *E Susx* 17 E3
Chainbridge *Cambs* 62 C5
Chainhurst *Kent* 17 H6
Chalbury *Dorset* 12 D5
Chalbury Common *Dorset* 12 D5
Chaldon *Surrey* 28 D2
Chale *IOW* 14 C1
Chale Green *IOW* 14 C1
Chalfont Common *Bucks* 28 A5
Chalfont St Giles *Bucks* 41 H4
Chalfont St Peter *Bucks* 28 A5
Chalford *Gloucs* 38 D5
Chalford *Oxon* 41 E4
Chalford *Wilts* 24 D4
Chalgrave *Beds* 50 A3
Chalgrove *Oxon* 41 E4
Chalk *Kent* 29 G3
Chalk End *Essex* 51 G2
Chalkhouse Green *Berks* 41 E2
Chalkway *Somset* 10 D5
Chalkwell *Kent* 30 C2
Challaborough *Devon* 6 D2
Challacombe *Devon* 21 G5
Challoch *D & G* 109 F1
Challock *Kent* 30 D1
Chalmington *Dorset* 11 F5
Chalton *Beds* 50 A3
Chalton *Beds* 50 B6
Chalton *Hants* 15 E5
Chalvey *Berks* 41 H2
Chalvington *E Susx* 17 F2
Chambers Green *Kent* 18 C6
Chandler's Cross *Herts* 28 B6
Chandler's Ford *Hants* 14 C6
Chandlers Cross *Worcs* 46 C3
Channel's End *Beds* 61 G1
Chantry *Somset* 24 C4
Chantry *Suffk* 53 E5
Chapel *Cumb* 103 F3
Chapel *Fife* 132 B4
Chapel Allerton *Somset* 23 G4
Chapel Allerton *W York* 90 D3
Chapel Amble *Cnwll* 4 D3
Chapel Brampton *Nhants* 60 C2
Chapel Chorlton *Staffs* 70 C4
Chapel Cross *E Susx* 17 G3
Chapel End *Beds* 50 B5
Chapel End *Beds* 61 G1
Chapel End *Cambs* 61 G4
Chapel End *Warwks* 59 F5
Chapel Field *Gt Man* 82 C5
Chapel Green *Warwks* 59 F4
Chapel Green *Warwks* 48 C5
Chapel Haddlesey *N York* 91 G2
Chapel Hill *Abers* 159 F3
Chapel Hill *Lincs* 74 B5
Chapel Hill *Mons* 37 F4
Chapel Hill *N York* 90 D4
Chapel Lawn *Shrops* 56 C3
Chapel le Dale *N York* 95 H2
Chapel Leigh *Somset* 22 D2
Chapel Milton *Derbys* 83 E3
Chapel of Garioch *Abers* 158 C1
Chapel Rossan *D & G* 100 B5
Chapel Row *Berks* 40 D1
Chapel Row *E Susx* 17 G3
Chapel Row *Essex* 30 B6
Chapel St Leonards *Lincs* 87 F2
Chapel Stile *Cumb* 94 D5
Chapel Town *Cnwll* 3 F5
Chapel-en-le-Frith *Derbys* 83 E3
Chapelbridge *Cambs* 62 B5
Chapelend Way *Essex* 51 H5
Chapelgate *Lincs* 74 D2
Chapelhall *N Lans* 120 B6
Chapelhope *Border* 121 G1
Chapelknowe *D & G* 111 G2
Chapels *Cumb* 94 C3
Chapelton *Angus* 141 F4
Chapelton *Devon* 21 F3
Chapelton *S Lans* 120 A4
Chapeltown *Lancs* 89 E1
Chapeltown *Moray* 156 D1
Chapeltown *Staffs* 84 A4
Chapmans Well *Devon* 5 G5
Chapmanslade *Wilts* 24 D4
Chapmore End *Herts* 50 D2
Chappel *Essex* 52 C3
Charaton *Cnwll* 5 F3
Chard *Somset* 10 D5
Chard Junction *Somset* 10 D5
Chardleigh Green *Somset* 10 D6
Chardstock *Devon* 10 C5
Charfield *Gloucs* 38 B3
Chargrove *Gloucs* 47 E1
Charing *Kent* 30 C1
Charing Heath *Kent* 30 C1
Charing Hill *Kent* 30 C1
Charingworth *Gloucs* 47 G3
Charlbury *Oxon* 48 B1
Charlcombe *Somset* 24 C6
Charlcutt *Wilts* 39 E2
Charlecote *Warwks* 47 H5
Charles *Devon* 21 G4
Charles Tye *Suffk* 52 D6
Charleshill *Surrey* 27 G4
Charleston *Angus* 140 D4
Charlestown *Aber C* 149 G4
Charlestown *Cnwll* 3 H5
Charlestown *Derbys* 83 E4
Charlestown *Dorset* 11 G2
Charlestown *Fife* 131 G3
Charlestown *Gt Man* 82 C5
Charlestown *Highld* 160 B1
Charlestown *Highld* 155 E4
Charlestown *W York* 90 A2
Charlestown *W York* 90 C3
Charlesworth *Derbys* 83 E4
Charlinch *Somset* 23 E3
Charlottetown *Fife* 132 B6
Charlton *Gt Lon* 29 E4
Charlton *Hants* 26 B4
Charlton *Herts* 50 C3
Charlton *Nhants* 48 D3
Charlton *Nthumb* 113 E3
Charlton *Oxon* 40 B3
Charlton *Shrops* 70 A1
Charlton *Somset* 23 F2
Charlton *Somset* 24 B4
Charlton *Somset* 24 B4
Charlton *Surrey* 28 B3
Charlton *W Susx* 15 G5
Charlton *Wilts* 25 E1
Charlton *Wilts* 38 D3
Charlton *Wilts* 25 G5
Charlton *Worcs* 58 A2
Charlton *Worcs* 47 F4
Charlton Abbots *Gloucs* 47 F2
Charlton Adam *Somset* 24 A2
Charlton Hill *Shrops* 57 F6
Charlton Horethorne *Somset* 24 B1
Charlton Kings *Gloucs* 47 E1
Charlton Mackrell *Somset* 23 H2
Charlton Marshall *Dorset* 12 C5
Charlton Musgrove *Somset* 24 C2
Charlton on the Hill *Dorset* 12 C5
Charlton-all-Saints *Wilts* 25 G2
Charlton-on-Otmoor *Oxon* 40 D6
Charlwood *Hants* 27 E2
Charlwood *Surrey* 16 C5
Charminster *Dorset* 11 G4
Charmouth *Dorset* 10 D4
Charndon *Bucks* 49 E2
Charney Bassett *Oxon* 40 B4
Charnock Green *Lancs* 88 D1
Charnock Richard *Lancs* 88 D1
Charsfield *Suffk* 65 E1
Chart Corner *Kent* 30 B1
Chart Hill *Kent* 30 B1
Chart Sutton *Kent* 30 B1
Charter Alley *Hants* 26 D5
Charterhall *Border* 123 E4
Charterhouse *Somset* 23 H5
Chartershall *Stirlg* 130 D4
Charterville Allotments *Oxon* 40 A5
Chartham *Kent* 31 E1
Chartham Hatch *Kent* 31 E2
Chartridge *Bucks* 41 G5
Chartway Street *Kent* 30 B1
Charwelton *Nhants* 48 D5
Chase Terrace *Staffs* 71 E1
Chasetown *Staffs* 58 C6
Chastleton *Oxon* 47 H2
Chasty *Devon* 5 G6
Chatburn *Lancs* 89 F4
Chatcull *Staffs* 70 C3
Chatham *Caerph* 36 C3
Chatham *Kent* 30 A3
Chatham Green *Essex* 51 H2
Chathill *Nthumb* 125 E4
Chatley *Worcs* 46 D5
Chatsworth House *Derbys* 83 G2
Chattenden *Kent* 30 A3
Chatter End *Essex* 51 F3
Chatteris *Cambs* 62 C4
Chatterton *Lancs* 89 F1
Chattisham *Suffk* 52 D5
Chatto *Border* 123 E1
Chatton *Nthumb* 124 D4
Chaul End *Beds* 50 B3
Chawleigh *Devon* 21 G2
Chawley *Oxon* 40 C5
Chawston *Beds* 61 G1
Chawton *Hants* 27 E3
Chaxhill *Gloucs* 38 B6
Chazey Heath *Oxon* 41 E2
Cheadle *Gt Man* 82 D3
Cheadle *Staffs* 71 E4
Cheadle Heath *Gt Man* 82 D4
Cheadle Hulme *Gt Man* 82 D3
Cheam *Gt Lon* 28 C2
Cheapside *Berks* 41 G1
Chearsley *Bucks* 41 E5
Chebsey *Staffs* 70 D3
Checkendon *Oxon* 41 E3
Checkley *Ches* 70 B5
Checkley *Staffs* 71 E4
Checkley Green *Ches* 70 B5
Chedburgh *Suffk* 63 G1
Cheddar *Somset* 23 G5
Cheddington *Bucks* 41 G6
Cheddleton *Staffs* 71 E5
Cheddleton Heath *Staffs* 71 E5
Cheddon Fitzpaine *Somset* 23 E2
Chedglow *Wilts* 38 D4
Chedgrave *Norfk* 65 F5
Chedington *Dorset* 11 E5
Chediston *Suffk* 65 F3
Chediston Green *Suffk* 65 F3
Chedworth *Gloucs* 39 E5
Chedzoy *Somset* 23 F3
Cheesden *Gt Man* 89 G1
Cheeseman's Green *Kent* 18 D5
Cheetham Hill *Gt Man* 82 C5
Cheetwood *Gt Man* 82 C5
Cheldon *Devon* 21 G2
Chelford *Ches* 82 C2
Chellaston *Derbys* 72 B3
Chellington *Beds* 49 H5
Chelmarsh *Shrops* 57 G4
Chelmick *Shrops* 57 E4
Chelmondiston *Suffk* 53 F4
Chelmorton *Derbys* 83 F2
Chelmsford *Essex* 51 H1
Chelmsley Wood *W Mids* 59 E4
Chelsea *Gt Lon* 28 D4
Chelsfield *Gt Lon* 29 F2
Chelsham *Surrey* 29 E2
Chelston *Somset* 22 D1
Chelsworth *Suffk* 52 C5
Cheltenham *Gloucs* 47 E1
Chelveston *Nhants* 61 F2
Chelvey *Somset* 37 F1
Chelwood *Somset* 24 B5
Chelwood Common *E Susx* 17 E4
Chelwood Gate *E Susx* 17 E4
Chelworth *Wilts* 38 D4
Chelworth Lower Green *Wilts* 39 E3
Chelworth Upper Green *Wilts* 39 E4
Cheney Longville *Shrops* 56 D4
Chenies *Bucks* 28 A6
Chepstow *Mons* 37 F4
Chequerbent *Gt Man* 82 B5
Chequers Corner *Norfk* 75 E1
Cherhill *Wilts* 39 E1
Cherington *Gloucs* 38 D4
Cherington *Warwks* 48 A3
Cheriton *Devon* 21 G5
Cheriton *Hants* 26 D2
Cheriton *Kent* 19 F5
Cheriton *Swans* 34 B4
Cheriton Bishop *Devon* 9 E4
Cheriton Fitzpaine *Devon* 9 E5
Cheriton or Stackpole Elidor *Pembks* 32 D1
Cherrington *Shrops* 70 B2
Cherry Burton *E R Yk* 92 D4
Cherry Hinton *Cambs* 62 D1
Cherry Orchard *Worcs* 46 D4
Cherry Willingham *Lincs* 85 H2
Chertsey *Surrey* 28 A3
Cheselbourne *Dorset* 12 B5

Chesham Coanwood

280

Chesham Bucks 41 H4
Chesham Gt Man 82 C6
Chesham Bois Bucks 41 H4
Cheshunt Herts 50 D1
Chesley Kent 30 B2
Cheslyn Hay Staffs 58 C6
Chessetts Wood Warwks 59 E3
Chessington Surrey 28 C2
Chessington World of Adventure Gt Lon 28 C2
Chester Ches 81 F1
Chester Cathedral Ches 81 F1
Chester Moor Dur 106 B6
Chester Zoo Ches 81 F2
Chester-le-Street Dur 106 B6
Chesterblade Somset 24 B3
Chesterfield Derbys 84 B2
Chesterfield Staffs 58 D6
Chesterhill Mdloth 132 C2
Chesters Border 122 C2
Chesters Border 112 C6
Chesterton Cambs 61 G5
Chesterton Cambs 62 D1
Chesterton Gloucs 39 E4
Chesterton Oxon 48 D1
Chesterton Shrops 57 H5
Chesterton Staffs 70 C5
Chesterton Green Warwks 48 B5
Chesterwood Nthumb 113 E1
Chestfield Kent 31 E3
Chestnut Street Kent 30 B2
Cheston Devon 6 D3
Cheswardine Shrops 70 B3
Cheswell Shrops 70 B2
Cheswick Nthumb 123 G4
Cheswick Green W Mids 58 D3
Chetnole Dorset 11 F5
Chettiscombe Devon 9 F6
Chettisham Cambs 63 E4
Chettle Dorset 12 C6
Chetton Shrops 57 G4
Chetwode Bucks 49 E2
Chetwynd Shrops 70 B2
Chetwynd Aston Shrops 70 C2
Cheveley Cambs 63 F1
Chevening Kent 29 F2
Cheverton IOW 14 C2
Chevington Suffk 63 G1
Chevington Drift Nthumb 114 D5
Chevithorne Devon 9 G6
Chew Magna Somset 24 A6
Chew Moor Gt Man 82 B5
Chew Stoke Somset 24 A5
Chewton Keynsham Somset 24 B6
Chewton Mendip Somset 24 B5
Chichacott Devon 8 C4
Chicheley Bucks 49 G4
Chichester W Susx 15 G4
Chickerell Dorset 11 G3
Chickering Suffk 65 E3
Chicklade Wilts 25 E3
Chickward Herefs 45 F4
Chidden Hants 15 E5
Chiddingfold Surrey 27 H3
Chiddingly E Susx 17 F3
Chiddingstone Kent 17 F6
Chiddingstone Causeway Kent 17 F6
Chideock Dorset 11 E4
Chidham W Susx 15 F4
Chidswell W York 90 D2
Chieveley Berks 40 C2
Chignall Smealy Essex 51 G2
Chignall St James Essex 51 G2
Chigwell Essex 29 E5
Chigwell Row Essex 29 E5
Chilbolton Hants 26 B3
Chilcomb Hants 26 C2
Chilcombe Dorset 11 F4
Chilcompton Somset 24 B4
Chilcote Leics 71 H1
Child Okeford Dorset 12 B6
Child's Ercall Shrops 70 B2
Childer Thornton Ches 81 F2
Childrey Oxon 40 B3
Childswickham Worcs 47 F3
Childwall Mersyd 81 F4
Childwick Bury Herts 50 B2
Childwick Green Herts 50 B2
Chilfrome Dorset 11 F4
Chilgrove W Susx 15 F5
Chilham Kent 30 D1
Chilhampton Wilts 25 F2
Chilla Devon 8 A5
Chillaton Devon 8 A3
Chillenden Kent 31 F1
Chillerton IOW 14 C2
Chillesford Suffk 53 G6
Chillingham Nthumb 124 D4
Chillington Devon 7 E2
Chillington Somset 10 D6
Chilmark Wilts 25 E2
Chilmington Green Kent 18 C5
Chilson Oxon 48 A1
Chilsworthy Cnwll 5 H3
Chilsworthy Devon 20 C1
Chiltern Green Beds 50 B3
Chilthorne Domer Somset 23 H1
Chilton Bucks 41 E5
Chilton Devon 9 E5
Chilton Dur 106 B4
Chilton Kent 19 F6
Chilton Oxon 40 C3
Chilton Suffk 52 C5
Chilton Candover Hants 26 D3
Chilton Cantelo Somset 24 A1
Chilton Foliat Wilts 40 A1
Chilton Polden Somset 23 F3
Chilton Street Suffk 52 A5
Chilton Trinity Somset 23 F3
Chilwell Notts 72 C4
Chilworth Hants 14 B5
Chilworth Surrey 16 A6
Chimney Oxon 40 B4
Chineham Hants 27 E5
Chingford Gt Lon 29 E5
Chinley Derbys 83 E3
Chinnor Oxon 41 F4
Chipchase Castle Nthumb 113 F2
Chipnall Shrops 70 B3
Chippenham Cambs 63 F2
Chippenham Wilts 38 D2
Chipperfield Herts 28 A6
Chipping Herts 50 D4
Chipping Lancs 89 E4
Chipping Campden Gloucs 47 G3
Chipping Hill Essex 52 B2
Chipping Norton Oxon 48 A2
Chipping Ongar Essex 51 F1
Chipping Sodbury Gloucs 38 B2
Chipping Warden Nhants 48 C4
Chipstable Somset 22 C2
Chipstead Kent 29 F2
Chipstead Surrey 28 D2
Chirbury Shrops 56 C5
Chirk Wrexhm 69 E4
Chirnside Border 123 F5
Chirnsidebridge Border 123 F5
Chirton Wilts 25 F5
Chisbury Wilts 26 A6
Chiselborough Somset 11 E6
Chiseldon Wilts 39 F2
Chiselhampton Oxon 40 D4
Chisholme Border 112 A6
Chislehurst Gt Lon 29 E3
Chislet Kent 31 F2
Chisley W York 90 A2
Chiswell Green Herts 50 B1
Chiswick Gt Lon 28 C4
Chiswick End Cambs 51 E5
Chisworth Derbys 83 E4
Chitcombe E Susx 18 B3
Chithurst W Susx 27 G1
Chittering Cambs 62 D2
Chitterne Wilts 25 E4
Chittlehamholt Devon 21 G3
Chittlehampton Devon 21 F3
Chittlehampton Devon 21 G2
Chittoe Wilts 25 E6
Chivelstone Devon 7 E1
Chivenor Devon 21 E4
Chlenry D & G 100 C6
Chobham Surrey 27 H5
Cholderton Wilts 25 H3
Cholesbury Bucks 41 G5
Chollerford Nthumb 113 F2
Chollerton Nthumb 113 F2
Cholmondeston Ches 70 A6
Cholsey Oxon 40 D3
Cholstrey Herefs 45 G5
Chop Gate N York 98 A5
Choppington Nthumb 114 D4
Chopwell T & W 114 C1
Chorley Ches 69 H5
Chorley Lancs 88 D1
Chorley Shrops 57 G4
Chorley Staffs 71 F1
Chorleywood Herts 28 A6
Chorleywood West Herts 28 A6
Chorlton Ches 70 B5
Chorlton Lane Ches 69 G5
Chorlton-cum-Hardy Gt Man 82 C4
Choulton Shrops 56 D4
Chowley Ches 69 G6
Chrishall Essex 51 E5
Chrisswell Inver 128 D2
Christ's Hospital W Susx 16 B4
Christchurch Cambs 62 D5
Christchurch Dorset 13 E4
Christchurch Gloucs 37 G6
Christchurch Mons 37 E3
Christian Malford Wilts 38 D2
Christleton Ches 81 G1
Christmas Common Oxon 41 E4
Christon Somset 23 G5
Christon Bank Nthumb 125 E3
Christow Devon 9 E3
Chuck Hatch E Susx 17 F5
Chudleigh Devon 9 E2
Chudleigh Knighton Devon 9 E2
Chulmleigh Devon 21 G2
Chunal Derbys 83 E4
Church Lancs 89 F2
Church Aston Shrops 70 B2
Church Brampton Nhants 60 C2
Church Brough Cumb 105 E1
Church Broughton Derbys 71 G3
Church Cove Cnwll 3 E1
Church Crookham Hants 27 F4
Church Eaton Staffs 70 C2
Church End Beds 49 H2
Church End Beds 49 H1
Church End Beds 50 A4
Church End Beds 61 F1
Church End Beds 61 G1
Church End Beds 50 C4
Church End Cambs 61 G3
Church End Cambs 62 A4
Church End Cambs 62 C3
Church End Cambs 62 D1
Church End Essex 51 G3
Church End Essex 51 H3
Church End Essex 52 A2
Church End Gt Lon 28 C5
Church End Hants 27 E5
Church End Herts 50 B2
Church End Herts 50 D4
Church End Herts 51 E3
Church End Lincs 74 C3
Church End Lincs 86 D4
Church End Warwks 59 E4
Church End Warwks 59 F5
Church Enstone Oxon 48 B2
Church Fenton N York 91 F3
Church Green Devon 10 B4
Church Gresley Derbys 71 H2
Church Hanborough Oxon 40 C6
Church Hill Ches 82 B1
Church Hill Staffs 71 E1
Church Houses N York 98 B5
Church Knowle Dorset 12 C3
Church Laneham Notts 85 F2
Church Langton Leics 60 C5
Church Lawford Warwks 59 G3
Church Lawton Staffs 70 C6
Church Leigh Staffs 71 E4
Church Lench Worcs 47 F4
Church Mayfield Staffs 71 F4
Church Minshull Ches 70 B6
Church Norton W Susx 15 G3
Church Preen Shrops 57 F5
Church Pulverbatch Shrops 57 E6
Church Stowe Nhants 49 E5
Church Street Essex 52 B5
Church Street Kent 29 H3
Church Street Suffk 65 G4
Church Stretton Shrops 57 E5
Church Town Lincs 85 E5
Church Village Rhondd 36 B3
Church Warsop Notts 84 C1
Church Wilne Derbys 72 B3
Churcham Gloucs 46 C1
Churchbridge Staffs 58 C6
Churchdown Gloucs 46 D1
Churchend Essex 30 D5
Churchfield W Mids 58 C5
Churchgate Herts 50 D1
Churchgate Street Essex 51 F2
Churchill Devon 21 F5
Churchill Devon 10 C5
Churchill Oxon 48 A2
Churchill Somset 23 G5
Churchill Worcs 58 B3
Churchill Worcs 47 E5
Churchinford Somset 10 C6
Churchover Warwks 60 A3
Churchstanton Somset 10 B6
Churchstoke Powys 56 C5
Churchstow Devon 6 D2
Churchthorpe Lincs 86 D4
Churchtown Derbys 83 G1
Churchtown Devon 21 G5
Churchtown Lancs 88 B4
Churchtown Lancs 88 C4
Churchtown Mersyd 88 B1
Churnsike Lodge Nthumb 112 D2
Churston Ferrers Devon 7 F3
Churt Surrey 27 G3
Churton Ches 69 F6
Churwell W York 90 D2
Chwilog Gwynd 66 D4
Chyandour Cnwll 2 B3
Chyanvounder Cnwll 2 D2
Chyeowling Cnwll 3 E4
Chysauster Cnwll 2 B3
Chyvarloe Cnwll 2 D2
Cil Powys 56 B6
Cilcain Flints 80 D1
Cilcennin Cerdgn 43 E5
Cilcewydd Powys 56 C6
Cilfrew Neath 35 E4
Cilfynydd Rhondd 36 B3
Cilgerran Pembks 42 B3
Cilgwyn Carmth 43 G2
Cilgwyn Gwynd 67 E5
Ciliau-Aeron Cerdgn 43 E5
Cilmaengwyn Neath 35 E5
Cilmery Powys 44 C4
Cilrhedyn Pembks 42 C3
Cilsan Carmth 43 F1
Ciltalgarth Gwynd 68 A4
Cilycwm Carmth 43 H3
Cimla Neath 35 E4
Cinder Hill W Mids 58 B5
Cinderford Gloucs 37 H6
Cippenham Berks 41 H2
Cirencester Gloucs 39 E4
Citadilla N York 97 E5
City Gt Lon 28 D4
City V Glam 35 G2
City Airport Gt Lon 29 E4
City Dulas IOA 78 D3
Clabhach Ag & B 134 D5
Clachaig Ag & B 128 C3
Clachan Ag & B 136 C2
Clachan Ag & B 136 C4
Clachan Ag & B 117 G6
Clachan Highld 151 E2
Clachan Mor Ag & B 134 B4
Clachan na Luib W Isls 168 b5
Clachan of Campsie E Duns 130 B3
Clachan-a-Luib W Isls 168 b5
Clachan-Seil Ag & B 136 B2
Clachaneasy D & G 109 E2
Clachnaharry Highld 155 E4
Clachtoll Highld 164 B1
Clackavoid P & K 140 B6
Clackmannan Clacks 131 E4
Clackmarras Moray 156 D5
Clacton-on-Sea Essex 53 E2
Cladich Ag & B 137 E2
Cladswell Worcs 47 F5
Claggan Highld 136 B5
Claigan Highld 150 B4
Clandown Somset 24 B5
Clanfield Hants 15 E5
Clanfield Oxon 39 G4
Clannaborough Devon 8 D5
Clanville Hants 26 A4
Clanville Somset 24 B2
Claonaig Ag & B 117 H6
Clap Hill Kent 18 D5
Clapgate Dorset 12 D5
Clapgate Herts 51 E3
Clapham Beds 50 A6
Clapham Devon 9 F3
Clapham Gt Lon 28 D4
Clapham N York 95 H2
Clapham W Susx 16 B2
Clapham Folly Beds 50 A6
Clappersgate Cumb 94 D5
Clapton Somset 10 D5
Clapton Somset 24 B5
Clapton-in-Gordano Somset 37 F2
Clapton-on-the-Hill Gloucs 39 F6
Clapworthy Devon 21 G3
Clarach Cerdgn 54 D4
Claravale T & W 114 C2
Clarbeston Pembks 33 E4
Clarbeston Road Pembks 32 D4
Clarborough Notts 85 E3
Clare Suffk 52 A5
Clarebrand D & G 110 B1
Clarencefield D & G 111 E2
Clareton N York 91 E5
Clarewood Nthumb 114 B2
Clarilaw Border 122 B1
Clark's Green Surrey 16 C5
Clarken Green Hants 26 D4
Clarkston E Rens 119 G5
Clashmore Highld 164 A1
Clashmore Highld 162 D3
Clashnessie Highld 164 B1
Clashnoir Moray 156 D1
Clathy P & K 139 G2
Clathymore P & K 139 G2
Clatt Abers 157 G2
Clatter Powys 55 G5
Clatterford End Essex 51 G2
Clatworthy Somset 22 C2
Claughton Lancs 88 D4
Claughton Lancs 95 F1
Claughton Mersyd 81 E3
Clavelshay Somset 23 E2
Claverdon Warwks 59 E2
Claverham Somset 23 G6
Clavering Essex 51 F4
Claverley Shrops 57 H5
Claverton Somset 24 C6
Claverton Down Somset 24 C6
Clawdd-coch V Glam 36 B2
Clawdd-newydd Denbgs 68 C5
Clawthorpe Cumb 95 F3
Clawton Devon 5 G6
Claxby Lincs 86 B4
Claxby Lincs 87 E2
Claxton N York 91 H6
Claxton Norfk 65 F6
Clay Common Suffk 65 G3
Clay Coton Nhants 60 B3
Clay Cross Derbys 84 B1
Clay End Herts 50 D3
Claybrooke Magna Leics 59 H4
Claydon Oxon 48 C4
Claydon Suffk 53 E6
Claygate D & G 112 A3
Claygate Kent 17 H6
Claygate Surrey 28 C2
Claygate Cross Kent 29 G2
Clayhall Gt Lon 29 E5
Clayhanger Devon 22 C1
Clayhanger W Mids 58 C6
Clayhidon Devon 10 B6
Clayhill E Susx 18 B4
Clayhill Hants 13 G5
Clayhithe Cambs 62 D2
Clayock Highld 167 E4
Claypit Hill Cambs 50 D6
Claypits Gloucs 38 B5
Claypole Lincs 73 F5
Claythorpe Lincs 86 D3
Clayton S York 84 B5
Clayton W Susx 16 D3
Clayton W York 90 B3
Clayton Green Lancs 88 D2
Clayton West W York 83 G6
Clayton-le-Moors Lancs 89 F3
Clayton-le-Woods Lancs 88 D2
Clayworth Notts 85 E3
Cleadale Highld 142 D3
Cleadon T & W 115 E2
Clearbrook Devon 6 C4
Clearwell Gloucs 37 G5
Clearwell Meend Gloucs 37 G5
Cleasby N York 106 B2
Cleat Ork 169 b1
Cleatlam Dur 105 H2
Cleator Cumb 102 D1
Cleator Moor Cumb 102 D2
Cleckheaton W York 90 C2
Clee St Margaret Shrops 57 F4
Cleedownton Shrops 57 F3
Cleehill Shrops 57 F3
Cleekhimin N Lans 120 B5
Cleestanton Shrops 57 F3
Cleethorpes Lincs 86 C6
Cleeton St Mary Shrops 57 F3
Cleeve Oxon 40 D2
Cleeve Somset 23 G6
Cleeve Hill Gloucs 47 E2
Cleeve Prior Worcs 47 F4
Cleghornie E Loth 133 E3
Clehonger Herefs 45 G3
Cleish P & K 131 G5
Cleland N Lans 120 C5
Clement Street Kent 29 F3
Clement's End Beds 50 A2
Clenamacrie Ag & B 136 D3
Clench Common Wilts 25 G6
Clenchwarton Norfk 75 F2
Clenerty Abers 158 D5
Clent Worcs 58 B3
Cleobury Mortimer Shrops 57 G3
Cleobury North Shrops 57 F4
Cleongart Ag & B 117 F4
Clephanton Highld 155 F4
Clerkhill D & G 111 G5
Cleuch-head D & G 110 C5
Clevancy Wilts 39 E2
Clevedon Somset 37 E1
Cleveley Oxon 48 B2
Cleveleys Lancs 88 B4
Clevelode Worcs 46 D4
Cleverton Wilts 38 D3
Clewer Somset 23 G4
Cley next the Sea Norfk 76 C4
Cliburn Cumb 104 C3
Cliddesden Hants 26 D4
Cliff Warwks 59 E5
Cliff End E Susx 18 B3
Cliffe Dur 106 B2
Cliffe Kent 30 A4
Cliffe Lancs 89 F3
Cliffe N York 91 H3
Cliffe Woods Kent 30 A3
Clifford Herefs 45 E4
Clifford W York 91 E4
Clifford Chambers Warwks 47 G4
Clifford's Mesne Gloucs 46 C1
Cliffsend Kent 31 G2
Clifton Beds 50 C5
Clifton Bristl 37 G2
Clifton Cumb 104 B3
Clifton Derbys 71 G4
Clifton Gt Man 82 C5
Clifton Lancs 88 C3
Clifton N York 90 C4
Clifton N York 91 G5
Clifton Notts 72 C3
Clifton Nthumb 114 D4
Clifton Oxon 48 C2
Clifton S York 84 C4
Clifton W York 90 C2
Clifton Worcs 46 D4
Clifton Campville Staffs 71 G1
Clifton Dykes Cumb 104 B3
Clifton Hampden Oxon 40 D4
Clifton Reynes Bucks 49 G4
Clifton upon Dunsmore Warwks 60 A3
Clifton upon Teme Worcs 46 C5
Cliftonville Kent 31 G3
Climping W Susx 16 A2
Clink Somset 24 C4
Clint N York 90 D6
Clint Green Norfk 76 C1
Clinterty Aber C 149 F5
Clintmains Border 122 C3
Clipiau Gwynd 67 H1
Clippesby Norfk 77 G1
Clipsham Rutlnd 73 G2
Clipston Nhants 60 C3
Clipston Notts 72 D3
Clipstone Beds 49 H2
Clipstone Notts 84 D1
Clitheroe Lancs 89 F4
Clive Shrops 69 G2
Clixby Lincs 86 A5
Cloatley Wilts 38 D3
Clocaenog Denbgs 68 C5
Clochan Moray 157 F5
Clochtow Angus 141 E5
Clock Face Mersyd 81 G4
Cloddiau Powys 68 D1
Clodock Herefs 45 F2
Cloford Somset 24 C4
Clola Abers 159 F3
Clophill Beds 50 B4
Clopton Nhants 61 G3
Clopton Suffk 53 F6
Clopton Corner Suffk 53 F6
Clopton Green Suffk 52 A6
Clopton Green Suffk 64 B1
Clos du Valle Guern 174 h3
Closeburn D & G 110 C4
Closeburnmill D & G 110 D4
Closeclark IOM 174 k2
Closworth Somset 11 F6
Clothall Herts 50 D4
Clotton Ches 81 G1
Cloudesley Bush Warwks 59 G4
Clough Gt Man 82 D6
Clough Foot W York 89 G2
Clough Head N York 90 B1
Cloughton N York 99 F4
Cloughton Newlands N York 99 F4
Clousta Shet 169 h3
Clova Angus 148 A2
Clovelly Devon 20 C3
Clovenfords Border 122 B3
Clovulin Highld 137 E6
Clow Bridge Lancs 89 G2
Clowne Derbys 84 C2
Clows Top Worcs 57 G3
Cloy Wrexhm 69 F4
Cluanie Inn Highld 144 C6
Cluanie Lodge Highld 144 C5
Clubworthy Cnwll 5 F5
Clugston D & G 101 E6
Clun Shrops 56 C3
Clunas Highld 155 G4
Clunbury Shrops 56 D3
Clune Highld 155 F2
Clunes Highld 144 D3
Clungunford Shrops 56 D3
Clunie Abers 158 B4
Clunie P & K 140 A4
Clunton Shrops 56 D3
Cluny Fife 132 A5
Clutton Ches 69 G5
Clutton Somset 24 B5
Clutton Hill Somset 24 B5
Clwt-y-bont Gwynd 79 E1
Clydach Mons 36 C6
Clydach Swans 34 D4
Clydach Vale Rhondd 35 G3
Clydebank W Duns 129 F2
Clydey Pembks 42 C3
Clyffe Pypard Wilts 39 E2
Clynder Ag & B 128 D3
Clynderwen Carmth 33 E4
Clyne Neath 35 E4
Clynnog-fawr Gwynd 66 D5
Clyro Powys 45 E4
Clyst Honiton Devon 9 G4
Clyst Hydon Devon 9 G5
Clyst St George Devon 9 G3
Clyst St Lawrence Devon 9 G5
Clyst St Mary Devon 9 G4
Cnoc W Isls 168 f8
Cnwch Coch Cerdgn 54 D3
Coad's Green Cnwll 5 F4
Coal Aston Derbys 84 A3
Coal Pool W Mids 58 C5
Coal Street Suffk 65 E2
Coalbrookdale Shrops 57 G6
Coalbrookvale Blae G 36 C5
Coalburn S Lans 120 C3
Coalburns T & W 114 C2
Coalcleugh Nthumb 105 E5
Coaley Gloucs 38 B4
Coalfell Cumb 104 C6
Coalhill Essex 30 A6
Coalmoor Shrops 57 G6
Coalpit Heath Gloucs 38 B2
Coalpit Hill Staffs 70 C5
Coalport Shrops 57 G6
Coalsnaughton Clacks 131 E5
Coaltown of Balgonie Fife 132 B5
Coaltown of Wemyss Fife 132 B5
Coalville Leics 72 B1
Coanwood Nthumb 104 D6

Coat

Coundon

Coat *Somset* 23 G1
Coatbridge *N Lans* 130 D2
Coatdyke *N Lans* 130 D2
Coate *Wilts* 25 F5
Coate *Wilts* 39 F2
Coates *Cambs* 62 B5
Coates *Gloucs* 38 D4
Coates *Lincs* 85 F3
Coates *Lincs* 85 G3
Coates *W Susx* 15 H5
Coatham *N York* 107 E3
Coatham Mundeville *Dur* 106 B3
Cobbaton *Devon* 21 F3
Coberley *Gloucs* 38 D6
Cobhall Common *Herefs* 45 G3
Cobham *Kent* 29 G3
Cobham *Surrey* 28 B2
Coblers Green *Essex* 51 H3
Cobley *Dorset* 25 F1
Cobnash *Herefs* 45 G5
Cobo *Guern* 174 g2
Cobridge *Staffs* 70 D5
Coburby *Abers* 159 E5
Cock & End *Suffk* 51 H6
Cock Alley *Derbys* 84 B2
Cock Bank *Wrexhm* 69 F5
Cock Bevington *Warwks* 47 F4
Cock Bridge *Abers* 147 G5
Cock Clarks *Essex* 52 B1
Cock Green *Essex* 51 H3
Cock Marling *E Susx* 18 B3
Cock Street *Kent* 30 A1
Cockayne *N York* 98 B5
Cockayne Hatley *Beds* 50 D6
Cockburnspath *Border* 133 G2
Cockenzie and Port Seton *E Loth* 132 C3
Cocker Bar *Lancs* 88 D2
Cocker Brook *Lancs* 89 F2
Cockerham *Lancs* 88 C5
Cockermouth *Cumb* 103 E3
Cockernhoe Green *Herts* 50 B3
Cockersdale *W York* 90 C3
Cockett *Swans* 34 D4
Cockfield *Dur* 105 H2
Cockfield *Suffk* 52 C6
Cockfosters *Gt Lon* 28 D6
Cocking *W Susx* 15 G5
Cocking Causeway *W Susx* 15 G6
Cockington *Devon* 7 F4
Cocklake *Somset* 23 G4
Cockle Park *Nthumb* 114 D5
Cockley Beck *Cumb* 94 C5
Cockley Cley *Norfk* 63 G6
Cockpole Green *Berks* 41 F2
Cocks *Cnwll* 3 E5
Cockshutford *Shrops* 57 F4
Cockshutt *Shrops* 69 G3
Cockthorpe *Norfk* 76 C4
Cockwells *Cnwll* 2 C3
Cockwood *Devon* 9 G3
Cockwood *Somset* 23 E3
Cockyard *Derbys* 83 E3
Cockyard *Herefs* 45 G3
Coddenham *Suffk* 53 E6
Coddington *Ches* 69 G6
Coddington *Herefs* 46 C3
Coddington *Notts* 73 F5
Codford St Mary *Wilts* 25 E3
Codford St Peter *Wilts* 25 E3
Codicote *Herts* 50 C2
Codmore Hill *W Susx* 16 B3
Codnor *Derbys* 72 B5
Codrington *Gloucs* 38 B2
Codsall *Staffs* 58 B6
Codsall Wood *Staffs* 58 A6
Coed Morgan *Mons* 37 E5
Coed Talon *Flints* 69 E6
Coed Ystumgwern *Gwynd* 67 E2
Coed-y-Bryn *Cerdgn* 42 D4
Coed-y-caerau *Newpt* 37 E3
Coed-y-paen *Mons* 36 D4
Coed-yr-ynys *Powys* 44 D1
Coedana *IOA* 78 D3
Coedely *Rhondd* 35 H3
Coedkernew *Newpt* 36 D3
Coedpoeth *Wrexhm* 69 E5
Coedway *Powys* 69 F1
Coelbren *Powys* 35 F5
Coffinswell *Devon* 7 F4
Coffle End *Beds* 61 F1
Cofton *Devon* 9 F3
Cofton Hackett *Worcs* 58 C3
Cogan *V Glam* 36 C1
Cogenhoe *Nhants* 49 F5
Cogges *Oxon* 40 B5
Coggeshall *Essex* 52 B3
Coggin's Mill *E Susx* 17 G4
Coignafearn *Highld* 146 B6
Coilacriech *Abers* 147 H4
Coilantogle *Stirlg* 130 B6
Coillore *Highld* 150 D2
Coiltry *Highld* 145 F5
Coity *Brdgnd* 35 G2
Col *W Isls* 168 f8
Colaboll *Highld* 162 C5
Colan *Cnwll* 4 B2
Colaton Raleigh *Devon* 10 A3
Colbost *Highld* 150 B4
Colburn *N York* 97 E5
Colbury *Hants* 13 G6
Colby *Cumb* 104 C2
Colby *IOM* 174 k2
Colby *Norfk* 77 E3
Colchester *Essex* 52 D3
Cold Ash *Berks* 40 C1
Cold Ashby *Nhants* 60 C3
Cold Ashton *Gloucs* 38 B1
Cold Aston *Gloucs* 47 G1
Cold Blow *Pembks* 33 E3
Cold Brayfield *Bucks* 49 G4
Cold Cotes *N York* 95 H2
Cold Green *Herefs* 46 B3
Cold Hanworth *Lincs* 85 H3
Cold Harbour *Herts* 50 B2
Cold Harbour *Oxon* 41 E2
Cold Harbour *Wilts* 24 D4
Cold Hatton *Shrops* 70 A2
Cold Hatton Heath *Shrops* 70 A2
Cold Hesledon *Dur* 106 D5
Cold Hiendley *W York* 84 A6
Cold Higham *Nhants* 49 E4
Cold Kirby *N York* 98 A3
Cold Newton *Leics* 60 C6
Cold Northcott *Cnwll* 5 F4
Cold Norton *Essex* 30 B6
Cold Overton *Leics* 73 F1
Cold Weston *Shrops* 57 F4
Coldbackie *Highld* 165 G4
Coldbeck *Cumb* 95 H5
Coldean *E Susx* 16 D2
Coldeast *Devon* 9 E2
Colden *W York* 89 H2
Colden Common *Hants* 26 C1
Coldfair Green *Suffk* 65 G1
Coldham *Cambs* 62 D6
Coldharbour *Cnwll* 3 E5
Coldharbour *Devon* 9 G6
Coldharbour *Gloucs* 37 G5
Coldharbour *Surrey* 16 B6
Coldingham *Border* 133 H2
Coldmeece *Staffs* 70 C3
Coldred *Kent* 19 F6
Coldridge *Devon* 8 D5
Coldstream *Border* 123 F3
Coldwaltham *W Susx* 16 A3
Coldwell *Herefs* 45 G3
Coldwells *Abers* 159 E3
Cole *Somset* 24 B3
Cole End *Warwks* 59 E4
Cole Green *Herts* 50 D2
Cole Green *Herts* 51 E4
Cole Henley *Hants* 26 C4
Cole's Cross *Devon* 7 E2
Colebatch *Shrops* 56 C4
Colebrook *Devon* 9 G5
Colebrook *Devon* 6 C3
Colebrooke *Devon* 9 E5
Coleby *Lincs* 92 C1
Coleby *Lincs* 73 G6
Coleford *Devon* 9 E5
Coleford *Gloucs* 37 G5
Coleford *Somset* 24 B4
Coleford Water *Somset* 22 D3
Colegate End *Norfk* 64 D4
Colehill *Dorset* 12 D5
Coleman Green *Herts* 50 C2
Coleman's Hatch *E Susx* 17 E5
Colemere *Shrops* 69 F3
Colemore *Hants* 27 E2
Colemore Green *Shrops* 57 G5
Colenden *P & K* 140 A3
Coleorton *Leics* 72 B2
Colerne *Wilts* 38 C1
Coles Cross *Dorset* 10 D5
Coles Green *Suffk* 53 E5
Colesbourne *Gloucs* 39 E6
Colesden *Beds* 61 G1
Coleshill *Bucks* 41 H4
Coleshill *Oxon* 39 G4
Coleshill *Warwks* 59 E4
Colestocks *Devon* 10 A5
Coley *Somset* 24 A5
Colgate *W Susx* 16 C5
Colinsburgh *Fife* 132 D5
Colinton *C Edin* 132 A2
Colintraive *Ag & B* 128 B2
Colkirk *Norfk* 76 B3
Collace *P & K* 140 B3
Collafirth *Shet* 169 h4
Collaton *Devon* 7 E1
Collaton *Devon* 7 E3
Collaton St Mary *Devon* 7 F4
College Green *Somset* 24 A3
College of Roseisle *Moray* 156 C6
College Town *Berks* 27 G5
Collessie *Fife* 140 C1
Colleton Mills *Devon* 21 G2
Collier Row *Gt Lon* 29 F5
Collier Street *Kent* 17 H6
Collier's End *Herts* 51 E3
Collier's Green *Kent* 18 B4
Colliers Green *Kent* 18 A5
Colliery Row *T & W* 106 C6
Collieston *Abers* 159 F2
Collin *D & G* 111 E2
Collingbourne Ducis *Wilts* 25 H5
Collingbourne Kingston *Wilts* 25 H5
Collingham *Notts* 85 F1
Collingham *W York* 91 E4
Collington *Herefs* 46 B5
Collingtree *Nhants* 49 F5
Collins Green *Ches* 81 H4
Collins Green *Worcs* 46 C5
Colliston *Angus* 141 F4
Colliton *Devon* 10 A5
Collyweston *Nhants* 61 F6
Colmonell *S Ayrs* 108 C3
Colmworth *Beds* 61 G1
Coln Rogers *Gloucs* 39 E5
Coln St Aldwyns *Gloucs* 39 F5
Coln St Dennis *Gloucs* 39 E5
Colnbrook *Berks* 28 A4
Colne *Cambs* 62 C3
Colne *Lancs* 89 G4
Colne Bridge *W York* 90 C2
Colne Edge *Lancs* 89 G4
Colne Engaine *Essex* 52 B4
Colney *Norfk* 64 D6
Colney Heath *Herts* 50 C1
Colney Street *Herts* 50 B1
Colpy *Abers* 158 B2
Colquhar *Border* 121 H4
Colquite *Cnwll* 4 D3
Colscott *Devon* 20 D2
Colsterdale *N York* 97 E3
Colsterworth *Lincs* 73 G2
Colston Bassett *Notts* 73 E3
Colt Hill *Hants* 27 F4
Colt's Hill *Kent* 17 G6
Coltfield *Moray* 156 C5
Coltishall *Norfk* 77 F2
Colton *Cumb* 94 D3
Colton *N York* 91 F4
Colton *Norfk* 76 D1
Colton *Staffs* 71 E2
Colton *W York* 91 E3
Columbjohn *Devon* 9 F5
Colva *Powys* 45 E4
Colvend *D & G* 102 C6
Colwall *Herefs* 46 C3
Colwell *Nthumb* 113 G2
Colwich *Staffs* 71 E2
Colwick *Notts* 72 D4
Colwinston *V Glam* 35 G2
Colworth *W Susx* 15 G4
Colwyn Bay *Conwy* 79 H3
Colyford *Devon* 10 C4
Colyton *Devon* 10 C4
Combe *Berks* 26 B5
Combe *Devon* 7 E1
Combe *Devon* 7 F2
Combe *Herefs* 56 D2
Combe *Oxon* 40 B6
Combe Almer *Dorset* 12 C4
Combe Common *Surrey* 27 H3
Combe Down *Somset* 24 C5
Combe Fishacre *Devon* 7 F4
Combe Florey *Somset* 22 D2
Combe Hay *Somset* 24 C5
Combe Martin *Devon* 21 F5
Combe Raleigh *Devon* 10 B5
Combe St Nicholas *Somset* 10 C6
Combeinteignhead *Devon* 7 F5
Comberbach *Ches* 82 A2
Comberford *Staffs* 59 E6
Comberton *Cambs* 62 C1
Comberton *Herefs* 57 E2
Combpyne *Devon* 10 C4
Combridge *Staffs* 71 F4
Combrook *Warwks* 48 A4
Combs *Derbys* 83 E2
Combs *Suffk* 64 C1
Combs Ford *Suffk* 64 C1
Combwich *Somset* 23 E3
Comers *Abers* 148 D5
Comhampton *Worcs* 58 A2
Commercial *Pembks* 33 F3
Commercial End *Cambs* 63 E2
Commins Coch *Powys* 55 F6
Common Edge *Lancs* 88 B3
Common End *Cumb* 102 D2
Common Moor *Cnwll* 5 F3
Common Platt *Wilts* 39 F3
Common Side *Derbys* 84 A2
Commondale *N York* 107 F2
Commonside *Ches* 81 H2
Commonside *Derbys* 71 G4
Commonwood *Shrops* 69 G3
Commonwood *Wrexhm* 69 F5
Compass *Somset* 23 F3
Compstall *Gt Man* 83 E4
Compstonend *D & G* 101 H5
Compton *Berks* 40 C2
Compton *Devon* 7 F4
Compton *Hants* 26 B2
Compton *Hants* 26 C2
Compton *Staffs* 58 A4
Compton *Surrey* 27 H4
Compton *W Susx* 15 F5
Compton *Wilts* 25 G4
Compton Abbas *Dorset* 24 D1
Compton Abdale *Gloucs* 39 E6
Compton Bassett *Wilts* 39 E1
Compton Beauchamp *Oxon* 39 G3
Compton Bishop *Somset* 23 G5
Compton Chamberlayne *Wilts* 25 F2
Compton Dando *Somset* 24 B6
Compton Dundon *Somset* 23 H2
Compton Durville *Somset* 23 G1
Compton Greenfield *Gloucs* 37 G2
Compton Martin *Somset* 24 A5
Compton Pauncefoot *Somset* 24 B2
Compton Valence *Dorset* 11 F4
Compton Verney *Warwks* 48 A4
Comrie *Fife* 131 F4
Comrie *P & K* 139 E2
Conaglen House *Highld* 144 C1
Conchra *Highld* 152 C2
Concraigie *P & K* 140 A4
Conder Green *Lancs* 88 C5
Conderton *Worcs* 47 E3
Condicote *Gloucs* 47 G2
Condorrat *N Lans* 130 D2
Condover *Shrops* 57 E6
Coney Hill *Gloucs* 38 C6
Coney Weston *Suffk* 64 B3
Coneyhurst Common *W Susx* 16 B4
Coneysthorpe *N York* 98 C2
Coneythorpe *W York* 91 E5
Conford *Hants* 27 F3
Congdon's Shop *Cnwll* 5 F4
Congerstone *Leics* 59 F6
Congham *Norfk* 75 G2
Conghurst *Kent* 18 A4
Congl-y-wal *Gwynd* 67 G4
Congleton *Ches* 82 D1
Congresbury *Somset* 23 G6
Congreve *Staffs* 70 D1
Conheath *D & G* 110 D2
Conicavel *Moray* 156 B4
Coningsby *Lincs* 74 C6
Conington *Cambs* 61 H4
Conington *Cambs* 62 B2
Conisbrough *S York* 84 C5
Conisholme *Lincs* 86 D4
Coniston *Cumb* 94 D5
Coniston *E R Yk* 93 E3
Coniston Cold *N York* 89 G5
Conistone *N York* 96 C2
Connah's Quay *Flints* 81 E2
Connel *Ag & B* 136 D3
Connel Park *E Ayrs* 109 H6
Connor Downs *Cnwll* 2 C4
Conon Bridge *Highld* 154 D5
Cononley *N York* 90 A4
Consall *Staffs* 71 E5
Consett *Dur* 105 H5
Constable Burton *N York* 97 E4
Constable Lee *Lancs* 89 F2
Constantine *Cnwll* 3 E3
Constantine Bay *Cnwll* 4 B3
Contin *Highld* 154 C5
Conwy *Conwy* 79 G2
Conyer *Kent* 30 C2
Conyer's Green *Suffk* 64 A2
Cooden *E Susx* 17 H2
Cook's Green *Essex* 53 E3
Cookbury *Devon* 20 D1
Cookbury Wick *Devon* 20 D1
Cookham *Berks* 41 G3
Cookham Dean *Berks* 41 G3
Cookham Rise *Berks* 41 G3
Cookhill *Warwks* 47 F5
Cookley *Suffk* 65 F3
Cookley *Worcs* 58 A3
Cookley Green *Oxon* 41 E3
Cookney *Abers* 149 F4
Cooks Green *Suffk* 52 C6
Cooksbridge *E Susx* 17 E3
Cooksey Green *Worcs* 58 B2
Cookshill *Staffs* 70 D4
Cooksland *Cnwll* 4 D3
Cooksmill Green *Essex* 51 G1
Cookson Green *Ches* 81 H2
Cookson's Green *Dur* 106 B4
Coolham *W Susx* 16 B4
Cooling *Kent* 30 A4
Cooling Street *Kent* 30 A3
Coombe *Cnwll* 2 D4
Coombe *Cnwll* 3 F4
Coombe *Devon* 9 E3
Coombe *Devon* 7 G5
Coombe *Devon* 10 A4
Coombe *Gloucs* 38 B4
Coombe *Hants* 15 E6
Coombe *Wilts* 25 G4
Coombe Bissett *Wilts* 25 F2
Coombe Cellars *Devon* 7 F5
Coombe Cross *Hants* 15 E6
Coombe End *Somset* 22 C2
Coombe Hill *Gloucs* 46 D2
Coombe Keynes *Dorset* 12 B3
Coombe Pafford *Devon* 7 F4
Coombe Street *Somset* 24 C2
Coombes *W Susx* 16 C2
Coombes-Moor *Herefs* 56 D2
Coombeswood *W Mids* 58 C4
Cooper Street *Kent* 31 G2
Cooper Turning *Gt Man* 82 A5
Cooper's Corner *Kent* 29 F1
Cooperhill *Moray* 156 B4
Coopers Green *E Susx* 17 F4
Coopers Green *Herts* 50 C2
Coopersale Common *Essex* 51 F1
Coopersale Street *Essex* 51 F1
Cootham *W Susx* 16 B3
Cop Street *Kent* 31 F2
Copdock *Suffk* 53 E5
Copford Green *Essex* 52 C3
Copgrove *N York* 97 G1
Copister *Shet* 169 j4
Cople *Beds* 50 B6
Copley *Dur* 105 G3
Copley *Gt Man* 83 E4
Copley *W York* 90 B2
Coplow Dale *Derbys* 83 F3
Copmanthorpe *N York* 91 G4
Copmere End *Staffs* 70 C3
Copp *Lancs* 88 C3
Coppathorne *Cnwll* 5 F6
Coppenhall *Staffs* 70 D2
Coppenhall Moss *Ches* 70 B6
Copperhouse *Cnwll* 2 C3
Coppicegate *Shrops* 57 G3
Coppingford *Cambs* 61 H3
Coppins Corner *Kent* 18 C6
Copplestone *Devon* 9 E5
Coppull *Lancs* 81 H6
Coppull Moor *Lancs* 81 H6
Copsale *W Susx* 16 C4
Copster Green *Lancs* 89 E3
Copston Magna *Warwks* 59 G4
Copt Heath *W Mids* 59 E3
Copt Hewick *N York* 97 G2
Copt Oak *Leics* 72 C1
Copthall Green *Essex* 29 E6
Copthorne *Cnwll* 5 F5
Copthorne *W Susx* 16 D5
Copy's Green *Norfk* 76 B4
Copythorne *Hants* 13 G6
Coram Street *Suffk* 52 D5
Corbets Tey *Gt Lon* 29 F5
Corbiere *Jersey* 174 a1
Corbridge *Nthumb* 113 G1
Corby *Nhants* 61 E4
Corby Glen *Lincs* 73 G2
Corby Hill *Cumb* 104 B6
Cordon *N Ayrs* 118 B2
Cordwell *Derbys* 83 H2
Coreley *Shrops* 57 F3
Cores End *Bucks* 41 G3
Corfe *Somset* 23 E1
Corfe Castle *Dorset* 12 C3
Corfe Mullen *Dorset* 12 D4
Corfton *Shrops* 57 E4
Corgarff *Abers* 147 H5
Corhampton *Hants* 14 D6
Corks Pond *Kent* 17 G5
Corley *Warwks* 59 F4
Corley Ash *Warwks* 59 F4
Corley Moor *Warwks* 59 F4
Cormuir *Angus* 147 H1
Cornard Tye *Suffk* 52 C5
Corndon *Devon* 8 D3
Corner Row *Lancs* 88 C3
Corney *Cumb* 94 B4
Cornforth *Dur* 106 C4
Cornhill *Abers* 158 B5
Cornhill-on-Tweed *Nthumb* 123 F3
Cornholme *W York* 89 G2
Cornish Hall End *Essex* 51 H4
Cornoigmore *Ag & B* 134 B4
Cornriggs *Dur* 105 E4
Cornsay *Dur* 105 H4
Cornsay Colliery *Dur* 106 A5
Corntown *Highld* 154 D5
Corntown *V Glam* 35 G2
Cornwell *Oxon* 48 A2
Cornwood *Devon* 6 C3
Cornworthy *Devon* 7 F3
Corpach *Highld* 144 C2
Corpusty *Norfk* 76 D3
Corrachree *Abers* 148 B5
Corran *Cnwll* 3 G4
Corran *Highld* 143 H5
Corran *Highld* 137 E6
Corrany *IOM* 174 m4
Corrie *D & G* 111 F3
Corrie *N Ayrs* 118 B4
Corriecravie *N Ayrs* 118 A2
Corriegills *N Ayrs* 118 B3
Corriegour Lodge Hotel *Highld* 145 E4
Corriemoille *Highld* 154 B5
Corrimony *Highld* 154 B2
Corringham *Essex* 29 H4
Corringham *Lincs* 85 F4
Corris *Gwynd* 55 E6
Corris Uchaf *Gwynd* 67 G1
Corrow *Ag & B* 128 C5
Corry *Highld* 151 F1
Cors-y-Gedol *Gwynd* 67 F2
Corscombe *Devon* 8 C4
Corscombe *Dorset* 11 E5
Corse *Gloucs* 46 C2
Corse Lawn *Gloucs* 46 D2
Corsham *Wilts* 38 C1
Corsindae *Abers* 148 D5
Corsley *Wilts* 24 D4
Corsley Heath *Wilts* 24 D4
Corsock *D & G* 110 B2
Corston *Somset* 24 C6
Corston *Wilts* 38 D3
Corstorphine *C Edin* 132 A2
Cortachy *Angus* 140 D6
Corton *Suffk* 65 H5
Corton *Wilts* 25 E3
Corton Denham *Somset* 24 B1
Coruanan Lodge *Highld* 144 C1
Corwen *Denbgs* 68 C4
Coryates *Dorset* 11 G3
Coryton *Devon* 8 B3
Coryton *Essex* 30 A4
Cosby *Leics* 60 B5
Coseley *W Mids* 58 B5
Cosford *Shrops* 58 A6
Cosgrove *Nhants* 49 F3
Cosham *Hants* 15 E4
Cosheston *Pembks* 32 D2
Coshieville *P & K* 139 E5
Cossall *Notts* 72 C4
Cossall Marsh *Notts* 72 B4
Cossington *Leics* 72 D1
Cossington *Somset* 23 F3
Costessey *Norfk* 77 E1
Costock *Notts* 72 C3
Coston *Leics* 73 F2
Coston *Norfk* 64 C6
Cote *Oxon* 40 B4
Cote *Somset* 23 F4
Cotebrook *Ches* 81 H1
Cotehill *Cumb* 104 A5
Cotes *Cumb* 95 F3
Cotes *Leics* 72 C2
Cotes *Staffs* 70 C3
Cotes Heath *Staffs* 70 C3
Cotesbach *Leics* 60 A4
Cotgrave *Notts* 72 D4
Cothal *Abers* 149 F6
Cotham *Notts* 73 F5
Cothelstone *Somset* 23 E2
Cotherstone *Dur* 105 G2
Cothill *Oxon* 40 C4
Cotleigh *Devon* 10 B5
Cotmanhay *Derbys* 72 B4
Coton *Cambs* 62 C1
Coton *Nhants* 60 C2
Coton *Shrops* 69 G3
Coton *Staffs* 70 C2
Coton *Staffs* 71 E3
Coton *Staffs* 59 E6
Coton Clanford *Staffs* 70 D2
Coton Hayes *Staffs* 71 E3
Coton Hill *Shrops* 69 G1
Coton in the Clay *Staffs* 71 G3
Coton in the Elms *Derbys* 71 G1
Coton Park *Derbys* 71 G2
Cott *Devon* 7 E4
Cottage End *Hants* 26 B4
Cottam *E R Yk* 99 F1
Cottam *Lancs* 88 C3
Cottam *Notts* 85 F3
Cottenham *Cambs* 62 D2
Cotterdale *N York* 96 B4
Cottered *Herts* 50 D4
Cotteridge *W Mids* 58 C3
Cotterstock *Nhants* 61 F4
Cottesbrooke *Nhants* 60 C3
Cottesmore *Rutlnd* 73 G1
Cottingham *E R Yk* 92 D3
Cottingham *Nhants* 60 D4
Cottingley *W York* 90 B3
Cottisford *Oxon* 48 D2
Cotton *Suffk* 64 C2
Cotton End *Beds* 50 B5
Cotton Tree *Lancs* 89 G4
Cottown *Abers* 157 G2
Cottown *Abers* 149 E6
Cottown of Gight *Abers* 158 D3
Cottrell *V Glam* 36 B2
Cotts *Devon* 6 B4
Cotwall *Shrops* 70 A2
Cotwalton *Staffs* 70 D3
Couch's Mill *Cnwll* 5 E2
Coughton *Herefs* 46 B1
Coughton *Warwks* 47 F5
Coulaghailtro *Ag & B* 127 F2
Coulags *Highld* 152 D4
Coulderton *Cumb* 102 D1
Coull *Abers* 148 C5
Coulport *Ag & B* 128 D4
Coulsdon *Gt Lon* 28 D2
Coulston *Wilts* 25 E5
Coulter *S Lans* 121 E3
Coultershaw Bridge *W Susx* 15 H6
Coultings *Somset* 23 E3
Coulton *N York* 98 B2
Coultra *Fife* 140 C2
Cound *Shrops* 57 F6
Coundlane *Shrops* 57 F6
Coundon *Dur* 106 B4

281

Coundon Grange
Culkerton
282

Coundon Grange Dur 106 B4
Countersett N York 96 B4
Countess Wilts 25 G3
Countess Cross Essex 52 B4
Countess Wear Devon 9 F3
Countesthorpe Leics 60 B5
Countisbury Devon 21 G6
Coup Green Lancs 88 D2
Coupar Angus P & K 140 B4
Coupland Cumb 104 D2
Coupland Nthumb 123 F2
Cour Ag & B 117 G5
Courance D & G 111 E4
Court Henry Carmth 43 F1
Court-at-Street Kent 18 D5
Courteachan Highld 143 F4
Courteenhall Nhants 49 F4
Courtsend Essex 30 D5
Courtway Somset 23 E3
Cousland Mdloth 132 C2
Cousley Wood E Susx 17 G5
Cove Ag & B 128 D3
Cove Border 133 G2
Cove Devon 22 B1
Cove Hants 27 G5
Cove Highld 160 B3
Cove Bay Aber C 149 G4
Cove Bottom Suffk 65 G3
Covehithe Suffk 65 H4
Coven Staffs 58 B6
Coven Lawn Staffs 58 B6
Coveney Cambs 62 D4
Covenham St Bartholomew Lincs 86 D4
Covenham St Mary Lincs 86 D4
Coventry W Mids 59 F3
Coventry Airport Warwks 59 F3
Coverack Cnwll 3 E2
Coverack Bridges Cnwll 2 D3
Coverham N York 96 D3
Covington Cambs 61 F2
Covington S Lans 120 D3
Cow Green Suffk 64 C2
Cow Honeybourne Worcs 47 G3
Cowan Bridge Lancs 95 G2
Cowbeech E Susx 17 G3
Cowbit Lincs 74 C2
Cowbridge V Glam 35 G2
Cowdale Derbys 83 F2
Cowden Kent 17 E5
Cowden Pound Kent 17 E6
Cowden Station Kent 17 F6
Cowdenbeath Fife 131 H4
Cowers Lane Derbys 71 H5
Cowes IOW 14 C3
Cowesby N York 97 H4
Cowesfield Green Wilts 25 H2
Cowfold W Susx 16 C4
Cowgill Cumb 96 A3
Cowhill Gloucs 37 G3
Cowie Stirlg 131 E4
Cowlam E R Yk 99 E1
Cowley Derbys 84 A2
Cowley Devon 9 F4
Cowley Gloucs 38 D6
Cowley Gt Lon 28 B4
Cowley Oxon 40 D5
Cowley Oxon 49 E2
Cowling Lancs 88 D1
Cowling N York 89 H4
Cowling N York 97 F4
Cowlinge Suffk 51 H6
Cowmes W York 90 C1
Cowpe Lancs 89 G2
Cowpen Nthumb 115 E4
Cowpen Bewley Dur 106 D3
Cowplain Hants 15 E5
Cowshill Dur 105 E4
Cowslip Green Somset 23 H5
Cowthorpe N York 91 E5
Cox Common Suffk 65 F4
Coxall Shrops 56 D3
Coxbank Ches 70 B4
Coxbench Derbys 72 A4
Coxbridge Somset 24 A3
Coxford Cnwll 5 E6
Coxford Norfk 76 B3
Coxgreen Staffs 58 A4
Coxheath Kent 30 A1
Coxhoe Dur 106 C4
Coxley Somset 23 H4
Coxley W York 90 D1
Coxley Wick Somset 23 H4
Coxpark Cnwll 5 H3
Coxtie Green Essex 29 F6
Coxwold N York 98 A3
Coychurch Brdgnd 35 G2
Coylton S Ayrs 119 F1
Coylumbridge Highld 146 D5
Coytrahen Brdgnd 35 F3
Crab Orchard Dorset 13 E5
Crabbs Cross Worcs 58 C2
Crabtree W Susx 16 C4
Crabtree Green Wrexhm 69 F4
Crackenthorpe Cumb 104 C2
Crackington Haven Cnwll 5 E6
Crackley Staffs 70 C5
Crackley Warwks 59 F3
Crackleybank Shrops 70 C1
Crackpot N York 96 C4
Cracoe N York 90 A6
Craddock Devon 10 A6
Cradle End Herts 51 E3
Cradley Herefs 46 C4
Cradley W Mids 58 B4
Cradley Heath W Mids 58 B4
Cradoc Powys 44 C2
Crafthole Cnwll 5 G1
Crafton Bucks 49 G1
Crag Foot Lancs 95 E2
Cragg Hill W York 90 D3
Cragg Vale W York 90 A2
Craggan Highld 156 B2
Craghead Dur 106 B6
Crai Powys 44 B2
Craibstone Moray 157 G5
Craichie Angus 141 E4
Craig Angus 141 G5
Craig Highld 153 F4
Craig Llangiwg Neath 35 E5
Craig Penllyn V Glam 35 G2
Craig's End Essex 51 H4
Craig-y-Duke Neath 35 E4
Craig-y-nos Powys 35 F6
Craigbank E Ayrs 109 H6
Craigburn Border 121 G5
Craigcefnparc Swans 34 D4
Craigcleuch D & G 111 H3
Craigdam Abers 158 D2
Craigdhu Ag & B 127 G6
Craigearn Abers 149 E6
Craigellachie Moray 157 E4
Craigend P & K 140 A2
Craigend Rens 129 F2
Craigendoran Ag & B 129 E3
Craighlaw D & G 100 D6
Craighouse Ag & B 126 D2
Craigie P & K 140 A4
Craigie S Ayrs 119 F3
Craigiefold Abers 159 E6
Craigley D & G 102 B6
Craiglockhart C Edin 132 A2
Craiglug Moray 157 E5
Craigmillar C Edin 132 B2
Craignant Shrops 69 E3
Craigneston D & G 110 B4
Craigneuk N Lans 130 D2
Craigneuk N Lans 120 B5
Craignure Ag & B 136 B3
Craigo Angus 141 G6
Craigrothie Fife 132 C6
Craigruie Stirlg 138 B2
Craigton Aber C 149 F5
Craigton Angus 141 E4
Craigton E Rens 119 G5
Craigton of Airlie Angus 140 C5
Crail Fife 133 E6
Crailing Border 122 D2
Craiselound Lincs 85 E4
Crakehall N York 97 F4
Crakehill N York 97 G2
Crakemarsh Staffs 71 F4
Crambe N York 98 C1
Cramlington Nthumb 114 D3
Cramond C Edin 132 A3
Cramond Bridge C Edin 131 H3
Crampmoor Hants 26 B1
Cranage Ches 82 C1
Cranberry Staffs 70 C4
Cranborne Dorset 12 D6
Cranbrook Kent 18 A5
Cranbrook Common Kent 18 B5
Crane Moor S York 83 H5
Crane's Corner Norfk 76 B1
Cranfield Beds 49 H3
Cranford Devon 20 D3
Cranford Gt Lon 28 B4
Cranford St Andrew Nhants 61 E3
Cranford St John Nhants 61 E3
Cranham Gloucs 38 D6
Cranham Gt Lon 29 G5
Cranhill Warwks 47 G4
Crank Mersyd 81 G5
Cranleigh Surrey 16 B5
Cranmer Green Suffk 64 C2
Cranmore IOW 14 B3
Cranmore Somset 24 B4
Cranoe Leics 60 D5
Cransford Suffk 65 F2
Cranshaws Border 122 D6
Cranstal IOM 174 n5
Cranswick E R Yk 92 D5
Crantock Cnwll 4 B2
Cranwell Lincs 73 H5
Cranwich Norfk 63 G5
Cranworth Norfk 64 B6
Craobh Haven Ag & B 127 G6
Crapstone Devon 6 B4
Crarae Ag & B 128 A5
Crask Inn Highld 162 B6
Crask of Aigas Highld 154 C3
Craster Nthumb 125 F3
Craswall Herefs 45 F3
Crateford Staffs 70 D1
Cratfield Suffk 65 F3
Crathes Abers 149 E4
Crathes Castle Abers 149 E4
Crathie Abers 147 G4
Crathie Highld 145 H4
Crathorne N York 106 D2
Craven Arms Shrops 57 E4
Crawcrook T & W 114 C2
Crawford Lancs 81 G5
Crawford S Lans 120 D1
Crawfordjohn S Lans 120 C2
Crawick D & G 110 B6
Crawley Hants 26 C3
Crawley Oxon 40 B5
Crawley W Susx 16 D5
Crawley Down W Susx 16 D5
Crawleyside Dur 105 F4
Crawshawbooth Lancs 89 F2
Crawton Abers 149 F2
Craxe's Green Essex 52 C3
Cray N York 96 C3
Cray's Pond Oxon 41 E2
Crayford Gt Lon 29 F3
Crayke N York 98 A2
Craymere Beck Norfk 76 D3
Crays Hill Essex 29 H5
Craythorne Staffs 71 G3
Craze Lowman Devon 9 G6
Crazies Hill Oxon 41 F2
Creacombe Devon 22 A1
Creag Ghoraidh W Isls 168 b4
Creagan Inn Ag & B 136 D4
Creagorry W Isls 168 b4
Creaguaineach Lodge Highld 145 E1
Creamore Bank Shrops 69 G3
Creaton Nhants 60 C2
Creca D & G 111 G2
Credenhill Herefs 45 G3
Crediton Devon 9 E5
Creebank D & G 109 E2
Creebridge D & G 109 F1
Creech Heathfield Somset 23 F2
Creech St Michael Somset 23 F2
Creed Cnwll 3 G4
Creedy Park Devon 9 E5
Creekmouth Gt Lon 29 E4
Creeting St Mary Suffk 64 C1
Creeton Lincs 73 H2
Creetown D & G 101 F6
Cregneash IOM 174 j2
Cregny Baa IOM 174 m3
Cregrina Powys 44 D4
Creich Fife 140 C2
Creigiau Cardif 36 B2
Crelly Cnwll 2 D3
Cremyll Cnwll 6 B3
Cressage Shrops 57 F6
Cressbrook Derbys 83 G2
Cresselly Pembks 33 E2
Cressex Bucks 41 F3
Cressing Essex 52 B3
Cresswell Nthumb 115 E5
Cresswell Pembks 33 E2
Cresswell Staffs 71 E4
Creswell Derbys 84 C2
Creswell Green Staffs 71 F1
Cretingham Suffk 65 E1
Cretshengan Ag & B 127 F2
Crew Green Powys 69 E2
Crewe Ches 69 F5
Crewe Ches 70 B6
Crewe Green Ches 70 B6
Crewkerne Somset 11 E6
Crews Hill Herefs 46 B1
Crews Hill Station Herts 28 D6
Crewton Derbys 72 B3
Crianlarich Stirlg 138 A2
Cribbs Causeway Gloucs 37 G2
Cribyn Cerdgn 43 E4
Criccieth Gwynd 67 E4
Crich Derbys 72 A5
Crich Carr Derbys 72 A5
Crich Common Derbys 72 A5
Crichton Mdloth 122 A6
Crick Mons 37 F3
Crick Nhants 60 B3
Crickadarn Powys 44 D3
Cricket St Thomas Somset 10 D5
Crickheath Shrops 69 E2
Crickhowell Powys 45 E1
Cricklade Wilts 39 F4
Cricklewood Gt Lon 28 C5
Cridling Stubbs N York 91 F2
Crieff P & K 139 F2
Criggan Cnwll 4 D2
Criggion Powys 69 E1
Crigglestone W York 90 D1
Crimble Gt Man 82 D6
Crimond Abers 159 F5
Crimplesham Norfk 63 F6
Crimscote Warwks 47 H4
Crinaglack Highld 154 C3
Crinan Ag & B 127 G4
Crindledyke N Lans 120 C5
Cringleford Norfk 64 D6
Cringles N York 90 B4
Crinow Pembks 33 E3
Cripp's Corner E Susx 18 A3
Cripplesease Cnwll 2 C3
Cripplestyle Dorset 13 E6
Crizeley Herefs 45 G2
Croachy Highld 155 E2
Croanford Cnwll 4 D3
Crochmore House D & G 110 C2
Crock Street Somset 10 D6
Crockenhill Kent 29 F3
Crocker End Oxon 41 E3
Crocker's Ash Herefs 37 F6
Crockerhill W Susx 15 G4
Crockernwell Devon 8 D4
Crockerton Wilts 24 D3
Crocketford D & G 110 C2
Crockey Hill N York 91 G4
Crockham Hill Kent 29 E1
Crockhurst Street Kent 17 G6
Crockleford Heath Essex 52 D3
Croes-goch Pembks 32 C5
Croes-lan Cerdgn 42 D4
Croes-y-mwyalch Torfn 36 D3
Croes-y-pant Mons 36 D5
Croeserw Neath 35 F4
Croesor Gwynd 67 F4
Croesyceiliog Carmth 34 B6
Croesyceiliog Torfn 36 D4
Croft Ches 82 A4
Croft Devon 8 B4
Croft Leics 60 A5
Croft Lincs 75 E6
Croft Michael Cnwll 2 D3
Croft-on-Tees Dur 106 B2
Croftamie Stirlg 129 F4
Crofton Cumb 103 G5
Crofton W York 91 E1
Crofton Wilts 25 H5
Crofts D & G 110 B1
Crofts Moray 157 E4
Crofts Bank Gt Man 82 C4
Crofts of Dipple Moray 157 E5
Crofts of Savoch Abers 159 F5
Crofty Swans 34 C4
Crogen Gwynd 68 B4
Croggan Ag & B 136 B2
Croglin Cumb 104 B5
Croik Highld 162 A3
Cromarty Highld 155 F6
Crombie Fife 131 G4
Cromdale Highld 156 C2
Cromer Herts 50 D3
Cromer Norfk 77 E4
Cromford Derbys 71 H6
Cromhall Gloucs 38 B3
Cromhall Common Gloucs 38 B3
Cromor W Isls 168 e7
Crompton Fold Gt Man 82 D6
Cromwell Notts 73 F6
Cronberry E Ayrs 119 H2
Crondall Hants 27 F4
Cronk-y-Voddy IOM 174 l4
Cronkbourne IOM 174 l3
Cronton Mersyd 81 G3
Crook Cumb 95 E4
Crook Dur 106 A4
Crook Inn Border 121 E2
Crook of Devon P & K 131 G5
Crookdake Cumb 103 F4
Crooke Gt Man 81 H5
Crooked End Gloucs 37 G6
Crooked Holme Cumb 112 B1
Crooked Soley Wilts 40 A1
Crookedholm E Ayrs 119 F3
Crookes S York 84 A3
Crookhall Dur 105 H5
Crookham Berks 26 D6
Crookham Nthumb 123 F3
Crookham Village Hants 27 F4
Crooklands Cumb 95 F3
Cropper Derbys 71 G3
Cropredy Oxon 48 C4
Cropston Leics 72 C1
Cropthorne Worcs 47 E4
Cropton N York 98 C4
Cropwell Bishop Notts 72 D4
Cropwell Butler Notts 72 D4
Cros W Isls 168 f9
Crosbie N Ayrs 118 D4
Crosbost W Isls 168 e7
Crosby Cumb 103 E4
Crosby IOM 174 l3
Crosby Lincs 85 F6
Crosby Mersyd 81 E4
Crosby Garret Cumb 95 H6
Crosby Ravensworth Cumb 104 C2
Crosby Villa Cumb 103 E4
Croscombe Somset 24 B4
Crosemere Shrops 69 G3
Crosland Edge W York 83 F6
Crosland Hill W York 90 B1
Cross Somset 23 G5
Cross Ash Mons 45 G1
Cross Coombe Cnwll 3 E5
Cross End Beds 61 G1
Cross End Essex 52 B4
Cross Flatts W York 90 B4
Cross Gates W York 91 E3
Cross Green Devon 5 G5
Cross Green Staffs 58 B6
Cross Green Suffk 52 B6
Cross Green Suffk 64 B1
Cross Green Suffk 52 C6
Cross Hands Carmth 34 C5
Cross Hands Pembks 33 E3
Cross Hill Derbys 72 B5
Cross Hills N York 90 A4
Cross Houses Shrops 57 F6
Cross Houses Shrops 57 G5
Cross in Hand E Susx 17 F3
Cross Inn Cerdgn 42 D5
Cross Inn Cerdgn 54 C2
Cross Inn Pembks 33 E2
Cross Inn Rhondd 36 B2
Cross Keys Ag & B 129 E4
Cross Keys Wilts 38 C1
Cross Lane IOW 14 C3
Cross Lane Head Shrops 57 G5
Cross Lanes Cnwll 2 D2
Cross Lanes Cnwll 3 E4
Cross Lanes N York 98 A1
Cross Lanes Wrexhm 69 F5
Cross o' th' hands Derbys 71 H5
Cross Oak Powys 44 D1
Cross of Jackston Abers 158 C2
Cross Roads Powys 44 C5
Cross Street Suffk 64 D3
Cross Town Ches 82 C2
Cross-at-Hand Kent 18 A6
Crossaig Ag & B 117 G5
Crossapoll Ag & B 134 B4
Crossbush W Susx 16 A2
Crosscanonby Cumb 103 E4
Crossdale Street Norfk 77 E4
Crossens Mersyd 88 B2
Crossford Fife 131 G4
Crossford S Lans 120 C4
Crossgate Cnwll 5 G5
Crossgate Lincs 74 C3
Crossgate Staffs 70 D4
Crossgatehall E Loth 132 C2
Crossgates E Ayrs 119 E4
Crossgates Fife 131 H4
Crossgates N York 99 F3
Crossgates Powys 56 A2
Crossgill Lancs 88 D6
Crosshands Carmth 33 F4
Crosshands E Ayrs 119 G2
Crosshill Fife 131 H5
Crosshill S Ayrs 109 E5
Crosshouse E Ayrs 119 F3
Crosskeys Caerph 36 C3
Crosskirk Highld 166 D5
Crosslands Cumb 94 D4
Crosslanes Shrops 69 E2
Crosslee Rens 129 E2
Crossley W York 90 C2
Crossmichael D & G 110 B1
Crosspost W Susx 16 C4
Crossroads Abers 148 C5
Crossroads Abers 149 E4
Crosston Angus 141 E5
Crossway Mons 45 G1
Crossway Pembks 42 B3
Crossway Powys 44 C5
Crossway Green Mons 37 F4
Crossway Green Worcs 58 A2
Crossways Dorset 12 B3
Crosswell Pembks 42 B3
Crosthwaite Cumb 95 E4
Croston Lancs 88 C1
Crostwick Norfk 77 E1
Crostwight Norfk 77 F3
Crouch Kent 30 D2
Crouch Kent 29 G2
Crouch End Gt Lon 28 D5
Crouch Hill Dorset 11 G6
Croucheston Wilts 25 F2
Crough House Green Kent 17 E6
Croughton Nhants 48 D2
Crovie Abers 158 D6
Crow Hants 13 E5
Crow Edge S York 83 G5
Crow End Cambs 62 C1
Crow Green Essex 29 G6
Crow Hill Herefs 46 B2
Crow's Green Essex 51 H3
Crow's Nest Cnwll 5 F3
Crowan Cnwll 2 D3
Crowborough E Susx 17 F4
Crowborough Town E Susx 17 F5
Crowcombe Somset 22 D3
Crowdecote Derbys 83 F1
Crowden Derbys 83 F5
Crowden Devon 8 B4
Crowdhill Hants 14 C6
Crowdleham Kent 29 F2
Crowell Oxon 41 F4
Crowfield Nhants 48 D3
Crowfield Suffk 64 D1
Crowfield Green Suffk 64 D1
Crowgate Street Norfk 77 F2
Crowhill E Loth 133 F2
Crowhole Derbys 84 A2
Crowhurst E Susx 18 A3
Crowhurst Surrey 17 E6
Crowhurst Lane End Surrey 17 E6
Crowland Lincs 74 C1
Crowland Suffk 64 C2
Crowlas Cnwll 2 C3
Crowle Lincs 85 E6
Crowle Worcs 47 E5
Crowle Green Worcs 47 E5
Crowmarsh Gifford Oxon 40 D3
Crown Corner Suffk 65 E2
Crownhill Devon 6 B3
Crownpits Surrey 27 H4
Crownthorpe Norfk 64 C6
Crowntown Cnwll 2 D3
Crows-an-Wra Cnwll 2 B2
Crowshill Norfk 64 B6
Crowsnest Shrops 56 D5
Crowthorne Berks 27 G6
Crowton Ches 81 H2
Croxall Staffs 71 G1
Croxby Lincs 86 B4
Croxdale Dur 106 B4
Croxden Staffs 71 F4
Croxley Green Herts 28 B6
Croxton Cambs 62 B1
Croxton Lincs 86 A6
Croxton Norfk 76 C3
Croxton Norfk 64 A4
Croxton Staffs 70 C3
Croxton Green Ches 69 H5
Croxton Kerrial Leics 73 F3
Croxtonbank Staffs 70 C3
Croy Highld 155 F4
Croy N Lans 130 D3
Croyde Devon 21 E4
Croyde Bay Devon 20 D5
Croydon Cambs 50 D6
Croydon Gt Lon 28 D3
Crubenmore Highld 146 B3
Cruckmeole Shrops 69 F1
Cruckton Shrops 69 F1
Cruden Bay Abers 159 G3
Crudgington Shrops 70 A2
Crudwell Wilts 38 D4
Crug Powys 56 B3
Crug-y-byddar Powys 56 B4
Crugmeer Cnwll 4 C4
Crugybar Carmth 43 G3
Crumlin Caerph 36 C4
Crumplehorn Cnwll 5 F1
Crumpsall Gt Man 82 C5
Crundale Kent 30 D1
Crundale Pembks 32 D3
Crunwear Pembks 33 F3
Cruwys Morchard Devon 9 F6
Crux Easton Hants 26 C5
Cruxton Dorset 11 F4
Crwbin Carmth 34 B6
Cryers Hill Bucks 41 G4
Crymmych Pembks 42 B3
Crynant Neath 35 E5
Crystal Palace Gt Lon 28 D3
Cuaig Highld 151 G4
Cuan Ferry Village Ag & B 136 B1
Cubbington Warwks 59 F2
Cubert Cnwll 4 B2
Cubley S York 83 G5
Cublington Bucks 49 G1
Cublington Herefs 45 G3
Cuckfield W Susx 16 D4
Cucklington Somset 24 C2
Cuckney Notts 84 C2
Cuckold's Green Kent 30 B4
Cuckoo Bridge Lincs 74 B2
Cuckoo's Corner Hants 27 F3
Cuckoo's Nest Ches 69 F6
Cuddesdon Oxon 40 D5
Cuddington Bucks 41 F5
Cuddington Ches 82 A2
Cuddington Heath Ches 69 G5
Cuddy Hill Lancs 88 C3
Cudham Gt Lon 29 E2
Cudliptown Devon 8 B2
Cudnell Dorset 12 D4
Cudworth S York 84 B6
Cudworth Somset 10 D6
Cudworth Common S York 84 B5
Cuerden Green Lancs 88 D2
Cuerdley Cross Ches 81 H3
Cufaude Hants 27 E5
Cuffley Herts 50 D1
Cuil Highld 136 D5
Culbokie Highld 154 D5
Culbone Somset 22 A4
Culburnie Highld 154 C3
Culcabock Highld 155 E3
Culcharry Highld 155 G4
Culcheth Ches 82 B4
Culdrain Abers 157 G2
Culduie Highld 151 G3
Culford Suffk 63 G2
Culgaith Cumb 104 C3
Culham Oxon 40 C4
Culkein Highld 164 A2
Culkein Drumbeg Highld 164 B2
Culkerton Gloucs 38 D4

Cullen Dizzard

Cullen Moray 157 G6
Cullercoats T & W 115 E3
Cullerlie Abers 149 E5
Cullicudden Highld 155 E5
Cullingworth W York 90 B3
Cullipool House Ag & B 136 B1
Cullivoe Shet 169 j5
Culloden Highld 155 E4
Cullompton Devon 9 G5
Culm Davy Devon 10 B6
Culmington Shrops 57 E4
Culmstock Devon 10 A6
Culnacraig Highld 161 E4
Culnaightrie D & G 102 B5
Culnaknock Highld 151 E5
Culpho Suffk 53 F6
Culrain Highld 162 C3
Culross Fife 131 F4
Culroy S Ayrs 109 E6
Culsalmond Abers 158 B2
Culscadden D & G 101 F5
Culshabbin D & G 100 D5
Culswick Shet 169 h2
Cultercullen Abers 159 E1
Cults Aber C 149 F5
Culverstone Green Kent 29 G2
Culverthorpe Lincs 73 H4
Culworth Nhants 48 D4
Culzean Castle S Ayrs 108 D6
Cumbernauld N Lans 130 D2
Cumbernauld Village N Lans 130 D3
Cumberworth Lincs 87 E2
Cumdivock Cumb 103 G5
Cuminestown Abers 158 D4
Cumledge Border 123 E5
Cummersdale Cumb 103 H5
Cummertrees D & G 111 F1
Cummingston Moray 156 C6
Cumnock E Ayrs 119 G1
Cumnor Oxon 40 C5
Cumrew Cumb 104 B5
Cumrue D & G 111 E3
Cumwhinton Cumb 104 A5
Cumwhitton Cumb 104 B5
Cundall N York 97 G2
Cunninghamhead N Ayrs 119 E4
Cupar Fife 140 D1
Cupar Muir Fife 140 D1
Curbar Derbys 83 G2
Curbridge Hants 14 C5
Curbridge Oxon 40 B5
Curdridge Hants 14 C5
Curdworth Warwks 59 E5
Curland Somset 23 F1
Curridge Berks 40 C1
Currie C Edin 131 H2
Curry Mallet Somset 23 F1
Curry Rivel Somset 23 G2
Curteis Corner Kent 18 B5
Curtisden Green Kent 18 A5
Curtisknowle Devon 7 E3
Cury Cnwll 2 D2
Cushnie Abers 148 C6
Cushuish Somset 23 E2
Cusop Herefs 45 E3
Cutcloy D & G 101 F4
Cutcombe Somset 22 B3
Cutgate Gt Man 82 D6
Cuthill Highld 162 D2
Cutiau Gwynd 67 F2
Cutler's Green Essex 51 G4
Cutmadoc Cnwll 5 E2
Cutmere Cnwll 5 G2
Cutnall Green Worcs 58 B2
Cutsdean Gloucs 47 F2
Cutsyke W York 91 E2
Cutthorpe Derbys 84 A2
Cuttivett Cnwll 5 G2
Cuxham Oxon 41 E4
Cuxton Kent 29 H3
Cuxwold Lincs 86 B5
Cwm Blae G 36 C5
Cwm Denbgs 80 C2
Cwm Capel Carmth 34 B4
Cwm Crawnon Powys 44 D1
Cwm Dulais Swans 34 D5
Cwm Irfon Powys 44 A4
Cwm Llinau Powys 55 F6
Cwm Morgan Carmth 42 C3
Cwm Penmachno Conwy 67 G5
Cwm-bach Carmth 34 B4
Cwm-celyn Blae G 36 C5
Cwm-Cewydd Gwynd 68 A1
Cwm-cou Cerdgn 42 C3
Cwm-Ifor Carmth 43 G2
Cwm-y-glo Carmth 34 C6
Cwm-y-glo Gwynd 79 E1
Cwmafan Neath 35 E3
Cwmaman Rhondd 35 G4
Cwmann Carmth 43 F4
Cwmavon Torfn 36 D5
Cwmbach Carmth 33 G4
Cwmbach Powys 44 D3
Cwmbach Rhondd 35 H4
Cwmbach Llechryd Powys 44 C5
Cwmbelan Powys 55 G3
Cwmbran Torfn 36 D4
Cwmbrwyno Cerdgn 55 E3
Cwmcarn Caerph 36 C4
Cwmcarvan Mons 37 F5
Cwmdare Rhondd 35 G5
Cwmdu Carmth 43 F2
Cwmdu Powys 45 E2
Cwmdu Swans 34 D4
Cwmduad Carmth 42 D2
Cwmdwr Carmth 43 G2
Cwmergyr Cerdgn 55 E4
Cwmfelin Brdgnd 35 F3
Cwmfelin Myr Td 36 B4
Cwmfelin Boeth Carmth 33 F4
Cwmfelin Mynach Carmth 33 F4
Cwmfelinfach Caerph 36 C3
Cwmffrwd Carmth 34 B6
Cwmgiedd Powys 35 E5
Cwmgorse Carmth 34 D5
Cwmgwili Carmth 34 C5
Cwmgwrach Neath 35 F5
Cwmhiraeth Carmth 42 D3
Cwmisfael Carmth 34 B6
Cwmllynfell Neath 35 E6
Cwmmawr Carmth 34 C5
Cwmparc Rhondd 35 G4
Cwmpengraig Carmth 42 D3
Cwmpennar Rhondd 36 B4
Cwmrhos Powys 45 E2
Cwmrhydyceirw Swans 34 D4
Cwmsychbant Cerdgn 43 E4
Cwmtillery Blae G 36 C5
Cwmyoy Mons 45 F1
Cwmystwyth Cerdgn 55 E3
Cwrt Gwynd 54 D5
Cwrt-newydd Cerdgn 43 E4
Cwrt-y-gollen Powys 36 C6
Cyfronydd Powys 56 B6
Cylibebyll Neath 35 E5
Cymer Neath 35 F4
Cymmer Rhondd 36 A3
Cynghordy Carmth 44 A3
Cynheidre Carmth 34 B5
Cynonville Neath 35 F4
Cynwyd Denbgs 68 C4
Cynwyl Elfed Carmth 42 D2

D

Daccombe Devon 7 F4
Dacre Cumb 104 A3
Dacre N York 90 C6
Dacre Banks N York 90 C6
Daddry Shield Dur 105 F4
Dadford Bucks 49 E3
Dadlington Leics 59 G5
Dafen Carmth 34 C4
Daffy Green Norfk 76 C1
Dagenham Gt Lon 29 F4
Daglingworth Gloucs 39 E5
Dagnall Bucks 41 H6
Dagworth Suffk 64 C1
Dailly S Ayrs 108 D5
Dainton Devon 7 F4
Dairsie Fife 140 D1
Daisy Hill Gt Man 82 B5
Daisy Hill W York 90 D2
Dalabrog W Isls 168 b3
Dalavich Ag & B 136 D1
Dalbeattie D & G 110 C1
Dalbury Derbys 71 G3
Dalby IOM 174 k3
Dalby Lincs 86 D2
Dalby N York 98 B2
Dalcapon P & K 139 G5
Dalchalm Highld 163 F4
Dalchreichart Highld 145 E6
Dalchruin P & K 138 D1
Dalcrue P & K 139 H2
Dalderby Lincs 86 C1
Dalditch Devon 9 G3
Dale Cumb 104 B4
Dale Derbys 72 B4
Dale Pembks 32 B2
Dale Bottom Cumb 103 G2
Dale End Derbys 71 G6
Dale End N York 89 H4
Dale Hill E Susx 17 H4
Dalehouse N York 107 G3
Dalgarven N Ayrs 119 E4
Dalgety Bay Fife 131 H3
Dalgig E Ayrs 109 G6
Dalginross P & K 139 E2
Dalguise P & K 139 G4
Dalhalvaig Highld 166 C4
Dalham Suffk 63 F1
Daliburgh W Isls 168 b3
Dalkeith Mdloth 132 B2
Dallas Moray 156 C4
Dallinghoo Suffk 53 F6
Dallington E Susx 17 G3
Dallington Nhants 49 E5
Dallow N York 97 E2
Dalmally Ag & B 137 F2
Dalmary Stirlg 129 G5
Dalmellington E Ayrs 109 F5
Dalmeny C Edin 131 H3
Dalmigavie Highld 155 F1
Dalmigavie Lodge Highld 155 F1
Dalmore Highld 155 E6
Dalmuir W Duns 129 F2
Dalnabreck Highld 143 F1
Dalnacardoch P & K 146 B1
Dalnahaitnach Highld 155 G1
Dalnaspidal P & K 146 A2
Dalnawillan Lodge Highld 166 D2
Daloist P & K 139 E5
Dalqueich P & K 131 G6
Dalquhairn S Ayrs 109 E4
Dalreavoch Lodge Highld 162 D5
Dalry N Ayrs 119 E4
Dalrymple E Ayrs 119 E1
Dalserf S Lans 120 C4
Dalsmeran Ag & B 117 E2
Dalston Cumb 103 H5
Dalston Gt Lon 28 D4
Dalswinton D & G 110 D3
Dalton Cumb 95 F2
Dalton D & G 111 F2
Dalton Lancs 81 G5
Dalton N York 96 D6
Dalton N York 97 G2
Dalton Nthumb 114 C3
Dalton S York 84 B4
Dalton Magna S York 84 B4
Dalton Parva S York 84 B4
Dalton Piercy Dur 106 D4
Dalton-in-Furness Cumb 94 C2
Dalton-le-Dale Dur 106 C6
Dalton-on-Tees N York 106 B2
Dalveen D & G 110 C5
Dalveich Stirlg 138 C2
Dalwhinnie Highld 146 A3
Dalwood Devon 10 C5
Dam Green Norfk 64 C4
Damask Green Herts 50 C4
Damerham Hants 13 E6
Damgate Norfk 77 G1
Danaway Kent 30 B2
Danbury Essex 52 A1
Danby N York 107 F2
Danby Bottom N York 98 C5
Danby Wiske N York 97 F5
Dandaleith Moray 157 E4
Danderhall Mdloth 132 B2
Dane End Herts 50 D3
Dane Hills Leics 60 B6
Dane Street Kent 30 D1
Danebridge Ches 83 E1
Danegate E Susx 17 F5
Danehill E Susx 17 E4
Danemoor Green Norfk 64 C6
Danesford Shrops 57 G4
Danesmoor Derbys 84 B1
Daniel's Water Kent 18 C5
Danshillock Abers 158 C5
Danskine E Loth 133 E2
Danthorpe E R Yk 93 F3
Danzey Green Warwks 58 D2
Dapple Heath Staffs 71 E3
Darby Green Hants 27 F5
Darcy Lever Gt Man 82 B5
Dardy Powys 45 E1
Daren-felen Mons 36 C5
Darenth Kent 29 F3
Daresbury Ches 81 H3
Darfield S York 84 B5
Darfoulds Notts 84 C2
Dargate Kent 30 D2
Darite Cnwll 5 F3
Darland Kent 30 A3
Darland Wrexhm 69 F6
Darlaston Staffs 70 D4
Darlaston W Mids 58 C5
Darlaston Green W Mids 58 C5
Darley N York 90 C6
Darley Abbey Derbys 72 A4
Darley Bridge Derbys 71 G6
Darley Dale Derbys 83 G1
Darley Green Warwks 59 E3
Darley Head N York 90 C5
Darleyhall Herts 50 B3
Darlingscott Warwks 47 H3
Darlington Dur 106 B2
Darliston Shrops 69 H3
Darlton Notts 85 E2
Darnford Staffs 71 F1
Darnick Border 122 C3
Darowen Powys 55 F6
Darra Abers 158 C4
Darracott Cnwll 20 C2
Darracott Devon 20 C2
Darracott Devon 21 E4
Darras Hall Nthumb 114 C2
Darrington W York 91 F2
Darsham Suffk 65 G2
Darshill Somset 24 B4
Dartford Kent 29 F3
Dartington Devon 7 E4
Dartmeet Devon 6 D5
Dartmouth Devon 7 F3
Darton S York 83 H6
Darvel E Ayrs 119 G3
Darwell Hole E Susx 17 H3
Darwen Lancs 89 E2
Datchet Berks 41 H2
Datchworth Herts 50 D3
Datchworth Green Herts 50 D2
Daubhill Gt Man 82 B5
Dauntsey Wilts 39 E2
Dava Highld 156 B3
Davenham Ches 82 B2
Davenport Gt Man 82 D3
Davenport Green Ches 82 C3
Davenport Green Gt Man 82 C3
Daventry Nhants 48 D5
David Street Kent 29 G2
Davidson's Mains C Edin 132 A3
Davidstow Cnwll 5 E5
Davington D & G 111 G5
Davington Hill Kent 30 D2
Daviot Abers 158 C2
Daviot Highld 155 E3
Daviot House Highld 155 E3
Davis's Town E Susx 17 F3
Davoch of Grange Moray 157 G4
Davyhulme Gt Man 82 C4
Daw End W Mids 58 C5
Daw's House Cnwll 5 G4
Dawesgreen Surrey 16 C6
Dawley Shrops 57 G6
Dawlish Devon 9 F2
Dawlish Warren Devon 9 G2
Dawn Conwy 80 A2
Daws Green Somset 23 E1
Daws Heath Essex 30 B5
Dawsmere Lincs 75 E3
Day Green Ches 70 C6
Daybrook Notts 72 C4
Dayhills Staffs 70 D3
Dayhouse Bank Worcs 58 C3
Daylesford Gloucs 47 H2
Ddol Flints 80 D2
Ddol-Cownwy Powys 68 B2
Deal Kent 31 G1
Dean Cumb 103 E3
Dean Devon 21 F5
Dean Devon 21 G5
Dean Devon 7 E4
Dean Dorset 12 D6
Dean Hants 26 C2
Dean Hants 14 D6
Dean Lancs 89 G2
Dean Oxon 48 B1
Dean Somset 24 B4
Dean Bottom Kent 29 G3
Dean Court Oxon 40 C5
Dean End Dorset 25 E1
Dean Head S York 83 G5
Dean Prior Devon 7 E4
Dean Row Ches 82 D3
Dean Street Kent 30 A1
Deanburnhaugh Border 112 A6
Deancombe Devon 7 E4
Deane Gt Man 82 B5
Deane Hants 26 D4
Deanhead W York 90 B1
Deanland Dorset 25 E1
Deanlane End W Susx 15 F5
Deanraw Nthumb 113 E1
Deans W Loth 131 F2
Deanscales Cumb 103 E3
Deanshanger Nhants 49 F3
Deanshaugh Moray 157 F4
Deanston Stirlg 130 C5
Dearham Cumb 103 E4
Dearnley Gt Man 89 H1
Debach Suffk 53 F6
Debden Essex 51 F4
Debden Essex 29 E6
Debden Green Essex 51 G4
Debenham Suffk 64 D2
Deblin's Green Worcs 46 D4
Dechmont W Loth 131 G2
Dechmont Road W Loth 131 F2
Deddington Oxon 48 C2
Dedham Essex 52 D4
Dedham Heath Essex 52 D4
Dedworth Berks 41 G2
Deene Nhants 61 E5
Deenethorpe Nhants 61 F5
Deepcar S York 83 H4
Deepcut Surrey 27 G5
Deepdale Cumb 95 H3
Deepdale N York 96 B3
Deeping Gate Lincs 74 B1
Deeping St James Lincs 74 B1
Deeping St Nicholas Lincs 74 C2
Deerhurst Gloucs 46 D2
Deerhurst Walton Gloucs 46 D2
Deerton Street Kent 30 C2
Defford Worcs 47 E3
Defynnog Powys 44 B2
Deganwy Conwy 79 G3
Degnish Ag & B 136 B1
Deighton N York 97 G5
Deighton N York 91 G4
Deighton W York 90 C1
Deiniolen Gwynd 79 E1
Delabole Cnwll 4 D4
Delamere Ches 81 H1
Delfrigs Abers 159 F1
Dell Quay W Susx 15 F4
Delley Devon 21 F3
Delliefure Highld 156 C2
Delly End Oxon 40 B6
Delmonden Green Kent 18 A4
Delnashaugh Inn Moray 156 D3
Delny Highld 162 D1
Delph Gt Man 83 E5
Delves Dur 105 H5
Delvine P & K 140 A4
Dembleby Lincs 73 H4
Demelza Cnwll 4 C2
Den of Lindores Fife 140 C1
Denaby S York 84 C5
Denaby Main S York 84 C5
Denbies Surrey 28 B1
Denbigh Denbgs 80 C1
Denbrae Fife 140 D2
Denbury Devon 7 F4
Denby Derbys 72 B5
Denby Bottles Derbys 72 B5
Denby Dale W York 83 G5
Denchworth Oxon 40 B3
Dendron Cumb 94 C2
Denel End Beds 50 A4
Denfield P & K 139 G1
Denford Nhants 61 F3
Dengie Essex 52 C1
Denham Bucks 28 A5
Denham Suffk 63 G1
Denham Suffk 64 D3
Denham End Suffk 63 G2
Denham Green Bucks 28 A5
Denham Green Suffk 64 D3
Denhead Abers 159 F4
Denhead Fife 141 E1
Denhead of Gray Dund C 140 C3
Denholm Border 122 C1
Denholme W York 90 B3
Denholme Clough W York 90 B3
Denio Gwynd 66 C4
Denmead Hants 15 E5
Denmore Aber C 149 G6
Denne Park W Susx 16 C4
Dennington Suffk 65 E2
Denny Falk 130 D3
Dennyloanhead Falk 130 D3
Denshaw Gt Man 83 E6
Denside Abers 149 F4
Densole Kent 19 F6
Denston Suffk 52 A6
Denstone Staffs 71 F4
Denstroude Kent 31 E2
Dent Cumb 95 H3
Denton Cambs 61 G4
Denton Dur 106 B3
Denton E Susx 17 E2
Denton Gt Man 82 D4
Denton Kent 29 G3
Denton Kent 19 F6
Denton Lincs 73 F3
Denton N York 90 C4
Denton Nhants 49 F5
Denton Norfk 65 E4
Denton Oxon 40 D4
Denver Norfk 63 E5
Denwick Nthumb 125 E2
Deopham Norfk 64 C5
Deopham Green Norfk 64 C5
Depden Suffk 63 G1
Depden Green Suffk 63 G1
Deptford Gt Lon 29 E4
Deptford Wilts 25 F3
Derby Derbys 72 A4
Derby Devon 21 F4
Derbyhaven IOM 174 i2
Derculich P & K 139 F5
Dereham Norfk 76 C1
Deri Caerph 36 B4
Derril Devon 20 C1
Derringstone Kent 31 F1
Derrington Staffs 70 D2
Derriton Devon 20 D1
Derry Hill Wilts 38 D1
Derrythorpe Lincs 85 F5
Dersingham Norfk 75 G3
Dervaig Ag & B 135 F5
Derwen Denbgs 68 C5
Derwen Fawr Carmth 43 F1
Derwenlas Powys 55 E5
Derwydd Carmth 34 D6
Desborough Nhants 60 D4
Desford Leics 59 H6
Deskford Moray 157 G5
Detchant Nthumb 123 H3
Detling Kent 30 B2
Deuxhill Shrops 57 G4
Devauden Mons 37 F4
Devil's Bridge Cerdgn 55 E3
Deviock Cnwll 5 G1
Devitts Green Warwks 59 F4
Devizes Wilts 25 F5
Devonport Devon 6 B3
Devonside Clacks 131 E5
Devoran Cnwll 3 E4
Dewarton Mdloth 132 C1
Dewlish Dorset 12 B4
Dewsbury W York 90 D2
Dewsbury Moor W York 90 C2
Deytheur Powys 69 E2
Dial Somset 23 H6
Dial Green W Susx 27 G2
Dial Post W Susx 16 B3
Dibberford Dorset 11 E5
Dibden Hants 14 B4
Dibden Purlieu Hants 14 B4
Dickens Heath W Mids 58 D3
Dickleburgh Norfk 64 D4
Didbrook Gloucs 47 F2
Didcot Oxon 40 C3
Didcot Railway Centre Oxon 40 C3
Diddington Cambs 61 H2
Diddlebury Shrops 57 E4
Didley Herefs 45 G2
Didling W Susx 15 F5
Didmarton Gloucs 38 C3
Didsbury Gt Man 82 C4
Didworthy Devon 6 D4
Digby Lincs 74 A5
Digg Highld 151 E6
Diggle Gt Man 83 E5
Digmoor Lancs 81 G5
Digswell Herts 50 C2
Digswell Water Herts 50 C2
Dihewyd Cerdgn 43 E5
Dilham Norfk 77 F2
Dilhorne Staffs 71 E4
Dillington Cambs 61 G2
Dilston Nthumb 113 G1
Dilton Wilts 24 D4
Dilton Marsh Wilts 24 D4
Dilwyn Herefs 45 G5
Dimple Derbys 71 H6
Dimple Gt Man 89 E1
Dinas Carmth 33 G5
Dinas Cnwll 4 C3
Dinas Gwynd 66 B4
Dinas Pembks 32 D6
Dinas Rhondd 35 G3
Dinas Dinlle Gwynd 66 D6
Dinas Powys V Glam 36 C1
Dinas-Mawddwy Gwynd 68 A1
Dinder Somset 24 A4
Dinedor Herefs 45 H3
Dingestow Mons 37 F5
Dingle Mersyd 81 F3
Dingleden Kent 18 B4
Dingley Nhants 60 D4
Dingwall Highld 154 D5
Dinham Mons 37 F3
Dinmael Conwy 68 B4
Dinnet Abers 148 B4
Dinnington S York 84 C3
Dinnington Somset 10 D6
Dinnington T & W 114 D3
Dinorwic Gwynd 67 E6
Dinton Bucks 41 F5
Dinton Wilts 25 F2
Dinwoodie D & G 111 F4
Dinworthy Devon 20 C2
Dipford Somset 23 E1
Dipley Hants 27 F5
Dippen Ag & B 117 G4
Dippen N Ayrs 118 B2
Dippenhall Surrey 27 F4
Dippermill Devon 8 A5
Dippertown Devon 5 H4
Dipple Moray 157 E5
Dipple S Ayrs 108 D5
Diptford Devon 7 E3
Dipton Dur 114 C1
Diptonmill Nthumb 105 F6
Dirleton E Loth 132 D3
Dirt Pot Nthumb 105 E5
Discoed Powys 56 C2
Diseworth Leics 72 B2
Dishforth N York 97 G2
Disley Ches 83 E3
Diss Norfk 64 D3
Disserth Powys 44 C5
Distington Cumb 102 D2
Ditchampton Wilts 25 F2
Ditchburn Nthumb 124 D3
Ditcheat Somset 24 B3
Ditchingham Norfk 65 F4
Ditchley Oxon 48 B1
Ditchling E Susx 16 D3
Ditherington Shrops 69 G1
Ditteridge Wilts 38 C1
Dittisham Devon 7 F3
Ditton Ches 81 G3
Ditton Kent 29 H2
Ditton Green Cambs 63 F1
Ditton Priors Shrops 57 F4
Dixton Gloucs 47 E2
Dixton Mons 37 F6
Dizzard Cnwll 5 E6

283

Dobcross
Earlston
284

Dobcross Gt Man 83 E5
Dobroyd Castle W York 89 H2
Dobwalls Cnwll 5 F2
Doccombe Devon 9 E3
Dochgarroch Highld 154 D3
Dockenfield Surrey 27 F3
Docker Lancs 95 F2
Docking Norfk 75 H4
Docklow Herefs 46 A5
Dockray Cumb 103 G5
Dockray Cumb 103 H2
Dod's Leigh Staffs 71 E3
Dodbrooke Devon 7 E2
Dodd's Green Ches 70 A4
Doddinghurst Essex 29 G6
Doddington Cambs 62 C4
Doddington Kent 30 C2
Doddington Lincs 85 G2
Doddington Nthumb 123 G3
Doddington Shrops 57 F3
Doddiscombsleigh Devon 9 E3
Doddshill Norfk 75 G3
Doddy Cross Cnwll 5 G2
Dodford Nhants 48 D5
Dodford Worcs 58 B3
Dodington Gloucs 38 B2
Dodington Somset 23 E3
Dodleston Ches 69 F6
Dodscott Devon 21 F2
Dodside E Rens 119 G5
Dodworth S York 83 H5
Dodworth Bottom S York 84 A5
Dodworth Green S York 83 H5
Doe Bank W Mids 58 D5
Doe Lea Derbys 84 B1
Dog Village Devon 9 G4
Dogdyke Lincs 74 B6
Dogley Lane W York 83 G6
Dogmersfield Hants 27 F4
Dogridge Wilts 39 E3
Dogsthorpe Cambs 62 A5
Dol-for Powys 55 F6
Dol-gran Carmth 42 D3
Dolanog Powys 68 C1
Dolau Powys 56 B2
Dolaucothi Carmth 43 G3
Dolbenmaen Gwynd 67 E4
Doley Shrops 70 B3
Dolfach Powys 55 G6
Dolfor Powys 56 A4
Dolgarrog Conwy 79 G1
Dolgellau Gwynd 67 G2
Dolgoch Gwynd 54 D6
Doll Highld 163 F4
Dollar Clacks 131 F5
Dollarfield Clacks 131 F5
Dolley Green Powys 56 C2
Dollwen Cerdgn 54 D3
Dolphin Flints 80 D2
Dolphinholme Lancs 88 D5
Dolphinton S Lans 121 E4
Dolton Devon 21 F2
Dolwen Conwy 80 A2
Dolwyddelan Conwy 67 G5
Dolybont Cerdgn 54 D4
Dolyhir Powys 45 E5
Domgay Powys 69 E2
Donaldson's Lodge Nthumb 123 F4
Doncaster S York 84 C5
Doncaster Carr S York 84 D5
Donhead St Andrew Wilts 25 E2
Donhead St Mary Wilts 25 E2
Donibristle Fife 131 H4
Doniford Somset 22 D3
Donington Lincs 74 B4
Donington on Bain Lincs 86 C3
Donington Southing Lincs 74 B3
Donisthorpe Leics 71 H2
Donkey Street Kent 19 E5
Donkey Town Surrey 27 G5
Donnington Berks 40 C1
Donnington Gloucs 47 G2
Donnington Herefs 46 C3
Donnington Shrops 57 F6
Donnington Shrops 70 B1
Donnington W Susx 15 G4
Donnington Wood Shrops 70 B1
Donyatt Somset 10 D6
Doomsday Green W Susx 16 C4
Doonfoot S Ayrs 119 E1
Doonholm S Ayrs 119 E1
Dorback Lodge Highld 147 F6
Dorchester Dorset 11 G4
Dorchester Oxon 40 D4
Dordon Warwks 59 E5
Dore S York 83 H3
Dores Highld 154 D2
Dorking Surrey 28 C1
Dorking Tye Suffk 52 C4
Dormans Land Surrey 17 E6
Dormans Park Surrey 17 E5
Dormington Herefs 46 A3
Dormston Worcs 47 E5
Dorn Gloucs 47 G3
Dorney Bucks 41 G2
Dornie Highld 152 C2
Dornoch Highld 163 E3
Dornock D & G 111 G1
Dorrery Highld 166 D4
Dorridge W Mids 59 E3
Dorrington Lincs 74 A5
Dorrington Shrops 57 E6
Dorrington Shrops 70 B4
Dorsington Warwks 47 G4
Dorstone Herefs 45 F3
Dorton Bucks 41 E6
Dosthill Staffs 59 E5
Dottery Dorset 11 E4
Doublebois Cnwll 5 E2
Doughton Gloucs 38 C3
Douglas IOM 174 m3
Douglas S Lans 120 C2
Douglas and Angus Dund C 140 D3
Douglas Castle S Lans 120 C3
Douglas Pier Ag & B 128 C5
Douglas Water S Lans 120 C3
Douglas West S Lans 120 C2
Douglastown Angus 140 D4
Doulting Somset 24 B4
Dounby Ork 169 b3
Doune Highld 162 A4
Doune Stirlg 130 D5
Dounepark S Ayrs 108 D4
Dounie Highld 162 C3
Dousland Devon 6 C4
Dovaston Shrops 69 F2
Dove Green Notts 72 B5
Dove Holes Derbys 83 F2
Dovenby Cumb 103 E3
Dover Gt Man 82 A5
Dover Kent 19 G6
Dover Castle Kent 19 G6
Dovercourt Essex 53 F4
Doverdale Worcs 58 B2
Doveridge Derbys 71 F3
Doversgreen Surrey 16 C6
Dowally P & K 139 G5
Dowbridge Lancs 88 C3
Dowdeswell Gloucs 47 E1
Dowlais Myr Td 36 B5
Dowland Devon 21 F2
Dowlish Ford Somset 10 D6
Dowlish Wake Somset 10 D6
Down Ampney Gloucs 39 F4
Down Hatherley Gloucs 46 D1
Down St Mary Devon 8 D5
Down Thomas Devon 6 B3
Downacarey Devon 5 G5
Downderry Cnwll 5 G1
Downe Gt Lon 29 E2
Downend Berks 40 C2
Downend Gloucs 37 G2
Downend Gloucs 38 C4
Downend IOW 14 D2
Downfield Dund C 140 D3
Downgate Cnwll 5 F3
Downgate Cnwll 5 G3
Downham Essex 29 H6
Downham Gt Lon 29 E3
Downham Lancs 89 F4
Downham Nthumb 123 F3
Downham Market Norfk 63 E6
Downhead Somset 24 A2
Downhead Somset 24 B4
Downhill Cnwll 4 B3
Downhill P & K 140 A3
Downholland Cross Lancs 81 F5
Downholme N York 96 D5
Downies Abers 149 G4
Downing Flints 80 D2
Downley Bucks 41 G4
Downside Somset 24 B4
Downside Somset 24 B4
Downside Surrey 28 B2
Downton Hants 13 F4
Downton Wilts 25 G1
Downton on the Rock Herefs 56 D3
Dowsby Lincs 74 B3
Dowsdale Lincs 74 C1
Dowsland Green Essex 52 B3
Doxey Staffs 70 D2
Doxford Nthumb 125 E3
Doynton Gloucs 38 B2
Draethen Caerph 36 C3
Draffan S Lans 120 B4
Dragonby Lincs 85 G6
Dragons Green W Susx 16 B4
Drakeholes Notts 85 E4
Drakelow Worcs 58 A3
Drakemyre N Ayrs 119 E4
Drakes Broughton Worcs 47 E4
Drakes Cross Worcs 58 D3
Drakewalls Cnwll 5 H3
Draughton N York 90 B5
Draughton Nhants 60 D3
Drax N York 91 H2
Drax Hales N York 91 H2
Draycot Foliat Wilts 39 F2
Draycote Warwks 59 G2
Draycott Derbys 72 B3
Draycott Gloucs 47 G3
Draycott Shrops 58 A5
Draycott Somset 23 G4
Draycott Somset 24 A1
Draycott Worcs 46 D4
Draycott in the Clay Staffs 71 F3
Draycott in the Moors Staffs 71 E4
Drayford Devon 21 H2
Draynes Cnwll 5 F3
Drayton Hants 15 E4
Drayton Leics 60 D5
Drayton Lincs 74 C4
Drayton Norfk 77 E1
Drayton Oxon 48 C3
Drayton Oxon 40 C4
Drayton Somset 23 G2
Drayton Worcs 58 B3
Drayton Bassett Staffs 59 E5
Drayton Beauchamp Bucks 41 G5
Drayton Manor Park Staffs 59 E5
Drayton Parslow Bucks 49 F2
Drayton St Leonard Oxon 40 D4
Drebley N York 90 B5
Dreemskerry IOM 174 n4
Dreen Hill Pembks 32 C3
Drefach Carmth 42 D3
Drefach Carmth 34 C6
Drefach Cerdgn 43 E4
Drefelin Carmth 42 D3
Dreghorn N Ayrs 119 E3
Drellingore Kent 19 F5
Drem E Loth 132 D3
Dresden Staffs 70 D4
Drewsteignton Devon 8 D4
Driby Lincs 86 D2
Driffield E R Yk 92 D5
Driffield Gloucs 39 E4
Driffield Cross Roads Gloucs 39 E4
Drift Cnwll 2 B3
Drigg Cumb 94 B5
Drighlington W York 90 C2
Drimnin Highld 135 G5
Drimpton Dorset 11 E5
Drimsallie Highld 144 B2
Dringhoe E R Yk 93 E5
Dringhouses N York 91 G4
Drinkstone Suffk 64 B1
Drinkstone Green Suffk 64 B1
Drinsey Nook Notts 85 F2
Drive End Dorset 11 F5
Driver's End Herts 50 C3
Drointon Staffs 71 E3
Droitwich Worcs 58 B2
Dron P & K 140 A1
Dronfield Derbys 84 A2
Dronfield Woodhouse Derbys 84 A2
Drongan E Ayrs 119 F1
Dronley Angus 140 C3
Droop Dorset 12 A5
Dropping Well S York 84 B4
Droxford Hants 14 D5
Droylsden Gt Man 82 D4
Druid Denbgs 68 C4
Druids Heath W Mids 58 D6
Druidston Pembks 32 C3
Druimachoish Highld 137 F4
Druimarbin Highld 144 C1
Druimdrishaig Ag & B 127 F2
Druimindarroch Highld 143 F2
Drum Ag & B 127 H3
Drum P & K 131 G5
Drumalbin S Lans 120 D3
Drumbeg Highld 164 B2
Drumblade Abers 158 B3
Drumbreddon D & G 100 B4
Drumbuie Highld 152 B2
Drumburgh Cumb 103 G6
Drumburn D & G 102 C6
Drumchapel C Glas 129 G2
Drumchastle P & K 138 D6
Drumclog S Lans 120 A3
Drumeldrie Fife 132 C5
Drumelzier Border 121 F3
Drumfearn Highld 143 F6
Drumfrennie Abers 149 E4
Drumguish Highld 146 C4
Drumhead Abers 148 D4
Drumin Moray 156 D2
Drumjohn D & G 109 G4
Drumlamford S Ayrs 109 E2
Drumlasie Abers 148 D5
Drumleaning Cumb 103 G5
Drumlemble Ag & B 117 F2
Drumlithie Abers 149 E2
Drummoddie D & G 101 E5
Drummore D & G 100 C4
Drummuir Moray 157 F3
Drumnadrochit Highld 154 C2
Drumnagorrach Moray 157 G4
Drumpark D & G 110 C3
Drumrunie Lodge Highld 161 F4
Drumshang S Ayrs 108 D6
Drumuie Highld 151 E3
Drumuillie Highld 156 B1
Drumvaich Stirlg 130 C5
Drunzie P & K 131 H6
Druridge Nthumb 114 D5
Drury Flints 81 E1
Dry Doddington Lincs 73 F5
Dry Drayton Cambs 62 C1
Dry Sandford Oxon 40 C4
Dry Street Essex 29 H5
Drybeck Cumb 104 C2
Drybridge Moray 157 F5
Drybridge N Ayrs 119 E3
Drybrook Gloucs 37 G6
Dryburgh Border 122 C3
Drym Cnwll 2 D3
Drymen Stirlg 129 F4
Drymuir Abers 159 E4
Drynoch Highld 150 D2
Dryslwyn Carmth 43 F1
Dryton Shrops 57 F6
Dubford Abers 158 D5
Dublin Suffk 64 D2
Duchally Highld 161 H5
Duck End Beds 50 B5
Duck End Cambs 62 B2
Duck End Essex 51 G3
Duck End Essex 51 H4
Duck's Cross Beds 61 G1
Duckend Green Essex 51 H3
Duckington Ches 69 G5
Ducklington Oxon 40 B5
Duddenhoe End Essex 51 E4
Duddingston C Edin 132 B2
Duddington Nhants 61 F5
Duddlestone Somset 23 E1
Duddleswell E Susx 17 E4
Duddlewick Shrops 57 G4
Duddo Nthumb 123 F4
Duddon Ches 81 G1
Duddon Bridge Cumb 94 C4
Dudleston Shrops 69 F4
Dudleston Heath Shrops 69 F4
Dudley T & W 114 D3
Dudley W Mids 58 B4
Dudley Hill W York 90 C3
Dudley Port W Mids 58 C4
Dudnill Shrops 57 G3
Dudsbury Dorset 13 E4
Dudswell Herts 41 H5
Duffield Derbys 72 A4
Duffryn Neath 35 F4
Dufftown Moray 157 E3
Duffus Moray 156 D6
Dufton Cumb 104 D3
Duggleby N York 98 D1
Duirinish Highld 152 B2
Duisdalemore Highld 143 F5
Duisky Highld 144 B2
Duke Street Suffk 52 D5
Dukestown Blae G 36 C5
Dukinfield Gt Man 82 D4
Dulas IOA 78 D4
Dulcote Somset 24 A4
Dulford Devon 10 A5
Dull P & K 139 E5
Dullatur N Lans 130 D3
Dullingham Cambs 63 E1
Dullingham Ley Cambs 63 F1
Dulnain Bridge Highld 156 B1
Duloe Beds 61 G1
Duloe Cnwll 5 F2
Dulverton Somset 22 B2
Dulwich Gt Lon 28 D3
Dumbarton W Duns 129 E3
Dumbleton Gloucs 47 F3
Dumfries D & G 110 D2
Dumgoyne Stirlg 129 G3
Dummer Hants 26 D4
Dumpton Kent 31 G3
Dun Angus 141 G6
Dunalastair P & K 138 D6
Dunan Ag & B 128 C2
Dunan Highld 151 F1
Dunan P & K 138 B5
Dunaverty Ag & B 117 F1
Dunball Somset 23 F3
Dunbar E Loth 133 F3
Dunbeath Highld 167 E1
Dunbeg Ag & B 136 C3
Dunblane Stirlg 130 D5
Dunbog Fife 140 C1
Dunbridge Hants 26 A2
Duncanston Highld 154 D5
Duncanstone Abers 158 B2
Dunchideock Devon 9 F3
Dunchurch Warwks 59 H2
Duncote Nhants 49 E4
Duncow D & G 110 D3
Duncrievie P & K 131 G6
Duncton W Susx 15 H5
Dundee Dund C 140 D3
Dundee Airport Dund C 140 D3
Dundon Somset 23 G2
Dundonald S Ayrs 119 E3
Dundonnell Highld 161 E2
Dundraw Cumb 103 F5
Dundreggan Highld 145 E6
Dundrennan D & G 102 B5
Dundry Somset 24 A6
Dunecht Abers 149 E5
Dunfermline Fife 131 G4
Dunfield Gloucs 39 F4
Dunford Bridge S York 83 F5
Dungate Kent 30 C2
Dungavel S Lans 120 A3
Dunge Wilts 24 D5
Dungworth S York 83 H4
Dunham Notts 85 F2
Dunham Town Gt Man 82 B3
Dunham Woodhouses Gt Man 82 B3
Dunham-on-the-Hill Ches 81 G2
Dunhampstead Worcs 47 E5
Dunhampton Worcs 58 A2
Dunholme Lincs 85 H3
Dunino Fife 132 D6
Dunipace Falk 130 D3
Dunk's Green Kent 29 G1
Dunkeld P & K 139 G4
Dunkerton Somset 24 C5
Dunkeswell Devon 10 B5
Dunkeswick W York 90 D4
Dunkirk Ches 81 F2
Dunkirk Gloucs 38 C3
Dunkirk Kent 30 D2
Dunkirk Staffs 70 C5
Dunkirk Wilts 25 E5
Dunlappie Angus 148 D1
Dunley Hants 26 C5
Dunley Worcs 57 H2
Dunlop E Ayrs 119 F4
Dunmaglass Highld 154 D1
Dunmere Cnwll 4 D3
Dunmore Falk 131 E4
Dunn Street Kent 30 B2
Dunnet Highld 167 F5
Dunnichen Angus 141 E5
Dunning P & K 139 G1
Dunnington E R Yk 93 E5
Dunnington N York 91 H5
Dunnington Warwks 47 F5
Dunnockshaw Lancs 89 G2
Dunoon Ag & B 128 C3
Dunphail Moray 156 B4
Dunragit D & G 100 C6
Duns Border 123 E5
Duns Tew Oxon 48 C2
Dunsa Derbys 83 G2
Dunsby Lincs 74 A3
Dunscar Gt Man 82 B6
Dunscore D & G 110 C3
Dunscroft S York 84 D6
Dunsdale N York 107 E3
Dunsden Green Oxon 41 E2
Dunsdon Devon 20 C1
Dunsfold Surrey 16 A5
Dunsford Devon 9 E3
Dunshalt Fife 132 B6
Dunshillock Abers 159 F4
Dunsill Notts 72 B6
Dunsley N York 107 H2
Dunsley Staffs 58 B4
Dunsmore Bucks 41 G5
Dunsop Bridge Lancs 89 E5
Dunstable Beds 50 A3
Dunstall Staffs 71 G2
Dunstall Common Worcs 46 D3
Dunstall Green Suffk 63 G1
Dunstan Nthumb 125 F3
Dunstan Steads Nthumb 125 E3
Dunster Somset 22 C4
Dunston Lincs 86 A1
Dunston Norfk 65 E6
Dunston Staffs 70 D2
Dunston T & W 114 D2
Dunston Heath Staffs 70 D2
Dunstone Devon 6 C3
Dunstone Devon 8 D2
Dunsville S York 84 D5
Dunswell E R Yk 93 E3
Dunsyre S Lans 121 E4
Dunterton Devon 5 G4
Dunthrop Oxon 48 B2
Duntisbourne Abbots Gloucs 38 D5
Duntisbourne Rouse Gloucs 39 E5
Duntish Dorset 11 G5
Duntocher W Duns 129 F2
Dunton Beds 50 C5
Dunton Bucks 49 F2
Dunton Norfk 76 B3
Dunton Bassett Leics 60 B4
Dunton Green Kent 29 F2
Dunton Wayletts Essex 29 G5
Duntulm Highld 150 D6
Dunure S Ayrs 118 D1
Dunvant Swans 34 C4
Dunvegan Highld 150 C3
Dunwich Suffk 65 G2
Dunwood Staffs 70 D6
Durdar Cumb 103 H5
Durgan Cnwll 3 E2
Durham Dur 106 B5
Durham Cathedral Dur 106 B5
Durisdeer D & G 110 C5
Durisdeermill D & G 110 C5
Durkar W York 90 D1
Durleigh Somset 23 F3
Durley Hants 14 C5
Durley Wilts 25 H6
Durley Street Hants 14 C5
Durlock Kent 31 F2
Durlock Kent 31 G2
Durlow Common Gloucs 46 B3
Durmgley Angus 140 D5
Durn Gt Man 89 H1
Durness Highld 165 E5
Duror Highld 137 E5
Durran Ag & B 128 A6
Durrington W Susx 16 B2
Durrington Wilts 25 G4
Durris Abers 149 E4
Dursley Gloucs 38 B4
Dursley Cross Gloucs 46 C1
Durston Somset 23 F2
Durweston Dorset 12 B5
Duston Nhants 49 E5
Duthil Highld 155 G1
Dutlas Powys 56 B3
Duton Hill Essex 51 G3
Dutson Cnwll 5 G4
Dutton Ches 81 H3
Duxford Cambs 51 F5
Duxford Oxon 40 B4
Duxford Aircraft Museum Cambs 51 E5
Dwygyfylchi Conwy 79 G2
Dwyran IOA 78 D1
Dyce Aber C 149 F6
Dyer's End Essex 51 H4
Dyfatty Carmth 34 B4
Dyffrydan Gwynd 67 F1
Dyffryn Brdgnd 35 F4
Dyffryn Myr Td 36 B5
Dyffryn V Glam 36 B1
Dyffryn Ardudwy Gwynd 67 E2
Dyffryn Castell Cerdgn 55 E4
Dyffryn Cellwen Neath 35 F5
Dyke Lincs 74 A2
Dyke Moray 156 B5
Dykehead Angus 140 B5
Dykehead Angus 140 D6
Dykehead N Lans 120 C5
Dykehead Stirlg 130 B5
Dykelands Abers 149 E1
Dykends Angus 140 C5
Dykeside Abers 158 C3
Dylife Powys 55 F5
Dymchurch Kent 19 E4
Dymock Gloucs 46 C2
Dyrham Gloucs 38 B2
Dysart Fife 132 B4
Dyserth Denbgs 80 C3

E

Eachway Worcs 58 C3
Eachwick Nthumb 114 C3
Eagland Hill Lancs 88 C4
Eagle Lincs 85 F1
Eagle Barnsdale Lincs 85 F1
Eagle Moor Lincs 85 F1
Eaglescliffe Dur 106 D2
Eaglesfield Cumb 103 E3
Eaglesfield D & G 111 G2
Eaglesham E Rens 119 G5
Eagley Gt Man 82 B6
Eairy IOM 174 l3
Eakley Lanes Bucks 49 F4
Eakring Notts 84 D1
Ealand Lincs 85 E6
Ealing Gt Lon 28 C4
Eals Nthumb 104 C6
Eamont Bridge Cumb 104 B3
Earby Lancs 89 G4
Earcroft Lancs 89 E2
Eardington Shrops 57 G4
Eardisland Herefs 45 G5
Eardisley Herefs 45 F4
Eardiston Shrops 69 F2
Eardiston Worcs 57 G2
Earith Cambs 62 C3
Earl Shilton Leics 59 G5
Earl Soham Suffk 65 E2
Earl Sterndale Derbys 83 F1
Earl Stonham Suffk 64 D1
Earl's Croome Worcs 46 D3
Earl's Down E Susx 17 G3
Earl's Green Suffk 64 C2
Earle Nthumb 124 C4
Earlestown Mersyd 81 H4
Earley Berks 41 F1
Earlham Norfk 64 D6
Earlish Highld 150 D5
Earls Barton Nhants 61 E2
Earls Colne Essex 52 B4
Earls Common Worcs 47 E5
Earlsditton Shrops 57 F3
Earlsdon W Mids 59 F3
Earlsferry Fife 132 D5
Earlsfield Gt Lon 28 C3
Earlsford Abers 158 D2
Earlsheaton W York 90 D2
Earlston Border 122 C3
Earlston E Ayrs 119 F3

Earlswood Elmers End
285

Earlswood Surrey 28 D1
Earlswood Warwks 58 D3
Earlswood Common Mons 37 F4
Earnley W Susx 15 F3
Earnshaw Bridge Lancs 88 D2
Earsdon Nthumb 114 D5
Earsdon T & W 115 E3
Earsham Norfk 65 F4
Earswick N York 91 G5
Eartham W Susx 15 G4
Earthcott Gloucs 37 G3
Easby N York 107 E2
Easdale Ag & B 136 B1
Easebourne W Susx 27 G1
Easenhall Warwks 59 G3
Eashing Surrey 27 H4
Easington Bucks 41 E5
Easington Dur 106 D5
Easington E R Yk 93 H1
Easington N York 107 G3
Easington Nthumb 124 D4
Easington Oxon 41 E4
Easington Colliery Dur 106 D5
Easington Lane T & W 106 C5
Easingwold N York 98 A2
Easole Street Kent 31 F1
Eassie and Nevay Angus 140 C4
East Aberthaw V Glam 22 C6
East Allington Devon 7 E2
East Anstey Devon 22 B2
East Anton Hants 26 B4
East Appleton N York 97 F4
East Ashey IOW 14 D2
East Ashling W Susx 15 F4
East Aston Hants 26 C4
East Ayton N York 99 F3
East Balsdon Cnwll 5 F6
East Bank Blae G 36 C5
East Barkwith Lincs 86 B3
East Barming Kent 29 H1
East Barnby N York 107 H2
East Barnet Gt Lon 28 D6
East Barns E Loth 133 F3
East Barsham Norfk 76 B3
East Beckham Norfk 77 E4
East Bedfont Gt Lon 28 B3
East Bergholt Suffk 52 D4
East Bierley W York 90 C2
East Bilney Norfk 76 C2
East Blatchington E Susx 17 F1
East Bloxworth Dorset 12 C4
East Boldon T & W 115 E2
East Boldre Hants 14 B4
East Bolton Nthumb 124 D3
East Bower Somset 23 F3
East Bradenham Norfk 64 B6
East Brent Somset 23 F4
East Bridgford Notts 73 E4
East Briscoe Dur 105 F2
East Buckland Devon 21 G4
East Budleigh Devon 9 G3
East Burnham Bucks 41 H3
East Burton Dorset 12 B3
East Butsfield Dur 105 H5
East Butterwick Lincs 85 F5
East Calder W Loth 131 G2
East Carleton Norfk 64 D6
East Carlton Nhants 60 D4
East Carlton W York 90 C4
East Chaldon (Chaldon Herring) Dorset 12 B3
East Challow Oxon 40 B3
East Charleton Devon 7 E2
East Chelborough Dorset 11 F5
East Chevington Nthumb 114 D5
East Chiltington E Susx 17 E3
East Chinnock Somset 11 E6
East Chisenbury Wilts 25 G4
East Cholderton Hants 26 A4
East Clandon Surrey 28 B1
East Claydon Bucks 49 F2
East Clevedon Somset 37 E1
East Coker Somset 11 F6
East Combe Somset 22 D2
East Compton Somset 24 B3
East Cornworthy Devon 7 F3
East Cote Cumb 103 E6
East Cottingwith E R Yk 91 H4
East Cowes IOW 14 C3
East Cowick E R Yk 91 H2
East Cowton N York 97 F5
East Cramlington Nthumb 114 D3
East Cranmore Somset 24 B4
East Creech Dorset 12 C3
East Curthwaite Cumb 103 G5
East Dean E Susx 17 F1
East Dean Gloucs 46 B1
East Dean Hants 26 A2
East Dean W Susx 15 G5
East Down Devon 21 F5
East Drayton Notts 85 E2
East Dulwich Gt Lon 28 D4
East Dundry Somset 24 A6
East Ella E R Yk 92 D2
East End Beds 49 H3
East End Beds 50 B6
East End Bucks 49 G4
East End E R Yk 93 F3
East End E R Yk 93 G2
East End Essex 51 E2
East End Hants 26 B5
East End Hants 14 B3
East End Herts 51 E3
East End Kent 18 B5
East End Kent 30 C3
East End Oxon 40 B6
East End Somset 37 F1
East End Somset 24 B4
East End Suffk 53 E4
East Everleigh Wilts 25 G5
East Farleigh Kent 30 A1
East Farndon Nhants 60 C4
East Ferry Lincs 85 F5
East Firsby Lincs 85 H3
East Fortune E Loth 132 D3
East Garforth W York 91 E3
East Garston Berks 40 B2
East Ginge Oxon 40 C3
East Goscote Leics 72 D1
East Grafton Wilts 25 H5
East Green Suffk 65 F2
East Grimstead Wilts 25 H2
East Grinstead W Susx 17 E5
East Guldeford E Susx 18 C3
East Haddon Nhants 60 C2
East Hagbourne Oxon 40 C3
East Halton Lincs 93 E2
East Ham Gt Lon 29 E4
East Hanney Oxon 40 B4
East Hanningfield Essex 30 A6
East Hardwick W York 91 F1
East Harling Norfk 64 B4
East Harlsey N York 97 G5
East Harnham Wilts 25 G2
East Harptree Somset 24 A5
East Hartburn Dur 106 D3
East Hartford Nthumb 114 D3
East Harting W Susx 15 F5
East Hatch Wilts 25 E2
East Hatley Cambs 50 D6
East Hauxwell N York 97 E4
East Haven Angus 141 F3
East Heckington Lincs 74 B4
East Hedleyhope Dur 106 A5
East Helmsdale Highld 163 G5
East Hendred Oxon 40 C3
East Heslerton N York 99 E2
East Hewish Somset 23 G6
East Hoathly E Susx 17 F3
East Holme Dorset 12 C3
East Horrington Somset 24 A4
East Horsley Surrey 28 B1
East Horton Nthumb 123 G2
East Howe Dorset 13 E4
East Huntington N York 91 G5
East Huntspill Somset 23 F4
East Hyde Beds 50 B2
East Ilkerton Devon 21 G5
East Ilsley Berks 40 C2
East Keal Lincs 86 D1
East Kennett Wilts 25 G6
East Keswick W York 91 E4
East Kilbride S Lans 119 H5
East Kimber Devon 8 B4
East Kirkby Lincs 86 D1
East Knighton Dorset 12 B3
East Knowstone Devon 22 A1
East Knoyle Wilts 24 D2
East Kyloe Nthumb 123 H3
East Lambrook Somset 23 G1
East Langdon Kent 19 G6
East Langton Leics 60 C5
East Laroch Highld 137 E6
East Lavant W Susx 15 G4
East Lavington W Susx 15 G5
East Layton N York 106 A2
East Leake Notts 72 C3
East Learmouth Nthumb 123 F3
East Leigh Devon 8 D5
East Leigh Devon 6 D3
East Leigh Devon 7 E3
East Lexham Norfk 76 B2
East Linton E Loth 133 E3
East Liss Hants 27 F2
East Lockinge Oxon 40 B3
East Lound Lincs 85 E5
East Lulworth Dorset 12 C3
East Lutton N York 99 E2
East Lydeard Somset 23 E2
East Lydford Somset 24 A2
East Malling Kent 29 H2
East Malling Heath Kent 29 H1
East Marden W Susx 15 F5
East Markham Notts 85 E2
East Martin Hants 25 F1
East Marton N York 89 G5
East Meon Hants 27 E1
East Mere Devon 9 G6
East Mersea Essex 52 D2
East Midlands Airport Leics 72 B3
East Molesey Surrey 28 B3
East Morden Dorset 12 C4
East Morton D & G 110 C5
East Morton W York 90 B4
East Ness N York 98 C3
East Newton E R Yk 93 F3
East Norton Leics 60 D5
East Ogwell Devon 7 F5
East Orchard Dorset 24 D1
East Ord Nthumb 123 G5
East Panson Devon 5 G5
East Parley Dorset 13 E4
East Peckham Kent 29 G1
East Pennar Pembks 32 D2
East Pennard Somset 24 B3
East Perry Cambs 61 G2
East Portlemouth Devon 7 E1
East Prawle Devon 7 E1
East Preston W Susx 16 B2
East Pulham Dorset 11 G6
East Putford Devon 20 D2
East Quantoxhead Somset 22 D4
East Rainham Kent 30 B3
East Rainton T & W 106 C6
East Ravendale Lincs 86 C5
East Raynham Norfk 76 B3
East Rigton W York 91 E4
East Rolstone Somset 23 G5
East Rounton N York 97 G5
East Rudham Norfk 76 A3
East Runton Norfk 77 E4
East Ruston Norfk 77 F3
East Saltoun E Loth 132 D2
East Scrafton N York 96 D3
East Sheen Gt Lon 28 C3
East Shefford Berks 40 B2
East Sleekburn Nthumb 114 D4
East Somerton Norfk 77 H2
East Stockwith Lincs 85 E4
East Stoke Dorset 12 C3
East Stoke Notts 73 E5
East Stour Dorset 24 D1
East Stourmouth Kent 31 F2
East Stowford Devon 21 F3
East Stratton Hants 26 D3
East Studdal Kent 31 G1
East Sutton Kent 30 B1
East Taphouse Cnwll 5 E2
East Thirston Nthumb 114 D5
East Tilbury Essex 29 H4
East Tisted Hants 27 E2
East Torrington Lincs 86 B3
East Tuddenham Norfk 76 D1
East Tytherley Hants 26 A2
East Tytherton Wilts 38 D2
East Village Devon 9 E5
East Wall Shrops 57 E5
East Walton Norfk 75 H2
East Water Somset 24 A4
East Week Devon 8 D4
East Wellow Hants 26 A1
East Wemyss Fife 132 B5
East Whitburn W Loth 131 F2
East Wickham Gt Lon 29 E4
East Williamston Pembks 33 E2
East Winch Norfk 75 G2
East Winterslow Wilts 25 H3
East Wittering W Susx 15 F3
East Witton N York 97 E3
East Woodburn Nthumb 113 F3
East Woodhay Hants 26 B5
East Woodlands Somset 24 C4
East Worldham Hants 27 F3
East Wretham Norfk 64 B4
East Youlstone Devon 20 C2
East-the-Water Devon 21 E3
Eastbourne Dur 106 B2
Eastbourne E Susx 17 G1
Eastbridge Suffk 65 G2
Eastbrook V Glam 36 C1
Eastburn W York 90 A4
Eastbury Berks 40 B2
Eastbury Herts 28 B5
Eastby N York 90 A5
Eastchurch Kent 30 C3
Eastcombe Gloucs 38 D5
Eastcote Gt Lon 28 B5
Eastcote Nhants 49 E5
Eastcote W Mids 59 E3
Eastcott Cnwll 20 C2
Eastcott Wilts 25 F5
Eastcourt Wilts 38 D3
Eastcourt Wilts 25 H5
Eastdown Devon 7 F2
Eastend Essex 30 C5
Eastend S Lans 120 D3
Easter Balmoral Abers 147 G4
Easter Compton Gloucs 37 G2
Easter Dalziel Highld 155 F4
Easter Howgate Mdloth 132 A1
Easter Kinkell Highld 154 D5
Easter Moniack Highld 154 D3
Easter Ord Abers 149 F5
Easter Pitkierie Fife 133 E6
Easter Skeld Shet 169 h2
Easter Softlaw Border 123 E3
Easter Suddie Highld 155 E5
Eastergate W Susx 15 G4
Easterhouse C Glas 130 C2
Eastern Green W Mids 59 F3
Easterton Wilts 25 F5
Easterton Somset 23 F5
Eastfield N Lans 131 E1
Eastfield N York 99 F3
Eastgate Dur 105 F4
Eastgate Lincs 74 A2
Eastgate Norfk 76 D2
Eastham Mersyd 81 F3
Eastham Ferry Mersyd 81 F3
Easthampstead Berks 27 G6
Easthampton Herefs 56 D2
Eastheath Berks 27 F6
Easthope Shrops 57 F5
Easthorpe Essex 52 C3
Easthorpe Notts 73 E5
Eastington Devon 8 D5
Eastington Gloucs 39 F6
Eastington Gloucs 38 C5
Eastlands D & G 110 C2
Eastleach Martin Gloucs 39 G5
Eastleach Turville Gloucs 39 G5
Eastleigh Devon 21 E3
Eastleigh Hants 14 C5
Eastling Kent 30 C2
Eastmoor Norfk 63 F6
Eastney Hants 15 E3
Eastnor Herefs 46 C3
Eastoft Lincs 92 B1
Easton Beds 40 B1
Easton Cambs 61 G2
Easton Cumb 103 G6
Easton Devon 8 D3
Easton Dorset 11 G2
Easton Hants 26 C2
Easton Lincs 73 G3
Easton Norfk 76 D1
Easton Somset 23 H4
Easton Suffk 65 E1
Easton Wilts 38 D1
Easton Grey Wilts 38 D3
Easton Maudit Nhants 49 G5
Easton on the Hill Nhants 61 F6
Easton Royal Wilts 25 G5
Easton-in-Gordano Somset 37 F2
Eastpeek Devon 5 G5
Eastrea Cambs 62 B5
Eastriggs D & G 111 G1
Eastrington E R Yk 92 B3
Eastrop Wilts 39 G3
Eastry Kent 31 G1
Eastshaw W Susx 27 G2
Eastville Bristl 37 G2
Eastville Lincs 74 D6
Eastwell Leics 73 E3
Eastwick Herts 51 E2
Eastwood Essex 30 B5
Eastwood Notts 72 B5
Eastwood W York 89 H2
Eastwood End Cambs 62 C5
Eathorpe Warwks 59 G2
Eaton Ches 81 H1
Eaton Ches 82 D1
Eaton Leics 73 F3
Eaton Norfk 64 D6
Eaton Notts 85 E2
Eaton Oxon 40 C5
Eaton Shrops 56 D4
Eaton Shrops 57 E4
Eaton Bishop Herefs 45 G3
Eaton Bray Beds 49 H1
Eaton Constantine Shrops 57 F6
Eaton Ford Beds 61 H1
Eaton Green Beds 49 H1
Eaton Hastings Oxon 39 G4
Eaton Mascott Shrops 57 F6
Eaton Socon Cambs 61 H1
Eaton upon Tern Shrops 70 B2
Eaves Brow Ches 82 A4
Eaves Green W Mids 59 E4
Ebberston N York 99 E3
Ebbesborne Wake Wilts 25 E2
Ebbw Vale Blae G 36 C5
Ebchester Dur 105 H6
Ebdon Somset 23 F6
Ebford Devon 9 G3
Ebley Gloucs 38 C5
Ebnal Ches 69 G5
Ebnall Herefs 45 G5
Ebrington Gloucs 47 G3
Ebsworthy Town Devon 8 B4
Ecchinswell Hants 26 C5
Ecclaw Border 133 F2
Ecclefechan D & G 111 F2
Eccles Border 123 E4
Eccles Gt Man 82 C4
Eccles Kent 29 H2
Eccles Green Herefs 45 G4
Eccles on Sea Norfk 77 G3
Eccles Road Norfk 64 C4
Ecclesall S York 83 H3
Ecclesfield S York 84 A4
Eccleshall Staffs 70 C3
Eccleshill W York 90 C3
Ecclesmachan W Loth 131 G2
Eccleston Ches 81 F1
Eccleston Lancs 88 D1
Eccleston Mersyd 81 G4
Eccleston Green Lancs 88 D1
Echt Abers 149 E5
Eckford Border 122 D2
Eckington Derbys 84 B3
Eckington Worcs 47 E3
Ecton Nhants 60 D2
Ecton Staffs 71 F6
Edale Derbys 83 F3
Eday Airport Ork 169 c3
Edburton W Susx 16 C2
Edderside Cumb 103 E5
Edderton Highld 162 D2
Eddington Kent 31 E3
Eddleston Border 121 G4
Eddlewood S Lans 120 B5
Eden Mount Cumb 95 E3
Eden Park Gt Lon 28 D3
Edenbridge Kent 17 E6
Edenfield Lancs 89 F1
Edenhall Cumb 104 B3
Edenham Lincs 74 A2
Edensor Derbys 83 G2
Edentaggart Ag & B 129 E4
Edenthorpe S York 84 D5
Edern Gwynd 66 B4
Edgarley Somset 23 H3
Edgbaston W Mids 58 D4
Edgcombe Cnwll 3 E3
Edgcott Bucks 49 E1
Edgcott Somset 22 A3
Edge Gloucs 38 C5
Edge Shrops 69 F1
Edge End Gloucs 37 G6
Edge Green Ches 69 G5
Edgebolton Shrops 69 H2
Edgefield Norfk 76 D3
Edgefield Green Norfk 76 D3
Edgefold Gt Man 82 B5
Edgehill Warwks 48 B4
Edgerley Shrops 69 F2
Edgerton W York 90 B1
Edgeside Lancs 89 G2
Edgeworth Gloucs 38 D5
Edgeworthy Devon 9 E6
Edgiock Worcs 47 F5
Edgmond Shrops 70 B2
Edgmond Marsh Shrops 70 B2
Edgton Shrops 56 D4
Edgware Gt Lon 28 C5
Edgworth Lancs 89 F1
Edial Staffs 58 D6
Edinbane Highld 150 D4
Edinburgh C Edin 132 B2
Edinburgh Airport C Edin 131 H2
Edinburgh Castle C Edin 132 B2
Edinburgh Zoo C Edin 132 A2
Edingale Staffs 71 G1
Edingham D & G 110 C1
Edingley Notts 72 D6
Edingthorpe Norfk 77 F3
Edingthorpe Green Norfk 77 F3
Edington Border 123 F5
Edington Nthumb 114 C4
Edington Somset 23 G3
Edington Wilts 25 E5
Edington Burtle Somset 23 G4
Edingworth Somset 23 F5
Edith Weston Rutlnd 61 E6
Edithmead Somset 23 F4
Edlesborough Bucks 49 H1
Edlingham Nthumb 124 D2
Edlington Lincs 86 C2
Edmond Castle Cumb 104 B6
Edmondsham Dorset 12 D6
Edmondsley Dur 106 B6
Edmondthorpe Leics 73 F2
Edmonton Cnwll 4 C3
Edmonton Gt Lon 28 D5
Edmundbyers Dur 105 G5
Ednam Border 123 E3
Ednaston Derbys 71 G4
Edradynate P & K 139 F5
Edrom Border 123 E5
Edstaston Shrops 69 G3
Edstone Warwks 47 G5
Edvin Loach Herefs 46 B5
Edwalton Notts 72 D4
Edwardstone Suffk 52 C5
Edwardsville Myr Td 36 B4
Edwinsford Carmth 43 F3
Edwinstowe Notts 84 D1
Edworth Beds 50 C5
Edwyn Ralph Herefs 46 B5
Edzell Angus 148 D1
Efail Isaf Rhondd 36 B3
Efail-fach Neath 35 E4
Efail-Rhyd Powys 68 D3
Efailnewydd Gwynd 66 C4
Efailwen Carmth 33 F4
Efenechtyd Denbgs 68 C6
Effgill D & G 111 G4
Effingham Surrey 28 B1
Efflinch Staffs 71 G2
Efford Devon 9 F5
Egbury Hants 26 C4
Egdean W Susx 15 H6
Egerton Gt Man 89 E1
Egerton Kent 18 C6
Eggbuckland Devon 6 B3
Eggesford Devon 21 G2
Eggington Beds 49 H2
Egginton Derbys 71 G3
Egglescliffe Dur 106 D2
Eggleston Dur 105 G2
Egham Surrey 28 A3
Egham Wick Surrey 41 H1
Eginswell Devon 7 F4
Egleton Rutlnd 61 E6
Eglingham Nthumb 124 D3
Egloshayle Cnwll 4 D3
Egloskerry Cnwll 5 F5
Eglwys Cross Wrexhm 69 G4
Eglwys Fach Cerdgn 54 D5
Eglwys-Brewis V Glam 35 G1
Eglwysbach Conwy 79 G2
Eglwyswrw Pembks 42 B3
Egmanton Notts 85 E1
Egremont Cumb 102 D1
Egremont Mersyd 81 E4
Egton N York 98 D5
Egton Bridge N York 98 D5
Eight and Forty E R Yk 92 B3
Eight Ash Green Essex 52 C3
Eilanreach Highld 143 G6
Elan Village Powys 55 G2
Elberton Gloucs 37 G3
Elbridge W Susx 15 G4
Elburton Devon 6 C3
Elcombe Wilts 39 F2
Elcot Berks 40 B1
Elder Street Essex 51 F4
Eldernell Cambs 62 B5
Eldersfield Worcs 46 C2
Elderslie Rens 129 F1
Eldmire N York 97 G2
Eldon Dur 106 B4
Eldwick W York 90 B4
Elfhill Abers 149 F3
Elford Nthumb 125 E4
Elford Staffs 71 G1
Elgin Moray 156 D5
Elgol Highld 143 E5
Elham Kent 19 E6
Elie Fife 132 D5
Elilaw Nthumb 124 C2
Elim IOA 78 C3
Eling Hants 14 B5
Elkesley Notts 85 E2
Elkstone Gloucs 38 D5
Ella Abers 158 B5
Ellacombe Devon 7 F4
Ellanbeich Ag & B 136 B1
Elland W York 90 B2
Elland Lower Edge W York 90 B2
Ellary Ag & B 127 F3
Ellastone Staffs 71 F4
Ellel Lancs 88 C5
Ellemford Border 122 D5
Ellen's Green Surrey 16 B5
Ellenborough Cumb 102 D4
Ellenbrook Gt Man 82 B5
Ellenhall Staffs 70 C3
Ellerbeck N York 97 G4
Ellerby N York 107 G2
Ellerdine Heath Shrops 70 A2
Ellerhayes Devon 9 G5
Elleric Ag & B 137 E5
Ellerker E R Yk 92 C2
Ellers N York 90 A4
Ellerton E R Yk 91 H4
Ellerton N York 97 F5
Ellerton Shrops 70 B3
Ellesborough Bucks 41 F5
Ellesmere Shrops 69 F3
Ellesmere Port Ches 81 F2
Ellicombe Somset 22 C4
Ellingham Hants 13 E5
Ellingham Norfk 65 F5
Ellingham Nthumb 125 E4
Ellingstring N York 97 E3
Ellington Cambs 61 G2
Ellington Nthumb 114 D5
Ellington Thorpe Cambs 61 G2
Elliots Green Somset 24 D4
Ellisfield Hants 27 E4
Ellishader Highld 151 E5
Ellistown Leics 72 B1
Ellon Abers 159 E2
Ellonby Cumb 104 A4
Ellough Suffk 65 G4
Elloughton E R Yk 92 C2
Ellwood Gloucs 37 G5
Elm Cambs 62 D6
Elm Green Essex 52 A1
Elm Grove Norfk 65 G6
Elm Park Gt Lon 29 F5
Elmbridge Worcs 58 B2
Elmdon Essex 51 E5
Elmdon W Mids 59 E4
Elmdon Heath W Mids 58 D3
Elmer W Susx 15 H4
Elmer's Green Lancs 81 G5
Elmers End Gt Lon 28 D3

Elmesthorpe

Ffairfach

286

Elmesthorpe Leics 59 G5
Elmhurst Staffs 71 F1
Elmley Castle Worcs 47 E3
Elmley Lovett Worcs 58 B2
Elmore Gloucs 38 C6
Elmore Back Gloucs 38 B6
Elms Green Worcs 57 G2
Elmscott Devon 20 C3
Elmsett Suffk 52 D5
Elmstead Heath Essex 52 D3
Elmstead Market Essex 52 D3
Elmstead Row Essex 52 D3
Elmsted Court Kent 19 E6
Elmstone Kent 31 F2
Elmstone Hardwicke Gloucs 47 E2
Elmswell E R Yk 92 D5
Elmswell Suffk 64 B2
Elmton Derbys 84 C2
Elphin Highld 161 F5
Elphinstone E Loth 132 C2
Elrick Abers 149 F5
Elrig D & G 101 E5
Elrington Nthumb 113 F1
Elsdon Nthumb 113 F4
Elsecar S York 84 B5
Elsenham Essex 51 F3
Elsfield Oxon 40 D5
Elsham Lincs 85 H6
Elsick House Abers 149 F4
Elsing Norfk 76 D2
Elslack N York 89 H4
Elson Hants 14 D4
Elson Shrops 69 F4
Elsrickle S Lans 121 E4
Elstead Surrey 27 G4
Elsted W Susx 15 F6
Elsthorpe Lincs 74 A2
Elstob Dur 106 C3
Elston Lancs 88 D3
Elston Notts 73 E5
Elston Wilts 25 F4
Elstone Devon 21 G2
Elstow Beds 50 A5
Elstree Herts 28 C6
Elstronwick E R Yk 93 F3
Elswick Lancs 88 C3
Elswick T & W 114 D2
Elsworth Cambs 62 B2
Elterwater Cumb 94 D5
Eltham Gt Lon 29 E3
Eltisley Cambs 62 B1
Elton Cambs 61 G5
Elton Ches 81 G2
Elton Derbys 71 G6
Elton Dur 106 C3
Elton Gloucs 38 B6
Elton Gt Man 82 C6
Elton Herefs 57 E2
Elton Notts 73 E4
Elton Green Ches 81 G2
Eltringham Nthumb 114 B2
Elvanfoot S Lans 120 D1
Elvaston Derbys 72 B3
Elveden Suffk 63 G3
Elvetham Heath Hants 27 F5
Elvingston E Loth 132 D2
Elvington Kent 31 F1
Elvington N York 91 H4
Elwell Devon 21 G4
Elwick Dur 106 D4
Elwick Nthumb 124 D5
Elworth Ches 70 B6
Elworthy Somset 22 D3
Ely Cambs 63 E3
Ely Cardif 36 C2
Emberton Bucks 49 G4
Embleton Cumb 103 F3
Embleton Dur 106 D4
Embleton Nthumb 125 E3
Embo Highld 163 E3
Embo Street Highld 163 E3
Emborough Somset 24 B4
Embsay N York 90 A5
Emery Down Hants 13 G5
Emley W York 83 G6
Emley Moor W York 83 G6
Emmbrook Berks 41 F1
Emmer Green Berks 41 E2
Emmett Carr Derbys 84 B2
Emmington Oxon 41 F4
Emneth Cambs 62 D6
Emneth Hungate Norfk 62 D6
Empingham Rutlnd 73 G1
Empshott Hants 27 F2
Empshott Green Hants 27 F2
Emsworth Hants 15 F4
Enborne Berks 26 C6
Enborne Row Hants 26 C6
Enchmarsh Shrops 57 E5
Enderby Leics 60 A5
Endmoor Cumb 95 F3
Endon Staffs 70 D5
Endon Bank Staffs 70 D5
Enfield Gt Lon 28 D6
Enfield Lock Gt Lon 28 D6
Enfield Wash Gt Lon 28 D6
Enford Wilts 25 G4
Engine Common Gloucs 38 B3
England's Gate Herefs 46 A4
Englefield Berks 40 D1
Englefield Green Surrey 41 H1
Englesea brook Ches 70 C5
English Bicknor Gloucs 37 G6
English Frankton Shrops 69 G3
Englishcombe Somset 24 C6
Engollan Cnwll 4 B3
Enham-Alamein Hants 26 B4
Enmore Somset 23 E3
Enmore Green Dorset 24 D1
Ennerdale Bridge Cumb 103 E2
Enniscaven Cnwll 4 C2
Enochdhu P & K 139 H6
Ensay Ag & B 135 E4
Ensbury Dorset 13 E4
Ensdon Shrops 69 F2
Ensis Devon 21 F3
Enson Staffs 70 D3
Enstone Oxon 48 B2
Enterkinfoot D & G 110 C5
Enterpen N York 97 H5
Enville Staffs 58 A4
Enys Cnwll 3 E3
Eolaigearraidh W Isls 168 b2
Epney Gloucs 38 B5
Epperstone Notts 72 D5
Epping Essex 51 E1
Epping Green Essex 51 E1
Epping Green Herts 50 D1
Epping Upland Essex 51 E1
Eppleby N York 106 A2
Eppleworth E R Yk 92 D3
Epsom Surrey 28 C2
Epwell Oxon 48 B3
Epworth Lincs 85 E5
Epworth Turbary Lincs 85 E5
Erbistock Wrexhm 69 F4
Erdington W Mids 58 D5
Eridge Green E Susx 17 F5
Eridge Station E Susx 17 F5
Erines Ag & B 127 G3
Erisey Cnwll 3 E1
Eriska Ag & B 136 D4
Eriswell Suffk 63 F3
Erith Gt Lon 29 F4
Erlestoke Wilts 25 E5
Ermington Devon 6 D3
Erpingham Norfk 77 E3
Erriottwood Kent 30 C2
Errogie Highld 154 D1
Errol P & K 140 B2
Erskine Rens 129 F2
Ervie D & G 108 B1
Erwarton Suffk 53 F4
Erwood Powys 44 D3
Eryholme N York 106 C2
Eryrys Denbgs 68 D6
Escalls Cnwll 2 A2
Escomb Dur 106 A4
Escott Somset 22 D3
Escrick N York 91 G4
Esgair Carmth 42 D2
Esgair Cerdgn 54 C2
Esgairgeiliog Powys 55 E6
Esgerdawe Carmth 43 F3
Esgyryn Conwy 79 G2
Esh Dur 106 A5
Esh Winning Dur 106 A5
Esher Surrey 28 B2
Esholt W York 90 C4
Eshott Nthumb 114 D5
Eshton N York 89 H5
Eskadale Highld 154 C3
Eskbank Mdloth 132 B2
Eskdale Green Cumb 94 B5
Eskdalemuir D & G 111 G4
Eskett Cumb 103 E2
Eskham Lincs 86 D4
Eskholme S York 91 G1
Esperley Lane Ends Dur 105 H2
Esprick Lancs 88 C3
Essendine Rutlnd 73 H1
Essendon Herts 50 D2
Essich Highld 155 E3
Essington Staffs 58 C6
Esslemont Abers 159 E2
Eston N York 107 E3
Etal Nthumb 123 F3
Etchilhampton Wilts 25 F5
Etchingham E Susx 17 H4
Etchinghill Kent 19 E5
Etchinghill Staffs 71 E2
Etchingwood E Susx 17 F4
Etherdwick E R Yk 93 F3
Etling Green Norfk 76 C1
Etloe Gloucs 38 B5
Eton Berks 41 H2
Eton Wick Berks 41 H2
Etruria Staffs 70 D5
Etteridge Highld 146 B4
Ettersgill Dur 105 E3
Ettiley Heath Ches 70 B6
Ettingshall W Mids 58 B5
Ettington Warwks 48 A4
Etton Cambs 61 G6
Etton E R Yk 92 D4
Ettrick Border 121 G1
Ettrickbridge Border 122 A2
Ettrickhill Border 111 G6
Etwall Derbys 71 G3
Eudon George Shrops 57 G4
Euston Suffk 64 B3
Euximoor Drove Cambs 62 D5
Euxton Lancs 88 D1
Evancoyd Powys 56 C2
Evanton Highld 154 D6
Evedon Lincs 74 A5
Evelith Shrops 57 H6
Evelix Highld 163 E3
Evenjobb Powys 45 E5
Evenley Oxon 48 D3
Evenlode Gloucs 47 H2
Evenwood Dur 106 A3
Evenwood Gate Dur 106 A3
Evercreech Somset 24 B3
Everingham E R Yk 92 B4
Everleigh Wilts 25 G5
Everley N York 99 E4
Eversfield Devon 8 B4
Eversholt Beds 49 H2
Evershot Dorset 11 F5
Eversley Hants 27 F5
Eversley Cross Hants 27 F5
Everthorpe E R Yk 92 C3
Everton Beds 50 C6
Everton Hants 13 G4
Everton Mersyd 81 F4
Everton Notts 85 E4
Evertown D & G 111 H2
Evesbatch Herefs 46 B4
Evesham Worcs 47 F4
Evington Leics 60 B6
Ewden Village S York 83 H4
Ewdness Shrops 57 G5
Ewell Surrey 28 C2
Ewell Minnis Kent 19 F6
Ewelme Oxon 41 E3
Ewen Gloucs 39 E4
Ewenny V Glam 35 F2
Ewerby Lincs 74 B5
Ewerby Thorpe Lincs 74 B5
Ewesley Nthumb 114 B5
Ewhurst Surrey 16 B5
Ewhurst Green E Susx 18 B4
Ewhurst Green Surrey 16 B5
Ewloe Flints 81 E1
Ewloe Green Flints 81 E1
Ewood Lancs 89 E2
Ewood Bridge Lancs 89 F2
Eworthy Devon 8 A4
Ewshot Hants 27 F4
Ewyas Harold Herefs 45 G2
Exbourne Devon 8 C5
Exbury Hants 14 C4
Exceat E Susx 17 F1
Exebridge Somset 22 B2
Exelby N York 97 F4
Exeter Devon 9 F4
Exeter Airport Devon 9 G4
Exford Somset 22 A3
Exfordsgreen Shrops 57 E6
Exhall Warwks 47 F5
Exhall Warwks 59 F4
Exlade Street Oxon 41 E2
Exley Head W York 90 B4
Exminster Devon 9 F3
Exmouth Devon 9 G3
Exning Suffk 63 E2
Exted Kent 19 E6
Exton Devon 9 G3
Exton Hants 14 D6
Exton Rutlnd 73 G1
Exton Somset 22 B3
Exwick Devon 9 F4
Eyam Derbys 83 G2
Eydon Nhants 48 D4
Eye Cambs 62 B6
Eye Herefs 57 E2
Eye Suffk 64 D3
Eye Green Cambs 62 B6
Eye Kettleby Leics 73 E2
Eyemouth Border 123 G6
Eyeworth Beds 50 C5
Eyhorne Street Kent 30 B1
Eyke Suffk 53 G6
Eynesbury Cambs 61 H1
Eynsford Kent 29 F3
Eynsham Oxon 40 C5
Eype Dorset 11 E4
Eyre Highld 150 D4
Eythorne Kent 31 F1
Eyton Herefs 45 G5
Eyton Shrops 69 F1
Eyton Shrops 69 G2
Eyton Shrops 56 D4
Eyton Wrexhm 69 F4
Eyton on Severn Shrops 57 F6
Eyton upon the Weald Moors Shrops 70 B1

F

Faccombe Hants 26 B5
Faceby N York 97 H5
Fachwen Powys 68 C2
Facit Lancs 89 G1
Fackley Notts 72 B6
Faddiley Ches 69 H5
Fadmoor N York 98 B4
Faerdre Swans 34 D4
Fagwyr Swans 34 D4
Faifley W Duns 129 F2
Failand Somset 37 F1
Failford S Ayrs 119 F2
Failsworth Gt Man 82 D5
Fair Oak Hants 14 C5
Fair Oak Green Hants 27 E5
Fairbourne Gwynd 67 F1
Fairburn N York 91 F2
Fairfield Derbys 83 F2
Fairfield Kent 18 C4
Fairfield Worcs 58 B3
Fairford Gloucs 39 F4
Fairford Park Gloucs 39 F4
Fairgirth D & G 102 C6
Fairhaven Lancs 88 B2
Fairlie N Ayrs 118 D5
Fairlight E Susx 18 B3
Fairmile Devon 10 A4
Fairmile Surrey 28 B2
Fairnilee Border 122 B3
Fairoak Staffs 70 C3
Fairseat Kent 29 G2
Fairstead Essex 52 A2
Fairstead Norfk 77 F2
Fairwarp E Susx 17 E4
Fairwater Cardif 36 C2
Fairy Cross Devon 20 D3
Fakenham Norfk 76 B3
Fakenham Magna Suffk 64 B3
Fala Mdloth 122 B5
Fala Dam Mdloth 122 B6
Falcondale Cerdgn 43 F4
Falcut Nhants 48 D3
Faldingworth Lincs 86 A3
Faldouet Jersey 174 d2
Falfield Gloucs 38 B4
Falkenham Suffk 53 F5
Falkirk Falk 131 E3
Falkland Fife 132 B6
Fallgate Derbys 72 A6
Fallin Stirlg 131 E4
Falloden Nthumb 125 E3
Fallowfield Gt Man 82 D4
Fallowfield Nthumb 113 F2
Falls of Blarghour Ag & B 137 E1
Falmer E Susx 16 D2
Falmouth Cnwll 3 F3
Falnash Border 112 A5
Falsgrave N York 99 F4
Falstone Nthumb 112 D3
Fanagmore Highld 164 C3
Fancott Beds 50 A3
Fanellan Highld 154 C3
Fangdale Beck N York 98 A4
Fangfoss E R Yk 92 B5
Fanmore Ag & B 135 F4
Fannich Lodge Highld 153 F6
Fans Border 122 C3
Far Bletchley Bucks 49 G3
Far Cotton Nhants 49 F5
Far End Cumb 94 D5
Far Forest Worcs 57 G3
Far Green Gloucs 38 C4
Far Moor Gt Man 81 G5
Far Oakridge Gloucs 38 D5
Far Sawrey Cumb 94 D4
Far Thorpe Lincs 86 C2
Farcet Cambs 62 A5
Farden Shrops 57 F3
Fareham Hants 14 D4
Farewell Staffs 71 F1
Farforth Lincs 86 D2
Faringdon Oxon 39 G4
Farington Lancs 88 D2
Farkhill P & K 139 H3
Farlam Cumb 104 B6
Farleigh Devon 7 E3
Farleigh Somset 37 F1
Farleigh Surrey 29 E2
Farleigh Hungerford Somset 24 D5
Farleigh Wallop Hants 26 D4
Farlesthorpe Lincs 87 E2
Farleton Cumb 95 F3
Farleton Lancs 95 F1
Farley Derbys 83 H1
Farley Staffs 71 F4
Farley Wilts 25 H2
Farley Green Suffk 52 A6
Farley Green Surrey 16 B6
Farley Hill Berks 27 F6
Farleys End Gloucs 38 B6
Farlington Hants 15 E4
Farlington N York 98 B2
Farlow Shrops 57 F3
Farm Town Leics 72 B2
Farmborough Somset 24 B5
Farmbridge End Essex 51 G2
Farmcote Gloucs 47 F2
Farmcote Shrops 57 H4
Farmers Carmth 43 G4
Farmington Gloucs 39 F6
Farmoor Oxon 40 C5
Farms Common Cnwll 2 D3
Farmtown Moray 157 G4
Farnachty Moray 157 F5
Farnah Green Derbys 72 A5
Farnborough Berks 40 C2
Farnborough Gt Lon 29 E2
Farnborough Hants 27 G5
Farnborough Warwks 48 C4
Farnborough Park Hants 27 G5
Farnborough Street Hants 27 G5
Farncombe Surrey 27 H4
Farndish Beds 61 E2
Farndon Ches 69 F5
Farndon Notts 73 E5
Farnell Angus 141 F5
Farnham Dorset 12 C6
Farnham Essex 51 F3
Farnham N York 91 E6
Farnham Suffk 65 F1
Farnham Surrey 27 F4
Farnham Common Bucks 41 H3
Farnham Green Essex 51 E3
Farnham Royal Bucks 41 H2
Farningham Kent 29 F3
Farnley N York 90 C4
Farnley W York 90 D3
Farnley Tyas W York 83 F6
Farnsfield Notts 72 D6
Farnworth Ches 81 G3
Farnworth Gt Man 82 B5
Farr Highld 166 A5
Farr Highld 155 E2
Farr Highld 146 C5
Farraline Highld 154 D1
Farringdon Devon 9 G4
Farrington Gurney Somset 24 B5
Farsley W York 90 C3
Farther Howegreen Essex 30 B6
Farthing Green Kent 18 B6
Farthing Street Gt Lon 29 E2
Farthinghoe Nhants 48 D3
Farthingloe Kent 19 F5
Farthingstone Nhants 48 D5
Fartown W York 90 C1
Fartown W York 90 C3
Farway Street Devon 10 B4
Fasnacloich Ag & B 137 E5
Fasnakyle Highld 153 G2
Fassfern Highld 144 C2
Fatfield T & W 115 E1
Faugh Cumb 104 B6
Fauld Staffs 71 G3
Fauldhouse W Loth 120 D5
Faulkbourne Essex 52 B2
Faulkland Somset 24 C5
Fauls Shrops 69 H3
Faversham Kent 30 D2
Fawdington N York 97 G2
Fawdon Nthumb 124 C3
Fawdon T & W 114 D2
Fawfieldhead Staffs 83 F1
Fawkham Green Kent 29 G3
Fawler Oxon 40 B6
Fawley Berks 40 B2
Fawley Bucks 41 F3
Fawley Hants 14 C4
Fawley Chapel Herefs 46 B2
Fawnog Flints 81 E1
Fawsley Nhants 48 D5
Faxfleet E R Yk 92 B2
Faygate W Susx 16 C5
Fazakerley Mersyd 81 F4
Fazeley Staffs 59 E6
Fearby N York 97 E3
Fearn Highld 163 E1
Fearnan P & K 138 D4
Fearnbeg Highld 151 G5
Fearnhead Ches 82 A4
Fearnmore Highld 151 G5
Fearnoch Ag & B 127 H3
Featherstone Staffs 58 B6
Featherstone W York 91 E2
Feckenham Worcs 47 F5
Feering Essex 52 B3
Feetham N York 96 C5
Feizor N York 96 A2
Felbridge Surrey 17 E5
Felbrigg Norfk 77 E4
Felcourt Surrey 17 E6
Felday Surrey 16 B6
Felden Herts 50 A1
Felin Fach Cerdgn 43 E5
Felin gwm Isaf Carmth 43 E1
Felin gwm Uchaf Carmth 43 E2
Felin-newydd Powys 44 D3
Felindre Carmth 43 F1
Felindre Carmth 43 G2
Felindre Carmth 42 D3
Felindre Cerdgn 43 F5
Felindre Powys 56 B3
Felindre Powys 45 E1
Felindre Swans 34 D4
Felindre Farchog Pembks 42 A3
Felinfach Powys 44 D2
Felinfoel Carmth 34 C4
Felixkirk N York 97 H3
Felixstowe Suffk 53 F4
Felixstowe Ferry Suffk 53 G4
Felkington Nthumb 123 G4
Felkirk W York 84 B6
Fell Foot Cumb 94 D5
Fell Lane W York 90 B4
Fell Side Cumb 103 G4
Felling T & W 114 D2
Felmersham Beds 49 H5
Felmingham Norfk 77 E3
Felpham W Susx 15 H3
Felsham Suffk 64 B1
Felsted Essex 51 G3
Feltham Gt Lon 28 B3
Felthamhill Gt Lon 28 B3
Felthorpe Norfk 77 E2
Felton Herefs 46 A4
Felton Nthumb 114 C6
Felton Somset 23 H6
Felton Butler Shrops 69 F2
Feltwell Norfk 63 F4
Fen Ditton Cambs 62 D1
Fen Drayton Cambs 62 C2
Fen End Lincs 74 C2
Fen End W Mids 59 E3
Fen Street Norfk 64 B5
Fen Street Suffk 64 D2
Fenay Bridge W York 90 C1
Fence Lancs 89 G3
Fence S York 84 B3
Fencehouses T & W 106 C6
Fencote N York 97 F4
Fencott Oxon 40 D6
Fendike Corner Lincs 75 E6
Fenham Nthumb 123 H3
Feniscliffe Lancs 89 E2
Feniscowles Lancs 89 E2
Feniton Devon 10 B4
Fenn Green Shrops 57 H4
Fenn Street Kent 30 B4
Fenny Bentley Derbys 71 G5
Fenny Bridges Devon 10 B4
Fenny Compton Warwks 48 B4
Fenny Drayton Leics 59 F5
Fenny Stratford Bucks 49 G3
Fenrother Nthumb 114 C5
Fenstanton Cambs 62 B2
Fenstead End Suffk 52 B6
Fenton Cambs 62 B3
Fenton Cumb 104 B6
Fenton Lincs 85 F2
Fenton Lincs 73 F5
Fenton Notts 85 E3
Fenton Nthumb 123 G3
Fenton Staffs 70 D4
Fenton Barns E Loth 132 D3
Fenwick E Ayrs 119 F4
Fenwick Nthumb 123 H3
Fenwick Nthumb 114 B3
Fenwick S York 91 G1
Feock Cnwll 3 F4
Feolin Ferry Ag & B 126 C2
Fergushill N Ayrs 119 E4
Feriniquarrie Highld 150 B4
Fermain Bay Guern 174 g1
Fern Angus 141 E6
Ferndale Rhondd 35 G4
Ferndown Dorset 13 E5
Ferness Moray 156 B4
Fernham Oxon 39 G3
Fernhill Heath Worcs 46 D5
Fernhurst W Susx 27 G2
Fernie Fife 140 C1
Ferniegair S Lans 120 B5
Fernilea Highld 150 D2
Fernilee Derbys 83 E2
Ferny Common Herefs 45 F4
Ferrensby N York 91 E6
Ferriby Sluice Lincs 92 D2
Ferrindonald Highld 143 F5
Ferring W Susx 16 B2
Ferry Point Highld 162 D2
Ferrybridge W York 91 F2
Ferryden Angus 141 G5
Ferryhill Dur 106 B4
Ferryside Carmth 33 H3
Ferrytown Highld 162 D2
Fersfield Norfk 64 C4
Fersit Highld 145 F2
Feshiebridge Highld 146 C5
Fetcham Surrey 28 B2
Fetterangus Abers 159 F4
Fettercairn Abers 148 D2
Fewcott Oxon 48 D2
Fewston N York 90 C5
Ffair Rhos Cerdgn 55 E2
Ffairfach Carmth 43 F1

Ffald-y-Brenin
Fundenhall
287

Ffald-y-Brenin *Carmth* 43 F4
Ffawyddog *Powys* 36 C6
Ffestiniog *Gwynd* 67 G4
Ffestiniog Railway *Gwynd* 67 F4
Ffordd-las *Denbgs* 80 C1
Fforest *Carmth* 34 C5
Fforest *Mons* 45 F1
Fforest Fach *Swans* 34 D4
Fforest Goch *Neath* 35 E4
Ffostrasol *Cerdgn* 42 D4
Ffrith *Flints* 69 E6
Ffynnon-Oer *Cerdgn* 43 E5
Ffynnonddewi *Cerdgn* 42 D4
Ffynnongroyw *Flints* 80 D3
Fiag Lodge *Highld* 165 F1
Fickleshole *Surrey* 29 E2
Fiddington *Gloucs* 47 E2
Fiddington *Somset* 23 E3
Fiddleford *Dorset* 12 B6
Fiddlers Green *Cnwll* 3 F5
Fiddlers Hamlet *Essex* 29 F6
Field *Staffs* 71 E3
Field Broughton *Cumb* 95 E3
Field Dalling *Norfk* 76 C4
Field Head *Leics* 72 C1
Fieldhead *Cumb* 104 A4
Fife Keith *Moray* 157 F4
Fifehead Magdalen *Dorset* 24 C1
Fifehead Neville *Dorset* 12 B6
Fifehead St Quintin *Dorset* 12 B6
Fifield *Berks* 41 G2
Fifield *Oxon* 47 H1
Fifield *Wilts* 25 G4
Figheldean *Wilts* 25 G4
Filands *Wilts* 38 D3
Filby *Norfk* 77 H1
Filey *N York* 99 G3
Filgrave *Bucks* 49 G4
Filkins *Oxon* 39 G5
Filleigh *Devon* 21 G3
Filleigh *Devon* 21 G2
Fillingham *Lincs* 85 G3
Fillongley *Warwks* 59 F4
Filmore Hill *Hants* 27 E2
Filton *Gloucs* 37 G2
Fimber *E R Yk* 92 C6
Finavon *Angus* 141 E5
Fincham *Norfk* 63 F6
Finchampstead *Berks* 27 F6
Fincharn *Ag & B* 127 H5
Finchdean *Hants* 15 F5
Finchingfield *Essex* 51 H4
Finchley *Gt Lon* 28 D5
Findern *Derbys* 71 H3
Findhorn *Moray* 156 C5
Findhorn Bridge *Highld* 155 F2
Findo Gask *P & K* 139 G2
Findochty *Moray* 157 G6
Findon *Abers* 149 G4
Findon *W Susx* 16 B2
Findon Mains *Highld* 154 D5
Findrack House *Abers* 148 D5
Finedon *Nhants* 61 E3
Fineshade *Nhants* 61 F5
Fingal Street *Suffk* 65 E2
Fingask *P & K* 140 B2
Fingest *Bucks* 41 F3
Finghall *N York* 97 E4
Fingland *Cumb* 103 F6
Fingland *D & G* 120 B1
Finglesham *Kent* 31 G1
Fingringhoe *Essex* 52 D3
Finkle Green *Essex* 51 H5
Finkle Street *S York* 83 H5
Finlarig *Stirlg* 138 C3
Finmere *Oxon* 49 E2
Finnart *P & K* 138 B5
Finningham *Suffk* 64 C2
Finningley *S York* 84 D5
Finsbay *W Isls* 168 d6
Finstall *Worcs* 58 C2
Finsthwaite *Cumb* 94 D4
Finstock *Oxon* 40 B6
Finstown *Ork* 169 b2
Fintry *Abers* 158 C4
Fintry *Stirlg* 130 B4
Finzean *Abers* 148 D4
Fionnphort *Ag & B* 135 E2
Fionnsbhagh *W Isls* 168 d6
Fir Tree *Dur* 105 H3
Firbank *Cumb* 95 G4
Firbeck *S York* 84 C3
Firby *N York* 97 F3
Firby *N York* 98 C1
Firgrove *Gt Man* 82 D6
Firsby *Lincs* 87 E1
Firsdown *Dorset* 25 G3
Fishbourne *IOW* 14 D3
Fishbourne *W Susx* 15 F4
Fishbourne Roman Palace *W Susx* 15 F4
Fishburn *Dur* 106 C4
Fishcross *Clacks* 131 E5
Fisher *W Susx* 15 G4
Fisher's Pond *Hants* 14 C6
Fisher's Row *Lancs* 88 C4
Fisherford *Abers* 158 C3
Fisherrow *E Loth* 132 B2
Fisherstreet *W Susx* 27 H2
Fisherton *Highld* 155 F4
Fisherton *S Ayrs* 119 E1
Fisherton de la Mere *Wilts* 25 E3
Fisherwick *Staffs* 59 E6
Fishery Estate *Berks* 41 G2
Fishguard *Pembks* 32 D5
Fishlake *S York* 84 D6
Fishleigh *Devon* 8 B5
Fishmere End *Lincs* 74 C4
Fishnish Pier *Ag & B* 136 A4
Fishpond Bottom *Dorset* 10 D4
Fishponds *Bristl* 37 G2
Fishpool *Gt Man* 82 C6
Fishtoft *Lincs* 74 D4
Fishtoft Drove *Lincs* 74 D5
Fishwick *Lancs* 88 D2
Fiskavaig *Highld* 150 C2
Fiskerton *Lincs* 85 H2
Fiskerton *Notts* 73 E5
Fitling *E R Yk* 93 F3
Fittleton *Wilts* 25 G4
Fittleworth *W Susx* 16 A3
Fitton End *Cambs* 75 E1
Fitz *Shrops* 69 G2
Fitzhead *Somset* 22 D2
Fitzroy *Somset* 23 E2
Fitzwilliam *W York* 91 E1
Five Ash Down *E Susx* 17 F4
Five Ashes *E Susx* 17 F4
Five Bells *Somset* 22 D3
Five Bridges *Herefs* 46 B4
Five Lanes *Mons* 37 E3
Five Oak Green *Kent* 17 G6
Five Oaks *Jersey* 174 c2
Five Oaks *W Susx* 16 B4
Five Roads *Carmth* 34 B5
Five Wents *Kent* 30 B1
Fivecrosses *Ches* 81 G2
Fivehead *Somset* 23 F1
Fivelanes *Cnwll* 5 F4
Flack's Green *Essex* 52 A2
Flackwell Heath *Bucks* 41 G3
Fladbury *Worcs* 47 E4
Fladdabister *Shet* 169 j2
Flagg *Derbys* 83 F1
Flamborough *E R Yk* 99 H2
Flamingo Land Theme Park *N York* 98 C3
Flamstead *Herts* 50 B2
Flansham *W Susx* 15 H4
Flanshaw *W York* 90 D2
Flappit Spring *W York* 90 B3
Flasby *N York* 89 H5
Flash *Staffs* 83 E1
Flashader *Highld* 150 D4
Flaunden *Herts* 28 A6
Flawborough *Notts* 73 E4
Flawith *N York* 97 H1
Flax Bourton *Somset* 37 F1
Flaxby *N York* 91 E5
Flaxley *Gloucs* 38 B6
Flaxmere *Ches* 81 H2
Flaxpool *Somset* 22 D3
Flaxton *N York* 91 H6
Fleckney *Leics* 60 C5
Flecknoe *Warwks* 60 A2
Fledborough *Notts* 85 F2
Fleet *Dorset* 11 G3
Fleet *Hants* 15 E4
Fleet *Hants* 27 F5
Fleet *Lincs* 74 D2
Fleet Hargate *Lincs* 74 D2
Fleetend *Hants* 14 C4
Fleetwood *Lancs* 88 B4
Flemingston *V Glam* 35 G1
Flemington *S Lans* 120 A5
Flempton *Suffk* 63 G2
Fletcher Green *Kent* 29 F1
Fletchersbridge *Cnwll* 5 E2
Fletchertown *Cumb* 103 F4
Fletching *E Susx* 17 E4
Fleur-de-lis *Caerph* 36 C4
Flexbury *Cnwll* 20 B1
Flexford *Surrey* 27 G4
Flimby *Cumb* 102 D3
Flimwell *E Susx* 17 H4
Flint *Flints* 81 E2
Flint Mountain *Flints* 81 E2
Flint's Green *W Mids* 59 E3
Flintham *Notts* 73 E5
Flinton *E R Yk* 93 F3
Flishinghurst *Kent* 18 A5
Flitcham *Norfk* 75 G3
Flitton *Beds* 50 B4
Flitwick *Beds* 50 A4
Flixborough *Lincs* 92 C1
Flixborough Stather *Lincs* 92 B1
Flixton *Gt Man* 82 B4
Flixton *N York* 99 F3
Flixton *Suffk* 65 F4
Flockton *W York* 90 D1
Flockton Green *W York* 90 D1
Flodden *Nthumb* 123 F3
Flodigarry *Highld* 151 E6
Flookburgh *Cumb* 94 D2
Flordon *Norfk* 64 D5
Flore *Nhants* 49 E5
Flotterton *Nthumb* 113 G5
Flowers Green *E Susx* 17 G2
Flowton *Suffk* 52 D5
Flushdyke *W York* 90 D2
Flushing *Cnwll* 3 F3
Fluxton *Devon* 10 A4
Flyford Flavell *Worcs* 47 E5
Fobbing *Essex* 29 H4
Fochabers *Moray* 157 E5
Fochriw *Caerph* 36 B5
Fockerby *Lincs* 92 B1
Foddington *Somset* 24 A2
Foel *Powys* 68 B1
Foel y Dyffryn *Brdgnd* 35 F4
Foelgastell *Carmth* 34 C6
Foggathorpe *E R Yk* 92 A3
Fogo *Border* 123 E4
Fogwatt *Moray* 156 D5
Foindle *Highld* 164 C3
Folda *Angus* 140 B6
Fole *Staffs* 71 E4
Foleshill *W Mids* 59 F4
Foliejon Park *Berks* 41 G2
Folke *Dorset* 11 G6
Folkestone *Kent* 19 F5
Folkingham *Lincs* 74 A3
Folkington *E Susx* 17 F2
Folksworth *Cambs* 61 G4
Folkton *N York* 99 F3
Folla Rule *Abers* 158 C2
Follifoot *N York* 91 E5
Folly Gate *Devon* 8 C4
Folly Hill *Surrey* 27 F4
Fonmon *V Glam* 22 C6
Font-y-gary *V Glam* 22 C6
Fonthill Bishop *Wilts* 25 E2
Fonthill Gifford *Wilts* 25 E2
Fontmell Magna *Dorset* 24 D1
Fontmell Parva *Dorset* 12 B6
Fontwell *W Susx* 15 H4
Foolow *Derbys* 83 G2
Foots Cray *Gt Lon* 29 F3
Forbestown *Abers* 148 A6
Forcett *N York* 106 A2
Ford *Ag & B* 127 G5
Ford *Bucks* 41 F5
Ford *Derbys* 84 B3
Ford *Devon* 20 D3
Ford *Devon* 6 D3
Ford *Devon* 7 E2
Ford *Gloucs* 47 F2
Ford *Nthumb* 123 G3
Ford *Shrops* 69 F1
Ford *Somset* 22 D2
Ford *Somset* 24 B5
Ford *Staffs* 71 F5
Ford *W Susx* 15 H4
Ford *Wilts* 38 C2
Ford *Wilts* 25 G2
Ford End *Essex* 51 H2
Ford Green *Lancs* 88 C4
Ford Heath *Shrops* 69 F1
Ford Street *Somset* 22 D1
Ford's Green *Suffk* 64 C2
Forda *Devon* 8 B4
Fordcombe *Kent* 17 F5
Fordell *Fife* 131 H4
Forden *Powys* 56 C5
Forder *Devon* 8 D4
Forder Green *Devon* 7 E4
Fordham *Cambs* 63 E2
Fordham *Essex* 52 C3
Fordham *Norfk* 63 E5
Fordham Heath *Essex* 52 C3
Fordingbridge *Hants* 13 E6
Fordon *E R Yk* 99 F2
Fordoun *Abers* 149 E2
Fordstreet *Essex* 52 C3
Fordton *Devon* 9 E4
Fordwells *Oxon* 40 A6
Fordwich *Kent* 31 E2
Fordyce *Abers* 158 B5
Forebridge *Staffs* 70 D2
Foremark *Derbys* 72 A3
Forest *Guern* 174 g1
Forest *N York* 97 F5
Forest Becks *Lancs* 89 F5
Forest Chapel *Ches* 83 E2
Forest Gate *Gt Lon* 29 E5
Forest Green *Surrey* 16 B5
Forest Hall *Cumb* 95 F5
Forest Hall *T & W* 114 D2
Forest Head *Cumb* 104 C6
Forest Hill *Gt Lon* 28 D3
Forest Hill *Oxon* 40 D5
Forest Lane Head *N York* 90 D5
Forest Lodge *Ag & B* 137 G4
Forest Mill *Clacks* 131 F4
Forest Row *E Susx* 17 E5
Forest Side *IOW* 14 C2
Forest Town *Notts* 84 C1
Forest-in-Teesdale *Dur* 105 E3
Forestburn Gate *Nthumb* 114 B5
Forestside *W Susx* 15 F5
Forfar *Angus* 140 D5
Forgandenny *P & K* 139 H2
Forge *Powys* 55 E5
Forge Hammer *Torfn* 36 D4
Forge Side *Torfn* 36 D5
Forgie *Moray* 157 F4
Forgieside *Moray* 157 F4
Forgue *Abers* 158 B4
Forhill *Worcs* 58 C3
Formby *Mersyd* 81 E5
Forncett End *Norfk* 64 D5
Forncett St Mary *Norfk* 64 D5
Forncett St Peter *Norfk* 64 D5
Fornham All Saints *Suffk* 63 G2
Fornham St Martin *Suffk* 63 H2
Fornside *Cumb* 103 G2
Forres *Moray* 156 B5
Forsbrook *Staffs* 71 E4
Forse *Highld* 167 F2
Forse House *Highld* 167 F2
Forshaw Heath *Warwks* 58 D3
Forsinard *Highld* 166 C3
Forston *Dorset* 11 G4
Fort Augustus *Highld* 145 F5
Fort Hommet *Guern* 174 f2
Fort le Marchant *Guern* 174 h3
Fort William *Highld* 144 C2
Forteviot *P & K* 139 H1
Forth *S Lans* 120 D5
Forthampton *Gloucs* 46 D2
Fortingall *P & K* 139 E4
Fortnighty *Highld* 155 G4
Forton *Hants* 26 B4
Forton *Lancs* 88 C5
Forton *Shrops* 69 F2
Forton *Somset* 10 D5
Forton *Staffs* 70 C2
Fortrie *Abers* 158 C4
Fortrose *Highld* 155 E5
Fortuneswell *Dorset* 11 G2
Forty Green *Bucks* 41 G3
Forty Hill *Gt Lon* 28 D6
Forward Green *Suffk* 64 D1
Fosbury *Wilts* 26 A5
Foscot *Oxon* 47 H1
Foscote *Nhants* 49 E4
Fosdyke *Lincs* 74 C3
Fosdyke Bridge *Lincs* 74 D3
Foss *P & K* 139 E6
Foss-y-ffin *Cerdgn* 43 E5
Fossebridge *Gloucs* 39 E5
Foster Street *Essex* 51 F2
Fosterhouses *S York* 91 G1
Foston *Derbys* 71 G3
Foston *Leics* 60 B5
Foston *Lincs* 73 F4
Foston *N York* 98 C1
Foston on the Wolds *E R Yk* 93 E5
Fotherby *Lincs* 86 C4
Fothergill *Cumb* 102 D3
Fotheringhay *Nhants* 61 F5
Foul End *Warwks* 59 E5
Foul Mile *E Susx* 17 G3
Foulbridge *Cumb* 104 A5
Foulby *W York* 91 E1
Foulden *Border* 123 F5
Foulden *Norfk* 63 G5
Foulridge *Lancs* 89 G4
Foulsham *Norfk* 76 C2
Fountainhall *Border* 122 B4
Four Ashes *Staffs* 58 B6
Four Ashes *Staffs* 58 A4
Four Ashes *Suffk* 64 C2
Four Ashes *W Mids* 58 D3
Four Cabots *Guern* 174 g2
Four Crosses *Powys* 69 E2
Four Crosses *Staffs* 70 D1
Four Elms *Kent* 29 E1
Four Foot *Somset* 24 A3
Four Forks *Somset* 23 E3
Four Gates *Gt Man* 82 A5
Four Gotes *Cambs* 75 E2
Four Lane End *S York* 83 H5
Four Lane Ends *Ches* 69 H6
Four Lanes *Cnwll* 2 D4
Four Marks *Hants* 27 E3
Four Mile Bridge *IOA* 78 B2
Four Oaks *E Susx* 18 B4
Four Oaks *Gloucs* 46 C2
Four Oaks *W Mids* 58 D5
Four Oaks *W Mids* 59 E3
Four Points *Berks* 40 D2
Four Roads *Carmth* 34 B5
Four Shire Stone *Warwks* 47 H2
Four Throws *Kent* 18 A4
Four Wents *Kent* 29 G1
Fourlanes End *Ches* 70 C6
Fourpenny *Highld* 163 E3
Fourstones *Nthumb* 113 F1
Fovant *Wilts* 25 F2
Foveran *Abers* 159 F1
Fowey *Cnwll* 5 E1
Fowley Common *Ches* 82 B4
Fowlhall *Kent* 17 H6
Fowlis *Angus* 140 C3
Fowlis Wester *P & K* 139 F2
Fowlmere *Cambs* 51 E5
Fownhope *Herefs* 46 A3
Fox Corner *Surrey* 27 H5
Fox Hatch *Essex* 29 G6
Fox Street *Essex* 52 D3
Foxbar *Rens* 119 F6
Foxcombe *Devon* 8 B3
Foxcote *Gloucs* 39 E6
Foxcote *Somset* 24 C5
Foxdale *IOM* 174 k3
Foxearth *Essex* 52 B5
Foxendown *Kent* 29 G3
Foxfield *Cumb* 94 C3
Foxham *Wilts* 38 D2
Foxhills *Hants* 13 G6
Foxhole *Cnwll* 3 G5
Foxhole *Swans* 34 D4
Foxholes *N York* 99 F2
Foxhunt Green *E Susx* 17 F3
Foxley *Nhants* 49 E4
Foxley *Norfk* 76 C2
Foxley *Wilts* 38 D3
Foxley Green *Wilts* 38 D3
Foxlydiate *Worcs* 58 C2
Foxt *Staffs* 71 E5
Foxton *Cambs* 51 E6
Foxton *Dur* 106 C3
Foxton *Leics* 60 C4
Foxton *N York* 97 G4
Foxup *N York* 96 B2
Foxwist Green *Ches* 82 A1
Foxwood *Shrops* 57 F3
Foy *Herefs* 46 B2
Foyers *Highld* 154 C1
Foynesfield *Highld* 155 G4
Fraddam *Cnwll* 2 C3
Fraddon *Cnwll* 4 C2
Fradley *Staffs* 71 G1
Fradswell *Staffs* 71 E3
Fraisthorpe *E R Yk* 93 E6
Framfield *E Susx* 17 F3
Framingham Earl *Norfk* 65 E6
Framingham Pigot *Norfk* 65 E6
Framlingham *Suffk* 65 E2
Frampton *Dorset* 11 G4
Frampton *Lincs* 74 D4
Frampton Cotterell *Gloucs* 37 H2
Frampton Mansell *Gloucs* 38 D4
Frampton on Severn *Gloucs* 38 B5
Frampton West End *Lincs* 74 C4
Framsden *Suffk* 64 D1
Framwellgate Moor *Dur* 106 B5
Frances Green *Lancs* 89 E3
Franche *Worcs* 58 A3
Frandley *Ches* 82 A3
Frankaborough *Devon* 5 G5
Frankby *Mersyd* 81 E3
Frankfort *Norfk* 77 F2
Franklands Gate *Herefs* 45 H4
Frankley *Worcs* 58 C3
Franksbridge *Powys* 44 D5
Frankton *Warwks* 59 G2
Frant *E Susx* 17 G5
Fraserburgh *Abers* 159 F6
Frating *Essex* 52 D3
Frating Green *Essex* 52 D3
Fratton *Hants* 15 E4
Freathy *Cnwll* 5 G1
Freckenham *Suffk* 63 F3
Freckleton *Lancs* 88 C2
Freebirch *Derbys* 83 H2
Freeby *Leics* 73 F2
Freefolk *Hants* 26 C4
Freehay *Staffs* 71 E4
Freeland *Oxon* 40 B5
Freethorpe *Norfk* 65 F6
Freethorpe Common *Norfk* 65 F6
Freiston *Lincs* 74 D4
Fremington *Devon* 21 E4
Fremington *N York* 96 D5
French Street *Kent* 29 E1
Frenchay *Gloucs* 37 G2
Frenchbeer *Devon* 8 D3
Frenich *P & K* 139 E6
Frensham *Surrey* 27 G4
Freshfield *Mersyd* 81 E5
Freshford *Somset* 24 C5
Freshwater *IOW* 13 G3
Freshwater Bay *IOW* 13 G3
Freshwater East *Pembks* 32 D1
Fressingfield *Suffk* 65 E3
Freston *Suffk* 53 E5
Freswick *Highld* 167 G5
Fretherne *Gloucs* 38 B5
Frettenham *Norfk* 77 E2
Freuchie *Fife* 132 B6
Freystrop *Pembks* 32 D3
Friar Waddon *Dorset* 11 G3
Friar's Gate *E Susx* 17 F5
Friars' Hill *N York* 98 C3
Friday Bridge *Cambs* 62 D6
Friday Street *E Susx* 17 G2
Friday Street *Suffk* 65 E1
Friday Street *Suffk* 53 G6
Friday Street *Suffk* 65 F1
Friday Street *Surrey* 16 B6
Fridaythorpe *E R Yk* 92 C5
Friden *Derbys* 71 G6
Friendly *W York* 90 B2
Friern Barnet *Gt Lon* 28 D5
Friesland Bay *Ag & B* 134 D5
Friesthorpe *Lincs* 86 A3
Frieston *Lincs* 73 G5
Frieth *Bucks* 41 F3
Friezeland *Notts* 72 B5
Frilford *Oxon* 40 C4
Frilsham *Berks* 40 D1
Frimley *Surrey* 27 G5
Frimley Green *Surrey* 27 G5
Frindsbury *Kent* 30 A3
Fring *Norfk* 75 H3
Fringford *Oxon* 48 D2
Frinsted *Kent* 30 C2
Frinton-on-Sea *Essex* 53 F3
Friockheim *Angus* 141 F5
Friog *Gwynd* 67 F1
Frisby on the Wreake *Leics* 73 E2
Friskney *Lincs* 75 E6
Friskney Eaudike *Lincs* 75 E6
Friston *E Susx* 17 F1
Friston *Suffk* 65 G1
Fritchley *Derbys* 72 A5
Frith Bank *Lincs* 74 C5
Frith Common *Worcs* 57 G2
Fritham *Hants* 13 F6
Frithelstock *Devon* 21 E2
Frithelstock Stone *Devon* 21 E2
Frithend *Hants* 27 F3
Frithsden *Herts* 50 A2
Frithville *Lincs* 74 C5
Frittenden *Kent* 18 B5
Frittiscombe *Devon* 7 E2
Fritton *Norfk* 65 G5
Fritton *Norfk* 65 E5
Fritwell *Oxon* 48 C2
Frizinghall *W York* 90 C3
Frizington *Cumb* 102 D2
Frocester *Gloucs* 38 C5
Frodesley *Shrops* 57 E5
Frodsham *Ches* 81 G2
Frog End *Cambs* 51 E5
Frog End *Cambs* 63 E1
Frog Pool *Worcs* 58 A2
Frogden *Border* 123 E2
Froggatt *Derbys* 83 G2
Froghall *Staffs* 71 E5
Frogham *Hants* 13 E6
Frogham *Kent* 31 F1
Frogmore *Devon* 7 E2
Frognall *Lincs* 74 B1
Frogpool *Cnwll* 3 E4
Frogwell *Cnwll* 5 G3
Frolesworth *Leics* 59 H4
Frome *Somset* 24 C4
Frome St Quintin *Dorset* 11 F5
Frome Whitfield *Dorset* 11 G4
Fromes Hill *Herefs* 46 B4
Fron *Denbgs* 80 C1
Fron *Gwynd* 66 C4
Fron *Gwynd* 67 E5
Fron *Powys* 56 C6
Fron *Powys* 56 B5
Fron Isaf *Wrexhm* 69 E4
Fron-goch *Gwynd* 68 A4
Froncysyllte *Denbgs* 69 E4
Frostenden *Suffk* 65 G3
Frosterley *Dur* 105 G4
Froxfield *Beds* 49 H2
Froxfield *Wilts* 39 G1
Froxfield Green *Hants* 27 E2
Fryern Hill *Hants* 14 C6
Fryerning *Essex* 29 G6
Fryton *N York* 98 C2
Fuinary *Highld* 135 H4
Fulbeck *Lincs* 73 G5
Fulbourn *Cambs* 62 D1
Fulbrook *Oxon* 39 G6
Fulflood *Hants* 26 C2
Fulford *N York* 91 G4
Fulford *Somset* 23 E2
Fulford *Staffs* 70 D4
Fulham *Gt Lon* 28 C4
Fulking *W Susx* 16 C2
Full Sutton *E R Yk* 92 A5
Fullaford *Devon* 21 G4
Fullarton *N Ayrs* 119 E3
Fuller Street *Essex* 52 A2
Fuller Street *Kent* 29 F2
Fuller's End *Essex* 51 F3
Fuller's Moor *Ches* 69 G5
Fullerton *Hants* 26 B3
Fulletby *Lincs* 86 C2
Fullready *Warwks* 48 A4
Fullwood *E Ayrs* 119 F4
Fulmer *Bucks* 41 H3
Fulmodeston *Norfk* 76 C3
Fulnetby *Lincs* 86 A3
Fulney *Lincs* 74 C2
Fulstone *W York* 83 G6
Fulstow *Lincs* 86 D4
Fulwell *Oxon* 48 B1
Fulwood *Lancs* 88 D3
Fulwood *Notts* 72 B6
Fulwood *S York* 83 H3
Fulwood *Somset* 23 E1
Fundenhall *Norfk* 64 D5

Funtington
Goose Green
288

Funtington W Susx 15 F4
Funtley Hants 14 D4
Funtullich P & K 139 E2
Furley Devon 10 C5
Furnace Ag & B 128 B5
Furnace Carmth 34 C4
Furnace Cerdgn 54 D5
Furnace End Warwks 59 E4
Furner's Green E Susx 17 E4
Furness Vale Derbys 83 E3
Furneux Pelham Herts 51 E3
Further Quarter Kent 18 C5
Furtho Nhants 49 F3
Furze Platt Berks 41 G2
Furzehill Devon 21 G5
Furzehill Dorset 12 D5
Furzehills Lincs 86 C2
Furzeley Corner Hants 15 E5
Furzley Hants 26 A1
Fyfett Somset 10 C6
Fyfield Essex 51 F1
Fyfield Hants 26 A4
Fyfield Oxon 40 B4
Fyfield Wilts 39 F1
Fyfield Wilts 25 G5
Fyfield Bavant Wilts 25 F2
Fyfield Wick Oxon 40 B4
Fylingthorpe N York 99 E5
Fyning W Susx 27 F2
Fyvie Abers 158 D3

G

Gabroc Hill E Ayrs 119 F4
Gaddesby Leics 72 D1
Gaddesden Row Herts 50 B2
Gadfa IOA 78 D4
Gadgirth S Ayrs 119 F2
Gadlas Shrops 69 F4
Gaer Powys 45 E1
Gaer-llwyd Mons 37 E4
Gaerwen IOA 78 D2
Gagingwell Oxon 48 B2
Gailes N Ayrs 119 E3
Gailey Staffs 70 D1
Gainford Dur 106 A2
Gainsborough Lincs 85 F4
Gainsford End Essex 51 H4
Gairloch Highld 160 B1
Gairlochy Highld 144 D3
Gairneybridge P & K 131 G5
Gaisby W York 90 C3
Gaisgill Cumb 95 G5
Gaitsgill Cumb 103 H5
Galashiels Border 122 B3
Galgate Lancs 88 C5
Galhampton Somset 24 B2
Gallanach Ag & B 136 C2
Gallantry Bank Ches 69 G5
Gallatown Fife 132 B4
Galley Common Warwks 59 F4
Galleywood Essex 51 H1
Gallovie Highld 145 H3
Gallowfauld Angus 140 D4
Gallowhill P & K 140 B3
Gallows Green Essex 52 C3
Gallows Green Worcs 58 B2
Gallowstree Common Oxon 41 E2
Gallt-y-foel Gwynd 79 E1
Galltair Highld 143 H6
Gally Hill Hants 27 F4
Gallypot Street E Susx 17 F5
Galmpton Devon 6 D2
Galmpton Devon 7 F3
Galphay N York 97 F2
Galston E Ayrs 119 G3
Galton Dorset 12 B3
Gamballs Green Staffs 83 E1
Gambles Green Essex 52 A2
Gamblesby Cumb 104 C4
Gamelsby Cumb 103 F5
Gamesley Gt Man 83 E4
Gamlingay Cambs 50 C6
Gamlingay Cinques Cambs 50 C6
Gamlingay Great Heath Beds 50 C6
Gammersgill N York 96 D3
Gamrie Abers 158 D5
Gamston Notts 85 E2
Gamston Notts 72 D4
Ganarew Herefs 37 F6
Ganavan Bay Ag & B 136 C3
Gang Cnwll 5 G3
Ganllwyd Gwynd 67 G2
Gannachy Angus 148 D1
Ganstead E R Yk 93 E3
Ganthorpe N York 98 C2
Ganton N York 99 F3
Ganwick Corner Herts 28 C6
Gappah Devon 9 E2
Garbity Moray 157 E4
Garboldisham Norfk 64 C3
Garchory Abers 147 H5
Garden City Flints 81 E2
Garden Village Derbys 83 G4
Gardeners Green Berks 27 F6
Gardenstown Abers 158 D5
Garderhouse Shet 169 h3
Gardham E R Yk 92 C4
Gare Hill Somset 24 C3
Garelochhead Ag & B 128 D4
Garford Oxon 40 C4
Garforth W York 91 E3
Garforth Bridge W York 91 E3
Gargrave N York 89 H5
Gargunnock Stirlg 130 C4
Garizim Conwy 79 F2
Garlic Street Norfk 65 E4
Garlieston D & G 101 F5
Garlinge Kent 31 G3
Garlinge Green Kent 31 E1
Garlogie Abers 149 E5
Garmond Abers 158 D4
Garmondsway Dur 106 C4
Garmouth Moray 157 E5
Garmston Shrops 57 F6
Garn Gwynd 66 B3
Garn-Dolbenmaen Gwynd 67 E4
Garnant Carmth 34 D6
Garnett Bridge Cumb 95 F5
Garnkirk N Lans 130 C2
Garnswllt Swans 34 D5
Garrabost W Isls 168 f8
Garrallan E Ayrs 119 G1
Garras Cnwll 3 E2
Garreg Gwynd 67 F4
Garrigill Cumb 104 D4
Garriston N York 97 E4
Garroch D & G 109 H3
Garrochtrie D & G 100 B4
Garrochty Ag & B 118 C5
Garros Highld 151 E5
Garrowby Hall E R Yk 92 B5
Garsdale Cumb 95 H4
Garsdale Head Cumb 96 A4
Garsdon Wilts 38 D3
Garshall Green Staffs 71 E3
Garsington Oxon 40 D4
Garstang Lancs 88 C4
Garston Herts 28 B6
Garston Mersyd 81 F3
Gartachossan Ag & B 126 B1
Gartcosh N Lans 130 C2
Garth Brdgnd 35 F3
Garth Denbgs 69 E4
Garth Mons 37 E3
Garth Powys 44 B4
Garth Powys 56 C3
Garth Penrhyncoch Cerdgn 54 D4
Garth Row Cumb 95 F5
Garthamlock C Glas 130 C2
Garthbrengy Powys 44 C2
Gartheli Cerdgn 43 F5
Garthmyl Powys 56 B5
Garthorpe Leics 73 F2
Garthorpe Lincs 92 B1
Garths Cumb 95 F4
Gartly Abers 157 G2
Gartmore Stirlg 129 G5
Gartness N Lans 130 D1
Gartness Stirlg 129 F4
Gartocharn W Duns 129 F4
Garton E R Yk 93 F3
Garton-on-the-Wolds E R Yk 92 D5
Gartymore Highld 163 G5
Garvald E Loth 133 E2
Garvan Highld 144 B2
Garvard Ag & B 126 C4
Garve Highld 154 B5
Garvestone Norfk 64 C6
Garvock Inver 128 D2
Garway Herefs 45 G1
Garway Common Herefs 45 G1
Garway Hill Herefs 45 G2
Garyvard W Isls 168 e7
Gasper Wilts 24 C2
Gastard Wilts 38 D1
Gasthorpe Norfk 64 B3
Gaston Green Essex 51 F2
Gatcombe IOW 14 C2
Gate Burton Lincs 85 F3
Gate Helmsley N York 91 H5
Gatebeck Cumb 95 F3
Gateford Notts 84 C3
Gateforth N York 91 G2
Gatehead E Ayrs 119 F3
Gatehouse Nthumb 113 E4
Gatehouse of Fleet D & G 101 G6
Gateley Norfk 76 C2
Gatenby N York 97 F4
Gates Heath Ches 69 G6
Gatesgarth Cumb 103 F2
Gateshaw Border 123 E2
Gateshead T & W 114 D2
Gateside Angus 140 D4
Gateside E Rens 119 G5
Gateside Fife 131 H6
Gateside N Ayrs 119 E5
Gateslack D & G 110 C5
Gathurst Gt Man 81 H5
Gatley Gt Man 82 C3
Gatton Surrey 28 D1
Gattonside Border 122 C3
Gatwick Airport W Susx 16 D5
Gaufron Powys 55 G2
Gaulby Leics 60 C5
Gauldry Fife 140 D2
Gauldswell P & K 140 B5
Gaulkthorn Lancs 89 F2
Gaultree Norfk 62 D6
Gaunt's Common Dorset 12 D5
Gaunt's End Essex 51 F3
Gaunton's Bank Ches 69 H5
Gautby Lincs 86 B2
Gavinton Border 123 E5
Gawber S York 84 A5
Gawcott Bucks 49 E2
Gawsworth Ches 82 D2
Gawthorpe W York 90 D2
Gawthrop Cumb 95 H4
Gawthwaite Cumb 94 C3
Gay Bowers Essex 52 B1
Gay Street W Susx 16 B3
Gaydon Warwks 48 B5
Gayhurst Bucks 49 G4
Gayle N York 96 B4
Gayles N York 96 D6
Gayton Mersyd 81 E3
Gayton Nhants 49 E5
Gayton Norfk 75 G2
Gayton Staffs 71 E3
Gayton le Marsh Lincs 87 E3
Gayton Thorpe Norfk 75 H2
Gaywood Norfk 75 G2
Gazeley Suffk 63 F2
Gear Cnwll 3 E2
Gearraidh Bhaird W Isls 168 e7
Geary Highld 150 C5
Gedding Suffk 64 B1
Geddington Nhants 61 E4
Gedling Notts 72 D4
Gedney Lincs 74 D2
Gedney Broadgate Lincs 74 D2
Gedney Drove End Lincs 75 E3
Gedney Dyke Lincs 74 D3
Gedney Hill Lincs 74 D1
Gee Cross Gt Man 82 D4
Geeston Rutlnd 61 F6
Geldeston Norfk 65 F4
Gelli Rhondd 35 G4
Gelli Torfn 36 D3
Gellifor Denbgs 80 D1
Gelligaer Caerph 36 B4
Gelligroes Caerph 36 C4
Gelligron Neath 35 E5
Gellilydan Gwynd 67 F4
Gellinudd Neath 35 E5
Gelly Carmth 33 E4
Gellyburn P & K 140 A4
Gellywen Carmth 33 G4
Gelston D & G 102 B6
Gelston Lincs 73 G5
Gembling E R Yk 93 E5
Gentleshaw Staffs 71 E1
George Green Bucks 28 A4
George Nympton Devon 21 G3
Georgefield D & G 111 G4
Georgeham Devon 21 E5
Georgetown Blae G 36 C5
Georgia Cnwll 2 B3
Georth Ork 169 b3
Gerlan Gwynd 79 F1
Germansweek Devon 8 A4
Germoe Cnwll 2 C3
Gerrans Cnwll 3 F3
Gerrards Cross Bucks 28 A5
Gerrick N York 107 F2
Gestingthorpe Essex 52 B4
Geuffordd Powys 68 D1
Gib Hill Ches 82 A2
Gibraltar Lincs 75 F6
Gibsmere Notts 73 E5
Giddeahall Wilts 38 C2
Giddy Green Dorset 12 B3
Gidea Park Gt Lon 29 F5
Gidleigh Devon 8 D3
Giffnock E Rens 119 G5
Gifford E Loth 132 D2
Giffordtown Fife 132 B6
Giggleswick N York 96 A1
Gilberdyke E R Yk 92 B2
Gilbert Street Hants 27 E2
Gilbert's Cross Staffs 58 A4
Gilbert's End Worcs 46 D3
Gilchriston E Loth 132 D2
Gilcrux Cumb 103 E4
Gildersome W York 90 D2
Gildingwells S York 84 C3
Gilesgate Moor Dur 106 B5
Gileston V Glam 22 C6
Gilfach Caerph 36 C4
Gilfach Goch Brdgnd 35 G3
Gilfachrheda Cerdgn 42 D5
Gilgarran Cumb 102 D2
Gill Cumb 104 A3
Gill's Green Kent 18 A5
Gillamoor N York 98 C4
Gillan Cnwll 3 E2
Gillen Highld 150 C5
Gillesbie D & G 111 F4
Gilling East N York 98 B2
Gilling West N York 97 E5
Gillingham Dorset 24 D2
Gillingham Kent 30 A3
Gillingham Norfk 65 F4
Gillock Highld 167 F4
Gillow Heath Staffs 70 D6
Gills Highld 167 G6
Gilmanscleuch Border 121 H2
Gilmerton C Edin 132 B2
Gilmerton P & K 139 F2
Gilmonby Dur 105 G1
Gilmorton Leics 60 B4
Gilsland Nthumb 112 D1
Gilson Warwks 59 E4
Gilstead W York 90 B3
Gilston Herts 51 E2
Gilston Mdloth 122 B5
Giltbrook Notts 72 C5
Gilwern Mons 36 D6
Gimingham Norfk 77 F4
Ginclough Ches 83 E2
Gingers Green E Susx 17 G3
Gipping Suffk 64 C2
Gipsey Bridge Lincs 74 C5
Girdle Toll N Ayrs 119 E3
Girlington W York 90 C3
Girlsta Shet 169 h3
Girsby N York 106 C2
Girtford Beds 50 C6
Girthon D & G 101 G5
Girton Cambs 62 C2
Girton Notts 85 F1
Girvan S Ayrs 108 D4
Gisburn Lancs 89 G4
Gisleham Suffk 65 G4
Gislingham Suffk 64 C2
Gissing Norfk 64 D4
Gittisham Devon 10 B4
Gladestry Powys 45 E5
Gladsmuir E Loth 132 D2
Glais Swans 34 D4
Glaisdale N York 98 C5
Glamis Angus 140 D4
Glan-Duar Carmth 43 E4
Glan-Dwyfach Gwynd 66 D4
Glan-rhyd Powys 35 E5
Glan-y-don Flints 80 D3
Glan-y-llyn Rhondd 36 B3
Glan-y-nant Powys 55 G4
Glan-yr-afon Gwynd 68 A4
Glan-yr-afon Gwynd 68 B4
Glan-yr-afon IOA 79 F3
Glan-yr-afon Swans 34 D5
Glanaber Gwynd 67 F5
Glanafon Pembks 32 D3
Glanaman Carmth 34 D6
Glandford Norfk 76 C4
Glandwr Pembks 33 F5
Glandyfi Cerdgn 55 E5
Glangrwyney Powys 36 D6
Glanllynfi Brdgnd 35 F3
Glanmule Powys 56 B4
Glanrhyd Pembks 42 B3
Glanton Nthumb 124 D2
Glanton Pike Nthumb 124 D2
Glanvilles Wootton Dorset 11 G5
Glapthorn Nhants 61 F4
Glapwell Derbys 84 B1
Glasbury Powys 45 E3
Glascoed Denbgs 80 B2
Glascoed Mons 36 D4
Glascote Staffs 59 E6
Glascwm Powys 44 D4
Glasfryn Conwy 68 B5
Glasgow C Glas 130 B2
Glasgow Airport C Glas 129 F2
Glasgow Science Centre C Glas 129 G2
Glasinfryn Gwynd 79 E1
Glasnacardoch Bay Highld 143 F4
Glasnakille Highld 143 E5
Glaspwll Powys 55 E5
Glass Houghton W York 91 E2
Glassenbury Kent 18 A5
Glasserton D & G 101 F4
Glassford S Lans 120 B4
Glasshouse Gloucs 46 C1
Glasshouse Hill Gloucs 46 C1
Glasshouses N York 97 E1
Glasson Cumb 103 F6
Glasson Lancs 88 C5
Glassonby Cumb 104 C4
Glasterlaw Angus 141 F5
Glaston Rutlnd 61 E5
Glastonbury Somset 23 H3
Glatton Cambs 61 G4
Glazebrook Ches 82 B4
Glazebury Ches 82 B4
Glazeley Shrops 57 G4
Gleadsmoss Ches 82 C1
Gleaston Cumb 94 C2
Glebe Highld 154 C1
Gledhow W York 90 D3
Gledpark D & G 101 G5
Gledrid Shrops 69 E4
Glemsford Suffk 52 B6
Glen Auldyn IOM 174 m4
Glen Clunie Lodge Abers 147 F3
Glen Maye IOM 174 k3
Glen Mona IOM 174 m4
Glen Nevis House Highld 144 D2
Glen Parva Leics 60 B5
Glen Trool Lodge D & G 109 F3
Glen Vine IOM 174 l3
Glenallachie Highld 157 E3
Glenancross Highld 143 F3
Glenaros House Ag & B 135 G4
Glenbarr Ag & B 117 F4
Glenbarry Abers 158 B4
Glenbeg Highld 135 H6
Glenbeg Highld 156 B2
Glenbervie Abers 149 E2
Glenboig N Lans 130 C2
Glenborrodale Highld 135 H5
Glenbranter Ag & B 128 C5
Glenbreck Border 121 E2
Glenbrittle House Highld 142 D6
Glenbuck E Ayrs 120 B2
Glencally Angus 140 D6
Glencaple D & G 110 D2
Glencarron Lodge Highld 153 E4
Glencarse P & K 140 B2
Glenceitlein Highld 137 F5
Glencoe Highld 137 F6
Glencothe Border 121 E2
Glencraig Fife 131 H5
Glencrosh D & G 110 B4
Glendale Highld 150 B4
Glendaruel Ag & B 128 B3
Glendevon P & K 131 F6
Glendoe Lodge Highld 145 F5
Glendoick P & K 140 B2
Glenduckie Fife 140 C2
Gleneagles P & K 131 E6
Gleneagles Hotel P & K 139 F1
Glenegedale Ag & B 116 B5
Glenelg Highld 143 H6
Glenerney Moray 156 B4
Glenfarg P & K 131 G6
Glenfeshie Lodge Highld 146 C4
Glenfield Leics 60 B6
Glenfinnan Highld 144 A2
Glenfintaig Lodge Highld 144 D3
Glenfoot P & K 140 B1
Glenfyne Lodge Ag & B 137 G1
Glengarnock N Ayrs 119 E5
Glengolly Highld 167 E5
Glengorm Castle Ag & B 135 F5
Glengrasco Highld 150 D3
Glenholm Border 121 E3
Glenhoul D & G 109 H3
Glenisla Angus 140 B6
Glenkin Ag & B 128 C3
Glenkindie Abers 148 B6
Glenlivet Moray 156 D2
Glenlochar D & G 110 B1
Glenlomond P & K 131 H6
Glenluce D & G 100 C6
Glenmassen Ag & B 128 C4
Glenmavis N Lans 130 D2
Glenmore Highld 150 D3
Glenmore Lodge Highld 147 E5
Glenquiech Angus 140 D6
Glenralloch Ag & B 127 G2
Glenridding Cumb 103 H2
Glenrothes Fife 132 B5
Glenshee P & K 139 G3
Glenshera Lodge Highld 145 H4
Glenstriven Ag & B 128 B3
Glentham Lincs 85 H4
Glentromie Lodge Highld 146 C4
Glentrool Village D & G 109 E3
Glentruim House Highld 146 B4
Glentworth Lincs 85 G3
Glenuig Highld 143 F2
Glenure Ag & B 137 E5
Glenvarragill Highld 151 E3
Glenwhilly D & G 108 D2
Glespin S Lans 120 C2
Glewstone Herefs 46 A1
Glinton Cambs 61 G6
Glooston Leics 60 D5
Glororum Nthumb 125 E4
Glossop Derbys 83 E4
Gloster Hill Nthumb 125 F1
Gloucester Gloucs 46 D1
Gloucestershire Airport Gloucs 46 D1
Glusburn N York 90 A4
Glutt Lodge Highld 166 D2
Gluvian Cnwll 4 C2
Glympton Oxon 48 C1
Glyn Ceiriog Wrexhm 68 D4
Glyn-Neath Neath 35 F5
Glynarthen Cerdgn 42 C4
Glyncorrwg Neath 35 F4
Glynde E Susx 17 E2
Glyndebourne E Susx 17 E2
Glyndyfrdwy Denbgs 68 D4
Glyntaff Rhondd 36 B3
Glyntawe Powys 35 F6
Glynteg Carmth 42 C3
Gnosall Staffs 70 C2
Gnosall Heath Staffs 70 C2
Goadby Leics 60 D5
Goadby Marwood Leics 73 E3
Goat Lees Kent 18 D6
Goatacre Wilts 39 E2
Goatfield Ag & B 128 B5
Goatham Green E Susx 18 B3
Goathill Dorset 24 B1
Goathland N York 98 D5
Goathurst Somset 23 E3
Goathurst Common Kent 29 F1
Gobowen Shrops 69 E3
Godalming Surrey 27 H4
Goddard's Corner Suffk 65 E2
Goddard's Green Kent 18 B5
Godford Cross Devon 10 B5
Godington Bucks 49 E2
Godley Gt Man 82 D4
Godmanchester Cambs 62 B2
Godmanstone Dorset 11 G4
Godmersham Kent 30 D1
Godney Somset 23 H3
Godolphin Cross Cnwll 2 D3
Godre'r-graig Neath 35 E5
Godshill Hants 13 F6
Godshill IOW 14 C2
Godstone Staffs 71 E3
Godstone Surrey 28 D1
Godsworthy Devon 8 B2
Godwinscroft Hants 13 F4
Goetre Mons 36 D5
Goff's Oak Herts 50 D1
Gofilon Mons 36 D6
Gogar C Edin 131 H2
Goginan Cerdgn 54 D3
Golan Gwynd 67 E4
Golant Cnwll 5 E1
Golberdon Cnwll 5 G3
Golborne Gt Man 82 A4
Golcar W York 90 B1
Gold Hill Cambs 63 E5
Gold Hill Dorset 12 B6
Goldcliff Newpt 37 E3
Golden Cross E Susx 17 F3
Golden Green Kent 17 G6
Golden Grove Carmth 43 F1
Golden Hill Pembks 32 D2
Golden Pot Hants 27 E4
Golden Valley Derbys 72 B5
Goldenhill Staffs 70 D5
Golders Green Gt Lon 28 C5
Goldfinch Bottom Berks 26 C6
Goldhanger Essex 52 C2
Golding Shrops 57 F6
Goldington Beds 50 B6
Golds Green W Mids 58 C5
Goldsborough N York 107 H2
Goldsborough N York 91 E5
Goldsithney Cnwll 2 C3
Goldstone Kent 31 F2
Goldstone Shrops 70 B3
Goldsworth Park Surrey 27 H5
Goldthorpe S York 84 B5
Goldworthy Devon 20 D3
Golford Kent 18 B5
Golford Green Kent 18 B5
Gollanfield Highld 155 F4
Gollinglith Foot N York 97 E3
Golly Wrexhm 69 F6
Golsoncott Somset 22 C3
Golspie Highld 163 E4
Gomeldon Wilts 25 G3
Gomersal W York 90 C2
Gomshall Surrey 16 B6
Gonalston Notts 72 D5
Gonerby Hill Foot Lincs 73 G4
Gonfirth Shet 169 h3
Good Easter Essex 51 G2
Goodameavy Devon 6 C4
Gooderstone Norfk 63 G6
Goodleigh Devon 21 F4
Goodmanham E R Yk 92 C4
Goodmayes Gt Lon 29 E5
Goodnestone Kent 30 D2
Goodnestone Kent 31 F1
Goodrich Herefs 46 A1
Goodrich Castle Herefs 46 A1
Goodrington Devon 7 F3
Goodshaw Lancs 89 F2
Goodshaw Fold Lancs 89 F2
Goodstone Devon 7 E5
Goodwick Pembks 32 D5
Goodworth Clatford Hants 26 B3
Goodyers End Warwks 59 F4
Goole E R Yk 92 A2
Goole Fields E R Yk 92 A2
Goom's Hill Worcs 47 F5
Goonbell Cnwll 3 E5
Goonhavern Cnwll 3 E5
Goonvrea Cnwll 3 E5
Goose Green Essex 53 E3
Goose Green Essex 53 E3
Goose Green Gloucs 38 B2

Goose Green
Gualachulain
289

Goose Green Gt Man 81 H5
Goose Green Kent 29 G1
Goose Green Kent 18 B5
Goose Green W Susx 16 B3
Goose Pool Herefs 45 G3
Goosecruives Abers 149 E3
Gooseford Devon 8 D4
Gooseham Cnwll 20 C2
Goosehill Green Worcs 47 E5
Goosemoor Somset 22 B3
Goosey Oxon 40 B3
Goosnargh Lancs 88 D3
Goostrey Ches 82 C2
Gorddinog Conwy 79 F2
Gordon Border 122 D4
Gordon Arms Hotel Border 121 G2
Gordonstown Abers 158 B5
Gordonstown Abers 158 C3
Gore Powys 45 E5
Gore Pit Essex 52 B3
Gore Street Kent 31 F2
Gorebridge Mdloth 121 H6
Gorefield Cambs 74 D1
Gores Wilts 25 G5
Gorey Jersey 174 d2
Goring Oxon 40 D2
Goring Heath Oxon 41 E2
Goring-by-Sea W Susx 16 B2
Gorleston on Sea Norfk 65 H6
Gorrachie Abers 158 C5
Gorran Cnwll 3 G4
Gorran Haven Cnwll 3 G4
Gorran High Lanes Cnwll 3 G4
Gorrig Cerdgn 42 D3
Gors Cerdgn 54 D3
Gorse Hill Wilts 39 F3
Gorsedd Flints 80 D2
Gorseinon Swans 34 C4
Gorseybank Derbys 71 H5
Gorsgoch Cerdgn 43 E4
Gorslas Carmth 34 C6
Gorsley Gloucs 46 B2
Gorsley Common Gloucs 46 B2
Gorst Hill Worcs 57 G3
Gorstage Ches 82 A2
Gorstan Highld 154 B5
Gorstello Ches 81 F1
Gorsty Hill Staffs 71 F3
Gorten Ag & B 136 B3
Gorthleck Highld 154 D1
Gorton Gt Man 82 D4
Gosbeck Suffk 64 D1
Gosberton Lincs 74 C3
Gosberton Clough Lincs 74 B3
Gosfield Essex 52 A4
Gosford Devon 10 A4
Gosforth Cumb 94 A5
Gosforth T & W 114 D2
Gosland Green Ches 69 H6
Gosling Street Somset 24 A2
Gosmore Herts 50 C3
Gospel End Staffs 58 B5
Gospel Green W Susx 27 G2
Gosport Hants 14 D4
Gossard's Green Beds 49 H4
Gossington Gloucs 38 B4
Goswick Nthumb 123 H4
Gotham Notts 72 C3
Gotherington Gloucs 47 E2
Gotton Somset 23 E2
Goudhurst Kent 17 H5
Goulceby Lincs 86 C3
Gourdas Abers 158 D3
Gourdie Angus 140 C3
Gourdon Abers 149 F1
Gourock Inver 128 D3
Govan C Glas 129 G2
Goveton Devon 7 E2
Gowdall E R Yk 91 G2
Gower Highld 154 C5
Gowerton Swans 34 C4
Gowkhall Fife 131 G4
Gowthorpe E R Yk 92 B5
Goxhill E R Yk 93 F4
Goxhill Lincs 93 E2
Grabhair W Isls 168 e7
Graby Lincs 74 A3
Grade Cnwll 3 E1
Gradeley Green Ches 69 H5
Graffham W Susx 15 G5
Grafham Cambs 61 G2
Grafham Surrey 16 A6
Grafton Herefs 45 H3
Grafton N York 97 G1
Grafton Oxon 39 G4
Grafton Shrops 69 F2
Grafton Worcs 46 A5
Grafton Worcs 47 E3
Grafton Flyford Worcs 47 E5
Grafton Regis Nhants 49 F4
Grafton Underwood Nhants 61 E3
Grafty Green Kent 30 B1
Graianrhyd Denbgs 68 D6
Graig Conwy 79 G2
Graig Denbgs 80 C2
Graig-fechan Denbgs 68 D5
Grain Kent 30 B4
Grains Bar Gt Man 83 E5
Grainsby Lincs 86 C5
Grainthorpe Lincs 86 D4
Grampound Cnwll 3 G5
Grampound Road Cnwll 3 G5
Gramsdal W Isls 168 b4
Gramsdale W Isls 168 b4
Granborough Bucks 49 F2
Granby Notts 73 E4
Grand Chemins Jersey 174 c2
Grand Prix Collection Donington Leics 72 B3
Grandborough Warwks 59 H2
Grandes Rocques Guern 174 g3
Grandtully P & K 139 F5
Grange Cumb 103 F2
Grange Kent 30 B3
Grange Mersyd 80 D3
Grange P & K 140 C2
Grange Crossroads Moray 157 G4
Grange Gate Dorset 12 C3
Grange Hall Moray 156 C5
Grange Hill Gt Lon 29 E5
Grange Moor W York 90 C1
Grange of Lindores Fife 140 C1
Grange Villa Dur 106 B6
Grange-over-Sands Cumb 95 E3
Grangehall S Lans 120 D4
Grangemill Derbys 71 G6
Grangemouth Falk 131 E3
Grangepans Falk 131 F3
Grangetown N York 107 E3
Grangetown T & W 115 F1
Gransmoor E R Yk 93 E5
Gransmore Green Essex 51 H3
Granston Pembks 32 C5
Grantchester Cambs 62 D1
Grantham Lincs 73 G4
Granton C Edin 132 A3
Grantown-on-Spey Highld 156 B2
Grantsfield Herefs 45 H5
Grantshouse Border 133 G2
Grappenhall Ches 82 A3
Grasby Lincs 86 A5
Grasmere Cumb 94 D6
Grass Green Essex 52 A4
Grasscroft Gt Man 83 E5
Grassendale Mersyd 81 F3
Grassgarth Cumb 103 G4
Grassington N York 96 C1
Grassmoor Derbys 84 B1
Grassthorpe Notts 85 F1
Grateley Hants 26 A3
Gratwich Staffs 71 E3
Graveley Cambs 62 B2
Graveley Herts 50 C3
Gravelly Hill W Mids 58 D4
Gravelsbank Shrops 56 D5
Graveney Kent 30 D2
Gravesend Kent 29 G3
Gravir W Isls 168 e7
Grayingham Lincs 85 G4
Grayrigg Cumb 95 F5
Grays Essex 29 G4
Grayshott Hants 27 G3
Grayson Green Cumb 102 D3
Grayswood Surrey 27 G3
Graythorpe Dur 107 E4
Grazeley Berks 27 E6
Greasbrough S York 84 B4
Greasby Mersyd 81 E3
Greasley Notts 72 C5
Great Abington Cambs 51 F6
Great Addington Nhants 61 F3
Great Alne Warwks 47 G5
Great Altcar Lancs 81 F5
Great Amwell Herts 51 E2
Great Asby Cumb 104 C1
Great Ashfield Suffk 64 C2
Great Ayton N York 107 E2
Great Baddow Essex 51 H1
Great Badminton Gloucs 38 C2
Great Bardfield Essex 51 G4
Great Barford Beds 50 B6
Great Barr W Mids 58 C5
Great Barrington Gloucs 39 G6
Great Barrow Ches 81 G1
Great Barton Suffk 64 A2
Great Barugh N York 98 C3
Great Bavington Nthumb 113 G3
Great Bealings Suffk 53 F6
Great Bedwyn Wilts 26 A6
Great Bentley Essex 53 E3
Great Billing Nhants 60 D2
Great Bircham Norfk 75 H3
Great Blakenham Suffk 53 E6
Great Blencow Cumb 104 A3
Great Bolas Shrops 70 B2
Great Bookham Surrey 28 B1
Great Bosullow Cnwll 2 B3
Great Bourton Oxon 48 C4
Great Bowden Leics 60 C4
Great Bradley Suffk 51 G6
Great Braxted Essex 52 B2
Great Bricett Suffk 52 D6
Great Brickhill Bucks 49 G2
Great Bridge W Mids 58 C5
Great Bridgeford Staffs 70 D3
Great Brington Nhants 60 C2
Great Bromley Essex 52 D3
Great Broughton Cumb 103 E3
Great Broughton N York 98 A5
Great Budworth Ches 82 B2
Great Burdon Dur 106 C2
Great Burstead Essex 29 H5
Great Busby N York 98 A5
Great Canfield Essex 51 G2
Great Carlton Lincs 86 D3
Great Casterton Rutlnd 73 G1
Great Chalfield Wilts 24 D6
Great Chart Kent 18 C6
Great Chatwell Staffs 70 C1
Great Chell Staffs 70 D5
Great Chesterford Essex 51 F5
Great Cheverell Wilts 25 E5
Great Chishill Cambs 51 E5
Great Clacton Essex 53 E2
Great Cliffe W York 90 D1
Great Clifton Cumb 102 D3
Great Coates Lincs 86 C6
Great Comberton Worcs 47 E3
Great Comp Kent 29 G2
Great Corby Cumb 104 B6
Great Cornard Suffk 52 B5
Great Cowden E R Yk 93 F4
Great Coxwell Oxon 39 G4
Great Cransley Nhants 60 D3
Great Cressingham Norfk 63 H6
Great Crosthwaite Cumb 103 G2
Great Cubley Derbys 71 F4
Great Dalby Leics 73 E1
Great Doddington Nhants 61 E2
Great Doward Herefs 37 F6
Great Dunham Norfk 76 B1
Great Dunmow Essex 51 G3
Great Durnford Wilts 25 G3
Great Easton Essex 51 G3
Great Easton Leics 60 D5
Great Eccleston Lancs 88 C4
Great Edstone N York 98 C3
Great Ellingham Norfk 64 C5
Great Elm Somset 24 C4
Great Englebourne Devon 7 E3
Great Everdon Nhants 48 D5
Great Eversden Cambs 51 E6
Great Finborough Suffk 64 C1
Great Fransham Norfk 76 B1
Great Gaddesden Herts 50 A2
Great Gidding Cambs 61 G4
Great Givendale E R Yk 92 B5
Great Glemham Suffk 65 F1
Great Glen Leics 60 C5
Great Gonerby Lincs 73 G4
Great Gransden Cambs 62 B1
Great Green Cambs 50 D5
Great Green Norfk 65 E4
Great Green Suffk 64 B1
Great Green Suffk 64 B2
Great Habton N York 98 C2
Great Hale Lincs 74 B4
Great Hallingbury Essex 51 F3
Great Harrowden Nhants 61 E2
Great Harwood Lancs 89 F3
Great Haseley Oxon 41 E4
Great Hatfield E R Yk 93 F4
Great Haywood Staffs 71 E2
Great Heck N York 91 G2
Great Henny Essex 52 B4
Great Hinton Wilts 25 E5
Great Hockham Norfk 64 B5
Great Holland Essex 53 F3
Great Horkesley Essex 52 C4
Great Hormead Herts 51 E4
Great Horton W York 90 C3
Great Horwood Bucks 49 F2
Great Houghton Nhants 49 F5
Great Houghton S York 84 B5
Great Hucklow Derbys 83 G2
Great Kelk E R Yk 93 E5
Great Kimble Bucks 41 F5
Great Kingshill Bucks 41 G4
Great Langdale Cumb 94 D5
Great Langton N York 97 F4
Great Leighs Essex 51 H2
Great Limber Lincs 86 B6
Great Linford Bucks 49 G3
Great Livermere Suffk 64 A2
Great Longstone Derbys 83 G2
Great Lumley Dur 106 B6
Great Lyth Shrops 57 E6
Great Malvern Worcs 46 C4
Great Maplestead Essex 52 B4
Great Marton Lancs 88 B3
Great Massingham Norfk 76 A2
Great Melton Norfk 64 D6
Great Meols Mersyd 81 E4
Great Milton Oxon 40 D4
Great Missenden Bucks 41 G4
Great Mitton Lancs 89 F3
Great Mongeham Kent 31 G1
Great Moulton Norfk 64 D4
Great Munden Herts 50 D3
Great Musgrave Cumb 104 D1
Great Ness Shrops 69 F2
Great Notley Essex 52 A3
Great Nurcott Somset 22 B3
Great Oak Mons 37 E5
Great Oakley Essex 53 E3
Great Oakley Nhants 61 E4
Great Offley Herts 50 B3
Great Ormside Cumb 104 D2
Great Orton Cumb 103 G6
Great Ouseburn N York 91 F6
Great Oxendon Nhants 60 C4
Great Oxney Green Essex 51 G1
Great Pattenden Kent 18 A6
Great Paxton Cambs 62 A2
Great Plumpton Lancs 88 B3
Great Plumstead Norfk 77 F1
Great Ponton Lincs 73 G3
Great Potheridge Devon 21 E2
Great Preston W York 91 E2
Great Purston Nhants 48 C3
Great Raveley Cambs 62 B3
Great Rissington Gloucs 39 G6
Great Rollright Oxon 48 B2
Great Rudbaxton Pembks 32 D4
Great Ryburgh Norfk 76 C3
Great Ryle Nthumb 124 C2
Great Ryton Shrops 57 E6
Great Saling Essex 51 H3
Great Salkeld Cumb 104 B4
Great Sampford Essex 51 G4
Great Sankey Ches 81 H3
Great Saredon Staffs 58 B6
Great Saughall Ches 81 F2
Great Saxham Suffk 63 G2
Great Shefford Berks 40 B2
Great Shelford Cambs 51 E6
Great Smeaton N York 97 G5
Great Snoring Norfk 76 C3
Great Somerford Wilts 38 D2
Great Soudley Shrops 70 B3
Great Stainton Dur 106 C3
Great Stambridge Essex 30 C5
Great Staughton Cambs 61 G2
Great Steeping Lincs 87 E1
Great Stoke Bristl 37 G2
Great Stonar Kent 31 G2
Great Strickland Cumb 104 B2
Great Stukeley Cambs 62 B3
Great Sturton Lincs 86 C2
Great Sutton Ches 81 F2
Great Sutton Shrops 57 E4
Great Swinburne Nthumb 113 F2
Great Tew Oxon 48 B2
Great Tey Essex 52 C3
Great Torrington Devon 21 E2
Great Tosson Nthumb 114 B6
Great Totham Essex 52 B2
Great Totham Essex 52 B2
Great Tows Lincs 86 C4
Great Urswick Cumb 94 C2
Great Wakering Essex 30 C5
Great Waldingfield Suffk 52 C5
Great Walsingham Norfk 76 B4
Great Waltham Essex 51 H2
Great Warford Ches 82 C2
Great Warley Essex 29 G5
Great Washbourne Gloucs 47 E3
Great Weeke Devon 8 D3
Great Weldon Nhants 61 E4
Great Welnetham Suffk 64 A1
Great Wenham Suffk 52 D5
Great Whittington Nthumb 113 G2
Great Wigborough Essex 52 C2
Great Wilbraham Cambs 63 E1
Great Wishford Wilts 25 F3
Great Witchingham Norfk 76 D2
Great Witcombe Gloucs 38 D6
Great Witley Worcs 57 H2
Great Wolford Warwks 47 H3
Great Wratting Essex 51 H5
Great Wymondley Herts 50 C4
Great Wyrley Staffs 58 C6
Great Wytheford Shrops 69 H2
Great Yarmouth Norfk 65 H6
Great Yeldham Essex 52 A5
Greatfield Wilts 39 E3
Greatford Lincs 74 A1
Greatgate Staffs 71 E4
Greatham Dur 106 D4
Greatham Hants 27 F2
Greatham W Susx 16 A3
Greatstone-on-Sea Kent 18 D4
Greatworth Nhants 48 D3
Grebby Lincs 87 E1
Greeba IOM 174 I3
Green Denbgs 80 C1
Green Bank Cumb 94 D3
Green Cross Surrey 27 G3
Green Down Somset 24 A5
Green End Beds 50 A5
Green End Beds 61 G2
Green End Beds 61 G2
Green End Beds 50 B6
Green End Cambs 62 B3
Green End Cambs 62 C1
Green End Cambs 62 D2
Green End Cambs 62 D1
Green End Cambs 61 H4
Green End Herts 50 D4
Green End Herts 50 D3
Green End Herts 50 D4
Green End Warwks 59 E4
Green Hammerton N York 91 F5
Green Head Cumb 103 H5
Green Heath Staffs 71 E1
Green Hill Wilts 39 E3
Green Lane Devon 9 E2
Green Lane Warwks 58 D2
Green Moor S York 83 H5
Green Oak E R Yk 92 B2
Green Ore Somset 24 A4
Green Quarter Cumb 95 E5
Green Street E Susx 18 A3
Green Street Gloucs 38 D6
Green Street Herts 51 E3
Green Street Herts 28 C6
Green Street Worcs 46 D4
Green Street Green Gt Lon 29 E2
Green Street Green Kent 29 G3
Green Tye Herts 51 E3
Greenburn W Loth 120 D5
Greencroft Hall Dur 106 A6
Greenend Oxon 48 B1
Greenfield Ag & B 128 D4
Greenfield Beds 50 B4
Greenfield Flints 80 D2
Greenfield Gt Man 83 E5
Greenfield Highld 144 D4
Greenfield Oxon 41 E3
Greenford Gt Lon 28 B4
Greengairs N Lans 130 D2
Greengates W York 90 C3
Greengill Cumb 103 E4
Greenhalgh Lancs 88 C3
Greenham Berks 26 C6
Greenham Somset 22 D1
Greenhaugh Nthumb 113 E3
Greenhead Nthumb 112 D1
Greenheys Gt Man 82 B5
Greenhill D & G 111 E3
Greenhill Falk 130 D3
Greenhill Herefs 46 C4
Greenhill Kent 31 E3
Greenhill S Lans 120 D3
Greenhillocks Derbys 72 B5
Greenhithe Kent 29 G3
Greenholm E Ayrs 119 G3
Greenholme Cumb 95 G5
Greenhouse Border 122 C2
Greenhow Hill N York 96 D1
Greenland Highld 167 F5
Greenland S York 84 B4
Greenlands Bucks 41 F3
Greenlaw Border 122 D4
Greenlea D & G 111 E2
Greenloaning P & K 131 E6
Greenmoor Hill Oxon 41 E2
Greenmount Gt Man 82 C6
Greenock Inver 128 D3
Greenodd Cumb 94 D3
Greens Norton Nhants 49 E4
Greensgate Norfk 76 D2
Greenshields S Lans 121 E4
Greenside T & W 114 C2
Greenside W York 90 C1
Greenstead Essex 52 D3
Greenstead Green Essex 52 B3
Greensted Essex 51 F1
Greenstreet Green Suffk 52 D6
Greenway Gloucs 46 C2
Greenway Somset 23 F2
Greenway V Glam 36 B2
Greenway Worcs 57 G2
Greenwich Gt Lon 29 E4
Greet Gloucs 47 F2
Greete Shrops 57 F2
Greetham Lincs 86 C2
Greetham Rutlnd 73 G1
Greetland W York 90 B2
Gregson Lane Lancs 88 D2
Greinton Somset 23 G3
Grenaby IOM 174 k2
Grendon Nhants 49 G5
Grendon Warwks 59 F5
Grendon Green Herefs 46 B5
Grendon Underwood Bucks 49 E1
Grenofen Devon 6 B5
Grenoside S York 84 A4
Greosabhagh W Isls 168 d5
Gresford Wrexhm 69 F5
Gresham Norfk 77 E4
Greshornish House Hotel Highld 150 D4
Gressenhall Norfk 76 C1
Gressenhall Green Norfk 76 C2
Gressingham Lancs 95 F2
Gresty Green Ches 70 B5
Greta Bridge Dur 105 G1
Gretna D & G 111 H1
Gretna Green D & G 111 H1
Gretton Gloucs 47 F2
Gretton Nhants 61 E5
Gretton Shrops 57 E5
Grewelthorpe N York 97 E2
Grey Friars Suffk 65 G2
Grey Green Lincs 85 E5
Greygarth N York 97 E2
Greylake Somset 23 G3
Greyrigg D & G 111 E4
Greys Green Oxon 41 E2
Greysouthen Cumb 103 E3
Greystoke Cumb 104 A3
Greystone Angus 141 E4
Greywell Hants 27 E4
Gribb Dorset 10 D5
Gribthorpe E R Yk 92 B3
Griff Warwks 59 F4
Griffithstown Torfn 36 D4
Griffydam Leics 72 B2
Griggs Green Hants 27 F2
Grimeford Village Lancs 82 A6
Grimesthorpe S York 84 A4
Grimethorpe S York 84 B6
Grimley Worcs 46 D5
Grimmet S Ayrs 109 E6
Grimoldby Lincs 86 D3
Grimpo Shrops 69 F3
Grimsargh Lancs 88 D3
Grimsby Lincs 86 C6
Grimscote Nhants 49 E5
Grimscott Cnwll 20 C1
Grimshader W Isls 168 e8
Grimshaw Lancs 89 E2
Grimshaw Green Lancs 81 G6
Grimsthorpe Lincs 73 H2
Grimston E R Yk 93 F3
Grimston Leics 72 D2
Grimston Norfk 75 G2
Grimston Hill Notts 84 D1
Grimstone Dorset 11 G4
Grimstone End Suffk 64 B2
Grinacombe Moor Devon 5 H5
Grindale E R Yk 99 G2
Grindle Shrops 57 H6
Grindleford Derbys 83 G2
Grindleton Lancs 89 F4
Grindley Brook Shrops 69 G4
Grindlow Derbys 83 G2
Grindon Dur 106 C3
Grindon Nthumb 123 F4
Grindon Staffs 71 F5
Grindon T & W 115 E1
Grindon Hill Nthumb 113 E2
Grindonrigg Nthumb 123 F4
Gringley on the Hill Notts 85 E4
Grinsdale Cumb 103 H6
Grinshill Shrops 69 G2
Grinton N York 96 D5
Griomaisiader W Isls 168 e8
Griomsaigh W Isls 168 b4
Grishipoll Ag & B 134 D5
Grisling Common E Susx 17 E4
Gristhorpe N York 99 F3
Griston Norfk 64 B5
Gritley Ork 169 c2
Grittenham Wilts 39 E2
Grittleton Wilts 38 C2
Grizebeck Cumb 94 C3
Grizedale Cumb 94 D4
Groby Leics 60 A6
Groes Conwy 80 B1
Groes-faen Rhondd 36 B2
Groes-Wen Caerph 36 B3
Groesffordd Gwynd 66 B4
Groesffordd Marli Denbgs 80 B2
Groesllwyd Powys 68 D1
Groeslon Gwynd 66 D6
Groeslon Gwynd 67 E6
Grogarry W Isls 168 b3
Grogport Ag & B 117 G5
Groigearraidh W Isls 168 b3
Gromford Suffk 65 F1
Gronant Flints 80 C3
Groombridge E Susx 17 F5
Grosebay W Isls 168 d6
Grosmont Mons 45 G2
Grosmont N York 98 D5
Groton Suffk 52 C5
Grotton Gt Man 83 E5
Grouville Jersey 174 d1
Grove Bucks 49 G1
Grove Dorset 11 G2
Grove Kent 31 F2
Grove Notts 85 E3
Grove Oxon 40 B3
Grove Pembks 32 D2
Grove Green Kent 30 A2
Grove Park Gt Lon 29 E3
Grove Vale W Mids 58 C5
Grovenhurst Kent 17 H5
Grovesend Gloucs 37 H3
Grovesend Swans 34 C4
Grubb Street Kent 29 G3
Gruinard Highld 160 D3
Gruinart Ag & B 126 B2
Grula Highld 150 D1
Gruline Ag & B 135 G3
Grumbla Cnwll 2 B3
Grundisburgh Suffk 53 F6
Gruting Shet 169 h3
Gualachulain Highld 137 F4

Guanockgate Hartwood

290

Guanockgate Lincs 74 D1
Guardbridge Fife 140 D2
Guarlford Worcs 46 D4
Guay P & K 139 G5
Guernsey Airport Guern 174 f1
Guestling Green E Susx 18 B3
Guestling Thorn E Susx 18 B3
Guestwick Norfk 76 D3
Guide Lancs 89 E2
Guide Bridge Gt Man 82 D4
Guide Post Nthumb 114 D4
Guilden Down Shrops 56 C4
Guilden Morden Cambs 50 D5
Guilden Sutton Ches 81 G1
Guildford Surrey 27 H4
Guildstead Kent 30 B2
Guildtown P & K 140 A3
Guilsborough Nhants 60 C3
Guilsfield Powys 68 D1
Guilton Kent 31 F2
Guiltreehill S Ayrs 109 E6
Guineaford Devon 21 F4
Guisborough N York 107 E2
Guiseley W York 90 C4
Guist Norfk 76 C3
Guiting Power Gloucs 47 F2
Gullane E Loth 132 D3
Gulling Green Suffk 63 G1
Gulval Cnwll 2 B3
Gulworthy Devon 6 B5
Gumfreston Pembks 33 E2
Gumley Leics 60 C4
Gummow's Shop Cnwll 4 B2
Gun Green Kent 18 A4
Gun Hill E Susx 17 F3
Gun Hill Warwks 59 F4
Gunby E R Yk 92 A3
Gunby Lincs 73 G2
Gunby Lincs 87 E1
Gundleton Hants 26 D3
Gunn Devon 21 F4
Gunnerside N York 96 C5
Gunnerton Nthumb 113 F2
Gunness Lincs 85 F6
Gunnislake Cnwll 6 B5
Gunnista Shet 169 j2
Gunthorpe Cambs 61 H6
Gunthorpe Lincs 85 F4
Gunthorpe Norfk 76 C3
Gunthorpe Notts 72 D4
Gunton Suffk 65 H5
Gunwalloe Cnwll 2 D2
Gupworthy Somset 22 C3
Gurnard IOW 14 C3
Gurnett Ches 82 D2
Gurney Slade Somset 24 B4
Gurnos Powys 35 E5
Gushmere Kent 30 D2
Gussage All Saints Dorset 12 D6
Gussage St Andrew Dorset 12 D6
Gussage St Michael Dorset 12 D6
Guston Kent 19 G6
Gutcher Shet 169 j5
Guthrie Angus 141 F5
Guy's Marsh Dorset 24 D1
Guyhirn Cambs 62 C6
Guyhirn Gull Cambs 62 C6
Guyzance Nthumb 125 E1
Gwaenysgor Flints 80 C3
Gwalchmai IOA 78 D2
Gwastadnant Gwynd 67 F6
Gwaun-Cae-Gurwen Carmth 34 D5
Gwbert on Sea Cerdgn 42 B4
Gwealavellan Cnwll 2 D4
Gwealeath Cnwll 2 D2
Gweek Cnwll 3 E2
Gwehelog Mons 37 E5
Gwenddwr Powys 44 D3
Gwendreath Cnwll 3 E1
Gwennap Cnwll 3 E4
Gwenter Cnwll 3 E1
Gwernaffield Flints 80 D1
Gwernesney Mons 37 E4
Gwernogle Carmth 43 E3
Gwernymynydd Flints 80 D1
Gwersyllt Wrexhm 69 E5
Gwespyr Flints 80 C3
Gwindra Cnwll 3 G5
Gwinear Cnwll 2 D3
Gwithian Cnwll 2 C4
Gwredog IOA 78 D3
Gwrhay Caerph 36 C4
Gwyddelwern Denbgs 68 C5
Gwyddgrug Carmth 43 E3
Gwynfryn Wrexhm 69 E5
Gwystre Powys 56 A2
Gwytherin Conwy 68 A6
Gyfelia Wrexhm 69 E5
Gyrn-goch Gwynd 66 D5

H

Habberley Shrops 56 D6
Habberley Worcs 58 A3
Habergham Lancs 89 F3
Habertoft Lincs 87 E2
Habin W Susx 27 F1
Habrough Lincs 86 B6
Hacconby Lincs 74 A2
Haceby Lincs 73 H4
Hacheston Suffk 65 E1
Hack Green Ches 70 B5
Hackbridge Gt Lon 28 D3
Hackenthorpe S York 84 B3
Hackford Norfk 64 C6
Hackforth N York 97 F4
Hackland Ork 169 b3
Hackleton Nhants 49 F5
Hacklinge Kent 31 G1
Hackman's Gate Worcs 58 B3
Hackness N York 99 E4
Hackness Somset 23 F4
Hackney Gt Lon 28 D4
Hackthorn Lincs 85 G3
Hackthorpe Cumb 104 B2
Hacton Gt Lon 29 F5
Hadden Border 123 E3
Haddenham Bucks 41 F5
Haddenham Cambs 62 D3
Haddington E Loth 132 D2
Haddington Lincs 85 G1
Haddiscoe Norfk 65 G5
Haddo Abers 158 D3
Haddon Cambs 61 G5
Hade Edge W York 83 F5
Hadfield Derbys 83 E4
Hadham Cross Herts 51 E3
Hadham Ford Herts 51 E3
Hadleigh Essex 30 B5
Hadleigh Suffk 52 D5
Hadleigh Heath Suffk 52 D5
Hadley Shrops 70 B1
Hadley Worcs 58 B2
Hadley End Staffs 71 F2
Hadley Wood Gt Lon 28 D6
Hadlow Kent 29 G1
Hadlow Down E Susx 17 F4
Hadnall Shrops 69 G2
Hadstock Essex 51 F5
Hadzor Worcs 47 E5
Haffenden Quarter Kent 18 B5
Hafod-y-bwch Wrexhm 69 E5
Hafod-y-coed Blae G 36 C4
Hafodunos Conwy 80 A1
Hafodyrynys Caerph 36 C4
Haggate Lancs 89 G3
Haggbeck Cumb 112 B2
Haggerston Nthumb 123 G4
Haggington Hill Devon 21 F5
Haggs Falk 130 D3
Hagley Herefs 46 A3
Hagley Worcs 58 B3
Hagmore Green Suffk 52 C5
Hagnaby Lincs 86 D1
Hagnaby Lincs 87 E3
Hagworthingham Lincs 86 D2
Haigh Gt Man 82 A6
Haighton Green Lancs 88 D3
Hail Weston Cambs 61 H2
Haile Cumb 94 A6
Hailes Gloucs 47 F2
Hailey Herts 51 E2
Hailey Oxon 41 E3
Hailey Oxon 40 B5
Hailsham E Susx 17 G2
Hainault Gt Lon 29 E5
Haine Kent 31 G3
Hainford Norfk 77 E2
Hainton Lincs 86 B3
Hainworth W York 90 B3
Haisthorpe E R Yk 99 G1
Hakin Pembks 32 C2
Halam Notts 72 D5
Halbeath Fife 131 G4
Halberton Devon 9 G6
Halcro Highld 167 F4
Hale Ches 81 G3
Hale Cumb 95 F3
Hale Gt Man 82 C3
Hale Hants 25 G1
Hale Somset 24 C2
Hale Surrey 27 G4
Hale Bank Ches 81 G3
Hale Green E Susx 17 F3
Hale Nook Lancs 88 B4
Hale Street Kent 29 G1
Halebarns Gt Man 82 C3
Hales Norfk 65 F5
Hales Staffs 70 B3
Hales Green Derbys 71 G4
Hales Place Kent 31 E2
Halesgate Lincs 74 D3
Halesowen W Mids 58 C4
Halesville Essex 30 C5
Halesworth Suffk 65 F3
Halewood Mersyd 81 G3
Halford Devon 7 E5
Halford Shrops 57 E4
Halford Warwks 47 H4
Halfpenny Cumb 95 F4
Halfpenny Green Staffs 58 A5
Halfpenny Houses N York 97 E3
Halfway Berks 40 B1
Halfway Carmth 43 G2
Halfway Carmth 44 A2
Halfway S York 84 B3
Halfway Bridge W Susx 27 G1
Halfway House Shrops 69 F1
Halfway Houses Kent 30 C3
Halifax W York 90 B2
Halkirk Highld 167 E4
Halkyn Flints 80 D2
Hall E Rens 119 F5
Hall Cliffe W York 90 D1
Hall Cross Lancs 88 C3
Hall Dunnerdale Cumb 94 C4
Hall End Beds 50 A5
Hall End Beds 50 B4
Hall End W Mids 58 C5
Hall Glen Falk 131 E3
Hall Green W Mids 58 D3
Hall's Green Essex 51 E1
Hall's Green Herts 50 D4
Hallam Fields Derbys 72 B4
Halland E Susx 17 F3
Hallaton Leics 60 D5
Hallatrow Somset 24 B5
Hallbankgate Cumb 104 C6
Hallbeck Cumb 95 G4
Hallen Gloucs 37 F2
Hallfield Gate Derbys 72 B6
Hallgarth Dur 106 C5
Hallin Highld 150 C5
Halling Kent 29 H2
Hallington Lincs 86 C3
Hallington Nthumb 113 G2
Halliwell Gt Man 82 B6
Halloughton Notts 73 E5
Hallow Worcs 46 D5
Hallow Heath Worcs 46 D5
Hallsands Devon 7 E1
Hallthwaites Cumb 94 C3
Halltoft End Lincs 74 D4
Hallworthy Cnwll 5 E5
Hallyne Border 121 F3
Halmer End Staffs 70 C5
Halmond's Frome Herefs 46 B4
Halmore Gloucs 38 B4
Halnaker W Susx 15 G4
Halsall Lancs 81 F6
Halse Nhants 48 D3
Halse Somset 22 D2
Halsetown Cnwll 2 C4
Halsham E R Yk 93 F2
Halsinger Devon 21 E4
Halstead Essex 52 B4
Halstead Kent 29 F2
Halstead Leics 60 D6
Halstock Dorset 11 F5
Halsway Somset 22 D3
Haltcliff Bridge Cumb 103 H4
Haltham Lincs 86 C1
Halton Bucks 41 G5
Halton Ches 81 H3
Halton Lancs 95 F1
Halton Nthumb 113 G1
Halton W York 91 E3
Halton Wrexhm 69 E4
Halton East N York 90 B5
Halton Fenside Lincs 87 E1
Halton Gill N York 96 B2
Halton Green Lancs 95 F1
Halton Holegate Lincs 86 D1
Halton Lea Gate Nthumb 104 C6
Halton Quay Cnwll 5 H2
Halton Shields Nthumb 113 G2
Halton West N York 89 G5
Haltwhistle Nthumb 112 D1
Halvergate Norfk 65 G6
Halwell Devon 7 E3
Halwill Devon 5 H6
Halwill Junction Devon 8 A5
Ham Devon 10 C5
Ham Gloucs 47 E1
Ham Gloucs 38 B4
Ham Gt Lon 28 C3
Ham Kent 31 G1
Ham Somset 23 F2
Ham Somset 24 B4
Ham Wilts 26 B5
Ham Common Dorset 24 D2
Ham Green Herefs 46 C4
Ham Green Kent 30 B3
Ham Green Kent 18 C4
Ham Green Somset 37 F2
Ham Green Worcs 58 C2
Ham Hill Kent 29 H2
Ham Street Somset 24 A3
Hamble-le-Rice Hants 14 C4
Hambleden Bucks 41 F3
Hambledon Hants 15 E5
Hambledon Surrey 27 H3
Hambleton Lancs 88 B4
Hambleton N York 91 G3
Hambleton Moss Side Lancs 88 B4
Hambridge Somset 23 G1
Hambridge Somset 24 B3
Hambrook Gloucs 37 G2
Hambrook W Susx 15 F4
Hameringham Lincs 86 C1
Hamerton Cambs 61 G3
Hamilton S Lans 120 B5
Hamlet Dorset 11 F5
Hamlins E Susx 17 G2
Hammerpot W Susx 16 B2
Hammersmith Gt Lon 28 C4
Hammerwich Staffs 58 D6
Hammerwood E Susx 17 E5
Hammond Street Herts 50 D1
Hammoon Dorset 12 B6
Hamnavoe Shet 169 h2
Hamnavoe Shet 169 j4
Hampden Park E Susx 17 G2
Hampden Row Bucks 41 G3
Hamperden End Essex 51 G4
Hampnett Gloucs 39 F6
Hampole S York 84 C6
Hampreston Dorset 12 D4
Hampsfield Cumb 95 E3
Hampson Green Lancs 88 C5
Hampstead Gt Lon 28 D5
Hampstead Norrey's Berks 40 D2
Hampsthwaite N York 90 D5
Hampt Cnwll 5 G3
Hampton Devon 10 C4
Hampton Gt Lon 28 B3
Hampton Kent 31 E3
Hampton Shrops 57 G4
Hampton Wilts 39 F3
Hampton Worcs 47 F3
Hampton Bishop Herefs 46 A3
Hampton Court Palace & Gardens Gt Lon 28 B3
Hampton Fields Gloucs 38 D4
Hampton Green Ches 69 G5
Hampton Heath Ches 69 G5
Hampton in Arden W Mids 59 E3
Hampton Loade Shrops 57 H4
Hampton Lovett Worcs 58 B2
Hampton Lucy Warwks 47 H5
Hampton Magna Warwks 59 E2
Hampton on the Hill Warwks 59 E2
Hampton Poyle Oxon 40 C6
Hampton Wick Gt Lon 28 C3
Hamptworth Wilts 25 H1
Hamrow Norfk 76 B2
Hamsey E Susx 17 E3
Hamsey Green Gt Lon 28 D2
Hamstall Ridware Staffs 71 F2
Hamstead IOW 14 B3
Hamstead W Mids 58 C5
Hamstead Marshall Berks 26 B6
Hamsterley Dur 105 H6
Hamsterley Dur 105 H3
Hamstreet Kent 18 D5
Hamwood Somset 23 F5
Hamworthy Dorset 12 D4
Hanbury Staffs 71 G3
Hanbury Worcs 58 C2
Hanby Lincs 73 H3
Hanchet End Suffk 51 G5
Hanchurch Staffs 70 C4
Hand and Pen Devon 9 G4
Hand Green Ches 69 H6
Handale N York 107 G2
Handbridge Ches 81 F1
Handcross W Susx 16 D4
Handforth Ches 82 D3
Handley Ches 69 G6
Handley Derbys 72 A6
Handley Green Essex 51 G1
Handsacre Staffs 71 F2
Handsworth S York 84 B3
Handsworth W Mids 58 C4
Handy Cross Bucks 41 G3
Hanford Dorset 12 B6
Hanford Staffs 70 D4
Hanging Houghton Nhants 60 D3
Hanging Langford Wilts 25 F3
Hangleton E Susx 16 D2
Hangleton W Susx 16 B2
Hanham Gloucs 37 G1
Hankelow Ches 70 B5
Hankerton Wilts 38 D3
Hankham E Susx 17 G2
Hanley Staffs 70 D5
Hanley Castle Worcs 46 D3
Hanley Child Worcs 57 G2
Hanley Swan Worcs 46 D3
Hanley William Worcs 57 G2
Hanlith N York 89 G6
Hanmer Wrexhm 69 G4
Hannaford Devon 21 F4
Hannah Lincs 87 E3
Hannington Hants 26 D5
Hannington Nhants 60 D2
Hannington Wilts 39 F4
Hannington Wick Wilts 39 F4
Hanscombe End Beds 50 B4
Hanslope Bucks 49 F4
Hanthorpe Lincs 74 A2
Hanwell Gt Lon 28 B4
Hanwell Oxon 48 C4
Hanwood Shrops 69 G1
Hanworth Gt Lon 28 B3
Hanworth Norfk 77 E4
Happendon S Lans 120 C3
Happisburgh Norfk 77 G3
Happisburgh Common Norfk 77 G3
Hapsford Ches 81 G2
Hapton Lancs 89 F3
Hapton Norfk 64 D5
Harberton Devon 7 E3
Harbertonford Devon 7 E3
Harbledown Kent 31 E2
Harborne W Mids 58 C4
Harborough Magna Warwks 59 H3
Harbottle Nthumb 113 F5
Harbourneford Devon 6 D4
Harbours Hill Worcs 58 C2
Harbridge Hants 13 E6
Harbridge Green Hants 13 E6
Harbury Warwks 48 B5
Harby Leics 73 E3
Harby Notts 85 F2
Harcombe Devon 9 F3
Harcombe Devon 10 B4
Harcombe Bottom Devon 10 D4
Harden W Mids 58 C5
Harden W York 90 B3
Hardenhuish Wilts 38 D2
Hardgate Abers 149 E5
Hardgate D & G 110 C1
Hardgate N York 90 D6
Hardgate W Duns 129 F2
Hardham W Susx 16 A3
Hardhorn Lancs 88 B3
Hardingham Norfk 64 C6
Hardingstone Nhants 49 F5
Hardington Somset 24 C4
Hardington Mandeville Somset 11 E6
Hardington Marsh Somset 11 E6
Hardington Moor Somset 11 E6
Hardisworthy Devon 20 C3
Hardley Hants 14 C4
Hardley Street Norfk 65 F5
Hardmead Bucks 49 G4
Hardraw N York 96 B4
Hardsough Lancs 89 F2
Hardstoft Derbys 84 B1
Hardway Hants 14 D4
Hardway Somset 24 C3
Hardwick Bucks 49 F1
Hardwick Cambs 62 C1
Hardwick Lincs 85 F2
Hardwick Nhants 60 D2
Hardwick Norfk 65 E4
Hardwick Oxon 40 B5
Hardwick Oxon 48 D2
Hardwick S York 84 C3
Hardwick W Mids 58 D5
Hardwick Green Worcs 46 D2
Hardwicke Gloucs 38 C5
Hardwicke Gloucs 47 E2
Hardy's Green Essex 52 C3
Hare Croft W York 90 B3
Hare Green Essex 53 E3
Hare Hatch Berks 41 F2
Hare Street Essex 51 E2
Hare Street Essex 29 F6
Hare Street Herts 51 E4
Harebeating E Susx 17 G2
Hareby Lincs 86 D1
Harefield Gt Lon 28 A5
Harehill Derbys 71 G4
Harehills W York 90 D3
Harehope Nthumb 124 D3
Harelaw Border 122 C2
Harelaw D & G 112 B3
Harelaw Dur 106 A6
Hareplain Kent 18 B5
Haresceugh Cumb 104 C4
Harescombe Gloucs 38 C5
Haresfield Gloucs 38 C5
Harestock Hants 26 C2
Harewood W York 90 D4
Harewood End Herefs 45 H2
Harford Devon 6 D3
Hargate Norfk 64 D4
Hargatewall Derbys 83 F2
Hargrave Ches 81 G1
Hargrave Nhants 61 F2
Hargrave Suffk 63 G1
Hargrave Green Suffk 63 G1
Harker Cumb 103 H6
Harkstead Suffk 53 E4
Harlaston Staffs 71 G1
Harlaxton Lincs 73 F3
Harle Syke Lancs 89 G3
Harlech Gwynd 67 E3
Harlescott Shrops 69 G2
Harlesden Gt Lon 28 C4
Harlesthorpe Derbys 84 C2
Harleston Devon 7 E2
Harleston Norfk 65 E4
Harleston Suffk 64 C1
Harlestone Nhants 60 C2
Harley S York 84 A4
Harley Shrops 57 F5
Harlington Beds 50 A4
Harlington Gt Lon 28 B4
Harlington S York 84 B5
Harlosh Highld 150 C3
Harlow Essex 51 E2
Harlow Hill Nthumb 114 B2
Harlthorpe E R Yk 92 A3
Harlton Cambs 51 E6
Harlyn Bay Cnwll 4 B3
Harman's Cross Dorset 12 D3
Harmby N York 96 D4
Harmer Green Herts 50 C2
Harmer Hill Shrops 69 G2
Harmondsworth Gt Lon 28 B4
Harmston Lincs 85 G1
Harnage Shrops 57 F6
Harnham Nthumb 114 B4
Harnhill Gloucs 39 E4
Harold Hill Gt Lon 29 F5
Harold Wood Gt Lon 29 F5
Haroldston West Pembks 32 C3
Haroldswick Shet 169 k5
Harome N York 98 B3
Harpenden Herts 50 B2
Harpford Devon 10 A4
Harpham E R Yk 93 E6
Harpley Norfk 76 A3
Harpley Worcs 46 B5
Harpole Nhants 49 E5
Harpsdale Highld 167 E4
Harpsden Oxon 41 F2
Harpswell Lincs 85 G4
Harpur Hill Derbys 83 F2
Harpurhey Gt Man 82 D5
Harraby Cumb 104 A6
Harracott Devon 21 F3
Harrapool Highld 151 F1
Harrietfield P & K 139 G3
Harrietsham Kent 30 B1
Harringay Gt Lon 28 D5
Harrington Cumb 102 D3
Harrington Lincs 86 D2
Harrington Nhants 60 D3
Harringworth Nhants 61 E5
Harriseahead Staffs 70 D6
Harriston Cumb 103 F4
Harrogate N York 90 D5
Harrold Beds 49 H5
Harrop Dale Gt Man 83 E5
Harrow Gt Lon 28 B5
Harrow Green Suffk 52 B6
Harrow on the Hill Gt Lon 28 B5
Harrow Weald Gt Lon 28 B5
Harrowbarrow Cnwll 5 G3
Harrowden Beds 50 B5
Harrowgate Village Dur 106 B3
Harston Cambs 51 E6
Harston Leics 73 F3
Harswell E R Yk 92 B4
Hart Dur 106 D4
Hart Station Dur 106 D4
Hartburn Nthumb 114 C4
Hartest Suffk 52 B6
Hartfield E Susx 17 F5
Hartford Cambs 62 B3
Hartford Ches 82 A2
Hartford Somset 22 B2
Hartford End Essex 51 H2
Hartfordbridge Hants 27 F5
Hartforth N York 97 E5
Hartgrove Dorset 24 D1
Harthill Ches 69 G6
Harthill N Lans 131 E1
Harthill S York 84 C3
Hartington Derbys 71 F6
Hartington Nthumb 114 B4
Hartland Devon 20 C3
Hartland Quay Devon 20 B3
Hartlebury Worcs 58 A2
Hartlepool Dur 106 D4
Hartley Cumb 96 A6
Hartley Kent 29 G3
Hartley Kent 18 A5
Hartley Nthumb 115 E3
Hartley Green Kent 29 G3
Hartley Green Staffs 71 E3
Hartley Wespall Hants 27 E5
Hartley Wintney Hants 27 F5
Hartlip Kent 30 B2
Hartlip Hill Kent 30 B2
Hartoft End N York 98 C4
Harton N York 91 H6
Harton Shrops 57 E4
Harton T & W 115 E2
Hartpury Gloucs 46 D2
Hartshead W York 90 C2
Hartshead Moor Side W York 90 C2
Hartshill Staffs 70 D5
Hartshill Warwks 59 F5
Hartshorne Derbys 72 A2
Hartside Nthumb 124 C3
Hartsop Cumb 103 H1
Hartswell Somset 22 D2
Hartwell Nhants 49 F4
Hartwith N York 90 C6
Hartwood N Lans 120 C5

Hartwoodmyres High Brooms

Hartwoodmyres Border 122 B2
Harvel Kent 29 G2
Harvington Worcs 58 B3
Harvington Worcs 47 F4
Harwell Notts 84 D4
Harwell Oxon 40 C3
Harwich Essex 53 F4
Harwood Dur 105 E3
Harwood Gt Man 82 B6
Harwood Nthumb 113 G4
Harwood Dale N York 99 E4
Harwood Lee Gt Man 82 B6
Harworth Notts 84 D4
Hasbury W Mids 58 C4
Hascombe Surrey 16 A5
Haselbech Nhants 60 C3
Haselbury Plucknett Somset 11 E6
Haseley Warwks 59 E2
Haseley Green Warwks 59 E2
Haseley Knob Warwks 59 E2
Haselor Warwks 47 G5
Hasfield Gloucs 46 D2
Hasguard Pembks 32 C3
Haskayne Lancs 81 F5
Hasketon Suffk 53 F6
Hasland Derbys 84 B2
Hasland Green Derbys 84 B1
Haslemere Surrey 27 G2
Haslingden Lancs 89 F2
Haslingden Grane Lancs 89 F2
Haslingfield Cambs 51 E6
Haslington Ches 70 B6
Hassall Ches 70 C6
Hassall Green Ches 70 C6
Hassell Street Kent 18 D6
Hassingham Norfk 65 F6
Hassness Cumb 103 F2
Hassocks W Susx 16 D3
Hassop Derbys 83 G2
Haste Hill Surrey 27 G2
Haster Highld 167 G3
Hasthorpe Lincs 87 E2
Hastingleigh Kent 18 D6
Hastings E Susx 18 B2
Hastings Somset 10 D6
Hastingwood Essex 51 F1
Hastoe Herts 41 G5
Haswell Dur 106 C5
Haswell Plough Dur 106 C5
Hatch Beds 50 B5
Hatch Beauchamp Somset 23 F1
Hatch End Beds 61 G1
Hatch End Gt Lon 28 B5
Hatchet Gate Hants 14 B4
Hatching Green Herts 50 B2
Hatchmere Ches 81 H2
Hatcliffe Lincs 86 B5
Hatfield Herefs 46 B5
Hatfield Herts 50 C2
Hatfield S York 84 D6
Hatfield Worcs 46 D4
Hatfield Broad Oak Essex 51 F2
Hatfield Heath Essex 51 F2
Hatfield Peverel Essex 52 B2
Hatfield Woodhouse S York 84 D5
Hatford Oxon 40 B4
Hatherden Hants 26 B4
Hatherleigh Devon 8 B5
Hathern Leics 72 C2
Hatherop Gloucs 39 F5
Hathersage Derbys 83 G3
Hathersage Booths Derbys 83 G3
Hatherton Ches 70 B5
Hatherton Staffs 71 E1
Hatley St George Cambs 50 D6
Hatt Cnwll 5 G2
Hattersley Gt Man 83 E4
Hattingley Hants 27 E3
Hatton Abers 159 F3
Hatton Angus 141 E4
Hatton Ches 82 A3
Hatton Derbys 71 G3
Hatton Gt Lon 28 B3
Hatton Lincs 86 B2
Hatton Shrops 57 E4
Hatton Warwks 59 E2
Hatton Heath Ches 69 G6
Hatton of Fintray Abers 149 F6
Haugh E Ayrs 119 G2
Haugh Lincs 86 D2
Haugh W York 82 D6
Haugh Head Nthumb 124 C4
Haugh of Glass Moray 157 F3
Haugh of Urr D & G 110 C1
Haugham Lincs 86 D3
Haughhead Inn E Duns 130 B3
Haughley Suffk 64 C2
Haughley Green Suffk 64 C2
Haughton Notts 84 D2
Haughton Powys 69 E2
Haughton Shrops 69 F3
Haughton Shrops 69 H2
Haughton Shrops 70 B1
Haughton Shrops 57 G5
Haughton Staffs 70 D2
Haughton Green Gt Man 82 D4
Haughton le Skerne Dur 106 C2
Haughton Moss Ches 69 H6
Haultwick Herts 50 D3
Haunton Staffs 71 G1
Hautes Croix Jersey 174 c3
Hauxley Nthumb 125 F1
Hauxton Cambs 51 E6
Havannah Ches 82 D1
Havant Hants 15 E4
Haven Herefs 45 G5
Haven Bank Lincs 74 C5
Haven Side E R Yk 93 F2
Havenstreet IOW 14 D3
Havercroft W York 84 B6
Haverfordwest Pembks 32 D3
Haverhill Suffk 51 G5
Haverigg Cumb 94 B3
Havering-atte-Bower Essex 29 F5
Haversham Bucks 49 F3
Haverthwaite Cumb 94 D3
Haverton Hill Dur 106 D3
Havyat Somset 23 G5
Havyatt Somset 23 H3
Hawarden Flints 81 E1
Hawbridge Worcs 47 E4
Hawbush Green Essex 52 B3
Hawcoat Cumb 94 C2
Hawe's Green Norfk 65 E5
Hawen Cerdgn 42 D4
Hawes N York 96 B4
Hawford Worcs 46 D5
Hawick Border 112 B6
Hawk Green Gt Man 83 E3
Hawkchurch Devon 10 D5
Hawkedon Suffk 52 B6
Hawkenbury Kent 18 B6
Hawkeridge Wilts 24 D5
Hawkerland Devon 9 G3
Hawkes End W Mids 59 F4
Hawkesbury Gloucs 38 B3
Hawkesbury Warwks 59 G4
Hawkesbury Upton Gloucs 38 C3
Hawkhill Nthumb 125 E2
Hawkhurst Kent 18 A4
Hawkhurst Common E Susx 17 F3
Hawkinge Kent 19 F5
Hawkley Hants 27 F2
Hawkridge Somset 22 B2
Hawksdale Cumb 103 H5
Hawkshaw Gt Man 89 F1
Hawkshead Cumb 94 D5
Hawkshead Hill Cumb 94 D5
Hawksland S Lans 120 C3
Hawkspur Green Essex 51 G4
Hawkstone Shrops 69 H3
Hawkswick N York 96 C2
Hawksworth Notts 73 E4
Hawksworth W York 90 C4
Hawkwell Essex 30 B5
Hawkwell Nthumb 114 B3
Hawley Hants 27 G5
Hawley Kent 29 F3
Hawling Gloucs 47 F1
Hawnby N York 98 A4
Haworth W York 90 B3
Hawridge Bucks 41 H5
Hawstead Suffk 63 H1
Hawstead Green Suffk 63 H1
Hawthorn Dur 106 D5
Hawthorn Hants 27 E3
Hawthorn Rhondd 36 B3
Hawthorn Hill Berks 41 G2
Hawthorn Hill Lincs 74 C6
Hawthorpe Lincs 73 H3
Hawton Notts 73 E5
Haxby N York 91 G5
Haxby Gates N York 91 G5
Haxey Lincs 85 E5
Haxey Turbary Lincs 85 E5
Haxted Surrey 17 E6
Haxton Wilts 25 G4
Hay Cnwll 3 F5
Hay Cnwll 3 G4
Hay Cnwll 3 G5
Hay Cnwll 4 C3
Hay Green Norfk 75 F2
Hay Street Herts 51 E3
Hay-on-Wye Powys 45 E3
Haydock Mersyd 81 H4
Haydon Dorset 11 G6
Haydon Somset 23 E2
Haydon Somset 24 B5
Haydon Bridge Nthumb 113 F1
Haydon Wick Wilts 39 F3
Haye Cnwll 5 G3
Hayes Gt Lon 28 B4
Hayes Gt Lon 29 E3
Hayes End Gt Lon 28 B4
Hayfield Ag & B 137 E2
Hayfield Derbys 83 E3
Haygate Shrops 70 A1
Hayhillock Angus 141 E4
Hayle Cnwll 2 C3
Hayley Green W Mids 58 B4
Haymoor Green Ches 70 B5
Hayne Devon 9 F6
Hayne Devon 8 D3
Haynes (Church End) Beds 50 B5
Haynes (Northwood End) Beds 50 B5
Haynes (Silver End) Beds 50 B5
Haynes (West End) Beds 50 B5
Hayscastle Pembks 32 C4
Hayscastle Cross Pembks 32 C4
Haysden Kent 17 F6
Hayton Cumb 103 E4
Hayton Cumb 104 B6
Hayton E R Yk 92 B4
Hayton Notts 85 E3
Hayton's Bent Shrops 57 E3
Haytor Vale Devon 9 E2
Haytown Devon 20 D2
Haywards Heath W Susx 16 D4
Haywood Herefs 45 H3
Haywood S York 84 D6
Haywood Oaks Notts 72 D5
Hazards Green E Susx 17 H3
Hazel Grove Gt Man 82 D3
Hazel Street Kent 17 H5
Hazel Stub Suffk 51 G5
Hazelbank S Lans 120 C4
Hazelbury Bryan Dorset 12 A5
Hazeleigh Essex 52 B1
Hazeley Hants 27 F5
Hazelford Notts 73 E5
Hazelhurst Gt Man 83 E5
Hazelslade Staffs 71 E1
Hazelton Walls Fife 140 C2
Hazelwood Derbys 72 A5
Hazlemere Bucks 41 G4
Hazlerigg T & W 114 D3
Hazles Staffs 71 E5
Hazleton Gloucs 39 E6
Heacham Norfk 75 G4
Headbourne Worthy Hants 26 C2
Headbrook Herefs 45 F5
Headcorn Kent 18 B6
Headingley W York 90 D3
Headington Oxon 40 D5
Headlam Dur 106 A3
Headland Dur 107 E4
Headless Cross Worcs 58 C2
Headlesscross N Lans 120 D5
Headley Hants 26 C5
Headley Hants 27 F3
Headley Surrey 28 C1
Headley Down Hants 27 F3
Headley Heath Worcs 58 D3
Headon Notts 85 E2
Heads S Lans 120 B4
Heads Nook Cumb 104 B6
Heage Derbys 72 A5
Healaugh N York 96 C5
Healaugh N York 91 F4
Heald Green Gt Man 82 C3
Heale Devon 21 G5
Heale Somset 23 E1
Heale Somset 23 G2
Healey Lancs 89 G1
Healey N York 97 E3
Healey Nthumb 114 B1
Healey W York 90 D1
Healeyfield Dur 105 G5
Healing Lincs 86 C6
Heamoor Cnwll 2 B3
Heanor Derbys 72 B5
Heanton Punchardon Devon 21 E4
Heapey Lancs 88 D2
Heapham Lincs 85 F3
Hearn Hants 27 F3
Hearts Delight Kent 30 B2
Heasley Mill Devon 21 G4
Heast Highld 143 F6
Heath Derbys 84 B1
Heath W York 91 E2
Heath and Reach Beds 49 G2
Heath Common W Susx 16 B3
Heath End Bucks 41 G4
Heath End Hants 26 B5
Heath End Leics 72 A2
Heath End Surrey 27 G4
Heath End Warwks 47 H5
Heath Green Worcs 58 D2
Heath Hall D & G 110 D3
Heath Hayes & Wimblebury Staffs 71 E1
Heath Hill Shrops 70 C1
Heath House Somset 23 G4
Heath Town W Mids 58 B5
Heathbrook Shrops 70 A3
Heathcote Derbys 71 F6
Heathcote Shrops 70 B3
Heathencote Nhants 49 E4
Heather Leics 72 B1
Heathfield Devon 9 E2
Heathfield E Susx 17 G3
Heathfield N York 97 E2
Heathfield Somset 22 D2
Heathfield Village Oxon 40 C6
Heathrow Airport Gt Lon 28 B4
Heathstock Devon 10 C5
Heathton Shrops 58 A5
Heatley Gt Man 82 B3
Heatley Staffs 71 F3
Heaton Gt Man 82 B6
Heaton Lancs 88 C6
Heaton Staffs 82 D1
Heaton T & W 114 D2
Heaton W York 90 C3
Heaton Chapel Gt Man 82 D4
Heaton Mersey Gt Man 82 D4
Heaton Norris Gt Man 82 D4
Heaton's Bridge Lancs 81 F6
Heaverham Kent 29 F2
Heaviley Gt Man 82 D4
Heavitree Devon 9 F4
Hebburn T & W 115 E2
Hebden N York 90 A6
Hebden Bridge W York 90 A2
Hebden Green Ches 82 A1
Hebing End Herts 50 D3
Hebron Carmth 33 F4
Hebron IOA 78 D3
Hebron Nthumb 114 D4
Heckfield Hants 27 E5
Heckfield Green Suffk 64 D3
Heckfordbridge Essex 52 C3
Heckington Lincs 74 B4
Heckmondwike W York 90 C2
Heddington Wilts 25 E6
Heddon-on-the-Wall Nthumb 114 C2
Hedenham Norfk 65 F5
Hedge End Hants 14 C5
Hedgerley Bucks 41 H3
Hedgerley Green Bucks 41 H3
Hedging Somset 23 F2
Hedley on the Hill Nthumb 114 B1
Hednesford Staffs 71 E1
Hedon E R Yk 93 F2
Hedsor Bucks 41 G3
Hegdon Hill Herefs 46 A5
Heglibister Shet 169 h3
Heighington Dur 106 B3
Heighington Lincs 85 H2
Heightington Worcs 57 H2
Heiton Border 122 D2
Hele Cnwll 5 F6
Hele Devon 21 E5
Hele Devon 9 G5
Hele Devon 7 E5
Hele Somset 23 E2
Hele Lane Devon 21 H2
Helebridge Cnwll 20 B1
Helensburgh Ag & B 128 D3
Helenton S Ayrs 119 F2
Helford Cnwll 3 E2
Helford Passage Cnwll 3 E2
Helhoughton Norfk 76 B3
Helions Bumpstead Essex 51 G5
Hell Corner Berks 26 B6
Hellaby S York 84 C4
Helland Cnwll 4 D3
Hellandbridge Cnwll 4 D3
Hellescott Cnwll 5 F5
Hellesdon Norfk 77 E1
Hellesveor Cnwll 2 C4
Hellidon Nhants 48 C5
Hellifield N York 89 G5
Hellingly E Susx 17 G3
Hellington Norfk 65 F6
Helm Nthumb 114 D5
Helmdon Nhants 48 D4
Helme W York 83 F6
Helmingham Suffk 64 D1
Helmington Row Dur 106 A4
Helmsdale Highld 163 G5
Helmshore Lancs 89 F2
Helmsley N York 98 B3
Helperby N York 97 G2
Helperthorpe N York 99 E2
Helpringham Lincs 74 B4
Helpston Cambs 61 G6
Helsby Ches 81 G2
Helsey Lincs 87 E2
Helston Cnwll 2 D2
Helstone Cnwll 4 D4
Helton Cumb 104 B2
Helwith N York 96 D5
Helwith Bridge N York 96 A2
Hemblington Norfk 77 F1
Hemel Hempstead Herts 50 B1
Hemerdon Devon 6 C3
Hemingbrough N York 91 H3
Hemingby Lincs 86 C2
Hemingfield S York 84 B5
Hemingford Abbots Cambs 62 B2
Hemingford Grey Cambs 62 B2
Hemingstone Suffk 53 E6
Hemington Nhants 61 G4
Hemington Somset 24 C5
Hemley Suffk 53 F5
Hemlington N York 106 D2
Hempholme E R Yk 93 E5
Hempnall Norfk 65 E5
Hempnall Green Norfk 65 E5
Hempriggs Moray 156 C5
Hempstead Essex 51 G4
Hempstead Kent 30 B2
Hempstead Norfk 76 D4
Hempstead Norfk 77 G3
Hempsted Gloucs 38 C6
Hempton Norfk 76 B3
Hempton Oxon 48 C2
Hemsby Norfk 77 H2
Hemswell Lincs 85 G4
Hemswell Cliff Lincs 85 G4
Hemsworth W York 84 B6
Hemyock Devon 10 B6
Henbury Bristl 37 G2
Henbury Ches 82 D2
Hendersyde Park Border 123 E3
Hendham Devon 7 E3
Hendomen Powys 56 B5
Hendon Gt Lon 28 C5
Hendon T & W 115 F1
Hendra Cnwll 3 E3
Hendra Cnwll 4 D3
Hendre Brdgnd 35 G2
Hendre Flints 80 D1
Hendre Mons 37 E6
Hendy Carmth 34 C5
Heneglwys IOA 78 D2
Henfield W Susx 16 C3
Henford Devon 5 G5
Henghurst Kent 18 C5
Hengoed Caerph 36 C4
Hengoed Powys 45 E4
Hengoed Shrops 69 E3
Hengrave Suffk 63 G2
Henham Essex 51 F3
Henhurst Kent 29 G3
Heniarth Powys 56 B6
Henlade Somset 23 E2
Henley Dorset 11 G5
Henley Gloucs 38 D6
Henley Shrops 57 E4
Henley Shrops 57 F3
Henley Somset 23 G2
Henley Suffk 53 E6
Henley W Susx 27 G2
Henley Green W Mids 59 F3
Henley Park Surrey 27 G4
Henley Street Kent 29 G3
Henley's Down E Susx 17 H3
Henley-in-Arden Warwks 58 D2
Henley-on-Thames Oxon 41 F2
Henllan Cerdgn 42 D3
Henllan Denbgs 80 C1
Henllan Amgoed Carmth 33 F4
Henllys Torfn 36 D3
Henlow Beds 50 C4
Hennock Devon 9 E3
Henny Street Essex 52 B4
Henry's Moat (Castell Hendre) Pembks 33 E4
Henryd Conwy 79 G2
Hensall N York 91 G2
Henshaw Nthumb 113 E1
Hensingham Cumb 102 D2
Henstead Suffk 65 G4
Hensting Hants 26 C1
Henstridge Somset 24 C1
Henstridge Ash Somset 24 C1
Henstridge Marsh Somset 24 C1
Henton Oxon 41 F4
Henton Somset 23 H4
Henwick Worcs 46 D5
Henwood Cnwll 5 F3
Henwood Oxon 40 C4
Heol Senni Powys 44 B1
Heol-las Swans 34 D4
Heol-y-Cyw Brdgnd 35 G3
Hepburn Nthumb 124 D3
Hepple Nthumb 113 G5
Hepscott Nthumb 114 D4
Heptonstall W York 90 A2
Hepworth Suffk 64 B3
Hepworth W York 83 F5
Herbrandston Pembks 32 C2
Hereford Herefs 45 H3
Hereson Kent 31 G3
Heribusta Highld 150 D6
Heriot Border 122 A5
Hermiston C Edin 131 H2
Hermit Hill S York 83 H5
Hermitage Berks 40 C1
Hermitage Border 112 B4
Hermitage Dorset 11 G5
Hermitage Hants 15 F4
Hermon IOA 78 D2
Hermon Pembks 42 B2
Herne Kent 31 E3
Herne Bay Kent 31 E3
Herne Common Kent 31 E2
Herne Hill Gt Lon 28 D3
Herne Pound Kent 29 G1
Herner Devon 21 F3
Hernhill Kent 30 D2
Herodsfoot Cnwll 5 F2
Heronden Kent 31 F1
Herongate Essex 29 G5
Heronsford S Ayrs 108 C3
Heronsgate Herts 28 A5
Herriard Hants 27 E4
Herring's Green Beds 50 B5
Herringfleet Suffk 65 G5
Herringswell Suffk 63 F2
Herringthorpe S York 84 B4
Herrington T & W 106 C6
Hersden Kent 31 F2
Hersham Cnwll 20 C1
Hersham Surrey 28 B2
Herstmonceux E Susx 17 G3
Herston Dorset 12 D2
Herston Ork 169 b1
Hertford Herts 50 D2
Hertford Heath Herts 50 D2
Hertingfordbury Herts 50 D2
Hesket Newmarket Cumb 103 G4
Hesketh Bank Lancs 88 C2
Hesketh Lane Lancs 89 E4
Heskin Green Lancs 88 D1
Hesleden Dur 106 D5
Hesleden N York 96 B2
Hesley S York 84 D4
Hesleyside Nthumb 113 E3
Heslington N York 91 G5
Hessay N York 91 F5
Hessenford Cnwll 5 G2
Hessett Suffk 64 B1
Hessle E R Yk 92 D2
Hessle W York 91 E1
Hest Bank Lancs 95 E1
Hestley Green Suffk 64 D2
Heston Gt Lon 28 B4
Hestwall Ork 169 a3
Heswall Mersyd 81 E3
Hethe Oxon 48 D2
Hethersett Norfk 64 D6
Hethersgill Cumb 112 B1
Hetherside Cumb 112 B1
Hetherson Green Ches 69 G5
Hethpool Nthumb 123 F2
Hett Dur 106 B4
Hetton N York 89 H5
Hetton Steads Nthumb 123 G3
Hetton-le-Hole T & W 106 C6
Heugh Nthumb 114 C3
Heugh Head Border 123 F6
Heughhead Abers 148 B6
Heveningham Suffk 65 F3
Hever Kent 17 F6
Heversham Cumb 95 F3
Hevingham Norfk 77 E2
Hewas Water Cnwll 3 G5
Hewelsfield Gloucs 37 G4
Hewenden W York 90 B3
Hewish Somset 23 G6
Hewish Somset 11 E5
Hewood Dorset 10 D5
Hexham Nthumb 113 F1
Hextable Kent 29 F3
Hexthorpe S York 84 C5
Hexton Herts 50 B4
Hexworthy Cnwll 5 G4
Hexworthy Devon 6 D5
Hey Lancs 89 G4
Hey Houses Lancs 88 B2
Heybridge Essex 52 B1
Heybridge Essex 29 G6
Heybridge Basin Essex 52 B1
Heybrook Bay Devon 6 B2
Heydon Cambs 51 E5
Heydon Norfk 76 D3
Heydour Lincs 73 H4
Heyhead Gt Man 82 C3
Heylipoll Ag & B 134 B4
Heylor Shet 169 h4
Heyrod Gt Man 83 E5
Heysham Lancs 88 C6
Heyshaw N York 90 C6
Heyshott W Susx 15 G5
Heyside Gt Man 82 D5
Heytesbury Wilts 25 E3
Heythrop Oxon 48 B2
Heywood Gt Man 82 D6
Heywood Wilts 24 D5
Hibaldstow Lincs 85 G5
Hickleton S York 84 B5
Hickling Norfk 77 G2
Hickling Notts 73 E3
Hickling Green Norfk 77 G2
Hickling Heath Norfk 77 G2
Hickmans Green Kent 30 D2
Hicks Forstal Kent 31 E2
Hickstead W Susx 16 D3
Hidcote Bartrim Gloucs 47 G3
Hidcote Boyce Gloucs 47 G3
High Ackworth W York 91 E1
High Angerton Nthumb 114 C4
High Ardwell D & G 100 B5
High Auldgirth D & G 110 D4
High Bankhill Cumb 104 B4
High Beach Essex 29 E6
High Bentham N York 95 G2
High Bewaldeth Cumb 103 F3
High Bickington Devon 21 F3
High Bickwith N York 96 A2
High Biggins Cumb 95 G3
High Blantyre S Lans 120 A5
High Bonnybridge Falk 131 E3
High Borrans Cumb 95 E5
High Bradley N York 90 A4
High Bray Devon 21 G4
High Brooms Kent 17 G6

291

High Bullen Hook

292

High Bullen *Devon* 21 E3
High Buston *Nthumb* 125 E2
High Callerton *Nthumb* 114 C3
High Casterton *Cumb* 95 G3
High Catton *E R Yk* 92 A5
High Close *N York* 106 A2
High Cogges *Oxon* 40 B5
High Common *Norfk* 64 B6
High Coniscliffe *Dur* 106 B2
High Crosby *Cumb* 104 A6
High Cross *Cnwll* 3 E3
High Cross *E Ayrs* 119 F4
High Cross *Hants* 27 E2
High Cross *Herts* 50 D3
High Cross *W Susx* 16 C3
High Cross *Warwks* 59 E2
High Cross Bank *Derbys* 71 H2
High Drummore *D & G* 100 C4
High Dubmire *T & W* 106 C6
High Easter *Essex* 51 G2
High Eggborough *N York* 91 G2
High Ellington *N York* 97 E3
High Ercall *Shrops* 70 A2
High Etherley *Dur* 106 A4
High Ferry *Lincs* 74 D5
High Flats *W York* 83 G5
High Garrett *Essex* 52 A3
High Grange *Dur* 106 A4
High Grantley *N York* 97 E2
High Green *Cumb* 95 E5
High Green *Norfk* 64 D6
High Green *Norfk* 64 D4
High Green *Norfk* 65 E5
High Green *S York* 84 A4
High Green *Shrops* 57 G4
High Green *Suffk* 63 H1
High Green *W York* 90 C1
High Green *Worcs* 46 D4
High Halden *Kent* 18 C5
High Halstow *Kent* 30 A4
High Ham *Somset* 23 G2
High Harrington *Cumb* 102 D3
High Harrogate *N York* 90 D5
High Haswell *Dur* 106 C5
High Hatton *Shrops* 70 A2
High Hawsker *N York* 99 E6
High Hesket *Cumb* 104 B5
High Hoyland *S York* 83 H6
High Hunsley *E R Yk* 92 C3
High Hurstwood *E Susx* 17 F4
High Hutton *N York* 98 C2
High Ireby *Cumb* 103 F4
High Kelling *Norfk* 76 D4
High Kilburn *N York* 98 A3
High Killerby *N York* 99 F3
High Knipe *Cumb* 104 B2
High Lands *Dur* 105 H3
High Lane *Gt Man* 82 D3
High Lanes *Cnwll* 2 C3
High Laver *Essex* 51 F2
High Legh *Ches* 82 B3
High Leven *N York* 106 D2
High Littleton *Somset* 24 B5
High Lorton *Cumb* 103 F3
High Marnham *Notts* 85 F2
High Melton *S York* 84 C5
High Mickley *Nthumb* 114 B2
High Moorsley *T & W* 106 C5
High Newport *T & W* 115 E1
High Newton *Cumb* 95 E3
High Nibthwaite *Cumb* 94 D4
High Offley *Staffs* 70 C3
High Ongar *Essex* 51 F1
High Onn *Staffs* 70 C2
High Park Corner *Essex* 52 D3
High Pennyvenie *E Ayrs* 109 G5
High Post *Wilts* 25 G3
High Roding *Essex* 51 G2
High Row *Cumb* 103 G4
High Row *Cumb* 103 H2
High Salter *Lancs* 88 D6
High Salvington *W Susx* 16 B2
High Scales *Cumb* 103 F5
High Seaton *Cumb* 102 D3
High Shaw *N York* 96 B4
High Side *Cumb* 103 F3
High Spen *T & W* 114 C1
High Stoop *Dur* 105 H4
High Street *Cnwll* 3 G5
High Street *Kent* 18 A4
High Street *Suffk* 65 G2
High Street *Suffk* 65 G1
High Throston *Dur* 106 D4
High Town *Staffs* 71 E1
High Toynton *Lincs* 86 C2
High Trewhitt *Nthumb* 113 G5
High Urpeth *Dur* 114 D1
High Valleyfield *Fife* 131 F4
High Warden *Nthumb* 113 F1
High Westwood *Dur* 105 H6
High Woolaston *Gloucs* 37 G4
High Worsall *N York* 106 C2
High Wray *Cumb* 94 D5
High Wych *Herts* 51 E2
High Wycombe *Bucks* 41 G4
Higham *Derbys* 72 B6
Higham *Kent* 17 G6
Higham *Kent* 29 H3
Higham *Lancs* 89 F3
Higham *S York* 83 H5
Higham *Suffk* 63 G2
Higham *Suffk* 52 D4
Higham Dykes *Nthumb* 114 C3
Higham Ferrers *Nhants* 61 F2
Higham Gobion *Beds* 50 B4
Higham Hill *Gt Lon* 28 D5
Higham on the Hill *Leics* 59 G5
Highampton *Devon* 8 B5
Highams Park *Gt Lon* 29 E5
Highbridge *Hants* 26 C1
Highbridge *Somset* 23 F4
Highbrook *W Susx* 16 D4
Highburton *W York* 83 G6
Highbury *Gt Lon* 28 D5
Highbury *Somset* 24 B4
Highclere *Hants* 26 C5
Highcliffe *Dorset* 13 F4
Highcross *Lancs* 88 B3
Higher Alham *Somset* 24 B3
Higher Ansty *Dorset* 12 B5
Higher Ballam *Lancs* 88 B3
Higher Bartle *Lancs* 88 C3
Higher Berry End *Beds* 49 H3
Higher Bockhampton *Dorset* 11 G4
Higher Brixham *Devon* 7 F3
Higher Burrowton *Devon* 9 G4
Higher Burwardsley *Ches* 69 G6
Higher Chillington *Somset* 10 D6
Higher Clovelly *Devon* 20 C3
Higher Combe *Somset* 22 B2
Higher Coombe *Dorset* 11 F4
Higher Disley *Ches* 83 E3
Higher Gabwell *Devon* 7 F4
Higher Halstock Leigh *Dorset* 11 E5
Higher Harpers *Lancs* 89 G3
Higher Heysham *Lancs* 88 C6
Higher Hurdsfield *Ches* 82 D2
Higher Irlam *Gt Man* 82 B4
Higher Kingcombe *Dorset* 11 F5
Higher Kinnerton *Flints* 69 F6
Higher Melcombe *Dorset* 12 A5
Higher Muddiford *Devon* 21 F4
Higher Nyland *Dorset* 24 C1
Higher Ogden *Gt Man* 82 D6
Higher Pentire *Cnwll* 2 D2
Higher Penwortham *Lancs* 88 D2
Higher Studfold *N York* 96 A2
Higher Town *Cnwll* 3 F4
Higher Town *Cnwll* 4 D2
Higher Town *IOS* 2 b2
Higher Tregantle *Cnwll* 5 G1
Higher Walton *Ches* 82 A3
Higher Walton *Lancs* 88 D2
Higher Wambrook *Somset* 10 C5
Higher Waterston *Dorset* 11 G4
Higher Whatcombe *Dorset* 12 B5
Higher Wheelton *Lancs* 88 D2
Higher Whiteleigh *Cnwll* 5 F5
Higher Whitley *Ches* 82 A3
Higher Wraxhall *Dorset* 11 F5
Higher Wych *Ches* 69 G4
Higherford *Lancs* 89 G4
Highfield *Devon* 8 D4
Highfield *E R Yk* 92 A3
Highfield *N Ayrs* 119 E4
Highfield *T & W* 114 C1
Highfields *S York* 84 C5
Highgate *E Susx* 17 E5
Highgate *Gt Lon* 28 D5
Highgate Head *Derbys* 83 E3
Highgreen Manor *Nthumb* 113 E4
Highland Wildlife Park *Highld* 146 C5
Highlane *Ches* 82 D1
Highlane *S York* 84 B3
Highlaws *Cumb* 103 E5
Highleadon *Gloucs* 46 C1
Highleigh *W Susx* 15 G3
Highley *Shrops* 57 G4
Highmoor *Cumb* 103 G5
Highmoor *Oxon* 41 E3
Highmoor Cross *Oxon* 41 E3
Highmoor Hill *Mons* 37 F3
Highnam *Gloucs* 46 C1
Highnam Green *Gloucs* 46 C1
Highridge *Somset* 24 A6
Highstead *Kent* 31 F3
Highsted *Kent* 30 C2
Highstreet *Kent* 30 D2
Highstreet Green *Essex* 52 A4
Highstreet Green *Surrey* 27 H3
Hightae *D & G* 111 E3
Highter's Heath *W Mids* 58 D3
Hightown *Ches* 82 D1
Hightown *Hants* 13 E5
Hightown *Mersyd* 81 E5
Hightown Green *Suffk* 64 B1
Highway *Herefs* 45 G4
Highway *Wilts* 39 E2
Highweek *Devon* 7 F5
Highwood *Staffs* 71 F3
Highwood Hill *Gt Lon* 28 C5
Highworth *Wilts* 39 G3
Hilborough *Norfk* 63 G5
Hilcote *Derbys* 72 B6
Hilden Park *Kent* 17 G6
Hildenborough *Kent* 29 F1
Hildersham *Cambs* 51 F6
Hilderstone *Staffs* 70 D3
Hilderthorpe *E R Yk* 99 G1
Hilfield *Dorset* 11 G5
Hilgay *Norfk* 63 E5
Hill *Gloucs* 37 G4
Hill *Warwks* 59 G2
Hill Brow *Hants* 27 F2
Hill Chorlton *Staffs* 70 C4
Hill Common *Norfk* 77 G2
Hill Common *Somset* 22 D2
Hill Deverill *Wilts* 24 D3
Hill Dyke *Lincs* 74 D5
Hill End *Dur* 105 G4
Hill End *Fife* 131 G5
Hill End *Gloucs* 47 E3
Hill Green *Kent* 30 B2
Hill Head *Hants* 14 D4
Hill of Beath *Fife* 131 H4
Hill of Fearn *Highld* 163 E1
Hill of Tarvit Mansion House *Fife* 140 D1
Hill Ridware *Staffs* 71 F2
Hill Side *W York* 90 C1
Hill Side *Worcs* 46 C5
Hill Top *Dur* 105 G2
Hill Top *Hants* 14 B4
Hill Top *S York* 84 B4
Hill Top *W Mids* 58 C5
Hill Top *W York* 83 F6
Hill Top *W York* 90 D1
Hillam *N York* 91 F2
Hillbeck *Dur* 105 E2
Hillborough *Kent* 31 F3
Hillbutts *Dorset* 12 D5
Hillcliffane *Derbys* 71 H5
Hillcott *Wilts* 25 G5
Hillend *Fife* 131 H3
Hillend *Mdloth* 132 B2
Hillend *N Lans* 131 E2
Hillend *Swans* 34 B3
Hillersland *Gloucs* 37 G6
Hillerton *Devon* 8 D4
Hillesden *Bucks* 49 E2
Hillesley *Gloucs* 38 B3
Hillfarrance *Somset* 22 D2
Hillgrove *W Susx* 27 G2
Hillhampton *Herefs* 46 B4
Hillhead *Devon* 7 F3
Hillhead *S Lans* 120 D3
Hillhead of Cocklaw *Abers* 159 G3
Hillhead of Durno *Abers* 158 C2
Hilliard's Cross *Staffs* 71 F1
Hilliclay *Highld* 167 E5
Hillingdon *Gt Lon* 28 B4
Hillington *C Glas* 129 G1
Hillington *Norfk* 75 G2
Hillis Corner *IOW* 14 C3
Hillmorton *Warwks* 60 A3
Hillock Vale *Lancs* 89 F2
Hillowton *D & G* 110 B1
Hillpool *Worcs* 58 B3
Hillpound *Hants* 14 D5
Hills Town *Derbys* 84 B2
Hillside *Abers* 149 G4
Hillside *Angus* 141 G6
Hillside *Devon* 6 D4
Hillstreet *Hants* 13 G6
Hillswick *Shet* 169 h4
Hilltown *Devon* 8 B3
Hilltown *E Loth* 132 B2
Hillwell *Shet* 169 h1
Hilmarton *Wilts* 39 E2
Hilperton *Wilts* 24 D5
Hilperton Marsh *Wilts* 24 D5
Hilsea *Hants* 15 E4
Hilston *E R Yk* 93 G3
Hilston Park *Mons* 45 G1
Hiltingbury *Hants* 26 C1
Hilton *Border* 123 F4
Hilton *Cambs* 62 B2
Hilton *Cumb* 104 D2
Hilton *Derbys* 71 G3
Hilton *Dorset* 12 B5
Hilton *Dur* 106 A3
Hilton *Highld* 163 E1
Hilton *N York* 106 D2
Hilton *Shrops* 57 H5
Himbleton *Worcs* 47 E5
Himley *Staffs* 58 B4
Hincaster *Cumb* 95 F3
Hinchley Wood *Surrey* 28 B3
Hinckley *Leics* 59 G5
Hinderclay *Suffk* 64 C3
Hinderwell *N York* 107 G2
Hindford *Shrops* 69 F3
Hindhead *Surrey* 27 G3
Hindle Fold *Lancs* 89 F3
Hindley *Gt Man* 82 A5
Hindley *Nthumb* 114 B1
Hindley Green *Gt Man* 82 A5
Hindlip *Worcs* 46 D5
Hindolveston *Norfk* 76 C3
Hindon *Wilts* 25 E2
Hindringham *Norfk* 76 C4
Hingham *Norfk* 64 C6
Hinksford *Staffs* 58 B4
Hinnington *Shrops* 57 H6
Hinstock *Shrops* 70 B3
Hintlesham *Suffk* 52 D5
Hinton *Gloucs* 38 B5
Hinton *Gloucs* 38 B2
Hinton *Hants* 13 F4
Hinton *Herefs* 45 F3
Hinton *Shrops* 56 D6
Hinton *Shrops* 57 G4
Hinton Admiral *Hants* 13 F4
Hinton Ampner *Hants* 26 D2
Hinton Blewett *Somset* 24 B5
Hinton Charterhouse *Somset* 24 C5
Hinton Green *Worcs* 47 F3
Hinton Marsh *Hants* 26 D2
Hinton Martell *Dorset* 12 D5
Hinton on the Green *Worcs* 47 F3
Hinton Parva *Wilts* 39 G3
Hinton St George *Somset* 11 E6
Hinton St Mary *Dorset* 12 B6
Hinton Waldrist *Oxon* 40 B4
Hinton-in-the-Hedges *Nhants* 48 D3
Hints *Shrops* 57 F3
Hints *Staffs* 58 D6
Hinwick *Beds* 49 G5
Hinxhill *Kent* 18 D6
Hinxton *Cambs* 51 F5
Hinxworth *Herts* 50 C5
Hipperholme *W York* 90 B2
Hipsburn *Nthumb* 125 E2
Hipswell *N York* 97 E5
Hirn *Abers* 149 E4
Hirnant *Powys* 68 C2
Hirst *Nthumb* 114 D4
Hirst Courtney *N York* 91 G2
Hirwaen *Denbgs* 68 D6
Hirwaun *Rhondd* 35 G5
Hiscott *Devon* 21 F3
Histon *Cambs* 62 D2
Hitcham *Suffk* 52 C6
Hitcham Causeway *Suffk* 52 C6
Hitcham Street *Suffk* 52 C6
Hitchin *Herts* 50 C4
Hither Green *Gt Lon* 29 E3
Hittisleigh *Devon* 8 D4
Hittisleigh Cross *Devon* 8 D4
Hive *E R Yk* 92 B3
Hixon *Staffs* 71 E3
Hoaden *Kent* 31 F2
Hoar Cross *Staffs* 71 F2
Hoarwithy *Herefs* 46 A2
Hoath *Kent* 31 F2
Hoathly *Kent* 17 G5
Hobarris *Shrops* 56 C3
Hobbles Green *Suffk* 51 H6
Hobbs Cross *Essex* 29 F6
Hobbs Cross *Essex* 51 F2
Hobkirk *Border* 112 C6
Hobland Hall *Norfk* 65 G5
Hobsick *Notts* 72 B5
Hobson *Dur* 114 C1
Hoby *Leics* 72 D2
Hoccombe *Somset* 22 D2
Hockering *Norfk* 76 D1
Hockerton *Notts* 73 E6
Hockley *Ches* 82 D3
Hockley *Essex* 30 B5
Hockley *Staffs* 59 E5
Hockley *W Mids* 59 F3
Hockley Heath *W Mids* 58 D3
Hockliffe *Beds* 49 H2
Hockwold cum Wilton *Norfk* 63 F4
Hockworthy *Devon* 22 C1
Hoddesdon *Herts* 51 E1
Hoddlesden *Lancs* 89 F2
Hoddom Cross *D & G* 111 F2
Hoddom Mains *D & G* 111 F2
Hodgehill *Ches* 82 C2
Hodgeston *Pembks* 32 D2
Hodnet *Shrops* 70 A3
Hodsall Street *Kent* 29 G2
Hodsock *Notts* 84 D3
Hodson *Wilts* 39 F2
Hodthorpe *Derbys* 84 C2
Hoe *Hants* 14 D5
Hoe *Norfk* 76 C2
Hoe Gate *Hants* 14 D5
Hoff *Cumb* 104 C2
Hog Hill *E Susx* 18 B3
Hogben's Hill *Kent* 30 D2
Hoggards Green *Suffk* 64 A1
Hoggeston *Bucks* 49 F2
Hoggrill's End *Warwks* 59 E5
Hoghton *Lancs* 89 E2
Hoghton Bottoms *Lancs* 89 E2
Hognaston *Derbys* 71 G5
Hogsthorpe *Lincs* 87 F2
Holbeach *Lincs* 74 D2
Holbeach Bank *Lincs* 74 D3
Holbeach Clough *Lincs* 74 D3
Holbeach Drove *Lincs* 74 D1
Holbeach Hurn *Lincs* 74 D3
Holbeach St Johns *Lincs* 74 D2
Holbeach St Mark's *Lincs* 74 D3
Holbeach St Matthew *Lincs* 74 D3
Holbeck *Notts* 84 C2
Holbeck Woodhouse *Notts* 84 C2
Holberrow Green *Worcs* 47 F5
Holbeton *Devon* 6 D3
Holborn *Gt Lon* 28 D4
Holborough *Kent* 29 H2
Holbrook *Derbys* 72 A4
Holbrook *S York* 84 B3
Holbrook *Suffk* 53 E4
Holbrook Moor *Derbys* 72 A5
Holburn *Nthumb* 123 G3
Holbury *Hants* 14 C4
Holcombe *Devon* 9 F2
Holcombe *Gt Man* 89 F1
Holcombe *Somset* 24 B4
Holcombe Brook *Gt Man* 89 F1
Holcombe Rogus *Devon* 22 C1
Holcot *Nhants* 60 D2
Holden *Lancs* 89 F4
Holden Gate *W York* 89 G2
Holdenby *Nhants* 60 C2
Holder's Green *Essex* 51 G4
Holdgate *Shrops* 57 F4
Holdingham *Lincs* 74 A5
Holditch *Dorset* 10 D5
Holdsworth *W York* 90 B2
Hole *Devon* 20 D1
Hole Park *Kent* 18 B5
Hole Street *W Susx* 16 B3
Hole-in-the-Wall *Herefs* 46 B2
Holehouse *Derbys* 83 E4
Holemoor *Devon* 20 D1
Holford *Somset* 22 D3
Holgate *N York* 91 G5
Holker *Cumb* 94 D2
Holkham *Norfk* 76 B4
Holkham Hall *Norfk* 76 B4
Hollacombe *Devon* 5 G6
Hollam *Somset* 22 B2
Holland Fen *Lincs* 74 C5
Holland Lees *Lancs* 81 G5
Holland-on-Sea *Essex* 53 E2
Hollandstoun *Ork* 169 d4
Hollee *D & G* 111 G2
Hollesley *Suffk* 53 G5
Hollicombe *Devon* 7 F4
Hollies Hill *Worcs* 58 B3
Hollin Green *Ches* 70 A5
Hollingbourne *Kent* 30 B1
Hollingbury *E Susx* 16 D2
Hollingdon *Bucks* 49 G2
Hollingthorpe *W York* 91 E3
Hollington *Derbys* 71 G4
Hollington *Staffs* 71 E4
Hollingworth *Gt Man* 83 E4
Hollinlane *Ches* 82 C3
Hollins *Derbys* 83 H2
Hollins *Gt Man* 82 C5
Hollins *Staffs* 71 E5
Hollins End *S York* 84 B3
Hollins Green *Ches* 82 B4
Hollins Lane *Lancs* 88 C5
Hollinsclough *Staffs* 83 F1
Hollinswood *Shrops* 70 B1
Hollinwood *Shrops* 69 G4
Holllingrove *E Susx* 17 H3
Hollocombe *Devon* 21 F2
Holloway *Derbys* 72 A6
Holloway *Gt Lon* 28 D5
Holloway *Wilts* 24 D2
Hollowell *Nhants* 60 C2
Hollowmoor Heath *Ches* 81 G1
Hollows *D & G* 112 A3
Holly End *Norfk* 62 D6
Holly Green *Worcs* 46 D3
Hollybush *Caerph* 36 C5
Hollybush *E Ayrs* 119 F1
Hollybush *Herefs* 46 C3
Hollyhurst *Ches* 69 H4
Hollym *E R Yk* 93 G2
Hollywood *Worcs* 58 D3
Holmbridge *W York* 83 F5
Holmbury St Mary *Surrey* 16 B6
Holmbush *Cnwll* 3 H5
Holmcroft *Staffs* 70 D2
Holme *Cambs* 61 H4
Holme *Cumb* 95 F3
Holme *Lincs* 85 G5
Holme *N York* 97 G3
Holme *Notts* 73 F6
Holme *W York* 83 F5
Holme Chapel *Lancs* 89 G2
Holme Green *N York* 91 G4
Holme Hale *Norfk* 64 A6
Holme Lacy *Herefs* 46 A3
Holme Marsh *Herefs* 45 F5
Holme next the Sea *Norfk* 75 G4
Holme on the Wolds *E R Yk* 92 C4
Holme Pierrepont *Notts* 72 D4
Holme St Cuthbert *Cumb* 103 E5
Holme upon Spalding Moor *E R Yk* 92 B3
Holmer *Herefs* 45 H3
Holmer Green *Bucks* 41 G4
Holmes Chapel *Ches* 82 C1
Holmes Hill *E Susx* 17 F3
Holmesfield *Derbys* 83 H2
Holmeswood *Lancs* 88 C1
Holmethorpe *Surrey* 28 D1
Holmewood *Derbys* 84 B1
Holmfield *W York* 90 B2
Holmfirth *W York* 83 F5
Holmgate *Derbys* 84 A1
Holmhead *E Ayrs* 119 G1
Holmpton *E R Yk* 93 G2
Holmrook *Cumb* 94 B5
Holmsey Green *Suffk* 63 F3
Holmshurst *E Susx* 17 G4
Holmside *Dur* 106 B6
Holmwrangle *Cumb* 104 B5
Holne *Devon* 6 D4
Holnest *Dorset* 11 G6
Holnicote *Somset* 22 B4
Holsworthy *Devon* 20 D1
Holsworthy Beacon *Devon* 20 D1
Holt *Dorset* 12 D5
Holt *Norfk* 76 D4
Holt *Wilts* 24 D5
Holt *Worcs* 58 A2
Holt *Wrexhm* 69 F5
Holt End *Worcs* 58 D2
Holt Fleet *Worcs* 58 A2
Holt Green *Lancs* 81 F5
Holt Heath *Dorset* 12 D5
Holt Heath *Worcs* 58 A2
Holt Street *Kent* 31 F1
Holtby *N York* 91 H5
Holton *Oxon* 40 D5
Holton *Somset* 24 B2
Holton *Suffk* 65 F3
Holton cum Beckering *Lincs* 86 B3
Holton Heath *Dorset* 12 C4
Holton Hill *E Susx* 17 G4
Holton le Clay *Lincs* 86 C5
Holton le Moor *Lincs* 86 A4
Holton St Mary *Suffk* 52 D4
Holtye *E Susx* 17 E5
Holway *Flints* 80 D2
Holwell *Dorset* 11 G6
Holwell *Herts* 50 C4
Holwell *Leics* 73 E2
Holwell *Oxon* 39 G5
Holwick *Dur* 105 F3
Holworth *Dorset* 12 B3
Holy Cross *Worcs* 58 B3
Holy Island *Nthumb* 124 D5
Holybourne *Hants* 27 E3
Holyfield *Essex* 51 E1
Holyhead *IOA* 78 B3
Holymoorside *Derbys* 84 A2
Holyport *Berks* 41 G2
Holystone *Nthumb* 113 G5
Holytown *N Lans* 120 B5
Holywell *Cambs* 62 C2
Holywell *Cnwll* 4 A2
Holywell *Dorset* 11 F5
Holywell *Flints* 80 D2
Holywell *Nthumb* 115 E3
Holywell *Warwks* 59 E2
Holywell Green *W York* 90 B1
Holywell Lake *Somset* 22 D1
Holywell Row *Suffk* 63 F3
Holywood *D & G* 110 D3
Holywood Village *D & G* 110 D3
Hom Green *Herefs* 46 A1
Homer *Shrops* 57 F5
Homer Green *Mersyd* 81 F5
Homersfield *Suffk* 65 E4
Homescales *Cumb* 95 F4
Homington *Wilts* 25 G2
Honey Hill *Kent* 31 E2
Honey Tye *Suffk* 52 C4
Honeyborough *Pembks* 32 D2
Honeybourne *Worcs* 47 G4
Honeychurch *Devon* 8 C5
Honeystreet *Wilts* 25 F5
Honiley *Warwks* 59 E3
Honing *Norfk* 77 F3
Honingham *Norfk* 76 D1
Honington *Lincs* 73 G4
Honington *Suffk* 64 B3
Honington *Warwks* 47 H3
Honiton *Devon* 10 B5
Honley *W York* 83 F6
Honnington *Shrops* 70 B1
Hoo *Kent* 31 F2
Hoo End *Herts* 50 C3
Hoo Green *Ches* 82 B3
Hoo Meavy *Devon* 6 C4
Hoo St Werburgh *Kent* 30 A3
Hoobrook *Worcs* 58 A3
Hood Green *S York* 83 H5
Hood Hill *S York* 84 A4
Hooe *Devon* 6 B3
Hooe *E Susx* 17 H2
Hoohill *Lancs* 88 B3
Hook *Cambs* 62 D5
Hook *Devon* 10 C5
Hook *E R Yk* 92 B2
Hook *Hants* 14 C4
Hook *Hants* 27 E5
Hook *Kent* 29 G3
Hook *Pembks* 32 D3

Hook Inverarnan

Hook Surrey 28 C2
Hook Wilts 39 E3
Hook Bank Worcs 46 D3
Hook End Essex 29 G6
Hook Green Kent 17 G5
Hook Norton Oxon 48 B2
Hook Street Gloucs 38 B4
Hook Street Wilts 39 E3
Hookagate Shrops 69 G1
Hooke Dorset 11 F5
Hookgate Staffs 70 B3
Hookway Devon 9 E4
Hookwood Surrey 16 D6
Hooley Surrey 28 D2
Hooley Bridge Gt Man 82 D6
Hooton Ches 81 F2
Hooton Levitt S York 84 C4
Hooton Pagnell S York 84 C5
Hooton Roberts S York 84 C4
Hop Pole Lincs 74 B1
Hopcrofts Holt Oxon 48 C2
Hope Derbys 83 G3
Hope Devon 6 D2
Hope Flints 69 E6
Hope Powys 56 C6
Hope Shrops 56 D5
Hope Shrops 57 F3
Hope Staffs 71 F5
Hope Bowdler Shrops 57 E5
Hope End Green Essex 51 G3
Hope Mansell Herefs 46 B1
Hope under Dinmore Herefs 45 H4
Hopehouse Border 121 G1
Hopeman Moray 156 D6
Hopesay Shrops 56 D4
Hopetown W York 91 E2
Hopgrove N York 91 G5
Hopperton N York 91 E5
Hopsford Warwks 59 G4
Hopstone Shrops 57 H5
Hopton Derbys 71 G5
Hopton Shrops 69 F2
Hopton Staffs 70 D3
Hopton Suffk 64 B3
Hopton Cangeford Shrops 57 F3
Hopton Castle Shrops 56 D3
Hopton on Sea Norfk 65 H5
Hopton Wafers Shrops 57 F3
Hoptonheath Shrops 56 D3
Hopwas Staffs 59 E6
Hopwood Gt Man 82 D6
Hopwood Worcs 58 C3
Horam E Susx 17 G3
Horbling Lincs 74 B3
Horbury W York 90 D1
Horcott Gloucs 39 F4
Horden Dur 106 D5
Horderley Shrops 56 D4
Hordle Hants 13 F4
Hordley Shrops 69 F3
Horeb Carmth 34 C5
Horeb Cerdgn 42 D3
Horfield Bristl 37 G2
Horham Suffk 65 E3
Horkesley Green Essex 52 C4
Horkesley Heath Essex 52 C4
Horkstow Lincs 92 D1
Horley Oxon 48 B4
Horley Surrey 16 D6
Horn Hill Bucks 28 A5
Horn Street Kent 19 E5
Hornblotton Green Somset 24 A3
Hornby Lancs 95 F2
Hornby N York 97 G5
Hornby N York 97 E4
Horncastle Lincs 86 C2
Hornchurch Gt Lon 29 F5
Horncliffe Nthumb 123 F4
Horndean Border 123 F4
Horndean Hants 15 E5
Horndon Devon 8 B3
Horndon on the Hill Essex 29 G4
Horne Surrey 16 D6
Horne Row Essex 52 A1
Horner Somset 22 B4
Horners Green Suffk 52 C5
Horney Common E Susx 17 E4
Horning Norfk 77 F2
Horninghold Leics 60 D5
Horninglow Staffs 71 G2
Horningsea Cambs 62 D2
Horningsham Wilts 24 D3
Horningtoft Norfk 76 B2
Horningtops Cnwll 5 F2
Horns Cross Devon 20 D3
Horns Cross E Susx 18 B4
Hornsbury Somset 10 D6
Hornsby Cumb 104 B5
Hornsbygate Cumb 104 B5
Hornsea E R Yk 93 F4
Hornsey Gt Lon 28 D5
Hornton Oxon 48 B4
Horpit Wilts 39 G3
Horra Shet 169 j5
Horrabridge Devon 6 C5
Horridge Devon 7 E5
Horringer Suffk 63 G1
Horringford IOW 14 D2
Horrocks Fold Gt Man 82 B6
Horrocksford Lancs 89 F4
Horsacott Devon 21 E4
Horsebridge Devon 5 G3
Horsebridge E Susx 17 G2
Horsebridge Hants 26 B2
Horsebridge Shrops 56 D6
Horsebridge Staffs 71 E5
Horsebrook Staffs 70 D1
Horsecastle Somset 23 G6
Horsedown Cnwll 2 D3
Horsegate Lincs 74 B1
Horsehay Shrops 57 G6
Horseheath Cambs 51 G5
Horsehouse N York 96 D3
Horsell Surrey 27 H5
Horseman's Green Wrexhm 69 G4
Horsenden Bucks 41 F4
Horsey Norfk 77 G2
Horsey Somset 23 F3
Horsey Corner Norfk 77 G2
Horsford Norfk 77 E2
Horsforth W York 90 D3
Horsham W Susx 16 C4
Horsham Worcs 46 C5
Horsham St Faith Norfk 77 E1
Horsington Lincs 86 B1
Horsington Somset 24 C2
Horsley Derbys 72 B4
Horsley Gloucs 38 C4
Horsley Nthumb 113 F4
Horsley Nthumb 114 C2
Horsley Cross Essex 53 E3
Horsley Woodhouse Derbys 72 B4
Horsley's Green Bucks 41 F4
Horsley-Gate Derbys 83 H2
Horsleycross Street Essex 53 E4
Horsleyhill Border 122 C1
Horsmonden Kent 17 H5
Horspath Oxon 40 D5
Horstead Norfk 77 F2
Horsted Keynes W Susx 17 E4
Horton Berks 28 A4
Horton Bucks 41 G5
Horton Dorset 12 D5
Horton Gloucs 38 B3
Horton Lancs 89 G5
Horton Nhants 49 F5
Horton Shrops 69 G3
Horton Shrops 70 B1
Horton Somset 10 D6
Horton Staffs 70 D6
Horton Surrey 28 C2
Horton Swans 34 B3
Horton Wilts 25 F6
Horton Cross Somset 10 D6
Horton Green Ches 69 G5
Horton Heath Hants 14 C5
Horton in Ribblesdale N York 96 A2
Horton Kirby Kent 29 F3
Horton-cum-Studley Oxon 40 D5
Horwich Gt Man 82 A6
Horwich End Derbys 83 E3
Horwood Devon 21 E3
Hoscar Lancs 81 G6
Hoscote Border 112 A6
Hose Leics 73 E3
Hosey Hill Kent 29 E1
Hosh P & K 139 F2
Hoswick Shet 169 h2
Hotham E R Yk 92 C3
Hothfield Kent 18 C6
Hoton Leics 72 C2
Hott Nthumb 113 E3
Hough Ches 70 B5
Hough Ches 82 D2
Hough End W York 90 D3
Hough Green Ches 81 G3
Hough-on-the-Hill Lincs 73 G5
Hougham Lincs 73 F4
Houghton Cambs 62 B3
Houghton Cumb 103 H6
Houghton Hants 26 B2
Houghton Nthumb 114 C2
Houghton Pembks 32 D2
Houghton W Susx 16 A2
Houghton Conquest Beds 50 A5
Houghton Gate T & W 106 B6
Houghton Green Ches 82 A4
Houghton Green E Susx 18 C4
Houghton le Side Dur 106 B3
Houghton le Spring T & W 106 C6
Houghton on the Hill Leics 60 C6
Houghton Regis Beds 50 A3
Houghton St Giles Norfk 76 B4
Hound Green Hants 27 E5
Houndslow Border 122 C4
Houndsmoor Somset 22 D2
Houndwood Border 133 G1
Hounslow Gt Lon 28 B4
Hounslow Green Essex 51 G2
Househill Highld 155 G5
Houses Hill W York 90 C1
Housesteads Roman Fort Nthumb 113 E2
Housieside Abers 159 E2
Houston Rens 129 E2
Houstry Highld 167 E2
Houton Ork 169 b2
Hove E Susx 16 D2
Hove Edge W York 90 C2
Hoveringham Notts 73 E5
Hoveton Norfk 77 F2
Hovingham N York 98 B2
How Caple Herefs 46 B2
How End Beds 50 A5
How Mill Cumb 104 B6
Howbrook S York 84 A4
Howden E R Yk 92 A2
Howden-le-Wear Dur 106 A4
Howe Highld 167 G5
Howe IOM 174 k2
Howe N York 97 G3
Howe Norfk 65 E5
Howe Bridge Gt Man 82 B5
Howe Green Essex 52 A1
Howe of Teuchar Abers 158 D4
Howe Street Essex 51 H2
Howe Street Essex 51 H4
Howegreen Essex 30 B6
Howell Lincs 74 B5
Howes D & G 111 F1
Howey Powys 44 C5
Howgate Mdloth 121 G5
Howgill N York 89 G4
Howick Nthumb 125 F3
Howle Dur 105 G3
Howle Shrops 70 B2
Howle Hill Herefs 46 B1
Howlett End Essex 51 G4
Howley Somset 10 C6
Howmore W Isls 168 b3
Hownam Border 123 E1
Howrigg Cumb 103 G5
Howsham Lincs 85 H5
Howsham N York 92 A6
Howt Green Kent 30 C3
Howtel Nthumb 123 F3
Howton Devon 8 D3
Howton Herefs 45 G2
Howtown Cumb 104 A2
Howwood Rens 119 F5
Hoxne Suffk 64 D3
Hoylake Mersyd 80 D4
Hoyland Common S York 84 A5
Hoyland Nether S York 84 A5
Hoyland Swaine S York 83 G5
Hoyle W Susx 15 G5
Hoyle Mill S York 84 A5
Hubberholme N York 96 C3
Hubberston Pembks 32 C2
Hubbert's Bridge Lincs 74 C4
Huby N York 90 D4
Huby N York 98 A1
Huccaby Devon 6 D5
Hucclecote Gloucs 38 C6
Hucking Kent 30 B2
Hucknall Notts 72 C5
Huddersfield W York 90 C1
Huddington Worcs 47 E5
Hudswell N York 97 E5
Huggate E R Yk 92 C5
Hugglescote Leics 72 B1
Hugh Town IOS 2 a1
Hughenden Valley Bucks 41 G4
Hughley Shrops 57 F5
Huish Devon 21 E2
Huish Wilts 25 G6
Huish Champflower Somset 22 C2
Huish Episcopi Somset 23 G2
Hulberry Kent 29 F3
Hulcote Beds 49 G3
Hulcott Bucks 41 G6
Hulham Devon 9 G3
Hull E R Yk 93 E2
Hulland Derbys 71 G5
Hulland Ward Derbys 71 G5
Hullavington Wilts 38 D2
Hullbridge Essex 30 B6
Hulme Ches 82 A4
Hulme Gt Man 82 C4
Hulme Staffs 70 D5
Hulme End Staffs 71 F6
Hulme Walfield Ches 82 C1
Hulse Heath Ches 82 B3
Hulton Lane Ends Gt Man 82 B5
Hulver Street Norfk 76 B1
Hulver Street Suffk 65 G4
Hulverstone IOW 14 B2
Humber Devon 9 F2
Humber Herefs 46 A5
Humberside Airport Lincs 86 A6
Humberston Lincs 86 C5
Humberstone Leics 60 B6
Humberton N York 97 G2
Humbie E Loth 122 B6
Humbleton E R Yk 93 F3
Humbleton Nthumb 124 C4
Humby Lincs 73 H3
Hume Border 122 D4
Humshaugh Nthumb 113 F2
Huna Highld 167 G6
Huncoat Lancs 89 F3
Huncote Leics 60 A5
Hundalee Border 122 D1
Hundall Derbys 84 B2
Hunderthwaite Dur 105 F2
Hundle Houses Lincs 74 C5
Hundleby Lincs 86 D1
Hundleton Pembks 32 D2
Hundon Suffk 52 A6
Hundred Acres Hants 14 D5
Hundred End Lancs 88 C2
Hundred House Powys 44 D5
Hungarton Leics 60 C6
Hungate End Bucks 49 F4
Hunger Hill Lancs 81 H6
Hungerford Berks 40 B1
Hungerford Hants 13 E6
Hungerford Somset 22 G3
Hungerford Newtown Berks 40 B1
Hungerstone Herefs 45 G3
Hungerton Lincs 73 F3
Hungryhatton Shrops 70 B3
Hunmanby N York 99 G3
Hunningham Warwks 59 G2
Hunnington Worcs 58 C3
Hunsdon Herts 51 E2
Hunsingore N York 91 E5
Hunslet W York 90 D3
Hunsonby Cumb 104 C4
Hunstanton Norfk 75 G4
Hunstanworth Dur 105 F5
Hunsterson Ches 70 B5
Hunston Suffk 64 B2
Hunston W Susx 15 G4
Hunston Green Suffk 64 B2
Hunstrete Somset 24 B5
Hunsworth W York 90 C2
Hunt End Worcs 58 C2
Hunt's Corner Norfk 64 C4
Hunt's Cross Mersyd 81 F3
Hunter's Inn Devon 21 G5
Hunter's Quay Ag & B 128 C3
Huntham Somset 23 F2
Hunthill Lodge Angus 148 B2
Huntingdon Cambs 62 B2
Huntingfield Suffk 65 F3
Huntingford Dorset 24 D2
Huntington Ches 81 F1
Huntington E Loth 132 D3
Huntington Herefs 45 E5
Huntington Herefs 45 H3
Huntington N York 91 G5
Huntington Staffs 71 E1
Huntley Gloucs 46 C1
Huntly Abers 157 G3
Hunton Hants 26 C3
Hunton Kent 29 H1
Hunton N York 97 E4
Hunton Bridge Herts 28 B6
Hunts Green Bucks 41 G5
Hunts Green Warwks 59 E5
Huntscott Somset 22 B4
Huntsham Devon 22 C1
Huntshaw Devon 21 E3
Huntshaw Cross Devon 21 E3
Huntspill Somset 23 F4
Huntstile Somset 23 E3
Huntworth Somset 23 F3
Hunwick Dur 106 A4
Hunworth Norfk 76 D4
Hurcott Somset 10 D6
Hurdcott Wilts 25 G3
Hurdsfield Ches 82 D2
Hurley Berks 41 F3
Hurley Warwks 59 E5
Hurley Bottom Berks 41 F3
Hurley Common Warwks 59 E5
Hurlford E Ayrs 119 F3
Hurlston Green Lancs 81 F6
Hurn Dorset 13 E4
Hurn's End Lincs 75 E5
Hursley Hants 26 C2
Hurst Berks 41 F1
Hurst Dorset 12 B4
Hurst N York 96 D5
Hurst Somset 23 G1
Hurst Green E Susx 18 A4
Hurst Green Essex 52 D2
Hurst Green Lancs 89 E3
Hurst Green Surrey 29 E1
Hurst Hill W Mids 58 B5
Hurst Wickham W Susx 16 D3
Hurstbourne Priors Hants 26 C4
Hurstbourne Tarrant Hants 26 B5
Hurstley Herefs 45 F4
Hurstpierpoint W Susx 16 D3
Hurstway Common Herefs 45 F4
Hurstwood Lancs 89 G3
Hurtiso Ork 169 c2
Hurtmore Surrey 27 H4
Hurworth Burn Dur 106 C4
Hurworth Place Dur 106 B2
Hurworth-on-Tees Dur 106 B2
Hury Dur 105 F2
Husbands Bosworth Leics 60 C4
Husborne Crawley Beds 49 H3
Husthwaite N York 98 A2
Hut Green N York 91 G2
Hutcherleigh Devon 7 E3
Huthwaite N York 97 H5
Huthwaite Notts 72 B6
Huttoft Lincs 87 E2
Hutton Border 123 F5
Hutton Cumb 104 A3
Hutton E R Yk 92 D5
Hutton Essex 29 G6
Hutton Lancs 88 C2
Hutton Somset 23 F5
Hutton Bonville N York 97 F5
Hutton Buscel N York 99 E3
Hutton Conyers N York 97 F2
Hutton Cranswick E R Yk 92 D5
Hutton End Cumb 104 A4
Hutton Hall N York 107 E2
Hutton Hang N York 97 E4
Hutton Henry Dur 106 D4
Hutton Lowcross N York 107 E2
Hutton Magna Dur 105 H1
Hutton Mulgrave N York 107 H2
Hutton Roof Cumb 103 H3
Hutton Roof Cumb 95 F3
Hutton Rudby N York 97 H5
Hutton Sessay N York 97 H2
Hutton Wandesley N York 91 F5
Hutton-le-Hole N York 98 C4
Huxham Devon 9 F4
Huxham Green Somset 24 B3
Huxley Ches 69 G6
Huyton Mersyd 81 G4
Hycemoor Cumb 94 B4
Hyde Gloucs 38 C4
Hyde Gt Man 82 D4
Hyde Hants 13 E6
Hyde End Berks 27 E6
Hyde Heath Bucks 41 G4
Hyde Lea Staffs 70 D2
Hyde Park Corner Somset 23 F2
Hydestile Surrey 27 H3
Hykeham Moor Lincs 85 G1
Hyndford Bridge S Lans 120 D4
Hynish Ag & B 134 B3
Hyssington Powys 56 C5
Hystfield Gloucs 37 H4
Hythe Hants 14 B4
Hythe Kent 19 E5
Hythe Somset 23 G4
Hythe End Berks 28 A3
Hyton Cumb 94 B4

I

Ibberton Dorset 12 B5
Ible Derbys 71 G6
Ibsley Hants 13 E5
Ibstock Leics 72 B1
Ibstone Bucks 41 F4
Ibthorpe Hants 26 B5
Iburndale N York 107 H1
Ibworth Hants 26 D5
Icelton Somset 23 F6
Ickburgh Norfk 63 G5
Ickenham Gt Lon 28 B5
Ickford Bucks 41 E5
Ickham Kent 31 F2
Ickleford Herts 50 C4
Icklesham E Susx 18 B3
Ickleton Cambs 51 F5
Icklingham Suffk 63 G3
Ickornshaw N York 89 H4
Ickwell Green Beds 50 B5
Ickworth Suffk 63 G1
Icomb Gloucs 47 G1
Idbury Oxon 47 H1
Iddesleigh Devon 8 C5
Ide Devon 9 F4
Ide Hill Kent 29 F1
Ideford Devon 9 F2
Iden E Susx 18 C4
Iden Green Kent 18 A5
Iden Green Kent 18 B5
Idle W York 90 C3
Idless Cnwll 3 F4
Idlicote Warwks 48 A4
Idmiston Wilts 25 G3
Idridgehay Derbys 71 H5
Idrigill Highld 150 D5
Idstone Oxon 39 G3
Iffley Oxon 40 C5
Ifield W Susx 16 C5
Ifold W Susx 16 A4
Iford Dorset 13 E4
Iford E Susx 17 E2
Ifton Mons 37 F3
Ifton Heath Shrops 69 E4
Ightfield Shrops 70 A4
Ightham Kent 29 G2
Iken Suffk 65 G1
Ilam Staffs 71 F5
Ilchester Somset 23 H1
Ilderton Nthumb 124 C3
Ilford Gt Lon 29 E5
Ilford Somset 23 F1
Ilfracombe Devon 21 E5
Ilkeston Derbys 72 B4
Ilketshall St Andrew Suffk 65 F4
Ilketshall St Margaret Suffk 65 F4
Ilkley W York 90 B4
Illand Cnwll 5 F4
Illey W Mids 58 C3
Illidge Green Ches 82 C1
Illingworth W York 90 B2
Illogan Cnwll 2 D4
Illston on the Hill Leics 60 C5
Ilmer Bucks 41 F5
Ilmington Warwks 47 G3
Ilminster Somset 10 D6
Ilsington Devon 9 E2
Ilsington Dorset 12 A4
Ilston Swans 34 C3
Ilton N York 97 E3
Ilton Somset 23 F1
Imachar N Ayrs 117 H4
Immingham Lincs 93 F1
Immingham Dock Lincs 93 F1
Impington Cambs 62 D2
Ince Ches 81 G2
Ince Blundell Mersyd 81 E5
Ince-in-Makerfield Gt Man 82 A5
Inchbae Lodge Hotel Highld 154 B6
Inchbare Angus 148 D1
Inchberry Moray 157 E5
Inchinnan Rens 129 F2
Inchlaggan Highld 144 D5
Inchmichael P & K 140 B2
Inchnacardoch Hotel Highld 145 F5
Inchnadamph Highld 161 G6
Inchture P & K 140 C3
Inchvuilt Highld 153 F3
Inchyra P & K 140 B2
Indian Queens Cnwll 4 C2
Ingate Place Suffk 65 G4
Ingatestone Essex 29 G6
Ingbirchworth S York 83 G5
Ingerthorpe N York 97 F1
Ingestre Staffs 71 E2
Ingham Lincs 85 G3
Ingham Norfk 77 G3
Ingham Suffk 63 H2
Ingham Corner Norfk 77 G3
Ingleborough Norfk 75 E1
Ingleby Derbys 72 A3
Ingleby Arncliffe N York 97 H5
Ingleby Barwick N York 106 D2
Ingleby Cross N York 97 H5
Ingleby Greenhow N York 98 B5
Ingleigh Green Devon 8 C5
Inglesbatch Somset 24 C5
Inglesham Wilts 39 G4
Ingleston D & G 110 D1
Ingleton Dur 106 A3
Ingleton N York 95 H2
Inglewhite Lancs 88 D4
Ingmire Hall Cumb 95 G4
Ingoe Nthumb 114 B3
Ingoldisthorpe Norfk 75 G3
Ingoldmells Lincs 87 F1
Ingoldsby Lincs 73 H3
Ingram Nthumb 124 C3
Ingrave Essex 29 G5
Ingrow W York 90 B3
Ings Cumb 95 E5
Ingst Gloucs 37 G3
Ingthorpe Lincs 61 F6
Ingworth Norfk 77 E3
Inkberrow Worcs 47 F5
Inkerman Dur 105 H4
Inkhorn Abers 159 E3
Inkpen Berks 26 B6
Inkstack Highld 167 F5
Inmarsh Wilts 25 E5
Innellan Ag & B 128 C2
Innerleithen Border 121 H3
Innerleven Fife 132 C5
Innermessan D & G 108 C1
Innerwick E Loth 133 F2
Innesmill Moray 157 E5
Insch Abers 158 B2
Insh Highld 146 C5
Inskip Lancs 88 C3
Inskip Moss Side Lancs 88 C3
Instow Devon 21 E4
Insworke Cnwll 5 H1
Intake S York 84 B3
Inver Abers 147 G4
Inver Highld 163 E2
Inver P & K 139 G4
Inver-boyndie Abers 158 C5
Inverailort Highld 143 G2
Inveralligin Highld 152 C5
Inverallochy Abers 159 F6
Inveran Highld 162 C3
Inveraray Ag & B 128 B6
Inverarish Highld 151 F2
Inverarity Angus 140 D4
Inverarnan Stirlg 137 H2

293

Inverasdale
King's Mills
294

Inverasdale Highld 160 B2
Inveravon Falk 131 F3
Inverawe Ag & B 137 E3
Inverbeg Ag & B 129 E5
Inverbervie Abers 149 F2
Inverbroom Highld 161 F2
Invercreran House Hotel Ag & B 137 E4
Inverdruie Highld 146 D5
Inveresk E Loth 132 B2
Inveresragan Ag & B 136 D3
Inverewe Garden Highld 160 C2
Inverey Abers 147 F3
Inverfarigaig Highld 154 C1
Inverfolla Ag & B 136 D4
Invergarry Highld 145 E4
Invergeldie P & K 139 E2
Invergloy Highld 144 D3
Invergordon Highld 155 E6
Invergowrie P & K 140 C3
Inverguseran Highld 143 G5
Inverhadden P & K 138 D5
Inverherive Hotel Stirlg 138 A2
Inverie Highld 143 G4
Inverinan Ag & B 136 D1
Inverinate Highld 152 C1
Inverkeilor Angus 141 G5
Inverkeithing Fife 131 G3
Inverkeithny Abers 158 B4
Inverkip Inver 128 D2
Inverkirkaig Highld 161 E6
Inverlael Highld 161 F2
Inverlair Highld 145 F2
Inverliever Lodge Ag & B 127 H6
Inverlochy Ag & B 137 F2
Invermark Angus 148 B2
Invermarkie Abers 157 F3
Invermoriston Highld 145 F6
Inverness Highld 155 E4
Inverness Dalcross Airport Highld 155 F4
Invernoaden Ag & B 128 C5
Inveroran Hotel Ag & B 137 G4
Inverquharity Angus 140 D5
Inverquhomery Abers 159 F4
Inverroy Highld 145 E3
Inversanda Highld 136 D6
Invershiel Highld 152 D1
Invershin Highld 162 C3
Invershore Highld 167 F2
Inversnaid Hotel Stirlg 129 E6
Inverugie Abers 159 G4
Inveruglas Ag & B 129 E6
Inveruglass Highld 146 C4
Inverurie Abers 158 D1
Inwardleigh Devon 8 C5
Inworth Essex 52 B2
Iochdar W Isls 168 b4
Iping W Susx 27 G1
Ipplepen Devon 7 F4
Ipsden Oxon 40 D3
Ipstones Staffs 71 E5
Ipswich Suffk 53 E5
Irby Mersyd 81 E3
Irby in the Marsh Lincs 87 E1
Irby upon Humber Lincs 86 B5
Irchester Nhants 61 E2
Ireby Cumb 103 F4
Ireby Lancs 95 G2
Ireland Beds 50 B5
Ireleth Cumb 94 C3
Ireshopeburn Dur 105 E4
Ireton Wood Derbys 71 H5
Irlam Gt Man 82 B4
Irnham Lincs 73 H3
Iron Acton Gloucs 38 B3
Iron Bridge Cambs 62 D5
Iron Bridge Museum Shrops 57 G6
Iron Cross Warwks 47 F4
Ironbridge Shrops 57 G6
Ironmacannie D & G 110 A2
Irons Bottom Surrey 16 C6
Ironville Derbys 72 B5
Irstead Norfk 77 G2
Irthington Cumb 112 B1
Irthlingborough Nhants 61 E2
Irton N York 99 F3
Irvine N Ayrs 119 E3
Isauld Highld 166 D5
Isbister Shet 169 h4
Isfield E Susx 17 E3
Isham Nhants 61 E3
Isington Hants 27 F3
Islandpool Worcs 58 B3
Islay Airport Ag & B 116 B5
Isle Abbotts Somset 23 F1
Isle Brewers Somset 23 F1
Isle of Dogs Gt Lon 29 E4
Isle of Man Ronaldsway Airport IOM 174 l2
Isle of Whithorn D & G 101 F4
Isleham Cambs 63 F3
Isleornsay Highld 143 F5
Isles of Scilly St Mary's Airport IOS 2 b1
Islesteps D & G 110 D2
Islet Village Guern 174 g3
Isleworth Gt Lon 28 C4
Isley Walton Leics 72 B2
Islibhig W Isls 168 c8
Islington Gt Lon 28 D4
Islip Nhants 61 F3
Islip Oxon 40 C6
Islivig W Isls 168 c8
Isombridge Shrops 70 A1
Istead Rise Kent 29 G3
Itchen Abbas Hants 26 D2
Itchen Stoke Hants 26 D2
Itchingfield W Susx 16 B4
Itchington Gloucs 37 H3
Itteringham Norfk 76 D3
Itton Devon 8 D4
Itton Mons 37 F4
Ivegill Cumb 103 H4
Ivelet N York 96 C5
Iver Bucks 28 A4
Iver Heath Bucks 28 A4
Iveston Dur 105 H5
Ivinghoe Bucks 41 G6
Ivinghoe Aston Bucks 41 H6
Ivington Herefs 45 G5
Ivington Green Herefs 45 G5
Ivy Cross Dorset 24 D2
Ivy Hatch Kent 29 G1
Ivy Todd Norfk 76 B1
Ivybridge Devon 6 D3
Ivychurch Kent 18 D4
Iwade Kent 30 C3
Iwerne Courtney or Shroton Dorset 12 B6
Iwerne Minster Dorset 12 C6
Ixworth Suffk 64 B2
Ixworth Thorpe Suffk 64 B3

J

Jack Green Lancs 88 D2
Jack Hill N York 90 C5
Jack's Bush Hants 26 A3
Jack-in-the-Green Devon 9 G4
Jacksdale Notts 72 B5
Jackson Bridge W York 83 G5
Jackton S Lans 119 H5
Jacobs Well Surrey 28 A1
Jacobstow Cnwll 5 E5
Jacobstowe Devon 8 C5
Jameston Pembks 33 E1
Jamestown Highld 154 C5
Jamestown W Duns 129 E3
Janets-town Highld 167 G3
Janetstown Highld 167 F2
Jardine Hall D & G 111 E4
Jarrow T & W 115 E2
Jarvis Brook E Susx 17 F4
Jasper's Green Essex 51 H3
Jawcraig Falk 131 E3
Jaywick Essex 53 E2
Jealott's Hill Berks 41 G2
Jeater Houses N York 97 G4
Jedburgh Border 122 D1
Jeffreyston Pembks 33 E2
Jemimaville Highld 155 E6
Jerbourg Guern 174 g1
Jersey Airport Jersey 174 b2
Jerusalem Lincs 85 G2
Jesmond T & W 114 D2
Jevington E Susx 17 F1
Jingle Street Mons 37 F5
Jockey End Herts 50 A2
Jodrell Bank Ches 82 C2
John o' Groats Highld 167 G6
John's Cross E Susx 18 A3
Johnby Cumb 104 A3
Johnshaven Abers 149 E1
Johnson's Street Norfk 77 G2
Johnston Pembks 32 D3
Johnstone D & G 111 G5
Johnstone Rens 129 F1
Johnstonebridge D & G 111 E4
Johnstown Carmth 42 D1
Johnstown Wrexhm 69 E5
Joppa C Edin 132 B2
Joppa Cerdgn 54 C2
Joppa S Ayrs 119 F1
Jordans Bucks 41 H3
Jordanston Pembks 32 C5
Jordanthorpe S York 84 A3
Joyden's Wood Kent 29 F3
Jubilee Corner Kent 18 B6
Jump S York 84 B5
Jumper's Town E Susx 17 E5
Juniper Nthumb 105 F6
Juniper Green C Edin 132 A2
Jurby IOM 174 l5
Jurston Devon 8 D3

K

Kaber Cumb 105 E1
Kaimend S Lans 120 D4
Kames Ag & B 128 A2
Kames E Ayrs 120 B2
Kea Cnwll 3 F4
Keadby Lincs 85 F6
Keal Cotes Lincs 74 D6
Kearby Town End N York 91 E4
Kearsley Gt Man 82 C5
Kearsley Nthumb 114 B3
Kearsney Kent 19 F6
Kearstwick Cumb 95 G3
Kearton N York 96 C5
Keasden N York 95 H1
Keason Cnwll 5 G3
Keaton Devon 6 D3
Keckwick Ches 81 H3
Keddington Lincs 86 D4
Keddington Corner Lincs 86 D4
Kedington Suffk 51 H5
Kedleston Derbys 71 H4
Keelby Lincs 86 B6
Keele Staffs 70 C5
Keele University Staffs 70 C4
Keeley Green Beds 50 A5
Keelham W York 90 B3
Keeston Pembks 32 C4
Keevil Wilts 25 E5
Kegworth Leics 72 C3
Kehelland Cnwll 2 D4
Keig Abers 158 B1
Keighley W York 90 B4
Keilarsbrae Clacks 131 E4
Keillour P & K 139 G2
Keiloch Abers 147 G4
Keils Ag & B 126 D2
Keinton Mandeville Somset 24 A2
Keir Mill D & G 110 C4
Keirsleywell Row Nthumb 104 D5
Keisby Lincs 73 H3
Keisley Cumb 104 D2
Keiss Highld 167 G4
Keith Moray 157 F4
Keithick P & K 140 B4
Keithock Angus 141 F6
Keithtown Highld 154 C5
Kelbrook Lancs 89 G4
Kelburn N Ayrs 118 D5
Kelby Lincs 73 H4
Keld Cumb 104 B1
Keld N York 96 B5
Keld Head N York 98 D3
Keldholme N York 98 C3
Kelfield Lincs 85 F5
Kelfield N York 91 G3
Kelham Notts 73 E6
Kelhead D & G 111 F2
Kellacott Devon 5 G5
Kellamergh Lancs 88 C2
Kellas Angus 140 D3
Kellas Moray 156 D4
Kellaton Devon 7 E1
Kelleth Cumb 95 G5
Kelling Norfk 76 D4
Kellington N York 91 G2
Kelloe Dur 106 C4
Kelloholm D & G 110 B6
Kells Cumb 102 D2
Kelly Devon 5 G4
Kelly Bray Cnwll 5 G3
Kelmarsh Nhants 60 C3
Kelmscot Oxon 39 G4
Kelsale Suffk 65 F2
Kelsall Ches 81 G1
Kelshall Herts 50 D4
Kelsick Cumb 103 F5
Kelso Border 122 D3
Kelstedge Derbys 84 A1
Kelstern Lincs 86 C4
Kelsterton Flints 81 E2
Kelston Somset 24 C6
Keltneyburn P & K 139 E5
Kelton D & G 110 D2
Kelty Fife 131 H4
Kelvedon Essex 52 B3
Kelvedon Hatch Essex 29 F6
Kelynack Cnwll 2 A3
Kemacott Devon 21 G5
Kemback Fife 140 D1
Kemberton Shrops 57 G6
Kemble Gloucs 39 E4
Kemble Wick Gloucs 38 D4
Kemerton Worcs 47 E3
Kemeys Commander Mons 37 E5
Kemnay Abers 149 E6
Kemp Town E Susx 16 D2
Kempe's Corner Kent 18 D6
Kempley Gloucs 46 B2
Kempley Green Gloucs 46 B2
Kemps Green Warwks 58 D2
Kempsey Worcs 46 D4
Kempsford Gloucs 39 F4
Kempshott Hants 26 D4
Kempston Beds 50 A5
Kempston Hardwick Beds 50 A5
Kempton Shrops 56 D4
Kemsing Kent 29 F2
Kemsley Kent 30 C3
Kemsley Street Kent 30 B2
Kenardington Kent 18 C5
Kenchester Herefs 45 G3
Kencot Oxon 39 G5
Kendal Cumb 95 F4
Kenderchurch Herefs 45 G2
Kendleshire Gloucs 38 A2
Kenfig Brdgnd 35 E2
Kenfig Hill Brdgnd 35 F2
Kenidjack Cnwll 2 A3
Kenilworth Warwks 59 F2
Kenley Gt Lon 28 D2
Kenley Shrops 57 F5
Kenmore Highld 152 B5
Kenmore P & K 139 E4
Kenn Devon 9 F3
Kenn Somset 37 E1
Kennacraig Ag & B 127 G1
Kennards House Cnwll 5 F4
Kenneggy Cnwll 2 C3
Kennerleigh Devon 9 E5
Kennessee Green Mersyd 81 F5
Kennet Clacks 131 E4
Kennethmont Abers 157 G2
Kennett Cambs 63 F2
Kennford Devon 9 F3
Kenninghall Norfk 64 C4
Kennington Kent 18 D6
Kennington Oxon 40 C4
Kennoway Fife 132 C5
Kenny Somset 23 F1
Kennyhill Suffk 63 F3
Kennythorpe N York 98 D1
Kenovay Ag & B 134 B4
Kensaleyre Highld 150 D4
Kensham Green Kent 18 B4
Kensington Gt Lon 28 C4
Kensworth Beds 50 A3
Kensworth Common Beds 50 A2
Kent End Wilts 39 E4
Kent Green Ches 70 C6
Kent Street E Susx 18 A3
Kent Street Kent 29 G1
Kent's Green Gloucs 46 C2
Kent's Oak Hants 26 A2
Kentallen Highld 137 E5
Kentchurch Herefs 45 G2
Kentford Suffk 63 F2
Kentisbeare Devon 10 A5
Kentisbury Devon 21 F5
Kentisbury Ford Devon 21 F5
Kentish Town Gt Lon 28 D4
Kentmere Cumb 95 E5
Kenton Devon 9 F3
Kenton Gt Lon 28 C5
Kenton Suffk 64 D2
Kenton T & W 114 D2
Kenton Bankfoot Nthumb 114 D2
Kentra Highld 143 F1
Kents Bank Cumb 95 E2
Kenwick Shrops 69 F3
Kenwyn Cnwll 3 F4
Kenyon Ches 82 A4
Keoldale Highld 165 E5
Keppoch Highld 152 C1
Kepwick N York 97 H4
Keresley W Mids 59 F4
Keresley Green Warwks 59 F4
Kergilliak Cnwll 3 E3
Kernborough Devon 7 E2
Kerne Bridge Herefs 46 A1
Kerridge Ches 82 D2
Kerridge-end Ches 82 D2
Kerris Cnwll 2 B2
Kerry Powys 56 B4
Kerrycroy Ag & B 118 C6
Kersall Notts 85 E1
Kersbrook Devon 10 A3
Kerscott Devon 21 F3
Kersey Suffk 52 D5
Kersey Tye Suffk 52 C5
Kersey Upland Suffk 52 C5
Kershader W Isls 168 e7
Kershopefoot Cumb 112 B3
Kersoe Worcs 47 E3
Kerswell Devon 10 A5
Kerswell Green Worcs 46 D4
Kerthen Wood Cnwll 2 C3
Kesgrave Suffk 53 F5
Kessingland Suffk 65 H4
Kessingland Beach Suffk 65 H4
Kestle Cnwll 3 G4
Kestle Mill Cnwll 4 B2
Keston Gt Lon 29 E2
Keswick Cumb 103 G2
Keswick Norfk 65 E6
Ketsby Lincs 86 D2
Kettering Nhants 61 E3
Ketteringham Norfk 64 D6
Kettins Angus 140 B4
Kettle Green Herts 51 E2
Kettlebaston Suffk 52 C6
Kettlebridge Fife 132 B6
Kettlebrook Staffs 59 E6
Kettleburgh Suffk 65 E1
Kettleholm D & G 111 F2
Kettleness N York 107 H2
Kettleshulme Ches 83 E3
Kettlesing N York 90 C5
Kettlesing Bottom N York 90 C5
Kettlestone Norfk 76 C3
Kettlethorpe Lincs 85 F2
Kettletoft Ork 169 d4
Kettlewell N York 96 C2
Ketton Rutlnd 61 F6
Kew Gt Lon 28 C4
Kew Gardens Gt Lon 28 C4
Kewstoke Somset 23 F6
Kexbrough S York 83 H6
Kexby Lincs 85 F3
Kexby N York 91 H5
Key Green Ches 82 D1
Key Green N York 98 D5
Key Street Kent 30 B2
Key's Toft Lincs 75 E6
Keyham Leics 60 C6
Keyhaven Hants 13 G4
Keyingham E R Yk 93 F2
Keymer W Susx 16 D3
Keynsham Somset 37 G1
Keysoe Beds 61 G2
Keysoe Row Beds 61 G1
Keyston Cambs 61 F3
Keyworth Notts 72 D3
Kibbear Somset 23 E1
Kibblesworth T & W 114 D1
Kibworth Beauchamp Leics 60 C5
Kibworth Harcourt Leics 60 C5
Kidbrooke Gt Lon 29 E4
Kidburngill Cumb 103 E2
Kidd's Moor Norfk 64 D6
Kiddemore Green Staffs 70 C1
Kidderminster Worcs 58 A3
Kiddington Oxon 48 B1
Kidlington Oxon 40 C6
Kidmore End Oxon 41 E2
Kidsdale D & G 101 F4
Kidsgrove Staffs 70 C5
Kidstones N York 96 C3
Kidwelly Carmth 34 B5
Kiel Crofts Ag & B 136 D4
Kielder Nthumb 112 C4
Kiells Ag & B 126 C2
Kilbarchan Rens 129 E1
Kilbeg Highld 143 F5
Kilberry Ag & B 127 F1
Kilbirnie N Ayrs 119 E5
Kilbride Ag & B 136 C2
Kilbride Ag & B 127 F3
Kilbride Ag & B 128 B2
Kilbuiack Moray 156 C5
Kilburn Derbys 72 B5
Kilburn Gt Lon 28 C4
Kilburn N York 98 A3
Kilby Leics 60 B5
Kilchamaig Ag & B 127 G1
Kilchattan Ag & B 126 C5
Kilchattan Ag & B 118 C5
Kilcheran Ag & B 136 C4
Kilchoan Highld 135 G6
Kilchoman Ag & B 126 A1
Kilchrenan Ag & B 137 E2
Kilconquhar Fife 132 D5
Kilcot Gloucs 46 C2
Kilcoy Highld 154 D4
Kilcreggan Ag & B 128 D3
Kildale N York 107 E2
Kildalloig Ag & B 117 G2
Kildary Highld 162 D1
Kildavaig Ag & B 128 A2
Kildavanan Ag & B 128 B2
Kildonan Highld 163 F6
Kildonan N Ayrs 118 B1
Kildonan Lodge Highld 163 F6
Kildonnan Highld 142 D2
Kildrochet House D & G 100 B6
Kildrummy Abers 148 B6
Kildwick N York 90 A4
Kilfinan Ag & B 127 H3
Kilfinnan Highld 145 E4
Kilford Denbgs 80 C1
Kilgetty Pembks 33 E2
Kilgrammie S Ayrs 108 D5
Kilgwrrwg Common Mons 37 F4
Kilham E R Yk 99 F1
Kilham Nthumb 123 F3
Kilkenneth Ag & B 134 A4
Kilkenzie Ag & B 117 F3
Kilkhampton Cnwll 20 C2
Killamarsh Derbys 84 B3
Killay Swans 34 C3
Killearn Stirlg 129 G4
Killen Highld 155 E5
Killerby Dur 106 A3
Killerton Devon 9 G5
Killichonan P & K 138 C6
Killiechronan Ag & B 135 G3
Killiecrankie P & K 139 F6
Killilan Highld 152 D2
Killin Stirlg 138 C3
Killinghall N York 90 D5
Killington Cumb 95 G4
Killington Devon 21 G5
Killingworth T & W 114 D3
Killiow Cnwll 3 E4
Killivose Cnwll 3 E5
Killochyett Border 122 B4
Kilmacolm Inver 129 E2
Kilmahog Stirlg 130 B6
Kilmahumaig Ag & B 127 G4
Kilmaluag Highld 150 D6
Kilmany Fife 140 D2
Kilmarnock E Ayrs 119 F3
Kilmartin Ag & B 127 G5
Kilmaurs E Ayrs 119 F4
Kilmelford Ag & B 136 C1
Kilmersdon Somset 24 C4
Kilmeston Hants 26 D2
Kilmichael Ag & B 117 F3
Kilmichael Glassary Ag & B 127 G4
Kilmichael of Inverlussa Ag & B 127 F4
Kilmington Devon 10 C4
Kilmington Wilts 24 C3
Kilmington Common Wilts 24 C3
Kilmington Street Wilts 24 C3
Kilmorack Highld 154 C3
Kilmore Ag & B 136 C2
Kilmore Highld 143 F5
Kilmory Ag & B 127 F3
Kilmory Highld 143 E1
Kilmory N Ayrs 118 B2
Kilmuir Highld 150 C3
Kilmuir Highld 150 D6
Kilmuir Highld 155 E4
Kilmuir Highld 162 D1
Kilmun Ag & B 128 C3
Kiln Green Berks 41 F2
Kiln Pit Hill Nthumb 105 G6
Kilnave Ag & B 126 B2
Kilncadzow S Lans 120 C4
Kilndown Kent 17 H5
Kilnhill Cumb 103 F3
Kilnhouses Ches 82 A1
Kilnhurst S York 84 B4
Kilninver Ag & B 136 C2
Kilnsea E R Yk 93 H1
Kilnsey N York 96 C2
Kilnwick E R Yk 92 D4
Kilnwick Percy E R Yk 92 B5
Kiloran Ag & B 126 C5
Kilpatrick N Ayrs 117 H3
Kilpeck Herefs 45 G2
Kilpin E R Yk 92 B2
Kilpin Pike E R Yk 92 B2
Kilrenny Fife 133 E6
Kilsby Nhants 60 B2
Kilspindie P & K 140 B2
Kilstay D & G 100 C4
Kilsyth N Lans 130 C3
Kiltarlity Highld 154 C3
Kilton N York 107 F3
Kilton Thorpe N York 107 F3
Kilvaxter Highld 150 D6
Kilve Somset 22 D3
Kilvington Notts 73 F4
Kilwinning N Ayrs 119 E4
Kimberley Norfk 64 C6
Kimberley Notts 72 C4
Kimberworth S York 84 B4
Kimble Wick Bucks 41 F5
Kimblesworth Dur 106 B6
Kimbolton Cambs 61 G2
Kimbolton Herefs 45 H5
Kimcote Leics 60 B4
Kimmeridge Dorset 12 C2
Kimmerston Nthumb 123 G3
Kimpton Hants 26 A4
Kimpton Herts 50 C2
Kimworthy Devon 20 C2
Kinbrace Highld 166 B1
Kinbuck Stirlg 130 D6
Kincaple Fife 141 E2
Kincardine Fife 131 F4
Kincardine Highld 162 C3
Kincardine O'Neil Abers 148 D4
Kinclaven P & K 140 B4
Kincorth Aber C 149 G5
Kincorth House Moray 156 B5
Kincraig Highld 146 C5
Kincraigie P & K 139 G5
Kindallachan P & K 139 G5
Kinerarach Ag & B 117 F6
Kineton Gloucs 47 F2
Kineton Warwks 48 B4
Kinfauns P & K 140 B2
Kinfold S Ayrs 119 E3
King Arthur's Labyrinth Gwynd 55 E6
King Sterndale Derbys 83 F2
King's Acre Herefs 45 G3
King's Bromley Staffs 71 F2
King's Cliffe Nhants 61 F5
King's Coughton Warwks 47 F5
King's Heath W Mids 58 D3
King's Hill Warwks 59 F3
King's Lynn Norfk 75 F2
King's Mills Guern 174 f2

King's Moss

Lancing

295

King's Moss Lancs 81 G5
King's Newton Derbys 72 B3
King's Norton Leics 60 C5
King's Norton W Mids 58 C3
King's Nympton Devon 21 G2
King's Pyon Herefs 45 G4
King's Somborne Hants 26 B2
King's Stag Dorset 11 G6
King's Stanley Gloucs 38 C5
King's Sutton Oxon 48 C3
King's Walden Herts 50 C3
Kingarth Ag & B 118 C5
Kingcausie Abers 149 F4
Kingcoed Mons 37 E5
Kingerby Lincs 85 H4
Kingford Devon 20 C1
Kingham Oxon 47 H2
Kingholm Quay D & G 110 D2
Kinghorn Fife 132 B4
Kinglassie Fife 132 A5
Kingoldrum Angus 140 C5
Kingoodie P & K 140 C3
Kings Bridge Swans 34 C4
Kings Caple Herefs 46 A2
Kings Green Gloucs 46 C3
Kings Hill Kent 29 G2
Kings Hill W Mids 58 C5
Kings House Hotel Highld 137 G5
Kings Langley Herts 50 B1
Kings Meaburn Cumb 104 C2
Kings Muir Border 121 G3
Kings Newnham Warwks 59 G3
Kings Ripton Cambs 62 B3
Kings Weston Bristl 37 F2
Kings Worthy Hants 26 C2
Kingsand Cnwll 6 B3
Kingsash Bucks 41 G5
Kingsbarns Fife 141 F1
Kingsbridge Devon 7 E2
Kingsbridge Somset 22 C3
Kingsburgh Highld 150 D4
Kingsbury Gt Lon 28 C5
Kingsbury Warwks 59 E5
Kingsbury Episcopi Somset 23 G1
Kingsclere Hants 26 C5
Kingscote Gloucs 38 C4
Kingscott Devon 21 E2
Kingscross N Ayrs 118 B2
Kingsdon Somset 23 H2
Kingsdown Kent 31 G1
Kingsdown Wilts 24 D6
Kingsdown Wilts 39 F3
Kingseat Fife 131 G4
Kingsey Bucks 41 F5
Kingsfold W Susx 16 C5
Kingsford Aber C 149 F5
Kingsford E Ayrs 119 F4
Kingsford Worcs 58 A3
Kingsgate Kent 31 G3
Kingshall Street Suffk 64 B1
Kingsheanton Devon 21 F4
Kingshouse Hotel Stirlg 138 C2
Kingshurst W Mids 59 E4
Kingside Hill Cumb 103 F5
Kingskerswell Devon 7 F4
Kingskettle Fife 132 B6
Kingsland Dorset 11 E4
Kingsland Herefs 45 G5
Kingsland IOA 78 B3
Kingsley Ches 81 H2
Kingsley Hants 27 F3
Kingsley Staffs 71 E5
Kingsley Green W Susx 27 G2
Kingsley Park Nhants 60 D2
Kingslow Shrops 57 H5
Kingsmead Hants 14 D5
Kingsmuir Angus 141 E5
Kingsmuir Fife 132 D6
Kingsnorth Kent 18 D5
Kingstanding W Mids 58 D5
Kingsteignton Devon 7 F5
Kingsthorne Herefs 45 H2
Kingsthorpe Nhants 60 D2
Kingston Cambs 50 D6
Kingston Cnwll 5 G3
Kingston Devon 6 D2
Kingston Devon 9 G3
Kingston Dorset 12 A6
Kingston Dorset 12 C2
Kingston E Loth 132 D3
Kingston E Susx 16 B2
Kingston Hants 13 E5
Kingston IOW 14 C2
Kingston Kent 31 E1
Kingston Bagpuize Oxon 40 B4
Kingston Blount Oxon 41 F4
Kingston Deverill Wilts 24 D3
Kingston Lisle Oxon 40 B3
Kingston near Lewes E Susx 17 E2
Kingston on Soar Notts 72 C3
Kingston on Spey Moray 157 E6
Kingston Russell Dorset 11 F4
Kingston Seymour Somset 23 G6
Kingston St Mary Somset 23 E2
Kingston Stert Oxon 41 E4
Kingston upon Thames Gt Lon 28 C3
Kingstone Herefs 45 G3
Kingstone Somset 10 D6
Kingstone Staffs 71 E3
Kingstone Winslow Oxon 39 G3
Kingstown Cumb 103 H6
Kingswear Devon 7 F3
Kingswells Aber C 149 F5
Kingswinford W Mids 58 B4
Kingswood Bucks 49 E1
Kingswood Gloucs 37 G2
Kingswood Gloucs 38 B3
Kingswood Kent 30 B1
Kingswood Powys 56 C6
Kingswood Somset 22 D3
Kingswood Surrey 28 C2
Kingswood Warwks 59 E2
Kingswood Brook Warwks 59 E2
Kingswood Common Herefs 45 F5
Kingswood Common Staffs 58 A6
Kingthorpe Lincs 86 B2
Kington Gloucs 37 G3
Kington Herefs 45 F5
Kington Worcs 47 E5
Kington Langley Wilts 38 D2
Kington Magna Dorset 24 C1
Kington St Michael Wilts 38 D2
Kingussie Highld 146 C4
Kingweston Somset 23 H2
Kinharrachie Abers 159 E2
Kinharvie D & G 110 D1
Kinkell Bridge P & K 139 F1
Kinknockie Abers 159 F3
Kinleith C Edin 131 H2
Kinlet Shrops 57 G3
Kinloch Highld 164 D2
Kinloch Highld 165 F4
Kinloch Highld 142 D4
Kinloch P & K 140 B4
Kinloch P & K 140 C4
Kinloch Hourn Highld 144 B5
Kinloch Rannoch P & K 138 D6
Kinlochard Stirlg 129 F5
Kinlochbervie Highld 164 C4
Kinlocheil Highld 144 B2
Kinlochewe Highld 152 D5
Kinlochlaggan Highld 145 G3
Kinlochleven Highld 137 F6
Kinlochmoidart Highld 143 G1
Kinlochnanuagh Highld 143 G2
Kinloss Moray 156 C5
Kinmel Bay Conwy 80 B3
Kinmuck Abers 158 D1
Kinmundy Abers 149 F6
Kinnabus Ag & B 116 B5
Kinnadie Abers 159 F3
Kinnaird P & K 139 G6
Kinnaird Castle Angus 141 F5
Kinneddar Moray 156 D6
Kinneff Abers 149 F2
Kinnelhead D & G 111 E5
Kinnell Angus 141 F5
Kinnerley Shrops 69 F2
Kinnersley Herefs 45 F4
Kinnersley Worcs 46 D4
Kinnerton Powys 56 C2
Kinnerton Shrops 56 D5
Kinnerton Green Flints 69 F6
Kinnesswood P & K 131 H5
Kinninvie Dur 105 G2
Kinnordy Angus 140 D5
Kinoulton Notts 72 D3
Kinross P & K 131 G5
Kinrossie P & K 140 B3
Kinsbourne Green Herts 50 B2
Kinsey Heath Ches 70 B4
Kinsham Herefs 56 D2
Kinsham Worcs 47 E3
Kinsley W York 91 E1
Kinson Dorset 13 E4
Kintbury Berks 26 B6
Kintessack Moray 156 B5
Kintillo P & K 140 A1
Kinton Herefs 56 D3
Kinton Shrops 69 F2
Kintore Abers 149 E6
Kintour Ag & B 116 D5
Kintra Ag & B 135 E2
Kintraw Ag & B 127 G6
Kinveachy Highld 155 G1
Kinver Staffs 58 A4
Kiplin N York 97 F5
Kippax W York 91 E3
Kippen Stirlg 130 C5
Kippford or Scaur D & G 102 B6
Kipping's Cross Kent 17 G5
Kirbister Ork 169 b2
Kirburd Border 121 F4
Kirby Bedon Norfk 65 E6
Kirby Bellars Leics 73 E2
Kirby Cane Norfk 65 F5
Kirby Corner W Mids 59 F3
Kirby Cross Essex 53 F3
Kirby Fields Leics 60 A6
Kirby Grindalythe N York 99 E2
Kirby Hill N York 97 E5
Kirby Hill N York 97 G2
Kirby Knowle N York 97 H4
Kirby le Soken Essex 53 F3
Kirby Misperton N York 98 C3
Kirby Muxloe Leics 60 A6
Kirby Row Norfk 65 F5
Kirby Sigston N York 97 G4
Kirby Underdale E R Yk 92 B5
Kirby Wiske N York 97 G3
Kirconnel D & G 110 D2
Kirdford W Susx 16 A4
Kirk Highld 167 F4
Kirk Bramwith S York 84 D6
Kirk Deighton N York 91 E5
Kirk Ella E R Yk 92 D2
Kirk Hallam Derbys 72 B4
Kirk Hammerton N York 91 F5
Kirk Ireton Derbys 71 G5
Kirk Langley Derbys 71 H4
Kirk Merrington Dur 106 B4
Kirk Michael IOM 174 I4
Kirk of Shotts N Lans 120 C6
Kirk Sandall S York 84 D5
Kirk Smeaton N York 91 F1
Kirk Yetholm Border 123 E2
Kirkabister Shet 169 j2
Kirkandrews D & G 101 G5
Kirkandrews upon Eden Cumb 103 G6
Kirkbampton Cumb 103 G6
Kirkbean D & G 102 D6
Kirkbride Cumb 103 F6
Kirkbridge N York 97 F4
Kirkbuddo Angus 141 E4
Kirkburn Border 121 G3
Kirkburn E R Yk 92 D5
Kirkburton W York 83 G6
Kirkby Lincs 86 A4
Kirkby Mersyd 81 F5
Kirkby N York 98 A5
Kirkby Fleetham N York 97 F4
Kirkby Green Lincs 74 A6
Kirkby Hall N York 97 F4
Kirkby in Ashfield Notts 72 C6
Kirkby la Thorpe Lincs 74 A5
Kirkby Lonsdale Cumb 95 G3
Kirkby Malham N York 89 G6
Kirkby Mallory Leics 59 G5
Kirkby Malzeard N York 97 E2
Kirkby Mills N York 98 C3
Kirkby on Bain Lincs 86 C1
Kirkby Overblow N York 90 D4
Kirkby Stephen Cumb 96 A6
Kirkby Thore Cumb 104 C3
Kirkby Underwood Lincs 74 A3
Kirkby Wharf N York 91 F4
Kirkby Woodhouse Notts 72 C5
Kirkby-in-Furness Cumb 94 C3
Kirkbymoorside N York 98 C3
Kirkcaldy Fife 132 B4
Kirkcambeck Cumb 112 C2
Kirkchrist D & G 101 H5
Kirkcolm D & G 108 B2
Kirkconnel D & G 110 B6
Kirkconnell D & G 101 H6
Kirkcowan D & G 101 E6
Kirkcudbright D & G 101 H5
Kirkdale Mersyd 81 F4
Kirkfieldbank S Lans 120 C4
Kirkgunzeon D & G 110 C1
Kirkham Lancs 88 C3
Kirkham N York 98 C1
Kirkhamgate W York 90 D2
Kirkharle Nthumb 113 G3
Kirkhaugh Nthumb 104 D5
Kirkheaton Nthumb 114 B3
Kirkheaton W York 90 C1
Kirkhill Highld 154 D4
Kirkhope S Lans 110 D5
Kirkhouse Cumb 104 B6
Kirkhouse Green S York 84 D6
Kirkibost Highld 143 E6
Kirkinch P & K 140 C4
Kirkinner D & G 101 E5
Kirkintilloch E Duns 130 C2
Kirkland Cumb 103 E2
Kirkland Cumb 104 C3
Kirkland D & G 110 B6
Kirkland D & G 110 C4
Kirkland D & G 111 E4
Kirkland Guards Cumb 103 F4
Kirkleatham N York 107 E3
Kirklevington N York 106 D2
Kirkley Suffk 65 H4
Kirklington N York 97 F3
Kirklington Notts 72 D6
Kirklinton Cumb 112 B1
Kirkliston C Edin 131 G2
Kirkmabreck D & G 101 F6
Kirkmaiden D & G 100 C4
Kirkmichael P & K 139 H6
Kirkmichael S Ayrs 109 E6
Kirkmuirhill S Lans 120 B4
Kirknewton Nthumb 123 F2
Kirknewton W Loth 131 G2
Kirkney Abers 157 G2
Kirkoswald Cumb 104 B4
Kirkoswald S Ayrs 108 D5
Kirkpatrick D & G 110 D4
Kirkpatrick IOM 174 k3
Kirkpatrick Durham D & G 110 B2
Kirkpatrick-Fleming D & G 111 G2
Kirksanton Cumb 94 B3
Kirkstall W York 90 D3
Kirkstead Lincs 86 B1
Kirkstile Abers 157 G3
Kirkstile D & G 111 H4
Kirkstone Pass Inn Cumb 95 E6
Kirkstyle Highld 167 G6
Kirkthorpe W York 91 E2
Kirkton Abers 158 B2
Kirkton Abers 158 D3
Kirkton D & G 110 D3
Kirkton Fife 140 D2
Kirkton Highld 152 B2
Kirkton Highld 152 C3
Kirkton P & K 139 G2
Kirkton Manor Border 121 G3
Kirkton of Airlie Angus 140 C5
Kirkton of Auchterhouse Angus 140 C4
Kirkton of Barevan Highld 155 F4
Kirkton of Collace P & K 140 B3
Kirkton of Glenbuchat Abers 148 A6
Kirkton of Logie Buchan Abers 159 F2
Kirkton of Menmuir Angus 141 E6
Kirkton of Monikie Angus 141 E4
Kirkton of Rayne Abers 158 C2
Kirkton of Skene Abers 149 F5
Kirkton of Strathmartine Angus 140 D3
Kirkton of Tealing Angus 140 D3
Kirktown Abers 159 F6
Kirktown Abers 159 G4
Kirktown of Bourtie Abers 158 D2
Kirktown of Fetteresso Abers 149 F3
Kirktown of Mortlach Moray 157 E3
Kirktown of Slains Abers 159 F2
Kirkwall Ork 169 b2
Kirkwall Airport Ork 169 c2
Kirkwhelpington Nthumb 113 G3
Kirmincham Ches 82 C1
Kirmington Lincs 86 A6
Kirmond le Mire Lincs 86 B4
Kirn Ag & B 128 C3
Kirriemuir Angus 140 D5
Kirstead Green Norfk 65 E5
Kirtlebridge D & G 111 G2
Kirtling Cambs 63 F1
Kirtling Green Suffk 63 F1
Kirtlington Oxon 48 C1
Kirtomy Highld 166 A5
Kirton Abers 148 D6
Kirton Lincs 74 C4
Kirton Notts 85 E2
Kirton Suffk 53 F5
Kirton End Lincs 74 C4
Kirton Holme Lincs 74 C4
Kirton in Lindsey Lincs 85 G4
Kirtonhill W Duns 129 E3
Kirwaugh D & G 101 E5
Kishorn Highld 152 C3
Kislingbury Nhants 49 E5
Kite Green Warwks 59 E2
Kitebrook Warwks 47 H2
Kites Hardwick Warwks 59 G2
Kitleigh Cnwll 5 F6
Kitt Green Gt Man 81 H5
Kittisford Somset 22 D1
Kittle Swans 34 C3
Kitts Green W Mids 58 D4
Kittybrewster Aber C 149 G5
Kitwood Hants 27 E2
Kivernoll Herefs 45 G2
Kiveton Park S York 84 C3
Knaith Lincs 85 F3
Knaith Park Lincs 85 F3
Knap Corner Dorset 24 D2
Knaphill Surrey 27 H5
Knaplock Somset 22 B3
Knapp Somset 23 F2
Knapp Hill Hants 26 B2
Knapthorpe Notts 73 E6
Knapton N York 91 G5
Knapton N York 98 D2
Knapton Norfk 77 F3
Knapton Green Herefs 45 G4
Knapwell Cambs 62 C2
Knaresborough N York 91 E5
Knarsdale Nthumb 104 C5
Knaven Abers 159 E3
Knayton N York 97 G4
Knebworth Herts 50 C3
Knedlington E R Yk 92 A2
Kneesall Notts 85 E1
Kneesworth Cambs 50 D5
Kneeton Notts 73 E5
Knelston Swans 34 B3
Knenhall Staffs 70 D4
Knettishall Suffk 64 B3
Knightacott Devon 21 G4
Knightcote Warwks 48 B5
Knightley Staffs 70 C2
Knightley Dale Staffs 70 C2
Knighton Devon 6 C2
Knighton Dorset 11 F6
Knighton Dorset 12 D4
Knighton Leics 60 B5
Knighton Powys 56 C3
Knighton Somset 23 E4
Knighton Staffs 70 B4
Knighton Staffs 70 C3
Knighton Wilts 39 G1
Knighton on Teme Worcs 57 F2
Knightsbridge Gloucs 46 D2
Knightsmill Cnwll 4 D4
Knightwick Worcs 46 C5
Knill Herefs 45 F5
Knipton Leics 73 E3
Knitsley Dur 105 H5
Kniveton Derbys 71 G5
Knock Cumb 104 D3
Knock Highld 143 F5
Knock Moray 157 G4
Knock W Isls 168 f8
Knock Castle N Ayrs 128 C1
Knockally Highld 167 E1
Knockan Highld 161 F5
Knockando Moray 156 D3
Knockbain Highld 154 D3
Knockbain Highld 154 D5
Knockdee Highld 167 E4
Knockdown Wilts 38 C3
Knockeen S Ayrs 109 E4
Knockenkelly N Ayrs 118 B2
Knockentiber E Ayrs 119 F3
Knockhall Kent 29 G3
Knockholt Kent 29 E2
Knockholt Pound Kent 29 F2
Knockin Shrops 69 F2
Knockinlaw E Ayrs 119 F3
Knockmill Kent 29 G2
Knocknain D & G 108 B1
Knocksheen D & G 109 G3
Knockvennie Smithy D & G 110 B2
Knodishall Suffk 65 G2
Knole Somset 23 H2
Knole Park Gloucs 37 G3
Knolls Green Ches 82 C3
Knolton Wrexhm 69 F4
Knook Wilts 25 E3
Knossington Leics 73 F1
Knott End-on-Sea Lancs 88 B4
Knotting Beds 61 F2
Knotting Green Beds 61 F2
Knottingley W York 91 F2
Knotty Ash Mersyd 81 F4
Knotty Green Bucks 41 G3
Knowbury Shrops 57 F3
Knowe D & G 109 E2
Knowehead D & G 109 H4
Knoweside S Ayrs 108 D6
Knowl Green Essex 52 A5
Knowl Hill Berks 41 F2
Knowle Bristl 37 G1
Knowle Devon 21 E4
Knowle Devon 9 E5
Knowle Devon 9 G5
Knowle Devon 9 G3
Knowle Shrops 57 F3
Knowle Somset 22 C4
Knowle W Mids 59 E3
Knowle Cross Devon 9 G4
Knowle Green Lancs 89 E3
Knowle Hill Surrey 27 H6
Knowle St Giles Somset 10 D6
Knowlefield Cumb 103 H6
Knowlton Dorset 12 D6
Knowlton Kent 31 F1
Knowsley Mersyd 81 G4
Knowsley Safari Park Mersyd 81 G4
Knowstone Devon 22 A1
Knox N York 90 D5
Knox Bridge Kent 18 B5
Knucklas Powys 56 C3
Knuston Nhants 61 E2
Knutsford Ches 82 C2
Knutton Staffs 70 C5
Knypersley Staffs 70 D6
Krumlin W York 90 B1
Kuggar Cnwll 3 E1
Kyle of Lochalsh Highld 152 B2
Kyleakin Highld 152 B2
Kylerhea Highld 143 G6
Kyles Scalpay W Isls 168 d6
Kylesku Highld 164 C2
Kylesmorar Highld 143 G3
Kylestrome Highld 164 C2
Kyloe Nthumb 123 H3
Kynaston Herefs 46 B3
Kynaston Shrops 69 F2
Kynnersley Shrops 70 B2
Kyre Green Worcs 46 B5
Kyre Park Worcs 57 F2
Kyrewood Worcs 57 F2
Kyrle Somset 22 C1

L

L'Ancresse Guern 174 g3
L'Eree Guern 174 f2
L'Etacq Jersey 174 a3
La Bellieuse Guern 174 g1
La Fontenelle Guern 174 h3
La Fosse Guern 174 g1
La Greve Guern 174 g3
La Greve de Lecq Jersey 174 a3
La Hougue Bie Jersey 174 d2
La Houguette Guern 174 f2
La Passee Guern 174 g3
La Pulente Jersey 174 a2
La Rocque Jersey 174 d1
La Rousaillerie Guern 174 g2
La Villette Guern 174 g1
Lacadal W Isls 168 f8
Lacasaigh W Isls 168 e7
Laceby Lincs 86 B5
Lacey Green Bucks 41 F4
Lach Dennis Ches 82 B2
Lackenby N York 107 E3
Lackford Suffk 63 G2
Lackford Green Suffk 63 G2
Lacock Wilts 38 D1
Ladbroke Warwks 48 B5
Ladderedge Staffs 71 E5
Laddingford Kent 17 H6
Lade Bank Lincs 74 D5
Ladock Cnwll 3 F5
Lady Hall Cumb 94 C3
Lady Village Ork 169 d4
Lady's Green Suffk 63 G1
Ladybank Fife 132 B6
Ladycross Cnwll 5 G5
Ladygill S Lans 120 D2
Ladykirk Border 123 F4
Ladyridge Herefs 46 B2
Ladywood W Mids 58 C4
Ladywood Worcs 46 D5
Lag D & G 110 C3
Laga Highld 136 A6
Lagavulin Ag & B 116 C5
Lagg N Ayrs 118 A2
Laggan Highld 145 E4
Laggan Highld 146 A4
Laid Highld 165 E4
Laide Highld 160 C3
Laig Highld 142 D3
Laigh Clunch E Ayrs 119 F4
Laigh Fenwick E Ayrs 119 F4
Laigh Glenmuir E Ayrs 119 H1
Laighstonehall S Lans 120 B5
Laindon Essex 29 H5
Lairg Highld 162 C4
Laisterdyke W York 90 C3
Laithes Cumb 104 A3
Lake Devon 21 F4
Lake Devon 8 B3
Lake Dorset 12 D4
Lake IOW 14 D2
Lake Wilts 25 G3
Lakenheath Suffk 63 F4
Laker's Green Surrey 16 A5
Lakesend Norfk 62 D5
Lakeside Cumb 94 D4
Laleham Surrey 28 A3
Laleston Brdgnd 35 F2
Lamancha Border 121 F5
Lamanva Cnwll 3 E3
Lamarsh Essex 52 B4
Lamas Norfk 77 E2
Lamb Roe Lancs 89 F3
Lambden Border 123 E4
Lamberhurst Kent 17 G5
Lamberhurst Down Kent 17 G5
Lamberton Border 123 G5
Lambeth Gt Lon 28 D4
Lambfair Green Suffk 51 H6
Lambley Notts 72 D5
Lambley Nthumb 104 C6
Lambourn Berks 40 B2
Lambourne End Essex 29 F5
Lambs Green W Susx 16 C5
Lambston Pembks 32 C3
Lamellion Cnwll 5 F2
Lamerton Devon 8 A2
Lamesley T & W 114 D1
Lamington S Lans 120 D2
Lamlash N Ayrs 118 B2
Lamonby Cumb 103 H4
Lamorick Cnwll 4 D2
Lamorna Cnwll 2 B2
Lamorran Cnwll 3 F4
Lampen Cnwll 5 E3
Lampeter Cerdgn 43 F4
Lampeter Velfrey Pembks 33 F3
Lamphey Pembks 32 D2
Lamplugh Cumb 103 E2
Lamport Nhants 60 D3
Lamyatt Somset 24 B3
Lana Devon 20 C1
Lana Devon 5 G6
Lanark S Lans 120 C4
Lanarth Cnwll 3 E2
Lancaster Lancs 88 C6
Lancaut Gloucs 37 F4
Lanchester Dur 106 A6
Lancing W Susx 16 C2

Land's End Linsidemore

296

Land's End Cnwll 2 A2
Land's End Airport Cnwll 2 A3
Land-hallow Highld 167 F2
Landbeach Cambs 62 D2
Landcross Devon 21 E3
Landerberry Abers 149 E5
Landford Wilts 25 H1
Landimore Swans 34 B3
Landkey Devon 21 F4
Landkey Town Devon 21 F4
Landore Swans 34 D4
Landrake Cnwll 5 G2
Landscove Devon 7 E4
Landshipping Pembks 32 D3
Landue Cnwll 5 G4
Landulph Cnwll 6 B4
Landwade Suffk 63 E2
Landywood Staffs 58 C6
Lane Cnwll 4 B2
Lane Bottom Lancs 89 G3
Lane End Bucks 41 F3
Lane End Ches 82 B4
Lane End Cnwll 4 D3
Lane End Hants 26 D2
Lane End Kent 29 F3
Lane End Lancs 89 G4
Lane End Wilts 24 D4
Lane End Waberthwaite Cumb 94 B4
Lane Ends Derbys 71 G3
Lane Ends Dur 106 A4
Lane Ends Lancs 89 F3
Lane Ends N York 90 A4
Lane Green Staffs 58 B6
Lane Head Dur 105 H1
Lane Head Gt Man 82 A4
Lane Head W Mids 58 C5
Lane Heads Lancs 88 C3
Lane Side Lancs 89 F2
Laneast Cnwll 5 F4
Laneham Notts 85 F2
Lanehead Dur 105 E4
Lanehead Nthumb 113 E3
Laneshaw Bridge Lancs 89 H4
Langaford Devon 5 H6
Langaller Somset 23 E2
Langar Notts 73 E3
Langbank Rens 129 E2
Langbar N York 90 B5
Langbaurgh N York 107 E2
Langcliffe N York 96 B1
Langdale End N York 99 E4
Langdon Cnwll 5 G5
Langdon Beck Dur 105 E3
Langdown Hants 14 B4
Langdyke Fife 132 B6
Langenhoe Essex 52 D3
Langford Beds 50 C5
Langford Devon 9 G5
Langford Essex 52 B2
Langford Notts 73 F6
Langford Oxon 39 G4
Langford Somset 23 G5
Langford Budville Somset 22 D1
Langford End Beds 50 C6
Langham Dorset 24 C2
Langham Essex 52 D4
Langham Norfk 76 C4
Langham RutInd 73 F1
Langham Suffk 64 B2
Langham Moor Essex 52 D4
Langham Wick Essex 52 D4
Langho Lancs 89 E3
Langholm D & G 111 H3
Langland Swans 34 D3
Langlee Border 122 B3
Langley Berks 28 A4
Langley Ches 82 D2
Langley Derbys 72 B5
Langley Gloucs 47 E2
Langley Gt Man 82 D5
Langley Hants 14 C4
Langley Herts 50 C3
Langley Kent 30 B1
Langley Nthumb 105 E6
Langley Oxon 39 H6
Langley Somset 22 D2
Langley W Susx 27 F2
Langley Warwks 59 E2
Langley Burrell Wilts 38 D2
Langley Castle Nthumb 113 E1
Langley Common Derbys 71 H4
Langley Green Derbys 71 H4
Langley Green Essex 52 B3
Langley Green Warwks 47 G5
Langley Lower Green Essex 51 E4
Langley Marsh Somset 22 D2
Langley Mill Derbys 72 B5
Langley Moor Dur 106 B5
Langley Park Dur 106 B5
Langley Street Norfk 65 F6
Langley Upper Green Essex 51 E4
Langleybury Herts 28 B6
Langney E Susx 17 G2
Langold Notts 84 D3
Langore Cnwll 5 F5
Langport Somset 23 G2
Langrick Lincs 74 C5
Langridge Somset 38 B1
Langridge Ford Devon 21 F3
Langrigg Cumb 103 F5
Langrish Hants 27 E2
Langsett S York 83 G5
Langside P & K 139 E1
Langstone Hants 15 E4
Langstone Newpt 37 E3
Langthorne N York 97 F4
Langthorpe N York 97 G2
Langthwaite N York 96 C5
Langtoft E R Yk 99 F1
Langtoft Lincs 74 B1
Langton Dur 106 A3
Langton Lincs 86 C1
Langton Lincs 86 D2
Langton N York 98 D1
Langton by Wragby Lincs 86 B2
Langton Green Kent 17 F5
Langton Green Suffk 64 D3
Langton Herring Dorset 11 F3
Langton Matravers Dorset 12 D2
Langtree Devon 21 E2
Langtree Week Devon 21 E2
Langwathby Cumb 104 B3
Langwell House Highld 163 H6
Langworth Lincs 86 A2
Langworthy Devon 8 B4
Lanhydrock House & Gardens Cnwll 4 D2
Lanivet Cnwll 4 D2
Lanjeth Cnwll 3 G5
Lank Cnwll 4 D3
Lanlivery Cnwll 4 D2
Lanner Cnwll 3 E4
Lanoy Cnwll 5 F4
Lanreath Cnwll 5 E2
Lansallos Cnwll 5 E1
Lanteglos Cnwll 4 D4
Lanteglos Highway Cnwll 5 E1
Lanton Border 122 C2
Lanton Nthumb 123 F2
Lapford Devon 8 D5
Laphroaig Ag & B 116 C5
Lapley Staffs 70 D1
Lapworth Warwks 59 E2
Larachbeg Highld 135 B5
Larbert Falk 131 E3
Larbreck Lancs 88 C4
Largie Abers 158 B2
Largiemore Ag & B 128 A4
Largoward Fife 132 D6
Largs N Ayrs 118 D5
Largybeg N Ayrs 118 B2
Largymore N Ayrs 118 B2
Larkbeare Devon 10 A4
Larkfield Inver 128 D3
Larkfield Kent 29 H2
Larkhall S Lans 120 B4
Larkhill Wilts 25 G4
Larling Norfk 64 B4
Lartington Dur 105 G2
Lasborough Gloucs 38 C4
Lasham Hants 27 E3
Lashbrook Devon 8 A5
Lashenden Kent 18 B5
Lask Edge Staffs 70 D6
Lassodie Fife 131 G4
Lasswade Mdloth 132 B2
Lastingham N York 98 C4
Latcham Somset 23 G4
Latchford Herts 51 E3
Latchford Oxon 41 E4
Latchingdon Essex 30 B6
Latchley Cnwll 5 H3
Latebrook Staffs 70 C5
Lately Common Gt Man 82 B4
Lathbury Bucks 49 G4
Latheron Highld 167 F2
Latheronwheel Highld 167 E2
Lathones Fife 132 D6
Latimer Bucks 28 A6
Latteridge Gloucs 37 H3
Lattiford Somset 24 C2
Latton Wilts 39 F4
Lauder Border 122 C4
Laugharne Carmth 33 G3
Laughterton Lincs 85 F2
Laughton E Susx 17 F3
Laughton Leics 60 C4
Laughton Lincs 85 F4
Laughton Lincs 74 A3
Laughton-en-le-Morthen S York 84 C3
Launcells Cnwll 20 C1
Launcells Cross Cnwll 20 C1
Launceston Cnwll 5 G4
Launton Oxon 48 D1
Laurencekirk Abers 149 E2
Laurieston D & G 110 A1
Laurieston Falk 131 E3
Lavendon Bucks 49 G5
Lavenham Suffk 52 C6
Lavernock V Glam 36 D1
Laversdale Cumb 112 B1
Laverstock Wilts 25 G2
Laverstoke Hants 26 C4
Laverton Gloucs 47 F3
Laverton N York 97 E2
Laverton Somset 24 C5
Lavister Wrexhm 69 F6
Law S Lans 120 C5
Law Hill S Lans 120 C5
Lawers P & K 138 D4
Lawford Essex 52 D4
Lawford Somset 22 D3
Lawgrove P & K 140 A2
Lawhitton Cnwll 5 G4
Lawkland N York 96 A1
Lawkland Green N York 96 A1
Lawley Shrops 70 B1
Lawnhead Staffs 70 C2
Lawrence End Herts 50 B3
Lawrenny Pembks 32 D2
Lawshall Suffk 52 B6
Lawshall Green Suffk 52 B6
Lawton Herefs 45 G5
Laxay W Isls 168 e7
Laxdale W Isls 168 f8
Laxey IOM 174 m3
Laxfield Suffk 65 E3
Laxford Bridge Highld 164 C3
Laxo Shet 169 j3
Laxton E R Yk 92 B2
Laxton Nhants 61 E5
Laxton Notts 85 E1
Laycock W York 90 B4
Layer Breton Essex 52 C2
Layer Marney Essex 52 C2
Layer-de-la-Haye Essex 52 C3
Layham Suffk 52 D5
Layland's Green Berks 26 B6
Laymore Dorset 10 D5
Layter's Green Bucks 41 H3
Laytham E R Yk 92 A3
Laythes Cumb 103 F6
Lazenby N York 107 E3
Lazonby Cumb 104 B4
Le Bigard Guern 174 f1
Le Bourg Guern 174 g1
Le Bourg Jersey 174 d1
Le Gron Guern 174 f1
Le Haguais Jersey 174 c1
Le Hocq Jersey 174 d1
Le Villocq Guern 174 g2
Lea Derbys 72 A6
Lea Herefs 46 B1
Lea Lincs 85 F3
Lea Shrops 69 F1
Lea Shrops 56 D4
Lea Wilts 38 D3
Lea Bridge Derbys 71 H6
Lea Heath Staffs 71 E3
Lea Marston Warwks 59 E5
Lea Town Lancs 88 C3
Lea Yeat Cumb 96 A3
Leachkin Highld 155 E4
Leadburn Mdloth 121 G5
Leaden Roding Essex 51 G2
Leadenham Lincs 73 G5
Leadgate Dur 105 H5
Leadgate Nthumb 114 C1
Leadhills S Lans 120 C1
Leadingcross Green Kent 30 C1
Leadmill Derbys 83 G3
Leafield Oxon 40 A6
Leagrave Beds 50 B3
Leahead Ches 82 B1
Leake N York 97 G4
Leake Common Side Lincs 74 D5
Lealholm N York 107 G2
Lealholm Side N York 107 G2
Lealt Highld 151 E5
Leam Derbys 83 G3
Leamington Hastings Warwks 59 G2
Leamington Spa Warwks 59 F2
Leamonsley Staffs 71 F1
Leamside Dur 106 C5
Leap Cross E Susx 17 G2
Leasgill Cumb 95 F3
Leasingham Lincs 74 A5
Leasingthorne Dur 106 B4
Leatherhead Surrey 28 C2
Leathley N York 90 C4
Leaton Shrops 69 G2
Leaton Shrops 70 A1
Leaveland Kent 30 D1
Leavenheath Suffk 52 C4
Leavening N York 92 B6
Leaves Green Gt Lon 29 E2
Lebberston N York 99 F3
Lechlade Gloucs 39 G4
Lecht Gruinart Ag & B 126 B2
Leck Lancs 95 G2
Leckbuie P & K 138 D4
Leckford Hants 26 B3
Leckhampstead Berks 40 C2
Leckhampstead Bucks 49 E3
Leckhampstead Thicket Berks 40 C2
Leckhampton Gloucs 47 E1
Leckmelm Highld 161 F3
Leckwith V Glam 36 C2
Leconfield E R Yk 92 D4
Ledaig Ag & B 136 D3
Ledburn Bucks 49 G1
Ledbury Herefs 46 C3
Leddington Gloucs 46 B3
Ledgemoor Herefs 45 G4
Ledicot Herefs 45 G5
Ledmore Junction Highld 161 G5
Ledsham Ches 81 F2
Ledsham W York 91 F2
Ledston W York 91 E2
Ledston Luck W York 91 E3
Ledstone Devon 7 E2
Ledwell Oxon 48 B2
Lee Devon 21 E5
Lee Gt Lon 29 E4
Lee Hants 14 B5
Lee Shrops 69 F3
Lee Brockhurst Shrops 69 H3
Lee Chapel Essex 29 H5
Lee Clump Bucks 41 G5
Lee Common Bucks 41 G5
Lee Green Ches 70 B6
Lee Mill Devon 6 C3
Lee Moor Devon 6 C4
Lee Street Surrey 16 D6
Lee-on-the-Solent Hants 14 D4
Leebotwood Shrops 57 E5
Leece Cumb 94 C2
Leedon Beds 49 G2
Leeds Kent 30 B1
Leeds W York 90 D3
Leeds Bradford Airport W York 90 C4
Leeds Castle Kent 30 B1
Leedstown Cnwll 2 D3
Leek Staffs 71 E6
Leek Wootton Warwks 59 F2
Leeming N York 97 F4
Leeming W York 90 B3
Leeming Bar N York 97 F4
Lees Derbys 71 G4
Lees Gt Man 82 D5
Lees W York 90 B3
Lees Green Derbys 71 G4
Lees Hill Cumb 112 C2
Leesthorpe Leics 73 E1
Leeswood Flints 69 E6
Leetown P & K 140 B2
Leftwich Ches 82 B2
Legar Powys 36 C6
Legbourne Lincs 86 D3
Legburthwaite Cumb 103 G2
Legerwood Border 122 C4
Legoland Berks 41 G2
Legsby Lincs 86 B3
Leicester Leics 60 B6
Leicester Forest East Leics 60 A6
Leigh Devon 21 G2
Leigh Dorset 11 F5
Leigh Gloucs 46 D2
Leigh Gt Man 82 B5
Leigh Kent 17 F6
Leigh Shrops 56 D6
Leigh Surrey 16 C6
Leigh Wilts 39 E3
Leigh Worcs 46 C5
Leigh Beck Essex 30 B4
Leigh Delamere Wilts 38 D2
Leigh Green Kent 18 C5
Leigh Knoweglass S Lans 119 H4
Leigh Park Dorset 12 D5
Leigh Sinton Worcs 46 C4
Leigh upon Mendip Somset 24 B4
Leigh Woods Somset 37 G1
Leigh-on-Sea Essex 30 B5
Leighland Chapel Somset 22 C3
Leighterton Gloucs 38 C3
Leighton N York 97 E3
Leighton Powys 56 C6
Leighton Shrops 57 F6
Leighton Somset 24 C4
Leighton Bromswold Cambs 61 G3
Leighton Buzzard Beds 49 G2
Leinthall Earls Herefs 57 E2
Leinthall Starkes Herefs 57 E2
Leintwardine Herefs 56 D3
Leire Leics 60 A4
Leiston Suffk 65 G2
Leitfie P & K 140 C4
Leith C Edin 132 B3
Leitholm Border 123 E4
Lelant Cnwll 2 C3
Lelley E R Yk 93 F3
Lem Hill Worcs 57 G3
Lemmington Hall Nthumb 124 D2
Lempitlaw Border 123 E3
Lemreway W Isls 168 e7
Lemsford Herts 50 C2
Lenchwick Worcs 47 F4
Lendalfoot S Ayrs 108 C4
Lendrick Stirlg 129 G6
Lendrum Terrace Abers 159 G3
Lenham Kent 30 C1
Lenham Heath Kent 30 C1
Lenie Highld 154 C2
Lennel Border 123 F3
Lennox Plunton D & G 101 G5
Lennoxtown E Duns 130 C3
Lent Bucks 41 G2
Lenton Lincs 73 H3
Lenton Notts 72 C4
Lenwade Norfk 76 D2
Lenzie E Duns 130 C2
Leochel-Cushnie Abers 148 C5
Leominster Herefs 45 H5
Leonard Stanley Gloucs 38 C5
Leoville Jersey 174 a3
Lepe Hants 14 C3
Lephin Highld 150 B4
Leppington N York 92 B6
Lepton W York 90 C1
Lerryn Cnwll 5 E2
Lerwick Shet 169 j2
Les Arquets Guern 174 f1
Les Hubits Guern 174 g1
Les Lohiers Guern 174 f2
Les Murchez Guern 174 f1
Les Nicolles Guern 174 g1
Les Quartiers Guern 174 g2
Les Quennevais Jersey 174 a2
Les Sages Guern 174 f1
Les Villets Guern 174 f1
Lesbury Nthumb 125 E2
Leslie Abers 158 B1
Leslie Fife 132 B5
Lesmahagow S Lans 120 C3
Lesnewth Cnwll 5 E5
Lessingham Norfk 77 G3
Lessonhall Cumb 103 F5
Lestowder Cnwll 3 E2
Leswalt D & G 108 B1
Letchmore Heath Herts 28 B6
Letchworth Herts 50 C4
Letcombe Bassett Oxon 40 B3
Letcombe Regis Oxon 40 B3
Letham Angus 141 E5
Letham Border 112 D6
Letham Falk 131 E4
Letham Fife 140 C1
Letham Grange Angus 141 F4
Lethendy P & K 140 A4
Lethenty Abers 158 B1
Lethenty Abers 158 D3
Letheringham Suffk 65 E1
Letheringsett Norfk 76 D4
Lett's Green Kent 29 E2
Lettaford Devon 8 D3
Letterewe Highld 152 D6
Letterfearn Highld 152 C1
Letterfinlay Lodge Hotel Highld 145 E3
Lettermorar Highld 143 G3
Letters Highld 161 F2
Lettershaw S Lans 120 C1
Letterston Pembks 32 D5
Lettoch Highld 156 B1
Lettoch Highld 156 C2
Letton Herefs 45 F4
Letton Herefs 56 D2
Letty Green Herts 50 D2
Letwell S York 84 C3
Leuchars Fife 140 D2
Leumrabhagh W Isls 168 e7
Leurbost W Isls 168 e8
Levalsa Meor Cnwll 3 G5
Levedale Staffs 70 D2
Level's Green Essex 51 F3
Leven E R Yk 93 E4
Leven Fife 132 C5
Levens Cumb 95 F3
Levens Green Herts 50 D3
Levenshulme Gt Man 82 D4
Levenwick Shet 169 h1
Leverburgh W Isls 168 c6
Leverington Cambs 75 E1
Leverstock Green Herts 50 B1
Leverton Lincs 74 D5
Levington Suffk 53 F5
Levisham N York 98 D4
Lew Oxon 40 B5
Lewannick Cnwll 5 F4
Lewdown Devon 8 A3
Lewes E Susx 17 E2
Leweston Dorset 11 G6
Leweston Pembks 32 D4
Lewis Wych Herefs 45 F5
Lewisham Gt Lon 29 E3
Lewiston Highld 154 C2
Lewknor Oxon 41 E4
Leworthy Devon 5 G6
Leworthy Devon 21 G4
Lewson Street Kent 30 C2
Lewth Lancs 88 C3
Lewtrenchard Devon 8 B3
Lexden Essex 52 C3
Lexworthy Somset 23 E3
Ley Cnwll 5 E2
Ley Hill Bucks 41 H4
Leybourne Kent 29 H2
Leyburn N York 96 D4
Leycett Staffs 70 C5
Leygreen Herts 50 C3
Leyland Lancs 88 D2
Leyland Green Mersyd 81 H5
Leylodge Abers 149 E6
Leys Abers 159 F4
Leys Angus 140 C3
Leys of Cossans Angus 140 D5
Leysdown-on-Sea Kent 30 D3
Leysmill Angus 141 F4
Leysters Herefs 57 F2
Leyton Gt Lon 29 E5
Leytonstone Gt Lon 29 E5
Lezant Cnwll 5 G4
Lezayre IOM 174 m4
Lezerea Cnwll 2 D3
Lhanbryde Moray 157 E5
Libanus Powys 44 C2
Libberton S Lans 120 D4
Liberton C Edin 132 B2
Lichfield Staffs 71 F1
Lickey Worcs 58 C3
Lickey End Worcs 58 C3
Lickey Rock Worcs 58 C3
Lickfold W Susx 27 G2
Liddaton Green Devon 8 B3
Liddesdale Highld 136 B6
Liddington Wilts 39 G2
Lidgate Derbys 83 H2
Lidgate Suffk 63 F1
Lidget S York 84 D5
Lidgett Notts 84 D1
Lidham Hill E Susx 18 B3
Lidlington Beds 49 H3
Lidsing Kent 30 B2
Liff Angus 140 C3
Lifford W Mids 58 C3
Lifton Devon 5 G4
Liftondown Devon 5 G4
Lighthazles W York 90 A2
Lighthorne Warwks 48 B5
Lighthorne Heath Warwks 48 B5
Lightwater Surrey 27 G5
Lightwood Staffs 70 D4
Lightwood Green Ches 70 A4
Lightwood Green Wrexhm 69 F4
Lilbourne Nhants 60 B3
Lilburn Tower Nthumb 124 C3
Lilleshall Shrops 70 B2
Lilley Berks 40 C2
Lilley Herts 50 B3
Lilliesleaf Border 122 C2
Lillingstone Dayrell Bucks 49 E3
Lillingstone Lovell Bucks 49 E3
Lillington Dorset 11 G6
Lilliput Dorset 12 D4
Lilstock Somset 22 D4
Lilyhurst Shrops 70 B1
Limbrick Lancs 88 D1
Limbury Beds 50 B3
Lime Street Worcs 46 D2
Limebrook Herefs 56 D2
Limefield Gt Man 82 C6
Limekilnburn S Lans 120 B4
Limekilns Fife 131 G3
Limerigg Falk 131 E2
Limerstone IOW 14 C2
Limestone Brae Nthumb 105 E5
Limington Somset 24 A1
Limmerhaugh E Ayrs 119 H2
Limpenhoe Norfk 65 F6
Limpley Stoke Wilts 24 C5
Limpsfield Surrey 29 E1
Limpsfield Chart Surrey 29 E1
Linby Notts 72 C5
Linchmere W Susx 27 G2
Lincluden D & G 110 D2
Lincoln Lincs 85 G2
Lincomb Worcs 58 A2
Lincombe Devon 7 E2
Lindal in Furness Cumb 94 C2
Lindale Cumb 95 E3
Lindfield W Susx 16 D4
Lindford Hants 27 F3
Lindley W York 90 B1
Lindley Green N York 90 C4
Lindow End Ches 82 C2
Lindridge Worcs 57 G2
Lindsell Essex 51 G3
Lindsey Suffk 52 C5
Lindsey Tye Suffk 52 C5
Liney Somset 23 F3
Linford Essex 29 G4
Linford Hants 13 F5
Lingbob W York 90 B3
Lingdale N York 107 F2
Lingen Herefs 56 D2
Lingfield Surrey 17 E6
Lingley Green Ches 81 H4
Lingwood Norfk 65 F6
Linicro Highld 150 D5
Linkend Worcs 46 D2
Linkenholt Hants 26 B5
Linkhill Kent 18 B4
Linkinhorne Cnwll 5 G3
Linktown Fife 132 B4
Linkwood Moray 156 D5
Linley Shrops 56 D5
Linley Green Herefs 46 C4
Linleygreen Shrops 57 G5
Linlithgow W Loth 131 F3
Linshiels Nthumb 113 F5
Linsidemore Highld 162 B4

Linslade
Llangelynin
297

Linslade Beds 49 G2
Linstead Parva Suffk 65 F3
Linstock Cumb 104 A6
Linthurst Worcs 58 C3
Linthwaite W York 90 B1
Lintlaw Border 123 E5
Lintmill Moray 157 G6
Linton Border 123 E2
Linton Cambs 51 F5
Linton Derbys 71 H2
Linton Herefs 46 B2
Linton Kent 30 A1
Linton N York 90 A6
Linton Nthumb 114 D5
Linton W York 91 E4
Linton Heath Derbys 71 H2
Linton Hill Gloucs 46 B2
Linton-on-Ouse N York 91 F6
Linwood Hants 13 F5
Linwood Lincs 86 B3
Linwood Rens 129 F2
Lionacleit W Isls 168 b4
Lional W Isls 168 f9
Lions Green E Susx 17 F3
Liphook Hants 27 F2
Lipley Shrops 70 B3
Liscard Mersyd 81 E4
Liscombe Somset 22 B2
Liskeard Cnwll 5 F2
Liss Hants 27 F2
Liss Forest Hants 27 F2
Lissett E R Yk 93 E5
Lissington Lincs 86 B3
Liston Essex 52 B5
Lisvane Cardif 36 C2
Liswerry Newpt 36 D3
Litcham Norfk 76 B2
Litchard Brdgnd 35 F2
Litchborough Nhants 48 D5
Litchfield Hants 26 C5
Litherland Mersyd 81 F4
Litlington Cambs 50 D5
Litlington E Susx 17 F1
Little Abington Cambs 51 F6
Little Addington Nhants 61 F3
Little Airies D & G 101 E5
Little Almshoe Herts 50 C3
Little Alne Warwks 47 G5
Little Altcar Mersyd 81 E5
Little Amwell Herts 50 D2
Little Asby Cumb 95 H6
Little Aston Staffs 58 D5
Little Atherfield IOW 14 C2
Little Ayton N York 107 E2
Little Baddow Essex 52 A1
Little Badminton Gloucs 38 C3
Little Bampton Cumb 103 G6
Little Bardfield Essex 51 G4
Little Barford Beds 61 H1
Little Barningham Norfk 76 D3
Little Barrington Gloucs 39 G5
Little Barrow Ches 81 G2
Little Barugh N York 98 C3
Little Bavington Nthumb 113 G3
Little Bayton Warwks 59 F4
Little Bealings Suffk 53 F5
Little Bedwyn Wilts 26 A6
Little Bentley Essex 53 E5
Little Berkhamsted Herts 50 D1
Little Billing Nhants 49 F5
Little Billington Beds 49 G1
Little Birch Herefs 45 H2
Little Bispham Lancs 88 B4
Little Blakenham Suffk 53 E6
Little Blencow Cumb 104 A3
Little Bloxwich W Mids 58 C6
Little Bognor W Susx 16 A3
Little Bolehill Derbys 71 H5
Little Bollington Ches 82 B3
Little Bookham Surrey 28 B1
Little Bourton Oxon 48 C4
Little Bowden Leics 60 C4
Little Bradley Suffk 51 H6
Little Brampton Herefs 45 F5
Little Brampton Shrops 56 D3
Little Braxted Essex 52 B2
Little Brechin Angus 141 F6
Little Brickhill Bucks 49 G2
Little Bridgeford Staffs 70 D3
Little Brington Nhants 60 C2
Little Bromley Essex 52 D4
Little Broughton Cumb 103 E3
Little Budworth Ches 82 A1
Little Burstead Essex 29 G5
Little Bytham Lincs 73 H2
Little Canfield Essex 51 G3
Little Carlton Lincs 86 D3
Little Carlton Notts 73 E6
Little Casterton Rutlnd 73 H1
Little Catwick E R Yk 93 E4
Little Catworth Cambs 61 G3
Little Cawthorpe Lincs 86 D3
Little Chalfield Wilts 24 D6
Little Chalfont Bucks 41 H4
Little Charlinch Somset 23 E3
Little Chart Kent 18 C6
Little Chesterford Essex 51 F5
Little Cheveney Kent 17 H6
Little Cheverell Wilts 25 E5
Little Chishill Cambs 51 E4
Little Clacton Essex 53 E3
Little Clanfield Oxon 39 G4
Little Clifton Cumb 103 E3
Little Coates Lincs 86 C6
Little Comberton Worcs 47 E3
Little Common E Susx 17 H2
Little Comp Kent 29 G2
Little Compton Warwks 47 H2
Little Corby Cumb 104 B6
Little Cornard Suffk 52 C5
Little Cowarne Herefs 46 B4
Little Coxwell Oxon 39 G4
Little Crakehall N York 97 F4
Little Cransley Nhants 60 D3
Little Cressingham Norfk 64 A5
Little Crosby Mersyd 81 E5
Little Crosthwaite Cumb 103 F3
Little Cubley Derbys 71 F4
Little Dalby Leics 73 E1
Little Dens Abers 159 F3
Little Dewchurch Herefs 45 H2
Little Ditton Cambs 63 F1
Little Doward Herefs 37 F6
Little Downham Cambs 62 D4
Little Driffield E R Yk 92 D5
Little Dunham Norfk 76 B1
Little Dunkeld P & K 139 G4
Little Dunmow Essex 51 G3
Little Durnford Wilts 25 G3
Little Easton Essex 51 G3
Little Eaton Derbys 72 A4
Little Ellingham Norfk 64 C5
Little Elm Somset 24 C4
Little Everdon Nhants 48 D5
Little Eversden Cambs 51 E6
Little Faringdon Oxon 39 G4
Little Fencote N York 97 F4
Little Fenton N York 91 F3
Little Fransham Norfk 76 B1
Little Gaddesden Herts 41 H6
Little Garway Herefs 45 G2
Little Gidding Cambs 61 G4
Little Glemham Suffk 65 F1
Little Gorsley Herefs 46 B2
Little Gransden Cambs 62 B1
Little Green Notts 73 E4
Little Green Somset 24 C4
Little Grimsby Lincs 86 D4
Little Gringley Notts 85 E3
Little Habton N York 98 C3
Little Hadham Herts 51 E3
Little Hale Lincs 74 B4
Little Hallam Derbys 72 B4
Little Hallingbury Essex 51 F2
Little Hanford Dorset 12 B6
Little Harrowden Nhants 61 E2
Little Haseley Oxon 41 E4
Little Hatfield E R Yk 93 E4
Little Hautbois Norfk 77 E2
Little Haven Pembks 32 C3
Little Hay Staffs 58 D6
Little Hayfield Derbys 83 E3
Little Haywood Staffs 71 E2
Little Heath Berks 41 E2
Little Heath Staffs 70 D2
Little Heath W Mids 59 F4
Little Hereford Herefs 57 F2
Little Hermitage Kent 29 H3
Little Horkesley Essex 52 C4
Little Hormead Herts 51 E4
Little Horsted E Susx 17 F3
Little Horton W York 90 C3
Little Horton Wilts 25 F5
Little Horwood Bucks 49 F2
Little Houghton Nhants 49 F5
Little Houghton S York 84 B5
Little Hucklow Derbys 83 F2
Little Hulton Gt Man 82 B5
Little Hungerford Berks 40 C2
Little Hutton N York 97 H2
Little Ingestre Staffs 71 E2
Little Irchester Nhants 61 E2
Little Kelk E R Yk 93 E5
Little Keyford Somset 24 C4
Little Kimble Bucks 41 F5
Little Kineton Warwks 48 B4
Little Kingshill Bucks 41 G4
Little Knox D & G 102 B6
Little Langdale Cumb 94 D5
Little Langford Wilts 25 F3
Little Lashbrook Devon 20 D1
Little Laver Essex 51 F2
Little Leigh Ches 82 A2
Little Leighs Essex 51 H2
Little Lever Gt Man 82 C5
Little Linford Bucks 49 G4
Little Linton Cambs 51 F5
Little Load Somset 23 G2
Little London Bucks 41 E5
Little London Cambs 62 C5
Little London E Susx 17 F3
Little London Essex 51 F4
Little London Essex 51 H4
Little London Gloucs 46 C1
Little London Hants 26 B4
Little London Hants 26 D5
Little London Lincs 74 C2
Little London Lincs 86 D2
Little London Lincs 75 E2
Little London Norfk 75 F2
Little London Powys 55 H4
Little London W York 90 C3
Little Longstone Derbys 83 G2
Little Madeley Staffs 70 C5
Little Malvern Worcs 46 C3
Little Mancot Flints 81 E1
Little Maplestead Essex 52 B4
Little Marcle Herefs 46 B3
Little Marland Devon 21 E2
Little Marlow Bucks 41 G3
Little Massingham Norfk 76 A2
Little Melton Norfk 64 D6
Little Mill Mons 36 D5
Little Milton Oxon 40 D4
Little Missenden Bucks 41 G4
Little Mongeham Kent 31 G1
Little Moor Somset 23 F2
Little Musgrave Cumb 104 D1
Little Ness Shrops 69 F2
Little Neston Ches 81 E2
Little Newcastle Pembks 32 D5
Little Newsham Dur 105 H2
Little Norton Somset 11 E6
Little Norton Staffs 58 C6
Little Oakley Essex 53 F4
Little Oakley Nhants 61 E4
Little Odell Beds 49 H5
Little Offley Herts 50 B3
Little Onn Staffs 70 C2
Little Ormside Cumb 104 D2
Little Orton Cumb 103 G6
Little Ouse Cambs 63 E4
Little Ouseburn N York 91 F6
Little Oxendon Nhants 60 C4
Little Packington Warwks 59 E4
Little Pattenden Kent 18 A6
Little Paxton Cambs 61 H2
Little Petherick Cnwll 4 C3
Little Plumpton Lancs 88 B3
Little Plumstead Norfk 77 F1
Little Ponton Lincs 73 G3
Little Posbrook Hants 14 D4
Little Potheridge Devon 21 E2
Little Preston Nhants 48 D5
Little Preston W York 91 E3
Little Raveley Cambs 62 B3
Little Reedness E R Yk 92 B2
Little Ribston N York 91 E5
Little Rissington Gloucs 47 G1
Little Rollright Oxon 48 A2
Little Rowsley Derbys 83 G1
Little Ryburgh Norfk 76 C3
Little Ryle Nthumb 124 C2
Little Ryton Shrops 57 E6
Little Salkeld Cumb 104 B4
Little Sampford Essex 51 G4
Little Sandhurst Berks 27 F5
Little Saredon Staffs 58 B6
Little Saughall Ches 81 F1
Little Saxham Suffk 63 G2
Little Scatwell Highld 154 B5
Little Sessay N York 97 H2
Little Shelford Cambs 51 E6
Little Silver Devon 9 E5
Little Silver Devon 9 F6
Little Singleton Lancs 88 B3
Little Skipwith N York 91 H3
Little Smeaton N York 91 F1
Little Snoring Norfk 76 C3
Little Sodbury Gloucs 38 B2
Little Sodbury End Gloucs 38 B3
Little Somborne Hants 26 B2
Little Somerford Wilts 38 D3
Little Soudley Shrops 70 B3
Little Stainforth N York 96 A1
Little Stainton Dur 106 C3
Little Stanney Ches 81 F2
Little Staughton Beds 61 G2
Little Steeping Lincs 87 E1
Little Stonham Suffk 64 D1
Little Stretton Leics 60 C5
Little Stretton Shrops 57 E5
Little Strickland Cumb 104 B2
Little Stukeley Cambs 62 A3
Little Sugnall Staffs 70 C3
Little Sutton Ches 81 F2
Little Sutton Shrops 57 E4
Little Swinburne Nthumb 113 G2
Little Sypland D & G 102 A5
Little Tew Oxon 48 B2
Little Tey Essex 52 C3
Little Thetford Cambs 63 E3
Little Thirkleby N York 97 H3
Little Thornage Norfk 76 D4
Little Thornton Lancs 88 B4
Little Thorpe Dur 106 D5
Little Thurlow Suffk 51 H6
Little Thurlow Green Suffk 51 H6
Little Thurrock Essex 29 G4
Little Torrington Devon 21 E2
Little Totham Essex 52 B2
Little Town Ches 82 A4
Little Town Cumb 103 F2
Little Town Lancs 89 E3
Little Twycross Leics 59 F6
Little Urswick Cumb 94 C2
Little Wakering Essex 30 C5
Little Walden Essex 51 F5
Little Waldingfield Suffk 52 C5
Little Walsingham Norfk 76 B4
Little Waltham Essex 51 H2
Little Warley Essex 29 G5
Little Washbourne Gloucs 47 E2
Little Weighton E R Yk 92 D3
Little Weldon Nhants 61 E4
Little Welnetham Suffk 64 A1
Little Welton Lincs 86 C3
Little Wenham Suffk 52 D5
Little Wenlock Shrops 57 G6
Little Weston Somset 24 B2
Little Whitefield IOW 14 D2
Little Whittington Nthumb 113 G2
Little Wilbraham Cambs 63 E1
Little Witcombe Gloucs 38 D6
Little Witley Worcs 57 H2
Little Wittenham Oxon 40 D4
Little Wolford Warwks 47 H3
Little Woodcote Surrey 28 D2
Little Wratting Suffk 51 H5
Little Wymington Beds 61 E2
Little Wymondley Herts 50 C3
Little Wyrley Staffs 58 C6
Little Wytheford Shrops 69 H2
Little Yeldham Essex 52 A5
Littlebeck N York 98 D5
Littleborough Devon 9 E6
Littleborough Gt Man 89 H1
Littleborough Notts 85 F3
Littlebourne Kent 31 F2
Littlebredy Dorset 11 F3
Littleburn Highld 155 E4
Littlebury Essex 51 F5
Littlebury Green Essex 51 F5
Littlecott Wilts 25 G4
Littledean Gloucs 38 B6
Littledown Hants 26 B5
Littleham Devon 21 E3
Littleham Devon 9 G3
Littlehampton W Susx 16 A2
Littleharle Tower Nthumb 113 G3
Littlehaven W Susx 16 C5
Littlehempston Devon 7 E4
Littlehoughton Nthumb 125 E3
Littlemill Abers 147 H4
Littlemill Highld 155 G4
Littlemoor Derbys 84 A1
Littlemore Oxon 40 D5
Littleover Derbys 72 A3
Littleport Cambs 63 E4
Littleport Bridge Cambs 63 E4
Littler Ches 82 A1
Littlestone-on-Sea Kent 18 D4
Littlethorpe Leics 60 B5
Littlethorpe N York 97 F2
Littleton Angus 140 C5
Littleton Ches 81 G1
Littleton D & G 101 G6
Littleton Dorset 12 C5
Littleton Hants 26 C2
Littleton Somset 23 H2
Littleton Somset 24 A6
Littleton Surrey 27 H4
Littleton Surrey 28 B3
Littleton Drew Wilts 38 C2
Littleton Pannell Wilts 25 E5
Littleton-on-Severn Gloucs 37 G3
Littletown Dur 106 C5
Littletown IOW 14 D3
Littlewick Green Berks 41 F2
Littlewindsor Dorset 11 E5
Littlewood Staffs 58 C6
Littleworth Bucks 49 G1
Littleworth Oxon 40 A4
Littleworth Staffs 70 D2
Littleworth Staffs 71 E1
Littleworth W Susx 16 C3
Littleworth Worcs 46 D4
Littleworth Worcs 58 C2
Littleworth Common Bucks 41 G3
Littleworth End Cambs 62 B2
Littley Green Essex 51 H2
Litton Derbys 83 G2
Litton N York 96 B2
Litton Somset 24 B5
Litton Cheney Dorset 11 F4
Liurbost W Isls 168 e8
Liverpool Mersyd 81 F4
Liverpool Airport Mersyd 81 F3
Liversedge W York 90 C2
Liverton Devon 9 E2
Liverton N York 107 F2
Liverton Mines N York 107 F3
Liverton Street Kent 30 B1
Livingston W Loth 131 G2
Livingston Village W Loth 131 G2
Lixton Devon 6 D3
Lixwm Flints 80 D2
Lizard Cnwll 3 E1
Llaingoch IOA 78 B3
Llaithddu Powys 56 A3
Llan Powys 55 F5
Llan-y-pwll Wrexhm 69 F5
Llanaber Gwynd 67 F2
Llanaelhaearn Gwynd 66 C4
Llanafan Cerdgn 54 D3
Llanafan-fechan Powys 44 C4
Llanallgo IOA 79 E3
Llanarmon Gwynd 66 D4
Llanarmon Dyffryn Ceiriog Wrexhm 68 D3
Llanarmon-yn-lal Denbgs 68 D6
Llanarth Cerdgn 42 D5
Llanarth Mons 37 E5
Llanarthne Carmth 43 E1
Llanasa Flints 80 C3
Llanbabo IOA 78 C3
Llanbadarn Fawr Cerdgn 54 D3
Llanbadarn Fynydd Powys 56 A3
Llanbadarn-y-garreg Powys 44 D4
Llanbadoc Mons 37 E4
Llanbadrig IOA 78 C4
Llanbeder Newpt 37 E3
Llanbedr Gwynd 67 E3
Llanbedr Powys 44 D4
Llanbedr Powys 45 E1
Llanbedr-Dyffryn-Clwyd Denbgs 68 D6
Llanbedr-y-Cennin Conwy 79 G2
Llanbedrgoch IOA 79 E3
Llanbedrog Gwynd 66 C3
Llanberis Gwynd 67 E6
Llanbethery V Glam 36 B1
Llanbister Powys 56 A3
Llanblethian V Glam 35 G2
Llanboidy Carmth 33 F4
Llanbradach Caerph 36 C3
Llanbrynmair Powys 55 F6
Llancadle V Glam 36 B1
Llancarfan V Glam 36 B1
Llancayo Mons 37 E5
Llancillo Herefs 45 F2
Llancloudy Herefs 45 H1
Llancynfelyn Cerdgn 54 D5
Llandaff Cardif 36 C2
Llandanwg Gwynd 67 E3
Llandawke Carmth 33 G3
Llanddanielfab IOA 79 E2
Llanddarog Carmth 34 C6
Llanddeiniol Cerdgn 54 C2
Llanddeiniolen Gwynd 79 E1
Llandderfel Gwynd 68 B4
Llanddeusant Carmth 43 H2
Llanddeusant IOA 78 C3
Llanddew Powys 44 C2
Llanddewi Swans 34 B3
Llanddewi Brefi Cerdgn 43 G5
Llanddewi Rhydderch Mons 37 E6
Llanddewi Velfrey Pembks 33 F3
Llanddewi Ystradenni Powys 56 A2
Llanddewi'r Cwm Powys 44 C4
Llanddoget Conwy 79 G1
Llanddona IOA 79 E3
Llanddowror Carmth 33 G3
Llanddulas Conwy 80 A2
Llanddwywe Gwynd 67 E2
Llanddyfnan IOA 79 E2
Llandecwyn Gwynd 67 F4
Llandefaelog Powys 44 C2
Llandefaelog-Trer-Graig Powys 44 D2
Llandefalle Powys 44 D3
Llandegfan IOA 79 E2
Llandegla Denbgs 68 D5
Llandegley Powys 56 B2
Llandegveth Mons 36 D4
Llandegwning Gwynd 66 B3
Llandeilo Carmth 43 F1
Llandeilo Graban Powys 44 D4
Llandeilo'r Fan Powys 44 B3
Llandeloy Pembks 32 C4
Llandenny Mons 37 E5
Llandevaud Newpt 37 E3
Llandevenny Mons 37 E3
Llandinabo Herefs 45 H2
Llandinam Powys 55 H4
Llandissilio Pembks 33 E4
Llandogo Mons 37 F5
Llandough V Glam 35 G1
Llandough V Glam 36 C1
Llandovery Carmth 43 H3
Llandow V Glam 35 G2
Llandre Carmth 43 G3
Llandre Cerdgn 54 D4
Llandre Isaf Pembks 33 E4
Llandrillo Denbgs 68 C4
Llandrillo-yn-Rhos Conwy 79 H3
Llandrindod Wells Powys 44 C5
Llandrinio Powys 69 E2
Llandudno Conwy 79 G3
Llandudno Junction Conwy 79 G2
Llandudwen Gwynd 66 B4
Llandulas Powys 44 B3
Llandwrog Gwynd 66 D6
Llandybie Carmth 34 D6
Llandyfaelog Carmth 34 B5
Llandyfan Carmth 34 D6
Llandyfriog Cerdgn 42 C3
Llandyfrydog IOA 78 D3
Llandygai Gwynd 79 F2
Llandygwydd Cerdgn 42 C4
Llandynan Denbgs 68 D5
Llandyrnog Denbgs 80 C1
Llandyssil Powys 56 B5
Llandysul Cerdgn 42 D3
Llanedeyrn Cardif 36 C2
Llanedi Carmth 34 C5
Llaneglwys Powys 44 C3
Llanegryn Gwynd 54 D6
Llanegwad Carmth 43 E1
Llaneilian IOA 78 D4
Llanelian-yn-Rhos Conwy 80 A2
Llanelidan Denbgs 68 C5
Llanelieu Powys 45 E3
Llanellen Mons 36 D5
Llanelli Carmth 34 C4
Llanelltyd Gwynd 67 G2
Llanelly Mons 36 C6
Llanelwedd Powys 44 C4
Llanenddwyn Gwynd 67 E2
Llanengan Gwynd 66 C3
Llanerch Gwynd 68 A2
Llanerch Powys 56 C5
Llanerchymedd IOA 78 D3
Llanerfyl Powys 68 C1
Llanfachraeth IOA 78 C3
Llanfachreth Gwynd 67 G2
Llanfaelog IOA 78 C2
Llanfaelrhys Gwynd 66 B3
Llanfaenor Mons 37 E6
Llanfaes IOA 79 F2
Llanfaes Powys 44 C2
Llanfaethlu IOA 78 C3
Llanfair Gwynd 67 E3
Llanfair Caereinion Powys 56 A6
Llanfair Clydogau Cerdgn 43 F4
Llanfair Dyffryn Clwyd Denbgs 68 D6
Llanfair Kilgeddin Mons 37 E5
Llanfair P G IOA 79 E2
Llanfair Talhaiarn Conwy 80 B2
Llanfair Waterdine Shrops 56 C3
Llanfair-is-gaer Gwynd 79 E1
Llanfair-Nant-Gwyn Pembks 42 B3
Llanfair-y-Cwmwd IOA 78 D1
Llanfair-yn-Neubwll IOA 78 C2
Llanfairfechan Conwy 79 F2
Llanfairynghornwy IOA 78 C4
Llanfallteg Carmth 33 F4
Llanfallteg West Carmth 33 F4
Llanfarian Cerdgn 54 C3
Llanfechain Powys 68 D2
Llanfechell IOA 78 C4
Llanferres Denbgs 68 D6
Llanfflewyn IOA 78 C4
Llanfigael IOA 78 C3
Llanfihangel Glyn Myfyr Conwy 68 B5
Llanfihangel Nant Bran Powys 44 B3
Llanfihangel Rhydithon Powys 56 B2
Llanfihangel Rogiet Mons 37 F3
Llanfihangel Tal-y-llyn Powys 44 D2
Llanfihangel yn Nhowyn IOA 78 C2
Llanfihangel-ar-Arth Carmth 43 E3
Llanfihangel-nant-Melan Powys 45 E5
Llanfihangel-uwch-Gwili Carmth 43 E1
Llanfihangel-y-Creuddyn Cerdgn 54 D3
Llanfihangel-y-pennant Gwynd 67 E4
Llanfihangel-y-pennant Gwynd 67 F1
Llanfihangel-y-traethau Gwynd 67 E3
Llanfihangel-yng-Ngwynfa Powys 68 C2
Llanfilo Powys 44 D2
Llanfoist Mons 36 D6
Llanfor Gwynd 68 B4
Llanfrechfa Torfn 36 D4
Llanfrothen Gwynd 67 F4
Llanfrynach Powys 44 D2
Llanfwrog Denbgs 68 C6
Llanfwrog IOA 78 C3
Llanfyllin Powys 68 D2
Llanfynydd Carmth 43 F2
Llanfynydd Flints 69 E6
Llanfyrnach Pembks 42 B2
Llangadfan Powys 68 B1
Llangadog Carmth 34 B5
Llangadog Carmth 43 G2
Llangadwaladr IOA 78 C2
Llangadwaladr Powys 68 D3
Llangaffo IOA 78 D1
Llangain Carmth 34 A6
Llangammarch Wells Powys 44 B4
Llangan V Glam 35 G2
Llangarron Herefs 45 H1
Llangasty-Talyllyn Powys 44 D2
Llangathen Carmth 43 F1
Llangattock Powys 36 C6
Llangattock Lingoed Mons 45 F1
Llangattock-Vibon-Avel Mons 37 F6
Llangedwyn Powys 68 D2
Llangefni IOA 78 D2
Llangeinor Brdgnd 35 G3
Llangeinwen IOA 78 D1
Llangeitho Cerdgn 43 F5
Llangeler Carmth 42 D3
Llangelynin Gwynd 54 C6

Llangendeirne
Lower Green

Llangendeirne Carmth 34 B6
Llangennech Carmth 34 C4
Llangennith Swans 34 B3
Llangenny Powys 36 D6
Llangernyw Conwy 80 A1
Llangian Gwynd 66 C3
Llangiwg Neath 35 E5
Llangloffan Pembks 32 C5
Llanglydwen Carmth 33 F4
Llangoed IOA 79 F3
Llangoedmor Cerdgn 42 B4
Llangollen Denbgs 68 D4
Llangolman Pembks 33 E4
Llangors Powys 44 D2
Llangovan Mons 37 F5
Llangower Gwynd 68 A3
Llangranog Cerdgn 42 C5
Llangristiolus IOA 78 D2
Llangrove Herefs 45 H1
Llangua Mons 45 G2
Llangunllo Powys 56 B2
Llangunnor Carmth 42 D1
Llangurig Powys 55 G3
Llangwm Conwy 68 B4
Llangwm Mons 37 E4
Llangwm Pembks 32 D3
Llangwm-isaf Mons 37 E4
Llangwnnadl Gwynd 66 B3
Llangwyfan Denbgs 80 C1
Llangwyllog IOA 78 D3
Llangwyryfon Cerdgn 54 D2
Llangybi Cerdgn 43 F4
Llangybi Gwynd 66 D4
Llangybi Mons 37 E4
Llangyfelach Swans 34 D4
Llangynhafal Denbgs 80 D1
Llangynidr Powys 44 D1
Llangynin Carmth 33 G4
Llangynllo Cerdgn 42 D4
Llangynog Carmth 33 G3
Llangynog Powys 68 C3
Llangynog Powys 44 C4
Llangynwyd Brdgnd 35 F3
Llanhamlach Powys 44 D2
Llanharan Rhondd 35 G3
Llanharry Rhondd 35 G2
Llanhennock Mons 37 E3
Llanhilleth Blae G 36 C4
Llanidan IOA 78 D1
Llanidloes Powys 55 G4
Llaniestyn Gwynd 66 B3
Llanigon Powys 45 E3
Llanilar Cerdgn 54 D3
Llanilid Rhondd 35 G2
Llanina Cerdgn 42 D5
Llanio Cerdgn 43 F5
Llanishen Cardif 36 C2
Llanishen Mons 37 F5
Llanllechid Gwynd 79 F1
Llanlleonfel Powys 44 B4
Llanllowell Mons 37 E4
Llanllugan Powys 55 H6
Llanllwch Carmth 42 D1
Llanllwchaiarn Powys 56 B5
Llanllwni Carmth 43 E3
Llanllyfni Gwynd 66 D5
Llanmadoc Swans 34 B4
Llanmaes V Glam 35 G1
Llanmartin Newpt 37 E3
Llanmerewig Powys 56 B5
Llanmihangel V Glam 35 G1
Llanmiloe Carmth 33 G2
Llanmorlais Swans 34 C4
Llannefydd Conwy 80 B2
Llannon Carmth 34 C5
Llannor Gwynd 66 C4
Llanon Cerdgn 54 C2
Llanover Mons 36 D5
Llanpumsaint Carmth 42 D2
Llanrhaeadr-ym-Mochnant Powys 68 D3
Llanrhian Pembks 32 B5
Llanrhidian Swans 34 B3
Llanrhos Conwy 79 G3
Llanrhychwyn Conwy 67 G6
Llanrhyddlad IOA 78 C4
Llanrhystud Cerdgn 54 C2
Llanrothal Herefs 45 G1
Llanrug Gwynd 79 E1
Llanrumney Cardif 36 C2
Llanrwst Conwy 67 G6
Llansadurnen Carmth 33 G3
Llansadwrn Carmth 43 G2
Llansadwrn IOA 79 E2
Llansaint Carmth 34 A5
Llansamlet Swans 34 D4
Llansanffraid Glan Conwy Conwy 79 G2
Llansannan Conwy 80 B1
Llansannor V Glam 35 G2
Llansantffraed Powys 44 D1
Llansantffraed-Cwmdeuddwr Powys 55 G2
Llansantffraed-in-Elvel Powys 44 D5
Llansantffraid Cerdgn 54 C2
Llansantffraid-ym-Mechain Powys 68 D2
Llansawel Carmth 43 F3
Llansilin Powys 68 D3
Llansoy Mons 37 E4
Llanspyddid Powys 44 C2
Llanstadwell Pembks 32 D2
Llansteffan Carmth 33 H3
Llanstephan Powys 44 D3
Llantarnam Torfn 36 D4
Llanteg Pembks 33 F3
Llanthewy Skirrid Mons 37 E6
Llanthony Mons 45 F2
Llantilio Pertholey Mons 36 D6
Llantilio-Crossenny Mons 37 E6
Llantrisant IOA 78 C3
Llantrisant Mons 37 E4
Llantrisant Rhondd 36 B3
Llantrithyd V Glam 36 B1
Llantwit Fardre Rhondd 36 B3
Llantwit Major V Glam 35 G1
Llantysilio Denbgs 68 D4
Llanuwchllyn Gwynd 68 A3
Llanvaches Newpt 37 E3
Llanvair Discoed Mons 37 E3
Llanvapley Mons 37 E6
Llanvetherine Mons 37 E6
Llanveynoe Herefs 45 F2
Llanvihangel Crucorney Mons 45 F1
Llanvihangel Gobion Mons 37 E5
Llanvihangel-Ystern-Llewern Mons 37 E6
Llanwarne Herefs 45 H2
Llanwddyn Powys 68 C2
Llanwenarth Mons 36 D6
Llanwenog Cerdgn 43 E4
Llanwern Newpt 37 E3
Llanwinio Carmth 33 G4
Llanwnda Gwynd 66 D6
Llanwnda Pembks 32 D6
Llanwnnen Cerdgn 43 E4
Llanwnog Powys 55 H5
Llanwonno Rhondd 36 A4
Llanwrda Carmth 43 G2
Llanwrin Powys 55 E6
Llanwrthwl Powys 55 G2
Llanwrtyd Powys 44 B4
Llanwrtyd Wells Powys 44 B4
Llanwyddelan Powys 56 A5
Llanyblodwel Shrops 69 E2
Llanybri Carmth 33 G3
Llanybydder Carmth 43 E4
Llanycefn Pembks 33 E4
Llanychaer Bridge Pembks 32 D5
Llanycrwys Carmth 43 F4
Llanymawddwy Gwynd 68 A2
Llanymynech Powys 69 E2
Llanynghenedl IOA 78 C3
Llanynys Denbgs 80 C1
Llanyre Powys 44 C5
Llanystumdwy Gwynd 66 D4
Llanywern Powys 44 D2
Llawhaden Pembks 33 E3
Llawnt Shrops 69 E3
Llawryglyn Powys 55 G4
Llay Wrexhm 69 F6
Llechcynfarwy IOA 78 C3
Llechfaen Powys 44 D2
Llechrhyd Caerph 36 B5
Llechryd Cerdgn 42 B4
Llechylched IOA 78 C2
Lledrod Cerdgn 54 D2
Llidiardau Gwynd 68 A4
Llidiart-y-parc Denbgs 68 C4
Llidiartnenog Carmth 43 E3
Llithfaen Gwynd 66 C4
Lloc Flints 80 D2
Llong Flints 81 E1
Llowes Powys 45 E3
Llwydcoed Rhondd 35 G5
Llwydiarth Powys 68 C2
Llwyn Denbgs 80 C1
Llwyn-drain Pembks 42 C3
Llwyn-du Mons 36 D6
Llwyn-on Myr Td 35 G5
Llwyn-y-brain Carmth 33 F3
Llwyn-y-groes Cerdgn 43 F5
Llwyncelyn Cerdgn 43 E5
Llwyndafydd Cerdgn 42 D5
Llwynderw Powys 56 B6
Llwyndyrys Gwynd 66 C4
Llwyngwril Gwynd 67 E1
Llwynhendy Carmth 34 C4
Llwynmawr Wrexhm 69 E4
Llwynypia Rhondd 35 G4
Llyn-y-pandy Flints 80 D1
Llynclys Shrops 69 E2
Llynfaes IOA 78 D2
Llys-y-fran Pembks 33 E4
Llysfaen Conwy 80 A2
Llyswen Cerdgn 43 E5
Llyswen Powys 44 D3
Llysworney V Glam 35 G2
Llywel Powys 44 B2
Load Brook S York 83 H3
Loan Falk 131 F3
Loanend Nthumb 123 G4
Loanhead Mdloth 132 B2
Loaningfoot D & G 102 D6
Loans S Ayrs 119 E3
Lobb Devon 21 E4
Lobhillcross Devon 8 B3
Loch Baghasdail W Isls 168 b2
Loch Euphoirt W Isls 168 b5
Loch Katrine Pier Stirlg 129 F6
Loch Maree Hotel Highld 152 C6
Loch nam Madadh W Isls 168 c5
Lochailort Highld 143 G2
Lochaline Highld 136 A4
Lochans D & G 100 B6
Locharbriggs D & G 110 D3
Lochavich Ag & B 136 D1
Lochawe Ag & B 137 F2
Lochboisdale W Isls 168 b2
Lochbuie Ag & B 135 H2
Lochcarron Highld 152 C3
Lochdon Ag & B 136 B3
Lochdonhead Ag & B 136 B3
Lochead Ag & B 127 F3
Lochearnhead Stirlg 138 C2
Lochee Dund C 140 D3
Locheilside Station Highld 144 B2
Lochend Highld 154 D3
Locheport W Isls 168 b5
Lochfoot D & G 110 C2
Lochgair Ag & B 127 H4
Lochgelly Fife 131 H4
Lochgilphead Ag & B 127 G4
Lochgoilhead Ag & B 128 C5
Lochieheads Fife 140 C1
Lochill Moray 157 E5
Lochindorb Lodge Highld 156 B3
Lochinver Highld 161 E6
Lochluichart Highld 153 G5
Lochmaben D & G 111 E3
Lochmaddy W Isls 168 c5
Lochore Fife 131 H5
Lochranza N Ayrs 118 A4
Lochside Abers 141 G6
Lochside D & G 110 D2
Lochside Highld 155 F4
Lochton S Ayrs 108 D3
Lochty Angus 141 E6
Lochty Fife 132 D6
Lochuisge Highld 136 C5
Lochwinnoch Rens 119 E5
Lochwood D & G 111 E4
Lockengate Cnwll 4 D2
Lockerbie D & G 111 F3
Lockeridge Wilts 25 G6
Lockerley Hants 26 A2
Locking Somset 23 F5
Locking Stumps Ches 82 A4
Lockington E R Yk 92 D4
Lockington Leics 72 B3
Lockleywood Shrops 70 B3
Locks Heath Hants 14 C4
Locksbottom Gt Lon 29 E2
Locksgreen IOW 14 C3
Lockton N York 98 D4
Loddington Leics 60 D6
Loddington Nhants 60 D3
Loddiswell Devon 7 E2
Loddon Norfk 65 F5
Lode Cambs 63 E2
Lode Heath W Mids 58 D3
Loders Dorset 11 E4
Lodge Green W Mids 59 E4
Lodsworth W Susx 27 G1
Lofthouse N York 96 D2
Lofthouse W York 90 D2
Lofthouse Gate W York 90 D2
Loftus N York 107 G3
Logan E Ayrs 119 H1
Loganbeck Cumb 94 C4
Loganlea W Loth 120 D6
Loggerheads Staffs 70 B4
Logie Angus 141 G6
Logie Fife 140 D2
Logie Moray 156 B4
Logie Coldstone Abers 148 B5
Logie Pert Angus 141 F6
Logierait P & K 139 G5
Logierieve Abers 159 E2
Login Carmth 33 F4
Lolworth Cambs 62 C2
Lon-las Swans 35 E4
Lonbain Highld 151 G4
Londesborough E R Yk 92 C4
London Gt Lon 28 D4
London Apprentice Cnwll 3 G5
London Beach Kent 18 B5
London Colney Herts 50 C1
London End Nhants 61 E2
Londonderry N York 97 F4
Londonthorpe Lincs 73 G4
Londubh Highld 160 C2
Lonemore Highld 160 B1
Long Ashton Somset 37 F1
Long Bank Worcs 57 H3
Long Bennington Lincs 73 F4
Long Bredy Dorset 11 F4
Long Buckby Nhants 60 B2
Long Cause Devon 7 E4
Long Clawson Leics 73 E3
Long Common Hants 14 C5
Long Compton Staffs 70 D2
Long Compton Warwks 48 A2
Long Crendon Bucks 41 E5
Long Crichel Dorset 12 D6
Long Ditton Surrey 28 C3
Long Drax N York 91 H2
Long Duckmanton Derbys 84 B2
Long Eaton Derbys 72 C3
Long Green Ches 81 G2
Long Green Worcs 46 D2
Long Hanborough Oxon 40 B6
Long Hedges Lincs 74 D5
Long Itchington Warwks 59 G2
Long Lane Shrops 70 A1
Long Lawford Warwks 59 G3
Long Load Somset 23 G1
Long Marston Herts 41 G6
Long Marston N York 91 F5
Long Marston Warwks 47 G4
Long Marton Cumb 104 C3
Long Meadow End Shrops 56 D4
Long Melford Suffk 52 B5
Long Newnton Gloucs 38 D3
Long Newton E Loth 132 D2
Long Preston N York 89 G5
Long Riston E R Yk 93 E4
Long Sight Gt Man 82 D5
Long Stratton Norfk 64 D5
Long Street Bucks 49 F4
Long Sutton Hants 27 F4
Long Sutton Lincs 75 E2
Long Sutton Somset 23 G2
Long Thurlow Suffk 64 C2
Long Waste Shrops 70 A1
Long Whatton Leics 72 B2
Long Wittenham Oxon 40 D4
Longbenton T & W 114 D2
Longborough Gloucs 47 G2
Longbridge W Mids 58 C3
Longbridge Warwks 59 F2
Longbridge Deverill Wilts 24 D3
Longburgh Cumb 103 G6
Longburton Dorset 11 G6
Longcliffe Derbys 71 G6
Longcombe Devon 7 F4
Longcot Oxon 39 G3
Longcroft Cumb 103 F6
Longcross Surrey 27 H6
Longden Shrops 57 E6
Longden Common Shrops 57 E6
Longdon Staffs 71 F1
Longdon Worcs 46 D3
Longdon Green Staffs 71 F1
Longdon Heath Worcs 46 D3
Longdon upon Tern Shrops 70 A2
Longdown Devon 9 E4
Longdowns Cnwll 3 E3
Longfield Kent 29 G3
Longford Derbys 71 G4
Longford Gloucs 46 D1
Longford Gt Lon 28 A4
Longford Kent 29 F2
Longford Shrops 70 A3
Longford Shrops 70 B2
Longford W Mids 59 F4
Longforgan P & K 140 C3
Longformacus Border 122 D5
Longframlington Nthumb 114 C6
Longham Dorset 12 D4
Longham Norfk 76 B2
Longhaven Abers 159 G3
Longhirst Nthumb 114 D4
Longhope Gloucs 46 B1
Longhope Ork 169 b1
Longhorsley Nthumb 114 C5
Longhoughton Nthumb 125 E2
Longlands Cumb 103 G4
Longlane Derbys 71 G4
Longleat Safari Park Wilts 24 D4
Longlevens Gloucs 46 D1
Longley W York 90 B2
Longley W York 83 F5
Longley Green Worcs 46 C4
Longleys P & K 140 C4
Longmanhill Abers 158 C5
Longmoor Camp Hants 27 F2
Longmorn Moray 156 D5
Longmoss Ches 82 D2
Longnewton Border 122 C2
Longnewton Dur 106 C2
Longney Gloucs 38 B5
Longniddry E Loth 132 C3
Longnor Shrops 57 E5
Longnor Staffs 83 F1
Longparish Hants 26 C4
Longpark Cumb 112 B1
Longridge Lancs 88 D3
Longridge Staffs 70 D1
Longridge W Loth 120 D6
Longriggend N Lans 130 D2
Longrock Cnwll 2 C3
Longsdon Staffs 71 E5
Longshaw Common Gt Man 81 G5
Longside Abers 159 F4
Longslow Shrops 70 B4
Longstanton Cambs 62 C2
Longstock Hants 26 B3
Longstone Pembks 33 F3
Longstowe Cambs 50 D6
Longstreet Wilts 25 G4
Longthorpe Cambs 61 H5
Longthwaite Cumb 104 A2
Longton Lancs 88 C2
Longton Staffs 70 D4
Longtown Cumb 112 A2
Longtown Herefs 45 F2
Longueville Jersey 174 c1
Longville in the Dale Shrops 57 F5
Longwick Bucks 41 F5
Longwitton Nthumb 114 B4
Longwood D & G 102 A6
Longwood Shrops 57 F6
Longwood House Hants 26 D2
Longworth Oxon 40 B4
Longyester E Loth 132 D2
Lonmay Abers 159 F5
Lonmore Highld 150 C3
Looe Cnwll 5 F1
Loose Kent 30 A1
Loosebeare Devon 8 D5
Loosegate Lincs 74 C3
Loosley Row Bucks 41 F4
Lootcherbrae Abers 158 B4
Lopcombe Corner Wilts 25 H3
Lopen Somset 11 E6
Loppington Shrops 69 G3
Lorbottle Nthumb 124 C2
Lordington W Susx 15 F5
Lords Wood Kent 30 A2
Lordsbridge Norfk 75 F1
Lornty P & K 140 B4
Loscoe Derbys 72 B5
Loscombe Dorset 11 E4
Lossiemouth Moray 156 D6
Lost Gardens of Heligan Cnwll 3 G4
Lostford Shrops 70 A3
Lostock Gralam Ches 82 B2
Lostock Green Ches 82 B2
Lostock Hall Lancs 88 D2
Lostock Hall Fold Gt Man 82 B6
Lostock Junction Gt Man 82 B5
Lostwithiel Cnwll 5 E2
Lothbeg Highld 163 F5
Lothersdale N York 89 H4
Lothmore Highld 163 F5
Loudwater Bucks 41 G3
Loughborough Leics 72 C2
Loughor Swans 34 C4
Loughton Bucks 49 F3
Loughton Essex 29 E6
Loughton Shrops 57 F4
Lound Lincs 74 A2
Lound Notts 85 E3
Lound Suffk 65 G5
Lounston Devon 9 E2
Lount Leics 72 B2
Louth Lincs 86 D3
Love Clough Lancs 89 F2
Lovedean Hants 15 E5
Lover Wilts 25 G1
Loversall S York 84 C4
Loves Green Essex 51 G1
Lovesome Hill N York 97 G5
Loveston Pembks 33 E2
Lovington Somset 24 B2
Low Ackworth W York 91 F1
Low Angerton Nthumb 114 C4
Low Barbeth D & G 108 B1
Low Barlings Lincs 86 A2
Low Bell End N York 98 C5
Low Bentham N York 95 G2
Low Biggins Cumb 95 G3
Low Borrowbridge Cumb 95 G5
Low Bradfield S York 83 G4
Low Bradley N York 90 A4
Low Braithwaite Cumb 104 A4
Low Burnham Lincs 85 E5
Low Buston Nthumb 125 E2
Low Catton E R Yk 91 H5
Low Coniscliffe Dur 106 B2
Low Crosby Cumb 104 A6
Low Dinsdale Dur 106 C2
Low Eggborough N York 91 G2
Low Ellington N York 97 E3
Low Fell T & W 114 D1
Low Gartachorrans Stirlg 129 F4
Low Gate Nthumb 113 F1
Low Gettbridge Cumb 104 B6
Low Grantley N York 97 F2
Low Green N York 90 C5
Low Habberley Worcs 58 A3
Low Ham Somset 23 G2
Low Harrogate N York 90 D5
Low Hawsker N York 99 E6
Low Hesket Cumb 104 A5
Low Hill Worcs 58 A3
Low Hutton N York 98 C2
Low Knipe Cumb 104 B2
Low Laithe N York 97 E1
Low Langton Lincs 86 B2
Low Leighton Derbys 83 E3
Low Lorton Cumb 103 E3
Low Marnham Notts 85 F2
Low Middleton Nthumb 124 D5
Low Mill N York 98 B4
Low Moor Lancs 89 F4
Low Moor W York 90 C2
Low Moorsley T & W 106 C5
Low Mowthorpe N York 99 E1
Low Newton Cumb 95 E3
Low Rogerscales Cumb 103 E3
Low Row Cumb 103 F5
Low Row Cumb 103 G4
Low Row Cumb 112 C1
Low Row N York 96 C5
Low Salchrie D & G 108 B1
Low Santon Lincs 85 G6
Low Street Essex 29 G4
Low Street Norfk 77 F2
Low Tharston Norfk 64 D5
Low Torry Fife 131 F4
Low Toynton Lincs 86 C2
Low Valley S York 84 B5
Low Walworth Dur 106 B3
Low Wood Cumb 94 D3
Low Worsall N York 106 C2
Low Wray Cumb 94 D5
Lowbands Gloucs 46 C2
Lowca Cumb 102 D2
Lowdham Notts 72 D5
Lowe Shrops 69 G3
Lowe Hill Staffs 71 E6
Lower Aisholt Somset 23 E3
Lower Ansty Dorset 12 B5
Lower Apperley Gloucs 46 D2
Lower Arncott Oxon 40 D6
Lower Ashton Devon 9 E3
Lower Assendon Oxon 41 F3
Lower Ballam Lancs 88 B3
Lower Barewood Herefs 45 G5
Lower Bartle Lancs 88 C3
Lower Basildon Berks 40 D2
Lower Beeding W Susx 16 C4
Lower Benefield Nhants 61 F4
Lower Bentley Worcs 58 C2
Lower Beobridge Shrops 57 H4
Lower Birchwood Derbys 72 B5
Lower Boddington Nhants 48 C4
Lower Boscaswell Cnwll 2 A3
Lower Bourne Surrey 27 G4
Lower Brailes Warwks 48 A3
Lower Breakish Highld 151 G1
Lower Bredbury Gt Man 82 D4
Lower Broadheath Worcs 46 D5
Lower Brockhampton Manor Herefs 46 B5
Lower Buckenhill Herefs 46 B2
Lower Bullingham Herefs 45 H3
Lower Burgate Hants 13 E6
Lower Burrowton Devon 9 G4
Lower Burton Herefs 45 G5
Lower Caldecote Beds 50 C5
Lower Cam Gloucs 38 B4
Lower Canada Somset 23 F5
Lower Catesby Nhants 48 C5
Lower Chapel Powys 44 C3
Lower Chicksgrove Wilts 25 E2
Lower Chute Wilts 26 A5
Lower Clapton Gt Lon 28 D5
Lower Clent Worcs 58 B3
Lower Clopton Warwks 47 G4
Lower Creedy Devon 9 E5
Lower Crossings Derbys 83 E3
Lower Cumberworth W York 83 G6
Lower Cwmtwrch Powys 35 E5
Lower Darwen Lancs 89 E2
Lower Dean Beds 61 F2
Lower Denby W York 83 G5
Lower Diabaig Highld 152 B5
Lower Dicker E Susx 17 F3
Lower Dinchope Shrops 57 E4
Lower Down Shrops 56 D4
Lower Dunsforth N York 97 G1
Lower Egleton Herefs 46 B4
Lower Elkstone Staffs 71 F6
Lower Ellastone Staffs 71 F4
Lower End Bucks 41 E5
Lower End Bucks 49 G3
Lower End Nhants 49 G5
Lower Everleigh Wilts 25 G5
Lower Exbury Hants 14 B3
Lower Eythorne Kent 31 F1
Lower Failand Somset 37 F2
Lower Farringdon Hants 27 E3
Lower Feltham Gt Lon 28 B3
Lower Fittleworth W Susx 16 A3
Lower Foxdale IOM 174 k3
Lower Frankton Shrops 69 F3
Lower Freystrop Pembks 32 D3
Lower Froyle Hants 27 F4
Lower Gabwell Devon 7 F5
Lower Gledfield Highld 162 C3
Lower Godney Somset 23 G3
Lower Gornal W Mids 58 B4
Lower Gravenhurst Beds 50 B4
Lower Green Gt Man 82 B5
Lower Green Herts 50 C4
Lower Green Herts 51 E4
Lower Green Kent 17 F5
Lower Green Kent 17 G6
Lower Green Nhants 49 F5
Lower Green Norfk 76 C4

Lower Green
Marrick
299

Lower Green Staffs 58 B6
Lower Green Suffk 63 G2
Lower Hacheston Suffk 65 F1
Lower Halliford Surrey 28 B3
Lower Halstock Leigh Dorset 11 F5
Lower Halstow Kent 30 B3
Lower Hamworthy Dorset 12 D4
Lower Hardres Kent 31 E1
Lower Harpton Herefs 45 F5
Lower Hartlip Kent 30 B2
Lower Hartshay Derbys 72 B5
Lower Hartwell Bucks 41 F5
Lower Hatton Staffs 70 C4
Lower Hawthwaite Cumb 94 C4
Lower Hergest Herefs 45 F5
Lower Heyford Oxon 48 C2
Lower Heysham Lancs 88 C6
Lower Higham Kent 29 H3
Lower Holbrook Suffk 53 E4
Lower Hordley Shrops 69 F3
Lower Horncroft W Susx 16 A3
Lower Howsell Worcs 46 C4
Lower Irlam Gt Man 82 B4
Lower Kilburn Derbys 72 A4
Lower Kilcott Gloucs 38 C3
Lower Killeyan Ag & B 116 B5
Lower Kingcombe Dorset 11 F4
Lower Kingswood Surrey 28 C1
Lower Kinnerton Ches 81 F1
Lower Langford Somset 23 G5
Lower Largo Fife 132 C5
Lower Leigh Staffs 71 E4
Lower Lemington Gloucs 47 H3
Lower Llanfadog Powys 55 G2
Lower Lovacott Devon 21 E3
Lower Loxhore Devon 21 F4
Lower Lydbrook Gloucs 37 G6
Lower Lye Herefs 56 D2
Lower Machen Newpt 36 C3
Lower Maes-coed Herefs 45 F2
Lower Mannington Dorset 12 D5
Lower Marston Somset 24 C4
Lower Meend Gloucs 37 G5
Lower Merridge Somset 23 E3
Lower Middleton Cheney Nhants 48 C3
Lower Milton Somset 24 A4
Lower Moor W Mids 47 E4
Lower Morton Gloucs 37 G3
Lower Nazeing Essex 51 E1
Lower Norton Warwks 59 E2
Lower Nyland Dorset 24 C1
Lower Penarth V Glam 36 C1
Lower Penn Staffs 58 B5
Lower Pennington Hants 13 G4
Lower Penwortham Lancs 88 D2
Lower Peover Ches 82 B2
Lower Place Gt Man 82 D6
Lower Pollicott Bucks 41 E6
Lower Quinton Warwks 47 G4
Lower Rainham Kent 30 B3
Lower Raydon Suffk 52 D4
Lower Roadwater Somset 22 C3
Lower Salter Lancs 95 G1
Lower Seagry Wilts 38 D2
Lower Sheering Essex 51 F2
Lower Shelton Beds 49 H3
Lower Shiplake Oxon 41 F2
Lower Shuckburgh Warwks 48 C5
Lower Slaughter Gloucs 47 G1
Lower Soothill W York 90 D2
Lower Soudley Gloucs 38 A5
Lower Standen Kent 19 F5
Lower Stanton St Quintin Wilts 38 D2
Lower Stoke Kent 30 B4
Lower Stone Gloucs 38 B4
Lower Stonnall Staffs 58 D6
Lower Stow Bedon Norfk 64 B5
Lower Street Dorset 12 B4
Lower Street E Susx 17 H3
Lower Street Norfk 77 F4
Lower Street Suffk 52 A6
Lower Street Suffk 53 E6
Lower Stretton Ches 82 A3
Lower Stroud Dorset 11 E4
Lower Sundon Beds 50 A3
Lower Swanwick Hants 14 C5
Lower Swell Gloucs 47 G2
Lower Tadmarton Oxon 48 B3
Lower Tale Devon 10 A5
Lower Tean Staffs 71 E4
Lower Thurlton Norfk 65 G5
Lower Town Cnwll 2 D3
Lower Town Devon 6 D5
Lower Town Herefs 46 B3
Lower Town Pembks 32 D5
Lower Trebullett Cnwll 5 G4
Lower Tregantle Cnwll 5 G1
Lower Treluswell Cnwll 3 E3
Lower Tysoe Warwks 48 B4
Lower Ufford Suffk 53 F6
Lower Upcott Devon 9 F3
Lower Upham Hants 14 C5
Lower Upnor Kent 30 A3
Lower Vexford Somset 22 D3
Lower Walton Ches 82 A3
Lower Waterston Dorset 11 H4
Lower Weare Somset 23 G5
Lower Weedon Nhants 48 D5
Lower Welson Herefs 45 F4
Lower Westmancote Worcs 47 E3
Lower Whatcombe Dorset 12 B5
Lower Whatley Somset 24 C4
Lower Whitley Ches 82 A3
Lower Wick Gloucs 38 B4
Lower Wick Worcs 46 D4
Lower Wield Hants 27 E3
Lower Wigginton Herts 41 G5
Lower Willingdon E Susx 17 G2
Lower Withington Ches 82 C2
Lower Woodend Bucks 41 F3
Lower Woodford Wilts 25 G3
Lower Wraxhall Dorset 11 F5
Lower Wyche Worcs 46 C4
Lower Wyke W York 90 C2
Lowerhouse Lancs 89 F3
Lowesby Leics 60 C6
Lowestoft Suffk 65 H5
Loweswater Cumb 103 E2
Lowfield Heath W Susx 16 D5
Lowgill Cumb 95 G5
Lowgill Lancs 95 G1
Lowick Cumb 94 D3
Lowick Nhants 61 F3
Lowick Nthumb 123 G3
Lowick Bridge Cumb 94 D3
Lowick Green Cumb 94 D3
Lowlands Dur 105 H3
Lowlands Torfn 36 D4
Lowsonford Warwks 59 E2
Lowther Cumb 104 B2
Lowther Castle Cumb 104 B2
Lowthorpe E R Yk 93 E6
Lowton Devon 8 D5
Lowton Gt Man 82 A4
Lowton Somset 23 E1
Lowton Common Gt Man 82 A4
Lowton St Mary's Gt Man 82 A4
Loxbeare Devon 9 F6
Loxhill Surrey 16 A5
Loxhore Devon 21 F4
Loxhore Cott Devon 21 F4
Loxley Warwks 47 H4
Loxley Green Staffs 71 F3
Loxter Herefs 46 C3
Loxton Somset 23 F5
Loxwood W Susx 16 A4
Loyal Lodge Highld 165 G3
Lubenham Leics 60 C4
Lucas Green Surrey 27 G5
Lucasgate Lincs 74 D5
Luccombe Somset 22 B4
Luccombe Village IOW 14 D1
Lucker Nthumb 125 E4
Luckett Cnwll 5 G3
Lucking Street Essex 52 B4
Luckington Wilts 38 C3
Lucknam Wilts 38 C1
Luckwell Bridge Somset 22 B3
Lucott Somset 22 B4
Lucton Herefs 57 E2
Lucy Cross N York 106 B2
Ludag W Isls 168 b2
Ludborough Lincs 86 C4
Ludbrook Devon 6 D3
Ludchurch Pembks 33 F3
Luddenden W York 90 B2
Luddenden Foot W York 90 B2
Luddenham Court Kent 30 D2
Luddesdown Kent 29 G3
Luddington Lincs 92 B1
Luddington Warwks 47 G4
Luddington in the Brook Nhants 61 G4
Ludford Lincs 86 B4
Ludford Shrops 57 E3
Ludgershall Bucks 41 E6
Ludgershall Wilts 25 H4
Ludgvan Cnwll 2 C3
Ludham Norfk 77 G2
Ludlow Shrops 57 E3
Ludney Somset 10 D6
Ludwell Wilts 25 E1
Ludworth Dur 106 C5
Luffenhall Herts 50 D4
Luffincott Devon 5 G5
Luffness E Loth 132 D3
Lugar E Ayrs 119 H2
Lugg Green Herefs 45 G5
Luggate Burn E Loth 133 E2
Luggiebank N Lans 130 D2
Lugsdale Ches 81 G3
Lugton E Ayrs 119 F5
Lugwardine Herefs 46 A3
Luib Highld 151 F1
Lulham Herefs 45 G3
Lullington Derbys 71 G1
Lullington E Susx 17 F2
Lullington Somset 24 C4
Lulsgate Bottom Somset 23 H6
Lulsley Worcs 46 C5
Lulworth Camp Dorset 12 B3
Lumb Lancs 89 G2
Lumb W York 90 B2
Lumbutts W York 89 H2
Lumby N York 91 F3
Lumloch E Duns 130 C2
Lumphanan Abers 148 C5
Lumphinnans Fife 131 H4
Lumsden Abers 157 G1
Lunan Angus 141 G5
Lunanhead Angus 141 E5
Luncarty P & K 140 A3
Lund E R Yk 92 D4
Lund N York 91 H3
Lundie Angus 140 C3
Lundie Stirlg 130 D6
Lundin Links Fife 132 C5
Lundin Mill Fife 132 C5
Lundy Green Norfk 65 E5
Lunna Shet 169 j4
Lunsford Kent 29 H2
Lunsford's Cross E Susx 17 H2
Lunt Mersyd 81 F5
Luntley Herefs 45 G5
Luppitt Devon 10 B5
Lupridge Devon 7 E3
Lupset W York 90 D1
Lupton Cumb 95 F3
Lurgashall W Susx 27 G2
Lurley Devon 9 F6
Lusby Lincs 86 D1
Luscombe Devon 7 E3
Luson Devon 6 C3
Luss Ag & B 129 E4
Lusta Highld 150 C4
Lustleigh Devon 9 E3
Luston Herefs 57 E2
Luthermuir Abers 148 D1
Luthrie Fife 140 C2
Lutley Worcs 58 B4
Luton Beds 50 B3
Luton Devon 10 A5
Luton Devon 9 F2
Luton Kent 30 A3
Luton Airport Beds 50 B3
Lutterworth Leics 60 B4
Lutton Devon 6 C3
Lutton Devon 6 D4
Lutton Lincs 75 E3
Lutton Nhants 61 G4
Luxborough Somset 22 C3
Luxulyan Cnwll 4 D2
Luzley Gt Man 83 E5
Lybster Highld 167 F2
Lydbury North Shrops 56 D4
Lydcott Devon 21 G4
Lydd Kent 18 D3
Lydd Airport Kent 18 D3
Lydden Kent 19 F6
Lydden Kent 31 G3
Lyddington Rutlnd 61 E5
Lyde Green Hants 27 E5
Lydeard St Lawrence Somset 22 D2
Lydeway Wilts 25 F5
Lydford Devon 8 B3
Lydford on Fosse Somset 24 A2
Lydgate Gt Man 89 H1
Lydgate W York 89 H2
Lydham Shrops 56 D4
Lydiard Green Wilts 39 E3
Lydiard Millicent Wilts 39 F3
Lydiard Tregoze Wilts 39 F3
Lydiate Mersyd 81 F5
Lydiate Ash Worcs 58 C3
Lydlinch Dorset 12 A6
Lydney Gloucs 37 G5
Lydstep Pembks 33 E1
Lye W Mids 58 B4
Lye Cross Somset 23 H5
Lye Green Bucks 41 H5
Lye Green E Susx 17 F5
Lye Green Warwks 59 E2
Lye Head Worcs 57 H3
Lye's Green Wilts 24 D4
Lyford Oxon 40 B4
Lymbridge Green Kent 19 E6
Lyme Regis Dorset 10 D4
Lyminge Kent 19 E5
Lymington Hants 13 G4
Lyminster W Susx 16 A2
Lymm Ches 82 B3
Lympne Kent 19 E5
Lympsham Somset 23 F5
Lympstone Devon 9 G3
Lynbridge Devon 21 G5
Lynch Somset 22 B4
Lynch Green Norfk 64 D6
Lynchat Highld 146 C5
Lyndhurst Hants 13 G5
Lyndon Rutlnd 61 E6
Lyndon Green W Mids 58 D4
Lyne Border 121 F3
Lyne Surrey 28 A3
Lyne Down Herefs 46 B2
Lyne of Skene Abers 149 E5
Lyneal Shrops 69 G3
Lyneham Devon 9 E2
Lyneham Oxon 48 A1
Lyneham Wilts 39 E2
Lyneham Airport Wilts 39 E2
Lyneholmford Cumb 112 B2
Lynemouth Nthumb 115 E5
Lyness Ork 169 b2
Lyng Norfk 76 D2
Lyng Somset 23 F2
Lynhales Herefs 45 F5
Lynmouth Devon 21 G5
Lynn Shrops 70 C2
Lynn Staffs 58 D6
Lynn of Shenval Moray 156 D2
Lynsted Kent 30 C2
Lynstone Cnwll 20 B1
Lynton Devon 21 G5
Lyon's Gate Dorset 11 G5
Lyonshall Herefs 45 F5
Lytchett Matravers Dorset 12 C4
Lytchett Minster Dorset 12 C4
Lyth Highld 167 F5
Lytham Lancs 88 B2
Lytham St Anne's Lancs 88 B2
Lythbank Shrops 57 E6
Lythe N York 107 H2
Lythmore Highld 166 D5

M

Mabe Burnthouse Cnwll 3 E3
Mabie D & G 110 D2
Mablethorpe Lincs 87 E3
Macclesfield Ches 82 D2
Macduff Abers 158 C6
Macharioch Ag & B 117 F1
Machen Caerph 36 C3
Machrie N Ayrs 117 H4
Machrihanish Ag & B 117 E2
Machrins Ag & B 126 C4
Machynlleth Powys 55 E5
Machynys Carmth 34 C4
Mackworth Derbys 71 H4
Macmerry E Loth 132 C2
Maddaford Devon 8 B4
Madderty P & K 139 G2
Maddington Wilts 25 F4
Maddiston Falk 131 F3
Madehurst W Susx 15 H5
Madeley Shrops 57 G6
Madeley Staffs 70 C4
Madeley Heath Staffs 70 C5
Madford Devon 10 B6
Madingley Cambs 62 C1
Madley Herefs 45 G3
Madresfield Worcs 46 D4
Madron Cnwll 2 B3
Maen-y-groes Cerdgn 42 D5
Maenaddwyn IOA 78 D3
Maenan Conwy 79 G1
Maenclochog Pembks 33 E4
Maendy V Glam 35 G2
Maenporth Cnwll 3 E3
Maentwrog Gwynd 67 F4
Maer Cnwll 20 B1
Maer Staffs 70 C4
Maerdy Carmth 43 G2
Maerdy Rhondd 35 G4
Maes-glas Newpt 36 D3
Maesbrook Shrops 69 E2
Maesbury Shrops 69 E3
Maesbury Marsh Shrops 69 E2
Maesgwynne Carmth 33 F4
Maeshafn Denbgs 68 D6
Maesllyn Cerdgn 42 D4
Maesmynis Powys 44 C4
Maesmynis Powys 44 C4
Maesteg Brdgnd 35 F3
Maesybont Carmth 34 C6
Maesycwmmer Caerph 36 C4
Magdalen Laver Essex 51 F1
Maggieknockater Moray 157 E4
Maggots End Essex 51 F3
Magham Down E Susx 17 G2
Maghull Mersyd 81 F5
Magor Mons 37 E3
Maiden Bradley Wilts 24 D3
Maiden Head Somset 24 A6
Maiden Law Dur 106 A6
Maiden Newton Dorset 11 F4
Maiden Wells Pembks 32 D2
Maidenbower W Susx 16 D5
Maidencombe Devon 7 F4
Maidenhayne Devon 10 C4
Maidenhead Berks 41 G2
Maidens S Ayrs 108 D6
Maidens Green Berks 41 G1
Maidenwell Lincs 86 D3
Maidford Nhants 48 D4
Maids Moreton Bucks 49 E3
Maidstone Kent 30 A2
Maidwell Nhants 60 D3
Maindee Newpt 36 D3
Mains of Balhall Angus 141 E6
Mains of Balnakettle Abers 148 D2
Mains of Dalvey Highld 156 C2
Mains of Haulkerton Abers 149 E2
Mainsforth Dur 106 C4
Mainsriddle D & G 102 C6
Mainstone Shrops 56 C4
Maisemore Gloucs 46 D1
Major's Green Worcs 58 D3
Makeney Derbys 72 A4
Malborough Devon 6 D1
Malcoff Derbys 83 F3
Malden Surrey 28 C3
Malden Rushett Gt Lon 28 C2
Maldon Essex 52 B1
Malham N York 89 G6
Mallaig Highld 143 F4
Mallaigvaig Highld 143 F4
Malleny Mills C Edin 131 H2
Mallows Green Essex 51 F3
Malltraeth IOA 78 D1
Mallwyd Gwynd 68 A1
Malmesbury Wilts 38 D3
Malmsmead Somset 21 H5
Malpas Ches 69 G5
Malpas Cnwll 3 F4
Malpas Newpt 36 D3
Malswick Gloucs 46 C2
Maltby Lincs 86 C3
Maltby N York 106 D2
Maltby S York 84 C4
Maltby le Marsh Lincs 87 E3
Malting Green Essex 52 C3
Maltman's Hill Kent 18 C6
Malton N York 98 D2
Malvern Link Worcs 46 C4
Malvern Wells Worcs 46 C3
Malzie D & G 101 E5
Mamble Worcs 57 G2
Mamhilad Mons 36 D5
Manaccan Cnwll 3 E2
Manafon Powys 56 A6
Manais W Isls 168 d6
Manaton Devon 8 D3
Manby Lincs 86 D3
Mancetter Warwks 59 F5
Manchester Gt Man 82 C4
Manchester Airport Gt Man 82 C3
Mancot Flints 81 E1
Mandally Highld 145 E4
Manderston House Border 123 E5
Manea Cambs 62 D4
Maney W Mids 58 D5
Manfield N York 106 B2
Mangerton Dorset 11 E4
Mangotsfield Gloucs 37 H2
Mangrove Green Herts 50 B3
Manhay Cnwll 2 D3
Manish W Isls 168 d6
Mankinholes W York 89 H2
Manley Ches 81 G2
Manmoel Caerph 36 C5
Mannel Ag & B 134 B3
Manning's Heath W Susx 16 C4
Manningford Bohune Wilts 25 G5
Manningford Bruce Wilts 25 G5
Manningham W York 90 C3
Mannington Dorset 12 D5
Manningtree Essex 53 E4
Mannofield Aber C 149 G5
Manor Park Gt Lon 29 E5
Manorbier Pembks 33 E1
Manorbier Newton Pembks 33 E2
Manordeilo Carmth 43 G2
Manorhill Border 122 D3
Manorowen Pembks 32 D5
Mansell Gamage Herefs 45 G4
Mansell Lacy Herefs 45 G4
Mansergh Cumb 95 G3
Mansfield E Ayrs 109 H6
Mansfield Notts 72 C6
Mansfield Woodhouse Notts 84 C1
Mansriggs Cumb 94 D3
Manston Dorset 12 B6
Manston Kent 31 G3
Manston W York 91 E3
Manston Airport Kent 31 G3
Manswood Dorset 12 D5
Manthorpe Lincs 73 G4
Manthorpe Lincs 74 A2
Manton Lincs 85 G5
Manton Notts 84 D2
Manton Rutlnd 61 E6
Manton Wilts 39 F1
Manuden Essex 51 F3
Manwood Green Essex 51 F2
Maperton Somset 24 B2
Maple Cross Herts 28 A5
Maplebeck Notts 73 E6
Mapledurham Oxon 41 E2
Mapledurwell Hants 27 E4
Maplehurst W Susx 16 C4
Maplescombe Kent 29 F2
Mapleton Derbys 71 F5
Mapleton Kent 29 E1
Mapperley Derbys 72 B4
Mapperley Park Notts 72 C4
Mapperton Dorset 11 E5
Mappleborough Green Warwks 58 D2
Mappleton E R Yk 93 F4
Mapplewell S York 84 A6
Mappowder Dorset 11 H5
Marazanvose Cnwll 3 E5
Marazion Cnwll 2 C3
Marbury Ches 69 H5
March Cambs 62 C5
March S Lans 110 D6
Marcham Oxon 40 C4
Marchamley Shrops 70 A3
Marchamley Wood Shrops 69 H3
Marchington Staffs 71 F3
Marchington Woodlands Staffs 71 F3
Marchros Gwynd 66 C3
Marchwiel Wrexhm 69 F5
Marchwood Hants 14 B5
Marcross V Glam 35 G1
Marden Herefs 45 H4
Marden Kent 18 A6
Marden Wilts 25 F5
Marden Ash Essex 51 F1
Marden Beech Kent 18 A6
Marden Thorn Kent 18 A6
Mardens Hill E Susx 17 F5
Mardlebury Herts 50 D2
Mardy Mons 36 D6
Marefield Leics 60 C6
Mareham le Fen Lincs 74 C6
Mareham on the Hill Lincs 86 C1
Marehay Derbys 72 B5
Marehill W Susx 16 B3
Maresfield E Susx 17 E4
Marfleet E R Yk 93 E2
Marford Wrexhm 69 F6
Margam Neath 35 E3
Margaret Marsh Dorset 24 D1
Margaret Roding Essex 51 G2
Margaretting Essex 29 G6
Margaretting Tye Essex 29 H6
Margate Kent 31 G3
Margnaheglish N Ayrs 118 B3
Margrie D & G 101 G5
Margrove Park N York 107 F2
Marham Norfk 75 G1
Marhamchurch Cnwll 20 B1
Marholm Cambs 61 G6
Marian-glas IOA 79 E3
Mariansleigh Devon 21 G3
Marine Town Kent 30 C3
Marionburgh Abers 149 E5
Marishader Highld 151 E5
Maristow Devon 6 B4
Maritime Centre Moray 119 E3
Marjoriebanks D & G 111 E3
Mark Somset 23 G4
Mark Causeway Somset 23 F4
Mark Cross E Susx 17 F2
Mark Cross E Susx 17 G4
Mark's Corner IOW 14 C3
Markbeech Kent 17 F6
Markby Lincs 87 E2
Markeaton Derbys 72 A4
Market Bosworth Leics 59 G6
Market Deeping Lincs 74 B1
Market Drayton Shrops 70 B3
Market Harborough Leics 60 C4
Market Lavington Wilts 25 F5
Market Overton Rutlnd 73 F2
Market Rasen Lincs 86 A4
Market Stainton Lincs 86 C3
Market Weighton E R Yk 92 C4
Market Weston Suffk 64 B3
Markfield Leics 72 C1
Markham Caerph 36 C4
Markham Moor Notts 85 E2
Markinch Fife 132 B5
Markington N York 97 F1
Markle E Loth 133 E3
Marks Tey Essex 52 C3
Marksbury Somset 24 B5
Markwell Cnwll 5 G2
Markyate Herts 50 B2
Marl Bank Worcs 46 C3
Marlborough Wilts 39 F1
Marlbrook Herefs 45 H5
Marlbrook Worcs 58 C3
Marlcliff Warwks 47 F4
Marldon Devon 7 F4
Marle Green E Susx 17 G3
Marlesford Suffk 65 F1
Marley Kent 31 E1
Marley Kent 31 G1
Marley Green Ches 69 H5
Marley Hill T & W 114 D1
Marlingford Norfk 76 D1
Marloes Pembks 32 B2
Marlow Bucks 41 G3
Marlow Herefs 56 D3
Marlow Bottom Bucks 41 G3
Marlpit Hill Kent 17 E6
Marlpits E Susx 17 E4
Marlpits E Susx 17 H3
Marlpool Derbys 72 B5
Marnhull Dorset 24 C1
Marple Gt Man 82 D3
Marple Bridge Gt Man 83 E4
Marr S York 84 C5
Marrick N York 96 D5

Marros
Millom
300

Marros Carmth 33 F2
Marsden T & W 115 F2
Marsden W York 83 E6
Marsden Height Lancs 89 G3
Marsett N York 96 B3
Marsh Bucks 41 F5
Marsh Devon 10 C6
Marsh W York 90 A3
Marsh Baldon Oxon 40 D4
Marsh Benham Berks 26 C6
Marsh Chapel Lincs 86 D5
Marsh Gibbon Bucks 49 E1
Marsh Green Devon 9 G4
Marsh Green Kent 17 E6
Marsh Green Shrops 70 A1
Marsh Green Staffs 70 D6
Marsh Lane Derbys 84 B3
Marsh Lane Gloucs 37 G5
Marsh Street Somset 22 C4
Marshall's Heath Herts 50 C2
Marshalswick Herts 50 C2
Marsham Norfk 77 E2
Marshborough Kent 31 G2
Marshbrook Shrops 57 E4
Marshfield Gloucs 38 C2
Marshfield Newpt 36 D2
Marshgate Cnwll 5 E5
Marshland Green Gt Man 82 B5
Marshland St James Norfk 75 E1
Marshside Mersyd 88 B1
Marshwood Dorset 10 D4
Marske N York 96 D5
Marske-by-the-Sea N York 107 F3
Marston Ches 82 B2
Marston Herefs 45 F5
Marston Lincs 73 F4
Marston Oxon 40 C5
Marston Staffs 70 C1
Marston Staffs 70 D3
Marston Warwks 59 E5
Marston Wilts 25 E5
Marston Green W Mids 59 E4
Marston Jabbet Warwks 59 G4
Marston Magna Somset 24 B1
Marston Meysey Wilts 39 F4
Marston Montgomery Derbys 71 F4
Marston Moretaine Beds 49 H3
Marston on Dove Derbys 71 G3
Marston St Lawrence Nhants 48 D3
Marston Stannett Herefs 46 A5
Marston Trussell Nhants 60 C4
Marstow Herefs 46 A1
Marsworth Bucks 41 G6
Marten Wilts 26 A5
Marthall Ches 82 C2
Martham Norfk 77 G2
Martin Hants 25 F1
Martin Kent 19 G6
Martin Lincs 74 B6
Martin Lincs 86 C1
Martin Dales Lincs 86 B1
Martin Drove End Hants 25 F1
Martin Hussingtree Worcs 46 D5
Martindale Cumb 104 A2
Martinhoe Devon 21 G5
Martinscroft Ches 82 B4
Martinstown Dorset 11 G3
Martlesham Suffk 53 F5
Martlesham Heath Suffk 53 F5
Martletwy Pembks 33 E3
Martley Worcs 46 C5
Martock Somset 23 G1
Marton Ches 82 A1
Marton Ches 82 C1
Marton Cumb 94 C3
Marton E R Yk 93 F3
Marton E R Yk 99 H2
Marton Lincs 85 F3
Marton N York 107 E2
Marton N York 91 E6
Marton N York 98 C3
Marton Shrops 56 C6
Marton Warwks 59 G2
Marton-le-Moor N York 97 G2
Martyr Worthy Hants 26 C2
Martyr's Green Surrey 28 B2
Marwick Ork 169 a3
Marwood Devon 21 F4
Mary Tavy Devon 8 B2
Marybank Highld 154 C4
Maryburgh Highld 154 D5
Maryculter Abers 149 F4
Marygold Border 123 E5
Maryhill Abers 158 D4
Maryhill C Glas 129 G2
Marykirk Abers 148 D1
Maryland Mons 37 F5
Marylebone Gt Lon 28 D4
Marylebone Gt Man 81 H5
Marypark Moray 156 D3
Maryport Cumb 102 D4
Maryport D & G 100 C4
Marystow Devon 8 A3
Maryton Angus 141 G5
Marywell Abers 148 C4
Marywell Abers 149 G4
Marywell Angus 141 F4
Masham N York 97 E3
Mashbury Essex 51 G2
Mason T & W 114 D3
Masongill N York 95 G2
Mastin Moor Derbys 84 B2
Matching Essex 51 F2
Matching Green Essex 51 F2
Matching Tye Essex 51 F2
Matfen Nthumb 114 B3
Matfield Kent 17 G6
Mathern Mons 37 F3
Mathon Herefs 46 C4
Mathry Pembks 32 C5
Matlask Norfk 76 D3
Matlock Derbys 71 H6
Matlock Bank Derbys 71 H6
Matlock Bath Derbys 71 H6
Matlock Dale Derbys 71 H6
Matson Gloucs 38 C6
Matterdale End Cumb 103 H2
Mattersey Notts 84 D4
Mattersey Thorpe Notts 84 D4
Mattingley Hants 27 E5
Mattishall Norfk 76 D1
Mattishall Burgh Norfk 76 D1
Mauchline E Ayrs 119 G2
Maud Abers 159 E4
Maufant Jersey 174 d2
Maugersbury Gloucs 47 G2
Maughold IOM 174 n4
Mauld Highld 154 B3
Maulden Beds 50 A4
Maulds Meaburn Cumb 104 C2
Maunby N York 97 G3
Maund Bryan Herefs 46 A4
Maundown Somset 22 C2
Mautby Norfk 77 H1
Mavesyn Ridware Staffs 71 F2
Mavis Enderby Lincs 86 D1
Maw Green Ches 70 B6
Maw Green W Mids 58 C5
Mawbray Cumb 103 E5
Mawdesley Lancs 88 C1
Mawdlam Brdgnd 35 E2
Mawgan Cnwll 3 E2
Mawgan Cross Cnwll 2 D2
Mawgan Porth Cnwll 4 B3
Mawla Cnwll 3 E4
Mawnan Cnwll 3 E2
Mawnan Smith Cnwll 3 E3
Mawthorpe Lincs 87 E2
Maxey Cambs 61 G6
Maxstoke Warwks 59 E4
Maxted Street Kent 19 E6
Maxton Border 122 C2
Maxton Kent 19 F5
Maxwell Town D & G 110 D2
Maxworthy Cnwll 5 F5
May Bank Staffs 70 D5
May's Green Oxon 41 F2
May's Green Surrey 28 B2
Mayals Swans 34 D3
Maybole S Ayrs 109 E6
Maybury Surrey 28 A2
Mayes Green Surrey 16 B5
Mayfield E Susx 17 G4
Mayfield Mdloth 132 C2
Mayfield Staffs 71 F5
Mayford Surrey 27 H5
Mayland Essex 30 C6
Maynard's Green E Susx 17 G3
Maypole Kent 31 F2
Maypole Mons 37 F6
Maypole W Mids 58 D3
Maypole Green Norfk 65 G5
Maypole Green Suffk 64 B1
Maypole Green Suffk 65 E2
Mead Devon 20 B2
Meadgate Somset 24 B5
Meadle Bucks 41 F5
Meadowfield Dur 106 B5
Meadowtown Shrops 56 C5
Meadwell Devon 5 G4
Meal Bank Cumb 95 F4
Mealrigg Cumb 103 E5
Mealsgate Cumb 103 F4
Meanwood W York 90 D3
Mearbeck N York 89 G6
Meare Somset 23 G3
Meare Green Somset 23 F2
Meare Green Somset 23 F1
Mearns E Rens 119 G5
Mears Ashby Nhants 60 D2
Measham Leics 72 A1
Meathop Cumb 95 E3
Meaux E R Yk 93 E3
Meavy Devon 6 C4
Medbourne Leics 60 D5
Meddon Devon 20 C2
Meden Vale Notts 84 D2
Medlam Lincs 74 C6
Medlar Lancs 88 C3
Medmenham Berks 41 F3
Medomsley Dur 105 H6
Medstead Hants 27 E3
Meer Common Herefs 45 F4
Meerbrook Staffs 71 E6
Meesden Herts 51 E4
Meeson Shrops 70 B2
Meeth Devon 8 B5
Meeting Green Suffk 63 G1
Meeting House Hill Norfk 77 F3
Meidrim Carmth 33 G4
Meifod Powys 68 D1
Meigle P & K 140 C4
Meikle Carco D & G 110 B6
Meikle Earnock S Lans 120 B5
Meikle Kilmory Ag & B 118 B5
Meikle Obney P & K 139 H3
Meikle Wartle Abers 158 C2
Meikleour P & K 140 B4
Meinciau Carmth 34 B5
Meir Staffs 70 D4
Meir Heath Staffs 70 D4
Melbourn Cambs 51 E5
Melbourne Derbys 72 B2
Melbourne E R Yk 92 A4
Melbury Devon 20 D2
Melbury Abbas Dorset 24 D1
Melbury Bubb Dorset 11 F5
Melbury Osmond Dorset 11 F5
Melbury Sampford Dorset 11 F5
Melchbourne Beds 61 F2
Melcombe Bingham Dorset 12 B5
Meldon Devon 8 C4
Meldon Nthumb 114 C4
Meldon Park Nthumb 114 C4
Meldreth Cambs 51 E5
Meldrum Stirlg 130 C5
Meledor Cnwll 3 G5
Melfort Ag & B 136 C1
Melgund Castle Angus 141 E5
Meliden Denbgs 80 C3
Melin Court Neath 35 F4
Melin-byrhedyn Powys 55 F5
Melin-y-coed Conwy 67 H6
Melin-y-ddol Powys 56 A6
Melin-y-wig Denbgs 68 C5
Melinau Pembks 33 F3
Melkinthorpe Cumb 104 B3
Melkridge Nthumb 113 E1
Melksham Wilts 25 E6
Mell Green Berks 40 C2
Mellangoose Cnwll 2 D2
Mellguards Cumb 104 A5
Melling Lancs 95 G2
Melling Mersyd 81 F5
Melling Mount Mersyd 81 F5
Mellington Powys 56 C5
Mellis Suffk 64 C3
Mellon Charles Highld 160 C3
Mellon Udrigle Highld 160 C3
Mellor Gt Man 83 E3
Mellor Lancs 89 E3
Mellor Brook Lancs 89 E3
Mells Somset 24 C4
Mells Suffk 65 F3
Melmerby Cumb 104 C4
Melmerby N York 96 D3
Melmerby N York 97 F2
Melness Highld 165 G5
Melon Green Suffk 63 H1
Melplash Dorset 11 E4
Melrose Border 122 C3
Melsetter Ork 169 a1
Melsonby N York 106 A2
Meltham W York 83 F6
Meltham Mills W York 83 F6
Melton E R Yk 92 D2
Melton Suffk 53 F6
Melton Constable Norfk 76 D3
Melton Mowbray Leics 73 E2
Melton Ross Lincs 86 A6
Meltonby E R Yk 92 B5
Melvaig Highld 160 B2
Melverley Shrops 69 F2
Melverley Green Shrops 69 F2
Melvich Highld 166 C5
Membury Devon 10 C5
Memsie Abers 159 F5
Memus Angus 140 D6
Menabilly Cnwll 5 E1
Menagissey Cnwll 3 E4
Menai Bridge IOA 79 E2
Mendham Suffk 65 E4
Mendlesham Suffk 64 D2
Mendlesham Green Suffk 64 C2
Menheniot Cnwll 5 F2
Menithwood Worcs 57 G2
Mennock D & G 110 C6
Menston W York 90 C4
Menstrie Clacks 131 E5
Menthorpe N York 91 H3
Mentmore Bucks 49 G1
Meoble Highld 143 G3
Meole Brace Shrops 69 G1
Meonstoke Hants 14 D6
Meopham Kent 29 G3
Meopham Green Kent 29 G3
Meopham Station Kent 29 G3
Mepal Cambs 62 D3
Meppershall Beds 50 B4
Mere Ches 82 B3
Mere Wilts 24 D2
Mere Brow Lancs 88 C1
Mere Green W Mids 58 D5
Mere Green Worcs 58 B2
Mere Heath Ches 82 B2
Mereclough Lancs 89 G3
Meresborough Kent 30 B2
Mereworth Kent 29 G1
Meriden W Mids 59 E4
Merkadale Highld 150 D2
Merley Dorset 12 D4
Merlin's Bridge Pembks 32 D3
Merrifield Devon 7 E2
Merrington Shrops 69 G2
Merrion Pembks 32 D1
Merriott Somset 11 E6
Merrivale Devon 8 B2
Merrow Surrey 28 A1
Merry Field Hill Dorset 12 D5
Merry Hill Herts 28 B5
Merry Lees Leics 59 G6
Merryhill W Mids 58 B5
Merrymeet Cnwll 5 F2
Mersham Kent 18 D5
Merstham Surrey 28 D1
Merston W Susx 15 G4
Merstone IOW 14 C2
Merther Cnwll 3 F4
Merthyr Carmth 33 H4
Merthyr Cynog Powys 44 C3
Merthyr Dyfan V Glam 36 B1
Merthyr Mawr Brdgnd 35 F2
Merthyr Tydfil Myr Td 36 B5
Merthyr Vale Myr Td 36 B4
Merton Devon 21 E2
Merton Gt Lon 28 C3
Merton Norfk 64 B5
Merton Oxon 40 D6
Meshaw Devon 21 H2
Messing Essex 52 C3
Messingham Lincs 85 F5
Metfield Suffk 65 E3
Metherell Cnwll 5 H3
Metherin Cnwll 5 E3
Metheringham Lincs 74 A6
Methil Fife 132 C5
Methilhill Fife 132 C5
Methleigh Cnwll 2 D2
Methley W York 91 E2
Methley Junction W York 91 E2
Methlick Abers 158 D3
Methven P & K 139 G2
Methwold Norfk 63 F5
Methwold Hythe Norfk 63 F5
Mettingham Suffk 65 F4
Metton Norfk 77 E4
Mevagissey Cnwll 3 G4
Mexborough S York 84 B5
Mey Highld 167 F6
Meylltyrn Gwynd 66 B3
Meysey Hampton Gloucs 39 F4
Miabhig W Isls 168 d8
Miavaig W Isls 168 d8
Michaelchurch Herefs 45 H2
Michaelchurch Escley Herefs 45 F3
Michaelchurch-on-Arrow Powys 45 E4
Michaelston-le-Pit V Glam 36 C1
Michaelstone-y-Fedw Newpt 36 C3
Michaelstow Cnwll 4 D4
Michelcombe Devon 6 D4
Micheldever Hants 26 C3
Micheldever Station Hants 26 C3
Michelmersh Hants 26 B2
Mickfield Suffk 64 D1
Mickle Trafford Ches 81 G2
Micklebring S York 84 C4
Mickleby N York 107 G2
Micklefield W York 91 E3
Micklefield Green Herts 28 A6
Mickleham Surrey 28 C1
Mickleover Derbys 71 H3
Micklethwaite Cumb 103 G5
Micklethwaite W York 90 B4
Mickleton Dur 105 F2
Mickleton Gloucs 47 G3
Mickletown W York 91 E2
Mickley Derbys 84 A3
Mickley N York 97 F2
Mickley Green Suffk 63 G1
Mickley Square Nthumb 114 B2
Mid Ardlaw Abers 159 E5
Mid Beltie Abers 148 D4
Mid Bockhampton Hants 13 F4
Mid Calder W Loth 131 G2
Mid Clyth Highld 167 G2
Mid Holmwood Surrey 16 C6
Mid Lavant W Susx 15 G4
Mid Mains Highld 154 C3
Mid Thorpe Lincs 86 C2
Mid Yell Shet 169 j4
Midbea Ork 169 b4
Middle Assendon Oxon 41 F3
Middle Aston Oxon 48 C2
Middle Barton Oxon 48 C2
Middle Chinnock Somset 11 E6
Middle Claydon Bucks 49 E2
Middle Duntisbourne Gloucs 38 D5
Middle Handley Derbys 84 B2
Middle Harling Norfk 64 B4
Middle Kames Ag & B 127 H4
Middle Littleton Worcs 47 F4
Middle Madeley Staffs 70 C4
Middle Maes-coed Herefs 45 F3
Middle Mayfield Staffs 71 F4
Middle Mill Pembks 32 B4
Middle Quarter Kent 18 C5
Middle Rasen Lincs 86 A4
Middle Rocombe Devon 7 F5
Middle Salter Lancs 88 D6
Middle Stoford Somset 23 E1
Middle Stoke Kent 30 B4
Middle Stoughton Somset 23 G4
Middle Street Gloucs 38 C5
Middle Taphouse Cnwll 5 E2
Middle Town IOS 2 a1
Middle Tysoe Warwks 48 B4
Middle Wallop Hants 26 A3
Middle Winterslow Wilts 25 H2
Middle Woodford Wilts 25 G3
Middle Yard Gloucs 38 C5
Middlebie D & G 111 G2
Middlebridge P & K 146 D1
Middlecliffe S York 84 B5
Middlecott Devon 8 D3
Middleham N York 96 D4
Middlehill Cnwll 5 F3
Middlehill Wilts 38 C1
Middlehope Shrops 57 E4
Middlemarsh Dorset 11 G5
Middlemore Devon 6 B5
Middlesbrough N York 106 D3
Middlesceugh Cumb 103 H4
Middleshaw Cumb 95 F4
Middlesmoor N York 96 D2
Middlestone Dur 106 B4
Middlestone Moor Dur 106 B4
Middlestown W York 90 D1
Middlethird Border 122 D4
Middleton Ag & B 134 A4
Middleton Cumb 95 G3
Middleton Derbys 83 G1
Middleton Derbys 71 H6
Middleton Essex 52 B5
Middleton Gt Man 82 D5
Middleton Hants 26 C4
Middleton Herefs 57 F2
Middleton Lancs 88 C5
Middleton N Ayrs 119 F5
Middleton N York 90 B4
Middleton N York 98 D3
Middleton Nhants 60 D4
Middleton Norfk 75 G2
Middleton Nthumb 124 D5
Middleton Nthumb 114 B4
Middleton P & K 131 G6
Middleton Shrops 69 E3
Middleton Shrops 57 F3
Middleton Suffk 65 G2
Middleton Swans 34 B3
Middleton W York 90 D2
Middleton Warwks 59 E5
Middleton Cheney Nhants 48 C3
Middleton Green Staffs 71 E3
Middleton Hall Nthumb 124 C4
Middleton Moor Suffk 65 G2
Middleton on the Hill Herefs 57 F2
Middleton on the Wolds E R Yk 92 C4
Middleton One Row Dur 106 C2
Middleton Priors Shrops 57 F4
Middleton Quernhow N York 97 F3
Middleton Scriven Shrops 57 G4
Middleton St George Dur 106 C2
Middleton Stoney Oxon 48 D1
Middleton Tyas N York 97 E5
Middleton-in-Teesdale Dur 105 F3
Middleton-on-Leven N York 106 D2
Middleton-on-Sea W Susx 15 H4
Middletown Cumb 102 D1
Middletown Powys 69 E1
Middletown Somset 37 F1
Middlewich Ches 82 B1
Middlewood Cnwll 5 F3
Middlewood Herefs 45 F4
Middlewood Green Suffk 64 C1
Middleyard E Ayrs 119 G3
Middlezoy Somset 23 G2
Middridge Dur 106 B3
Midford Somset 24 C5
Midge Hall Lancs 88 D2
Midgeholme Cumb 104 C6
Midgham Berks 26 D6
Midgley W York 90 B2
Midgley W York 90 D1
Midhopestones S York 83 G5
Midhurst W Susx 15 G6
Midlem Border 122 B2
Midney Somset 23 H2
Midpark Ag & B 118 B5
Midsomer Norton Somset 24 B5
Midtown Highld 165 G5
Midville Lincs 74 D6
Midway Ches 82 D3
Migvie Abers 148 B5
Milborne Port Somset 24 B1
Milborne St Andrew Dorset 12 B4
Milborne Wick Somset 24 B1
Milbourne Nthumb 114 C3
Milbourne Wilts 38 D3
Milburn Cumb 104 C3
Milbury Heath Gloucs 38 B3
Milby N York 97 G2
Milcombe Oxon 48 B3
Milden Suffk 52 C5
Mildenhall Suffk 63 F3
Mildenhall Wilts 39 G1
Mile Elm Wilts 39 E1
Mile End Essex 52 C3
Mile End Gloucs 37 G5
Mile End Suffk 65 F4
Mile Oak E Susx 16 C2
Mile Oak Kent 17 H6
Mile Oak Staffs 59 E6
Mile Town Kent 30 C3
Milebrook Powys 56 C3
Milebush Kent 18 A6
Mileham Norfk 76 B2
Miles Hope Herefs 57 F2
Miles Platting Gt Man 82 D5
Milesmark Fife 131 G4
Milfield Nthumb 123 F3
Milford Derbys 72 A4
Milford Devon 20 C3
Milford Powys 56 A4
Milford Staffs 71 E2
Milford Surrey 27 H3
Milford Haven Pembks 32 C2
Milford on Sea Hants 13 G4
Milkwall Gloucs 37 G5
Mill Bank W York 90 B2
Mill Brow Gt Man 83 E4
Mill Common Norfk 65 F6
Mill Common Suffk 65 F3
Mill Cross Devon 7 E4
Mill End Bucks 41 F3
Mill End Cambs 62 B3
Mill End Herts 50 D4
Mill Green Cambs 51 G5
Mill Green Essex 29 G6
Mill Green Herts 50 C2
Mill Green Lincs 74 C2
Mill Green Norfk 64 D4
Mill Green Staffs 71 F2
Mill Green Suffk 52 C5
Mill Green Suffk 64 C1
Mill Green Suffk 64 D1
Mill Green Suffk 65 F1
Mill Green W Mids 58 D5
Mill Hill E Susx 17 G2
Mill Hill Gt Lon 28 C5
Mill Meece Staffs 70 C3
Mill of Drummond P & K 139 F1
Mill of Haldane W Duns 129 E3
Mill Side Cumb 95 E3
Mill Street Kent 29 H2
Mill Street Norfk 76 C2
Mill Street Norfk 76 D2
Mill Street Suffk 64 C3
Millais Jersey 174 a3
Milland W Susx 27 F2
Milland Marsh W Susx 27 F2
Millbeck Cumb 103 F3
Millbreck Abers 159 F3
Millbrex Abers 158 D3
Millbridge Surrey 27 G3
Millbrook Beds 50 A5
Millbrook Cnwll 5 H1
Millbrook Gt Man 83 E5
Millbrook Hants 14 B5
Millbrook Jersey 174 b2
Millbuie Abers 149 F5
Millbuie Highld 154 D4
Millburn S Ayrs 119 F2
Millcombe Devon 7 E3
Millcorner E Susx 18 B4
Millcraig Highld 155 E6
Milldale Staffs 71 F5
Millend Gloucs 37 G5
Millend Gloucs 38 B4
Miller's Dale Derbys 83 F2
Miller's Green Essex 51 G1
Millerhill Mdloth 132 B2
Millers Green Derbys 71 H5
Millerston N Lans 130 C2
Millgate Lancs 89 G1
Millgreen Shrops 70 B3
Millhalf Herefs 45 F4
Millhayes Devon 10 C5
Millhead Lancs 95 F2
Millheugh S Lans 120 B4
Millhouse Ag & B 128 A2
Millhouse Cumb 103 G4
Millhouse Green S York 83 G5
Millhousebridge D & G 111 E3
Millhouses S York 84 B5
Millhouses S York 84 A3
Milliken Park Rens 119 F6
Millin Cross Pembks 32 D3
Millington E R Yk 92 B5
Millness Cumb 95 F3
Millom Cumb 94 B3

Millook Nannerch

Millook Cnwll 5 E6
Millpool Cnwll 2 C3
Millpool Cnwll 5 E3
Millport N Ayrs 118 C5
Millthorpe Derbys 83 H2
Millthrop Cumb 95 G4
Milltimber Aber C 149 F5
Milltown Abers 147 G5
Milltown Abers 148 B6
Milltown Cnwll 5 E2
Milltown D & G 111 H2
Milltown Derbys 72 A6
Milltown Devon 21 F4
Milltown of Campfield Abers 148 D4
Milltown of Edinvillie Moray 157 E3
Milltown of Learney Abers 148 D5
Milnathort P & K 131 G6
Milngavie W Duns 129 G3
Milnrow Gt Man 82 D6
Milnthorpe Cumb 95 F3
Milnthorpe W York 90 D1
Milovaig Highld 150 B4
Milson Shrops 57 G3
Milstead Kent 30 C2
Milston Wilts 25 G4
Milthorpe Lincs 74 B3
Milthorpe Nhants 48 D4
Milton Cambs 62 D2
Milton Cumb 104 B6
Milton D & G 100 C6
Milton D & G 110 C2
Milton Derbys 71 H3
Milton Highld 167 G3
Milton Highld 151 G3
Milton Highld 154 C2
Milton Highld 154 D4
Milton Highld 162 D1
Milton Inver 129 E2
Milton Kent 29 G3
Milton Moray 157 G5
Milton Newpt 37 E3
Milton Notts 85 E2
Milton Oxon 48 C3
Milton Oxon 40 C3
Milton P & K 140 A5
Milton Pembks 33 E2
Milton Somset 23 F5
Milton Somset 23 G1
Milton Staffs 70 D5
Milton Stirlg 129 F5
Milton W Duns 129 F2
Milton Abbas Dorset 12 B5
Milton Abbot Devon 5 H4
Milton Bridge Mdloth 121 G6
Milton Bryan Beds 49 H2
Milton Clevedon Somset 24 B3
Milton Combe Devon 6 B4
Milton Common Oxon 41 E5
Milton Damerel Devon 20 D2
Milton End Gloucs 38 B5
Milton End Gloucs 39 F4
Milton Ernest Beds 61 F1
Milton Green Ches 69 G6
Milton Hill Oxon 40 C3
Milton Keynes Bucks 49 G3
Milton Lilbourne Wilts 25 G5
Milton Malsor Nhants 49 E5
Milton Morenish P & K 138 C3
Milton of Auchinhove Abers 148 C5
Milton of Balgonie Fife 132 B5
Milton of Buchanan Stirlg 129 F4
Milton of Campsie E Duns 130 C3
Milton of Leys Highld 155 E3
Milton of Tullich Abers 148 B4
Milton on Stour Dorset 24 D2
Milton Regis Kent 30 C2
Milton Street E Susx 17 F2
Milton-under-Wychwood Oxon 47 H1
Milverton Somset 22 D2
Milverton Warwks 59 F2
Milwich Staffs 71 E3
Milwr Flints 80 D2
Minard Ag & B 128 A5
Minchington Dorset 12 D6
Minchinhampton Gloucs 38 C4
Mindrum Nthumb 123 E3
Mindrum Mill Nthumb 123 F3
Minehead Somset 22 C4
Minera Wrexhm 69 E5
Minety Wilts 39 E3
Minffordd Gwynd 67 E4
Mingarrypark Highld 143 F1
Miningsby Lincs 86 D1
Minions Cnwll 5 F3
Minishant S Ayrs 109 E6
Minllyn Gwynd 67 H1
Minnigaff D & G 109 F1
Minnis Bay Kent 31 F3
Minnonie Abers 158 D5
Minskip N York 97 G1
Minstead Hants 13 G6
Minsted W Susx 15 G6
Minster Kent 30 C3
Minster Kent 31 G2
Minster Lovell Oxon 40 A5
Minsteracres Nthumb 105 G6
Minsterley Shrops 56 D6
Minsterworth Gloucs 38 C6
Minterne Magna Dorset 11 G5
Minterne Parva Dorset 11 G5
Minting Lincs 86 B2
Mintlaw Abers 159 F4
Minto Border 122 C1
Minton Shrops 57 E4
Minwear Pembks 33 E3
Minworth W Mids 58 D5
Mirehouse Cumb 102 D2
Mirfield W York 90 C2
Miserden Gloucs 38 D5
Miskin Rhondd 36 B3
Miskin Rhondd 36 B4
Misson Notts 84 D4
Misterton Lincs 60 B4
Misterton Notts 85 E4
Misterton Somset 11 E5
Mistley Essex 53 E4
Mistley Heath Essex 53 E4
Mitcham Gt Lon 28 D3
Mitchel Troy Mons 37 F5
Mitcheldean Gloucs 46 B1
Mitchell Cnwll 3 F5
Mitchellslacks D & G 110 D4
Mitford Nthumb 114 C4
Mithian Cnwll 3 E5
Mitton Staffs 70 D1
Mixbury Oxon 48 D3
Mixenden W York 90 B2
Mixon Staffs 71 E6
Moats Tye Suffk 52 D6
Mobberley Ches 82 C3
Mobberley Staffs 71 E4
Moccas Herefs 45 F3
Mochdre Conwy 79 H2
Mochdre Powys 56 A4
Mochrum D & G 101 E5
Mockbeggar Hants 13 E5
Mockbeggar Kent 17 H6
Mockerkin Cumb 103 E2
Modbury Devon 6 D3
Moddershall Staffs 70 D4
Moel Tryfan Gwynd 67 E6
Moelfre IOA 79 E3
Moelfre Powys 68 D3
Moffat D & G 111 E5
Mogerhanger Beds 50 B6
Moira Leics 71 H1
Mol-chlach Highld 142 D5
Molash Kent 30 D1
Mold Flints 81 E1
Moldgreen W York 90 C1
Molehill Green Essex 51 F3
Molehill Green Essex 51 H3
Molescroft E R Yk 92 D4
Molesden Nthumb 114 C4
Molesworth Cambs 61 G3
Molland Devon 22 A2
Mollington Ches 81 F2
Mollington Oxon 48 C4
Mollinsburn N Lans 130 C2
Monachty Cerdgn 43 E5
Mondynes Abers 149 E2
Monewden Suffk 65 E1
Moneydie P & K 139 H3
Moneyrow Green Berks 41 G2
Moniaive D & G 110 B4
Monifieth Angus 141 E3
Monikie Angus 141 E4
Monimail Fife 140 C1
Monington Pembks 42 B4
Monk Bretton S York 84 A5
Monk Fryston N York 91 F2
Monk Sherborne Hants 26 D5
Monk Soham Suffk 65 E2
Monk Soham Green Suffk 65 E2
Monk Street Essex 51 G4
Monk's Gate W Susx 16 C4
Monken Hadley Gt Lon 28 C6
Monkhide Herefs 46 B4
Monkhill Cumb 103 G6
Monkhopton Shrops 57 F5
Monkland Herefs 45 G5
Monkleigh Devon 21 E3
Monknash V Glam 35 G1
Monkokehampton Devon 8 C5
Monks Eleigh Suffk 52 C5
Monks Heath Ches 82 C2
Monks Horton Kent 19 E5
Monks Kirby Warwks 59 G4
Monks Risborough Bucks 41 F5
Monkseaton T & W 115 E3
Monksilver Somset 22 D3
Monkspath W Mids 58 D3
Monksthorpe Lincs 87 E1
Monkswood Mons 37 E4
Monkton Devon 10 B5
Monkton Kent 31 F2
Monkton S Ayrs 119 E2
Monkton T & W 115 E2
Monkton V Glam 35 G1
Monkton Combe Somset 24 C5
Monkton Deverill Wilts 24 D3
Monkton Farleigh Wilts 24 D6
Monkton Heathfield Somset 23 E2
Monkton Up Wimborne Dorset 12 D6
Monkton Wyld Dorset 10 D4
Monkwearmouth T & W 115 F1
Monkwood Hants 27 E2
Monmore Green W Mids 58 B5
Monmouth Mons 37 F6
Monnington on Wye Herefs 45 F3
Monreith D & G 101 E4
Mont Saint Guern 174 f2
Montacute Somset 23 H1
Montcliffe Gt Man 82 B6
Montford Shrops 69 F1
Montford Bridge Shrops 69 F1
Montgarrie Abers 148 C6
Montgarswood E Ayrs 119 G2
Montgomery Powys 56 C5
Montgreenan N Ayrs 119 E4
Monton Gt Man 82 C5
Montrose Angus 141 G6
Monxton Hants 26 A4
Monyash Derbys 83 F1
Monymusk Abers 148 D6
Monzie P & K 139 F2
Moodiesburn N Lans 130 C2
Moonzie Fife 140 C1
Moor Allerton W York 90 D3
Moor Crichel Dorset 12 D5
Moor End Beds 49 H1
Moor End Devon 8 D5
Moor End E R Yk 92 B3
Moor End Lancs 88 B4
Moor End N York 91 G3
Moor End W York 90 B2
Moor Green Herts 50 D3
Moor Head W York 90 D2
Moor Monkton N York 91 F5
Moor Row Cumb 102 D1
Moor Row Cumb 103 F5
Moor Row Dur 106 A2
Moor Side Lancs 88 C3
Moor Side Lancs 88 C3
Moor Side Lincs 74 C6
Moor Street Kent 30 B3
Moor Street W Mids 58 C4
Moorbath Dorset 11 E4
Moorby Lincs 86 C1
Moorcot Herefs 45 F5
Moordown Dorset 13 E4
Moore Ches 81 H3
Moorend Gloucs 38 B5
Moorends S York 91 H1
Moorgreen Hants 14 C5
Moorgreen Notts 72 C5
Moorhall Derbys 83 H2
Moorhampton Herefs 45 G4
Moorhead W York 90 C3
Moorhouse Cumb 103 F5
Moorhouse Cumb 103 G6
Moorhouse Notts 85 E1
Moorhouse W York 84 C6
Moorhouse Bank Surrey 29 E1
Moorland Somset 23 F2
Moorlinch Somset 23 G3
Moorsholm N York 107 F2
Moorside Cumb 94 B5
Moorside Dorset 24 D1
Moorside Gt Man 82 D5
Moorside W York 90 D3
Moorstock Kent 19 E5
Moorswater Cnwll 5 F2
Moorthorpe W York 84 B6
Moortown Devon 6 C5
Moortown Hants 13 E5
Moortown IOW 14 B2
Moortown Lincs 86 A5
Moortown Shrops 70 A2
Moortown W York 90 D3
Morangie Highld 162 D2
Morar Highld 143 F3
Morborne Cambs 61 G4
Morchard Bishop Devon 9 E5
Morcombelake Dorset 10 D4
Morcott Rutlnd 61 E5
Morda Shrops 69 E3
Morden Dorset 12 C4
Morden Gt Lon 28 C3
Mordiford Herefs 46 A3
Mordon Dur 106 C3
More Shrops 56 D4
Morebath Devon 22 B2
Morebattle Border 123 E2
Morecambe Lancs 95 E1
Moredon Wilts 39 F3
Morefield Highld 161 E3
Morehall Kent 19 F5
Moreleigh Devon 7 E3
Morenish P & K 138 C3
Moresby Cumb 102 D2
Moresby Parks Cumb 102 D2
Morestead Hants 26 C2
Moreton Dorset 12 B3
Moreton Essex 51 F1
Moreton Herefs 57 E2
Moreton Mersyd 81 E4
Moreton Oxon 41 E5
Moreton Staffs 70 C2
Moreton Staffs 71 F3
Moreton Corbet Shrops 69 H2
Moreton Jeffries Herefs 46 B4
Moreton Morrell Warwks 48 A5
Moreton on Lugg Herefs 45 H4
Moreton Paddox Warwks 48 A5
Moreton Pinkney Nhants 48 D4
Moreton Say Shrops 70 A3
Moreton Valence Gloucs 38 C5
Moreton-in-Marsh Gloucs 47 G2
Moretonhampstead Devon 8 D3
Moretonmill Shrops 69 H2
Morfa Cerdgn 42 C4
Morfa Bychan Gwynd 67 E4
Morfa Dinlle Gwynd 66 D6
Morfa Glas Neath 35 F5
Morfa Nefyn Gwynd 66 C4
Morgan's Vale Wilts 25 G1
Morganstown Cardif 36 B2
Morham E Loth 132 D2
Moriah Cerdgn 54 D3
Morland Cumb 104 C2
Morley Ches 82 C3
Morley Derbys 72 B4
Morley Dur 105 H3
Morley W York 90 D2
Morley Green Ches 82 C3
Morley St Botolph Norfk 64 C5
Mornick Cnwll 5 G3
Morningside C Edin 132 A2
Morningside N Lans 120 C5
Morningthorpe Norfk 65 E5
Morpeth Nthumb 114 D4
Morphie Abers 141 G6
Morrey Staffs 71 F2
Morridge Side Staffs 71 E5
Morridge Top Staffs 83 E1
Morriston Swans 34 D4
Morston Norfk 76 C4
Mortehoe Devon 21 E5
Morthen S York 84 B4
Mortimer Berks 27 E6
Mortimer Common Berks 27 E6
Mortimer West End Hants 27 E6
Mortimer's Cross Herefs 56 D2
Mortlake Gt Lon 28 C4
Morton Cumb 103 H6
Morton Cumb 104 A4
Morton Derbys 72 B6
Morton IOW 14 D2
Morton Lincs 85 F4
Morton Lincs 74 A2
Morton Notts 73 E5
Morton Shrops 69 E2
Morton Hall Lincs 85 F1
Morton on the Hill Norfk 76 D2
Morton Tinmouth Dur 106 A3
Morton-on-Swale N York 97 F4
Morvah Cnwll 2 B3
Morval Cnwll 5 F2
Morvich Highld 152 D1
Morville Shrops 57 G5
Morville Heath Shrops 57 G5
Morwellham Quay Devon 6 B5
Morwenstow Cnwll 20 B2
Mosborough S York 84 B3
Moscow E Ayrs 119 G3
Mose Shrops 57 H4
Mosedale Cumb 103 G3
Moseley W Mids 58 B5
Moseley W Mids 58 D4
Moseley Worcs 46 D5
Moses Gate Gt Man 82 B5
Moss Ag & B 134 B4
Moss S York 84 D6
Moss Wrexhm 69 E5
Moss Bank Mersyd 81 G4
Moss Edge Lancs 88 C4
Moss End Ches 82 B2
Moss Side Cumb 103 F5
Moss Side Lancs 88 B3
Moss Side Mersyd 81 F5
Moss Side Mersyd 81 E5
Moss-side Highld 155 G5
Mossat Abers 157 G1
Mossbank Shet 169 j4
Mossbay Cumb 102 D3
Mossblown S Ayrs 119 F2
Mossbrow Gt Man 82 B4
Mossburnford Border 122 D1
Mossdale D & G 110 A2
Mossdale E Ayrs 109 G5
Mossend N Lans 120 B5
Mosser Mains Cumb 103 E3
Mossley Ches 70 D6
Mossley Gt Man 83 E5
Mosspaul Hotel Border 112 A5
Mosstodloch Moray 157 E5
Mossy Lea Lancs 81 G6
Mossyard D & G 101 G5
Mosterton Dorset 11 E5
Moston Gt Man 82 D5
Moston Shrops 69 H3
Moston Green Ches 70 B6
Mostyn Flints 80 D3
Motcombe Dorset 24 D2
Mothecombe Devon 6 C2
Motherby Cumb 104 A3
Motherwell N Lans 120 B5
Motspur Park Gt Lon 28 C3
Mottingham Gt Lon 29 E3
Mottisfont Hants 26 B2
Mottistone IOW 14 B2
Mottram in Longdendale Gt Man 83 E4
Mottram St Andrew Ches 82 D2
Mouilpied Guern 174 g1
Mouldsworth Ches 81 G2
Moulin P & K 139 G6
Moulsecoomb E Susx 16 D2
Moulsford Oxon 40 D3
Moulsoe Bucks 49 G3
Moultavie Highld 155 E6
Moulton Ches 82 B2
Moulton Lincs 74 C2
Moulton N York 97 E5
Moulton Nhants 60 D2
Moulton Suffk 63 F2
Moulton V Glam 36 B1
Moulton Chapel Lincs 74 C2
Moulton Seas End Lincs 74 D3
Moulton St Mary Norfk 65 F6
Mount Cnwll 3 E5
Mount Cnwll 5 E3
Mount W York 90 B1
Mount Ambrose Cnwll 3 E4
Mount Bures Essex 52 C4
Mount Hawke Cnwll 3 E4
Mount Hermon Cnwll 2 D1
Mount Lothian Mdloth 121 G5
Mount Pleasant Ches 70 C6
Mount Pleasant Derbys 72 A5
Mount Pleasant Dur 106 B4
Mount Pleasant E Susx 17 E3
Mount Pleasant Norfk 64 B5
Mount Pleasant Suffk 52 A5
Mount Pleasant Worcs 58 C2
Mount Sorrel Wilts 25 F2
Mount Tabor W York 90 B2
Mountain W York 90 B3
Mountain Ash Rhondd 36 B4
Mountain Cross Border 121 F4
Mountain Street Kent 30 D1
Mountfield E Susx 18 A3
Mountgerald House Highld 154 D5
Mountjoy Cnwll 4 B2
Mountnessing Essex 29 G6
Mounton Mons 37 F4
Mountsorrel Leics 72 C1
Mousehill Surrey 27 G3
Mousehole Cnwll 2 B2
Mouswald D & G 111 E2
Mow Cop Ches 70 D6
Mowhaugh Border 123 E1
Mowmacre Hill Leics 60 B6
Mowsley Leics 60 C4
Mowtie Abers 149 F3
Moy Highld 155 F2
Moy Highld 145 F3
Moye Highld 152 C1
Moyles Court Hants 13 E5
Moylgrove Pembks 42 A4
Muasdale Ag & B 117 F4
Much Birch Herefs 45 H2
Much Cowarne Herefs 46 B4
Much Dewchurch Herefs 45 H2
Much Hadham Herts 51 E3
Much Hoole Lancs 88 C2
Much Hoole Town Lancs 88 C2
Much Marcle Herefs 46 B2
Much Wenlock Shrops 57 F5
Muchalls Abers 149 G4
Muchelney Somset 23 G2
Muchelney Ham Somset 23 G2
Muchlarnick Cnwll 5 F2
Mucking Essex 29 H4
Muckingford Essex 29 G4
Muckleburgh Collection Norfk 76 D4
Muckleford Dorset 11 G4
Mucklestone Staffs 70 B4
Muckley Shrops 57 G5
Muckton Lincs 86 D3
Mud Row Kent 30 D3
Muddiford Devon 21 F4
Muddles Green E Susx 17 F3
Mudeford Dorset 13 F4
Mudford Somset 24 A1
Mudford Sock Somset 24 A1
Mudgley Somset 23 G4
Mugdock Stirlg 129 G3
Mugeary Highld 150 D3
Mugginton Derbys 71 H4
Muggintonlane End Derbys 71 H4
Muggleswick Dur 105 G5
Muir of Fowlis Abers 148 C6
Muir of Miltonduff Moray 156 D5
Muir of Ord Highld 154 C4
Muir of Thorn P & K 139 H3
Muirden Abers 158 C4
Muirdrum Angus 141 F3
Muiresk Abers 158 C4
Muirhead Angus 140 C3
Muirhead Fife 132 B6
Muirhead N Lans 130 C2
Muirkirk E Ayrs 120 B2
Muirmill Stirlg 130 D3
Muirshearlich Highld 144 D2
Muirtack Abers 159 F3
Muirton P & K 139 F1
Muirton Mains Highld 154 C4
Muirton of Ardblair P & K 140 B4
Muker N York 96 B5
Mulbarton Norfk 64 D5
Mulben Moray 157 F4
Mulfra Cnwll 2 B3
Mullacott Cross Devon 21 E5
Mullion Cnwll 2 D2
Mullion Cove Cnwll 2 D1
Mumby Lincs 87 E2
Munderfield Row Herefs 46 B4
Munderfield Stocks Herefs 46 B4
Mundesley Norfk 77 F4
Mundford Norfk 63 G5
Mundham Norfk 65 F5
Mundon Hill Essex 52 B1
Mundy Bois Kent 18 C6
Mungrisdale Cumb 103 H3
Munlochy Highld 155 E4
Munnoch N Ayrs 118 D4
Munsley Herefs 46 B3
Munslow Shrops 57 E4
Murchington Devon 8 D3
Murcot Worcs 47 F3
Murcott Oxon 40 D6
Murcott Wilts 38 D3
Murkle Highld 167 E5
Murlaggan Highld 144 B4
Murrell Green Hants 27 F5
Murroes Angus 141 E3
Murrow Cambs 62 C6
Mursley Bucks 49 F2
Murston Kent 30 C2
Murthill Angus 141 E5
Murthly P & K 140 A4
Murton Cumb 104 D2
Murton Dur 106 C6
Murton N York 91 G5
Murton Nthumb 123 G4
Murton T & W 115 E3
Musbury Devon 10 C4
Muscoates N York 98 C3
Musselburgh E Loth 132 B2
Muston Leics 73 F4
Muston N York 99 G3
Mustow Green Worcs 58 B3
Muswell Hill Gt Lon 28 D5
Mutehill D & G 102 A5
Mutford Suffk 65 G4
Muthill P & K 139 F1
Mutterton Devon 9 G5
Muxton Shrops 70 B1
Mybster Highld 167 E4
Myddfai Carmth 43 H2
Myddle Shrops 69 G2
Mydroilyn Cerdgn 43 E5
Mylor Cnwll 3 F3
Mylor Bridge Cnwll 3 E3
Mynachlog ddu Pembks 33 F5
Myndd-llan Flints 80 D2
Myndtown Shrops 56 D4
Mynydd Buch Cerdgn 55 E3
Mynydd Isa Flints 81 E1
Mynydd Llandygai Gwynd 79 F1
Mynydd-bach Mons 37 F4
Mynydd-Bach Swans 34 D4
Mynyddgarreg Carmth 34 B5
Mynytho Gwynd 66 C3
Myrebird Abers 149 E4
Myredykes Border 112 C5
Mytchett Surrey 27 G5
Mytholm W York 90 A2
Mytholmroyd W York 90 A2
Mythop Lancs 88 B3
Myton-on-Swale N York 97 G1

N

Na Buirgh W Isls 168 c6
Naast Highld 160 B2
Nab's Head Lancs 89 E2
Naburn N York 91 G4
Naccolt Kent 18 D6
Nackington Kent 31 E1
Nacton Suffk 53 F5
Nafferton E R Yk 92 D5
Nag's Head Gloucs 38 D4
Nailbridge Gloucs 37 G6
Nailsbourne Somset 23 E2
Nailsea Somset 37 F1
Nailstone Leics 59 G6
Nailsworth Gloucs 38 C4
Nairn Highld 155 G5
Nalderswood Surrey 16 C6
Nancegollan Cnwll 2 D3
Nancledra Cnwll 2 C3
Nanhoron Gwynd 66 B3
Nannerch Flints 80 D2

301

Nanpantan
Newton Toney
302

Nanpantan Leics 72 C2
Nanpean Cnwll 3 G5
Nanquidno Cnwll 2 A3
Nanstallon Cnwll 4 D3
Nant Gwynant Gwynd 67 F5
Nant Peris Gwynd 67 F6
Nant-ddu Powys 35 G6
Nant-glas Powys 55 G2
Nant-y-Bwch Blae G 36 B5
Nant-y-caws Carmth 34 B6
Nant-y-derry Mons 36 D5
Nant-y-gollen Shrops 69 E3
Nant-y-moel Brdgnd 35 G3
Nant-y-pandy Conwy 79 F2
Nanternis Cerdgn 42 D5
Nantgaredig Carmth 43 E1
Nantgarw Rhondd 36 B3
Nantglyn Denbgs 68 B6
Nantgwyn Powys 55 G3
Nantlle Gwynd 67 E5
Nantmawr Shrops 69 E2
Nantmel Powys 55 H2
Nantmor Gwynd 67 F5
Nantwich Ches 70 B5
Nantyffyllon Brdgnd 35 F3
Nantyglo Blae G 36 C5
Naphill Bucks 41 G4
Napleton Worcs 46 D4
Nappa N York 89 G5
Napton on the Hill Warwks 48 C5
Narberth Pembks 33 E3
Narborough Leics 60 B5
Narborough Norfk 75 H1
Narkurs Cnwll 5 G1
Nasareth Gwynd 66 D5
Naseby Nhants 60 C3
Nash Bucks 49 F3
Nash Gt Lon 29 E2
Nash Herefs 45 F5
Nash Newpt 36 D3
Nash Shrops 57 F2
Nash End Worcs 57 H4
Nash Lee Bucks 41 G5
Nash Street Kent 29 G3
Nash's Green Hants 27 E4
Nassington Nhants 61 G5
Nastend Gloucs 38 C5
Nasty Herts 50 D3
Nateby Cumb 96 A5
Nateby Lancs 88 C4
National Shire Horse Centre Devon 6 C3
National Space Science Centre Leics 60 B6
Natland Cumb 95 F4
Naughton Suffk 52 D6
Naunton Gloucs 47 G1
Naunton Worcs 46 D3
Naunton Beauchamp Worcs 47 E4
Navenby Lincs 73 G6
Navestock Essex 29 F6
Navestock Side Essex 29 F6
Navidale House Hotel Highld 163 G5
Navity Highld 155 F6
Nawton N York 98 B3
Nayland Suffk 52 C4
Nazeing Essex 51 E1
Nazeing Gate Essex 51 E1
Neacroft Hants 13 F4
Neal's Green Warwks 59 F4
Neap Shet 169 j3
Near Cotton Staffs 71 F5
Near Sawrey Cumb 94 D4
Neasden Gt Lon 28 C5
Neasham Dur 106 C2
Neath Neath 35 E4
Neatham Hants 27 F3
Neatishead Norfk 77 F2
Nebo Cerdgn 54 C2
Nebo Conwy 67 H6
Nebo Gwynd 66 D5
Nebo IOA 78 D4
Necton Norfk 76 B1
Nedd Highld 164 B2
Nedderton Nthumb 114 D4
Nedging Suffk 52 D5
Nedging Tye Suffk 52 D6
Needham Norfk 65 E3
Needham Market Suffk 52 D6
Needham Street Suffk 63 F2
Needingworth Cambs 62 C3
Neen Savage Shrops 57 G3
Neen Sollars Shrops 57 G3
Neenton Shrops 57 G4
Nefyn Gwynd 66 C4
Neilston E Rens 119 G5
Nelson Caerph 36 B4
Nelson Lancs 89 G3
Nemphlar S Lans 120 C4
Nempnett Thrubwell Somset 23 H5
Nenthall Cumb 104 D5
Nenthead Cumb 104 D4
Nenthorn Border 122 D3
Neopardy Devon 9 E4
Nep Town W Susx 16 C3
Nercwys Flints 69 E6
Nereabolls Ag & B 116 A6
Nerston S Lans 120 A5
Nesbit Nthumb 123 G3
Nesfield N York 90 B5
Ness Ches 81 E2
Ness Botanic Gardens Ches 81 E2
Nesscliffe Shrops 69 F2
Neston Ches 81 E2
Neston Wilts 38 C1
Netchwood Shrops 57 F4
Nether Alderley Ches 82 C2
Nether Blainslie Border 122 C4
Nether Broughton Notts 73 E3
Nether Cerne Dorset 11 G4
Nether Compton Dorset 24 B1
Nether Crimond Abers 158 D1
Nether Dallachy Moray 157 F5
Nether Exe Devon 9 F5
Nether Fingland S Lans 110 D6
Nether Handley Derbys 84 B2
Nether Handwick Angus 140 D4
Nether Haugh S York 84 B4
Nether Headon Notts 85 E2
Nether Heage Derbys 72 A5
Nether Heyford Nhants 49 E5
Nether Howcleugh S Lans 111 E6
Nether Kellet Lancs 95 F2
Nether Kinmundy Abers 159 F3
Nether Langwith Notts 84 C2
Nether Moor Derbys 84 B1
Nether Padley Derbys 83 G2
Nether Poppleton N York 91 G5
Nether Row Cumb 103 G4
Nether Silton N York 97 H4
Nether Skyborry Shrops 56 C3
Nether Stowey Somset 23 E3
Nether Street Essex 51 G2
Nether Wallop Hants 26 A3
Nether Wasdale Cumb 94 B5
Nether Welton Cumb 103 G5
Nether Westcote Gloucs 47 H1
Nether Whitacre Warwks 59 E5
Nether Whitecleuch S Lans 120 C1
Nether Winchendon Bucks 41 E5
Netheravon Wilts 25 G4
Netherbrae Abers 158 D5
Netherburn S Lans 120 C4
Netherbury Dorset 11 E4
Netherby Cumb 112 A2
Netherby N York 90 D4
Nethercleuch D & G 111 F3
Nethercote Warwks 60 A2
Nethercott Devon 21 E4
Nethercott Devon 5 G6
Netherend Gloucs 37 G4
Netherfield E Susx 17 H3
Netherfield Leics 72 D2
Netherfield Notts 72 D4
Netherfield Road E Susx 18 A3
Nethergate Lincs 85 E5
Nethergate Norfk 76 D3
Netherhampton Wilts 25 F2
Netherhay Dorset 10 D5
Netherland Green Staffs 71 F3
Netherlaw D & G 102 B5
Netherley Abers 149 F4
Nethermill D & G 111 E3
Nethermuir Abers 159 E3
Netheroyd Hill W York 90 C1
Netherplace E Rens 119 G5
Netherseal Derbys 71 H1
Netherstreet Wilts 25 E6
Netherthong W York 83 F6
Netherthorpe Derbys 84 B2
Netherton Angus 141 E5
Netherton Devon 7 F5
Netherton Hants 26 B5
Netherton Herefs 45 H2
Netherton N Lans 120 B5
Netherton Nthumb 124 C2
Netherton Oxon 40 B4
Netherton P & K 140 A5
Netherton Shrops 57 G4
Netherton Stirlg 129 G3
Netherton W Mids 58 B4
Netherton W York 83 F6
Netherton W York 90 D1
Netherton Worcs 47 E3
Nethertown Cumb 102 D1
Nethertown Highld 167 G6
Nethertown Lancs 89 F3
Nethertown Staffs 71 F2
Netherurd Border 121 F4
Netherwitton Nthumb 114 C4
Nethy Bridge Highld 156 B1
Netley Hants 14 C4
Netley Marsh Hants 13 G6
Nettacott Devon 9 F5
Nettlebed Oxon 41 E3
Nettlebridge Somset 24 B4
Nettlecombe Dorset 11 E4
Nettlecombe IOW 14 C1
Nettleden Herts 50 A2
Nettleham Lincs 85 H2
Nettlestead Kent 29 H1
Nettlestead Green Kent 29 H1
Nettlestone IOW 14 D3
Nettlesworth Dur 106 B6
Nettleton Lincs 86 B5
Nettleton Wilts 38 C2
Nettleton Shrub Wilts 38 C2
Netton Devon 6 C2
Netton Wilts 25 G3
Neuadd Carmth 43 G1
Neuadd Fawr Carmth 43 H3
Neuadd-ddu Powys 55 G3
Nevendon Essex 30 A5
Nevern Pembks 42 A3
Nevill Holt Leics 60 D5
New Abbey D & G 110 D1
New Aberdour Abers 159 E5
New Addington Gt Lon 29 E2
New Alresford Hants 26 D2
New Alyth P & K 140 B4
New Arram E R Yk 92 D4
New Ash Green Kent 29 G3
New Balderton Notts 73 F5
New Barn Kent 29 G3
New Barnet Gt Lon 28 D6
New Barton Nhants 61 E2
New Bewick Nthumb 124 D3
New Bilton Warwks 59 H3
New Bolingbroke Lincs 74 C6
New Boultham Lincs 85 G2
New Bradwell Bucks 49 F3
New Brampton Derbys 84 A2
New Brancepeth Dur 106 B5
New Bridge N York 98 D3
New Brighton Flints 81 E1
New Brighton Mersyd 81 E4
New Brinsley Notts 72 B5
New Brotton N York 107 F3
New Broughton Wrexhm 69 E5
New Buckenham Norfk 64 C4
New Bury Gt Man 82 B5
New Byth Abers 158 D4
New Costessey Norfk 77 E1
New Cowper Cumb 103 E5
New Crofton W York 91 E1
New Cross Cerdgn 54 D3
New Cross Gt Lon 28 D4
New Cross Somset 23 G1
New Cumnock E Ayrs 109 H6
New Cut E Susx 18 B3
New Deer Abers 159 E4
New Delaval Nthumb 115 E3
New Delph Gt Man 83 E5
New Denham Bucks 28 A4
New Duston Nhants 60 C2
New Earswick N York 91 G5
New Eastwood Notts 72 B5
New Edlington S York 84 C5
New Elgin Moray 156 D5
New Ellerby E R Yk 93 E3
New Eltham Gt Lon 29 E3
New End Worcs 47 F5
New England Cambs 61 H5
New Farnley W York 90 D3
New Ferry Mersyd 81 F3
New Fletton Cambs 61 H5
New Fryston W York 91 F2
New Galloway D & G 109 H2
New Gilston Fife 132 C6
New Grimsby IOS 2 a2
New Hartley Nthumb 115 E3
New Haw Surrey 28 B2
New Hedges Pembks 33 E2
New Herrington T & W 106 C6
New Holkham Norfk 76 B3
New Holland Lincs 93 E2
New Houghton Derbys 84 C1
New Houghton Norfk 76 A3
New Houses Gt Man 81 H5
New Houses N York 96 A2
New Hutton Cumb 95 F4
New Hythe Kent 29 H2
New Inn Carmth 43 E3
New Inn Torfn 36 D4
New Invention Shrops 57 E6
New Lakenham Norfk 65 E6
New Lanark S Lans 120 C4
New Lane Lancs 81 F6
New Lane End Ches 82 A4
New Langholm D & G 111 H3
New Leake Lincs 74 D6
New Leeds Abers 159 F4
New Lodge S York 84 A6
New Longton Lancs 88 D2
New Luce D & G 108 D1
New Malden Gt Lon 28 C3
New Marske N York 107 E3
New Marston Oxon 40 C5
New Marton Shrops 69 F3
New Mill Abers 149 E3
New Mill Cnwll 2 B3
New Mill Herts 41 G5
New Mill W York 83 F6
New Mills Cnwll 3 F5
New Mills Derbys 83 E3
New Mills Powys 56 A5
New Milton Hants 13 F4
New Mistley Essex 53 E4
New Moat Pembks 33 E4
New Ollerton Notts 84 D1
New Oscott W Mids 58 D5
New Pitsligo Abers 159 E5
New Polzeath Cnwll 4 C4
New Prestwick S Ayrs 119 E2
New Quay Cerdgn 42 D5
New Quay Essex 52 D3
New Rackheath Norfk 77 F1
New Radnor Powys 45 E5
New Rent Cumb 104 A4
New Ridley Nthumb 114 B1
New Road Side N York 89 H4
New Romney Kent 18 D4
New Rossington S York 84 D4
New Row Cerdgn 55 E3
New Row Lancs 89 E3
New Sauchie Clacks 131 E5
New Sharlston W York 91 E2
New Shoreston Nthumb 125 E4
New Silksworth T & W 106 C6
New Skelton N York 107 F3
New Somerby Lincs 73 G4
New Spilsby Lincs 86 D1
New Springs Gt Man 82 A5
New Stevenston N Lans 120 B5
New Street Herefs 45 F5
New Swannington Leics 72 B2
New Thundersley Essex 30 A5
New Town Beds 50 C5
New Town Dorset 12 C6
New Town Dorset 12 D5
New Town Dorset 25 E1
New Town E Loth 132 C2
New Town E Susx 17 F3
New Town Nhants 61 F3
New Town Wilts 39 G1
New Tredegar Caerph 36 C5
New Trows S Lans 120 C3
New Tupton Derbys 84 B1
New Village E R Yk 92 B3
New Walsoken Cambs 75 E1
New Waltham Lincs 86 C5
New Whittington Derbys 84 B2
New Winton E Loth 132 C2
New Yatt Oxon 40 B6
New York Lincs 74 C6
New York N York 90 C6
New York T & W 115 E2
Newall W York 90 C4
Newark Cambs 62 A5
Newark Ork 169 d4
Newark-on-Trent Notts 73 F5
Newarthill N Lans 120 B5
Newbarn Kent 19 E5
Newbattle Mdloth 132 B2
Newbie D & G 111 F1
Newbiggin Cumb 104 A3
Newbiggin Cumb 104 B5
Newbiggin Cumb 104 C3
Newbiggin Cumb 94 B4
Newbiggin Cumb 94 C2
Newbiggin Dur 105 F3
Newbiggin Dur 106 A6
Newbiggin N York 96 C4
Newbiggin N York 96 C3
Newbiggin-by-the-Sea Nthumb 115 E4
Newbiggin-on-Lune Cumb 95 H5
Newbigging Angus 140 C4
Newbigging Angus 140 D3
Newbigging Angus 141 E3
Newbigging S Lans 121 E4
Newbold Derbys 84 A2
Newbold Leics 72 B2
Newbold on Avon Warwks 59 H3
Newbold on Stour Warwks 47 H4
Newbold Pacey Warwks 48 A5
Newbold Revel Warwks 59 G3
Newbold Verdon Leics 59 G6
Newborough Cambs 62 A6
Newborough IOA 78 D1
Newborough Staffs 71 F2
Newbottle Nhants 48 C3
Newbottle T & W 106 C6
Newbourne Suffk 53 F5
Newbridge C Edin 131 G2
Newbridge Caerph 36 C4
Newbridge Cerdgn 43 E5
Newbridge Cnwll 2 B3
Newbridge Cnwll 3 E4
Newbridge D & G 110 D3
Newbridge Hants 13 G6
Newbridge IOW 14 B2
Newbridge Oxon 40 B4
Newbridge Pembks 32 D5
Newbridge Wrexhm 69 E4
Newbridge Green Worcs 46 D3
Newbridge on Wye Powys 44 C5
Newbridge-on-Usk Mons 37 E4
Newbrough Nthumb 113 F1
Newbuildings Devon 9 E5
Newburgh Abers 159 E5
Newburgh Abers 159 F2
Newburgh Fife 140 B2
Newburgh Lancs 81 G6
Newburgh Priory N York 98 A2
Newburn T & W 114 C2
Newbury Berks 26 C6
Newbury Somset 24 C4
Newbury Wilts 24 D3
Newbury Park Gt Lon 29 E5
Newby Cumb 104 C2
Newby Lancs 89 G4
Newby N York 106 D2
Newby N York 95 H2
Newby N York 99 F4
Newby Bridge Cumb 94 D3
Newby Cross Cumb 103 H5
Newby East Cumb 104 B6
Newby Head Cumb 104 C2
Newby West Cumb 103 H5
Newby Wiske N York 97 G4
Newcastle Mons 37 E6
Newcastle Shrops 56 C4
Newcastle Airport Nthumb 114 C3
Newcastle Emlyn Carmth 42 C3
Newcastle upon Tyne T & W 114 D2
Newcastle-under-Lyme Staffs 70 C5
Newcastleton Border 112 B3
Newchapel Pembks 42 B3
Newchapel Staffs 70 D5
Newchapel Surrey 16 D6
Newchurch Blae G 36 C5
Newchurch Herefs 45 F4
Newchurch IOW 14 D2
Newchurch Kent 18 D4
Newchurch Mons 37 F4
Newchurch Powys 45 E4
Newchurch Staffs 71 F2
Newchurch in Pendle Lancs 89 G3
Newcraighall C Edin 132 B2
Newdigate Surrey 16 C6
Newell Green Berks 41 G1
Newenden Kent 18 B4
Newent Gloucs 46 C2
Newfield Dur 106 B4
Newfield Dur 106 B6
Newfield Highld 163 E1
Newfound Hants 26 D4
Newgale Pembks 32 C4
Newgate Norfk 76 D4
Newgate Street Herts 50 D1
Newhall Ches 70 A5
Newhall Derbys 71 H2
Newham Nthumb 125 E4
Newhaven Derbys 71 G6
Newhaven E Susx 17 E1
Newhey Gt Man 82 D6
Newholm N York 107 H2
Newhouse N Lans 120 B6
Newick E Susx 17 E3
Newingreen Kent 19 E5
Newington Kent 30 B2
Newington Kent 19 E5
Newington Oxon 40 D4
Newington Shrops 56 D4
Newington Bagpath Gloucs 38 C4
Newland Cumb 94 D3
Newland E R Yk 92 B2
Newland E R Yk 92 D3
Newland Gloucs 37 F5
Newland N York 91 H2
Newland Oxon 40 B5
Newland Somset 22 A3
Newland Worcs 46 C4
Newlandrig Mdloth 121 H6
Newlands Border 112 B4
Newlands Cumb 103 G4
Newlands Nthumb 105 G6
Newlands of Dundurcas Moray 157 E4
Newlyn Cnwll 2 B3
Newlyn East Cnwll 3 F5
Newmachar Abers 159 E1
Newmains N Lans 120 C5
Newman's End Essex 51 F2
Newman's Green Suffk 52 B5
Newmarket Suffk 63 F2
Newmarket W Isls 168 e8
Newmill Border 112 B6
Newmill Moray 157 F4
Newmill of Inshewan Angus 140 D6
Newmillerdam W York 90 D1
Newmills C Edin 131 H2
Newmills Fife 131 F4
Newmills Mons 37 F5
Newmiln P & K 140 A3
Newmilns E Ayrs 119 G3
Newnes Shrops 69 F3
Newney Green Essex 51 G1
Newnham Gloucs 38 B5
Newnham Hants 27 E5
Newnham Herts 50 C4
Newnham Kent 30 C2
Newnham Nhants 48 D5
Newnham Worcs 57 G2
Newnham Paddox Warwks 59 H4
Newport Cnwll 5 G4
Newport Devon 21 F4
Newport Dorset 12 C4
Newport E R Yk 92 B3
Newport Essex 51 F4
Newport Gloucs 38 B4
Newport Highld 163 H6
Newport IOW 14 C2
Newport Newpt 36 D3
Newport Norfk 77 H2
Newport Pembks 33 E6
Newport Shrops 70 B2
Newport Pagnell Bucks 49 G3
Newport-on-Tay Fife 140 D2
Newpound Common W Susx 16 B4
Newquay Cnwll 4 B2
Newquay Airport Cnwll 4 B2
Newsam Green W York 91 E3
Newsbank Ches 82 C1
Newseat Abers 158 C2
Newsham Lancs 88 D3
Newsham N York 96 D6
Newsham N York 97 G3
Newsham Nthumb 115 E3
Newsholme E R Yk 92 A2
Newsholme Lancs 89 G5
Newstead Border 122 C3
Newstead Notts 72 C5
Newstead Nthumb 125 E4
Newtack Moray 157 F4
Newthorpe N York 91 F3
Newthorpe Notts 72 B5
Newtimber W Susx 16 D3
Newtoft Lincs 85 H3
Newton Ag & B 128 B5
Newton Beds 50 C5
Newton Border 122 C1
Newton Brdgnd 35 F2
Newton Cambs 75 E1
Newton Cambs 51 E6
Newton Cardif 36 C2
Newton Ches 81 F1
Newton Ches 69 G6
Newton Ches 81 G2
Newton Cumb 94 C2
Newton Derbys 72 B6
Newton Herefs 45 F2
Newton Herefs 56 D2
Newton Herefs 45 H5
Newton Highld 154 D4
Newton Highld 155 F4
Newton Highld 155 F6
Newton Lancs 88 B3
Newton Lancs 95 G2
Newton Lancs 89 E5
Newton Lincs 73 H4
Newton Mdloth 132 B2
Newton Moray 156 D5
Newton Moray 157 E5
Newton N York 99 E2
Newton Nhants 61 E4
Newton Norfk 76 A2
Newton Notts 72 D4
Newton Nthumb 124 C2
Newton Nthumb 114 B2
Newton S Lans 120 A5
Newton S Lans 120 D3
Newton Shrops 69 F3
Newton Somset 22 D3
Newton Staffs 71 E2
Newton Suffk 52 C5
Newton W Loth 131 G3
Newton W Mids 58 C5
Newton W York 91 F2
Newton Warwks 60 A3
Newton Wilts 25 H1
Newton Abbot Devon 7 F5
Newton Arlosh Cumb 103 F6
Newton Aycliffe Dur 106 B3
Newton Bewley Dur 106 D3
Newton Blossomville Bucks 49 G4
Newton Bromswold Beds 61 F2
Newton Burgoland Leics 72 A1
Newton by Toft Lincs 85 H3
Newton Ferrers Cnwll 5 G2
Newton Ferrers Devon 6 C2
Newton Ferry W Isls 168 c5
Newton Flotman Norfk 65 E5
Newton Green Mons 37 F3
Newton Harcourt Leics 60 B5
Newton Heath Gt Man 82 D5
Newton Hill W York 90 D2
Newton Kyme N York 91 F4
Newton Longville Bucks 49 G2
Newton Mearns E Rens 119 G5
Newton Morrell N York 106 B2
Newton Mountain Pembks 32 D2
Newton Mulgrave N York 107 G2
Newton of Balcanquhal P & K 131 H6
Newton of Balcormo Fife 132 D6
Newton on Ouse N York 91 F6
Newton on the Hill Shrops 69 G2
Newton on Trent Lincs 85 F2
Newton Poppleford Devon 10 A4
Newton Purcell Oxon 48 D2
Newton Regis Warwks 59 F6
Newton Reigny Cumb 104 B3
Newton Row Highld 167 G3
Newton Solney Derbys 71 H3
Newton St Cyres Devon 9 F4
Newton St Faith Norfk 77 E2
Newton St Loe Somset 24 C6
Newton St Petrock Devon 20 D2
Newton Stacey Hants 26 B3
Newton Stewart D & G 109 F1
Newton Toney Wilts 25 H3

Newton Tracey

Ockbrook

Newton Tracey Devon 21 E3
Newton under Roseberry N York 107 E2
Newton Underwood Nthumb 114 C4
Newton upon Derwent E R Yk 92 A4
Newton Valence Hants 27 E2
Newton Wamphray D & G 111 F4
Newton with Scales Lancs 88 C3
Newton-by-the-Sea Nthumb 125 E4
Newton-le-Willows Mersyd 81 H4
Newton-le-Willows N York 97 E4
Newton-on-Rawcliffe N York 98 D4
Newton-on-the-Moor Nthumb 125 E1
Newtongarry Croft Abers 158 B3
Newtongrange Mdloth 132 B1
Newtonhill Abers 149 G4
Newtonloan Mdloth 121 H6
Newtonmill Angus 141 F6
Newtonmore Highld 146 B4
Newtown Blae G 36 C5
Newtown Ches 70 A5
Newtown Ches 70 D6
Newtown Ches 81 G2
Newtown Cnwll 2 C3
Newtown Cnwll 3 E2
Newtown Cnwll 5 E1
Newtown Cnwll 5 F4
Newtown Cumb 103 E5
Newtown Cumb 112 B1
Newtown Cumb 104 B2
Newtown Cumb 112 A1
Newtown D & G 110 B6
Newtown Derbys 83 E3
Newtown Devon 9 G4
Newtown Devon 21 H3
Newtown Dorset 11 E5
Newtown Dorset 12 D4
Newtown Gloucs 38 B4
Newtown Gt Man 81 H5
Newtown Hants 13 F6
Newtown Hants 26 C6
Newtown Hants 14 D5
Newtown Herefs 45 G5
Newtown Herefs 45 H2
Newtown Herefs 46 B4
Newtown Herefs 46 C3
Newtown Highld 145 F5
Newtown IOW 14 B3
Newtown Lancs 88 D1
Newtown Nthumb 123 G4
Newtown Nthumb 114 B6
Newtown Nthumb 124 D3
Newtown Powys 56 A4
Newtown Rhondd 36 B4
Newtown Shrops 69 F2
Newtown Shrops 69 G3
Newtown Somset 10 C6
Newtown Staffs 58 C6
Newtown Wilts 25 E2
Newtown Wilts 26 A6
Newtown Worcs 46 D5
Newtown Worcs 58 B3
Newtown Linford Leics 72 C1
Newtown of Beltrees Rens 119 F5
Newtown St Boswells Border 122 C3
Newtown Unthank Leics 59 H6
Newtyle Angus 140 C4
Newyears Green Gt Lon 28 B5
Newyork Ag & B 128 A6
Nextend Herefs 45 F5
Neyland Pembks 32 D2
Niarbyl IOM 174 k3
Nibley Gloucs 38 A5
Nibley Gloucs 38 B2
Nibley Green Gloucs 38 B4
Nicholashayne Devon 10 B6
Nicholaston Swans 34 C3
Nickies Hill Cumb 112 C1
Nidd N York 90 D6
Nigg Aber C 149 G5
Nigg Highld 163 E1
Nightcott Somset 22 B2
Nimlet Somset 38 B1
Nine Elms Wilts 39 F3
Nine Wells Pembks 32 B4
Ninebanks Nthumb 104 D5
Nineveh Worcs 57 F2
Ninfield E Susx 17 H3
Ningwood IOW 14 B2
Nisbet Border 122 D2
Nisbet Hill Border 123 E4
Niton IOW 14 C1
Nitshill C Glas 119 G5
No Man's Heath Ches 69 G5
No Man's Heath Warwks 71 H1
No Man's Land Cnwll 4 C3
No Man's Land Cnwll 5 F2
Noah's Ark Kent 29 F2
Noak Bridge Essex 29 H5
Noak Hill Essex 29 F5
Noblethorpe W York 83 H5
Nobold Shrops 69 G1
Nobottle Nhants 60 C2
Nocton Lincs 85 H1
Nogdam End Norfk 65 F5
Noke Oxon 40 D6
Nolton Pembks 32 C3
Nolton Haven Pembks 32 C4
Nomansland Devon 9 E6
Nomansland Wilts 25 H1
Noneley Shrops 69 G3
Nonington Kent 31 F1
Nook Cumb 112 B3
Nook Cumb 95 F3
Norbiton Gt Lon 28 C3
Norbreck Lancs 88 B4
Norbridge Herefs 46 C4
Norbury Ches 69 H5
Norbury Derbys 71 F4
Norbury Gt Lon 28 D3
Norbury Shrops 56 D5
Norbury Staffs 70 C2
Norbury Common Ches 69 H5
Norbury Junction Staffs 70 C2
Norchard Worcs 58 B2
Norcott Brook Ches 82 A3
Norcross Lancs 88 B4
Nordelph Norfk 63 E5
Norden Gt Man 89 G1
Nordley Shrops 57 G5
Norham Nthumb 123 F4
Norland Town W York 90 B2
Norley Ches 81 H2
Norleywood Hants 14 B3
Norlington E Susx 17 E3
Norman Cross Cambs 61 G4
Norman's Bay E Susx 17 H2
Norman's Green Devon 9 G5
Normanby Lincs 92 C1
Normanby Lincs 85 G3
Normanby N York 107 E3
Normanby N York 98 C3
Normanby le Wold Lincs 86 B4
Normandy Surrey 27 G4
Normanton Derbys 72 A3
Normanton Leics 73 F4
Normanton Lincs 73 G5
Normanton Notts 73 E5
Normanton Rutlnd 61 E6
Normanton W York 91 E2
Normanton Wilts 25 G3
Normanton le Heath Leics 72 A1
Normanton on Soar Notts 72 C2
Normanton on the Wolds Notts 72 D3
Normanton on Trent Notts 85 E1
Normoss Lancs 88 B3
Norney Surrey 27 G4
Norrington Common Wilts 24 D6
Norris Green Cnwll 5 H3
Norristhorpe W York 90 C2
North Anston S York 84 C3
North Aston Oxon 48 C2
North Baddesley Hants 14 B6
North Ballachulish Highld 137 E6
North Barrow Somset 24 B2
North Barsham Norfk 76 B3
North Benfleet Essex 30 A5
North Bersted W Susx 15 G4
North Berwick E Loth 132 D4
North Bitchburn Dur 106 A4
North Blyth Nthumb 115 E4
North Boarhunt Hants 14 D5
North Bockhampton Hants 13 F4
North Bovey Devon 8 D3
North Bradley Wilts 24 D5
North Brentor Devon 8 B3
North Brewham Somset 24 C3
North Bridge Surrey 27 H3
North Brook End Cambs 50 D5
North Buckland Devon 21 E5
North Burlingham Norfk 77 G1
North Cadbury Somset 24 B2
North Carlton Lincs 85 G2
North Carlton Notts 84 D3
North Cave E R Yk 92 C3
North Cerney Gloucs 39 E5
North Chailey E Susx 17 E3
North Charford Hants 25 G1
North Charlton Nthumb 125 E3
North Cheam Gt Lon 28 C3
North Cheriton Somset 24 B2
North Chideock Dorset 11 E4
North Cliffe E R Yk 92 C3
North Clifton Notts 85 F2
North Close Dur 106 B4
North Cockerington Lincs 86 D4
North Connel Ag & B 136 D3
North Cornelly Brdgnd 35 F2
North Corner Cnwll 3 E2
North Corry Highld 136 C5
North Cotes Lincs 86 D5
North Country Cnwll 2 D4
North Cove Suffk 65 G4
North Cowton N York 97 F5
North Crawley Bucks 49 G4
North Cray Gt Lon 29 F3
North Creake Norfk 76 B4
North Curry Somset 23 F2
North Dalton E R Yk 92 C5
North Deighton N York 91 E5
North Duffield N York 91 H3
North Duntulm Highld 150 D6
North Elham Kent 19 E6
North Elkington Lincs 86 C4
North Elmham Norfk 76 C2
North Elmsall W York 84 B6
North End Cumb 103 G6
North End Dorset 24 D2
North End E R Yk 93 F4
North End E R Yk 93 G3
North End Essex 51 G3
North End Hants 25 F1
North End Hants 26 D2
North End Hants 15 E4
North End Leics 72 C1
North End Lincs 93 E2
North End Lincs 86 C5
North End Lincs 85 H5
North End Lincs 74 C4
North End Lincs 87 E4
North End Mersyd 81 E5
North End Nhants 61 F2
North End Norfk 64 C5
North End Nthumb 114 C6
North End Somset 23 G6
North End W Susx 15 H4
North End W Susx 16 B2
North Erradale Highld 160 B2
North Evington Leics 60 B6
North Fambridge Essex 30 B6
North Ferriby E R Yk 92 D2
North Frodingham E R Yk 93 E5
North Gorley Hants 13 E6
North Green Norfk 65 E4
North Green Suffk 65 F2
North Green Suffk 65 F2
North Grimston N York 98 D2
North Halling Kent 29 H3
North Hayling Hants 15 E4
North Hazelrigg Nthumb 123 H3
North Heasley Devon 21 G4
North Heath W Susx 16 B3
North Hele Somset 22 C1
North Hill Cnwll 5 F4
North Hillingdon Gt Lon 28 B4
North Hinksey Oxon 40 C5
North Holmwood Surrey 16 C6
North Huish Devon 6 D3
North Hykeham Lincs 85 G1
North Kelsey Lincs 85 H5
North Kessock Highld 155 E4
North Killingholme Lincs 93 E1
North Kilvington N York 97 G3
North Kilworth Leics 60 B4
North Kingston Hants 13 E5
North Kyme Lincs 74 B5
North Landing E R Yk 99 H2
North Lee Bucks 41 F5
North Lees N York 97 F2
North Leigh Kent 19 E6
North Leigh Oxon 40 B6
North Leverton with Habblesthorpe Notts 85 E3
North Littleton Worcs 47 F4
North Lopham Norfk 64 C4
North Luffenham Rutlnd 61 E6
North Marden W Susx 15 F5
North Marston Bucks 49 F1
North Middleton Mdloth 121 H5
North Middleton Nthumb 124 C3
North Milmain D & G 100 B5
North Molton Devon 21 G4
North Moreton Oxon 40 D3
North Mundham W Susx 15 G4
North Muskham Notts 73 F6
North Newbald E R Yk 92 C3
North Newington Oxon 48 B3
North Newnton Wilts 25 G5
North Newton Somset 23 F2
North Nibley Gloucs 38 B4
North Oakley Hants 26 D5
North Ockendon Gt Lon 29 G5
North Ormesby N York 106 D3
North Ormsby Lincs 86 C4
North Otterington N York 97 G4
North Owersby Lincs 86 A4
North Perrott Somset 11 E5
North Petherton Somset 23 F2
North Petherwin Cnwll 5 F5
North Pickenham Norfk 63 H6
North Piddle Worcs 47 E5
North Pool Devon 7 E2
North Poorton Dorset 11 F4
North Poulner Hants 13 E5
North Quarme Somset 22 B3
North Queensferry C Edin 131 G3
North Radworthy Devon 21 H4
North Rauceby Lincs 73 H5
North Reston Lincs 86 D3
North Rigton N York 90 D4
North Ripley Hants 13 E5
North Rode Ches 82 D1
North Ronaldsay Airport Ork 169 d4
North Row Cumb 103 F3
North Runcton Norfk 75 G2
North Scale Cumb 94 C2
North Scarle Lincs 85 F1
North Seaton Nthumb 115 E4
North Seaton Colliery Nthumb 114 D4
North Shian Ag & B 136 D4
North Shields T & W 115 E2
North Shoebury Essex 30 C5
North Shore Lancs 88 B3
North Side Cambs 62 B5
North Side Cumb 102 D3
North Skelton N York 107 F3
North Somercotes Lincs 87 E4
North Stainley N York 97 F2
North Stainmore Cumb 105 E2
North Stifford Essex 29 G4
North Stoke Oxon 40 D3
North Stoke Somset 38 B1
North Stoke W Susx 16 A2
North Street Berks 41 E1
North Street Cambs 63 E2
North Street Hants 25 G1
North Street Hants 27 E3
North Street Kent 30 B3
North Street Kent 30 D2
North Sunderland Nthumb 125 E4
North Tamerton Cnwll 5 G6
North Tawton Devon 8 D5
North Third Stirlg 130 D4
North Thoresby Lincs 86 C4
North Tidworth Wilts 25 H4
North Town Berks 41 G2
North Town Devon 21 E1
North Town Somset 24 A3
North Tuddenham Norfk 76 C1
North Walbottle T & W 114 C2
North Walsham Norfk 77 F3
North Waltham Hants 26 D4
North Warnborough Hants 27 E4
North Weald Bassett Essex 51 F1
North Wheatley Notts 85 E3
North Whilborough Devon 7 F4
North Wick Somset 24 A6
North Widcombe Somset 24 A5
North Willingham Lincs 86 B3
North Wingfield Derbys 84 B1
North Witham Lincs 73 G2
North Wootton Dorset 11 G6
North Wootton Norfk 75 G2
North Wootton Somset 24 A3
North Wraxall Wilts 38 C2
North Wroughton Wilts 39 F2
Northacre Norfk 64 B5
Northall Bucks 49 H1
Northall Green Norfk 76 C1
Northallerton N York 97 G4
Northam Devon 21 E3
Northam Hants 14 C5
Northampton Nhants 49 F5
Northampton Worcs 58 A2
Northaw Herts 50 D1
Northay Somset 10 C6
Northborough Cambs 61 G6
Northbourne Kent 31 G1
Northbridge Street E Susx 18 A4
Northbrook Hants 26 C3
Northbrook Oxon 48 C1
Northchapel W Susx 27 H2
Northchurch Herts 41 H5
Northcott Devon 10 A6
Northcott Devon 10 B5
Northcott Devon 5 G5
Northcourt Oxon 40 C4
Northdown Kent 31 G3
Northedge Derbys 84 A1
Northend Bucks 41 E3
Northend Warwks 48 B4
Northend Woods Bucks 41 G3
Northenden Gt Man 82 C4
Northfield Aber C 149 G5
Northfield E R Yk 92 D2
Northfield W Mids 58 C3
Northfields Lincs 61 F6
Northfleet Kent 29 G3
Northiam E Susx 18 B4
Northill Beds 50 B5
Northington Gloucs 38 B5
Northington Hants 26 D3
Northlands Lincs 74 D5
Northleach Gloucs 39 F6
Northleigh Devon 21 F4
Northleigh Devon 10 B4
Northlew Devon 8 B4
Northload Bridge Somset 23 H3
Northmoor Oxon 40 B4
Northmoor Somset 22 B2
Northmuir Angus 140 D5
Northney Hants 15 E4
Northolt Gt Lon 28 B4
Northop Flints 81 E1
Northop Hall Flints 81 E1
Northorpe Lincs 85 F4
Northorpe Lincs 74 A2
Northorpe Lincs 74 B4
Northorpe W York 90 C2
Northover Somset 23 H3
Northover Somset 23 H2
Northowram W York 90 B2
Northport Dorset 12 C3
Northrepps Norfk 77 E4
Northton W Isls 168 c6
Northway Somset 22 D2
Northway Swans 34 C3
Northwich Ches 82 B2
Northwick Gloucs 37 G3
Northwick Somset 23 F4
Northwick Worcs 46 D5
Northwold Norfk 63 G5
Northwood Derbys 83 G1
Northwood Gt Lon 28 B5
Northwood IOW 14 C3
Northwood Shrops 69 G3
Northwood Staffs 70 D5
Northwood Green Gloucs 38 B6
Norton Ches 81 H3
Norton Cnwll 4 D3
Norton Dur 106 D3
Norton E Susx 17 F1
Norton Gloucs 46 D2
Norton Herts 50 C4
Norton IOW 13 G3
Norton Mons 45 G1
Norton N York 98 D2
Norton Nhants 60 B2
Norton Notts 84 C2
Norton Powys 56 C2
Norton S York 91 G1
Norton S York 84 A3
Norton Shrops 69 H1
Norton Shrops 57 G5
Norton Shrops 57 E3
Norton Shrops 57 G4
Norton Somset 23 F6
Norton Suffk 64 B2
Norton Swans 34 D3
Norton W Susx 15 G4
Norton Wilts 38 D3
Norton Worcs 46 D4
Norton Worcs 47 F4
Norton Bavant Wilts 25 E4
Norton Bridge Staffs 70 D3
Norton Canes Staffs 58 C6
Norton Canon Herefs 45 G4
Norton Corner Norfk 76 D3
Norton Disney Lincs 73 F6
Norton Ferris Wilts 24 C3
Norton Fitzwarren Somset 23 E2
Norton Green IOW 13 G3
Norton Green Staffs 58 C6
Norton Hawkfield Somset 24 B6
Norton Heath Essex 51 G1
Norton in Hales Shrops 70 B4
Norton in the Moors Staffs 70 D5
Norton Lindsey Warwks 59 E2
Norton Little Green Suffk 64 B2
Norton Malreward Somset 24 B6
Norton Mandeville Essex 51 G1
Norton St Philip Somset 24 C5
Norton sub Hamdon Somset 11 E6
Norton Subcourse Norfk 65 G5
Norton Wood Herefs 45 F4
Norton-Juxta-Twycross Leics 59 F6
Norton-le-Clay N York 97 G2
Norwell Notts 73 E6
Norwell Woodhouse Notts 85 E1
Norwich Norfk 77 E1
Norwich Airport Norfk 77 E1
Norwich Cathedral Norfk 77 E1
Norwick Shet 169 k6
Norwood Clacks 131 E4
Norwood Kent 18 D4
Norwood S York 84 B3
Norwood End Essex 51 F2
Norwood Green Gt Lon 28 B4
Norwood Green W York 90 C2
Norwood Hill Surrey 16 D6
Norwoodside Cambs 62 C5
Noseley Leics 60 C5
Noss Mayo Devon 6 C2
Nosterfield N York 97 F3
Nosterfield End Cambs 51 G5
Nostie Highld 152 C2
Notgrove Gloucs 47 F1
Nottage Brdgnd 35 F2
Notter Cnwll 5 G2
Nottingham Notts 72 C4
Nottington Dorset 11 G3
Notton W York 84 A6
Notton Wilts 38 D1
Nottswood Hill Gloucs 46 C1
Nounsley Essex 52 B2
Noutard's Green Worcs 58 A2
Nowton Suffk 63 H1
Nox Shrops 69 F1
Nuffield Oxon 41 E3
Nun Monkton N York 91 F5
Nunburnholme E R Yk 92 B4
Nuncargate Notts 72 C5
Nunclose Cumb 104 B5
Nuneaton Warwks 59 F5
Nuneham Courtenay Oxon 40 D4
Nunhead Gt Lon 28 D4
Nunkeeling E R Yk 93 E5
Nunney Somset 24 C4
Nunney Catch Somset 24 C4
Nunnington Herefs 46 A3
Nunnington N York 98 B3
Nunnykirk Nthumb 114 B5
Nunsthorpe Lincs 86 C5
Nunthorpe N York 91 G5
Nunthorpe N York 107 E2
Nunthorpe Village N York 107 E2
Nunton Wilts 25 G2
Nunwick N York 97 F2
Nunwick Nthumb 113 F2
Nup End Bucks 49 G1
Nupdown Gloucs 37 G4
Nupend Gloucs 38 C5
Nuptow Berks 41 G2
Nursling Hants 14 B5
Nursted Hants 15 F6
Nursteed Wilts 25 F5
Nurton Staffs 58 A5
Nutbourne W Susx 15 F4
Nutbourne W Susx 16 B3
Nutfield Surrey 28 D1
Nuthall Notts 72 C4
Nuthampstead Herts 51 E4
Nuthurst W Susx 16 C4
Nutley E Susx 17 E4
Nutley Hants 26 D4
Nuttal Lane Gt Man 89 F1
Nutwell S York 84 D5
Nybster Highld 167 G5
Nyetimber W Susx 15 G3
Nyewood W Susx 27 F1
Nymet Rowland Devon 8 D5
Nymet Tracey Devon 8 D5
Nympsfield Gloucs 38 C4
Nynehead Somset 22 D1
Nythe Somset 23 G3
Nyton W Susx 15 G4

O

Oad Street Kent 30 B2
Oadby Leics 60 B5
Oak Cross Devon 8 B4
Oak Tree Dur 106 C2
Oakall Green Worcs 46 D5
Oakamoor Staffs 71 E4
Oakbank W Loth 131 G2
Oakdale Caerph 36 C4
Oake Somset 22 D2
Oaken Staffs 58 B6
Oakenclough Lancs 88 D4
Oakengates Shrops 70 B1
Oakenholt Flints 81 E2
Oakenshaw Dur 106 A5
Oakenshaw W York 90 C2
Oaker Side Derbys 71 H6
Oakerthorpe Derbys 72 B5
Oakford Cerdgn 43 E5
Oakford Devon 22 B1
Oakfordbridge Devon 22 B1
Oakgrove Ches 82 D2
Oakham Rutlnd 61 E6
Oakhanger Ches 70 C5
Oakhanger Hants 27 F3
Oakhill Somset 24 B4
Oakhurst Kent 29 F1
Oakington Cambs 62 C2
Oaklands Powys 44 C4
Oakle Street Gloucs 38 B6
Oakley Beds 50 A5
Oakley Bucks 41 E5
Oakley Dorset 12 D4
Oakley Fife 131 F4
Oakley Hants 26 D4
Oakley Oxon 41 F4
Oakley Suffk 64 D3
Oakley Green Berks 41 G2
Oakley Park Powys 55 G4
Oakridge Gloucs 38 D5
Oaks Dur 106 A3
Oaks Lancs 89 E3
Oaks Shrops 56 D6
Oaks Green Derbys 71 F3
Oaksey Wilts 39 E4
Oakshaw Cumb 112 B2
Oakshott Hants 27 F2
Oakthorpe Leics 71 H1
Oakwood Derbys 72 B4
Oakwood Nthumb 113 F1
Oakwoodhill Surrey 16 B5
Oakworth W York 90 B3
Oare Kent 30 D2
Oare Somset 21 H5
Oare Wilts 25 G6
Oasby Lincs 73 H4
Oath Somset 23 G2
Oathlaw Angus 141 E5
Oatlands Park Surrey 28 B2
Oban Ag & B 136 C3
Obley Shrops 56 D3
Obney P & K 139 G3
Oborne Dorset 24 B1
Obthorpe Lincs 74 A1
Occold Suffk 64 D2
Occumster Highld 167 F2
Ochiltree E Ayrs 119 G1
Ockbrook Derbys 72 B4

303

Ocker Hill
Patchacott
304

Ocker Hill W Mids 58 C5
Ockeridge Worcs 46 C5
Ockham Surrey 28 B2
Ockle Highld 143 E1
Ockley Surrey 16 B5
Ocle Pychard Herefs 46 B4
Octon E R Yk 99 F2
Odcombe Somset 11 E6
Odd Down Somset 24 C5
Oddingley Worcs 47 E5
Oddington Gloucs 47 H2
Oddington Oxon 40 D6
Odell Beds 49 H5
Odham Devon 8 B5
Odiham Hants 27 F4
Odsal W York 90 C2
Odsey Herts 50 D5
Odstock Wilts 25 G2
Odstone Leics 59 G6
Offchurch Warwks 59 F2
Offenham Worcs 47 F4
Offerton T & W 115 E1
Offham E Susx 17 E3
Offham Kent 29 G2
Offham W Susx 16 A2
Offleymarsh Shrops 70 C3
Offord Cluny Cambs 62 B2
Offord Darcy Cambs 62 B2
Offton Suffk 52 D6
Offwell Devon 10 B4
Ogbourne Maizey Wilts 39 F1
Ogbourne St Andrew Wilts 39 F1
Ogbourne St George Wilts 39 G2
Ogden W York 90 B3
Ogle Nthumb 114 C3
Oglet Mersyd 81 G3
Ogmore V Glam 35 F2
Ogmore Vale Brdgnd 35 G3
Ogmore-by-Sea V Glam 35 F2
Ogwen Bank Gwynd 79 F1
Okeford Fitzpaine Dorset 12 B6
Okehampton Devon 8 C4
Olchard Devon 9 F2
Old Nhants 60 D3
Old Aberdeen Aber C 149 G5
Old Alresford Hants 26 D3
Old Auchenbrack D & G 110 B4
Old Basford Notts 72 C4
Old Basing Hants 27 E4
Old Bewick Nthumb 124 D3
Old Bolingbroke Lincs 86 D1
Old Bracknell Berks 41 G1
Old Bramhope W York 90 C4
Old Brampton Derbys 84 A2
Old Bridge of Urr D & G 110 B1
Old Buckenham Norfk 64 C4
Old Burghclere Hants 26 C5
Old Byland N York 98 A3
Old Cantley S York 84 D5
Old Cassop Dur 106 C5
Old Castle Brdgnd 35 F2
Old Churchstoke Powys 56 C5
Old Clee Lincs 86 C5
Old Cleeve Somset 22 C3
Old Clipstone Notts 84 D1
Old Colwyn Conwy 80 A2
Old Dailly S Ayrs 108 D5
Old Dalby Leics 72 D2
Old Dam Derbys 83 F3
Old Deer Abers 159 F4
Old Ditch Somset 23 H4
Old Edlington S York 84 C4
Old Eldon Dur 106 B4
Old Ellerby E R Yk 93 E3
Old Felixstowe Suffk 53 G4
Old Fletton Cambs 62 A5
Old Forge Herefs 46 A1
Old Furnace Herefs 45 H1
Old Glossop Derbys 83 E4
Old Goole E R Yk 92 A2
Old Grimsby IOS 2 a2
Old Hall Green Herts 51 E3
Old Hall Street Norfk 77 F3
Old Harlow Essex 51 F2
Old Heath Essex 52 D3
Old Hunstanton Norfk 75 G4
Old Hurst Cambs 62 B3
Old Hutton Cumb 95 F4
Old Kea Cnwll 3 F4
Old Kilpatrick W Duns 129 F2
Old Knebworth Herts 50 C3
Old Lakenham Norfk 65 E6
Old Langho Lancs 89 E3
Old Laxey IOM 174 m3
Old Leake Lincs 74 D5
Old Malton N York 98 D2
Old Micklefield W York 91 E3
Old Milverton Warwks 59 F2
Old Newton Suffk 64 C2
Old Quarrington Dur 106 C5
Old Radford Notts 72 C4
Old Radnor Powys 45 E5
Old Rayne Abers 158 C2
Old Romney Kent 18 D4
Old Shoreham W Susx 16 C2
Old Soar Kent 29 G1
Old Sodbury Gloucs 38 B2
Old Somerby Lincs 73 G3
Old Stratford Nhants 49 F3
Old Swinford W Mids 58 B4
Old Tebay Cumb 95 G5
Old Thirsk N York 97 G3
Old Town Cumb 104 B4
Old Town Cumb 95 G3
Old Town E Susx 17 G1
Old Town IOS 2 b1
Old Town Nthumb 113 F4
Old Town W York 90 A2
Old Trafford Gt Man 82 C4
Old Tupton Derbys 84 B1
Old Warden Beds 50 B5
Old Weston Cambs 61 G3
Old Wick Highld 167 G3
Old Windsor Berks 41 H2
Old Wives Lees Kent 30 D1
Old Woking Surrey 28 A2
Old Wolverton Bucks 49 F3
Old Woods Shrops 69 G2
Oldany Highld 164 B2
Oldberrow Warwks 58 D2
Oldburry Kent 29 G2
Oldbury Shrops 57 G5
Oldbury W Mids 58 C4
Oldbury Warwks 59 F5
Oldbury Naite Gloucs 37 G4
Oldbury on the Hill Gloucs 38 C3
Oldbury-on-Severn Gloucs 37 G3
Oldcastle Mons 45 F2
Oldcastle Heath Ches 69 G5
Oldcotes Notts 84 D3
Oldfield W York 90 A3
Oldfield Worcs 58 A2
Oldford Somset 24 C4
Oldhall Green Suffk 64 B1
Oldham Gt Man 82 D5
Oldhamstocks E Loth 133 F2
Oldland Gloucs 38 B1
Oldmeldrum Abers 158 D2
Oldmill Cnwll 5 G3
Oldmixon Somset 23 F5
Oldridge Devon 9 E4
Oldshoremore Highld 164 C4
Oldstead N York 98 A3
Oldwall Cumb 112 B1
Oldwalls Swans 34 B3
Oldways End Somset 22 B2
Olive Green Staffs 71 F2
Oliver Border 121 E2
Oliver's Battery Hants 26 C2
Ollaberry Shet 169 h4
Ollach Highld 151 E2
Ollerton Ches 82 C2
Ollerton Notts 84 D1
Ollerton Shrops 70 B2
Olmarch Cerdgn 43 F5
Olmstead Green Cambs 51 G5
Olney Bucks 49 G4
Olrig House Highld 167 F5
Olton W Mids 58 D4
Olveston Gloucs 37 G3
Ombersley Worcs 58 A2
Ompton Notts 84 D1
Once Brewed Nthumb 113 E1
Onchan IOM 174 m3
Onecote Staffs 71 E6
Onehouse Suffk 64 C1
Onen Mons 37 E6
Ongar Street Herefs 56 D2
Onibury Shrops 57 E3
Onich Highld 137 E6
Onllwyn Neath 35 F5
Onneley Staffs 70 C4
Onslow Village Surrey 27 H4
Onston Ches 81 H2
Openwoodgate Derbys 72 A5
Opinan Highld 160 B1
Orbliston Moray 157 E5
Orbost Highld 150 C3
Orby Lincs 87 E1
Orchard Portman Somset 23 E1
Orcheston Wilts 25 F4
Orcop Herefs 45 G2
Orcop Hill Herefs 45 G2
Ord Abers 158 B5
Ordhead Abers 148 D5
Ordie Abers 148 B5
Ordiequish Moray 157 E5
Ordley Nthumb 105 F6
Ordsall Notts 85 E3
Ore E Susx 18 B2
Oreleton Common Herefs 57 E2
Oreton Shrops 57 G3
Orford Ches 82 A4
Orford Suffk 53 H6
Organford Dorset 12 C4
Orgreave Staffs 71 F2
Orlestone Kent 18 D5
Orleton Herefs 57 E2
Orleton Worcs 57 G2
Orlingbury Nhants 61 E3
Ormathwaite Cumb 103 G3
Ormesby N York 107 E2
Ormesby St Margaret Norfk 77 H1
Ormesby St Michael Norfk 77 H1
Ormiscaig Highld 160 C3
Ormiston E Loth 132 C2
Ormsaigmore Highld 135 G6
Ormsary Ag & B 127 F2
Ormskirk Lancs 81 F5
Ornsby Hill Dur 106 A6
Oronsay Ag & B 126 B4
Orphir Ork 169 b2
Orpington Gt Lon 29 E3
Orrell Gt Man 81 G5
Orrell Mersyd 81 F4
Orrell Post Gt Man 81 G5
Orrisdale IOM 174 l4
Orroland D & G 102 B5
Orsett Essex 29 G4
Orslow Staffs 70 C2
Orston Notts 73 E4
Orthwaite Cumb 103 F3
Ortner Lancs 88 D5
Orton Cumb 95 G6
Orton Nhants 60 D3
Orton Staffs 58 B5
Orton Longueville Cambs 61 H5
Orton Rigg Cumb 103 G5
Orton Waterville Cambs 61 G5
Orton-on-the-Hill Leics 59 F6
Orwell Cambs 50 D6
Osbaldeston Lancs 89 E3
Osbaldeston Green Lancs 89 E3
Osbaldwick N York 91 G5
Osbaston Leics 59 G6
Osbaston Shrops 69 E2
Osborne IOW 14 C3
Osborne House IOW 14 C3
Osbournby Lincs 74 A4
Oscroft Ches 81 G1
Ose Highld 150 C3
Osgathorpe Leics 72 B2
Osgodby Lincs 86 A4
Osgodby N York 91 G3
Osgodby N York 99 F3
Oskaig Highld 151 E2
Oskamull Ag & B 135 F3
Osmaston Derbys 71 G4
Osmington Dorset 11 G3
Osmington Mills Dorset 11 H3
Osmondthorpe W York 90 D3
Osmotherley N York 97 H5
Osney Oxon 40 C5
Ospringe Kent 30 D2
Ossett W York 90 D2
Ossington Notts 85 E1
Ostend Essex 30 C6
Osterley Gt Lon 28 C4
Oswaldkirk N York 98 B3
Oswaldtwistle Lancs 89 F2
Oswestry Shrops 69 E3
Otford Kent 29 F2
Otham Kent 30 B1
Otham Hole Kent 30 B1
Othery Somset 23 G2
Otley Suffk 65 E1
Otley W York 90 C4
Otley Green Suffk 65 E1
Otter Ferry Ag & B 127 H3
Otterbourne Hants 26 C1
Otterburn N York 89 G5
Otterburn Nthumb 113 F4
Otterham Cnwll 5 E5
Otterham Quay Kent 30 B3
Otterhampton Somset 23 E4
Otternish W Isls 168 c5
Ottershaw Surrey 28 A2
Otterswick Shet 169 j4
Otterton Devon 10 A3
Otterwood Hants 14 B4
Ottery Devon 8 A2
Ottery St Mary Devon 10 A4
Ottinge Kent 19 E6
Ottringham E R Yk 93 F2
Oughterby Cumb 103 G6
Oughtershaw N York 96 B3
Oughterside Cumb 103 E4
Oughtibridge S York 83 H4
Oughtrington Ches 82 B3
Oulston N York 98 A2
Oulton Cumb 103 F5
Oulton Norfk 76 D3
Oulton Staffs 70 C2
Oulton Staffs 70 D4
Oulton Suffk 65 H5
Oulton W York 91 E2
Oulton Broad Suffk 65 H5
Oulton Street Norfk 76 D3
Oundle Nhants 61 F4
Ounsdale Staffs 58 B5
Ousby Cumb 104 C4
Ousden Suffk 63 G1
Ousefleet E R Yk 92 B2
Ouston Dur 114 D1
Out Elmstead Kent 31 F1
Out Newton E R Yk 93 G2
Out Rawcliffe Lancs 88 C4
Outchester Nthumb 124 D4
Outgate Cumb 94 D5
Outhgill Cumb 96 A5
Outhill Warwks 58 D2
Outlands Staffs 70 C3
Outlane W York 90 B1
Outwell Norfk 62 D6
Outwick Hants 25 G1
Outwood Surrey 16 D6
Outwood W York 90 D2
Outwood Gate Gt Man 82 C5
Outwoods Leics 72 B2
Outwoods Staffs 70 C2
Outwoods Warwks 59 E4
Ouzlewell Green W York 90 D2
Ovenden W York 90 B2
Over Cambs 62 C2
Over Ches 82 A1
Over Gloucs 46 D1
Over Gloucs 37 G2
Over Burrows Derbys 71 G4
Over Compton Dorset 24 A1
Over End Cambs 61 G5
Over Green Warwks 59 E5
Over Haddon Derbys 83 G1
Over Kellet Lancs 95 F2
Over Kiddington Oxon 48 B1
Over Monnow Mons 37 F5
Over Norton Oxon 48 A2
Over Peover Ches 82 C2
Over Silton N York 97 H4
Over Stowey Somset 23 E3
Over Stratton Somset 11 E6
Over Tabley Ches 82 B3
Over Wallop Hants 26 A3
Over Whitacre Warwks 59 E4
Over Woodhouse Derbys 84 B2
Over Worton Oxon 48 C2
Overbury Worcs 47 E3
Overcombe Dorset 11 G3
Overgreen Derbys 83 H2
Overleigh Somset 23 H3
Overley Staffs 71 F2
Overpool Ches 81 F2
Overscaig Hotel Highld 162 A6
Overseal Derbys 71 H1
Oversland Kent 30 D2
Oversley Green Warwks 47 F5
Overstone Nhants 60 D2
Overstrand Norfk 77 E4
Overstreet Wilts 25 F3
Overthorpe Nhants 48 C3
Overton Aber C 149 F6
Overton Ches 81 G2
Overton Hants 26 C4
Overton Lancs 88 C5
Overton N York 91 G5
Overton Shrops 57 E3
Overton Swans 34 B3
Overton W York 90 D1
Overton Wrexhm 69 F4
Overton Bridge Wrexhm 69 F4
Overton Green Ches 70 C6
Overtown Lancs 95 G2
Overtown N Lans 120 C5
Overtown W York 91 E1
Overtown Wilts 39 F2
Overy Oxon 40 D4
Oving Bucks 49 F1
Oving W Susx 15 G4
Ovingdean E Susx 16 D2
Ovingham Nthumb 114 C2
Ovington Dur 105 H2
Ovington Essex 52 A5
Ovington Hants 26 D2
Ovington Norfk 64 B6
Ovington Nthumb 114 B2
Ower Hants 26 B1
Ower Hants 14 C4
Owermoigne Dorset 12 B3
Owl's Green Suffk 65 E2
Owlbury Shrops 56 C4
Owlerton S York 84 A4
Owlpen Gloucs 38 C4
Owlsmoor Berks 27 G5
Owlswick Bucks 41 F5
Owmby Lincs 86 A5
Owmby Lincs 85 H3
Owslebury Hants 26 C2
Owston Leics 60 D6
Owston S York 84 C6
Owston Ferry Lincs 85 F5
Owstwick E R Yk 93 F3
Owthorne E R Yk 93 G2
Owthorpe Notts 72 D3
Oxborough Norfk 63 G5
Oxbridge Dorset 11 E4
Oxcombe Lincs 86 C2
Oxcroft Derbys 84 B2
Oxen End Essex 51 G4
Oxen Park Cumb 94 D4
Oxenholme Cumb 95 F4
Oxenhope W York 90 B3
Oxenpill Somset 23 G3
Oxenton Gloucs 47 E2
Oxenwood Wilts 26 A5
Oxford Oxon 40 C5
Oxhey Herts 28 B6
Oxhill Dur 106 A6
Oxhill Warwks 48 A4
Oxley W Mids 58 B6
Oxley Green Essex 52 C2
Oxley's Green E Susx 17 H3
Oxlode Cambs 62 D4
Oxnam Border 122 D1
Oxnead Norfk 77 E2
Oxshott Surrey 28 B2
Oxshott Heath Surrey 28 B2
Oxspring S York 83 G5
Oxted Surrey 29 E1
Oxton Border 122 B5
Oxton N York 91 F4
Oxton Notts 72 D5
Oxwich Swans 34 C3
Oxwich Green Swans 34 B3
Oxwick Norfk 76 B2
Oykel Bridge Hotel Highld 161 H4
Oyne Abers 158 C2
Oystermouth Swans 34 D3
Ozleworth Gloucs 38 C4

P

Pabail W Isls 168 f8
Packers Hill Dorset 11 G6
Packington Leics 72 A1
Packmoor Staffs 70 D5
Packmores Warwks 59 F2
Padanaram Angus 140 D5
Padbury Bucks 49 E2
Paddington Ches 82 A4
Paddington Gt Lon 28 D4
Paddlesworth Kent 29 H2
Paddlesworth Kent 19 E5
Paddock Wood Kent 17 G6
Paddolgreen Shrops 69 G3
Padeswood Flints 81 E1
Padfield Derbys 83 E4
Padgate Ches 82 A4
Padhams Green Essex 29 G6
Padiham Lancs 89 F3
Padside N York 90 C5
Padstow Cnwll 4 C3
Padworth Berks 26 D6
Page Bank Dur 106 B4
Pagham W Susx 15 G3
Paglesham Essex 30 C5
Paignton Devon 7 F4
Pailton Warwks 59 G3
Paine's Cross E Susx 17 G4
Painleyhill Staffs 71 E3
Painscastle Powys 44 D4
Painshawfield Nthumb 114 B1
Painsthorpe E R Yk 92 B5
Painswick Gloucs 38 C5
Painter's Forstal Kent 30 D2
Paisley Rens 129 F1
Pakefield Suffk 65 H4
Pakenham Suffk 64 B2
Pale Gwynd 68 B4
Pale Green Essex 51 G5
Palestine Hants 25 H3
Paley Street Berks 41 G2
Palfrey W Mids 58 C5
Palgrave Suffk 64 D3
Pallington Dorset 12 B4
Palmers Green Gt Lon 28 D5
Palmersbridge Cnwll 5 E4
Palmerston E Ayrs 119 G1
Palmerstown V Glam 36 B1
Palnackie D & G 102 B6
Palnure D & G 109 F1
Palterton Derbys 84 B1
Pamber End Hants 26 D5
Pamber Green Hants 26 D5
Pamber Heath Hants 26 D5
Pamington Gloucs 47 E2
Pamphill Dorset 12 D5
Pampisford Cambs 51 F5
Panborough Somset 23 G4
Panbride Angus 141 F3
Pancrasweek Devon 20 C1
Pancross V Glam 36 B1
Pandy Caerph 36 C3
Pandy Gwynd 54 D6
Pandy Gwynd 68 A3
Pandy Mons 45 F1
Pandy Powys 55 F6
Pandy Wrexhm 68 D4
Pandy Tudur Conwy 79 H1
Pandy'r Capel Denbgs 68 C5
Panfield Essex 52 A3
Pangbourne Berks 41 E2
Pangdean W Susx 16 D3
Panks Bridge Herefs 46 B4
Pannal N York 90 D5
Pannal Ash N York 90 D5
Pannanich Wells Hotel Abers 148 B4
Pant Shrops 69 E2
Pant Glas Gwynd 66 D5
Pant Mawr Powys 55 F4
Pant-ffrwyth Brdgnd 35 G3
Pant-Gwyn Carmth 43 F2
Pant-lasau Swans 34 D4
Pant-pastynog Denbgs 68 C6
Pant-y-dwr Powys 55 G3
Pant-y-ffridd Powys 56 B6
Pant-y-gog Brdgnd 35 F3
Pant-y-mwyn Flints 80 D1
Pantasaph Flints 80 D2
Panteg Pembks 32 C5
Pantersbridge Cnwll 5 E3
Pantglas Powys 55 E5
Panton Lincs 86 B3
Pantperthog Gwynd 55 E6
Pantyffynnon Carmth 34 D5
Pantygaseg Torfn 36 D4
Pantymenyn Carmth 33 F4
Panxworth Norfk 77 F1
Papa Westray Airport Ork 169 c4
Papcastle Cumb 103 E3
Papigoe Highld 167 G4
Papple E Loth 133 E2
Papplewick Notts 72 C5
Papworth Everard Cambs 62 B2
Papworth St Agnes Cambs 62 B2
Par Cnwll 4 D1
Paramour Street Kent 31 F2
Parbold Lancs 81 G6
Parbrook Somset 24 A3
Parbrook W Susx 16 B4
Parc Gwynd 68 A3
Parc Seymour Newpt 37 E3
Parclyn Cerdgn 42 C4
Pardshaw Cumb 103 E3
Parham Suffk 65 E1
Park Abers 149 E4
Park D & G 110 D4
Park Nthumb 112 D1
Park Bottom Cnwll 2 D4
Park Bridge Gt Man 82 D5
Park Corner Berks 41 G2
Park Corner E Susx 17 F5
Park Corner Oxon 41 E3
Park End Beds 49 H4
Park End Nthumb 113 F2
Park End Staffs 70 C5
Park Gate Hants 14 C4
Park Gate W York 90 C4
Park Gate Worcs 58 B2
Park Green Essex 51 E4
Park Green Suffk 64 D2
Park Head Cumb 104 C4
Park Head Derbys 72 A5
Park Hill Gloucs 37 G4
Park Royal Gt Lon 28 C4
Park Street Herts 50 B1
Park Street W Susx 16 B4
Parkend Gloucs 37 G5
Parkers Green Kent 29 G1
Parkeston Essex 53 F4
Parkeston Quay Essex 53 F4
Parkfield Cnwll 5 G3
Parkgate Ches 81 E2
Parkgate Cumb 103 F5
Parkgate D & G 111 E4
Parkgate E Susx 17 H3
Parkgate Essex 51 H4
Parkgate Kent 29 F2
Parkgate Kent 18 B5
Parkgate Surrey 16 C6
Parkhall W Duns 129 F2
Parkham Devon 20 D3
Parkham Ash Devon 20 D3
Parkhill Notts 73 E5
Parkhill House Abers 149 F6
Parkhouse Mons 37 F5
Parkmill Swans 34 C3
Parkside Dur 106 D6
Parkside N Lans 120 C5
Parkside Wrexhm 69 F6
Parkstone Dorset 12 D4
Parley Green Dorset 13 E4
Parlington W York 91 E3
Parmoor Bucks 41 F3
Parndon Essex 51 E1
Parracombe Devon 21 G5
Parson Drove Cambs 62 C6
Parson's Cross S York 84 A4
Parson's Heath Essex 52 D3
Parson's Hill Derbys 71 H3
Parsonby Cumb 103 E4
Partick C Glas 129 G2
Partington Gt Man 82 B4
Partney Lincs 86 D1
Parton Cumb 102 D2
Partridge Green W Susx 16 C3
Partrishow Powys 45 F1
Parwich Derbys 71 G5
Paslow Wood Common Essex 51 G1
Passenham Nhants 49 F3
Passfield Hants 27 F3
Passingford Bridge Essex 29 F6
Paston Cambs 61 H6
Paston Norfk 77 F3
Pasturefields Staffs 71 E2
Patchacott Devon 8 B4

Patcham Plaistow

Patcham E Susx 16 D2
Patchetts Green Herts 28 B6
Patching W Susx 16 B2
Patchole Devon 21 F5
Patchway Gloucs 37 G2
Pateley Bridge N York 97 E1
Paternoster Heath Essex 52 C2
Pateshall Herefs 45 H5
Path of Condie P & K 139 H1
Pathe Somset 23 G2
Pathhead Fife 132 B4
Pathhead Mdloth 132 C1
Pathlow Warwks 47 G5
Patmore Heath Herts 51 E3
Patna E Ayrs 109 F6
Patney Wilts 25 F5
Patrick Brompton N York 97 E4
Patricroft Gt Man 82 C4
Patrington E R Yk 93 G2
Patrixbourne Kent 31 E1
Patterdale Cumb 103 H2
Pattingham Staffs 58 A5
Pattishall Nhants 49 E5
Pattiswick Green Essex 52 B3
Patton Shrops 57 F5
Paul Cnwll 2 B2
Paul's Dene Wilts 25 G2
Paulerspury Bucks 49 E4
Paull E R Yk 93 E2
Paulton Somset 24 B5
Paunton Herefs 46 B4
Pauperhaugh Nthumb 114 C5
Pave Lane Shrops 70 C2
Pavenham Beds 49 H5
Pawlett Somset 23 F3
Pawston Nthumb 123 F3
Paxford Gloucs 47 G3
Paxton Border 123 F5
Payden Street Kent 30 C1
Payhembury Devon 10 A5
Paythorne Lancs 89 G5
Paytoe Herefs 56 D2
Peacehaven E Susx 17 E1
Peak Dale Derbys 83 F2
Peak Forest Derbys 83 F3
Peak Hill Lincs 74 C2
Peakirk Cambs 61 H6
Peanmeanach Highld 143 G2
Pearson's Green Kent 17 H6
Peartree Green Herefs 46 B2
Pease Pottage W Susx 16 D5
Peasedown St John Somset 24 C5
Peasehill Derbys 72 B5
Peaseland Green Norfk 76 D2
Peasemore Berks 40 C2
Peasenhall Suffk 65 F2
Peaslake Surrey 16 B6
Peasley Cross Mersyd 81 G4
Peasmarsh E Susx 18 B4
Peasmarsh Somset 10 D6
Peasmarsh Surrey 27 H4
Peat Inn Fife 132 C6
Peathill Abers 159 E6
Peatling Magna Leics 60 B5
Peatling Parva Leics 60 B4
Peaton Shrops 57 E4
Pebmarsh Essex 52 B4
Pebworth Worcs 47 G4
Pecket Well W York 90 A2
Peckforton Ches 69 H6
Peckham Gt Lon 28 D4
Peckleton Leics 59 G5
Pedairffordd Powys 68 C2
Pedlinge Kent 19 E5
Pedmore W Mids 58 B4
Pedwell Somset 23 G3
Peebles Border 121 G3
Peel IOM 174 k3
Peel Lancs 88 B3
Peel Common Hants 14 D4
Peene Kent 19 E5
Peening Quarter Kent 18 B4
Peggs Green Leics 72 B2
Pegsdon Beds 50 B4
Pegswood Nthumb 114 D4
Pegwell Kent 31 G2
Peinchorran Highld 151 E2
Peinlich Highld 150 D5
Pelcomb Pembks 32 C3
Pelcomb Bridge Pembks 32 D3
Pelcomb Cross Pembks 32 C3
Peldon Essex 52 C2
Pell Green E Susx 17 G5
Pelsall W Mids 58 C6
Pelsall Wood W Mids 58 C6
Pelton Dur 106 B6
Pelton Fell Dur 106 B6
Pelutho Cumb 103 E5
Pelynt Cnwll 5 F1
Pemberton Carmth 34 C4
Pemberton Gt Man 81 H5
Pembles Cross Kent 18 C6
Pembrey Carmth 34 B4
Pembridge Herefs 45 G5
Pembroke Pembks 32 D2
Pembroke Dock Pembks 32 D2
Pembury Kent 17 G5
Pen Rhiwfawr Neath 35 E5
Pen-bont Rhydybeddau Cerdgn 54 D4
Pen-ffordd Pembks 33 E4
Pen-groes-oped Mons 36 D5
Pen-llyn IOA 78 C3
Pen-lon IOA 78 D1
Pen-rhiw Pembks 42 C3
Pen-twyn Caerph 36 C4
Pen-twyn Mons 37 F5
Pen-twyn Torfn 36 D5
Pen-y-bont Powys 68 D2
Pen-y-bont-fawr Powys 68 C2
Pen-y-bryn Neath 35 F3
Pen-y-bryn Pembks 42 B3
Pen-y-cae Powys 35 F6
Pen-y-cae-mawr Mons 37 E4
Pen-y-cefn Flints 80 C2
Pen-y-clawdd Mons 37 F5
Pen-y-coedcae Rhondd 36 B3
Pen-y-cwn Pembks 32 C4
Pen-y-darren Myr Td 36 B5
Pen-y-fai Brdgnd 35 F2
Pen-y-felin Flints 80 D2
Pen-y-garn Cerdgn 54 D4
Pen-y-Garnedd Powys 68 C2
Pen-y-genffordd Powys 45 E2
Pen-y-graig Gwynd 66 B3
Pen-y-Gwryd Gwynd 67 F6
Pen-y-lan V Glam 35 G2
Pen-y-pass Gwynd 67 F6
Pen-y-stryt Denbgs 68 D5
Pen-yr-Heol Mons 37 E5
Pen-yr-Heolgerrig Myr Td 36 B5
Penair Cnwll 3 F4
Penallt Mons 37 F5
Penally Pembks 33 E1
Penalt Herefs 46 A2
Penare Cnwll 3 G4
Penarth V Glam 36 C1
Penblewin Pembks 33 E3
Penbryn Cerdgn 42 C4
Pencader Carmth 43 E3
Pencaenewydd Gwynd 66 D4
Pencaitland E Loth 132 C2
Pencalenick Cnwll 3 F4
Pencarnisiog IOA 78 C2
Pencarreg Carmth 43 E4
Pencarrow Cnwll 5 E4
Pencelli Powys 44 D2
Penclawdd Swans 34 C4
Pencoed Brdgnd 35 G2
Pencombe Herefs 46 B4
Pencoyd Herefs 45 H2
Pencraig Herefs 46 A1
Pencraig Powys 68 C3
Pendeen Cnwll 2 A3
Penderyn Rhondd 35 G5
Pendine Carmth 33 F2
Pendlebury Gt Man 82 C5
Pendleton Lancs 89 F3
Pendock Worcs 46 C2
Pendoggett Cnwll 4 D4
Pendomer Somset 11 F6
Pendoylan V Glam 36 B2
Pendre Brdgnd 35 F2
Penegoes Powys 55 E5
Penelewey Cnwll 3 F4
Pengam Caerph 36 C4
Pengam Cardif 36 C2
Penge Gt Lon 28 D3
Pengelly Cnwll 3 F5
Pengelly Cnwll 4 D4
Pengorffwysfa IOA 78 D4
Pengover Green Cnwll 5 F2
Pengrugla Cnwll 3 G4
Pengwern Denbgs 80 C2
Penhale Cnwll 2 D2
Penhale Cnwll 4 C2
Penhale Cnwll 4 D2
Penhale Cnwll 5 H1
Penhallow Cnwll 3 E5
Penhalurick Cnwll 3 E4
Penhalvean Cnwll 3 E4
Penhill Wilts 39 F3
Penhow Newpt 37 E3
Penhurst E Susx 17 H3
Peniarth Gwynd 54 D6
Penicuik Mdloth 121 G5
Peniel Carmth 42 D2
Peniel Denbgs 80 C1
Penifiler Highld 151 E3
Peninver Ag & B 117 G3
Penisar Waun Gwynd 79 E1
Penistone S York 83 G5
Penjerrick Cnwll 3 E3
Penkelly Cnwll 5 E1
Penketh Ches 81 H3
Penkill S Ayrs 108 D5
Penkridge Staffs 70 D1
Penlean Cnwll 5 F6
Penley Wrexhm 69 F4
Penllergaer Swans 34 D4
Penllyn V Glam 35 G2
Penmachno Conwy 67 G5
Penmaen Caerph 36 C4
Penmaen Swans 34 C3
Penmaenan Conwy 79 G2
Penmaenmawr Conwy 79 G2
Penmaenpool Gwynd 67 F2
Penmark V Glam 36 B1
Penmon IOA 79 F3
Penmorfa Gwynd 67 E4
Penmynydd IOA 79 E2
Penn Bucks 41 G4
Penn W Mids 58 B5
Penn Street Bucks 41 G4
Pennal Gwynd 55 E5
Pennan Abers 158 D6
Pennant Cerdgn 54 C2
Pennant Denbgs 68 C3
Pennant Powys 55 F5
Pennant-Melangell Powys 68 C3
Pennard Swans 34 C3
Pennerley Shrops 56 D5
Pennicott Devon 9 F5
Pennington Cumb 94 C3
Pennington Hants 13 G4
Pennington Green Gt Man 82 A5
Pennorth Powys 44 D2
Pennsylvania Gloucs 38 B2
Penny Bridge Cumb 94 D3
Penny Bridge Pembks 32 D2
Penny Green Notts 84 C2
Penny Hill Lincs 74 D3
Pennycross Ag & B 135 G2
Pennygate Norfk 77 F2
Pennyghael Ag & B 135 G2
Pennyglen S Ayrs 108 D6
Pennymoor Devon 9 E6
Penparc Cerdgn 42 B4
Penparcau Cerdgn 54 C3
Penpedairheol Caerph 36 C4
Penpedairheol Mons 36 D5
Penperlleni Mons 36 D5
Penpethy Cnwll 4 D4
Penpillick Cnwll 4 D1
Penpol Cnwll 3 F4
Penpoll Cnwll 5 E1
Penponds Cnwll 2 D4
Penpont Cnwll 4 D3
Penpont D & G 110 C4
Penpont Powys 44 C2
Penquit Devon 6 D3
Penrest Cnwll 5 G4
Penrherber Carmth 42 C3
Penrhiw-pal Cerdgn 42 D4
Penrhiwceiber Rhondd 36 B4
Penrhiwllan Cerdgn 42 D3
Penrhos Gwynd 66 C3
Penrhos IOA 78 B3
Penrhos Mons 37 E5
Penrhos Powys 35 E5
Penrhos garnedd Gwynd 79 E2
Penrhyn Bay Conwy 79 H3
Penrhyn Castle Gwynd 79 F2
Penrhyn-side Conwy 79 H3
Penrhyncoch Cerdgn 54 D4
Penrhyndeudraeth Gwynd 67 F4
Penrice Swans 34 B3
Penrioch N Ayrs 117 H5
Penrith Cumb 104 B3
Penrose Cnwll 4 B3
Penrose Cnwll 5 F5
Penruddock Cumb 104 A3
Penryn Cnwll 3 E3
Pensarn Carmth 42 D1
Pensarn Conwy 80 B2
Pensax Worcs 57 G2
Pensby Mersyd 81 E3
Penselwood Somset 24 C2
Pensford Somset 24 B6
Pensham Worcs 47 E4
Penshaw T & W 106 C6
Penshurst Kent 17 F6
Penshurst Station Kent 17 F6
Pensilva Cnwll 5 F3
Pensnett W Mids 58 B4
Penstone Devon 9 E5
Penstrowed Powys 56 A4
Pentewan Cnwll 3 H4
Pentir Gwynd 79 E1
Pentire Cnwll 4 B2
Pentlepoir Pembks 33 E2
Pentlow Essex 52 B5
Pentlow Street Essex 52 B5
Pentney Norfk 75 G1
Penton Grafton Hants 26 B4
Penton Mewsey Hants 26 B4
Pentonbridge Cumb 112 B2
Pentraeth IOA 79 E2
Pentre Denbgs 80 C1
Pentre Flints 81 E1
Pentre Mons 36 D5
Pentre Powys 56 A4
Pentre Powys 56 B4
Pentre Powys 56 C5
Pentre Rhondd 35 G4
Pentre Shrops 69 F2
Pentre Wrexhm 69 E4
Pentre Bach Cerdgn 43 F4
Pentre Bach Flints 80 D2
Pentre Berw IOA 78 D2
Pentre Ffwrndan Flints 81 E2
Pentre Gwynfryn Gwynd 67 E3
Pentre Halkyn Flints 80 D2
Pentre Hodrey Shrops 56 D3
Pentre Isaf Conwy 80 B2
Pentre Llanrhaeadr Denbgs 80 C1
Pentre Llifior Powys 56 B5
Pentre Meyrick V Glam 35 G2
Pentre Saron Denbgs 68 C6
Pentre ty gwyn Carmth 44 A3
Pentre'r Felin Conwy 79 H2
Pentre'r-felin Cerdgn 43 F4
Pentre'r-felin Powys 44 B2
Pentre'rbryn Cerdgn 42 D5
Pentre-bach Powys 44 B2
Pentre-bont Conwy 67 G5
Pentre-cagel Cerdgn 42 D3
Pentre-celyn Denbgs 68 D5
Pentre-celyn Powys 55 F6
Pentre-chwyth Swans 34 D4
Pentre-clawdd Shrops 69 E3
Pentre-cwrt Carmth 42 D3
Pentre-dwr Swans 34 D4
Pentre-Gwenlais Carmth 34 D6
Pentre-llwyn-llwyd Powys 44 B5
Pentre-llyn Cerdgn 54 D3
Pentre-llyn-cymmer Conwy 68 B5
Pentre-Maw Powys 55 F6
Pentre-piod Torfn 36 D4
Pentre-poeth Newpt 36 D3
Pentre-tafarn-y-fedw Conwy 79 H1
Pentrebach Myr Td 36 B5
Pentrebeirdd Powys 68 D1
Pentredwr Denbgs 68 D5
Pentrefelin Gwynd 67 E4
Pentrefelin IOA 78 D4
Pentrefoelas Conwy 68 A5
Pentregalar Pembks 42 B2
Pentregat Cerdgn 42 D4
Pentrich Derbys 72 B5
Pentridge Hill Dorset 25 F1
Pentwynmaur Caerph 36 C4
Pentyrch Cardif 36 B2
Penwithick Cnwll 3 H5
Penwood Hants 26 C5
Penwyllt Powys 35 F6
Penybanc Carmth 43 F2
Penybont Powys 56 A2
Penycae Wrexhm 69 E4
Penycaerau Gwynd 66 B3
Penyffordd Flints 69 E6
Penygraig Rhondd 35 G3
Penygroes Carmth 34 C6
Penygroes Gwynd 66 D5
Penysarn IOA 78 D4
Penywaun Rhondd 35 G5
Penywern Neath 35 E5
Penzance Cnwll 2 B3
Penzance Heliport Cnwll 2 B3
Peopleton Worcs 47 E4
Peover Heath Ches 82 C2
Peper Harow Surrey 27 G4
Peplow Shrops 70 A2
Pepper's Green Essex 51 G2
Peppershill Oxon 41 E5
Pepperstock Beds 50 B2
Perceton N Ayrs 119 E3
Percie Abers 148 D4
Percyhorner Abers 159 E6
Perelle Guern 174 f2
Periton Somset 22 B4
Perivale Gt Lon 28 C4
Perkins Village Devon 9 G4
Perkinsville Dur 114 D1
Perlethorpe Notts 84 D2
Perran Wharf Cnwll 3 E4
Perranarworthal Cnwll 3 E4
Perranporth Cnwll 3 E5
Perranuthnoe Cnwll 2 C3
Perranwell Cnwll 3 E4
Perranwell Cnwll 3 E5
Perranzabuloe Cnwll 3 E5
Perrott's Brook Gloucs 39 E5
Perry W Mids 58 D5
Perry Barr W Mids 58 D4
Perry Green Essex 52 B3
Perry Green Herts 51 E2
Perry Green Wilts 38 D3
Perry Street Somset 10 D5
Pershall Staffs 70 C3
Pershore Worcs 47 E4
Pertenhall Beds 61 G2
Perth P & K 140 A2
Perthy Shrops 69 F3
Perton Herefs 46 B3
Perton Staffs 58 B5
Pertwood Wilts 24 D3
Pet Street Kent 18 D6
Peter Tavy Devon 8 B2
Peter's Green Herts 50 B3
Peterborough Cambs 62 A5
Peterchurch Herefs 45 F3
Peterculter Aber C 149 F4
Peterhead Abers 159 G4
Peterlee Dur 106 D5
Peters Marland Devon 21 E2
Petersfield Hants 27 F2
Petersham Gt Lon 28 C3
Peterston-super-Ely V Glam 36 B2
Peterstone Wentlooge Newpt 36 D2
Peterstow Herefs 46 A2
Petham Kent 31 E1
Petherwin Gate Cnwll 5 F5
Petrockstow Devon 8 B5
Petsoe End Bucks 49 G4
Pett E Susx 18 B3
Pett Bottom Kent 31 E1
Pettaugh Suffk 64 D1
Petterden Angus 140 D4
Pettinain S Lans 120 D4
Pettistree Suffk 53 F6
Petton Devon 22 C2
Petton Shrops 69 F3
Petts Wood Gt Lon 29 E3
Petty France Gloucs 38 C3
Pettycur Fife 132 B4
Pettymuk Abers 159 E1
Pevensey E Susx 17 G2
Pevensey Bay E Susx 17 G2
Pewsey Wilts 25 G5
Pheasant's Hill Bucks 41 F3
Phepson Worcs 47 E5
Philadelphia T & W 106 C6
Philham Devon 20 C3
Philiphaugh Border 122 B2
Phillack Cnwll 2 C4
Philleigh Cnwll 3 F4
Philpot End Essex 51 G2
Philpstoun W Loth 131 G3
Phocle Green Herefs 46 B2
Phoenix Green Hants 27 F5
Phoines Highld 146 B4
Pibsbury Somset 23 G2
Pica Cumb 102 D2
Piccadilly Warwks 59 E5
Piccotts End Herts 50 A2
Pickburn S York 84 C5
Pickering N York 98 D3
Picket Piece Hants 26 B4
Picket Post Hants 13 F5
Pickford W Mids 59 F3
Pickford Green W Mids 59 F3
Pickhill N York 97 G3
Picklescott Shrops 57 E5
Pickmere Ches 82 B2
Pickney Somset 23 E2
Pickstock Shrops 70 B2
Pickup Bank Lancs 89 F2
Pickwell Devon 21 E5
Pickwell Leics 73 E1
Pickwick Wilts 38 C1
Pickworth Lincs 73 G1
Pickworth Lincs 73 H3
Pict's Cross Herefs 46 A2
Pictillum Abers 149 E6
Picton Ches 81 G2
Picton Flints 80 C3
Picton N York 106 D1
Picton Ferry Carmth 33 G3
Piddinghoe E Susx 17 E2
Piddington Bucks 41 F4
Piddington Nhants 49 F5
Piddington Oxon 41 E6
Piddlehinton Dorset 11 G4
Piddletrenthide Dorset 11 G5
Pidley Cambs 62 C3
Pie Corner Herefs 46 B5
Piercebridge Dur 106 B2
Pierowall Ork 169 b4
Piff's Elm Gloucs 46 D2
Pig Oak Dorset 12 D5
Pig Street Herefs 45 F4
Pigdon Nthumb 114 C4
Pigeon Green Warwks 47 H5
Pikehall Derbys 71 G6
Pilford Dorset 12 D5
Pilgrims Hatch Essex 29 G6
Pilham Lincs 85 F4
Pill Somset 37 F2
Pillaton Cnwll 5 G2
Pillatonmill Cnwll 5 G2
Pillerton Hersey Warwks 48 A4
Pillerton Priors Warwks 48 A4
Pilleth Powys 56 C2
Pilley Hants 13 G4
Pilley S York 84 A5
Pilley Bailey Hants 13 G4
Pillgwenlly Newpt 36 D3
Pillhead Devon 21 E3
Pilling Lancs 88 C4
Pilling Lane Lancs 88 B4
Pilning Gloucs 37 G3
Pilot Inn Kent 18 D3
Pilsbury Derbys 83 F1
Pilsdon Dorset 10 D4
Pilsgate Cambs 61 G6
Pilsley Derbys 83 G2
Pilsley Derbys 84 B1
Pilson Green Norfk 77 G1
Piltdown E Susx 17 E4
Pilton Devon 21 F4
Pilton Nhants 61 F4
Pilton RutInd 61 E6
Pilton Somset 24 B3
Pilton Green Swans 34 B3
Pimlico Lancs 89 F4
Pimlico Nhants 48 D3
Pimperne Dorset 12 C5
Pin Green Herts 50 C3
Pinchbeck Lincs 74 C3
Pinchbeck Bars Lincs 74 B2
Pinchbeck West Lincs 74 B2
Pincheon Green S York 91 H1
Pinchinthorpe N York 107 E2
Pincock Lancs 88 D1
Pindon End Bucks 49 F4
Pinfold Lancs 81 F6
Pinford End Suffk 63 H1
Pinged Carmth 34 B5
Pingewood Berks 41 E1
Pinhoe Devon 9 F4
Pinkett's Booth W Mids 59 F3
Pinkney Wilts 38 C3
Pinley W Mids 59 F3
Pinley Green Warwks 59 E2
Pinmill Suffk 53 F4
Pinminnoch S Ayrs 108 D4
Pinmore S Ayrs 108 D4
Pinn Devon 10 A3
Pinner Gt Lon 28 B5
Pinner Green Gt Lon 28 B5
Pinsley Green Ches 69 H5
Pinvin Worcs 47 E4
Pinwherry S Ayrs 108 D3
Pinxton Derbys 72 B5
Pipe and Lyde Herefs 45 H4
Pipe Gate Shrops 70 B4
Pipehill Staffs 58 D6
Piperhill Highld 155 G4
Pipers Pool Cnwll 5 F4
Pipewell Nhants 60 D4
Pippacott Devon 21 E4
Pippin Street Lancs 88 D2
Pipton Powys 44 D3
Pirbright Surrey 27 H5
Pirbright Camp Surrey 27 G5
Pirnie Border 122 D2
Pirnmill N Ayrs 117 H5
Pirton Herts 50 B4
Pirton Worcs 46 D4
Pishill Oxon 41 E3
Pistyll Gwynd 66 C4
Pitagowan P & K 146 C1
Pitblae Abers 159 F6
Pitcairngreen P & K 139 H2
Pitcalnie Highld 163 E1
Pitcaple Abers 158 C2
Pitcarity Angus 148 A1
Pitch Green Bucks 41 F5
Pitch Place Surrey 27 G3
Pitch Place Surrey 27 H4
Pitchcombe Gloucs 38 C5
Pitchcott Bucks 49 F1
Pitcher Row Lincs 74 C3
Pitchford Shrops 57 E6
Pitchroy Moray 156 D3
Pitcombe Somset 24 B2
Pitcot V Glam 35 F2
Pitcox E Loth 133 E3
Pitfichie Abers 148 D6
Pitglassie Abers 158 C3
Pitgrudy Highld 163 E3
Pitkennedy Angus 141 E5
Pitlessie Fife 132 B6
Pitlochry P & K 139 G6
Pitmachie Abers 158 C2
Pitmain Highld 146 B4
Pitmedden Abers 159 E2
Pitmedden Garden Abers 159 E2
Pitmuies Angus 141 F5
Pitmunie Abers 148 D6
Pitney Somset 23 G2
Pitroddie P & K 140 B2
Pitscottie Fife 140 D1
Pitsea Essex 30 A5
Pitses Gt Man 82 D5
Pitsford Nhants 60 D2
Pitstone Bucks 41 G6
Pitt Devon 9 G6
Pitt Hants 26 C2
Pitt Court Gloucs 38 B4
Pitt's Wood Kent 29 G1
Pittarrow Abers 149 E2
Pittenweem Fife 132 D5
Pitteuchar Fife 132 B5
Pittington Dur 106 C5
Pittodrie House Hotel Abers 158 C1
Pitton Wilts 25 G2
Pittulie Abers 159 E6
Pity Me Dur 106 B5
Pityme Cnwll 4 C4
Pivington Kent 18 C6
Pixey Green Suffk 65 E3
Pixham Surrey 28 C1
Plain Street Cnwll 4 C4
Plains N Lans 130 D2
Plaish Shrops 57 E5
Plaistow Derbys 72 A6
Plaistow Gt Lon 29 E4
Plaistow Herefs 46 C3

305

Plaistow Pyworthy

306

Plaistow W Susx 16 A4
Plaitford Hants 26 A1
Plank Lane Gt Man 82 A5
Plas Cymyran IOA 78 C2
Plastow Green Hants 26 D5
Platt Kent 29 G2
Platt Bridge Gt Man 82 A5
Platt Lane Shrops 69 G4
Platts Heath Kent 30 B1
Plawsworth Dur 106 B6
Plaxtol Kent 29 G1
Play Hatch Oxon 41 F2
Playden E Susx 18 C4
Playford Suffk 53 F5
Playing Place Cnwll 3 F4
Playley Green Gloucs 46 C2
Plealey Shrops 56 D6
Plean Stirlg 131 E4
Pleasance Fife 140 B1
Pleasington Lancs 89 E2
Pleasley Derbys 84 C1
Pleasleyhill Notts 84 C1
Pleck Dorset 11 G6
Pledgdon Green Essex 51 F3
Pledwick W York 90 D1
Pleinheaume Guern 174 g3
Plemont Jersey 174 a3
Plemstall Ches 81 G2
Plenmeller Nthumb 112 D1
Pleshey Essex 51 G2
Plockton Highld 152 B2
Plowden Shrops 56 D4
Plox Green Shrops 56 D6
Pluckley Kent 18 C6
Pluckley Station Kent 18 C6
Pluckley Thorne Kent 18 C6
Plucks Gutter Kent 31 F2
Plumbland Cumb 103 E4
Plumgarths Cumb 95 F4
Plumley Ches 82 B2
Plumpton Cumb 104 B4
Plumpton Cumb 94 D3
Plumpton E Susx 16 D3
Plumpton Nhants 48 D4
Plumpton End Nhants 49 E4
Plumpton Green E Susx 16 D3
Plumpton Head Cumb 104 B4
Plumstead Gt Lon 29 E4
Plumstead Norfk 76 D3
Plumstead Green Norfk 76 D3
Plumtree Notts 72 D3
Plumtree Green Kent 18 B6
Plungar Leics 73 E3
Plurenden Kent 18 C5
Plush Dorset 11 G5
Plusha Cnwll 5 F4
Plushabridge Cnwll 5 F3
Plwmp Cerdgn 42 D4
Plymouth Devon 6 B3
Plymouth Airport Devon 6 C4
Plympton Devon 6 C3
Plymstock Devon 6 C3
Plymtree Devon 9 G5
Pockley N York 98 B3
Pocklington E R Yk 92 B4
Pode Hole Lincs 74 C2
Podimore Somset 24 A2
Podington Beds 49 G5
Podmore Staffs 70 C4
Point Clear Essex 53 E2
Pointon Lincs 74 B3
Pokesdown Dorset 13 E4
Polapit Tamar Cnwll 5 G5
Polbain Highld 160 D5
Polbathic Cnwll 5 G2
Polbeth W Loth 131 F1
Polbrock Cnwll 4 D3
Poldark Mine Cnwll 2 D3
Pole Elm Worcs 46 D4
Pole Moor W York 90 B1
Polebrook Nhants 61 G4
Polegate E Susx 17 G2
Polelane Ends Ches 82 A3
Polesworth Warwks 59 E6
Polgigga Cnwll 2 A2
Polglass Highld 160 D4
Polgooth Cnwll 3 G5
Polgown D & G 110 B5
Poling W Susx 16 A2
Poling Corner W Susx 16 A2
Polkerris Cnwll 4 D1
Pollard Street Norfk 77 F3
Pollington E R Yk 91 G1
Polloch Highld 143 G1
Pollokshaws C Glas 119 G6
Pollokshields C Glas 130 B1
Polmassick Cnwll 3 G4
Polmear Cnwll 4 D1
Polmont Falk 131 F3
Polnish Highld 143 G2
Polperro Cnwll 5 F1
Polruan Cnwll 5 E1
Polsham Somset 23 H3
Polstead Suffk 52 C5
Polstead Heath Suffk 52 D5
Poltalloch Ag & B 127 G5
Poltescoe Cnwll 3 E1
Poltimore Devon 9 F4
Polton Mdloth 132 B1
Polwarth Border 123 E4
Polyphant Cnwll 5 F4
Polzeath Cnwll 4 C4
Pomathorn Mdloth 121 G5
Pomeroy Derbys 83 F1
Ponde Powys 44 D3
Ponders End Gt Lon 28 D6
Pondersbridge Cambs 62 B5
Ponsanooth Cnwll 3 E3
Ponsonby Cumb 94 A5
Ponsongath Cnwll 3 E1
Ponsworthy Devon 6 D5
Pont Cyfyng Conwy 67 G6
Pont Dolgarrog Conwy 79 G1
Pont Morlais Carmth 34 C5
Pont Pen-y-benglog Gwynd 67 F6
Pont Rhyd-sarn Gwynd 67 H3
Pont Rhyd-y-cyff Brdgnd 35 F3
Pont Robert Powys 68 C1
Pont Walby Neath 35 F5
Pont-ar-gothi Carmth 43 E1
Pont-ar-Hydfer Powys 44 B2
Pont-ar-llechau Carmth 43 G2
Pont-Ebbw Newpt 36 D3
Pont-faen Powys 44 C3
Pont-Nedd-Fechan Neath 35 F5
Pont-rhyd-y-fen Neath 35 E4
Pont-rug Gwynd 79 E1
Pont-y-blew Wrexhm 69 E4
Pont-y-pant Conwy 67 G5
Pont-yr-hafod Pembks 32 C4
Pont-yr-Rhyl Brdgnd 35 F3
Pontac Jersey 174 d1
Pontamman Carmth 34 D5
Pontantwn Carmth 34 B6
Pontardawe Neath 35 E5
Pontarddulais Swans 34 C5
Pontarsais Carmth 43 E2
Pontblyddyn Flints 69 E6
Pontdolgoch Powys 55 H5
Pontefract W York 91 F2
Ponteland Nthumb 114 C3
Ponterwyd Cerdgn 55 E3
Pontesbury Shrops 56 D6
Pontesbury Hill Shrops 56 D6
Pontesford Shrops 56 D6
Pontfadog Wrexhm 69 E4
Pontfaen Pembks 32 D5
Pontgarreg Cerdgn 42 D5
Pontgarreg Pembks 42 B3
Ponthenry Carmth 34 B5
Ponthir Torfn 36 D3
Ponthirwaun Cerdgn 42 C4
Pontllanfraith Caerph 36 C4
Pontlliw Swans 34 D4
Pontlottyn Caerph 36 B5
Pontlyfni Gwynd 66 D5
Pontnewydd Torfn 36 D4
Pontnewynydd Torfn 36 D4
Pontop Dur 105 H5
Pontrhydfendigaid Cerdgn 55 E2
Pontrhydygroes Cerdgn 55 E3
Pontrhydyrun Torfn 36 D4
Pontrilas Herefs 45 G2
Ponts Green E Susx 17 G3
Pontshaen Cerdgn 43 E4
Pontshill Herefs 46 B1
Pontsticill Powys 36 B5
Pontwelly Carmth 42 D3
Pontyates Carmth 34 B5
Pontyberem Carmth 34 C5
Pontybodkin Flints 69 E6
Pontyclun Rhondd 36 B2
Pontycymer Brdgnd 35 F3
Pontyglasier Pembks 42 B3
Pontygwaith Rhondd 35 G4
Pontygynon Pembks 42 B3
Pontymoel Torfn 36 D4
Pontypool Torfn 36 D4
Pontypool Road Torfn 36 D4
Pontypridd Rhondd 36 B3
Pontywaun Caerph 36 C3
Pool Cnwll 2 D4
Pool IOS 2 a2
Pool W York 90 D4
Pool Head Herefs 46 A4
Pool of Muckhart Clacks 131 F5
Pool Quay Powys 69 E1
Pool Street Essex 52 A4
Poole Dorset 12 D4
Poole Keynes Gloucs 39 E4
Poolewe Highld 160 C2
Pooley Bridge Cumb 104 B2
Pooley Street Norfk 64 C3
Poolfold Staffs 70 D6
Poolhill Gloucs 46 C2
Pooting's Kent 29 E1
Popham Hants 26 D4
Poplar Gt Lon 29 E4
Poplar Street Suffk 65 G2
Porchbrook Worcs 57 G2
Porchfield IOW 14 C3
Poringland Norfk 65 E5
Porkellis Cnwll 2 D3
Porlock Somset 22 B4
Porlock Weir Somset 22 B4
Port Appin Ag & B 136 D4
Port Askaig Ag & B 126 C2
Port Bannatyne Ag & B 128 B2
Port Carlisle Cumb 111 G1
Port Charlotte Ag & B 126 A1
Port Clarence Dur 106 D3
Port Driseach Ag & B 128 A2
Port e Vallen IOM 174 n4
Port Einon Swans 34 B3
Port Ellen Ag & B 116 C5
Port Elphinstone Abers 158 D1
Port Erin IOM 174 k2
Port Gaverne Cnwll 4 D4
Port Glasgow Inver 129 E2
Port Henderson Highld 160 B1
Port Isaac Cnwll 4 D4
Port Logan D & G 100 B4
Port Mor Highld 142 D2
Port Mulgrave N York 107 G3
Port nan Giuran W Isls 168 f8
Port nan Long W Isls 168 c5
Port Nis W Isls 168 f9
Port of Menteith Stirlg 130 B5
Port of Ness W Isls 168 f9
Port Quin Cnwll 4 C4
Port Ramsay Ag & B 136 C4
Port Soderick IOM 174 l2
Port Solent Hants 14 D4
Port St Mary IOM 174 k2
Port Sunlight Mersyd 81 F3
Port Talbot Neath 35 E3
Port Tennant Swans 34 D4
Port Wemyss Ag & B 116 A5
Port William D & G 101 E4
Port-an-Eorna Highld 152 B2
Portachoillan Ag & B 117 G6
Portavadie Ag & B 127 H2
Portbury Somset 37 F2
Portchester Hants 14 D4
Porteath Cnwll 4 C4
Portencalzie D & G 108 B2
Portencross N Ayrs 118 D4
Portesham Dorset 11 F3
Portessie Moray 157 F6
Portfield Gate Pembks 32 C3
Portgate Devon 5 H4
Portgordon Moray 157 F5
Portgower Highld 163 G5
Porth Cnwll 4 B2
Porth Rhondd 36 A3
Porth Dinllaen Gwynd 66 B4
Porth Navas Cnwll 3 E2
Porth-y-Waen Shrops 69 E2
Porthallow Cnwll 3 E2
Porthallow Cnwll 5 F1
Porthcawl Brdgnd 35 F2
Porthcothan Cnwll 4 B3
Porthcurno Cnwll 2 A2
Porthgain Pembks 32 B5
Porthgwarra Cnwll 2 A2
Porthill Staffs 70 C5
Porthkea Cnwll 3 F4
Porthkerry V Glam 22 D6
Porthleven Cnwll 2 D2
Porthmadog Gwynd 67 E4
Porthmeor Cnwll 2 B3
Portholland Cnwll 3 G4
Porthoustock Cnwll 3 F2
Porthpean Cnwll 3 H5
Porthtowan Cnwll 2 D4
Porthwgan Wrexhm 69 F5
Porthyrhyd Carmth 34 C6
Portincaple Ag & B 128 D4
Portinfer Jersey 174 a3
Portington E R Yk 92 B3
Portinnisherrich Ag & B 136 D1
Portinscale Cumb 103 F2
Portishead Somset 37 F2
Portknockie Moray 157 G6
Portletten Abers 149 G4
Portling D & G 102 C5
Portloe Cnwll 3 G4
Portlooe Cnwll 5 F1
Portmahomack Highld 163 F2
Portmeirion Gwynd 67 E4
Portmellon Cnwll 3 H4
Portmore Hants 13 G4
Portnacroish Ag & B 136 D4
Portnaguran W Isls 168 f8
Portnahaven Ag & B 116 A6
Portnalong Highld 150 D2
Portobello C Edin 132 B2
Portobello T & W 114 D1
Portobello W Mids 58 C5
Porton Wilts 25 G3
Portontown Devon 5 H4
Portpatrick D & G 100 A5
Portreath Cnwll 2 D4
Portree Highld 151 E3
Portscatho Cnwll 3 F3
Portsea Hants 15 E4
Portskerra Highld 166 C5
Portskewett Mons 37 F3
Portslade E Susx 16 C2
Portslade-by-Sea E Susx 16 D2
Portslogan D & G 100 A6
Portsmouth Hants 15 E4
Portsmouth W York 89 G2
Portsonachan Hotel Ag & B 137 E2
Portsoy Abers 158 B6
Portswood Hants 14 C5
Portuairk Highld 135 F6
Portway Herefs 45 H4
Portway Herefs 45 H3
Portway W Mids 58 C4
Portway Worcs 58 D3
Portwrinkle Cnwll 5 G1
Portyerrock D & G 101 F4
Posbury Devon 9 E4
Posenhall Shrops 57 G6
Poslingford Suffk 52 A5
Posso Border 121 F3
Post Green Dorset 12 C4
Postbridge Devon 8 C2
Postcombe Oxon 41 E4
Postling Kent 19 E5
Postwick Norfk 65 E6
Potarch Abers 148 D4
Pothole Cnwll 3 G5
Potsgrove Beds 49 H2
Pott Row Norfk 75 G2
Pott Shrigley Ches 82 D3
Pott's Green Essex 52 C3
Potten End Herts 50 A2
Potten Street Kent 31 F3
Potter Brompton N York 99 E3
Potter Heigham Norfk 77 G2
Potter Row Bucks 41 G4
Potter Somersal Derbys 71 F4
Potter's Cross Staffs 58 A4
Potter's Forstal Kent 18 C6
Potter's Green E Susx 17 F4
Potter's Green Herts 50 D3
Pottergate Street Norfk 64 D4
Potterhanworth Lincs 85 H1
Potterhanworth Booths Lincs 86 A1
Potterne Wilts 25 E5
Potterne Wick Wilts 25 E5
Potters Bar Herts 28 C6
Potters Brook Lancs 88 C5
Potters Crouch Herts 50 B1
Potters Green W Mids 59 G4
Potters Marston Leics 59 H5
Pottersheath Herts 50 C2
Potterspury Nhants 49 F3
Potterton Abers 149 G6
Potterton W York 91 E3
Potthorpe Norfk 76 B2
Pottle Street Wilts 24 D3
Potto N York 97 H5
Potton Beds 50 C6
Poughill Cnwll 20 B1
Poughill Devon 9 E5
Poulner Hants 13 E5
Poulshot Wilts 25 E5
Poulston Devon 7 E3
Poulton Gloucs 39 F4
Poulton Mersyd 81 E4
Poulton Priory Gloucs 39 F4
Poulton-le-Fylde Lancs 88 B3
Pound Bank Worcs 57 G3
Pound Green E Susx 17 F4
Pound Green Suffk 51 H6
Pound Green Worcs 57 H3
Pound Hill W Susx 16 D5
Pound Street Hants 26 C5
Poundffald Swans 34 C4
Poundgate E Susx 17 F4
Poundon Bucks 49 E2
Poundsbridge Kent 17 F6
Poundsgate Devon 6 D5
Poundstock Cnwll 5 F6
Pounsley E Susx 17 F4
Pouton D & G 101 F5
Pouy Street Suffk 65 F2
Povey Cross Surrey 16 D6
Pow Green Herefs 46 C4
Powburn Nthumb 124 D3
Powderham Devon 9 F3
Powerstock Dorset 11 E4
Powfoot D & G 111 F1
Powhill Cumb 103 F6
Powick Worcs 46 D4
Powmill P & K 131 F5
Poxwell Dorset 11 H3
Poyle Surrey 28 A4
Poynings W Susx 16 D3
Poynter's Lane End Cnwll 2 D4
Poyntington Dorset 24 B1
Poynton Ches 82 D3
Poynton Shrops 69 H2
Poynton Green Shrops 69 H2
Poyston Cross Pembks 32 D4
Poystreet Green Suffk 64 B1
Praa Sands Cnwll 2 C3
Pratt's Bottom Gt Lon 29 F2
Praze-an-Beeble Cnwll 2 D3
Predannack Wollas Cnwll 2 D1
Prees Shrops 69 H3
Prees Green Shrops 69 H3
Prees Heath Shrops 69 H4
Prees Higher Heath Shrops 69 H4
Prees Lower Heath Shrops 69 H3
Preesall Lancs 88 B4
Preesgweene Shrops 69 E4
Pren-gwyn Cerdgn 42 D4
Prendwick Nthumb 124 C2
Prenteg Gwynd 67 E4
Prenton Mersyd 81 E3
Prescot Mersyd 81 G4
Prescott Devon 10 A6
Prescott Shrops 69 F2
Prescott Shrops 57 G3
Presnerb Angus 147 G1
Pressen Nthumb 123 E3
Prestatyn Denbgs 80 C3
Prestbury Ches 82 D2
Prestbury Gloucs 47 E2
Presteigne Powys 56 C2
Prestleigh Somset 24 B3
Prestolee Gt Man 82 C5
Preston Border 123 E5
Preston Devon 7 E3
Preston Devon 7 F5
Preston Devon 7 F4
Preston Dorset 11 G3
Preston E Loth 133 E3
Preston E R Yk 93 F3
Preston E Susx 16 D2
Preston Gloucs 46 B3
Preston Gloucs 39 E4
Preston Herts 50 C3
Preston Kent 30 D2
Preston Kent 31 F2
Preston Lancs 88 D3
Preston Nthumb 125 E4
Preston Rutlnd 61 E6
Preston Shrops 69 G1
Preston Somset 22 D3
Preston Suffk 52 C6
Preston Wilts 39 G2
Preston Bagot Warwks 59 E2
Preston Bissett Bucks 49 E2
Preston Bowyer Somset 22 D2
Preston Brockhurst Shrops 69 H2
Preston Brook Ches 81 H3
Preston Candover Hants 26 D3
Preston Capes Nhants 48 D5
Preston Crowmarsh Oxon 40 D3
Preston Deanery Nhants 49 F5
Preston Green Warwks 59 E2
Preston Gubbals Shrops 69 G2
Preston Montford Shrops 69 F1
Preston on Stour Warwks 47 G4
Preston on Tees Dur 106 D2
Preston on the Hill Ches 81 H3
Preston on Wye Herefs 45 G3
Preston Patrick Cumb 95 F3
Preston Plucknett Somset 11 F6
Preston Street Kent 31 F2
Preston upon the Weald Moors Shrops 70 B1
Preston Wynne Herefs 46 A4
Preston-under-Scar N York 96 D4
Prestonpans E Loth 132 C2
Prestwich Gt Man 82 C5
Prestwick Nthumb 114 C3
Prestwick S Ayrs 119 G2
Prestwick Airport S Ayrs 119 E2
Prestwood Bucks 41 G4
Prestwood Staffs 58 B4
Price Town Brdgnd 35 G3
Prickwillow Cambs 63 E4
Priddy Somset 23 H4
Priest Hutton Lancs 95 F2
Priestacott Devon 20 D1
Priestcliffe Derbys 83 F2
Priestcliffe Ditch Derbys 83 F2
Priestend Bucks 41 E5
Priestland E Ayrs 119 G3
Priestley Green W York 90 C2
Priestweston Shrops 56 C5
Priestwood Green Kent 29 G2
Primethorpe Leics 60 A5
Primrose Green Norfk 76 D2
Primrose Hill Cambs 62 C4
Primrose Hill Derbys 72 B6
Primrose Hill Lancs 81 F6
Primrose Hill W Mids 58 B4
Primrosehill Border 123 E5
Primsidemill Border 123 E2
Princes Gate Pembks 33 F3
Princes Risborough Bucks 41 F5
Princethorpe Warwks 59 G2
Princetown Devon 6 C5
Prinsted W Susx 15 F4
Prion Denbgs 80 C1
Prior Rigg Cumb 112 B2
Priors Halton Shrops 57 E3
Priors Hardwick Warwks 48 C5
Priors Marston Warwks 48 C5
Priors Norton Gloucs 46 D2
Priory Wood Herefs 45 E4
Prisk V Glam 35 G2
Priston Somset 24 C5
Pristow Green Norfk 64 D4
Prittlewell Essex 30 B5
Privett Hants 27 E2
Prixford Devon 21 F4
Probus Cnwll 3 F4
Prora E Loth 132 D3
Prospect Cumb 103 E4
Prospidnick Cnwll 2 D3
Protstonhill Abers 158 D5
Providence Somset 37 F1
Prudhoe Nthumb 114 C2
Prussia Cove Cnwll 2 C3
Publow Somset 24 B6
Puckeridge Herts 51 E3
Puckington Somset 23 F1
Pucklechurch Gloucs 38 B2
Puckrup Gloucs 46 D3
Puddinglake Ches 82 B2
Puddington Ches 81 E2
Puddington Devon 9 E6
Puddledock Norfk 64 C5
Puddlehill Herts 50 A3
Puddletown Dorset 12 A4
Pudleston Herefs 46 A5
Pudsey W York 90 C3
Pulborough W Susx 16 A3
Puleston Shrops 70 B2
Pulford Ches 69 F6
Pulham Dorset 11 G5
Pulham Market Norfk 64 D4
Pulham St Mary Norfk 65 E4
Pullens Green Gloucs 37 G3
Pulley Shrops 69 G1
Pulloxhill Beds 50 B4
Pumpherston W Loth 131 G2
Pumsaint Carmth 43 G3
Puncheston Pembks 32 D5
Puncknowle Dorset 11 F3
Punnett's Town E Susx 17 G3
Purbrook Hants 15 E4
Purfleet Essex 29 F4
Puriton Somset 23 F3
Purleigh Essex 52 B1
Purley Berks 41 E2
Purley Gt Lon 28 D2
Purlogue Shrops 56 C3
Purlpit Wilts 24 D6
Purls Bridge Cambs 62 D4
Purse Caundle Dorset 24 C1
Purshull Green Worcs 58 B2
Purslow Shrops 56 D3
Purston Jaglin W York 91 E1
Purtington Somset 10 D5
Purton Gloucs 38 B5
Purton Gloucs 38 B5
Purton Wilts 39 F3
Purton Stoke Wilts 39 F3
Pury End Nhants 49 E4
Pusey Oxon 40 B4
Putley Herefs 46 B3
Putley Green Herefs 46 B3
Putloe Gloucs 38 C5
Putney Gt Lon 28 C3
Putron Village Guern 174 g1
Putsborough Devon 21 E5
Puttenham Herts 41 G6
Puttenham Surrey 27 G4
Puttock End Essex 52 B5
Puttock's End Essex 51 F3
Putton Dorset 11 G3
Puxley Nhants 49 F3
Puxton Somset 23 G6
Pwll Carmth 34 B4
Pwll Trap Carmth 33 G3
Pwll-du Mons 36 D5
Pwll-glas Denbgs 68 C5
Pwll-y-glaw Neath 35 E4
Pwllcrochan Pembks 32 C2
Pwllgloyw Powys 44 C3
Pwllheli Gwynd 66 C3
Pwllmeyric Mons 37 F3
Pydew Conwy 79 H3
Pye Bridge Derbys 72 B5
Pye Corner Herts 51 E2
Pye Corner Newpt 37 E3
Pye Green Staffs 71 E1
Pyecombe W Susx 16 D3
Pyle Brdgnd 35 F2
Pyleigh Somset 22 D2
Pylle Somset 24 B3
Pymoor Cambs 62 D4
Pymore Dorset 11 E4
Pyrford Surrey 28 A2
Pyrton Oxon 41 E4
Pytchley Nhants 61 E3
Pyworthy Devon 5 G6

Quabbs Rising Bridge
307

Q

Quabbs Shrops 56 B3
Quadring Lincs 74 C3
Quadring Eaudike Lincs 74 C3
Quainton Bucks 49 F1
Quaker's Yard Myr Td 36 B4
Quaking Houses Dur 106 A6
Quarley Hants 26 A4
Quarndon Derbys 72 A4
Quarr Hill IOW 14 D3
Quarrier's Village Inver 129 E2
Quarrington Lincs 74 A4
Quarrington Hill Dur 106 C5
Quarry Bank W Mids 58 B4
Quarrybank Ches 81 H1
Quarrywood Moray 156 D5
Quarter N Ayrs 118 D6
Quarter S Lans 120 B5
Quatford Shrops 57 G4
Quatt Shrops 57 H4
Quebec Dur 106 A5
Quedgeley Gloucs 38 C6
Queen Adelaide Cambs 63 E3
Queen Camel Somset 24 B2
Queen Charlton Somset 24 B6
Queen Dart Devon 22 A1
Queen Oak Dorset 24 C2
Queen Street Kent 17 H6
Queen Street Wilts 39 E3
Queen's Bower IOW 14 D2
Queen's Head Shrops 69 F3
Queen's Park Beds 50 A6
Queen's Park Nhants 49 F5
Queenborough Kent 30 C3
Queenhill Worcs 46 D3
Queensbury W York 90 B3
Queensferry Flints 81 E1
Queenslie C Glas 130 C2
Queenzieburn N Lans 130 C3
Quendon Essex 51 F4
Queniborough Leics 72 D1
Quenington Gloucs 39 F5
Quernmore Lancs 88 D6
Quernmore Park Hall Lancs 88 D6
Queslett W Mids 58 D5
Quethiock Cnwll 5 G2
Quick's Green Berks 40 D2
Quidenham Norfk 64 C4
Quidhampton Hants 26 C4
Quidhampton Wilts 25 F2
Quina Brook Shrops 69 G3
Quinbury End Nhants 48 D4
Quinton Nhants 49 F5
Quinton W Mids 58 C4
Quinton Green Nhants 49 F4
Quintrell Downs Cnwll 4 B2
Quither Devon 8 A3
Quixhall Staffs 71 F4
Quixwood Border 133 G1
Quoditch Devon 5 H6
Quorn Leics 72 C2
Quothquan S Lans 120 D3
Quoyburray Ork 169 c2
Quoyloo Ork 169 a3

R

Rabbit's Cross Kent 18 A6
Rableyheath Herts 50 C3
Raby Cumb 103 F5
Raby Mersyd 81 E3
Rachan Mill Border 121 F3
Rachub Gwynd 79 F1
Rackenford Devon 22 A1
Rackham W Susx 16 A3
Rackheath Norfk 77 F1
Racks D & G 111 E2
Rackwick Ork 169 a2
Radbourne Derbys 71 H4
Radcliffe Gt Man 82 C5
Radcliffe Nthumb 114 D6
Radcliffe on Trent Notts 72 D4
Radclive Bucks 49 E3
Radcot Oxon 39 G4
Raddery Highld 155 E5
Raddington Somset 22 C2
Radernie Fife 132 D6
Radford Semele Warwks 59 F2
Radlet Somset 23 E3
Radlett Herts 28 C6
Radley Devon 21 G3
Radley Oxon 40 D4
Radley Green Essex 51 G1
Radmore Green Ches 70 A6
Radnage Bucks 41 F4
Radstock Somset 24 B5
Radstone Nhants 48 D3
Radway Warwks 48 B4
Radway Green Ches 70 C5
Radwell Beds 61 F1
Radwell Herts 50 C4
Radwinter Essex 51 G4
Radwinter End Essex 51 G5
Radyr Cardif 36 B2
RAF College (Cranwell) Lincs 73 H5
Rafford Moray 156 C5
Ragdale Leics 72 D2
Ragdon Shrops 57 E4
Raginnis Cnwll 2 B2
Raglan Mons 37 E5
Ragnall Notts 85 F2
Raigbeg Highld 155 F2
Rainbow Hill Worcs 46 D5
Rainford Mersyd 81 G5
Rainham Gt Lon 29 F4
Rainham Kent 30 B3
Rainhill Mersyd 81 G4
Rainhill Stoops Mersyd 81 G4
Rainow Ches 82 D2
Rainsough Gt Man 82 C5
Rainton N York 97 G2
Rainworth Notts 72 D6
Raisbeck Cumb 95 G6
Raise Cumb 104 D5
Raisthorpe N York 92 B6
Rait P & K 140 B2
Raithby Lincs 86 C3
Raithby Lincs 86 D1
Raithwaite N York 107 H2
Rake W Susx 27 F2
Rakewood Gt Man 89 H1
Ralia Highld 146 B4
Ram Carmth 43 F4
Ram Hill Gloucs 38 B2
Ram Lane Kent 18 C6
Ramasaig Highld 150 B3
Rame Cnwll 3 E3
Rame Cnwll 5 H1
Rampisham Dorset 11 F5
Rampside Cumb 94 C1
Rampton Cambs 62 D2
Rampton Notts 85 F2
Ramsbottom Gt Man 89 F1
Ramsbury Wilts 39 G1
Ramscraigs Highld 167 E1
Ramsdean Hants 27 E1
Ramsdell Hants 26 D5
Ramsden Oxon 40 B6
Ramsden Worcs 47 E4
Ramsden Bellhouse Essex 29 H5
Ramsden Heath Essex 29 H6
Ramsey Cambs 62 B4
Ramsey Essex 53 F4
Ramsey IOM 174 m4
Ramsey Forty Foot Cambs 62 B4
Ramsey Heights Cambs 62 B4
Ramsey Island Essex 52 C1
Ramsey Mereside Cambs 62 B4
Ramsey St Mary's Cambs 62 B4
Ramsgate Kent 31 G2
Ramsgill N York 96 D2
Ramshaw Dur 105 F5
Ramsholt Suffk 53 G5
Ramshope Nthumb 112 D5
Ramshorn Staffs 71 F4
Ramsley Devon 8 C4
Ramsnest Common Surrey 27 H2
Ranby Lincs 86 C3
Ranby Notts 84 D3
Rand Lincs 86 A2
Randwick Gloucs 38 C5
Ranfurly Rens 129 E2
Rangemore Staffs 71 G2
Rangeworthy Gloucs 38 B3
Rank's Green Essex 52 A2
Rankinston E Ayrs 109 F6
Ranksborough Rutlnd 73 F1
Rann Lancs 89 F2
Rannoch Station P & K 138 B5
Ranscombe Somset 22 B4
Ranskill Notts 84 D3
Ranton Staffs 70 D2
Ranton Green Staffs 70 C2
Ranworth Norfk 77 F1
Raploch Stirlg 130 D5
Rapness Ork 169 c4
Rapps Somset 23 F1
Rascarrel D & G 102 B5
Rashfield Ag & B 128 C3
Rashwood Worcs 58 B2
Raskelf N York 97 H2
Rassau Blae G 36 C5
Rastrick W York 90 C2
Ratagan Highld 152 C1
Ratby Leics 60 A6
Ratcliffe Culey Leics 59 F5
Ratcliffe on Soar Notts 72 C3
Ratcliffe on the Wreake Leics 72 D1
Ratfyn Wilts 25 G3
Rathen Abers 159 F5
Rathillet Fife 140 D2
Rathmell N York 89 F6
Ratho C Edin 131 H2
Rathven Moray 157 F6
Ratlake Hants 26 B2
Ratley Warwks 48 B4
Ratling Kent 31 F1
Ratlinghope Shrops 56 D5
Rattan Row Norfk 75 E1
Rattar Highld 167 F6
Ratten Row Cumb 103 G4
Ratten Row Cumb 103 H5
Ratten Row Lancs 88 C4
Rattery Devon 7 E4
Rattlesden Suffk 64 B1
Ratton Village E Susx 17 G1
Rattray P & K 140 B4
Raughton Cumb 103 H5
Raughton Head Cumb 103 H5
Raunds Nhants 61 F3
Raven Meols Mersyd 81 E5
Ravenfield S York 84 C4
Ravenglass Cumb 94 B4
Ravenhills Green Worcs 46 C5
Raveningham Norfk 65 F5
Ravenscar N York 99 E5
Ravenscliffe Staffs 70 C5
Ravensdale IOM 174 l4
Ravensden Beds 50 B6
Ravenshead Notts 72 C5
Ravensmoor Ches 70 A5
Ravensthorpe Nhants 60 C2
Ravensthorpe W York 90 C2
Ravenstone Bucks 49 G4
Ravenstone Leics 72 B1
Ravenstonedale Cumb 95 H5
Ravenstruther S Lans 120 D4
Ravensworth N York 97 E6
Raw N York 99 E5
Rawcliffe E R Yk 91 H2
Rawcliffe N York 91 G5
Rawcliffe Bridge E R Yk 91 H2
Rawdon W York 90 C3
Rawling Street Kent 30 C2
Rawmarsh S York 84 B4
Rawnsley Staffs 71 E1
Rawreth Essex 30 A5
Rawridge Devon 10 B5
Rawtenstall Lancs 89 F2
Raydon Suffk 52 D5
Raylees Nthumb 113 F4
Rayleigh Essex 30 B5
Raymond's Hill Devon 10 D4
Rayne Essex 51 H3
Raynes Park Gt Lon 28 C3
Rea Gloucs 38 C6
Reach Cambs 63 E2
Read Lancs 89 F3
Reading Berks 41 E2
Reading Street Kent 18 C4
Reading Street Kent 31 G3
Reagill Cumb 104 C2
Rearquhar Highld 162 D3
Rearsby Leics 72 D1
Rease Heath Shrops 70 A5
Reay Highld 166 C5
Reculver Kent 31 F3
Red Ball Somset 22 D1
Red Bull Ches 70 C5
Red Cross Cambs 51 F6
Red Cross Cnwll 20 C1
Red Dial Cumb 103 F5
Red Hill Dorset 13 E4
Red Hill Warwks 47 G5
Red Lodge Suffk 63 F2
Red Lumb Gt Man 89 G1
Red Rock Gt Man 81 H6
Red Roses Carmth 33 F3
Red Row T & W 114 D5
Red Street Staffs 70 C5
Red Wharf Bay IOA 79 E3
Redberth Pembks 33 E2
Redbourn Herts 50 B2
Redbourne Lincs 85 G5
Redbrook Gloucs 37 F5
Redbrook Wrexhm 69 G4
Redbrook Street Kent 18 C5
Redburn Highld 156 B4
Redburn Nthumb 113 E1
Redcar N York 107 E3
Redcastle D & G 110 C1
Redcastle Highld 154 D4
Redding Falk 131 E3
Reddingmuirhead Falk 131 E3
Reddish Gt Man 82 D4
Redditch Worcs 58 C2
Rede Suffk 63 G1
Redenhall Norfk 65 E4
Redenham Hants 26 A4
Redesmouth Nthumb 113 F3
Redford Abers 149 E1
Redford Angus 141 F4
Redford W Susx 27 G2
Redfordgreen Border 121 H1
Redgate Rhondd 35 G3
Redgorton P & K 139 H3
Redgrave Suffk 64 C3
Redhill Abers 149 E5
Redhill Herts 50 D4
Redhill Somset 23 H6
Redhill Surrey 28 D1
Redisham Suffk 65 F4
Redland Bristl 37 G2
Redland Ork 169 b3
Redlingfield Suffk 64 D2
Redlingfield Green Suffk 64 D2
Redlynch Somset 24 C3
Redlynch Wilts 25 G1
Redmain Cumb 103 E3
Redmarley Worcs 57 H2
Redmarley D'Abitot Gloucs 46 C2
Redmarshall Dur 106 C3
Redmile Leics 73 F4
Redmire N York 96 D4
Redmyre Abers 149 E2
Rednal Shrops 69 F3
Rednal W Mids 58 C3
Redpath Border 122 C3
Redpoint Highld 151 G6
Redruth Cnwll 2 D4
Redstocks Wilts 25 E5
Redstone P & K 140 B3
Redstone Cross Pembks 33 E3
Redvales Gt Man 82 C6
Redwick Gloucs 37 F3
Redwick Newpt 37 E3
Redworth Dur 106 B3
Reed Herts 51 E4
Reedham Norfk 65 G6
Reedness E R Yk 92 B2
Reeds Beck Lincs 86 B1
Reeds Holme Lancs 89 F2
Reepham Lincs 85 H2
Reepham Norfk 76 D2
Reeth N York 96 D5
Reeves Green W Mids 59 E3
Regaby IOM 174 m5
Reiff Highld 160 D5
Reigate Surrey 28 C1
Reighton N York 99 G2
Reisque Abers 159 E1
Reiss Highld 167 G4
Rejerrah Cnwll 3 E5
Releath Cnwll 2 D3
Relubbus Cnwll 2 C3
Relugas Moray 156 B4
Remenham Berks 41 F3
Remenham Hill Berks 41 F2
Rempstone Notts 72 C2
Rendcomb Gloucs 39 E5
Rendham Suffk 65 F2
Rendlesham Suffk 53 G6
Renfrew Rens 129 F2
Renhold Beds 50 B6
Renishaw Derbys 84 B2
Rennington Nthumb 125 E3
Renton W Duns 129 E3
Renwick Cumb 104 C4
Repps Norfk 77 G2
Repton Derbys 71 H3
Resaurie Highld 155 E4
Rescassa Cnwll 3 G4
Rescorla Cnwll 3 G5
Resipole Highld 136 B6
Reskadinnick Cnwll 2 D4
Resolis Highld 155 E6
Resolven Neath 35 F4
Rest and be thankful Ag & B 128 D6
Reston Border 123 F6
Restronguet Cnwll 3 F3
Reswallie Angus 141 E5
Reterth Cnwll 4 C2
Retew Cnwll 3 G5
Retford Notts 85 E3
Retire Cnwll 4 D2
Rettendon Essex 30 A6
Retyn Cnwll 4 B2
Revesby Lincs 74 C6
Rew Devon 7 E5
Rew Devon 6 D1
Rew Street IOW 14 C3
Rewe Devon 9 F4
Rexon Devon 5 H5
Reydon Suffk 65 G3
Reymerston Norfk 64 C6
Reynalton Pembks 33 E2
Reynoldston Swans 34 B3
Rezare Cnwll 5 G4
Rhadyr Mons 37 E4
Rhandirmwyn Carmth 43 H4
Rhayader Powys 55 G2
Rheindown Highld 154 C4
Rhes-y-cae Flints 80 D2
Rhewl Denbgs 68 C6
Rhewl Denbgs 68 D4
Rhewl Mostyn Flints 80 D3
Rhewl-fawr Flints 80 D3
Rhicarn Highld 164 B1
Rhiconich Highld 164 D4
Rhicullen Highld 162 D1
Rhigos Rhondd 35 G5
Rhireavach Highld 160 D3
Rhives Highld 163 E4
Rhiwbina Cardif 36 C2
Rhiwbryfdir Gwynd 67 F5
Rhiwderyn Newpt 36 D3
Rhiwen Gwynd 79 E1
Rhiwinder Rhondd 35 H3
Rhiwlas Gwynd 79 E1
Rhiwlas Gwynd 68 B4
Rhiwlas Powys 68 D3
Rhiwsaeson Cardif 36 B2
Rhode Somset 23 F3
Rhoden Green Kent 17 H6
Rhodes Gt Man 82 C5
Rhodes Minnis Kent 19 E6
Rhodesia Notts 84 C3
Rhodiad-y-brenin Pembks 32 B4
Rhonehouse D & G 102 B6
Rhoose V Glam 22 C6
Rhos Carmth 42 D3
Rhos Denbgs 68 D6
Rhos Neath 35 E5
Rhos Powys 45 E2
Rhos Haminiog Cerdgn 54 C2
Rhos Lligwy IOA 78 D3
Rhos y-brithdir Powys 68 D2
Rhos-fawr Gwynd 66 C4
Rhos-on-Sea Conwy 79 H3
Rhos-y-garth Cerdgn 54 D3
Rhos-y-gwaliau Gwynd 68 B3
Rhos-y-llan Gwynd 66 B4
Rhos-y-meirch Powys 56 C2
Rhosbeirio IOA 78 D4
Rhoscefnhir IOA 79 E2
Rhoscolyn IOA 78 B2
Rhoscrowther Pembks 32 C2
Rhosesmor Flints 80 D1
Rhosgadfan Gwynd 67 E6
Rhosgoch IOA 78 D4
Rhosgoch Powys 45 E4
Rhoshill Pembks 42 B3
Rhoshirwaun Gwynd 66 B3
Rhoslan Gwynd 66 D4
Rhoslefain Gwynd 54 C6
Rhosllanerchrugog Wrexhm 69 E5
Rhosmaen Carmth 43 F2
Rhosmeirch IOA 78 D2
Rhosneigr IOA 78 C2
Rhosnesni Wrexhm 69 F5
Rhosrobin Wrexhm 69 E5
Rhossili Swans 34 B3
Rhostryfan Gwynd 67 E6
Rhostyllen Wrexhm 69 E5
Rhosybol IOA 78 D4
Rhosygadfa Shrops 69 E3
Rhosymedre Wrexhm 69 E4
Rhu Ag & B 128 D3
Rhualt Denbgs 80 C2
Rhubodach Ag & B 128 B2
Rhuddall Heath Ches 81 H1
Rhuddlan Cerdgn 43 E3
Rhuddlan Denbgs 80 C2
Rhulen Powys 44 D4
Rhunahaorine Ag & B 117 F5
Rhyd Gwynd 67 F5
Rhyd-Ddu Gwynd 67 E5
Rhyd-lydan Conwy 68 A5
Rhyd-uchaf Gwynd 68 A4
Rhyd-y pennau Cerdgn 54 D4
Rhyd-y-clafdy Gwynd 66 C3
Rhyd-y-foel Conwy 80 A2
Rhyd-y-groes Gwynd 79 E1
Rhyd-y-meirch Mons 36 D5
Rhyd-y-sarn Gwynd 67 F4
Rhyd-yr-onnen Gwynd 54 D6
Rhydargaeau Carmth 43 E2
Rhydcymerau Carmth 43 F3
Rhydd Worcs 46 D4
Rhydding Neath 35 E4
Rhydgaled Conwy 80 B1
Rhydlanfair Conwy 67 H5
Rhydlewis Cerdgn 42 D4
Rhydlios Gwynd 66 B3
Rhydowen Cerdgn 43 E4
Rhydrosser Cerdgn 54 C2
Rhydspence Herefs 45 E4
Rhydtalog Flints 69 E5
Rhydycroesau Shrops 69 E3
Rhydyfelin Cerdgn 54 C3
Rhydyfelin Rhondd 36 B3
Rhydyfro Neath 35 E5
Rhydymain Gwynd 67 G2
Rhydymwyn Flints 80 D1
Rhyl Denbgs 80 B3
Rhymney Caerph 36 B5
Rhynd P & K 140 B2
Rhynie Abers 157 G2
Rhynie Highld 163 E2
Ribbesford Worcs 57 H3
Ribbleton Lancs 88 D3
Ribby Lancs 88 C3
Ribchester Lancs 89 E3
Riber Derbys 71 H6
Riby Lincs 86 B5
Riccall N York 91 G3
Riccarton Border 112 C4
Riccarton E Ayrs 119 F3
Rich's Holford Somset 22 D3
Richards Castle Herefs 57 E2
Richings Park Bucks 28 A4
Richmond Gt Lon 28 C3
Richmond N York 97 E5
Richmond S York 84 B3
Richmond Fort Guern 174 f2
Rickerscote Staffs 70 D2
Rickford Somset 23 H5
Rickham Devon 7 E1
Rickinghall Suffk 64 C3
Rickling Essex 51 F4
Rickling Green Essex 51 F4
Rickmansworth Herts 28 B5
Riddell Border 122 B2
Riddings Cumb 112 A2
Riddings Derbys 72 B5
Riddlecombe Devon 21 F2
Riddlesden W York 90 B4
Ridge Dorset 12 C3
Ridge Herts 28 C6
Ridge Somset 24 A5
Ridge Wilts 25 E2
Ridge Green Surrey 28 D1
Ridge Lane Warwks 59 F5
Ridge Row Kent 19 F6
Ridgebourne Powys 44 C5
Ridgehill Somset 24 A5
Ridgeway Derbys 72 A5
Ridgeway Derbys 84 B3
Ridgeway Worcs 47 F5
Ridgeway Cross Herefs 46 C4
Ridgewell Essex 52 A5
Ridgewood E Susx 17 F3
Ridgmont Beds 49 H3
Riding Mill Nthumb 114 B2
Ridley Kent 29 G2
Ridley Nthumb 113 E1
Ridley Green Ches 69 H5
Ridlington Norfk 77 F3
Ridlington Rutlnd 60 D6
Ridlington Street Norfk 77 F3
Ridsdale Nthumb 113 F3
Rievaulx N York 98 B3
Rievaulx Abbey N York 98 B3
Rigg D & G 111 G1
Riggend N Lans 130 D2
Righoul Highld 155 G4
Rigmadon Park Cumb 95 G3
Rigsby Lincs 87 E2
Rigside S Lans 120 C3
Riley Green Lancs 89 E2
Rileyhill Staffs 71 F1
Rilla Mill Cnwll 5 F3
Rillaton Cnwll 5 F3
Rillington N York 98 D2
Rimington Lancs 89 F4
Rimpton Somset 24 B1
Rimswell E R Yk 93 G2
Rinaston Pembks 32 D4
Rindleford Shrops 57 G5
Ring o'Bells Lancs 81 G6
Ring's End Cambs 62 C6
Ringford D & G 102 A6
Ringinglow Derbys 83 H3
Ringland Norfk 76 D1
Ringles Cross E Susx 17 F4
Ringlestone Kent 30 B2
Ringley Gt Man 82 C5
Ringmer E Susx 17 E3
Ringmore Devon 6 D2
Ringmore Devon 7 G5
Ringorm Moray 157 E3
Ringsfield Suffk 65 F4
Ringsfield Corner Suffk 65 F4
Ringshall Bucks 41 H6
Ringshall Suffk 52 D6
Ringshall Stocks Suffk 52 D6
Ringstead Nhants 61 F3
Ringstead Norfk 75 G4
Ringwood Hants 13 E5
Ringwould Kent 19 G6
Rinsey Cnwll 2 C2
Rinsey Croft Cnwll 2 D3
Ripe E Susx 17 F2
Ripley Derbys 72 B5
Ripley Hants 13 E4
Ripley N York 90 D6
Ripley Surrey 28 A2
Riplingham E R Yk 92 C3
Riplington Hants 27 E2
Ripon N York 97 F2
Rippingale Lincs 74 A3
Ripple Kent 31 G1
Ripple Worcs 46 D3
Ripponden W York 90 B1
Risabus Ag & B 116 B5
Risbury Herefs 46 A5
Risby Lincs 92 C1
Risby Suffk 63 G2
Risca Caerph 36 C3
Rise E R Yk 93 E4
Riseden E Susx 17 G4
Riseden Kent 17 H5
Risegate Lincs 74 C3
Riseholme Lincs 85 G2
Risehow Cumb 102 D4
Riseley Beds 61 F2
Riseley Berks 27 E6
Rishangles Suffk 64 D2
Rishton Lancs 89 F3
Rishworth W York 90 B1
Rising Bridge Lancs 89 F2

Risley St Johns

308

Risley Ches 82 B4
Risley Derbys 72 B4
Risplith N York 97 F2
Rivar Wilts 26 A5
Rivenhall End Essex 52 B2
River Kent 19 F6
River W Susx 27 G1
River Bank Cambs 63 E2
Riverford Highld 154 D5
Riverhead Kent 29 F2
Rivers Corner Dorset 12 B6
Rivington Lancs 89 E1
Roachill Devon 22 A1
Road Ashton Wilts 24 D5
Road Green Norfk 65 E5
Roade Nhants 49 F4
Roadhead Cumb 112 B2
Roadmeetings S Lans 120 C4
Roadside E Ayrs 119 G1
Roadside Highld 167 E4
Roadwater Somset 22 C3
Roag Highld 150 C3
Roan of Craigoch S Ayrs 109 E5
Roast Green Essex 51 E4
Roath Cardif 36 C2
Roberton Border 112 B6
Roberton S Lans 120 D2
Robertsbridge E Susx 18 A4
Roberttown W York 90 C2
Robeston Wathen Pembks 33 E3
Robgill Tower D & G 111 G2
Robin Hill Staffs 70 D6
Robin Hood Lancs 81 G6
Robin Hood W York 90 D2
Robin Hood's Bay N York 99 E5
Robinhood End Essex 51 H4
Roborough Devon 21 F2
Roborough Devon 6 B4
Roby Mersyd 81 G4
Roby Mill Lancs 81 G5
Rocester Staffs 71 F4
Roch Pembks 32 C4
Roch Gate Pembks 32 C4
Rochdale Gt Man 82 D6
Roche Cnwll 4 C2
Rochester Kent 30 A3
Rochester Nthumb 113 E5
Rochford Essex 30 B5
Rochford Worcs 57 F2
Rock Cnwll 4 C3
Rock Neath 35 E4
Rock Nthumb 125 E3
Rock W Susx 16 B3
Rock Worcs 57 G2
Rock Ferry Mersyd 81 F3
Rock Hill Worcs 58 B2
Rockbeare Devon 9 G4
Rockbourne Hants 25 G1
Rockcliffe Cumb 111 H1
Rockcliffe D & G 102 C5
Rockcliffe Cross Cumb 111 H1
Rockend Devon 7 F4
Rockestal Cnwll 2 A2
Rockfield Highld 163 F2
Rockfield Mons 37 F6
Rockford Devon 21 H5
Rockford Hants 13 E5
Rockgreen Shrops 57 E3
Rockhampton Glocus 37 G4
Rockhead Cnwll 4 D4
Rockhill Shrops 56 C3
Rockingham Nhants 61 E4
Rockland All Saints Norfk 64 B5
Rockland St Mary Norfk 65 F6
Rockland St Peter Norfk 64 B5
Rockley Notts 85 E2
Rockley Wilts 39 F1
Rockliffe Lancs 89 G2
Rockville Ag & B 128 D4
Rockwell End Bucks 41 F3
Rockwell Green Somset 22 D1
Rodborough Gloucs 38 C5
Rodbourne Wilts 39 F3
Rodbourne Wilts 38 D3
Rodd Herefs 45 F5
Roddam Nthumb 124 C3
Rodden Dorset 11 F3
Roddymoor Dur 106 A4
Rode Somset 24 D5
Rode Heath Ches 70 C6
Rode Heath Ches 82 D1
Rodel W Isls 168 c6
Roden Shrops 69 H2
Rodhuish Somset 22 C3
Rodington Shrops 69 H1
Rodington Heath Shrops 69 H1
Rodley Gloucs 38 B5
Rodley W York 90 C3
Rodmarton Gloucs 38 D4
Rodmell E Susx 17 E2
Rodmersham Kent 30 C2
Rodmersham Green Kent 30 C2
Rodney Stoke Somset 23 H4
Rodsley Derbys 71 G4
Rodway Somset 23 E3
Roe Cross Gt Man 83 E4
Roe Green Gt Man 82 C5
Roe Green Herts 50 C1
Roe Green Herts 50 D4
Roecliffe N York 97 G1
Roehampton Gt Lon 28 C3
Roffey W Susx 16 C5
Rogart Highld 162 D4
Rogate W Susx 27 F2
Roger Ground Cumb 94 D5
Rogerstone Newpt 36 D3
Roghadal W Isls 168 c6
Rogiet Mons 37 F3
Roke Oxon 40 D4
Roker T & W 115 F1
Rollesby Norfk 77 G2
Rolleston Leics 60 C5
Rolleston Notts 73 E5
Rolleston Staffs 71 G3
Rolston E R Yk 93 F4
Rolstone Somset 23 G5
Rolvenden Kent 18 B4
Rolvenden Layne Kent 18 B4
Romaldkirk Dur 105 G2
Roman Amphitheatre Caerleon Newpt 36 D3
Roman Baths & Pump Room Somset 24 C6
Romanby N York 97 G4
Romanno Bridge Border 121 F4
Romansleigh Devon 21 G3
Romden Castle Kent 18 C6
Romesdal Highld 150 D4
Romford Dorset 13 E6
Romford Gt Lon 29 F5
Romiley Gt Man 82 D4
Romney Street Kent 29 F2
Romsey Hants 14 B6
Romsley Shrops 57 H4
Romsley Worcs 58 C3
Ronachan Ag & B 117 F6
Rookhope Dur 105 F4
Rookley IOW 14 C2
Rookley Green IOW 14 C2
Rooks Bridge Somset 23 F4
Rooks Nest Somset 22 D3
Rookwith N York 97 E3
Roos E R Yk 93 G3
Roose Cumb 94 C2
Roosebeck Cumb 94 C2
Roothams Green Beds 61 G1
Ropley Hants 27 E2
Ropley Dean Hants 26 D2
Ropley Soke Hants 27 E3
Ropsley Lincs 73 G3
Rora Abers 159 F4
Rorrington Shrops 56 C5
Rosarie Moray 157 F4
Roscroggan Cnwll 2 D4
Rose Cnwll 3 E5
Rose Ash Devon 21 H3
Rose Green Essex 52 C3
Rose Green Suffk 52 C4
Rose Green Suffk 52 C5
Rose Green W Susx 15 G3
Rose Hill E Susx 17 E3
Rose Hill Lancs 89 G3
Roseacre Lancs 88 C3
Rosebank S Lans 120 C4
Rosebush Pembks 33 E5
Rosecare Cnwll 5 E5
Rosecliston Cnwll 4 B2
Rosedale Abbey N York 98 C4
Rosehall Highld 162 B4
Rosehearty Abers 159 E6
Rosehill Shrops 69 G2
Roseisle Moray 156 C6
Roselands E Susx 17 G1
Rosemarket Pembks 32 D2
Rosemarkie Highld 155 F5
Rosemary Lane Devon 10 B6
Rosemount P & K 140 B4
Rosenannon Cnwll 4 C2
Rosenithon Cnwll 3 E2
Roser's Cross E Susx 17 F3
Rosevean Cnwll 4 D2
Rosevine Cnwll 3 F3
Rosewarne Cnwll 2 D3
Rosewell Mdloth 121 G6
Roseworth Dur 106 D3
Roseworthy Cnwll 2 D4
Rosgill Cumb 104 B2
Roskhill Highld 150 C3
Roskorwell Cnwll 3 E2
Roskrow Cnwll 3 E3
Rosley Cumb 103 G5
Roslin Mdloth 132 B1
Rosliston Derbys 71 G2
Rosneath Ag & B 128 D3
Ross D & G 101 H5
Ross Nthumb 124 D5
Ross-on-Wye Herefs 46 B2
Rossett Wrexhm 69 F6
Rossett Green N York 90 D5
Rossington S York 84 D4
Rossland Rens 129 F2
Roster Highld 167 F2
Rostherne Ches 82 B3
Rosthwaite Cumb 103 F2
Roston Derbys 71 F4
Rosudgeon Cnwll 2 C3
Rosyth Fife 131 G3
Rothbury Nthumb 114 B6
Rotherby Leics 72 D2
Rotherfield E Susx 17 F4
Rotherfield Greys Oxon 41 E2
Rotherfield Peppard Oxon 41 E2
Rotherham S York 84 B4
Rothersthorpe Nhants 49 E5
Rotherwick Hants 27 E5
Rothes Moray 157 E4
Rothesay Ag & B 128 B1
Rothiebrisbane Abers 158 C3
Rothiemay Moray 157 G4
Rothiemurchus Lodge Highld 146 D5
Rothienorman Abers 158 C3
Rothley Leics 72 C1
Rothley Nthumb 114 B4
Rothmaise Abers 158 C2
Rothwell Lincs 86 B5
Rothwell Nhants 60 D3
Rothwell W York 91 E2
Rothwell Haigh W York 90 D2
Rotsea E R Yk 92 D5
Rottal Lodge Angus 148 A1
Rottingdean E Susx 17 E2
Rottington Cumb 102 D1
Rou Island Cumb 94 C1
Roucan D & G 111 E3
Roud IOW 14 C2
Rough Close Staffs 70 D4
Rough Common Kent 31 E2
Rougham Norfk 76 A2
Rougham Green Suffk 64 B1
Roughlee Lancs 89 G4
Roughley W Mids 58 D5
Roughpark Abers 148 A6
Roughton Lincs 86 C1
Roughton Norfk 77 E4
Roughton Shrops 57 H5
Roughway Kent 29 G1
Round Bush Herts 28 B6
Round Green Beds 50 B3
Round Street Kent 29 G3
Roundbush Essex 30 B6
Roundbush Green Essex 51 G2
Roundham Somset 11 E6
Roundhay W York 90 D3
Rounds Green W Mids 58 C4
Roundstreet Common W Susx 16 A4
Roundway Wilts 25 F6
Roundyhill Angus 140 D5
Rous Lench Worcs 47 F5
Rousdon Devon 10 C4
Rousham Oxon 48 C2
Rout's Green Bucks 41 F4
Routenbeck Cumb 103 F3
Routenburn N Ayrs 118 D6
Routh E R Yk 93 E4
Row Cnwll 5 E4
Row Cumb 104 C4
Row Cumb 95 E4
Row Ash Hants 14 D5
Row Green Essex 52 A3
Row Town Surrey 28 A2
Rowanburn D & G 112 A2
Rowardennan Hotel Stirlg 129 E5
Rowardennan Lodge Stirlg 129 E5
Rowarth Derbys 83 E4
Rowberrow Somset 23 G5
Rowborough IOW 14 C2
Rowde Wilts 25 E5
Rowden Devon 8 C4
Rowen Conwy 79 G2
Rowfield Derbys 71 G5
Rowfoot Nthumb 104 D6
Rowford Somset 23 E2
Rowhedge Essex 52 D3
Rowhook W Susx 16 B5
Rowington Warwks 59 E2
Rowland Derbys 83 G2
Rowland's Castle Hants 15 E5
Rowland's Gill T & W 114 C1
Rowledge Surrey 27 F4
Rowley Dur 105 G5
Rowley E R Yk 92 D3
Rowley Shrops 56 C6
Rowley Green W Mids 59 F4
Rowley Hill W York 90 C1
Rowley Regis W Mids 58 C4
Rowlstone Herefs 45 F2
Rowly Surrey 16 A5
Rowner Hants 14 D4
Rowney Green Worcs 58 C2
Rownhams Hants 14 B5
Rowrah Cumb 103 E2
Rows of Trees Ches 82 C3
Rowsham Bucks 41 G6
Rowsley Derbys 83 G1
Rowstock Oxon 40 C3
Rowston Lincs 74 A6
Rowthorne Derbys 84 B1
Rowton Ches 81 G1
Rowton Shrops 69 F1
Rowton Shrops 70 A2
Rowton Shrops 56 D3
Roxburgh Border 122 D2
Roxby Lincs 92 C1
Roxby N York 107 G2
Roxton Beds 50 B6
Roxwell Essex 51 G1
Roy Bridge Highld 145 E2
Royal Botanic Gardens C Edin 141 E1
Royal Oak Dur 106 B3
Royal Oak Lancs 81 F5
Royal's Green Ches 70 A4
Roydhouse W York 83 G6
Roydon Essex 51 E2
Roydon Norfk 75 G2
Roydon Norfk 64 D3
Roydon Hamlet Essex 51 E1
Royston Herts 50 D5
Royston S York 84 A6
Royton Gt Man 82 D5
Rozel Jersey 174 d3
Ruabon Wrexhm 69 E4
Ruaig Ag & B 134 C4
Ruan High Lanes Cnwll 3 F4
Ruan Lanihorne Cnwll 3 F4
Ruan Major Cnwll 3 E1
Ruan Minor Cnwll 3 E1
Ruardean Gloucs 37 G6
Ruardean Hill Gloucs 37 G6
Ruardean Woodside Gloucs 37 G6
Rubery Worcs 58 C3
Rubha Ban W Isls 168 b2
Ruckcroft Cumb 104 B4
Ruckhall Herefs 45 G3
Ruckhall Common Herefs 45 G3
Ruckinge Kent 18 D5
Ruckland Lincs 86 D2
Ruckley Shrops 57 E5
Rudby N York 97 H5
Rudchester Nthumb 114 C2
Ruddington Notts 72 C3
Ruddle Gloucs 38 B5
Ruddlemoor Cnwll 3 G5
Rudford Gloucs 46 C1
Rudge Somset 24 D4
Rudgeway Gloucs 37 G3
Rudgwick W Susx 16 B5
Rudhall Herefs 46 B2
Rudheath Ches 82 B2
Rudley Green Essex 52 B1
Rudloe Wilts 38 C1
Rudry Caerph 36 C3
Rudston E R Yk 99 G2
Rudyard Staffs 70 D6
Ruecastle Border 122 C1
Rufford Lancs 88 C1
Rufforth N York 91 F5
Rug Denbgs 68 C4
Rugby Warwks 60 A3
Rugeley Staffs 71 E2
Ruggaton Devon 21 F5
Ruishton Somset 23 E2
Ruislip Gt Lon 28 B5
Rumbach Moray 157 F4
Rumbling Bridge P & K 131 F5
Rumburgh Suffk 65 F3
Rumby Hill Dur 106 A4
Rumford Cnwll 4 C3
Rumford Falk 131 F3
Rumney Cardif 36 C2
Rumwell Somset 23 E2
Runcorn Ches 81 G3
Runcton W Susx 15 G4
Runcton Holme Norfk 75 F1
Runfold Surrey 27 G4
Runhall Norfk 64 C6
Runham Norfk 77 G1
Runham Norfk 65 H6
Runnington Somset 22 D1
Runsell Green Essex 52 B1
Runshaw Moor Lancs 88 D1
Runswick N York 107 G2
Runtaleave Angus 147 H1
Runwell Essex 30 A5
Ruscombe Berks 41 F2
Rush Green Ches 82 B3
Rush Green Essex 53 E2
Rush Green Gt Lon 29 F5
Rush Green Herts 50 C3
Rush Green Herts 50 D3
Rushall Herefs 46 B3
Rushall Norfk 64 D4
Rushall W Mids 58 C5
Rushall Wilts 25 G5
Rushbrooke Suffk 64 B1
Rushbury Shrops 57 E5
Rushden Herts 50 D4
Rushden Nhants 61 F2
Rushenden Kent 30 C3
Rusher's Cross E Susx 17 G4
Rushett Common Surrey 16 A6
Rushford Devon 8 A2
Rushford Norfk 64 B3
Rushlake Green E Susx 17 G3
Rushmere Suffk 65 G4
Rushmere St Andrew Suffk 53 E5
Rushmoor Surrey 27 G3
Rushock Herefs 45 F5
Rushock Worcs 58 B2
Rusholme Gt Man 82 D4
Rushton Ches 81 H1
Rushton Nhants 60 D4
Rushton Shrops 57 F6
Rushton Spencer Staffs 82 D1
Rushwick Worcs 46 D5
Rushyford Dur 106 B4
Ruskie Stirlg 130 C5
Ruskington Lincs 74 A5
Rusland Cumb 94 D4
Rusper W Susx 16 C5
Ruspidge Gloucs 37 H5
Russ Hill Surrey 16 C5
Russel's Green Suffk 65 E3
Russell Green Essex 52 A2
Russell's Water Oxon 41 E3
Rusthall Kent 17 F5
Rustington W Susx 16 A2
Ruston N York 99 E3
Ruston Parva E R Yk 92 D6
Ruswarp N York 99 E6
Ruthall Shrops 57 F4
Rutherford Border 122 D2
Rutherglen S Lans 119 H6
Ruthernbridge Cnwll 4 D3
Ruthin Denbgs 68 D6
Ruthrieston Aber C 149 G5
Ruthven Abers 157 G4
Ruthven Angus 140 C5
Ruthven Highld 146 C4
Ruthven House Angus 140 C4
Ruthvoes Cnwll 4 C2
Ruthwaite Cumb 103 F4
Ruthwell D & G 111 E1
Ruxley Corner Gt Lon 29 F3
Ruxton Green Herefs 46 A1
Ruyton-XI-Towns Shrops 69 F2
Ryal Nthumb 114 B3
Ryall Dorset 10 D4
Ryall Worcs 46 D3
Ryarsh Kent 29 G2
Rycote Oxon 41 E5
Rydal Cumb 94 D5
Ryde IOW 14 D3
Rye E Susx 18 C3
Rye Cross Worcs 46 C3
Rye Foreign E Susx 18 C4
Rye Harbour E Susx 18 C3
Rye Street Worcs 46 C3
Ryebank Shrops 69 G3
Ryeford Herefs 46 B1
Ryehill E R Yk 93 F2
Ryeish Green Nhants 27 E6
Ryhall Rutlnd 73 H1
Ryhill W York 91 E1
Ryhope T & W 106 C6
Rylah Derbys 84 B1
Ryland Lincs 85 H3
Rylands Notts 72 C4
Rylstone N York 89 H5
Ryme Intrinseca Dorset 11 F6
Ryther N York 91 G3
Ryton N York 98 D2
Ryton Shrops 57 H6
Ryton T & W 114 C2
Ryton Warwks 59 G4
Ryton Woodside T & W 114 C2
Ryton-on-Dunsmore Warwks 59 G3

S

Sabden Lancs 89 F3
Sabine's Green Essex 29 F6
Sacombe Herts 50 D3
Sacombe Green Herts 50 D3
Sacriston Dur 106 B6
Sadberge Dur 106 C2
Saddell Ag & B 117 G4
Saddington Leics 60 C4
Saddle Bow Norfk 75 F2
Saddlescombe W Susx 16 D2
Sadgill Cumb 95 F5
Saffron Walden Essex 51 F4
Sageston Pembks 33 E2
Saham Hills Norfk 64 B6
Saham Toney Norfk 64 B6
Saighton Ches 81 G1
St Abbs Border 133 H2
St Agnes Border 133 F1
St Agnes Cnwll 3 E5
St Albans Herts 50 B1
St Allen Cnwll 3 F5
St Andrew Guern 174 g2
St Andrew's Major V Glam 36 C1
St Andrews Fife 141 E1
St Andrews Well Dorset 11 E4
St Ann's D & G 111 E4
St Ann's Chapel Cnwll 5 H3
St Ann's Chapel Devon 6 D2
St Anne's Lancs 88 B2
St Anthony Cnwll 3 E2
St Anthony's Hill E Susx 17 G1
St Arvans Mons 37 F4
St Asaph Denbgs 80 C2
St Athan V Glam 22 C6
St Aubin Jersey 174 b2
St Austell Cnwll 3 H5
St Bees Cumb 102 D1
St Blazey Cnwll 3 H5
St Blazey Gate Cnwll 3 H5
St Boswells Border 122 C2
St Brelade Jersey 174 a2
St Brelade's Bay Jersey 174 a1
St Breock Cnwll 4 C3
St Breward Cnwll 5 E4
St Briavels Gloucs 37 G5
St Bride's Major V Glam 35 F2
St Brides Pembks 32 B3
St Brides Netherwent Mons 37 E3
St Brides super-Ely V Glam 36 B2
St Brides Wentlooge Newpt 36 D2
St Budeaux Devon 6 B3
St Buryan Cnwll 2 B2
St Catherine Somset 38 C1
St Catherines Ag & B 128 C6
St Chloe Gloucs 38 C4
St Clears Carmth 33 G3
St Cleer Cnwll 5 F3
St Clement Cnwll 3 F4
St Clement Jersey 174 d1
St Clether Cnwll 5 F4
St Colmac Ag & B 128 B2
St Columb Major Cnwll 4 C2
St Columb Minor Cnwll 4 B2
St Columb Road Cnwll 4 C2
St Combs Abers 159 F5
St Cross South Elmham Suffk 65 E4
St Cyrus Abers 141 G6
St David's P & K 139 G2
St David's Pembks 32 B4
St Day Cnwll 3 E4
St Decumans Somset 22 D3
St Dennis Cnwll 4 C2
St Devereux Herefs 45 G2
St Dogmaels Cerdgn 42 B4
St Dogwells Pembks 32 D4
St Dominick Cnwll 5 G3
St Donats V Glam 35 G1
St Edith's Marsh Wilts 25 E6
St Endellion Cnwll 4 D4
St Enoder Cnwll 3 F5
St Erme Cnwll 3 F5
St Erney Cnwll 5 G2
St Erth Cnwll 2 C3
St Erth Praze Cnwll 2 C3
St Ervan Cnwll 4 C3
St Ewe Cnwll 3 G4
St Fagans Cardif 36 B2
St Fagans Welsh Life Museum Cardif 36 B2
St Fergus Abers 159 G4
St Fillans P & K 138 D2
St Florence Pembks 33 E2
St Gennys Cnwll 5 E6
St George Conwy 80 B2
St George's V Glam 36 B2
St George's Hill Surrey 28 B2
St Georges Somset 23 F5
St Germans Cnwll 5 G2
St Giles in the Wood Devon 21 E2
St Giles-on-the-Heath Cnwll 5 G5
St Gluvia's Cnwll 3 E3
St Harmon Powys 55 G3
St Helen Auckland Dur 106 A3
St Helena Norfk 77 E2
St Helens Cumb 102 D3
St Helens E Susx 18 B3
St Helens IOW 14 D2
St Helens Mersyd 81 G4
St Helier Gt Lon 28 C3
St Helier Jersey 174 c2
St Hilary Cnwll 2 C3
St Hilary V Glam 35 G1
St Hill Devon 10 A5
St Hill W Susx 17 E5
St Illtyd Blae G 36 C4
St Ippollitts Herts 50 C3
St Ishmael's Pembks 32 C2
St Issey Cnwll 4 C3
St Ive Cnwll 5 G3
St Ives Cambs 62 B2
St Ives Cnwll 2 C4
St Ives Dorset 13 E5
St James Norfk 77 F2
St James South Elmham Suffk 65 F3
St James's End Nhants 49 F5
St John Cnwll 5 H1
St John Jersey 174 b3
St John's IOM 174 k3
St John's Chapel Devon 21 E3
St John's Chapel Dur 105 E4
St John's Fen End Norfk 75 F1
St John's Highway Norfk 75 F1
St John's Kirk S Lans 120 D3
St John's Town of Dalry D & G 109 H3
St John's Wood Gt Lon 28 D4
St Johns Dur 105 G3

St Johns

Shadforth

St Johns Kent 29 F2
St Johns Surrey 27 H5
St Johns Worcs 46 D5
St Jude's IOM 174 m5
St Just Cnwll 2 A3
St Just Lane Cnwll 3 F3
St Just-in-Roseland Cnwll 3 F3
St Katherines Abers 158 D2
St Keverne Cnwll 3 E2
St Kew Cnwll 4 D4
St Kew Highway Cnwll 4 D3
St Keyne Cnwll 5 F2
St Lawrence Cnwll 4 D3
St Lawrence Essex 52 C1
St Lawrence IOW 14 D1
St Lawrence Jersey 174 b2
St Lawrence Kent 31 G3
St Leonard's Street Kent 29 G2
St Leonards Bucks 41 G5
St Leonards Dorset 13 E5
St Leonards E Susx 18 B2
St Levan Cnwll 2 A2
St Lythans V Glam 36 B1
St Mabyn Cnwll 4 D3
St Madoes P & K 140 B2
St Margaret South Elmham Suffk 65 F4
St Margaret's at Cliffe Kent 19 G6
St Margaret's Hope Ork 169 b2
St Margarets Herefs 45 F3
St Margarets Herts 51 E2
St Marks IOM 174 l2
St Martin Cnwll 5 F1
St Martin Cnwll 3 E2
St Martin Guern 174 g1
St Martin Jersey 174 d2
St Martin's P & K 140 B3
St Martin's Moor Shrops 69 E4
St Martins Shrops 69 E4
St Mary Jersey 174 b3
St Mary Bourne Hants 26 B4
St Mary Church V Glam 35 G1
St Mary Cray Gt Lon 29 F3
St Mary Hill V Glam 35 G2
St Mary in the Marsh Kent 18 D4
St Mary's Ork 169 c2
St Mary's Bay Kent 18 D4
St Mary's Grove Somset 37 F1
St Mary's Hoo Kent 30 B4
St Marychurch Devon 7 F4
St Maughans Mons 37 F6
St Maughans Green Mons 37 F6
St Mawes Cnwll 3 F3
St Mawgan Cnwll 4 B2
St Mellion Cnwll 5 G2
St Mellons Cardif 36 C2
St Merryn Cnwll 4 C3
St Mewan Cnwll 3 G5
St Michael Caerhays Cnwll 3 G4
St Michael Church Somset 23 F2
St Michael Penkevil Cnwll 3 F4
St Michael South Elmham Suffk 65 F4
St Michael's on Wyre Lancs 88 C4
St Michaels Kent 18 B5
St Michaels Worcs 57 F2
St Minver Cnwll 4 C4
St Monans Fife 132 D5
St Neot Cnwll 5 E3
St Neots Cambs 61 H1
St Nicholas Pembks 32 C5
St Nicholas V Glam 36 B2
St Nicholas at Wade Kent 31 F3
St Ninians Stirlg 130 D4
St Olaves Norfk 65 G5
St Osyth Essex 53 E2
St Ouen Jersey 174 a2
St Owens Cross Herefs 46 A2
St Paul's Walden Herts 50 C3
St Pauls Cray Gt Lon 29 F3
St Peter Jersey 174 b2
St Peter Port Guern 174 g2
St Peter's Guern 174 f1
St Peter's Kent 31 G3
St Peter's Hill Cambs 62 B3
St Petrox Pembks 32 D1
St Pinnock Cnwll 5 F2
St Quivox S Ayrs 119 E2
St Ruan Cnwll 3 E1
St Sampson Guern 174 h3
St Saviour Guern 174 f2
St Saviour Jersey 174 c2
St Stephen Cnwll 3 G5
St Stephen's Coombe Cnwll 3 G5
St Stephens Cnwll 5 G4
St Stephens Cnwll 5 H2
St Teath Cnwll 4 D4
St Tudy Cnwll 4 D4
St Twynnells Pembks 32 D1
St Veep Cnwll 5 E1
St Vigeans Angus 141 F4
St Wenn Cnwll 4 C2
St Weonards Herefs 45 H2
St y-Nyll V Glam 36 B2
Saintbury Gloucs 47 G3
Salachail Ag & B 137 E5
Salcombe Devon 7 E1
Salcombe Regis Devon 10 B3
Salcott Essex 52 C2
Sale Gt Man 82 C4
Sale Green Worcs 47 E5
Saleby Lincs 87 E2
Salehurst E Susx 18 A4
Salem Carmth 43 F2
Salem Cerdgn 54 D4
Salem Gwynd 67 E6
Salen Ag & B 135 H4
Salen Highld 136 B6
Salesbury Lancs 89 E3
Salford Beds 49 G3
Salford Gt Man 82 C4
Salford Oxon 48 A2
Salford Priors Warwks 47 F4
Salfords Surrey 16 D6
Salhouse Norfk 77 F1
Saline Fife 131 F4
Salisbury Wilts 25 G2
Salisbury Cathedral Wilts 25 G2
Salkeld Dykes Cumb 104 B4
Salle Norfk 76 D2
Salmonby Lincs 86 D2
Salperton Gloucs 47 F1
Salph End Beds 50 B6
Salsburgh N Lans 120 C6
Salt Staffs 70 D3
Salt Cotes Cumb 103 F5
Salta Cumb 103 E5
Saltaire W York 90 C3
Saltash Cnwll 5 H2
Saltburn Highld 155 E6
Saltburn-by-the-Sea N York 107 F3
Saltby Leics 73 F3
Saltcoats Cumb 94 B5
Saltcoats N Ayrs 118 D4
Saltcotes Lancs 88 B2
Saltdean E Susx 17 E2
Salterbeck Cumb 102 D3
Salterforth Lancs 89 G4
Salterswall Ches 82 A1
Salterton Wilts 25 G3
Saltfleet Lincs 87 E4
Saltfleetby All Saints Lincs 87 E4
Saltfleetby St Clement Lincs 87 E4
Saltfleetby St Peter Lincs 87 E4
Saltford Somset 24 B6
Salthouse Norfk 76 D4
Saltley W Mids 58 D4
Saltmarsh Newpt 37 E2
Saltmarshe E R Yk 92 B2
Saltney Flints 81 F1
Salton N York 98 C3
Saltrens Devon 21 E3
Saltwick Nthumb 114 C3
Saltwood Kent 19 E5
Salvington W Susx 16 B2
Salwarpe Worcs 46 D5
Salwayash Dorset 11 E4
Sambourne Warwks 47 F5
Sambrook Shrops 70 B2
Samlesbury Lancs 88 D3
Samlesbury Bottoms Lancs 89 E2
Sampford Arundel Somset 22 D1
Sampford Brett Somset 22 D3
Sampford Courtenay Devon 8 C5
Sampford Moor Somset 22 D1
Sampford Peverell Devon 9 G6
Sampford Spiney Devon 6 C5
Samson's Corner Essex 52 D2
Samsonlane Ork 169 c3
Samuelston E Loth 132 D2
Sanaigmore Ag & B 126 A2
Sancreed Cnwll 2 B3
Sancton E R Yk 92 C3
Sand Somset 23 G4
Sand Hills W York 91 E3
Sand Hole E R Yk 92 B3
Sand Hutton N York 91 H5
Sand Side Cumb 94 C3
Sandaig Highld 143 G4
Sandal Magna W York 91 E1
Sandale Cumb 103 F4
Sandavore Highld 142 D2
Sanday Airport Ork 169 d4
Sandbach Ches 70 C6
Sandbank Ag & B 128 C3
Sandbanks Dorset 12 D3
Sandend Abers 157 G6
Sanderstead Gt Lon 28 D2
Sandford Cumb 104 D2
Sandford Devon 9 E5
Sandford Dorset 12 C3
Sandford Hants 13 E5
Sandford IOW 14 D2
Sandford S Lans 120 B4
Sandford Shrops 69 F2
Sandford Shrops 69 H3
Sandford Somset 23 G5
Sandford Orcas Dorset 24 B1
Sandford St Martin Oxon 48 B2
Sandford-on-Thames Oxon 40 D4
Sandgate Kent 19 E5
Sandhaven Abers 159 E6
Sandhead D & G 100 B5
Sandhill S York 84 B4
Sandhills Dorset 11 F5
Sandhills Dorset 11 G6
Sandhills Oxon 40 D5
Sandhills Surrey 27 G3
Sandhills W Mids 58 D6
Sandhoe Nthumb 113 G1
Sandhole Ag & B 128 B5
Sandholme E R Yk 92 B3
Sandholme Lincs 74 D4
Sandhurst Berks 27 F5
Sandhurst Gloucs 46 D1
Sandhurst Kent 18 B4
Sandhurst Cross Kent 18 B4
Sandhutton N York 97 G3
Sandiacre Derbys 72 B4
Sandilands Lincs 87 F3
Sandiway Ches 82 A2
Sandleheath Hants 13 E6
Sandleigh Oxon 40 C4
Sandley Dorset 24 C2
Sandling Kent 30 A2
Sandlow Green Ches 82 C1
Sandness Shet 169 g3
Sandon Essex 52 A1
Sandon Herts 50 D4
Sandon Staffs 70 D3
Sandon Bank Staffs 70 D3
Sandown IOW 14 D2
Sandplace Cnwll 5 F2
Sandridge Herts 50 C2
Sandridge Wilts 25 E6
Sandringham Norfk 75 G3
Sands Bucks 41 G4
Sandsend N York 107 H2
Sandside Cumb 95 E3
Sandtoft Lincs 85 E5
Sandway Kent 30 C1
Sandwich Kent 31 G2
Sandwick Cumb 104 A2
Sandwick Shet 169 j2
Sandwick W Isls 168 f8
Sandwith Cumb 102 D2
Sandwith Newtown Cumb 102 D1
Sandy Beds 50 C6
Sandy Bank Lincs 74 C5
Sandy Cross E Susx 17 G3
Sandy Cross Herefs 46 B5
Sandy Haven Pembks 32 C2
Sandy Lane W York 90 B3
Sandy Lane Wilts 38 D1
Sandy Lane Wrexhm 69 F4
Sandy Park Devon 8 D4
Sandycroft Flints 81 F1
Sandyford D & G 111 F4
Sandygate Devon 9 E2
Sandygate IOM 174 m5
Sandyhills D & G 102 C6
Sandylands Lancs 88 C6
Sandylane Staffs 70 B4
Sandylane Swans 34 C3
Sandysike Cumb 112 A1
Sandyway Herefs 45 H2
Sangobeg Highld 165 E5
Sangomore Highld 165 E5
Sankey Bridges Ches 81 H3
Sankyn's Green Worcs 57 H2
Sanna Bay Highld 142 D1
Sanndabhaig W Isls 168 f8
Sannox N Ayrs 118 B4
Sanquhar D & G 110 B6
Santon Cumb 94 B5
Santon IOM 174 l2
Santon Bridge Cumb 94 B5
Santon Downham Suffk 63 G4
Sapcote Leics 59 H5
Sapey Common Herefs 57 G2
Sapiston Suffk 64 B3
Sapley Cambs 62 B3
Sapperton Derbys 71 G3
Sapperton Gloucs 38 D5
Sapperton Lincs 73 H3
Saracen's Head Lincs 74 D3
Sarclet Highld 167 G3
Sarisbury Hants 14 C4
Sarn Brdgnd 35 F3
Sarn Gwynd 66 B3
Sarn Powys 55 G5
Sarn Powys 56 B4
Sarn-bach Gwynd 66 C3
Sarn-wen Powys 69 E2
Sarnau Carmth 33 G3
Sarnau Cerdgn 42 C4
Sarnau Gwynd 68 B4
Sarnau Powys 69 E2
Sarnau Powys 44 C2
Sarnesfield Herefs 45 F4
Saron Carmth 42 D3
Saron Carmth 34 D5
Saron Gwynd 79 E1
Saron Gwynd 66 D6
Sarratt Herts 28 A6
Sarre Kent 31 F2
Sarsden Oxon 48 A1
Sarson Hants 26 A4
Satley Dur 105 H4
Satmar Kent 19 F5
Satron N York 96 C5
Satterleigh Devon 21 G3
Satterthwaite Cumb 94 D4
Satwell Oxon 41 E3
Sauchen Abers 149 E5
Saucher P & K 140 B3
Sauchieburn Abers 148 D1
Saul Gloucs 38 B5
Saundby Notts 85 E3
Saundersfoot Pembks 33 F2
Saunderton Bucks 41 F4
Saunton Devon 21 E4
Sausthorpe Lincs 86 D2
Saveock Water Cnwll 3 E4
Saverley Green Staffs 71 E4
Savile Town W York 90 D2
Sawbridge Warwks 59 H2
Sawbridgeworth Herts 51 F2
Sawdon N York 99 E3
Sawley Derbys 72 B3
Sawley Lancs 89 F4
Sawley N York 97 F2
Sawston Cambs 51 F6
Sawtry Cambs 61 H4
Saxby Leics 73 F2
Saxby Lincs 85 H3
Saxby All Saints Lincs 92 D1
Saxelbye Leics 73 E2
Saxham Street Suffk 64 C1
Saxilby Lincs 85 F2
Saxlingham Norfk 76 C4
Saxlingham Green Norfk 65 E5
Saxlingham Nethergate Norfk 65 E5
Saxlingham Thorpe Norfk 65 E5
Saxmundham Suffk 65 F2
Saxon Street Cambs 63 F1
Saxondale Notts 72 D4
Saxtead Suffk 65 E2
Saxtead Green Suffk 65 E2
Saxtead Little Green Suffk 65 E2
Saxthorpe Norfk 76 D3
Saxton N York 91 F3
Sayers Common W Susx 16 D3
Scackleton N York 98 B2
Scaftworth Notts 84 D4
Scagglethorpe N York 98 D2
Scalasaig Ag & B 126 C4
Scalby E R Yk 92 B2
Scalby N York 99 F4
Scald End Beds 61 F1
Scaldwell Nhants 60 D3
Scale Houses Cumb 104 C5
Scaleby Cumb 112 B1
Scalebyhill Cumb 112 B1
Scales Cumb 103 G3
Scales Cumb 94 C2
Scalesceugh Cumb 104 A5
Scalford Leics 73 E2
Scaling N York 107 G2
Scaling Dam N York 107 G2
Scalloway Shet 169 h2
Scamblesby Lincs 86 C2
Scammonden W York 90 B1
Scamodale Highld 143 H1
Scampston N York 98 D2
Scampton Lincs 85 G3
Scaniport Highld 154 D3
Scapegoat Hill W York 90 B1
Scarborough N York 99 F4
Scarcewater Cnwll 3 G5
Scarcliffe Derbys 84 C1
Scarcroft W York 91 E4
Scarcroft Hill W York 91 E4
Scarfskerry Highld 167 F6
Scargill Dur 105 G1
Scarinish Ag & B 134 B4
Scarisbrick Lancs 81 F6
Scarness Cumb 103 F3
Scarning Norfk 76 C1
Scarrington Notts 73 E4
Scarth Hill Lancs 81 F5
Scarthingwell N York 91 F3
Scartho Lincs 86 C5
Scatsta Airport Shet 169 h4
Scawby Lincs 85 G5
Scawsby S York 84 C5
Scawthorpe S York 84 C5
Scawton N York 98 A3
Scayne's Hill W Susx 17 E4
Scethrog Powys 44 D2
Scholar Green Ches 70 C6
Scholes Gt Man 82 A5
Scholes S York 84 B4
Scholes W York 83 F5
Scholes W York 90 C2
Scholes W York 91 E3
Scholey Hill W York 91 E2
School Aycliffe Dur 106 B3
School Green Ches 82 A1
School Green W York 90 B3
School House Dorset 10 D5
Schoolgreen Berks 27 E6
Scissett W York 83 G6
Scleddau Pembks 32 D5
Sco Ruston Norfk 77 F2
Scofton Notts 84 D3
Scole Norfk 64 D3
Scone P & K 140 A2
Sconser Highld 151 E2
Scoonie Fife 132 C5
Scopwick Lincs 74 A6
Scoraig Highld 160 D3
Scorborough E R Yk 92 D4
Scorrier Cnwll 3 E4
Scorriton Devon 6 D4
Scorton Lancs 88 C4
Scorton N York 97 F5
Scot Hay Staffs 70 C5
Scot Lane End Gt Man 82 A6
Scot's Gap Nthumb 114 B4
Scotby Cumb 104 A6
Scotch Corner N York 97 E5
Scotforth Lancs 88 C5
Scothern Lincs 85 H2
Scotland Lincs 73 G3
Scotland W York 90 C4
Scotland Gate T & W 114 D4
Scotlandwell P & K 131 H5
Scotscalder Station Highld 167 E4
Scotsdike Cumb 112 A2
Scotsmill Abers 158 B1
Scotstoun C Glas 129 G2
Scotswood T & W 114 D2
Scott Willoughby Lincs 73 H4
Scotter Lincs 85 F5
Scotterthorpe Lincs 85 F5
Scottlethorpe Lincs 73 H2
Scotton Lincs 85 F5
Scotton N York 97 E4
Scotton N York 90 D6
Scottow Norfk 77 F2
Scoulton Norfk 64 B5
Scounslow Green Staffs 71 F3
Scourie Highld 164 C3
Scourie More Highld 164 C3
Scousburgh Shet 169 h1
Scouthead Gt Man 83 E5
Scrabster Highld 167 E5
Scraesburgh Border 122 D1
Scrafield Lincs 86 C2
Scrainwood Nthumb 124 C2
Scrane End Lincs 74 D4
Scraptoft Leics 60 C6
Scratby Norfk 77 H1
Scrayingham N York 92 A6
Scrays E Susx 18 A3
Scredington Lincs 74 A4
Scremby Lincs 87 E1
Scremerston Nthumb 123 G4
Screveton Notts 73 E4
Scrivelsby Lincs 86 C1
Scriven N York 91 E5
Scrooby Notts 84 D4
Scropton Derbys 71 G3
Scrub Hill Lincs 74 C6
Scruschloch Angus 140 B5
Scruton N York 97 F4
Scuggate Cumb 112 B2
Scullomie Highld 165 G4
Sculthorpe Norfk 76 B3
Scunthorpe Lincs 85 F6
Scurlage Swans 34 B3
Sea Somset 10 D6
Sea Palling Norfk 77 G3
Seaborough Dorset 11 E5
Seabridge Staffs 70 C4
Seabrook Kent 19 E5
Seaburn T & W 115 F1
Seacombe Mersyd 81 E4
Seacroft Lincs 75 F6
Seacroft W York 91 E3
Seadyke Lincs 74 D4
Seafield Highld 151 E3
Seafield W Loth 131 F2
Seaford E Susx 17 F1
Seaforth Mersyd 81 E4
Seagrave Leics 72 D2
Seagry Heath Wilts 39 E3
Seaham Dur 106 D6
Seahouses Nthumb 125 E4
Seal Kent 29 F2
Seal Sands Dur 107 E3
Seale Surrey 27 G4
Seamer N York 106 D2
Seamer N York 99 F3
Seamill N Ayrs 118 D4
Searby Lincs 86 A5
Seasalter Kent 30 D2
Seascale Cumb 94 A5
Seathwaite Cumb 103 F1
Seathwaite Cumb 94 C4
Seatle Cumb 94 D3
Seatoller Cumb 103 F1
Seaton Cnwll 5 G1
Seaton Cumb 102 D3
Seaton Devon 10 C4
Seaton Dur 106 C6
Seaton E R Yk 93 E4
Seaton Kent 31 F2
Seaton Nthumb 115 E3
Seaton Rutlnd 61 E5
Seaton Burn T & W 114 D3
Seaton Carew Dur 107 E4
Seaton Delaval Nthumb 115 E3
Seaton Ross E R Yk 92 B4
Seaton Sluice Nthumb 115 E3
Seatown Dorset 11 E4
Seave Green N York 98 A5
Seaview IOW 14 D3
Seaville Cumb 103 F5
Seavington St Mary Somset 10 D6
Seavington St Michael Somset 10 D6
Sebastopol Torfn 36 D4
Sebergham Cumb 103 G4
Seckington Warwks 59 E6
Sedbergh Cumb 95 G4
Sedbury Gloucs 37 F4
Sedbusk N York 96 B4
Sedge Fen Suffk 63 F4
Sedgeberrow Worcs 47 F3
Sedgebrook Lincs 73 F4
Sedgefield Dur 106 C4
Sedgeford Norfk 75 G4
Sedgehill Wilts 24 D2
Sedgley W Mids 58 B5
Sedgley Park Gt Man 82 C5
Sedgwick Cumb 95 F3
Sedlescombe E Susx 18 A3
Sedrup Bucks 41 F5
Seed Kent 30 C2
Seend Wilts 25 E5
Seend Cleeve Wilts 25 E5
Seer Green Bucks 41 H3
Seething Norfk 65 F5
Sefton Mersyd 81 F5
Sefton Town Mersyd 81 F5
Seghill Nthumb 114 D3
Seighford Staffs 70 D2
Seion Gwynd 79 E1
Seisdon Staffs 58 A5
Selattyn Shrops 69 E3
Selborne Hants 27 F3
Selby N York 91 G3
Selham W Susx 15 G6
Selhurst Gt Lon 28 D3
Selkirk Border 122 B2
Sellack Herefs 46 A2
Sellafirth Shet 169 j5
Sellan Cnwll 2 B3
Sellick's Green Somset 23 E1
Sellindge Kent 19 E5
Selling Kent 30 D2
Sells Green Wilts 25 E5
Selly Oak W Mids 58 C4
Selmeston E Susx 17 F2
Selsdon Gt Lon 28 D2
Selsey W Susx 15 G3
Selsfield Common W Susx 16 D5
Selside Cumb 95 F5
Selside N York 96 A2
Selsley Gloucs 38 C5
Selsted Kent 19 F6
Selston Notts 72 B5
Selworthy Somset 22 B4
Semer Suffk 52 D5
Semington Wilts 24 D5
Semley Wilts 24 D2
Sempringham Lincs 74 B3
Send Surrey 28 A2
Send Marsh Surrey 28 A2
Senghenydd Caerph 36 B3
Sennen Cnwll 2 A2
Sennen Cove Cnwll 2 A2
Sennybridge Powys 44 B2
Serlby Notts 84 D4
Sessay N York 97 H2
Setchey Norfk 75 G1
Setley Hants 13 G5
Seton Mains E Loth 132 C3
Settle N York 96 A1
Settlingstones Nthumb 113 F2
Settrington N York 98 D2
Seven Ash Somset 22 D3
Seven Kings Gt Lon 29 E5
Seven Sisters Neath 35 F5
Seven Springs Gloucs 38 D6
Seven Star Green Essex 52 C3
Seven Wells Gloucs 47 G3
Sevenhampton Gloucs 47 F1
Sevenhampton Wilts 39 G3
Sevenoaks Kent 29 F1
Sevenoaks Weald Kent 29 F1
Severn Beach Gloucs 37 F3
Severn Stoke Worcs 46 D4
Sevick End Beds 50 B6
Sevington Kent 18 D5
Sewards End Essex 51 F4
Sewardstonebury Gt Lon 29 E6
Sewell Beds 49 H1
Sewerby E R Yk 99 H2
Seworgan Cnwll 3 E3
Sewstern Leics 73 F2
Sexhow N York 97 H5
Sezincote Gloucs 47 G2
Sgiogarstaigh W Isls 168 f9
Shabbington Bucks 41 E5
Shackerstone Leics 59 G6
Shacklecross Derbys 72 B3
Shackleford Surrey 27 G4
Shade W York 89 H2
Shader W Isls 168 e9
Shadforth Dur 106 C5

Shadingfield
Sloothby
310

Shadingfield Suffk 65 G4
Shadoxhurst Kent 18 C5
Shadwell Norfk 64 B4
Shadwell W York 91 E4
Shaftenhoe End Herts 51 E4
Shaftesbury Dorset 24 D1
Shaftholme S York 84 C5
Shafton S York 84 B6
Shafton Two Gates S York 84 B6
Shalbourne Wilts 26 A6
Shalcombe IOW 14 B2
Shalden Hants 27 E3
Shalden Green Hants 27 E4
Shaldon Devon 7 G5
Shalfleet IOW 14 B2
Shalford Essex 51 H4
Shalford Surrey 16 A6
Shalford Green Essex 51 H3
Shallowford Staffs 70 D3
Shalmsford Street Kent 31 E1
Shalstone Bucks 49 E3
Shamley Green Surrey 16 A6
Shandford Angus 141 E6
Shandon Ag & B 128 D4
Shandwick Highld 163 E1
Shangton Leics 60 C5
Shankhouse Nthumb 114 D3
Shanklin IOW 14 D2
Shap Cumb 104 B2
Shapwick Dorset 12 C5
Shapwick Somset 23 G3
Shard End W Mids 58 D4
Shardlow Derbys 72 B3
Shareshill Staffs 58 B6
Sharlston W York 91 E1
Sharlston Common W York 91 E1
Sharman's Cross W Mids 58 D3
Sharnal Street Kent 30 B3
Sharnbrook Beds 49 H5
Sharneyford Lancs 89 G2
Sharnford Leics 59 H4
Sharnhill Green Dorset 11 G5
Sharoe Green Lancs 88 D3
Sharow N York 97 F2
Sharp Green Norfk 77 G2
Sharpenhoe Beds 50 B4
Sharperton Nthumb 113 G5
Sharpness Gloucs 38 A4
Sharpthorne W Susx 17 E5
Sharptor Cnwll 5 F3
Sharpway Gate Worcs 58 B2
Sharrington Norfk 76 C4
Shatterford Worcs 57 H3
Shatterling Kent 31 F2
Shaugh Prior Devon 6 C4
Shave Cross Dorset 10 D4
Shavington Ches 70 B5
Shaw Berks 40 C1
Shaw Gt Man 82 D6
Shaw W York 90 A3
Shaw Wilts 24 D6
Shaw Wilts 39 F3
Shaw Common Gloucs 46 B2
Shaw Green Herts 50 D4
Shaw Green Lancs 88 D1
Shaw Green N York 90 D5
Shaw Hill Lancs 88 D2
Shaw Mills N York 90 D6
Shawbost W Isls 168 e9
Shawbury Shrops 69 H2
Shawclough Gt Man 89 G1
Shawdon Hill Nthumb 124 D2
Shawell Leics 60 B3
Shawford Hants 26 C2
Shawforth Lancs 89 G2
Shawhead D & G 110 C2
Shawsburn S Lans 120 B4
Shear Cross Wilts 24 D3
Shearington D & G 111 E1
Shearsby Leics 60 B4
Shearston Somset 23 F2
Shebbear Devon 8 A5
Shebdon Staffs 70 C3
Shebster Highld 166 D5
Sheddens E Rens 119 G5
Shedfield Hants 14 D5
Sheen Derbys 71 F6
Sheep Hill Dur 114 C1
Sheep-ridge W York 90 C1
Sheepbridge Derbys 84 A2
Sheepscar W York 90 D3
Sheepscombe Gloucs 38 D5
Sheepstor Devon 6 C4
Sheepwash Devon 8 B5
Sheepwash Nthumb 114 D4
Sheepway Somset 37 F2
Sheepy Magna Leics 59 F5
Sheepy Parva Leics 59 F5
Sheering Essex 51 F2
Sheerness Kent 30 C3
Sheerwater Surrey 28 A2
Sheet Hants 27 F2
Sheffield Cnwll 2 B2
Sheffield S York 84 A3
Sheffield Bottom Berks 41 E1
Sheffield City Airport S York 84 B3
Sheffield Green E Susx 17 E4
Shefford Beds 50 B5
Sheigra Highld 164 C4
Sheinton Shrops 57 F6
Shelderton Shrops 56 D3
Sheldon Derbys 83 G1
Sheldon Devon 10 B5
Sheldon W Mids 58 D4
Sheldwich Kent 30 D2
Sheldwich Lees Kent 30 D2
Shelf W York 90 B2
Shelfanger Norfk 64 D4
Shelfield W Mids 58 C6
Shelfield Warwks 58 D2
Shelfield Green Warwks 47 G5
Shelford Notts 72 D4
Shelford Warwks 59 G4
Shellacres Border 123 F4
Shelley Essex 51 F1
Shelley Suffk 52 D5
Shelley W York 83 G6
Shelley Far Bank W York 83 G6
Shellingford Oxon 40 A4
Shellow Bowells Essex 51 G1
Shelsley Beauchamp Worcs 57 G2
Shelsley Walsh Worcs 57 G2
Shelton Beds 61 F2
Shelton Norfk 65 E4
Shelton Notts 73 E4
Shelton Shrops 69 G1
Shelton Green Norfk 65 E4
Shelton Lock Derbys 72 A3
Shelton Under Harley Staffs 70 C4
Shelve Shrops 56 D5
Shelwick Herefs 45 H3
Shenfield Essex 29 G6
Shenington Oxon 48 B3
Shenley Herts 28 C6
Shenley Brook End Bucks 49 F3
Shenley Church End Bucks 49 F3
Shenleybury Herts 50 C1
Shenmore Herefs 45 G3
Shennanton D & G 109 E1
Shenstone Staffs 58 D6
Shenstone Worcs 58 B3
Shenstone Woodend Staffs 58 D5
Shenton Leics 59 G5
Shepeau Stow Lincs 74 C1
Shephall Herts 50 D3
Shepherd's Bush Gt Lon 28 C4
Shepherd's Green Oxon 41 E3
Shepherds Cnwll 3 F5
Shepherds Patch Gloucs 38 B5
Shepherdswell Kent 19 F6
Shepley W York 83 G6
Shepperdine Gloucs 37 G4
Shepperton Surrey 28 B3
Shepperton Green Surrey 28 B3
Shepreth Cambs 51 E5
Shepshed Leics 72 B2
Shepton Beauchamp Somset 23 G1
Shepton Mallet Somset 24 B4
Shepton Montague Somset 24 B2
Shepway Kent 30 A1
Sheraton Dur 106 D4
Sherborne Dorset 24 B1
Sherborne Gloucs 39 F6
Sherborne Somset 24 A5
Sherborne Causeway Dorset 24 D1
Sherborne St John Hants 26 D5
Sherbourne Warwks 47 H5
Sherburn Dur 106 C5
Sherburn N York 99 E2
Sherburn Hill Dur 106 C5
Sherburn in Elmet N York 91 F3
Shere Surrey 16 B6
Shereford Norfk 76 B3
Sherfield English Hants 26 A1
Sherfield on Loddon Hants 27 E5
Sherfin Lancs 89 F2
Sherford Devon 7 E2
Sherford Dorset 12 C4
Sheriff Hutton N York 98 B1
Sheriffhales Shrops 70 C1
Sheringham Norfk 77 E4
Sherington Bucks 49 G4
Shermanbury W Susx 16 C3
Shernborne Norfk 75 G3
Sherrington Wilts 25 E3
Sherston Wilts 38 C3
Sherwood Notts 72 C4
Shettleston C Glas 130 C1
Shevington Gt Man 81 H6
Shevington Moor Gt Man 81 H6
Shevington Vale Gt Man 81 G6
Sheviock Cnwll 5 G1
Shibden Head W York 90 B2
Shide IOW 14 C2
Shidlaw Nthumb 123 E3
Shiel Bridge Highld 152 D1
Shieldaig Highld 152 B4
Shieldhill D & G 111 E3
Shieldhill Falk 131 E3
Shieldhill House Hotel S Lans 121 E3
Shields N Lans 120 B5
Shielfoot Highld 143 F1
Shielhill Angus 140 D5
Shielhill Inver 128 D2
Shifford Oxon 40 B4
Shifnal Shrops 57 H6
Shilbottle Nthumb 125 E2
Shildon Dur 106 B3
Shillford E Rens 119 F5
Shillingford Devon 22 C2
Shillingford Oxon 40 D3
Shillingford Abbot Devon 9 F3
Shillingford St George Devon 9 F3
Shillingstone Dorset 12 B6
Shillington Beds 50 B4
Shillmoor Nthumb 113 F6
Shilton Oxon 39 G5
Shilton Warwks 59 G4
Shilvinghampton Dorset 11 G3
Shimpling Norfk 64 D4
Shimpling Suffk 52 B6
Shimpling Street Suffk 52 B6
Shincliffe Dur 106 B5
Shiney Row T & W 106 C6
Shinfield Berks 41 E1
Shingay Cambs 50 D5
Shingle Street Suffk 53 G5
Shinnersbridge Devon 7 E4
Shinness Highld 162 B5
Shipbourne Kent 29 G1
Shipbrookhill Ches 82 B2
Shipdham Norfk 64 B6
Shipham Somset 23 G5
Shiphay Devon 7 F4
Shiplake Oxon 41 F2
Shiplake Row Oxon 41 F2
Shiplate Somset 23 F5
Shipley Derbys 72 B4
Shipley Shrops 58 A5
Shipley W Susx 16 B4
Shipley W York 90 C3
Shipley Bridge Surrey 16 D5
Shipley Hatch Kent 18 D5
Shipmeadow Suffk 65 F4
Shippea Hill Station Cambs 63 F4
Shippon Oxon 40 C4
Shipston on Stour Warwks 47 H3
Shipton Bucks 49 F2
Shipton Gloucs 47 F1
Shipton N York 91 G5
Shipton Shrops 57 F5
Shipton Bellinger Hants 25 H4
Shipton Gorge Dorset 11 E4
Shipton Green W Susx 15 F4
Shipton Moyne Gloucs 38 D3
Shipton-on-Cherwell Oxon 40 C6
Shipton-under-Wychwood Oxon 39 G6
Shiptonthorpe E R Yk 92 B4
Shirburn Oxon 41 E4
Shirdley Hill Lancs 81 F6
Shire Cumb 104 C4
Shire Oak W Mids 58 C6
Shirebrook Derbys 84 C1
Shiregreen S York 84 A4
Shirehampton Bristl 37 F2
Shiremoor T & W 115 E3
Shirenewton Mons 37 F4
Shireoaks Notts 84 C3
Shirkoak Kent 18 C5
Shirl Heath Herefs 45 G5
Shirland Derbys 72 B6
Shirlett Shrops 57 G5
Shirley Derbys 71 G4
Shirley Gt Lon 28 D3
Shirley Hants 14 B5
Shirley W Mids 58 D3
Shirrell Heath Hants 14 D5
Shirvan Ag & B 127 G3
Shirwell Devon 21 F4
Shirwell Cross Devon 21 F4
Shiskine N Ayrs 118 A2
Shittlehope Dur 105 G4
Shobdon Herefs 45 G5
Shobley Hants 13 F5
Shobrooke Devon 9 E5
Shoby Leics 72 D2
Shocklach Ches 69 G5
Shocklach Green Ches 69 F5
Shoeburyness Essex 30 C5
Sholden Kent 31 G1
Sholing Hants 14 C5
Shoose Cumb 102 D3
Shoot Hill Shrops 69 F1
Shop Cnwll 20 B2
Shop Cnwll 4 B3
Shop Street Suffk 65 E2
Shopwyke W Susx 15 G4
Shore Gt Man 89 H1
Shoreditch Gt Lon 28 D4
Shoreditch Somset 23 E1
Shoreham Kent 29 F2
Shoreham Airport W Susx 16 C2
Shoreham-by-Sea W Susx 16 C2
Shoreswood Nthumb 123 F4
Shorley Hants 26 D2
Shorncote Gloucs 39 E4
Shorne Kent 29 H3
Shorne Ridgeway Kent 29 H3
Short Heath W Mids 58 C5
Short Heath W Mids 58 D5
Shorta Cross Cnwll 5 F2
Shortbridge E Susx 17 E3
Shortfield Common Surrey 27 G3
Shortgate E Susx 17 F3
Shortheath Hants 27 F3
Shortlanesend Cnwll 3 F4
Shortstown Beds 50 B5
Shorwell IOW 14 C2
Shoscombe Somset 24 C5
Shotesham Norfk 65 E5
Shotgate Essex 30 A5
Shotley Suffk 53 F4
Shotley Bridge Dur 105 G5
Shotley Gate Suffk 53 F4
Shotley Street Suffk 53 F4
Shotleyfield Nthumb 105 G5
Shottenden Kent 30 D1
Shottermill Surrey 27 G2
Shottery Warwks 47 G5
Shotteswell Warwks 48 C4
Shottisham Suffk 53 G5
Shottle Derbys 71 H5
Shottlegate Derbys 71 H5
Shotton Dur 106 C3
Shotton Dur 106 D5
Shotton Flints 81 E1
Shotton Nthumb 123 F2
Shotton Nthumb 114 D3
Shotton Colliery Dur 106 C5
Shotts N Lans 120 C5
Shotwick Ches 81 F2
Shougle Moray 156 D5
Shouldham Norfk 75 G1
Shouldham Thorpe Norfk 63 F6
Shoulton Worcs 46 D5
Shover's Green E Susx 17 G4
Shraleybrook Staffs 70 C5
Shrawardine Shrops 69 F1
Shrawley Worcs 58 A2
Shreding Green Bucks 28 A4
Shrewley Warwks 59 E2
Shrewsbury Shrops 69 G1
Shrewton Wilts 25 F4
Shripney W Susx 15 G4
Shrivenham Oxon 39 G3
Shropham Norfk 64 B5
Shrub End Essex 52 C3
Shucknall Herefs 46 A3
Shudy Camps Cambs 51 G5
Shurdington Gloucs 47 E1
Shurlock Row Berks 41 F2
Shurnock Worcs 47 F5
Shurrery Highld 166 D4
Shurrery Lodge Highld 166 D4
Shurton Somset 23 E4
Shustoke Warwks 59 E4
Shut Heath Staffs 70 D2
Shute Devon 9 F5
Shute Devon 10 C4
Shutford Oxon 48 B3
Shuthonger Gloucs 46 D3
Shutlanger Nhants 49 E4
Shutt Green Staffs 70 D1
Shutterton Devon 9 F2
Shuttington Warwks 59 E6
Shuttlewood Derbys 84 B2
Shuttlewood Common Derbys 84 B2
Shuttleworth Lancs 89 F1
Siabost W Isls 168 e9
Siadar W Isls 168 e9
Sibbertoft Nhants 60 C4
Sibdon Carwood Shrops 56 D4
Sibford Ferris Oxon 48 B3
Sibford Gower Oxon 48 B3
Sible Hedingham Essex 52 A4
Sibley's Green Essex 51 G4
Siblyback Cnwll 5 F3
Sibsey Lincs 74 D5
Sibsey Fenside Lincs 74 D5
Sibson Cambs 61 G5
Sibson Leics 59 F5
Sibster Highld 167 G4
Sibthorpe Notts 85 E2
Sibthorpe Notts 73 E5
Sibton Suffk 65 F2
Sicklesmere Suffk 64 A1
Sicklinghall N York 91 E4
Sid Cop S York 84 B6
Sidbrook Somset 23 E2
Sidbury Devon 10 B4
Sidbury Shrops 57 G4
Sidcot Somset 23 G5
Sidcup Gt Lon 29 E3
Siddick Cumb 102 D3
Siddington Ches 82 C2
Siddington Gloucs 39 E4
Sidemoor Worcs 58 B2
Sidestrand Norfk 77 F4
Sidford Devon 10 B4
Sidlesham W Susx 15 G3
Sidlesham Common W Susx 15 G4
Sidley E Susx 18 A2
Sidmouth Devon 10 B3
Siefton Shrops 57 E4
Sigford Devon 7 E5
Sigglesthorne E R Yk 93 E4
Sigingstone V Glam 35 G1
Signet Oxon 39 G5
Silchester Hants 26 D5
Sileby Leics 72 D1
Silecroft Cumb 94 B3
Silfield Norfk 64 D5
Silian Cerdgn 43 F4
Silk Willoughby Lincs 74 A4
Silkstead Hants 26 C2
Silkstone S York 83 H5
Silkstone Common S York 83 H5
Silksworth T & W 106 C6
Silloth Cumb 103 E5
Silpho N York 99 E4
Silsden W York 90 B4
Silsoe Beds 50 B4
Silton Dorset 24 C2
Silver End Essex 52 B3
Silver Street Kent 30 B2
Silver Street Somset 24 A2
Silverburn Mdloth 121 F5
Silverdale Lancs 95 E2
Silverdale Staffs 70 C5
Silverdale Green Lancs 95 E2
Silverford Abers 158 D5
Silvergate Norfk 77 E3
Silverlace Green Suffk 65 F1
Silverley's Green Suffk 65 E3
Silverstone Nhants 49 E4
Silverton Devon 9 F5
Silverwell Cnwll 3 E5
Silvington Shrops 57 F3
Simmondley Derbys 83 E4
Simonburn Nthumb 113 F2
Simons Burrow Devon 22 D1
Simonsbath Somset 21 H4
Simonstone Lancs 89 F3
Simonstone N York 96 B4
Simprim Border 123 F4
Simpson Bucks 49 G3
Simpson Cross Pembks 32 C4
Sinclair's Hill Border 123 E4
Sinclairston E Ayrs 119 F1
Sinderby N York 97 G3
Sinderhope Nthumb 105 E5
Sinderland Green Gt Man 82 B4
Sindlesham Berks 41 F1
Sinfin Derbys 72 A3
Single Street Gt Lon 29 E2
Singleborough Bucks 49 F2
Singleton Lancs 88 B3
Singleton W Susx 15 G5
Singlewell Kent 29 G3
Sinkhurst Green Kent 18 B6
Sinnarhard Abers 148 B6
Sinnington N York 98 C3
Sinton Worcs 46 D5
Sinton Green Worcs 46 D5
Sipson Gt Lon 28 B4
Sirhowy Blae G 36 C5
Sissinghurst Kent 18 B5
Siston Gloucs 38 B2
Sitcott Devon 5 G5
Sithney Cnwll 2 D3
Sithney Common Cnwll 2 D3
Sithney Green Cnwll 2 D3
Sittingbourne Kent 30 C2
Six Ashes Staffs 57 H4
Six Bells Blae G 36 C5
Six Mile Bottom Cambs 63 E1
Six Rues Jersey 174 b3
Sixhills Lincs 86 B3
Sixmile Cottages Kent 19 E6
Sixpenny Handley Dorset 25 E1
Sizergh Castle Cumb 95 F4
Sizewell Suffk 65 G2
Skaill Ork 169 c2
Skares E Ayrs 119 G1
Skateraw Abers 149 G4
Skateraw E Loth 133 F3
Skeabost Highld 150 D3
Skeeby N York 97 E5
Skeffington Leics 60 C6
Skeffling E R Yk 93 G1
Skegby Notts 72 C6
Skegby Notts 85 E2
Skegness Lincs 87 F1
Skelbo Highld 163 E3
Skelbo Street Highld 163 E3
Skelbrooke S York 84 C6
Skeldyke Lincs 74 D4
Skellingthorpe Lincs 85 G2
Skellorn Green Ches 82 D3
Skellow S York 84 C6
Skelmanthorpe W York 83 G6
Skelmersdale Lancs 81 G5
Skelmorlie N Ayrs 128 C2
Skelpick Highld 166 A4
Skelston D & G 110 C3
Skelton Cumb 104 A4
Skelton E R Yk 92 B2
Skelton N York 96 D5
Skelton N York 107 F3
Skelton N York 97 G2
Skelton N York 91 G5
Skelwith Bridge Cumb 94 D5
Skendleby Lincs 87 E2
Skene House Abers 149 E5
Skenfrith Mons 45 G1
Skerne E R Yk 92 D5
Skerray Highld 165 G5
Skerricha Highld 164 C3
Skerton Lancs 95 E1
Sketchley Leics 59 G5
Sketty Swans 34 D3
Skewen Neath 35 E4
Skewsby N York 98 B2
Skeyton Norfk 77 E3
Skeyton Corner Norfk 77 E3
Skiall Highld 166 D5
Skidbrooke Lincs 87 E4
Skidbrooke North End Lincs 87 E4
Skidby E R Yk 92 D3
Skigersta W Isls 168 f9
Skilgate Somset 22 C2
Skillington Lincs 73 F3
Skinburness Cumb 103 E6
Skinflats Falk 131 E3
Skinidin Highld 150 B3
Skinners Green Berks 26 C6
Skinningrove N York 107 F3
Skipness Ag & B 117 H6
Skipper's Bridge Cumb 112 A3
Skiprigg Cumb 103 H5
Skipsea E R Yk 93 E5
Skipsea Brough E R Yk 93 E5
Skipton N York 90 A5
Skipton-on-Swale N York 97 G3
Skipwith N York 91 H3
Skirlaugh E R Yk 93 E3
Skirling Border 121 E3
Skirmett Bucks 41 F3
Skirpenbeck E R Yk 92 A5
Skirwith Cumb 104 C3
Skirwith N York 95 H2
Skirza Highld 167 G5
Skitby Cumb 112 B1
Skittle Green Bucks 41 F5
Skulamus Highld 151 G1
Skyborry Green Shrops 56 C3
Skye Green Essex 52 B3
Skye of Curr Highld 156 B1
Skyreholme N York 90 B6
Slack Derbys 84 A1
Slack W York 90 A2
Slack Head Cumb 95 F3
Slackcote Gt Man 83 E6
Slackholme End Lincs 87 F2
Slacks of Cairnbanno Abers 158 D4
Slad Gloucs 38 C5
Slade Devon 21 E5
Slade Devon 10 B5
Slade Somset 22 A2
Slade End Oxon 40 D3
Slade Green Kent 29 F4
Slade Heath Staffs 58 B6
Slade Hooton S York 84 C4
Slades Green Worcs 46 D3
Sladesbridge Cnwll 4 D3
Slaggyford Nthumb 104 C5
Slaid Hill W York 90 D4
Slaidburn Lancs 89 E5
Slaithwaite W York 83 F6
Slaley Derbys 71 H6
Slaley Nthumb 105 F6
Slamannan Falk 131 E2
Slapton Bucks 49 G1
Slapton Devon 7 F2
Slapton Nhants 49 E4
Slattocks Gt Man 82 D5
Slaugham W Susx 16 C4
Slaughterford Wilts 38 C2
Slawston Leics 60 D5
Sleaford Hants 27 F3
Sleaford Lincs 74 A5
Sleagill Cumb 104 C2
Sleap Shrops 69 G3
Sleapford Shrops 70 A2
Sleasdairidh Highld 162 C3
Sledge Green Worcs 46 D3
Sledmere E R Yk 99 E1
Sleight Dorset 12 D4
Sleightholme Dur 96 C6
Sleights N York 107 H2
Slepe Dorset 12 C4
Slickly Highld 167 G5
Sliddery N Ayrs 118 A2
Sligachan Highld 151 E2
Sligrachan Ag & B 128 C4
Slimbridge Gloucs 38 B5
Slindon Staffs 70 C3
Slindon W Susx 15 H4
Slinfold W Susx 16 B4
Sling Gwynd 79 F1
Slingsby N York 98 C2
Slip End Beds 50 B2
Slip End Herts 50 D4
Slipton Nhants 61 E3
Slitting Mill Staffs 71 E2
Slockavullin Ag & B 127 G5
Slogarie D & G 110 A2
Sloley Norfk 77 F2
Sloncombe Devon 8 D3
Sloothby Lincs 87 E2

Slough Stanford Bridge 311

Slough Berks 41 H2
Slough Green Somset 23 E1
Slough Green W Susx 16 D4
Slumbay Highld 152 C3
Slyfield Green Surrey 28 A1
Slyne Lancs 95 E1
Smailholm Border 122 D3
Small Dole W Susx 16 C3
Small Heath W Mids 58 D4
Small Hythe Kent 18 C4
Small Wood Hey Lancs 88 B4
Smallbridge Gt Man 89 G1
Smallbrook Devon 9 E4
Smallbrook Gloucs 37 G4
Smallburgh Norfk 77 F2
Smalldale Derbys 83 F2
Smalldale Derbys 83 G3
Smalley Derbys 72 B4
Smalley Common Derbys 72 B4
Smalley Green Derbys 72 B4
Smallfield Surrey 16 D6
Smallridge Devon 10 C5
Smallthorne Staffs 70 D5
Smallways N York 105 H1
Smallwood Ches 70 C6
Smallworth Norfk 64 C3
Smannell Hants 26 B4
Smardale Cumb 95 H6
Smarden Kent 18 B6
Smarden Bell Kent 18 B6
Smart's Hill Kent 17 F6
Smeafield Nthumb 124 D5
Smearisary Highld 143 F2
Smeatharpe Devon 10 B6
Smeeth Kent 18 D5
Smeeton Westerby Leics 60 C5
Smelthouses N York 97 E1
Smerral Highld 167 E2
Smestow Staffs 58 B5
Smethwick W Mids 58 C4
Smethwick Green Ches 82 C1
Smisby Derbys 72 A2
Smith End Green Worcs 46 C4
Smith Green Lancs 88 C5
Smith's End Herts 51 E4
Smith's Green Essex 51 G3
Smith's Green Essex 51 G5
Smitheclose IOW 14 D3
Smithfield Cumb 112 B1
Smithies S York 84 A5
Smithincott Devon 9 G6
Smithstown Highld 160 B1
Smithton Highld 155 E4
Smithy Bridge Gt Man 89 H1
Smithy Green Ches 82 B2
Smithy Green Gt Man 82 D3
Smithy Houses Derbys 72 B5
Smockington Leics 59 G4
Smoo Highld 165 E5
Smythe's Green Essex 52 C3
Snade D & G 110 C3
Snailbeach Shrops 56 D6
Snailwell Cambs 63 F2
Snainton N York 99 E3
Snaith E R Yk 91 G2
Snake Pass Inn Derbys 83 F4
Snape N York 97 F3
Snape Suffk 65 F1
Snape Green Mersyd 81 F6
Snape Street Suffk 65 F1
Snaresbrook Gt Lon 29 E5
Snarestone Leics 72 A1
Snarford Lincs 85 H3
Snargate Kent 18 C4
Snave Kent 18 D4
Sneachill Worcs 47 E4
Snead Powys 56 C5
Sneath Common Norfk 64 D4
Sneaton N York 99 E6
Sneatonthorpe N York 99 E5
Snelland Lincs 86 A3
Snelson Ches 82 C2
Snelston Derbys 71 F4
Snetterton Norfk 64 B4
Snettisham Norfk 75 G3
Snibston Leics 72 B1
Snig's End Gloucs 46 C2
Snitter Nthumb 124 C1
Snitterby Lincs 85 G4
Snitterfield Warwks 47 H5
Snitterton Derbys 71 H6
Snittlegarth Cumb 103 F4
Snitton Shrops 57 F3
Snoadhill Kent 18 C6
Snodhill Herefs 45 F3
Snodland Kent 29 H2
Snoll Hatch Kent 17 G6
Snow End Herts 51 E4
Snow Street Norfk 64 C3
Snowden Hill S York 83 G5
Snowshill Gloucs 47 F3
Soake Hants 15 E5
Soar Cardif 36 B3
Soar Devon 6 D1
Soar Powys 44 C2
Soberton Hants 14 D5
Soberton Heath Hants 14 D5
Sockbridge Cumb 104 B3
Sockburn Dur 97 G6
Sodom Denbgs 80 C2
Sodylt Bank Shrops 69 F4
Soham Cambs 63 E3
Soham Cotes Cambs 63 E3
Solas W Isls 168 b5
Solbury Pembks 32 C3
Soldon Devon 20 C2
Soldon Cross Devon 20 C2
Soldridge Hants 27 E3
Sole Street Kent 29 G3
Sole Street Kent 31 E1
Solihull W Mids 58 D3
Sollers Dilwyn Herefs 45 G5
Sollers Hope Herefs 46 B2
Sollom Lancs 88 C1
Solva Pembks 32 B4
Solwaybank D & G 111 G2
Somerby Leics 73 E1
Somerby Lincs 86 A5
Somercotes Derbys 72 B5
Somerford Dorset 13 F4
Somerford Keynes Gloucs 39 E4
Somerley W Susx 15 F3
Somerleyton Suffk 65 G5
Somersal Herbert Derbys 71 F3
Somersby Lincs 86 D2
Somersham Cambs 62 C3
Somersham Suffk 52 D6
Somerton Oxon 48 C2
Somerton Somset 23 H2
Somerton Suffk 52 B6
Somerwood Shrops 69 H1
Sompting W Susx 16 C2
Sonning Berks 41 F2
Sonning Common Oxon 41 E2
Sonning Eye Oxon 41 F2
Sontley Wrexhm 69 F5
Sopley Hants 13 E4
Sopworth Wilts 38 C3
Sorbie D & G 101 F5
Sordale Highld 167 E5
Sorisdale Ag & B 135 E6
Sorn E Ayrs 119 G2
Sortat Highld 167 F5
Sosgill Cumb 103 E2
Sotby Lincs 86 B2
Sots Hole Lincs 86 B1
Sotterly Suffk 65 G4
Soughton Flints 81 E1
Soulbury Bucks 49 G2
Soulby Cumb 104 A3
Soulby Cumb 104 D1
Souldern Oxon 48 C2
Souldrop Beds 49 H5
Sound Muir Moray 157 F4
Soundwell Gloucs 37 G2
Sourton Devon 8 B4
Soutergate Cumb 94 C3
South Acre Norfk 76 A1
South Alkham Kent 19 F6
South Allington Devon 7 E1
South Alloa Falk 131 E4
South Ambersham W Susx 15 G6
South Anston S York 84 C3
South Ascot Berks 27 G6
South Ashford Kent 18 D6
South Baddesley Hants 14 B3
South Bank N York 107 E3
South Bank N York 91 G5
South Barrow Somset 24 B2
South Beddington Gt Lon 28 D2
South Beer Cnwll 5 G5
South Benfleet Essex 30 A5
South Bersted W Susx 15 G4
South Bockhampton Dorset 13 F4
South Bowood Dorset 11 E4
South Bramwith S York 84 D6
South Brent Devon 6 D4
South Brewham Somset 24 C3
South Broomhill Nthumb 114 D5
South Burlingham Norfk 65 F6
South Cadbury Somset 24 B2
South Carlton Lincs 85 G2
South Carlton Notts 84 D3
South Cave E R Yk 92 C3
South Cerney Gloucs 39 E4
South Chailey E Susx 17 E3
South Chard Somset 10 D5
South Charlton Nthumb 125 E3
South Cheriton Somset 24 C2
South Church Dur 106 B4
South Cleatlam Dur 105 H2
South Cliffe E R Yk 92 C3
South Clifton Notts 85 F2
South Cockerington Lincs 86 D4
South Cornelly Brdgnd 35 F2
South Cove Suffk 65 G3
South Creake Norfk 76 B4
South Crosland W York 83 F6
South Croxton Leics 72 D1
South Dalton E R Yk 92 C4
South Darenth Kent 29 F3
South Duffield N York 91 H3
South Elkington Lincs 86 C3
South Elmsall W York 84 B6
South End E R Yk 93 H1
South End Hants 13 E6
South End Herefs 46 C4
South End Lincs 93 E2
South End Norfk 64 B4
South Erradale Highld 152 B6
South Fambridge Essex 30 B5
South Fawley Berks 40 B2
South Ferriby Lincs 92 D2
South Field E R Yk 92 D2
South Godstone Surrey 28 D1
South Gorley Hants 13 E6
South Gosforth T & W 114 D2
South Green Essex 52 D3
South Green Essex 29 H5
South Green Kent 30 B2
South Green Norfk 76 D1
South Green Suffk 64 D3
South Gyle C Edin 131 H2
South Hanningfield Essex 30 A6
South Harting W Susx 15 F5
South Hayling Hants 15 E4
South Hazelrigg Nthumb 123 H3
South Heath Bucks 41 G4
South Heighton E Susx 17 E2
South Hetton Dur 106 C5
South Hiendley W York 84 B6
South Hill Cnwll 5 G3
South Hill Somset 23 G2
South Hinksey Oxon 40 C5
South Hole Devon 20 C3
South Holmwood Surrey 16 C6
South Hornchurch Gt Lon 29 F4
South Huish Devon 6 D2
South Hykeham Lincs 85 G1
South Hylton T & W 115 E1
South Kelsey Lincs 85 H4
South Kessock Highld 155 E4
South Killingholme Lincs 93 E1
South Kilvington N York 97 G3
South Kilworth Nhants 60 B3
South Kirkby W York 84 B6
South Knighton Devon 7 E5
South Kyme Lincs 74 B5
South Lawn Oxon 39 G6
South Leigh Oxon 40 B5
South Leverton Notts 85 E3
South Littleton Worcs 47 F4
South Lopham Norfk 64 C3
South Luffenham Rutlnd 61 E6
South Malling E Susx 17 E2
South Marston Wilts 39 G3
South Merstham Surrey 28 D1
South Middleton Nthumb 124 C3
South Milford N York 91 F3
South Milton Devon 6 D2
South Mimms Herts 28 C6
South Molton Devon 21 G3
South Moor Dur 106 A6
South Moreton Oxon 40 D3
South Mundham W Susx 15 G4
South Muskham Notts 73 E6
South Newbald E R Yk 92 C3
South Newington Oxon 48 B2
South Newton Wilts 25 F3
South Normanton Derbys 72 B6
South Norwood Gt Lon 28 D3
South Nutfield Surrey 28 D1
South Ockendon Essex 29 G4
South Ormsby Lincs 86 D2
South Ossett W York 90 D1
South Otterington N York 97 G4
South Owersby Lincs 86 A4
South Park Surrey 28 C1
South Perrott Dorset 11 E5
South Petherton Somset 23 G1
South Petherwin Cnwll 5 G4
South Pickenham Norfk 63 H6
South Pill Cnwll 5 H2
South Pool Devon 7 E2
South Poorton Dorset 11 F4
South Quarme Somset 22 B3
South Queensferry C Edin 131 G3
South Radworthy Devon 21 G4
South Rauceby Lincs 73 H5
South Raynham Norfk 76 B2
South Reddish Gt Man 82 D4
South Reston Lincs 86 D3
South Runcton Norfk 75 G1
South Scarle Notts 85 F1
South Shian Ag & B 136 D4
South Shields T & W 115 E2
South Shore Lancs 88 B3
South Somercotes Lincs 86 D4
South Stainley N York 97 F1
South Stifford Essex 29 G4
South Stoke Lincs 73 G3
South Stoke Oxon 40 D3
South Stoke Somset 24 C5
South Stoke W Susx 16 A2
South Stour Kent 18 D5
South Street Kent 29 G2
South Street Kent 30 D2
South Street Kent 31 E3
South Tarbrax S Lans 121 E5
South Tawton Devon 8 C4
South Thoresby Lincs 86 D2
South Thorpe Dur 105 H1
South Town Hants 27 E3
South Walsham Norfk 77 G1
South Warnborough Hants 27 E4
South Weald Essex 29 F5
South Weston Oxon 41 E4
South Wheatley Cnwll 5 F5
South Widcombe Somset 24 A5
South Wigston Leics 60 B5
South Willesborough Kent 18 D5
South Willingham Lincs 86 B3
South Wingate Dur 106 D4
South Wingfield Derbys 72 A6
South Witham Lincs 73 G2
South Wonston Hants 26 C3
South Woodham Ferrers Essex 30 B6
South Wootton Norfk 75 G2
South Wraxall Wilts 24 D6
South Zeal Devon 8 C4
Southall Gt Lon 28 B4
Southam Gloucs 47 E2
Southam Warwks 48 B5
Southampton Hants 14 B5
Southampton Airport Hants 14 C5
Southborough Gt Lon 29 E3
Southborough Kent 17 G6
Southbourne Dorset 13 E4
Southbourne W Susx 15 F4
Southbrook Dorset 12 B4
Southburgh Norfk 64 C6
Southburn E R Yk 92 D5
Southchurch Essex 30 C5
Southcott Cnwll 5 E5
Southcott Devon 21 E2
Southcott Devon 8 B4
Southcott Devon 8 D3
Southcott Wilts 25 G5
Southcourt Bucks 41 F5
Southease E Susx 17 E2
Southend Ag & B 117 F1
Southend Wilts 39 G2
Southend Airport Essex 30 B5
Southend-on-Sea Essex 30 B5
Southernby Cumb 103 H4
Southernden Kent 18 B6
Southerndown V Glam 35 F2
Southerness D & G 102 D6
Southerton Devon 10 A4
Southery Norfk 63 E5
Southfield Falk 131 E2
Southfleet Kent 29 G3
Southford IOW 14 C1
Southgate Gt Lon 28 D5
Southgate Norfk 75 G3
Southgate Norfk 76 B3
Southgate Norfk 76 D2
Southgate Swans 34 C3
Southill Beds 50 B5
Southington Hants 26 C4
Southleigh Devon 10 B4
Southminster Essex 30 C6
Southmoor Oxon 40 B4
Southmuir Angus 140 D5
Southoe Cambs 61 H2
Southolt Suffk 64 D2
Southorpe Cambs 61 G6
Southover Dorset 11 F4
Southover E Susx 17 G4
Southowram W York 90 B2
Southport Mersyd 88 B1
Southrepps Norfk 77 E4
Southrey Lincs 86 B1
Southrop Gloucs 39 G5
Southrope Hants 27 E4
Southsea Hants 15 E3
Southsea Wrexhm 69 E5
Southside Dur 105 H3
Southtown Norfk 65 H6
Southtown Somset 23 F1
Southwaite Cumb 104 A5
Southwark Gt Lon 28 D4
Southwater W Susx 16 B4
Southwater Street W Susx 16 B4
Southway Somset 23 H3
Southwell Dorset 11 G2
Southwell Notts 73 E5
Southwick Hants 14 D4
Southwick Nhants 61 F5
Southwick Somset 23 F4
Southwick T & W 115 E1
Southwick W Susx 16 C2
Southwick Wilts 24 D5
Southwold Suffk 65 G3
Southwood Norfk 65 F6
Southwood Somset 24 A3
Sowe Common W Mids 59 G4
Sower Carr Lancs 88 B4
Sowerby N York 97 G3
Sowerby W York 90 B2
Sowerby Bridge W York 90 B2
Sowerby Row Cumb 103 H4
Sowerhill Somset 22 B2
Sowhill Torfn 36 D4
Sowley Green Suffk 51 H6
Sowood W York 90 B1
Sowton Devon 6 B4
Sowton Devon 9 G4
Soyland Town W York 90 B2
Spa Common Norfk 77 F3
Spain's End Essex 51 G4
Spalding Lincs 74 C2
Spaldington E R Yk 92 B3
Spaldwick Cambs 61 G3
Spalford Notts 85 F2
Spanby Lincs 74 A4
Spanish Green Hants 27 E5
Sparham Norfk 76 D2
Sparhamill Norfk 76 D2
Spark Bridge Cumb 94 D3
Sparket Cumb 104 A3
Sparkford Somset 24 B2
Sparkhill W Mids 58 D4
Sparkwell Devon 6 C3
Sparrow Green Norfk 76 C1
Sparrowpit Derbys 83 F3
Sparrows Green E Susx 17 G5
Sparsholt Hants 26 C2
Sparsholt Oxon 40 B3
Spartylea Cumb 105 E5
Spath Staffs 71 F4
Spaunton N York 98 C4
Spaxton Somset 23 E3
Spean Bridge Highld 144 D3
Spear Hill W Susx 16 B3
Spearywell Hants 26 A2
Speen Berks 26 C6
Speen Bucks 41 G4
Speeton N York 99 G2
Speke Mersyd 81 G3
Speldhurst Kent 17 F6
Spellbrook Herts 51 F2
Spelmonden Kent 17 H5
Spelsbury Oxon 48 B1
Spen W York 90 C2
Spen Green Ches 70 C6
Spencers Wood Berks 27 E6
Spennithorne N York 97 E4
Spennymoor Dur 106 B4
Spernall Warwks 47 F5
Spestos Devon 8 D4
Spetchley Worcs 46 D5
Spetisbury Dorset 12 C5
Spexhall Suffk 65 F3
Spey Bay Moray 157 F6
Speybridge Highld 156 B2
Speyview Moray 157 E3
Spilsby Lincs 86 D1
Spindlestone Nthumb 125 E4
Spinkhill Derbys 84 B2
Spinningdale Highld 162 D3
Spion Kop Notts 84 C1
Spirthill Wilts 39 E2
Spital Mersyd 81 F3
Spital Hill S York 84 D4
Spital in the Street Lincs 85 G4
Spithurst E Susx 17 E3
Spittal E Loth 132 D3
Spittal E R Yk 92 B5
Spittal Highld 167 E4
Spittal Nthumb 123 G5
Spittal Pembks 32 D4
Spittal of Glenmuick Abers 147 H3
Spittal of Glenshee P & K 147 F1
Spittal-on-Rule Border 122 C1
Spittalfield P & K 140 A4
Spixworth Norfk 77 E1
Splatt Cnwll 4 C4
Splatt Cnwll 5 F5
Splatt Devon 8 C5
Splayne's Green E Susx 17 E4
Splottlands Cardif 36 C2
Spodegreen Ches 82 B3
Spofforth N York 91 E5
Spon Green Flints 81 E1
Spondon Derbys 72 B4
Spooner Row Norfk 64 C5
Sporle Norfk 76 B1
Spott E Loth 133 F3
Spottiswoode Border 122 C4
Spratton Nhants 60 C2
Spreakley Surrey 27 F3
Spreyton Devon 8 D4
Spriddlestone Devon 6 C3
Spridlington Lincs 85 H3
Spring Gardens Dur 106 A3
Spring Vale S York 83 G5
Springburn C Glas 130 B2
Springfield D & G 111 H2
Springfield Essex 51 H1
Springfield Fife 140 C1
Springhill Staffs 58 C6
Springhill Staffs 58 D6
Springholm D & G 110 C2
Springside N Ayrs 119 E3
Springthorpe Lincs 85 F4
Springwell T & W 114 D1
Sproatley E R Yk 93 F3
Sproston Green Ches 82 B1
Sprotbrough S York 84 C5
Sproughton Suffk 53 E5
Sprouston Border 123 E3
Sprowston Norfk 77 E1
Sproxton Leics 73 F2
Sproxton N York 98 B3
Sprytown Devon 5 H4
Spunhill Shrops 69 F3
Spurstow Ches 69 H6
Spyway Dorset 11 F4
Square & Compass Pembks 32 C5
Stableford Shrops 57 H5
Stableford Staffs 70 C4
Stacey Bank Derbys 83 H4
Stackhouse N York 96 A1
Stackpole Pembks 32 D1
Stacksford Norfk 64 C4
Stacksteads Lancs 89 G2
Staddiscombe Devon 6 C3
Staddlethorpe E R Yk 92 B2
Staden Derbys 83 F2
Stadhampton Oxon 40 D4
Stadhlaigearraidh W Isls 168 b3
Staffield Cumb 104 B4
Staffin Highld 151 E5
Stafford Staffs 70 D2
Stagsden Beds 49 H4
Stainborough S York 84 A5
Stainburn Cumb 102 D3
Stainburn N York 90 D4
Stainby Lincs 73 G2
Staincross S York 84 A6
Staindrop Dur 105 H2
Staines Surrey 28 A3
Stainfield Lincs 74 A2
Stainfield Lincs 86 B2
Stainforth N York 96 B2
Stainforth S York 84 D6
Staining Lancs 88 B3
Stainland W York 90 B1
Stainsacre N York 99 E6
Stainsby Derbys 84 B1
Stainton Cumb 103 H6
Stainton Cumb 104 B3
Stainton Cumb 95 F3
Stainton Dur 105 G2
Stainton N York 106 D2
Stainton N York 96 D4
Stainton S York 84 C4
Stainton by Langworth Lincs 86 A2
Stainton le Vale Lincs 86 B4
Stainton with Adgarley Cumb 94 C2
Staintondale N York 99 F5
Stair Cumb 103 F2
Stair E Ayrs 119 F2
Stair Haven D & G 100 C5
Stairfoot S York 84 A5
Staithes N York 107 G3
Stake Pool Lancs 88 C4
Stakeford Nthumb 114 D4
Stakes Hants 15 E4
Stalbridge Dorset 24 C1
Stalbridge Weston Dorset 24 C1
Stalham Norfk 77 G2
Stalham Green Norfk 77 G2
Stalisfield Green Kent 30 C1
Stallen Dorset 24 B1
Stalling Busk N York 96 B3
Stallingborough Lincs 86 B6
Stallington Staffs 70 D4
Stalmine Lancs 88 B4
Stalmine Moss Side Lancs 88 B4
Stalybridge Gt Man 83 E4
Stambourne Essex 51 H5
Stambourne Green Essex 51 H4
Stamford Lincs 61 F6
Stamford Nthumb 125 E3
Stamford Bridge Ches 81 G1
Stamford Bridge E R Yk 92 A5
Stamford Hill Gt Lon 28 D5
Stamfordham Nthumb 114 B3
Stanah Lancs 88 B4
Stanborough Herts 50 C2
Stanbridge Beds 49 H2
Stanbridge Dorset 12 D5
Stanbury W York 90 A3
Stand Gt Man 82 C5
Stand N Lans 130 D2
Standburn Falk 131 E3
Standeford Staffs 58 B6
Standen Kent 18 B5
Standen Street Kent 18 B4
Standerwick Somset 24 D4
Standford Hants 27 F3
Standingstone Cumb 102 D3
Standish Gloucs 38 C5
Standish Gt Man 81 H6
Standish Lower Ground Gt Man 81 H5
Standlake Oxon 40 B5
Standon Hants 26 C2
Standon Herts 51 E3
Standon Staffs 70 C3
Standon Green End Herts 50 D3
Standwell Green Suffk 64 D2
Stane N Lans 120 C5
Stanfield Norfk 76 B2
Stanford Beds 50 C5
Stanford Kent 19 E5
Stanford Shrops 69 F1
Stanford Bishop Herefs 46 B4
Stanford Bridge Shrops 70 B2

Stanford Bridge

Stretton

312

Stanford Bridge *Worcs* 57 G2
Stanford Dingley *Berks* 40 D1
Stanford in the Vale *Oxon* 40 B4
Stanford le Hope *Essex* 29 H4
Stanford on Avon *Nhants* 60 B3
Stanford on Soar *Notts* 72 C2
Stanford on Teme *Worcs* 57 G2
Stanford Rivers *Essex* 29 F6
Stanfree *Derbys* 84 B2
Stanghow *N York* 107 F2
Stanground *Cambs* 62 A5
Stanhill *Lancs* 89 F2
Stanhoe *Norfk* 76 A4
Stanhope *Border* 121 F2
Stanhope *Dur* 105 G4
Stanhope Bretby *Derbys* 71 H2
Stanion *Nhants* 61 E4
Stanklin *Worcs* 58 B3
Stanley *Derbys* 72 B4
Stanley *Dur* 106 A6
Stanley *Notts* 84 B1
Stanley *P & K* 140 A3
Stanley *Shrops* 57 H4
Stanley *Staffs* 70 D5
Stanley *W York* 91 E2
Stanley Common *Derbys* 72 B4
Stanley Crook *Dur* 106 A5
Stanley Ferry *W York* 91 E2
Stanley Gate *Lancs* 81 G5
Stanley Moor *Staffs* 70 D5
Stanley Pontlarge *Gloucs* 47 E2
Stanmer *E Susx* 16 D2
Stanmore *Berks* 40 C2
Stanmore *Gt Lon* 28 C5
Stanmore *Hants* 26 C2
Stannersburn *Nthumb* 112 D3
Stanningfield *Suffk* 64 A1
Stanningley *W York* 90 C3
Stannington *Nthumb* 114 D3
Stannington *S York* 83 H3
Stannington Station *Nthumb* 114 D4
Stansbatch *Herefs* 45 F5
Stansfield *Suffk* 52 A6
Stanshope *Staffs* 71 F5
Stanstead *Suffk* 52 B6
Stanstead Abbotts *Herts* 51 E2
Stanstead Street *Suffk* 52 B6
Stansted *Kent* 29 G2
Stansted Airport *Essex* 51 F3
Stansted Mountfitchet *Essex* 51 F3
Stanton *Derbys* 71 H2
Stanton *Devon* 6 D3
Stanton *Gloucs* 47 F3
Stanton *Mons* 45 F1
Stanton *Nthumb* 114 C4
Stanton *Staffs* 71 F5
Stanton *Suffk* 64 B3
Stanton Butts *Cambs* 62 B3
Stanton by Bridge *Derbys* 72 A3
Stanton by Dale *Derbys* 72 B4
Stanton Drew *Somset* 24 B6
Stanton Fitzwarren *Wilts* 39 F3
Stanton Harcourt *Oxon* 40 B5
Stanton Hill *Notts* 72 B6
Stanton in Peak *Derbys* 83 G1
Stanton Lacy *Shrops* 57 E3
Stanton Lees *Derbys* 83 G1
Stanton Long *Shrops* 57 F4
Stanton on the Wolds *Notts* 72 D3
Stanton Prior *Somset* 24 B5
Stanton St Bernard *Wilts* 25 F5
Stanton St John *Oxon* 40 D5
Stanton St Quintin *Wilts* 38 D2
Stanton Street *Suffk* 64 B2
Stanton under Bardon *Leics* 72 B1
Stanton upon Hine Heath *Shrops* 69 H2
Stanton Wick *Somset* 24 B5
Stantway *Gloucs* 38 B6
Stanwardine in the Field *Shrops* 69 F2
Stanwardine in the Wood *Shrops* 69 F3
Stanway *Essex* 52 C3
Stanway *Gloucs* 47 F2
Stanway Green *Essex* 52 C3
Stanway Green *Suffk* 65 E2
Stanwell *Surrey* 28 B3
Stanwell Moor *Surrey* 28 A3
Stanwick *Nhants* 61 F2
Stanwix *Cumb* 103 H6
Staoinebrig *W Isls* 168 b3
Stape *N York* 98 D4
Stapehill *Dorset* 12 D5
Stapeley *Ches* 70 B5
Stapenhill *Staffs* 71 G2
Staple *Kent* 31 F2
Staple *Somset* 22 D3
Staple Cross *Devon* 22 C1
Staple Cross *E Susx* 18 A4
Staple Fitzpaine *Somset* 23 E1
Staple Hill *Worcs* 58 C3
Staplefield *W Susx* 16 D4
Stapleford *Cambs* 51 F6
Stapleford *Herts* 50 D2
Stapleford *Leics* 73 F2
Stapleford *Lincs* 73 F6
Stapleford *Notts* 72 C4
Stapleford *Wilts* 25 F3
Stapleford Abbotts *Essex* 29 F5
Stapleford Tawney *Essex* 29 F6
Staplegrove *Somset* 23 E2
Staplehay *Somset* 23 E1
Staplehurst *Kent* 18 A6
Staplers *IOW* 14 C2
Staplestreet *Kent* 30 D2
Staplet *Cumb* 112 B2
Stapleton *Herefs* 56 D2
Stapleton *Leics* 59 G5
Stapleton *N York* 106 B2
Stapleton *Shrops* 57 E6
Stapleton *Somset* 23 G1
Stapley *Somset* 10 B6
Staploe *Beds* 61 G1
Staplow *Herefs* 46 C3
Star *Fife* 132 B5
Star *Pembks* 42 C3
Star *Somset* 23 G5
Starbeck *N York* 90 D5
Starbotton *N York* 96 C2
Starcross *Devon* 9 G3
Stareton *Warwks* 59 F2
Starkholmes *Derbys* 71 H6
Starling *Gt Man* 82 C6
Starlings Green *Essex* 51 E4
Starr's Green *E Susx* 18 A3
Starston *Norfk* 65 E4
Start *Devon* 7 E2
Startforth *Dur* 105 G2
Startley *Wilts* 38 D2
Statenborough *Kent* 31 G2
Statham *Ches* 82 B3
Stathe *Somset* 23 F2
Stathern *Leics* 73 E3
Station Town *Dur* 106 C4
Staughton Green *Cambs* 61 G2
Staughton Highway *Cambs* 61 G2
Staunton *Gloucs* 37 F5
Staunton *Gloucs* 46 C2
Staunton Green *Herefs* 45 F5
Staunton in the Vale *Notts* 73 F4
Staunton on Arrow *Herefs* 45 F5
Staunton on Wye *Herefs* 45 F4
Staveley *Cumb* 94 D3
Staveley *Cumb* 95 E5
Staveley *Derbys* 84 B2
Staveley *N York* 91 E6
Staverton *Devon* 7 E4
Staverton *Gloucs* 46 D1
Staverton *Nhants* 48 D5
Staverton *Wilts* 24 D5
Staverton Bridge *Gloucs* 46 D1
Stawell *Somset* 23 F3
Stawley *Somset* 22 C1
Staxigoe *Highld* 167 G4
Staxton *N York* 99 F3
Staylittle *Cerdgn* 54 D4
Staylittle *Powys* 55 F5
Staynall *Lancs* 88 B4
Staythorpe *Notts* 73 E5
Stead *W York* 90 C4
Stean *N York* 96 D2
Steane *Nhants* 48 D3
Stearsby *N York* 98 B2
Steart *Somset* 23 E4
Stebbing *Essex* 51 G3
Stebbing Green *Essex* 51 H3
Stebbing Park *Essex* 51 G3
Stechford *W Mids* 58 D4
Stede Quarter *Kent* 18 B5
Stedham *W Susx* 27 G1
Steel *Nthumb* 105 F6
Steel Cross *E Susx* 17 F4
Steel Green *Cumb* 94 B3
Steel Heath *Shrops* 69 H4
Steele Road *Border* 112 B4
Steelend *Fife* 131 G4
Steen's Bridge *Herefs* 46 A5
Steep *Hants* 27 F2
Steep Lane *W York* 90 B2
Steephill *IOW* 14 D1
Steeple *Dorset* 12 C3
Steeple *Essex* 52 C1
Steeple Ashton *Wilts* 25 E5
Steeple Aston *Oxon* 48 C2
Steeple Barton *Oxon* 48 C2
Steeple Bumpstead *Essex* 51 H5
Steeple Claydon *Bucks* 49 E2
Steeple Gidding *Cambs* 61 G3
Steeple Langford *Wilts* 25 F3
Steeple Morden *Cambs* 50 D5
Steeton *W York* 90 B4
Stein *Highld* 150 C4
Stella *T & W* 114 C2
Stelling Minnis *Kent* 19 E6
Stembridge *Somset* 23 G1
Stenalees *Cnwll* 3 G5
Stenhouse *D & G* 110 C4
Stenhousemuir *Falk* 131 E3
Stenigot *Lincs* 86 C3
Stenscholl *Highld* 151 E5
Stenton *E Loth* 133 E2
Steornabhagh *W Isls* 168 f8
Stepaside *Pembks* 33 F2
Stepney *Gt Lon* 28 D4
Stepping Hill *Gt Man* 82 D3
Steppingley *Beds* 50 A4
Stepps *N Lans* 130 C2
Sternfield *Suffk* 65 F1
Sterridge *Devon* 21 F5
Stert *Wilts* 25 F5
Stetchworth *Cambs* 63 F1
Steven's Crouch *E Susx* 17 H3
Stevenage *Herts* 50 C3
Stevenston *N Ayrs* 118 D4
Steventon *Hants* 26 D4
Steventon *Oxon* 40 C3
Steventon End *Essex* 51 G5
Stevington *Beds* 49 H4
Stewartby *Beds* 50 A4
Stewartfield *S Lans* 119 H5
Stewarton *E Ayrs* 119 F4
Stewkley *Bucks* 49 G2
Stewley *Somset* 23 F1
Stewton *Lincs* 86 D3
Steyne Cross *IOW* 15 E2
Steyning *W Susx* 16 C2
Steynton *Pembks* 32 C2
Stibb *Cnwll* 20 B2
Stibb Cross *Devon* 20 D2
Stibb Green *Wilts* 25 H5
Stibbard *Norfk* 76 C3
Stibbington *Cambs* 61 G5
Stichill *Border* 122 D3
Sticker *Cnwll* 3 G5
Stickford *Lincs* 74 D6
Sticklepath *Devon* 8 C4
Sticklepath *Somset* 22 C3
Stickling Green *Essex* 51 F4
Stickney *Lincs* 74 D6
Stiff Street *Kent* 30 B2
Stiffkey *Norfk* 76 C4
Stifford's Bridge *Herefs* 46 C4
Stile Bridge *Kent* 18 A6
Stileway *Somset* 23 G3
Stilligarry *W Isls* 168 b3
Stillingfleet *N York* 91 G4
Stillington *Dur* 106 C3
Stillington *N York* 98 B2
Stilton *Cambs* 61 G4
Stinchcombe *Gloucs* 38 B4
Stinsford *Dorset* 11 G4
Stiperstones *Shrops* 56 D5
Stirchley *Shrops* 57 G6
Stirchley *W Mids* 58 C3
Stirling *Abers* 159 G3
Stirling *Stirlg* 130 D4
Stirtloe *Cambs* 62 A2
Stirton *N York* 89 H5
Stisted *Essex* 52 B3
Stitchcombe *Wilts* 39 G1
Stithians *Cnwll* 3 E3
Stivichall *W Mids* 59 F3
Stixwould *Lincs* 86 B1
Stoak *Ches* 81 F2
Stobo *Border* 121 F3
Stoborough *Dorset* 12 C3
Stoborough Green *Dorset* 12 C3
Stobs Castle *Border* 112 B6
Stobswood *Nthumb* 114 D5
Stock *Essex* 29 H6
Stock *Somset* 23 G5
Stock Green *Worcs* 47 E5
Stock Wood *Worcs* 47 E5
Stockbridge *Hants* 26 B3
Stockbriggs *S Lans* 120 B3
Stockbury *Kent* 30 B2
Stockcross *Berks* 40 C1
Stockdale *Cnwll* 3 E3
Stockdalewath *Cumb* 103 H5
Stocker's Hill *Kent* 30 C1
Stockerston *Leics* 60 D5
Stocking *Herefs* 46 B2
Stocking Green *Bucks* 49 F4
Stocking Pelham *Herts* 51 E4
Stockingford *Warwks* 59 F4
Stockland *Devon* 10 C5
Stockland Bristol *Somset* 23 E4
Stockland Green *Kent* 17 F6
Stockleigh English *Devon* 9 E5
Stockleigh Pomeroy *Devon* 9 F5
Stockley *Wilts* 25 E6
Stockley Hill *Herefs* 45 F3
Stocklinch *Somset* 23 G1
Stockmoor *Herefs* 45 G5
Stockport *Gt Man* 82 D4
Stocksbridge *S York* 83 G4
Stocksfield *Nthumb* 114 B2
Stockstreet *Essex* 52 B3
Stockton *Herefs* 45 H5
Stockton *Norfk* 65 F5
Stockton *Shrops* 56 C5
Stockton *Shrops* 70 C2
Stockton *Shrops* 57 G5
Stockton *Warwks* 59 G2
Stockton *Wilts* 25 E3
Stockton Brook *Staffs* 70 D5
Stockton Heath *Ches* 82 A3
Stockton on Teme *Worcs* 57 G2
Stockton on the Forest *N York* 91 H5
Stockton-on-Tees *Dur* 106 D3
Stockwell *Gloucs* 38 D6
Stockwell End *W Mids* 58 B5
Stockwell Heath *Staffs* 71 E2
Stockwood *Bristl* 37 G1
Stockwood *Dorset* 11 F5
Stodday *Lancs* 88 C5
Stodmarsh *Kent* 31 F2
Stody *Norfk* 76 D3
Stoer *Highld* 164 B1
Stoford *Somset* 11 F6
Stoford *Wilts* 25 F3
Stogumber *Somset* 22 D3
Stogursey *Somset* 23 E3
Stoke *Devon* 20 C3
Stoke *Hants* 26 B4
Stoke *Hants* 15 E4
Stoke *Kent* 30 B3
Stoke *W Mids* 59 G3
Stoke Abbott *Dorset* 11 E5
Stoke Albany *Nhants* 60 D4
Stoke Ash *Suffk* 64 D2
Stoke Bardolph *Notts* 72 D4
Stoke Bliss *Worcs* 57 G2
Stoke Bruerne *Nhants* 49 F4
Stoke by Clare *Suffk* 52 A5
Stoke Canon *Devon* 9 F4
Stoke Charity *Hants* 26 C3
Stoke Climsland *Cnwll* 5 G3
Stoke Cross *Herefs* 46 B4
Stoke D'Abernon *Surrey* 28 B2
Stoke Doyle *Nhants* 61 F4
Stoke Dry *Rutlnd* 61 E5
Stoke Edith *Herefs* 46 B3
Stoke End *Warwks* 59 E5
Stoke Farthing *Wilts* 25 F2
Stoke Ferry *Norfk* 63 F5
Stoke Fleming *Devon* 7 F2
Stoke Gabriel *Devon* 7 F3
Stoke Gifford *Gloucs* 37 G2
Stoke Golding *Leics* 59 G5
Stoke Goldington *Bucks* 49 F4
Stoke Green *Bucks* 41 H2
Stoke Hammond *Bucks* 49 G2
Stoke Heath *Shrops* 70 B3
Stoke Heath *W Mids* 59 F3
Stoke Heath *Worcs* 58 B2
Stoke Holy Cross *Norfk* 65 E6
Stoke Lacy *Herefs* 46 B4
Stoke Lyne *Oxon* 48 D2
Stoke Mandeville *Bucks* 41 F5
Stoke Newington *Gt Lon* 28 D5
Stoke Orchard *Gloucs* 47 E2
Stoke Poges *Bucks* 41 H2
Stoke Pound *Worcs* 58 C2
Stoke Prior *Herefs* 45 H5
Stoke Prior *Worcs* 58 B2
Stoke Rivers *Devon* 21 F4
Stoke Row *Oxon* 41 E3
Stoke St Gregory *Somset* 23 F2
Stoke St Mary *Somset* 23 E1
Stoke St Michael *Somset* 24 B4
Stoke St Milborough *Shrops* 57 F4
Stoke sub Hamdon *Somset* 23 G1
Stoke Talmage *Oxon* 41 E4
Stoke Trister *Somset* 24 C2
Stoke upon Tern *Shrops* 70 A3
Stoke Wake *Dorset* 12 B5
Stoke Wharf *Worcs* 58 B2
Stoke-by-Nayland *Suffk* 52 C4
Stoke-on-Trent *Staffs* 70 D5
Stoke-upon-Trent *Staffs* 70 D5
Stokeford *Dorset* 12 C3
Stokeham *Notts* 85 E2
Stokeinteignhead *Devon* 7 F5
Stokenchurch *Bucks* 41 F4
Stokenham *Devon* 7 E2
Stokesay *Shrops* 57 E3
Stokesay Castle *Shrops* 57 E3
Stokesby *Norfk* 77 G1
Stokesley *N York* 107 E2
Stolford *Somset* 23 E4
Ston Easton *Somset* 24 B5
Stondon Massey *Essex* 29 G6
Stone *Bucks* 41 F5
Stone *Gloucs* 38 B4
Stone *Kent* 29 G3
Stone *Kent* 18 C4
Stone *S York* 84 C4
Stone *Somset* 24 A3
Stone *Staffs* 70 D3
Stone *Worcs* 58 B3
Stone Allerton *Somset* 23 G4
Stone Bridge Corner *Cambs* 62 B5
Stone Chair *W York* 90 B2
Stone Cross *E Susx* 17 F4
Stone Cross *E Susx* 17 G2
Stone Cross *E Susx* 17 G4
Stone Cross *Kent* 17 F5
Stone Cross *Kent* 18 D5
Stone Cross *Kent* 31 G2
Stone Hill *S York* 84 D6
Stone House *Cumb* 96 A3
Stone Street *Kent* 29 G1
Stone Street *Suffk* 52 C5
Stone Street *Suffk* 52 D5
Stone Street *Suffk* 65 F4
Stone-edge-Batch *Somset* 37 F1
Stonea *Cambs* 62 D5
Stonebridge *Norfk* 64 B4
Stonebridge *Somset* 23 G5
Stonebridge *W Mids* 59 E4
Stonebroom *Derbys* 72 B6
Stonecross Green *Suffk* 63 G1
Stonecrouch *Kent* 17 H5
Stoneferry *E R Yk* 93 E3
Stonefield Castle Hotel *Ag & B* 127 G2
Stonegate *E Susx* 17 G4
Stonegate *N York* 107 G2
Stonegrave *N York* 98 B3
Stonehall *Worcs* 46 D4
Stonehaugh *Nthumb* 113 E2
Stonehaven *Abers* 149 F3
Stonehenge *Wilts* 25 G3
Stonehill Green *Gt Lon* 29 F3
Stonehouse *Ches* 81 G2
Stonehouse *D & G* 110 C2
Stonehouse *Devon* 6 B3
Stonehouse *Gloucs* 38 C5
Stonehouse *Nthumb* 104 D6
Stonehouse *S Lans* 120 B4
Stoneleigh *Warwks* 59 F3
Stoneley Green *Ches* 70 A5
Stonely *Cambs* 61 G2
Stoner Hill *Hants* 27 E2
Stones Green *Essex* 53 E3
Stonesby *Leics* 73 F2
Stonesfield *Oxon* 40 B6
Stonestreet Green *Kent* 18 D5
Stonethwaite *Cumb* 103 G1
Stonewells *Moray* 157 E6
Stonewood *Kent* 29 G3
Stoney Cross *Hants* 13 F6
Stoney Middleton *Derbys* 83 G2
Stoney Stanton *Leics* 59 H5
Stoney Stoke *Somset* 24 C2
Stoney Stratton *Somset* 24 B3
Stoney Stretton *Shrops* 69 F1
Stoneybridge *W Isls* 168 b3
Stoneybridge *Worcs* 58 B3
Stoneyburn *W Loth* 120 D6
Stoneygate *Leics* 60 B6
Stoneyhills *Essex* 30 C6
Stoneykirk *D & G* 100 B5
Stoneywood *Aber C* 149 F5
Stoneywood *Falk* 130 D3
Stonham Aspal *Suffk* 64 D1
Stonnall *Staffs* 58 D6
Stonor *Oxon* 41 E3
Stonton Wyville *Leics* 60 C5
Stony Cross *Herefs* 57 F2
Stony Cross *Herefs* 46 C4
Stony Houghton *Derbys* 84 C1
Stony Stratford *Bucks* 49 F3
Stonyford *Hants* 13 G6
Stonywell *Staffs* 71 F1
Stoodleigh *Devon* 21 G4
Stoodleigh *Devon* 22 B1
Stopham *W Susx* 16 A3
Stopsley *Beds* 50 B3
Stoptide *Cnwll* 4 C3
Storeton *Mersyd* 81 E3
Storeyard Green *Herefs* 46 C4
Stormy Corner *Lancs* 81 G5
Stornoway *W Isls* 168 f8
Stornoway Airport *W Isls* 168 f8
Storridge *Herefs* 46 C4
Storrington *W Susx* 16 B3
Storth *Cumb* 95 E3
Storwood *E R Yk* 92 A4
Stotfield *Moray* 156 D6
Stotfold *Beds* 50 C4
Stottesdon *Shrops* 57 G4
Stoughton *Leics* 60 B6
Stoughton *Surrey* 27 H4
Stoughton *W Susx* 15 F5
Stoul *Highld* 143 G3
Stoulton *Worcs* 47 E4
Stour Provost *Dorset* 24 C1
Stour Row *Dorset* 24 D1
Stourbridge *W Mids* 58 B4
Stourpaine *Dorset* 12 C6
Stourport-on-Severn *Worcs* 58 A2
Stourton *Staffs* 58 B4
Stourton *W York* 90 D3
Stourton *Warwks* 48 A3
Stourton *Wilts* 24 C3
Stourton Caundle *Dorset* 11 G6
Stout *Somset* 23 G2
Stove *Shet* 169 h2
Stoven *Suffk* 65 G3
Stow *Border* 122 B4
Stow *Lincs* 85 F3
Stow Bardolph *Norfk* 63 E6
Stow Bedon *Norfk* 64 B5
Stow Longa *Cambs* 61 G2
Stow Maries *Essex* 30 B6
Stow-cum-Quy *Cambs* 62 D1
Stow-on-the-Wold *Gloucs* 47 G2
Stowbridge *Norfk* 63 E6
Stowe *Gloucs* 37 G5
Stowe *Shrops* 56 C3
Stowe by Chartley *Staffs* 71 E3
Stowehill *Nhants* 49 E5
Stowell *Somset* 24 B1
Stowey *Somset* 24 B5
Stowford *Devon* 8 A4
Stowford *Devon* 21 G5
Stowford *Devon* 8 A3
Stowford *Devon* 10 B4
Stowlangtoft *Suffk* 64 B2
Stowmarket *Suffk* 64 C1
Stowting *Kent* 19 E6
Stowting Common *Kent* 19 E6
Stowupland *Suffk* 64 C1
Straanruie *Moray* 147 E6
Strachan *Abers* 148 D4
Strachur *Ag & B* 128 B5
Stracthro Hospital *Angus* 148 D1
Stradbroke *Suffk* 65 E3
Stradbrook *Wilts* 25 E4
Stradishall *Suffk* 52 A6
Stradsett *Norfk* 63 F6
Stragglethorpe *Lincs* 73 G5
Stragglethorpe *Notts* 72 D4
Straight Soley *Wilts* 40 A1
Straiton *Mdloth* 132 B2
Straiton *S Ayrs* 109 F5
Straloch *Abers* 158 D1
Straloch *P & K* 139 H6
Stramshall *Staffs* 71 F4
Strang *IOM* 174 I3
Strangford *Herefs* 46 A2
Stranraer *D & G* 100 B6
Strata Florida *Cerdgn* 55 E2
Stratfield Mortimer *Berks* 27 E6
Stratfield Saye *Hants* 27 E5
Stratfield Turgis *Hants* 27 E5
Stratford *Beds* 50 C5
Stratford *Gt Lon* 29 E4
Stratford St Andrew *Suffk* 65 F1
Stratford St Mary *Suffk* 52 D4
Stratford sub Castle *Wilts* 25 G2
Stratford Tony *Wilts* 25 F2
Stratford-upon-Avon *Warwks* 47 G5
Strath *Highld* 160 B1
Strathan *Highld* 161 E6
Strathan *Highld* 165 G5
Strathaven *S Lans* 120 B4
Strathblane *Stirlg* 129 G3
Strathcanaird *Highld* 161 F4
Strathcarron Station *Highld* 152 D3
Strathcoil *Ag & B* 136 B3
Strathdon *Abers* 148 A6
Strathkinness *Fife* 141 E1
Strathloanhead *W Loth* 131 E2
Strathmashie House *Highld* 145 H4
Strathmiglo *Fife* 132 A6
Strathpeffer *Highld* 154 C5
Strathtay *P & K* 139 F5
Strathwhillan *N Ayrs* 118 B3
Strathy *Highld* 166 B5
Strathy Inn *Highld* 166 B5
Strathyre *Stirlg* 138 C1
Stratton *Cnwll* 20 C1
Stratton *Dorset* 11 G4
Stratton *Gloucs* 39 E5
Stratton Audley *Oxon* 48 D2
Stratton St Margaret *Wilts* 39 F3
Stratton St Michael *Norfk* 64 D5
Stratton Strawless *Norfk* 77 E2
Stratton-on-the-Fosse *Somset* 24 B4
Strathvithie *Fife* 141 E1
Stream *Somset* 22 D3
Streat *E Susx* 16 D3
Streatham *Gt Lon* 28 D3
Streatley *Beds* 50 B3
Streatley *Berks* 40 D2
Street *Devon* 10 B3
Street *Lancs* 88 D5
Street *N York* 98 C5
Street *Somset* 23 H3
Street Ashton *Warwks* 59 G4
Street Dinas *Shrops* 69 F4
Street End *E Susx* 17 G4
Street End *Kent* 31 E1
Street End *W Susx* 15 G3
Street Gate *T & W* 114 D1
Street Houses *N York* 107 G3
Street Houses *N York* 91 F4
Street Lane *Derbys* 72 B5
Street on the Fosse *Somset* 24 B3
Streethay *Staffs* 71 F1
Streetlam *N York* 97 F5
Streetly *W Mids* 58 D5
Streetly End *Cambs* 51 G5
Strefford *Shrops* 57 E4
Strelitz *P & K* 140 B3
Strelley *Notts* 72 C4
Strensall *N York* 91 G6
Strensham *Worcs* 47 E3
Stretcholt *Somset* 23 F4
Strete *Devon* 7 F2
Stretford *Gt Man* 82 C4
Stretford *Herefs* 45 G5
Stretford *Herefs* 45 H5
Strethall *Essex* 51 F5
Stretham *Cambs* 62 D3
Strettington *W Susx* 15 G4
Stretton *Ches* 69 G5
Stretton *Ches* 82 A3
Stretton *Derbys* 72 B6
Stretton *Rutlnd* 73 G2

Stretton
Tetsworth
313

Stretton Staffs 70 D1
Stretton Staffs 71 G3
Stretton en le Field Leics 71 H1
Stretton Grandison Herefs 46 B4
Stretton Heath Shrops 69 F1
Stretton on Fosse Warwks 47 H3
Stretton Sugwas Herefs 45 G3
Stretton under Fosse Warwks 59 G3
Stretton Westwood Shrops 57 F5
Stretton-on-Dunsmore Warwks 59 G3
Strichen Abers 159 E5
Strines Gt Man 83 E3
Stringston Somset 23 E3
Strixton Nhants 49 G5
Stroat Gloucs 37 G4
Stromeferry Highld 152 C2
Stromness Ork 169 a2
Stronachlachar Stirlg 129 E6
Stronafian Ag & B 128 B3
Stronchrubie Highld 161 G6
Strone Ag & B 128 C3
Strone Highld 144 D2
Stronenaba Highld 144 D3
Stronmilchan Ag & B 137 F3
Stronsay Airport Ork 169 c3
Strontian Highld 136 C6
Strood Kent 29 H3
Strood Kent 18 B5
Strood Green Surrey 16 C6
Strood Green W Susx 16 A4
Stroud Gloucs 38 C5
Stroud Hants 27 E2
Stroud Green Essex 30 B5
Stroud Green Gloucs 38 C5
Stroude Surrey 28 A3
Stroxton Lincs 73 G3
Struan Highld 150 D2
Struan P & K 146 C1
Strubby Lincs 87 E3
Strumpshaw Norfk 65 F6
Strutherhill S Lans 120 B4
Struthers Fife 132 C6
Struy Highld 154 B3
Stryd-y-Facsen IOA 78 C3
Stryt-issa Wrexhm 69 E5
Stuartfield Abers 159 F4
Stubbers Green W Mids 58 C5
Stubbington Hants 14 D4
Stubbins N York 89 F1
Stubbs Green Norfk 65 E5
Stubhampton Dorset 12 C6
Stubley Derbys 84 A3
Stubshaw Cross Gt Man 81 H5
Stubton Lincs 73 F5
Stuchbury Nhants 48 D4
Stuckeridge Devon 22 B1
Stuckton Hants 13 E6
Stud Green Berks 41 G2
Studfold N York 96 A2
Studham Beds 50 A2
Studholme Cumb 103 F6
Studland Dorset 12 D3
Studley Warwks 58 D2
Studley Wilts 38 D1
Studley Common Warwks 58 D2
Studley Roger N York 97 F2
Studley Royal N York 97 F2
Stump Cross Cambs 51 F5
Stuntney Cambs 63 E3
Stunts Green E Susx 17 G3
Sturbridge Staffs 70 C3
Sturgate Lincs 85 F4
Sturmer Essex 51 H5
Sturminster Common Dorset 12 B6
Sturminster Marshall Dorset 12 C5
Sturminster Newton Dorset 12 B6
Sturry Kent 31 E2
Sturton Lincs 85 G5
Sturton by Stow Lincs 85 F3
Sturton le Steeple Notts 85 E3
Stuston Suffk 64 D3
Stutton N York 91 F4
Stutton Suffk 53 E4
Styal Ches 82 C3
Stydd Lancs 89 E3
Stynie Moray 157 E5
Styrrup Notts 84 D4
Succoth Ag & B 128 D6
Suckley Worcs 46 C4
Suckley Green Worcs 46 C5
Sudborough Nhants 61 F4
Sudbourne Suffk 53 H6
Sudbrook Lincs 73 G4
Sudbrook Mons 37 F3
Sudbrooke Lincs 85 H2
Sudbury Derbys 71 F3
Sudbury Gt Lon 28 C5
Sudbury Suffk 52 B5
Sudden Gt Man 82 D6
Suddington Worcs 58 A2
Sudgrove Gloucs 38 D5
Suffield N York 99 E4
Suffield Norfk 77 E3
Sugdon Shrops 70 A1
Sugnall Staffs 70 C3
Sugwas Pool Herefs 45 G3
Suisnish Highld 143 E6
Sulby IOM 174 m4
Sulgrave Nhants 48 D4
Sulgrave Manor Nhants 48 D4
Sulham Berks 41 E2
Sulhamstead Berks 40 D1
Sulhamstead Abbots Berks 27 E6
Sulhamstead Bannister Berks 41 E1
Sullington W Susx 16 B3
Sullom Shet 169 h4
Sullom Voe Shet 169 h4
Sully V Glam 36 C1
Sumburgh Airport Shet 169 h1
Summer Heath Bucks 41 F3
Summer Hill Wrexhm 69 E5
Summerbridge N York 90 C6
Summercourt Cnwll 3 F5
Summerfield Norfk 75 H4
Summerfield Worcs 58 A2
Summerhouse Dur 106 A3
Summerlands Cumb 95 F3
Summerley Derbys 84 A2
Summersdale W Susx 15 G4
Summerseat Gt Man 89 F1
Summertown Oxon 40 C5
Summit Gt Man 82 D6
Summit N York 89 H1
Sunbiggin N York 95 G6
Sunbury Surrey 28 B3
Sundaywell D & G 110 C3
Sunderland Ag & B 126 A1
Sunderland Cumb 103 F4
Sunderland Lancs 88 C5
Sunderland T & W 115 F1
Sunderland Bridge Dur 106 B5
Sundhope Border 121 H2
Sundon Park Beds 50 B3
Sundridge Kent 29 F1
Sunk Island E R Yk 93 F1
Sunningdale Berks 27 H6
Sunninghill Surrey 27 G6
Sunningwell Oxon 40 C4
Sunniside Dur 105 H4
Sunniside T & W 114 D1
Sunny Bank Lancs 89 F2
Sunny Brow Dur 106 A4
Sunnyhill Derbys 72 A3
Sunnyhurst Lancs 89 E2
Sunnylaw Stirlg 130 D5
Sunnymead Oxon 40 C5
Sunton Wilts 25 H5
Surbiton Gt Lon 28 C3
Surfleet Lincs 74 C3
Surfleet Seas End Lincs 74 C3
Surlingham Norfk 65 F6
Surrex Essex 52 B3
Sustead Norfk 77 E4
Susworth Lincs 85 F5
Sutcombe Devon 20 D2
Sutcombemill Devon 20 D2
Suton Norfk 64 C5
Sutterby Lincs 86 D2
Sutterton Lincs 74 C4
Sutton Beds 50 C5
Sutton Cambs 61 G5
Sutton Cambs 62 D3
Sutton Devon 8 D5
Sutton Devon 6 D2
Sutton E Susx 17 F1
Sutton Gt Lon 28 C2
Sutton Kent 31 G1
Sutton Mersyd 81 G4
Sutton N York 91 F2
Sutton Norfk 77 G2
Sutton Notts 73 E4
Sutton Oxon 40 B5
Sutton Pembks 32 C3
Sutton S York 84 C6
Sutton Shrops 69 F3
Sutton Shrops 69 G1
Sutton Shrops 70 B3
Sutton Shrops 57 G4
Sutton Staffs 70 C2
Sutton Suffk 53 G5
Sutton W Susx 15 H5
Sutton at Hone Kent 29 F3
Sutton Bassett Nhants 60 D4
Sutton Benger Wilts 38 D2
Sutton Bingham Somset 11 F6
Sutton Bonington Notts 72 C2
Sutton Bridge Lincs 75 E2
Sutton Cheney Leics 59 G5
Sutton Coldfield W Mids 58 D5
Sutton Courtenay Oxon 40 C4
Sutton Crosses Lincs 75 E2
Sutton cum Lound Notts 84 D3
Sutton Fields Notts 72 C3
Sutton Grange N York 97 F2
Sutton Green Oxon 40 B5
Sutton Green Surrey 28 A1
Sutton Green Wrexhm 69 F5
Sutton Howgrave N York 97 F3
Sutton in Ashfield Notts 72 C6
Sutton in the Elms Leics 60 A5
Sutton Lane Ends Ches 82 D2
Sutton Maddock Shrops 57 G5
Sutton Mallet Somset 23 F3
Sutton Mandeville Wilts 25 E2
Sutton Manor Mersyd 81 G4
Sutton Marsh Herefs 46 A4
Sutton Montis Somset 24 B2
Sutton on Sea Lincs 87 E3
Sutton on the Hill Derbys 71 G3
Sutton on Trent Notts 85 F1
Sutton Poyntz Dorset 11 G3
Sutton Scotney Hants 26 C3
Sutton St Edmund Lincs 74 D1
Sutton St James Lincs 74 D2
Sutton St Nicholas Herefs 45 H4
Sutton Street Kent 30 B2
Sutton upon Derwent E R Yk 92 A4
Sutton Valence Kent 30 B1
Sutton Veny Wilts 24 D3
Sutton Waldron Dorset 12 C6
Sutton Weaver Ches 81 H3
Sutton Wick Oxon 40 C4
Sutton Wick Somset 24 A5
Sutton-in-Craven N York 90 A4
Sutton-on-Hull E R Yk 93 E3
Sutton-on-the-Forest N York 98 B1
Sutton-under-Brailes Warwks 48 A3
Sutton-under-Whitestonecliffe N York 97 H3
Swaby Lincs 86 D2
Swadlincote Derbys 71 H2
Swaffham Norfk 76 A1
Swaffham Bulbeck Cambs 63 E2
Swaffham Prior Cambs 63 E2
Swafield Norfk 77 F3
Swainby N York 97 H5
Swainshill Herefs 45 G3
Swainsthorpe Norfk 65 E5
Swainswick Somset 38 B1
Swalcliffe Oxon 48 B3
Swalecliffe Kent 31 E3
Swallow Lincs 86 B5
Swallow Beck Lincs 85 G1
Swallow Nest S York 84 B3
Swallowcliffe Wilts 25 E2
Swallowfield Berks 27 E6
Swallows Cross Essex 29 G6
Swampton Hants 26 B4
Swan Green Ches 82 B2
Swan Street Essex 52 C3
Swan Village W Mids 58 C5
Swanage Dorset 12 D2
Swanbourne Bucks 49 F2
Swanbridge V Glam 22 D6
Swancote Shrops 57 H5
Swanland E R Yk 92 D2
Swanley Kent 29 F3
Swanley Village Kent 29 F3
Swanmore Hants 14 D5
Swannington Leics 72 B2
Swannington Norfk 76 D2
Swanpool Garden Suburb Lincs 85 G2
Swanscombe Kent 29 G3
Swansea Swans 34 D3
Swansea Airport Swans 34 C3
Swanton Abbot Norfk 77 F3
Swanton Morley Norfk 76 C2
Swanton Novers Norfk 76 C3
Swanton Street Kent 30 B2
Swanwick Derbys 72 B5
Swanwick Hants 14 C4
Swarby Lincs 73 H4
Swardeston Norfk 64 D6
Swarkestone Derbys 72 A3
Swarland Nthumb 114 C6
Swarland Estate Nthumb 125 E1
Swarraton Hants 26 D3
Swartha W York 90 B4
Swarthmoor Cumb 94 C3
Swaton Lincs 74 B4
Swavesey Cambs 62 C2
Sway Hants 13 G4
Swayfield Lincs 73 G2
Swaythling Hants 14 C5
Sweet Green Worcs 46 B5
Sweetham Devon 9 F4
Sweethaws E Susx 17 F4
Sweetlands Corner Kent 18 B6
Sweets Cnwll 5 E5
Sweetshouse Cnwll 4 D2
Swefling Suffk 65 F2
Swepstone Leics 72 A1
Swerford Oxon 48 B2
Swettenham Ches 82 C1
Swffryd Blae G 36 C4
Swift's Green Kent 18 B6
Swilland Suffk 53 E6
Swillbrook Lancs 88 C3
Swillington W York 91 E3
Swimbridge Devon 21 F4
Swimbridge Newland Devon 21 F4
Swinbrook Oxon 39 G5
Swincliffe N York 90 D5
Swincliffe W York 90 C2
Swincombe Devon 21 G5
Swinden N York 89 G5
Swinderby Lincs 85 F1
Swindon Gloucs 47 E2
Swindon Nthumb 113 G5
Swindon Staffs 58 B4
Swindon Wilts 39 F3
Swine E R Yk 93 E3
Swinefleet E R Yk 92 B2
Swineford Gloucs 38 B1
Swineshead Beds 61 F2
Swineshead Lincs 74 C4
Swineshead Bridge Lincs 74 C4
Swiney Highld 167 F2
Swinford Leics 60 B3
Swinford Oxon 40 C5
Swingfield Minnis Kent 19 F6
Swingfield Street Kent 19 F6
Swingleton Green Suffk 52 C5
Swinhoe Nthumb 125 E4
Swinhope Lincs 86 C4
Swinithwaite N York 96 D4
Swinmore Common Herefs 46 B3
Swinscoe Staffs 71 F5
Swinside Cumb 103 F2
Swinstead Lincs 73 H2
Swinthorpe Lincs 86 A3
Swinton Border 123 E4
Swinton Gt Man 82 C5
Swinton N York 97 E3
Swinton N York 98 C2
Swinton S York 84 B5
Swithland Leics 72 C1
Swordale Highld 154 D6
Swordland Highld 143 G3
Swordly Highld 166 A5
Sworton Heath Ches 82 B3
Swyddffynnon Cerdgn 54 D2
Swynnerton Staffs 70 C4
Swyre Dorset 11 F3
Sycharth Powys 68 D2
Sychnant Powys 55 G3
Sychtyn Powys 55 G6
Sydallt Flints 69 E6
Syde Gloucs 38 D5
Sydenham Gt Lon 28 D3
Sydenham Oxon 41 E4
Sydenham Damerel Devon 5 H3
Sydenhurst Surrey 27 H3
Syderstone Norfk 76 A3
Sydling St Nicholas Dorset 11 G4
Sydmonton Hants 26 C5
Sydnal Lane Shrops 58 A6
Syerston Notts 73 E5
Sygun Copper Mine Gwynd 67 F5
Syke Gt Man 89 G1
Sykehouse S York 91 G1
Syleham Suffk 65 E3
Sylen Carmth 34 C5
Symbister Shet 169 j3
Symington S Ayrs 119 F2
Symington S Lans 120 D3
Symonds Yat Herefs 37 G6
Symondsbury Dorset 11 E4
Sympson Green W York 90 C3
Synderford Dorset 10 D5
Synod Inn Cerdgn 42 D5
Syre Highld 165 H3
Syreford Gloucs 47 F1
Syresham Nhants 48 D3
Syston Leics 72 D1
Syston Lincs 73 G4
Sytchampton Worcs 58 A2
Sywell Nhants 60 D2

T

Tabley Hill Ches 82 B3
Tackley Oxon 48 C1
Tacolneston Norfk 64 D5
Tadcaster N York 91 F4
Taddington Derbys 83 F2
Taddington Gloucs 47 F2
Taddiport Devon 21 E2
Tadley Hants 26 D5
Tadlow Cambs 50 D5
Tadmarton Oxon 48 B3
Tadwick Somset 38 B1
Tadworth Surrey 28 C2
Tafarn-y-bwlch Pembks 42 A3
Tafarn-y-Gelyn Denbgs 68 D6
Tafarnaubach Blae G 36 B5
Taff's Well Cardif 36 B3
Tafolwern Powys 55 F6
Tai'r Bull Powys 44 C2
Taibach Neath 35 E3
Tain Highld 167 F5
Tain Highld 163 E2
Tairbeart W Isls 168 d6
Takeley Essex 51 F3
Takeley Street Essex 51 F3
Tal-y-bont Cerdgn 54 D4
Tal-y-Bont Conwy 79 G1
Tal-y-bont Gwynd 67 E2
Tal-y-bont Gwynd 79 F2
Tal-y-Cafn Conwy 79 G2
Tal-y-coed Mons 37 E6
Tal-y-garn Rhondd 36 A2
Tal-y-llyn Gwynd 67 G1
Tal-y-Waun Torfn 36 D5
Talachddu Powys 44 D2
Talacre Flints 80 C3
Talaton Devon 9 G5
Talbenny Pembks 32 C3
Talbot Green Rhondd 36 B2
Talbot Village Dorset 13 E4
Taleford Devon 10 A4
Talerddig Powys 55 G5
Talgarreg Cerdgn 42 D4
Talgarth Powys 44 D3
Talisker Highld 150 C2
Talke Staffs 70 C5
Talke Pits Staffs 70 C5
Talkin Cumb 104 B6
Talla Linnfoots Border 121 F1
Talladale Highld 152 C6
Tallaminnock S Ayrs 109 F5
Tallarn Green Wrexhm 69 G4
Tallentire Cumb 103 E4
Talley Carmth 43 F2
Tallington Lincs 61 G6
Tallwrn Wrexhm 69 E5
Talmine Highld 165 G5
Talog Carmth 33 G4
Talsarn Cerdgn 43 F5
Talsarnau Gwynd 67 F4
Talskiddy Cnwll 4 C2
Talwrn IOA 78 D2
Talwrn Wrexhm 69 F5
Talybont-on-Usk Powys 44 D1
Talysarn Gwynd 66 D5
Talywern Powys 55 F5
Tamer Lane End Gt Man 82 A5
Tamerton Foliot Devon 6 B4
Tamworth Staffs 59 E6
Tamworth Green Lincs 74 D4
Tan Hill N York 96 B5
Tan-y-Bwlch Gwynd 67 F4
Tan-y-fron Conwy 80 B1
Tan-y-fron Wrexhm 69 E5
Tan-y-Grisiau Gwynd 67 F5
Tan-y-groes Cerdgn 42 C4
Tancred N York 91 F5
Tancredston Pembks 32 C4
Tandridge Surrey 29 E1
Tanfield Dur 114 C1
Tanfield Lea Dur 114 D1
Tangiers Pembks 32 D3
Tangley Hants 26 B4
Tangmere W Susx 15 G4
Tangusdale W Isls 168 a2
Tankerness Ork 169 c2
Tankersley S York 84 A5
Tankerton Kent 31 E3
Tannach Highld 167 G3
Tannachie Abers 149 E3
Tannadice Angus 141 E6
Tanner's Green Worcs 58 D3
Tannington Suffk 65 E2
Tannochside N Lans 120 B6
Tansley Derbys 71 H6
Tansor Nhants 61 F4
Tantobie Dur 114 C1
Tanton N York 107 E2
Tanwood Worcs 58 B3
Tanworth in Arden Warwks 58 D2
Taobh Tuath W Isls 168 c6
Taplow Bucks 41 G2
Tarbert Ag & B 117 F6
Tarbert Ag & B 127 G2
Tarbert W Isls 168 d6
Tarbet Ag & B 129 E6
Tarbet Highld 164 C3
Tarbet Highld 143 G3
Tarbock Green Mersyd 81 G3
Tarbolton S Ayrs 119 F2
Tarbrax S Lans 121 E5
Tardebigge Worcs 58 C2
Tarfside Angus 148 C2
Tarland Abers 148 C5
Tarleton Lancs 88 C2
Tarlscough Lancs 81 G6
Tarlton Gloucs 38 D4
Tarnock Somset 23 G4
Tarns Cumb 103 E5
Tarnside Cumb 95 E4
Tarporley Ches 81 H1
Tarr Somset 22 B2
Tarr Somset 22 D2
Tarrant Crawford Dorset 12 C5
Tarrant Gunville Dorset 12 C6
Tarrant Hinton Dorset 12 C6
Tarrant Keyneston Dorset 12 C5
Tarrant Launceston Dorset 12 C6
Tarrant Monkton Dorset 12 C5
Tarrant Rawston Dorset 12 C5
Tarrant Rushton Dorset 12 C5
Tarring Neville E Susx 17 E2
Tarrington Herefs 46 B3
Tarskavaig Highld 143 E5
Tarves Abers 159 E2
Tarvie P & K 139 G6
Tarvin Ches 81 G1
Tarvin Sands Ches 81 G1
Tasburgh Norfk 64 D5
Tasley Shrops 57 G5
Taston Oxon 48 B1
Tatenhill Staffs 71 G2
Tathall End Bucks 49 F4
Tatham Lancs 95 G2
Tathwell Lincs 86 D3
Tatsfield Surrey 29 E2
Tattenhall Ches 69 G6
Tatterford Norfk 76 B3
Tattersett Norfk 76 B3
Tattershall Lincs 74 C6
Tattershall Bridge Lincs 74 B6
Tattershall Thorpe Lincs 74 C6
Tattingstone Suffk 53 E4
Tattingstone White Horse Suffk 53 E4
Tatworth Somset 10 D5
Tauchers Moray 157 F4
Taunton Somset 23 E2
Taverham Norfk 77 E1
Taverners Green Essex 51 F2
Tavernspite Pembks 33 F3
Tavistock Devon 6 B5
Taw Green Devon 8 C4
Tawstock Devon 21 F4
Taxal Derbys 83 E3
Taychreggan Hotel Ag & B 137 E2
Tayinloan Ag & B 117 F5
Taynton Gloucs 46 C1
Taynton Oxon 39 G6
Taynuilt Ag & B 137 E3
Tayport Fife 141 E3
Tayvallich Ag & B 127 F4
Tealby Lincs 86 B4
Team Valley T & W 114 D1
Teangue Highld 143 F5
Teanord Highld 154 D6
Tebay Cumb 95 G5
Tebworth Beds 49 H2
Tedburn St Mary Devon 9 E4
Teddington Gloucs 47 E2
Teddington Gt Lon 28 C3
Tedstone Delamere Herefs 46 C5
Tedstone Wafer Herefs 46 B5
Teesport N York 107 E3
Teesside Airport Dur 106 C2
Teesside Park N York 106 D3
Teeton Nhants 60 C2
Teffont Evias Wilts 25 E2
Teffont Magna Wilts 25 E2
Tegryn Pembks 42 B2
Teigh Rutlnd 73 F2
Teigncombe Devon 8 D3
Teigngrace Devon 7 F5
Teignmouth Devon 7 G5
Teindside Border 112 B6
Telford Shrops 70 B1
Tellisford Somset 24 D5
Telscombe E Susx 17 E2
Telscombe Cliffs E Susx 17 E1
Tempar P & K 138 D5
Templand D & G 111 E3
Temple Cnwll 5 E3
Temple Mdloth 121 G5
Temple Balsall W Mids 59 E3
Temple Bar Cerdgn 43 E5
Temple Cloud Somset 24 B5
Temple End Suffk 51 G6
Temple Ewell Kent 19 F6
Temple Grafton Warwks 47 G5
Temple Guiting Gloucs 47 F2
Temple Hirst N York 91 G2
Temple Normanton Derbys 84 B1
Temple of Fiddes Abers 149 F2
Temple Pier Highld 154 D2
Temple Sowerby Cumb 104 C3
Templecombe Somset 24 C1
Templeton Devon 9 F6
Templeton Pembks 33 E3
Templetown Dur 105 H5
Tempsford Beds 50 C6
Ten Mile Bank Norfk 63 E5
Tenbury Wells Worcs 57 F2
Tenby Pembks 33 E2
Tendring Essex 53 E3
Tendring Green Essex 53 E3
Tendring Heath Essex 53 E3
Tenpenny Heath Essex 52 D3
Tenterden Kent 18 B5
Terling Essex 52 A2
Tern Shrops 70 A2
Ternhill Shrops 70 A3
Terregles D & G 110 D2
Terrington N York 98 B2
Terrington St Clement Norfk 75 F2
Terrington St John Norfk 75 F1
Terry's Green Warwks 58 D3
Teston Kent 29 H1
Testwood Hants 14 B5
Tetbury Gloucs 38 D4
Tetbury Upton Gloucs 38 D4
Tetchill Shrops 69 F3
Tetcott Devon 5 G6
Tetford Lincs 86 D2
Tetney Lincs 86 C5
Tetney Lock Lincs 86 D5
Tetsworth Oxon 41 E4

Tettenhall
Tong Street
314

Tettenhall W Mids 58 B5
Tettenhall Wood W Mids 58 B5
Tetworth Cambs 50 C6
Teversal Notts 72 C6
Teversham Cambs 62 D1
Teviothead Border 112 A5
Tewin Herts 50 D2
Tewkesbury Gloucs 46 D2
Teynham Kent 30 C2
Thackley W York 90 C3
Thackthwaite Cumb 103 E2
Thackthwaite Cumb 104 A3
Thakeham W Susx 16 B3
Thame Oxon 41 E5
Thames Ditton Surrey 28 C3
Thamesmead Gt Lon 29 F4
Thanington Kent 31 E2
Thankerton S Lans 120 D3
Tharston Norfk 64 D5
Thatcham Berks 26 C6
Thatto Heath Mersyd 81 G4
Thaxted Essex 51 G4
The Bank Ches 70 C6
The Bank Shrops 57 F5
The Beeches Gloucs 39 E4
The Blythe Staffs 71 E3
The Bog Shrops 56 D5
The Bourne Worcs 47 E5
The Braes Highld 151 E2
The Bratch Staffs 58 B5
The Broad Herefs 45 H5
The Brunt E Loth 133 F2
The Bungalow IOM 174 m4
The Butts Gloucs 38 D6
The Camp Gloucs 38 D5
The Chequer Wrexhm 69 G4
The City Beds 61 G1
The City Bucks 41 F4
The Common Oxon 48 A2
The Common Wilts 25 H2
The Common Wilts 39 E3
The Corner Kent 17 H6
The Corner Shrops 57 E4
The Cronk IOM 174 I5
The Den N Ayrs 119 E5
The Eden Project Cnwll 3 H5
The Flatt Cumb 112 C3
The Forge Herefs 45 F5
The Forstal E Susx 17 F5
The Forstal Kent 18 C6
The Forstal Kent 18 D5
The Fouralls Shrops 70 B3
The Green Cumb 94 C3
The Green Essex 52 A3
The Green N York 98 C5
The Grove Worcs 46 D3
The Haven W Susx 16 B4
The Haw Gloucs 46 D2
The Hill Cumb 94 C3
The Holt Berks 41 F2
The Hundred Herefs 57 E2
The Leacon Kent 18 C5
The Lee Bucks 41 G5
The Lhen IOM 174 m5
The Lochs Moray 157 E5
The Marsh Powys 56 C5
The Middles Dur 106 B6
The Moor Kent 18 A4
The Mumbles Swans 34 D3
The Murray S Lans 119 H5
The Mythe Gloucs 46 D3
The Narth Mons 37 F5
The Neuk Abers 149 E4
The Quarry Gloucs 38 B4
The Quarter Kent 18 B6
The Reddings Gloucs 47 E1
The Rookery Staffs 70 C6
The Ross P & K 139 E2
The Sands Surrey 27 G4
The Shoe Wilts 38 C2
The Smithies Shrops 57 G5
The Spike Cambs 51 F5
The Spring Warwks 59 F3
The Square Torfn 36 D4
The Stair Kent 17 G6
The Stocks Kent 18 C4
The Straits Hants 27 F3
The Strand Wilts 25 E5
The Towans Cnwll 2 C4
The Vauld Herefs 45 H4
The Wyke Shrops 57 G6
Theakston N York 97 F3
Thealby Lincs 92 C1
Theale Berks 41 E1
Theale Somset 23 G4
Thearne E R Yk 93 E3
Theberton Suffk 65 G2
Thedden Grange Hants 27 E3
Theddingworth Leics 60 C4
Theddlethorpe All Saints Lincs 87 E3
Theddlethorpe St Helen Lincs 87 E4
Thelbridge Cross Devon 21 H2
Thelnetham Suffk 64 C3
Thelveton Norfk 64 D3
Thelwall Ches 82 B3
Themelthorpe Norfk 76 D2
Thenford Nhants 48 C3
Theobald's Green Wilts 39 E1
Therfield Herts 50 D4
Thetford Norfk 64 A4
Thethwaite Cumb 103 H4
Theydon Bois Essex 29 E6
Thicket Priory E R Yk 91 H4
Thickwood Wilts 38 C1
Thimbleby Lincs 86 C2
Thimbleby N York 97 H4
Thingwall Mersyd 81 E3
Thirkleby N York 97 H3
Thirlby N York 97 H3
Thirlestane Border 122 C4
Thirlspot Cumb 103 G2
Thirn N York 97 E3
Thirsk N York 97 G3
Thirtleby E R Yk 93 E3
Thistleton Lancs 88 C3
Thistleton Rutlnd 73 G2
Thistley Green Suffk 63 F3
Thixendale N York 92 B6
Thockrington Nthumb 113 G3
Tholomas Drove Cambs 62 C6
Tholthorpe N York 97 H1
Thomas Chapel Pembks 33 E2
Thomas Close Cumb 104 A4
Thomas Town Warwks 58 D2
Thomastown Abers 158 B3
Thompson Norfk 64 B5
Thong Kent 29 G3
Thoralby N York 96 C3
Thoresby Notts 84 D2
Thoresthorpe Lincs 87 E2
Thoresway Lincs 86 B4
Thorganby Lincs 86 B4
Thorganby N York 91 H4
Thorgill N York 98 C4
Thorington Suffk 65 G3
Thorington Street Suffk 52 D4
Thorlby N York 89 H5
Thorley Herts 51 F3
Thorley IOW 14 B2
Thorley Houses Herts 51 E3
Thorley Street IOW 14 B2
Thormanby N York 97 H2
Thornaby-on-Tees N York 106 D3
Thornage Norfk 76 D4
Thornborough Bucks 49 F2
Thornborough N York 97 F3
Thornbury Devon 20 D1
Thornbury Gloucs 37 G3
Thornbury Herefs 46 B5
Thornbury W York 90 C3
Thornby Cumb 103 G5
Thornby Nhants 60 C3
Thorncliff Staffs 71 E6
Thorncombe Dorset 10 D5
Thorncombe Street Surrey 27 H3
Thorncott Green Beds 50 B5
Thorncross IOW 14 C2
Thorndon Suffk 64 D2
Thorndon Cross Devon 8 B4
Thorne S York 84 D6
Thorne Somset 23 H1
Thorne St Margaret Somset 22 D1
Thornecroft Devon 7 E4
Thornehillhead Devon 20 D2
Thorner W York 91 E4
Thornes Staffs 58 D6
Thornes W York 90 D1
Thorney Bucks 28 A4
Thorney Cambs 62 B6
Thorney Notts 85 F2
Thorney Somset 23 G1
Thorney Hill Hants 13 F5
Thorney Toll Cambs 62 C6
Thornfalcon Somset 23 F2
Thornford Dorset 11 F6
Thorngrafton Nthumb 113 E1
Thorngrove Somset 23 F2
Thorngumbald E R Yk 93 F2
Thornham Norfk 75 H4
Thornham Magna Suffk 64 D2
Thornham Parva Suffk 64 D3
Thornhaugh Cambs 61 G5
Thornhill Caerph 36 C3
Thornhill D & G 110 C4
Thornhill Derbys 83 G3
Thornhill Hants 14 C5
Thornhill Stirlg 130 C5
Thornhill W York 90 D1
Thornhill Lees W York 90 D1
Thornhills W York 90 C2
Thornholme E R Yk 93 E6
Thornicombe Dorset 12 C5
Thornington Nthumb 123 F3
Thornley Dur 105 H4
Thornley Dur 106 C5
Thornley Gate Cumb 105 E6
Thornliebank E Rens 119 G5
Thorns Suffk 63 G1
Thorns Green Gt Man 82 C3
Thornsett Derbys 83 E3
Thornthwaite Cumb 103 F3
Thornthwaite N York 90 C5
Thornton Angus 140 D4
Thornton Bucks 49 F3
Thornton E R Yk 92 B4
Thornton Fife 132 B5
Thornton Lancs 88 B4
Thornton Leics 59 G6
Thornton Lincs 86 C1
Thornton Mersyd 81 F5
Thornton N York 106 D2
Thornton Nthumb 123 G4
Thornton Pembks 32 C2
Thornton W York 90 B3
Thornton Curtis Lincs 93 E1
Thornton Green Ches 81 G2
Thornton Heath Gt Lon 28 D3
Thornton Hough Mersyd 81 E3
Thornton in Lonsdale N York 95 G2
Thornton le Dale N York 98 D3
Thornton le Moor Lincs 85 H4
Thornton Rust N York 96 C4
Thornton Steward N York 97 E4
Thornton Watlass N York 97 E3
Thornton-in-Craven N York 89 G4
Thornton-le-Beans N York 97 G4
Thornton-le-Clay N York 98 C1
Thornton-le-Moor N York 97 G4
Thornton-le-Moors Ches 81 G2
Thornton-le-Street N York 97 G3
Thorntonhall S Lans 119 H5
Thorntonloch E Loth 133 F2
Thornwood Common Essex 51 E1
Thornydykes Border 122 C4
Thornythwaite Cumb 103 H2
Thoroton Notts 73 E4
Thorp Arch W York 91 E4
Thorpe Derbys 71 F5
Thorpe E R Yk 92 D4
Thorpe Lincs 87 E3
Thorpe N York 90 A6
Thorpe Norfk 65 G5
Thorpe Notts 73 E5
Thorpe Surrey 28 A3
Thorpe Abbotts Norfk 64 D3
Thorpe Acre Leics 72 C2
Thorpe Arnold Leics 73 E2
Thorpe Audlin W York 91 F1
Thorpe Bassett N York 98 D2
Thorpe Bay Essex 30 C5
Thorpe by Water Rutlnd 61 E5
Thorpe Common S York 84 B4
Thorpe Constantine Staffs 59 E6
Thorpe End Norfk 77 F1
Thorpe Green Essex 53 E3
Thorpe Green Lancs 88 D2
Thorpe Green Suffk 52 C6
Thorpe Hesley S York 84 B4
Thorpe in Balne S York 84 D6
Thorpe in the Fallows Lincs 85 G3
Thorpe Langton Leics 60 C5
Thorpe Larches Dur 106 C3
Thorpe le Street E R Yk 92 B4
Thorpe Lea Surrey 28 A3
Thorpe Malsor Nhants 60 D3
Thorpe Mandeville Nhants 48 D4
Thorpe Market Norfk 77 E4
Thorpe Morieux Suffk 52 C6
Thorpe on the Hill Lincs 85 G1
Thorpe on the Hill W York 90 D2
Thorpe Park Surrey 28 A3
Thorpe Salvin S York 84 C3
Thorpe Satchville Leics 73 E1
Thorpe St Andrew Norfk 65 E6
Thorpe St Peter Lincs 75 E6
Thorpe Thewles Dur 106 C3
Thorpe Tilney Lincs 74 B6
Thorpe Underwood N York 91 F5
Thorpe Underwood Nhants 60 D3
Thorpe Waterville Nhants 61 F3
Thorpe Willoughby N York 91 G3
Thorpe-le-Soken Essex 53 E3
Thorpeness Suffk 65 G1
Thorpland Norfk 75 F1
Thorrington Essex 52 D3
Thorverton Devon 9 F5
Thrales End Beds 50 B2
Thrandeston Suffk 64 D3
Thrapston Nhants 61 F3
Threapland Cumb 103 F4
Threapland N York 90 A6
Threapwood Ches 69 G4
Threapwood Staffs 71 E4
Threapwood Head Staffs 71 E4
Threave S Ayrs 109 E5
Threave Castle D & G 110 B1
Three Ashes Herefs 45 H1
Three Bridges W Susx 16 D5
Three Burrows Cnwll 3 E4
Three Chimneys Kent 18 B5
Three Cocks Powys 45 E3
Three Crosses Swans 34 C4
Three Cups Corner E Susx 17 G3
Three Gates Worcs 46 B5
Three Hammers Cnwll 5 F5
Three Holes Norfk 62 D5
Three Lane Ends Gt Man 82 C6
Three Leg Cross E Susx 17 H4
Three Legged Cross Dorset 13 E5
Three Mile Cross Berks 27 E6
Three Mile Stone Cnwll 3 E4
Three Miletown W Loth 131 G3
Three Oaks E Susx 18 B3
Threehammer Common Norfk 77 F2
Threekingham Lincs 74 A4
Threepwood Border 122 B4
Threlkeld Cumb 103 G3
Threshfield N York 96 C1
Thrigby Norfk 77 G1
Thringarth Dur 105 F2
Thringstone Leics 72 B2
Thrintoft N York 97 F4
Thriplow Cambs 51 E5
Throapham S York 84 C3
Throckenhalt Lincs 74 D1
Throcking Herts 50 D4
Throckley T & W 114 C2
Throckmorton Worcs 47 E4
Throop Dorset 12 B4
Throop Dorset 13 E4
Throphill Nthumb 114 C4
Thropton Nthumb 114 B6
Throsk Stirlg 131 E4
Througham Gloucs 38 D5
Throughgate D & G 110 C3
Throwleigh Devon 8 D4
Throwley Kent 30 C2
Throwley Forstal Kent 30 C1
Thrumpton Notts 72 C3
Thrumpton Notts 85 E3
Thrumster Highld 167 G3
Thrunscoe Lincs 86 C5
Thrunton Nthumb 124 D2
Thrup Oxon 39 G4
Thrupp Gloucs 38 C5
Thrupp Oxon 40 C6
Thrushelton Devon 8 A3
Thrushesbush Essex 51 F2
Thrussington Leics 72 D2
Thruxton Hants 26 A4
Thruxton Herefs 45 G3
Thrybergh S York 84 B4
Thulston Derbys 72 B3
Thundersley Essex 30 B5
Thurcaston Leics 72 C1
Thurcroft S York 84 C4
Thurdon Cnwll 20 C2
Thurgarton Norfk 77 E3
Thurgarton Notts 73 E5
Thurgoland S York 83 H5
Thurlaston Leics 59 H5
Thurlaston Warwks 59 G2
Thurlbear Somset 23 E1
Thurlby Lincs 73 G6
Thurlby Lincs 74 A2
Thurlby Lincs 87 E2
Thurleigh Beds 61 F1
Thurlestone Devon 6 D2
Thurlow Suffk 51 H6
Thurloxton Somset 23 F2
Thurlstone S York 83 G5
Thurlton Norfk 65 G5
Thurlwood Ches 70 C6
Thurmaston Leics 72 D1
Thurnby Leics 60 C6
Thurne Norfk 77 G2
Thurnham Kent 30 B2
Thurning Nhants 61 G4
Thurning Norfk 76 D3
Thurnscoe S York 84 B5
Thursby Cumb 103 G5
Thursden Lancs 89 G3
Thursford Norfk 76 C3
Thursley Surrey 27 G3
Thurso Highld 167 E5
Thurstaston Mersyd 81 E3
Thurston Suffk 64 B2
Thurston Clough Gt Man 83 E5
Thurston Planch Suffk 64 B2
Thurstonfield Cumb 103 G6
Thurstonland W York 83 F6
Thurton Norfk 65 F5
Thurvaston Derbys 71 G4
Thuxton Norfk 64 C6
Thwaite N York 96 B5
Thwaite Suffk 64 D2
Thwaite Head Cumb 94 D4
Thwaite St Mary Norfk 65 F5
Thwaites W York 90 B4
Thwaites Brow W York 90 B4
Thwing E R Yk 99 F2
Tibbermore P & K 139 H2
Tibbers D & G 110 C4
Tibberton Gloucs 46 C1
Tibberton Shrops 70 B2
Tibberton Worcs 47 E5
Tibbie Shiels Inn Border 121 G1
Tibenham Norfk 64 D4
Tibshelf Derbys 72 B6
Tibthorpe E R Yk 92 C5
Ticehurst E Susx 17 H4
Tichborne Hants 26 D2
Tickencote Rutlnd 73 G1
Tickenham Somset 37 F1
Tickford End Bucks 49 G3
Tickhill S York 84 D4
Ticklerton Shrops 57 E4
Ticknall Derbys 72 A2
Tickton E R Yk 92 D4
Tidbury Green W Mids 58 D3
Tidcombe Wilts 26 A5
Tiddington Oxon 41 E5
Tiddington Warwks 47 H5
Tidebrook E Susx 17 G4
Tideford Cnwll 5 G2
Tideford Cross Cnwll 5 G2
Tidenham Gloucs 37 G4
Tideswell Derbys 83 F2
Tidmarsh Berks 41 E2
Tidmington Warwks 47 H3
Tidpit Hants 25 F1
Tiers Cross Pembks 32 C3
Tiffield Nhants 49 E4
Tigerton Angus 141 E6
Tigh a Ghearraidh W Isls 168 b5
Tigharry W Isls 168 b5
Tighnabruaich Ag & B 128 A2
Tigley Devon 7 E4
Tilbrook Cambs 61 G2
Tilbury Essex 29 G4
Tilbury Green Essex 52 A5
Tile Cross W Mids 59 E4
Tile Hill W Mids 59 F3
Tilehouse Green W Mids 59 E3
Tilehurst Berks 41 E2
Tilford Surrey 27 G4
Tilgate W Susx 16 D5
Tilgate Forest Row W Susx 16 D5
Tilham Street Somset 24 A3
Tillers Green Gloucs 46 C2
Tillicoultry Clacks 131 E5
Tillietudlem S Lans 120 C4
Tillingham Essex 52 C1
Tillington Herefs 45 G4
Tillington W Susx 27 H1
Tillington Common Herefs 45 G4
Tillybirloch Abers 148 D5
Tillycairn Abers 148 B4
Tillyfourie Abers 148 D6
Tillygreig Abers 159 E1
Tillyrie P & K 131 G6
Tilmanstone Kent 31 F1
Tiln Notts 85 E3
Tilney All Saints Norfk 75 F2
Tilney High End Norfk 75 F2
Tilney St Lawrence Norfk 75 F1
Tilshead Wilts 25 F4
Tilstock Shrops 69 H4
Tilston Ches 69 G5
Tilstone Bank Ches 69 H6
Tilstone Fearnall Ches 69 H6
Tilsworth Beds 49 H2
Tilton on the Hill Leics 60 C6
Tiltups End Gloucs 38 C4
Tilty Essex 51 G3
Timberland Lincs 74 B6
Timbersbrook Ches 82 D1
Timberscombe Somset 22 B3
Timble N York 90 C5
Timewell Devon 22 C2
Timpanheck D & G 111 H2
Timperley Gt Man 82 C4
Timsbury Hants 26 B2
Timsbury Somset 24 B5
Timsgarry W Isls 168 d8
Timsgearraidh W Isls 168 d8
Timworth Suffk 63 H2
Timworth Green Suffk 63 H2
Tincleton Dorset 12 B4
Tindale Cumb 104 C6
Tindale Crescent Dur 106 A4
Tingewick Bucks 49 E2
Tingley W York 90 D2
Tingrith Beds 50 A4
Tingwall Airport Shet 169 h3
Tinhay Devon 5 G4
Tinker's Hill Hants 26 B4
Tinkersley Derbys 83 G1
Tinsley S York 84 B4
Tinsley Green W Susx 16 D5
Tintagel Cnwll 4 D5
Tintagel Castle Cnwll 4 D5
Tintern Abbey Mons 37 F4
Tintern Parva Mons 37 F4
Tintinhull Somset 23 H1
Tintwistle Derbys 83 E4
Tinwald D & G 110 D3
Tinwell Rutlnd 61 F6
Tipp's End Norfk 62 D5
Tippacott Devon 21 H5
Tiptoe Hants 13 F4
Tipton W Mids 58 B5
Tipton Green W Mids 58 B5
Tipton St John Devon 10 A4
Tiptree Essex 52 C2
Tiptree Heath Essex 52 B2
Tir-y-fron Flints 69 E6
Tirabad Powys 44 B3
Tiree Airport Ag & B 134 B4
Tiretigan Ag & B 127 F1
Tirley Gloucs 46 D2
Tirphil Caerph 36 C5
Tirril Cumb 104 B3
Tisbury Wilts 25 E1
Tisman's Common W Susx 16 B5
Tissington Derbys 71 G5
Titchberry Devon 20 C3
Titchfield Hants 14 D4
Titchfield Common Hants 14 C4
Titchmarsh Nhants 61 F3
Titchwell Norfk 75 H4
Tithby Notts 73 E4
Titley Herefs 45 F5
Titmore Green Herts 50 C3
Titsey Surrey 29 E1
Titson Cnwll 20 C1
Tittensor Staffs 70 D4
Tittleshall Norfk 76 B2
Titton Worcs 58 A2
Tiverton Ches 69 H6
Tiverton Devon 9 F6
Tivetshall St Margaret Norfk 64 D4
Tivetshall St Mary Norfk 64 D4
Tivington Somset 22 B4
Tivy Dale S York 83 H5
Tixall Staffs 71 E2
Tixover Rutlnd 61 F5
Toadhole Derbys 72 B6
Toadmoor Derbys 72 A5
Tobermory Ag & B 135 G5
Toberonochy Ag & B 127 F6
Tobha Mor W Isls 168 b3
Tocher Abers 158 C2
Tochieneal Moray 157 G6
Tockenham Wilts 39 E2
Tockenham Wick Wilts 39 E2
Tocketts N York 107 F3
Tockholes Lancs 89 E2
Tockington Gloucs 37 G3
Tockwith N York 91 F5
Todber Dorset 24 D1
Todburn Nthumb 114 C5
Toddington Beds 50 A4
Toddington Gloucs 47 F2
Todds Green Herts 50 C3
Todenham Gloucs 47 H3
Todhills Angus 140 D4
Todhills Cumb 112 A1
Todhills Dur 106 B4
Todmorden W York 89 H2
Todwick S York 84 C3
Toft Cambs 62 C1
Toft Ches 82 C2
Toft Lincs 74 A2
Toft Shet 169 j4
Toft Warwks 59 H2
Toft Hill Dur 106 A4
Toft Hill Lincs 86 C1
Toft Monks Norfk 65 G5
Toft next Newton Lincs 85 H3
Toftrees Norfk 76 B3
Toftwood Norfk 76 C1
Togston Nthumb 114 D6
Tokavaig Highld 143 F5
Tokers Green Oxon 41 E2
Tolastadh W Isls 168 f9
Toldish Cnwll 4 C2
Toll Bar S York 84 C5
Tolland Somset 22 D2
Tollard Farnham Dorset 12 C6
Tollard Royal Wilts 25 E1
Tollbar End W Mids 59 F3
Toller Fratrum Dorset 11 F4
Toller Porcorum Dorset 11 F4
Toller Whelme Dorset 11 E5
Tollerton N York 98 A1
Tollerton Notts 72 D3
Tollesbury Essex 52 C2
Tolleshunt D'Arcy Essex 52 C2
Tolleshunt Knights Essex 52 C2
Tolleshunt Major Essex 52 C2
Tolob Shet 169 h1
Tolpuddle Dorset 12 B4
Tolsta W Isls 168 f9
Tolvan Cnwll 3 E3
Tolver Cnwll 2 B3
Tolworth Gt Lon 28 C3
Tomatin Highld 155 F2
Tomchrasky Highld 145 E6
Tomdoun Highld 144 D4
Tomich Highld 162 C4
Tomich Highld 153 G2
Tomich Highld 154 D4
Tomich Highld 155 E6
Tomintoul Moray 156 D1
Tomlow Warwks 59 G2
Tomnacross Highld 154 C3
Tomnavoulin Moray 156 D2
Tompkin Staffs 70 D5
Ton Mons 36 D4
Ton Mons 37 E4
Ton-teg Rhondd 36 B3
Tonbridge Kent 17 G6
Tondu Brdgnd 35 F3
Tonedale Somset 22 D1
Tong Kent 30 C2
Tong Shrops 57 H6
Tong W York 90 C3
Tong Green Kent 30 C1
Tong Norton Shrops 57 H6
Tong Street W York 90 C3

Tonge
Tushingham cum Grindley
315

Tonge Leics 72 B2
Tongham Surrey 27 G4
Tongland D & G 102 A6
Tongue Highld 165 G4
Tongue End Lincs 74 B2
Tongwynlais Cardif 36 B2
Tonna Neath 35 E4
Tonwell Herts 50 D2
Tonypandy Rhondd 35 G3
Tonyrefail Rhondd 35 G3
Toot Baldon Oxon 40 D4
Toot Hill Essex 51 F1
Toot Hill Hants 14 B5
Toothill Wilts 39 F3
Tooting Gt Lon 28 D3
Tooting Bec Gt Lon 28 D3
Top End Beds 61 F2
Top of Hebers Gt Man 82 D5
Top-y-rhos Flints 69 E6
Topcliffe N York 97 G2
Topcroft Norfk 65 E5
Topcroft Street Norfk 65 E5
Topham S York 91 G1
Toppesfield Essex 52 A4
Toppings Gt Man 82 B6
Toprow Norfk 64 D5
Topsham Devon 9 F3
Torbeg N Ayrs 117 H3
Torboll Highld 162 D4
Torbreck Highld 155 E3
Torbryan Devon 7 F4
Torcastle Highld 144 D2
Torcross Devon 7 F2
Tore Highld 154 D4
Torfrey Cnwll 5 E1
Torinturk Ag & B 127 G1
Torksey Lincs 85 F2
Tormarton Gloucs 38 B2
Tormore N Ayrs 117 H4
Tornagrain Highld 155 F4
Tornaveen Abers 148 D5
Torness Highld 154 D2
Tornewton Devon 7 E4
Toronto Dur 106 A4
Torosay Castle Ag & B 136 B3
Torpenhow Cumb 103 F4
Torphichen W Loth 131 F2
Torphins Abers 148 D5
Torpoint Cnwll 6 B3
Torquay Devon 7 F4
Torquhan Border 122 B4
Torr Devon 6 C3
Torran Highld 151 F4
Torrance E Duns 130 C2
Torranyard N Ayrs 119 E4
Torre Somset 22 C3
Torridon Highld 152 C5
Torridon House Highld 152 C5
Torrin Highld 143 E6
Torrisdale Ag & B 117 G4
Torrisdale Highld 165 H5
Torrish Highld 163 F6
Torrisholme Lancs 95 E1
Torrobull Highld 162 C4
Torry Aber C 149 G5
Torryburn Fife 131 F4
Tortan Worcs 58 A3
Torteval Guern 174 f1
Torthorwald D & G 111 E3
Tortington W Susx 16 A2
Tortworth Gloucs 38 B4
Torvaig Highld 151 E3
Torver Cumb 94 D4
Torwood Falk 131 E4
Torwoodlee Border 122 B3
Torworth Notts 84 D3
Toscaig Highld 151 G2
Toseland Cambs 62 B2
Tosside N York 89 F5
Tostock Suffk 64 B2
Totaig Highld 150 B4
Tote Highld 150 D4
Tote Highld 151 E5
Tote Hill W Susx 27 G2
Tothill Lincs 86 D3
Totland IOW 13 G3
Totley S York 83 H3
Totley Brook S York 83 H3
Totnes Devon 7 E4
Toton Notts 72 C3
Totronald Ag & B 134 D5
Totscore Highld 150 D5
Tottenham Gt Lon 28 D5
Tottenhill Norfk 75 G1
Totteridge Gt Lon 28 C5
Totternhoe Beds 49 H1
Tottington Gt Man 82 C6
Tottleworth Lancs 89 F3
Totton Hants 14 B5
Touchen End Berks 41 G2
Toulston N York 91 F4
Toulton Somset 23 E2
Toulvaddie Highld 163 F2
Tovil Kent 30 A1
Tow Law Dur 105 H4
Towan Cnwll 4 B3
Towan Cnwll 3 H5
Toward Ag & B 128 C2
Toward Quay Ag & B 128 C2
Towcester Nhants 49 E4
Towednack Cnwll 2 B4
Towersey Oxon 41 E5
Towie Abers 148 B6
Town End Cambs 62 C5
Town End Cumb 94 C4
Town End Cumb 94 D6
Town End Cumb 104 C3
Town End Cumb 94 D4
Town End Cumb 95 E3
Town Green Lancs 81 F5
Town Green Norfk 77 G1
Town Head Cumb 95 E5
Town Head N York 89 G5
Town Head N York 90 C4
Town Kelloe Dur 106 C4
Town Lane Gt Man 82 B5
Town Littleworth E Susx 17 E3
Town of Lowdon Mersyd 82 A4
Town Row E Susx 17 F4
Town Street Suffk 63 G4
Town Yetholm Border 123 E2
Townend W Duns 129 E3
Towngate Cumb 104 B5
Towngate Lincs 74 B1
Townhead Cumb 103 E4
Townhead Cumb 104 C3
Townhead D & G 110 D4
Townhead S York 83 G5
Townhead of Greenlaw D & G 110 B1
Townhill Fife 131 G4
Townlake Devon 5 H3
Towns End Hants 26 D5
Townsend Somset 10 D6
Townshend Cnwll 2 C3
Townwell Gloucs 38 B3
Towthorpe E R Yk 92 C6
Towthorpe N York 91 G5
Towton N York 91 F3
Towyn Conwy 80 B3
Toxteth Mersyd 81 F3
Toy's Hill Kent 29 F1
Toynton All Saints Lincs 86 D1
Toynton Fen Side Lincs 74 D6
Toynton St Peter Lincs 86 D1
Trabboch E Ayrs 119 F2
Trabbochburn E Ayrs 119 F2
Traboe Cnwll 3 E2
Tracebridge Somset 22 D1
Tradespark Highld 155 G5
Traethsaith Cerdgn 42 C4
Trallong Powys 44 C2
Tramway Museum Derbys 72 A6
Tranent E Loth 132 C2
Tranmere Mersyd 81 E3
Trannack Cnwll 2 C3
Trantelbeg Highld 166 C4
Trantlemore Highld 166 C4
Tranwell Nthumb 114 C4
Trap's Green Warwks 58 D2
Trapp Carmth 43 G1
Traprain E Loth 133 E3
Trapshill Berks 26 B6
Traquair Border 121 H3
Trash Green Berks 41 E1
Traveller's Rest Devon 21 F3
Trawden Lancs 89 G3
Trawscoed Cerdgn 54 D3
Trawsfynydd Gwynd 67 G4
Tre Aubrey V Glam 36 B1
Tre Taliesin Cerdgn 54 D4
Tre'r-ddol Cerdgn 54 D5
Tre-gagle Mons 37 F5
Tre-Gibbon Rhondd 35 G5
Tre-groes Cerdgn 42 D4
Tre-Mostyn Flints 80 D3
Tre-Vaughan Carmth 42 D1
Tre-wyn Mons 45 F1
Trealaw Rhondd 35 G3
Treales Lancs 88 C3
Treamble Cnwll 3 E5
Trearddur Bay IOA 78 B3
Treaslane Highld 150 D4
Treator Cnwll 4 C3
Trebanog Rhondd 35 G3
Trebanos Neath 35 E5
Trebartha Cnwll 5 F4
Trebarvah Cnwll 3 E3
Trebarwith Cnwll 4 D4
Trebeath Cnwll 5 F5
Trebehor Cnwll 2 A2
Trebelzue Cnwll 4 B2
Trebetherick Cnwll 4 C4
Treborough Somset 22 C3
Trebudannon Cnwll 4 C2
Trebullett Cnwll 5 G4
Treburgett Cnwll 4 D4
Treburick Cnwll 4 C3
Treburley Cnwll 5 G4
Treburrick Cnwll 4 B3
Trebyan Cnwll 4 D2
Trecastle Powys 44 B2
Trecogo Cnwll 5 G4
Trecott Devon 8 C5
Trecwn Pembks 32 D5
Trecynon Rhondd 35 G5
Tredaule Cnwll 5 F4
Tredavoe Cnwll 2 B3
Tredegar Blae G 36 C5
Tredethy Cnwll 4 D3
Tredington Gloucs 47 E2
Tredington Warwks 47 H4
Tredinnick Cnwll 4 C3
Tredinnick Cnwll 4 D2
Tredinnick Cnwll 5 E2
Tredinnick Cnwll 5 F2
Tredinnick Cnwll 5 F2
Tredomen Powys 44 D2
Tredrissi Pembks 42 A3
Tredrizzick Cnwll 4 C4
Tredunhock Mons 37 E4
Tredustan Powys 44 D2
Treen Cnwll 2 B3
Treen Cnwll 2 B2
Treesmill Cnwll 4 D1
Treeton S York 84 B3
Trefasser Pembks 32 C5
Trefdraeth IOA 78 D2
Trefecca Powys 44 D2
Trefeglwys Powys 55 G4
Trefenter Cerdgn 54 D2
Treffgarne Pembks 32 D4
Treffgarne Owen Pembks 32 C4
Trefforest Rhondd 36 B3
Treffynnon Pembks 32 C5
Trefil Blae G 36 B5
Trefilan Cerdgn 43 F5
Trefin Pembks 32 C5
Treflach Wood Shrops 69 E3
Trefnannau Powys 69 E2
Trefnant Denbgs 80 C2
Trefonen Shrops 69 E3
Trefor Gwynd 66 C5
Trefor IOA 78 C3
Treforda Cnwll 4 D5
Trefrew Cnwll 5 E4
Trefriw Conwy 79 G1
Tregadillett Cnwll 5 F4
Tregaian IOA 78 D3
Tregare Mons 37 E5
Tregarne Cnwll 3 E2
Tregaron Cerdgn 43 G5
Tregarth Gwynd 79 F1
Tregaswith Cnwll 4 C2
Tregatta Cnwll 4 D5
Tregawne Cnwll 4 D2
Tregear Cnwll 3 F5
Tregeare Cnwll 5 F5
Tregeiriog Wrexhm 68 D3
Tregele IOA 78 C4
Tregellist Cnwll 4 D4
Tregenna Cnwll 3 F4
Tregenna Cnwll 4 D3
Tregeseal Cnwll 2 A3
Tregew Cnwll 3 F3
Tregidden Cnwll 3 E2
Tregiddle Cnwll 2 D2
Tregidgeo Cnwll 3 G4
Tregiskey Cnwll 3 G4
Treglemais Pembks 32 B5
Tregole Cnwll 5 E6
Tregolls Cnwll 3 E3
Tregonce Cnwll 4 C3
Tregonetha Cnwll 4 C2
Tregony Cnwll 3 G4
Tregoodwell Cnwll 5 E4
Tregoose Cnwll 2 D2
Tregoss Cnwll 4 C2
Tregowris Cnwll 3 E2
Tregoyd Powys 45 E3
Tregrehan Mills Cnwll 3 H5
Tregullon Cnwll 4 D2
Tregunna Cnwll 4 C3
Tregunnon Cnwll 5 F4
Tregurrian Cnwll 4 B2
Tregustick Cnwll 4 C2
Tregynon Powys 56 A5
Trehafod Rhondd 36 B3
Trehan Cnwll 5 G2
Treharris Myr Td 36 B4
Treharrock Cnwll 4 D4
Trehemborne Cnwll 4 B3
Treherbert Carmth 43 F4
Treherbert Rhondd 35 G4
Treheveras Cnwll 3 F4
Trehunist Cnwll 5 G2
Trekelland Cnwll 5 G4
Trekenner Cnwll 5 G4
Treknow Cnwll 4 D5
Trelan Cnwll 3 E2
Trelash Cnwll 5 E5
Trelassick Cnwll 3 F5
Trelawne Cnwll 5 F1
Trelawnyd Flints 80 C3
Treleague Cnwll 3 E2
Treleaver Cnwll 3 E1
Trelech Carmth 33 G5
Trelech a'r Betws Carmth 33 G4
Treleddyd-fawr Pembks 32 B4
Trelew Cnwll 3 F3
Trelewis Myr Td 36 B4
Treligga Cnwll 4 D4
Trelights Cnwll 4 C4
Trelill Cnwll 4 D4
Trelinnoe Cnwll 5 G4
Trelion Cnwll 3 G5
Trelissick Cnwll 3 F4
Trelissick Garden Cnwll 3 F4
Trelleck Mons 37 F5
Trelleck Grange Mons 37 F4
Trelogan Flints 80 C3
Trelonk Cnwll 3 F4
Trelow Cnwll 4 C3
Trelowarren Cnwll 3 E2
Trelowia Cnwll 5 F2
Treluggan Cnwll 3 F4
Trelystan Powys 56 C6
Tremadog Gwynd 67 E4
Tremail Cnwll 5 E5
Tremain Cerdgn 42 C4
Tremaine Cnwll 5 F5
Tremar Cnwll 5 F3
Trematon Cnwll 5 G2
Trembraze Cnwll 5 F2
Tremeirchion Denbgs 80 C2
Tremethick Cross Cnwll 2 B3
Tremollett Cnwll 5 F3
Tremore Cnwll 4 D2
Trenance Cnwll 3 E2
Trenance Cnwll 4 B3
Trenance Cnwll 4 C3
Trenance Cnwll 2 D2
Trenarren Cnwll 3 H5
Trenault Cnwll 5 F4
Trench Shrops 70 B1
Trench Green Oxon 41 E2
Trencreek Cnwll 4 B2
Trencreek Cnwll 5 E6
Trendeal Cnwll 3 F5
Trendrine Cnwll 2 B4
Treneague Cnwll 4 C3
Trenear Cnwll 2 D3
Treneglos Cnwll 5 F5
Trenerth Cnwll 2 D3
Trenewan Cnwll 5 E1
Trenewth Cnwll 4 D4
Trengune Cnwll 5 E5
Treninnick Cnwll 4 B2
Trenowah Cnwll 4 B2
Trenoweth Cnwll 3 E3
Trent Dorset 24 B1
Trent Port Lincs 85 F3
Trent Vale Staffs 70 D4
Trentham Staffs 70 D4
Trentishoe Devon 21 G5
Trentlock Derbys 72 C3
Treoes V Glam 35 G2
Treorchy Rhondd 35 G4
Trequite Cnwll 4 D4
Trerhyngyll V Glam 35 G2
Trerulefoot Cnwll 5 G2
Tresahor Cnwll 3 E3
Tresawle Cnwll 3 F4
Tresco Heliport IOS 2 a2
Trescott Staffs 58 A5
Trescowe Cnwll 2 C3
Tresean Cnwll 4 B2
Tresham Gloucs 38 C3
Tresillian Cnwll 3 F4
Tresinney Cnwll 5 E4
Treskinnick Cross Cnwll 5 F6
Treslea Cnwll 5 E3
Tresmeer Cnwll 5 F5
Tresparrett Cnwll 5 E5
Tressait P & K 139 E6
Tresta Shet 169 h3
Tresta Shet 169 j4
Treswell Notts 85 E3
Treswithian Cnwll 2 D4
Trethawle Cnwll 5 F2
Trethevey Cnwll 4 D5
Trethewey Cnwll 2 A2
Trethomas Caerph 36 C3
Trethosa Cnwll 3 G5
Trethurgy Cnwll 3 H5
Tretio Pembks 32 B5
Tretire Herefs 45 H2
Tretower Powys 45 E1
Treuddyn Flints 69 E6
Trevadlock Cnwll 5 F4
Trevague Cnwll 5 F4
Trevalga Cnwll 4 D5
Trevalyn Wrexhm 69 F6
Trevanger Cnwll 4 C4
Trevanson Cnwll 4 C3
Trevarrack Cnwll 2 B3
Trevarren Cnwll 4 C2
Trevarrian Cnwll 4 B2
Trevarrick Cnwll 3 G4
Trevarth Cnwll 3 E4
Trevaughan Carmth 33 F3
Treveal Cnwll 2 B4
Treveal Cnwll 4 B2
Treveale Cnwll 3 F5
Treveighan Cnwll 4 D4
Trevellas Downs Cnwll 3 E5
Trevelmond Cnwll 5 F2
Trevemper Cnwll 4 B2
Treveneague Cnwll 2 C3
Treveor Cnwll 3 G4
Treverbyn Cnwll 3 F5
Treverbyn Cnwll 3 H5
Treverva Cnwll 3 E3
Trevescan Cnwll 2 A2
Trevethin Torfn 36 D4
Trevia Cnwll 5 E4
Trevigro Cnwll 5 G3
Trevilla Cnwll 3 F4
Trevilledor Cnwll 4 C3
Trevilson Cnwll 3 F5
Treviscoe Cnwll 3 G5
Treviskey Cnwll 3 G4
Trevissick Cnwll 3 H5
Trevithal Cnwll 2 B2
Trevithick Cnwll 4 B2
Trevithick Cnwll 3 G4
Trevivian Cnwll 5 E4
Trevoll Cnwll 4 B2
Trevone Cnwll 4 C3
Trevor Denbgs 69 E4
Trevorgans Cnwll 2 B2
Trevorrick Cnwll 4 B3
Trevorrick Cnwll 4 C3
Trevose Cnwll 4 B3
Trew Cnwll 2 D3
Trewalder Cnwll 4 D4
Trewalkin Powys 44 D2
Trewarlett Cnwll 5 G4
Trewarmett Cnwll 4 D5
Trewarthenick Cnwll 3 F4
Trewassa Cnwll 5 E5
Trewavas Cnwll 2 D2
Treween Cnwll 5 F4
Trewellard Cnwll 2 A3
Trewen Cnwll 5 F4
Trewen Cnwll 4 D4
Trewennack Cnwll 2 D3
Trewent Pembks 32 D1
Trewern Powys 69 E1
Trewetha Cnwll 4 D4
Trewethern Cnwll 4 D4
Trewidland Cnwll 5 F2
Trewillis Cnwll 3 E1
Trewince Cnwll 3 F3
Trewint Cnwll 5 E3
Trewint Cnwll 5 F4
Trewint Cnwll 5 F2
Trewirgie Cnwll 3 F4
Trewithian Cnwll 3 F3
Trewoodloe Cnwll 5 G3
Trewoofe Cnwll 2 B2
Trewoon Cnwll 2 D2
Trewoon Cnwll 3 G5
Treworgan Cnwll 3 F5
Treworlas Cnwll 3 F4
Treworld Cnwll 5 E5
Treworthal Cnwll 3 F4
Treyarnon Cnwll 4 B3
Treyford W Susx 15 F5
Triangle W York 90 B2
Trickett's Cross Dorset 13 E5
Triermain Cumb 112 C1
Triffleton Pembks 32 D4
Trillacott Cnwll 5 F5
Trimdon Dur 106 C4
Trimdon Colliery Dur 106 C4
Trimdon Grange Dur 106 C4
Trimingham Norfk 77 F4
Trimley Suffk 53 F4
Trimley Lower Street Suffk 53 F4
Trimpley Worcs 57 H3
Trims Green Herts 51 F2
Trimsaran Carmth 34 B5
Trimstone Devon 21 E5
Trinafour P & K 138 D6
Trinant Caerph 36 C4
Tring Herts 41 G5
Tring Wharf Herts 41 G6
Tringford Herts 41 G6
Trinity Angus 141 F6
Trinity Jersey 174 c3
Trinity Gask P & K 139 G2
Triscombe Somset 22 B3
Triscombe Somset 22 D3
Trislaig Highld 144 C2
Trispen Cnwll 3 F5
Tritlington Nthumb 114 D5
Troan Cnwll 4 C2
Trochry P & K 139 G4
Troedrhiwfuwch Caerph 36 B5
Troedyraur Cerdgn 42 C4
Troedyrhiw Myr Td 36 B4
Trofarth Conwy 80 A2
Trois Bois Jersey 174 b2
Troon Cnwll 2 D4
Troon S Ayrs 119 E2
Tropical World Roundhay Park W York 90 D3
Troston Suffk 64 B3
Troswell Cnwll 5 F5
Trotshill Worcs 46 D5
Trottiscliffe Kent 29 G2
Trotton W Susx 27 F1
Trough Gate Lancs 89 G2
Troughend Nthumb 113 F4
Troutbeck Cumb 103 H3
Troutbeck Cumb 95 E5
Troutbeck Bridge Cumb 95 E5
Troway Derbys 84 B3
Trowbridge Wilts 24 D5
Trowell Notts 72 C4
Trowle Common Wilts 24 D5
Trowse Newton Norfk 65 E6
Troy W York 90 D3
Trudoxhill Somset 24 C4
Trull Somset 23 E1
Trumfleet S York 84 D6
Trumpan Highld 150 B5
Trumpet Herefs 46 B3
Trumpington Cambs 51 E6
Trumpsgreen Surrey 27 H6
Trunch Norfk 77 F5
Trunnah Lancs 88 B4
Truro Cnwll 3 F4
Truro Cathedral Cnwll 3 F4
Truscott Cnwll 5 F4
Trusham Devon 9 E3
Trusley Derbys 71 G4
Trusthorpe Lincs 87 E3
Trysull Staffs 58 B5
Tubney Oxon 40 C4
Tuckenhay Devon 7 E3
Tuckhill Shrops 57 H4
Tuckingmill Cnwll 2 D4
Tuckingmill Wilts 25 E2
Tuckton Dorset 13 E4
Tucoyse Cnwll 3 G4
Tuddenham Suffk 63 F2
Tuddenham Suffk 53 E6
Tudeley Kent 17 G6
Tudhoe Dur 106 B4
Tudorville Herefs 46 B1
Tudweiloig Gwynd 66 B4
Tuesley Surrey 27 H3
Tuffley Gloucs 38 C6
Tufton Hants 26 C4
Tufton Pembks 33 E4
Tugby Leics 60 D5
Tugford Shrops 57 F4
Tughall Nthumb 125 E4
Tullibody Clacks 131 E5
Tullich Highld 155 E2
Tullich Highld 163 E1
Tulliemet P & K 139 G5
Tulloch Abers 158 D2
Tulloch Stirlg 138 B2
Tulloch Station Highld 145 F2
Tullochgorm Ag & B 128 A5
Tullybeagles Lodge P & K 139 G3
Tullynessle Abers 158 B1
Tulse Hill Gt Lon 28 D3
Tumble Carmth 34 C5
Tumbler's Green Essex 52 B3
Tumby Lincs 74 C6
Tumby Woodside Lincs 74 C6
Tummel Bridge P & K 139 E6
Tunbridge Wells Kent 17 G5
Tundergarth D & G 111 F3
Tungate Norfk 77 F3
Tunley Somset 24 C5
Tunstall E R Yk 93 G3
Tunstall Kent 30 C2
Tunstall Lancs 95 G2
Tunstall N York 97 E4
Tunstall Norfk 65 G6
Tunstall Staffs 70 C3
Tunstall Staffs 70 D5
Tunstall Suffk 65 F1
Tunstall T & W 106 C6
Tunstead Derbys 83 F2
Tunstead Norfk 77 F2
Tunstead Milton Derbys 83 E3
Tunworth Hants 27 E4
Tupsley Herefs 45 H3
Tur Langton Leics 60 C5
Turgis Green Hants 27 E5
Turkdean Gloucs 39 F6
Turleigh Wilts 24 D5
Turleygreen Shrops 57 H4
Turn Lancs 89 F1
Turnastone Herefs 45 F3
Turnberry S Ayrs 108 D5
Turnchapel Devon 6 B3
Turnditch Derbys 71 H5
Turner Green Lancs 88 D3
Turner's Green E Susx 17 G3
Turner's Green Warwks 59 E2
Turner's Hill W Susx 16 D5
Turners Puddle Dorset 12 B4
Turnford Herts 50 D1
Turnhouse C Edin 131 H2
Turnworth Dorset 12 B5
Turriff Abers 158 C4
Turton Bottoms Gt Man 89 F1
Turves Cambs 62 C5
Turvey Beds 49 G4
Turville Bucks 41 F3
Turville Heath Bucks 41 F3
Turweston Bucks 48 D3
Tushielaw Inn Border 121 G1
Tushingham cum Grindley Ches 69 G5

Tutbury Walditch
316

Tutbury Staffs 71 G3
Tutnall Worcs 58 C2
Tutshill Gloucs 37 F4
Tuttington Norfk 77 E3
Tutwell Cnwll 5 G3
Tuxford Notts 85 E2
Twatt Ork 169 a3
Twatt Shet 169 h3
Twechar E Duns 130 C3
Tweedmouth Nthumb 123 G5
Tweedsmuir Border 121 E2
Twelve Oaks E Susx 17 H3
Twelveheads Cnwll 3 E4
Twemlow Green Ches 82 C1
Twenty Lincs 74 B2
Twerton Somset 24 C6
Twickenham Gt Lon 28 C3
Twigworth Gloucs 46 D1
Twineham W Susx 16 C3
Twineham Green W Susx 16 C3
Twinhoe Somset 24 C5
Twinstead Essex 52 B4
Twitchen Devon 21 H4
Twitchen Shrops 56 D3
Twitham Kent 31 F2
Two Bridges Devon 8 C2
Two Dales Derbys 83 H1
Two Gates Staffs 59 E5
Two Mile Oak Cross Devon 7 F4
Two Pots Devon 21 E5
Two Waters Herts 50 B1
Twycross Leics 59 F6
Twycross Zoo Leics 59 F6
Twyford Berks 41 F2
Twyford Bucks 49 E2
Twyford Hants 26 C2
Twyford Leics 73 E1
Twyford Lincs 73 G2
Twyford Norfk 76 C2
Twyford Common Herefs 45 H3
Twyn-carno Caerph 36 B5
Twyn-y-Sheriff Mons 37 E5
Twyn-yr-Odyn V Glam 36 B2
Twynholm D & G 101 H5
Twyning Gloucs 46 D3
Twyning Green Gloucs 47 E3
Twynllanan Carmth 43 H2
Twywell Nhants 61 E3
Ty'n-dwr Denbgs 69 E4
Ty'n-y-bryn Rhondd 35 G3
Ty'n-y-coedcae Caerph 36 C3
Ty'n-y-Groes Conwy 79 G2
Ty-nant Conwy 68 B4
Ty-nant Gwynd 68 A3
Tyberton Herefs 45 G3
Tyburn W Mids 58 D4
Tycroes Carmth 34 D5
Tycrwyn Powys 68 C2
Tydd Gote Lincs 75 E2
Tydd St Giles Cambs 75 E2
Tydd St Mary Lincs 75 E2
Tye Hants 15 E4
Tye Green Essex 51 F3
Tye Green Essex 51 G4
Tye Green Essex 52 A3
Tyersal W York 90 C3
Tyldesley Gt Man 82 B5
Tyler Hill Kent 31 E2
Tyler's Green Essex 51 F1
Tylers Green Bucks 41 G4
Tylers Green Surrey 28 D1
Tylorstown Rhondd 35 G4
Tylwch Powys 55 G3
Tyn-y-nant Rhondd 36 B3
Tyndrum Stirlg 137 H3
Tynemouth T & W 115 E2
Tynewydd Rhondd 35 G4
Tyninghame E Loth 133 E3
Tynron D & G 110 C4
Tynygongl IOA 79 E3
Tynygraig Cerdgn 54 D2
Tyringham Bucks 49 G4
Tyseley W Mids 58 D4
Tythegston Brdgnd 35 F2
Tytherington Ches 82 D2
Tytherington Gloucs 38 A3
Tytherington Somset 24 C4
Tytherington Wilts 25 E3
Tytherleigh Devon 10 D5
Tytherton Lucas Wilts 38 D2
Tywardreath Cnwll 4 D1
Tywardreath Highway Cnwll 4 D1
Tywyn Conwy 79 G2
Tywyn Gwynd 54 C5

U

Ubbeston Green Suffk 65 F2
Ubley Somset 23 H5
Uckerby N York 97 F5
Uckfield E Susx 17 F3
Uckinghall Worcs 46 D3
Uckington Gloucs 47 E2
Uckington Shrops 69 H1
Uddingston S Lans 120 B5
Uddington S Lans 120 C3
Udimore E Susx 18 B3
Udny Green Abers 159 E2
Udny Station Abers 159 E1
Uffcott Wilts 39 F2
Uffculme Devon 10 A6
Uffington Lincs 61 F6
Uffington Oxon 39 H3
Uffington Shrops 69 G1
Ufford Cambs 61 G6
Ufford Suffk 53 F6
Ufton Warwks 48 B5
Ufton Nervet Berks 27 E6
Ugadale Ag & B 117 G3
Ugborough Devon 6 D3
Uggeshall Suffk 65 G3
Ugglebarnby N York 107 H1
Ughill Derbys 83 G4
Ugley Essex 51 F4
Ugley Green Essex 51 F4
Ugthorpe N York 107 G2
Uig Ag & B 134 D5
Uig Highld 150 B4
Uig Highld 150 D5
Uig W Isls 168 d8
Uigshader Highld 150 D3
Uisken Ag & B 135 F1
Ulbster Highld 167 G2
Ulcat Row Cumb 103 H2
Ulceby Lincs 93 E1
Ulceby Lincs 87 E2
Ulceby Cross Lincs 86 D2
Ulceby Skitter Lincs 93 E1
Ulcombe Kent 30 B1
Uldale Cumb 103 E4
Uley Gloucs 38 C4
Ulgham Nthumb 114 D5
Ullapool Highld 161 E3
Ullenhall Warwks 58 D2
Ullenwood Gloucs 38 D6
Ulleskelf N York 91 F4
Ullesthorpe Leics 59 H4
Ulley S York 84 B3
Ullingswick Herefs 46 B4
Ullinish Lodge Hotel Highld 150 C2
Ullock Cumb 103 E2
Ulpha Cumb 94 C4
Ulpha Cumb 95 E3
Ulrome E R Yk 93 E5
Ulsta Shet 169 j4
Ulting Wick Essex 52 B2
Ulverley Green W Mids 58 D4
Ulverston Cumb 94 D3
Ulwell Dorset 12 D3
Umachan Highld 151 F4
Umberleigh Devon 21 F3
Unapool Highld 164 C2
Under Burnmouth Border 112 B3
Under River Kent 29 F1
Underbarrow Cumb 95 E4
Undercliffe W York 90 C3
Underdale Shrops 69 G1
Underley Hall Cumb 95 G3
Underling Green Kent 18 A6
Underwood Notts 72 B5
Undley Suffk 63 F3
Undy Mons 37 E3
Union Mills IOM 174 l3
Union Street E Susx 17 H4
Unstone Derbys 84 A2
Unstone Green Derbys 84 A2
Unsworth Gt Man 82 C5
Unthank Cumb 103 H5
Unthank Cumb 104 A4
Unthank Cumb 104 C4
Unthank Derbys 83 H2
Unthank Nthumb 123 G4
Unthank End Cumb 104 A4
Up Cerne Dorset 11 G5
Up Exe Devon 9 F5
Up Holland Lancs 81 G5
Up Marden W Susx 15 F5
Up Mudford Somset 24 A1
Up Nately Hants 27 E4
Up Somborne Hants 26 B2
Up Sydling Dorset 11 G5
Upavon Wilts 25 G5
Upchurch Kent 30 B3
Upcott Devon 21 F4
Upcott Devon 21 H3
Upcott Herefs 45 F4
Upcott Somset 22 B2
Updown Hill Surrey 27 G6
Upend Cambs 63 F1
Upgate Norfk 76 D2
Upgate Street Norfk 64 C5
Upgate Street Norfk 65 E4
Uphall Dorset 11 F5
Uphall W Loth 131 G2
Upham Devon 9 F5
Upham Hants 14 D6
Uphampton Herefs 56 D2
Uphampton Worcs 58 A2
Uphill Somset 23 F5
Uplawmoor E Rens 119 F5
Upleadon Gloucs 46 C2
Upleatham N York 107 F3
Uplees Kent 30 D2
Uploders Dorset 11 E4
Uplowman Devon 9 G6
Uplyme Devon 10 D4
Upminster Gt Lon 29 F5
Upottery Devon 10 B5
Uppaton Devon 8 A3
Upper & Lower Stondon Beds 50 B4
Upper Affcot Shrops 57 E4
Upper Ardchronie Highld 162 C3
Upper Arley Worcs 57 H3
Upper Arncott Oxon 40 D6
Upper Astrop Nhants 48 C3
Upper Basildon Berks 40 D2
Upper Batley W York 90 D2
Upper Beeding W Susx 16 C2
Upper Benefield Nhants 61 F4
Upper Bentley Worcs 58 C2
Upper Bighouse Highld 166 C4
Upper Birchwood Derbys 72 B5
Upper Boat Rhondd 36 B3
Upper Boddington Nhants 48 C4
Upper Borth Cerdgn 54 D4
Upper Brailes Warwks 48 A3
Upper Breakish Highld 151 G1
Upper Breinton Herefs 45 G3
Upper Broadheath Worcs 46 D5
Upper Broughton Notts 72 D3
Upper Bucklebury Berks 40 D1
Upper Burgate Hants 13 E6
Upper Bush Kent 29 H3
Upper Caldecote Beds 50 C5
Upper Canada Somset 23 F5
Upper Canterton Hants 13 F6
Upper Catesby Nhants 48 C5
Upper Catshill Worcs 58 C3
Upper Chapel Powys 44 C3
Upper Cheddon Somset 23 E2
Upper Chicksgrove Wilts 25 E2
Upper Chute Wilts 26 A5
Upper Clapton Gt Lon 28 D5
Upper Clatford Hants 26 B4
Upper Clynnog Gwynd 66 D5
Upper Coberley Gloucs 38 D6
Upper Cokeham W Susx 16 C2
Upper Cotton Staffs 71 E5
Upper Cound Shrops 57 F6
Upper Cudworth S York 84 B6
Upper Cumberworth W York 83 G6
Upper Cwmtwrch Powys 35 E5
Upper Dallachy Moray 157 F5
Upper Deal Kent 31 G1
Upper Dean Beds 61 F2
Upper Denby W York 83 G5
Upper Denton Cumb 112 C1
Upper Dicker E Susx 17 F2
Upper Dinchope Shrops 57 E4
Upper Dounreay Highld 166 D5
Upper Dovercourt Essex 53 F4
Upper Drumbane Stirlg 130 C6
Upper Dunsforth N York 91 E6
Upper Eashing Surrey 27 H4
Upper Eathie Highld 155 F5
Upper Egleton Herefs 46 B4
Upper Elkstone Staffs 71 E6
Upper Ellastone Staffs 71 F4
Upper End Derbys 83 F2
Upper Enham Hants 26 B4
Upper Farmcote Shrops 57 H5
Upper Farringdon Hants 27 E3
Upper Framilode Gloucs 38 B5
Upper Froyle Hants 27 F3
Upper Godney Somset 23 H3
Upper Gravenhurst Beds 50 B4
Upper Green Berks 26 B6
Upper Green Essex 51 G4
Upper Green Mons 45 G1
Upper Green Suffk 63 G2
Upper Grove Common Herefs 46 A2
Upper Hackney Derbys 71 H6
Upper Hale Surrey 27 F4
Upper Halliford Surrey 28 B3
Upper Halling Kent 29 H2
Upper Hambleton Rutlnd 61 E6
Upper Harbledown Kent 31 E2
Upper Hardres Court Kent 31 E1
Upper Hardwick Herefs 45 G5
Upper Hartfield E Susx 17 E5
Upper Hartshay Derbys 72 B5
Upper Hatherley Gloucs 47 E1
Upper Hatton Staffs 70 C4
Upper Haugh S York 84 B4
Upper Hayton Shrops 57 E3
Upper Heaton W York 90 C1
Upper Helmsley N York 91 H5
Upper Hergest Herefs 45 E5
Upper Heyford Nhants 49 E5
Upper Heyford Oxon 48 C2
Upper Hill Herefs 45 G4
Upper Hockenden Kent 29 F3
Upper Hopton W York 90 C1
Upper Howsell Worcs 46 C4
Upper Hulme Staffs 71 E6
Upper Ifold Surrey 16 A5
Upper Inglesham Wilts 39 G4
Upper Kilcott Gloucs 38 C3
Upper Killay Swans 34 C3
Upper Kinchrackine Ag & B 137 F2
Upper Lambourn Berks 40 A2
Upper Landywood Staffs 58 C6
Upper Langford Somset 23 G5
Upper Langwith Derbys 84 C2
Upper Largo Fife 132 C5
Upper Leigh Staffs 71 E4
Upper Ley Gloucs 38 B6
Upper Littleton Somset 24 A6
Upper Longdon Staffs 71 F1
Upper Ludstone Shrops 58 A5
Upper Lybster Highld 167 F2
Upper Lydbrook Gloucs 37 G6
Upper Lyde Herefs 45 H4
Upper Lye Herefs 56 D2
Upper Maes-coed Herefs 45 F3
Upper Midhope Derbys 83 G5
Upper Milton Worcs 58 A3
Upper Minety Wilts 39 E3
Upper Moor Worcs 47 E4
Upper Moor Side W York 90 D3
Upper Mulben Moray 157 F4
Upper Netchwood Shrops 57 F5
Upper Nobut Staffs 71 E3
Upper Norwood W Susx 15 G5
Upper Padley Derbys 83 G3
Upper Pennington Hants 13 G4
Upper Pickwick Wilts 38 C1
Upper Pollicott Bucks 41 E6
Upper Poppleton N York 91 G5
Upper Quinton Warwks 47 G4
Upper Ratley Hants 26 B2
Upper Rochford Worcs 57 F2
Upper Ruscoe D & G 109 G1
Upper Sapey Herefs 57 G2
Upper Seagry Wilts 38 D2
Upper Shelton Beds 49 H3
Upper Sheringham Norfk 76 D4
Upper Shuckburgh Warwks 48 C5
Upper Skelmorlie N Ayrs 128 C2
Upper Slaughter Gloucs 47 G1
Upper Soudley Gloucs 37 H5
Upper Spond Herefs 45 F4
Upper Standen Kent 19 F5
Upper Staploe Beds 61 G1
Upper Stepford D & G 110 C3
Upper Stoke Norfk 65 E6
Upper Stowe Nhants 49 E5
Upper Street Hants 25 G1
Upper Street Norfk 77 F2
Upper Street Norfk 77 F2
Upper Street Norfk 64 D3
Upper Street Suffk 52 A6
Upper Street Suffk 53 E6
Upper Street Suffk 53 E4
Upper Strensham Worcs 46 D3
Upper Sundon Beds 50 A3
Upper Swell Gloucs 47 G2
Upper Tankersley S York 84 A5
Upper Tasburgh Norfk 65 E5
Upper Tean Staffs 71 E4
Upper Threapwood Ches 69 G4
Upper Town Derbys 71 G5
Upper Town Derbys 71 G6
Upper Town Dur 105 G4
Upper Town Herefs 46 A4
Upper Town Somset 23 H6
Upper Town Suffk 64 B2
Upper Tumble Carmth 34 C5
Upper Tysoe Warwks 48 B4
Upper Ufford Suffk 53 F6
Upper Upham Wilts 39 G2
Upper Upnor Kent 30 A3
Upper Victoria Angus 141 E3
Upper Vobster Somset 24 C4
Upper Wardington Oxon 48 C4
Upper Weald Bucks 49 F3
Upper Weedon Nhants 48 D5
Upper Wellingham E Susx 17 E3
Upper Weston Somset 24 C6
Upper Weybread Suffk 65 E3
Upper Wick Worcs 46 D4
Upper Wield Hants 26 D3
Upper Winchendon Bucks 41 F6
Upper Woodford Wilts 25 G3
Upper Wootton Hants 26 D5
Upper Wraxall Wilts 38 C2
Upper Wyche Worcs 46 C4
Upperby Cumb 103 H5
Upperglen Highld 150 C4
Uppermill Gt Man 83 E5
Upperthong W York 83 F5
Upperthorpe Derbys 84 B3
Upperthorpe Lincs 85 E5
Upperton W Susx 27 H1
Uppertown Derbys 83 H1
Uppertown Highld 167 G6
Upperup Gloucs 39 E4
Upperwood Derbys 71 H6
Uppincott Devon 9 F5
Uppingham Rutlnd 61 E5
Uppington Dorset 12 D5
Uppington Shrops 70 A1
Upsall N York 97 H3
Upsettlington Border 123 F4
Upshire Essex 29 E6
Upstreet Kent 31 F2
Upthorpe Suffk 64 B3
Upton Berks 41 H2
Upton Bucks 41 F5
Upton Cambs 61 G5
Upton Cambs 61 H3
Upton Ches 81 F2
Upton Ches 81 G3
Upton Cnwll 20 B1
Upton Cnwll 5 F3
Upton Cumb 103 G4
Upton Devon 10 A5
Upton Devon 6 D2
Upton Dorset 11 H3
Upton Dorset 12 D4
Upton E R Yk 93 E5
Upton Hants 26 B5
Upton Hants 14 B5
Upton Leics 59 F5
Upton Lincs 85 F3
Upton Mersyd 81 E3
Upton Nhants 49 E5
Upton Norfk 77 G1
Upton Notts 73 E5
Upton Notts 85 E2
Upton Oxon 39 G6
Upton Oxon 40 C3
Upton Pembks 32 D2
Upton Somset 22 C2
Upton Somset 23 G2
Upton W York 84 B6
Upton Warwks 47 G5
Upton Wilts 24 D2
Upton Bishop Herefs 46 B2
Upton Cheyney Gloucs 38 B1
Upton Cressett Shrops 57 G5
Upton Crews Herefs 46 B2
Upton Cross Cnwll 5 F3
Upton End Beds 50 B4
Upton Grey Hants 27 E4
Upton Heath Ches 81 F2
Upton Hellions Devon 9 E5
Upton Lovell Wilts 25 E3
Upton Magna Shrops 69 H1
Upton Noble Somset 24 C3
Upton Pyne Devon 9 F4
Upton Scudamore Wilts 24 D4
Upton Snodsbury Worcs 47 E5
Upton St Leonards Gloucs 38 C6
Upton Towans Cnwll 2 C4
Upton upon Severn Worcs 46 D3
Upton Warren Worcs 58 B2
Upwaltham W Susx 15 G5
Upware Cambs 63 E2
Upwell Norfk 62 D6
Upwey Dorset 11 G3
Upwick Green Herts 51 E3
Upwood Cambs 62 B4
Urchfont Wilts 25 F5
Urdimarsh Herefs 45 H4
Ure Bank N York 97 F2
Urlay Nook Dur 106 C2
Urmston Gt Man 82 C4
Urquhart Moray 157 E5
Urra N York 98 A5
Urray Highld 154 C4
Usan Angus 141 G5
Ushaw Moor Dur 106 B5
Usk Mons 37 E4
Usselby Lincs 86 A4
Usworth T & W 115 E1
Utkinton Ches 81 H1
Utley W York 90 B4
Uton Devon 9 E4
Utterby Lincs 86 C4
Uttoxeter Staffs 71 F3
Uwchmynydd Gwynd 66 A3
Uxbridge Gt Lon 28 B4
Uyeasound Shet 169 j5
Uzmaston Pembks 32 D3

V

Vale Guern 174 g3
Vale of Rheidol Railway Cerdgn 55 E3
Valley IOA 78 C3
Valley End Surrey 27 H6
Valley Truckle Cnwll 5 E4
Valtos Highld 151 E5
Valtos W Isls 168 d8
Van Caerph 36 C3
Vange Essex 29 H5
Varteg Torfn 36 D5
Vatsetter Shet 169 j4
Vatten Highld 150 C3
Vaynor Myr Td 36 B5
Vazon Bay Guern 174 f2
Velindre Powys 45 E3
Vellow Somset 22 D3
Velly Devon 20 C3
Venn Cnwll 20 C1
Venn Devon 7 F3
Venn Ottery Devon 10 A4
Venngreen Devon 20 D2
Vennington Shrops 69 F1
Venny Tedburn Devon 9 E4
Venterdon Cnwll 5 G3
Ventnor IOW 14 D1
Venton Devon 6 C3
Vernham Dean Hants 26 B5
Vernham Street Hants 26 B5
Vernolds Common Shrops 57 E3
Verwood Dorset 13 E5
Veryan Cnwll 3 G4
Veryan Green Cnwll 3 G4
Vickerstown Cumb 94 C2
Victoria Blae G 36 C5
Victoria Cnwll 4 C2
Victoria S York 83 G5
Vidlin Shet 169 j3
Viewfield Moray 157 E5
Viewpark N Lans 120 B6
Vigo Kent 29 G2
Ville la Bas Jersey 174 a3
Villiaze Guern 174 f1
Vinehall Street E Susx 18 A3
Vines Cross E Susx 17 G3
Virginia Water Surrey 28 A3
Virginstow Devon 5 G5
Virley Essex 52 C2
Vobster Somset 24 C4
Voe Shet 169 h3
Vowchurch Herefs 45 F3
Vulcan Village Lancs 81 H4

W

Wackerfield Dur 106 A3
Wacton Norfk 64 D5
Wadborough Worcs 47 E4
Waddesdon Bucks 41 F6
Waddeton Devon 7 F3
Waddicar Mersyd 81 F5
Waddingham Lincs 85 G4
Waddington Lancs 89 F4
Waddington Lincs 85 G1
Waddon Devon 9 F2
Waddon Dorset 11 F3
Wadebridge Cnwll 4 D3
Wadeford Somset 10 C6
Wadenhoe Nhants 61 F4
Wadesmill Herts 50 D2
Wadhurst E Susx 17 G5
Wadshelf Derbys 83 H2
Wadswick Wilts 24 D6
Wadworth S York 84 C4
Waen Denbgs 80 B1
Waen Denbgs 80 C1
Waen Powys 69 E2
Waen Fach Powys 68 D2
Waen-pentir Gwynd 79 E1
Waen-wen Gwynd 79 E1
Wagbeach Shrops 56 D6
Wainfelin Torfn 36 D4
Wainfleet All Saints Lincs 75 E6
Wainfleet Bank Lincs 75 E6
Wainford Norfk 65 F4
Wainhouse Corner Cnwll 5 E5
Wains Hill Somset 37 E1
Wainscott Kent 30 A3
Wainstalls W York 90 B2
Waitby Cumb 95 H6
Waithe Lincs 86 C5
Wake Green W Mids 58 D4
Wakefield W York 90 D2
Wakerley Nhants 61 E5
Wakes Colne Essex 52 C4
Wal-wen Flints 80 D2
Wal-wen Flints 80 D2
Walberswick Suffk 65 G3
Walberton W Susx 15 H4
Walbottle T & W 114 C2
Walbutt D & G 110 B2
Walby Cumb 104 A6
Walcombe Somset 24 A4
Walcot Lincs 92 C2
Walcot Lincs 74 A3
Walcot Shrops 69 H1
Walcot Shrops 56 D4
Walcot Warwks 47 G5
Walcot Wilts 39 F3
Walcot Green Norfk 64 D3
Walcote Leics 60 B4
Walcott Lincs 74 B6
Walcott Norfk 77 F3
Walden N York 96 C3
Walden Head N York 96 C3
Walden Stubbs N York 91 G1
Walderslade Kent 30 A2
Walderton W Susx 15 F5
Walditch Dorset 11 E4

Waldley West End 317

Waldley Derbys 71 F4
Waldridge Dur 106 B6
Waldringfield Suffk 53 F5
Waldron E Susx 17 F3
Wales S York 84 C3
Wales Somset 24 A2
Walesby Lincs 86 B4
Walesby Notts 84 D2
Walford Herefs 56 D3
Walford Herefs 46 A1
Walford Shrops 69 G2
Walford Staffs 70 C3
Walford Heath Shrops 69 G2
Walgherton Ches 70 B5
Walgrave Nhants 60 D2
Walhampton Hants 13 G4
Walk Mill Lancs 89 G2
Walkden Gt Man 82 B5
Walker T & W 114 D2
Walker Fold Lancs 89 E4
Walker's Green Herefs 45 H4
Walker's Heath W Mids 58 C3
Walkerburn Border 121 H3
Walkeringham Notts 85 E4
Walkerith Lincs 85 E4
Walkern Herts 50 D3
Walkerton Fife 132 A5
Walkford Dorset 13 F4
Walkhampton Devon 6 C5
Walkington E R Yk 92 D3
Walkley S York 84 A3
Walkwood Worcs 58 C2
Wall Cnwll 2 D3
Wall Nthumb 113 F2
Wall Staffs 58 D6
Wall End Cumb 94 C3
Wall End Herefs 45 G5
Wall Heath W Mids 58 B4
Wall Houses Nthumb 114 B2
Wall under Haywood Shrops 57 E5
Wallacetown S Ayrs 109 E5
Wallacetown S Ayrs 119 E2
Wallands Park E Susx 17 E2
Wallasey Mersyd 81 E4
Wallend Kent 30 B4
Waller's Green Herefs 46 B3
Wallhead Cumb 104 A6
Wallingford Oxon 40 D3
Wallington Gt Lon 28 D2
Wallington Hants 14 D4
Wallington Herts 50 D4
Wallington Heath W Mids 58 C6
Wallis Pembks 32 D4
Wallisdown Dorset 12 D4
Walliswood W Susx 16 B5
Walls Shet 169 g3
Wallsend T & W 115 E2
Wallthwaite Cumb 103 G3
Wallyford E Loth 132 C2
Walmer Kent 31 G1
Walmer Bridge Lancs 88 C2
Walmersley Gt Man 82 C6
Walmestone Kent 31 F2
Walmley W Mids 58 D5
Walmley Ash W Mids 58 D5
Walmsgate Lincs 86 D2
Walpole Somset 23 F3
Walpole Suffk 65 F3
Walpole Cross Keys Norfk 75 E2
Walpole Highway Norfk 75 E1
Walpole St Andrew Norfk 75 E2
Walpole St Peter Norfk 75 E2
Walrow Somset 23 F4
Walsall W Mids 58 C5
Walsall Wood W Mids 58 C6
Walsden W York 89 H2
Walsgrave on Sowe W Mids 59 G3
Walsham le Willows Suffk 64 C2
Walshaw Gt Man 82 C6
Walshaw W York 89 H3
Walshford N York 91 E5
Walsoken Norfk 75 E1
Walston S Lans 121 E4
Walsworth Herts 50 C4
Walter's Ash Bucks 41 F4
Walters Green Kent 17 F5
Walterston V Glam 36 B1
Walterstone Herefs 45 F2
Waltham Kent 31 E1
Waltham Lincs 86 C5
Waltham Abbey Essex 29 E6
Waltham Chase Hants 14 D5
Waltham Cross Herts 28 D6
Waltham on the Wolds Leics 73 F2
Waltham St Lawrence Berks 41 F2
Waltham's Cross Essex 51 H4
Walton Bucks 49 G3
Walton Cambs 61 H6
Walton Cumb 112 B1
Walton Derbys 84 A2
Walton Leics 60 B4
Walton Powys 45 E5
Walton Shrops 69 H2
Walton Shrops 57 E3
Walton Somset 23 G3
Walton Staffs 70 D3
Walton Staffs 70 D3
Walton Suffk 53 F4
Walton W Susx 15 F4
Walton W York 91 E1
Walton W York 91 E4
Walton Warwks 48 A4
Walton Cardiff Gloucs 47 E2
Walton East Pembks 32 D4
Walton Elm Dorset 24 C1
Walton Grounds Nhants 48 C3
Walton on the Hill Surrey 28 C1
Walton on the Naze Essex 53 F3
Walton on the Wolds Leics 72 D2
Walton Park Somset 37 E1
Walton West Pembks 32 C3
Walton-in-Gordano Somset 37 E2
Walton-le-Dale Lancs 88 D2
Walton-on-Thames Surrey 28 B3
Walton-on-the-Hill Staffs 70 D2
Walton-on-Trent Derbys 71 G2
Walwen Flints 80 D2
Walwick Nthumb 113 F2
Walworth Dur 106 B3
Walworth Gt Lon 28 D4
Walworth Gate Dur 106 B3
Walwyn's Castle Pembks 32 C3
Wambrook Somset 10 C5
Wampool Cumb 103 F6
Wanborough Surrey 27 G4
Wanborough Wilts 39 G2
Wandon End Herts 50 B3
Wandsworth Gt Lon 28 C3
Wangford Suffk 65 G3
Wanlip Leics 72 D1
Wanlockhead D & G 110 C6
Wannock E Susx 17 G2
Wansford Cambs 61 G5
Wansford E R Yk 92 D5
Wanshurst Green Kent 18 A6
Wanstead Gt Lon 29 E5
Wanstrow Somset 24 C3
Wanswell Gloucs 38 B4
Wantage Oxon 40 B3
Wants Green Worcs 46 C5
Wapley Gloucs 38 B2
Wappenbury Warwks 59 G2
Wappenham Nhants 48 D4
Warbleton E Susx 17 G3
Warborough Oxon 40 D4
Warboys Cambs 62 B3
Warbreck Lancs 88 B3
Warbstow Cnwll 5 F5
Warburton Gt Man 82 B4
Warcop Cumb 104 D2
Ward End W Mids 58 D4
Ward Green Suffk 64 C2
Warden Kent 30 D3
Warden Nthumb 113 F1
Warden Law T & W 106 C6
Warden Street Beds 50 B5
Wardhedges Beds 50 B4
Wardington Oxon 48 C4
Wardle Ches 70 A6
Wardle Gt Man 89 G1
Wardley Gt Man 82 C5
Wardley Rutlnd 60 D5
Wardley T & W 115 E2
Wardlow Derbys 83 G2
Wardsend Ches 82 D3
Wardy Hill Cambs 62 D4
Ware Herts 50 D2
Ware Street Kent 30 B2
Wareham Dorset 12 C3
Warehorne Kent 18 C5
Waren Mill Nthumb 125 E4
Warenford Nthumb 124 D4
Warenton Nthumb 124 D4
Wareside Herts 51 E2
Waresley Cambs 50 C6
Waresley Worcs 58 A2
Warfield Berks 41 G1
Warfleet Devon 7 F3
Wargate Lincs 74 C3
Wargrave Berks 41 F2
Warham Herefs 45 H3
Warham All Saints Norfk 76 C4
Warham St Mary Norfk 76 B4
Wark Nthumb 123 E3
Wark Nthumb 113 F2
Warkleigh Devon 21 F3
Warkton Nhants 61 E3
Warkworth Nhants 48 C3
Warkworth Nthumb 125 F2
Warlaby N York 97 G4
Warland W York 89 H2
Warleggan Cnwll 5 E3
Warleigh Somset 24 C6
Warley Town W York 90 B2
Warlingham Surrey 29 E2
Warmanbie D & G 111 F2
Warmbrook Derbys 71 H5
Warmfield W York 91 E2
Warmingham Ches 70 B6
Warmington Nhants 61 G4
Warmington Warwks 48 B4
Warminster Wilts 24 D4
Warmley Gloucs 38 A2
Warmsworth S York 84 C5
Warmwell Dorset 12 A3
Warndon Worcs 46 D5
Warnford Hants 26 D1
Warnham W Susx 16 B5
Warnham Court W Susx 16 C5
Warningcamp W Susx 16 A2
Warninglid W Susx 16 C4
Warren Ches 82 D2
Warren Pembks 32 D1
Warren Row Berks 41 F2
Warren Street Kent 30 C1
Warren's Green Herts 50 D4
Warrenby N York 107 E3
Warrenhill S Lans 120 D3
Warrington Bucks 49 G5
Warrington Ches 82 A3
Warriston C Edin 132 B3
Warsash Hants 14 C4
Warslow Staffs 71 F6
Warsop Notts 84 C1
Warsop Vale Notts 84 C1
Warter E R Yk 92 C5
Warter Priory E R Yk 92 B4
Warthermaske N York 97 E3
Warthill N York 91 H5
Wartling E Susx 17 G2
Wartnaby Leics 73 E2
Warton Lancs 88 C2
Warton Lancs 95 F2
Warton Nthumb 113 G5
Warton Warwks 59 F6
Warwick Cumb 104 A6
Warwick Warwks 59 F2
Warwick Bridge Cumb 104 B6
Warwick Castle Warwks 59 F2
Warwicksland Cumb 112 B2
Wasbister Ork 169 b3
Wasdale Head Cumb 94 C6
Wash Derbys 83 F3
Wash Devon 7 E4
Washall Green Herts 51 E4
Washaway Cnwll 4 D3
Washbourne Devon 7 E3
Washbrook Somset 23 G4
Washbrook Suffk 53 E5
Washfield Devon 9 F6
Washfold N York 96 D5
Washford Somset 22 C3
Washford Pyne Devon 9 E6
Washingborough Lincs 85 H2
Washington T & W 115 E1
Washington W Susx 16 B3
Washwood Heath W Mids 58 D4
Wasing Berks 26 D6
Waskerley Dur 105 G5
Wasperton Warwks 48 A5
Wasps Nest Lincs 86 A1
Wass N York 98 A3
Watchet Somset 22 D4
Watchfield Oxon 39 G3
Watchfield Somset 23 F4
Watchgate Cumb 95 F5
Watchill Cumb 103 F4
Watcombe Devon 7 F4
Watendlath Cumb 103 G2
Water Devon 8 D3
Water Lancs 89 G2
Water Eaton Oxon 40 C5
Water Eaton Staffs 70 D1
Water End Beds 50 B4
Water End Beds 50 B5
Water End Beds 50 B6
Water End E R Yk 92 B3
Water End Essex 51 G5
Water End Herts 50 A2
Water End Herts 50 C1
Water Fryston W York 91 F2
Water Newton Cambs 61 G5
Water Orton Warwks 59 E4
Water Stratford Bucks 49 E3
Water Street Neath 35 E3
Water Yeat Cumb 94 D4
Water's Nook Gt Man 82 B5
Waterbeach Cambs 62 D2
Waterbeach W Susx 15 G4
Waterbeck D & G 111 G2
Watercombe Dorset 12 A3
Waterden Norfk 76 B4
Waterend Cumb 103 E2
Waterfall Staffs 71 F5
Waterfoot Lancs 89 G2
Waterfoot S Lans 119 G5
Waterford Herts 50 D2
Watergate Cnwll 5 E4
Waterhead Cumb 94 D5
Waterhead E Ayrs 109 G6
Waterheads Border 121 G4
Waterhouses Dur 106 A5
Waterhouses Staffs 71 F5
Wateringbury Kent 29 H1
Waterlane Gloucs 38 D5
Waterloo Cnwll 5 E3
Waterloo Derbys 84 B1
Waterloo Dorset 12 D4
Waterloo Herefs 45 F4
Waterloo Highld 151 G1
Waterloo Mersyd 81 E4
Waterloo N Lans 120 C5
Waterloo Norfk 77 E2
Waterloo P & K 139 H3
Waterloo Pembks 32 D2
Waterloo Cross Devon 9 G6
Waterloo Port Gwynd 78 D1
Waterlooville Hants 15 E5
Watermillock Cumb 104 A2
Waterperry Oxon 40 D5
Waterrow Somset 22 C2
Waters Upton Shrops 70 A2
Watersfield W Susx 16 A3
Waterside Bucks 41 H4
Waterside Cumb 103 F5
Waterside E Ayrs 109 F6
Waterside E Ayrs 119 G4
Waterside E Duns 130 C2
Waterside Lancs 89 E2
Waterside S York 84 D6
Waterstein Highld 150 B3
Waterstock Oxon 41 E5
Waterston Pembks 32 D2
Watford Herts 28 B6
Watford Nhants 60 B2
Wath N York 97 E2
Wath N York 97 F2
Wath upon Dearne S York 84 B5
Watlington Norfk 75 F1
Watlington Oxon 41 E4
Watnall Notts 72 C5
Watten Highld 167 F4
Wattisfield Suffk 64 C3
Wattisham Suffk 52 D6
Watton Dorset 11 E4
Watton E R Yk 92 D5
Watton Norfk 64 B5
Watton Green Norfk 64 B5
Watton-at-Stone Herts 50 D3
Wattons Green Essex 29 F6
Wattston N Lans 130 D2
Wattstown Rhondd 35 H4
Wattsville Caerph 36 C3
Wauldby E R Yk 92 C2
Waulkmill Abers 148 D4
Waunarlwydd Swans 34 D4
Waunfawr Cerdgn 54 D4
Waunfawr Gwynd 67 E6
Waungron Swans 34 C4
Waunlwyd Blae G 36 C5
Wavendon Bucks 49 G3
Waverbridge Cumb 103 F5
Waverton Ches 81 G1
Waverton Cumb 103 F5
Wawne E R Yk 93 E3
Waxham Norfk 77 G3
Waxholme E R Yk 93 G3
Way Kent 31 G2
Way Village Devon 9 F6
Way Wick Somset 23 G5
Waye Devon 7 E5
Wayford Somset 10 D5
Waytown Dorset 11 E4
Weacombe Somset 22 D3
Weald Oxon 39 H4
Wealdstone Gt Lon 28 B5
Weardley W York 90 D4
Weare Somset 23 G4
Weare Giffard Devon 21 E3
Wearhead Dur 105 E4
Wearne Somset 23 G2
Weasdale Cumb 95 H5
Weasenham All Saints Norfk 76 B2
Weasenham St Peter Norfk 76 B2
Weaste Gt Man 82 C4
Weatheroak Hill Worcs 58 D3
Weaverham Ches 82 A2
Weaverslake Staffs 71 F2
Weaverthorpe N York 99 E2
Webb's Heath Gloucs 38 B2
Webbington Somset 23 G5
Webheath Worcs 58 C2
Webton Herefs 45 G3
Wedderlairs Abers 158 D2
Wedding Hall Fold N York 89 H4
Weddington Kent 31 F2
Weddington Warwks 59 F5
Wedhampton Wilts 25 F5
Wedmore Somset 23 G4
Wednesbury W Mids 58 C5
Wednesfield W Mids 58 B5
Weecar Notts 85 F1
Weedon Bucks 49 F1
Weedon Nhants 48 D5
Weedon Lois Nhants 48 D4
Weeford Staffs 58 D6
Week Devon 21 F3
Week Devon 21 G2
Week Devon 7 E4
Week St Mary Cnwll 22 B3
Week St Mary Cnwll 5 F6
Weeke Devon 8 D5
Weeke Hants 26 C2
Weekley Nhants 61 E3
Weel E R Yk 92 D3
Weeley Essex 53 E3
Weeley Heath Essex 53 E3
Weem P & K 139 F5
Weeping Cross Staffs 70 D2
Weethley Warwks 47 F5
Weeting Norfk 63 G4
Weeton E R Yk 93 G2
Weeton Lancs 88 B3
Weeton N York 90 D4
Weetwood W York 90 D3
Weir Lancs 89 G2
Weir Quay Devon 6 B4
Weirbrook Shrops 69 F2
Welbeck Abbey Notts 84 C2
Welborne Norfk 76 D1
Welbourn Lincs 73 G5
Welburn N York 98 C2
Welbury N York 97 G5
Welby Lincs 73 G4
Welches Dam Cambs 62 D4
Welcombe Devon 20 C2
Weldon Bridge Nthumb 114 C5
Welford Berks 40 B1
Welford Nhants 60 B3
Welford-on-Avon Warwks 47 G4
Welham Leics 60 D5
Welham Notts 85 E3
Welham Green Herts 50 C1
Well Hants 27 F4
Well Lincs 87 E2
Well N York 97 F3
Well End Bucks 41 G3
Well End Herts 28 C6
Well Fold W York 90 C2
Well Head Herts 50 C3
Well Hill Kent 29 F2
Well Town Devon 9 F6
Welland Worcs 46 C3
Welland Stone Worcs 46 D3
Wellbank Angus 141 E3
Wellbury Herts 50 B4
Wellesbourne Warwks 48 A5
Wellesbourne Mountford Warwks 48 A5
Wellhouse Berks 40 C1
Welling Gt Lon 29 E4
Wellingborough Nhants 61 E2
Wellingham Norfk 76 B2
Wellingore Lincs 73 G6
Wellington Cumb 94 B5
Wellington Herefs 45 H4
Wellington Shrops 70 B1
Wellington Somset 22 D1
Wellington Heath Herefs 46 C3
Wellington Marsh Herefs 45 H4
Wellow IOW 14 B2
Wellow Notts 84 D1
Wellow Somset 24 C5
Wellpond Green Herts 51 E3
Wells Somset 24 A4
Wells Green Ches 70 B5
Wells Head W York 90 B3
Wells-next-the-sea Norfk 76 B4
Wellsborough Leics 59 F6
Wellstye Green Essex 51 G3
Welltree P & K 139 G2
Wellwood Fife 131 G4
Welney Norfk 62 D5
Welsh Bicknor Herefs 37 G6
Welsh End Shrops 69 G4
Welsh Frankton Shrops 69 F3
Welsh Hook Pembks 32 D4
Welsh Newton Herefs 37 F6
Welsh St Donats V Glam 36 A2
Welshampton Shrops 69 G3
Welshpool Powys 56 C6
Welton Cumb 103 G5
Welton E R Yk 92 C2
Welton Lincs 85 H3
Welton Nhants 60 B2
Welton le Marsh Lincs 87 E1
Welton le Wold Lincs 86 C3
Welwick E R Yk 93 G2
Welwyn Herts 50 C2
Welwyn Garden City Herts 50 C2
Wem Shrops 69 G3
Wembdon Somset 23 F3
Wembley Gt Lon 28 C5
Wembury Devon 6 C2
Wembworthy Devon 21 G1
Wemyss Bay Inver 128 C2
Wenallt Cerdgn 54 D2
Wendens Ambo Essex 51 F4
Wendlebury Oxon 48 D1
Wendling Norfk 76 B1
Wendover Bucks 41 G5
Wendron Cnwll 2 D3
Wendy Cambs 50 D5
Wenfordbridge Cnwll 4 D3
Wenhaston Suffk 65 G3
Wennington Cambs 62 B3
Wennington Gt Lon 29 F4
Wennington Lancs 95 G2
Wensley Derbys 71 G6
Wensley N York 96 D4
Wentbridge W York 91 F1
Wentnor Shrops 56 D5
Wentworth Cambs 62 D3
Wentworth S York 84 B4
Wentworth Castle S York 83 H5
Wenvoe V Glam 36 B1
Weobley Herefs 45 G4
Weobley Marsh Herefs 45 G4
Wepham W Susx 16 A2
Wereham Norfk 63 F5
Wergs Staffs 58 B5
Wern Gwynd 67 E4
Wern Powys 68 B1
Wern Powys 69 E1
Wern Powys 36 B6
Wern Shrops 69 E3
Wern-y-gaer Flints 80 D1
Werneth Low Gt Man 83 E4
Wernffrwd Swans 34 C4
Werrington Cambs 61 H6
Werrington Cnwll 5 G5
Werrington Staffs 70 D5
Wervin Ches 81 F2
Wesham Lancs 88 C3
Wessington Derbys 72 A6
West Aberthaw V Glam 22 C6
West Acre Norfk 75 H1
West Allerdean Nthumb 123 G4
West Alvington Devon 7 E2
West Amesbury Wilts 25 G3
West Anstey Devon 22 A2
West Appleton N York 97 E4
West Ashby Lincs 86 C2
West Ashling W Susx 15 F4
West Ashton Wilts 24 D5
West Auckland Dur 106 A3
West Ayton N York 99 F3
West Bagborough Somset 23 E3
West Balsdon Cnwll 5 F6
West Bank Blae G 36 C5
West Bank Ches 81 G3
West Barkwith Lincs 86 B3
West Barnby N York 107 G2
West Barns E Loth 133 E3
West Barsham Norfk 76 B3
West Bay Dorset 11 E4
West Beckham Norfk 76 D4
West Bedfont Surrey 28 B3
West Bergholt Essex 52 C3
West Bexington Dorset 11 F3
West Bilney Norfk 75 G1
West Blatchington E Susx 16 D2
West Boldon T & W 115 E2
West Bourton Dorset 24 C2
West Bowling W York 90 C3
West Brabourne Kent 18 D6
West Bradenham Norfk 64 B6
West Bradford Lancs 89 F4
West Bradley Somset 24 A3
West Bretton W York 83 H6
West Bridgford Notts 72 C4
West Briscoe Dur 105 F2
West Bromwich W Mids 58 C4
West Buccleuch Hotel Border 111 H6
West Buckland Devon 21 G4
West Buckland Somset 23 E1
West Burton N York 96 C3
West Burton W Susx 16 A3
West Butsfield Dur 105 H5
West Butterwick Lincs 85 F5
West Byfleet Surrey 28 A2
West Cairngaan D & G 100 C3
West Caister Norfk 77 H1
West Calder W Loth 131 F1
West Camel Somset 24 A2
West Chaldon Dorset 12 B3
West Challow Oxon 40 B3
West Charleton Devon 7 E2
West Chelborough Dorset 11 F5
West Chevington Nthumb 114 D5
West Chiltington W Susx 16 B3
West Chinnock Somset 11 E6
West Chisenbury Wilts 25 G4
West Clandon Surrey 28 A1
West Cliffe Kent 19 G6
West Coker Somset 11 E6
West Combe Devon 7 E4
West Compton Somset 24 B3
West Compton Abbas Dorset 11 F4
West Cottingwith N York 91 H4
West Cowick E R Yk 91 G2
West Cross Swans 34 D3
West Curry Cnwll 5 F5
West Curthwaite Cumb 103 G5
West Dean W Susx 15 G5
West Dean Wilts 25 H2
West Deeping Lincs 74 A1
West Derby Mersyd 81 F4
West Dereham Norfk 63 F5
West Down Devon 21 E5
West Drayton Gt Lon 28 B4
West Drayton Notts 85 E2
West Dunnet Highld 167 F6
West Ella E R Yk 92 D2
West End Beds 49 H5
West End Berks 41 F2
West End Berks 41 G1
West End Caerph 36 C4
West End Cambs 62 B2
West End Cumb 103 G6
West End E R Yk 92 C3

West End
Whiteshill
318

West End E R Yk 93 F3
West End E R Yk 93 F2
West End Gloucs 38 B3
West End Hants 14 C5
West End Hants 27 E3
West End Herts 50 D1
West End Herts 50 C3
West End Lancs 89 F2
West End Lincs 86 D4
West End N York 90 C5
West End N York 91 F4
West End Norfk 76 B1
West End Norfk 77 H1
West End Oxon 40 D3
West End Somset 37 F1
West End Somset 24 B3
West End Surrey 27 H5
West End Surrey 28 B2
West End W Susx 16 C3
West End W York 90 C3
West End Wilts 25 E2
West End Wilts 38 D2
West End Wilts 25 E2
West End Green Hants 27 E5
West Ewell Surrey 28 C2
West Farleigh Kent 29 H1
West Farndon Nhants 48 C4
West Felton Shrops 69 F2
West Firle E Susx 17 F2
West Firsby Lincs 85 G3
West Flotmanby N York 99 F3
West Garforth W York 91 E3
West Ginge Oxon 40 C3
West Grafton Wilts 25 H5
West Green Hants 27 E5
West Grimstead Wilts 25 G2
West Grinstead W Susx 16 C4
West Haddlesey N York 91 G2
West Haddon Nhants 60 B2
West Hagbourne Oxon 40 C3
West Hagley Worcs 58 B3
West Hallam Derbys 72 B4
West Hallam Common Derbys 72 B4
West Halton Lincs 92 C2
West Ham Gt Lon 29 E4
West Handley Derbys 84 B2
West Hanney Oxon 40 B3
West Hanningfield Essex 30 A6
West Harnham Wilts 25 G2
West Harptree Somset 24 A5
West Harting W Susx 15 F6
West Hatch Somset 23 F1
West Hatch Wilts 25 E2
West Haven Angus 141 F3
West Head Norfk 63 E6
West Heath Hants 26 D5
West Heath W Mids 58 C3
West Helmsdale Highld 163 G5
West Hendred Oxon 40 C3
West Heslerton N York 99 E2
West Hewish Somset 23 G6
West Hill Devon 10 A4
West Hoathly W Susx 16 D5
West Holme Dorset 12 C3
West Horndon Essex 29 G5
West Horrington Somset 24 A4
West Horsley Surrey 28 B1
West Horton Nthumb 123 G2
West Hougham Kent 19 F5
West Howe Dorset 12 D4
West Howetown Somset 22 B3
West Huntingtower P & K 139 H2
West Huntspill Somset 23 F4
West Hyde Beds 50 B2
West Hyde Herts 28 A5
West Hythe Kent 19 E5
West Ilkerton Devon 21 G5
West Ilsley Berks 40 C2
West Itchenor W Susx 15 F4
West Keal Lincs 86 D1
West Kennett Wilts 39 F1
West Kilbride N Ayrs 118 D4
West Kingsdown Kent 29 F2
West Kington Wilts 38 C2
West Kirby Mersyd 80 D3
West Knapton N York 98 D2
West Knighton Dorset 11 H3
West Knoyle Wilts 24 D2
West Lambrook Somset 23 G1
West Langdon Kent 19 G6
West Laroch Highld 137 E6
West Lavington W Susx 15 G6
West Lavington Wilts 25 F4
West Layton N York 97 E6
West Leake Notts 72 C3
West Learmouth Nthumb 123 F3
West Lees N York 97 H5
West Leigh Devon 8 D5
West Leigh Devon 7 E3
West Leigh Somset 22 D2
West Lexham Norfk 76 B2
West Lilling N York 98 B1
West Linton Border 121 F5
West Littleton Gloucs 38 B2
West Lockinge Oxon 40 B3
West Lulworth Dorset 12 B3
West Lutton N York 99 E2
West Lydford Somset 24 A2
West Lyn Devon 21 G5
West Lyng Somset 23 F2
West Lynn Norfk 75 F2
West Malling Kent 29 H2
West Malvern Worcs 46 C4
West Marden W Susx 15 F5
West Markham Notts 85 E2
West Marsh Lincs 86 C6
West Marton N York 89 G5
West Melbury Dorset 24 D1
West Melton S York 84 B5
West Meon Hants 27 E2
West Meon Hut Hants 27 E2
West Meon Woodlands Hants 27 E2
West Mersea Essex 52 D2
West Mickley Nthumb 114 B2
West Midlands Safari Park Worcs 58 A3
West Milton Dorset 11 E4
West Minster Kent 30 C3
West Molesey Surrey 28 B3
West Monkton Somset 23 E2
West Moors Dorset 13 E5
West Morden Dorset 12 C4
West Morriston Border 122 C3
West Morton W York 90 B4
West Mudford Somset 24 A1
West Ness N York 98 C3
West Newbiggin Dur 106 C3
West Newton E R Yk 93 F3
West Newton Norfk 75 G3
West Newton Somset 23 F2
West Norwood Gt Lon 28 D3
West Ogwell Devon 7 F5
West Orchard Dorset 24 D1
West Overton Wilts 25 G6
West Panson Devon 5 G5
West Parley Dorset 13 E4
West Peckham Kent 29 G1
West Pelton Dur 106 B6
West Pennard Somset 24 A3
West Pentire Cnwll 4 A2
West Perry Cambs 61 G2
West Porlock Somset 22 B4
West Prawle Devon 7 E1
West Pulham Dorset 11 G5
West Putford Devon 20 D2
West Quantoxhead Somset 22 D3
West Raddon Devon 9 F5
West Rainton Dur 106 C6
West Rasen Lincs 86 A4
West Ravendale Lincs 86 C5
West Raynham Norfk 76 B2
West Retford Notts 85 E3
West Rounton N York 97 G5
West Row Suffk 63 F3
West Rudham Norfk 76 A3
West Runton Norfk 77 E4
West Saltoun E Loth 132 D2
West Sandford Devon 9 E5
West Sandwick Shet 169 j4
West Scrafton N York 96 D3
West Sleekburn Nthumb 114 D4
West Somerton Norfk 77 H2
West Stafford Dorset 11 G4
West Stockwith Notts 85 E4
West Stoke W Susx 15 F4
West Stonesdale N York 96 B5
West Stoughton Somset 23 G4
West Stour Dorset 24 C1
West Stourmouth Kent 31 F2
West Stow Suffk 63 G2
West Stowell Wilts 25 G5
West Stratton Hants 26 D3
West Street Kent 29 H4
West Street Kent 30 C1
West Street Kent 31 G1
West Street Suffk 64 B2
West Tanfield N York 97 F3
West Taphouse Cnwll 5 E2
West Tarbert Ag & B 127 G2
West Tarring W Susx 16 B2
West Thirston Nthumb 114 C5
West Thorney W Susx 15 F4
West Thorpe Notts 72 D2
West Thurrock Essex 29 G4
West Tilbury Essex 29 G4
West Tisted Hants 27 E2
West Torrington Lincs 86 B3
West Town Hants 15 E3
West Town Herefs 45 G5
West Town Somset 37 F1
West Town Somset 23 H5
West Town Somset 24 A3
West Town Somset 24 C3
West Tytherley Hants 26 A2
West Walton Norfk 75 E1
West Walton Highway Norfk 75 E1
West Wellow Hants 26 A1
West Wembury Devon 6 C2
West Wemyss Fife 132 B5
West Wick Somset 23 F5
West Wickham Cambs 51 G6
West Wickham Gt Lon 29 E3
West Williamston Pembks 33 E2
West Winch Norfk 75 G2
West Winterslow Wilts 25 H2
West Wittering W Susx 15 F3
West Witton N York 96 D4
West Woodburn Nthumb 113 F3
West Woodhay Berks 26 B6
West Woodlands Somset 24 C4
West Woodside Cumb 103 G5
West Worldham Hants 27 F3
West Worthing W Susx 16 B2
West Wratting Essex 51 G6
West Wycombe Bucks 41 F4
West Wylam Nthumb 114 C2
West Yatton Wilts 38 C2
West Yoke Kent 29 G3
West Youlstone Cnwll 20 C2
Westbere Kent 31 E2
Westborough Lincs 73 F4
Westbourne Dorset 13 E4
Westbourne W Susx 15 F4
Westbrook Berks 40 C1
Westbrook Kent 31 G3
Westbrook Wilts 25 E6
Westbury Bucks 48 D3
Westbury Shrops 69 F1
Westbury Wilts 24 D4
Westbury Leigh Wilts 24 D4
Westbury on Severn Gloucs 38 B6
Westbury-on-Trym Bristl 37 G2
Westbury-sub-Mendip Somset 23 H4
Westby Lancs 88 B3
Westcliff-on-Sea Essex 30 B5
Westcombe Somset 24 B3
Westcote Gloucs 47 H1
Westcote Barton Oxon 48 C2
Westcott Bucks 41 E6
Westcott Devon 9 G5
Westcott Somset 22 B1
Westcott Surrey 28 B1
Westcourt Wilts 25 H5
Westdean E Susx 17 F1
Westdown Camp Wilts 25 F4
Westdowns Cnwll 4 D4
Wested Kent 29 F3
Westend Gloucs 38 C5
Westend Town Nthumb 113 E1
Westenhanger Kent 19 E5
Wester Drumashie Highld 154 D2
Wester Ochiltree W Loth 131 F3
Wester Pitkierie Fife 132 D6
Westerdale Highld 167 E4
Westerdale N York 98 B5
Westerfield Suffk 53 E5
Westergate W Susx 15 G4
Westerham Kent 29 E1
Westerhope T & W 114 D2
Westerland Devon 7 F4
Westerleigh Gloucs 38 B2
Westerton Angus 141 G5
Westerton W Susx 15 G4
Westfield Cumb 102 D3
Westfield E Susx 18 B3
Westfield Highld 166 D5
Westfield N Lans 130 D2
Westfield Norfk 76 C1
Westfield Somset 24 B5
Westfield W Loth 131 F2
Westfield Sole Kent 30 A2
Westfields Dorset 11 G5
Westfields Herefs 45 H3
Westfields of Rattray P & K 140 B4
Westford Somset 22 D1
Westgate Dur 105 F4
Westgate Lincs 85 E5
Westgate Norfk 76 C4
Westgate Hill W York 90 C2
Westgate on Sea Kent 31 G3
Westgate Street Norfk 77 E2
Westhall Suffk 65 G3
Westham Dorset 11 G2
Westham E Susx 17 G2
Westham Somset 23 G4
Westhampnett W Susx 15 G4
Westhay Somset 23 G3
Westhead Lancs 81 G5
Westhide Herefs 46 A4
Westhill Abers 149 F5
Westholme Somset 24 A3
Westhope Herefs 45 G4
Westhope Shrops 57 E4
Westhorp Nhants 48 C4
Westhorpe Lincs 74 C3
Westhorpe Suffk 64 C2
Westhoughton Gt Man 82 B5
Westhouse N York 95 G2
Westhouses Derbys 72 B6
Westhumble Surrey 28 C1
Westlake Devon 6 D3
Westland Green Herts 51 E3
Westleigh Devon 21 E3
Westleigh Devon 22 C1
Westleton Suffk 65 G2
Westley Shrops 56 D6
Westley Suffk 63 G2
Westley Waterless Cambs 63 E1
Westlington Bucks 41 F5
Westlinton Cumb 112 A1
Westmarsh Kent 31 F2
Westmeston E Susx 16 D3
Westmill Herts 51 E3
Westminster Gt Lon 28 D4
Westmuir Angus 140 D5
Westnewton Cumb 103 E4
Westoe T & W 115 E2
Weston Berks 40 B2
Weston Ches 81 G3
Weston Ches 70 B5
Weston Devon 10 B5
Weston Devon 10 B3
Weston Dorset 11 G2
Weston Hants 27 E1
Weston Herefs 45 F5
Weston Herts 50 C4
Weston Lincs 74 C2
Weston N York 90 C4
Weston Nhants 48 D4
Weston Notts 85 E1
Weston Shrops 57 F5
Weston Shrops 69 E3
Weston Shrops 56 D3
Weston Somset 24 C6
Weston Staffs 71 E3
Weston Beggard Herefs 46 A3
Weston by Welland Nhants 60 D4
Weston Colley Hants 26 C3
Weston Colville Cambs 51 G6
Weston Corbett Hants 27 E4
Weston Coyney Staffs 70 D4
Weston Favell Nhants 49 F5
Weston Green Cambs 51 G6
Weston Heath Shrops 70 C1
Weston Hills Lincs 74 C2
Weston in Arden Warwks 59 G4
Weston Jones Staffs 70 C2
Weston Longville Norfk 76 D2
Weston Lullingfields Shrops 69 F2
Weston Patrick Hants 27 E4
Weston Rhyn Shrops 69 E4
Weston Subedge Gloucs 47 G3
Weston Turville Bucks 41 G5
Weston under Penyard Herefs 46 B1
Weston under Wetherley Warwks 59 F2
Weston Underwood Bucks 49 G4
Weston Underwood Derbys 71 H4
Weston-in-Gordano Somset 37 F2
Weston-on-the-Green Oxon 48 D1
Weston-Super-Mare Somset 23 F5
Weston-under-Lizard Staffs 70 C1
Weston-under-Redcastle Shrops 69 H3
Weston-upon-Trent Derbys 72 B3
Westonbirt Gloucs 38 C3
Westoning Beds 50 A4
Westoning Woodend Beds 50 A4
Westonzoyland Somset 23 F3
Westow N York 98 C1
Westpeek Devon 5 G5
Westport Somset 23 G1
Westquarter Falk 131 E3
Westra V Glam 36 C1
Westray Airport Ork 169 b4
Westridge Green Berks 40 D2
Westrigg W Loth 131 E2
Westrop Wilts 39 G4
Westruther Border 122 D4
Westry Cambs 62 C5
Westthorpe Derbys 84 B3
Westward Cumb 103 G5
Westward Ho! Devon 20 D3
Westwell Kent 18 C6
Westwell Oxon 39 G5
Westwell Leacon Kent 18 C6
Westwick Cambs 62 C2
Westwick Dur 105 G2
Westwick Norfk 77 F3
Westwood Devon 9 G4
Westwood Kent 29 G3
Westwood Kent 31 G3
Westwood Notts 72 B5
Westwood Nthumb 113 E1
Westwood Wilts 24 D5
Westwood Heath W Mids 59 F3
Westwoodside Lincs 85 E5
Wetham Green Kent 30 B3
Wetheral Cumb 104 A6
Wetherby W York 91 E4
Wetherden Suffk 64 C2
Wetheringsett Suffk 64 D2
Wethersfield Essex 51 H4
Wetherup Street Suffk 64 D2
Wetley Rocks Staffs 71 E5
Wettenhall Ches 70 A6
Wetton Staffs 71 F6
Wetwang E R Yk 92 C5
Wetwood Staffs 70 C3
Wexcombe Wilts 26 A5
Wexham Bucks 41 H2
Wexham Street Bucks 41 H3
Weybourne Norfk 76 D4
Weybread Suffk 65 E3
Weybread Street Suffk 65 E3
Weybridge Surrey 28 B2
Weycroft Devon 10 C5
Weydale Highld 167 E5
Weyhill Hants 26 A4
Weymouth Dorset 11 G2
Whaddon Bucks 49 F3
Whaddon Cambs 50 D5
Whaddon Gloucs 38 C6
Whaddon Wilts 24 D5
Whaddon Wilts 25 G2
Whale Cumb 104 B2
Whaley Derbys 84 C2
Whaley Bridge Derbys 83 E3
Whaley Thorns Derbys 84 C2
Whaligoe Highld 167 G2
Whalley Lancs 89 F3
Whalley Banks Lancs 89 F3
Whalton Nthumb 114 C4
Whaplode Lincs 74 D2
Whaplode Drove Lincs 74 D1
Wharf Warwks 48 C4
Wharfe N York 96 A2
Wharles Lancs 88 C3
Wharley End Beds 49 G3
Wharmley Nthumb 113 F1
Wharncliffe Side S York 83 H4
Wharram-le-Street N York 98 D1
Wharton Ches 82 B1
Wharton Herefs 45 H5
Whashton N York 97 E5
Whashton Green N York 97 E5
Whasset Cumb 95 F3
Whatcote Warwks 48 A4
Whateley Warwks 59 E5
Whatfield Suffk 52 D5
Whatley Somset 10 D5
Whatley Somset 24 C4
Whatley's End Gloucs 37 H2
Whatlington E Susx 18 A3
Whatsole Street Kent 19 E6
Whatstandwell Derbys 72 A5
Whatton Notts 73 E4
Whauphill D & G 101 E5
Whaw N York 96 C5
Wheal Rose Cnwll 3 E4
Wheatacre Norfk 65 G5
Wheatfield Oxon 41 E4
Wheathampstead Herts 50 C2
Wheathill Shrops 57 F4
Wheathill Somset 24 A2
Wheatley Hants 27 F3
Wheatley Oxon 40 D5
Wheatley W York 90 B2
Wheatley Hill Dur 106 C5
Wheatley Hills S York 84 D5
Wheatley Lane Lancs 89 G3
Wheaton Aston Staffs 70 C1
Wheatsheaf Wrexhm 69 E5
Wheddon Cross Somset 22 B3
Wheel Inn Cnwll 2 D2
Wheelbarrow Town Kent 19 E6
Wheeler's Green Oxon 41 F1
Wheeler's Street Kent 18 B6
Wheelerend Common Bucks 41 F4
Wheelerstreet Surrey 27 H3
Wheelock Ches 70 C6
Wheelock Heath Ches 70 C6
Wheelton Lancs 88 D2
Wheldale W York 91 F2
Wheldrake N York 91 H4
Whelford Gloucs 39 F4
Whelpley Hill Bucks 50 A1
Whelpo Cumb 103 G4
Whelston Flints 80 D2
Whempstead Herts 50 D3
Whenby N York 98 B2
Whepstead Suffk 63 G1
Wherstead Suffk 53 E5
Wherwell Hants 26 B3
Wheston Derbys 83 F2
Whetsted Kent 17 G6
Whetstone Gt Lon 28 D5
Whetstone Leics 60 B5
Wheyrigg Cumb 103 F5
Whicham Cumb 94 B3
Whichford Warwks 48 A3
Whickham T & W 114 D2
Whiddon Devon 8 B5
Whiddon Down Devon 8 D4
Whight's Corner Suffk 53 E5
Whigstreet Angus 141 E4
Whilton Nhants 60 B2
Whimble Devon 20 D1
Whimple Devon 9 G4
Whimpwell Green Norfk 77 G3
Whin Lane End Lancs 88 B4
Whinburgh Norfk 76 C1
Whinnie Liggate D & G 102 A5
Whinnow Cumb 103 G5
Whinny Hill Dur 106 C3
Whinnyfold Abers 159 G2
Whippingham IOW 14 C3
Whipsnade Beds 50 A2
Whipsnade Wild Animal Park Bucks 50 A2
Whipton Devon 9 F4
Whirlow S York 83 H3
Whisby Lincs 85 G1
Whissendine Rutlnd 73 F1
Whissonsett Norfk 76 B2
Whistlefield Ag & B 128 D4
Whistlefield Inn Ag & B 128 C4
Whistley Green Berks 41 F2
Whiston Mersyd 81 G4
Whiston Nhants 49 G5
Whiston S York 84 B4
Whiston Staffs 70 D1
Whiston Staffs 71 E5
Whiston Cross Shrops 57 H6
Whiston Eaves Staffs 71 E5
Whiston Lane End Mersyd 81 G4
Whitacre Fields Warwks 59 E5
Whitbeck Cumb 94 B3
Whitbourne Herefs 46 C5
Whitburn T & W 115 F2
Whitburn W Loth 131 F2
Whitby Ches 81 F2
Whitby N York 99 E6
Whitbyheath Ches 81 F2
Whitchester Border 122 D5
Whitchurch Bucks 49 F1
Whitchurch Cardif 36 C2
Whitchurch Devon 6 B5
Whitchurch Hants 26 C4
Whitchurch Herefs 37 F6
Whitchurch Oxon 41 E2
Whitchurch Pembks 32 B4
Whitchurch Shrops 69 H4
Whitchurch Somset 24 B6
Whitchurch Canonicorum Dorset 10 D4
Whitchurch Hill Oxon 41 E2
Whitcombe Dorset 11 G3
Whitcot Shrops 56 D4
Whitcott Keysett Shrops 56 C4
White Ball Somset 22 D1
White Chapel Lancs 88 D4
White Chapel Worcs 47 F3
White Colne Essex 52 B4
White Coppice Lancs 89 E1
White Cross Cnwll 2 D2
White End Worcs 46 C3
White Kirkley Dur 105 G4
White Lackington Dorset 11 G4
White Ladies Aston Worcs 47 E4
White Mill Carmth 43 E1
White Notley Essex 52 A2
White Ox Mead Somset 24 C5
White Pit Lincs 86 D2
White Roding Essex 51 F2
White Stake Lancs 88 D2
White Stone Herefs 46 A3
White Waltham Berks 41 G2
White-le-Head Dur 114 C1
Whiteacre Kent 19 E6
Whiteacre Heath Warwks 59 E5
Whiteash Green Essex 52 B4
Whitebirk Lancs 89 E2
Whitebridge Highld 145 G6
Whitebrook Mons 37 F5
Whitecairns Abers 149 G6
Whitechapel Gt Lon 28 D4
Whitechurch Pembks 42 B3
Whitecliffe Gloucs 37 G5
Whitecraig E Loth 132 B2
Whitecroft Gloucs 37 G5
Whitecrook D & G 100 C6
Whitecross Cnwll 2 C3
Whitecross Cnwll 4 C3
Whitecross Falk 131 F3
Whiteface Highld 162 D3
Whitefarland N Ayrs 117 H5
Whitefaulds S Ayrs 109 E6
Whitefield Devon 21 G4
Whitefield Gt Man 82 C5
Whitefield Somset 22 D2
Whitefield Lane End Mersyd 81 G4
Whiteford Abers 158 C2
Whitegate Ches 82 A2
Whitehall Hants 27 F4
Whitehall Ork 169 c3
Whitehall W Susx 16 B3
Whitehaven Cumb 102 D2
Whitehill Hants 27 F3
Whitehill Kent 30 D2
Whitehill Leics 72 B1
Whitehills Abers 158 B6
Whitehouse Abers 148 D6
Whitehouse Ag & B 127 G1
Whitehouse Common W Mids 58 D5
Whitekirk E Loth 133 E3
Whitelackington Somset 10 D6
Whiteley Hants 14 D5
Whiteley Bank IOW 14 D2
Whiteley Green Ches 82 D2
Whiteley Village Surrey 28 B2
Whitemans Green W Susx 16 D4
Whitemire Moray 156 B4
Whitemoor Cnwll 4 C2
Whitemoor Derbys 72 A5
Whitemoor Notts 72 C4
Whitemoor Staffs 70 D6
Whiteness Shet 169 h2
Whiteoak Green Oxon 40 B6
Whiteparish Wilts 25 H2
Whiterashes Abers 158 D1
Whiterow Highld 167 G3
Whiterow Moray 156 B5
Whiteshill Gloucs 38 C5

Whitesmith Woodend

Whitesmith E Susx 17 F3
Whitestaunton Somset 10 C6
Whitestone Devon 9 E4
Whitestone Cross Devon 9 F4
Whitestreet Green Suffk 52 C5
Whitewall Corner N York 98 D2
Whiteway Gloucs 38 D5
Whiteway Somset 24 C6
Whitewell Lancs 89 E4
Whiteworks Devon 6 C5
Whitfield Gloucs 38 B3
Whitfield Kent 19 F6
Whitfield Nhants 48 D3
Whitfield Nthumb 104 D6
Whitfield Hall Nthumb 104 D6
Whitford Devon 10 C4
Whitford Flints 80 D2
Whitgift E R Yk 92 B2
Whitgreave Staffs 70 D3
Whithorn D & G 101 F4
Whiting Bay N Ayrs 118 B2
Whitkirk W York 91 E3
Whitland Carmth 33 F3
Whitlaw Border 112 B6
Whitletts S Ayrs 119 E2
Whitley Berks 41 E1
Whitley N York 91 G2
Whitley S York 84 A4
Whitley Wilts 24 D6
Whitley Bay T & W 115 E3
Whitley Chapel Nthumb 105 F6
Whitley Heath Staffs 70 C3
Whitley Lower W York 90 C1
Whitley Row Kent 29 F1
Whitlock's End W Mids 58 D3
Whitminster Gloucs 38 C5
Whitmore Dorset 12 D5
Whitmore Staffs 70 C4
Whitnage Devon 9 G6
Whitnash Warwks 59 F2
Whitney-on-Wye Herefs 45 E4
Whitrigg Cumb 103 F4
Whitrigg Cumb 103 F6
Whitrigglees Cumb 103 F6
Whitsbury Hants 25 G1
Whitsford Devon 21 G4
Whitsome Border 123 F4
Whitson Newpt 37 E3
Whitstable Kent 31 E3
Whitstone Cnwll 5 F6
Whittingham Nthumb 124 D2
Whittingslow Shrops 57 E4
Whittington Derbys 84 B2
Whittington Gloucs 47 F1
Whittington Lancs 95 G2
Whittington Norfk 63 F5
Whittington Shrops 69 E3
Whittington Staffs 58 D6
Whittington Staffs 58 B4
Whittington Warwks 59 F5
Whittington Worcs 46 D4
Whittington Moor Derbys 84 A2
Whittle-le-Woods Lancs 88 D2
Whittlebury Nhants 49 E4
Whittlesey Cambs 62 B5
Whittlesford Cambs 51 F5
Whittlestone Head Lancs 89 F1
Whitton Dur 106 C3
Whitton Lincs 92 C2
Whitton Nthumb 114 B6
Whitton Powys 56 C2
Whitton Shrops 57 F3
Whitton Suffk 53 E5
Whittonditch Wilts 39 G1
Whittonstall Nthumb 105 G6
Whitway Hants 26 C5
Whitwell Derbys 84 C2
Whitwell Herts 50 C3
Whitwell IOW 14 C1
Whitwell N York 97 F5
Whitwell Rutlnd 73 G1
Whitwell Street Norfk 76 D2
Whitwell-on-the-Hill N York 98 C1
Whitwick Leics 72 B2
Whitwood W York 91 E2
Whitworth Lancs 89 G1
Whixall Shrops 69 G3
Whixley N York 91 E5
Whorlton Dur 105 H2
Whorlton N York 97 H5
Whyle Herefs 46 A5
Whyteleafe Surrey 28 D2
Wibdon Gloucs 37 G4
Wibsey W York 90 C3
Wibtoft Warwks 59 H4
Wichenford Worcs 46 C5
Wichling Kent 30 C2
Wick Devon 10 B5
Wick Dorset 13 E4
Wick Gloucs 38 B1
Wick Highld 167 G3
Wick Somset 23 E4
Wick Somset 23 G2
Wick V Glam 35 G1
Wick W Susx 16 A2
Wick Wilts 25 G1
Wick Worcs 47 E4
Wick Airport Highld 167 G4
Wick End Beds 49 H4
Wick St Lawrence Somset 23 F6
Wicken Cambs 63 E2
Wicken Nhants 49 F3
Wicken Bonhunt Essex 51 F4
Wickenby Lincs 86 A3
Wicker Street Green Suffk 52 C5
Wickersley S York 84 B4
Wickford Essex 30 A5
Wickham Berks 40 B1
Wickham Hants 14 D5
Wickham Bishops Essex 52 B2
Wickham Green Berks 40 B1
Wickham Green Suffk 64 C2
Wickham Heath Berks 40 B1
Wickham Market Suffk 65 E1
Wickham Skeith Suffk 64 C2
Wickham St Paul Essex 52 B4
Wickham Street Suffk 52 A6
Wickham Street Suffk 64 C2
Wickhambreaux Kent 31 F2
Wickhambrook Suffk 52 A6
Wickhamford Worcs 47 F3
Wickhampton Norfk 65 G6
Wicklewood Norfk 64 C6
Wickmere Norfk 77 E3
Wickstreet E Susx 17 F2
Wickwar Gloucs 38 B3
Widdington Essex 51 F4
Widdop Lancs 89 H3
Widdrington Nthumb 114 D5
Widdrington Station T & W 114 D5
Wide Open T & W 114 D3
Widecombe in the Moor Devon 8 D2
Widegates Cnwll 5 F2
Widemouth Bay Cnwll 5 F6
Widford Essex 51 H1
Widford Herts 51 E2
Widford Oxon 39 G5
Widham Wilts 39 F3
Widley Hants 15 E4
Widmer End Bucks 41 G4
Widmerpool Notts 72 D3
Widmore Gt Lon 29 E3
Widnes Ches 81 G3
Widworthy Devon 10 C4
Wigan Gt Man 81 H5
Wigborough Somset 11 E6
Wiggaton Devon 10 A4
Wiggenhall St Germans Norfk 75 F1
Wiggenhall St Mary Magdalen Norfk 75 F1
Wiggenhall St Mary the Virgin Norfk 75 F1
Wiggens Green Essex 51 G5
Wiggenstall Staffs 71 F6
Wiggington Shrops 69 F4
Wigginton Herts 41 G5
Wigginton N York 91 G5
Wigginton Oxon 48 B2
Wigginton Staffs 59 E6
Wigglesworth N York 89 F5
Wiggold Gloucs 39 E5
Wiggonby Cumb 103 G4
Wiggonholt W Susx 16 B3
Wighill N York 91 F4
Wighton Norfk 76 B4
Wightwick Staffs 58 B5
Wigley Derbys 83 H2
Wigley Hants 26 B1
Wigmore Herefs 56 D2
Wigmore Kent 30 B2
Wigsley Notts 85 F2
Wigsthorpe Nhants 61 F4
Wigston Leics 60 B5
Wigston Fields Leics 60 B5
Wigston Parva Leics 59 G4
Wigthorpe Notts 84 D3
Wigtoft Lincs 74 C4
Wigton Cumb 103 F5
Wigtown D & G 101 F6
Wigtwizzle S York 83 G4
Wike W York 90 D4
Wilbarston Nhants 60 D4
Wilberfoss E R Yk 92 A5
Wilburton Cambs 62 D3
Wilby Nhants 61 E2
Wilby Norfk 64 C4
Wilby Suffk 65 E3
Wilcot Wilts 25 G5
Wilcott Shrops 69 F2
Wilcrick Newpt 37 E3
Wilday Green Derbys 84 A2
Wildboarclough Ches 83 E1
Wilden Beds 50 B6
Wilden Worcs 58 A3
Wildhern Hants 26 B4
Wildhill Herts 50 D1
Wildmanbridge S Lans 120 C5
Wildmoor Worcs 58 C3
Wildsworth Lincs 85 F4
Wilford Notts 72 C4
Wilkesley Ches 70 A4
Wilkhaven Highld 163 F2
Wilkieston W Loth 131 G2
Wilkin's Green Herts 50 C1
Wilksby Lincs 86 C1
Willand Devon 9 G6
Willards Hill E Susx 17 H4
Willaston Ches 81 F2
Willaston Ches 70 B5
Willen Bucks 49 G3
Willenhall W Mids 58 C5
Willenhall W Mids 59 F3
Willerby E R Yk 92 D3
Willerby N York 99 F3
Willersey Gloucs 47 F3
Willersley Herefs 45 F4
Willesborough Kent 18 D6
Willesborough Lees Kent 18 D6
Willesden Gt Lon 28 C4
Willesleigh Devon 21 F4
Willesley Wilts 38 C3
Willett Somset 22 D3
Willey Shrops 57 G5
Willey Warwks 59 H4
Willey Green Surrey 27 G4
Williamscot Oxon 48 C4
Williamstown Rhondd 35 G3
Willian Herts 50 C4
Willicote Warwks 47 G4
Willingale Essex 51 G1
Willingdon E Susx 17 G2
Willingham Cambs 62 C2
Willingham by Stow Lincs 85 F3
Willingham Green Cambs 51 G6
Willington Beds 50 B6
Willington Derbys 71 H3
Willington Dur 106 A4
Willington Kent 30 A1
Willington Warwks 48 A3
Willington Corner Ches 81 G1
Willington Quay T & W 115 E2
Willitoft E R Yk 92 A3
Williton Somset 22 D3
Willoughby Lincs 87 E2
Willoughby Warwks 60 A2
Willoughby Hills Lincs 74 D5
Willoughby Waterleys Leics 60 B5
Willoughby-on-the-Wolds Notts 72 D2
Willoughton Lincs 85 G4
Willow Green Ches 82 A2
Willows Green Essex 51 H3
Willsbridge Gloucs 38 A1
Willsworthy Devon 8 B3
Willtown Somset 23 G2
Wilmcote Warwks 47 G5
Wilmington Devon 10 C5
Wilmington E Susx 17 F2
Wilmington Kent 29 F3
Wilmington Somset 24 C5
Wilmslow Ches 82 C3
Wilnecote Staffs 59 E5
Wilpshire Lancs 89 E3
Wilsden W York 90 B3
Wilsford Lincs 73 H4
Wilsford Wilts 25 F5
Wilsford Wilts 25 G3
Wilsham Devon 21 H5
Wilshaw W York 83 F6
Wilsill N York 97 E1
Wilsley Green Kent 18 A5
Wilsley Pound Kent 18 A5
Wilson Herefs 46 A1
Wilson Leics 72 B2
Wilsontown S Lans 120 D5
Wilstead Beds 50 B5
Wilsthorpe Lincs 74 A1
Wilstone Herts 41 G6
Wilstone Green Herts 41 G6
Wilton Cumb 102 D1
Wilton Herefs 46 A2
Wilton N York 107 E3
Wilton N York 98 D3
Wilton Wilts 25 F2
Wilton Wilts 25 H5
Wilton Dean Border 122 B1
Wimbish Essex 51 G4
Wimbish Green Essex 51 G4
Wimbledon Gt Lon 28 C3
Wimblington Cambs 62 C5
Wimboldsley Ches 82 B1
Wimborne Minster Dorset 12 D5
Wimborne St Giles Dorset 12 D6
Wimbotsham Norfk 63 E6
Wimpole Cambs 50 D6
Wimpstone Warwks 47 H4
Wincanton Somset 24 C2
Winceby Lincs 86 D1
Wincham Ches 82 B2
Winchburgh W Loth 131 G3
Winchcombe Gloucs 47 F2
Winchelsea E Susx 18 C3
Winchelsea Beach E Susx 18 C3
Winchester Hants 26 C2
Winchet Hill Kent 18 A5
Winchfield Hants 27 F5
Winchmore Hill Bucks 41 G4
Winchmore Hill Gt Lon 28 D5
Wincle Ches 83 E1
Wincobank S York 84 B4
Winder Cumb 102 D2
Windermere Cumb 95 E5
Winderton Warwks 48 B3
Windhill Highld 154 D4
Windlehurst Gt Man 82 D3
Windlesham Surrey 27 G6
Windmill Cnwll 4 C3
Windmill Derbys 83 G2
Windmill Hill E Susx 17 G3
Windmill Hill Somset 23 F1
Windrush Gloucs 39 G6
Windsole Abers 158 B5
Windsor Berks 41 H2
Windsor Castle Berks 41 H2
Windsor Green Suffk 52 C6
Windsoredge Gloucs 38 C4
Windy Arbour Warwks 59 F2
Windy Hill Wrexhm 69 E5
Windygates Fife 132 B5
Windyharbour Ches 82 C2
Wineham W Susx 16 C3
Winestead E R Yk 93 G2
Winewall Lancs 89 G4
Winfarthing Norfk 64 D4
Winford IOW 14 D2
Winford Somset 24 A6
Winforton Herefs 45 F4
Winfrith Newburgh Dorset 12 B3
Wing Bucks 49 G1
Wing Rutlnd 61 E6
Wingate Dur 106 C4
Wingates Gt Man 82 B5
Wingates Nthumb 114 C5
Wingerworth Derbys 84 B1
Wingfield Beds 50 A3
Wingfield Suffk 65 E3
Wingfield Wilts 24 D5
Wingfield Green Suffk 65 E3
Wingham Kent 31 F2
Wingmore Kent 19 E6
Wingrave Bucks 49 G1
Winkburn Notts 73 E6
Winkfield Berks 41 G1
Winkfield Row Berks 41 G1
Winkfield Street Berks 41 G1
Winkhill Staffs 71 E5
Winkhurst Green Kent 29 F1
Winkleigh Devon 8 C5
Winksley N York 97 F2
Winkton Dorset 13 E4
Winlaton T & W 114 C2
Winlaton Mill T & W 114 C2
Winless Highld 167 G4
Winllan Powys 68 D2
Winmarleigh Lancs 88 C4
Winnall Hants 26 C2
Winnall Worcs 58 A2
Winnersh Berks 41 F1
Winnington Ches 82 A2
Winscales Cumb 102 D3
Winscombe Somset 23 G5
Winsford Ches 82 B1
Winsford Somset 22 B3
Winsham Devon 21 E4
Winsham Somset 10 D5
Winshill Staffs 71 G2
Winshwen Swans 34 D4
Winskill Cumb 104 C4
Winslade Hants 27 E4
Winsley Wilts 24 D5
Wisley Gardens Surrey 28 B2
Winslow Bucks 49 F2
Winson Gloucs 39 F5
Winsor Hants 13 G6
Winster Cumb 95 E4
Winster Derbys 71 G6
Winston Dur 105 H2
Winston Suffk 64 D1
Winston Green Suffk 64 D1
Winstone Gloucs 38 D5
Winswell Devon 21 E2
Winterborne Came Dorset 11 G3
Winterborne Clenston Dorset 12 B5
Winterborne Herringston Dorset 11 G3
Winterborne Houghton Dorset 12 B5
Winterborne Kingston Dorset 12 C4
Winterborne Monkton Dorset 11 G3
Winterborne Stickland Dorset 12 B5
Winterborne Tomson Dorset 12 C4
Winterborne Whitechurch Dorset 12 B5
Winterborne Zelston Dorset 12 C4
Winterbourne Berks 40 C1
Winterbourne Gloucs 37 G2
Winterbourne Abbas Dorset 11 F4
Winterbourne Bassett Wilts 39 F2
Winterbourne Dauntsey Wilts 25 G3
Winterbourne Earls Wilts 25 G3
Winterbourne Gunner Wilts 25 G3
Winterbourne Monkton Wilts 39 F1
Winterbourne Steepleton Dorset 11 G4
Winterbourne Stoke Wilts 25 F3
Winterbrook Oxon 40 D3
Winterburn N York 89 H5
Winteringham Lincs 92 C2
Winterley Ches 70 B6
Wintersett W York 91 E1
Winterslow Wilts 25 H2
Winterton Lincs 92 C1
Winterton-on-Sea Norfk 77 H2
Winthorpe Lincs 87 F1
Winthorpe Notts 73 F6
Winton Cumb 96 A6
Winton Dorset 13 E4
Winton E Susx 17 F2
Winton N York 97 G4
Wintringham N York 99 E2
Winwick Cambs 61 G3
Winwick Ches 82 A4
Winwick Nhants 60 B3
Wirksworth Derbys 71 H5
Wirswall Ches 69 H4
Wisbech Cambs 75 E1
Wisbech St Mary Cambs 62 C6
Wisborough Green W Susx 16 A4
Wiseman's Bridge Pembks 33 F2
Wiseton Notts 85 E4
Wishanger Gloucs 38 D5
Wishaw N Lans 120 B5
Wishaw Warwks 59 E5
Wisley Surrey 28 B2
Wispington Lincs 86 B2
Wissenden Kent 18 C5
Wissett Suffk 65 F3
Wissington Norfk 63 F5
Wissington Suffk 52 C4
Wistanstow Shrops 57 E4
Wistanswick Shrops 70 B3
Wistaston Ches 70 B5
Wistaston Green Ches 70 B5
Wisterfield Ches 82 C2
Wiston Pembks 32 D3
Wiston S Lans 120 D3
Wiston W Susx 16 B3
Wistow Cambs 62 B3
Wistow Leics 60 C5
Wistow N York 91 G3
Wiswell Lancs 89 F3
Witcham Cambs 62 D3
Witchampton Dorset 12 D5
Witchford Cambs 62 D3
Witcombe Somset 23 G1
Witham Essex 52 B2
Witham Friary Somset 24 C3
Witham on the Hill Lincs 73 H2
Withcall Lincs 86 C3
Withdean E Susx 16 D2
Witherenden Hill E Susx 17 G4
Witheridge Devon 9 E6
Witherley Leics 59 F5
Withern Lincs 87 E3
Withernsea E R Yk 93 G2
Withernwick E R Yk 93 F4
Withersdale Street Suffk 65 E3
Withersfield Essex 51 G5
Witherslack Cumb 95 E3
Witherslack Hall Cumb 95 E3
Withiel Cnwll 4 D2
Withiel Florey Somset 22 C3
Withielgoose Cnwll 4 D2
Withington Gloucs 39 E6
Withington Gt Man 82 C4
Withington Herefs 46 A3
Withington Shrops 69 H1
Withington Staffs 71 E3
Withington Green Ches 82 C2
Withington Marsh Herefs 46 A4
Withleigh Devon 9 F6
Withnell Lancs 89 E2
Withy Mills Somset 24 B5
Withybed Green Worcs 58 C3
Withybrook Warwks 59 G4
Withycombe Somset 22 C3
Withyham E Susx 17 F5
Withypool Somset 22 A3
Withywood Bristl 24 A6
Witley Surrey 27 H3
Witnesham Suffk 53 E6
Witney Oxon 40 B5
Wittering Cambs 61 F6
Wittersham Kent 18 C4
Witton Norfk 77 F1
Witton Norfk 77 F3
Witton W Mids 58 D4
Witton Gilbert Dur 106 B5
Witton Green Norfk 65 G6
Witton le Wear Dur 105 H3
Witton Park Dur 106 A4
Wiveliscombe Somset 22 D2
Wivelrod Hants 27 E3
Wivelsfield E Susx 16 D3
Wivelsfield Green E Susx 16 D3
Wivelsfield Station W Susx 16 D3
Wivenhoe Essex 52 D3
Wivenhoe Cross Essex 52 D3
Wiveton Norfk 76 C4
Wix Essex 53 E4
Wix Green Essex 53 E3
Wixford Warwks 47 F5
Wixhill Shrops 69 H3
Wixoe Essex 51 H5
Woburn Beds 49 H2
Woburn Abbey Beds 49 H2
Woburn Sands Bucks 49 G3
Wokefield Park Berks 27 E6
Woking Surrey 28 A2
Wokingham Berks 41 F1
Wolborough Devon 7 F5
Wold Newton E R Yk 99 F2
Wold Newton Lincs 86 C4
Woldingham Surrey 29 E2
Wolf Hills Nthumb 104 D6
Wolf's Castle Pembks 32 D4
Wolfclyde S Lans 121 E3
Wolferlow Herefs 46 B5
Wolferton Norfk 75 G3
Wolfhampcote Warwks 60 A2
Wolfhill P & K 140 B3
Wolfsdale Pembks 32 D4
Wollaston Nhants 61 E2
Wollaston Shrops 69 E1
Wollaston W Mids 58 B4
Wollaton Notts 72 C4
Wolleigh Devon 9 E3
Wollerton Shrops 70 A3
Wollescote W Mids 58 B4
Wolseley Bridge Staffs 71 E2
Wolsingham Dur 105 G4
Wolstanton Staffs 70 D5
Wolstenholme Gt Man 89 G1
Wolston Warwks 59 G3
Wolsty Cumb 103 E5
Wolvercote Oxon 40 C5
Wolverhampton W Mids 58 B5
Wolverley Shrops 69 G3
Wolverley Worcs 58 A3
Wolverton Bucks 49 F3
Wolverton Hants 26 D5
Wolverton Kent 19 F6
Wolverton Warwks 47 G5
Wolverton Wilts 24 C2
Wolverton Common Hants 26 D5
Wolvesnewton Mons 37 F4
Wolvey Warwks 59 G4
Wolvey Heath Warwks 59 G4
Wolviston Dur 106 D3
Wombleton N York 98 B3
Wombourne Staffs 58 B5
Wombwell S York 84 B5
Womenswold Kent 31 F1
Womersley N York 91 F1
Wonastow Mons 37 F5
Wonersh Surrey 16 A6
Wonford Devon 9 F4
Wonson Devon 8 D4
Wonston Hants 26 C3
Wooburn Bucks 41 G3
Wooburn Green Bucks 41 G3
Wooburn Moor Bucks 41 G3
Wood Bevington Warwks 47 F5
Wood Burcot Nhants 49 E4
Wood Dalling Norfk 76 D3
Wood Eaton Staffs 70 C2
Wood End Beds 50 A5
Wood End Beds 61 G2
Wood End Cambs 62 C3
Wood End Gt Lon 28 B4
Wood End Herts 50 D3
Wood End W Mids 58 B5
Wood End Warwks 58 D2
Wood End Warwks 59 E5
Wood End Warwks 59 F4
Wood Enderby Lincs 86 C1
Wood Green Gt Lon 28 D5
Wood Hayes W Mids 58 B6
Wood Lane Shrops 69 F3
Wood Lane Staffs 70 C5
Wood Norton Norfk 76 C3
Wood Row W York 91 E2
Wood Street Norfk 77 G2
Wood Street Surrey 27 H4
Wood Top Lancs 88 D4
Wood Walton Cambs 62 A3
Wood's Corner E Susx 17 G3
Wood's Green E Susx 17 G5
Woodale N York 96 C3
Woodall S York 84 B3
Woodbastwick Norfk 77 F1
Woodbeck Notts 85 E2
Woodborough Notts 72 D5
Woodborough Wilts 25 G5
Woodbridge Devon 10 B4
Woodbridge Dorset 24 D1
Woodbridge Suffk 53 F6
Woodbury Devon 9 G3
Woodbury Salterton Devon 9 G3
Woodchester Gloucs 38 C5
Woodchurch Kent 18 C5
Woodchurch Mersyd 81 E3
Woodcombe Somset 22 B4
Woodcote Gt Lon 28 D2
Woodcote Oxon 41 E2
Woodcote Shrops 70 C1
Woodcote Green Worcs 58 B3
Woodcott Hants 26 C5
Woodcroft Gloucs 37 F4
Woodcutts Dorset 25 E1
Woodditton Cambs 63 F1
Woodeaton Oxon 40 D5
Wooden Pembks 33 E2
Woodend Highld 136 B6
Woodend Nhants 48 D4

319

Woodend — Zouch

Place	Page	Grid
Woodend Staffs	71	G3
Woodend W Loth	131	E2
Woodend W Susx	15	F4
Woodend Green Essex	51	F4
Woodfalls Wilts	25	G1
Woodford Devon	7	E3
Woodford Gloucs	38	B4
Woodford Gt Lon	29	E5
Woodford Gt Man	82	D3
Woodford Nhants	61	F3
Woodford Bridge Gt Lon	29	E5
Woodford Halse Nhants	48	D4
Woodford Wells Gt Lon	29	E5
Woodgate Devon	10	B6
Woodgate Norfk	76	B1
Woodgate Norfk	76	C2
Woodgate W Mids	58	C4
Woodgate W Susx	15	G4
Woodgate Worcs	58	C2
Woodgreen Hants	25	G1
Woodgreen Oxon	40	B5
Woodhall Lincs	86	C1
Woodhall N York	96	C4
Woodhall Hill W York	90	C3
Woodhall Spa Lincs	86	B1
Woodham Bucks	49	E1
Woodham Dur	106	B3
Woodham Surrey	28	A2
Woodham Ferrers Essex	30	B6
Woodham Mortimer Essex	52	B1
Woodham Walter Essex	52	B1
Woodhead Abers	158	D3
Woodhill Somset	23	F2
Woodhorn Nthumb	115	E4
Woodhorn Demesne Nthumb	115	E4
Woodhouse Leics	72	C1
Woodhouse S York	84	B3
Woodhouse W York	90	D3
Woodhouse W York	91	G2
Woodhouse Eaves Leics	72	C1
Woodhouse Green Staffs	82	D1
Woodhouse Mill S York	84	B3
Woodhouselee Mdloth	132	A1
Woodhouselees D & G	112	A2
Woodhouses Cumb	103	G5
Woodhouses Gt Man	82	D5
Woodhouses Staffs	71	F1
Woodhouses Staffs	71	F2
Woodhuish Devon	7	F3
Woodhurst Cambs	62	B3
Woodingdean E Susx	16	D2
Woodkirk W York	90	D2
Woodland Abers	159	E1
Woodland Devon	7	E4
Woodland Devon	6	D3
Woodland Dur	105	G3
Woodland Kent	19	E5
Woodland S Ayrs	108	D4
Woodland Head Devon	9	E4
Woodland Street Somset	24	A3
Woodland View S York	83	H3
Woodlands Abers	149	E4
Woodlands Dorset	12	D5
Woodlands Hants	13	G6
Woodlands Kent	29	F2
Woodlands N York	90	D5
Woodlands S York	84	C5
Woodlands Somset	22	D3
Woodlands Park Berks	41	G2
Woodlands St Mary Berks	40	B2
Woodleigh Devon	7	E2
Woodlesford W York	91	E2
Woodley Berks	41	F2
Woodley Gt Man	82	D4
Woodmancote Gloucs	47	E2
Woodmancote Gloucs	39	E5
Woodmancote Gloucs	38	B4
Woodmancote W Susx	15	F4
Woodmancote W Susx	16	C3
Woodmancote Worcs	47	E3
Woodmancott Hants	26	D3
Woodmansey E R Yk	92	D3
Woodmansgreen W Susx	27	G2
Woodmansterne Surrey	28	D2
Woodmanton Devon	9	G3
Woodmarsh Wilts	24	D5
Woodmill Staffs	71	F2
Woodminton Wilts	25	F1
Woodnesborough Kent	31	G2
Woodnewton Nhants	61	F5
Woodnook Notts	72	B5
Woodplumpton Lancs	88	C3
Woodrising Norfk	64	B6
Woodrow Worcs	58	B3
Woodseaves Shrops	70	B3
Woodseaves Staffs	70	B3
Woodsend Wilts	39	G2
Woodsetts S York	84	C3
Woodsford Dorset	12	B4
Woodside Berks	41	G1
Woodside Cumb	102	D3
Woodside Essex	51	F1
Woodside Fife	132	C6
Woodside Gt Lon	28	D3
Woodside Hants	13	G4
Woodside Herts	50	C1
Woodside P & K	140	D3
Woodside Green Kent	30	C1
Woodstock Oxon	40	C6
Woodstock Pembks	33	E4
Woodston Cambs	61	H5
Woodthorpe Derbys	84	B2
Woodthorpe Leics	72	C2
Woodthorpe Lincs	87	E3
Woodton Norfk	65	E5
Woodtown Devon	20	D3
Woodvale Mersyd	81	E6
Woodville Derbys	71	H2
Woodwall Green Staffs	70	C3
Woody Bay Devon	21	G5
Woodyates Dorset	25	F1
Woofferton Shrops	57	E2
Wookey Somset	23	H4
Wookey Hole Somset	23	H4
Wool Dorset	12	B3
Woolacombe Devon	21	E5
Woolage Green Kent	31	F1
Woolage Village Kent	31	F1

Place	Page	Grid
Woolaston Gloucs	37	G4
Woolaston Common Gloucs	37	G4
Woolavington Somset	23	F3
Woolbeding W Susx	27	G1
Woolbrook Devon	10	B3
Woolcotts Somset	22	C2
Wooldale W York	83	F6
Wooler Nthumb	124	C4
Woolfardisworthy Devon	20	D3
Woolfardisworthy Devon	9	E5
Woolfold Gt Man	82	C6
Woolfords S Lans	121	E5
Woolhampton Berks	26	D6
Woolhanger Devon	21	G5
Woolhope Herefs	46	B3
Woolland Dorset	12	B5
Woollard Somset	24	B6
Woollensbrook Herts	50	D2
Woolley Cambs	61	G3
Woolley Cnwll	20	C2
Woolley Derbys	72	A6
Woolley Somset	38	B1
Woolley W York	83	H6
Woolley Bridge Derbys	83	E4
Woolley Green Berks	41	G2
Woolmer Green Herts	50	C3
Woolmere Green Worcs	58	C2
Woolmerston Somset	23	F3
Woolminstone Somset	10	D5
Woolpack Kent	18	B5
Woolpit Suffk	64	B2
Woolpit Green Suffk	64	B1
Woolscott Warwks	59	H2
Woolsgrove Devon	9	E5
Woolsington T & W	114	D2
Woolstaston Shrops	57	E5
Woolsthorpe Lincs	73	F3
Woolsthorpe-by-Colsterworth Lincs	73	G2
Woolston Ches	82	B4
Woolston Devon	7	E2
Woolston Devon	7	E3
Woolston Hants	14	C5
Woolston Shrops	69	E2
Woolston Shrops	56	D4
Woolston Somset	22	D3
Woolston Somset	24	B2
Woolston Green Devon	7	E4
Woolstone Bucks	49	G3
Woolstone Gloucs	47	E2
Woolstone Oxon	39	G3
Woolton Mersyd	81	F3
Woolton Hill Hants	26	C5
Woolverstone Suffk	53	E5
Woolverton Somset	24	C5
Woolwich Gt Lon	29	E4
Woonton Herefs	45	F4
Woonton Herefs	46	A5
Wooperton Nthumb	124	D3
Woore Shrops	70	B4
Wootten Green Suffk	65	E3
Wootton Beds	50	A5
Wootton Hants	13	F4
Wootton Herefs	45	F4
Wootton IOW	14	D3
Wootton Kent	19	F6
Wootton Lincs	93	E1
Wootton Nhants	49	F5
Wootton Oxon	48	C1
Wootton Oxon	40	C4
Wootton Shrops	69	F3
Wootton Staffs	70	C3
Wootton Staffs	71	F4
Wootton Bassett Wilts	39	E2
Wootton Bridge IOW	14	D3
Wootton Broadmead Beds	50	A5
Wootton Common IOW	14	D3
Wootton Courtenay Somset	22	B4
Wootton Fitzpaine Dorset	10	D4
Wootton Rivers Wilts	25	G6
Wootton St Lawrence Hants	26	D5
Wootton Wawen Warwks	58	D2
Worcester Worcs	46	D5
Worcester Park Gt Lon	28	C3
Wordsley W Mids	58	B4
Worfield Shrops	57	H5
Worgret Dorset	12	C3
Workhouse End Beds	50	B6
Workington Cumb	102	D3
Worksop Notts	84	C3
Worlaby Lincs	85	H6
Worlaby Lincs	86	C3
World's End Berks	40	C2
Worlds End Bucks	41	H5
Worlds End Hants	14	D5
Worlds End W Susx	16	D3
Worle Somset	23	F6
Worleston Ches	70	B6
Worlingham Suffk	65	G4
Worlington Devon	21	H2
Worlington Suffk	63	F3
Worlingworth Suffk	65	E2
Wormald Green N York	97	F1
Wormbridge Herefs	45	G2
Wormegay Norfk	75	G1
Wormelow Tump Herefs	45	H2
Wormhill Derbys	83	F2
Wormhill Herefs	45	G3
Worminghall Bucks	41	E5
Wormington Gloucs	47	F3
Worminster Somset	24	A3
Wormit Fife	140	D2
Wormleighton Warwks	48	C5
Wormley Herts	50	D1
Wormley Hill S York	91	H1
Wormleybury Herts	50	D1
Wormshill Kent	30	B2
Wormsley Herefs	45	H5
Wormsley Herefs	45	H5
Worplesdon Surrey	27	H5
Worrall S York	83	H4
Worrall Hill Gloucs	37	G6
Worsbrough S York	84	A5
Worsbrough Bridge S York	84	A5
Worsbrough Dale S York	84	A5
Worsley Gt Man	82	C5
Worsley Mesnes Gt Man	81	H5

Place	Page	Grid
Worstead Norfk	77	F3
Worsthorne Lancs	89	G3
Worston Devon	6	C3
Worston Lancs	89	F4
Worth Kent	31	G2
Worth Somset	23	H4
Worth W Susx	16	D5
Worth Abbey Surrey	16	D5
Worth Matravers Dorset	12	D2
Wortham Suffk	64	C3
Worthen Shrops	56	D6
Worthenbury Wrexhm	69	F5
Worthing Norfk	76	C2
Worthing W Susx	16	B2
Worthington Leics	72	B2
Worthybrook Mons	37	F5
Worting Hants	26	D4
Wortley S York	83	H5
Wortley W York	90	D3
Worton N York	96	C4
Worton Wilts	25	E5
Wortwell Norfk	65	E4
Wotherton Shrops	56	C5
Wothorpe Cambs	61	F6
Wotter Devon	6	C4
Wotton Surrey	16	B3
Wotton Underwood Bucks	41	E6
Wotton-under-Edge Gloucs	38	B4
Woughton on the Green Bucks	49	G3
Wouldham Kent	29	H2
Woundale Shrops	57	H5
Wrabness Essex	53	E4
Wrafton Devon	21	E4
Wragby Lincs	86	B2
Wragby W York	91	E1
Wramplingham Norfk	64	D6
Wrangaton Devon	6	D3
Wrangbrook W York	84	C6
Wrangle Lincs	75	E5
Wrangle Common Lincs	75	E5
Wrangle Lowgate Lincs	75	E5
Wrangway Somset	22	D1
Wrantage Somset	23	G5
Wrawby Lincs	85	H6
Wraxall Somset	37	F1
Wraxall Somset	23	H3
Wray Lancs	95	G2
Wray Castle Cumb	94	D5
Wraysbury Berks	28	A3
Wrayton Lancs	95	G2
Wrea Green Lancs	88	B3
Wreaks End Cumb	94	C3
Wreay Cumb	104	A5
Wreay Cumb	104	A2
Wrecclesham Surrey	27	F4
Wrekenton T & W	114	D1
Wrelton N York	98	C3
Wrenbury Ches	70	A5
Wrench Green N York	99	E4
Wrentham Suffk	65	G4
Wrenthorpe W York	90	D2
Wrentnall Shrops	56	D6
Wressle E R Yk	92	A3
Wressle Lincs	85	G6
Wrestlingworth Beds	50	C5
Wretton Norfk	63	F5
Wrexham Wrexhm	69	F5
Wribbenhall Worcs	57	H3
Wrickton Shrops	57	G4
Wright's Green Essex	51	F2
Wrightington Bar Lancs	81	G6
Wrinehill Staffs	70	C5
Wrington Somset	23	G5
Wringworthy Cnwll	5	F2
Writhlington Somset	24	C5
Writtle Essex	51	H1
Wrockwardine Shrops	70	A1
Wroot Lincs	85	E5
Wrose W York	90	C3
Wrotham Kent	29	G2
Wrotham Heath Kent	29	G2
Wrottesley Staffs	58	A2
Wroughton Wilts	39	F2
Wroxall IOW	14	D1
Wroxall Warwks	59	E2
Wroxeter Shrops	57	F6
Wroxham Norfk	77	F2
Wroxton Oxon	48	B3
Wyaston Derbys	71	G4
Wyatt's Green Essex	29	G6
Wyberton East Lincs	74	D1
Wyberton West Lincs	74	C4
Wyboston Beds	61	H1
Wybunbury Ches	70	B5
Wych Dorset	11	E4
Wych Cross E Susx	17	E5
Wychbold Worcs	58	B2
Wychnor Staffs	71	G2
Wyck Hants	27	F3
Wyck Rissington Gloucs	47	G5
Wycliffe Dur	105	H1
Wycoller Lancs	89	H3
Wycomb Leics	73	E2
Wycombe Marsh Bucks	41	G3
Wyddial Herts	51	E4
Wyck Kent	18	D6
Wyesham Mons	37	F5
Wyfordby Leics	73	E2
Wyke Devon	9	F5
Wyke Devon	10	C4
Wyke Dorset	24	D2
Wyke Shrops	57	G6
Wyke Surrey	27	G4
Wyke W York	90	C2
Wyke Champflower Somset	24	B3
Wyke Regis Dorset	11	G2
Wykeham N York	98	D2
Wykeham N York	99	E3
Wyken Shrops	57	H5
Wyken W Mids	59	G3
Wykey Shrops	69	F2
Wykin Leics	59	G5
Wylam Nthumb	114	C2
Wylde Green W Mids	58	D5
Wylye Wilts	25	F3
Wymeswold Leics	72	D2
Wymington Beds	61	F2

Place	Page	Grid
Wymondham Leics	73	F2
Wymondham Norfk	64	D5
Wyndham Brdgnd	35	G3
Wynford Eagle Dorset	11	F4
Wynyard Park Dur	106	D3
Wyre Piddle Worcs	47	E4
Wysall Notts	72	D2
Wyson Herefs	57	E2
Wythall Worcs	58	D3
Wytham Oxon	40	C5
Wythburn Cumb	103	G1
Wythenshawe Gt Man	82	C3
Wythop Mill Cumb	103	F3
Wyton Cambs	62	B3
Wyton E R Yk	93	F3
Wyverstone Suffk	64	C2
Wyverstone Street Suffk	64	C2
Wyville Lincs	73	F3

Y

Place	Page	Grid
Y Felinheli Gwynd	79	E1
Y Ferwig Cerdgn	42	B4
Y Ffor Gwynd	66	D4
Y Gyffylliog Denbgs	68	C6
Y Maerdy Conwy	68	B4
Y Nant Wrexhm	69	E5
Y Rhiw Gwynd	66	B3
Yaddlethorpe Lincs	85	F5
Yafford IOW	14	C2
Yafforth N York	97	G4
Yalberton Devon	7	F3
Yalding Kent	29	H1
Yanwath Cumb	104	B3
Yanworth Gloucs	39	E6
Yapham E R Yk	92	B5
Yapton W Susx	15	H4
Yarborough Somset	23	G5
Yarbridge IOW	14	D2
Yarburgh Lincs	86	D5
Yarcombe Devon	10	C5
Yard Devon	21	H3
Yardley W Mids	58	D4
Yardley Gobion Nhants	49	F4
Yardley Hastings Nhants	49	G5
Yardley Wood W Mids	58	D3
Yardro Powys	45	E2
Yarford Somset	23	E2
Yarkhill Herefs	46	B3
Yarley Somset	23	H4
Yarlington Somset	24	B2
Yarlsber N York	95	H2
Yarm N York	106	C2
Yarmouth IOW	14	B2
Yarnacott Devon	21	F4
Yarnbrook Wilts	24	D5
Yarner Devon	9	E2
Yarnfield Staffs	70	D2
Yarnscombe Devon	21	F3
Yarnton Oxon	40	C5
Yarpole Herefs	57	E2
Yarrow Border	121	H2
Yarrow Somset	23	G4
Yarrow Feus Border	121	H2
Yarrowford Border	122	A2
Yarsop Herefs	45	G4
Yarwell Nhants	61	G5
Yate Gloucs	38	B2
Yateley Hants	27	F5
Yatesbury Wilts	39	E1
Yattendon Berks	40	D2
Yatton Herefs	57	E2
Yatton Herefs	46	B2
Yatton Somset	23	G6
Yatton Keynell Wilts	38	C2
Yaverland IOW	14	D2
Yawl Devon	10	D4
Yawthorpe Lincs	85	F4
Yaxham Norfk	76	C1
Yaxley Cambs	61	H5
Yaxley Suffk	64	D3
Yazor Herefs	45	G4
Yeading Gt Lon	28	B4
Yeadon W York	90	C4
Yealand Conyers Lancs	95	F2
Yealand Redmayne Lancs	95	F2
Yealand Storrs Lancs	95	F2
Yealmbridge Devon	6	C3
Yealmpton Devon	6	C3
Yearby N York	107	E3
Yeargill Cumb	103	E4
Yearsley N York	98	B2
Yeaton Shrops	69	G2
Yeaveley Derbys	71	G4
Yeavering Nthumb	123	F2
Yedingham N York	99	E3
Yelford Oxon	40	B5
Yelland Devon	21	E4
Yelling Cambs	62	B2
Yelvertoft Nhants	60	B3
Yelverton Devon	6	C4
Yelverton Norfk	65	E6
Yenston Somset	24	C1
Yeo Mill Somset	22	A2
Yeo Vale Devon	20	D3
Yeoford Devon	9	E4
Yeolmbridge Cnwll	5	G5
Yeovil Somset	24	A1
Yeovil Marsh Somset	24	A1
Yeovilton Somset	24	A1
Yeovilton Fleet Air Arm Museum Somset	24	A2
Yerbeston Pembks	33	E3
Yesnaby Ork	169	a3
Yetlington Nthumb	124	C2
Yetminster Dorset	11	F6
Yetson Devon	7	E3
Yettington Devon	9	G3
Yetts o' Muckhart Clacks	131	F5
Yew Green Warwks	59	E2
Yews Green W York	90	B3

Place	Page	Grid
Yieldshields S Lans	120	C4
Yiewsley Gt Lon	28	B4
Ynysboeth Rhondd	36	B4
Ynysddu Caerph	36	C3
Ynysforgan Swans	34	G4
Ynyshir Rhondd	35	H3
Ynyslas Cerdgn	54	D5
Ynysmaerdy Rhondd	36	B3
Ynysmeudwy Neath	35	G2
Ynystawe Swans	34	G4
Ynyswen Powys	35	F6
Ynyswen Rhondd	35	G4
Ynysybwl Rhondd	36	B4
Ynysymaengwyn Gwynd	54	D6
Yockenthwaite N York	96	B3
Yockleton Shrops	69	F1
Yokefleet E R Yk	92	B2
Yoker C Glas	129	F2
York Lancs	89	E3
York N York	91	G5
York Minster N York	91	G5
York Town Surrey	27	G5
Yorkletts Kent	30	D2
Yorkley Gloucs	37	G2
Yorton Heath Shrops	69	G2
Youlgreave Derbys	83	G1
Youlthorpe E R Yk	92	B5
Youlton N York	97	H1
Young's End Essex	52	A3
Youngsbury Herts	51	E2
Yoxall Staffs	71	F2
Yoxford Suffk	65	F2
Yoxford Little Street Suffk	65	F2
Ysbyty Cynfyn Cerdgn	55	E3
Ysbyty Ifan Conwy	67	H5
Ysbyty Ystwyth Cerdgn	55	E2
Ysceifiog Flints	80	D2
Ysgubor-y-Coed Cerdgn	54	D5
Ystalyfera Powys	35	E5
Ystrad Rhondd	35	G4
Ystrad Aeron Cerdgn	43	E5
Ystrad Ffin Carmth	43	H4
Ystrad Meurig Cerdgn	55	E2
Ystrad Mynach Caerph	36	C4
Ystradfellte Powys	35	G6
Ystradgynlais Powys	35	E5
Ystradowen V Glam	35	G2
Ystumtuen Cerdgn	55	E3
Ythanbank Abers	159	F2
Ythanwells Abers	158	B3
Ythsie Abers	159	E2

Z

Place	Page	Grid
Zeal Monachorum Devon	8	D4
Zeals Wilts	24	D2
Zelah Cnwll	3	F5
Zennor Cnwll	2	B4
Zoar Cnwll	3	E2
Zouch Notts	72	C2